CONTROVERSIES IN
SOCIOLOGY

A Canadian Introduction

CONTROVERSIES IN
SOCIOLOGY

A Canadian Introduction

SECOND EDITION

Sylvia M. Hale

St Thomas University

Copp Clark Ltd.
Toronto

ISBN: 0-7730-5356-5

managing editor: Barbara Tessman
executive editor: Jeff Miller
editor: Pamela Erlichman
photo research: Richard Dunlop
index: Sarah Robertson
cover and text design: Kyle Gell
cover illustration: Helen D'Souza
cover photo: Ray Boudreau
typesetting: Marnie Benedict
printing and binding: Best Book Manufacturers

Canadian Cataloguing in Publication Data

Hale, Sylvia Marion, 1945–
   Controversies in sociology

2nd ed.
Includes bibliographical references and index.
ISBN 0-7730-5356-5

1. Sociology.   2. Canada - Social conditions.
I. Title.

HM22.C3H35 1995   301   C95-930592-0

Copp Clark Ltd.
2775 Matheson Blvd. East
Mississauga, Ontario
L4W 4P7

Printed and bound in Canada

1 2 3 4 5   5356-5   99 98 97 96 95

LIST OF CHAPTERS

CONTENTS

Chapter 5   Gender Relations: Competing Perspectives   85

▦ PART III   Social Cohesion and Order in Industrial Society   119

Chapter 6   Cohesion and Morality: A Critical Look at Durkheim   121

Chapter 7   Anomie: The Roots of Industrial Conflict and Crime   153

◼ PART IV   Political Economy: Challenging Capitalism   189

Chapter 8   Karl Marx and the Analysis of Capitalism   191

Chapter 9   The Political Economy of Canada: "The Main Business"   213

Acknowledgments

In the preparation of this second edition I owe a special debt of thanks to Peter Weeks, a colleague and associate professor at St Thomas University. He prepared a detailed draft of the section on the social construction of schooling that has been incorporated into the revised chapter on education. The chapter on the microsociology of everyday life that Peter wrote for the first edition is now incorporated into Part VII of this edition, which focusses on the sociology of knowledge. This edition is also greatly enlivened by Peter's selection of new cartoons. I am also indebted to Gary Kinsman, currently in the department of sociology at Laurentian University, for his very detailed and critical review of an early draft of the new chapter on gender relations. Gary shared his extensive knowledge of research on gay and lesbian experience, and he contributed significantly to the development of the theoretical frameworks for this chapter. Colm Kelly provided many helpful suggestions in the preparation of the new chapter on postmodernism, as did Gerry Coulter for the chapter on culture and communications.

In closing, I would like to express my thanks to Pamela Erlichman of Copp Clark. As senior editor responsible for the preparation of the second edition, Pamela contributed immeasurably to its overall coherence. Many times, her critical questioning forced me to address areas of confusion in my own thinking and to clarify ideas, particularly as I struggled to incorporate new developments in social constructionist theory into all chapters of the text. She kept encouraging me along even as I fell far behind schedule in preparing new materials.

Sylvia Hale
St Thomas University
Fredericton

Preface to the First Edition

The initial impetus for this text came from a plan to develop a Canadian edition of a British text, *The Problem of Sociology* by David Lee and Howard Newby (1983). The Canadianization seemed warranted by the outstanding qualities of the original British text. In many ways, it represented a radical departure from the traditional format of North American introductions to sociology. Gone were the token chapters on "great names" and the ubiquitous lists of social institutions. Instead, students were introduced to sociology as a theoretical discipline, grounded in a long historical and intellectual tradition in which controversies and empirical research are fundamental.

Each section of the British book presented a sophisticated, in-depth treatment of theory. Institutions such as education, family, religion, bureaucracy, deviance, and so on, were all represented, but as empirical tests of theory rather than as specialized entities within a structural model of society. The major achievement of the text was that it systematically applied sociological theory to the analysis of contemporary industrial capitalist society. The consistently high quality of Lee and Newby's book, their organizing focus around theories of industrial society, and their empirical testing of theories with contemporary data, all provided a challenging framework for an introductory course.

Using this text for an introductory sociology course in a Canadian university, however, proved frustrating. The historical order of the presentation of theories, combined with their complexity and the absence of specifically Canadian data, made it difficult for the average Canadian student to absorb the material. The historical framework that was used by Lee and Newby meant that contemporary theories came last. We thought it desirable to engage students in actively debating the comparative merits of different perspectives right from the beginning. Not only was it necessary to introduce structural functionalism—which has long dominated North American sociology and introductory sociology texts—right at the outset, but feminist and social constructionist theories had to be presented as well. In this way, students could relate their immediate personal experiences to what they were studying because these interactive perspectives in effect bridge the gap between micro- and macrosociological theory.

These changes, combined with the need to include Canadian data, were too far-reaching to be accomplished by the cut-and-paste Canadianization. Hence, *Controversies in Sociology*. Even the chapters on classical theorists such as Durkheim, Marx, and Weber, which still bear some structural resemblance to the corresponding chapters in Lee and Newby, had to be substantially altered. They had to reflect the present text's concern with integrating the four theoretical approaches of structural functionalism, Marxism, feminism, and social constructionism into each section of the book.

The data that we present in this book are not treated as "facts," but as tests of different sociological theories. Throughout this text, students are encouraged to develop their critical skills instead of passively absorbing material. We believe that such a goal constitutes a striking difference between *Controversies in Sociology* and other Canadian sociology textbooks. It is in this regard that the book remains true to the fundamental conception of Lee and Newby that students should be introduced to sociology as the study of a body of theory, rather than as a collection of rapidly changing descriptive data.

Introduction to the Second Edition

This text presents sociology as a way of questioning experience rather than as an accumulation of factual knowledge. The objective is to stimulate discussion and to assist students in developing their capacity to think critically about society rather than simply to memorize facts. Theory is accorded central importance and is utilized throughout the text as the basis for exploring all substantive issues.

The text is organized around the comparative application of a range of contemporary theories to problems of industrial capitalist society, with special reference to Canada. It introduces the four broad theoretical perspectives of functionalism, political economy, the social construction of reality, and feminism, tracing their roots in the works of Durkheim, Marx, Parsons, and Weber. We study the founding fathers' contribution to, and continuing relevance for, a variety of contemporary theories and analyses. The main body of the text combines theory, methodology, and evidence throughout and tries to explain the basis of controversies in sociology. Different chapters present a comparative application of the four major theoretical approaches to the substantive issues of community life in rural and urban contexts, gender, religion, suicide, crime and industrial conflict, political economy, development and change, bureaucracy, family, stratification, education, racial and ethnic relations, the microsociology of everyday life, culture and communications, and postmodernism. Each of these topics is studied as an arena for debate between competing theories rather than as a body of factual knowledge that can be taken as given. The text has no chapter devoted exclusively to women's issues. Such issues are treated as an integral part of human concerns and are given systematic attention in each chapter.

Each substantive chapter illustrates the close relationship between theory, method, and what is taken to be factual information. The theoretical perspectives focus on different aspects of a problem or conceptualize the nature of the problem in very different ways. Hence, the major critique of one approach or one body of data is to juxtapose it systematically with contrasting theories that search for different kinds of data. Throughout the text, the critique of ethnomethodology—that there can be no such thing as disembodied facts separate from the interpretive frameworks that give them meaning—is taken seriously. Feminist theory is similarly critical in showing that much that has been taken for objective information about humanity is in reality ideological, serving to cover up the experiences of half of humanity and to distort the experience of the other half.

The goal of the text is not to propound one theoretical perspective over others. Rather, the text presents substantive material in such a way that students can see how sociologists use their theories and their research techniques to investigate topics. It shows how the assumptions that underlie these different approaches systematically influence how questions are asked and what kind of data is sought. The ultimate aim is to challenge students to debate competing explanations and theories and so to encourage them to participate actively in sociology as critical readers of theory and research.

This second edition of *Controversies in Sociology* has been substantially revised to reflect theoretical advances since the last edition. Social constructionist theory and discourse analysis have gained prominence in contemporary Canadian sociology, emerging as distinctive approaches within interpretive theory that differ markedly from earlier symbolic interactionist theory. Feminist theory has also been changing rapidly, both in analytical clarity and in diversity of approaches. Traditional Marxist theory has evolved in new directions, particularly in the wake of the collapse of communist regimes in Eastern Europe. The pivotal second chapter that provides an overview of major theoretical perspectives in sociology has been rewritten to reflect these developments. The discussion of interpretive theory is now organized in subsections that focus on symbolic interaction, ethnomethodology, social constructionism, and discourse analysis, highlighting the distinctions between them. The overview of feminist theory has also been essentially rewritten to incorporate a more detailed discussion of analytical frameworks and diverse schools of thought. The section on political economy theory has also been substantially changed to give greater attention to the Marxist model of capitalism in this overview chapter and to introduce theoretical developments within Marxist thought. In this edition the perspective of traditional political economy theory is distinguished from broader Marxist and neo-Marxist theoretical work, which is often associated with constructionist and feminist analysis. All the subsequent chapters of the text have been revised, many of them radically, to show how these theoretical developments have influenced research in the different substantive areas.

This second edition introduces three new areas of research. Chapter 5 focusses on the burgeoning literature in gender relations. True to the format adopted throughout the text, the chapter critically compares research and analysis from functionalist, political economy, constructionist, and feminist perspectives. The new chapter 19 on culture and communications fills an important gap in the first edition. It contrasts the functionalist view of culture as an integrative force with the political economy view of hegemony and the manufacturing of consent, and controversial research in the areas of the social construction of meaning and feminist analysis of patriarchal cultural discourse. The following chapter 20 introduces postmodernism, with both critics and defenders offering their contradictory visions for the future of sociology.

Material carried over from the first edition has been substantially rearranged, with topics organized in relation to seven parts. The three chapters in Part I, *An Overview of Sociology*, introduce the sociological imagination, an overview of theories, and a critical look at methodologies. Part II, *Testing the Perspectives*, is designed to give students an earlier introduction to substantive research that utilizes the four major theoretical perspectives. It includes a revised version of the former chapter on the rural-urban debate and the new chapter on gender relations. Part III, *Social Cohesion and Order in Industrial Society*,

follows the first edition in focussing on Durkheim's contribution and competing theoretical perspectives on the study of suicide, religion, labour relations, and crime. Part IV, *Political Economy: Challenging Capitalism*, includes a chapter on the work of Karl Marx, a considerably shortened and updated analysis of the political economy of Canada, and concludes with the chapter on competing theories of international and Canadian economic development. Analyses of the implications of the North American Free Trade Agreements, and the restructuring of socialist economies are introduced here. Part V, *Rationality and Bureaucratic Society* brings forward the discussion of Weber's work and competing perspectives on bureaucracy. Part VI, *Traditional Theory Under Attack*, begins with the work of Talcott Parsons, followed by the four chapters on family, stratification, education, and race and ethnic relations. This last chapter has been the most radically revised to reflect major shifts in theoretical analysis. The text concludes with the new Part VII, *The Sociology of Knowledge*, which comprises Peter Weeks' original chapter on ethnomethodology and the microsociology of everyday life, as well as the two new chapters on culture and communications and postmodernism. Peter's chapter has been modified to shift most of the material on the social construction of gender to the new chapter 5 on gender relations.

All chapters in this second edition conclude with suggested readings and a list of ten questions designed as a study guide and foci for class discussions about materials in the chapter. A comprehensive essay and test bank has also been prepared for this edition by Norman Okihiro of the department of sociology, Mount Saint Vincent University.

PART I

An Overview of Sociology

The Sociological Imagination

What is **sociology**? A deceptively simple definition is that sociology sets out to investigate the happenings of human society. But, what exactly is **society**? It is not a tangible entity, a system that exists independently of the behaviours of the people who constitute it. Rather, it is the set of forces "exerted by people over one another and over themselves" (Elias 1970, 17). Sociology is concerned with the source and form of these forces. During certain periods, as when countries go to war, or when the economy collapses leaving hundreds of thousands of people adrift without jobs, forces may seem overwhelming, sweeping people along as helpless victims. Yet these are still human forces, pressures that people in groups bring to bear upon each other. Sometimes people resist, fighting back against such pressures and forcing changes. People continue to assert themselves, even within the most oppressive social institutions. Goffman (1961a) describes how a patient, stripped of almost all autonomy in a large, closed ward of an asylum,

still managed to assert himself against the system by urinating on the radiator—an ideal location for the act to produce maximum effect.

The Promise of Sociology

In a brilliant essay, C. Wright Mills (1959, ch. 1) notes that people are both victims and creators of society. He describes people's sense of ambivalence that stems from this dualism. Mills observes that people often believe that they are in a series of traps in their personal lives. They feel, often correctly, that they cannot overcome their personal problems. It seems that individuals do not control the forces that affect their lives. These forces are located far beyond the immediate, personal settings in which people live, and it is difficult for people to see beyond their own private reality: their jobs, their neighbourhoods, their families. The more that these threatening forces transcend their direct experience, the more trapped people feel. How do steel workers in Cape Breton feel when foreign companies stop building supertankers and the world market for steel founders? Or residents of a small Ontario town when its major employer, a multinational corporation, closes local operations and moves to the United States? Or parents who see their children's lives bombarded by war toys, pornography, drugs, sex, the threat of AIDS? All these forces are more or less beyond the immediate control of the people who are affected by them.

When we as individuals are faced with forces that we do not understand and cannot control, we often react by withdrawal. We retreat into our private lives, tell ourselves that the problems are not our responsibility, and try to forget them and get on with our own lives. When we cannot avoid the threats, we tend to react with fear, resentment, and hostility. Moral insensitivity can result from people's sense of being overwhelmed by historical changes that they do not understand and

that may challenge cherished values. This may help to explain a news item about a homeless old man who was set ablaze as he slept on a bench in an affluent Chicago neighbourhood. Middle-class residents had apparently become exasperated with having to face this dishevelled man every day and, unable to understand the forces that foster such poverty amid such affluence, they reacted violently to his presence.

The mass media bring coverage of worldwide upheavals into our living rooms on a daily basis. It is almost impossible to escape from a sense of overwhelming global crises that threaten to engulf us. We hear about the civil wars in the former Yugoslavia, Northern Ireland, the Middle East, Somalia, and Rwanda; we see political turmoil across Latin America and pervasive crises in developed as well as impoverished Third World countries. People fleeing from civil war, dictatorship, and persecution abroad seek refugee status in Canada almost daily. Still more come to escape grinding poverty at home, only to be faced with Canada's own unemployment problem.

The forces that led to the closure of the Newfoundland fishery lie far beyond the control of the individuals most affected.

Although the media increase our awareness, they do not necessarily increase our understanding of events. When we are unable to understand what is happening or why, we desperately try to interpret events in personal terms. Some people believe, for example, that the street people huddling over heating grates and lining up outside soup kitchens are inferior or lazy or alcoholic and could pull themselves up if they wanted to. They believe that riots are caused by a few trouble-makers, outside agitators who should be put in prison. But these individual explanations are inadequate.

People need much more than information to overcome their sense of being trapped. We live in the age of the information revolution, with satellite printing of national newspapers, instantaneous around-the-world coverage of events on radio and television, and a plethora of magazines. The media flood us with information, but they do not ensure that we have the capacity to handle it, make sense of it, and distinguish the reliable information from that which is misleading.

For C. Wright Mills, the special promise of sociology as a discipline is its capacity to process information. He uses the term the **sociological imagination** to describe "a quality of mind that will help [people] to use information and to develop reason in order to achieve lucid summations of what is going on in the world and of what may be happening within themselves" (Mills 1959, 5).

The basic assumption of sociology is that an individual's life chances are understandable only within a historical situation, through comparisons with the life chances of others in similar situations. One's chances of having a job, getting rich, dying from cancer, going to war, being a Catholic, a Buddhist, or an atheist, are socially situated. Sociology as a discipline tries to grasp the nature of the relationship between individual biography and social-historical forces within society. The way in which people tend to answer the question, "Who are you?"—in terms of their sex, age, profession, ethnicity—situates them on a social map. Given information about a couple's occupations and income, one can predict a great deal about them: where they live, what kind of home and furnishings they have, what they read, what music they listen to, how they speak, how they vote, even whether they prefer sex with the light on or off (Berger 1963, 80–81).

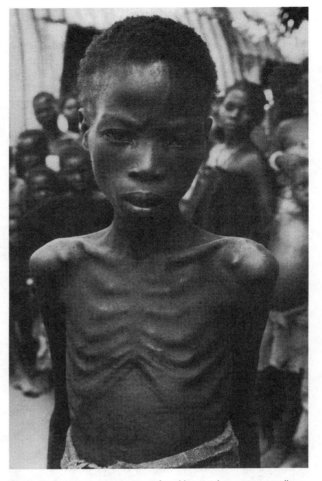

The media increase our awareness of world events but not necessarily our understanding of them.

According to Mills (1959, 6–7), the sociological endeavour entails three fundamental kinds of questions. The first category focusses on the structure of society: What is the structure of a particular society? What are its major parts? How are these—education, church, polity, economy—interrelated? How does Canada differ from other societies and why? All of us have immediate experience of how different elements of society affect each other. We know that the economy affects education, influencing decisions about whether to go to university or to take a job and about what course of studies to follow. Religion affects voting patterns, the number of children people have, the chance that a person will commit suicide. Work life affects family life, dictating the standard of living and also the time available for parenting. Canada differs from other societies in multiple ways. Some of these are immediately obvious, like the dependence of our economy on trends in the United States. Others, such as attitudes toward multiculturalism, social security, and federalism, are less obvious. The elements of our society interact in different ways from those of the rest of the world. Exploring how these relationships work is a major concern of sociology.

The second type of question turns on patterns of social change: Where does our society stand in human history? How did Canada get to be the way it is and how is it changing? How do events in Canadian history fit into the present situation? To answer such questions, one needs to dig deep into Canada's past as a colony of France and Britain to explore the kinds of people who settled here, the values that they brought with them, their relations with the old countries and with their neighbours in the more recent past. One must also try to understand the forces for change in contemporary Canada: the impact of the baby

Canada's history as a colony of France, and the Catholic values that missionaries brought with them, tell us much about contemporary Canada.

boom, feminism, increasing numbers of elderly people, and so on. Sociology looks both backwards and forwards in an effort to understand contemporary society.

The third type of question focusses on the characteristics of the people who form society: What kinds of women and men make up our society? How are people formed? How are they liberated and repressed? How are their sensitivities sharpened or blunted? What does the experience of years of unemployment do to young people who are out of work, and what does the constant fear of possible layoffs do to people who are working? The 1960s were known for hippies, flower power, and campus radicalism, but students of the 1990s seem more conservative and conformist than their earlier counterparts. Why? People fear that the sensitivities of children are being blunted by violence on television or excited in negative ways by war toys and pornography. The feminist movement seems in some respects to be radically altering the lives of women and men but, on the other hand, there are signs that many schoolgirls do not identify with the movement. Is this because feminism is only a passing fad, or because sensitivity to its message only comes with age? Sociology explores the multiple ways in which social experiences structure the characteristics of individual people.

The basic message of sociology is that our society has not always been the way it is, nor is it inevitably this way, and it probably will not be so in the future. For this reason alone, sociology can be deeply disturbing to people who benefit from the status quo and who do not want change or want it only in a particular direction.

An important distinction drawn in sociology is between **personal troubles** and **public issues** (Mills 1959, 8–10). Troubles stem from private matters that lie within an individual's character and immediate relations with friends and family. Issues, by contrast, go beyond the personal, local setting, to broader social forces that affect the life experiences of many people. An important part of learning to do sociology is learning to generalize from personal experience to broader social forces that this experience reflects. Consider unemployment. When only a few individuals are unemployed in a large city, it can reasonably be viewed as a private trouble, reflecting the particular problems of the unemployed individuals, and it can perhaps best be dealt with

Many kinds of women and men make up our Canadian society.

using an individual casework approach. But when 15 million people are unemployed out of a labour force of 50 million, for example, unemployment is a public issue. It cannot be solved by helping individual cases. The structure of opportunities has collapsed.

The student of sociology has to be able to shift perspectives—to switch from looking at the family to looking at politics or the economy—to see their interconnections. It is not an easy discipline. The sociological imagination frequently makes the ordinary world look incredible. We commonly think of family relations, for example, as part of our uniquely private lives. It comes as a shock to see how deeply these intimate relations are shaped by wider social forces.

Mills argues that it is the sociological imagination, the capacity to understand the relationships between elements of society and their impact on individual life chances that has become the central feature of modern society. It dominates how people think, how histories are written, the kinds of art we view and literature we read. Contemporary literature and art express the uneasiness that people feel, but they cannot provide answers, except insofar as they may suggest new ways of seeing. Science and technology remain powerful forces in society, but they are no longer central to how people think because they have failed us in important ways. In many respects, technology has conquered nature. We know how to get to the moon and beyond, how to create a human embryo

in a test tube, how to transmit thousands of conversations simultaneously on optical fibres. But technology has not solved our problems. It has become, instead, part of what traps us. It is the sociological imagination that seeks to explain social processes, the nature of our traps, and the underlying structural factors that give rise to them (Mills 1959, 14–15).

Sociology and the Scientific Ideal

Sociological explanations are more difficult and more elusive than explanations in the physical sciences because society is not a tangible, fixed entity ready for objective experimental research. The very sociological knowledge we generate is likely to alter the sets of relationships we are trying to study. In another sense, however, sociology may be easier and more rewarding than the physical sciences in that we ourselves are part of it, creators of the societies in which we live, able to understand social processes subjectively as participants in their production.

As a science, sociology is concerned fundamentally with the search for knowledge about society, but this search is both difficult and dangerous. It involves the study of people who, as members of a society, generate their own sense of truth about the social world. The kinds of ideas or ways of thinking that prevail in any society can be grouped into two categories. First, they take the form of **common-sense understandings**, or assumptions about how things work and why, based upon immediate experience. Secondly, they involve more coherent **ideologies**, or systems of values that justify certain kinds of actions or ways of life, sometimes to the detriment of the interests of other people. These ideologies strongly influence the way we see social reality. They tend to sensitize us in certain ways and to blind us in others.

Sociological analysis must typically confront and challenge ideologies. A major problem is that sociologists may be as blinded by ideologies as are other people, since they are themselves part of the society that they study, and they tend to accept the assumptions of people like themselves. Smith (1974a, 40) has conceptualized ideology, not as a specific set of beliefs, but as a biased *method* of inquiry that entails in its effects a systematic means *not* to know and *not* to see the situations of others. Given that sociologists are predominantly well-educated, reasonably well-paid professionals, and until recently were predominantly male, it should come as no surprise that the values of such people tend to be represented in sociology to a greater extent than those of less privileged people. Poorly educated women living on welfare or people working in unskilled jobs, for example, do not tend to publish in sociology journals. The scientific search for knowledge in sociology entails a major struggle to see past the taken-for-granted understandings and justifications of the professional middle-class world.

It is always easier to see through the ideologies of other groups than to see through one's own. The Nazi ideology of the superiority of the "Aryan race" has been widely discredited, but the ideology of capitalism and the work ethic are readily accepted by most Canadians as common-sense. The ideology of "free market" and "free trade," for example, implicitly justifies price wars to crush small competitors; the ideology of profit justifies charging higher prices to poor people who often do not have access to alternative markets; it justifies laying off employees when the going gets tough and charging high interest rates on money that poor people have to borrow. The ideology that effort and ability lead to success justifies labelling the unemployed as lazy or stupid. The Christian ideology that "man" was made in the image of God and given dominion over the beasts justifies the exploitation by humans of everything on the planet, and so on. It is important to remember, however, that we are

not merely blind victims of ideologies. We are also their creators and interpreters, and we can learn to analyse them, to challenge them, and to change them.

The major problem with common-sense interpretations of the world, and with most ideologies, is not that they are totally wrong, but that they can be biased and partial. Common-sense knowledge is inevitably self-centred. It tends to deal with very narrow individual concerns, not with the broader interests of other people in other situations. Common sense is incomplete, based on limited personal experience with only a hazy idea of what other people's lives are like. Ideology, too, has its limitations and can lead to intolerance. We often have a great deal invested in our beliefs, and it can be difficult to question and to change them, especially when change can have disturbing consequences. If we abandon the ideology that effort and ability lead to success, for example, it changes our responsibilities to the poor and the disadvantaged. We begin to feel uncomfortable about our own wealth and about the system that allows such discrepancies to exist.

Science attempts to provide explanations based upon impartial evidence. Impartiality is particularly difficult in the social sciences because people who are the subjects of research react to findings in a conscious way, and the theories themselves affect their behaviour. Even the physical sciences do not escape this social imprint because human society itself reacts with and alters the physical world. Socially learned values and ways of thinking also profoundly influence how research questions come to be asked.

In sociology, the problem of **objectivity** lies, in part, in the fact that sociologists cannot be impartial to what they study. Our own preconceptions and biases are hard to break. For example, sociologists commonly define prostitution as a social problem. There are, however, other ways of looking at the subject. From the perspective of the prostitutes themselves, the fact that powerful sectors of society define what they do as a "problem" makes their work vastly more difficult. One might instead see the "real" problem as the sexual frustration of the men who seek out prostitutes, or the fact that soliciting is illegal, which makes the prostitutes prey to protection rackets and pimps. Perhaps the problem is the double standard, which leads to the arrest and prosecution of prostitutes while their customers go free.

Perhaps there is no problem at all. Perhaps prostitution should just be seen as a service industry like any other and be left to operate freely as in the red light district of Amsterdam.

Notwithstanding the values of researchers, a measure of objectivity is possible in social science. At root, it is not the values that matter so much as the research methods used to collect the evidence. There are many different techniques, some of which are discussed in chapter 3. None of them guarantees the elimination of bias, but there are important principles of research that can reduce it.

It is relatively easy to find evidence to support an argument. Even stupid theses can usually be backed up by some examples. It is important, therefore, to test an argument by deliberately searching for information and evidence that, if found, would show the argument to be wrong. Consider, for example, a researcher who is interested in studying divorce because she strongly disapproves of it and feels that it harms children. Such a researcher could still provide impartial evidence by deliberately allowing for the reverse data, the possibility that dissolution of an unhappy marriage is a good thing for the children involved. A minimum requirement for such a study would be comparative data from four types of families: those where the parents describe themselves as happily married; those where the parents describe their marriage as unhappy but say that they intend to stay together for the children; divorced families that describe themselves as happier since the divorce; and divorced families that describe themselves as unhappier since the divorce. If data are gathered concerning children in all these sorts of families, the researcher allows for the possibility that children of divorced parents turn out to be happier and healthier than children living with parents in stressful, unhappy marriages. Useful research tests for the possibility that the researcher's starting assumptions might be wrong.

The important element here is reasoned procedure, the disciplined, rigorous collection of evidence that deliberately tests for the opposite of the initial assumptions. Good research, of course, will attempt much more than this. Given that divorce, like marriage, does not always bring the same results, it is important to explain the conditions under which different outcomes are likely. Again, the ideal is that explanations will be tested, rather than assumed and supported with only selective examples.

Three general principles are involved in all scientific practice, regardless of the particular theories and methodologies adopted. The first is the need for systematic and public accumulation of experience and observations. It involves a search for materials and the incorporation of a variety of people's experiences, not just those of one's own group. It is important to be clear about how the evidence was collected so that others can do similar research to check or challenge the results.

A second important principle of research is comparative investigation, incorporating data on people in different situations or different societies. A comparative focus is critically important in avoiding **ethnocentrism**, the tendency to assume that one's own group's way of doing things is more natural and proper than that of others. A sociological study of families, for example, might look at how family life is managed in other countries, other ethnic groups, or at other times in history. Through such comparative evidence, the study might explore the effects that different patterns seem to have on family members.

The third principle, and for philosophers of science the most important, is systematic doubt. Whatever the evidence looks like, it could be false, or misleading, or biased, or badly collected. Key factors may have been overlooked. Assumptions on which the research was based may turn out to be wrong. One may spend decades researching the effects of divorce upon children, only to conclude in the end that divorce is not the key issue at all—it is the poverty that so often accompanies divorce.

It can be very difficult to discover the "real" factors underlying a phenomenon. For example, in the Hawthorne experiment researchers spent three years studying the effects of illumination, rest pauses, and length of the working day on productivity of workers in a telephone assembly factory, only to conclude that these variables had next to nothing to do with productivity. The "real" factor was the attention that workers were getting from the researchers, which made each one feel valued instead of just one of a mass on the shopfloor (Mayo [1933] 1960). Sceptical researchers later disputed this result. They argued that the "real" factors influencing productivity were the onset of the economic depression of the 1930s and the desperate need of two of the five women in the experimental group for money to support large families when other relatives were unemployed (Carey 1967).

Facts can be elusive things. The ideal approach to an issue is to scrutinize the evidence, to question the theories and assumptions of any research, and to ask how the research was carried out and whether alternative strategies or additional data might have made the picture look different. Science is essentially a style of rigorous, systematic, critical thought, not a collection of facts to be memorized.

In sociological endeavour, controversy is critical. Given the biases and blind spots of researchers, the goal of systematic testing for the opposite of one's beliefs is often not attained. Researchers are often more concerned with supporting their theories than with testing them. Scientific journals are reluctant to publish articles that seem to show that starting assumptions were proven incorrect, as if it somehow meant that there must be something wrong with the research. For a long time, the assumption of differences between women and men was so strongly accepted that research that failed to substantiate behavioural differences between the sexes was simply discarded (Nicholson 1984, 4). It is important that research that challenges established theories, whether those of the researcher or of larger groups, be conducted and be available to other researchers.

Although it is essential that individual sociologists test their own data and theories, it is also important that the discipline encourages controversy among sociologists. When researchers disagree among themselves, it leads to a search for new evidence. New questions that might never have been thought of from one point of view can be brought forward by another researcher who started with different assumptions. Mutually incompatible assumptions provide the best challenge to each other. If your theory says that village life is happier and less isolating than cities, and my theory is that city life is best and villages are stifling, our combined evidence is likely to be the best test of each other's assumptions. This is true of all science, not merely the social sciences. The philosopher Feyerabend (1970) has argued that, whenever strong consensus emerges among a body of scientists that they have found the truth, the likely result will be **dogmatism**. More and more research will be done supporting the

same assumptions, and it will be increasingly difficult for anyone to come up with alternative theories. Evidence that might well show the errors in the dominant theory is likely never to come to light because no one will be looking for it. In effect, controversy or lack of agreement over theories in sociology is not a problem, but an asset. For Feyerabend, such controversy is a precondition for creative research.

Current sociology is in no danger of sinking into dogmatic consensus. As will be evident from the next chapter, there is no one theoretical approach that dominates sociological research, but rather a number of schools of thought that begin from very different assumptions and are often very critical of each other's work. To be valuable for science, however, controversy should be organized, not just shouted opinions. Organized controversy entails checking the assumptions of different perspectives and challenging them with alternative evidence. Clarity of basic assumptions is essential.

This textbook sets out to present the controversies of sociology in an organized way. The theories of classical sociologists are presented in detail. We explore their basic assumptions, the logic behind them, and the consequences or predictions to which they give rise. These consequences are then tested by looking at relevant evidence, drawn mostly from contemporary Canadian research. Controversy among different theorists is used to clarify the strengths and the limitations of different theoretical assumptions by comparing the research results from studies based on different perspectives.

As students, you are encouraged to react to, not to accept, the text. You should challenge arguments by examining their underlying assumptions, thinking up alternatives, and exploring counterevidence. The goal is to develop a capacity to shift perspectives and to question assumptions in a systematic way. Howard Boughey (1978, ix), in the introduction to his delightful little book *The Insights of Sociology*, comments that the beginning scholar in the Sanskrit tradition must have the capacity to be aware of eight things simultaneously. This text is not quite so ambitious: it explores only four approaches to a problem. The basic philosophy of the text is that it is more important for you to develop the capacity for **critical literacy** than to amass facts.

Suggested Reading

The best introduction to the study of sociology is still C. Wright Mills' essay "The Promise," found in his book *The Sociological Imagination* (1959). This essay is now three decades old, but it still conveys the conviction that we must first understand society in order to change it. We need to know what our society is like and be aware of the processes that are shaping it. Mills speaks of the promise of sociology to empower people to bring their hopes for a better world closer to reality.

An excellent and concise introduction to sociology, which is inspired by Mills' essay, is Anthony Giddens, *Sociology: A Brief but Critical Introduction* (1982). Giddens begins with an introduction to the sociological imagi-

nation and then shows how questions are raised concerning competing interpretations of industrial society or capitalism, and issues of class, the state, the city, family and gender, and capitalism. This short, readable book is a very good place to start in gaining a feel for sociology as a critical discipline.

Another book that gives a succinct, readable introduction to the discipline of sociology is Peter Berger, *Invitation to Sociology: A Humanistic Perspective* (1963). Berger describes how people actively create their social world through interaction. He introduces many of the issues and approaches to sociology that we examine in this text.

Questions

1. In the view of C.W. Mills, what critical problem might underlie widespread evidence of cruel and insensitive behaviour?

2. What does Mills see as the central problem with mass media as sources of news?

3. What does Mills see as the special promise of the sociological imagination?

4. According to Mills, what three fundamental questions are central to sociology?

5. Why is the science of sociology potentially much easier than natural sciences such as physics?

6. Why is the science of sociology potentially much more difficult than natural sciences such as physics?

7. Summarize the two meanings of *ideology*— the general meaning and that proposed by Smith.

8. List the three critical requirements of science.

9. In what sense can controversies in science be considered an advantage rather than a sign of confusion and ignorance?

10. What is the distinction in sociology between personal troubles and public issues?

CHAPTER

An Overview of Theories

The relationship between individuals and the society in which they live has given rise to very different understandings of how social reality is maintained and reproduced over time. This chapter presents an overview of the major contemporary approaches to sociology, their assumptions, and the differences and similarities among them. Their comparative strengths and limitations are examined through critical questions that sociologists, inspired by different approaches, have directed toward each other. Different perspectives start with different problems, ask different questions, see and ignore different things. It is important to try to understand how they complement each other, to learn to challenge the contradictions, and thus to explore for the truth. However deep the differences between approaches, all share the same fundamental concern with developing our knowledge of the character of social life.

Controversies in Sociological Thought

This chapter's overview of approaches to sociology begins with a consideration of the two concepts of **structure** and **agency**. This discussion helps to pull together the diverse approaches to sociology as interrelated aspects of the same complex field of study, however different they might seem from each other at first reading. We then examine four major perspectives in sociological theory, beginning with the classical approach of functionalism, or systems theory, which focusses primarily upon the question of order. The second approach we examine is political economy theory, which challenges the notion of **equilibrium** and **order** in society. The next broad perspective, which is loosely called interpretive sociology, encompasses various approaches that focus less on the large-scale system and structures of society than on how individuals create their social reality in ongoing interaction. The last perspective, feminist theory, offers a radical critique of the male-centred biases built into virtually all existing approaches to mainstream or "male-stream" sociology.

Structure and Agency: The View of Sociology as History

A perennial problem in sociology is reconciling two seemingly contradictory views of people. Proponents of one perspective see people as agents who choose between different courses of action and so consciously create their social world. Advocates of the other approach see people as part of a **social system**, an existing set of structures that constrains and in many ways determines their actions. We have a sociology of *action* and a sociology of *systems* and tend to shuffle uneasily between the two. Some theorists stress free human actions and choice, while others stress how the structures of society determine people's lives. When these alternative views are pushed to their extremes, they appear to be so different that it is hard to see how they could be reconciled or even how they could be part of the same discipline of sociology. Even words like *society*, *social structure*, and *social system* are used in such different ways that definitions favoured in one approach are hotly disputed in the other.

The goal of theorists such as Abrams and Giddens is to bridge these two extremes by rethinking the relationship between human agency and deterministic social systems. They do so by giving central attention to the passage of time in their analysis of social action. In essence, they argue for a view of sociology as history, or **historical sociology**. Abrams (1982) refers to the concept of "processes in time" while Giddens (1979) refers to the "*durée* [continuance] of human agency." They both argue that human actions produce the structures of society that people later experience as constraining or deter-

mining their actions, e.g., "the capitalist system." Abrams and Giddens accept the classical Marxist notion that we make our own history, but not in circumstances of our own choosing. They emphasize the critical point that these circumstances were produced by other people, or perhaps even by ourselves, through choices made at earlier points in time. When social theorists focus on a narrow, fixed period of time, it makes sense to analyse human actions as constrained by social structures. But, given a longer time frame, we see that these structures were themselves produced by human actions.

The dilemma of whether to think of human actions as free or as determined is resolved by recognizing that, within historical time, human actions are shaped by prior human actions. Structures comprise actions taken collectively in the past. Actions produce structures for the future. What we choose to do now will shape the circumstances that our children inherit.

Giddens and Abrams maintain that explanations based on this idea of human agency over time holds for all levels of analysis, both sweeping historical changes such as the rise of industrialization, as well as intimate **microhistories** of interaction at the level of factories and schools, families and friends. Individual actions are moments in a sequence of actions, not isolated events. Even conversations can be thought of as historical

The rise of industrialization reflects the interdependence of human agency and deterministic social structures.

processes in that what one person says only makes sense in terms of what someone else previously said.

This broad conception of the interdependence of social structures and individual actions is generally accepted in sociology, but with deeply divergent views of its implications for analysis. A host of secondary questions arise as we try to apply the formula to develop explanations for social behaviour (Sharrock 1987, 126–27). We might agree that human beings make history, but this begs the question of how far and in what ways is this true? On the one hand, we could say that the weight of accumulated history and social constraints is such that people only have a marginal capacity to influence anything. On the other hand, we could hold that human beings are capable of overcoming the limitations of the circumstances they find themselves in and reshaping those circumstances. Either way, we come up against another set of difficult questions. It is all very well to say that human beings are dominated by their circumstances, but we still have to show how this works. Just how do circumstances, or history, or environments dominate people? If we take the more optimistic view that people are not just victims of circumstances, but are capable of overcoming their situations and actively making their own lives, then we have to show how they are able to do this.

The four major perspectives in current sociology struggle with the yin and the yang of structure and agency, and propose very different models. Functionalist and political economy perspectives give greater emphasis to the social world as comprised of structures that people can influence in only limited ways at any one time, and that constrain human agency into a narrow range of choices. The interpretive perspective gives greater emphasis to human agency, especially to the meanings that people bring to the circumstances in which they find themselves. The range of choices that people have are constrained more by how they come to understand and interpret their situation than by the weight of historical organization of the circumstances they encounter. Feminist theory draws on both these traditions. On the one hand, the theory draws attention to the crushing power of social structures to limit women's lives, but at the same time it reinterprets and undermines these structures and points the way to radical social change.

Functionalism: Society as a System

Classical functionalist analysis in sociology was first modelled on the science of biology. Society is seen as a **system** of interrelated parts, existing within an environment, much as a biologist might view an organism. The terms **systems theory** or **structural functionalism** are commonly used to refer to this approach.

Structural functionalism has a long history. It grew out of the work of the founding fathers of the discipline of sociology, particularly Comte, Spencer, and Durkheim. Its development in contemporary sociology is identified with Talcott Parsons. The individual contributions of these theorists are explored in later chapters, particularly chapter 6 on cohesion and morality and chapter 13 on Parsonian functionalism. Here we give brief summaries of their basic ideas as a background to understanding **functionalism**.

Auguste Comte (1798–1857) lived and worked in Paris just after the French Revolution. He shared with Hobbes a concern with the need for order and structure. He is widely regarded as the father of sociology. He first coined the term *sociology* and tried to establish it as an independent science of social systems. He viewed sociology as the last great science developed after biology. Comte originated a model of the evolution of societies, suggesting that they evolved through theological, military, and industrial stages, much as biological organisms passed through evolutionary stages from fish and reptiles to birds and mammals.

Herbert Spencer (1820–1903), writing in the very different context of capitalist expansion following the American Civil War, carried Comte's early ideas on the evolution of societies much further. He analysed the development of industrial society in terms of evolutionary processes of adaptive selection and the **survival of the fittest**. Spencer's ideas made him extremely popular with the emerging business class because business people liked to think of themselves as the best adapted members of the human species, dominating the social world since they were the fittest to do so.

Emile Durkheim (1858–1917) shared this fascination with the scientific study of the evolution of industrial society and its special characteristics as a system. He was especially concerned with understanding the moral basis of order in industrial society. He viewed morality as the essential mechanism that maintained the stability of a social system. His work has had a much more profound impact on contemporary sociology than that of either Comte or Spencer.

Within functionalist theory, however, it is undoubtedly Talcott Parsons (1902–1979) who ranks as the central figure, sometimes described as the high priest of American sociology. Parsons systematized the work of many early sociologists in his *The Structure of Social Action* ([1937] 1968) and *Essays in Sociological Theory* (1949) and then went on to develop his own abstract model of society as a functioning system. He stressed that society could be studied as an operating system viewed at one point in time, without concern for evolution, origin of parts, or even developmental processes. His goal was to elaborate an abstract model of society that would provide a framework for systematic and comparative social science.

Basic Assumptions of Functionalist Theory

The basic unit of functionalist analysis is society, conceptualized as a system that has identifiable needs that must be met for it to continue in a healthy, balanced state, and a set of specific structural arrangements for meeting these needs. In an early statement of the foundations of functionalist theory, Aberle et al. offer the following definition of society: "A society is a group of human beings sharing a self-sufficient system of action which is capable of existing longer than the life-span of an individual, the group being recruited at least in part by the sexual reproduction of the members" (1950, 100). Smaller social systems, such as a monastery, a church or a town, exist as parts of a wider society but do not meet all the critical conditions of recruitment through sexual reproduction of its members or self-sufficiency as systems of action. Aberle et al. suggest that four critical conditions would lead to the termination of a society as defined: the biological extinction or dispersion of the members; apathy or cessation of motivation of members; the war of each against all; or lastly absorption into another society. The four conditions that

would lead to the death of a society also imply the conditions needed for a society to survive.

Using these conditions and a theory of human action elaborated by Parsons, the authors suggest a set of functional prerequisites that any society has to meet to continue as a going concern.

1. Any society must physically sustain its members by working with the nonhuman environment, and must pattern heterosexual relationships to ensure a sufficient rate of reproduction. It must also deal with other societies in its environment to permit the persistence of its own system of action.

2. Any society has activities that must be done regularly and dependably and this requires that they be broken down and assigned to capable individuals trained and motivated to carry them out. Hence all societies require some system of role differentiation and role assignment. The two critical problems of scarcity and need for order seem impossible to handle without unequal distribution of resources and authority to get things done. It is also essential that the mass of people in a society accept such inequality as legitimate, if stability is to be maintained rather than permanent conflict.

3. A system of communication is essential for such differentiation to function adequately.

4. Members also need a shared cognitive orientation to make stable, meaningful, and predictable the social situations in which they are engaged.

5. Members need a shared, articulated range of goals. Without such shared definitions and goals the inevitable result would be mutually incompatible actions, failure to perform all socially necessary activities, extreme levels of frustration, and internal fighting.

6. Any society must also determine how its goals are to be met by regulating socially acceptable means.

7. It must also regulate the emotions or affective expression of members. Emotions need to be mutually communicable and comprehensible to allow stable expectations between members. Certain destructive emotions must be suppressed or repressed. Ungoverned expression of lust and rage, for example, would disrupt relationships and lead ultimately to the

war of each against all. Other emotions must be fostered, particularly affection within families to ensure their survival and the nurturing of young people.

8. A critical problem for the long-term survival of any society is to ensure that its structure of action is learned by new members. Each individual must learn the appropriate modes of dealing with the total situation, the modes of communication, shared cognitive frames of reference, goal systems, attitudes involved in the regulation of means, modes of emotional expression, and the like, so as to be capable of adequate performance in life roles. This learning process is called *socialization.*

9. Lastly, any society must ensure the effective control of disruptive forms of behaviour.

In summary, this list of prerequisites serves as a guide for constructing a theory that tells us how functional needs may be met and provides a basis for comparing the structure and functioning of specific societies. Talcott Parsons' work addresses how a society is organized to ensure that functional needs are met.

When one starts with a notion of society as the basic unit of analysis, the questions that arise are how large numbers of individual people come to be integrated into the system, and how this integration can be smoothly perpetuated from one generation to another so that a stable, orderly society is maintained. The twin concepts of **roles** and **socialization** provide the answers. As noted above, role differentiation is a functional prerequisite for society. Within the functionalist model of society, roles are analysed in terms of how they perform their functions for the society of which they are a part. Organized collections of interacting roles constitute the **institutions** of society—a university, a school, a family, a church. These organized relations can be analysed in terms of functional subsystems of society, such as the educational system, the child-care system, the economic system, the administrative system, and so on. Particular institutions may have multiple functions in different subsystems of action. Schools, for example, are part of the child-care system, the education system, and the economic system. The same is true of families.

People are seen as **actors** or role-players within a system of roles. An actor's position or **status** is set by the social context. The important feature of social roles in functionalist theory is that they are seen as existing independently of any single actor. They are predefined, and new generations of role-incumbents are trained to fit them. This does not mean that all people play the same role in exactly the same way, but rather that the role itself has typical aspects that are common to all incumbents, regardless of individual idiosyncrasies. It is this typicality that makes **social order** possible and ensures continuity from one generation to another.

Roles vary in the degree of detail with which they are laid down. Bureaucratic work roles are generally defined in the highest detail and require exact conformity. A job description, for example, sets out what the incumbent must do. If he or she does it willingly, all is well, but if not, then rules are invoked to force compliance. The role of motherhood is much vaguer, but there are still set minimums. A mother must clean, feed, and clothe her children and get them to school every day. If not, social workers will intervene to force closer compliance with society's minimum expectations. The role of professor includes expectations that the incumbent will arrive on time, come prepared, lecture for set periods of time, and not be drunk. Students are expected to attend classes, not to talk privately during the lecture, or at least not loud enough for others to hear them, and so on. The **norms** or standards associated with being a student are much more flexible than those required of a professor. Role interactions between professors and students are also defined very differently from those among students themselves. Sexual advances between professor and student, for example, are proscribed, while flirting among students is permitted and even expected.

Sets of roles are the sum of the roles with which one actor interacts. For example, a school teacher, in the performance of the teacher role, interacts with students, the school principal, other teachers, the school board, and parents. All have expectations of the teacher role, and one can locate the job in the centre of these overlapping expectations. The sum of all the patterned role interactions constitutes the **social system**. At the other extreme, the **personality system** comprises the system that integrates the different roles that one person plays, both simultaneously and throughout life. Research into this system is the domain of psychology.

Society must motivate people to play their allotted roles and to meet the typical expectations for minimal role performance. Berger (1963, 68–78) refers to **circles of social control** to describe the mechanisms by which such conformity is produced (see figure 2-1). The innermost circle, and probably the most powerful, is guilt. We come to want to conform, to see conformity as morally proper, and nonconformity makes us feel guilty. For most of our social roles, most of our lives, this internalized sense of guilt may be all that is necessary to ensure conformity.

Figure 2-1

Circles of Social Control

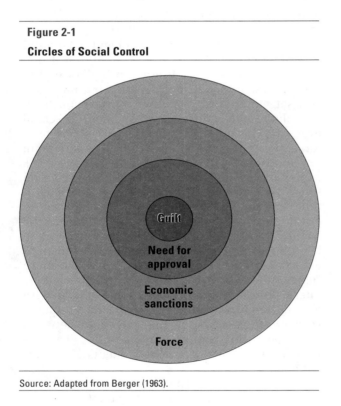

Source: Adapted from Berger (1963).

Closely supporting these innermost feelings are our relations with family and friends, our primary group. Because our relationships with these people matter to us, we usually want to conform to their expectations. We feel unhappy if we disappoint them by not playing our roles in relation to them in ways that they have come to expect. Only when these intimate pressures fail, or in more impersonal aspects of our lives where friendship ties are not involved, do more formal societal sanctions come into play. These may be economic

sanctions, in that we may risk losing our jobs or not being hired if we do not conform at least minimally to the expectations that employers have of us. Students who do not do assignments or perform in class as expected will not pass the course and will face sanctions of not being eligible for promotion or for jobs that require such courses. In such cases we conform out of economic self-interest, meeting role demands so that other needs of our own are met. As a last resort, formal sanctions and laws punish those who refuse to conform minimally to the expectations of others as to how roles must be played.

The process by which people in society learn new roles is called **socialization**. As children, we learn primarily by watching and emulating our parents. Later we learn by watching and playing teacher and the many other roles that we encounter. Because we want others to approve of us, we come to want to behave in ways that earn their approval. Reciprocally, we tend to give approval to others who behave in their roles as we expect them to. This learning and **internalization** process is most intense during childhood, when almost all roles are new, but it continues throughout life. As adults, we learn our job roles both by formal training and by on-the-job learning through watching and emulating others. Even in old age we learn to retire, sometimes taking courses on retirement in which we are trained in what to expect and how to cope. In the final analysis, what we are as people is constituted by the sum of all the social roles we play. Certain roles are more important in defining our identity than others. Traditionally, men have been defined by their work roles, and women by their wife-mother roles. We all play many other roles simultaneously, but they are tailored to fit these dominant roles.

Through internalization we become the role, and it becomes part of us, part of our identity. Playing a role becomes not merely a set of learned behaviours or doing what is expected of us. It becomes a duty. Being a good doctor, a good mechanic, or a good student becomes central to our sense of ourselves. Our body image, our **presentation of ourselves** is intimately tied to the roles we play. It is frequently possible to tell what work people do just by looking at them.

The centrality of jobs to self-identity in our society is especially apparent when we change work roles. People who change their jobs tend to change their personalities as well to better conform to new role expectations. For example, a private who is newly promoted to the rank of officer may initially feel embarrassed before his old peers. But a new uniform, new terms of address, and new expectations of others all work towards him coming to see himself as an officer. Before long he not only comes to expect a salute from former friends, but to feel angry if such deference is not shown (Lieberman 1956). Stages in life that entail major changes in role sets are often marked by public ceremonies. Marriage ceremonies, graduation days, ceremonial investitures into higher ranks, all mark role transfers and serve as rites of passage into new lifestyles.

Marriage ceremonies mark major role transfers and serve as rites of passage into new lifestyles.

Over a lifetime, a person performs a series of roles that mark the passage of time. You may begin life within your family as a baby, but very quickly you become younger sibling, older sibling, child-minder, daughter or son, spouse, parent, breadwinner, grandparent, retiree. We play multiple roles that overlap, such as career and family roles. The sum of all these roles together constitutes the social self. Research in the **role-theory** tradition studies individual role sets, the expectations associated with roles, systems of roles as they interrelate, and the socialization processes by which roles are learned and internalized throughout life. Another area that is studied by role theorists is **role strain**. Role strain can occur when different actors in a system of roles have conflicting expectations of what a particular role entails or when an individual experiences conflict within personal roles, such as between career and parental roles.

Culture and Role Integration

Each social role is recognizable as a set of unique behavioural expectations or norms, but there are also broader patterns of expectations that many roles have in common. The overarching **values** of a society or collectivity of people constitute a **culture**, the set of shared ideas about what comprises appropriate behaviour within a given society. People may not always live up to these values, but they generally know what they are and tend to use them to evaluate their own behaviour and the behaviour of others. It is through culture that a society meets the functional requirements of shared cognitive orientation, shared sets of goals, and socially accepted regulation of means, and of emotions, that ensure the long-term stability of the society. Through internalizing the culture of a community, actors are already aware of appropriate patterns of behaviour even before learning details of specific roles.

A culture serves to integrate roles within a society and to minimize friction between them. When roles have very different values, such as work roles requiring aggressive, competitive behaviour, and family roles requiring supportive and co-operative behaviour, they are typically separated both in time and space. People perform work roles at one time of day in one context and family roles at another time and in another place. Alternatively, mothers with young children at home may give up paid work altogether to devote themselves full-time to nurturing roles while fathers devote the major part of their days to earning money.

A culture typically includes ideals concerning appropriate masculine and feminine behaviour, ideals that tend to circumscribe behaviour, from early childhood through to old age. Such ideals can become an influential part of our self-concepts. We deviate from these generalized values only with difficulty and with considerable insecurity and fear of disapproval and/or sanctions from friends and elders. In our culture, fathers are typically expected to be breadwinners and mothers to be homemakers, whatever other roles they might have. A man who would like to be a full-time homemaker is likely to face considerable ridicule from other males, and indeed from females as well. Conversely, if a home is not kept clean to the level of conventional standards it is typically the woman who will be blamed. Women who do not want to become mothers often face strong criticism from relatives.

Subgroups within a society tend to develop distinctive subsets of values or **subcultures**, typically related to the dominant roles that they play. Durkheim argued that occupational specialization necessarily produces cultural diversity, even without major differences in ethnic background. As societies become more complex and differentiated in terms of occupational roles, so subcultural differences become more common. Members of such occupational subcultures share **dominant values** with the rest of society but differ on important subsets of values. Jazz musicians, for example, develop a jazz-linked subculture of values. Within this subculture, musicians value spontaneity, reject the 9-to-5 work ethic, wear unconventional clothes, have an intense commitment to playing music, and sometimes take illicit drugs (Becker 1963, 85–100). Such values set the musicians apart from the rest of society and help to confirm their identity as a distinct subgroup. Outsiders tend to expect them to behave differently from the average person. These expectations help to reinforce distinctive behaviour. It can take a long time to learn the elements of a subculture. First-year students who live in residence, for example, may spend more time learning the student subculture than learning coursework.

A particular form of subculture is that associated with ethnic minorities. Typically, such subcultures share a dominant set of values with the wider society and share norms concerning public work roles. But they have distinctive subcultural values in terms of the family and religion, and perhaps in dress and food habits. The degree of subcultural differences may vary from minor aspects of private life to broad patterns of private and public behaviour that serve to set one group

of people apart from the majority. The term *assimilation* denotes the process of change as individuals or groups of people lose their distinctive minority group patterns of behaviour and adopt the norms and values of the majority. Learning a new language or a new jargon is a major step in this transition, which might also include changes in dress, family relations, and so on.

Ethnic minorities have distinctive subcultural values.

Individual roles constitute the lowest or most personal level of the social order. At a higher level, sets of roles combine into institutions, or established patterns of action organized around a central function. Institutions in a sociological sense constitute typical ways of **structuring** social relations. The institution of the family, for example, constitutes the typical role relations between relatives. In some instances, family boundaries may take in "adopted" aunts and uncles who are treated as kin. The institution of a university comprises a set of roles including those of professors, students, secretaries, administrators, cooks, and caretakers. It is embedded in a broader set of roles that constitutes the education system.

Sets of institutions and the socially accepted ways of regulating relations among them constitute the social system as a whole. Each member institution has a distinct set of social functions and together they fulfil the overall system requirements. The institution of the family produces and nurtures young people and socializes them into adult roles. Economic institutions produce and distribute goods and integrate occupational roles. Political institutions set common beliefs in the legitimacy of power structures and organize collective goals. Religious institutions reinforce moral values, which integrate roles. The education system builds on the specialized role of family by socializing young people, teaching adult role skills, and reinforcing collective values. Administrative and legal systems serve to integrate institutions and to discourage noncompliance with collective values.

Institutions change primarily by becoming more specialized and differentiated from each other. In simple societies, the family may perform almost all social functions but, in complex industrial societies, families specialize in nurturing roles while most other functions are performed by specialized institutions outside the family.

The functions of some institutionalized patterns may not always be immediately obvious (Merton 1967, 73–138). Largely unrecognized or **latent functions** may occasionally be more important than the more obvious or **manifest functions**. Veblen (1928, 25), for example, has pointed out that the manifest function of buying all kinds of expensive or luxurious goods is the enjoyment that comes from using them. Such goods as Rolls Royce cars, caviar, and rare art serve the manifest functions of mobility, satisfaction of hunger, and ornamentation. But the latent reason why many people buy such goods is **conspicuous consumption**: not direct gratification, but a desire to demonstrate their wealth to others and so enhance their social status. The manifest function of funerals is to bury the dead, but their more important latent function is to bring family members together to reinforce the identity and solidarity of the family in the face of loss that might otherwise tear it apart. The manifest function of magic rituals, such as blessing the boats of fishermen before they set off, is to appease the gods, but their latent function may be to relieve anxiety (Merton 1967, 88).

In summary, the systems approach to sociology sees society in a form analogous to an organism, comprising interrelated parts that perform specialized functions for the whole. These parts, or institutions, in turn are made up of interrelated sets of roles that are learned through socialization. Social order requires that most actors within the society be motivated to fulfil their roles adequately and that they share a culture that defines the minimum expectations for proper behaviour. The reactions of others, of approval or disapproval, and an internalized sense of guilt, serve to keep most people conforming most of the time. Harsher control mechanisms of force and coercion are used only as a last resort. Social systems are normally in a state of **dynamic equilibrium**; that is, a state of orderly self-regulation and replication in relatively stable form over generations. Parsons explicitly identifies his model as a **voluntaristic theory** of society in which individual agency and choice behaviour are central features. Society as a system functions because individuals are motivated to fulfil their expectations of each other.

The systems perspective is the dominant approach to sociology in North America. The major kinds of research done in this tradition tend to centre on the study of specialized institutions such as family, education, religion, ethnic relations, and so on. Research is strongly empirical and is particularly associated with a survey approach and with the analysis of cultural norms and values as they influence social behaviour. The research also tends to emphasize **positivism**, a scientific approach that bases conclusions upon evidence that is taken to be objective, factual, and subject to statistical testing.

Political Economy Theory: The Problem of Conflict

Political economy theory, also widely referred to as Marxist theory or **conflict theory**, begins from different assumptions than functionalism and generates a very different model of society and social processes. It is strongly identified with the work of Karl Marx (1818–1883). Although born in Germany, Marx did most of his writing in England. His first-hand observation of the suffering of working-class people in nineteenth-century London inspired him to write *Capital*, his famous critical analysis of the prevailing economic system known as capitalism.

This approach to sociology takes as its point of departure the basic premise that people must produce in order to live. As Marx expresses it, "life involves before everything else eating and drinking, a habitation, clothing and many other things" (Marx and Engels [1846] 1970, 48). The first historical act by people is thus the production of the means to satisfy these needs, the production of material life itself. The relations of this production form the privileged starting point for analysis of society (Frisby and Sayer 1986, ch. 5). Production involves two kinds of relations, natural and social. Firstly, the natural resources available form basic constraints on all human existence. Through the labour process, people work with the aid of instruments of production of one sort or another, to transform natural raw materials into products that meet their needs. Secondly, production involves relations among people. People produce through working together in specific ways and by exchanging their activities. The totality of these relations of production constitute the foundations of society, out of which political structures arise. The natural resources, the production tools available, and the ways in which production has been organized, have varied in significant respects, giving rise historically to very different forms of society. As production technologies advanced, people were able to produce a surplus over their immediate subsistence needs. Control over this surplus production, and how surplus labour is extracted from the direct producers, constitute, for Marx, the **class** relations of society, the basis of inequality. From this material base emerges the prevailing system of laws and values, or the **superstructure** of society.

Political economy theory thus starts with the study of prevailing economic relations and works outwards to understand all other aspects of social life. Marx's writings focussed particularly on the analysis of capitalism as a mode of production. His ideas are explored in depth in a later chapter of this text. Here we will sketch only a broad framework, as a guide to understanding political economy analysis in sociology.

Marx saw the capitalist mode of production as an inherently inegalitarian system. Society is divided into two great classes, those who own the means of industrial production—the **capitalists** or **bourgeoisie**—and those who do not—the wageworkers or **proletariat**. There is a smaller intermediate class of business people or the **petite bourgeoisie**, comprising those who have sufficient means of production to work for themselves, but who hire few employees beyond their own family members. Wageworkers, who make up by far the majority of people in capitalist economies, compete for jobs on the basis of whatever skills and abilities they can offer. They are paid wages but what they produce through their labour belongs to their employers. The gap between the value of wages paid to them and the market value of the products they have made constitutes the surplus value or profits that accrue to their employer.

Capitalists compete in the market to sell the commodities produced. There is a built-in incentive to increase profits by reducing labour costs, especially by investment in labour-saving technology. The most innovative capitalists can thus reduce the unit costs of their commodities, and undercut competitors in the market. Those capitalists who fall behind in technological development risk bankruptcy.

This process has contradictory effects. The tremendous technological innovation generated within capitalist societies has resulted in an exponential increase in productive capacity, and an abundance of goods that have materially raised the living standards of workers. But it comes at a high cost. Wealth, and thus the capacity to invest in still better technology is highly concentrated. Weaker capitalists struggle to stave off bankruptcy when they cannot keep up with technological change. Labour-saving technology results in recurring cycles of severe structural unemployment, competition for jobs, and falling average wages. Rising unemployment in turn creates crises of overproduction, as purchasing power falls across the market. Capitalists cut back production, or strive to produce cheaper goods with even less labour input, and recession results. These great disparities in wealth and recurring cycles of booms and slumps cause enormous insecurity and suffering for many people. People who live in impoverished Third World countries, or in peripheral regions, experience the worst exploitation. For the most part they can compete in world markets only by offering cheap labour and cheap raw materials to industrialized capitalist centres. They are caught in a vicious trap from which it is very difficult to escape.

Marx argued further that societies and world economies that are based on such inequality would be inherently unstable, tending not towards equilibrium as in the functionalist model, but towards conflict and change. Members of the disprivileged class, who do not own the means of

People who live in impoverished Third World countries experience capitalism's worst exploitation.

production, have a permanent reason to pressure for change. Marx saw the history of all societies as the history of class struggle. From this perspective the French Revolution can be understood as the struggle of landless peasants to take land away from the nobility. In capitalist societies the class of propertyless labourers has most to gain from the overthrow of the owners of capital. Marx suggested that this might be the final battle of history. With the collective ownership of all means of industrial production within a communist system, the last major source of class conflict would be eliminated. Social equilibrium based on genuine consensus might then be possible.

In more recent formulations of political economy theory the Marxist concept of class has been modified to take into account other kinds of resources, including specialized skills that give people more bargaining power in the labour market. Skills can be seen as a form of means of production in their own right. Middle-class professionals have very different experiences from unskilled manual workers when they seek employment, and they generally command higher incomes. In other respects, however, the underlying class relations remain unchanged. Even pro-

fessionals are still at the mercy of employers who want their services. In the 1980s, as big oil companies curtailed their activities, Canada saw the crisis of unemployment hitting professional workers such as geologists, scientists, and managers in the oil industry. During the hard recession of the 1990s, professionals in many fields were made redundant as a result of "lean and mean" corporate restructuring. Highly educated people found themselves competing for limited numbers of insecure, contract jobs. In the crunch, class differences based on skills may be more apparent than real, and more tenuous than many middle-class people care to think.

To the extent that there are shared values and expectations in an unequal society, **consensus** is likely to be manipulated rather than freely adopted. A central tenet of political economy theory is that the prevailing or **dominant culture** of a given society is the values of the dominant class. Within capitalism this is the class of capitalists or big business. Stinchcombe (1968, 108–17) points to a number of mechanisms through which people in powerful positions perpetuate their values among succeeding generations with more success than their opponents. Members of the dominant class may control the socialization process by influencing both school curricula and the appointment of teachers, clergy, and other influential people. They may be able to determine not only the rules governing how subsequent incumbents must perform in prescribed roles but also the kinds of people who will or will not be permitted to take up important jobs. As successful figureheads of society, they are more likely to attract hero worship and serve as **role models** for the younger generation. They are in a better position than others to influence the content of mass media, either because they own media outlets directly or because they control the advertising revenues on which such outlets depend. As noted in chapter 1, disprivileged people such as the ill-educated and the unemployed rarely write books. They may well have conflicting values concerning what is functional or dysfunctional for the mass of people, but they are scarcely in a position to shape the knowledge and values of many other individuals. The powerful people, at any given time, are those whose actions can determine the kind of structures that a society will have. The more powerful a class, the more influential it is as a cause of social structures (Stinchcombe 1968, 94).

The concept of **alienation** is central to political economy theory. People experience alienation when they feel powerless to control central aspects of their lives, such as how to make a living; when they are forced into work that is demeaning or is meaningless to them; when they are exploited by being paid less for their labour than the true value of what they produce. At the individual level this alienation is experienced as a sense of entrapment.

Unequal power relations are evident even in intimate interpersonal relations. A wife who is economically dependent upon her husband may find herself constantly deferring to his wishes over her own. Girls may defer to the wishes of their boyfriends because the boys have more money to pay for a night out. In our society, young people remain under the authority of their parents until well beyond puberty because our economy is not set up in a way that allows adolescents to provide for themselves. Recession makes all of these problems worse.

Political Economy and Functionalism

The vision of society that emerges from political economy analysis is very different from the stable and orderly system conceptualized within functionalism. The crucial explanatory variable becomes, not internalized norms and values, but organized relations of power that determine access to and control over the important resources of a society. This focus leads to the study of asymmetrical relationships and hierarchies of power and dependency. Inequality, injustice, and the resulting conflict, competition, aggression, and war, are as much features of society as is peaceful co-operation.

Political economy theory shares with functionalism a general conception of interrelated sets of roles at the level of interpersonal relations, but it draws attention to the frequently forced character of role incumbency, and the marked inequality in prestige and social and financial rewards that accrue to different roles. Factory workers, for example, often find themselves trapped in dull, routine work that offers little intrinsic interest and few other rewards. Worse still, they may find themselves trapped in unemployment, their energies and skills not wanted by local employers. Young women in small mining towns, where there are few jobs for women, are forced into marriage and the role of dependent wife because nothing else is available. Internalization of the values and expectations of roles seems at best inadequate to explain the behaviour of such people. At worst, such an explanation constitutes a cruel distortion of these people's situations in life. It covers up what is really happening to people. The fact that people have few if any viable options in life can be masked by the argument that they do what they do because they have internalized the appropriate values.

Within the political economy framework, evidence of subcultural differences in values and attitudes are analysed in very different ways from functionalism. They are seen more as the effect of people's class location in society than as the cause of behaviour. One critical example is the so-called culture of poverty. Within functionalist theory the attitudes commonly associated with poor people, such as apathy, dependency, limited goals or aspirations, a hand-out mentality, and the like, are all seen as responsible for the failure of poor people to take advantage of opportunities to get ahead. Their reproduction in the children through family socialization is a critical contributing factor in the poverty trap where children who grew up in poverty are more likely to continue to live in poverty as adults. From the perspective of political economy, the attitude set associated with the **culture of poverty** is seen as the effect of experience rather than the cause of behaviour. It is the workings of the capitalist economic system that produces the underclass of chronically un- and underemployed people, and which generates the soul-destroying alienation that manifests itself in a poverty culture. Immigrants and members of ethnic minority groups are particularly likely to experience subtle or overt discrimination in the labour market, and to find themselves pushed out onto the periphery of the economy, into the least desirable jobs. This experience, not their ethnic cultural characteristics, may generate the attitudes of apathy, withdrawal, or delinquency that others see as the cause of their situation.

Political economy theory also acknowledges a functional interrelation among social institutions, but raises a further question—functional for whom? Such institutions are not necessarily or even usually of equal benefit to all sectors of society. What is more likely is that the institutions and practices within a society are those that favour the interests of the dominant class. Within functionalist theory, for example, the legal system is analysed for its function of upholding shared values and expectations for appropriate behaviour and thus ensuring order in the society as a whole. But political economy theory directs attention to different questions. When society is viewed as inherently inegalitarian, this same system of laws can be analysed for its function of protecting the property of the haves from the have-nots. Quinney (1975) argues that laws function primarily to defend the interests of the propertied classes. In Canada, for example, laws to protect property are more prolific and are enforced to a far greater degree than laws to protect the environment or workers' health. Similarly, with respect to educational institutions, analysis from a political economy perspective probes the "corporate agenda" of business interests that underlie much curriculum planning, notwithstanding the language of concern with the interests of children. What is functional for the labour-market considerations of members of the corporate business class is not necessarily functional for the interests of other social groups. Notions of the functional efficiency of organizations are similarly open to challenge for not specifying the class interests in terms of which efficiency is defined. Practices that may be functional for reducing labour costs may well have negative consequences for many other goals.

In all these examples, political economy theory takes class relations as the point of departure for analysing particular institutions and practices. The goal is to make visible the underlying processes by which the exploitative relations of production for private profit are sustained. The central issues explored concern the workings of industrial capitalism, the international relations of capital, and how particular societies such as Canada fit into this world system. The new reality of late twentieth-century capitalism is that the world economy is dominated by **multinational corporations** that may actually control more resources than do nation-states. In the light of this new reality, contemporary theorists are having to re-evaluate their notions of "societies" as self-contained systems that can be understood totally through their internal functioning.

Crisis in Marxist Predictions

Two further, closely related questions remain central to political economy theory; the apparent failure of communism, manifest in the collapse of the Soviet Union, and the absence of revolt and revolution within advanced capitalist societies. With respect to the first question, it has been obvious to political economists for decades that communism was not working out as hoped. The reality of stagnant economies, monolithic bureaucracies, inequality, and limited human rights, did not fit the image of workers in control of their own lives and production. In 1968, the event known as "The Prague Spring," when the Soviet army invaded Czechoslovakia to crush a working-class revolt, shattered what was left of the hope of international solidarity among workers. Many Marxist intellectuals in Europe left the Communist Party after this event. The problems within communist societies constitute a specialized area of research with respect to which most Western sociologists have limited expertise. It will not concern us in this text, except as it raises questions for Marxist theories of the state and bureaucracy, and for understanding the dynamics of managing complex industrial economies in general.

The second question has attracted more immediate attention in Western sociology. Given the obvious inequalities and suffering in capitalist societies, why has there been no sustained rebellion by members of the disprivileged classes against the system? While the East looks to the West to learn about market principles and model democracies, what they are likely to find are a series of social crises, unemployment, recession, and struggles over how to meet the most basic needs for food, shelter, and health care for the poor. Marx was largely correct in his prediction of chronic instability in capitalist economies. Since his death just over a century ago, we have experienced two world wars, separated by the Great Depression of the 1930s, and a never-ending series of smaller, regional wars in which conflicting economic interests play a major role. Cycles of booms and slumps, recession, and unemployment are endemic to capitalism. Yet the system remains intact.

A branch of political economy theory known as **The Frankfurt School** or as **critical theory** shifts the focus of analysis from the structure of class relations to the superstructure of ideas and culture that prevail in advanced capitalist societies (Harland 1987, ch. 4). Our most basic cultural concepts of *individual freedom*, *free choice*, and *equal opportunity* are challenged as ideology—a form of thinking that serves to conceal the true exploitative character of capitalism as an economic system. Such ideas translate the evidence of inequality back into "natural differences" in individual abilities and effort. Crises and recession, and poverty on an international scale, appear as the natural and inevitable outcome of competitive market forces, rather than as the unnecessary effects of exploitative relations of production geared to profit instead of meeting human needs. Hence, in Althusser's conceptualization of Marxist theory, there is no room for individual agency at all. The historically organized structures of capitalism determine individual consciousness. The voluntarism emphasized in Parsons' model of functionalism is illusory. Notions such as the "free individual" and "free choice" do not arise out of individual experience, but are constructed by society and imposed onto consciousness so that our individual "I-hood" seems obvious, as do free enterprise economies (Althusser 1971, 171). They form such basic categories of thought and language that they are absorbed into the unconscious mind and simply taken for granted (Althusser 1969, 233). It becomes impossible to make political objection to the status quo when it seems so natural.

In summary, while functionalist theory still predominates in Canadian sociology, political economy theory, with its focus on class analysis, is fast gaining ground. Richardson and Wellman (1985, 774) suggest that the visible dependency of Canada on the American economy may be largely responsible for the emergence of a strong political economy tradition among Canadian academics. Americans, at the centre of international capitalism, have tended to ignore the power links that bind others to them and to stress instead the valuable traits of their own society. The powerful influence of American sociological traditions on Canadian academics can be traced to the major influx of Americans into expanding Canadian universities in the 1960s, and by the United States domination of the publishing industry. The pattern of American sociology may change if the prognosis proves correct that the American economy is losing its pre-eminence in international capitalism, as multinational corporations pull their investments out of the United States and direct capital to other parts of the world where labour is cheap and taxes and environmental controls are minimal (Marchak 1985, 694–96).

Interpretive Theory: From Symbolic Interaction to Social Constructionism

Interpretive theory begins from the recognition that people "interpret" and make sense of their social world, and experience their actions as meaningful. Instead of beginning with a global theory of society as a system, they focus on how what we think of as "society" emerges through interaction. Like functionalists, theorists in this tradition also conceive of people as playing roles and reacting to each other's expectations, but these roles are not preprogrammed or available independently of the role incumbents. Rather, they are actively created and negotiated, sustained or abandoned, in ongoing interaction. They are continually subject to reinterpretation both by the people involved, and by onlookers. Terms such as "roles" and "reality" are frequently placed in quotation marks by interpretive theorists to emphasize that they are not seen as factual entities but as interpretations that people use to make sense of what they perceive to be happening.

Interpretive theory can be loosely subdivided into three broad approaches. Symbolic interaction theory is the earliest and still the most widely used approach. It has its roots in social psychology and focusses particularly on the meanings and intentions that people bring to situations and how they communicate and negotiate expectations of each other. The second approach is ethnomethodology, which developed in the late sixties, and treats as problematic what symbolic interactionism takes as given. Rather than starting with actors' meanings, ethnomethodology explores how actors collectively produce a sense of meaning; that is, the common-sense methods of reasoning that people use to decide what is going on, prior to formulating expectations about a situation, and how they organize conversations so as to sustain a sense of orderly, shared meaning. The third approach of social constructionism, which became influential in sociology in the early eighties, takes a much broader focus on what people do collectively to accomplish what we think of in common-sense reasoning as "social reality." All aspects of social life are explored as processes that people accomplish, the outcome of practical activities rather than entities that can be described.

Interpretive theory, especially as it has developed into ethnomethodology and social constructionism, assumes the extreme position on the structure-agency debate. There are no pre-established structures to which people respond, only human agency. Our sense of social relations as being structured is continually being produced through people's ongoing activities.

The interpretive perspective generally is difficult to grasp because it involves such a different way of thinking about what we usually take for granted as factual knowledge about society. We usually think that **facts** exist and we describe them, but now we are being asked to see how the work we do in coming up with descriptions serves to create what we refer to as facts. We begin this overview of interpretive theory with several examples of just how powerful descriptions can be in constructing facts.

Boughey's (1978) example of cards night in a church illustrates how differently interpretive theory and traditional functionalist theory use the notion of "social roles." Men at one table are laughing raucously and a woman admonishes them, "Shush, you are in church you know." If the men subsequently quieten down we would conclude that the role of "church member" is being played, but if they continue to be raucous, then they must be playing the role of "card-players." The important point is that no matter how clearly we know the expectations associated with church member or card-player roles, we cannot predict what the men will do. Only after the people involved have taken some action, can we make inferences about which of the roles they were engaged in. Reference to role expectations thus does not explain behaviour, so much as provide a convenient after-the-fact way of giving an account of it.

It may take only a small shift in interpretation for one's entire sense of what is going on to change. Consider a simple situation. A woman wearing spike heels steps on your toe. What actu-ally happened depends on your interpretation— whether you see yourself as the deliberate target of an angry woman, or as the victim of someone who has a careless disregard for others, or as an unfortunate participant in an accidental event. Perhaps you are being warned of some social blunder she feared you were about to make, or she may have created the incident in the hope of getting your attention and a chance to talk to you. "What happened" could be literally anything imaginable. What interpretation you come to will affect your response and the interaction that follows.

It is difficult, perhaps impossible, to give a description of a social situation and to make it totally free of interpretation. Consider the kinds of words that newspapers commonly use to talk about some public disturbance. The people involved may be identified as "terrorists," "freedom fighters," "bandits," "hoodlums," or "members of . . . ." The nature of the reality that is being talked about is altered by the choice of words. Terrorists are evil people who terrorize the innocent for illegitimate reasons; freedom fighters are good people striving to liberate others who are wrongfully oppressed; bandits are simply out to rob people for private gain; hoodlums are irrational people who hurt others and damage property for no clear motives; "members of" implies an organized group of people acting on orders rather than individuals acting on frustrations or motivations of their own; and so on. The reality behind the words is by no means obvious. When we accept a particular description as accurate, we are also accepting a theory of motives and causation. In a sense, people actively create reality in the process of describing it. Descriptions offered by sociologists are no exception. Moreover, as we will see in the section on social constructionism, they may be particularly influential in structuring how ordinary people come to interpret and account for what is going on.

The interpretive approach to sociology is closely associated with the philosophical approach of **phenomenology** and particularly the work of Alfred Schutz (1967). Phenomenology studies the ways in which sensory information becomes meaningful. Sensory experience means nothing until it is interpreted. A classic example of this is the picture that looks either like a white vase on a dark background, or the silhouette of two dark faces on a white background (see figure 2-2). Another example comes from the children's book

Figure 2-2

Interpreting Sensory Experience

The Little Prince, by Antoine de Saint-Exupéry, in which the hero laments that he has drawn a picture of a boa constrictor that has swallowed an elephant, but people keep mistaking it for a picture of a hat (see figure 2-3). The difference lies not in the sensory experience, but what is attended to.

Figure 2-3

Interpreting Sensory Experience

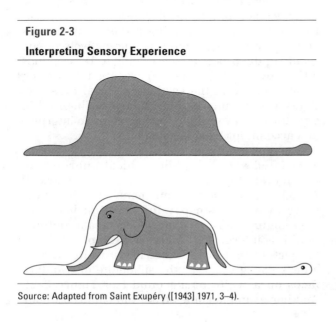

Source: Adapted from Saint Exupéry ([1943] 1971, 3–4).

Symbolic Interaction

Early approaches to interpretive sociology, which can loosely be referred to as **symbolic interaction** theory, complement functionalism by exploring the interactive processes involved in socialization. Theorists such as Charles Horton Cooley (1864–1929), George Herbert Mead (1863–1931), and their many followers at the University of Chicago during the 1930s and 1940s were particularly interested in the social processes through which an individual's sense of self emerge (Cooley 1964; Mead 1934). Cooley popularized the concept of the **looking-glass self** to describe the dependency of self-image upon the reactions of others. Even as infants, he suggests, we learn that we can influence other people, and we are also deeply concerned with how others see us. We learn to see and to respond to ourselves as objects through the eyes of others. This reflected image invokes feelings of pride or shame. Some people are more significant to us than others in this development of self. Intimate family members are most important initially, but later in life a variety of other people take on significance. This process is flexible in that we can to some extent choose our **significant others**; that is, those who are most important to us. People may change their friends when they change their beliefs, seeking out people who support them and avoiding those who are overly critical.

Mead developed the concepts of **self** and **other**, arguing that they were inseparable parts of individual identity. The self comprises the **I** and the **Me**. The I is the unique, impulsive, and spontaneous aspects of a person, while the Me is the internalized other, formed through how we see ourselves mirrored in the reactions of significant others. The process of acquiring a language and learning how we are addressed by others, is a central mechanism through which we learn to see ourselves as objects.

Personality, Mead suggests, develops in stages. At first, young children imitate the behaviour of others without understanding it, as when they pretend to read. Later, they begin to take on the role of the other, as when they play at being mothers and fathers. **Role-taking** involves imagining and trying to empathize with the experiences and expectations of other. More complicated role-taking involves assuming a number of roles together. In team games, for example, each player must be able to imagine the expectations of all the others, so as to respond appropriately as a team member. Eventually, we develop an inner sense of a **generalized other**, which is the synthesis of expectations and attitudes of the group or community with which we identify.

Berger and Luckmann (1966) incorporate the insights of symbolic interactionism and phenomenology into a general model of how social reality is constructed. They draw on Schutz's argument that the problem of **intersubjectivity**—of knowing what the other person actually intended—can be solved for all practical purposes by **recipe knowledge**. People refer to typical patterns of actions that they have learned to recognize and to associate with particular motives and goals. Berger and Luckmann describe the hypothetical meeting of Robinson Crusoe and Man Friday, two isolated people who have no prior language or culture in common. How are they to develop meaningful, intersubjective understanding of each other? First they watch each other, looking for patterns. Actions soon become **typified** ("there he goes again") and routinized ("this is the way we do things"). When such patterns are transmitted to a second generation, they acquire legitimation and are accepted as rationales for why people like us do things in a particular way. Eventually such patterns and legitimations become reified and objectified, as if they existed independently of people. Yet this social reality remains, at root, nothing more than patterns of behaviour that people justify to themselves. Interactions with others may reaffirm this reality, or may change it by expressing doubts. Social reality is thus inherently unstable, open to change whenever its justifications are called into question.

The development of symbolic interactionism at the University of Chicago became associated with a special style of research that emphasizes participant observation, detailed ethnographies and individual life histories, all designed to reveal their subjects' own interpretative understanding of their lives. Students were encouraged "to go and live in the slums and the ghettos, to hang around street corners, bars, and pool halls, to visit the 'other side of the tracks' as well as to talk to officials, examine public records and official statistics" (Hitchcock and Hughes 1989, 30). A model study in this tradition is *The Jack-Roller: A Delinquent Boy's Own Story* in which Shaw ([1930] 1966) records the autobiographical life story of a teenage mugger, a text described by Denzin and others as "one of symbolic interactionism's mythical texts" (Denzin 1992, 36).

The next generation of symbolic interactionist work focussed on the way that individuals actively manipulate the features of their environment to create images of themselves for others. The works of Erving Goffman, which span more than two decades from 1959 to the early 1980s, command special respect. In his first major work *The Presentation of Self in Everyday Life* (1959) Goffman develops the metaphor of theatre into a **dramaturgical model** of society. Seen from Goffman's perspective, roles are not so much learned as created and maintained by people. The bare outlines of role expectations may be common to all actors, but the details are not. Moreover, many social interactions do not take the form of predefined roles at all. Goffman describes the practices of secrecy, deference, demeanour, team work, backstage collusions, and consensual performances before potentially critical audiences, that characterize informal encounters. We see the importance of the private or backstage area where people can drop their act and check performances, or recover from social blunders. Even people engaged in well-defined roles—Goffman uses riding a merry-go-round (1961b, 97)—may play the role in strikingly different ways to display different self-images, from the scared toddler who displays total absorption, to nonchalant teenagers who ride the horse backwards and jump off and on to give the message that they are really too old for this game, to displays of casual mastery of the moving machinery by the person running the roundabout.

Most of Goffman's extensive studies focus on informal settings of parties and social gatherings, but wider structures are still apparent in some of his studies in the form of hierarchical relations that set constraints on individual performances. In his famous study of asylums (1961a), Goffman shows us doctors, nurses, and patients playing out their roles in an institution in positions of very unequal power. Goffman gets himself admitted to the mental hospital in order to participate directly in the lives of the patients and give a patient's eye view of seemingly bizarre behaviour.

Labelling theory is an important branch of symbolic interactionism that directs attention to the opposite process of how individuals can be actively influenced or manipulated by the images that others have of them, especially when these others are in positions of power to impose these images as public labels. It is a theory of interaction that involves an often negative spiral of action and reaction. People act on the basis of the label or reputation and so treat the labelled person differently than they might otherwise have done, and the labelled person in turn reacts to the differential treatment. This may be especially significant when a person is labelled as a deviant. Others typically respond to deviants by avoidance or ostracism, and the very experience of being ostracized or singled out for special treatment, may make the labelled person act in angry or unusual ways and so reinforce the original deviant label. Howard Becker (1963) is particularly associated with this analysis of "the outsiders," a study of how stigmatized people tend to gravitate towards others in similar circumstances and so form a subcultural group in which the label provides a focus for a more positive self-image.

The complexity of the labelling process is illustrated by Daniels' (1972) example of the situation of an army doctor faced with a soldier whose marriage has just broken up. The soldier appears depressed, marginally suicidal, delusional, and is drinking heavily. Several potential interpretations are possible. If the doctor decides that the behaviour is a reaction to a stressful situation, he is saying in essence that the condition is temporary and the soldier not seriously ill. If he decides that the problems stem from the soldier's character, then he is laying the blame on the man. But if he labels the behaviour "psychotic," then it indicates that he considers the soldier mentally ill and so not responsible for the behaviour. The consequences that follow from each label will be very different. In the first instance, the soldier may get an honourable discharge on compassionate grounds; in the second case, a dishonourable discharge or other punishment, including loss of pension rights; in the third case, specialized care and a disability pension. Daniels suggests that the label chosen may depend more on what the doctor wants to happen to the man, based on how long he has been in the army, what he seems to deserve, and what facilities exist to treat someone labelled psychotic, than on what the symptoms are. Once labelled, however, the person is typified in a way that will strongly influence how others react to him. The very expectations that others have of the mentally ill may pressure the person so labelled to act in ways that confirm their impressions. Subsequent deviant behaviour will be the effect rather than the cause of the deviant label.

Ethnomethodology

Ethnomethodology is a distinctive approach within interpretive theory that was developed by Harold Garfinkel and his associates at the University of California in the late sixties. The term *ethno* refers to people or members of a society. Ethnomethodology concerns members' methods of making sense or the common-sense reasoning that underlies everyday interaction. This is usually taken for granted and unnoticed by participants, and yet arguably forms the foundation for all social order. One way of getting a feel for what ethnomethodology entails is to contrast it with the approach of symbolic interactionism. Ethnomethodologist Psathas (1980) suggests the kind of analysis of everyday interaction that Goffman, and other symbolic interactionists, provides has serious limitations. Goffman continually switches back and forth between actor-subject and actor-observer in a two-person interaction, treating first one and then the other as acting or interpreting the other's actions. Goffman also continually imputes acts of interpretation, as distinct from observable acts, to the participants. But acts of interpretation cannot be directly observed—only imputed. In effect, we never do get to see how actor-subject and actor-observer are interpreting each other's moves. What we DO see is the perspective of the third-party sociologist-observer (in this case Goffman himself) who imputes interpretations to both the actors under observation. This is not visible in the text because the same word *observer* is used to cover both the actor-observer and the sociologist-observer, without distinction. The sense of illumination that we get when reading Goffman's accounts, Psathas suggests, is based on our unquestioned assumption of common-sense reasoning, evidence, and example (1980, 73). Our impression that we have gained an understanding of previously perceived but un-understandable complex events serves merely to keep us ignorant of the basis of the "understanding" and thus to keep us dependent on Goffman to provide further "illumination." We do not learn how to do such analysis for ourselves. Nor do we learn how Goffman does it.

The question that ethnomethodology raises is precisely what Goffman, and symbolic interactionism generally, take for granted. What are the common-sense reasoning practices by which people, in everyday interaction, manage to make interpretations? How do we accomplish this intersubjective understanding for practical purposes? How do social actors come to know, and to know in common, what they are doing and the circumstances in which they are doing it? How do you come to know what role I am playing? How do I know that you know it? How do we both know that each of us shares and will sustain the definition of reality that we are trying to produce? Garfinkel asks us to suspend the **natural attitude**—the assumption that we know what is going on and that it makes sense—and to ask ourselves HOW we know.

Garfinkel designed **breaching experiments** to expose the rules underlying familiar everyday activities and to show how these rules and activities are mutually sustained. His students were asked to disrupt the taken-for-granted order in very simple ways and to describe what happened (Garfinkel 1967, 41–49). In one case, simply asking for clarification of a routine question like "How are you?" was sufficient to destroy the entire interaction. When the student asked, "How am I in regard to what? My health, my finances, my school work, my peace of mind, my . . . ," the other person lost his temper and shouted back, "Look! I was just trying to be polite. Frankly I don't give a damn how you are." A bus driver exploded with anger when asked if he were sure he knew where the bus was going. When their normally noisy, exuberant, and cheeky kids are suddenly quiet, solicitous, and polite, the first reaction of most parents is to think something's wrong; they assume the kids must have done something bad like dent the car.

These experiments reveal the inherent fragility of social order. The moral outrage that these breaching experiments engendered reveals also the power of sanctions sustaining that order. Garfinkel argues that it was the threat to people's sense of reality, and not the actual behaviour, that invoked the indignation. People calmed down as soon as they could find some alternative set of motives to make sense of what was going on like, "It's okay Dad, I was just doing a sociology experiment." Clearly, for any sense of social reality to be sustained, we have to rely upon assumptions that other people will use their **background understandings**, will trust appearances as corresponding to intentions, will be willing to anticipate the sense of conversations, using future remarks to clarify what is being talked about, and so on. Otherwise, interaction is impossible.

The technique of "suspending the natural attitude" that Garfinkel advocates in breaching experiments, is a powerful method of making visible how important these background understandings are in sustaining interaction. The students experienced for themselves how quickly interaction broke down and tempers flared when they deliberately stopped using their background understandings and asked for clarification, and when they behaved in ways they knew would violate the background understandings of others.

Another experiment showed just how much and what kind of work people do to create a sense of what is happening (Garfinkel 1967, 79–94). Students were asked to participate in what they were told was an experiment in alternative methods of counselling in a psychiatry department. They were asked to describe a

HERMAN

© 1991 Jim Unger/Distributed by Universal Press Syndicate

10/3

"I put these on the ones I haven't done yet."

serious situation for which they were seeking advice and then ask ten questions. The counsellor could answer yes or no to the questions, but could not offer further advice. In fact, the counselling was literally nonsense; the yes/no answers were entirely random. Yet students stayed for the entire "counselling" session, made sense out of each of the yes or no answers, even when they were blatantly contradictory, interpreted the counsellor's reasoning, and came away for the most part actually thinking they had received useful advice. Sense was imposed entirely by the students' imagination. They interpreted random utterances as meaningful conversation because this was what they were expecting.

These experiments have far-reaching implications for sociology as a scientific discipline. They raise the very real possibility that the order that sociologists purport to describe may be nothing more than the one that sociologists themselves impose. The methods that they use and the theories they invoke to make sense of the data actually create the order that they describe. How do we know whether the order that sociologists describe constitutes an order inherent in the reality being observed or an abstract order produced by sociologists themselves as they try to make sense of the random utterances they gather? There is no easy answer.

Social Constructionism

Social constructionist theory explores how people, in their routine everyday activities, actually create the versions of reality that are taken for granted in common-sense reasoning as "the way things are," or as "social facts." The approach takes a much broader view of sense-making practices than ethnomethodology, but shares the same theoretical idea that "meaning" is not inherent in social interaction but produced through work that people do. All aspects of social life are treated as processes that people accomplish, not entities that can be described. Social constructionist research continually strives to translate nouns into verbs, descriptions into activities. The following examples give a sense of how this translation process works in particular settings.

Suppose you hear or read that X percent of men who leave the Canadian army are officially discharged for reasons of mental illness. In common-sense reasoning this is taken to be a statement of fact, particularly if it appears in a reputable "official" document such as a government report. The social constructionist perspective might translate this fact into a verb by asking what is it that some people must have done to produce evidence that looks like this? Some army physicians must have signed a number of discharge certificates in which the category "mentally ill" is checked, or they may have provided some account of symptoms in a form that fits a notion of "mental illness." That begs the question further, how do army physicians, in their routine work, make decisions about how to fill in discharge forms? What do they look for when someone comes into their office? As we noted above in Daniels' description of labelling, many other outcomes are possible, including the decision that the person in question is a philanderer or a lazy drunkard, and not mentally ill at all. How do physicians manage the talk, what kinds of questions do they ask, how do they process the answers, so as to come to a decision? How do individuals accomplish themselves as "mentally ill" for the immediate practical purpose of getting a certain kind of discharge, or conversely, how do they accomplish themselves as mentally "normal" but temporarily stressed out or misunderstood by others?

A similar research question might focus on the social construction of grading student assignments. Suppose you learn that on the first assignment in an introductory sociology course, 7 percent of students gained a grade of A– or better, 20 percent scored B– to B+, and so on. What have people been doing, individually and collectively, to produce this as an outcome? Again we might begin by exploring how lecturers, in the routine performance of their work, accomplish the grading of assignments. Do they, as student mythology has it, throw them down the stairs and give As to the heavy ones that land on the bottom? Most lecturers will tell you that grading essays involves an agonizing process of trying to decide what "comprehension of course materials" looks like, as distinct from "summary of lecture notes," or what constitutes "clear development of an argument." Teaching-effectiveness seminars at the university level commonly devote many hours of debate to such issues. One way of beginning to make visible how such work gets done is to have several lecturers grade the same student paper and then discuss the reasoning behind different evaluations. Students typically engage in similar debates and comparative readings to learn what "good" or "poor" papers look like. These practices constitute a small part of the work that goes into accomplishing what is recognizably "an A paper."

Social constructionist theory emphasizes that a great deal of what we think we know about our society is the outcome of work practices, either by individuals, or groups of people (Smith 1974b). Through radio, television, newspapers, and various publications and speeches, we come to learn about "facts" such as rates of illness, crime waves, unemployment levels, protests, wars, world markets, and the like. These accounts are, in Smith's words, "**worked up**" by people, usually government bureaucrats. They appear to provide us with factual knowledge of features of our society. But they are all social constructions, the products of peoples' work. Every one of these "facts" can be translated into verbs through the same research technique of asking what are people doing to accomplish this particular feature? The goal of social constructionist analysis is to make these practices visible as work activities enacted by particular people in concrete situations (Smith 1990c; 1990d).

In principle, social constructionist analysis can be applied to any situation, to explore the mundane practices by which all aspects of social reality are accomplished. In practice, however, much of the research we will explore in different chapters of this text has focussed on the work activities of professionals. The main reason is that professionals as a class have special authority to make interpretations or diagnoses of situations that become "the way things are" for other people. In the above example, students are deeply involved in the process of accomplishing themselves as people who appear to comprehend course materials, but it is the lecturer's determination of what "comprehension of course materials" looks like that is definitive for assigning the grade.

From the social constructionist perspective, much of what professionals do appears as authoritative "reality-creating" work. While everyone is engaged in reality-constructing, professionals are particularly useful as a focus for research because their work is routinely documented. It thus becomes possible to track back through the documents to discover how the process works. For example, in chapter 12 of this text we discuss the construction of individuals as clients of social service agencies. In common-sense reasoning, clients exist and they receive assistance when the facts of their situation fit the criteria for eligibility for services. But when we translate these facts or nouns into verbs we become aware of how much work goes into their accomplishment. In their everyday work with clients, social service workers face the messy, ambiguous, and changing situations of people in their local settings. It is by no means obvious who should or should not constitute a "case." What workers do involves complicated processes of selecting, abstracting, highlighting, discarding, and arranging of concrete particulars to fit them into official categories so as to construct unique individuals as typical "cases." Social constructionist research involves intensive, detailed investigation of how such work practices get done. The people who are trying to accomplish themselves as "cases" for the purposes of receiving assistance are engaged in a complementary process of working up their accounts of themselves in ways they hope will appear to the social workers as what "clients" look like.

Power and Resistance in Social Constructionism

In social constructionist theory the notion of "power," like all other aspects of social reality, is understood as a process that is accomplished rather than a fact of life. Power is not something that people *have*, but something that they *do*. Power is accomplished through reality-construction practices that serve to interpret "what is going on" in ways that mandate appropriate courses of action, as matters of administration, punishment, treatment, and so on (McKendy 1992, 62). The work of professionals, especially in the social sciences, is central to these processes in that their interpretations carry the authority of science and specialized expertise. In the above example, it is relatively straightforward to trace how the construction of an individual's life experiences into a "case" constitutes the basis for a series of other professionals to take actions appropriate to such cases.

The successful exercise of such power depends not on coercion, but on people generally accepting the outcomes of reality-construction work as accurately representing "the way things are" and so adjusting their attitudes and behaviour accordingly. As McKendy expresses it, people commonly do come to accept the accounts of their lives offered by professionals as reasonable, accurate, and helpful, and this is indeed what most professionals are trying to offer (1992, 63). The learning and evaluating relationship between students and lecturer, for example, works only to the extent that both parties believe in the lecturer's competence to define and to recognize what competence is.

The power embedded in reality-construction practices is very difficult to resist, precisely because it seems so reasonable, so grounded in objective, factual evidence. While coercion generates resentment, expertise generates willing compliance. Resistance seems irrational or even mad. It seems to be going against factual knowledge and the weight of objective scientific evidence. Hence it tends to be muted and easily discredited. Foucault's scathing critique of traditional social science expertise rests on this view of the ubiquitous power of the disciplines to control how people think, and to subordinate immediate subjective and emotional experiences to the stranglehold of supposed "objective" knowledge (Foucault 1980, 126–33; Beechey and Donald 1985, xiv).

The critical objective of much social constructionist analysis is to make visible the work practices that produce versions of reality, to provide a basis for challenging those practices. Interpretive theory generally recognizes that any description of a social situation necessarily entails interpretation, but social constructionist analysis pushes the questioning further to explore how particular interpretations are accomplished and imposed. Such analysis also focusses attention on interpretations as the site of struggles and contestations, particularly with respect to political movements. These struggles over meaning are variously referred to in the literature as "reality-defining contests" (Loseke 1987, 235), "contestations over naming" (McKendy 1992, 60), and "the politics of interpretation" (Denzin 1992). One example of such struggle is the women's movement's effort to introduce the term *wife battery* to replace *family conflict*, as a way of identifying the underlying problem as one of institutionalized male dominance rather than interpersonal frictions (Walker 1990a; 1990b). A successful shift in interpretation would mandate very different courses of action with respect to treatment and punishment.

Discourse Analysis

There is some disagreement within the social constructionist perspective over how to think about the relations of power associated with reality-constructing practices. Theorists who draw particularly on the Marxist tradition use the term **ideology** to convey a sense that people are victims of inaccurate and perhaps deliberately distorted versions of reality. Such distortions undermine the capacity of the mass of people to achieve a fuller understanding of their lives based on their own subjective experience (Smith 1990c, 4; Habermas 1987a, 355). The term *ideology* in effect presupposes that there is a "truth," or a nondistorted account, that accurately describes reality the way it really is.

Other theorists are sceptical of the possibility of ever arriving at "truth" based on experience. If reality is truly socially constructed through people's practices, then there is no objective, factual, accurate reality that can stand outside of the meanings that people accomplish (Game 1991, 4). Theorists who think in these terms advocate the term **discourse** to refer to prevailing ways of thinking about or interpreting social experiences that in themselves are neither true nor false (Beechey and Donald 1985, xiv).

The analysis of discourse focusses on **texts**, especially those that are seen as authoritative accounts. Texts are understood very broadly to cover all forms of communication, including books, articles, newspapers, government documents and forms, and also films, television programs, and conversations recorded on tape or video. These are analysed not simply for the interpretations they place on social issues, but also for how the texts themselves are organized, how interpretations are put together, how truth claims are established and sustained, and how they work to mandate certain courses of action. The detailed investigation of how texts achieve their meanings is known as **deconstruction**.

Discourse analysis within the discipline of sociology has prompted critical reflection back onto sociological texts—studies, reports, articles, textbooks—in an attempt to deconstruct them to reveal how they produce the appearance of truth. In such analysis the texts are not treated as sources of factual information about some feature of society under investigation. They are studied as discursive practices, for which we can ask the conceptually awkward question, "How does this particular social text mean?" (Game 1991, 5). What matters is not "what does it say," but how does it manage to convey the impression that the content constitutes information that is objectively correct and believable, rather than the figment of someone's imagination?

Denzin (1992, 65–69) subjects earlier work in the tradition of symbolic interaction to this intensive deconstructive analysis. He particularly focusses on Goffman's writings that analyse various face-to-face encounters as dramatic performances. Denzin cites Clough's (1991) reading of these texts as novels, to display how they create the impression that the reader can see and feel what the writer has seen, including the interior qualities of the subjects being observed. What we begin to see are the practices that Goffman as writer employs to get his readers to interpret his texts as social science accounts and not as novels.

In his own work Denzin (1992, ch. 4) carries the analysis a step further to investigate how readers react to what they interpret to be social science accounts; how they take up the theoretical explanations they find therein, and apply them as explanations for their own personal experiences. Denzin focusses particularly on social science accounts of the lives of alcoholics and adult children of alcoholics and their popularization in the media. He shows how people use the frameworks provided in these accounts to organize how they think and talk about their own personal life stories. These accounts work by first informing readers that they need help in identifying their problem, then that they must re-open the door on their childhood, and then find emotional release through telling their stories. The texts also identify the ingredients to be expected in such autobiographies. Readers who have had any brush with alcohol learn from these texts how to think scientifically about their childhood, what remembered features to find significant, and how to organize telling others about their lives so that these features are strung together in some scientifically credible account of themselves as "people with alcohol problems." The circle of scientific practices is complete when individuals construct accounts of their life stories for sociologists engaged in doing ethnographies, and these sociologists construct their interviews in ways that further prompt the individuals in how to tell their stories. These stories are then written up as

ethnographic research that "proves" the relevance of the theoretical frameworks found in earlier texts. These texts thus "create" their subjects, constructing the meanings and the relevances that people use to make sense of their social world, which then become visible as "members' meanings" in the descriptive research practices of symbolic interaction. The hero in *The Jack-Roller* does just this when he was re-interviewed some fifty years later. He agreed fervently with the theory that personal makeup mentally is established in early years, adding, "I must have had some awful experiences before I was conscious of them" (Denzin 1992, 40, citing Snodgrass 1982, 171). The hero seems to have read sociopsychological texts on deviance, learned the prevailing discourse that deviant personalities are the result of childhood trauma or unhappiness, and learned how to incorporate this discourse into the account of his life story that he tells to Snodgrass. Hence the anomalous statement that even though he cannot remember any awful experiences in his childhood, he is certain he must have had them. Denzin concludes that it is not possible for ethnographers to record peoples' lived experiences in some pristine or direct manner because peoples' descriptions already have sociological frameworks built into them. People have already learned how to talk about themselves from authoritative accounts that they have encountered in television documentaries or in books and magazines. Through such practices, the social sciences can be seen as creating the social realities they attempt to describe.

Denzin (1992, ch. 7) further challenges early examples of symbolic interactionism, particularly the Chicago School version for what he calls a structural blindness, a failure to see how greatly their work was influenced by the values of capitalism. The focus on individual members' meanings implicitly endorses middle-class views on the importance of the individual and family backgrounds, and conservative cultural values about proper behaviour, and how to present oneself so as to impress others. The detailed descriptions of individual life experiences, which is the stuff of ethnographies, can also be seen as a crude way of exploiting people by treating their private lives as commodities for public consumption.

From the social constructionist perspective, however, such challenges can in turn be deconstructed. Denzin is open to the criticism that he is doing exactly what he sees the Jack-Roller as doing—namely, using explanatory frameworks learned from earlier sociology texts to provide a scientifically credible framework for organizing his own account. He uses sociological notions like "the ideology of late capitalism" just as the Jack-Roller uses sociopsychological notions like "early childhood trauma" as an organizing tool. Ann Game challenges such writing by pointing out "the significance of the fact that sociological concepts are necessarily used to account for sociology" (1991, 23). For her, there is still no extradiscursive reality outside the interpretive system itself.

In conclusion, it is difficult to apply the standard concepts of structure and agency to social constructionist work. On the one hand, it seems that there is no structure, only human agency. Structures seem to be nothing more than interpretations that people use to create meaningful accounts. But on the other hand, the discursive practices through which interpretations are communicated in texts powerfully structure how individuals construct meaning in their own experience.

Feminist Theory

The feminist perspective in Canadian sociology is fairly recent, beginning only in the 1970s, although it grew out of a much longer history of struggles by women to challenge the **sexism** and the disadvantages that women experienced. It has strong roots in both Marxism and interpretive theory. It shares with Marxism a central concern with structures of power and inequality; however, **feminist theory** examines not only relations of capitalism and production, but also those of **patriarchy**, or male power over women, and the social relations of reproduction. The social relations of production comprise the way in which people organize themselves to produce material goods. Relations of reproduction comprise the way in which people organize themselves to produce children and raise them to maturity. Feminism shares with interpretive theory, and especially with ethnomethodology, a sensitivity to the ways in which intimate personal relations create the social world and continually reproduce male dominance within the workplace,

the family, the kitchen, and the bedroom. It also shares the focus on discourse, and the power of language not only to express ideas, but also to structure how people interpret and make sense of their social world.

Variants of feminist theory take very different positions with respect to the structure/agency debate. At one extreme, the pre-existing structures of patriarchal capitalism are seen as having a determining impact on women's lives, so much so that major political and economic revolution seems necessary before the inferior status of women can be substantially changed. At the other extreme, feminist work that is allied with interpretive and social constructionist perspectives sees human agency as paramount. The appearance of social life as patriarchal is the outcome of meanings and interpretations that people construct, and these meanings can be radically altered through a shift in consciousness.

Feminist theory, by its very existence, has drawn stark attention to inadequacies in mainstream sociological perspectives, which have pervasively excluded, trivialized, and marginalized the experiences and the viewpoints of women. Feminism showed that much of what we believed to be objective and universally valid knowledge about society was partial and biased, specific only to the experiences of men, and only to men in particular historical situations. It turned out to be impossible to merely "add women and stir." The central theories of sociology and the main concepts within them had to change. This feminist rethinking of sociology has been a long and complicated task, and by the mid-1990s it is still very much in progress rather than a completed body of theory.

This process can be seen as roughly divided into three main stages—the discovery of women as objects of study, learning to view the world through the subjective experiences of women, and exploring differences among women (Lengermann and Niebrugge-Brantley 1990). In common with Simone de Beauvoir's seminal book *The Second Sex* (1953), feminist scholars have sought to discover the "other." They raised the basic question "and what about the women?" Where are they in any situation being studied by any scholar in any discipline? If they are not present, why not? If they are present, in what ways? This led to further pointed questions about the scholarship itself. Why were scholars so blind for so long to women's presence? What were and are the processes that make women invisible? The common explanation has been that the social sciences have necessarily been concerned with understanding the most important roles in the public realm of society. These are the roles that concern leadership, decision making, the professions, the economy, the running of complex organizations, and the like. Objectively, all these roles have been occupied overwhelmingly by males, and hence it seems entirely reasonable that males have been the centre of research interests. Until very recently, women have been present only in secondary support roles, and otherwise preoccupied with domestic concerns in the private realm.

In her guide to nonsexist research methods, Eichler (1988b) has many examples of women's invisibility to social scientists. She gives a description of intergroup warfare cited in an anthropology text as "a rational means of gaining livestock, women and slaves." Within this image of society, women appear only as property. Discussion of hunting and gathering societies typically gives central attention to how male-dominated hunting parties are organized, and how these may determine the evolution of community structures. The potential importance of how women organize to gather food is ignored, despite evidence that gathered food may comprise close to 80 percent of what is eaten in such societies. In sociology, studies of stratification focus on the relative statuses of father and son, with the role of mothers considered irrelevant. The status of women is measured only through fathers and husbands. In virtually every subfield of sociology, with the exception of research on families, women have tended to be invisible, or noticed only as they deviate from the male norm. Even in the area of the family, where women have been the centre of attention, their contribution has been trivialized. Only recently has housework come to be thought of as work at all. Meanwhile, it has been men who are seen as active in the public realm, the realm where "important things" happen. Feminist historians have had to develop new research techniques to find women in history, using such sources as letters, diaries, and petitions, rather than formal political, military, religious, and educational documents.

In the next phase of feminist scholarship, women became not only objects of inquiry, but

Feminist theory has drawn attention to the exclusion of women from mainstream sociology.

subjects—subjectivities through which the world could be viewed (Lengermann and Niebrugge-Brantley 1990, 322). In this process, males became "other," the strangers no longer taken-for-granted as naturally the way they were, but as socially and historically specific. Feminist research, ironically, provided the foundations for what is now developing as "men's studies."

Taking the standpoint of women, to understand how women themselves experience and see their social worlds, has not been easy because the established viewpoints are overwhelmingly male. As Smith (1975) expresses it, women in general, along with other disprivileged people, have been systematically excluded from the creation of culture. Historically, women have played little part in the creation or circulation of dominant ideas in society. It is predominantly white, middle- and upper-class males who have been most directly involved in producing, debating, and developing ideas. Their perspectives came to prevail in the professions of medicine, psychology, law, and education, as well as in the social sciences and humanities. Historically, a primary mechanism for excluding women from the creation of culture was their exclusion from higher education, combined with laws barring the entry of women into most of the professions. Students in any of the above fields will find very little written or produced by women before the 1960s. Smith (1992b) describes the electric effect of teaching, or rather collaborating with, students in the first ever Women's Studies course offered at the University of British Columbia in the seventies. She comments that there was nothing to teach in the ordinary academic sense because there was no literature. She and her students together had to draw upon their immediate experiences as women to challenge conventional knowledge, to explore, contend, expand, discover. It was a very different way of doing sociology, and it illuminated for Smith both the male biases built into standard sociology and its inability to explain the social relations that structure women's lives.

The third phase in feminist scholarship is associated with the broader exploration of differences among women, in recognition of the white middle-class biases in earlier work. It has been stimulated particularly by the work of women of colour, and their efforts to articulate women's experiences that have been shaped not only by sexism, but also by the oppressive relations of colonialism and racism (see Moraga and Anzaluda 1981). It has fostered a growing appreciation of and attention to differences among women, reflecting age, ethnicity, class, sexual preference, nationality, and culture. Exploring differences among women as a way of viewing the world from multiple vantage points, is the central concern of what is currently known as postmodern feminist theory. This perspective warns of the danger of perpetuating the category "woman" itself, as an intellectual straightjacket (Parr 1990, 8; Hamilton forthcoming). The concept of *woman* and the standpoint of women was important in the early development of feminist theory, to make visible what had been left unexamined. But in continuing to use the category "woman," feminist theory itself risks perpetuating the sexism inherent in the oppositional characterization of woman and man, with women defined as what men are not. Women are associated with private, micro, emotional, passive, dependent, while men are associated with public, macro, rational, active, independent, and the like. It also risks collapsing

differences among women into an unwarranted uniformity. A central thrust of feminist work has been to challenge all such dualistic and stereotyped thinking as patriarchal ideology that legitimates the subordination of women to men.

Smith has elaborated on her earlier concept of the *standpoint* of women to get away from the notion of a singular, gendered viewpoint. In the earlier phases of feminist work the notion of a woman's standpoint was an important tool for discovering the "other"—the suppressed experiences of women and what women shared in common. Central to this experience Smith suggests, was our sense of "our sexed bodies . . . [as] the site of women's oppression, whether of violence, of rape, or lack of control over our choices to have children, through our connectedness to our children, or through childbirth and suckling" (1992c, 89).

It was also, very importantly, a different method of sociological inquiry. In consciousness-raising groups, like the women's studies course described above, research did not begin with the abstract and formal categories of sociological theory; it began with women as subjects, as knowers, confronting and testing theory against their own immediate, embodied experiences in the practical activities of their lives. What they struggled to make sense of was their mundane, ordinary everyday and everynight lives as women, and how these lives are hooked into and shaped by social relations, organization, and powers beyond the scope of direct experience. It was a kind of inquiry that was far removed from the conventional approaches of mainstream sociology. Smith argues that this is what the notion of the standpoint of women ultimately means. It is a standpoint that treats the mundane and practical activities of the everyday world as problematic. It begins with people as knowers who are actually located in a particular place, and where their everyday bodily existence is not forgotten. As such it is neither gender-specific nor singular. It permits a great variety of human experiences to be explored.

This shift in focus, to bring the mundane and the ordinary to centre stage, entails much more than adding new variables to some existing list of topics. It involves a fundamental revision of basic models of social organization. It became apparent how the everyday worlds of women were both embedded in and organized through relations of capitalism and patriarchy that spread far beyond the range of immediate experience. It also became evident how important the formerly invisible and unrecognized work of women is to the functioning of these macro societal organizations. As we will see later, feminist theory has challenged as ideological such basic sociological concepts as private and public, macro and micro, and has proposed a radical redefinition of notions of economy, politics, and organization (see chapter 9).

Social Organization in Feminist Theory

Within feminist theory, gender is not conceptualized as a role, but as a system of stratification. This gender stratification is seen as rooted in relations of social production. Whereas Marxist theory analyses relations of production with respect to material goods, feminist theory focusses on the total web of relations involved in the continual production and reproduction of social life itself, bringing into central view such activities as childbearing and -rearing, maintaining households and their members, the creation and maintenance of health, and the sexual and emotional work that these entail, as well as the production of economic commodities (Lengermann and Niebrugge-Brantley 1990, 323–24). From this perspective, the work traditionally done by women no longer appears as marginal to or merely supportive of "the main business" of society, but as fundamental. Analysis of relations of social production requires the creation of a new vocabulary to describe the fluid interrelationships between everyday interactions and structural arrangements.

A basic assumption of the feminist perspective is that the personal is political. The concept of *political* is used here in its broadest sense to refer to relations of authority and control. Feminist theory explores how these are structured in intimate personal interaction within ordinary everyday activities. Smith (1979a, 16) gives an example of how personal relations within the home affect macro political activities, in her analysis of problems experienced in a trade union local that includes both women and men. People are complaining that women who are on the executive never seem to do anything, and that women members never come to meetings. The prevailing explanation offered is that

women are apathetic. They are not interested in union politics and leave men to run things. But when the women begin to talk among themselves about what they feel is happening on the executive and to female members, a very different sense of reality emerges. Women speak of meetings being held at times and in places where it is hard for them to attend when they also have to care for children. Women go home from their paid jobs to take up their other responsibilities for preparing dinner, giving time and attention to children, bedding them down, and cleaning the house. It is precisely because women are shouldering primary responsibility for domestic work that men are free to go to union meetings after working hours. Moreover, when women do attend union meetings and speak out, they find that they are commonly not listened to at all, or that what they say is not taken seriously. When seen from the standpoint of the intimate, everyday experiences of these women, the relative absence and the silence of women at the union meetings can no longer be accounted for as the effect of women's political apathy, but as the outcome of their socially organized exclusion. Seemingly trivial issues such as when and where to hold a meeting, whose opinion is responded to, who talks with whom during a coffee break, become critical factors in silencing women and promoting policies favoured by men. Who takes responsibility for preparing food, cleaning up, and being with children directly affects who will or will not appear at union and other meetings. How domestic work is divided up within the family demarcates important lines of authority. Feminists have drawn direct parallels between the exploitation of women's labour time within the home and exploitation of workers within capitalist enterprises. An abstract language that tries to separate the public political sphere from the supposedly private and interpersonal relations within families is a distortion, not a description, of reality (see chapter 13).

Diversity in Feminist Thought

All feminist theory shares the broad perspective of the critique of patriarchy, the complex interrelation of ideas and practices that perpetuate the subordination of women. Within this framework there is much diversity in approaches to analysis of the origins and persistence of gender

hierarchy (Jaggar and Rothenberg 1984; Tong 1989; Hamilton forthcoming). Here we will briefly trace through the main themes that link this body of literature. Details of the different arguments and the major theorists associated with them will be covered in later chapters.

Early work in the feminist tradition stressed the intellectual and moral equality of women and men, and campaigned for the abolition of barriers to equal opportunities for women to participate in the public arenas of society. This **liberal feminism** tends to be seen as an oversimplification in contemporary theory, but it contains the seeds of the more radical critique of the gendered category "woman" that was to follow, and a recognition that differences between women and men may be more socially constructed than natural.

Marxist feminism emphasizes the role of economy and private property in the subordination of women, along with others who suffer exploitation under capitalism. They elaborate the propositions developed by Marx and Engels that, historically, male control over private property and surplus production within agricultural and herding societies gave men as a class the leverage to dominate women and appropriate their labour power and their children within families. This control is perpetuated in contemporary capitalist societies through the economic dependence of women and children on male income earners. Women's unpaid domestic labour maintains and reproduces the *labour power* on which relations of capitalism depend.

Socialist feminism broadens this focus to emphasize the linkages between the economy and division of labour within families. More than a transition to socialism, or access to good jobs, seems to be needed to achieve the goal of equality for women. As long as women carry the major responsibility for child care and domestic work they will not be able to compete as equals in the labour market.

Radical feminism shifts the focus more directly onto relations within families, suggesting that male control over sexuality and reproduction is a more potent force in the subordination of women than control over economic relations alone. Historically, this has been institutionalized in marriage laws which subsumed a woman and her children under the legal status of her husband. Male control over women's bodies is expressed in more extreme form in pornography,

prostitution, rape and incest, and is reflected in a pervasive fear among women of going out alone after dark. A branch of feminist theory that draws on **psychoanalysis** explores the roots of aggressive sexuality in primary experiences of sexual competition between male infant and the all-powerful father (the oedipus complex) and in penis envy and the devaluation of pregnancy.

There is considerable debate and disagreement within feminist theory over the importance to be accorded to biological differences in the subordination of women. But all variants of feminist theory concur in challenging recourse to such differences as justification for pervasive gender inequality. While pregnancy and suckling infants are clearly rooted in female biology, the conditions under which they occur are social, not natural arrangements. So also are responsibilities for caring for children and maintaining a home. Arguments that cite biology as justification for women shouldering the bulk of domestic labour while males dominate all public arenas of society are seen as ideology, not factual truth.

Feminist analysis of discourse, or the ways in which people conceptualize and talk about gender issues, is revealing the power of language, not only to express a gendered reality, but also to construct and legitimate that reality. Out of such work is emerging the critique of a vast array of concepts once taken for granted by sociologists, including the gender-linked dualisms noted. A familiar example is the term *working mother*, which came into the English language during the 1970s with the great influx into the paid labour force of women with young children. The term carries a host of emotional and conceptual baggage, including the notion of neglected children and normal or "unhyphenated" mothers who stay home (Hamilton forthcoming). There is no parallel term *working father*, with connotations of children neglected because their father goes off to work. We speak of unemployed fathers but not of unemployed mothers. Hamilton notes that the term *working mother* is pejorative in other senses as well. It may implicate women in taking jobs away from men, and so contributing to unemployed fathers, especially during recessionary periods. It also connotes women who have relatively low status and low-paying jobs. Women who work in more prestigious roles tend to be referred to as *professionals* rather than working mothers.

Epistemology and Feminist Theory

Feminist theory, in conjunction with the interpretive perspective, raises critical questions about what constitutes knowledge. If so much of what was once taken for granted as objective knowledge has been discredited as the gender-biased assertions of privileged male speakers, then what remains? Is feminist theory doomed to be as much gender-biased as malestream theory? There is no one feminist method of doing research, but there are certain guiding principles. Objective factual knowledge, or a "god's eye view" of society, uncontaminated by the situation and interests of the viewer is rejected as unattainable. In its place is a recognition that we construct our knowledge of the world from the accounts of differently situated social actors, and hence that we need approaches to research that will make these accounts visible.

Eichler (1985a, 629–31) defines four guiding principles of feminist contributions to sociology. The first is that knowledge is socially constructed. As we have seen, women's systematic exclusion from the professions where books, legislation, media, art, history, and religion are produced, has had a profound impact on the culture of our society. From this recognition comes the second principle, that what is accepted as the dominant ideology is that of the ruling group, the people whose opinions count, who are quoted as authority figures, and who formulate policies. Only a tiny minority of these people have been women. The third principle is that there is no such thing as a value-free social science. The knowledge we create is human knowledge and stems from our position within our social world. The fourth principle is that perspectives vary systematically with location in society. What it means, for example, for a man to work for wages while his wife remains at home, is not what it means for a woman to work at home, without directly earning any money, while her husband is away all day.

The widely expressed goal of feminist research is to engage with the subjects of their research in a process of inter-viewing, in which the researcher is as much a participant in the discussion as the subjects (Oakley 1981; Lengermann and Niebrugge-Brantley 1990, 325). The intent is to enable people to express their experiences as they understand them, and to translate these accounts into the generalizable terms of a sociological analysis of those experiences. This is never easy since women, along with other marginalized and disempowered people, commonly lack a language to name their own experience, because other conceptions have been imposed over them in advance. The example we gave is of women talking about their experience of being members of a union. The prevailing organizational perspective accounts for their silence and absence from meetings as instances of apathy. Questioning women about why they are apathetic only further silences them. Another way of talking has to be found to allow these women to describe their experiences so that the full pattern of the relationships in which they are embedded can come into view.

Prospects for Incorporation of Feminism in Sociology

Feminist theories have not won easy acceptance in any of the established disciplines, and at times they have met outright rejection and open hostility from nonfeminist scholars. Even by the mid-1990s, most standard textbooks for introductory sociology courses in North American give little attention to feminist theory. Smith (1992d) uses the phrase "regime of rationality" to describe the set of practices within universities that have worked to "masculinize" knowledge, and to exclude women and the kinds of knowledge represented by feminist work. Following from Descartes, she suggests, rational knowledge became identified with specialized thought, the detached viewpoint separating the "mind" from the local particularities of humdrum everyday life in which most women were embedded. With Rousseau and Hegel, reason came to be associated with combat and conflict in debate, in which one side wins and the other caves in. Women came to be seen as incapable of such rationality, and a very different form of education was prescribed for them. When Kant maintained that learning, meditation, and reflection would harm women and destroy the merits proper to their sex, he raised scarcely a murmur of dissent. There were deep contradictions between the principle of universal reason and the practices of gender exclusiveness, but they did not appear on the surface of academic discourses and texts. The convention of reading the masculine subject "man" as the impersonal, aided the pretence of universalism. Barriers to education for women stifled challenge to prevailing views. The universities and the professions, or what Denzin refers to as "the meaning-making institutions" of society remained almost exclusively male bastions (Denzin 1992, 74).

Times have changed. In the 1990s the proportions of male and female students in Canadian universities are approximately equal, with women sometimes exceeding men in the humanities and social sciences. But within these disciplines, the dominant **paradigms**, the analytical frameworks, and the major questions have already been set up from male perspectives, and they have been slow to change. What junior women scholars write is typically evaluated—approved of or ignored—in terms of what their work adds to existing bodies of knowledge and theory. For Smith (1992d, 221) the myth of universities as the site of rationality and objectivity was shattered by the rage unleashed when feminist thought began to challenge the masculine subtexts. Students who incorporated feminist thought in their papers risked having them rejected as nonsense. In her own efforts to establish the first women's studies course at the University of British Columbia in the 1970s, Smith recounts encountering "prejudice, questioning of our professional competence, insults and threats variously veiled and unveiled. We went through thirteen committees when the normal process was two or at most three" (1992b, 127). Law students at Queen's University in Kingston, Ontario, openly threatened and harassed law professor Sheila McIntyre when she introduced feminist issues in her tort class (McIntyre 1986).

Within the discipline of sociology, gender issues have been most readily incorporated as a distinct subfield, allotted a separate chapter in standard introductory texts. Women have been widely introduced as objects of study within sub-specialties, but with limited inclusion as subjects with distinctive viewpoints on social life. The radical revisioning of the social world implied by feminist theory is only beginning to make a significant impact on sociological theory.

Conclusion

This text takes seriously the notion developed within interpretive theory that sociology as a discipline is at least partially responsible for the active creation of reality through its influence over how people make sense of social experience. It also takes seriously the notion that pushing for a unified version of social science can turn it into dogmatism, closing off one's ability to think in alternative ways. The aim of this text is to show the power of sociological analysis in discovering and making sense of the social world, but without the dogmatism. The process of questioning experience from very different perspectives helps to make visible in practice how starting assumptions and categories of thought actively structure what we see. It may feel confusing and unsettling at first not to find the right answer or the correct version, but it is also empowering to understand how and why the different conceptions of the social world take the forms that they do. The goal of this text is to create space for different voices to be heard.

Suggested Reading

There are many books available that give detailed summaries of each of the approaches outlined in this chapter, but at this stage the goal is to give you a feel for the variety of theories and the controversies in sociology. Particular approaches are studied in later chapters in more depth.

A simple but lively and critical introduction to three perspectives in sociology—order theory, conflict theory, and interpretive theory—is

Harold Boughey, *The Insights of Sociology: An Introduction* (1978). Boughey continually pits the different approaches against each other, encouraging his readers to take sides and join the fray. Sociology for Boughey is not for people who like to sit passively on the sidelines and collect facts. Boughey has a large blind spot, however, in that he gives no attention to feminist theory. Margrit Eichler fills this gap with her book *The Double Standard: A*

Feminist Critique of Feminist Social Science (1980). She shows how many theories in sociology have to be revised to take into account the situation of women.

The best way to get a feel for sociology in practice is to read some studies. Below is a list of material that you might browse through. Most are designed for the general reader rather than the specialist.

Among the finest works in the functionalist tradition are studies of community life. They show how the various institutions of society, economy, family, education, and religion are integrated into a total system. A series that includes many studies of communities in eastern Canada is published by the Institute of Social and Economic Research, Memorial University of Newfoundland. Selected titles include T. Philbrook, *Fisherman, Logger, Merchant, Miner: Social Change and Industrialism in Three Newfoundland Communities* (1966) and N. Iverson and R. Matthews, *Communities in Decline: An Examination of Household Resettlement in Newfoundland* (1968).

Holt, Rinehart and Winston have produced a series of short community studies. Some of the studies that are of particular interest to Canadian readers are N. A. Chance, *The Eskimo of North Alaska* (1966); E. A. Hoebel, *The Cheyennes: Indians of the Great Plains* (1960); and J. A. Hostetler and G. E. Huntington, *The Hutterites in North America* (1965).

An old but excellent functionalist study of a work situation is William Foote Whyte's *Human Relations in the Restaurant Industry* (1948). Whyte describes in intimate detail how all the different employees' roles function together to make up the food-delivery system.

Jean Briggs' *Never in Anger: Portrait of an Eskimo Family* (1970) describes how the Eskimo build a satisfying system of life centred on a subsistence hunting and gathering economy in a harsh environment.

For a critical approach, which focusses particularly on the effects of economic relations on people's lives, a valuable and very readable collection of articles is by Gary Burrill and Ian McKay, *People, Resources, and Power: Critical Perspectives on Underdevelopment and Primary Industries in the Atlantic Region* (1987). These articles look at life in the Atlantic region of Canada, organized around the four issues of agriculture, fishing, forestry, and mining and energy. They speak with anger of how deeply the communities within Atlantic Canada are being damaged by corporate capitalist business practices over which they have no control. The publication *This Magazine* also provides general interest articles on contemporary issues, mostly from a critical perspective. The study by Joan Kuyek, *The Phone Book: Working at the Bell* (1979), provides a worker's view of life in the Bell Telephone Company and how the class relations of capitalism work.

Meg Luxton's *More than a Labour of Love: Three Generations of Women's Work in the Home* (1980), is both Marxist and feminist in orientation. Luxton describes life in the single-industry town of Flin Flon, Manitoba. In one sense Luxton's book is a community study like those suggested above, but the kind of questions she raises about how the lives of people are integrated around the mining economy are very different from traditional functionalist studies.

The many studies by Erving Goffman of everyday interaction and how people create and negotiate definitions of themselves, provide an excellent introduction to interpretive sociology. Some of his smaller and very readable books include *The Presentation of Self in Everyday Life* (1959); *Interaction Ritual: Essays on Face-to-Face Behavior* (1967); *Stigma: Notes on the Management of Spoiled Identity* (1963); and *Strategic Interaction* (1969). When reading studies by Goffman, try to place yourself in the situations of his characters and see how you would have negotiated similar interactions.

Ethnomethodology is an approach that many people initially have difficulty understanding. One fascinating essay is by Harold Garfinkel, "Passing and the Managed Achievement of Sex Status in an Intersexed Person" in *Studies in Ethnomethodology* (1967). Garfinkel describes how a person who was born biologically male, but who chose to be a female, manipulated the entire range of her adolescent relationship to maintain the status of a female. Garfinkel uses the study to show how definitions of masculine and feminine identity are socially constructed in everyday life.

An excellent collection of articles by ethnomethodologists is Roy Turner, ed., *Ethnomethodology* (1974). Part three, "Practical Reasoning in Organizational Settings," is particularly useful in providing examples of how ethnomethodologists do their research.

Gillian Walker's study of "The Conceptual Politics of Struggle" (1990a) is a good example of a social constructionist approach to the analysis of social movements. So is John McKendy's study "Ideological Practices and the Management of Emotions: The Case of 'Wife Abusers'" (1992) which examines the discourse of counsellors in a therapy group for wife batterers and the men's emotional resistance to it.

For a feeling of the feminist approach and the enormous difference that women's studies can make to sociological analysis, see Dorothy Smith's article "Remaking a Life, Remaking Sociology: Reflections of a Feminist" (1992b). She describes the electrifying effect it had on both herself and her students when she first taught a women's studies course.

Questions

1. According to functionalist theory, what two key concepts account for relative stability and order in society?

2. Explain Berger's concept of *circles of social control*.

3. How does political economy theory reinterpret the functionalist concept of consensus in society?

4. List five mechanisms by which members of the dominant class are able to influence prevailing cultural values in a society.

5. What is the relationship between labour-saving technology, abstract labour time, and falling rates of profit?

6. How does interpretive theory modify the functionalist theory of social roles?

7. What is meant by the reflexive character of interaction?

8. In what sense are "facts" about society always worked up?

9. Explain the differences between relations of production and social relations of reproduction.

10. How does feminist theory conceptualize *culture* as essentially masculine?

CHAPTER

3

A Critical Look at Methodologies

Given the variety of theoretical perspectives in sociology, it should come as no surprise that there are also a great many research techniques to choose from. These can be used individually or in combination. No one technique is either better or worse than any other. They are rather more or less appropriate for different kinds of research contexts and different theoretical questions. No fixed correspondence exists between theory and type of methodology, although certain combinations of theory and methods tend to be more common than others. Systems theory, for example, is widely associated with a *positivist* approach that, like the physical sciences, stresses quantitative, objective data rather than subjective or impressionistic research. Those who turn a critical eye on systems theory accuse such sociologists of being "number crunchers," of creating the social world out of surveys, census data, and statistical analysis of trends. Yet systems theory is also associated with the approach of participant observation in

anthropology, in which researchers try to live as participants in another culture, learning from the inside how the complex web of social institutions comes together as a total culture of a people.

Certain writers in the feminist tradition have argued that feminist research necessitates a new and qualitatively different approach in order to get beyond the abstractions of mainstream theory to uncover the intensely personal, intimate experience of women (Duelli Klein 1980). Such methods include listening to women, and encouraging them to speak from their own standpoint and experiences, while imposing the minimum of prior expectations. Other feminists, however, advocate methods to explore the structural patterns that generate such experiences, patterns that may not be immediately visible to the people involved (G. Smith 1990). Yet other feminists have used surveys, census data, and statistical techniques to test generalizations about the situation of large numbers of women (Eichler 1985a, 632–33). The important question is not which method one might prefer, but which is more appropriate for the particular kinds of evidence one is trying to get. As you will see, no method is foolproof. Each has its particular strengths and utility and its particular weaknesses and blind spots. The ideal, therefore, is to have a number of researchers coming at similar issues from different perspectives and starting points. Their studies then will not only complement each other and increase our overall understanding, but will reveal the limitations and blind spots of specific approaches.

This chapter surveys a variety of techniques and gives brief examples of the kinds of research topics that have used them. It examines the value of techniques for gaining knowledge of the social world, and the problems to which each approach is prone. Techniques can be loosely divided into quantitative and qualitative methods. **Quantitative methods** try to establish generalizations that apply to large numbers of people. **Qualitative methods** explore smaller settings in depth with the goal of gaining insight that may subsequently form the basis for broader generalizations.

The objective of this chapter is not to teach you how to do research, but rather to convey a sense of how to be intelligent readers of research. You should not just passively absorb "facts." Rather, it is important to learn to be constructively critical of research findings by developing an awareness both of the strengths of good research and of the inevitable limitations of knowledge.

Experiments

For researchers in the physical sciences, **experiments** are virtually the defining characteristic of the "scientific" method. There is no better technique for testing precise causal relationships. The ideal experiment controls, or holds constant, everything that could possibly influence the phenomenon of interest, then allows one **variable** to change. If there is a change in the phenomenon, and the experiment was done properly, one knows that the manipulated variable, and only that one, could have caused the change. In the terminology of experimental research, the **independent variable** is the presumed cause. This is the one that is manipulated in the experiment to see the effect of its presence or absence. The

dependent variable is the phenomenon that is thought to depend on or be influenced by the other variable.

One interesting sociological experiment began with the observation that students who habitually sat near the front of classrooms tended to get higher marks on average than students who habitually sat near the back (Dooley 1984, 20–23). Two plausible hypotheses were suggested. The phenomenon could be due to "self-selection"; that is, that the more interested and able students chose to sit near the front. Alternatively, it could be that increased interaction and eye contact with the professor stimulated higher performance from students who sat at the front. An experiment was designed to test these theories. The professor let students choose where to sit on the first day of classes, then asked them to stay in that place for the next three weeks until he gave the first test. Then he randomly mixed everybody up, with some of the back-row people moving to the front and some of the front-row people sitting at the back. Three weeks later he tested the students again. The theory was that if self-selection caused the association, then making some of the better students sit at the back would make no difference to their test results. But if sitting at the front under the close eye of the professor was the real cause, then there should be noticeable changes in test results after students were moved.

The results supported the self-selection **hypothesis**, showing that moving people randomly seemed to make little difference to test results. Good students choose to sit at the front and poor students at the back. It was interesting to note, however, that the level of participation, measured by their asking questions and getting involved in class discussions, did change as students were moved from back to front and vice versa. Closeness to the professor rather than personality characteristics of the students seemed to be the major factor in class participation.

This study has all the elements of a true experiment. It includes a clear theory that either self-selection or proximity to professors causes grades to be higher among students who sit near the front. In this experiment, the dependent variable is grades. There are two independent variables—proximity to professor and self-selection. Two logical predictions are derived from this theory. If the theory of self-selection is correct, then moving the students will make no difference to their marks. If proximity to the professor is the correct theory, then moving students will make a clear difference. The researcher changes one variable—where people sit—and everything else is held constant. All students receive the same lectures and tests. The researcher observes what happens and decides which theory is correct on the basis of whether the results were as predicted.

Other experiments can be more exploratory, investigating how people react to controlled situations or stimuli. Such experiments are frequently used in the area of social psychology. Researchers often make use of **small groups laboratories** for such experiments. These are specially equipped rooms designed so that researchers can control key variables such as seating arrangements, lighting, noise, whether subjects in the experiment can or cannot communicate with each other, and so on. The room may be equipped with a one-way mirror so that subjects in the experiment can be observed without being distracted by the visible presence of the researcher.

An example of this kind of experimental research is the study of coalitions and bargaining in competitive three-person games. Experiments suggest that what commonly happens is that two people join together in a partnership that brings them the highest individual outcome rather than agree to a three-person coalition that would make the outcome more equal, but mean less for themselves individually. In games with two women and one man, or with two men and one woman, the two members in the majority sex appear to compete for the member of the opposite sex. Each of the two men, for example, would try to get the woman on his side against the other man. All-female groups tended to be less egoistic than men in coalition formation games and were more likely to form a three-way rather than a two-against-one coalition, dividing the outcomes equally (Archibald 1978, ch. 7). Archibald suggests that the competitive behaviour revealed in these games may not necessarily hold as a universal human trait, but may be more a characteristic of people who live in competitive capitalist societies rather than ones based on co-operative forms of economy.

Experiments have one major advantage over other forms of research in that they provide clear tests of theoretical predictions. Their limitation as a tool in sociological research is that it is rarely possible to control all the variables in a social situation. Experiments can only be done under very particular circumstances. Results may be fascinating, but the question always arises whether it is valid to generalize from what people do in artificial and simplified contexts to how they will behave in complex social institutions in the wider society. Very commonly it is students from large undergraduate courses in sociology and psychology who are used as subjects for experimental research because they are readily available and easily persuaded to participate. The results of experiments that use such specialized subjects cannot necessarily be generalized to the behaviour of others. Feminists in particular have argued that serious distortions are introduced when conclusions from experiments using male subjects are applied as explanations for the behaviour of women.

Another problem peculiar to social science experiments is that of the subjects guessing the purpose of the experiment and accommodating their responses to what they think the experimenter wants. Garfinkel's breaching experiments, where he tried to disturb the taken-for-granted rules of behaviour, failed once too many people have heard of ethnomethodology. A student in Vancouver who nervously tried to breach customary rules for privacy and public space by sitting right next to a stranger on a nearly empty beach was taken aback when the stranger smiled and said, "You must be taking the ethnomethodology class." The stranger's new set of accounting procedures made perfect sense out of the behaviour and robbed it of the bizarre element that the student was trying to create.

Part of the problem of subjects guessing the intent of the experiment stems from the impressions that experimenters themselves can unwittingly give off. A self-fulfilling prophesy can come about whereby people act in such a way that they produce the expected results. This is graphically illustrated by one experiment where psychology students were asked to do learning experiments with rats. Six students were told that they had "maze-bright" rats—that is, rats genetically bred to be particularly bright—while six had "maze-dull" rats. True to expectations, the maze-bright rats learned much faster and made fewer mistakes than the dull ones (Rosenthal and Fode 1963). What is curious is the fact that the animals were randomly distributed: no one set of rats was brighter than the other. The performance differences stemmed entirely from the students' expectations, not from the abilities of the rats. Somehow when students thought they had bright rats, they related to them in ways that stimulated the curiosity of the rats, while those who thought they had stupid animals actually depressed them. In the case of the experiment with student performance and seating arrangements, the professor may also have contributed to the self-fulfilling prophecy by modifying—whether consciously or unconsciously—the way he interacted with his class after he had moved the good students to the back of the room.

It is clear that caution must be exercised in interpreting experimental data. There are also ethical questions to be considered. Do researchers have the right to perform experiments on students when there is at least some risk that certain students may get lower grades because they were made to sit at the back of the classroom? Can people be treated like rats? This, of course, raises the issue of whether rats should be made to live out their lives in psychology laboratories just so students can experiment on them.

Nonscientific factors also come into play in influencing which experiments get published and which are disregarded. Experiments that disprove accepted theory are likely to be dismissed as invalid. A music student taking a biology elective described carefully controlled experiments that seemed to demonstrate that plants not only can hear music, but actually have preferences and are particularly attracted to Beethoven and Ravi Shankar (Tompkins and Bird 1973, 168–75). Standard biology journals refused to publish the results on the grounds that the experiments must be rubbish because plants cannot hear.

Experiments clearly can provide a valuable tool for social research, especially in the interdisciplinary area of social psychology, but they have limited applicability in sociology. The majority of issues that are central to sociological theory are not amenable to experimental testing, although they may draw on some of the insights of experimental results in psychology.

Survey Research

Questionnaires

Survey research is so commonly associated with sociology as to be virtually synonymous with the discipline in the minds of many people. Typically, surveys involve the use of **questionnaires** or structured interviews in which a series of questions is asked of large numbers of people. In theory, one could approach every person in a population when doing a survey, as when a census is taken. But in practice this is so expensive and time-consuming that usually only a sample of people is used. A **sample** comprises a small proportion of people carefully selected from a wider population. On a university campus with 30 000 students, for example, a researcher might interview a selected sample of 300 students (a one percent sample) to study aspects of student life. The goal is to use information gained from the sample to generalize to the wider population it represents.

It is very important that the sample be selected carefully so that it fairly represents the range of experience and characteristics in the population. The data garnered from a survey of 300 students

PEANUTS

PEANUTS reprinted by permission of UFS, Inc.

in a local pub, for example, would not be representative of the student body as a whole since these students differ in important respects from others who rarely or never go to pubs and hence would not be included in the sample.

The ideal way to select a sample is through a random process. A random sample is one in which every member of a population has an equal chance of being selected, leaving no possibility that researchers can select their friends or particular types of people who might be easily available. To draw a random one percent sample of university students, we might get the registrar's list of students, close our eyes and stick a pin in the list to choose the first person for our sample, and then select every hundredth name thereafter, until we had the number of names we wanted for our survey.

One important advantage that surveys have over experiments is that they permit **multivariate analysis**. As we have seen, an experiment studies the effect of change in one variable while all others remain the same. Surveys, in contrast, can gather information about a number of variables at the same time and explore how combinations of variables influence the issue of interest to the researcher. In a survey of students, for example, we might be interested in finding out why some maintain a high grade point average while others fail or barely scrape by. We have good reason to believe that no single variable can explain this. Multiple variables may be involved. We might want to find out not only about students' IQs, but also about how many classes they attend, how many hours a week they study, how often they visit a pub, what kind of family background they have, and so on. Do less intelligent students who study long hours do better or worse on average than highly intelligent students who spend more time socializing than studying? What difference does it make if we also take into account that some students come to university straight from school while others have not been in full-time education for years? With the aid of computers and statistical techniques it is possible to see how sets of variables interact in combination.

One example of large-scale survey research explored patterns of immigrant settlement and race relations in an English city (Richmond et al. 1973). It used a questionnaire with 172 questions, covering such topics as housing conditions and overcrowding, social and economic status,

local slang and idioms, work experience, including discrimination in getting a job and possible prejudice experienced from fellow workers, satisfaction with the neighbourhood, interaction between residents of different ethnic origins, and continuing relations between immigrants and people in their country of origin. The survey also covered the topic of **acculturation**, the extent to which immigrants have adopted the culture—lifestyle, behaviour patterns, values, and attitudes—that prevails among local people.

Responses to a range of questions provided a wealth of material for understanding the life experiences of immigrants and their neighbours and allowed researchers to explore a multitude of hypotheses concerning how variables might relate to each other. Do relations with neighbours improve with acculturation? Are immigrants measurably worse off than indigenous people with respect to housing? Does the level of co-operation or conflict with neighbours vary with ethnic group, social class, or family size and structure? Does it vary in terms of whether immigrants keep their houses in good repair?

Since a complete **enumeration** of the 2633 households in the chosen area was used as the basis for the sample, one can be confident that the results are based on a representative cross-section of the community, free from the biased coverage that would occur if any volunteers or personal friends and contacts of the researchers had been used as sources of information. This particular study was carried out by a team of researchers who went door-to-door, called back many times, took great pains to encourage people to be interviewed because it was so important to learn how everyone felt, and arranged for foreign-language interviews whenever necessary. Virtually no other research technique could have provided the quality of information derived from this survey. Even living within the area as a member of the community would have been less effective, since friendship patterns and acquaintances are invariably limited and selective. Mailed questionnaires or forms that people are left to fill in themselves also could not have achieved this very high level of coverage.

Not all survey research is conducted like this. Such exhaustive surveys take a great deal of time, skill, and money. Under the broad term *survey*, there is a wide variety of techniques that can be used to contact people. At one extreme, tightly structured questionnaires can be mailed out for people to fill in themselves and post back to the research headquarters. Such an approach may be particularly valuable for collecting data on topics that are sensitive or embarrassing. People may feel more comfortable answering questions about their sexual behaviour, for example, in an anonymous questionnaire than with an interviewer facing them. Mailed questionnaires are also quick, relatively cheap to administer, and can be mailed out to very large numbers of people simultaneously.

There are problems, however, that make questionnaires unsuitable for many kinds of research. Clearly, they cannot be sent to illiterate people. They are also unsuitable for many less-educated people who, while able to read and write, may have difficulty understanding the language of the questionnaire and expressing themselves in writing. More importantly, if the questions are the least bit vague or ambiguous, there is no way for the recipient to ask for clarification. Another common problem is inappropriate answer categories that do not fit the person's peculiar circumstances so that she or he is unable to answer accurately. Since recipients cannot explain to the researcher what the problem is, they are likely to answer randomly or pick an inappropriate response and leave it to the researcher to work out what they meant. In addition, the researcher has no way of knowing what people answering the questionnaire meant by their answers and can only assume that what they meant is what the researcher would have meant. If you recall what happened in the experiment described in chapter 2, in which students made sense of the random utterances of a counsellor, you can see why the major critique of survey research raised by ethnomethodologists is that researchers are simply reading into the answers the patterns that they are determined to find. In reality, these patterns might not be there at all. There is much evidence that the wording of the questions themselves can determine, at least in part, the kind of answers given.

Experiments designed to test how people respond to questionnaires suggest that people routinely try to read meanings into questions and construct appropriate answers, even when they cannot possibly know the answer. To oblige the researcher, subjects have been known to rank what, unbeknownst to them, were fictitious television programs. The resulting order is entirely the product of the researcher's question. It is possible that other rank orders, such as ethnic preferences, may be equally artificial, with people actually having no particular preferences, just obliging the researcher.

Other questions distort reality by imposing false answer categories. Consider a question on the quality of relations between siblings that provides the following answer categories: (1) warm, co-operative, supportive relations; (2) helpful and co-operative much of the time; (3) strained, mildly competitive relations; (4) much competition and tension. The problem is that answer categories do not allow for the possibility that people may have very warm and supportive relations that are also very competitive, or tense relations that are not competitive. According to this questionnaire, competition is bad by definition, whatever the respondent might think.

Another problem with questionnaires is that the meaning of answers to questions is commonly context-dependent. For example, attitudes toward the desirability of large families depend heavily on whether one is thinking about family parties or education costs. The coded answer may be meaningless if interpreted out of context (Cicourel 1974).

Distortions can arise when researchers assume they know what the respondent meant by an answer to a particular question, as illustrated by Eichler's (1988a, 82–88) studies of sex-role stereotyping. One question asked the respondent to agree or disagree with the following statement: "If a married woman has to stay away from home for long periods of time in order to have a career, she had better give up the career." More working-class people responded by agreeing with this statement than did middle-class people. This was interpreted as greater sex-role stereotyping among the working classes. However, when a second statement was added, "If a married man has to stay away from home for long periods of time in order to have a career, he had better give up the career," more working-class than middle-class people also agreed with this. The two questions together suggested that what working-class people really meant by their yes response was not sex-role stereotyping of women's work in the home, but rather a generalized sense that family life is more important than jobs for both men and women. In contrast, middle-class people were more inclined to put jobs before family. The interpretive pattern was imposed by the researcher and did not reflect the values of the people being studied.

Surveys are only as useful as the quality of the questions asked. A critical reading of research must involve taking a hard look at the questions used to see whether the researcher's interpretation of the answers is warranted or whether some other meaning could reasonably be applied. The same question with slightly modified wording can quite easily mean different things to different people. In the previous example, if the word *job* had replaced the word *career*, middle-class people might have reacted to the question differently, since giving up a career does not mean quite the same thing as giving up a job.

Interviews

In some respects, interviews are better than questionnaires at clarifying meanings because the interviewer is there to correct ambiguities and misunderstandings. Response rates are also likely to be much higher. People may simply throw a questionnaire into the waste basket, or never get around to answering it, but they will talk to someone standing in front of them, particularly if they get on well with the researcher and actually enjoy the interaction. Researchers can also gather much additional, subtle information by watching the respondents' facial expressions, body language, and so on. People commonly dislike admitting that they do not understand a question for fear of looking stupid. They would rather mutter a vague agreement and let it pass. Vague answers and a confused facial expression may alert the interviewer to the need for a more detailed explanation of what the questions mean. Likewise, when people avert their eyes while answering a question, it may signal that they are not telling the truth.

The very sensitivity of the interview situation, however, may prove its downfall. **Interviewer bias** can become a factor. This is particularly true when the interviewer is unskilled or uninterested. Some interviewers show their feelings to the extent that respondents can guess the kind of answers that would please or disappoint them. Respondents may alter their answers accordingly. In extreme cases, answers may tell us more about the attitudes of the interviewer than those of the respondent.

The distortions that can occur between what a person meant and what their comments are interpreted to mean by a researcher is evident in the reaction of one housewife to the race relations survey referred to earlier. She said that she did not want to be interviewed because she felt researchers always jump to the conclusion that people are prejudiced even if they raise legitimate complaints. She explained carefully that she did not dislike immigrants but hated the way that the immigrant men living in a rooming house on her street would whistle and shout sexual remarks when she walked past them, as if she were one of the local prostitutes. She was also disturbed and intimidated by the noise these men made as they crowded onto the steps outside their house on warm summer evenings. The female interviewer assured the woman that she could understand her feelings. But when the interviewer discussed these remarks with a senior researcher, he responded bluntly that the woman obviously was prejudiced against immigrants and was merely rationalizing her responses. Perhaps he was right. But the problem is that if the woman meant what she said—that she was distressed, not by their racial characteristics, but by the sexual taunts from a crowd of frustrated single men—there was absolutely no way she could say this so that researchers, out to prove their theory that English people are prejudiced, would believe her. There is the risk that researchers' conclusions on the extent of prejudice among the local people stem from the predetermined interpretive scheme used by the researchers rather than from the internally experienced values of the people being studied.

Census Data and Government Records

Census data are immensely valuable for social science research. These comprehensive surveys of the entire population of a country, carried out with government funding, and with the force of law to compel people to answer all the questions, provide a wealth of information about the social, economic, and **demographic** characteristics of a people, which no other form of research can parallel. Since censuses are carried out every ten years in Canada, and within the vast majority of countries in the world, government data banks provide comprehensive historical and comparative information that permits analysis of patterns of social change. Armstrong and Armstrong (1984), among others, have used census data to show changes in the economic status of women in Canada during the twentieth century, tracing proportions of women in different occupations. In addition, reports prepared by Statistics Canada include a labour force study of the relative importance of age, marital status, and education as factors influencing participation of women in the work force (Report 71-509) and a study exploring patterns of job search and success for persons in the labour market (Report 71-525). Reports under the general heading of education, health, and welfare include vital statistics on births, marriages, and deaths, and causes of death and suicide rates by age, sex, and province, with international comparisons (Report 84-528). Other reports can provide detailed information on home values, rents, household facilities, population distribution, education, ethnic groups, religion, language, migration, occupation, income, and so on (Report 95-703).

Many sociologists use the census as their primary source of data for studies of social change. The comprehensiveness of coverage of the population and the huge numbers involved make possible statistical analysis of the interaction between multiple variables. There is no substitute for these kinds of data, and it is consequently a matter of great concern to social scientists what kinds of questions are included in the census. The omission of a simple question such as ethnic origin of parents, for example, would greatly hamper the study of assimilation, migration, and discrimination in the labour market. When one Canadian prime minister even hinted at not carrying out the regular census in order to save money, it was sufficient to have all associations of social scientists start lobbying efforts to retain it. Luckily for sociologists, the business community also wanted the census since demographic data help them in deciding market patterns. The census survived.

Other less comprehensive sources of information are government agency statistics including, for example, crime statistics from the Department of Justice or poverty statistics from the Department of Health and Welfare. These statistics are often released as annual reports.

A famous classical study based entirely upon decades of government statistics is Emile Durkheim's analysis of *Suicide* ([1897] 1951). As we will see in more detail in chapter 6, he showed that suicide rates per 100 000 people varied markedly for different groups. From these patterns, Durkheim tested his thesis that human happiness depends upon social cohesion: the more cohesive the group, the lower the proportion of people too unhappy to live.

As with any other data, the problem with using census data and government statistics for sociological research is that the results are only as good as the methods used to collect the original statistics. If statistics are gathered in a sloppy or biased manner, then the resulting research will also be inaccurate and biased, no matter how carefully the researcher tries to handle the data. The social world comes to us already worked up by somebody else for certain specific purposes, usually those of a bureaucracy (Smith 1974b, 257). We have access to the end product of the statistical rates but not normally to the procedures by which the rates were counted up in the first place. Even census data is not necessarily "factual." During the 1975 mini-census, I was asked how many hours a week I worked. Since this was my first year of university teaching, I estimated it to be about 120 hours a week. The interviewer smiled and said, "For professors, we always put 60 hours." If this was indeed common practice, then any research that correlates hours of work by profession will be invalid. The data might not be any more correct if the estimates given by professors themselves were recorded at face value. Those professors who actually do no more than the minimum nine hours of formal lectures per week are unlikely to admit that they are so lazy, even in a census!

Census data are inadequate in other respects in that the categories used to collect the information may not be those appropriate for the research interests. The census, for example, records the total number of marriages for the period under consideration, but does not indicate whether a given marriage is a first or a subsequent one for the persons involved. It thus becomes impossible to determine how many **reconstituted families** may exist within a community. Similarly, the census records the number of single parents who have children living with them, but does not record the number of men who have fathered children without a long-term attachment to the mother. Records of family income as units give no information on how much money the wife might actually have to call her own. Hence, many interesting questions about family life simply cannot be answered using census data because the recording categories do not permit it (Eichler 1988a, 21–23).

Worse problems can arise, in that it is by no means always obvious how particular experiences are coded into categories used for the statistics. Different record keepers may make these decisions quite differently. Suicide rates for a particular region jumped by fifty percent in one year when government bureaucrats replaced Catholic priests as keepers of the rates (Douglas 1967).

Researchers who mistake the apparent increase in counted suicides as evidence of a real increase in the numbers of people choosing to kill themselves may be building up complex explanations for something that never happened. The statistical "facts" are "socially constructed" by the people doing the original counting. It thus becomes important to study exactly how the data are collected, in order to interpret what the resulting categories actually mean.

As with questionnaires, the actual definitions of categories used by people doing the counting fundamentally determine the resulting rates. The Badgley report on child abuse in Canada (1984, 116) concludes bluntly that it is simply impossible to determine the actual rate of abuse because different methods of counting have produced huge variations in estimates. Reports that state that X percent of children are abused, without indicating precisely the methods used for counting, may be seriously distorting people's grasp of what is actually going on.

Statistics on emotional issues such as child abuse or wife battering are particularly prone to distortion. This distortion can take the form of underreporting, with people trying to keep such behaviour secret, or overreporting, with people using such accusations as powerful mechanisms for social control over others, ammunition in child custody cases, or justification for professional intrusion upon families. Premarital sex was once such a taboo practice that people were reluctant to mention it. Now, in order to appear sophisticated, high-school students may even brag about sexual experiences they have not had.

Statistical Analysis

Statistical analysis in sociology has reached a high level of sophistication with the aid of computers. It is possible to model sets of data to explore the relative impact of many variables upon each other. Such analyses, particularly when based upon large amounts of data, are important tools for exploring social reality, but like all other forms of research, the results are only as valuable as the quality of the original data. As computer analysts are fond of saying, "garbage in, garbage out." It is important to gain some understanding of statistics and how useful they can be, but at the same time to avoid the trap of assuming that, just because evidence is presented in numerical form, it is somehow any more scientific or rigorous or objectively true than any other form of presentation. Darrell Huff, in his book *How to Lie with Statistics* (1954), gives many examples of how numbers can be deliberately used to convey false impressions, particularly in advertising. "Four out of five doctors . . ." gives the impression that one is talking about 80 percent of the medical profession, when in fact one may be discussing only four hand-picked quacks.

Correlations also do not prove **causality**. It may be possible to show that two variables are correlated, in that as one variable increases so does the other, without there being any causal relationship between them. There is a strong association, for example, between increases in the price of rum and increases in the incomes of Presbyterian ministers. Does this mean the ministers are rum-running? Not necessarily. It may reflect merely that both salaries and prices of liquor are affected by inflation in the economy. Bernard Shaw pointed out a strong correlation between age of British men at death and what type of hat they wore. Men who wore top hats seemed to live much longer than men who wore cloth caps. Does this mean we should all start wearing top hats if we want to live longer? Of course not. The association reflects the fact that top hats were worn largely by upper-class men who had much better living conditions and healthier diets than the working-class men who generally wore cloth caps.

The important point with statistics, then, is to read them critically and to question how they have been manipulated from the original counting and what they mean. Numbers do not mean anything in themselves. They have to be interpreted, and this involves critical reading.

Participant Observation

Participant observation involves varying degrees of personal involvement in the everyday lives of the people being studied. Through intimately sharing in their activities on a face-to-face level, observing, questioning, and learning how to participate in their world, the researcher is in a uniquely valuable position to develop a sympathetic understanding of social reality from the perspectives of the people themselves. This is pre-eminently the methodology of anthropology, since it is ideally suited to developing an understanding of the total culture of a people who live in a different society from one's own.

In sociology, **participant observation** has been adapted to the study of distinctive subgroups or interaction within specific social locations or activity groups such as work groups, churches, group homes, and the like. This technique enables sociologists to study the patterns of socialization involved in membership in these subcultures.

The observer can adopt different methods, from concealing the research to openly playing the researcher role. One example of concealed research is Hochschild's (1973) study of old people in a senior citizens' housing project. Hochschild did the research while working as a reporter for the project's monthly newsletter. Through regular involvement in the daily activities of the old people, she was able to gain intimate insights into the complexity of their lives, as no survey or questionnaire could have done. Other sociologists have researched the groups of which they were active members. Becker, for example, studied the lives of jazz musicians in the band in which he himself played. His book, *The Outsiders* (1963), provides a fascinating account of the subcultural values of the musicians who perceived themselves as deviants, set apart from the squares. Through Becker's study we come to see how the musicians view us as audience, and the mechanisms by which they protect themselves and their musical forms from the demands of nonmusicians who hire them to play.

In the case of both the musicians and senior citizens, the people being studied were unaware that they were actually subjects of research. This minimized the likelihood that their consciousness of being observed would influence their behaviour. Other researchers have openly revealed their research interests, trading the value of anonymity for the advantage of being able to question people more directly for insider information. A classic study of this type is Whyte's analysis of *Street Corner Society* (1943). Whyte joined a group of unemployed Italians in Boston, hanging around with them on the streets and participating in their daily activities. His intrusion into their group undoubtedly influenced behaviour initially, but the experience of most researchers is that, as time passes and friendships develop, people soon forget about the fact that they are being researched, and the pre-established routines of behaviour re-emerge. Jules Henry (1971) was able to attain this level of acceptance as an unobtrusive observer while actually living with the families of disturbed children. Within a very short time, family members seemed to fall back into the routines of everyday behaviour with its intimacies, bickering, and fights, as if oblivious of the quiet observer.

Participant observation has the potential, unmatched by any other research technique, for providing a depth of understanding of the lived experience of the people being studied. But it also has its limitations. For a start, it requires a special form of dedication on the part of researchers to be willing to disrupt their own lives in order to immerse themselves in the lives of others. It is immensely time-consuming. Learning by participating takes many months. In anthropology it typically takes two years or more of fieldwork to feel close to achieving competent membership knowledge of another culture.

Participant observation can take a tremendous psychological toll on researchers. Jean Briggs' account of her anthropological fieldwork, *Never in Anger* (1970), describes the emotional stress she experienced while living through one winter with an isolated Inuit community. She recounts her at times desperate efforts to protect her own privacy from the intensely curious and sometimes reproachful gaze of all the members of the community as they, in their turn, studied her.

There is also the risk that the presence of the researcher may alter the interaction being studied. Within the Inuit community, for example, it subsequently became clear to Briggs that the people accommodated to her presence in a number of ways in order to protect her. They left women behind in the camp so that she would not be alone, shortened the distances they travelled so that she could keep up, and hid from her their growing resentment at some of her own behaviour, such as hoarding food supplies, which was anathema to the Inuit.

The biases that result from interaction between researcher and respondents are not peculiar to participant observation but what is problematic, especially given the public character of scientific knowledge, is that participatory research is very difficult to replicate. The complex sets of experiences through which a researcher gains insight into the group that she or he is studying are essentially unique, and the quality of the final analysis depends very heavily upon the personal resources and sensitivities of the individual researcher. Another researcher, joining the group at another time, may draw very different conclusions or impressions of its social reality. The question then arises whether one researcher is correct and the other mistaken, or whether the group culture itself has changed in the meantime.

Margaret Mead has been accused of painting an overly harmonious picture of adolescent life in Samoa, failing to see the teenage strife, delinquency, and illegitimacy that actually occurred (Mead 1928; Freeman 1983). The people themselves may have gone out of their way to hide this seamier side of Samoan life from the gaze of a stranger.

In summary, then, participatory research has both strengths and weaknesses. As a technique, it offers unparalleled depth of insight, but it lacks some of the systematic controls and potential for replication and checking of other techniques. Its greatest strength lies in exploratory studies that open up new areas of knowledge. Subsequent testing of these insights may benefit from more structured approaches. Participant observation is often combined with elements of survey research to provide quantifiable measures of early insights.

Like some other types of research, participant observation studies raise difficult ethical questions. Do sociologists have the right to conduct research on or in a group of people without their prior consent or knowledge? Is it very different if people know that the research is going on but do

The work of Margaret Mead, a pioneer of social research, raised questions of concern about participatory research.

not understand exactly what it is that the researcher is looking for? If we conclude that people should always be told everything, and that their consent should be obtained beforehand, how do we get around the problem that all research would be biased in favour of the kind of people who like the idea of being researched and against the many other kinds of people who, for whatever reason, may decide not to participate? If we are researching an entire village community, whose consent should we obtain? Practical and political considerations usually dictate that we get the permission of the leaders or elders. But it is hard to argue on moral grounds that such people can legitimately speak for everyone else in the community. There are no easy answers to such questions, but we still have an obligation to raise them and to deal with them as best we can. We can state that, at the very least, research should not be carried out in ways that might reasonably be expected to harm the subjects. We will return to this question again at the end of this chapter where we discuss research ethics.

Unobtrusive Measures

In the arsenal of social science research techniques, there are few that avoid the risk of interaction biases between researcher and subjects by focussing upon traces or records of events that have already been completed. Very occasionally some of these **unobtrusive measures** have found their way into sociological studies (Webb et al. 1966). A survey of community tombstones may reveal much about migration patterns, ethnic mix, and relative wealth or poverty of families in different communities, and some hints as to the status of women through the size of lettering accorded to them on family gravestones. A study of janitors (Gold 1951–52) revealed how they sometimes amused themselves by drawing inferences about the lives of tenants from the composition of their garbage. One can potentially learn quite a lot about people from what they throw out. Unopened mail may indicate financial difficulty or unpaid bills, torn letters suggest thwarted love affairs, empty bottles a secret alcoholic, and pet food tins, in the absence of pets, indicate severe poverty.

Other simple research devices have included counting the height and number of nose prints on the glass surrounding museum exhibits to determine the relative popularity of different exhibits and the age range of those most interested. In much the same way, the grubbiest sections of bound journals in a library indicate where the most useful articles are located. Advertisers may survey the settings on car radios in a parking lot to determine which radio station people listen to on the way to work. All such techniques have the value of being unobtrusive, of not disturbing the interaction or the behaviour that is being studied, and of providing rough quantitative data on incidence. Their limitations include the selective survival of traces and sometimes a considerable element of guesswork as to what the traces mean.

Documentary and Textual Analysis

Techniques that focus on written documents provide much greater scope for unobtrusive research into the social reality of the writers. Writing is in essence an intentional form of communication of facts or records and impressions by the authors, often for specific audiences. The social scientist is frequently as interested in reading between the lines to explore the underlying assumptions of the authors as in reading the overt text. An early study by Thomas and Znaniecki, *The Polish Peasant* ([1919] 1971), used the letters and diaries written by Polish immigrants to America to piece together what life was like for these people. The problem, however, is that one cannot be certain that what the immigrants wrote was, or was intended to be, an accurate description of their experience. Immigrants may feel under pressure not to worry family members left behind, to make their accounts more rosy than their experiences really were, and to leave out references to activities of which relatives might disapprove. In the same way, letters that students write home may not be accurate accounts of what they have actually been doing at university. What written records do provide, however, is evidence of the patterns that the authors themselves chose to impose upon their social reality as they tried to make their experiences accountable to others. It is frequently this aspect, as much as factual data, that interests the social science researcher.

A specialized research technique known as **content analysis** has been developed to aid this kind of study of written materials. In such analysis, the content of samples of written material is counted in predefined categories determined by the theoretical hypotheses. Depending on the researchers' interests, this may involve counting the number of times particular topics are raised in newspapers, or in letters and diaries, with a given time frame, the number of column inches devoted to these topics, the number of positive or negative adjectives used to convey approval or disapproval of the topic, and so on. This technique has been used very effectively to study sex **stereotypes** in children's picture books. Researchers count the numbers of stories devoted to activities by girls versus boys, active and passive characters by sex, and the variety of roles in which characters are displayed (Weitzman et al. 1972). The general pattern has been that girls are referred to less often and are usually in passive roles or in situations where they need to be helped by a boy. Similar studies have been done of ethnic and racial stereotypes in literature. The technique can also be adapted to analyse television programs for cultural content and biases.

Textual analysis involves a more sophisticated study of the form, as distinct from the content, of particular pieces of writing, to reveal in detail how meaning is constructed by the **text**. As it concerns the manner in which documents, including written accounts by sociologists, serve to construct definitions of social reality, this method is associated particularly with the theoretical approach of ethnomethodology.

Smith (1974b, 258–59), for example, analyses the way in which texts convey to readers that certain statements, and not others, are to be taken as facts. The factual property of a statement is not intrinsic but is conveyed by the social organization of the text. If a statement is prefaced by the words "in fact" or "the fact of the matter is" or is bluntly stated without qualification—"X is a conservative"—then the statement comes across to the reader as unarguably factual. If the same statement is prefaced by "I think," "I believe," or "she said that X is a conservative," then it comes to the reader as an opinion that can be subject to questioning and interpretation. These subtle changes fundamentally alter the relationship between the reader and the text. The factual form conveys the impression that the statements are fixed and eternal—the same for everyone—while the nonfactual form invites the reader to participate in questioning the underlying social reality.

Smith demonstrates other techniques by which different versions of reality are textually constructed. A powerful tool is the location of "brackets," or the cutting-off points that one chooses to take as the beginning and end of an account of an event. For example, if brackets are placed at one time frame, a confrontation between police and street people may appear as an instance of people throwing rocks at police who then have to defend themselves. But if the brackets are expanded to include events several days earlier, then the same event may appear as police harassment of people who eventually fight back. Police accounts are likely to be presented in factual form as depersonalized aggregate knowledge of what happened. Accounts from other bystanders will be presented in the "I saw" or "it seemed to me" form. Given that most of our knowledge of our social world comes to us in the form of documents, either written or spoken on radio or television, textual analysis has critically important implications for our understanding of how we come to think about our society.

Conversation Analysis

The development of **conversation analysis** is currently at the leading edge of ethnomethodological research, exploring at the most intimate level of interaction how people construct and maintain definitions of social reality. This research examines in minute detail the shape of conversations or sequences of **adjacency pairs** of **utterances** produced by different speakers. The basic assumption is that conversations are structurally organized so that no order is accidental or irrelevant. One example of this type of research includes the analysis of the invitation and acceptance/denial sequence (Heritage 1984, 260–79). The tendency for acceptance to be immediate and refusals to be prefaced by a pause allows the first speaker to add a comment to embellish the invitation or to suggest acceptable excuses such as, "If you have time." These basic forms of interaction are regarded by ethnomethodologists as the foundations of social order. People need to be able to carry on orderly talk before any other level of meaningful interaction can take place. Conversation analysis can play an important part in research involving interviews. Abrupt changes in flow of the talk can signal contradictory and conflicting emotions. The emotional content of the voice also contributes significantly to the implications of what is said (Opie 1992).

Conversation analysis generally relies on tape-recordings rather than memory or re-enactments because of the precision and detail required for the analysis.

Interpreting Evidence

It is fitting that this brief survey of research techniques concludes with content, textual, and conversation analysis. Textual analysis alerts us to the fact that sociology texts, like other forms of writing, are socially constructed, and written to intend their own interpretation. Intelligent reading requires analysis of the bases of factual assertions and the mechanisms by which accounts of social reality are put together. Reading sociology is itself a form of research requiring an active interaction with the text. This does not mean that facts and data are nonexistent, but that they get their importance from what is made of them in interpretation (Said 1981, 154–56). Interpretation occurs not just after the data are collected, but through the entire research process—the kind of questions the researcher thinks important to ask and the way they are asked. Researchers actively construct meanings. There is no such thing as objective factual knowledge simply "out there" to be found. That is why it is often considered very important that researchers include their own commitments and understanding as an explicit part of their research reports (Kirby and McKenna 1989, 7).

Ethics of Research

The responsibility of the researcher to protect informants or subjects of research constitutes the basic ethic of sociology. The Code of Ethics of the Canadian Sociology and Anthropology Association emphasizes that informants should not be damaged by research. In addition, subjects' anonymity must be protected; they have the right to refuse to participate in the research; they should be informed as clearly as is possible of the objectives of the research; and they should have access to the results. The code insists that students in particular should be protected and should not be forced to be subjects of research against their will as a condition of passing their courses. The general ethical guidelines also include the recommendation that, wherever possible, researchers should offer to provide subjects with the results of their study.

The basic ethic of not harming respondents is largely adhered to, but sociology is not without its horror stories of researchers who have shown callous disregard for the well-being of their informants. One piece of research that was considered ethically borderline was a study of homosexuality where the researcher posed as a look-out for men meeting in a public washroom. He then used his vantage point as an opportunity to take down the licence plate numbers of the men in order to learn their identity and to do follow-up interviews with them (Humphreys 1970). There was some debate at the time whether the researcher's doctorate should be withheld, although it was eventually accepted that he had scrupulously protected the anonymity of the men involved. If his research files had come into the wrong hands, however, the men could have been seriously hurt. All research in Canada that is carried out with the aid of university or government funding now has to receive prior approval from a research committee indicating that the techniques proposed are ethically acceptable.

Ethical issues for sociology, however, do not stop at consideration of the well-being of informants. They also include responsibility for the consequences of the final report. All social science research has political implications because of the central role that such research plays in structuring perceptions of social reality of the people being studied. Sociological research is capable of fundamentally influencing the choices people make, the alternatives they perceive, and their understanding of how others relate to them.

Sociological reports are capable of generating self-fulfilling prophesies if sufficient numbers of people come to believe the analysis and orientate their behaviour in accordance with it. White homeowners, for example, are liable to react to nonwhite neighbours quite differently if sociological reports convince them that other people are open-minded and tolerant, than if such reports suggest that other people are sufficiently prejudiced for property values to fall when nonwhite neighbours move in.

A deeper ethical problem concerns the possible uses to which the results of research might be put, particularly by people who have the power to influence social policies. A proposed study of political insurgency in Latin America, known as Project Camelot, was halted on precisely the grounds that such knowledge, in the wrong hands could be dangerous (Horowitz 1968). The project had been conceived as large-scale, fundamental research into social conflict, designed to "predict and influence politically significant aspects of social change, to assess the potential for internal war, . . . and to assess government actions to relieve this." The problem was not that such a topic was not valuable social science, but that the U.S. Army wanted to fund the project and to have access to the results. Mounting political protest halted the study on the grounds that the Army wanted to use the information to crush opposition groups. Closer to home, research into worker satisfaction and productivity in factories has provided management with valuable information on how to manipulate workers to increase their output. Given that managers are in a better position to manipulate the mechanisms for controlling social structures than are workers, it is more likely that managers will benefit from the information than that workers will.

Certain radical and critical social scientists have taken the stand that they have an obligation to redress this imbalance by directing their work toward empowering subordinate groups in society to understand and to manipulate social structures in their own interests (Meis 1983, 123; Kirby and McKenna 1989, ch. 1). Feminist scholars make this commitment when they strive for a sociology *for* rather than *of* women, a sociology that will expose the roots of women's subordination in society as a first step toward changing it. Kirby and McKenna (1989) go further, explicitly striving to design a research methods text that would help ordinary people without special expertise to carry out research for themselves. Then they might participate in creation of knowl-edge instead of being subjects of research carried out by and for dominant groups in society.

Part of this commitment to a noncolonial, nonexploitative way of conducting social science research involves actively recognizing all informants as equals in the research process, sharing their knowledge and information through a process of intersubjectivity or inter-viewing (Oakley 1981, 48) and who may well have much to contribute towards a reshaping of research questions and reflection upon data. This ideal of equality between researcher and participants is not easily achieved. Research commonly involves interaction between people with marked differences in education, status, and power. McRobbie (1991, ch. 4) describes young women on welfare as almost desperate in their compliance and their eagerness to be interviewed. No one had ever taken an interest in their lives or viewpoints before. This is very different from Gayle MacDonald's experience of interviewing female lawyers, who insisted on receiving written copies of questions in advance and on their right to edit resulting transcripts (MacDonald 1993).

The goal of providing subjects with the results of a study is also not easy to achieve. I am well aware that my own research in rural India has helped my career far more directly than it will benefit the village people who taught me so much. There are no easy answers to ethical questions. They constitute an ongoing personal and professional struggle.

Suggested Reading

This chapter is not designed to teach you how to do research. The goal is only to convey a feeling for the variety of research techniques available and the limitations associated with each of them.

There are many textbooks available on research methods in sociology. Some of them are referred to in this chapter, but they tend to be technical and difficult to read. One book stands out as a very readable and straightforward guide to good research practice, Kirby and McKenna's text on *Experience, Research, Social Change* (1989). They share a commitment to making the basic skills of research accessible to nonspecialists, and particularly to subordinated groups or "people on the margins" of social power. They also emphasize the essentially interpretive processes of meaning-construction involved in any research.

Another valuable text is Margrit Eichler's *Nonsexist Research Methods: A Practical Guide* (1988b). Eichler presents an overview of many kinds of research, showing how the ways in which various studies were conducted have distorted the results. She is particularly interested in sexism, but her insights have much broader relevance. She teaches how to read research in a critical way, rather than taking results for granted.

Questions

1. What two very different methods of research are associated with systems theory?

2. Distinguish between qualitative and quantitative research. List two examples of each.

3. List one major advantage and two major disadvantages of using experiments in research.

4. What do we learn from the evidence that rats identified as intelligent learned to run mazes faster than other rats?

5. Define the following terms:
   a. *multivariate analysis*
   b. *random sample*

6. List the principal advantage and the principal disadvantage of doing interviews rather than giving people questionnaires to fill out.

7. Why do correlations not prove causality in statistical analysis?

8. What two critical factors limit the use of an unobtrusive measure like counting instances of some phenomenon?

9. Define what is meant by *adjacency pairs* in conversation analysis. List three such pairs.

10. How does textual analysis differ in principle from content analysis?

PART  II

Testing the Perspectives

4

Loss of Community? The Rural-Urban Debate

The question mark in the title of this chapter is very significant. It is a signal that what you will find here is not a collection of factual knowledge. Rather you will confront evidence and interpretations concerning the nature of rural and urban communities, both now and in the past. This ongoing debate surrounding the patterns of social change calls into question many fundamental assumptions about the structure and functioning of human communities.

The methodology of social science is a critical issue in this chapter. We will trace the processes of formulating a theory, spelling out its basic assumptions, testing them against evidence, and framing conclusions about whether the original theory worked and how it might be modified or replaced by alternative theories that seem better able to account for the evidence at hand.

The loss of community thesis, which we will look at here, originated in the ideology of conservatism in the late nineteenth and early twentieth centuries. The assumptions implicit in this worldview were spelled out in a theory concerning the fundamental characteristics of community life and how they were being threatened. This theory has empirical consequences, and it is these consequences that can be compared with evidence collected through research. In principle, evidence that conflicts with the expected consequences challenges the assumptions on which the initial theory was based and so prompts its revision. In practice, however, this linear progress is complicated by the development of competing theories, which search for very different kinds of evidence. What is particularly problematic is that theories can easily generate blind spots and distortions in the amassing of evidence. As a result, new research may generate more and more evidence. Such evidence can seem to lend overwhelming support for the prevailing body of theory. Competing theories face a major battle in reinterpreting what is perceived as existing "knowledge."

Loss of Community

The loss of community thesis is rooted in the belief that, from the nineteenth century onwards, human communities underwent very profound changes with the development of industrialized, urban centres. This thesis posits a fundamental division between "then" and "now"; it sees a cleft rather than continuity in social history. As the concept of loss implies, the thesis also includes a moral critique of this cleft. The thesis is accompanied by a nostalgia for the past and a vision of a more humane form of **community** based on harmonious, integrated, and stable relationships and collective sentiments of loyalty and belonging. By contrast, the present world is defined in terms of growing individualism, with concomitant disharmony, disintegration, instability, disloyalty, and lack of a sense of belonging. In effect, the thesis constitutes a basic critique of **industrialization** and urban life.

Gemeinschaft and Gesellschaft: Community and Association

The German theorist Ferdinand Tönnies was the first major exponent of the loss of community thesis, which was set out in his study entitled *Gemeinschaft und Gesellschaft* (1887). The term **Gemeinschaft** can loosely be translated into English as *community* and **Gesellschaft** as *association*. Tönnies argues that, with the development of modern industrial society, a very distinctive pattern of social life began to emerge, which differed in almost all respects from the kind of society that it replaced. Preindustrial social life is characterized by what Tönnies refers to as "natural will." Relations among people in preindustrial society are governed by natural ties of kinship and long-established friendship, by familiarity and liking, and by age-old habit and customary ways of doing things. Industrial society, by contrast, is characterized by "rational will." Relations among people are governed by careful deliberation and evaluation of means and ends, or the advantages that people expect to gain from others.

The *gemeinschaft* community, as conceptualized by Tönnies, is akin to the natural community of a living organism. It involves an underlying consensus based on kinship, on residence in a common locality, and on friendship. Relations exist for their own sake and cannot be arbitrarily terminated. Tönnies assumes that this pattern of relations is characteristic of preindustrial society. Social position or status in such a community is clearly defined from birth. It is based on who one is, who one's parents and ancestors were, and one's sex and age. Personal achievements, education, property, and so on, matter little compared with status ascribed by birth. By and large, people in *gemeinschaft* communities are socially immobile, remaining within the same status group, as peasants or nobles, throughout life. People are also geographically immobile, staying in or close by the same locality.

These stable communities are generally homogeneous. People are descended from the same racial stock, and they share the same ethnic identity, religion, language, and way of life, all rigidly enforced by the central institutions of church and family. Both of these institutions derive their strength from the people's unquestioned acceptance of them as natural. Core values within this culture are the sanctity of kinship ties, solidarity as a community, and attachment to the locality. People share a sentimental attachment to conventions handed down through generations of ancestors. Their community operates through dense networks of interaction among people who are highly interrelated through marriage, who know each other well, and who know that they hold cherished values in common.

The *gesellschaft* pattern of relations differs so greatly from this traditional form as scarcely to warrant the term *community*. Tönnies refers to this form as an association of people based on principles of contract and exchange. He conceptualized such a society as merely a mechanical aggregate rather than a living organism, an artificial society that is transitory and superficial. It emerges out of competitive struggles among individuals who do not feel themselves bound together by either kinship or religion. People are geographically mobile and, hence, tend to be heterogeneous with respect to racial and ethnic origins and religious beliefs. Relations among individuals are impersonal, based on rational calculation of advantage. In such calculations the spirit of neighbourly love and the virtues and morality of community life are lost. People tend to collect in large-scale agglomerations rather than in small local groups.

Tönnies' vision of *gesellschaft*—the collapse of community life into an association of individuals motivated by calculated self-interest—was intended as a critique of the order of society underlying industrialization. The fundamental value of capitalism—the rational pursuit of profit and individual advantage—generates dehumanized and artificial relations. George Simmel, a German theorist who was a contemporary of Tönnies, modified Tönnies' ideas to apply more specifically to rural versus urban settings. Simmel identified *gemeinschaft* patterns with rural communities and *gesellschaft* trends with urban settings. He proposed further that a unidirectional process of change was occurring from rural to urban type. Urban life appeared essentially rational, with only weak emotional attachments. Diverse interests further weakened local controls. Like Tönnies, Simmel feared that this weakening of communal solidarity in urban areas would lead to the collapse of a stable social order. Rural community life appeared to be superior to urban lifestyles.

The Chicago School

A number of sociologists working together at the University of Chicago in the late 1920s and 1930s developed a broad body of theory and research that became known as **The Chicago School** of urban sociology. Louis Wirth, Robert Redfield, Robert Park, and Ernest Burgess are important individual theorists in this group. They developed a number of specific theories about different aspects of urban life within the broad functionalist perspective. These theorists accepted the basic classification of rural and urban types and tried to develop them further into theories of change.

One of these theorists, Louis Wirth, in his essay "Urbanism as a Way of Life" (1938) set out a formal theory in which he suggests that the characteristics of the city as a city explain the patterns of culture identified by Tönnies and others. Wirth identified three critical variables as causal determinants of the *gesellschaft* type of community: size, density, and heterogeneity.

The large *size* of urban centres inevitably gives rise to differentiation between people. It becomes impossible to know and to interact with everyone over a wide variety of concerns. Hence, the interactions inevitably become limited and specialized, and therefore superficial, transitory, and

anonymous. The result, suggests Wirth, is the experience of individual loneliness within the urban crowd.

The second key variable is *density*. People are concentrated in a limited space, where they experience overcrowding and pollution. Like rats artificially crowded together in laboratories, people are forced into a competitive struggle for space. Laboratory rats, housed in a spacious cage, live peacefully together. But as more and more animals are crowded into the same space, their behaviour changes. They become increasingly aggressive and more likely to inflict injuries on each other (see studies by Hall 1966, ch. 1; Calhoun 1963; Michelson 1970, 6–7). The Chicago School theorists reasoned that overcrowding in cities would generate similar antisocial behaviour among people.

The third variable is *heterogeneity*. People with different racial and ethnic backgrounds and different occupations and statuses are mixed together. In the face of such heterogeneity, people have divided allegiances and hence cannot form a secure sense of belonging, either to their locality or to the people around them.

In this model, the relation between urban setting and values reverses the original association proposed by Tönnies. For Tönnies, the values of rational, calculated self-interest led to the breakup of community life and to the impetus to gather in cities that offered economic advantages. In the Chicago School model, it was the gathering in cities that led to the loss of community values and their replacement by calculations of individual advantage.

The Chicago School thesis is modelled directly on the functionalist perspective. In this perspective, shared culture and moral consensus are the foundations of social order. **Culture** comprises the complex of language, history, symbol systems, values, attitudes, and behavioural expectations. Broad cultural values, along with patterned expectations for behaviour in specific roles, are internalized through early socialization within families, and reinforced by the institutions of church and school. The central social controls that reinforce conformity are internalized sense of guilt, and desire for acceptance and approval. These moral bases for order and control are weak or absent in the urban agglomeration. *Heterogeneity* of social backgrounds means that urban residents lack a common core of culture and moral consensus. Individuals cannot assume that other people have internalized the same behavioural expectations and values. Distrust and fear in interpersonal relations are the likely result of this unpredictability. Moreover, *large size* and the resulting prevalence of limited and specialized interaction among strangers, weakens traditional sanctions on behaviour. People have less concern with social approval and acceptance from strangers. The other variable, *high density*, increases frustrations and competition and so promotes aggression and crime. In terms of Berger's model of circles of social control (see figure 2-1), the intimate controls of guilt and need for social approval cannot be expected to work in context. With these sanctions weakened, control increasingly has to take the form of force—the option of last resort.

The overwhelming impression that comes through these theories of urbanism is a sense of loss and regress, rather than positive change for the better. The term *loss of community* expresses dissatisfaction with the quality of contemporary urban life and a desire to return to a more humane society where individuals were integrated into a stable and harmonious community of family, friends, and neighbours. The past may well not have been as rosy as this idealized image of integrated community life. But the feelings of loss cannot be dismissed as merely misguided nostalgia, for what they articulate is a deep criticism of the present.

Summary: Predictions that Follow from the Theory

The focus in this chapter is on testing theories in rural and urban sociology. We explore the predictions or consequences that can be logically derived from traditional theories and compare them with the predictions that can be derived from alternative systems of explanation. You should keep in mind that plausible arguments, however convincing they might sound, are not necessarily correct. They need to be tested in a systematic way against evidence, and the evidence itself has to be scrutinized for the biases and distortions that preconceived notions can impose.

A central prediction of Wirth's theory is that, where population settlement is small in size, of low density, and relatively homogeneous, as in

rural areas, one can expect the sense of community to be strong and characterized by intimacy, co-operation, and a clear sense of security and personal identity. Alternatively, in large cities such as Toronto and Montreal, and more so in metropolises such as New York, London, and Tokyo, relationships will be superficial and competitive, with limited sense of belonging to a cohesive and satisfying community. In effect, one can expect to find a rural-to-urban continuum with the sense of community being strongest in the smallest settlements and steadily weaker as the size of the city and overcrowding increase.

Wirth predicted that sense of community is weakest in large, dense cities, but some theorists suggest this is a myth.

An Alternative Theory: Political Economy

As we argued in chapter 2, the most useful and productive way to test a theory is to compare it with an alternative theory that begins from different assumptions and makes different predictions.

In this chapter the most important alternative theory to the Chicago School is the political economy perspective, which draws heavily on the work of Karl Marx. It starts out from different assumptions and makes different predictions about the changing quality of rural and urban community life. This theory finds the same evidence of dehumanization—loss of community and dissatisfaction among people in contemporary industrial society—but explains it in terms of different causes. The dehumanizing effects of capitalism are seen as crucial, with insecurity stemming from poverty, inflation, and unemployment, and exploitation at work. This theory does not predict that people living in small towns or rural areas will be any more or less happy than people in urban areas. It predicts rather that people who have economic security, and who control their own means of production, will develop satisfying social relations with others, while this sense of community will collapse when fundamental economic security is undermined. To the extent that villages are comprised of farmers or small producers who have both security and independence, such communities are likely to be contented and cohesive. But economically insecure rural poor are as likely as the urban poor to experience a breakdown in sense of community. Political economy theory is closer to the original ideas of Tönnies than is the Chicago School model. It implies an indictment not of cities as such, but of the values of rational, calculated self-interest that pervade industrial capitalist society at all levels.

In the following review of research in rural and urban sociology in Canada, we explore first the contribution of traditional theory to the analysis of folk society or precapitalist rural life in Quebec. This is followed by studies of contemporary rural and urban communities. With respect to each broad area, we draw attention to evidence that seems to contradict the basic assumptions of the Chicago School model. Similar research contexts are re-examined from the perspective of political economy theory to test the extent to which it can account for these apparent contradictions. Later in the chapter, we explore the contribution of the social constructionist perspective, and the closely related work of feminist urban geography.

Folk Society: A Test of the Chicago School Thesis

Robert Redfield (1947), another contributor to the Chicago School, elaborated an **ideal-type model** of **folk society** to contrast with urban society, based on the work of Tönnies, Simmel, and Wirth. An ideal-type model is designed as a tool for research to highlight typical features of the kind of society or social institution being studied. Any particular case may not have all the features listed in the model, but the broad characteristics should be visible. Redfield was particularly interested in the folk communities typical of relatively isolated rural areas. In his model he highlighted five key features: (1) folk communities are organized around family and kinship ties; (2) they involve intimate face-to-face relations; (3) they have minimal specialization or division of labour; (4) people are united by a strong sense of local identity, loyalties, and obligations; and (5) the members support a deep commitment to shared cultural values and ways of behaviour.

The model of an urban society incorporates the opposite of these key features, namely, (1) weak family ties; (2) superficial relations between strangers; (3) a high degree of specialization of occupations; (4) limited cohesion; and (5) readiness to adopt new and changing values and ways of behaving. Redfield suggests that the typical differences between a hamlet, a village, a trading centre, and a city can be described in terms of a systematic and linear process of change from folk to urban characteristics.

Redfield (1930) found strong support for his thesis that rural communities are more cohesive than urban centres in his pioneering study of life in Mexico in the 1930s. He describes the small village of Tepoztlan as a homogeneous, smoothly functioning, well-integrated, contented, stable, and harmonious community. He compared it favourably with a neighbouring town, which he characterized as heterogeneous and faction-ridden.

This powerful support for his folk society model was not to go unchallenged, however. A study of the same village by Oscar Lewis (1949), conducted less than twenty years later, shattered the harmonious image and, with it, some of the credibility of Redfield's thesis. Lewis argues that Redfield biased his research by focussing only on co-operative and unifying factors. He charges Redfield with glossing over evidence of violence, cruelty, disease, suffering, poverty, economic and social maladjustment, and political schisms. Redfield later attempted to defend himself by arguing that Lewis had imposed his own value judgments on his research. Lewis wanted to find support for the Marxist argument that the low material standard of living in Tepoztlan gave rise to social maladjustment. Hence he went out of his way to look for evidence of suffering and stress in the community, and then overemphasized the problems that he found. Whatever the validity of this response by Redfield, Lewis's work did challenge the image of the village as an ideal-type *gemeinschaft* community.

Quebec Folk Society

In Canadian research, studies of the folk society of rural Quebec offer powerful and convincing descriptions of life that accord closely with the *gemeinschaft* image. But these studies, too, have been subject to the criticism that researchers found just what they were looking for, rather than what was actually there. A widely cited study of French-Canadian folk society is that by Horace Miner (1939) on the parish of St Denis. Robert Redfield wrote the introduction to the book, and he leaves no doubt that he views St Denis as the epitome of a folk society: "Habitants live in terms of common understandings which are rooted in tradition. . . . Fundamental views of life are shared by everyone, and these views find consistent expression in the beliefs, institutions, rituals, and manners of the people" (Redfield 1964, 58). Sanctions have a strongly sacred character in St Denis. The way of life of the people is endorsed by the priest, but followed because of deeply felt convictions of the people themselves rather than due to any pressure from outside authority. The family system is also strong, pervasive, and certain in its effects. Almost all aspects of life—work, getting married, finding a career, politics—are largely determined by position in a family. There is minimal social disorganization.

Redfield and Miner acknowledge that the fact that St Denis is not an isolated peasant community, but part of a modern urbanized world, cannot be ignored. But this can be discounted in large measure. Although people do have connections with the city, and even relatives who live there, this exposure to alien influences is mediated by the Catholic Church, which "has stood between the changing world and the habitant, preventing admission of elements which she [the church] condemns and interpreting admitted elements in accordance with the faith and with the local culture" (Redfield 1964, 60). When local ways are threatened, the church minimizes the

influence of outside forces and so helps to preserve the folk character of the community.

The only threat to this way of life has come from the structural problem of land pressure (Miner 1964, 66), a consequence of traditionally large families, indivisible small farms, and limited supply of land. Farmers needed money to educate sons for alternative city jobs or to buy farms for them. The result, suggests Miner, was the gradual erosion of independent subsistence farming as a way of life. Farmers slowly became more dependent on the outside economy. The only other solution to the land pressure problem would have been to cut the birth rate, but Miner argues that this was strongly opposed by the Catholic Church, which has always played a vital role in the rural parish. Birth rates declined rapidly in urban areas during the interwar years, but not in the villages, suggesting to Miner that the old culture of religion and **familism**—or life centring on the family—was not disrupted.

Hubert Guindon (1964) and Marcel Rioux (1964) similarly defend the appropriateness of the folk society model as applied to rural Quebec until well into the twentieth century. They cite evidence of strong family ties, low geographic and social mobility, the central importance of inherited land, and the powerful moral leadership of the clergy in perpetuating the folk character of communities such as St Denis. Rioux characterizes rural Quebec as made up of small communities, with few outside contacts, and with people bound together by organic ties of family, culture, and church. It is this folk cultural identity, Rioux suggests, that underlies contemporary Quebec nationalism and sense of French-Canadian identity. Although Quebec has an urban population, Rioux argues that the province can still be characterized as essentially a rural folk culture.

It is Philippe Garigue (1964) who challenges the validity of this folk society thesis in the context of rural Quebec, notwithstanding the wealth of data in its support. Garigue, like Oscar Lewis, argues that the model has led researchers to overemphasize evidence that supports it, and to minimize the relevance of empirical data not related to the definition. He suggests that the concept of *folk society* is not valid in French-Canadian history nor is it appropriate for contemporary rural Quebec. Historically, he argues, there never were the equivalent of close-knit, self-contained, traditionalist, organic communities in rural Quebec. The land was colonized by a process of ribbon development out from small towns, which acted as colonial trading posts. Individual farms were established in parallel rows, first fronting a river and then on an interior road built for the purpose.

This pattern of settlement militated against the development of close-knit communities, suggests Garigue. Farmers were fiercely individualistic. They built houses in the middle of their own individual plots about three miles away from neighbours in either direction. Only much later did communities or villages begin to emerge once a church was built in the district. The church provided an initial gathering place around which other buildings were established. Old people tended to move near the church when they retired, and the locality slowly began to function as a service centre for the district. Only at this stage could a village be said to exist. But the development of such a village centre did not substantially alter the private family individualism of independent farmers. In 1663, Louis XIV of France tried, for administrative convenience, to force settlers or habitants to build houses in village groups rather than on their own land (Falardeau 1964, 20). But such edicts were strongly resisted. Farm families refused to move. People maintained social relationships with the families living on neighbouring plots, but had no desire to form village communities. Parishes were not formed until long after colonial settlement, and they constituted only huge administrative areas. Throughout most of Quebec's history, they could not be equated with rural communities.

Tenancies were frequently bought and sold (Garigue 1964, 126). This, too, challenges the notion of cohesive, long-settled folk communities. In addition, one researcher found that entire families had moved away from parishes to seek their fortune elsewhere. Nobody seemed to find this unusual or regrettable (Gérin 1964, 36).

The structural constraints of large families, indivisible farms, and limited land meant that the majority of children in any large family could not settle near home. They had to seek a livelihood elsewhere. Thus, there was considerable geographic mobility within families, contradicting the folk society model, despite the near truism that there was low mobility among the people who stayed behind. Usually only the youngest son would inherit the family farm when the parents

were too old to farm it themselves. Older sons left. Only the lucky ones among them got farms in neighbouring parishes. This accounts for the observation that rural families in the 1950s were not usually centred in one community but were spread all over the province of Quebec and beyond (Garigue 1964, 134).

Garigue challenges even the notion of an all-embracing church with a subservient flock of parishioners. He cites evidence of widespread accounts of laypersons who refused to obey their priests, or even the bishop, over such matters as building a church and paying dues (Garigue 1964, 129–30). Thus, in multiple ways, Garigue argues that rural settlement in Quebec does not conform to the folk society model. The concept, he suggests, is a myth, an ideology imposed on the data by the researchers. The intensely individualistic, independent farmers that Garigue found have more in common with the image of nuclear family individualism, characteristic of urban life, than with the Chicago School caricature of people embedded within an organic folk society.

The Myth of Quebec Motherhood

Another strong challenge to the notion of folk culture in Quebec comes from an unlikely source, a re-evaluation of fertility data. Marie Lavigne (1986) questions the image of the fertile French-Canadian mother, dominated by the Catholic clergy and local political elites advocating a large French-speaking population. Québécois women have been portrayed as fertile mothers, responding not only to Catholic admonitions to have as many children as possible but also to nationalistic propaganda exhorting "the revenge of the cradle." Lavigne questions how we can reconcile this image with the history of the women's movement in Quebec from the nineteenth century onwards. Her answer is that this fertile mother image is largely a myth, applying at best to about one-fifth of all Quebec women from the 1850s onwards, when her data begin. Folk culture values, admonitions from the clergy, lack of access to modern contraceptives, and their illegality prior to 1968 notwithstanding, the birth rate in Quebec fell steadily every decade between 1850 and 1961.

As table 4-1 shows, of the women born during the years 1887, 1903, and 1913, at least 25 percent never became mothers. Most of these childless women remained unmarried, and only a small minority of them became nuns. A further 15 to 25 percent of women made only a minimal contribution to fertility rates by having one or two children. At the other extreme, the ideal-typical large family of ten or more children was produced by less than one-fifth of the 1887 **cohort**. This ratio dropped to about one in fifteen women by 1913. The percentage of women having six or more children also dropped from almost 40 percent to just over 20 percent in the same period. This sharp drop indicates that many girls whose mothers had large numbers of children did not see this model of motherhood as one they wanted to copy.

Table 4-1

Birth Cohorts of Women by Marital Status and Number of Children, Quebec			
	Birth Cohort		
Number of Children	1887	1903	1913
0	10.8	13.7	11.9
1–2	15.8	21.2	25.2
3–5	21.9	22.8	27.4
6–9	19.7	16.3	14.7
10 or more	17.7	11.0	6.5
Unmarried women	14.1	15.0	14.3
Total	100	100	100

Source: Lavigne (1986). Calculations based on Henripin (1968).

Clearly, large numbers of women did practise contraception, regardless of the church's teachings on the subject. Interviews in 1950 with elderly women who had their families at the turn of the century, indicated that they had not been particularly influenced by church doctrine, despite outward conformity. They practised contraception and still went to church. Lavigne argues from these data that we have to revise our view of the influence of religion on family life in Quebec. It appears to have been considerably shallower than the folk culture model would lead us to believe. We only have to compare these data with Redfield's commentary at the beginning of the study of St Denis—with his references to the sacred character of sanctions, the deeply felt convictions of the people, and the family system as "strong, pervasive, and certain in its effects"—to

realize how significant a challenge Lavigne's work presents to taken-for-granted theories.

We still need to ask where the image of fertile French-Canadian women comes from, if the majority of women did not conform to it. Lavigne points out that the collective memory that all Québécois ancestors had large families derives from the fact that most people remember the same minority of women. For example, if, hypothetically, ten women have one child each and one woman has ten children, half of the resulting twenty children in the second generation will have grown up in a large family, even though 90 percent of families did not conform to this pattern.

From Lavigne's article we learn that strong convictions, even when they appear well substantiated by evidence, may still give a false overall picture. The folk society concept of large families, inherited land, and overarching religious control by the Catholic Church is not wholly false, in that it does apply to a portion of people. The problem is that it may not fit more than half the members of the community. The majority of women and men made decisions about their family size that conflicted with the teachings of the church. It cannot even be assumed that women with large families were mindlessly following church edicts. Lavigne suggests the economic factors, like the usefulness of child labour on farms and in the textile mills or the disadvantages of large families once schooling became compulsory, played a role in decisions about family size. Women make

Critics of the folk society model argue that large families were not as common in French society as the myth of the fertile Québécoise would suggest.

rational choices in historical-economic circumstances, Lavigne suggests, rather than conforming unquestioningly to cultural norms. It would seem, then, that the folk culture model obscures more than it reveals about life in rural Quebec.

Contemporary Rural Communities

The second stage of our critical review of rural-urban sociology in Canada turns from historical research to more contemporary studies of village communities. The main questions are the same. Do the characteristics described by researchers fit the Chicago School model? Is there sufficient contradictory evidence to suggest that the basic assumptions of the model are false?

In this section we will focus on Louis Wirth's causal model of the determinants of *gemeinschaft* and *gesellschaft* communities. As we saw earlier in this chapter, Wirth argues that three critical variables—large size, high density, and heterogeneity—generate *gesellschaft* types of association. *Gesellschaft* patterns include superficial, anonymous, and transitory relations, competitive struggle, divided allegiances, and limited sense of belonging, either to a locality or with the neighbouring people. The logical obverse of Wirth's three variables—small size, low density, and homogeneity—should maximize the probability of *gemeinschaft* relations. These are characterized by close-knit communities based on the sanctity of kinship ties, solidarity, attachment to the locality and to the core of shared cultural values. How well does this model stand up to contemporary research on rural communities?

Samuel Clark's controversial study of four selected villages in the Miramichi and Bathurst areas of New Brunswick, conducted during 1972–73, offers little to support the image of *gemeinschaft* communities. The villages have the characteristics of small size, low population density, and homogeneity, but the social life described by Clark (1978, ch. 3) is anything but well-integrated and cohesive. Instead he gives a picture of rural society in a state of deterioration, with little evidence of any rich social life. The impression is one of people shut in on themselves. Not only did residents have little contact

with the outside world, many of them indicated that they did scarcely any visiting among neighbours. "No one ever visits," said one respondent. "Television ruined that," said another. "People visit less now, got no reason to visit. . . . I'm not one for visiting." Many residents complained about the lack of social activity in their area, yet they gave no indication of any inclination to do anything about it. "There's not much social life here. People don't try to get together," was a typical response.

Two sets of ties did have some meaning: kinship and church. Almost everyone in the communities was either a relative or a neighbour of a relative of someone else in the community, and few new people moved in. Yet Clark found that kinship obligations appeared shallow and rarely extended beyond the immediate family circle. In Catholic communities virtually everyone went to mass, while in Protestant areas church attendance tended to be associated with higher status. But in either case church did not form the focus of much active social life.

Apart from what limited social life developed around kinship and church, the communities appeared to lack anything in the character of a social structure. A few residents in these villages indicated that they belonged to clubs or bought a newspaper, but most did not. Clark concludes that what generally obtained was "what might be described as a state of social anomie." **Anomie** is a state of social breakdown, characterized by weak bonds between people, a limited sense of meaningful relations, and the lack of any strong commitment to shared norms and regulations guiding interactions. Most residents appeared to have little feelings for their social obligations; that is, what they owed to their local community or to the society at large. There was nothing to support the view of idyllic contentment. Mostly people gave vent to their grievances, discouragement, and at times despair. The dominant attitude was a fatalistic acceptance of things as they were.

The two other communities in the study, located on the outskirts of large towns, showed similarly impoverished social life. There was evidence of a good deal of animosity and little visiting among neighbours. One person described her neighbours as "a God-damned bad crowd—from way back in the woods where they never see no people, only bear and fox. Maybe is good people. We can't tell" (Clark 1978, 92). Insecurity and fear of crime were widely felt in these communities. Interviewing was actually cut short because "the field-workers had reason to fear for their physical safety had they attempted any extensive interviewing in the more congested parts of the inner area" (Clark 1978, 73). People were suspicious that interviewers on the project might be government agents, checking on them with the intention of cutting off their welfare payments.

We will return to this study later, and the responses of local people that suggest this pervasive image of anomie may have been overdrawn and overgeneralized. But something clearly is at odds with the Chicago School thesis. According to Louis Wirth's theory of causality, the small, low-density, and homogeneous kinship-related areas in New Brunswick ought to have been harmonious and integrated communities. But they were not. Clark's study is not alone in finding that small size, low-density living, and homogeneity do not ensure close community ties. The image of idyllic rustic communities may be part of our collective cultural mythology, but it is not part of the contemporary reality of village and small-town life. A 1983 study of towns and villages in Canada concludes that, while Gallup polls may show that people still express preferences for farm and small community living, citing the appeal of peace and friendliness and simplicity of life in the countryside for city-weary, ecology-conscious, and independent urbanites, there is little evidence to support these images (Hodge and Qadeer 1983, 131). The study suggests that, while individual towns and villages differ widely from each other, patterns of daily life show minimal differences between rural and metropolitan centres.

Small communities are not necessarily safer places than big cities. The per capita incidence of crimes of violence may actually be higher in small towns than in cities. To the outside world, small towns and villages may present a face of serenity, but internally they are communities with a fair degree of individualism and social division (Hodge and Qadeer 1983, 143). Smallness results in high visibility, and hence familiarity between residents, but this does not necessarily lead to sociability and friendliness. Often small towns harbour a hard core of poverty that is combined with a general indifference toward the poor. Prejudice is also often present. Racial and ethnic minorities may be tolerated, but they are often made to feel unwelcome.

These negative accounts of social disorganization in rural communities should not be taken to imply that all or even most rural communities are characterized by social anomie. Towns and villages vary widely. There are innumerable small settlements that provide satisfying community life for the residents. The critical point here is that smallness and homogeneity by themselves do not guarantee integrated community spirit. To explain such patterns we need more complex explanations than the Chicago School model provides.

Urban Communities: The Myth of Anomie

Chicago School theorists saw cities as made up of distinctive zones or "ecological areas" that emerged and changed as the population expanded with successive waves of migrants. This approach is particularly associated with the work of Robert Park (1916; 1936) and Ernest Burgess. Park argued that the most recent migrants would necessarily have to compete for space with existing residents. Economically dominant groups would be able to command their space, or invade favourable new areas, while others are crowded out. The weakest groups become concentrated in the poorest zones, usually in deteriorating older properties in the city centre. Here, housing is surrounded by office blocks and factories for light manufacturing. Working-class families would be housed in somewhat better housing around this inner core, with middle-class homes located further out, and spacious higher-class housing farthest away from the deteriorating city core. These early ecological models—seeing people in relation to their distinctive habitat zones within cities— have been revised and adapted to the experience of individual cities, and have been used extensively to plot ethnic migration patterns (Driedger 1991, ch. 4).

In this chapter our central interest will be with testing Wirth's model of urbanism as a way of life with respect to different residential zones. If many rural communities do not fit the folk image, can it be argued that the metropolitan environment, characterized by large size, high-density living, and heterogeneity, necessarily results in a loss of community? Research in urban sociology in Canada leads to a convincing "no." The Chicago School zones theory predicted that local neighbourhoods would decline in significance in urban centres. Nuclear families would be mobile and hence isolated, detached from strong allegiance to kinship ties beyond those of husband, wife, and dependent children. Social disorganization would increase with the demise of traditional bases of social solidarity.

Middle-Class Boroughs

Research in the Metropolitan Toronto borough of East York did not bear out these predictions (Wellman 1978; Shulman 1976). A study of a small sample of young, native-born, anglophone, lower middle-class couples found that these people did not live isolated lives. Geographic integration between generations was quite high. People valued being near to other family members and wanted frequent interaction with them. Three-quarters of the sample visited kin in the metropolitan area at least once a week. The minority whose parents lived farther away saw them less frequently. Couples expressed a sense of obligation to keep in contact with other family members. They regularly initiated contacts and participated in common ritual activities such as birthdays and anniversaries. Almost one-third saw their parents more than any other persons. The telephone was also a common means of contact.

The studies of East York note that mutual aid was very important between young couples and their parents. Almost half the young couples lived with one set of parents during the early years of marriage, before they could afford a place of their own. Common forms of aid included young people caring for sick parents, and grandparents babysitting their grandchildren. Parents also gave financial aid in crises, while young adults helped their parents with house repairs and with other needs of older people. The prediction that urban life would result in the breakdown of kinship ties was not substantiated in East York.

The prediction that high mobility would result in social isolation was similarly not supported by the data from studies in Fredericton and Montreal (McGahan 1982, 239–41). Geographic mobility did not reduce the size of the **kin universe**. The average number of kin contacted did not differ between the mobile and nonmobile urbanites. The nonmobile people had more face-to-face contacts, while the others used letters and telephones to keep in touch with relatives. There was no difference between them in the importance that accorded to the kinship bond. The death of central connecting relatives was more important than geographic mobility in terminating kin ties.

Because of the strength of the image of large, traditional, rural families, French-Canadian families provide a particularly valuable test of the thesis that family ties decline with urban residence. One would expect city families to present a very different picture from rural ones, but in fact we do not find this. The data totally contradict the prediction that nuclear family isolation would be evident in urban areas. People in the Montreal sample were able to name, on average, 215 relatives. Women were generally able to name more relatives than could men in the sample, and wives could often name more of their husbands' relatives than the husbands knew themselves (Garigue 1956). Women had much greater knowledge of the affairs of the kin group and interacted with the group more frequently. Contact with both parents and siblings was sustained regardless of geographic location. In the French-Canadian community in St Boniface, Manitoba, mobility also did not disrupt kinship bonds (Piddington 1965). Instead, migrant kin tended to cluster together, and chain migration was common. Intermarriage among distant kin was not unusual.

Zones Within the City Centre

The strongest predictions of urban anomie and blight in the Chicago School thesis are directed at the inner city, seen as the locality with the highest density and the most mobile and heterogeneous populations. The term **inner city**, referring to the central areas of old properties within large cities, actually encompasses a wide variety of neighbourhoods, including the commercial core of office blocks, stable working-class areas, slums and "skid row." The inner city has increasingly come to include revitalized areas where more affluent middle-class people have bought up and renovated old properties. Clearly these different neighbourhoods vary widely in community character.

Working-Class Zones

Stable working-class areas in large cities show a consistent pattern of close identification with neighbourhood and kin. McGahan (1982) cites the example of Toronto's Cabbagetown, a locality then inhabited predominantly by Anglo-Saxon, blue-collar, semiskilled or unskilled workers with below average incomes (Lorimer and Phillips 1971). Family roles were very traditional and were segregated along age and sex lines, but family ties were strong, with mutual support and obligations. Circles of close friends commonly included kin, often parents and adult children.

This pattern confirms what many other studies have found. A famous one is Young and Willmott's study (1957) of the working-class area of Bethnal Green in East London. In the heart of one of the largest cities in the world, they found not an anonymous *gesellschaft* but a stable, homogeneous, and very close-knit community. On a shopping trip, for example, one of their respondents met sixty-three people she knew, thirty-eight of whom were relatives. Herbert Gans (1962) found a similar pattern in the Italian neighbourhood in Boston.

Over the past decades in many cities in Canada and the United States, the cohesiveness of these old working-class communities has been disrupted by middle-class renovators looking for the convenience of downtown residence. This influx can erode the cohesiveness of the inner-city working-class and ethnic communities. Tensions in Cabbagetown in Toronto have resulted as middle-class renovators buy up neighbourhood houses. Relations between the long-term residents and the renovators are described as cautious but edgy, with a mutual recognition that they are quite different types of people. The newcomers tend to be less noisy and "troublesome" than some working-class residents, but on the other hand these newcomers cause more annoyance by making a fuss about such things as the congestion created by neighbours parking on the street (McGahan 1982, 273). Nonetheless, the impression from the research is that the working-class residents derive much satisfaction from living in Cabbagetown, and have a sense of identity with the neighbourhood. This is shown in their organized opposition to the city's urban renewal plans. Their middle-class neighbours may think them disorganized, but the image they give of themselves is one of strong community cohesion.

Urban Slums

A central presumption among town planners is that physical deterioration goes with social deterioration and that urban slums are dangerous areas that should be avoided. Yet even in the slums one can find some evidence of integrated social order based on loyalties to ethnic group and to territory. One famous study was conducted in the mid-1960s in the Addams area in Chicago. This area comprised half a square mile and had a population of 20 000 people including Italians, blacks, Mexicans, and Puerto Ricans (Suttles 1968, 1972). Even in this area of high density, heterogeneity, and poverty, an underlying social order existed with territoriality and ethnicity providing bases for association and integration. A certain mutual trust and predictability developed among the various groups, which were subdivided by ethnicity, territory, age, and sex. Sectors opposed each other at times but were also able to co-operate against a common enemy from outside the neighbourhood. Street life was critical for forming personal acquaintances. People got to know each other as they lounged on street corners or met informally in local businesses and corner stores. In effect the middle-class view of the slums was not supported by the residents themselves. For most it was a viable community with which they could identify.

Skid Row Areas

A study of hobos, or the men on skid row, reflects the same discovery that, behind the appearance of destitution and personal disorganization, there is nonetheless a recognizable and, in some measure, supportive social organization (Harper 1979). When the researcher spent two weeks living and travelling with a hobo companion, he found that the man had a network of lifelong friends, and that together they had their own complex system of stratification and moral obligations.

An important word of caution here is that, just as Redfield found what he was looking for in describing harmonious village relations, so other researchers may be overemphasizing the sense of social organization to the exclusion of tensions and hostilities. In an effort to counter the middle-class bias that too easily equates poverty with disorganization, they may be overstating the opposite image. Nonetheless, these studies demonstrate that, just as a village environment does not guarantee cohesive community relations, neither does a densely populated, mobile, and heterogeneous urban environment preclude integrated community relations, local loyalties, and strong kinship ties. The predictions of the Chicago School theory are not borne out.

In Regent Park, Toronto, residents experienced a sense of community despite poor living conditions. The city's urban renewal plans to build high density housing met with organized neighbourhood opposition.

The Limitations of Chicago School Theory

This overview of the findings of rural-urban research—into the "folk" society of Quebec, contemporary life in villages and small towns, and conditions in different urban areas points to the general failure of the Chicago School thesis. The model predicts that small and homogeneous villages will function as integrated and cohesive communities. Loneliness, isolation, and social disorganization will increase steadily as size, density, and heterogeneity increase, and will reach their worst extreme in the centre of metropolitan cities. No doubt instances can be found to fit the model, but these are not sufficient for the theory to be retained. What matters is that there is clear evidence that these predictions have failed in many instances. We have examples of villages where residents described their lives in terms of loneliness, isolation, and distrust; alternatively we have examples of residential areas in the heart of some of the largest metropolitan centres in Canada where people describe their lives in terms of integrated, cohesive neighbourhood ties and strong kinship links. The theoretical model that has guided a great deal of this research cannot account for such results.

A Reorientation of Theory: Political Economy Analysis

The dominant alternative perspective of political economy theory is beginning to fill this theoretical vacuum. Researchers working in this tradition are offering new insights into the economic determinants of loss of community and why it seems much more in evidence in some contexts than in others. They focus not on the demographic characteristics of different localities, but on the surrounding economy and the destructive impact of economic insecurity, poverty, and exploitation. Political economy theory predicts that, regardless of size or location, the communities that will show the most evidence of social disorganization and demoralization will be in areas of relatively severe poverty or, more importantly, where people are losing their basic sense of economic security and control over their life situation.

The study of villages in the Miramichi region of New Brunswick in the early 1970s gives ample evidence of prolonged economic decline, which is consistent with the conditions of social anomie found by researchers. Clark suggests that the poor quality of farmland, with the exception of isolated pockets of fertile soil near the region could support only a **subsistence** level of living. In other words, the farms might provide sufficient food, fuel, and building materials to meet the basic necessities of life for a family, but they provided little surplus produce that could be marketed. Most farmers depended on supplementing their farm income with part-time work as woods-men, fishermen, or labourers. Some farms became more prosperous as the opening of nearby urban markets promoted commercial farming, but success was not possible for all, and many were ruined by debt (Clark 1978).

Clark himself tends to blame impoverishment, minimal levels of education, and lack of experience of industrial work for the apparent inability of many Miramichi residents to move in search of better opportunities. A few of the more enterprising people did get out, but the remainder are trapped by cheap housing, unemployment insurance or welfare payments, and the absence of any social or educational skills that might equip them to survive in a city such as Toronto.

William Dunn, a sociologist who worked directly with Clark on the study, and who is himself a native of this area, disagrees strongly with the historical-cultural perspective adopted by Clark. While he supports all the quotations in the book and the experience of anomie that the people expressed, Dunn argues strongly for a more critical neo-Marxist perspective to analyse the findings. In particular, he stresses the high level of poverty and welfare that the researchers found in three of the four villages studied. He comments, "that the very poor should lack interest in literature is not surprising. When one struggles day by day to survive, there is not time for literature, or any other interests that middle-class folk take for granted" (*Miramichi Leader*, 9 March 1988, 5). Dunn notes further that research data may exaggerate the small proportion of Maritime natives who went to Toronto but failed to integrate, because it is precisely these people who tend to be concentrated in low-income housing projects where they can be readily identified and contacted for research. The majority who succeeded bought homes and are scattered all over the city.

Political economy theory can also offer some explanation for the changing character of rural and urban communities, as reflecting changes in economic conditions. The economy of the Miramichi region of New Brunswick has undergone much change since 1972–73 when Clark's study was conducted. Federal and provincial support for the Chatham Air Base, the expansion of jobs in the pulp and paper industry around Newcastle, increased mining activities around Bathurst, and government subsidies to small

fishermen along the North Shore have all helped to provide a viable economic base in the area. With this support the small communities have pulled through.

Is their future secure? There are important questions hanging over the future of the regional economy, with the livelihood of people in these small communities dependent on the vagaries of capitalist practices and government policies. In 1989, the federal Conservative government threatened to close the Chatham Air base, but pulled back from its implementation. In February 1994, the new federal Liberal government announced again that the Chatham base would be closed, with the loss of all 620 military and 240 civilian jobs. Other sources of employment in the fishery and in pulp and paper manufacture are far from secure.

The Marxist theorist James Sacouman (1980; 1981) similarly rejects Clark's notion that poverty might be accounted for by an inadequate rural culture, arguing instead that the uneven development of farming, fishing, and forestry in the Maritimes was the result of organized capitalist policies. This process he terms the **semiproletarianization** of the domestic mode of production. What he means by this is that people who once worked for themselves as small farmers, woodlot owners, or small fishermen, or some combination of these activities, have been pushed into a situation where they have to take part-time wagework to survive. The jobs made available to them are seasonal, insecure, and at the bottom of the wage scale, so that it is impossible to survive on wages alone. The fact that people in the region could provide for themselves, at least in part, through subsistence farming has meant that employers in big corporations have been able to exploit them ruthlessly, paying below **subsistence wages** or extremely low prices for the raw materials. Merchants also benefited from unequal exchange: they bought products from rural producers at low prices and sold supplies at high prices. The result was that merchants always came out on top, and the rural population was unable to accumulate any wealth.

A collection of articles on farming, fishing, forestry, mining, and energy in the Atlantic region (Burrill and McKay 1987) documents the extensive destruction of the rural Maritime economy to the state of near catastrophe for many communities. Between 1941 and 1981, for example, the number of farms in New Brunswick dropped from 26 000 to 4000, as highly mechanized corporate capitalist farming took over the potato industry. What happened to the 22 000 displaced farmers and their families? Where did they go? Many of the young people with options migrated from the region, going to Alberta and Toronto. Others went to Moncton and Saint John. Many more people, who lacked the financial and educational resources to move long distances, drifted into the outskirts of smaller towns in the Miramichi area, forming the settlements described in Clark's study. They survived as best they could on intermittent, low-wage work and welfare. Thousands of families lived below the poverty line in the substandard housing that still dots the area.

People on welfare, people who have lost their means of independent subsistence, do not tend to give generously to the local United Way or the Red Cross. Nor do they generally show much interest in literature and the arts. They cannot. They are victims of the system. From this perspective, the "social anomie" described by Clark has little do with the culture of the people, or with "a few bad apples." The quality of community life suffers through no fault of the people themselves. Powerlessness, dependency, and loss of hope for the future breed anger, frustration, and sometimes violence. The underlying factor is fear. It was precisely such feelings that led residents in one community to threaten researchers, for fear that they might be collecting evidence that could be used to cut welfare cheques, the only source of meagre economic security for many local families in the early 1970s. These people had already lost their dignity as independent farmers and farm workers. They probably could not take much more.

The expansion of factory freezer trawlers also threatens the survival of the small inshore fishery in the Atlantic region, and has cost many jobs in fish packing. Local women could juggle the dual demands of domestic work and wagework so long as the packing plant was near where they lived. But this is no longer possible when freezer trawlers require that they be away at sea for forty days at a stretch. Families that survived on a semiproletarian lifestyle may fall back onto welfare without the added income that women brought home. These economic downturns impose major strains on small Maritime communities. Young people who cannot find work in the region may be compelled to leave.

Native Reservations

The political economy thesis similarly predicts a high level of anomie in many Native Indian communities, despite the structural advantages of small size, low density, and cultural homogeneity. Indian reserves in Canada are commonly so lacking in an economic base that they cannot provide a standard of living above welfare for the residents. Welfare dependency, loss of dignity, and the absence of hope for the future manifest themselves in exceptionally high rates of alcoholism, glue and gasoline sniffing, suicide, and violence. Kellough (1980, 352) described Indians as "a permanent underclass of unemployment people within capitalism." This situation, too, is not due to the culture of the Indian people. One does not have to dig far into Canadian history to find the evidence of a multitude of Indian bands driven from their land by white settlers and forced back onto the poorest quality land, which white settlers did not want. Indians were cheated repeatedly out of the lands they did possess, and their capacity to run their own affairs was constantly undermined by the patriarchal powers vested in agents from the Department of Indian Affairs.

High levels of poverty among Native peoples are partly due to government policies that herded Native bands onto the poorest quality land.

Community Life as Social Construction: Insights of Feminist Analysis

The functionalist approach of the Chicago School and the traditional political economy approach both rely on essentially deterministic explanations for the character of community life. Abstract structures and forces seem to determine human communities—either the forces of size, density, and heterogeneity, or the vagaries of capitalist market forces. In both approaches the activities of people who live in these communities seem largely irrelevant to the analysis. They appear as victims rather than creators of these structural patterns.

The social constructionist perspective addresses the issue of community in a fundamentally different way. A community is not an entity with characteristics, that somehow does things to people, but rather a field of social practice, continually accomplished through what people do. We need to shift the notion of community from a noun to a verb, thinking of people as "doing community" rather than being in one.

This approach has not yet been widely incorporated into rural and urban sociology. It tends to come through as small sections or insights in research that is not primarily organized within this theoretical framework. Where it is most in evidence is in recent feminist work, particularly feminist urban geography. Hence, the following discussion merges the exploration of the social construction of community with feminist research. This confluence is not accidental. Prevailing concepts that dichotomize activities into private and public, domestic work and productive work, family and occupation, have selectively blinded traditional research to women's networks and productive activities. The efforts of feminists to explore these issues have promoted innovative ways of theorizing and researching community.

The kinds of issues explored here include what women do to maintain farming as a way of life, women's practices in the accomplishment of kinship networks, women's resource networks that accomplish the transformation of suburban "dormitories" into centres of production, the processes involved in constructing alternative economies in a declining resource-extraction town, and coping strategies in relation to the dis-organizing practices of urban planning.

Farm Life as Accomplishment

In the traditional model of rural or folk society, farming is associated with almost mystical notions of a way of life, with farmers as independent producers working their own lands, in close harmony with nature. Political economy theory shifts the focus from agriculture to agribusiness. Farms become businesses, pressured into adopting large-scale and highly mechanized farming practices to respond to market demand. They manage heavy investment debts and large payrolls for hired labour. Communities disappear as thousands of farmers sell out or go bankrupt.

What we do not see in either of these accounts are the active strategies and choices worked out by the people involved. Machum's (1992) study of women's work in potato farming in New Brunswick describes two very different survival strategies, one geared to preserving farming as "a way of life" and the other geared to commerce. The shift in focus from *what* farm women do to *why* they do it was prompted by one of her respondents exclaiming, "Why are we doing this? Are we crazy?" (1992, 92). The desire to preserve family farming as a way of life motivated this woman and many like her to do a tremendous range of income-generating and income-conserving work to support the farm—planting several acres of vegetables, canning and freezing a year's supply of food, producing eggs, milk, and butter, participating in other farm work and often also holding a paid job to cover family consumption costs, and otherwise minimizing expenditure on household goods. These families actively resisted mechanizing their farms, against persistent government and agribusiness pressures, to hold on to these ideals. When families made their choices differently, to focus on running a business, they bought extra land and invested heavily in farm machines. Women connected with the farm largely ceased to be "farm women." They were more likely to have careers or businesses that were unconnected with the farm, and if they became involved in farm bookkeeping and accounting they drew salaries. Their homes had all the modern equipment of an urban household. Their goal for their children was often not to continue the farm, but to "go where the money is." The preservation or demise of family farming as a way of life is thus neither automatic or inevitable. It is the outcome of such active strategizing.

Doing Kinship

We gain some insights into the community-making work of women in the descriptive studies of East York, Montreal, and East London boroughs. The East York Study noted interesting differences between women and men in their social relationships with kin and neighbours, although this was not itself a central focus of the research. Wives telephoned their parents more frequently than did their husbands. Most of the emotional contacts and interaction were organized by women. This finding suggests a certain sex bias in theories of urbanism. Generalizations prompted by research in the Chicago School tradition tend to be based on expectations about the behaviour of urban male workers. Female networks, and how these might vary for housewives compared with employed women, receive little attention. But current research in urban geography by feminist theorists suggests that this is a critical blind spot in traditional functionalist and political economy theory and has resulted in distorted perceptions of urban social relations.

The extensive networks of kin and friends, sometimes estimated at upwards of 200 people, do not happen by biological accident. They have to be worked at. This is especially true when families are mobile, and kin spread out geographically across provinces and cities where meetings would not occur by chance. We only have glimpses of the work involved in maintaining these networks, letters, regular telephone calls, keeping track of birthdays, actively organizing get-togethers, the special location of older family members in the centre of networks of contact, gossip, and services that tie other relatives together. We have even less information on the practices through which networks of nonkin friendships are constituted and how these practices change across stages in family life-cycles. With further investigation we may find that the notion of community as tied to locality is less relevant for contempory community-making strategies than in the past.

The Accomplishment of Suburbia

Recent work in feminist urban geography is beginning to uncover the extensive practices through which people, particularly women, negotiate around the dis-organizing practices of urban planning to constitute **suburbs** as centres of production. Suburbs were themselves constituted through the organized practices of city planners, during the late nineteenth and early twentieth century to address problems of co-ordinating production and reproduction in industrial cities (Mackenzie 1986b, 87). City planners were strongly influenced by Chicago School theories that portrayed the high density and artificial environment of industrial city centres as unconducive to stable community life. Suburbs seemed to provide a solution, offering relatively low-density, single-family homes, with open spaces and parks, and with transportation routes that would carry workers to and from their city jobs in the mornings and evenings. Integral to the design of suburbs were fundamental notions about the segregation of home from work, and the concomitant separation of women's activities from those of men. Planners assumed that women as housewives and mothers would remain within the suburban home with children, while the husband-father commuted to the city each day as family breadwinner. Suburbs worked as places to live, Mackenzie suggests, only so long as these assumptions held.

The crunch came for many suburban women in the early 1960s when the costs of purchasing and maintaining a suburban home became greater than one income could sustain. As women began to seek income-earning work in greater numbers, they had to develop strategies to combat the segregating practices built into suburban layouts (Mackenzie 1986b, 92–93). Women who wanted to run small businesses from their homes had to convert rooms and garages designed for family recreation to make them function as work stations—places in which they could manufacture crafts, food, or other goods for sale, or organize play centres, tutorial classrooms, drop-in centres, and the like. These women studied by Mackenzie reversed the patterns associated with industrialization, of transferring work from home to factory. In their lives, the distinctions between homemaking, housework, employment, and work could not be drawn. Domestic work was simultaneously productive and income-generating work.

More and more women in the suburbs began to seek out and set up networks to assist them in their dual homemaking/income-earning activities. Contacts among friends and neighbours were redesigned as working networks, sources of contact, advice, and assistance. Through such networks women could disseminate information about the quality of goods and services provided by homemakers. The networks also operated as referral systems, linking child-minders with mothers needing the service, and knitters and dressmakers with their clientele, for example. Women also organized mutual aid networks to develop facilities such as drop-in centres and playgrounds to support their "domestic-community work."

Women have also had to struggle with the implicit gender-role biases built into the organization of public transit. Women on average use public transit three times more frequently than men, but the system designs rarely take their needs into account (Michelson 1988, 89). Most suburban bus routes are radial; that is, they are arranged like spokes of a wheel, going into the downtown centre from outlying suburbs. Bus timetables are geared to "business hours" with the majority of vehicles going from suburb to city centre in the mornings and from city centre to suburb in early evenings. This arrangement of bus routes and schedules can be very inconvenient for women. Their income-earning activities often require lateral movement from one suburban district to another at irregular hours. Women who earn money by selling cosmetics or clothing or other home-produced goods, or who do domestic work or child care in other people's homes, or who tutor in the evenings, for example, are all likely to find the bus service extremely inconvenient if not useless. The Toronto transit system, with its interconnected grid of routes, very frequent services, and monthly passes that allow unlimited transfers, may be one of the few exceptions to this general pattern. Most urban transit systems tend not to be geared to women's erratic and multistop movements between child care, shops, children's teachers, and so on. It is perhaps only when one has tried to leave work, stop off to buy groceries, run other errands, pick up a child from day-care before it shuts, and bundle all of this onto a bus to get home that one realizes just how frustrating public transit can be. When families can only afford one car, it is typically the husband who uses it to get to work, leaving the wife to contend with all the inflexibilities of transit systems (Michelson 1988, 88).

Research into the working lives and the "hidden economy" of women highlights how different the experience of suburban living can be for men and women. Most men leave the suburb to go to work in the morning and return at night, finding it a convenient place to relax after work and play with children. Most women spend their working day in the suburb and find it a frustrating and restricting place in which to make a living. On the other hand, people who work elsewhere may develop few ties within the suburbs while people who are trying to transform them into work centres may find them teaming with networks of support services and clientele.

It is with these kinds of complexities in mind, and the very different experiences of women and men in appropriating their environment that prompts Mackenzie to press for a transition from the special interest field of the "geography of women" to a feminist geography with a distinctive theoretical and methodological basis (Mackenzie 1986a).

Constituting an Alternative Economy

Research into women's domestic-work economy took on special significance in the community of Nelson, in the British Columbia interior (Mackenzie 1987b). Nelson is located in a resource-extraction area that underwent severe economic recession in the 1980s. Almost all industrial plants either closed down or "modernized" their operations resulting in significant cuts in their labour force. This occurred at the same time as massive cuts in resource extraction and related industries in mining, smelting, and forestry.

Secure, highly paid, unionized jobs for men disappeared. What remained were the once economically marginal activities largely done by women, such as caring for children, maintaining homes, cooking meals, growing food, and manufacturing goods and crafts in the home. People involved in this informal economy mobilized all their energies to expand their operations to meet this economic crisis. As unions, employers' groups, and chambers of commerce contracted, women's networks expanded. The local Doukhobour community revived its farming and food processing co-operatives, largely inactive since 1940. They joined forces with two groups to generate small businesses based on skills and existing resources. These two groups were the politically active and articulate feminist movement and the back-to-the-landers, comprising relatively well-educated people with city backgrounds, who were attracted to a self-sufficient rural lifestyle. Together they organized a variety of alternative employment, including woodworking, home renovation, machinery maintenance, food processing co-operatives, artisans' co-operatives, home childcare services, and related nursery education classes. They used the deserted university buildings to develop a Summer School of the Arts and to promote tourism and the sale of artwork.

Women strengthened and restructured old networks in the process of developing this home and community sector economy, generating a strong sense of community spirit. Various groups worked together under the umbrella of the West Kootenay Women's Association, to provide support and resources for small enterprises, holding seminars on business management and grant applications, sharing employment grants, and holding skill-development seminars. They also worked actively with what was left of the men's union groups to sponsor projects.

The outcome, suggests Mackenzie, was a radical transformation of a formerly gender-segregated, resource-based, male-working-force town. The definitions of public and private locations, and of what constitutes unskilled and private activity versus marketable and public skills, broke down. Women gained prominence in community activities as the informal economy became the public economy. This did not happen smoothly or without a struggle. Conservative local groups argued that attention should be focussed on *men's* jobs, not just any job, and the conditions for re-establishment of "normal" family life, meaning the male breadwinner/female-homemaker pattern. Notwithstanding the naysayers, Mackenzie suggests feminist strategies kept the community going when the formal economy pulled out.

Mackenzie (1987a, 248–49) draws on this research into the hidden economy of domestic-community work and the importance of women's activities in the life of communities, to critique the prevailing assumptions of functionalist and political economy theory that dichotomize analysis of industrial society into economic sector versus home and community sector. Traditionally, the home and community sector is conceptualized as dependent upon the public economy and therefore irrelevant to research on the determinants of community survival. The experience of Nelson challenges that view.

Urban Anomie: The Dis-organizing of Local Networks

If people living in suburbs and declining resource-extraction towns have been able to form support networks, the question remains why people do not always pull together to create community networks in localities that are characterized by anomie. Are there certain conditions or practices that inhibit networking or community-forming activities? Given the limited research available, only tentative answers can be suggested here. The first is that women may well have formed such networks but researchers have not seen them. The second is that such networks may have been undermined by practices that promote dependency or make people feel powerless to control their environment.

The urban zones for which there is some consensus in applying descriptions such as "urban anomie" and "social disorganization" are the areas to which people have been relocated after slum clearance programs and concentrated areas of subsidized housing, particularly where the housing takes the form of high-rise apartments.

Subsidized housing projects for low-income families typically reflect many of the characteristics associated with anomie, including high crime rates, and vandalism. Tenants feel the stigma of public housing, and complain of swearing, drinking, fighting, noisy and destructive people, and few social controls, particularly over children. Alice Coleman's work (1985), in typical Chicago School fashion, identifies three characteristics of public housing that make it easy for criminals to operate and hard for residents to control or defend their territory; anonymity, lack of surveillance, and availability of several alternative escape routes. Her solution is to design public housing with no more than three to four residences accessible from any one entrance, apartment entrances open to surveillance from residents and from the street, restricted access points with no public shortcuts through the estate, and the elimination of public play areas. Criminal behaviour may be somewhat deterred by such designs, but what Coleman does not address is why such a propensity for crime exists in the first place.

The objective of city planners in slum clearance projects is generally to improve the lot of the residents, but rarely does this seem to have worked. Economically disadvantaged people are uprooted and bundled together into subsidized housing complexes, under the patriarchal authority of government agencies. It may well be that this uprooting from the slum districts, while it gives people better quality housing, also destroys the existing community support and working networks that made it possible for people to make a living in the inner city. City planners are generally not trained to notice or to look favourably on such networks. Indeed, those trained in Chicago School theory are actively trained *not* to look for and *not* to see such networks, especially among dependent women. In an effort to help, planners may have destroyed the people's means to help themselves, made them "grateful" recipients of welfare housing, and actually produced the social collapse that they then blame on the character of the residents. People have been unable to reproduce the cohesiveness of old slum communities (McGahan 1982, 278–82).

An example of such a slum clearance project is the relocation in 1964 of eighty black families living in an enclave of Halifax, Nova Scotia, locally known as Africville (Clairmont and Magill 1974, 19). This collection of shacks was isolated from the rest of Halifax behind the railroad and the city dump, and it lacked even such basic amenities as sewerage and lighting. The city forced the residents to move, promising the relocatees safe, sanitary, and decent housing. Most were relo-

Africville residents in Halifax felt they lost their freedom and their sense of belonging when the city demolished their community in the 1960s.

cated in a two-storey, public housing project. In interviews nearly a decade later, many still regretted the move and look back with nostalgia to Africville days. Although they now had better housing, they felt they had lost their freedom because they had to rent from the city rather than being squatters on their own land. Over half felt they could no longer count on their neighbours for help. They had lost a sense of belonging, and felt that the friendliness and trustworthiness of neighbours had declined (Clairmont and Magill 1974, 223).

It is an open question whether the slum clearance could have been organized differently, so as to utilize to the full the existing resourcefulness and networks among the people of Africville. Perhaps if they had been given full control over the organization and planning of the improved housing, with only the financing from outside, the sense of community might have survived.

Caution is needed here. The studies cited above describe the absence of social networks in these areas, but fall short of a social constructionist analysis that would assess the systematic practices that accomplish this sense of powerlessness. Some insights come from personal discussions with people, mostly single-parent women, who lived in subsidized housing projects. Among other experiences, these women described city housing officers giving them certain semilegal privileges, such as paying them to do small jobs without having to declare the money as income. Once they accepted such a perk they were under obligation to the official, and also subject to the threat that disclosure could mean losing their accommodation. Several women felt trapped in a vicious circle of compliance, including providing sex, because they had accepted such favours. Women who were not certain of their rights as tenants were easily intimidated, and would not risk openly trying to assert control over their lives in the housing project, for fear of being evicted on some technicality. Teenaged children may also face heavy pressure to prove themselves part of the local gang, or face reprisals. These brief comments suggest that there may well be systematic practices that sustain the powerlessness of residents in housing projects as an ongoing accomplishment, but we need much more detailed research to explore them.

Certain parallels can be drawn between the experiences of people in subsidized housing and those of people living in single-industry, nonrenewable resource-extraction towns in Canada. Both have a reputation for fatalism. Superficially, the two contexts are very different. The towns are generally prosperous, with men employed by the local company, and their families housed in company-owned property. But the sense of powerlessness and long-term insecurity of town residents is a central theme of Lucas's study *Minetown, Milltown, Railtown* (1971). The economic roots of fatalism appear straightforward. Many of these towns face uncertain futures because mines depend upon extraction of a nonrenewable resource. They are also vulnerable to changes in technology and markets. But what they particularly have in common with residents of subsidized housing projects is subjection to the control of the companies. Critical economic decisions are made by head office personnel, government policies, and international trading agreements, with townspeople removed from the decision-making processes. At home, even small decisions about community facilities or land use are subject to the paternalistic control of company personnel. The extent of this power is evidenced in the comment of one company executive concerning why there were so few women employed in the town. In the early days, he opined, the company had both husbands and wives working, but the children were running wild and the police were moving in. So the company laid down new rules by which married women were not permitted to work (Lucas 1971). This man's opinions about appropriate gender-roles and the proper place of women in the home was sufficient to block the employment opportunities of an entire community of women. Meg Luxton (1980) describes in depth the entrapment experienced by women in the northern Manitoba town of Flin Flon, where early marriage and dependence on a male breadwinner offer virtually the only option for women to survive in the town.

Conclusion

The study of rural and urban sociology has a long history, but many questions remain unanswered, and the developing approaches of social constructionism and feminism indicate that there are still many more questions yet to be formulated. The folk-urban thesis popularized by Chicago School theorists has not stood the test of comparative research. Rural communities are not uniformly or even generally characterized by the close-knit, integrated social life envisioned in the notion of folk society. Neither do urban residential areas fit the image of shallow and detached associations between strangers. The predictions of political economy theory that link community integration with economic security have a better fit with evidence. But such explanations fail to take account of the tenacity with which people fight to hold viable communities together in the face of economic hardship. The practical activities of people involved in creating and sustaining community integration have only recently begun to be explored, mostly under the impetus of feminist research. We still know relatively little about community life as ongoing accomplishment.

The most valuable lesson to be learned from the classical loss of community debate is the importance of subjecting evidence to a critical evaluation. The folk-urban model sounds convincing. It fits the preconceptions that most of us have about simple rural life, where people care about each other, and about anonymous crowds in the city, where self-interest prevails. But however convincing this argument sounds, when the assumptions are systematically tested against the evidence, they do not hold up. It is essential to adopt the same critical approach to all other theories in sociology, and indeed, in all other fields of study.

Suggested Reading

Two short essays that give a good introduction to the Chicago School approach to rural-urban sociology are Louis Wirth, "Urbanism as a Way of Life" (1938), and Robert Redfield, "The Folk Society" (1947). Both authors support the theory that rural community life will be highly cohesive and integrated around shared values and commitments of kinship and religion. Urban life, in contrast, is characterized by shallow associations between strangers.

The collection of articles edited by Marcel Rioux and Yves Martin, *French-Canadian Society*, Volume 1 (1964), provides an excellent overview of the folk-society thesis as applied historically to rural Quebec. Articles by Guindon, Rioux, and Redfield strongly support the folk-society argument, while the article by Garigue and, to a lesser extent, those by Falardeau and Gérin, challenge it. A contemporary challenge to the folk-society thesis is provided by Marie Lavigne in "Feminist Reflections on the Fertility of Women in Quebec" (1986). Lavigne questions whether Quebec women as a whole ever internalized the traditional Catholic emphasis on large families and the church's opposition to contraception.

The study by Samuel D. Clark, *The New Urban Poor* (1978), provides a largely functionalist view of community life in rural New Brunswick in the early 1970s. Clark explores the problems of social and economic decline associated with widespread, if temporary, migration from New Brunswick to Toronto and the West.

The text by Peter McGahan, *Urban Sociology in Canada* (1982), provides an excellent and comprehensive overview of research on urban communities in Canada. Different sections of the book cover such topics as the inner-city areas, middle-class and working-class sub-urbs, and comparisons between Toronto and Montreal.

A political economy perspective on life in single-industry towns is provided by Rex Lucas in *Minetown, Milltown, Railtown* (1971) and Meg Luxton in *More than a Labour of Love* (1980). Lucas shows how all aspects of life in small Canadian towns are dictated by the policies of major corporations that dominate the local economies. Inhabitants are relatively powerless to influence the future of their town. Many of these towns, especially those that rely on extraction industries, have an uncertain future, and that insecurity carries over into community life in a sense of fatalism and dependency upon the corporation. Luxton focusses particularly upon the lives of women in such towns.

A series of articles by Suzanne Mackenzie explores how women, both in suburbs and economically declining small towns, actively create new social and economic relations of community life. Her articles include "Women's Response to Economic Restructuring: Changing Gender, Changing Space" (1986) and "Neglected Spaces in Peripheral Places: Homeworkers and the Creation of a New Economic Centre" (1987).

Questions

1. List the stages in the process of theorizing in social science.

2. What is the major problem scientists face in proposing a new theory?

3. List the three variables in the Chicago School thesis on rural-urban differences.

4. List four arguments Garigue cites to challenge the folk society model of rural Quebec.

5. How does Lavigne's work challenge the notion of the influence of the church in rural Quebec society?

6. Define *anomie*.

7. How did geographic mobility affect the frequency of contact with kin in studies of people living in Fredericton and Montreal?

8. List three kinds of evidence cited to suggest that inner-city slums might not be as disorganized as one might expect?

9. How does Marxist theory challenge the historical-cultural theory of anomie in the Miramichi region of New Brunswick?

10. What practices is Mackenzie referring to in her model of domestic-community work?

CHAPTER 5

Gender Relations: Competing Perspectives

Gender relations are moving into the centre of cultural, social, and political struggles in the 1990s. Much of the taken-for-granted character of relations between women and men, and also between men and men, and women and women, have been challenged by feminist theory, the active politics of the women's movement, and emerging struggles around gay and lesbian sexual orientation, and men's liberation movements.

Contraception changed the character of intimate sexual relations, increasing the possibilities for sexual expression outside of procreation. But a host of new problems and questions have emerged alongside sexual liberation. The reduced risk of pregnancy has changed the moral debate around adolescent sexual activity, but the potential for "liberation" has also increased the potential for coercive and exploitative relationships as girls in particular find themselves under increased pressure to be sexually active and available. Medical concerns have arisen around the spread of virulent forms of sexually transmitted diseases, particularly the epidemic of acquired immune-deficiency syndrome (AIDS). Other concerns have focussed around the commercialization of sexuality in advertising, pornography, and prostitution, and associated struggles around public definitions of morality, censorship, and freedom of speech. The 1980s were also marked by heightened awareness of the sometimes exploitative and violent character of sexual relations, reflected in the proliferation of accounts of battery within the home, sexual abuse of children, sexual assault and date rape, sexual harassment, and violent attacks against gay men, and also increasing anger and frustration directed against campaigns focussing on these issues.

Sexual politics have brought to light new patterns of power, interest, and conflict. Within the economy, struggles have focussed on employment equity policies, affirmative action, and nondiscrimination on the basis of gender and sexual orientation. These, in turn, are associated with a questioning of the appropriateness of traditional division of domestic responsibilities, child care, and breadwinning within families. Patterns of change have been neither unidirectional nor uncontested. Alongside the politics of feminism and gay liberation are the politics of religious fundamentalism and the "New Right" concerned with the reinforcement of traditional family and sexual values.

These arenas of confrontation reflect profound confusion over the appropriateness of emerging patterns of sexuality and gender relations. The goal of this chapter is to explore this contested terrain of gender relations through four major theoretical perspectives within current sociology—functionalism, political economy, social constructionism, and feminism—comparing and contrasting the different explanatory frameworks.

The study of gender relations is particularly useful for giving a sense of how the focus of sociological analysis differs from approaches of biology and psychology. The sex dichotomy of male and female is commonly viewed as an immutable biological state, but contemporary analyses in sociology have challenged this assumption as ideological rather than factual, developing a different conceptualization of sex differences and gender relations as socially constructed rather than given. We begin this discussion with a brief overview of biological theories of gender as the background against which specifically sociological theories have developed.

Biology or Social Learning: The Foundations of Gender

Functionalist theory in sociology stays closest to the biological view of sex differences, but with an important qualification. Functionalism begins with the assumption that there is a biological basis to the specialization of functions for males and females in society, but it sees this specialization as structured by socialization. Typically, in functionalist writing the terms **sex** and **sex roles** are used to refer to differences in male and female bodies and reproductive capacities that are presumed to be universal. The terms **gender** and **gender roles** refer to socially acquired behavioural differences that vary across cultures and historical periods. In

practice, as we will see below, much controversy surrounds this distinction.

Functionalist theory argues that the long dependency of human infants, necessitating many years of adult care, is the biological root of gender relations (Goode 1982). The reproductive strategy of having few offspring and caring intensively for them is held to predispose long pairing relationships in family settings, since the nurturing female depends on her male partner for support and protection. These biological imperatives are also seen as dictating fundamental differences in the roles of adult males and females. Females are seen as physically handicapped by long pregnancy and breast-feeding and are home-bound with dependent infants and young children. Hence, they are more tied to the domestic arena. This was especially so in the era before widespread use of contraception when women could expect to be either pregnant or breast-feeding for most of their adult lives. Males, in contrast, are freer to move away from the home, and since they are also physically stronger, they are best suited biologically to perform the roles of hunter and protector. With industrialization, the importance of physical strength declined, but males are still freer to work away from home every day as principal breadwinners while females are seen as biologically better suited to remain at home as principal caregivers for small children. These roles can certainly overlap with fathers giving some time to child care and mothers some time to work outside the home, especially when children are older, but the basic predispositions and principal responsibilities remain. In some feminist writings, particularly those of Shulamith Firestone, liberation for women is seen as ultimately requiring a technological revolution that would free women from the biological imperatives of pregnancy.

The thesis of Social Darwinism elaborates on the biological roots of behaviour, maintaining that many of the differences in average behaviour between men and women emerged through a long evolutionary process that selectively developed traits conducive to survival. While males and females produce both testosterone and estrogens, the higher average levels of the hormone testosterone in males compared to females is seen as predisposing males to greater aggressiveness, a trait that enhances their survival as hunters. Aggressiveness would not have the same adaptive value for females who do not participate in the hunt. Conversely, higher average levels of estrogens in females may predispose them to the more passive, nurturing behaviour necessary in caring for infants. Some theorists argue further that the relative sexual promiscuity of males reflects the biological evolution of traits that increase the survival of the male's gene stock (Dawkins 1976). Promiscuity has little reproductive value for females since they can bear only a limited number of offspring. Conversely, females have a strong need to form pairing relationships to support them during pregnancy and the care of infants. Lionel Tiger (1969) argues further that males selectively evolved the traits of teamwork and male bonding as adaptive to their survival as hunters, and this predisposition now gives males an advantage over women in business and politics, or other similar activities in the public arena that involve teamwork. The argument has been expanded to assert that patriarchy or domination by males over females in society, is biologically determined, since males have a competitive edge over females in all assertive, public leadership roles (Goldberg 1973).

Studies of differences in male and female behaviour among animals is widely cited as supporting evidence for the biological roots of human behaviour. A common example is Harlow's studies of infant rhesus monkeys who had been separated from their mothers. The males appeared to be naturally more aggressive, to engage in more rough and tumble play, and to initiate more games (Harlow 1962; 1965).

Current work in the field of **sociobiology**, the study of the biological bases of social behaviour, goes beyond speculative evolutionary arguments to explore differences in brain functioning of males and females. These include studies that suggest that girls on average are predisposed to be better than boys at verbal skills and the recognition of interrelated patterns. Boys are generally better than girls in thinking that involves linear logic and mathematical skills. The gender-inversion theory of homosexuality suggests that the hormones and brain patterning of homosexuals may be congenitally those of the opposite biological sex. This theory is held to account for the tendency of gay men to display "effeminate" characteristics and for their concentration in careers in the arts. Lesbians are seen as congenitally predisposed towards masculine characteristics.

The Limitations of Biological Explanations

Much of the early sociobiological theories concerning evolutionary traits cannot be tested scientifically against evidence. They are based on imaginative speculation, not biological research. Elaine Morgan, in her book *The Descent of Women* (1972), offers a critique that is partly serious and partly a parody of what she sees as essentially "male-centred" theories of evolution. She speculates that evolutionary functions can be thought up for all kinds of traits that distinguish women from men, with female traits generally having greater survival value for the species. Take, for example, the evidence that baldness is common among men but rare among women. Morgan speculates that during the prehistorical period when our human ancestors lived in shallow coastal waters, it would have been very important for the survival of infants that their mothers had long hair. Naked apes are slippery when wet and the infants of bald mothers would be more likely to drown. Baldness in males would have no evolutionary consequences. Similarly, it might have been advantageous for females to develop fat on their buttocks since they would have had to sit on sharp rocks at the water's edge to breast-feed their young.

The main value of Morgan's work lies not in these proposals as such, but how they illustrate the speculative character and the male bias of more widely accepted versions of evolutionary functions. Whatever the appeal of certain arguments about evolutionary traits, their usefulness in understanding the contemporary social behaviour of men or women is minimal. The conditions under which male hunting packs had any survival value have long gone. So, at least within Western societies, have conditions under which women could expect to be pregnant and suckling infants throughout their adult lives. As Connell puts it, evolutionary theories are about 2 million years out of date (1987, 72).

Other aspects of sociobiology have been supported by evidence from studies of animal behaviour, but there are several serious problems with extrapolating from animals to humans. In the first place, the animals chosen are often selected to make the point in question. Rhesus monkeys, for example, are known to be a particularly aggressive primate species. Male baboons are much more docile and might be cited to support very different conclusions about innate male behaviour with respect to aggression. Analogies drawn between animal and human behaviour leave out what is most characteristic of the human species—the capacity for language, intellect, imagination, and learning. These attributes play such an overwhelmingly important part in the social behaviour of people that comparison with primates in which such attributes are minimal or nonexistent can have little explanatory value.

Efforts to link biological differences between males and females to differences in behaviour have generally been inconclusive. A common argument is that boys and men are generally more aggressive than girls and women because they have more of the hormone testosterone. But other evidence reverses this cause and effect relationship, suggesting that social context, and emotions of aggression and anger produce fluctuations in testosterone levels. Rather than the body determining behaviour, social relationships are seen as producing characteristics of the body.

The argument advanced by Goldberg (1973) that patriarchy is inevitable because males enjoy an aggressive advantage over women in competition is seriously flawed in other ways. It assumes that there is open competition between women and men and that women lose. The historical experience of women in most societies, however, is that they have never been given the opportunity to compete on equal terms with men for positions of power in society. The institutional arrangements that feminists refer to as "patriarchy" are precisely those that block opportunities for women to compete. Biological evidence of small average differences between women and men in hormones, body size, or mathematical abilities, even if taken at face value, are not adequate to explain why so few women are found in positions of major political authority and economic power in most contemporary societies. The extensive overlapping of characteristics and abilities among women and men would support the prediction of far greater social equality than is actually found.

In general, theories that try to account for gender differences by reference to biological factors tend to be both too weak and too strong. On the one hand, the connections established between biology and human behaviour are generally very weak. On the other hand, theories that rely on biological explanations assume a uniformity within the categories of male and female that cannot account for tremendous variation in gender behaviour. This variation is evident among people with homosexual orientations as well as heterosexual. The images of "butch-femme" women and effeminate men implied by the gender-inversion theory of homosexuality at best applies to only a small minority of people who would identify themselves as homosexuals. To account for such variation we need to shift focus from biology to social learning as the basis of gender relations.

Psychoanalysis

Psychoanalysis, as a branch of psychiatry, lies midway between biological and social explanations for gender relations. In the classic theory first proposed by Sigmund Freud (1856–1939), the biological fact that boys possess a penis, while girls "only" have a clitoris, is seen as a central determinant of different temperament and personality of adult males and females (Freud [1905] 1976). Freud suggests that during the phallic stage of development, beginning around three to four years of age, a boy experiences strong urges to compete with his father sexually for possession of his mother. He learns to repress this drive, and later to displace it onto other women, out of fear that his father might retaliate and castrate him. Infant girls, in contrast, experience a sense of mutilation and sexual powerlessness at not having a penis, which accounts for their relative passivity.

Freud's work has been widely criticized for its deterministic, ahistorical, and male-biased assumptions. Contemporary re-reading of Freud's thesis suggests that what Freud interpreted as universal features of human sexuality are better understood as the historically specific characteristics of sexuality developed within late nineteenth- and early twentieth-century patriarchal bourgeois families—the family background of most of the patients that Freud treated for neurosis in his Vienna clinic. Mechanisms of repression and displacement of sexual drives that are central to Freudian theory, have been reconceptualized as deep psychological responses to power relations within families dominated by an all-powerful husband-father figure. Feminist re-

reading of stories told by female patients suggest that these are not merely childhood fantasies, as Freud surmised, but accounts of incest. The neurosis displayed by these patients seems more likely to reflect the trauma of sexual abuse than displaced penis envy. Feminist psychoanalysis has generated further theoretical interest in the potential effects on gender-identity formation in families where a powerful father figure is absent (Chodorow 1978). The theoretical insights of psychoanalysis have also been incorporated into theories of homosexuality, drawing on the Freudian notion that children have inherently bisexual instincts and drives that are moulded and channelled into socially acceptable heterosexual forms through early childhood experiences within the nuclear family. The mechanisms of psychological repression and displacement are seen as controlling bisexual drives but never fully erasing them.

In general these re-readings of Freud's work retain the insights concerning the importance of the unconscious mind, and mechanisms of repression and displacement, but with a significant change in underlying assumptions. The explanatory focus has shifted away from notions of innate biological drives and toward a greater emphasis on the role of historically changeable family forms and patterns of culture in the development of adult gender identity. This shift in focus has facilitated the incorporation of aspects of psychoanalytic theory into contemporary sociological perspectives on gender relations.

A fuller discussion of contemporary readings of Freud's work and the importance of psychoanalytic theory in understanding patriarchal culture is presented in chapter 19 of this text on feminist theories of culture and communications.

Functionalist Theory of Gender Roles

Functionalist theory of gender relations incorporates a decisive shift to focus on social environment and social learning, an approach often referred to as *socialization theory*. Infants are assumed to have sex but not gender. Gender roles do not depend upon innate biological or psychological drives. They are learned through the processes of **gender-role socialization**. The basic

idea of functionalism is that people in society can be thought of as occupying social positions, to which a set of expectations are assigned. These expectations or norms define which actions are appropriate to given positions. Individuals acquire and internalize norms and these guide behaviour, much like actors in a play conform to a script. Becoming a man or a woman means taking on a general role ascribed to one's sex, such that in almost all social contexts there are two distinctive sets of roles corresponding to different social expectations of males and females. Individuals are inserted into social relations through learning the role behaviour appropriate to their sex. Functionalist theory is centrally interested in the people and institutions responsible for this learning—the "agents of socialization"—including parents, family, teachers, peers, religious leaders, mass media, and the like. Research focusses on the scripts—the gender patterns and stereotypes that are taught, the different treatment of boys and girls, and the ways in which models of femininity and masculinity are conveyed to children. Deviance from acceptable gender behaviour is understood in terms of faulty socialization, especially in early childhood experience. This approach has the advantage over sociobiology of offering an explanation for both the variation and the consistency in patterns of male and female behaviour within a given culture. It also offers a policy for reforming gender relations through changing expectations, and challenging stereotyped attitudes.

Variations Among Cultures

Margaret Mead's (1935) classic study of three New Guinea tribes, the Arapesh, the Mundugamore, and the Tschambuli, emphasized the malleability of human gender-role behaviour and the importance of socialization over biology. She described marked differences in the specific behaviours ascribed to males and females in the three cultures. Among the Arapesh, both males and females were socialized to be gentle, nurturing, responsive, co-operative, and willing to subordinate themselves to the needs of others. Both men and women participated actively in childbirth. They were both said to "bear the child," and it was believed that only through the continual caring and participation of the father could the child grow in the mother's womb or continue into healthy adulthood. According to Mead, authority and aggression were repugnant to both Arapesh men and women. Arapesh men did not provoke fights, and rape was unknown. Among the Mundugamore, in contrast, both men and women were expected to be aggressive rather than nurturing. The people practised headhunting, and emotions of hostility, hatred, and suspicion permeated their relationships. Even their families were organized on the basis of the theory of natural hostility among members of the same sex. Fathers and daughters formed one rival group against mothers and sons. Within the third culture, the Tschambuli, women were expected to be more dominant, impersonal, and managing than men, while men were expected to be less responsible and more emotionally dependent than women, in effect the opposite of feminine and masculine expected in Western societies. Later studies have modified Mead's findings, suggesting that she overstated the cultural differences, but her general thesis that the gender-role behaviour of women and men are powerfully influenced by upbringing and cultural expectations remains.

Functionalist theory assumes that individuals come to internalize the gender-role behaviour patterns appropriate for their biological sex through socialization. Primary socialization occurs within the family. It is principally here that infants acquire language and gender identity, and learn the basic norms, and appropriate attitudes and values of their sex. Secondary socialization involves learning and teaching in the public arenas of school, church, work, and mass media. The two spheres of socialization are directly connected during childhood since parents commonly select the day-cares, churches, and schools that their children attend, and monitor their friendships and the mass media to which they are exposed. Socialization continues in some degree throughout adult life as individuals enter new roles and form new associations, but the influence of parents in early childhood learning is considered decisive in gender identity formation. We know from studies of young children that they learn to accurately define their own gender and that of others from a very early age (Mackie 1991, 79).

Behavioural Traits Within a Culture

Primary socialization into gender roles in Western cultures begins from the moment of birth as infants are assigned an identity as male or female on the basis of genitals. Sex-typing may begin even before birth, as parents speculate that an active fetus is most likely to be male and a quiet one female. From the first day of life parents tend to see, and to respond to, boy and girl babies differently. Girls are more often described as little, beautiful, cute, weak, and delicate, whereas boys are described as firmer, larger, more alert, stronger, and hardier. This occurs despite objective evidence that male and female babies are on average of equal size and activity level, and female neonates are generally more robust than males.

The behavioural traits identified as specifically male or female are actively promoted and reinforced by parents. For example, a study of the content of rooms that parents provide for

BACK BENCH

WE'RE *NOT* PLAYING DOCTOR... WE'RE ESTABLISHING GENDER DIFFERENCES...

children (Rheingold and Cook 1975; Greenglass 1992, 208) showed that boys' rooms tended to have vehicles of all kinds, building blocks, toy tools, sports equipment, machines, and military toys. Girls' rooms most often had dolls, doll houses, stuffed animals, and domestic toys of all kinds for playing house.

Activities and interests encouraged by parents commonly emphasize the same gender-typing. Domestic chores are commonly allocated to boys and girls differently. Boys tend to be encouraged more than girls to be independent, for example by being allowed to cross streets alone at a younger age, to play away from home for long periods without first telling parents where they would be, and using sharp scissors without adult supervision. There is no objective evidence that boys are any more advanced than girls at such skills. If anything, boys tend to be more impulsive and less mature (Hoffman 1977; Greenglass 1992, 210). Parents also see female toddlers as needing more help, encourage them to ask for more help, and restrict and supervise them more. As a result, boys and girls develop different kinds of competence and coping skills. As adults, men strive for success and take risks to attain it, while women are socialized not to take risks and to perceive risks as threatening failure. Early in life they learn not to have high expectations for themselves and so as adults they tend to be less self-confident, less assertive, and more timid than men. They tend to rely more on others than do boys, and have a greater need for social approval, and are more likely to break down or cry under stress. All these traits are seen as detrimental to women who try to function in adult work roles that require leadership or management skills (Hale 1987a, 491; Hennig and Jardim 1981; Fenn 1980; Larwood and Wood 1977). On the positive side, girls are encouraged to be more nurturing, to display emotions, to be open to others, to be skilled listeners, and more empathetic than boys, traits that prepare them well for adult roles as caregivers.

There is much evidence to suggest that gender-typing is more rigidly enforced for boys than for girls. Boys are under greater pressure not to be "sissies" than are girls not to be "tomboys," and boys are subject to much more physical and non-physical punishments, as well as more praise, in pressuring them to behave in a "masculine" way. Fathers are also more likely to emphasize gen-der-typing in their interaction with children than are mothers (Greenglass 1992, 209; Lynn 1974; Mackie 1991, 109–10). Fathers worry when boys seem unaggressive and unwilling to defend themselves, while they do not worry about unaggressive girls. David and Brannon (1976, 12) summarize the traditional requirements of the masculine gender role as (1) no sissy stuff—with a stigma on all stereotypically feminine characteristics; (2) the big wheel—the need to be looked up to and to have symbols of success and status, especially as a breadwinner looked up to by his wife, if no one else; (3) the sturdy oak—portraying a manly air of toughness, confidence, and self-reliance; and (4) "Give 'em Hell"—the aura of aggression, violence, and daring. The most important of all is no sissy stuff—not behaving like girls. Boys are socialized to suppress emotions that suggest vulnerability, and especially not to cry. The involvement of boys in sports is widely cited as critical in the development of appropriate masculinity. Male athletes commonly report feeling pressured, even bullied, into participation in sports by their fathers (Messner 1992). Teamwork, competition, winning at any cost, and aggression, are important aspects of organized sports for boys. There is no comparable pressure on girls to become

Gender traits are often promoted by parents who encourage boys to play with vehicles, tools, machines, and sports and war toys.

involved in sports, and if they do, the aspects of having fun tend to be stressed over competition and winning.

Problems in Family Socialization

From the perspective of socialization theory, failure to exhibit appropriate adult gender-role behaviour can be accounted for primarily by faulty upbringing, especially within the family. A central cause for concern in studies addressing the notion of a "masculinity crisis" is the gender confusion that boys may experience when appropriate male role models are absent from their families (Brittan 1989, 25–26). Young boys may scarcely see their father when he is working away from home all day or working very long hours. High levels of unemployment may mean that fathers are home for longer periods, but inability to hold a steady job undermines a father's ability to provide an appropriate male role model for his sons. The erosion of the father's authority and status within the home may be further exacerbated if the wife-mother is employed. Of particular concern within research on socialization is the growing numbers of single-parent, female-headed households. In functionalist theory this deviation from the traditional nuclear family form is seen as likely to result in deviant psychological development, especially for boys. The fear is that fatherless boys may find it difficult to achieve proper gender identity, and may act out their resulting insecurities and anxieties in negative ways, through delinquency, violence, and hostility towards women. Chodorow (1978) and Dinnerstein (1976) link psychoanalysis and functionalism in their theory that the masculinity crisis may be generated by the extreme differentiation and specialization in gender roles in Western societies, which leave mothers almost totally responsible for child care. Boys, they suggest, are engulfed in the overflowing influence of women, the combination of maternal care and discipline that translates into power over boys. They suggest that boys resent and try to escape from women's power, rather than struggling to repress oedipal conflicts with respect to an all-powerful father figure. The key problem is not a too-powerful father, but a weak or absent father, or a too-powerful mother.

The challenge of raising sons to be appropriately masculine is a difficult one for feminist mothers. Van Gelder and Carmichael (1975) studied the attitudes of mothers, including those in leadership positions in feminist organizations. As many as one-third of these mothers worried that they might unwittingly be responsible for their sons "unnecessarily" becoming homosexual. None of them worried that a liberated or feminist upbringing would turn girls into lesbians, but they feared that it might turn boys into homosexuals. They gave serious thought to nonsexist child-rearing for their girls, but not for their boys. Among their peers, boys who fail to display appropriately masculine behaviour, who are unathletic or bookish, or who enjoy "effeminate" activities like dance, knitting, or even cooking, are likely to be taunted by such gibes as "What are you, a fag?" Such homophobic taunting seems to function as a powerful technique for enforcing conformity to stereotypically masculine gender-role behaviour (Fine 1992, 138; Lehne 1976).

Those concerned with promoting the advancement of women in prestigious and better-paid careers in business and management see the prevailing pattern of socialization for girls as a critical limiting factor. Studies of women in management roles suggest that competitive team sports, particularly football, are important in socializing boys into skills of leadership and teamwork, and notions of planning, tactics, strategies, and playing to win (Hennig and Jardim 1981; Fenn 1980; Larwood and Wood 1977). Girls who have no comparable socialization experience are severely handicapped as adults if they try to enter roles in politics, business, and management, where skills of leadership and teamwork are very important. Liberal feminists, working within the functionalist perspective, have focussed attention on restrictive stereotypes of adult roles for women, especially in mass media and school textbooks. They stress the importance of nontraditional role models for girls in changing the distribution of gender roles for women and men.

The Limitations of Socialization Theory

Socialization theory offers major advantages over biological explanations for gender relations in that it provides a workable explanation for broad differences between cultures and it places at the centre of analysis the specifically human characteristics of social learning. It is, however, open to criticism as an overly simplistic form of explanation that ignores much of the complexity of gender relations.

The model relies on an implicit notion of normal male and female gender-role behaviour, and implies that there is consensus among agents of socialization as to what these norms are. Critics argue that neither assumption fits the evidence. There seems to be too much variation in how women and men behave. If we were to use what we know about normative expectations to predict actual behaviour of males and females in specific situations, we would be wrong more often than correct. A study conducted in rural India tried to predict women's responses to new employment opportunities on the basis of prevailing norms for women's behaviour that emphasized domesticity and strict seclusion within the home (Hale 1988a). All the predictions failed. Cultural norms did predict what women thought other people thought, but not at all what the women had internalized as standards for themselves. This discrepancy between the prevailing culture and what women actually wanted to do, calls into question the meaning of "culture" as the accepted set of norms, attitudes, and values of the people. It suggests that the culture of rural India reflects more how men want women to behave than the internalized values of women themselves.

There is also extensive evidence of inconsistencies, conflict, and contradictions between different agents of socialization that belies the notion of normative standards. They may teach conflicting messages about gender-role expectations to children. What parents teach may differ from school teachers, and both may differ from mass media or peers, or religious teachings. Consistency among all socialization agents in a given community may be the exception rather than the rule. Moreover, individual agents are themselves often inconsistent in what they teach. Studies of families suggest that contradictory pressures and demands are routinely placed on children (Connell 1987, 192–93). Mass media similarly offer contradictory messages about appropriate gender-role behaviour. The notion of distinctive patterns of socialization for boys and girls also seems to have been overdrawn. The body of research on parent-child interaction with babies and preschoolers that was reviewed by Maccoby and Jacklin (1974) failed to find clear-

cut differences in either the amount or kind of parental talk or nurturing behaviour toward sons and daughters.

The unquestioned assumption within functionalist theory that there are distinctive male and female gender roles has promoted extensive research into differences in upbringing and behaviour of boys and girls. As we noted in chapter 1, however, for every published study that confirms expected differences, several more are discarded as flawed because no significant differences were found. Connell suggests that were it not for the powerful influence of gender-role theory on research, we would be focussing on sex similarity studies rather than sex differences (1987, 170).

Critics also challenge the assumption that deviation from normative standards for gender-role behaviour can be accounted for in terms of faulty socialization (Brittan 1989, 23–24). The bookish and unathletic boys, the male ballet dancers, the women with leadership and management skills, cannot all be explained away by reference to malfunctioning socialization. The assumption that children mechanically internalize standards that they are taught ignores both choice and resistance in human behaviour. Children may reject what they are taught, or they may choose to mix gender traits in ways that conflict partially or perhaps fundamentally with how they were brought up. The theory that homosexuality is the result of faulty parental role modelling loads unnecessary guilt onto parents, without any evidence of specific parenting practices being linked to the sexual orientation of children. It also denies any agency to individuals who come to identify themselves as homosexual.

There is, furthermore, a strongly conservative ideology embedded in the assumptions that specific feminine and masculine gender identities are necessary for psychological health and that boys who lack immediate male role models will be disturbed and deviant in their own self-identity. Such assumptions imply that there is only one way to be psychologically healthy and all other patterns are sick.

There seems to be something seriously wrong with the theory. It seems that normative standards do exist for male and female behaviour. Most of us know what they are and can list them when asked. Yet the majority of people we know do not seem to have internalized them in the way that the functionalist theory of socialization predicts. The normative pattern of the nuclear family with male breadwinner and female homemaker is not the prevailing form of gender-role behaviour. Connell suggests that what we begin to see here is that what is "normative" is not a definition of normality, but a definition of what holders of social power wish to have accepted (1987, 51–52). Yet this analysis of power is precisely what is missing from functionalist theory.

We do not speak of "race roles" or "class roles" because in such relations power differentials are obvious. But the assumption that gender roles reflect natural differences between women and men functions to obscure the dimension of power in the structuring of gender relations. Socialization theory implicitly assumes that all problems of inequality in relations between women and men can be accounted for by upbringing, with the corollary that if society were to alter the prevailing role models all such inequities could be eliminated. Critics reject such arguments as simplistic at best, and at worst as ideological distortions that legitimate inequality. Critics argue that the pervasive inequalities in occupational status, income, and political influence between women and men cannot be reduced simply to learned psychological predispositions; all the difficulties encountered by the token few women in management positions cannot be meaningfully attributed to lack of experience on football teams. Nor can the prevalence of pornography, violence against women within families, or rape be accounted for simply by boys' resentfulness at the authority of mothers during their infancy. Such explanations ignore the vested interests in the maintenance of relations of domination and the active strategies and power dynamics that shore them up (Connell 1987, ch. 9; Brittan 1989).

Once we come to see gender-role stereotypes as embedded in power relations, we are led to question the interests that structure and maintain them. Socialization theory describes how males and females are supposedly trained to fit the mould of acceptable masculine and feminine behaviour, but it does not address the question of why the moulds have the characteristics that they do. Why are boys raised to be aggressive and competitive? Why are girls not also raised like this? Such questions point to issues of social and economic structures that are not addressed within socialization theory itself. The force of such criticism is not that socialization has no influence on adult behaviour or gender relations, but that it is too limited and too individualistic in focus to account for complex structural patterns of gender-based inequality in society. A different kind of analysis seems to be needed to explain the structural patterns of gendered inequality.

The Political Economy of Gender Relations

Political economy theory focusses on patterns of economic organization and their importance in shaping all other social relationships, including gender. The contemporary Canadian economy is part of a global system of advanced corporate capitalism. This means that it is characterized by private enterprise that is dominated by giant corporations that compete on world markets to sell commodities for profit, with smaller sectors of small-business people and primary producers in farming, fishing, and forestry. The majority of people in Canada's labour force do not work for themselves, but find careers in corporations or state bureaucracies. An individual's social class is defined in terms of their relationship to the system of production, whether they own or control capital, and their situation with respect to the labour market.

A central argument within political economy theory is that the attitudes and values that people hold are shaped by their immediate practical experiences in the daily processes of survival or earning a living. Attitudes and values are thus effects rather than principal causes of behaviour. Analysis of gender relations, and the different attitudes, values, and behaviour of women and men, is embedded in the understanding of class relations within capitalism.

The Influence of Gender on Class Situation

Frederich Engels, a long-time collaborator with Karl Marx, suggests in his classic essay on the rise of private property, the family, and the state ([1884] 1978) that in the earliest hunting and gathering economies, authority and descent within kinship systems were probably organized around women as the only known parent. Men most likely played a secondary role within extended matriarchal households. However, Engels argues, this probably changed dramatically with the introduction of more advanced means of production, such as domesticated animals and cultivated land. As men gained control over these means of production they would have been able to break the authority of women and organize descent and inheritance through the male rather than the female line. Men would have been in a position to control and enslave women because women and their children would be economically dependent upon them. Women's work was still essential, but socially subordinate. They worked for their husbands. Engels refers to this point in history as the world historical defeat of the female sex, and the first example of class relations. The solution to the subordination of women to men, in Engels' view, would be to draw women into the labour force, and to abolish the bourgeois pattern in which men control the family wealth. **Communism**—the communal ownership of all means of production—promised ultimate equality for all members of society.

Prior to industrialization, most economic production took place in households, with no clear division between domestic and productive work, or between family production and consumption. With the rise of industrial capitalism this pattern changed dramatically. Production shifted into centralized factories, and households became units of consumption. Increasingly, men went out of the home to work for wages, while women remained within the home, taking principal responsibility for child care and domestic work. This shifting pattern of economic production is widely seen as decisively important in structuring gender relations. It liberated many people from the confines of the old households and made possible new forms of independence and sexual expression, but it simultaneously trapped others in a narrow private realm.

Women's involvement in the paid labour force has varied greatly with the economic situation of their families and shifting labour demands. But such involvement has not provided a basis for economic independence for women, with the exception of a minority in professional careers. With the development of industrial capitalism,

women from the wealthier capitalist and upper middle classes were expected to remain within the home devoting themselves to domestic duties, the management of servants, and the care and moral upbringing of children. For women from the poorer classes, however, some means of supplementing family income was essential. Men's wages were commonly so low that it was impossible for a family to survive on them. While the cult of gentile domesticity for women and notions of childhood as the age of innocence prevailed as ideals among the upper classes, working-class women and children were more likely to experience the drudgery of working appallingly long hours under bad conditions and for very low incomes (Synnott 1992, 196–97).

Historical records of women's employment in Canada are sparse and unreliable (Wilson 1986, ch. 5). There were generally no records kept of women's unpaid farm labour in the preindustrial rural economy. In the cities, until the beginning of the twentieth century, the two major occupations open to working-class women were domestic service or labour in their own homes for the developing textile and clothing industries. Under the "putting out" system, women and children sewed in their homes or in small shops for a middle man who sold the completed goods to a manufacturer. Women could supplement the family income through such work, but could not achieve any financial or social independence. Women who worked in domestic service had no privacy and were under the constant control of their employers. By the end of the nineteenth century, textile and garment factories were expanding in Canada, while demand for domestic servants was declining with the introduction of electricity and home appliances. Accounts suggest that women gladly traded the isolation and controls of domestic service for factory work, but conditions of work and levels of pay remained abysmal. A Royal Commission on the Textile Industry, published in 1938, described women and young girls working seventy-five to eighty hours a week in conditions thick with dust, heat, fumes and gases, and for weekly wages of fifty cents to three dollars, often cut on the pretext of "flawed work" (Wilson 1986, 86–87). Such wages were insufficient to live on, even as a single person.

There is scattered evidence of women's involvement in unions and strikes in the nineteenth century, but efforts to improve working conditions for women were isolated and of short duration (Prentice 1988). Women were concentrated in unskilled jobs, or scattered in small workshops or in domestic service, which made it very difficult for them to organize collectively. Most reformers of the day, together with trade unionists, employers, and fellow labourers saw women's labour-force participation as undesirable at best. Government policies to regulate women's employment focussed on morality, and the importance of segregating women from men in the factories. Working conditions and wages were ignored. Employment for women was described as temporary and secondary, and their incomes merely supplemental to the man as the main family breadwinner. The cheap labour of women and children was generally seen as unfair competition that dragged down men's average wages. A few voices were raised in favour of the argument that equal pay for women and men would eliminate this problem (Prentice 1988, 137). But most unions focussed their efforts on attaining "**family wages**" for male employees so that women would not have to work. The plight of women who had no male protector was overlooked.

Women from the lower middle classes who had access to some education had a somewhat wider range of employment options. Many found work as nurses and teachers, but at the turn of the century these were not the kind of professions we think of today. Nursing schools were connected to hospitals and provided a constant source of unpaid labour. In the early 1900s, for example, the entire nursing staff of Toronto General Hospital were unpaid nurses in training. This meant there were limited jobs for graduate nurses—they mostly did home nursing, with sporadic employment and very low pay (Wilson 1986, 84). Women teachers were paid half of a male teacher's salary, on the excuse that they were temporary workers who would soon quit their jobs. In many jurisdictions this was ensured by legislation that prohibited hiring married women as teachers. The assumption was that women ought to be supported by husbands. The plight of women who had to support themselves was not addressed.

Current patterns of employment for women in Canada emerged during the period of prosperity following the Second World War. The growth of corporate capitalism and the associated expansion of bureaucracies and government adminis-

tration increased demand for labour in offices, sales, and service. Women were available to meet these demands. While the number and range of jobs available to women increased, however, the organization of the dual labour force has changed little. By the mid-1980s, approximately two-thirds of single women and half of married women with children were employed. But women remain concentrated within a much more limited range of jobs than do men. In 1983, 60 percent of all women worked in three occupational categories, clerical, service, and sales, all of them relatively low paid. A further 15 percent worked in medicine and health, and teaching. Only a tiny minority of women work as executives or in positions of decision-making power within corporations. The 1982 figures show that average salaries of women employed full-time equalled about 64 percent of average salaries for men. Professional women fared the best but they are far from typical. Women working in factory and service jobs earned only 54 to 56 percent of men's wages. Moreover, a quarter of all women are employed only part-time so that their actual incomes are very low. Most of those working part-time are married. Half of all married women are not employed at all: they are full-time homemakers.

What these figures mean is that notwithstanding all the changes in labour-force participation, the majority of women remain dependent on a man's wages to maintain a decent standard of living. They either are not employed at all, work part-time, or work in jobs where they do not earn sufficient income to support themselves and one child. Legislation requiring that women and men receive the same pay for the same job has little effect in a system where most women are employed in jobs that men rarely do. The lives of women who have to support themselves continue to be very difficult, particularly when they have children. Single mothers are often considered a welfare problem. Unless they are part of the small minority of women who have professional careers, the kind of jobs they can expect to get will provide an income little better than welfare if they have to deduct child care, medical and dental expenses, and pay for clothes and transportation to get to work. Government policies focus on trying to force absent fathers to pay maintenance. The question of whether women with children ought to be dependent on men is rarely raised. It is taken for granted.

The institutionalized organization of women as secondary members of the paid labour force assumes that all women are tied to men, and that they are financially dependent upon men. These structures and their justification in social values constitute what is termed **heterosexism** in lesbian politics. For a woman to declare herself publicly a lesbian means to accept that she will not be tied to a man, and will therefore have to support herself for the rest of her life. It means learning to cope in a society that is not materially organized to incorporate women alone (Bunch 1975). The gendered character of class relations has a special immediacy for lesbians, Bunch argues, because its impact is inescapable. Lesbians need to develop political consciousness as a matter of survival, not merely idealism. Women who are tied to men by material interests may be committed in principle to fighting

Lesbians need to develop political consciousness as a matter of survival, not merely idealism.

discrimination against women in the job market, but tend to back away when it is their man's job prospects that are threatened by feminist hiring practices. Women who have experienced marital breakdown may experience the force of heterosexism with similar intensity, although it is easier for ex-wives to shift blame onto individual men rather than onto the institutionalized structures of heterosexism.

The rise of capitalism in Europe is closely associated with the historical emergence of homosexual men as a distinct social category (Kinsman 1987b, ch. 2). Kinsman argues that capitalism afforded these men avenues for personal freedom that were not available to lesbians. By separating work from household, capitalist relations created social space in which young men could earn their own discretionary income and live autonomously. This made it possible for men who engaged in same-gender sex to congregate, and to develop networks that provided places where they could meet for sex and where they could develop a distinctive identity and self-awareness. By the early eighteenth century, such networks of gay men were clearly established in London and Paris. Opportunities for young women to achieve financial autonomy from the household were much more restricted. Kinsman estimates that it was only towards the end of the nineteenth century that equivalent lesbian networks began to emerge.

The Influence of Class on Gender Relations

A central idea in Marxist thought is that it is not consciousness that determines existence, but rather existence that determines consciousness. The notion of existence refers to experience of the daily struggle to survive, while consciousness refers to how people come to understand the social world around them and the attitudes and values they have towards it. Marx also argued that the dominant ideas in any society, those that receive public backing and support by agents of socialization, are the ideas of the dominant class.

Prevailing gender stereotypes can be linked directly to how different classes of women and men experience the struggle for economic survival. The idealized version of masculinity described in functionalist theory incorporates many of the values pressured into executives within the corporate capitalist system, where competitiveness, aggression, and hard-nosed, unemotional decision-making, are considered good business practice. Ruthless executives who are capable of firing fifty men at a shot and imposing their will on subordinates are widely admired (David and Brannon 1976, 27). Young executives are expected to prove themselves by fitting into the corporate image and working long hours, including evenings and weekends. Men who break the stereotype by balking at decisions that hurt others, not being highly competitive, and especially by avoiding working overtime to give more of themselves to family and children, risk jeopardizing their careers and their family's economic future. Currently only a very small proportion of all corporate executives are women, but the same pressures apply to them. Many find it extremely difficult to meet these demands and to cope with the pressures of running a home and raising a family (Maynard and Brouse 1988).

Working-class factory jobs carry different pressures. They commonly entail endless days of physically demanding work, often under conditions of dirt, fumes and noise, and demanding mindless obedience to machine-paced tasks. Typically, factory work forces have been segregated on gender lines, with textiles and light assembly work overwhelmingly female and heavy industry overwhelmingly male. Gray (1987) suggests that male blue-collar workers typically develop shopfloor cultures that value toughness, swearing and rough behaviour, and exaggerated maleness that gives their work status as "man's work." The alienation generated by such work, and by the emotional coldness of competitive capitalism, has been cited as an important factor in domestic violence, as men displace repressed emotions and anger onto weaker targets in the home (Luxton 1980, ch. 6). The wretched conditions endured by women in nineteenth-century textile factories, however, were not cited as precipitating abusive behaviour by women.

The application of political economy theory to women's behaviour draws attention to how particular conceptions of "femininity" are organized into work requirements in many of the jobs that are typically considered "women's work" (Connell 1987, 103; Hochschild 1983). Receptionists, secretaries, flight attendants, and others in similar jobs are pressured to smile at those they serve, to speak in honeyed tones, to be sexually attractive and to put up with sexual overtures at work, in order to sell the company product or to keep offices running smoothly. Women in part-time, low-paid, and insecure jobs tend to acquire histories and attitudes that reflect this experience; these can readily be attributed back onto them as justification for their economic position. Women, not jobs, become associated with high labour turnover and low ambition (Wilson 1986, 122–23).

The occupation that is most stereotypically defined as women's work is homemaking. Approximately half of all married women in Canada are full-time homemakers, and most of the others assume principal responsibility for it in addition to their paid jobs. As work, it involves multiple services for family members including the standard tasks of cooking, cleaning, and shopping, the less visible "expressive" work of emotional support and tension management, and the physical, emotional, and tutorial care of children. It is performed in relative isolation in private homes. A Statisics Canada Report, published in April of 1994, estimated that the dollar value of unpaid housework would amount to $319 billion annually if all services rendered had to be purchased on the open market. But this does not alter the fact that women who do housework full-time are defined as outside the labour force and ineligible even for minimal Canada pension benefits. From the perspective of political economy theory, the defining characteristic of housework is that it is unpaid, and those who do such work are dependent on the income-earning labour of others. It is outside the capitalist market system, notwithstanding its importance in maintaining and reproducing the labour force. Many of the traits defined as typically feminine: putting the needs of others first, being emotional rather than task-oriented or rational, being followers rather than leaders, deferring to men in important decisions, and the like, can be seen as appropriate responses to the lifetime experience of being financially dependent and powerless.

In summary, what functionalist theory interprets as appropriate gender-role behaviour for males and females in different social classes, political economy theory interprets as the structural demands placed on male and female workers by corporate capitalism. It makes good economic sense that boys in school concentrate on training for jobs while girls in school concentrate on getting married. Girls who look around them are likely to see very few women earning incomes that make them financially independent of a male wage. Only girls who make top marks in school can reasonably aspire to professional careers with large salaries. The "cult of femininity" among working-class girls—their preoccupation with makeup, clothes, and getting a boyfriend—is not based on a romanticized view of love and marriage so much as fear of being a "maiden-aunt" struggling to get by in a low-paying job and dependent on the generosity and pity of their parents (McRobbie 1991). Efforts by teachers toward a new kind of socialization that discourages gender stereotyping and promotes feminist consciousness-raising have little impact in the face of what girls and their parents see as the realistic options open to them (Gaskell 1988, 166; Gaskell, McLaren, and Novogrodsky 1989).

The Limitations of Political Economy Theory

Political economy theory describes the gendered character of class relations and draws attention to its importance in structuring gender relations. But the framework does not adequately account for how or why this gendered class structure exists. Why is it that male workers earn substantially higher average incomes than female workers, even when obvious factors linked to labour productivity, such as level of education, years on the job, and working full- or part-time are controlled? Why are women ghettoized in such a limited range of jobs? How did the economy come to be organized so that women rather than men assume principal responsibility for unpaid, domestic work?

The classic explanation offered within political economy theory for such patterns takes a functionalist form. The dual labour market exists because it is functional for the capitalist system. Business people need the cheap labour of women to increase profits. They also need the reserve army of women who can be hired and fired easily in order to ride out fluctuations in the market. Capitalism needs the unpaid domestic labour done by women to maintain current workers and reproduce the next generation of workers. But there are a number of logical and practical flaws with such arguments. Relations of subordination of women to men long predate the rise of capital-

ism. Capitalism was shaped by and also took advantage of pre-existing patriarchal relations, but did not produce them. Women's labour may have been essential to the preindustrial patterns of production organized around large family households. But this did not afford them equal status with men. Legally and politically, women had few rights. Household authority rested squarely with men. The rise of capitalism made life generally easier for women by reducing domestic drudgery and providing at least some opportunities for financial independence.

The argument that capitalism needs and therefore perpetuates the status of women as secondary, marginal, and cheap workers contradicts the logic of a profit-driven economy. In principle, if women in general are a cheap labour pool, and if they are as productive as men, then it would make good business sense to hire *only* women. If women are discriminated against by other, irrational employers, then their labour would be cheap. It makes good business sense to hire the people that others discriminate against to reduce one's own labour costs. Either way, demand for women's labour should rise, which would increase their wage-bargaining power and the differential price of male and female labour should decrease (Wilson 1986, 114). This generally does not happen, suggesting that the roots of the dual labour market do not rest solely in the play of business interests in the market.

Marxist analysis, with its focus on class and wage labour, provides a powerful explanation of the development of class society, and the reproduction of class domination, but its categories are fundamentally gender-blind. The theory does not address the question of why particular people fill particular jobs, or specifically why women are systematically subordinated in the labour market relative to men (Hartmann 1984). What remains to be analysed is why and how women are available to be exploited as cheap labour by capitalists, and the complicity of trade unions and male co-workers in these practices.

Political economy theory similarly fails to treat as problematic the division of labour that places principal responsibility for homemaking on women. Marx himself regarded how men and women organize to reproduce children within families as natural or biologically determined, and hence as not warranting the kind of critical analysis that he directed to how people organize to produce commodities. Current feminist theory challenges this naturalness as ideology that obscures complex relations of power between men and women. Engels argued that patriarchal family relations arose when men gained control of means of production ([1884] 1978). But the theory fails to explain how and why it was men and not women who took such control, particularly when women supposedly held power in the communal, matriarchal households, and commonly did much of the work of cultivation and caring for domesticated animals. The theory presupposes male dominance in the process of trying to explain it.

Political economy theory suggests that the alienating conditions of work under capitalism and the aggressive, competitive behaviour that the system promotes, may be important in generating the frustrations and aggression that are manifest in domestic violence. But it is a large intellectual jump to assert that class oppression and alienation produce rapists, gay bashers, and child molesters (Brittan 1989, 69). The incidence of wife battering may well increase with unemployment, but it is not confined to such conditions. The predispositions that facilitate wife battering or attacks on gays and lesbians exist prior to the unemployment or to the job frustration, constructing particular categories of people, and marking them as acceptable targets.

The prevalence of sexual harassment against women in the workplace, and similar patterns of hostility and violence directed against gay men and lesbians, also cannot readily be accounted for within the framework of political economy theory. Discrimination in employment on the grounds of sexual orientation has been explicitly declared illegal under the Human Rights Code of Ontario since 1986, yet lesbian teachers still fear to identify themselves, under the very real expectation of harassment (Khayatt 1990). One school board voted to drop all reference to nondiscrimination clauses in their hiring policy rather than acknowledge that they might possibly hire lesbians as teachers. Gay men similarly face discrimination and harassment in employment. It is very difficult to be openly gay and hold an executive position. If they cannot be fired directly for sexual orientation, other excuses are likely to be used (Kinsman 1987b, ch. 8).

In summary, while political economy theory seems to offer important insights into the organi-

zation of gender relations, there is much that remains outside its focus. Sexual politics have brought to light patterns of power, interests, and conflicts that cannot readily be understood in terms of conventional class analysis. Gender inequality is clearly linked to class inequality, but cannot be simply subsumed under it. We need an expanded theoretical framework to understand the interrelationship between patriarchal and capitalist relations.

Sex and Gender as Social Constructions

The social constructionist perspective challenges much of what we generally take for granted as factual characteristics of people and society. All aspects of social life are regarded as processes that people accomplish rather than entities that can be described. Sex and gender are no exception. In our common-sense thinking, we tend to view a person's sex as given, as a biological fact of life. Someone is either a male or a female; males display the gender characteristics of masculinity and females display femininity. Social constructionist theory pressures us to set these common-sense assumptions aside. It continually translates nouns into verbs, entities into practices. Instead of taking the two sex categories male and female as obvious, it asks "How do people do categorizing work such that they end up with two unambiguous groupings?"

Similarly, rather than treating male or female as nouns, constructionists ask "How are maleness and femaleness accomplished? How do people, in their practical, everyday interactions, accomplish themselves as male or female?" The study of what we customarily think of as gender attributes of masculinity and femininity also shifts the focus from describing characteristics to describing what people do to accomplish for themselves and for others the sense of being masculine or being feminine. How do we come to know, and know in common, what is recognizably being masculine or being feminine, and how do we accomplish such categorizing work for practical purposes?

Terminology becomes confusing at this point. Earlier we defined *sex* as biological attributes and *gender* as associated behavioural expectations that are socially learned. But this distinction no longer works. Some theorists use the term *gender* exclusively to convey the meaning that everything is socially accomplished, including what we usually think of as biologically determined. But this tends to obscure what aspect of common-sense thinking is being challenged at any particular point. We will use the term *sex* when the discussion focusses specifically on challenges to what are commonly thought of as biological states or attributes. However, this usage is not followed with any consistency in the literature being cited.

Sex as Social Construction

We opened this chapter with a discussion of biological theories about the foundations of male and female roles in society, where at least the notion that there are males and females could be taken as given, and that it is obvious which category an individual fits into. Probably most of you read this section without the thought even crossing your mind that there might be anything problematic about it. However, the ethnomethodological study by Kessler and McKenna (1978) makes precisely such obviousness problematic. As explained in chapter 2, and elaborated in chapter 18 of this text, ethnomethodology involves the study of members' methods of making sense of what seems to be going on. This includes how people draw on background understandings and practical reasoning in a continual process of formulating and reformulating accounts of what is happening that seem to make sense for the purposes at hand. Kessler and McKenna apply this approach to the question of how people, in their everyday reasoning, come to decide whether someone is male or female. They first tried a simple experiment with stick drawings to see what features a sample of 950 people would use to label the figure as male or female, and how many features had to change before people changed their label. What they found was that once people had categorized the sex of the figure, almost any surface features could be changed without affecting the label. Once people labelled a particular figure male, for example, the addition of a series of typically female characteristics, including breasts, narrow waist, broad hips, long hair, low muscle mass, and absence of facial hair, were not sufficient to prompt people to change their labels.

Common-sense suggests that we see surface features and then form a decision about a person's sex, but in practice reasoning seems to work the other way around. People decide what sex someone is, and then interpret surface features to be consistent with that categorization. For example, suppose we were told that person X has a female gender identity, prefers male sex partners, wears skirts and dresses, has some facial hair, and has feminine interests. Would this be sufficient to determine conclusively whether the person is male or female? The answer is no. We need to have attributed the category male or female to the person *before* we could evaluate the information. If we were told that this person is a female, we would see all the information as consistent with a typical woman who perhaps has a cosmetic problem with facial hair. However, if we were told that this person is a male, we would see the same information as consistent with a male transvestite, perhaps with a different kind of hormone imbalance.

Kessler and McKenna's experiments with stick drawings indicated that the presence of a penis was often decisive in people's reasoning. If the stick figure had a penis it was generally labelled male no matter what other features were added, even a vagina. This reasoning that gender attribution is genital attribution, and specifically that having a penis determines maleness, was put into medical practice in 1984 when conjoined twins were surgically separated at the pelvis in a Toronto hospital. The twin boys had only one penis between them. From the moment of separation, the twin without the penis was called a girl, her testicle was removed, and a "vagina" constructed from a piece of colon. "She" was thereafter shown in pictures with a ribbon or barrettes in her hair and wearing a dress. In terms of this practical reasoning, being female does not seem to have any positive status. It is defined by the lack of a penis, notwithstanding that the child had male chromosomes and a testicle, and lacked any female genitalia or reproductive capabilities.

The irony in everyday life is that classification of people by sex is almost always made without seeing a person's genitals. The surface features that people so readily discounted when looking at stick figures are all we have to go on. This leaves open the question of how do we accomplish gender attribution. You might try an experiment for

Conjoined boy twins became a girl and a boy after surgical separation in a Toronto hospital, despite the fact that the "girl" lacked female genitals.

yourselves. Instead of assuming you know what sex someone is, put this in doubt. Go to a shopping mall, particularly during a winter noon hour when high-school students tend to congregate there. Now suppose you are told that at least one teenager is a transvestite, claiming a sex category incongruent with genitals. Concentrate on how you do the work of categorizing the teenagers by sex, and trying to find the anomalies. How often are you not quite certain? How would you test your conclusions—knowing that transvestites would angrily deny your insinuation that they might be other than they appear, and that non-transvestites would be equally angry if you made such a suggestion to them?

A famous description of cross-sex passing is Garfinkel's study of Agnes (1967, ch. 5). Agnes was apparently born and raised as a male, but decided at puberty that she wished to be female. So she forged her mother's prescriptions for estrogen to promote growth of breasts, copied all the behaviour patterns that she thought were "typically feminine," and was successful in getting all her acquaintances, including her boyfriend, to think of her as female. As a young adult she underwent a sex-change operation to have her penis converted into a vagina.

Kessler and McKenna suggest that transsexuals and transvestites can manage to "pass" relatively easily in our society because we so readily assume that individuals have to be either one sex or the other, and that they are what they appear to be. The Olympic games is one context in which concerns have been raised that men might try to pass as women in order to gain an unfair advantage. It was even considered possible that some countries might be so set on winning medals that they would surgically alter male athletes to look like females. In the early 1960s a chromosome test was developed, using cells from an athlete's mouth. Evidence of a Y chromosome is taken as proof that an athlete is not female and cannot compete as a woman. One woman who competed in the 1964 Olympic games, winning several medals, was banned in 1967 when Y chromosomes were detected in her cells. However, she continued to live, in her own and other's eyes, as a female.

Three or More Sexes? Opening up Options

The above discussion has been based on the assumption that there are only two sex categories and they are mutually exclusive, however tricky it might be in practice to slot everybody exclusively into one of them. But why be so certain that there can be only two? We have some evidence that people in other societies have not taken it for granted that sex is dichotomous, or determined solely by presence or absence of male genitals. Prior to colonization, some North American Indian tribes, including the Zuni, the Navajo, and the Mojave, accepted and revered individuals who were thought of as having a third sex that incorporated aspects of both male and female (Midnight Sun 1988; Roscoe 1988). In anthropological literature this third sex is often referred to as the **berdache**. The term cannot be translated into contemporary Western notions such as "homosexual." The berdache were thought of in very different ways. They had culturally defined, multidimensional social roles, and were accorded status and prestige in terms of their religious, economic, kinship, and political roles, not the single dimension of sexual orientation. Among the Mojave, such third-sex individuals often attained high prestige as shamans, or as the partners of shamans or chiefs. Biologically female berdache who adopted the male sex observed the menstruation taboos of their female partners rather than of themselves, and at social gatherings they sat with the men. Biologically male berdache would feign pregnancy and still-birth, and scratch their legs to draw blood to imitate menstruation. The sexual partners of these individuals retained the gender identity associated with their own biological sex.

Enforcing Two Sexes: Closing Options

If it is possible in principle to categorize people in terms of three or perhaps more sexes, and far from straightforward to categorize them exclusively into either male or female, then how is it that we take for granted the rigid categorization of male or female? How do we accomplish and sustain the social construction of our world as made up of two distinct sexes, despite the failure of human reality on almost any count to be strictly dimorphic (Connell 1987, 75)? Connell's answer is that this definitely does not come naturally. It has to be worked at. Sustained effort to exaggerate differences between people categorized as male and female is needed precisely because biological logic cannot sustain the gender categories (1987, 83). Similarities far outweigh differences. Children have their sex categorization vehemently imposed upon them long before this has any relevance for purposes of sexual reproduction. Obsessive efforts go into the sex-typing of clothes and adornment, and the production of body images that exaggerate muscular physique for males and physical slimness and beauty for females. Frank (1992, 275–76) describes how teenaged boys actively worked on their bodies to produce desired effects, especially through involvement in sports and weight training. Until relatively recently in Western societies, girls were actively discouraged from involvement in muscle-building programs. When women did become

involved in intensive sports training, the magnitude of supposed biological differences in the strength, endurance, and speed of male and female athletes dwindled to a fraction of their former size. Women who currently participate in Olympic sports can beat all but a small minority of men. They routinely shatter world records set by men at the turn of the century.

In summary, in social constructionist theory, bodies are not "givens." We are not simply born with our bodies. They are sites of action that men and women work on by a multitude of practices including sports, training, diet, and clothing. Surgical intervention is an extreme form of action on a continuum that has included such instruments of torture as whale-bone corsets, spike-heeled shoes, and other forms of clothing that restrict, twist, and shape bodies into the moulds considered naturally male or naturally female.

Gender as Social Construction

Members' methods for establishing the categorization of individuals into male and female are directly implicated in members' methods for accomplishing the recognition of masculinity and femininity as distinctive behavioural patterns. Much social science literature in the functionalist tradition is preoccupied with identifying sex-based differences in behaviour. Typically, such work begins with sex dimorphism as given, describes sets of traits associated with the two categories, conceptualizes these as typically male and typically female normative patterns, and defines these as the cultural norms for the group or groups with which the individuals are identified.

From the perspective of social constructionist theory, there are serious problems with this approach. The research process appears to be circular in two respects. Firstly, behavioural traits are commonly used in practical reasoning to decide the sex category in which to place the individuals being studied. Secondly, the methods used to discover typical traits actively work to create the realities of masculinity and femininity that such research is intended to describe. Psychological scales designed to measure masculinity and femininity, such as those developed by Bem (1974), provide valuable illustrations of such circularity. Social constructionist analysis focusses not on the accuracy of such scales for describing reality, but on the detailed methods used by scientists to produce the scales themselves (Connell 1987, 171–74; Eichler 1980, 62). A common approach is to develop long lists of adjectives describing behavioural traits and then ask a large sample of people to classify each adjective as more typical for a male, or more typical for a female. Bem used a checklist of 400 adjectives. The final scale includes only those adjectives that are consistently identified by judges as typical for one sex with a high level of statistical accuracy. Further trials are used to eliminate adjectives or "items" that seem inconsistent with the others on the scale, in how people respond to them. Finally, when used to measure the supposed masculinity or femininity of particular people, responses to all items are added together and averaged, since any one item alone might be unreliable as a measure of the underlying gender trait.

The systematic deconstruction of these scales reveals the practices that produce the "reality" of gender traits that they supposedly describe. In the first stage, the selection of adjectives deemed to constitute gender-specific traits depends heavily on the view of the panel of judges. Typically, these comprise undergraduate psychology students. Eichler suggests that what poor, black women from American inner cities might recognize as "typical for a male" or "typical for a female" are likely to be very different from what psychology students pick out. But their opinions are not normally asked. Hypothetically, a wide enough variety of judges might result in no consistent list of gender-linked adjectives. The next step in scale formation accomplishes the construction of masculine and feminine as opposing categories. The vast majority of adjectives were seen by judges as commonly applying to both males and females, from which we might reasonably conclude that there is no gender dimorphism. But all these adjectives are eliminated. The scale devised by Bem, for example, includes only 40 of the original 400 adjectives, 20 for the masculinity measure and 20 for femininity. These practices construct gender traits as residual terms. Gender is what is left over when all the characteristics that men and women share are eliminated. "Masculine" thus necessarily constitutes what "femininity" is not, and vice versa. Final confirmation of sex-linked "gender" traits is achieved when researchers routinely discard as faulty those studies that do not find expected gender dimorphism.

These scales carry the aura of scientific objectivity backed by precise statistical data, which gives them considerable influence. Individual men and women who do not score higher or lower on the appropriate masculinity or femininity scale, may appear in the eyes of themselves and others to be gender deviants. But such apparent **deviance** or conformity to supposed gender traits are entirely an artifact of the scale's construction. The core of the constructionist critique of such measures is that they are inherently flawed because the underlying conceptualization of gender is false. Gender is not an essence or entity that can be abstracted and measured, but rather an ongoing accomplishment in social interaction. With this shift in focus, the central research question becomes how do people accomplish gender. What are the practices that individuals use to accomplish themselves as recognizably, accountably masculine or feminine for practical purposes in particular social situations?

Accomplishing Masculinity

Conversations with fourteen young men about what it means to be a man, revealed a high level of anxiety and doubt (Frank 1992). Most were not at all sure of their own masculinity, and went to considerable lengths to try to assert it, to themselves as much as to others. The boys talked of the strategies they adopted to accomplish themselves as recognizably, accountably masculine in everyday interaction. Most of them worked on their bodies, trying to build up muscle. Frank describes them as "using their bodies like suits of armour that they carry with them for protection" (1992, 275–76). Those who could usually did some sports, or otherwise they made a point of hanging around with bigger boys who did. They generally avoided friendships with girls lest they might compromise their appearance of being masculine, but at the same time they tried to get a girlfriend to establish themselves as heterosexual. They were well aware that there was no clear way to establish themselves conclusively as heterosexual, and felt continually under pressure to display their claims to "proper" masculinity. Typically, they engaged in "dirty talk" about girls and exaggerated heterosexist posturing with other boys. Another study of boys in Little League baseball teams revealed that they constantly taunted each other with comments like "You're a faggot," "What a queer," and "Kiss my ass" (Fine 1992). Most of the boys had only the vaguest notion of gay sexual behaviour and had never met anyone they knew to be gay. The taunts were mostly directed at boys who did not display the bodywork, sports, and sex talk associated with masculinity claims. The main intent of such taunts, Fine suggests, is to reinforce the generally shaky sense of what proper masculinity should look like. The most insecure boys used such taunting the most to assert to themselves and to other boys their own accomplished masculinity.

Participation on sports teams is one way that young men work at accomplishing masculinity.

Many of the boys who talked to Frank (1992) spoke of the gap they sensed between their public facade of exaggerated masculinity claims and the private practices and fantasies that they kept to themselves, or shared with only close confidants. Some were heterosexual in both practice and fantasies, while others had homosexual fantasies; others engaged in homosexual practices while maintaining a surface of heterosexuality. For those boys who do recognize homosexual desires in themselves, the exaggerated heterosexist taunting can be painful and even frightening (G. Smith 1992). The term *heterosexism* generally refers to the practices and the patterns of discourse, or ways of thinking and talking, that enforce heterosexual masculinity as "normal" and all other forms of sexual desire as aberrant. Heterosexism organizes the relations within which homophobic attitudes emerge as hostile personal attitudes toward gays, often by people

who have never met any. Such an attitude set often co-exists with a rigid demarcation of male versus female tasks and activities, and a view of girls and women as inferior to boys and men (Fine 1992; Lehne 1976). Racism, or rigid notions about racial distinctions and relative superiority and inferiority of such groupings, is also a common corollary of homophobia.

Accomplishing Femininity

For young women, the practical accomplishment of themselves as recognizably feminine is complicated by the particularly amorphous and contradictory character of the concept. Scientific models of femininity in gender-trait scales generally portray it in passive or indirect forms as less aggressive and assertive, and less associated with initiative or risk-taking than masculinity. The women's movement has openly challenged traditional models of appropriate roles for women, to the point that being considered feminine is not necessarily complimentary. Smith (1990a) suggests that the fashion industry may play a pivotal role in organizing ways of thinking and talking about femininity, supported by an array of mass media that include women's magazines, television, advertising, retail displays of cosmetics and fashion, and romantic novels. The ubiquitous presence of the media makes it possible for total strangers to strike up conversations about fashions and the fashion industry's conception of femininity, and understand each other. They are likely also to understand how the fashion industry codes particular clothing styles and body shapes to convey certain messages about femininity. Preoccupation with clothes and cosmetics arguably plays a similar part in accomplishing femininity for young women as sports do for young men. But the relationship does not appear to be one of straightforwardly copying fashion images. We have some evidence of how girls actively manipulate fashion images and even consciously choose to get fat to create oppositional versions of femininity (Orbach 1979; Findlay 1975, 59). A group of working-class girls in Britain saw fashion and cosmetics as a way of asserting their independence from school and their superiority over middle-class girls who wore "horrible" school uniforms (McRobbie 1978). Conversely, working-class girls on the Yonge Street strip in Toronto flaunted the standard fashion by cross-dressing in black leather (Smith 1990a). The problem is that the meanings attached to such behaviour are continually in flux. It is also unclear whether women follow fashions or fashions follow women. The fashion industry is fine-tuned to pick up cues about innovations in clothing and to reproduce them in new styles, in an endless effort to keep women as fashion consumers. No sooner do teenagers take to ripping holes in their jeans and patching them with coloured rags, than the fashion industry produces jeans with holes and patches already made.

In summary, the view of masculinity and femininity that emerges from constructionist theory is very different from the traditional functionalist approach of socialization theory. There is no predefined set of cultural norms that individuals internalize and express in behaviour. Rather, the notions of what being a male and being a female might mean are actively constituted by the participants in ongoing interaction. Any subsequent description of behaviour as conforming to subcultural norms is an after-the-fact accounting. In effect, ethnographers in the functionalist tradition create the reality of norms in the process of observing, categorizing, and assigning normative labels to the behaviour they describe. This is a circular process in that whatever people do becomes what the cultural norms are. This descriptive labelling of patterns as cultural norms, however, misses the processes involved in their constitution.

Currently, we lack a body of research that explores in intimate ways how young men and women accomplish what it means to be a man or a woman. Frank's study is limited to a small number of boys and we do not have information on their class background or social situation. Strategies adopted by other groups of boys may differ widely from the pattern of bodywork, sports, and girlfriend that these boys describe. We also have very little understanding of the strategies by which girls accomplish being female, with or without the contradictory image of being feminine and fashion-conscious.

Sexuality as Social Construction

In common-sense accounting, sexuality is a biological fact of life. The experience of erotic desires, the intensity of attendant emotions, and the preoccupation with attracting members of the opposite sex, are thought to reflect the surge of sex hormones at the onset of puberty. But conflicting and contradictory accounts of what has been understood to be natural sexuality in different historical periods and societies cannot be easily reconciled with the notion of biological determination. During the Victorian era in Europe and North America, the official view of what constitutes natural sexuality defined people as procreators rather than erotic beings (Katz 1990). Prevailing notions of true love, true womanhood, and true manhood stressed purity and freedom from sexuality. In the medical discourse of the Victorian era, erotic impulses and desires to masturbate, especially when displayed by women, were defined as physiological disorders of such seriousness as to warrant surgical intervention to cure them. In 1906 a gynaecological surgeon estimated that some 150 000 American women had undergone ovariotomy—removal of the ovaries—to control female personality disorders (Carby 1982, 222). The last recorded clitoridectomy—removal of a woman's clitoris—was performed in the United States in 1948 on a five-year-old child as a cure for masturbation.

Such views stand in stark contrast to those prevailing in contemporary North America where the absence of erotic desire is considered abnormal. Far from being a diseased state, eroticism is heralded. Advertisers routinely exploit it to sell commodities, striving to identify their products with sex appeal. Media idols and pop stars who can incite erotic passions in mass audiences stand to reap huge profits.

Social constructionist theory does not address the issue of which version of sexuality is "natural," or which version might best describe subcultural views of appropriate sexuality. It raises questions about how prevailing notions of sexuality come to be constituted in particular historical periods, and especially the role of experts in the construction of common-sense reasoning. The objective is to deconstruct discourses about sexuality, to reveal how they sustain the appearance of truth. **Discourses** are the prevailing ways of thinking and talking about an issue such as sexuality. Expert discourses within medicine and the social sciences have a powerful impact on common-sense reasoning. They appear to have scientific credibility as factual descriptions of the way things are. People draw on them in constructing accounts of their own experiences, both for themselves and for others. Discourses do not provide descriptions of normal or typical behaviour, but rather conceptualizations that serve to "normalize" and legitimate certain behaviour patterns and to subordinate others. Relations of power are embedded in the authoritative interpretations of experts. When these interpretations gain ascendancy, they mandate courses of action to bring people in conformity with them. As noted above, Victorian medical discourse about sexuality justified actions that would now be considered grievous bodily mutilation. Successful normalization sustains the uniformity that functionalist research can describe as "norms" for the society or the subgroups being studied.

The work of Michel Foucault on *The History of Sexuality* (1978) is a formative study in this field. Foucault traces broad historical shifts in discourses around sexuality, linking them to changing economic relations, and the state's increasing concern to control the behaviour of the emergent working-class masses who flooded the cities in the late nineteenth-century. With the rise of capitalism, families changed from centres of production to privatized units of consumption. Individuals worked for wages outside the home, creating the possibility for young men, and occasionally young women, to become financially independent. They had more opportunities than ever before to live alone and to experiment with sex for pleasure, outside of procreation. New forms of authority emerged to control this freedom.

Foucault argues that experts within medicine and the social sciences took over the traditional authority of churches and family elders in the management of sexuality. A virtual obsession with sexuality emerged in these disciplines behind the mask of Victorian prudery and repression, with sex increasingly proposed as the cause of any and everything. This, in turn, justified extensive inquisition into it. Sex was conceptualized as a **taboo** topic, a powerful psychic force that was hidden from people or repressed into their unconscious. Hence experts were justified in extracting hidden sexual drives and preoccupations through forced confession. Confession, in turn, came to be treated as therapy, required for diagnosis and "normalization."

Within medical discourse, erotic heterosexual desire became defined as normal with all other forms of sexuality as illnesses or perversions that should be subject to treatment. Categories of sexual "types" proliferated in medical and psychiatric

discourses: types of women included the indifferent or obsessive mother, the frigid wife, or the nervous and neurotic woman; types of men included the impotent, the perverse, and the sadistic husband; children were categorized as the masturbating child, or the precocious and already-exhausted child. In 1869, the term *homosexual* was introduced as a category within the discourses of psychology, psychiatry, medicine, and law. Formerly sodomy was considered just a form of nonprocreative sexual practice proscribed by the church. It became transformed in medical discourse from an activity to a particular type of person. Such persons thereby became subject to the power and control of experts in the professions.

These professional discourses were not simply objective or detached scientific theorizing. They mandated courses of action that subjected people to intensive surveillance and control, justified by the powerful ideology of scientific rationality. Foucault maintains that the goal behind the professional fixation on sex was to attain deeper power and control over the body. Norms of sexual development were defined from childhood to old age, with all possible deviations described and labelled as forms of illness to be treated. Children were conceptualized as latent sexual beings who must be continually controlled and repressed through perpetual surveillance, discipline, precautions, and punishments.

Educators, doctors, school administrators, and parents were all implicated in this discourse. Parents were used to spread new notions of sexuality, and then for monitoring it under the guidance of experts. Masturbation by children was constituted as a secret and forced into hiding as a form of abnormality. Then it became possible to justify compelling children to admit to practising it so that they could be subjected to correction and treatment. This, in turn, multiplied the power exerted by experts in medicine, law, and education. Foucault suggests that this fixation on childhood sexuality and its repression, monitored by segregation and surveillance in the family, created the very environment that would promote incest. The family thus became constituted as the focus of still more intensive monitoring, confession, and therapy. Donzelot (1979) documents two centuries of government intervention in families justified through the discourses of medical and social work experts. The status of women's work as homemakers was improved, but at the same time that work was subordinated to directives from experts as to how it should be performed (Ehrenreich and English 1979).

The practice of confession is embedded in relations of power. The person who confesses is seen as ignorant of his own psychic processes, or at best as having only incomplete knowledge. It is the listener—the priest, doctor, psychologist, social worker, or educator—who is seen as having the knowledge to interpret what is said, and to treat the person with the aim of normalizing their behaviour. Techniques of knowledge and strategies for power are thus tightly interrelated.

People who engaged in forms of same-gender sex were subjected to a combination of legal punishments and forced therapy that amounted to psychological and social terrorism (Kinsman 1987a, 106). They were portrayed as types of people who threatened social order. Military elites saw intense friendships between men as undermining discipline; gay men were hounded from government jobs as potential national security risks. It was not until 1969 that homosexual acts conducted in private between consenting adults aged twenty-one and over became decriminalized in Canada, two years after a similar legal amendment was passed in Britain. Since then the struggle over policing has centred around the definition of *private*. Any living spaces within the armed forces, gay bath houses, even closed toilet cubicles, could be declared "public" areas for purposes of policing. Even a photograph could constitute evidence of public sex, in that a third person, the photographer, must have been present. During the four years after homosexual acts were decriminalized in Britain, the conviction rate for homosexual offences increased by 160 percent (Kinsman 1987b, 143).

Power and Resistance

Power is always an ongoing accomplishment, never absolute, or attained once and for all. For Foucault, any exercise of power inevitably generates resistance because people never can be reduced to the socialized, normative role-players envisioned in functionalist theory.

The power of scientific expertise is no exception. But it is unique in that it is generally not experienced as force imposed from above, but rather as normal, rational activity generated in ordinary, everyday interaction. Parents and educa-

tors turn to experts to learn how to do a better job of parenting and teaching children. Psychologists and social workers study their disciplines in order to help people overcome their problems and feel "normal." Resistance seems irrational. It is difficult even to be sure what one is rebelling against when the mechanisms of power—confession, exposure, and therapy—are themselves often presented as rebellion against Victorian prudery and repression.

Nonetheless, people do resist the force of scientific rationality. The medical and scientific discourses that defined homosexual activity in terms of aberrant personality types also provided a focus for self-identity, and for resistance to forced therapy and to the deviantizing practices of policing. People involved in same-gender sex adopted the label *homosexual* as a basis for claiming a distinct identity and therefore grounds for some recognition, and human rights protection (Foucault 1978, 101; Kinsman 1987a, 111). Demands for "gay liberation" challenged the assumed naturalness of heterosexuality. Gay networks slowly transformed into ghetto communities in cities such as Toronto and Montreal, organized around gay commerce and markets. They fostered the emergence of distinctive cultural values and claims to respectability as a quasi-ethnic group, with a new stratum of "experts" who act as spokespersons for the "gay community" (Kinsman 1987b, ch. 10). Lesbians have not emerged to the same extent as gay men, in part reflecting their more limited access to economic resources.

The rise of gay culture and attendant claims to quasi-ethnic status have brought important gains in the form of greater public acceptance, but not without costs. Pressures to establish respectability by emphasizing masculinity or macho-style gay behaviour marginalizes those who do not fit the ascendant gay-cultural definitions. The political dilemma is that in accepting the categorizing of homosexuality as a personality type, people who engage in same-gender sex adopt the hegemonic heterosexual discourse that defines them as a deviant minority. On the other hand, in deconstructing the category to challenge the notion of "types of people" they undermine the basis for political activism in naming their own sexual experiences and resisting oppression. Activists argue that the deconstruction of the category "homosexual" must await the deconstruction of the category "heterosexual."

The Limitations of Social Constructionism

The social constructionist perspective avoids the deterministic implications of the functionalist theory of socialization into gender roles, and also simplified versions of economic relations determining gender. The conceptualization of sex and gender relations as ongoing accomplishments allows for enormous variation in their expression and for rapid, dynamic change. Discourse analysis holds up for inspection whatever is taken to be factual statements about human nature as socially constructed and subject to negotiation.

The main criticism launched against this perspective is that it does not go far enough in its own investigation of the dynamics of power that structure discourse. The central feature of sexuality and gender relations is inequality—the privileging of a particular expression of male sexuality and the generalized dominance of males over females. Social constructionist analysis exposes the power of such myths to structure the practices that constitute gender relations. But such analysis does not by itself explain why it is male sexuality, and a particular form of masculinity, that becomes privileged in this discourse. We have to look outside the discourse itself to explore the relations of male domination that the talk reflects. Male sexuality, gender inequality, and the privileging of male sexuality in discourse is not itself the effect of discourse, although this is a potent mechanism through which such patterns are maintained. What needs further investigation is the institutionalized and systemic character of gender inequality. This is the central focus of feminist theories of gender relations.

Feminist Theories of Gender Relations

When **feminist theory** is viewed in its broadest sense as an approach that asks questions about women in society and makes their presence visible in the theory and practices of sociology, then everything discussed in this chapter can be classified under the rubric of *feminist*. The sociology of gender relations, including the study of masculinity and men's roles, had its origins in the **feminist movement**.

In this section, however, we will go beyond the inclusion of women as a topic, to concentrate on the second stage in development of feminist theory that seeks to explore the social world from the standpoint of women. In particular, we will explore the thesis specific to feminist theory, namely that the social world can be meaningfully understood as organized in terms of **patriarchy**. The patriarchy thesis asserts that there is a systematic and institutionalized complex of relations and practices that organize and perpetuate the subordination of women to men. This pattern cannot be reduced to the voluntary behaviour or attitudes of individuals. It is systemic to how social relations are organized.

There is much diversity within feminist thought. The liberal, Marxist, socialist, and radical feminist perspectives approach the study of women's subordination in different ways and are associated with different political strategies for transforming patriarchal structures. These labels, however, are not precise and they tend to be used inconsistently in feminist literature. As conceptual divisions, they are useful for ordering the overview of feminist literature on gender relations, but as we will see the approaches overlap considerably in practice.

Liberal Feminism: The Struggle for Equal Opportunity

Liberal feminist thought focusses on the issue of equal rights for women and men in the public arena, with a special emphasis on legal reforms. Historically, it was a long and bitter struggle to win recognition for any independent legal status and political rights for women. Prior to 1929, women in Canada were not fully recognized as "persons" under the British North America Act. Even thereafter, the inclusion of women under "persons" was only selectively applied by the courts. With few exceptions, Canadian women were systematically and universally disenfranchised. It was 1918 before women were granted the right to vote in federal elections. Most of the provinces extended the franchise to women over the six-year period 1916 to 1922, but Quebec did not do so until 1940.

For the majority of women, the most important legislation defining their status was probably the marriage contract. In British and Canadian marital law until the latter half of the nineteenth century, married women were subsumed under the legal personhood of their husband. They were barred from owning or disposing of property in their own names. Their husband's authorization in writing was required before they signed any legal contracts. All children born to a married woman were the legal heirs of her husband. If the marriage broke down for whatever reason, and the woman separated from her husband, he retained absolute legal custody of any children (Smart 1984).

Piecemeal changes in these laws were won only very slowly, and often in forms that made it difficult for the majority of women to benefit. In the 1890s, married women gained the right to own and dispose of their own property. For women from wealthier families who inherited property, this was a significant change. It meant that they did not automatically relinquish control of it to their husband on marriage. But few women had any means to earn money or amass property in their own name. Any property that the husband brought with him into the marriage belonged legally only to him. So also did all the property that the couple amassed during the marriage. In the infamous Murdoch case, in 1975, the Supreme Court of Canada decided that a wife who had worked alongside her husband to run the family ranch for more than twenty years, had done "just about what the ordinary rancher's wife does" and had "no right to a share in it" upon dissolution of her twenty-five-year marriage to an abusive husband (Bissett-Johnson 1988). Only in the 1980s were marital property laws in Canada amended to state that the work of homemakers in nurturing the family entitled them to an equal share in family property.

Changes in legislation governing divorce and custody of children came equally slowly. By the late 1880s in Canada, mothers were granted the right to petition for a custody order, but to be successful they had to prove their exemplary character. Desire to leave a marriage was in itself evidence of being a bad mother, unless extreme abuse could be demonstrated. Also, any suggestion of adultery on the mother's part was considered sufficient to disqualify her, although no such strictures were applied to adulterous fathers (Backhouse 1991, ch. 7).

A feminist review of Canadian legal history provides ample evidence of institutionalized patriarchy, but by the 1980s most of the obvious examples of discriminatory laws had been repealed. The enactment of the Canadian Charter of Rights and Freedoms in 1981 seemed to epitomize the triumph of liberal feminism. It enshrines absolute legal equality for male and female persons, together with endorsement of affirmative action to ameliorate social inequalities. Section 15 of the Charter states:

(1) Every individual is equal before and under the law and has the right to equal protection and equal benefit of the law, without discrimination and, in particular, without discrimination based on race, national or ethnic origin, colour, religion, sex, age, or mental or physical disability.

(2) Subsection (1) does not preclude any law, program or activity that has as its object the amelioration of conditions of disadvantaged individuals or groups including those that are disadvantaged because of race, national or ethnic origin, colour, religion, sex, age, or mental or physical disability.

Section 28 of the Charter further states:

Notwithstanding anything in this Charter, the rights and freedoms referred to in it are guaranteed equally to male and female persons.

The aftermath of the Charter, as with many of the legal reforms that preceded it, has been disappointment and disillusionment with the power of law to radically change gender inequalities. In practice, the rights of women are always subject to interpretation and to counterclaims from other interests. Gender bias still appears to be pervasive within the Canadian justice system (Brockman and Chunn 1993). In addition, hard-won rights are not necessarily permanent. The National Action Committee on the Status of Women (NAC) came out strongly against the proposed Charlottetown Accord in 1992 that would have amended the Canadian Constitution. Among other serious reservations, NAC specifically feared that the Canada Clause included in this Accord would have permitted Section 28 of the Charter to be overridden in the interests of language and culture. Native women would also have had their Charter protection removed under the new proposals for aboriginal self-government.

The central problem for liberal feminist analysis is that guarantees of legal equality have not been sufficient to overcome pervasive economic and social inequalities between women and men. Women vote, but they are not voted for as often as men. Women are entitled to an equal share in marital property and have the right to sue for divorce and custody of children equally with men, but this does not solve the financial problems facing women who are single parents. As we have seen, women typically earn incomes almost 40 percent below the average incomes for men. Commonly, divorced women find they cannot afford the mortgage payments on the half of a house they might receive. Broad estimates suggest that divorce typically results in a 73 percent decline in the living standards for women with young children in the first year after divorce, and a 43 percent rise in men's incomes in the same period (Eichler 1988a, 249). The strict application of gender neutrality in custody disputes can also readily result in fathers looking like the better parent; they are more likely to have a stable job, a higher income, and to remarry and so to have a new wife to act as caregiver for the children (Boyd 1993, 172–75). True gender equality in society seems to be much more complex than legal equality.

Marxist Feminism: Challenging Exploitation in the Economy

Marxist feminist thought focusses particularly on the exploitative character of capitalist relations and the superexploitation of women as cheap, part-time, and temporary labour power. This perspective tries to redress the gender blindness of traditional Marxist theory, and the inadequacy of mainstream or "malestream" attempts to add women as a topic without rethinking the theoretical frameworks. Hartmann laments that "The 'marriage' of marxism and feminism has been like the marriage of husband and wife depicted in English common law: marxism and feminism are one, and that one is marxism" (Hartmann 1984, 172).

Feminist research into the history of women's labour-force participation has documented the systematic practices by male-dominated unions and by employers that have contributed to the subordination of women workers. Male workers had good reason to fear that the availability of women as cheap labour would undermine

their own ability to command high wages. They responded by restricting the access of women to apprenticeships, and by promoting protective legislation to limit the hours that women and children could work (White 1980, 12–18; Hartmann 1984, 182). Such legislation did help women who had little bargaining power to protect themselves but it simultaneously made them less attractive to employers relative to men. Historically, it was also common practice for male-dominated unions to bargain for lower wages and lower increases for women workers within their own ranks. The justification was that men needed a family wage, whereas women should be supported by men.

By the 1970s, such practices had largely disappeared in Canada. The Canadian Labour Congress (CLC) endorsed principles of equal opportunity for women, equal pay for work of equal value, paid maternity leave without loss of seniority or benefits, and affirmative action policies for women (White 1980, 65–73). By the mid-1980s, the CLC also endorsed free choice on abortion. The problems, however, remain. A relatively small proportion of employed women are union members, provision for maternity and parenting responsibility are very limited, and there are wide discrepancies in the average pay of women and men.

Women are typically employed in sectors of the labour market that have always been hard to unionize, namely services, retail trades, and finance, especially banks, and they are isolated and fragmented in a myriad of small offices. From such locations it is extremely difficult even to communicate with fellow workers, let alone to organize collectively. Where women have tried to unionize they have often met ferocious resistance from employers fearful of losing their pool of cheap labour. Banks have a particularly notorious reputation for breaking unions. In 1980 there were 7600 bank branches in Canada and only 65 were unionized. Unions that had formed had frequently been broken by intimidation and penalties, including the proliferation of expensive and long-drawn-out grievances, contracts that were worse than agreements in nonunionized branches, and the transfer of union members to other branches (Warskett 1988). Contract clauses of particular interest to women, such as maternity leave and flexible hours, are very hard to win even by established unions, because employers often cut back on pay raises when improved benefits are demanded. Few union members, women included, want to accept such conditions.

The gender-segregated character of the labour force makes it possible for large discrepancies in average pay for women and men to continue despite tough equal pay legislation. Discrimination is hard to demonstrate when there are no comparison groups of identically situated men to measure against women. Female-dominated professions like nursing, kindergarten teaching, and secretarial work thus continue to be among the lowest paid relative to the levels of education and job skills required. To counter the problem of job segregation, feminists have fought for legislation to guarantee "equal pay for work of equal value." Such legislation is now law in the Canadian federal government and the Ontario provincial government. In principle, jobs are compared on a points system that quantifies such characteristics as skill level, experience, responsibilities, hazards, and the like. In practice, such schemes are very difficult to operationalize because so much subjective judgment goes into assessments (Armstrong and Armstrong 1992). The private sector has so far largely resisted such evaluations. The prevailing cry is that any enforcement of such policies would bankrupt employers (Breckenridge 1985). The cheap labour of women seems to be a requirement for capitalists to be competitive.

Marxist feminist analysis of patriarchy has served to highlight many of the practices that constitute the subordination of women within the labour force. But like liberal feminism, the strategies for transforming these practices are still far from achieving the goal of substantive equality for women and men. The systemic nature of patriarchal relations goes deeper than a reorganization of opportunities within the labour force can resolve.

Socialist Feminism: The Double System of Social Production

Socialist feminism explores the complex ways in which **relations of reproduction** within the family are interlinked with **relations of production** within the economy. Relations of reproduction refers to how people organize to produce children and raise them to maturity. Relations of production refers to how people organize to produce

goods. The core argument is that transformation of relations in both fields of human practices are needed to substantially alleviate the subordination of women. Patriarchy, in other words, is multifaceted and not confined to the public arena.

The organization of reproduction within the home forms part of the explanation for women's disadvantaged position within the wage-labour market. Studies suggest that even when women are employed full-time in paid jobs they still do the bulk of domestic, child-care, and people-servicing work at home (Armstrong and Armstrong 1990, 72–74). In effect, men take advantage of the labour power of women so that they can return to their jobs relaxed and refreshed while women return exhausted from their double day. Legislation to prevent discrimination against women employees does nothing to resolve the built-in discriminatory practices that assume that "normal" employees are not responsible for child care. Hence when particular employees—usually female—ask for child-care leave or flexible working hours, it sounds like an appeal for special treatment (Mackinnon 1989, 219). Similarly, potential employees who have a combination of undesirable traits, such as being older, lacking in current work experience, having large gaps in their employment careers, and who seem likely to quit the job after a few years, are less likely to be selected than applicants with few or none of these negative traits. Strictly gender-neutral hiring practices will do nothing to resolve the fact that typically it is women rather than men who manifest all of these negative traits. These patterns are rooted in the domestic division of labour, and their transformation would require systemic changes that are much more complex than law reform. Eisenstein (1984) argues that the women's movement has precipitated a crisis in liberal thought precisely because the principles of individual freedom and equality do not work when applied to women and men.

The elimination of systemic disadvantages that women face in employment would entail a reorganization both of domestic labour and paid employment so as to make childbirth and caring for children inconsequential for education and career opportunities of women and men. Some of the changes in the social relations of child care that feminists have proposed include provision of extended parenting leave for both mothers and fathers with full incomes and guaranteed job security, child-sick-leave days, flexible working hours, universally accessible, quality day-care facilities, and guaranteed income support for children and homemakers. But such proposals are contrary to the traditional discourses of mothering that idealize full-time caring for children in the home. They have been strongly resisted by the powerful "New Right" or moral conservative movement as undermining a man's responsibility to support mothers and children, and hence threatening family life and social order itself (Eichler 1985b). In a sense, the New Right is correct. Socialist feminist theory exposes the extent to which traditional patterns of organizing domestic relations work to perpetuate a social order in which the majority of women are socially marginalized in private homes and economically dependent. This patriarchal social order is precisely what is being challenged.

Radical Feminism: The Struggle Against Exploitative Sexuality

Radical feminist theory carries the exploration of domestic relations more deeply than socialist feminist concerns with division of labour, to highlight the sphere of private and intimate relations between women and men. The core argument is that the root of patriarchy lies in sexuality—specifically in the systemic institutionalization and legitimation of male sexual dominance. In a multiplicity of ways, laws and social practices can be shown as organized to protect and defend male ownership, control, and use of female sexuality and reproductive power. Sexual oppression of women parallels and perhaps even surpasses in importance the exploitation of women's labour power, with women's economic dependence being a critical strategy used by men to secure women's sexual subordination (O'Brien 1981).

Historically, the marriage contract did not merely give the husband effective control over material property. It defined wives explicitly as the sexual property of their husband. Until as recently as the 1980s, rape in marriage was a legal impossibility in British and Canadian law. A husband had the legal right to the sexual services of his wife as and when he chose. But there was no reciprocal responsibility on the husband's part to meet his wife's sexual needs (Smart 1984, 94–95). A wife's refusal to have sexual inter-

course constituted grounds for divorce as an act of cruelty, but a husband's refusal to have intercourse with his wife constituted only "natural disinclination" and not cruelty. Not until 1966 did the Courts of Appeal in Britain begin to apply the principle of sexual frustration equally to wives in considering divorce. Adultery was always considered a more serious offence for a wife than a husband.

Historically also, both the authority of the Catholic Church and British common law recognized the right of a husband to beat his wife for her moral betterment, or in effect to enforce his right to her obedience. This is the origin of "the rule of thumb" that refers to the convention that such beatings were proper so long as the stick used was no thicker than a man's thumb. Fathers had the same acknowledged right to thrash children into obedience. Wives have never been accorded the religious or legal right to beat their husbands, no matter what their behaviour. Canadian law no longer condones the thrashing of wives and children but domestic violence is still endemic in many families. It was the early 1970s, thanks in large measure to the women's movement, that wife battery received public attention. It is exceptionally difficult to measure the incidence with any accuracy, but the physical evidence of battered women in transition houses, and the results of many surveys, suggest that some 10 percent of women have been beaten at least once by their male partner. An important effect, and arguably the main intent behind wife battery is the woman's subservience to the man's will.

The crime of rape is regarded in feminist jurisprudence as the most extreme expression of male power to subordinate and exploit women as sexual objects for their use. But historically, it was not regarded as a crime against women at all, but a violation of a man's property right over his chaste wife or virginal daughter. Theoretically, the sexual violation of women who had transgressed the norms of chastity was unimportant, because such women had no value to lose (Clark and Lewis 1977, ch. 7). Subsequently, under the impact of more liberal sexual mores and the women's movement, legislation was changed to focus on a woman's right to consent to sexual intercourse. This shift in thinking, however, did not significantly alter courtroom practices. The onus of proof was placed on women to demonstrate to the court that she did not consent to intercourse. Judges and jurors were predisposed to believe that any woman who was not a chaste wife or virgin probably did consent to have sex, or that the alleged rapist could reasonably have assumed that she was consenting, and hence that he was not guilty. In 1983 in Canada, the crime of rape was redefined as "sexual assault" shifting the focus from penetration by a penis to unwanted sexual touching. The new law removes the legal exemption against a victim's husband being charged with rape and also incorporates sexual assaults against males (DeKeseredy and Hinch 1991, 62–65). The term *rape*, however, is still widely used and defended as a stronger and descriptively more accurate term to describe most of the offences.

Radical feminist studies of courtroom practices suggest that while the laws may have changed, the old notions that a virgin or chaste married woman is valuable, whereas other women are "open territory," still prevail in the minds of police, jurors, and judges. A woman's sexual history remains critical in a defendant's claim that he had an honest-if-mistaken belief that the woman consented to sexual intercourse with him because she had consented with other men in the past. Feminists denounce such arguments as ludicrous, and contend that sexual history has no bearing on the critical question of whether the woman might be lying about having consented to sex with the man on trial. Arguably, it is women with chaste reputations rather than sexually active women who would be more likely to misrepresent consensual sex as rape (Boyle and Rowley 1987). But this is not typically how judges and jurors reason. Many studies suggest that in rape trials the woman's character is on trial more than the defendant's. The publicity surrounding such trials helps to constitute the discourse around acceptable feminine behaviour. Women who do not abide by the rules can expect little protection from courts if they are sexually violated. In principle, prostitutes are entitled to the same legal protection from sexual assault as other women, but in practice they have little hope of winning their case.

Prostitution is condemned within radical feminist theory as a trade in women's bodies that expresses and reinforces their status as objects for male use. A double standard has always prevailed in the laws that govern its management and prosecution to target the women who sell their sex, not their male customers. Historically, the major concern behind vigilance and control over prostitutes was fear that they would spread diseases to young men—particularly to soldiers (Bland 1985). Few worried that soldiers might spread diseases to women. Efforts by feminist groups in the nineteenth century to protect women from false entrapment and forced vaginal inspections under the Contagious Diseases Act only seemed to strengthen patriarchal relations, providing justification for increased custodial control over women (Walkowitz 1983, 423–24).

Current legislation in Canada makes prostitution semilegal. It is not illegal to sell sex, but it is illegal to solicit customers in a public place, to communicate for the purposes of prostitution, to create a public nuisance, or to keep a bawdy house. The net result of such legislation is to give police broad powers to arrest and prosecute women while customers are left alone. These laws significantly increase the risks to women from sometimes deranged or violent male customers. To avoid a charge of soliciting in a public place, the women must get into a customer's car before negotiating a deal or being able to check him out. Similarly, to avoid a charge of keeping a bawdy house, the woman must go to a customer's room rather than bringing different customers back to the same room in which the woman might arrange some protection for herself. Even having a boyfriend is risky because he can be charged with living on the avails of her work. The semilegal status of prostitution means that the women who do this work have no legal recourse for crimes committed against them (Scott 1987).

In radical feminist theory, pornography ranks alongside prostitution as trade in women's bodies, a multibillion-dollar industry that sells women as sexual objects for men. The extreme position is that any erotica can be seen as problematic in that by packaging women as objects it serves to normalize and naturalize sexism (Mackinnon 1989, ch. 11; Dworkin 1980). It is morally easier to rape an object than a person, and easier to see women who complain as unnaturally frigid, manipulative, or lying. Others, however, see no problem with nonexploitative erotica depicting sex between consenting adults, and argue against any policing of sexuality for pleasure (Valverde 1987).

There is greater consensus among feminists on the evils of that segment of hard core pornography that depicts the violent penetration, bondage, and dismemberment of women's bodies as a sexual release for men. But there remains a sharp division of opinion about strategies for dealing with it. Activists such as Mackinnon and Dworkin argue strongly in favour of censorship and prosecution on the grounds that it constitutes hate literature. But many others argue against censorship on practical grounds. Violent pornography is a symptom, not a cause, of sexism and in a deeply sexist society censorship rarely works as feminist advocates intend. On the one hand, illicit materials only increase in value. They do not disappear. On the other hand, experience indicates that censors often ban materials that women themselves want, like information on contraceptives and sex education. The main targets of censorship by the Canadian customs have been bookstores that carry lesbian and gay erotica. Ironically, even Dworkin's book opposing violent pornography has been banned because it discusses violent sex (*Globe and Mail*, 12 Feb. 1994, D1, D5).

Men's Liberation or Antisexism

Feminist analysis of gender relations as patriarchy raises difficult questions for the relationship of men generally to the women's movement. Responses within the men's movement have varied from active hostility and backlash against feminism (Faludi 1991) to challenges to hegemonic forms of masculinity, and to attempts to deal with issues of male privilege and power in relations with women. From the feminist perspective, any approach to men's liberation that does not directly address this power imbalance constitutes antifeminism. Much of the literature on **men's liberation** has focussed on the oppressive character of male socialization. Men are invited to learn how to become more nurturing and emotionally expressive, and more involved with children. The problem with this focus is that it rarely incorporates an analysis of sexism as political action (Lyttleton 1990). In its extreme form, oppression disappears altogether; it is men who are oppressed while women are conceptualized as having the power of motherhood, or the power to engulf and humiliate men behind the scenes. Men's liberation becomes part of the discourse of sexism that challenges women's struggle towards social equality. From the feminist perspective, an antisexist men's movement has to begin with the recognition of power and incorporate the intention to counteract it. The power of hegemonic heterosexist masculinity to marginalize and subordinate other expressions of masculinity is part of this antisexist struggle.

Drawing by Cheney; © 1992 The New Yorker Magazine, Inc.

Limitations of Feminist Theory

Taking the standpoint of women has illuminated aspects of the social world that were invisible to mainstream social theories. The concept of patriarchy has proven a powerful analytical tool in challenging the taken-for-grantedness of gender relations and turning the spotlight on practices of gender inequality. The problem with this spotlight approach, however, is that many of the subtleties and inconsistencies of social life disappear from view.

Feminist theorizing is prone to categoricalism, the tendency to view social relations in terms of two internally undifferentiated categories of male and female, related by power and conflicts of interest. This singular view of a woman's standpoint is being challenged by women from many different minority group backgrounds as itself an oppressive form of theorizing that reflects white, middle-class, heterosexist bias. Women of colour have argued that systemic racism—the inequalities organized along lines of racial and ethnic differences—has as profound an impact as gender inequalities upon their lives and those of their family members (Kline 1989). They cannot simply align themselves politically with women and against men. Other women cite classism and the social organization of poverty as more central to their lives than gender. Women who never excelled in school find little to interest them in the preoccupation of academic feminists with gender equality in professional careers. Lesbian women describe their sense of oppression and ostracism as they struggle against the heterosexism within the mainstream feminist movement (Bunch 1975; Kinsman 1991, 93). A typical response within feminist analysis has been to try to incorporate diversity by adding categories to the theory of gender. But as the "isms" proliferate, the analytical utility of division into categories itself comes into question. A more dynamic analysis of practical politics seems needed.

An implicit functionalism underlies much feminist theorizing, particularly radical feminism. Analysis tends to be framed in terms of how the social system is organized for a purpose, and that purpose is male control of women's sexuality. The function of elements within the system are understood through the contribution they make to the maintenance of this pattern. The conceptualization of the state as a patriarchal system organized to protect and defend male dominance is an extreme statement of this position (Mackinnon 1989). This approach, however, has all the limitations and the rigidities of systems theory. It posits a level of systematization and singularity of purpose that do not reflect experience. It is by no means evident that state repression is directed principally at women. When the state is repressive, young men are much more likely to be the targets than are women (Connell 1987, 128). In Canadian prisons, for example, men outnumber women by a ratio of more than nine to one. Although it may be true that women are more likely to be attacked by men than men are to be attacked by women, it is also true that other males are far more likely to be targets of male violence than are women. The notion of patriarchy offers little to the understanding of men's experience of other men (Frank 1992, 297).

The relationship between state institutions and the women's movement is full of inconsistencies. Universal franchise, affirmative action policies in employment, and Charter protection are only some examples of state support for cherished goals of the women's movement and these co-exist with policies to reduce child support or day-care programs. The legal system is similarly full of inconsistencies and contradictory practices. Like the state, it is more usefully understood as the site of multiple practices and struggles than as the unified and purposive agent of sexist policy (Smart 1989, ch. 1). Women's experiences within nuclear families are similarly so diverse and multifaceted that they cannot be captured solely by the notion of family as a patriarchal institution.

The active agency of women themselves is curiously understated in some feminist writings. They are sometimes portrayed as the passive victims of male aggression and dominance than as actively constructing their own lives. This has been especially true with respect to the analysis of sexuality. Some of the women who work as prostitutes describe their ambivalent relationship to feminism, rejecting the patronizing image of themselves as victims (Scott 1987; Kinsman 1986). Underneath the radical feminist critique of prostitution and pornography they suggest is a puritanical conception of female passionlessness and male sexual control.

These disagreements seem to stem less from the intent of feminist analysis than the effect of an overly simplistic conceptualization of power. While power is recognized in feminist theory, the practical politics of choice, doubt, strategy, planning, error and transformation are often not adequately developed (Connell 1987, 61). The current trend in feminist sociology within Canada is toward a merging of social constructionist and feminist analysis that seeks to retain the insights into gender inequality that the concept of patriarchy provides, while avoiding the rigidities of systems theory analysis.

Suggested Reading

Elaine Morgan's book *The Descent of Women* (1972) gives a very entertaining and insightful critique of sociobiological explanations of gender differences and human evolution. She speculates on a woman-centred sociobiology and in the process reveals the biases inherent in much of this literature. Esther Greenglass's article on "Socialization of Girls and Boys" (1992) provides many illustrations of how mothers and fathers interact differently with sons and daughters and how these experiences may be linked to distinctive gender traits.

Susannah Wilson's book *Women, The Family and the Economy* (1986), especially part 3 on women's work, gives a powerful historical analysis of how women have been exploited in the Canadian labour force, and what the impact is on other aspects of women's lives. Meg Luxton's study of the lives of women in the small mining town of Flin Flon, *More than A Labour of Love* (1980), is a deeply moving account of the impact of virtual lifelong economic dependency on relationships between husbands and wives in the town.

Harold Garfinkel's study of Agnes in *Studies in Ethnomethodology* (1967, ch. 5) is an unusual and fascinating account of the social construction of an alternative gender. Agnes describes how she accomplished "being normally and naturally a female all along" for years before her sex-change operation.

Jonathan Katz's article on "The Invention of Heterosexuality" (1990) pushes us to recognize how what we currently assume to be "natural" heterosexual desires and feelings are quite recent inventions that reflect specific historical and cultural conditions. Gary Kinsman's article "Men Loving Men: The Challenge of Gay Liberation" (1987) pushes us to recognize and to question heterosexist assumptions concerning what is "normal." Didi Khayatt's study of "Legalized Invisibility: The Effect of Bill 7 on Lesbian Teachers" (1990) reveals how vulnerable and secretive are the lives of lesbian teachers, notwithstanding legislation that formally prohibits discrimination on the basis of sexual orientation.

Heidi Hartmann's article on "The Unhappy Marriage of Marxism and Feminism" (1984) provides a detailed historical account of the organized discrimination practised by male workers against women co-workers. Mackinnon's text *Toward a Feminist Theory of the State* (1989) offers a series of essays from a stridently radical feminist perspective that document the power and the violence associated with patriarchy.

Questions

1. Distinguish between *sex role* and *gender role*. What is problematic about this distinction?

2. What key observation is used to support the theory of biological determinism in role behaviour?

3. In functionalist theory, what key process is held to account both for variation and for stability in gender-role behaviour?

4. How do sociobiology and functionalism differentially explain the apparent predisposition for females to do domestic work?

5. In feminist psychoanalysis, what single factor is seen as explaining the ambivalence and hostility of many men towards women?

6. What problem challenges the prediction that gender equality would follow women's entry into the paid labour force?

7. Contrast functionalist and Marxist explanation for evidence that girls appear less motivated than boys to do advanced school work.

8. What is the goal of ethnomethodological analysis with respect to gender?

9. List three mechanisms by which Eichler feels the Bem scale produces a distorted view of gender behaviour.

10. List two ways in which Foucault sees the "knowledge" of experts as a power mechanism.

 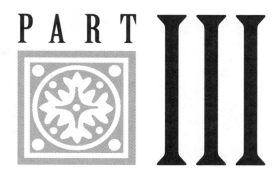

PART III

Social Cohesion and Order in Industrial Society

Cohesion and Morality: A Critical Look at Durkheim

The development of sociological theory in the eighteenth and nineteenth centuries was powerfully influenced by belief in the inevitability of progress and in the **evolution** of social and biological forms from simpler to more advanced states. From these perspectives, the industrial and political revolutions occurring in Europe and North America reflected not the breakdown of social order but the emergence of a new and potentially better order, one based on science and reason and the liberation of individuals from the crushing yolk of superstition and feudalism. A central question concerned how individuals, once freed from feudal constraints, could nonetheless cohere into a greater whole called society.

The Emergence of the Scientific Study of Society

The challenge for early theorists of society was to account for cultural diversity, for the spectacular advance of science, and for its corollary, the Industrial Revolution, in European societies. The theories of progress that emerged focussed on stages through which societies pass in a struggle to survive and adapt. The comparative study of contemporary nonindustrial societies, conceptualized as being at earlier stages of development than Western European cities, promised to yield insights into the origins and course of development of technologically advanced societies. Such theories gathered momentum under the impact of colonialism. Following the European conquest of Africa and Asia, and of the Native peoples of America, the colonizers and missionaries began to study these societies. The superiority of European societies tended to be taken for granted, and other peoples were seen as more "primitive" or "uncivilized."

Auguste Comte and Positive Society

The system of sociology developed by Auguste Comte (1798–1857) represents one of the earliest and most famous theories of societal progress. Comte wrote during the period of French history following the revolution, the final defeat of Napoleon in 1815, and the return of the Bourbon monarchy. Despite the restoration of the Bourbons, there was not a return to the order that had prevailed before the revolution. Comte sought to understand the basis of this new order, in which he saw that the old powers of absolute monarchy, military, and church had become bankrupt.

Comte's argument is that changes at the societal level reflect fundamental changes in forms of thought or stages in the search for understanding. He proposed a law of three stages in which the development of distinctive types of knowledge and belief is associated with typical forms of organization of society and social institutions.

The **theological stage** is a form of society dominated by primitive religious thought. People seek to explain events and phenomena in terms of supernatural forces such as gods or spirits. Such a society is based on intuition, sentiment, and feelings. It is ruled by priests and by military personnel, and its moral structure is centred around blood ties.

The **metaphysical stage** of society is associated with a limited development of critical thought. It is marked by a transition to belief in a single deity and the search for some kind of ultimate reality. Phenomena come to be explained in terms of abstract forces rather than irrational spirits. Such forms of thought are conducive to a unified concept of society. The notion of the state

and its defence are central principles of social organization.

The third stage is **positive society** based on scientific **empiricism**. Science seeks to establish such relations through the accumulation of factual knowledge derived by means of observation, experiment, comparison, and prediction. It involves the rejection of the religious search for final ends and reasons. Scientists, not priests, become the new intellectual and spiritual leaders. This mode of thought is associated with industrial society.

Changes in patterns of thought are thus mirrored in changing social structures. Social organization changes from a military state, where progress is based on conquest and plunder, to an industrial state where wealth is generated by rational, scientific organization of work. Comte hypothesized that war would have no place in industrial societies where plunder was no longer the basis of wealth. For Comte the decisive characteristics of progress include the scientific character of industry, especially the way in which labour is organized, the unparalleled development of wealth and resources arising from scientific applications, and the new social phenomenon of large-scale organization of work in factories.

What was needed to complete the transition to a positive society was a science of society itself— *sociology*. Sociology would complete the study of **natural laws**, which had begun with the physical world. It would have a critical role in the reorganization of society in more rational ways through the scientific study of the laws of society. Comte is credited with being one of the first exponents of positivism as an approach to the study of society. This is an approach to knowledge through the search for lawlike relations between observable phenomena established by empirical and experimental research. For Comte, the tremendous value of such an approach lay in its practical applicability. Sociology held the promise of providing a factual basis for controlled change of social organization.

Problems with Comte

There are many limitations to Comte's system of sociology. As a theory of progress it provides a fascinating classification of stages of intellectual and social development, but it does not explain the mechanisms behind such changes or account for why either reason or society itself should develop in the observed direction. Comte is vague not only as to what he means by "observables," but also as to how one might distinguish between empirical regularities and the unobservable scientific laws hypothesized to explain them. The main value of his thought lies in his insistence that the extent and form of variations in human nature and social organization are empirical questions that can in principle be settled by scientific investigation.

Herbert Spencer and Social Evolution

Herbert Spencer (1820–1903) was a British philosopher who was strongly influenced by Comte's classification of stages in the development of societies and by his positivist approach to the study of social organization. He went beyond Comte's descriptive model to explore the mechanisms behind the phenomenon of progress. Spencer's theory of evolution involves a grand scheme that unifies all realms of the universe, inanimate and animate, biological and social (Keat and Urry 1982, 80).

All matter, he argues, tends to move from a state of disorganized flux to one of order and relative stability. In the course of this movement, simple forms and structures give rise to more complex ones by means of two simultaneous processes: differentiation and integration. **Differentiation** refers to the breakdown of simple, unspecialized structures into many separate specialized parts. **Integration** means the development of a specialized function, organ, or bond preserving unity among the differentiated parts. Societies evolve toward even greater institutional complexity based on greater specialization of tasks or division of labour. With this complexity comes the development of some central co-ordinating agency, such as the modern state.

For Spencer, the fundamental mechanism governing this evolutionary change in both organic and social systems is competitive struggle. This struggle encourages more complex and specialized forms to emerge out of simpler ones. The chances of survival in a highly competitive environment are enhanced if an organism can adapt to a specialized niche that few other organisms inhabit, or if it can develop specialized ways of obtaining food and other scarce resources that give it a competitive edge. Such specialized adaptation required great flexibility over a wide range of activities. Competitive struggle between social groups similarly heightens the degree of differentiation and intensifies the need for regulation and integration. Groups that cannot make the necessary adaptations will be eliminated in favour of those that can. It was Spencer, not Darwin, who first coined the phrase "survival of the fittest" to describe this process.

From this idea of competitive adaptation, Spencer developed the notion of **function**. To judge whether an adaptation is successful, one needs to evaluate it in relation to essential conditions or functions that must be met if the social system is to survive. Three important functions include: the *sustaining system*, which comprises economic arrangements, such as agricultural and industrial production, that provide a means of livelihood for members of society; the *distribution system*, which allocates products and services between members; and the *regulation system*, which manages and co-ordinates these separate activities. More advanced societies are those with more voluntary, less compulsive systems of regulation since they allow the greatest flexibility.

The impact of Spencer upon the society of his time was enormous. His ideas won widespread acclaim, and when he travelled through the United States in 1882 he was welcomed by leading industrialists such as the Carnegies and the Rockefellers. His model of competitive advantage fit perfectly with their liberal philosophy of laissez-faire individualism and the survival of the fittest in the market. If unbridled competition leaves some individuals worse off than others, this is merely the price of allowing the struggle for survival to perform its progressive function.

Problems with Spencer

Spencer's grandiose system of classification of societies along an evolutionary continuum has come under criticism. Other theorists have challenged his idea of an unvarying sequence of development, suggesting that different societies may take different paths, and that convergence of social forms is not inevitable. Spencer's comparative method, which assumes that the prehistory of all societies was the same, is particularly suspect. Anthropologists have pointed out that supposedly "primitive" societies themselves have long histories. Impoverished societies may have regressed into that state due to exploitative colonialism rather than weak adaptation mechanisms.

Spencer's main contribution to the development of sociology lies in his biological analogy that conceptualizes society as a functioning system. He is notable for his elaboration of processes of differentiation and specialization in societal development, his analysis of specialized functions, and his comparative analysis of social forms. He had a major influence on the development of structural functionalist theory, which is explored in chapter 13.

Emile Durkheim (1858–1917).

◉ Durkheim's Theory of Morality and Cohesion

Emile Durkheim (1858–1917) shared with Comte and Spencer a concern with the comparative evolution of societal forms and a commitment to a positivist methodology that seeks to identify and to establish lawlike relations of cause and effect within the sphere of social behaviour (Keat and Urry 1982, 81–82). He rejected the notion that metaphysical forces could be responsible for the character of the empirically observable social world. At the same time, however, he acknowledged the importance of the internal mental states of individuals, their states of consciousness, their moral beliefs and values, and their motives and reasons for acting, in the structuring of social order. His influence upon the subsequent development of sociology far exceeds that of Comte and Spencer.

Details of Durkheim's personal life give valuable insights into his sociology. He was born a Jew in the Rhineland province of Alsace, a territory that was the focus of prolonged disputes between France and Prussia during the nineteenth century. Durkheim's family moved to France and became French citizens but, as a Jewish immigrant, Durkheim always felt himself to be a somewhat marginal member of French society. France at that time was just emerging from a long period of political instability that had begun with the

French Revolution of 1789. This was followed by the rise of Napoleon and the Napoleonic wars, the restoration of the Bourbon monarchy, further revolutions in 1830 and 1848, followed by the coup d'état of Napoleon's nephew Louis Napoleon. Two events of 1870 ended this period: a crushing military defeat by Prussia and the last brief flowering of the Parisian insurrection known as the Paris Commune, which Marx regarded as a true proletarian uprising. The Third Republic, inaugurated in 1871, was to last until the German invasion of 1940. Durkheim strongly supported the Third Republic and the promise of stability that it brought. He saw himself as a socialist but rejected revolutionary politics in favour of a more administrative form of socialism.

As a Jew in predominantly Catholic France, Durkheim experienced prejudice and oppression at first hand. Although an atheist himself, he understood the intense commitment of Jews to their community and the power of the religion of Judaism as a social force. He was very concerned with religious tolerance, and he insisted that in a highly diversified, multiracial, and multiethnic society, such tolerance for individual differences was essential. This belief motivated his political involvement in the Dreyfus case in 1894. Dreyfus, an Alsatian Jew like Durkheim, was a French army officer. He was falsely accused of selling information to the Germans and was convicted on the basis of minimal evidence. After a counter-intelligence review concluded he was innocent, it was a full two years before his case was re-opened and he was pardoned. All France took sides in what came to be seen as a blatant case of **anti-Semitism**. Durkheim's argument was that anti-Semitism threatened the cohesion of modern multiethnic society, directly undermining social solidarity.

The themes of intense commitment to community, and the religious character of this commitment, together with his insistence on the sanctity of the individual person and individual rights, and the necessity of tolerance for diversity, are central to all of Durkheim's sociological writings. Each of his major works addresses the question of the origins and nature of **morality** as the expression of the relationship between individuals and society. In his first major work, *The Division of Labour in Society* ([1893] 1964), Durkheim develops his theory of the evolution of society from relatively simple, undifferentiated, small-scale communities to complex and heterogeneous industrial societies. His central theme traces the evolution of a new form of social cohesion. His most significant contributions to contemporary sociology are his pioneering work in the application of scientific methods to the study of society, his focus on macrosocietal structures as the basis for understanding individual happiness, his explication of the foundations of social order in industrial society, and his seminal concept of *anomie* or moral breakdown. These contributions are examined in detail below.

The Scientific Study of Morality

The first premise of Durkheim's methodological approach to the study of society is that social forces exist as a distinctive level of reality. Sociology, which takes these forces as its subject matter, is therefore a legitimate and meaningful scientific discipline. The guiding rule of his methodological teachings is that the sociologist must treat **social facts** as if they were things ([1895] 1964, 14). By this rule, Durkheim does not mean that aspects of social life can literally be observed in the same way as physical objects can in the natural sciences. Nonetheless, they have the characteristics of things in two respects: they are external to individuals, and they exercise constraint over individual behaviour. Social facts comprise anything that people experience as external constraints on their behaviour. The sense of being constrained provides a sign of the presence of social facts. These facts, or external constraints, cannot be understood in terms of individual personality and circumstances alone, nor will wishful thinking make them disappear.

In the preface to *The Division of Labour in Society* ([1893] 1964, 32), Durkheim proposes to "treat the facts of moral life according to the methods of the positive sciences." His goal then, is to study the facts of moral life scientifically and to look for the laws explaining them. His central argument is that the conditions under which people live give rise to moral rules, and these rules change when society changes. The nature of morality underlying complex industrial society is necessarily very different from the morality of simpler societies, but it nonetheless does have a moral base.

The moral order, for Durkheim, refers to two central aspects of society. The first is a sense of **solidarity** with others or the achievement of cohesiveness and integration. The second is **regulation**, which involves restraint—including self-restraint or **altruism**—upon the pursuit of self-interest. Durkheim's basic thesis in *The Division of Labour in Society* is that there are two fundamentally different kinds of solidarity and therefore of morality. First, there is **mechanical solidarity**, which is based on sameness and shared conditions. This idea is captured in the saying that "birds of a feather flock together." People feel closer to others who share very similar backgrounds and experiences than to those who seem very different. The other form of solidarity is **organic solidarity**. This is based on recognition of differences that complement and complete us and that are experienced in exchange and mutual dependence. Durkheim gives the example of the bonding between a woman and a man in marriage, where their differences and resulting dependence unites them. Durkheim argues that, ultimately, organic solidarity based on complementary differences is stronger than the simpler mechanical solidarity based on sameness.

Law and Morality

The fundamental character of solidarity or moral order of a society can be studied objectively through the ways in which members of the society intervene to regulate each other's behaviour. For Durkheim, any form of behaviour that threatens the solidarity of a community will be experienced as immoral and will be subject to sanctions. Law constitutes the codified morality of a society, and hence the study of law provides for Durkheim an objective basis for the scientific study of the underlying moral life of the society.

Durkheim argues that the two kinds of solidarity are reflected in two very different kinds of law. Mechanical solidarity based on sameness promotes penal or **repressive law**. Such law is concerned with the punishment of offenders who have transgressed the shared values of the community. He then uses the French words *conscience collective* to refer to this sense of collective moral awareness and mutual obligation. He defines **conscience collective** as "the totality of beliefs and sentiments common to the average citizens of the same society" (Durkheim [1893] 1964, 79).

There is some dispute as to whether *conscience collective* should be translated into English as "collective conscience"—referring to people's sense of what is right or wrong—or as "collective consciousness"—referring to people's sense of involvement in a community. The French term implies both meanings. Many sociologists who write about Durkheim's work prefer to use the French form to alert readers that the term has this dual meaning.

Durkheim emphasizes that the totality of beliefs and sentiments associated with the *conscience collective* forms a determinant system that has its own life and that exists independently of the particular conditions in which individuals are placed. Any one member of a society encounters these beliefs and sentiments as social facts, as constraints upon behaviour that are above and beyond individual whims or feelings. Repressive law is oriented toward behaviour that violates the collective conscience of the community of people. The societal function of punishment is not primarily to take revenge against the perpetrator of crime, but to publicly reaffirm collective values and thus to strengthen the collec-

tive conscience itself. This is what is codified as repressive law.

Organic solidarity, based on differences and mutual dependence, promotes **restitutive law** or contract law. This is exemplified by civil law, encompassing commercial, contractual, constitutional, and administrative regulations. Restitutive law is less concerned with punishment than with the return of things as they were or with the re-establishment of reciprocal obligations between members of a society. As such, civil law presupposes a division of labour among people who have specialized functions and who therefore depend upon each other to perform these functions in definite, reciprocal ways.

Durkheim uses these two models—mechanical solidarity and repressive law versus organic solidarity and restitutive law—to develop a theory of the evolution of society from simple agricultural to complex industrial patterns.

Societies Based on Mechanical Solidarity

Durkheim argues that simpler, preindustrial societies are characterized by mechanical solidarity, the form of cohesion that is based fundamentally on sameness. Most of the members of such societies live very similar lives, with little specialization or division of labour beyond that associated with age and sex. Members feel bonded by their shared beliefs and sentiments, their common conscience and consciousness. The stronger the uniformity of beliefs and practices in such communities, the stronger the social solidarity—hence the intensity with which these beliefs and practices are defended against diversity.

For Durkheim, any stronger convictions that are shared by members of a community take on a religious character because they inspire reverence. Violation of these convictions is sin. The system of law associated with such intensely felt values is essentially repressive. Religion is critically important and tends to regulate all details of social life. Repressive or penal law is thus, at root, religious law. Nonconformity in such communities constitutes a threat precisely because uniformity of beliefs is the basis of solidarity. If such beliefs are allowed to weaken through tolerance for nonconformity, then the very cohesion of the community itself is threatened.

Transition in Forms of Society

Mechanical solidarity can be very powerful in relatively isolated and homogeneous communities, but it cannot retain its hold over individual consciousness in the face of rapid social change or in the context of heterogeneous, multiethnic, and multireligious societies such as the France of Durkheim's time. The erosion of mechanical solidarity as a unifying force is the inevitable result of the cultural, demographic, and economic changes that preceded industrialization.

Durkheim proposes three factors as critical in generating the transition to industrial society. The first is the development of communication over vast areas, which allows information to reach previously isolated segments. The second factor is demographic: an increase in population size. As population pressure increases, people are forced to diversify in order to survive. This necessity gives rise to the third major factor: division of labour. Durkheim likens this process to biological evolution where plants and animals adapt so as to occupy different niches. As population density increases, people are pressured to develop in increasingly divergent directions, which allows them to co-operate rather than compete.

The combined effects of these three factors upon the social order are far-reaching. The common consciousness of shared beliefs and sentiments becomes more abstract "as it rises over" local diversities. The God of humanity is necessarily less concrete than the god of an individual clan. As Durkheim expresses it, "the gods take leave of space." This process in itself makes possible individual emancipation. There is more room for variation and for diversity of beliefs and sentiments. Durkheim argues that, once experienced, liberty becomes increasingly more necessary and inevitable. There can be no turning back. The social basis of individual emancipation is division of labour. As people develop specialized functions, they have different life experiences, and so develop different perspectives on life.

Societies Based on Organic Solidarity

Durkheim argues that complex, industrialized societies are characterized by organic solidarity, the form of social cohesion that is based on division of labour and interdependence. As people become more specialized, they also become more dependent upon each other. A homesteading family engaged in subsistence farming, for example, may survive with little or no help from similar homesteaders, but specialized workers in a garment factory cannot survive without a host of other specialized workers supplying their basic needs. Members of a society characterized by advanced division of labour are united by mutual obligations, and not merely by sentiments of sameness. Their ties to each other are based on co-operation that cannot be neglected.

Some of the theories of urbanism that we explored in chapter 4 saw size, density, and heterogeneity as negative features of society, leading to the breakdown or weakening of social cohesion. Durkheim rejects this interpretation. He argues in contrast that the earlier homogeneous forms of society, made up of relatively undifferentiated family groupings, were actually more fragile. The parts, or family groupings, that made up such societies, could break away from each other and remain relatively independent on their homesteads, or in their small villages or kin communities. Although modern, heterogeneous, urban societies foster a far greater degree of individualism, they are also more interdependent. The specialized parts need each other and cannot break away. Heterogeneity thus presupposes differences and specialization. These differences give rise to ties of mutual obligation and co-operation that grow progressively stronger as specialization increases.

In such societies, repressive or religious law necessarily declines because the core of common beliefs and sentiments declines. Restitutive or contract law expands in its place. Restitutive law regulates the rules of justice that cannot be violated by individual contracts. Respect for the individual and for individual rights constitutes the fundamental ground of justice, or what Durkheim calls the **precontractual basis of contract**, that expresses morality in highly specialized societies. Respect for the individual and for individual rights is not merely "good." It is essential for solidarity in modern society.

The grip of religious dogma on everyday life declines, and the *conscience collective*—the shared beliefs and sentiments—becomes more abstract. What replaces it is the religion of individualism, or **humanism**. Such moral individualism is not to be equated with selfish self-interest, but rather with reciprocal obligations and mutual respect. This recognition of the fundamental moral role of the division of labour in society is Durkheim's most important theoretical contribution. He totally rejects the arguments of Spencer and utilitarian economists who suggest that a stable society could be based upon unbridled self-interest. Durkheim argues that "there is nothing less constant than interest. Today it unites me to you; tomorrow it will make me your enemy. Such a cause can only give rise to transient relations and passing associations" ([1893] 1964, 204). Even purely economic contracts presuppose a precontractual basis of moral standards that underlies and regulates the agreements between people and determines standards of justice.

Problems with Durkheim

Durkheim's analysis of division of labour and moral order was an important advance over theories that viewed this division as entirely negative and destructive; however, it is open to a number of criticisms. His early formulation of the transition from mechanical to organic solidarity as a unilinear process is seriously overdrawn. Anthropological studies have shown that there is much division of labour and contractual obligation in nonspecialized, simple societies. Similarly, mechanical solidarity is still deeply embedded in industrial societies, manifested in strong identification with religious and ethnic groups. A related point is that repressive, penal law has by no means disappeared in modern societies. It is not difficult in the late twentieth century to point out authoritarian regimes that demand conformity to dominant political doctrines. Many such regimes are arguably the direct result of the exploitative economic interest of advanced industrialized nations.

The first criticism based on the transition from mechanical to organic solidarity can be deflected if one measures the type of solidarity in terms of relative preponderance rather than in an absolute either/or manner. As a member of the Jewish community in France, Durkheim was certainly well aware of strong religious and ethnic affiliations, and he probably never intended his formulation to be interpreted rigidly. Specialization and differentiation certainly exist in nonindustrialized societies, but not to the same extent as in industrial societies. In Canada in the 1990s, even rural areas are totally tied to specialized mono-crop production, and farmers are as dependent as industrial workers upon the market economy for their subsistence needs.

Restitutive or contract law impinges on almost every aspect of market transactions. In China, for example, economic reforms under Deng Xiaoping permit peasant farmers to sign contracts in which they agree to deliver fixed amounts of produce to the state in return for the right to farm a plot of land for themselves. One result of this policy has been an explosion in the number of restitutive laws, just as Durkheim predicted. It has been followed by an explosion in the number of lawyers needed to handle contracts and disputes. Law schools in China are booming. In 1991, there were 41 639 lawyers in China, a substantial increase from 3000 in 1980. Since 1978, two hundred new economic laws have been promulgated. Some people argue that China is now on the road to Western "rule of law" and is experiencing a rapid expansion of legal rights for individuals and families, as newly wealthy peasants seek legal ways to protect their property (*Globe and Mail*, 13 Nov. 1985).

The second criticism, that repressive law has not disappeared, is harder to deal with. Division of labour has the potential for sustaining organic solidarity based on mutual obligation and duty, with humanism as the supreme religion. Yet this state is far from being realized. The struggle to establish a universal commitment to human rights is one of the most pressing international moral issues of our time. The recognition of basic human rights is an important requirement for political stability in the interdependent world community, but it is not yet achieved. Like the Marxist vision of a socialist utopia, Durkheim's vision of a cohesive, co-operative world community has nowhere been realized.

Anomic Division of Labour

Durkheim's lasting contribution to sociology has been his development of the concept of **anomie** as an explanation for the moral ills of contemporary industrial society. Anomie is a complex concept, not easily defined. In general, it refers to a relative absence or confusion of values and to a corresponding lack of clear regulations or norms for behaviour. People feel lost, disorganized, unsure of how to behave or what to believe in, so that their lives come to feel meaningless or purposeless.

In his analysis of **anomic division of labour**, Durkheim anticipates much modern writing on the meaninglessness and routine character of industrial work and on the moral breakdown that threatens to occur because of the injustices of factory life. Durkheim recognized that industrial and commercial crises were becoming more frequent, and the conflict between labour and capital more apparent. But he argued that these were not a necessary result of industrialized society, nor could they be resolved by a retreat to the mechanical solidarity of nationalism. One cannot force moral uniformity in the face of functional diversity. The key problem, he argues, is lack of regulation. At the societal level, the absence of necessary regulation means that the parts of the social order are insufficiently co-ordinated. The consequence of this for the individual is a sense of isolation and meaninglessness of life and work. The economic structure of a **laissez-faire system**, with its powerful inducements to self-interested behaviour, hurts people. They lose a sense of being tied to others in ongoing relations and so feel separated and alone.

A major cause of anomie is forced or unjust division of labour. To be just, division of labour or specialization must fit natural talents. People must be able to choose their occupations freely. This sense of natural co-operation is destroyed when rules constrain people by force. Fair contracts require that both parties be equal so that both may freely enter the contract. This basis for justice is violated by inherited wealth; hence hereditary privilege should be abolished. There cannot be rich and poor at birth, Durkheim argues, without there being unjust contracts (Durkheim [1893] 1964, 384).

A further cause of anomie is fractionalized work. This is precisely the kind of work pattern produced by **scientific management**, which aims to maximize control and productivity of labour for the benefit of management. Under scientific management, operations are broken down into their separate components. Workers specialize in a discrete task rather than following the operation through. Labour becomes fragmented, lacking unity, co-ordination, and coherence. As a result, workers lose the feeling of the solidarity and continuity of work essential to the sense of organic community. They also lose their sense of pride in their own contribution. Work becomes meaning-

less when individual workers are reduced to machines, subjected to monotonous routines without intrinsic interest. Normal specialization does not require this level of **fragmentation**.

Durkheim concludes that the objective of ensuring justice in the treatment of workers in industrial society is a critical task facing most technologically advanced societies. Liberty for individuals can only be attained through just regulations. It is not enough that there be rules governing contracts; the rules must be just.

The basic question that Durkheim does not address, however, is whether such justice would ever be possible within a capitalist economic structure. It is at this juncture that Marxist theorists diverge from Durkheim. While Durkheim describes the factors that give rise to "abnormal forms" of division of labour, Marxists seek to examine the origins of these forms within the exploitative structures of capitalism. The Marxist thesis is that justice is impossible within a profit-motivated system where a small class of people controls the means of production upon which others depend. From this perspective, capitalism itself creates the lack of regulation, the **egoism**, and the immorality in collective life that Durkheim identifies as abnormal.

Chapter 7 explores at more length the concepts of anomie and alienation in the study of social disorder and conflict within industrial society. We now turn to two major studies that Durkheim himself undertook as a test and elaboration of his conception of the nature of social solidarity and of anomie: *Suicide* ([1897] 1951) and *The Elementary Forms of Religious Life* ([1915] 1976). Both studies have had a seminal influence on sociological analysis in these two areas.

❖ Suicide

Suicide and the Loss of Social Cohesion

Durkheim's study of suicide is fundamentally a test of his central hypothesis that human happiness depends upon social cohesion. The corollary of this assertion is that, whenever social solidarity weakens or breaks down, the level of unhappiness among members of that community will rise. The difficult task for Durkheim as a positivist was to find some scientifically acceptable, objective method for studying essentially intangible and subjective states such as cohesion and unhappiness. Durkheim's brilliantly innovative proposal was to use data on suicide rates to measure the level of unhappiness within a society. He defines suicide as "intentional self-death by any action known to have that effect" (Durkheim [1897] 1951, 44).

The act of committing suicide is a supremely individual and private act, but suicide *rates* are social facts. The suicide rate is the actual number of people per 100 000 population recorded as having intentionally killed themselves. It is regularly published by government agencies. Suicide, thankfully, occurs relatively rarely, and it is almost impossible to observe directly. When statistics are kept for large populations and over long periods of time, however, it becomes possible to study patterns and to compare differences in rates among nations and among subgroups. For Durkheim, therefore, officially recorded suicide rates provide objective facts that can stand as indicators of the general level of happiness of members of different communities.

As a sociologist, Durkheim is not interested in the precipitating factors for each individual suicide. He is interested in the conditions that would increase the general level of unhappiness and hence increase the proportion of people unhappy enough to consider killing themselves. He carefully examines individual factors such as mental illness, but argues that such factors tend to occur randomly and do not explain differences in rates of suicide between social groups. One needs more than individual explanations to account for these differences. Durkheim's theory is that specific kinds of social conditions that lead to a weakening of social solidarity generate increasing unhappiness and higher suicide rates.

Durkheim outlines three categories of suicide: egoistic, anomic, and altruistic. **Egoistic suicide** occurs when society is poorly integrated; that is, when people lack a sense of strong social bonds linking them to each other. To test this hypothesis, Durkheim needed **indicators** of the strength of social bonding. A series of comparisons based on religious affiliation and marital status provided just such indicators. Durkheim first compares Catholics and Protestants. He argues that Catholics have a ready-made faith and relative certainty of beliefs, whereas Protestants emphasize free inquiry by individuals. Thus, Catholics would appear to have greater social cohesion than Protestants. Durkheim predicted that Catholics should have lower suicide rates than Protestants. Official suicide rates kept for Catholic and Protestant administrative areas over many decades confirmed this prediction. In Catholic areas the recorded suicide rates were much lower than in Protestant areas.

Secondly, Durkheim argues that marriage and children tie people into social life and reflect greater social bonding than the state of being single or childless. Almost all the comparative data on rates of suicide confirmed his predictions that suicide rates would be lower when people are married and have children. Married men committed suicide less often than single men, married men with children less than husbands without children, widowers with children less than widowers without children.

Similarly, he argues that rural communities are more cohesive than urban areas because people know each other more. Again his prediction was supported: rural communities did have lower rates of suicide than urban ones.

A particularly significant comparison is between Jews and gentiles. Jews are predominantly urban dwellers and are highly educated. Both factors are associated with higher suicide rates in general. As a persecuted religious minority, however, they tend to be intensely cohesive. Durkheim hypothesizes that the internal cohesion would counteract the divisive forces of urbanism and education. The data confirm his prediction that Jews would have lower suicide rates than non-Jews.

There is only one statistic that goes against Durkheim's predictions. Women had higher suicide rates when married than when never married, although the rates were lower when they had children than when they were without children. Durkheim concludes that marriage benefits men more than women. Men, he suggests, need restraints more than women. Divorced men are more prone to go on drunken sprees, consort with many different women, and then fall into despair and suicide. The explanation is only guesswork on Durkheim's part, but the statistical difference has stood the test of time. In general, however, the recorded suicide rates were strongly consistent with Durkheim's theoretical prediction that, under conditions where bonds of social cohesion are relatively weak, suicide rates are relatively high.

Anomic suicide is closely related to egoistic suicide and occurs when people experience a loss of regulation. When people have a clear sense of their position in life, have meaningful goals and realistic expectations as to what they should be and should become, then they are contented and happy. But when these constraints are vague, and the limits unclear, people tend to become dissatisfied with their lot, unhappy, and frustrated. Durkheim predicts that the suicide rate, reflecting the proportion of people too unhappy to live, will increase as social regulation declines.

The main data with which he tests this prediction are periods of economic boom or bust compared with periods of relative stability. One might expect that people may become depressed during periods of economic collapse, but Durkheim shows that boom times are equally disturbing. The scales are upset, regulations are lacking, goals appear limitless and meaningless. Enough is never enough; people cannot stop running. Durkheim shows that during such times suicide rates go up.

A comparable source of stress is family disruption. Divorced people have a four to five times higher rate of suicide than do married people. Again, divorced men seem to suffer more than divorced women, judging from their higher propensity to commit suicide.

Altruistic suicide is qualitatively different from the other two forms. It is associated with too much cohesion or overly strong social bonds, rather than with the weakening of such bonds. In this extreme situation, society is so tight and cohesive that individuals are totally obedient to it and are willing to die for the honour of the group. Altruistic suicide is thus voluntary death as an obligation to one's group. Old or sick Inuit people would walk out of the camp to die rather than be a burden on younger people during periods of famine. Japanese kamikaze pilots during World War II flew their planes directly into their target, knowing that they would die, but willing to do so for the success of their country in war. More recent examples of altruistic suicide include hunger strikers in the Irish Republican Army who chose to die for their cause rather than bow to the will of the English government, and Palestinians who drove trucks loaded with bombs into American military camps.

Durkheim suggests that altruistic suicide is comparatively rare in modern society because individualism is valued more intensely than religion—egoistic or anomic suicide is more likely. The only context where he finds rates of altruistic suicide to be quite high is in the army. He found that army personnel have higher suicide rates than civilians, volunteers more than conscripts, officers more than privates, and re-enlisted men more than newcomers. If the hard life of the army were the main explanation for suicide, one would expect all these rates to be reversed. Durkheim concludes that higher rates for volunteers, officers, and re-enlisted men reflect the greater subordination of their individuality to the group. They are willing to die for their country.

This study of suicide rates has had a tremendous impact upon sociology. Durkheim demonstrated conclusively the relation between intensely individual acts and social conditions. He also showed the critical importance of treating societal forces as a distinct level of reality. He pioneered the methodological approach of using statistical data as objectively visible indicators of abstract concepts such as happiness and cohesion, thus opening them to empirical research.

The work is now dated, and subsequent researchers have shown flaws in his analysis. Pope, in particular, has used more sophisticated statistical analysis to show that some of the relationships claimed by Durkheim are suspect. The association between bankruptcy and suicide and between relative severity of economic crisis and suicide has been shown to be a small negative rather than positive relationship. In other words, suicide rates decline somewhat as the crisis period worsens. Pope also points out that the theoretical distinction between egoistic and anomic suicide is vague. Suicide rates among divorced people can readily be classified under either type, suggesting that the differences between them are a matter of emphasis rather than clear-cut distinctions (Pope 1976, 16–17). The high rates of suicide in the army would also seem to contradict Durkheim's own predictions that strong cohesion would reduce the rates. That scholars can find flaws in Durkheim's work nearly a century after he completed it, however, does not detract from its brilliance as a pioneering analysis of its kind.

The Political Economy of Suicide Rates

The political economy perspective draws on the Marxist critique of capitalism to understand variation in suicide rates. Boughey (1978, ch. 1) contrasts the Marxist approach with Durkheim's analysis in the following ways. Both make use of statistical rates in their analyses, but they focus upon different underlying factors. While Durkheim stressed the breakdown of moral order, Marxist theory draws attention to the underlying exploitative relations of capitalism, which may precipitate such breakdown, and in particular to the social problems associated with poverty. We saw in chapter 4 how crime, depression, and defeatism were high in the impoverished regions of northeastern New Brunswick and among low-income and unemployed people living in subsidized housing in pockets of Canada's large cities. The central prediction of Marxist theory is that poverty and unemployment will correlate positively with suicide rates and also with marital stress and divorce. Class oppression causes the anomie that drives people to despair.

Political economy theory maintains that class oppression causes the anomie that drives people to despair.

Current data bear out this prediction. Horwitz (1984) finds a consistent association between economic deprivation and psychological distress. Being unemployed can be an extremely stressful experience. People who have experienced a period of unemployment are far more likely to report feelings of unhappiness, dissatisfaction with life, and high levels of personal strain. Studies of unemployed workers show that this experience is associated with many forms of distress such as depression, fear, loneliness, anxiety, insomnia, headaches, and stomach problems. Unemployment rates correlate positively with mental hospital admission rates. There is a consistent association between economic decline and a subsequent rise in suicide rates in five separate studies cited by Horwitz (1984, 102).

The relationship between economic prosperity and suicide rates, first noted by Durkheim, is an ambiguous one. Several studies using aggregate data suggest that rising per capita income rates are related to long-term increases in suicide, homicide, rates of imprisonment, and alcohol consumption. At first glance it seems that people who get richer must also experience anomie and be prone to suicide. But this conclusion does not follow from the data. Such reasoning involves what is called an **ecological fallacy**. In other words, one cannot argue from aggregate data on rates to individual inferences. The apparent association between generally high levels of affluence and suicide may be the result of the great strain upon and misery of the poorest people who do not share the prosperity. Their sense of **relative deprivation** gets worse as they have to watch other people enjoying luxuries that they cannot afford for themselves or their families. They also experience a sense of personal failure and blame because they are not "successful."

Studies based on individual-level data support this interpretation. A study of lottery winners failed to support Durkheim's contention that sudden prosperity would generate anomie. The lottery winners did not score high on a series of questions designed to measure anomie (Abrahamson 1978). On the other hand, a study of unemployed workers indicates that they have a suicide rate thirty times higher than the national average (Stillman 1980). More microstudies are needed to inspect which groups are affected by suicide in times of unemployment: whether it is the unemployed person directly, immediate family members, those who fear losing their jobs, or new entrants and re-entrants to the labour force who cannot find good jobs (Stack 1982). Aggregate census data showing rates of employment and suicide rates cannot answer such questions.

In summary, there are important parallels between the Durkheimian and Marxist approaches to the study of suicide. Essentially, while Durkheim describes the symptoms of anomic division of labour, the approach of political economy explores the origins of these symptoms in the capitalist mode of production. This is a system of production in which the mass of workers are exploited by a minority of capitalists, or those who own the means of production. This system produces anomie by reducing human relations to the level of inhuman cash payments. Workers are hired when their labour power is useful to the capitalist, and fired when it is no longer needed. In a society in which division of labour provides the central social and moral bond between people through a sense of mutual obligation and interdependence, unemployment does not merely produce financial difficulties for the victims. It deals a devastating blow to one's sense of self-worth and belonging to a society. The right to work has become a fundamental human need, a moral obligation of society. But under the capitalist mode of production, when the rate of profit falls, workers are laid off. Women especially find themselves shut out at such times. Typically, women are the last hired and first fired when the job market is tight.

Suicide Among Women

Data that show lower rates of suicide for women generally, compared with men, are also ambiguous in their meaning. The differences in themselves are impressive. Suter (1976, 129) indicates that males commit suicide about three times more frequently than females. Others confirm this pattern, suggesting that it holds for all age groups, from approximately one woman to every two men at age twenty to twenty-five, to one woman to every ten men in the group sixty years or older. The gap is so large that suicide has been called "a masculine behaviour" (Neuringer and Lettieri 1982, 14, 15). The difference in suicide rates between men and women in Canada is shown in figure 6-1 (see also tables 6-1 and 6-2).

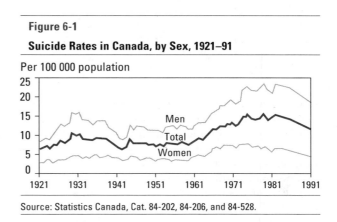

Figure 6-1

Suicide Rates in Canada, by Sex, 1921–91

Per 100 000 population

Source: Statistics Canada, Cat. 84-202, 84-206, and 84-528.

Are we to conclude from these rates that women are much happier than men? That men's lives in the rat race of industrial society are more anomic than the lives of housewives protected within their homes? Not necessarily. The catch is that women *attempt* suicide far more frequently than men. Suter suggests that females attempt suicide two to three times more often than males. Suicide attempts generally are six to ten times more frequent than completions. Altogether, women seem considerably more suicidal than men, although they are less likely to complete the act. One straightforward explanation for this

Table 6-1

Suicide Rate by Age and Sex, Selected Provinces, 1981 (per 100 000 population)					
	15–19 Years			20–24 Years		
	Male	Female	Total	Male	Female	Total
Nova Scotia	11.4	9.6	10.5	33.1	–	16.6
Manitoba	39.0	2.1	20.8	44.5	10.7	27.7
Saskatchewan	41.4	17.1	29.5	42.3	15.9	29.2
Alberta	32.8	3.8	18.7	34.3	3.1	19.3
British Columbia	22.9	4.3	13.8	33.6	7.9	20.7

Source: Lapierre and Aylwin (1985, 87).

Table 6-2

Hospital Separation Related to Attempted Suicide or "Self-inflicted Injuries" by Age and Sex, Selected Provinces, 1980–81 (per 100 000 population)

	15–19 Years			20–24 Years		
	Male	Female	Total	Male	Female	Total
Nova Scotia	22.4	35.2	28.6	27.8	38.7	33.1
Manitoba	148.9	243.3	195.5	154.7	167.4	161.0
Saskatchewan	53.1	90.5	71.5	80.2	86.4	83.2
Alberta	98.5	211.7	154.1	125.0	191.8	157.1
British Columbia	161.5	303.7	231.2	212.7	272.2	231.5

Source: Lapierre and Aylwin (1985, 87).

difference may be that men are trained to be more aggressive than women and have easier access to the favoured technique of using a gun. Women are more likely to use barbiturates or poison, methods that have a greater margin for error.

The explanation as to why women in general appear more suicidal than men remains unsatisfactory. From the Marxist feminist perspective, however, the generalized subordination of women to men, their relative poverty and powerlessness, and their entrapment in marriages that they lack the economic resources to leave, would go far toward explaining these patterns. Many of these issues will be explored in subsequent chapters. For now, the most important message is methodological. Statistical rates, treated in isolation, can lead to erroneous conclusions.

The Social Construction of Suicide Rates

The interpretive approach to the study of suicide raises questions of a qualitatively different kind from either Durkheim or the Marxist theorists. It has prompted the most far-reaching and, in some respects, devastating critique of Durkheim's study. Theorists in this tradition challenge the basic assumption that statistical rates produced by government agents can be unambiguously treated as a factual counting of the actual incidence of suicides among different groups and societies. They point out that such rates are socially constructed. Ethnomethodological studies have directed attention from "why people commit suicide" to the practices that coroners use to recognize and classify particular deaths as suicides, as distinct from accidents, murders, or natural causes. They study how coroners actively employ Durkheimian theories about conditions conducive to suicides to make such categorizing decisions.

It may seem simple and unambiguous enough at first glance to make such decisions, but consider some of the following situations. A man dies by crashing his car at high speed into a tree; a young man apparently gets heavily drunk, falls asleep in the car with the engine running in a closed garage, and dies from carbon monoxide poisoning; a women takes an overdose of sleeping pills; an old woman is found dead in her room with the doors and windows stuffed shut and the gas coming from an unlit heater.

A coroner who assigns the label *suicide* to such cases is, in effect, assigning responsibility for the death to the individual who has died. It becomes an excuse for no further action by the law. But how does one make such decisions? Was the car crash just an accident, or was the person driving full speed into a stationary object on the very realistic expectation that this would end it all, while still permitting the family to claim his life insurance? Did the woman take an overdose of pills deliberately in order to die, or did she simply wake up in the night confused and half drugged and take some more pills without being conscious of what she was doing? Or again, did she intend only to take a nonlethal dose as a cry for attention or help? Did the old woman intend to gas herself, or had she simply stuffed the cracks to keep out the cold and become a victim when the gas fire did not ignite properly or blew out? Suicide, by definition, means intentional self-death, but did these people intend to die? We can never know because we cannot ask the dead.

The label *suicide* imputes motives after the fact, and coroners can only do this by guesswork, by asking witnesses or close family members, or by looking for suicide notes, and then coming to a decision whether it was likely that this person might have wanted to die. The procedure leads to other questions. How many witnesses were consulted? Who was consulted with respect to assumed motives? One might get different answers from an estranged wife or from a Catholic priest. Suicide rates are the outcome of decisions such as these. Their "factual" character is much more problematic than the neat tables in Statistics Canada reports would have us believe.

Douglas's (1967) ethnomethodological critique of Durkheim's study challenges all the evidence that Durkheim used. As a first step, Douglas shows conclusively that huge changes in suicide rates occur when the method of counting changes. In Prussia in 1868, for example, Catholic priests kept the records of suicides. The rate jumped 50 percent in one year when the methods were reformed and civilian officials began keeping the rates. Similar jumps occurred in the official statistics in Austria, Hungary, and Italy when methods of record keeping changed. Douglas concludes that changes of between 10 and 50 percent were because of methods of collection alone. Durkheim's tests of his theory rely on smaller differences than these and so might be caused by nothing more than differences in how rates were counted.

Douglas goes on to show that all the reasons hypothesized by Durkheim as causes of low social cohesion, and hence higher suicide rates, are the same reasons that influence coroners to make their decisions one way rather than the other. During the period in which Durkheim did his study, suicide was considered a mortal sin for Catholics and was sufficient grounds for denying them a Christian burial. One can realistically expect that when Catholic priests kept the rates, they would go to great lengths to give the benefit of the doubt to the deceased and list the death as accidental, and that Catholic family members would do likewise. Protestant record keepers and witnesses would not be under such pressure. Douglas shows that Catholic cantons in Switzerland recorded fewer suicides than did Protestant cantons, but more accidents. Douglas concludes that different rates may reflect different concealment and not real dif-

ferences in the propensity of Catholics and Protestants to kill themselves.

He suggests, similarly, that all the conditions of higher social integration listed by Durkheim are associated with a higher propensity, and ability, to cover up a suicide. When a person is married and has children, these family members are likely to want to influence a coroner to see the death as accidental, while a divorced person living alone has no one to speak for him or her. A small rural community is more likely to close ranks and cover up damning evidence of a suicide in their midst than are neighbours in a loosely integrated city area. Durkheim was correct in claiming that the number of deaths officially classified as suicides is lower among Catholics, married people, and villagers, but differences in rates may be solely an artifact of how coroners were influenced to make their decisions.

Smith (1983a) goes further than Douglas in demonstrating the essential circularity of theory and data in studies of suicide. She cites work to show that not only coroners, but witnesses and family members themselves, rely upon theories about motives for committing suicide when they produce accounts of what happened. Consider the man who crashes his car into a tree. People generally believe that a married man with children is unlikely to commit suicide, but that a divorced man who keeps to himself might well be miserable and potentially suicidal. Thus, if the victim were a married man, friends might well comment, when questioned by a coroner, that he was a happy man, a bit reckless with the car, perhaps, and so assure themselves and the coroner that it was an accident. If the victim were divorced, friends would be much more likely to comment that they had always feared that he would do something terrible to himself, poor man, how miserable he must have been, and thus convince themselves and the coroner that his death was probably a suicide.

All that is needed for people to become convinced of the truth of their speculation is for like-minded people to reinforce their interpretation. People tend retrospectively to pick out the incidents that support their emerging theory, and they downplay evidence to the contrary. Experts who analyse such accounts for features of suicidal behaviour are likely to discover in them the theories that people use when they put the accounts together.

Smith presents several analyses of written texts to show how their authors selectively structure details of events into accounts that are consistent with their interpretation of what happened. In one case, a psychiatrist's clinical report described a woman as sitting behind a door staring vacantly into space for long periods of time. She was diagnosed as suffering from psychotic depression. Another account describes the same woman as working hard to provide for her children, keeping them neat and healthy, and taking them for long walks in the park every day, even though she was living in great poverty that was exacerbated by the oppressive and irresponsible behaviour of her husband. The family was crammed into one room that offered no space for privacy. Sometimes the woman would sit behind the door in a corner and stare vacantly across the room. When the account is written in this broader form we are drawn to the different conclusion that this is a psychologically healthy woman living under extremely stressful and depressing conditions.

The issue here is not which account is the correct version. What is significant is the way in which the author's interpretive scheme or theory directs how each account is put together such that we as readers will come to the conclusion that the author intended. The account, or text, *intends* the interpretive schema that has entered into its creation (Smith 1983a, 322). We have no possibility of knowing "the facts of the matter," listed in some uninterpreted form, on the basis of which we might draw our own independent conclusions. We only have access to the facts as the tellers of the tales recount them to us. So it is with coroners, or anyone else trying to find out what might have happened. The facts come to us already worked up, already organized in a certain way. The patterns that we find in them are not the patterns necessarily inherent in the occurrences. They are the patterns that the tellers unavoidably impose in the effort to make the vague flux of experience accountable, to themselves and to others, as what happened.

These ethnomethodological critiques do not necessarily mean that Durkheim's conclusions about suicide being associated with egoistic or anomic social circumstances, or Marxist conclusions about poverty and exploitation as precipitating suicides, are wrong. They do show, however, that neither case is proven because what these theorists take as factual statistics are no more than coroners' biased interpretations of shaky evidence. Ethnomethodologists insist that we need detailed observational studies of exactly how coroners do their work of classification of deaths before we can draw any firm conclusions about what suicide rates actually mean.

❖ Religion

Elementary Forms of Religious Life

Durkheim's last major work, *The Elementary Forms of Religious Life* ([1915] 1976), still represents a milestone in the sociology of religion. In this study he ties the analysis of religion intimately to his conception of the nature of social cohesion and, in effect, to the foundations of society itself. His first premise is that something like religion, which people of virtually all societies on earth have accepted, could not be based on illusion or superstition. It is not merely a response to the unknown or to fear of the unexpected, or it would never survive discovery of the truth. Like magic, it would be replaced by science.

Many theorists predicted that religion would lose its hold over people in the modern, industrial world. In some senses it has. Churches have become less dogmatic, adherence to religion has declined, and the church has lost its power to prohibit people from doing such things as opening stores, gambling, or going to ball games on Sundays.

Yet the predictions of a steady trend toward the total secularism and rationalism are clearly false. In the United States, a country with one of the highest levels of education, science, and technology in the world, religion has not only not disappeared, it has gained in strength and has become a powerful influence in politics (Collins 1982, ch. 2). There are religious groups of many kinds, including fundamentalist sects that take the Bible as literally true, and evangelical programs on radio and television. Oriental religions have made a greater influx into Western societies than at any previous time, with Hindu gurus, Buddhist monks, and followers of Krishna appearing in large numbers (Collins 1982, 31). Religion is clearly not a spent force, although the forms that it is taking may differ from the past.

Durkheim concludes from a comparison of major religions that there is no one doctrine that all have in common. Some religions believe in a single god, but many others believe in a multiplicity of gods and goddesses. Nor do all religions share the concept of god. Buddhism is a religion, but its basic concept of enlightenment is completely nontheistic. In many tribal religions there are no gods, only **totem** animals, plants, or rocks that constitute cult objects.

Yet, there are central characteristics that all religions have in common. Firstly, they all comprise certain shared beliefs that are held by all adherents, and secondly, they all have certain rituals that all believers collectively perform. From these characteristics Durkheim derives his fundamental definition of **religion**: "Religion is a unified system of belief and practices, relative to sacred things, which unite into a single moral community called a church, all those who adhere to them" (Durkheim [1915] 1976, 10). A central element of all religious thought is the distinction drawn between the **sacred** and the **profane** or worldly. The distinction is absolute and is manifest in ritual prescriptions and prohibitions surrounding the sacred realm. All religions have a church, in the sense of an organization that performs rituals and ceremonies on a regular basis for a particular group of worshippers (Giddens 1971, 107).

What does this sacred realm refer to? What is it in people's normal, everyday experience that is so powerful that it could give rise to the sacred? For Durkheim, the one reality that has all the characteristics people attribute to the divine is society itself. Society is a force far greater than any individual. It brought us to life, and it can kill us. It has tremendous power over us. Everyone depends on it. Our sense of ourselves and the concepts and the language through which we think and communicate come to us through society. The community, omnipresent and omnipotent, comprises an anonymous, impersonal force to which all belong. *God* is the symbolic expression of the intensity of our feeling of community with others. It is this human community that arouses in us the sense of the divine and that has moral authority over us. The duality of the human person and the *soul* is, like religion, found

everywhere, and so cannot be illusory. For Durkheim, the concept of soul symbolizes the force of the group within the self, the duality of human nature as both individual and social.

We derive a tremendous sense of emotional energy from belonging with a group. It gives us courage beyond any level that we could muster alone. It makes us capable of heroism and sacrifice and gives us confidence to achieve things we could not otherwise reach. Such energy can also become fanatical, powerful, and potentially dangerous (Collins 1982, 39–41). These intangible but very real forces are part of what religion expresses.

Durkheim's own study focusses on the most primitive form of religion—totemism among the aboriginal hunting and gathering societies of Australia. His central argument is that the conceptual structure of aboriginal religion can be understood as mirroring the structure of their clan communities. They have no wealth and no

The sacredness of a totem, according to Durkheim, is found in its symbolic, religious nature.

hierarchy, and the different clans that make up the tribe are equal. Each clan has a sacred totem that gives the clan its name and is the centre of its special rituals and beliefs. The totem is the emblem of the clan and has sacred force because it transcends the individual in representing the group. The sacred force is not intrinsic to the animal or plant selected as a totem, any more than a Christian cross is sacred. The sacredness resides in its nature as a symbol. Just as all clans within the hunting and gathering society are equal, so all the totems of the different clans are religiously equal. Durkheim goes on to describe the seasonal rituals that draw together all the disparate groups within the clan. All the different totems play a role in these deeply sacred ceremonies, in which all the totems have a ritual part, reinforce the unity of the clan and hold people together during the long seasons when members must separate into small wandering groups in search of food.

Durkheim was aware that, as social life becomes more diversified, the shared values of mechanical solidarity can no longer form a central unifying force. In societies characterized by advanced division of labour, religion must take a very different form. As we noted above, Durkheim knew at first hand how deeply divisive religious intolerance could be in a multiethnic society like France. He argued that the core values of organic solidarity must be respect for individuality and human rights. People develop a sense of belonging to highly differentiated societies not through sameness with others, but through awareness of mutual interdependence and moral obligation. This develops despite, or in fact because of, the tremendous diversity of lifestyles and values in the world community. For Durkheim, the religion that best expressed such core values was humanism, a religion in which tolerance for diversity would be a basic premise (Neyer 1960). This was a utopian vision that Durkheim hoped might eventually be achieved.

Durkheim's anthropological data with respect to aboriginal social structures and religious practices were somewhat limited, and a number of his specific descriptive claims have been criticized. But his overall conception of the nature of religious experience and its grounding in the everyday experience of communal life still stands as a seminal argument in the sociology of religion.

Durkheim and Contemporary Functionalist Theory of Religion

Durkheim's analysis remains central to the study of religion from the functionalist perspective. Functionalist theory does not address the question of whether religious ideas represent some ultimate reality; it focusses on the immediate practical issue of the functions that religion might have for human society. A starting point for analysis is the working assumption that any societal institution that persists over time does so only because it serves some function for the social system of which it is a part. A phenomenon such as religion, which is found in all known societies, must therefore be crucial for the maintenance of society; it must have some indispensable function. Durkheim conceptualized religion as arising from and reflecting social cohesion. Functionalist theory modifies this view to see religion as an essential element in fostering that cohesion. The notion of a "common consciousness" of shared beliefs and sentiments that Durkheim saw as uniting people in societies characterized by mechanical solidarity is generalized within functionalist theory to all forms of society, simple and highly differentiated. Religion is that common consciousness. It functions to integrate society in the face of the suffering and death of its members (Yinger 1957, 7–12). Society, it is argued, requires a unifying value system to legitimate social order. At the individual level, all human desires—for power, love, knowledge, consolation—find expression in religious beliefs. Above all, religion helps people to grapple with death. The hope of salvation eases suffering while the rituals surrounding death draw people together.

Religious rituals have a special power to draw us together. The sacred taboos and ceremonials reinforce the sense of cohesion with others in the moral community. Rites such as Communion within the Christian tradition, and similar ceremonies involving the sharing of sacred foods in other traditions, reinforce the bonds of kinship between us. *Representative rites*—the dramas and myths that repeat the actions of our ancestors—perpetuate tradition and reinforce a sense of belonging to the past and to the future of our community. Other rites such as funerals draw us together and so reaffirm consciousness of our moral community.

Functionalist theory also draws upon Durkheim's notion of stages in societal evolution with a corresponding evolution of more complex forms of religion. Different types of societies should have different types of gods, reflecting their own unique structures. The very simple, nonhierarchical patterns of totemic religion can promote cohesion in aboriginal societies, but more complex and abstract systems of beliefs and rituals are required in societies that are more highly differentiated.

In agricultural communities, which are larger than hunting and gathering societies and have some accumulated wealth, the nature of religious belief is different (Collins 1982, 48–50). In particular, Collins argues, the role of kinship ties and inheritance and, hence, the position of women is more important, and this is reflected in fertility rites and the worship of goddesses. As societies become more hierarchically organized, the gods are likely to be thought of as arranged in a hierarchy as well. Finally, in literate, cosmopolitan civilizations, the concept of God as a single, transcendent reality emerges. This type of religion aims to be universal. It reflects a rationalized, literate society with sufficient political power that it can foster the idea of a universal state.

Problems with Functionalist Theory

The functionalist perspective, which posits that religion reinforces social cohesion, has been extensively criticized. Critics maintain that the functionalist argument's weakest link is its underlying view of society itself as a unified, cohesive system. This view might be valid for the very small-scale hunting and gathering societies associated with Durkheim's study of elementary forms of religion. But complex industrial societies are ethnically heterogeneous and rife with class divisions and conflict. Fundamental divisions of power and inequality cannot be glossed over by Durkheim's appeal to humanism. His utopian vision of an integrative humanistic religion that would encompass all diversity within an organic solidarity has not materialized. If one overarching religion is maintained in the face of societal diversity, that religion is likely to reflect an imposed consensus that suppresses other reli-

gions. Alternatively, the presence of more than one religious tradition in a given society can reinforce divisions rather than promote cohesion.

The Political Economy of Religion

Political economy theory relates the analysis of religion to the material, physical situation in which people find themselves, and especially their experience of how production is organized in a given society. A central assumption in Marxist thought is that existence determines consciousness. To understand the prevailing ideas in any given society one has to understand the prevailing economic relations. This approach to the study of religion also focusses centrally on the issue of class divisions within society, and the power of the dominant class to promote and sustain religious ideas that reinforce its own class values, values that commonly function to legitimate and perpetuate inequality.

Marx himself addressed the issue of religion only in a fragmentary way. Much of what now stands as the political economy of religion was developed by later theorists who extrapolated on Marxist thought. Marx characterized religion as a powerful form of ideology that legitimates and strengthens class domination by inculcating among subordinate people an acceptance of subordination. In the Marxist critique of functionalist theory, religion functions as an "opiate of the masses." Religions that stress acceptance of suffering, with reward in the life after death, drug people into passivity and submission. As we will see, **puritanism**, which prevailed in nineteenth-century England during the period when Marx was writing, was a particularly notorious target for such criticism. It was an ethic that justified the wealth and power of capitalists as somehow ordained by God or merited on the basis of holy grace, while poor people were enjoined to endure suffering or hardship as trials that would prove their worthiness for ultimate salvation in the life beyond death.

Early Marxist writings did not entirely discount the radical potential of religion. However distorted its particular message might be, Marx recognized that "religious distress is at the same time real distress and the protest against real distress" (Baum 1979, 30). The problem for Marx was that religion was all too often a powerful force that prevented people from recognizing their real situation and rebelling against it.

Engels ([1884] 1978), a close confederate of Marx, recognized the affinity between the ideas underlying communism and Christianity, particularly as reflected in early Christian communities. Christianity appeared as a religion of slaves and emancipated slaves, of poor people deprived of all rights. Like **socialism**, it promised forthcoming salvation from bondage and misery. The major difference between them was that Christianity did not want to accomplish the transformation in this world, but beyond it, in heaven, in eternal life after death. Engels accounts for this difference by reference to the historical condition of slaves and the absence of a strong working-class structure that would have made the socialist revolution possible at the time that Christianity first took hold. It expressed people's practical experience of powerlessness to alter their material conditions on earth. Christianity subsequently became the dominant religion of the Roman Empire, and its promise of salvation after death was tied to a message of passivity and submission to earthly rulers. Traditional Christian notions of God as "lord" and "master" who demanded total obedience was again a realistic expression of people's experience of feudalism. Relations of economic production in Europe would have to change markedly before alternative conceptions of God could take root in the minds of the mass of people.

Max Weber's Contribution

Much of Max Weber's work was acknowledged to be a conversation with the ghost of Marx, an effort both to elaborate Marx's ideas and to go beyond them. Weber's contribution was to undertake a historical, comparative study of world religions and of the varied forms of religious expression among different social classes within Western industrial societies. Weber documents how closely the patterns of religious expression reflect diverse life experiences. The road to salvation varies markedly with social position (Weber [1922] 1964, chs. 6 and 7). People who do different kinds of work and who occupy different places within a society, whether as peasants, warriors, intellectuals, or business people, have

very different religious tendencies, even with the same overarching religious tradition such as Christianity.

Peasants have a secure relation to the land but experience the vagaries of weather and unpredictable natural forces. They have little interest in rationalized theology and are more inclined toward magic. The ethic of warriors, on the other hand, is not compatible with a kindhearted divinity. Concepts of an otherworldly god with systematic ethical demands have little or no appeal. Warriors are drawn toward an image of a god of power and toward a religion that allows them to view their adversaries as morally depraved. The Old Testament god Yahweh, for example, is essentially a god bent upon war, revenge, and punishment. The New Testament religion of Jesus is, in contrast, the religion of a subordinate people under the Roman Empire. Here the salvation ethic rather than justification of war is paramount. The self-esteem and honour of disprivileged people rest on a promise for the future and on their significance in the eyes of a divine authority who has values different from those of the world. For such people, breakaway sects and cults of heroes and saints have special appeal.

The Distinctive Religion of the Capitalist Class

Weber's most famous study in the sociology of religion, *The Protestant Ethic and the Spirit of Capitalism* ([1904] 1930), explores in depth the ethic of the business class in Europe. Weber observed that members of the business class in Europe were disproportionately adherents of a puritanical Calvinist form of Protestantism, even though the dominant religion of Europe at that time was Catholicism. The religious dogma of **Calvinism** advocated a sober, frugal style of living, and prohibited alcohol, dancing, and luxuries. It also stressed a disciplined obligation to work as a means to serve God. The Calvinist conception of God was of a harsh, all-knowing, all-powerful being, incomprehensible to humans. From the assumption that God knew in advance who would be damned, and who saved, came the doctrine of **predestination**. There could be no salvation through the church or magical sacraments or human actions, only through grace. Such beliefs generated intense psychological feelings of insecurity and concern with finding indications of whether one might be among the damned or the blessed. Success in economic activities came to be seen as pre-eminently a sign of God's grace, while poverty or failure was a measure of lack of moral fervour and of damnation.

Such ideas, Weber argues, provided unique encouragement to capitalism. Work was a duty, and amassing wealth a sign of grace, but self-indulgence, or spending such wealth on idle consumption was a sign of damnation. The only moral option was to invest wealth in expanding business. The Catholic Church of the period forbade usury, or lending money with interest, as profiting from the distress of others, but Calvinism supported it as morally proper business behaviour.

Weber does not address the issue of whether Calvinist religion promoted capitalism or capitalism promoted Calvinism. Rather, he speaks of an *elective affinity* between the two. By elective affinity, Weber means the mutual attraction between the business lifestyle and the **Protestant ethic**, the tendency for this kind of ethic to promote behaviour and values conducive to good business practices, and the propensity for people who spend their lives in business to be attracted to this kind of moral teaching. Business people were drawn to, and stimulated by, the ethic of work as a duty and economic success as a sign of grace. This ethic provided a moral justification for wealth. Poverty, on the other hand, was a sign

of moral depravity, and to help the poor would be akin to helping the devil. Such dogma justified harsh and punitive treatment of destitute people to force them to become more industrious and self-sufficient.

Puritanism and the Working Class

Calvinist doctrines held little appeal outside the business class. It was **Methodism** that spread the puritan message to the working classes in Europe. Puritanism as a general philosophy advocated scrupulous moral behaviour and extreme strictness in adherence to details of religious practice. Many forms of spontaneous enjoyment and leisure, including parties, dancing, and especially sex, were seen as sinful and were either banned or very strictly controlled. Methodist tracts stressed the sinfulness of youth, the threat of eternal damnation, and the state of humans as blind, fallen, helpless sinners, but for divine grace. These doctrines translated into an extremely harsh edict of repression and inhibition. "A more appalling system of religious terrorism, one more fitted to unhinge a tottering intellect and to darken and embitter a sensitive nature, has seldom existed" (Thompson 1963, 410, quoting Lecky 1891). E.P. Thompson (1963, ch. 11) leaves no doubt that the puritanical doctrines embodied in Methodism fit the Marxist vision of religion as imposing on the masses the values of the dominant capitalist class. The religious discipline of Methodism was very effective in controlling the industrial working class. The major problem for employers during the early stages of industrialization was the immense resistance of workers to the unnatural and hateful restraints of machine-paced work. What was needed, from the employers' viewpoint, was education not only in methodical habits, but also in punctilious attention to instructions, fulfilment of contracts on time, and the sinfulness of embezzling materials. Mere wage payment could never secure "zealous service." An inner compulsion was needed, and this is what Methodism provided.

The question still to be answered is how the repressive doctrines of Methodism came to appeal to wide sections of the working class. Thompson (1963, 391) argues that Methodism spread among the poor because it stressed spiritual egalitarianism and religion of the heart rather than the intellect. The simplest and least

"Where in heaven's name does he get these bizarre 'left wing' notions? 'The meek shall inherit the earth,' indeed!"

educated might attain grace through sincere repentance and forgiveness of sin. This forgiveness, however, was always conditional and provisory, lasting only so long as the penitent went and sinned no more. Perpetual service to the church itself and methodical discipline in all aspects of life were demanded. In return, membership within the Methodist Church provided a kind of community for people uprooted by the Industrial Revolution. The church offered much mutual aid, some recognition for sobriety, chastity, and piety, and could contribute to family stability. It also provided an emotional opiate, not unlike the real opiates that were widely consumed during this period. Methodism offered religious consolation to people oppressed by war and the wretched conditions of industrial working-class life.

The Social Gospel in Canada

The success of Methodism in incorporating the poor contained the seeds of a more radical spiritual message. While mainstream Methodism was a puritanical, pro-business establishment church, it also promoted an egalitarian, social justice fringe that embraced socialist doctrines of collective social responsibility. Socialist-Methodist leaders such as J.S. Woodsworth conducted extensive research into the appalling conditions of the poor in Winnipeg at the beginning of the twentieth century. What he saw convinced him that the churches could not hope to minister to the spiritual needs of the working classes without also caring for the physical conditions of their lives.

The **Social Gospel movement** that flourished in Canada during the period between 1880 and 1920 stressed the links between Christianity and socialism (Allen 1975). The meaning of sin and salvation was translated in social rather than individual terms, so that social justice became central to the Christian message. Under the leadership of radical ministers from Methodist, Anglican, and Presbyterian churches, adherents of the Social Gospel promoted trade unions, and lobbied for the Lord's Day Observance Act to grant Sundays off for workers. By 1913, the church union became the Social Services Council of Canada, which was active in the provision of schools, libraries, savings banks, nurseries, and clubrooms for the working classes.

By the 1920s, however, the Social Gospel movement was in decline. Orthodox sectors of the churches withdrew their support, especially after the Russian Revolution and Winnipeg General Strike. They feared growing labour power and strikes. Methodists as a whole grew richer and tended to place more stress on individualism and entrepreneurship than collective responsibility. Within the establishment churches the Social Gospel movement retreated to a radical fringe role. The spirit of the movement found more direct political expression of the prairies in the formation of the Co-operative Commonwealth Federation (CCF) led by Woodsworth and Tommy Douglas, a Baptist minister turned political reformer. The CCF later became the New Democratic Party.

Liberation Theology

The Catholic Church worldwide has also manifested this internal struggle with a radical Social Gospel movement known as **liberation theology**, which has emerged as an important fringe group. The lived experience of Catholics in Latin America, struggling against repressive political regimes, has been an extremely powerful force for radical theology within Catholicism. Liberation theology seeks to integrate the radical social theory of Marxism with the central Christian message of God's love for humanity.

Gregory Baum (1979; 1981), a Catholic priest, theologian, and sociologist in Canada, takes pains to emphasize that this radical Social Gospel is a liberation *theology*, and not merely, or even primarily, a secular political movement. Concern with spirituality and the concept of divinity is at the heart of this Catholic message. Liberation theology seeks, above all, to deprivatize the Christian message. It rejects the interpretation of salvation, sin, and conversion in individual terms. In contrast, it emphasizes the social dimension of the Christian message and the social covenant of the Old Testament between God and the people of Israel in which God fulfils the promise to deliver the Israelites, as a nation, from bondage. It conceptualizes God as one who takes the side of the oppressed, the excluded, the outcasts, the Hebrew slaves. The gospel message of hope is linked with the practices of Jesus who took the place of the poor, shifting them to the centre of his ministry (Betto 1993).

Liberation theology is thus "this-worldly" in Weber's sense, but also transcendent, a Christian, mystical, divine call for justice (Baum 1981).

Baum argues that Pope John Paul II's encyclical on labour and the dignity of human work, together with the Catholic bishops' pastoral letters on the economy and social justice, express a Christian option for the poor that integrates the one-sided Marxist emphasis on economic infrastructure with an essential spiritual and cultural dimension, working together for the transformation of society.

The problem is that the Social Gospel message remains as ephemeral and as marginal to the establishment churches now as during the last century. It exists on the fringes of the Christian community, vulnerable, occasionally isolated and attacked. At worst, liberation theology has been reduced to just another consumer item for intellectuals (Green 1979, 38–39), a program filler for organizations whose comfortable middle-class patrons do penance merely by listening to the hard words of the activists. In Latin America also, the establishment church largely supports the repressive governments, while movements such as Christians for Socialism now exist only in exile. Liberation theologians have been censured by the Catholic hierarchy in Rome, and discredited by the collapse of socialist states in Eastern Europe. But the movement has not been silenced. The crises of poverty and oppression that liberation theology addresses have not gone away, and the need for its challenge to the complacency of institutionalized Christianity are as potent as ever (Betto 1993; Assmann 1993). Its very existence within all the established churches is a reminder that culture is not a monolithic, nor a fixed, unchanging entity, and that wherever there is repression there will also be resistance.

Religion as Social Construction

The social constructionist perspective involves a critical shift in the way in which we conceptualize religion. In both functionalism and political economy theory, religion is viewed as a societal institution, comprising identifiable elements of beliefs and practices that people adopt through processes of socialization or conversion. Social constructionism, however, conceptualizes religion as ongoing accomplishment. Religion is not something that people *have*. It is something that they

do. This gives rise to very different kinds of questioning around how the intersubjective understanding of religion is negotiated and sustained, and struggles around the naming and interpretation of religious experience.

Religion as Discourse

The possibility that social science discourse actually creates the reality of the religious categories that it describes has become a major issue in the study of Native peoples spirituality. At the centre of the debate among scholars who focus on the study of Native religions is the hotly disputed claim by social constructionists that Euro-American ethnographers have projected Western versions of "primitive" cultures and religions into their studies of Native peoples, producing in the process a "timeless noble savage stereotype" that has little basis in reality.

The myth of the noble savage has a very long history in Western thought, evident even in Homer's treatment of the Scythians in the *Iliad*. The idea of religious thought evolving from primitive naturist myths to abstract metaphysics and theology is also central to early sociological accounts of social evolution proposed by Comte, Spencer, and Durkheim. It was easy to identify the indigenous peoples of North America as the embodiment of primitive naivety, in contrast with civilized man. The Jesuit Fathers who worked among the Huron characterized them as purer, natural, childlike souls, uncorrupted with the vices of civilization (Simard 1990, 336).

Daniel (1992) argues that notions of "Indian" culture and spirituality that have gained credence in white Canadian society are largely an invention of Europeans. Since the 1960s, he suggests, we have been inundated with books and films celebrating the spiritual side of Indian life, the wisdom of the elders, the secret practices of sorcerers and shamans. In his discussion of "plastic shamans" (1992, ch. 6) he gives many examples of non-Native individuals appropriating a fictitious Indian image and claiming spiritual wisdom. They were readily believed within white society because they conformed to the white stereotype of what Indians are supposed to be like. Spiritualists, hippies, disaffected white youth, writers of popular fiction, many ethnographers, and other interested people were drawn to these images. Feeling an absence of the sacred in modern life, many non-Natives from a wide variety of social backgrounds look to Indian culture for values they find lacking in their own. But the images of Native people that white Canadians have manufactured are reflections of white rather than Native cultural history. Daniel uses the term *Indian* to refer to images of aboriginal people invented by Europeans and *Native* to refer to the people themselves (Daniel 1992, 5).

Euro-American ethnographers often projected Western versions of "primitive" cultures onto Native peoples.

A recurring theme in Western accounts of Native spirituality is the notion of "Gaia" or the Mother Earth goddess, expressing Native people's primordial closeness to the land. Greedy, civilized men rape her, tearing ores from her womb and crops from her bosom, while the Natives respect her, taking only the wild fruits and fauna that she lovingly provides (Gill 1982; 1990; Kehoe 1990). In Gill's view, however, this romantic vision is largely a creation of the writers themselves, with minimal supporting evidence from historical or ethnographic data. Although there are many female figures in Native stories, almost none has been understood as a deity personifying the earth. Gill traces details of the Gaia myth to a story told in 1886 by a man named Smohalla, a Native American protesting the efforts of Euro-Americans to drive indigenous peoples from the land in order to exploit it for mining, lumber, and agriculture. Kehoe (1990, 196–98) similarly recounts how Oglala tribal rituals were codified, with ethnographer and Indian storyteller produc-

ing the theme of symbolic correspondence between the peace pipe and the crucifix. The naturistic vision of Mother Earth, often paired with Father Sky, the Great Spirit or the Creator, has won widespread respect among Native peoples. New Age devotees, feminists, and non-Natives who present themselves within white society as Native spiritualists—often referred to as "plastic medicine men"—have also been attracted by the vision of Natives as repositories of authentic primal spirituality. But, Kehoe maintains, this vision is rooted in Western, not Native mythology (see also chapter 17).

Controversial Issues in Constructionist Analysis

The thesis proposed by anthropologists such as Clifton, Gill, Kehoe, and other contributors to Clifton's anthology—that much of what passes in scholarly literature as accounts of Native spirituality are constructs of Western cultural myths rather than the authentic sacred myths of Native peoples—has provoked intense and angry debate. Many scholars and Native peoples who interpret these myths as genuine reflections of contemporary Native spirituality feel that their professional competence and/or their religious identity are under attack (Parkhill 1995 forthcoming; Paper 1993; Clifton 1990; Churchill 1992). Churchill rejects Clifton's work outright as a new form of racism, designed to discredit all Native spirituality and social accomplishments as unsubstantiated and therefore fiction (Churchill 1992, 163–83).

Several critical issues for constructionist theory underlie this conflict. Firstly, the analysis of how ethnographic and popular media accounts of Indian spirituality are socially constructed is conceptually quite distinct from how Native participants themselves come to develop and identify with a meaningful religious tradition. Some of the conflict arises from a failure to keep these issues separate. A second more general issue concerns the conceptualization of tradition and religion that is accepted both by those who challenge and those who defend the authenticity of particular myths and rituals. The classic conception of tradition that comes out of functionalist theory is that it embodies a set of beliefs and practices that are internalized by adherents, are relatively stable over long periods of time, and are followed by people without much reflection or questioning. Religious traditions involve beliefs and practices relative to sacred things and hence are classically viewed as more deeply internalized and invariant than other traditions.

Once this view of religious tradition is assumed, then any evidence that a particular aspect of tradition, such as the Gaia myth, is of relatively recent origin or can be traced to some specific event or person implies that the "tradition" is not authentic and must be sham. Similarly, evidence that certain beliefs postdate colonial contact or the influence of Christian missionaries appears to discredit the beliefs as not bona fide Native expressions of spirituality. Such assumptions presuppose that there is or was an ancient, unchanging or "true" set of Native religious beliefs and practices, in relation to which other accounts can be assessed as "bogus."

This classic conception of religion was utilized by the Canadian prison authorities and Native elders in the struggle to gain recognition of Native rituals as constituting religion with respect to providing services for prison inmates. In order to have the Indian peace-pipe ceremony accepted as a bona fide spiritual ceremony equivalent to other religions, Native elders felt obliged to call on the services of an ethnographer to demonstrate that the ceremony was of ancient origin (Paper 1993, 369). Paper struggles to prove that the pan-Indian pipe-smoking ceremonies are implicated in ritual artifacts throughout a wide geographic region two millennia in the past (Paper 1989). He offers such evidence as defence against Gill and Parkhill's contention that pan-Indian rituals postdate colonization and are thus not authentically Native.

The social constructionist perspective challenges the classical conceptions of tradition and religion, and in so doing shifts the ground of the debate surrounding Native spirituality. All traditions, including religions, are viewed not as entities but as ongoing, practical accomplishments that are always in the process of being constituted by what people do. This shifts the focus from a listing of elements supposedly contained in a tradition, to the question of how people, in their everyday activities, produce for themselves a sense of religious identity and how it is constituted as tradition. Reference to the historical origins or duration of specific beliefs and practices is itself a social construction. People selectively stress and negotiate such linkages with past practices to serve as legitimation for current practices.

From this perspective, evidence relating to the recent origins of certain Native rituals or colonial influences on Native belief systems in no way challenges their authenticity as components of Native spirituality. Such spirituality is always accomplished in the present, not in the distant past. Religious practices that showed no adaptation or response to several centuries of colonial experience and monumental economic, social, and political change in the lives of Native peoples would not be "authentic" living traditions at all. They would be dead. The notion that authentic Native culture was fixed in a mode that predates colonialism, and that all evidence of change represents assimilation or loss of Native identity can itself be seen as a construct of the white Canadian myth of noble savages (Daniel 1992, 58–60).

Religion and Identity Formation

Constructionist theory maintains that the transformative processes of invention and reinterpretation involved in the construction of religious identity and tradition occur continually, although perhaps with heightened intensity during periods of rapid social change. Winland's case study of Mennonite communities in Southern Ontario highlights their struggle to redefine their sense of peoplehood as they shift from living in tightly knit village communities to being dispersed throughout urban centres, many in professional occupations. Mennonite leaders and scholars for the most part have adopted the classic conceptualization of religious tradition as a ready set of endowments and have tried to codify a singular unifying definition of Mennonite identity. The irony, Winland suggests, is that these efforts have only succeeded in creating a plethora of competing interpretations. Attempts to identify a historic Anabaptist heritage only served to highlight the problem that Mennonite religious identity never was clear, even in the distant past (Winland 1993, 118–19). Historical evidence suggests a plurality of Mennonite origins, and continuous migration, conflicts and schism over issues of faith and culture. Mennonite scholars are engaged in a process of "manufacturing a usable past," selectively stressing historical records to support a perception of the past that provides continuity with the present. Strong attachment to the *idea* of a "Mennonite community," for example, continues undiminished, but with the meaning of the term transformed from a geographically bounded social entity to a symbolic community of believers. Winland concludes that there is no definitive answer to the question "What is a Mennonite?" and there never was such an answer. How people express their sense of Mennonite identity varies with the context in which they find themselves and the form in which questions are asked.

This constructionist analysis of identity formation among Mennonites suggests a different way of understanding processes to create a Native spiritual identity. The debate regarding the authenticity of Gaia symbolism or of peace-pipe ceremonies loses its significance. What becomes important are the processes by which Native peoples and spiritual leaders are actively constituting a meaningful spiritual identity in their contemporary situation, and the creative transformation of the past into a living tradition. This is not a process that works from the top down, with scholars producing accounts that others adopt, although others may draw on this scholarship in making positive identifications with the past. As with the Mennonites, the richer the historical fabric, the greater the potential for selection and reinterpretation in response to the contemporary situations of Native peoples. The shared experience of the majority of Native peoples in North and South America, for example, is of colonialism, poverty, and exclusion on rural reservations. It is perhaps this context that gives the symbolism of Mother Earth raped by colonial oppressors its power in pan-Indian discourse. It speaks to their material experience.

Constructionist and Marxist analysis of religion are complementary in drawing attention to the practical and political significance of identity formation. Thompson's analysis of the spread of Methodism among the working classes in nineteenth-century Europe suggests that despite its repressive puritanical doctrines, it contained the seeds of political radicalism (Thompson 1963, 428–37). Methodist chapels, by their very existence, tended to assume a class-conscious form, expressing nonconformity to the establishment church and the political authority associated with it. Through laypreaching and tumultuous bible camps, working-class people gained experience in local organization that spilled over into labour unions. The doctrine of spiritual egalitarianism

promoted demands for political action, supported by doctrinal justification in the allegory of the Children of Israel, and the vengeful God who punished corrupt and oppressive governments. Burridge (1969, 79–80) offers a similar analysis of the Ghost Dance rituals that spread among Native peoples in North America as they were driven from the plains, their buffalo-hunting economies destroyed. The self-torture and trances that promoted union with the glorious dead of their warrior past also promoted political self-awareness and organization. All religions, Burridge suggests, are concerned fundamentally with principles of power and the moral basis of people's obligations towards society. New religious interpretations emerge particularly during periods of social unrest when these principles are called into question (Burridge 1969, 4–7).

Feminist Critiques of Religion

Feminist analysis of religion has been strongly influenced by the Marxist thesis that dominant ideas and values within a society provide a justification for the ruling-class position. Feminism shifts the focus, however, from economic classes to patriarchy or male dominance. Engels ([1884] 1978) defines the male subjugation of women as the first oppressor-oppressed relation and the foundation of all other class and property relations. Ruether suggests it is also the last inequality to be challenged by established religions, after racism and slavery (Ruether 1975, 3). Mary Daly argues that religion is a potent force in the perpetuation of women's subordinate social status, by a conditioning process of sex-role socialization, in which the consent of the victims as well as the dominant sex is obtained (Daly 1973, 2). Religious doctrine concerning the appropriate behaviour and responsibilities of women functions as an opiate for the mass of women, dulling the pain of subordination and the capacity to rebel and change things.

Feminist theologians stress that the fundamental symbolic systems of Judaic and Christian religions, and the conceptual apparatus and linguistic instruments for communication that go with them, have been male creations, formulated under conditions of patriarchy, and they serve the purposes of a patriarchal social order. The dominant symbol of God as male—as Father—contributes to the view of societal oppression of women as right and fitting. It renders it "natural" and according to divine plan. The husband dominating his wife represents God "Himself" (Daly 1973, 3, 13), and the husband's authority over his wife is sanctioned by God's command in the Book of Genesis.

The roots of this symbolism lie deep in Greco-Roman philosophy. A fundamental element of this heritage is the philosophical separation of mind and body. Rational powers, associated with men, are seen as superior to the faculties of the body and nature, associated with women (Kolbenschlag 1979, 183). Within this intellectual system, even the myths of primitive **matriarchy**—where women commanded the highest authority by virtue of being the only known parent—and the mother goddess associated with mother nature do not promote female equality. They serve rather as a stage in the co-optation of the female into a male-defined power system (Ruether 1975, 6–14).

Ruether's argument is that as men sought to free themselves from dependence on nature, they downplayed not only the generative aspects of women as mothers, but also the overall position of women as well. Men developed a philosophy that males were created from above, and were identified with intellectuality and spirituality, while femaleness was identified with the bodily world and was seen as dependent upon, and inferior to, maleness. The myth of the creation of woman through Adam's rib is a classic portrayal of this. The male, Adam, is the human prototype, and he "gives birth" to the woman with the help of a father God. Similarly, in Aristotle's theory of biology, women are denied all generative potency. They are not seen as actively contributing anything to the creation of a baby; they are merely the passive carriers or incubators of male seed.

Women were denigrated in other ways. Menstruating women came to be seen as "unclean" as maternal power was undercut and suppressed culturally. Canon law in the fourth century cited the uncleanliness of women as a major reason for eliminating the office of deaconess. Even lay women were advised to stay away from Communion during menstruation (Ruether 1975, 16, 70). These old ideas linger on, manifest in the 1980 edict of Pope John Paul II banning altar girls. This edict has been quietly ignored in many Catholic churches but, in June 1987, an eleven-year-old girl who had served as altar girl at Sacre Coeur Church in Toronto for four years was banned from a special mass to mark the hundredth anniversary of the parish, on the orders of Emmett Cardinal Carter (*Globe and Mail*, 19 June 1987, A1).

Ruether argues that Christianity has a dual view of women, represented by the Virgin Mary, who symbolizes sublimated spiritual femininity, and the Fallen Eve, who symbolizes the actual fleshly woman. Mariology, or the love of the Virgin Mary, presupposes that real woman are feared and hated (Ruether 1975, 18–19). If real women can only be loved when they have no sexual desires of their own and remain chaste virgins, except for submitting to pregnancy through some form of artificial insemination, then no real woman would ever be loved. To be a normal, fleshly woman, with normal sexual desires and sexual attractiveness, is to be a failure, a fallen woman. When Uta Ranke-Heinemann, the world's first female Catholic theology professor, challenged this vision of the pure, holy, asexual Virgin Mary by daring to dispute the virgin birth, the church withdrew her authority to teach theology (*Globe and Mail*, 20 June 1987, A10).

When, in 1971, the Episcopal bishop of California denied the capacity of women for ordination on the grounds that only males possess the capacity for "initiative" that represents the "potency" of God, he had a long history of clerical **misogyny**, or woman hating, behind him. He could cite the lines of 1 Timothy 2:13–14 that women are "to learn in silence with all submissiveness. I permit no woman to teach or to have authority over men; she is to keep silent." One could recite a litany of antifeminism in Christian history. He might also have cited one of the church fathers, Tertullian, who writes: "Women, do you not know that you are Eve? You are the devil's gateway." Saint Augustine opined that women are not made in the image of God, and the Decretum of Gratian in 1140, the first enduring systematization of church laws, assumed this with impunity (Kolbenschlag 1979, 183). St Thomas Aquinas defined women as misbegotten males who do not possess the image of God by themselves, but only when taken together with the male who is their "head" (Ruether 1975, 72). Martin Luther held that God created Adam lord over all living creatures, but Eve spoiled this early idyll. John Knox composed a "First Blast of the Trumpet against the Monstrous Regiment of

Women." The theologians Barth and Bonhoeffer insisted that women should be subordinate to their husbands (Daly 1973, 5). The list goes on and on. What angers Daly most is that it is possible for scholars to acknowledge the blatant misogyny of these theologians and at the same time to treat their unverified opinions on far more imponderable matters with the utmost reverence and respect (Daly 1973, 20). They do not seem to see any serious credibility gap.

It is important to see such pronouncements as social constructions rather than innate principles of Christianity. Ruether (1975, 64) notes that Jesus himself can be seen, in some respects, as a feminist, challenging the stereotypes of his time. He had close female friends who accompanied him on his preaching and teaching trips, including Mary Magdalene, Joanna, and Susanna. He praised the faith of poor widows and outcast women against the faithlessness of the religious establishment. He performed his first miracles for women, women were the first witnesses of his resurrection. Women also seem to have been prominent as teachers in the early period of the church. Such historical evidence provides a basis for a feminist reinterpretation of Christian tradition, according the status of authenticity to the equal participation of women in the ministry.

What they struggle against is the authenticity of patriarchal interpretations that gained ascendancy within the Catholic Church establishment as early as the fourth century A.D. The misogyny of the early church fathers became deeply entrenched in the dogma and practices of the church, and women were officially excluded from any teaching or leadership roles. The maleness of Christ and the twelve disciples provided the doctrinal basis for this reinterpretation of the appropriate roles of women within the church.

The period from the fifteenth to the seventeenth centuries was marked by the systematic persecution and slaughter of women as witches, with the authority of the church. The *Malleus Maleficarum (The Hammer of Witches)*, written in 1486 by two Dominican inquisitors, was used as a guide for witch hunters. This document makes very clear the perceived link between witchcraft and sex. It claims that "All witchcraft comes from carnal lust, which is in women insatiable. . . . Wherefore for the sake of fulfilling their lust they consort even with devils" (Jong 1981, 69). According to Jong, the book gave credence to every misogynist myth: women cause impotence; women are weak-willed,

weak-minded, carnal temptresses; women are unfit to rule or to have professions; midwives kill babies, and so on. Theological justification for witch hunts came from the Lateran council decree of 1215 that all heretics should be punished with death (Jong 1981, 51).

The women most at risk of being targeted as witches were those who did not conform to the male idea of proper female behaviour; assertive, independent women, particularly those who did not nurture men or children, were particularly in danger (Larner 1984, 84). There is some evidence that homosexual men were also disproportionately likely to be seen as witches.

Women in Contemporary Christian Churches

The established Christian churches no longer engage in witch hunts or inquisitions, but the basic structures of male dominance within the churches remains largely unchallenged. Women are still banned from all but the lowest rungs of the Catholic Church hierarchy. Some Protestant churches are, in theory, more open and permit the ordination of women, but women are far from achieving equal stature.

During the 1980s, there was a slow but steady increase in the number of women ordained to the ministry (McAteer 1989). Churches that refused to ordain women were still in the majority; of the eighty denominations surveyed in Canada in 1987, only twenty-nine ordained women to the full ministry. But where women are admitted, their numbers are rising. The United Church of Canada led the way. In 1993, 23 percent of its ministers were women; of the fifty-three ministers ordained that year, thirty-five were women.

Women in the Pentecostal churches in the United States have also been able to draw upon traditional notions of a calling from God, to subvert religious injunctions against ministry by women (Lawless 1991). Lawless describes the active processes of "rescripting their lives and narratives" by which women establish their authenticity as preachers. Typically, their life stories are divided into stages. First, they experience a calling from God, but as women who are not encouraged to preach, they are too astonished or humble to believe it. So they "test" God who then affirms them in their calling. Such self-narratives draw on certain aspects of Pentecostal tradition to creatively subvert other aspects of that tradition (Lawless 1991, 70).

The Anglican Church of Canada approved the ordination of women in 1975, but the mother church in England held out for another nineteen years. In 1994, the Church of England ordained its first women priests after years of divisive debate, court challenges, and intense agonizing among members of the church hierarchy over whether the church community could withstand the potential divisive impact of this break with tradition. Many compromises were made, including giving parishes the right to refuse women priests, and assuring men that opposition to women priests would not be a barrier to their own priesthood or election as bishop. Hundreds of male priests declared their intention to leave the church over the issue, many of them planning to join the Roman Catholic faith. The official position of the Church of Rome remains that women cannot be called to the priesthood because they cannot represent the manhood of Christ on earth. Among rank and file members of the Catholic Church and within the hierarchy itself, however, the ferment of debate continues.

The numbers of women who have officially joined the ministries of various Christian churches, however, do not tell the full story of women's struggles for acceptance in the churches. Most ordained women are still concentrated in administrative posts rather than in the ministry. Those who aspire to the ministry itself have to battle discrimination and sexism. A survey of ordained women in Canada reported widespread bitterness, unhappiness, and anger in women who were trying to find a place in the ministry. Fully one-third of the women surveyed in the United Church said they had been sexually harassed in their ministry.

Women ministers continue to face an uphill struggle. They tend to minister to very small congregations. They tend to experience the exodus from their congregations of a number of people who dislike women in leadership positions. Most of the liturgy, hymns, rituals, and symbols of the churches still remain sexist. The battle for **inclusive language** has yet to be won in most churches. The United Church of Canada is making more headway than most in this respect with the publication of a language manual to guide the introduction of nonsexist terms.

For Madonna Kolbenschlag, a Catholic nun, the question of women's position within the church hierarchy is not the major concern. For her, the most damaging of all the misogynist pronouncements of the church is the mutilation of the spirit that the image of God as Male has wrought in the lives of women. Woman, she says, has adapted herself to a relationship with a transcendent Being who is radically Other than herself. The closer she comes to this God, the more she loses her own soul. She concludes that "a woman has no choice but to be an atheist" (Kolbenschlag 1979, 184). Kolbenschlag means this statement in a positive sense. For her, the rejection of the image of God as Father is a necessary prelude to spiritual maturity and to the rediscovery of an autonomous image of God that is experienced as transpersonal and as a ground of personality. She chooses to continue to live as a nun and to work for change within the Catholic Church.

Mary Daly takes the much more radical option of leaving the established Christian churches altogether. In a lecture at the University of New Brunswick in 1984, she commented that, while she would not oppose the ordination of women in the Catholic Church, she would not recommend it, since it would be like inviting blacks to join the Ku Klux Klan. She draws upon more ancient, pre-Christian traditions that she calls *Gyn/Ecology*, the ancient sciences of womankind. In a stand that is strongly reminiscent of Native spirituality, she rejects what she sees as "the phallo-centric value system imposed by patriarchy," a value system that glorifies the power of male sexuality and that ultimately threatens to rape the earth of its life. She writes a "croneology," "dis-covering" the hidden history of thought of her foresisters, the Great Hags or witches "who the institutionally powerful but privately impotent patriarchs found too threatening for co-existence and whom historians erase" (Daly 1978, 14). The word *Hag* comes from an old English word meaning "an evil or frightening spirit," but frightening to whom? These are women who frighten the patriarchs. Hags are often "haggard," in the sense of the word's ancient meaning of "intractable, wilful, wanton, unchaste," and especially "a woman reluctant to yield to wooing." The Great Hags live to be Crones, or the "long-lasting ones." Daly defines herself as a revolting hag and a *spinster*, meaning one who spins complex webs of thought in new directions, participating in the whirling movement of creation.

One example of her journey of "discovery" and "re-membering" of the ancient religions of women concerns the antecedent myths and symbols that underlie the Christian concept of the Holy Trinity. These are the symbols of the Triple Goddess, which are omnipresent in early mythology (Daly 1978, 75). Kolbenschlag (1979, 187) also notes that in the Gnostic or mystical tradition of early Christianity, the Holy Spirit was equated with god the mother. The suppression of these heretical scriptures is linked more to the ecclesiastical suppression of women than to dogmatic interpretation.

Kolbenschlag and Daly are far apart in their level of tolerance for existing Christian churches, but both concur in seeing the emergence of feminism as a critical turning point for civilization. The feminist movement challenges the entire culture and the religious expressions of our social order.

Conclusion

Durkheim's insight that religion fundamentally expresses our deepest experience of our human community, and reflects in its dogmas the deepest values of the community, has stood the test of nearly a century of sociological theory. In future decades, we can expect radical changes in our faith as the changing status of women transforms our society, and as the "catholicization" of capitalism, global pollution, poverty, starvation, and the reality of religious wars in Europe and the Middle East, force us toward a more Durkheimian conception of an all-inclusive humanism. Sociologists of religion have as yet only begun the work of understanding the social construction of religious identity.

Many of those who study the sociology of religion are themselves deeply religious people. Critical sociology, like liberation theology, may challenge many taken-for-granted assumptions of traditional teaching, but ultimately there is no conflict between faith and sociological analysis for they are concerned with different levels of human experience. Sociology does not seek to provide answers to ultimate questions of value or the meaning of life. What it reveals is that the ways in which people all over the world struggle with such questions are grounded in their human experience, which is social. As Durkheim acknowledged, all churches are, by definition, communities of believers, and all religions comprise a shared social experience. The sociology of religion explores the relation between forms of thought and religious expression and the grounds of human experience in social life. For those who are willing to share in this exploration, the sociological imagination is not a threat but a gift.

Suggested Reading

Durkheim's first major work, *The Division of Labour in Society* ([1893] 1964), provides the theoretical foundation for his later studies. In this text he develops his ideas concerning the transition from traditional society based on mechanical solidarity to modern society based on organic solidarity. This is a large and complex book. For an excellent introduction to Durkheim's work see Robert Bierstedt, *Emile Durkheim* (1966). Bierstedt provides an overview of Durkheim's life, followed by selections from each of his major works: *The Division of Labour*; *The Rules of Sociological Method*; *Suicide*; and *The Elementary Forms of Religious Life*.

Jack Douglas's study, *The Social Meanings of Suicide* (1967) revolutionized the analysis of suicide rates. Douglas systematically challenges each of Durkheim's conclusions on the grounds that the patterns that Durkheim found in the data on suicide rates reflect, not concrete evidence, but the outcome of coroners' decisions. Durkheim discovers the theories used by coroners to decide how to classify suspicious deaths.

Two short essays by Garfinkel and Sudnow that show how ethnomethodologists approach the study of suicide are in the edited collection by Roy Turner, *Ethnomethodology: Selected Readings* (1974).

An article by Dorothy Smith, "No One Commits Suicide: Textual Analysis of Ideological Practices" (1983a) explores how people necessarily impose patterns on evidence in the process of accounting for what they think happened.

With respect to religion, Durkheim is best known for his study of *The Elementary Forms* of Religious Life ([1915] 1976), in which he discusses aboriginal society and religion. Durkheim's view of the nature of religion in complex societies is discussed by J. Neyer in "Individualism and Socialism in Durkheim" (1960). Neyer explores Durkheim's argument that in complex industrial societies religion must rise over all ethnic diversity. The most all-encompassing religion is humanism, with respect for human rights as its central people.

A functionalist perspective on religion as providing an integrative force in society can be found in J.M. Yinger's *Religion, Society and the Individual: An Introduction to the Sociology of Religion* (1957). The first chapter presents a useful overview of this approach.

A famous and controversial thesis on the relation between social class and religion is Max Weber's *The Protestant Ethic and the Spirit of Capitalism* ([1904] 1930). Weber argues that the Calvinist doctrine of individual salvation by the grace of God, manifest through worldly success, is ideally suited to capitalist enterprise. This is not, however, an easy book to read. A valuable selection from Weber's work on religion is provided by Stanislav Andreski, ed., *Max Weber on Capitalism, Bureaucracy and Religion: A Selection of Texts* (1983). See particularly chapters 6 and 7 on "Protestantism and the Spirit of Capitalism" and "Religion and Other Factors in the Development of Modern Capitalism."

A radical Marxist perspective on religion is provided in a special edition of *Canadian Dimension*, "The Left Hand of God" (Jan.–Feb. 1979). Articles by Baum, Green, Jungueira, and Smillie argue that a living religion does not merely function to provide social integration. The radical gospel message of social justice implies that religion must be at the centre of revolutionary movements to change societies in which justice is not respected. Frei Betto's article "Did Liberation Theology Collapse with the Berlin Wall "(1993) explores the continuing importance of Liberation Theology in the aftermath of the collapse of socialist states in Eastern Europe.

Winland's analysis of *The Quest for Mennonite Peoplehood* (1993) offers a valuable example of the social constructionist approach to the understanding of religious identity formation. Alice Kehoe's (1990) article on "Primal Gaia: Primitivists and Plastic Medicine Men" explores the influence of Euro-American myths in construction of accounts of Native spirituality.

Radical feminist writers apply the social justice message of Marxist analysis to women. They challenge traditional forms of Christianity, along with other world religions, for fostering a patriarchal ideology. Studies by Mary Daly, *Beyond God the Father* (1973), and Rosemary Ruether, *New Woman New Earth* (1975), explore new forms of religious expression inspired by feminism.

Questions

1. What three distinctive modes of explanation did Comte link with the three stages of societal evolution?

2. Why did Spencer's theory appeal to American capitalists?

3. According to Durkheim, what two critical features identify societal "facts" as things?

4. With respect to the two forms of solidarity, what does Durkheim see as the basis of solidarity in:
   a) mechanical?
   b) organic?

5. Define *conscience collective*. Indicate the two distinct meanings in English translation.

6. How can the concepts of *anomie* and *alienation* be linked?

7. What was Durkheim's precise definition of religion?

8. How does functionalist theory adapt and yet distort Durkheim's conception of *religion*?

9. Why does Kolbenschlag, a Catholic nun, recommend that women become atheists?

10. How are constructionist and Marxist analyses of religion similar?

Anomie: The Roots of Industrial Conflict and Crime

To summarize from chapter 6, the central focus of Durkheim's theoretical work concerns the moral basis of social cohesion. In complex industrial societies, characterized by extensive division of labour, an alternative form of moral order, which has its roots in interdependence, gains prominence. The moral order breaks down, however, under conditions of anomic division of labour. This occurs when the division of labour is not based upon the different interests and abilities of the people concerned, but is forced upon them and experienced as unjust. It also occurs when work becomes so fractionalized that all sense of meaningful co-operation in the work process is lost. Under these conditions, people become isolated from each other rather than integrated. Unhappiness increases when people experience egoism and anomie, that is, when social ties with others weaken, and they lack a sense of meaningful values and moral regulation. In extreme cases, such unhappiness can lead to suicide.

Anomie and Alienation

Marxist analysis focusses upon the specific characteristics of division of labour within the capitalist system of economic production. When a minority of people own the means of production upon which others depend for their livelihood, the result is class conflict, exploitation, and alienation. Alienation refers to the dehumanizing character of social relations under capitalism. When the majority of people are denied access to any means of producing for themselves, they are reduced to a state of chronic insecurity and powerlessness. They survive by selling their labour power for wages, but there are no further obligations between workers and employers. Workers are laid off whenever their labour power is no longer useful or profitable for employers, such as when new technology makes their labour redundant. It is in the interests of employers to minimize labour requirements and to routinize and simplify tasks so that they can be done by unskilled, and therefore cheap, easily replaceable workers. Work is reduced to a meaningless, demoralizing activity. From the Marxist perspective, the capitalist system itself precludes justice and creates the selfish egoism and fractionalized work that give rise to anomie.

The concepts of anomie and alienation thus have complementary aspects, notwithstanding the very different concerns of Durkheimian and Marxist analyses. Durkheim was concerned primarily with social order and the foundations of cohesion and morality, while Marx focussed upon conflict and the foundations of revolution. But these can be seen as two sides of the same issue: the factors that threaten social cohesion are also those that promote conflict. Contemporary work in social constructionist and feminist perspectives further elaborates Durkheim's basic concept of anomie in the exploration of questions of justice. This chapter explores the relevance of these theories of social cohesion and conflict in the analysis of industrial unrest, deviance, and crime in contemporary Canadian society.

✖ Disorder and Conflict in Labour Relations

The Human Relations School of Management

The early application of Durkheim's ideas to the study of industrial relations was decidedly conservative in orientation, focussing upon the human need for social ties and ignoring the concern with social justice implied in Durkheim's own analysis of anomic division of labour. Elton Mayo ([1933] 1960) pioneered this approach in his lengthy study of the Hawthorne Electrical Company in Chicago from 1927 to 1932. The focus of the study was how to improve productivity of workers engaged in the assembly of telephone relays. The researchers' initial experimental interest was on fatigue and monotony and how they affected production. A series of experiments, carried out over two years, systematically varied rest pauses, hours worked per day, provision of free lunches, and intensity of lighting. Five young women were selected from the factory floor and set to work in the experimental test room. Their output had been measured without their knowledge for two weeks prior to the experiment. This provided the base line for measurement of subsequent changes in productivity.

To the surprise of the researchers, output increased with every change. With shorter hours, more rest pauses, more lunch breaks, output went up. Then, when they returned to the original working conditions, output went up higher than ever before. The researchers concluded that increased output was not due to the experimental variables at all. They theorized that it was due to changes in the social situation of the workers. Instead of being a part of an anonymous mass of workers on the factory floor, they had become the centre of attention in a small work group. They were also directly consulted and involved in organizing the various changes in work schedules that took place during the years of the study. Mayo's research is frequently referred to as the origin of the **human relations school of management** theory. The basic assumption of this theory is that workers are happier and thus more productive when they belong to small cohesive, familylike work communities and when they are consulted by management and are encouraged to participate in decisions affecting their working lives.

A second influential study, conducted in 1948, was of young women in a pyjama factory, doing the routine work of sewing, folding, and packaging pyjamas. The management noticed that even small changes in job specifications resulted in marked resentment and lost productivity among the workers. When they experimented with **participatory management** styles, however, allowing the women to be involved in planning the changes in work patterns, the result was a rapid increase in productivity, with no signs of aggression or labour turnover (Coch and French 1949). The researchers concluded that the original problem was anomie. The workers were suffering from noninvolvement in their work community and a lack of group cohesion. Again, the thesis is that a human relations approach to management, which encourages democratic involvement, would resolve industrial conflicts and create a productive work community.

Such research appeared to take all the teeth out of Marxist analyses of capitalism. No fundamental changes in the social order seemed to be required to resolve industrial conflicts and anomie. Only a more humane, participatory style of management seemed necessary. Theorists concerned with order and consensus latched onto these and similar studies as providing empirical justification for conservative theoretical models concerned with the maintenance of existing institutions. Durkheimian analysis came to be seen as radically different from Marxist analysis.

These early experimental data, however, turned out to be flawed. Subsequent **secondary analyses**, especially of Mayo's Hawthorne study, led to the conclusion that both the data and the theoretical conclusions reached by the researchers were erroneous (Landsberger 1958; Carey 1967). Carey convincingly argues that change in **piece-rate payments**, and not the move to smaller work groups, was the major factor behind the initial rise in productivity among the five women selected for participation in Mayo's experiments. When they were paid on the basis of the average output as a group of five workers, their own personal productivity could directly affect their wages. This was not possible when their pay was calculated on the basis of the average output of the entire shopfloor of over one hundred workers. When other workers not in the experiment heard about the change in piece-rate payments, they began to demand that they also be paid on the basis of small-group or individual output.

Carey also shows that the participatory supervision and the familylike atmosphere within the experimental work group was a myth. The experimenters had selected five highly co-operative women in the first place. When two of the women talked too much and did not work hard enough, they were reprimanded and then fired. They protested that they had been told to "work as they feel," but they learned to their cost that this was not the case. The two women who replaced them in the experimental group were both desperate for money. One was the sole supporter of a large family after her father had lost his job. She drove the other women to work harder and cursed them when they seemed to ease up and so threaten the group's average productivity rate, which determined her wages. Carey also noted that Mayo's research took place during the early years of the Depression of the 1930s when workers feared losing their jobs. Mass layoffs from the Hawthorne works occurred in 1932, which was

the point when the Mayo study finished. Carey's general conclusion is that the Hawthorne experiments are scientifically worthless since too many variables were not controlled.

The study of change in the pyjama factory was likewise suspect in that it focussed on young female workers from rural Virginia who had no industrial work experience. Later, when a union organizer illustrated how exploited and underpaid the women were, labour unrest escalated and management became more harsh. When a similar experiment in participatory management was tried among male workers in a Norwegian shoe factory, it had no effect (French, Israel, and As 1960). These male workers were already unionized and had some experience of bargaining over working conditions. They were not impressed by the invitation from management to participate in minor decisions about work tasks. They perhaps understood better than did the young women in the pyjama factory that true industrial democracy would require a much more radical sharing of power between management and workers.

These critiques raise some basic questions. How did the original researchers draw such erroneous conclusions from their data? Why were these studies so readily accepted by later sociologists? More importantly, why is the Hawthorne study still so widely praised in literature on management more than thirty years after its flaws were exposed by critics such as Carey? Carey argues that the studies served the ideological interests of management and perhaps also of sociological theorists committed to the order perspective.

Durkheim's analysis of anomic division of labour draws attention to political issues that human relations theory ignores. Durkheim's fundamental premise is that social cohesion presupposes **distributive justice** as a precondition of contractual relations. Friendly supervision without such justice cannot allay conflicts indefinitely.

The Synthesis of Anomie and Alienation

A valuable synthesis of the concepts of anomie and alienation is developed in Blauner's thesis on alienation and freedom among factory workers. Blauner (1964) combines the ideas of emotional detachment and a loss of commitment to core values, which are central to Durkheim's concept of anomie, with the experience of economic oppression and powerlessness, which is central to the Marxist concept of alienation.

In his comparative study of work settings, Blauner develops measures of degree of alienation with respect to four elements that derive from the work situations in which anomie develops. **Powerlessness** involves job insecurity, fear of unemployment, and lack of control over the task itself. **Meaninglessness** derives from overly fragmented jobs where the individual worker's contribution is so small that the worker loses any sense of co-operating meaningfully with others in a total product. Social **isolation** may result from workers being along on the job but, more importantly, Blauner links it to absence of a sense of loyalty and commitment to the workplace. A critical aspect of this is the breakdown of normative integration, when workers no longer accept the rules that govern the relations between employees and employers. These rules include practices for disciplining and laying off workers, assigning wages relative to the earnings of others, and awarding promotions (Blauner 1964, 25). When these are perceived as fundamentally unjust, social integration breaks down. The last element, **self-estrangement**, occurs when jobs are so monotonous and boring that workers cannot develop a sense of personal involvement or pride in what they do. This again is directly related to Durkheim's conception of a forced and fragmented anomic division of labour. The epitome of alienating work, for Blauner, is labour on car assembly lines. Workers are little more than

appendages to the machine, doing totally monotonous, repetitive work, while tied to a noisy assembly line that precludes any camaraderie on the job. The only plus is that the pay is generally good.

Blauner suggests that **automation** might reduce alienation at work. In the chemical plant that he studied, workers were needed principally to watch the dials on the computers regulating the production process. They enjoyed more control over their own tasks, less fragmented work, more freedom of movement and interaction, and also better promotion prospects than car assembly workers. Other researchers dispute these claims. For many workers, automation had brought only isolation as a result of greatly reduced work forces, chronic job insecurity, and shift work, which interferes with family life and leisure activities.

Automation and computers may have the potential to enrich the lives of workers and reduce drudgery, but frequently such technology has served only to intensify managerial control. Bell Telephone workers, for example, find themselves totally monitored by machines, which record the number of seconds they take to respond to incoming calls and the amount of "downtime" workers take (Kuyek 1979, 18). Computer operators find that every keystroke and every error can be counted and recorded. Such close monitoring results in near intolerable levels of stress for employees. Under such working conditions, anomie takes a new form as old norms of regulative justice and old concepts of humane working conditions are undermined.

The most far-reaching effect of automation for the mass of workers has been chronic job insecurity. There is an ever-present threat that labour-saving technology will make old jobs redundant, and there is no guarantee that new types of jobs will replace them. Given the moral basis of division of labour in interdependence, the issue of unemployment has become a major moral concern. An unemployed worker's loss of a sense of integration with others in a productive community may generate a deeper experience of emotional stress than does lack of money, difficult though this is.

Anomie and Unjust Contracts

Anomie, for Durkheim, has its roots in the breakdown of social regulations. Anomie does not simply mean a lack of rules. Rather, it is the state that results when the moral preconditions for

The epitome of alienating work, for Blauner, is labour on car assembly lines.

contracts have been undermined and thus when the rules that regulate the division of labour are experienced as fundamentally unjust. Flanders and Fox (1969, ch. 15) argue that anomie in industrial relations occurs when two types of norms—procedural and substantive—are undermined. **Procedural norms** include legal provisions for negotiations and dispute settlements, while **substantive norms** regulate the content of collective bargaining such as standard wage rates, working hours, and so on.

Marxist analysts link the escalation of conflicts in industrial relations to economic factors, particularly to the effects of labour-saving technology, rising unemployment, inflation, declining markets, and declining profit margins. The emotional consequence of cycles of boom and bust within capitalist economies is anomie. Anomie also results when people see the degree of economic inequality—and the reasons for that inequality—as unfair. For Durkheim, when inequality of wealth appears unjust, it promotes dissatisfaction and conflict between classes. Within the working class itself, different levels of bargaining power create inequalities. Rising frustration and resentment among workers who lack the power to pressure for their demands in wage disputes split them from more powerful workers.

Canadian Labour Relations

In Canadian labour relations, as in those of many other industrialized countries, both procedural and substantive norms have come under increasing criticism. Provincial and federal governments have been directly drawn into the resulting conflicts.

Procedural Justice

Jamieson (1968) draws attention to a basic contradiction in ideology and policy in Canadian labour relations. Both employers and union spokespersons express a shared liberal ideology, demanding maximum freedom for free enterprise and free collective bargaining; however, a rigid and highly complex system of laws and administrative procedures has come to govern relations between the two groups. Business enterprises want maximum freedom of competition and freedom to determine investments, prices, and output

policies, including the freedom to close down plants and lay off workers when business is unprofitable. Ironically, such freedom has led employers to depend upon government to enact and enforce laws to protect them against organized labour. On the other hand, unions uphold the freedom of workers to organize into unions, to strike, to picket, and to boycott. They depend upon government to enact and enforce laws to protect them against employers and anti-union policies and practices. But such protection has been accompanied by laws on behalf of employers, which sharply restrict unions' freedom of action. Pressure from both sides has resulted in such an extremely complex system of laws, suggests Jamieson, that violations and recourse to illegal actions are frequent and unavoidable.

Warskett's (1988) study of the largely failed attempt to unionize bank workers in Canada throughout the 1980s is particularly insightful in this regard. She demonstrates how the labour laws restricted the freedom of action of union organizers and effectively shifted the locus of struggle from workers themselves to a team of legal experts. A seemingly endless series of litigations, challenges, appeals, and counteraccusations of unfair labour practices was sufficient to tie up the certification procedures for years.

The centrality of law to the class struggle has far-reaching effects on union ideology and practice. It creates dependency on legal experts and serves to obscure the basis of union power, making it appear as if this power derived from legal processes rather than from the unity of union members. The right to strike appears to have been granted to workers by the liberal democratic state, instead of being the outcome of long historical struggles. The laws appear to be neutral, but in fact they are profoundly political, and their ultimate intention is to ensure the smooth working of capitalism.

Warskett argues that this appearance of neutrality is not merely a distortion. Workers are inclined to obey labour laws, partly because their repressive aspects are relatively hidden behind claims to neutrality and equality of treatment, but also because the laws embody gains won by subordinate classes over time. Workers can look to the laws to protect their rights to unionize, to bargain, and to arbitrate grievances without being threatened with dismissal or other reprisals. But in return, workers' potential for political action is blunted by the requirement that they obey the laws or be punished by the state. Control is taken from the workers and vested in legal experts in the hearing rooms of the Labour Relations Board and the courts.

The succession of bitter and occasionally violent confrontations between labour and management, both in private and government enterprises in Canada, can be understood as the expression of deep-rooted anomie in industrial relations. Procedural laws regulating strikes, lockouts, and strikebreakers are the formal expression of fundamental moral questions concerning legitimacy of these procedural laws that is challenged by workers. In 1986, workers protested what they saw as draconian antilabour legislation in Alberta with a protracted and very bitter strike at Gainers meat packing plant. The company was able to hire strikebreakers during a period of high unemployment, leaving former workers with little or no leverage in contract negotiations and with a very real threat that they would permanently lose their jobs. In Ontario, newly unionized workers at Eatons stores faced similar risks and had to settle for a poor contract. Nationally, post office workers walked picket lines during the summers of 1987 and 1988, attempting to intimidate the busloads of strikebreakers who were themselves unemployed and frequently desperate to earn money or to take over the stable jobs that the postal workers seemed unhappy with.

In all these disputes it is much more than money that matters. National consensus on the issue of procedural justice is at stake. The moral dilemmas are real. Employers feel that their rights to run their own businesses in a free market are being undermined by powerful unions and efforts to establish closed shops in which employers are prohibited from hiring anyone who is not a union member. Employed workers feel that their right to bargain collectively for terms and conditions of employment is being undermined by laws that weaken their limited means to apply pressure during negotiations with vastly more powerful employers. During the nine-month strike of INCO workers in Sudbury in 1978, for example, workers found themselves unable to get management to negotiate seriously because the market for nickel was weak, and the company had been stockpiling supplies for several months before the strike began (Clement 1981, ch. 9). Striking newspaper workers at the

Times in London, England, found themselves up against the Thomson corporate empire, which, during the strike, made the biggest profits in its history from its diverse holdings.

People other than employers and workers are also affected by labour disputes. Unemployed people feel that their rights to bargain for work are being undermined by the unions from which they are excluded. Police become targets for frustration and anger when they are called in by governments to keep the peace on picket lines. People who are dependent upon the services once provided by the striking workers pressure for their rights to transportation, educational, postal, or medical services.

Industrial anomie in Canada has at times reached the level of pitched battles between opposing forces with mass arrests of strikers by police. More than a decade of labour unrest, punctuated by increasingly violent strikes, preceded the Winnipeg General Strike of 1919. Mounted police were used to quell strikers during this major confrontation. Panitch and Swartz (1988) indicate that coercion against strikers was the norm in Canada prior to the 1940s. The right of workers to free collective bargaining was only recognized by the Canadian state in 1945. This was precipitated by the unprecedented expansion of trade unions during World War II and the increasing militancy of workers, bolstered by war mobilization and full employment. The authors argue, however, that during the 1980s, collective bar-

Industrial anomie in Canada led to labour unrest and violence in the Winnipeg General Strike in 1919.

gaining rights eroded. The right to strike was conspicuously not enshrined in the Charter of Rights and Freedoms of 1982. Since then, both federal and provincial governments have frequently passed antistrike and back-to-work legislation. The trend is toward increasing state coercion of unions through both the police and the courts.

Changes in the structure of the labour market in the 1990s are also making old union strategies and labour laws increasingly irrelevant (Armstrong and Armstrong 1992, 310–13). Many new jobs, particularly in the state sector, involve service—caring for people, teaching, providing assistance and information. The nature of such jobs encourages employees to identify with the goals of their employer and with their clients. Strikes hurt clients, and also hurt the long-term working climate of employees. Also, when the employer is the state, strikes save the employer money. Other new jobs are in small workplaces, or in large enterprises that are divided into dispersed shops. Jobs are often part-time, short-term, done in the home, or contracted out. The Armstrongs suggest that the very success of large-scale union organizing in the past has encouraged employers to adopt such decentralized labour patterns. Management control can be maintained by new computer technology and networks rather than direct supervision. Appropriate strategies for maintaining procedural justice under these changed conditions have yet to be worked out. Pressure for legislative changes through political action and extra-work coalitions, such as the women's movement, community action groups, and special interest lobby groups, may become more significant than union bargaining in labour-market reform.

Substantive Justice

Like those governing procedural justice, the norms for judging the merits of claims to financial and other rewards are in dispute, creating further divisions within Canadian society. Durkheim argued that, to avoid anomie, it is not sufficient that there be rules; the rules must be accepted as just. In his view, inequalities in rewards are justifiable only in a **meritocracy**; that is, in a system where inequalities directly reflect the natural capabilities and interests of different people. Marxists dispute this, arguing that hours of labour time expended should be the primary cri-

terion for rewards. People should not expect a higher standard of living simply because they happen to have more intelligence or stronger bodies than others. From this perspective, moral justice dictates that people should work according to their abilities and be rewarded according to their needs. This is a fundamental difference in basic moral principles that cannot be resolved by logical arguments alone.

Employment Equity as Social Construction

Social constructionist theory raises sensitivity to how notions such as "job skills" are created and the common-sense reasoning that accomplishes understanding of such terms as *equity* and *value*. It alerts us also to how systems of measuring and categorizing job characteristics create versions of reality, and to the power wielded by experts whose work it is to design job evaluation schemes for the purposes of pay equity comparisons. Definitions of the relative value of different jobs are themselves the sites of political struggle, but sites increasingly controlled by legal and technical experts rather than employees who actually do the work. To arrive at an understanding of how pay equity is accomplished requires us to deconstruct the categories that describe jobs. **Deconstruction** involves the detailed investigation of texts that set out job descriptions, to see precisely how they produce their results; that is, how job categories are set up, exactly what features of particular jobs are deemed relevant and what features are ignored in the official forms used to classify and evaluate jobs, and how equivalences and differentials among jobs are produced. Such work is still very much in the early stages of development.

In Canada, the prevailing consensus is that merit provides the moral basis for differential rewards within the economy. People who do the same job, or jobs of equivalent value, should receive equivalent rewards without discrimination on the basis of such factors as ethnicity or gender. In 1978, the Canadian Human Rights Act was amended to state that: "It is a discriminatory practice for an employer to establish or maintain differences in wages between male and female employees employed in the same establishment who are performing work of equal value." In March 1985, the Mulroney government authorized a Joint Union Management Initiative on Pay Equity in the federal civil service. In the same year the NDP in Ontario pressured the minority Liberal government to enact proactive equal pay legislation. Implementation of these Acts, however, has been slow, and the impact on pay differentials minimal. In part this has been due to deliberate stalling tactics by government and private employers. Complaints filed under the Human Rights Act have been subject to years of costly litigation, appeals and counterappeals in the courts, and decisions favourable to employees have been very narrowly interpreted (Butler and Brookfield 1992; Armstrong and Armstrong 1992).

It is easy to see why employers would be reluctant to co-operate with **employment equity** schemes. They stand to lose traditional management control over wages and salaries, and also to lose an important source of cheaper labour. Small employers gained exemption from the Ontario Pay Equity Act on the grounds that they could not afford to pay equal wages to women. In the process they admitted that they did discriminate against female employees. Large employers argued that Canada's competitive edge in world markets would be threatened and foreign investments would drop (Breckenridge 1985). Breckenridge warns that firms will do everything possible to avoid **pay equity** laws, including refusing to hire women. In her argument, competitive advantage is accorded higher importance than is the moral imperative to end the discrimination by which women on average earn only 60 percent of what men earn.

The Ontario Pay Equity Legislation has been extensively modified under pressure from business groups, to significantly reduce its potential impact. Firms with ten or fewer employees are exempted completely, and those with between eleven and ninety-nine employees are not required to have a Pay Equity Plan, although they may be subject to complaints procedures activated by employees. In establishments where the Act does apply, permissible comparisons for pay equity claims are strictly limited. Women must establish that they are in a job class and compare themselves with a male job class in the same establishment, with the same employer, in the

same geographic location, and, where feasible, within the same bargaining unit. Such details exclude workers in geographically widespread chains such as McDonald's; exclude subcontracted jobs, or workers hired through agencies; and block provincewide implementation of any pay equity adjustments to women doing the same job for different employers (Armstrong and Armstrong 1992, 300–1).

These overt class-interested practices are at least obvious targets for political action by women's groups and organized labour. But there are deeper theoretical and conceptual problems inherent in the notion of "equal pay for work of equal value" that have scarcely begun to be worked through. What does *equity* mean? What does *equal value* mean? How are they to be determined or measured? Such questions shift the focus from equity as a demonstrable state of affairs to equity as social construction. Differential pay levels have their origin in the outcome of negotiations, bargaining, and control over techniques of production. They do not arise from measurable components of different jobs, yet pay equity legislation requires that such measurements be decisive.

Common-sense reasoning generally gives high priority to level of training required in deciding the relative merits of different jobs. But length of training is itself directly related to the power of different workers to protect apprenticeship schemes, against employer incentives to circumvent them. Male workers in many trades such as electrician, plumber, carpenter, welder, and the like, were influential enough to insist that any person hired to do such work had to have completed lengthy apprenticeship schemes. Men who learned such skills informally from watching friends and relatives at work could not qualify for trade papers and so were barred from applying to many jobs. Women workers, however, were generally less successful at protecting their skills. In the nineteenth century, for example, clerical training was a recognized apprenticeship scheme run by employers, and women who completed such training could claim to be skilled workers. At the turn of the century, however, clerical training was shifted into the public school curriculum. Girls who completed such training came to be seen merely as high-school graduates with no specialized credentials and warranting only low levels of pay (Gaskell 1986). Gaskell suggests that this pattern developed largely because clerical workers are generally nonunionized and fragmented and thus unable to protect their trade skills as successfully as workers in predominantly male trades.

Professional job evaluation schemes typically focus on such job requirements as responsibility, effort, skill, and working conditions. The goal is to develop gender-neutral measurements that can provide objective ranking for a wide variety of jobs. The problem is that each of these dimensions has subjective judgments and gender biases built into it, the results of years of contract negotiations and power relations. Many schemes order factors hierarchically, assuming some more important than others. Responsibility for money and employees tends to be at the top, while responsibility for clients, patients, students, and customers tends to be at the bottom. Supervision of subordinate employees counts as management skill, whereas supervision of children and patients does not. Directing the work of others has higher value than co-ordinating activities with other workers. With respect to working conditions, the objectionable nature of garbage, for example, has justified higher salaries for refuse collectors, but the objectionable nature of human waste and vomit has not been invoked to justify higher salaries for nurses' aides. The effort required to lift heavy patients is calculated into the salaries of male nurses more readily than the emotional effort required of other nurses to comfort complaining, sick, and dying patients. Some skills are not factored in at all. The skill required to handle multilevel activities may not be recognized in clerical job descriptions—for example, workers in a health insurance office switch constantly from keyboarding, to interpreting complex legislation, to translating it for clients who are often distressed after illness or bereavement and whose command of English may be limited, to communicating with civil servants. In all the preceding examples, women typically predominate in the kinds of jobs that are accorded low evaluations. Women have also learned to place a low value on their work and to describe their work in terms of formal job descriptions in which much of the complexity of what they do is not recognized.

The value of job evaluation schemes in achieving pay equity depends on just such a multiplicity of subjective judgments made by experts. These experts work in a context of power relations in which pay evaluation schemes are typically management tools, paid for by management, and oriented to what managers want measured. They can work to rigidify job descriptions and increase management control, and job fragmentation, rather than enhancing the rewards to employees.

In these processes, women employees have limited power, but they are not passive victims. As Foucault stresses, the exercise of power itself generates resistance. Pay equity legislation has served to legitimate women's demands for better pay, and to reconceptualize the problem of gender bias as systemic rather than a problem of individual workers or the attitudes of individual employers. The legislation requires disclosure of information on salary scales that were formerly kept secret. As women struggle to fill out job evaluation questionnaires that do not describe their work, political awareness increases. Courts are hearing more and more cases in which unions challenge the validity of evaluation schemes. Common-sense understandings and discourse around employment equity are changing. Real gains transform the conditions and consciousness of the people involved, which in turn gives rise to new contradictions and new struggles (Armstrong and Armstrong 1992, 296).

▣ Deviance and Crime

The sociological study of deviant behaviour and crime has been profoundly influenced by Durkheim's theoretical analysis of the relationship between law and social structure. Durkheim argues that law expresses the moral basis of social cohesion, the shared values and the fundamental rules of orderly contractual relations that are essential for the maintenance of industrial society. Crime, as the violation of law, challenges the foundations of the social order itself. Crime rates, much like suicide rates, reflect the level of anomie or moral breakdown within any given society. Variation in these rates between subgroups within society reveal the stress points in the social system.

In this section we will first examine functionalist theories of crime and **deviance**, which are drawn directly from Durkheim's work. Then we explore how these ideas are being modified and challenged by political economy, social constructionist, and feminist perspectives. Each perspective can be assessed for its usefulness in accounting for data concerning crime rates in Canada. Among these data is evidence that people in trouble with the law are disproportionately drawn from the lower class and have below-average levels of education and income. Members of economically disprivileged minority groups, such as Native peoples and blacks, are especially overrepresented among those charged with offences, as are young people between the ages of fifteen and twenty-five. Criminals are also overwhelmingly male, notwithstanding evidence that crime rates among women have been rising in recent years. This pattern differs little from the patterns found in the United States, Britain, and other industrialized societies.

Functionalist Theories of Deviance and Crime

Functionalist theories focus on socialization and consensus with reference to the values and behavioural norms of society. Learned consensus assures the maintenance of stability and order within any social system. The purpose or role of the criminal justice system, which includes the framework of laws, the police, the courts and prisons, is to protect the members of society from the minority of deviants who might otherwise threaten this order. Various theoretical approaches to the study of deviance and crime within this broad perspective include anomie theory of crime, differential opportunity theory, differential association theory, and deviant subculture theory.

The Anomie Theory of Crime

As we have seen, the concept of anomie, as developed by Durkheim, refers to a relative absence or confusion of values and a corresponding lack of clear regulations or norms for behaviour. People feel lost and unsure of what to believe in or how to behave. Robert Merton (1968) systematizes this broad concept into a general model, the **anomie theory of crime**. Merton's central hypothesis is that deviance is a symptom of the dissociation between the goals that people are taught to aspire

to and the means through which they can be achieved. All societies, Merton argues, teach culturally valued goals and socially approved behaviour to achieve them. Strains develop in such value systems because not everyone has access to the means needed to attain valued goals.

Merton has developed a typology of possible responses to goals and means (see table 7-1). In this typology, **conformists** accept cultural values and are able to achieve them by socially acceptable means. Such people must constitute a majority in any given society for that society to be stable or orderly. **Innovators** accept cultural goals such as material success and money, but they lack legitimate opportunities to attain them. They seek alternative, illicit means such as theft, prostitution, or drug trafficking. Merton suggests that this category best accounts for the relatively high crime rates found among the poor. **Ritualists** are people who give up on cultural goals, no longer even trying to attain them. They ritualistically obey the rules and conform to outward behaviour patterns, but they have no motivation to succeed. This category includes people who live as petty cogs in the bureaucratic machine. **Retreatists** reject both goals and means. They essentially withdraw into a form of apathy. Merton suggests that hobos, dropouts, skid row alcoholics, and drug addicts fit into this category. Drugs provide a retreat for those who have failed in society. Finally, **rebels** are people who generate new goals and new means. They are the revolutionaries and political activists who aspire to a new social order. They reject the value placed on money, individualism, and competition in North American society and favour new values such as co-operation, communal welfare, and equality.

Table 7-1

Typology of Modes of Adaptation		
Mode of Adaptation	Culturally Valued Goals	Socially Approved Means
Conformist	accept	accept
Innovator	accept	reject
Ritualist	reject	accept
Retreatist	reject	reject
Rebel	replace	replace

Source: Merton (1968, 194).

The value of Merton's typology is that it focusses directly upon social structural variables and not on individual pathology. By drawing attention to unequal opportunities and the strains that such inequality generates, it implies a criticism of industrial society. It suggests that lower-class people and members of disadvantaged minority groups seem particularly likely to engage in deviant or illegal behaviour, not because they have innately criminal characters, but because they face more obstacles to achieving the success goals of the dominant culture.

The **differential opportunity theory** of delinquency developed by Cloward and Ohlin (1960) modifies Merton's formulation to explain why members of one group rather than another are more likely to turn to crime. People who can get what they want legally have little incentive to turn to crime. They are likely to be the conformists. For potential nonconformists to become deviant innovators, rather than ritualists or retreatists, they have to have criminal opportunities. It helps, when embezzling funds, for example, to be a bookkeeper or an accountant.

Subcultural Variations in Crime

Alternative theories developed within the functionalist perspective suggest ways in which Merton's model can be adapted to account for subcultural variations in crime rates. They share the basic assumption that socialization and value consensus are critical mechanisms explaining behaviour, but they focus on distinctive subcultures rather than assuming a uniform pattern of values.

Sutherland's theory of **differential association** developed out of his attempt to explain the culture of professional thieves (Sutherland 1937; Sutherland and Cressey 1960). Rather than viewing professional thieves as deviants from a broader system, he analysed their lifestyles in terms of a cohesive cultural system, much as an anthropologist might study a tribe. In his differential association model, he suggests that deviant behaviour is socially learned in interaction with close associates. Deviants learn both the motives and the techniques of crime, or to use Merton's terminology, they learn both deviant goals and deviant means. From Sutherland's perspective, deviants appear as normal conformists; the only difference is that they are conforming to an unusual minority group culture.

A criminal lifestyle, suggests Sutherland, presupposes specific values and attitudes. People who are surrounded by others who violate the law tend to copy them. Sutherland concludes that early childhood experiences are likely to be the most significant factors in developing an allegiance to a criminal lifestyle. Children who live in areas with a high delinquency rate are particularly likely to conform to such behaviour patterns and so become delinquents themselves. This, he argues, might explain the perpetuation of high crime rates in certain areas.

Sutherland ([1949] 1961) also applies the model to **white-collar crime**; this is crime among people in business, professional, and managerial roles. He suggests that business people often learn contempt for legal regulations that restrict misleading advertising, infringing patents, unfair labour practices, and the like. Hence, they can engage in such activities without feeling like deviants. Even prosecution for such acts is unlikely to result in loss of status among corporate associates.

Gang Subculture

Alternative versions of a **subcultural theory of deviance** have been developed out of Merton's anomie theory specifically to account for behaviour of members of working-class gangs found in many large urban centres in North America (Cohen 1955; Thrasher 1963; Miller 1958). The motivation for youths to join gangs is seen to stem from the status frustration of lower-class males who are exposed to middle-class expectations they cannot hope to achieve. The gang culture turns traditional cultural values such as ambition, responsibility, skills development, and respect for property upside down. Gang culture grants prestige to those who rebel, get into trouble, outsmart others, take risks, and are tough and autonomous. Violation of legal norms for its own sake is a respected part of gang culture, and to gang members it represents conformity rather than rebellion. Descriptions of gang life read like studies of exotic tribes with their own internal social organization, moral codes, and sanctions.

Greenberg (1981b) argues that the theory of gangs as a reflection of lower-class subculture needs to be modified to apply more specifically to adolescents, since almost all gang members are under twenty-one. Lower-class teenagers, he suggests, have very specific aspirations and thwarted expectations that lead them to rebel against the dominant middle-class culture. They are denied the adult status, required to stay in school much longer than previous generations, and have few opportunities to earn much money. Yet participation in teen social life requires financial resources for such things as clothes, cosmetics, cigarettes, cars, motorbikes, CDs, and often liquor and drugs. Young lower-class males may doubt their ability ever to fulfil traditional male sex-role expectations of finding work and supporting a family, particularly if they live in neighbourhoods where many men are unemployed. Exaggerated concern with toughness, fighting, vandalism, sexual conquests, joy-riding in stolen cars, and smoking, can all be seen as compensating behaviour for status anxiety and lack of legitimate opportunities for attaining the prerogatives of adulthood. Interest in gang membership drops off sharply as boys reach school-leaving age.

The Limitations of Functionalist Theories of Crime

In functionalist theory, deviance is accounted for primarily as the effect of unequal opportunities, which compel disadvantaged individuals to adopt illegal means to achieve their goals. Alternatively, deviance is seen as reflecting socialization and conformity to subcultural goals that are perceived as deviant from those of the wider society.

Merton's original formulation of the anomie theory of crime, particularly his model of types of crime, has been criticized for a number of flaws that limit its usefulness in analysing deviance. The five categories are vaguely defined and difficult to apply. Rebellion and innovation, for example, are very similar. Merton lists groups such as hippies within the category of retreatists, but they might equally well be categorized as rebels, rejecting both the goals and the means of a consumer-oriented society. Marxists criticize Merton for a superficial treatment of rebellion. His model avoids the issue of an alienating social order that should be overthrown. Feminists argue that the categories cannot be unambiguously applied to crimes commonly committed by women. Are prostitutes retreatists who reject the goals and means thought appropriate for women, or are

they rebels whose primary goal is money (Leonard 1982, 61)? Alternatively, are they innovators who accept financial success goals but have unorthodox means to achieve them?

A more general criticism is that Merton's model assumes the background of a basically stable and homogeneous community with clearly defined goals and means, in terms of which deviance can be clearly recognized. It does not allow for the possibility that goals might differ between subcultures. Indulgence in drugs or alcohol, for example, may be deviant for people in certain social groups, but may represent conformity to peer group norms for others. Moreover, cultural goals are socially learned and they vary widely over time and between groups. They cannot simply be assumed as given for the purpose of developing theories about crime. Lastly, the focus upon lack of legitimate opportunities as the explanation for crime also takes it for granted that most crimes are committed by disadvantaged or lower-class people. White-collar crimes committed by members of the business and professional classes are not readily explained.

Sutherland's revised model of differential association has not been widely adopted. The situations in which it might be usefully applied to explain crime rates seem limited. Leonard (1982, 91–105) argues that the view of crime as merely like any other form of learned behaviour is too deterministic. It leaves unanswered the basic question of how and why people choose the associations they do. By no means do all people in high-crime areas adopt criminal lifestyles. This observation challenges the assumption that deviant lifestyles constitute merely a minority group cultural variation. The model also seems to offer little explanation of white-collar crime beyond giving some insight into how people are able to rationalize self-serving behaviour.

The application of subcultural theory to gang behaviour is also problematic. The concept of value inversion is based largely on speculation, with little evidence to support it. Much gang culture, Leonard suggests (1982, 124–28), seems to reflect an exaggerated emphasis on masculine values of power and autonomy rather than a reversal of dominant cultural values. Gang members, moreover, clearly know that their behaviour is deviant, and they can experience guilt as well as defiance when caught. The notion of conformity to alternative cultural values does not adequately explain this sense of guilt. The theory seems to function primarily as a rationalization and neutralization of behaviour that frequently has clear victims and is rational, calculated, and utilitarian. Leonard sees gang behaviour as an innovative way of achieving the goals of money and power rather than as the expression of exotic cultural diversity.

A further criticism from the perspective of Marxist theory is that while anomie theory incorporates an implicit critique of an inegalitarian social order, this is not developed into any broader analysis of the social structures that generate crime. Feminists also point out that differences between males and females with respect to crime rates are either ignored or dismissed under the argument that the two sexes are socialized into different roles and values and that only male roles are sufficiently problematic to generate much deviance.

The Political Economy of Crime

The political economy perspective within criminology places the structure of capitalism at the centre of the analysis of law and the criminal justice system. The central assumption is that crime reflects contradictions or irresolvable problems within the capitalist economic system. The functionalist emphasis on individual pathology or deviant socialization at best touches only on the symptoms, not the causes of crime. Human action, including criminal behaviour, is shaped by the socially structured inequalities of wealth and power. Under capitalism, which is discussed in more detail in chapters 8 and 9, capitalists strive to beat competitors in the market. Labour-saving technology serves to boost productivity, reduce labour costs, and so raise profits. But such competition generates exploitation, unemployment, continuous cycles of booms and slumps in the economy, and misery for the mass of workers who sell their labour power. An underclass of chronically unemployed or temporary and **marginal workers** bears the brunt of this exploitative system. This class is disproportionately composed of racial and ethnic minorities. People from this underclass also predominate among the prison populations in capitalist countries. A high crime rate among these people is not evidence of any inherent degeneracy or antisocial culture, but an understandable reaction to material conditions.

Marxism and Anomie

Marxist theorists argue that the anomie at the centre of functionalist explanations for crime is directly produced by capitalism. Even those who escape the grinding poverty and insecurity of the underclass of marginal workers still suffer the alienating effects of fragmented, meaningless jobs under conditions that give little scope for pride or fulfilment. Most adolescents grow up to a future in which they can expect to spend eight hours a day doing pointless work and to come home afterwards to be entertained by mindless television. Goodman (1956) suggests that crime and delinquency among adolescents do not reflect merely transitory problems of adjustment to adult role responsibilities. They express the pervasive moral emptiness of capitalist society, which adults only partially manage to push from their thoughts when coping with the routine of earning a living. Adolescents grow up into a world that is absurd. Few jobs are intrinsically worth doing in the sense that they provide goods or services that people need or that improve the quality of life. In the contemporary North American economy, jobs are often worse than useless. They involve products designed to harm people. As many as one-third of all jobs in the United States are, directly or indirectly, connected to the military. For example, military funding is a significant source of university research grants, both in the United States and in Canada.

In 1986, the Nova Scotia government began negotiations with a German armaments company to build tanks in Cape Breton for export to Saudi Arabia. German laws prohibit the sale of armaments made in Germany to any foreign government that potentially might use them against Israel. Editorials in Maritime newspapers, however, scoffed at the argument that Cape Bretoners might also view such trade as morally repugnant. All that counted was that Cape Bretoners needed the four hundred jobs the tank factory might provide. An editorial (*The Daily Gleaner* [Fredericton], 28 Feb. 1986) pointed out that Canadians had benefited from thousands of jobs, and had made millions of dollars in profits selling armaments to the Americans during the Vietnam War. Why, then, should they be concerned about making tanks destined to be used in the Arab-Israeli conflict or any other theatre of war? The editorial concluded that "to moralize on the backs of the jobless is unconscionable." The basic message behind the editorials is that concern with moral issues has no place in capitalist business deals. Wars are welcome when they provide opportunities for jobs and profits.

If this argument is accepted, it would seem that anomie, or the undermining of moral order, occurs at the heart of the capitalist system. The origin of this immorality lies not with the workers but with capitalism itself. When the economy is based on competition, and workers are exploited to make profits, everyone comes to see everyone else as a potential competitor, an enemy. The consequence is social war (Greenberg 1981a, 40). Capitalism reduces altruism and compassion and promotes a spirit of domination and insensitivity to others that is conducive to crime (Leonard 1982, 146).

Laws for the Capitalist Class

The link between capitalism and crime goes much deeper than generating an atmosphere in which moral issues have low priority, however. Capitalism originated in larceny of the largest scale imaginable (Greenberg 1981a, 39). The feudal system in Europe in which **peasants** had hereditary rights to live on and work the land, ended when it became profitable for large landowners to raise sheep for market. Landowners converted croplands into pasture and drove peasants off the land. Laws were pushed through the British parliament to deprive villagers of their customary rights to use common lands to graze their own livestock, gather wood, and so on, so that the big landowners could use the land to graze sheep. Church lands were confiscated, depriving paupers of their legal right to share in the harvest or rental incomes from these lands. In effect, common lands were stolen from peasants to enlarge the estates of rural landlords.

The important point for Marxist criminology is that laws were enacted almost entirely to protect the interests of the people who were stealing the lands, not the people who had traditional land-use rights. Law within capitalist societies is thus rooted in class struggle. The Marxist historian E.P. Thompson (1975) analyses the use of law in the class struggle that marked this transition from feudal to capitalist forms of property ownership in eighteenth-century England. One such law was called the Black Act. Passed in 1723, it imposed the death sentence for the seemingly innocuous act of blacking one's face. The reason behind the penalty was that such blacking was widely used by peasants as a disguise while hunting deer in the king's forests and other land that had been enclosed. The death sentence also covered such acts as poaching, hurting cattle, cutting down trees, and burning haystacks or barns on the estates.

On the surface, the laws imposed an unbelievably harsh sentence for minor felonies, but they reflected a class struggle of profound importance. The new estates enclosed vast acres of common lands that earlier generations of village people had the right to use. The common lands were decreed to be the private, inalienable property of the nobles, politicians, and other favoured persons. One legal decision after another emphasized the absolute property rights vested in the big estate owners over the coincident land-use rights of local people. The laws appeared, in their wording, to be neutral and impartial. They merely protected property held by one individual against damage or theft by another. Yet underneath this neutral terminology was class war. The laws simultaneously created and defended two classes: people who owned no property and those who owned the means of production.

Capitalism and the Spread of Crime in Canada

Comparable processes to the expropriation of feudal lands by capitalists in Europe also took place in Canada and the United States several centuries later. Huge land grants were given by government decree to businessmen, railway tycoons, politicians, and loyalists, with scant regard for the rights of Native peoples. Settlers were exploited by bankers and landowners who speculated on real estate for huge profits. New homesteaders were forced into virtual debt bondage to pay mortgages, and compelled to adopt cash cropping and wage-labour to raise money for the bankers.

Native peoples fared the worst. Most were displaced from their traditional hunting and trapping grounds and herded onto reservations, commonly established on the least desirable tracts of land unsuitable for settlement. Without a viable economic base, many have been reduced to welfare. Others have turned to crime, exploiting the minor vices of Canadians and Americans. Simard (1990, 345) suggests that most of the tribes in the United States, and some in Canada, especially in reservations close to or straddling the Canadian-American border, have started selling taxfree cigarettes and contraband alcohol, but the real money-makers in both countries are high-stakes bingo emporiums and gambling casinos. There is also a more sinister cross-border trade in machine guns, which are illegal in Canada. The peculiar legal status of the reservations makes them havens for groups of people involved in these illicit activities.

The Native peoples themselves are the primary victims of these activities, through the divisiveness and violence that they generate. The Akwesasne Mohawk reservation near Montreal is deeply divided between the progambling forces, among them the militant Warrior Society, and antigambling factions, many of whom live on the Canadian side of the reserve. A *Globe and Mail* report (Lysiane Gagnon, 19 Feb. 1994, D3) states that in the eight years between 1986 and 1994 there have been seventy-five violent deaths on the reserve, most of them not investigated by police. The violent faction involved in contraband gained control of the reservation over these years. Opponents are intimidated by the threat and the exercise of violence, or reprisals by the band government. During the Oka crisis in July 1990, armed Mohawk Warriors blocked the road through the reservation for five weeks in a confrontation with Quebec police. The crisis seems to have been precipitated in part over police raids on the reserve in the guise of looking for contraband, as well as a dispute over rights to land once used as a Native burial ground. Whatever the immediate factors, however, the long-term problem is the dearth of economic opportunities within the reservations, outside of welfare or crime.

A small proportion of reservations in Canada have made windfall profits from the exploitation of minerals, timber, and hydro-electric power on their lands. But the spread of capitalism into these communities seems to have brought anomie and despair rather than prosperity and peace for the majority of people. In the 1980s, the Lubicon in Alberta, the Haida Nation in British Columbia, and the Dene in northern

Confrontations between Mohawk Warriors and Quebec police became violent during the Oka crisis in 1990.

Quebec found themselves fighting to defend their traditional land-use rights and means of livelihood against logging firms, the oil industry, and hydro-electric companies. Members of the James Bay Cree community at Chisasibi became marginal workers in the Hydro-Quebec project in 1980, after the community moved from its old location on Fort George Island to avoid flooding and erosion caused by the damming of the La Grande River. Within a decade the community changed from peaceful and crimefree, to a society characterized by vandalism, drug and alcohol abuse, family violence, teenaged pregnancies, and high suicide rates; there was a virtual explosion in juvenile crime, particularly break and enter, and theft (Niezen 1993). The families of unemployed people were four times as likely to be in trouble with the law than those of employed people, but even among the latter, crime rates were far above those of a similar Cree community of comparable size where most people continued their traditional occupations as hunters and trappers. Niezen concludes that the continued spread of capitalism into the Cree communities of the North is likely to promote further social dislocation and anomie that will not be resolved merely by giving jobs or financial subsidies to the Cree.

Defining Crime: Illegal Behaviour or Social Harm?

Marxist theory holds that the rule of law in a capitalist society is never neutral. The power and vested interests of the elite class, and not the collective morality of the community as a whole, determine the character of laws. Laws are mechanisms by which the dominant class exercises control over subordinate classes.

Quinney (1975) proposes four hypotheses in which he juxtaposes the Marxist view of law with the functionalist interpretation developed from Durkheim's work.

1. Acts are labelled as criminal, not because they offered morality, but because they offend the interests of the ruling class.

2. Acts are labelled deviant, not when they are beyond public tolerance, but when they threaten the interests of the ruling class.

3. Lower-class people are arrested more, not because they commit more crimes, but because middle-class people control law enforcement.

4. Contractual law protects, not justice in contracts, but capitalist property interests.

Quinney argues further that the processes that favour the interests of the dominant class within the criminal justice system work at the state of enactment and enforcement of legislation. Laws protecting property owners are the most prevalent and tend to be diligently enforced with strong penalties. Conversely, laws to protect workers against the capitalist class are few, they are laxly enforced, and their infringement generally results in lenient penalties, with little regard for the level of harm involved. Criminal behaviour by the powerful is likely to be lightly punished, if punished at all.

Marxists argue that the traditional functionalist approach to criminology, which defines crime as the violation of state legislation, constitutes an ideology that serves to legitimate an often unjust and fundamentally class-biased system of laws. The functionalist perspective also excludes from scrutiny many forms of harmful behaviour by members of the propertied class because they are not defined as against the law. Analysis that accepts official statistics on people in prison as a measure of the number of criminals in society perpetuates the myth that lower-class people are bad or antisocial, while middle-class people are good, law-abiding citizens.

Marxists challenge the traditional definition of crime and propose an alternative meaning in terms of violation of human rights. One definition of human rights includes the right to well-being; to food, shelter, clothes, and medicine; to challenging work; and to social, sexual, and economic equality. It also includes freedom from predatory and repressive social elites (Schwendinger and Schwendinger 1975).

When crime is defined as a violation of these human rights, it is clear that state agencies are guilty of much criminal behaviour. Greenberg (1981a, 6) points out that the overwhelming majority of murders in this century have been carried out by government during wartime. To such deaths can be added killings by police that go unprosecuted. In North America the largest forcible plunder of property has been the government-sanctioned takeover of Native lands. The largest mass kidnapping in Canada was the government internment of Japanese Canadians during World War II; these people were also robbed of their property. More recently, hundreds of innocent people in Quebec were arrested under the War Measures Act in 1970. None of these actions fall within the scope of traditional criminology because they are not technically in violation of the law.

The largest mass kidnapping in Canada was the government internment of Japanese Canadians during World War II.

Some radical criminologists broaden the definition of crime to include corporate behaviour that clearly harms the well-being of workers, consumers, and other members of society, even though such behaviour may not be prohibited under the criminal law (Greenberg 1981a, 9). A list of such behaviour includes polluting the environment, failing to improve hazardous working conditions, profiteering, marketing unsafe products, or taking advantage of professional status and expertise to cheat clients.

We owe the limited research that has been done on white-collar crime primarily to Marxist criminologists. Such violations of the law tend to be committed by professional people and rarely find their way into official statistics. Practices include misappropriating public funds, padding expense accounts, bribery, influence peddling, tax fraud, insider trading, and illegally acquiring funds through padding payrolls or through kickbacks from appointees. Labour union bosses may likewise misappropriate union funds, act in collusion with employers to the disadvantage of members, or engage in fraudulent means to maintain control.

People who commit such offences tend to see themselves as respectable citizens rather than common criminals, and they are able to rationalize their behaviour as smart business practice (Sutherland [1949] 1961). The dollar figures involved in such illicit activities may vastly exceed the amounts stolen by poor people during break-and-enter offences, yet the perpetrators tend to be treated more leniently. A welfare recipient who fails to disclose additional income is far more likely to go to prison than is a professional person who cheats on an income tax return.

White-collar crime is often not punished or is dealt with by civil and administrative action rather than criminal prosecution. Those who are convicted tend to get small sentences, served under relatively good prison conditions. John Dean, convicted of playing a leading role in the Watergate affair during the Nixon administration in the United States, was sentenced to five years, but he served only eighteen months, and this in a small, comfortable institution that he shared mainly with Mafia figures.

Companies convicted of major pollution offences routinely meet with only token fines while taxpayers cover the costs of the cleanup. In March 1989, the supertanker *Exxon Valdez* ran aground, spilling 38 million litres of crude oil into Prince William Sound, off the coast of Alaska. After the accident, an Exxon spokesperson confidently announced that the cleanup would not cost the company anything because all costs could be written off against taxes as legitimate business expenses. No one contradicted him.

Boughey argues that the biggest crooks and swindlers may be found at the top of society's power ladder. People most often labelled deviant are those powerless to assert their respectability. He concludes that, "in an age that exposed the crookedness of former President Richard Nixon and Vice-President Spiro Agnew, and proved the top officials of the largest corporations guilty of multi-million-dollar bribery and other scandals, to continue to study petty thieves, vandals, and pot smokers as social deviants is an absurdity" (Boughey 1978, 107).

Capitalism and the Politics of Crime Control

From the Marxist perspective, crime and crime control in capitalist societies are political acts. Criminal behaviour can be seen as a form of protest against oppressive social conditions, a refusal to play the game by the established rules or to accept the unjust distribution of property and the spoils of capitalist social war (Greenberg 1981a, 9). The thesis acknowledges that the majority of people in prison have committed selfish and unpleasant acts such as stealing or breaking and entering other people's homes. Individually these are not political activists. But it is nonetheless a political decision to treat these kinds of acts as deserving penal sanctions while other forms of social harm committed by big corporations and powerful figures are not subject to penal sanction, even though the actual extent of social damage may be many times greater (Smith and Fried 1974, 140).

Drug Wars as Class War

Within Marxist analysis, the so-called war on drugs waged by the Reagan and Bush administrations is the epitome of class war, both within the United States and internationally. The problem of drug addiction is seen as first and foremost a consequence of the economic devastation in American inner cities. People try to lose themselves in drugs when they see no future for themselves. There are no decent jobs, no health care, no education worth the name in the black and Chicano ghettoes, and infant mortality rates approach Third World levels (Ransom 1991, 6).

The war on drugs translates social problems into a crime problem. In 1991, for example, the New York City government opted to reduce its massive budget deficit by closing walk-in clinics, drug rehabilitation centres, homeless shelters, and libraries, laying off 10 000 workers, and by cutting back child immunization, AIDS programs, and garbage recycling. But at the same time it opted to spend $1.2 billion to hire 5000 police officers and to increase prison occupancy by 5500 (Cockburn and Cohen 1991, 22).

The policy of zero tolerance for drugs gives both a justification and a mechanism for controlling the marginalized underclass, providing the rationale for expanding police powers of surveillance, search and seizure, and for suspending civil liberties. An estimated one-quarter of all young black males in New York City have criminal records for drug-related offences. Whites make up 30 percent of arrests for sale and possession of drugs but less than 10 percent of all commitments to state prison for drug-related crime. Blacks make up 10 percent of the population of New York State, but 50 percent of prison inmates (Cockburn and Cohen 1991).

Internationally, the war on drugs becomes a war on the powerless and impoverished peasant farmers in South American countries such as Bolivia, Peru, and Colombia. In the mid-1980s the world price of tin collapsed, causing 30 000 Bolivian tin-miners to lose their jobs. Wracked by debt and collapsing commodity prices, and unable to compete with multinational agribusiness corporations, peasants on marginal hill farms in countries like Bolivia and Peru have turned to growing coca as the one crop for which they can get a good price. Americans have responded by financing fleets of aircraft to spray the crops with harmful defoliants such as *Agent Orange*, extensively used in the Vietnam war (Ransom 1991; Rance 1991). Ransom comments that it is hard to see what immediate purpose such persecution serves, since the United States is itself the largest producer of marijuana and amphetamines (speed). In the face of this reality, efforts to eradicate coca growing in the Andes seem as irrelevant as they are futile.

The hypocrisy of the American government's war on drugs in Latin America is highlighted by evidence that implicates the American Central Intelligence Agency directly in drug trafficking as a means of funding the Contra rebels in Nicaragua (Ransom 1991; Cockburn and Cohen 1991). At the same time the overt war on drugs has provided justification for extensive American government interference in the internal politics of Latin American countries. The main beneficiaries have been military governments, bank-rolled on the promise of repressing coca farmers (Rance 1991). Meanwhile, profits from the drug trade that approach $122 billion per year in the United States and Europe have to be "laundered" to give the appearance of legitimate investment funds. This is accomplished through banks in Switzerland and Luxembourg, as well as offshore islands like the Bahamas, Cayman Islands, and Virgin Islands. These governments reap huge revenues from laws that guarantee the secrecy of bank records (Benn 1991).

The blinkered focus of traditional criminology on prison inmates excludes from analysis all evidence of criminal involvement and violence perpetrated by governments of capitalist societies. Hence, Marxists challenge that criminology as an ideological discourse serves to not know and to not see what is happening.

The Limitations of Marxist Theory

The main criticism of the Marxist theory of crime is not that it is wrong, but that, like functionalism, it suffers from tunnel vision. It overgeneralizes from some valid observations to propose an all-encompassing theory that distorts the complex reality of criminal behaviour and the legal system. The notion that all crime can be attributed to capitalism is not persuasive (Greenberg 1981a, 11–14; Leonard 1982, 161–75). Quinney presents a grand scheme of law as defined and enforced in the interests of capitalism, but his hypotheses are too vague to be tested. Almost any findings can be construed somehow or another as in the interests of capitalism. His assumption that crime will disappear under socialism is particularly unconvincing. The persistence of criminal behaviour in noncapitalist communities makes it clear that Quinney's spotlight is too narrowly focussed to provide a general theory of crime.

Marxist theory is more broadly criticized for romanticizing crime and for seeing deviants as rebels engaged in purposeful and rational behaviour. As Currie (1974, 139) expresses it, "an approach to deviance that cannot distinguish between politically progressive and politically regressive forms of deviance is not much of a basis for real understanding of political action." This tendency to view deviance as a progressive force grew out of the cultural milieu of the late 1960s and early 1970s in the United States when Black Power and the hippie **counterculture** were prominent. But such a view cannot readily be applied to racist, ultraright-wing forms of deviance such as neo-Nazi groups, skinheads, and gangs that take pleasure in attacking immigrants and nonwhites. What is needed is a theoretical framework that will help to explain the conditions under which deviance is or is not politically progressive.

A further criticism of Marxist criminology concerns its characterization of law and law enforcement as nothing more than a weapon used by the capitalist class to preserve its domination over workers. The extreme version of this argument dismisses fear of crime and popular support for law enforcement as the distorted thinking of people duped by capitalist propaganda. The notion that all law is merely manipulation with no legitimacy amongst the mass of working-class people is untenable—their fear of crime is based in real experience and not illusion.

E.P. Thompson (1975, 258–66) identifies himself as a Marxist, but he is highly critical of what he sees as oversimplified, deterministic versions of Marxist theory. He argues that the rule of law is not the same as rule by brute force. In order to function as support for ruling-class power, law has to be seen by subordinates as legitimate. In order to retain this aura of legitimacy, the law must be experienced as just, at least a significant part of the time. Laws may well be devised by members of the propertied class to defend their interests and property against other people, but law is also used by others to limit the arbitrary power of property owners. Common people fought tenaciously for their legal rights to use grazing lands, and not without effect. Native peoples in Canada have similarly used aboriginal treaties to fight a long and bitter, but not entirely hopeless, battle for land claims. Law, argues Thompson, is not an instrument of class power so much as the central arena of class conflict. Law cannot be reserved for the exclusive use of the powerful. They are also bound by the rules.

In conclusion, Marxist criminology is valuable in that it exposes the capitalist underpinnings of demoralization that foster criminal behaviour among the underclass of marginalized workers. It also exposes the class-biased character of many laws and law enforcement policies. What is needed is a broader approach to criminology that retains these insights while breaking out of the tunnel vision of cruder versions of Marxist theory. In particular, we need to explore the processes through which definitions of crime are socially constructed and how they are challenged and changed over time.

Crime as Social Construction

In social constructionist theory, crime is not viewed as an entity. Crime emerges through accounting processes, as the outcome of decisions about how to categorize experience. This perspective focusses attention on discourse, the prevailing system of interpretation, through which crime comes to be defined and recognized. The work of professionals in the criminal justice system involves making interpretations and transforming this discourse into the organized practices of control and management of crime. These interpretive and transformative practices constitute the site of ongoing struggle and contestation.

The origins of social constructionist theories of crime can be traced to Durkheim's observation ([1893] 1964, 102) that crime is a natural social activity that will be found in all healthy societies. Crime is that behaviour which violates the *conscience collective* or the shared beliefs and sentiments of a community. Any definition of what is valued and appropriate behaviour in a community simultaneously defines what is unacceptable. Crime is functional, and perhaps even essential for a society, because in their collective reaction to it people are drawn together in a reaffirmation of the values that underlie their social cohesion. The Puritans who settled in Massachusetts in the 1630s, for example, created an extaordinarily strict and law-abiding community. They labelled many activities that were commonplace among other people, including playing card games and dancing, as deviant for people like themselves. Erikson (1962; 1966) argues that in doing so, they effectively drew **symbolic brackets** around their community, defining the behavioural boundaries between themselves and others, and thus identifying their group as distinct. Their intense preoccupation with rooting out all forms of deviance served an important function for members of the community in reinforcing their distinctive group identity.

When a community feels conformity to particular values are very important, it spends more time and energy rooting out and punishing violations. This produces the ironic result that crime tends to occur precisely where members most fear it. The emphasis placed on conformity precipitates nonconformity in exactly these areas. Thief and victim, for example, share the same high value on private property; heretic and religious fanatic relate to the same sensitive points of religion (Erikson 1966, 20).

The symbolic boundaries defining group identity are never static. They change as the situation of group members changes, and they have to be taught anew to each generation. Hence the work of identifying certain behaviours as crimes and punishing them constitutes an ongoing accomplishment, never a finished event. Crimes that go unpunished weaken the symbolic boundaries defining group identity. Censure must be public. Judges help to stabilize crime rates by tending to give harsh sentences when rates are high and lighter ones when they are low. Erikson concludes that, in principle, even if a community were to lop off all marginal people and expel them, as when Britain banished prisoners and heretics to the colonies, the size of the deviant population would not diminish. People would merely draw the boundaries of appropriate behaviour more strictly, and look for new examples of deviant behaviour. A society of cloistered nuns or monks, for example, will magnify trivial faults into major sins.

Morality and Deviantizing Discourse

Constructionist theory is especially valuable in understanding morality crimes, those often referred to as **victimless crimes**. These are transactional crimes where the persons involved in exchanging illicit goods and services do not see themselves as either criminals or victims, and are very unlikely to complain to the police. Such offences include virtually all sexual behaviour involving willing adult partners, prostitution, buying and using marijuana and other banned drugs, and illegal gambling (Schur 1965; 1971; Schur and Bedau 1974). The prevailing discourses that identify such behaviour as deviant legitimate the subjection of participants to a variety of disciplinary practices.

Same-Gender Sex

As we have seen in chapter 5, the discourse of heterosexual hegemony produced from multiple expert sources in the state, the criminal justice system, medicine, and social sciences, defines heterosexuality as normal and natural, and homosexuality as sick, abnormal, and criminal. People who engage in same-gender sex have been subject to practices of surveillance and control that have been likened to "psychological and social terrorism" (Kinsman 1987a, 106). In England, the decriminalization of same-gender sex in private came into law in 1967, but this generated a protracted legal struggle around the definition of *private*. The closed cubicles of washrooms and bath houses were deemed "public" and subject to intensified police surveillance. In the four years following 1967, the conviction rate for homosexual offences rose 160 percent (Kinsman 1987b, 142).

In Canada, too, surveillance increased during the 1950s and sixties as gay networks expanded in the cities of Toronto, Montreal, and Vancouver. In 1963, as a result of police entrapment in a public washroom, eight men were charged with "indecent acts." One of the arrested men hanged himself. In a critical test case in 1965, Everett Klippert was charged with four counts of "gross indecency" after he told police he had been a practising homosexual for twenty-four years. All acts were consensual and not public, but he was convicted on the basis of his own testimony. Psychiatrists declared him a "dangerous sexual offender" on the grounds that he would be likely to repeat his homosexual offences if released. The Supreme Court of Canada affirmed this judgment, which in effect deemed all sexually active homosexuals dangerous offenders liable to incarceration for life. The then Justice Minister Pierre Trudeau responded by introducing legislation to decriminalize homosexual acts in private, which passed into law in 1969. As in England, however, the site of struggle shifted to contesting the definition of *private*. In 1981 in Toronto, a bath house frequented by gay men was raided and three hundred men arrested. Few of these arrests resulted in convictions, or more than small fines, and public protest was sufficient to deter such large-scale raids in future. Disciplinary tactics have changed with police using overcrowding charges against gay bars, and obscenity charges against gay bookstores and magazines. The closed cubicles of washrooms, and the interiors of moving cars, have been deemed public areas subject to surveillance. Even a photograph of a gay couple having sex can be deemed to violate the privacy act in that a third person, the photographer, must have been present. All areas of military bases were deemed public, including bedrooms. In January 1985, another man committed suicide after being arrested for a brief homosexual encounter in a washroom (*Globe and Mail*, 8 Jan. 1985). A family man, he could not face the shame of public exposure as a homosexual, even though a conviction would probably have resulted only in a minor fine.

The politics of discourse and practices around same-gender sexuality took a new turn early in 1994 with a number of European governments agreeing to recognize same-gender couples as equivalent to heterosexual couples for the purposes of administering family benefits. In most of Canada same-gender couples have no legal status. When a partner dies, biological relatives have been able to establish prior legal claim to possessions that might have been built up over years of a couple living together. The surviving partner may not even be entitled to time off work to attend the funeral. In May 1994, the New Democratic Party government of Ontario introduced a Bill that would have recognized same-sex partnerships as families, but it was defeated on second reading.

Discourse and Practices Around AIDS

The presentation of gay men as deviant, sick, and a threat to society gained new momentum with the outbreak of AIDS in the 1980s, a disease that readily became characterized in the media as "the gay plague." Extremist discourse even likened it to a biblical curse on sinners. Court cases in 1994 focussed on the plight of "innocent victims" who contracted the immuno-deficiency virus through blood transfusions, or from a spouse who received a "tainted" blood transfusion. The direct implication of such discourse is that the thousands of people who became infected through sexual intercourse or sharing needles are "guilty" victims who somehow deserve their fate, even though this may have happened long before the specifics of the virus or of how it can be transmitted were understood. AIDS activists have taken up the struggle to shift this conceptualization from one in which "being a gay male" is the

source of the problem to an issue of safe sexual practices (Canadian AIDS Society n.d.).

The discourse through which the problem of AIDS is conceptualized organizes the practices of government agencies through which the problem is handled. For people who are living with AIDS or carrying the virus, what matters is how to treat the condition, how to find well-informed doctors, and how to ensure swift access to experimental drugs. Frustration at the seeming slowness of government response to their needs has fostered widespread accusations of "red tape" and "homophobia." From the perspective of government, however, the AIDS crisis is being handled through the Health Protection Agency whose principal concern is to control the spread of contagious diseases. The agency has no mandate to facilitate the distribution of experimental drugs, and actually has a formal mandate to ensure that all drugs are meticulously tested through long-term double-blind and placebo experiments prior to their release. George Smith (1990) argues that the attitudes of government bureaucrats, homophobic or otherwise, have no bearing on how the agency operates. What is required is not attitude change, but the establishment of treatment centres with a different legal mandate that would be more appropriate for the AIDS crisis.

Sex for Sale

The criminalization of prostitution in Canada, as elsewhere, has long been justified on the dual grounds that it violates religious and moral standards of the community, and it endangers public health, especially the health of soldiers through the spread of venereal diseases. In nineteenth-century Britain, government regulation of prostitution under the Contagious Diseases Act provided for the sanitary inspection of prostitutes in military depots (Walkowitz 1983). In Cardiff, during the First World War, the government assumed the powers to impose a curfew on "women of a certain class" between 7 P.M. and 8 A.M., and banned all women from pubs after 7 P.M. This was done in the name of protecting troops from "infesting harpies." No consideration was given to controlling troops to prevent them from preying on or infecting local women (Bland 1985).

Efforts by feminists of the day to protect young women from false entrapment and "instrumental rape" largely backfired. The discourse of innocent female victims and individual evil men encouraged more repressive political initiatives with the support of puritanical religious groups. Working-class men were encouraged to assume custodial powers over "their" women, and police were granted extended powers of summary jurisdiction over poor women and girls. Residential brothels were closed down, forcing the women onto the streets where they became prey to pimps.

In Canada in 1985, Bill C-49 extended the criminalization of street prostitution by decreeing that "every person, who, in a public place, or in any place open to public view, stops or attempts to stop any person or in any manner communicates or attempts to communicate with any person for the purpose of engaging in prostitution or of obtaining the services of a prostitute is guilty of an offence punishable on summary conviction" (Scott 1987, 100). Subsequent to the Act being passed, the arrest rate shot up. Women and male hustlers have to work extra hard to pay off the resulting fines, or to bribe police to look the other way. Scott points out that the wording of the law is so vague that it grants police extensive powers to determine what constitutes "for the purposes of prostitution"—even flagging a taxi can be seen as an attempt to communicate. The law prevents women who offer sex for sale to organize or even to communicate with each other for protection or to refer clients. All the techniques by which prostitutes could work together, look out for each other by noting the licence plate numbers of clients, or using a room in a house where they could arrange protection, have been outlawed. A prostitute cannot even have a boyfriend, or be married, for any person who is habitually in the company of a prostitute can be charged with being a pimp, or living on the avails of prostitution. Scott is a member of the Canadian Organization for the Rights of Prostitutes (CORP) that lobbies for the decriminalization of prostitution. Only when their trade is legal, will prostitutes be able to apply to the courts for protection against exploitation from pimps, or violent clients. CORP was started in reaction to a woman being arrested under the bawdy-house laws for working out of her own home.

Drugs: Contesting Criminalization

A third major focus of morality crime is use of illegal drugs—marijuana, LSD, cocaine, crack, and similar narcotics. Narcotics have assumed almost mystical proportions in the discourse on crime in the United States, for their supposed power in creating addiction and precipitating a life of crime. But much of the popular wisdom used to justify the criminalization of drugs is unsubstantiated or wrong. Alexander (1990) cites extensive research that indicates that illegal drugs are no more harmful or addictive than legal drugs like alcohol and tobacco, and no more likely to cause anybody to go out of control. Opium sticks used to be sold at corner shops in England in the nineteenth century, without addiction becoming an overwhelming problem. Legal regulation and controlled distribution of drugs, similar to policies adopted in Holland, or the methadone maintenance programs provided for some addicts in England, seem more likely to be successful in undermining the harm caused by criminal drug rings, than the prosecution of users. Alexander concludes that the war on drugs continues because it meets other psychological and social needs that have little to do with the use of drugs as such. People live in a real world characterized by horrifying violence—perpetrated by criminals, disappointed lovers, soldiers, guerillas, religious fanatics, reckless drivers, police, parents, spouses and so on, and they also face the threat of environmental pollution on a huge scale from nuclear waste, industrial chemicals, sewage, growth hormones, oil spills, and multiple other sources. Illegal drugs provide a scapegoat, something concrete to blame, and around which members of a society can mobilize their emotions. The intensification of moral panic around drugs, like the seventeenth-century crusade against wayward Puritans, helps to reinforce a sense of social cohesion and order in the face of divisive social forces.

Stigmatization and Secondary Deviance

Each of these examples has in common the pattern that the people affected by the proscribed behaviour are the persons labelled as deviant and criminal, rather than some other people who feel victimized or harmed. The labelling process itself produces the crime. In Becker's words, "Social groups create deviance by making the rules whose infraction constitutes deviance and by applying those rules to particular people and labelling them outsiders" (1963, 9).

The experiences of being arrested and subjected to criminal trial function as **status degradation ceremonies** (Garfinkel 1956) and signal a

"Basically you're not bad, it's just that everybody expects you to be bad, and that makes you bad."

fundamental change in social status from that of normal citizen to deviant outsider. The label *deviant* or *criminal* can undermine a person's self-esteem and set off a cycle of reaction and counteraction that drives the deviantized person into further acts of nonconformity and eventually total separation from the group. The person is transformed from someone who occasionally did wrong things into a deviant or criminal person (Lemert 1951). Becker (1963) emphasizes how the experience of being treated as a degraded **outsider** can drive people to associate more extensively with other outsiders and begin to form a collective identity around a deviant subculture. Negative social reactions towards stigmatized people can thus function to promote rather than inhibit the development of deviant careers (Schur and Bedau 1974, 29).

The war on drugs in the United States may well be serving to aggravate all the problems associated with drugs by generating a process of **secondary deviance**. The prosecution and imprisonment of drug users turns them into social outcasts who are forced into closer and more exclusive association with each other. At the same time, drug prohibition promotes criminal mobsters who run the trade, and it forces up the cost of drugs, which further pushes users to turn to crime to get the money to buy them. Another sinister side effect of the so-called zero tolerance for drugs is the rampant spread of AIDS among drug users. The distribution of clean needles to addicts is a criminal offence.

In contrast, in the Netherlands prohibitionist drug laws are no longer enforced. The state offers help and treatment to people in trouble with drugs, rather than prosecuting them. Clean needles are liberally distributed to addicts. Cannibis, heroin, and cocaine are on sale openly, yet drug violence is minimal, and the use of hard drugs is declining (Ransom 1991). Drug mobsters do not operate in this controlled market.

Policing Practices and Deviantizing Work

In principle, policing work involves the apprehension of people who violate laws. But complex decision making and categorizing practices are entailed in recognizing how and when such violations have occurred. What constitutes public or private space for the purposes of sex, or what behaviour constitutes communicating or attempting to communicate for the purposes of prostitution, are by no means obvious. To understand what deviance means in practice, we need to study how the people who enforce the rules make decisions about what to react to and what to ignore. Studies of how police carry out patrol work suggest that they routinely react to situations in terms of practical notions of what seems to be "suspicious for this time and place" (Boughey 1978, 116; Bittner 1967; Sacks 1972) and a set of stereotypes about the kinds of people who constitute typical criminals. Even such ostensibly innocuous actions as standing on a street corner or sitting on a park bench, when performed by certain types of people at certain times of day, may be sufficient grounds for these people to be picked up and taken in for a police check. Young males from lower-class areas of town, particularly those from visible minority groups, are common targets for suspicion. Ontario police stop bikers and hippies for identity checks with far greater frequency than people who fit the conventional middle-class stereotype (Ericson 1982). Ericson suggests that the primary objective of such identity checks is not to catch criminals, but to assert control over marginal people. The majority of routine checks do not find anything, and officers do not appear to expect that they should. But when officers stop such people, make them get out of their vehicles, surrender their wallets, and submit to identity checks, they visibly display and achieve intimidation and submission to police powers. Marginalized people pay a high price for this control in terms of status degradation, and are especially vulnerable to the cycle of negative reactions and counteractions that promote a criminal self-definition. They are more likely to be criminalized, not because they necessarily commit more crimes than other people, but because they fit the criminal stereotypes that guide police in the apprehension of offenders. To the extent that they are more often stopped, searched, and checked, they stand a greater risk of being caught and charged with some offence.

In Canada, the position of a visible, criminalized marginal group has been filled overwhelmingly by Native peoples, and to a lesser extent, by blacks in the areas of Nova Scotia and Toronto where they are concentrated. The proportion of Native peoples who are in trouble with the law is six to ten times higher than their proportion in the population at large. Table 7-2 shows the overrepresentation of Native peoples in federal prisons.

Racism as social accomplishment is constituted through these circular processes in which such statistics produce the notion of a typical criminal, and this in turn guides police officers in the performance of policing. The attitudes of individual officers towards Natives or blacks, whether sympathetic or hostile, may have little bearing on how these policing practices work. The cycle of suspicion, anger, fear and hostility may be very hard to resist. Public inquiries into racism in the police force typically cite multiple instances of racist language and attitudes that poison the environment of prisons (Gittens and Cole 1994). Systemic racism is reflected in the routine racial segregation of prisoners among living units and the failure to address the distinctive needs of black and other racial minorities in the provision of prison services. As we noted in chapter 6, it took a protracted struggle by Native elders before Native spiritual ceremonies were permitted in Canadian prisons. Prisoners from minority groups who struggle for better services risk being viewed as overassertive or as "troublemakers."

Table 7-2

Overrepresentation of Native Peoples in Federal Prisons, June 1989*

Province	All Inmates	Native Inmates	Percent Native Inmates	Natives as Percentage of Total Population
Newfoundland	204	8	3.9	0.8
Prince Edward Island	39	1	2.6	0.5
Nova Scotia	551	10	1.8	0.9
New Brunswick	365	15	4.1	0.8
Quebec	3 888	29	0.7	1.3
Ontario	3 454	165	0.5	1.9
Manitoba	689	241	35.0	8.1
Saskatchewan	584	286	49.0	7.8
Alberta	1 462	359	24.6	4.4
British Columbia	1 840	260	14.1	4.4
Yukon	18	9	50.0	21.4
Northwest Territories	60	54	90.0	58.7
Outside Canada	48	2	4.1	–
Missing data	22	1	4.5	–
Total Canada	13 224	1 440	10.9	2.8

*There are no accurate figures available concerning the overrepresentation of Natives in provincial prisons because local prison officials do not collect data on the ethnic background of inmates. However, many informal surveys suggest that the rates are much higher. In Saskatchewan, for example, Natives are estimated to comprise fully 70 percent of inmates in provincial prisons. See LaPrairie (1984).

Source: Management Information Services, Correctional Services Canada. Population Profile Report and Native Population Profile Report. Population on Register 30/06/89, p. A002; Department of Indian Affairs customized census count 1986. Figures provided by Indian and Inuit Affairs Atlantic Region, 6 Oct. 1989.

"Making a Case"

Once a suspicious person has been apprehended, the next stage in the policing process entails making a case that will stand up in court and result in a conviction. Facts never speak for themselves. They have to be worked up. They must be linked together in a network of meaning through which the conclusion of "guilty" seems warranted. Police present the particulars of the case in a form that intends the conclusion that they have indeed apprehended the right person. The accused person, or lawyers acting for the defence, must respond to the particulars as presented by the prosecution and try to provide an alternative account for the observations (Smith 1990c, ch. 4). To the extent that judges and jurors share similar notions about typical criminals as do the police, members of stigmatized minorities may have greater than normal difficulty in sustaining an alternative account of their behaviour, and they may also be financially unable to hire an experienced lawyer.

Such routine courtroom practices of "making a case" resulted in the serious miscarriage of justice when Donald Marshall, a Micmac Indian, was wrongly convicted of murder and spent eleven years in prison before an alternative account of what happened could be successfully upheld. A public inquiry into the case in 1988 heard evidence that the police may have bullied witnesses into perjuring themselves in the original trial to secure the conviction. Subsequent evidence pointing to Marshall's innocence was covered up.

These case-making practices constitute routine aspects of courtroom work that cannot be understood simply as aberrant examples of racism. Very similar accounts of bullied testimony and failure to disclose subsequent evidence that cast doubt on the original conviction surfaced in 1992 with respect to David Milgaard's murder conviction. Investigators hired by his mother, Joyce Milgaard, eventually gained public support for an alternative account of the murder in which they argued that the web of reasoning pointing to Milgaard's guilt, could be seen as more strongly implicating another man as the murderer. Milgaard was freed on a pardon after serving more than twenty years of a life sentence. Individual police officers associated with each of these cases commented on the routineness of the procedures used, their own certainty that they had apprehended a guilty person, and the neces-

David Milgaard spent more than twenty years in prison after being convicted of a murder he did not commit.

sity of working up evidence to convince a jury. In 1994, Joyce Milgaard founded an organization of lawyers and other experts dedicated to the reinvestigation of cases for people serving life sentences for murders who claim evidence that points to their innocence.

"Not Making a Case"

The web of practical reasoning that sustains certain cases as credible, also works to constitute other cases as not credible, or unfounded. Feminist work has focussed attention on the difficulties involved at every stage of making the case for a sexual assault charge. A study of 116 rape cases reported to the Toronto police in 1970 revealed that the police rejected two-thirds as unfounded (Clark and Lewis 1977). The realistic fear that police would respond negatively also deters many victims from reporting sexual assaults. A victimization survey carried out in the early 1980s found that only 38 percent of incidents of sexual aggression were reported to the police, with 44 percent of victims expressing fear that police would respond negatively (Roberts 1990, 3–4). Amendments to the Criminal Code in 1983 were designed to address these problems, to encourage people to report aggression, and to increase the number of cases going to trial. Roberts reports that between 1982 and 1988 the number of reported sexual assault cases more than doubled and the proportions deemed unfounded averaged 15 percent over this period (1990, 9, 32). The unfounded rates varied widely by province, however, with a low of 7 percent in Quebec, 14 percent in neighbouring Ontario, and fully 29 percent in the Yukon. Roberts acknowledges that little is known about the attitudes of police officers to the new crimes of sexual assault, or the classification procedures employed by police officers that might explain regional variations. In their study of 1970 data, Clark and Lewis found that the probability of a case appearing "founded" depended heavily on who raised the complaint. All the professional women who reported being raped had their allegations treated as founded, but only half the students, and none of the women who were on welfare. Black and Native women were particularly likely to find their stories not treated as credible. Police also routinely advised women not to press charges if they were over seventeen, not a virgin, and on the pill. The reasoning was that jurors would not return a guilty verdict in such cases. Data from 1988 suggest that much has changed in the wake of the law reforms of 1983. By 1988, 85 percent of cases reported to the police went to trial, and 49 percent resulted in conviction (Roberts 1990, 6).

The probability that cases will result in conviction still seems to be strongly influenced by stereotyped notions about what rape is and who can be raped (Morris 1987, ch. 7). A study of six hundred Minnesota residents in 1980 revealed that more than half of these potential jurors held common-sense assumptions about rape that would lead them to dismiss most charges. They reasoned that any healthy woman can resist, that a rape victim is usually promiscuous, and it is usually her fault for letting things get out of hand, for leading him on or dressing in a seductive way, asking for it by being alone in an inappropriate place such as a pub, or trying to hitchhike (Morris 1987, 170). Morris cites a male gynaecologist as saying "there is one type of woman I would have a hard time believing has been raped; a woman between 16 and 25, on the

pill, and no longer a virgin" (ibid.). As an expert witness in a trial, or as a jury member, this man would dismiss out of hand the majority of cases he would encounter. Judges also take such reasoning into account in their sentencing judgments. In 1988, a Sault Ste Marie man who pleaded guilty to sexual assault was sentenced to thirty days in jail to be served on weekends. The judge reasoned that the man was from a good family and the woman had been drunk at the time and was hitchhiking (Stone 1993).

Feminists have long been struggling against such courtroom practices, striving to use both mass media and scholarly legal journals to promote an alternative web of reasoning. The hope is that feminist discourse will permeate back into the decision-making processes of jurors and experts in the criminal justice system. A major triumph for feminists was the Criminal Code amendment in 1983, known as the rape-shield law, that limited the right of defence council in sexual assault trials to grill women about past sexual behaviour. This amendment was struck down by the Supreme Court of Canada in 1991 as a violation of a person's right to a fair trial, but replaced in 1992 with new guidelines that limit such cross-examinations to exceptional cases. Since then, lawyers for the defence have begun to shift their focus to the woman's psychological history. Evidence of the woman having sought psychological counselling, especially if related to sexual abuse in childhood, can be used to imply that she may be emotionally confused and falsely projecting fantasies about abuse onto the defendant (*Globe and Mail*, 16 June 1994, A1–2).

The abuse of children is another contested area in which until recently it has been very difficult to make a case, particularly when the alleged perpetrators hold positions of trust in the community. In 1989, widespread media coverage was given to the alleged sexual abuse of boys in Newfoundland by Roman Catholic priests, former priests, and members of a Roman Catholic lay order of teachers in an orphanage (*Globe and Mail*, 19 April 1989; 26 April 1989). Records showed that reports of abuse at the orphanage surfaced in 1975, but they were apparently hushed up by the combined actions of the church elders, the police, and the Newfoundland Department of Justice and Social Services. A flood of similar allegations have followed, many dating back to the 1970s and earlier.

A major difficulty in cases involving children is how to establish their credibility as witnesses in court. Much skilled work is required to teach children how to testify, and how to translate their experiences into categories of legal discourse. The irony is that the very success of officers investigating such cases in opening up the discourse for children gives rise to the opposite problem that bizarre allegations of abuse may themselves be a product of the investigations. Children may be coaxed and prodded into telling stories that implicate the accused. Several cases alleging widespread sexual abuse of children in day-care centres have been dismissed when it became obvious that children were wildly embellishing whatever happened in response to repeated encouragement to tell more and more to the investigators. Certain overzealous investigations have been likened to the Salem witch trials in creating a form of group contagion fostering beliefs in ritual-satanic cult abuse of children that never really happened (*Globe and Mail*, 19 Feb. 1994, D1–3; 1 May 1993, D3). In Salem, Massachusetts, in 1692, twenty-seven people were convicted of practising witchcraft, largely on the basis of testimony from adolescents. Nineteen were hanged and four more died in prison. Another was stoned. Months later, when the mass hysteria died down, the convictions were revoked.

The work of judges involves sifting through such competing claims. The discourse of law claims for itself a special status as neutral arbiter of truth (Smart 1989, ch. 1). But we are only beginning the investigation of the common-sense reasoning and courtroom practices of judges, lawyers, and jurors involved in the social construction of verdicts.

The Limitations of Social Constructionist Analysis

Classic labelling theory, which was the basis for early social constructionist theory, has been most effective in the analysis of offences against morality, developing Durkheim's view of crime as natural, occurring wherever a given community draws the boundaries of shared beliefs and sentiments concerning acceptable behaviour. It draws attention to the arbitrary character of much that is defined as criminal. In particular, labelling theory has increased understanding of the negative psychological and social effects of **stigmatization**, and of its role in creating and reinforcing deviant careers.

The strength of this approach to criminology, however, has also been its weakness. It focusses too narrowly on crimes against morality. Concern with stigmatization makes sense in relation to what are essentially victimless crimes, but much crime is not of this form. Most behaviour that is labelled criminal clearly involves victims. Offenders know in advance that the behaviour will damage others and that they will face sanctions if caught. The critical question here is why certain people engage in such criminal behaviour. Their reaction to subsequent stigmatization as deviants or criminals is of secondary interest.

Other theorists fault the approach for not carrying the analysis further to explore the structures of power that underlie labelling processes. Critical Marxist theorists suggest that the problem populations that are targeted as deviants and controlled under capitalism are those whose position threatens the interests of capitalists in accumulating profits (Spitzer 1975, 642; Schur 1980, 77). The poor and economically marginalized people are criminalized to a far greater extent than the wealthy. The war on drugs in the United States is pre-eminently a war on young black males and Chicanos living in inner-city ghettoes. The labelling theory approach suggests that if drugs were legalized the problems associated with them would disappear. But legalization by itself does nothing to address the misery of the inner cities, or the poverty and despair on many Native reservations that drive people to use drugs. The sniffing of legally available substances like glue and gasoline have proven substitutes for narcotics among adolescents on some of the impoverished and isolated northern reservations where they have neither the money nor the contacts needed to purchase narcotics.

Critical feminist theory, on the other hand, focusses attention on patriarchal relations and the victimization of women through practices that are commonly not labelled as criminal offences.

The contemporary social constructionist approach to criminology is taking up these issues, conceptualizing the discourse of crime as the site of struggle between interest groups. Relations of power are embedded in the transformative practices through which control and management of crime is accomplished. This approach is having a powerful influence on both critical Marxist and feminist theory, which we explore now.

Crime and Patriarchy: The Feminist Critique of Criminology

Criminology is fundamentally sexist. This is the main conclusion of feminist theorists such as Leonard (1982) and Morris (1987) in their overview of contemporary literature. None of the major perspectives—functionalist, political economy, labelling theory—gives more than cursory attention to the issue of women and crime—either as perpetrators or victims. In explanations of criminal behaviour proposed by these perspectives, the standard criminal they have in mind is male.

The problem is that theories designed with reference to male offenders fail conspicuously when they are applied to women. Women do not display the same behaviour as men in comparable situations. The analytical weakness of criminology becomes particularly apparent when explanations given for higher crime rates among certain kinds of men are used to predict the opposite rates among women: lower-class men commit crimes because of their sense of powerlessness, their frustrated success goals, and their lack of legitimate opportunities; lower-class women do not commit crimes because they are powerless, learn to fear and abandon success goals, and lack legitimate opportunities to enter positions that facilitate criminal behaviour.

Most criminologists do not even notice the contradictions because they do not notice women. As Adelberg and Currie (1987a) express it, women are "too few to count" in criminology. They make up less than 10 percent of the prison population of Canada, and their offences tend to be less serious. Nonetheless, any theory that adequately explains male crime rates must necessarily explain the differences between male and female rates (see figure 7-1). This goal is a long way off.

Women and Crime in Functionalist Theory

The anomie theory of crime proposed by Merton stresses the gap between success goals and legitimate means, with crime rates predicted to be highest among people with least access to legiti-mate means to achieve culturally valued goals. The theory, however, does not provide a workable explanation for the markedly different crime rates for males and females. Women face multiple barriers to career success and are more likely than men to live in poverty, yet women as a whole are responsible for very little crime (Leonard 1982, 57–62). Greenberg offers a modified anomie theory to account for teenage gang behaviour as reflecting the thwarted aspirations and expectations of adolescents who are denied the power and privileges of adulthood. But if we concede that girls and young women experience similar frustrations and anxieties as do boys, then the critical question of differential crime rates by gender remains unanswered: Why do so many adolescent boys turn to gangs, violence, and sexual aggression when girls do not? The typical explanations offered within socialization theory are that girls are socialized to stay home more, are more closely supervised and chaperoned, and are more oriented toward families. This implies that if boys were more closely supervised and encouraged to focus on fathering rather than earning money, adolescent male problems would be resolved.

Another modification of anomie theory, proposed by Ruth Morris (1964), focusses specifically on women. Morris suggests that women generally experience less anomie than men because they have different success goals, being oriented more to relationships than to economic achievement. Success for women means getting married and having children. Since such goals are easy to achieve, the argument goes, women suffer less frustration and hence commit less crime. Morris argues further that the growing influence of the women's movement in recent years may encourage more women to aspire to economic success goals, and hence frustration levels and crime rates among women may rise.

Feminist theorists challenge Morris's arguments as unsubstantiated by evidence and as distorting reality for many women. Even if it were to be shown that women have primarily relational goals, it is by no means obvious that such goals are easily achieved. Children may grow up to be delinquents; marriages may be miserable. Conservative estimates of wife abuse in Canada suggest that 10 percent of women are beaten by their mates (Canada 1982). Between 30 and 40 percent of marriages end in divorce.

Figure 7-1

Percentage of All Offences Committed by Men and Women, 1985

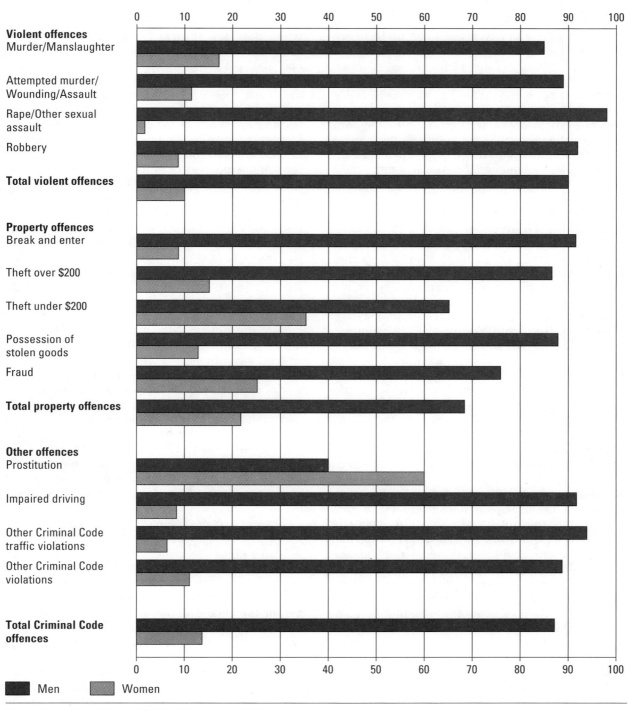

Source: Adapted from Johnson (1987); Statistics Canada (1986).

Morris's theory would predict high crime rates for women in these circumstances, but statistics do not bear this out (Morris 1987, 7; Leonard 1982, 57). Allison Morris (1987) further argues that, despite the fact that they are more likely than men to live in poverty, women do have economic success goals.

Related theories of differential association and deviant subculture that see criminal behaviour as learned through interaction similarly fail to account for the lower crime rates among girls compared with boys. Girls grow up in the same neighbourhoods, and often in the same families, yet commit fewer crimes than boys and are markedly less inclined to join youth gangs.

Women and Crime in Political Economy Theory

Criminology from the political economy perspective has also been faulted by feminists for lack of attention to the issue of women and crime. Women are almost totally ignored in major collections of writings on critical criminology (see Taylor, Walton, and Young 1975; Greenberg 1981a). It is assumed that theories that apply to men can be generalized to women, but the broad arguments of critical criminology fare little better than functionalist theory in accounting for gender differences in crime rates. The main theory that links crime to the material experience of economic injustice, poverty, and powerlessness implies that crime rates for women should equal or exceed crime rates for men. A related argument within Marxist theory is that the brutalizing and exploitative conditions of working life under capitalism are principally responsible for promoting anomie and antisocial behaviour. This suggests that women who work at home rather than in the paid labour force may be spared the most directly harmful effects of capitalism and so be less driven to crime. Leonard (1982, 170), however, rejects this notion, pointing to the dehumanizing experience of economic dependency, and the prevalence of wife abuse and child abuse in capitalist societies. The relative noncriminality of women cannot be accounted for by the absence of suffering or conflict in their lives.

Political economy theory also fails to account for the prevalence of crimes committed by men against women. The crime of rape, Leonard observes, cannot be romanticized as a form of struggle against the capitalist system. Class analysis does not explain women's oppression, which cuts across class lines.

Women tend to be unnoticed in analysis even when they are central figures in the criminal behaviour. Leyton (1986) uses concepts of anomie and alienation to develop a class analysis of the rising number of serial killers or multiple murderers in the United States. He argues that serial killers are mostly socially ambitious upper-working-class or lower-middle-class workers who feel excluded from the American dream of secure middle-class status. They wreak vengeance on the symbol and source of their exclusion, drawing their victims mostly from middle-class neighbourhoods, university students, aspiring models, and pedestrians in middle-class shopping malls. The questions that Leyton's analysis leave unanswered are why virtually all serial killers in the twentieth century are males and why the vast majority of their victims are females. Ted Bundy, for example, did not hunt humans in general. He hunted women, and especially women whose social status was higher than his own. Marc Lepine did not gun down *any* engineering students in Montreal in 1989. He gunned down women, screaming at them that they were feminists who had ruined his life. Leyton's theoretical model cannot account for why women do not get involved in serial killings. Neither does it explain why males should choose female victims. He does not ask why it might be that men with acute status anxiety should feel most threatened by women. If he had considered the question, it might have shifted his theoretical analysis toward a study of patriarchy and the women's movement.

Constructionist Theories of Women and Crime

Social constructionist and labelling theory perspectives in criminology come closer to accounting for the gender differential in crime rates. The official statistics that work against Native peoples work in favour of women. To the extent that police patrol work is oriented to practical notions about typical criminals, women in general are less likely than men to attract attention in random stop-and-search procedures, and so less likely to be caught and charged for minor offences. They are also less likely to get caught up in the cycle of stigmatization that promotes secondary deviance and a criminal self-image. The main exception to this generalization is women who conform to the police stereotype of a typical prostitute. They may be subject to continual surveillance and frequent arrest on suspicion of attempting to communicate for the purposes of prostitution.

Research into gender differences in how offences are categorized challenges the notion that girls and women somehow escape negative labelling, suggesting instead that they may be labelled as sick or mentally disturbed individuals, rather than criminal. The cycle of response to the mentally disturbed label is different from the criminal label and results in different overall outcomes for women and men. Morris (1987, 52–53) cites data that indicate that, while male criminals outnumber females by five to one, females labelled mentally ill outnumber men so labelled by three to one. An important reason behind this, Morris suggests, is that the typical standard of mental health is male. The model for a healthy adult is a healthy male. A healthy female is typified as excitable, submissive, emotional, and dependent. Such characteristics are the opposite of those attributed to healthy adults. Women tend to outnumber men mostly in the vague categories of mental illness such as "neurotic" and "depressed."

The tendency to label female offenders as sick or mentally disturbed rather than as criminal has a long history in criminology. Early theoretical speculation about the character of female offenders leaves little doubt that women were stereotyped in very negative ways (Smart 1977, 91). Caesar Lombroso (1895) opined, on the basis of interviews with prostitutes, that women were inherently evil and prone to crime. Their criminal potential was generally kept in check by their natural passivity, lack of intelligence, and especially by their "maternal instincts." Lack of maternal instinct in a woman was a sure sign of a criminal character. Otto Pollak (1950) similarly believed that women were naturally criminal, prone to lying, deceit, and trickery. Women instigated crimes and manipulated gullible males into enacting them. Women had lower crime rates only because of their success at concealment.

These early theories of covert criminal dispositions in women gave way to more explicitly biological explanations for female crime rates.

Female crime, it is argued, is linked to hormonal imbalances associated with menstruation, pregnancy, childbirth, and menopause (Cowie, Cowie, and Slater 1968; Smart 1977, 91). Morris concludes from a review of psychological studies that there is little reliable evidence to support the notion that premenstrual tension (PMS) is a significant factor in mood fluctuations; but she notes that courts are still receptive to arguments positing such tension as a mitigating factor in crimes of violence committed by women (Morris 1987, 46–51). The "illness" label, she suggests, functions as an alternative to a criminal label and implies a different kind of treatment. Females are far more likely to be remanded for psychiatric evaluation before sentencing than are men (Morris 1987, 53).

The tendency to conceptualize female offenders as sick or mentally disturbed rather than criminal does not necessarily result in greater leniency toward them. Females may actually be subject to more stringent controls. Smart (1977, 96–98) found that **double standards** regarding appropriate sex-role behaviour frequently result in girls being punished for behaviour that is not considered deviant for boys. For example, girls who display promiscuous behaviour are considered to be in need of treatment and control; boys displaying similar behaviour are considered to be normal. Girls are also more likely to be punished for being "incorrigible" or "out of control" than boys. In Canada, under the Juvenile Delinquents Act, which was in force from 1908 to 1984, adolescents could be brought to court for numerous offences that were not crimes for adults, including truancy from school, running away from home, sexual immorality, and incorrigibility—a catch-all category for juveniles considered unmanageable or very badly behaved. Girls were far more likely to be charged with such offences than boys, and sent to training schools (Geller 1987, 114–17).

The Young Offenders Act, which came into force in 1984, promised to change such practices. Under the new Act, young people can only be charged with offences for which adults can be charged. But Geller suggests that female adolescents are still being controlled indirectly. They are more likely than boys to be charged with a trivial criminal offence, enabling authorities to gain power over them and to deal with other problem behaviour such as promiscuity and running away from home. Child welfare, drug and alcohol, and mental health legislation are also being used to punish girls who are considered unmanageable (Geller 1987, 119–23), or who are promiscuous (Leschied and Jaffe 1991). Most provinces enacted legislation outside the Young Offenders Act to enable youth court to prosecute status offences such as truancy (Markwart and Corrado 1989, 256). Bell's study (1994) of sentencing practices in an Ontario family court during 1986–87 suggests that a quarter of the cases concerned status offenders, essentially young people designated out of control.

Smart argues that belief in chivalry and leniency acts as an ideology that conceals stereotypes about women and real injustice meted out under the guise of humanitarianism. Behind the notion of chivalry is the unequal distribution of power between the sexes. A woman should depend on a man for her protection and should be deserving of such protection. Women who are labelled as having bad moral character are open to the full force of outraged male morality. Women from visible minority groups are particularly likely to be targets for harsh treatment (Leonard 1982, 86). Smart concludes that the theoretical analysis of female criminality in terms of individual pathology, hormonal imbalance, and mental illness, carries an inherently political message. Such analysis locates the causes of the problem within the individual and the solution in technical controls and psychiatric treatment programs, rather than in the social emancipation of women.

A Feminist Reorientation of Criminology

The feminist critique of traditional criminology goes beyond the demand that more attention be paid to female offenders, to challenge the conceptualization of the discourse of criminology itself as sexist. Critical Marxist theory pressured for a redefinition of crime in terms of social harm, incorporating much that is considered legitimate business practice. Feminist theory pressures for the incorporation of harm inflicted on women in a patriarchal social order, that until recently has not been recognized as criminal.

When criminologists study crime, particularly crimes of violence against individuals, what they typically have in mind is street crime. This is the kind of crime in which people are victimized by strangers in public places. Surveys designed to

measure the incidence of crime and fear of crime within a population use questions concerning how safe people feel on the street, or after dark, or when they are alone in their neighbourhood (Stanko 1988, 76–79). Typical victims of such crimes are males who are under thirty years of age, who tend to go out several nights a week, who drink heavily, and assault others (Morris 1987, 161). Women tend to have more fear of crime than men but appear less likely to be victims.

Stanko criticizes such research as inherently sexist because it ignores private violence, and in so doing, it ignores much of the reality of women's experience of violence. Women are far more likely to be victimized at home, in private, than on the streets. They are most likely to be attacked by a member of their own family, or someone they know, someone who has access to them in their homes. The fear generated by being attacked within this supposedly safe place and by someone familial and familiar is worse than fear of attack by strangers, because the victims have literally no safe place to go.

Interpersonal violence against women involves battery and sexual assault by partners and intimate companions. Historically, wife beating was approved by the church and the state in Britain and North America. Until the end of the nineteenth century, a husband could beat his wife for her own spiritual and moral betterment, provided the stick he used were no bigger in width than his thumb. In Canada, before changes in the sexual assault legislation in 1983, it was legally impossible for a wife to be raped by her husband. Most sexual violence is still not considered a crime unless the resulting injuries are so severe that the victim requires hospitalization. Even then the batterer is not automatically charged with a criminal offence.

A crucial mechanism inhibiting the recognition of sexual and domestic violence as crime was the lack of names to apply to such acts. Terms like *battered women* and *sexual harassment*, for example, did not exist before the 1960s. As a result, these experiences remained amorphous and unnamed, felt but not seen for what they were, and women were silenced. It took the full force of the women's movement during the 1960s and 1970s to have these assaults labelled as crimes and to begin to protect the victim herself from being blamed. The true extent of domestic violence is unknown. Official statistics do not exist in Canada because it is not a reportable offence. Doctors, social workers, or others who may know or suspect that wife battery has occurred, are not under any legal obligation to report such occurrences to the police. The evidence we do have is of many thousands of women seeking shelter in transition houses all across Canada. In Ontario alone, in 1981, over 30 000 women sought help from transition houses. Only a tiny minority of all such violence ever results in criminal charges. There is some evidence that police in Canada respond to only about half the domestic disturbance calls they receive (Canada 1982, 10), and then they are trained to calm the situation down and leave, rather than to press assault charges. Morris suggests that police typically see such cases as nuisance calls or "rubbish work" that interferes with their "real work" of controlling crime (Morris 1987, 185). This pattern may be changing with the recruitment of more women as police officers. They are widely acknowledged to be more adept at handling situations of domestic violence than male officers.

The crime of rape, or sexual assault as it is now called, is an offence under the Criminal Code, but as we have seen above, powerful nonlabelling mechanisms intervene to inhibit most instances of forced sex from being recognized and labelled as criminal assault. When charges were laid, it was typically the woman's character rather than the alleged male offender that was on trial. If she could be discredited as sexually promiscuous or as having led him on, then he was presumed innocent. Feminist lawyers and activists succeeded in lobbying for changes in legislation that would shift the focus onto assault rather than sex. Legislation passed in Canada in 1983 redefined the crime of rape to "sexual assault." The new law also removed the legal exemption against a victim's husband being charged with rape, and also incorporated sexual assaults against males (DeKeseredy and Hinch 1991, 62–65). The law also precluded questions about prior sexual activity of the woman, "unless the judge determined that the exclusion of such evidence would prevent a just determination of the case" (Boyle and Rowley 1987, 319–20). However, since the most common grounds for defence in a sexual assault trial is that the accused believed the woman consented because she had consented on previous occasions or with other men, lawyers commonly did ask for prior sexual behaviour to be admissable, and most of the time such requests were granted (Morris 1987, 171). In 1991, the Supreme Court struck down the legislation as a violation of the man's right to a fair trial. Radical feminists interpret this reversal as yet one more instance of the state supporting patriarchy. The struggle continues around the formulation of new legislation that will be consistent with the Charter of Rights and Freedoms and the guarantee of a fair trial, but requiring some positive evidence of having received consent to sexual advances, rather than evidence of past sexual practices of the woman to infer consent.

The Limitations of Feminist Theory

In her overview of the state of criminology in 1987, Morris concludes that there is as yet no feminist theory of crime (1987, 15). Her ideal is to develop a criminology that avoids the sexism of conventional wisdom, that makes women visible, and that acknowledges the fear of oppression that women feel. The ultimate goal of a feminist criminology is not to generate a separate theory that applies only to women, or to have a "criminology of women" chapter in standard textbooks. The goal is rather to develop an integrated body of theory that can explain both male and female experience of crime, and the connections between them. That ideal is still a long way from being achieved. But the discourses of criminology have nonetheless been radically influenced by feminist theory. Definitions of crime have shifted to incorporate domestic violence. Feminist views on sexual assault legislation are part of the media discourses. Stone's research on the Toronto press (1993) suggests that while feminist views were generally absent from press coverage of violence against women, there were also openings where feminists could achieve a significant amount of access to the press to express their views on the issue. The presence of feminists in law, criminology, sociology, and journalism, generates the contradictions that create opportunities for alternative views to find expression.

Conclusion

Contemporary studies of the breakdown of social order still owe much to Durkheim's original analysis of social cohesion in industrial society. Durkheim insists that justice, based on respect for individual human rights, constitutes the essential moral foundation of social order in societies based on the interdependence and mutual obligations of specialists. This concept of justice must transcend racial, ethnic, and occupational diversity if it is to hold complex societies together in relative harmony. Failure to establish a regulative order that members perceive to be just results in anomie. That anomie is reflected in suicide, conflict, and crime.

The prevalence of industrial conflict in contemporary Canada suggests that this sense of justice is still far from being realized. The central Marxist critique of Durkheim's work is that he gives inadequate attention to the structure of capitalism. Marxists argue that this structure precludes the possibility of social justice. They point to the law as a central arena of class struggle in which the outcome is heavily biased in favour of capitalists.

Feminist theory is also forcing a reappraisal of justice in labour relations in terms of inequalities associated with gender. In Durkheim's analysis, gendered division of labour is accepted as natural and therefore compatible with principles of justice. But such assumptions of natural order are now being questioned. The contemporary struggle in the arena of labour law focusses on affirmative action for gender equality as well as for distributive justice along the lines of class, race and ethnicity, and sexual orientation. More recently, activists have recognized the importance of incorporating the demands of handicapped people. These struggles are complicated by the fact that the terms of the debate are not consistently defined. For feminists, justice requires affirmative action to redress systematic inequality. Meanwhile, their opponents see affir-

mative action as institutionalized discrimination on the basis of sex, and therefore as unjust.

High crime rates in Canada suggest that anomie is prevalent in many other spheres of social life. The functionalist theory of anomie regards crime as the expression of frustration felt by disprivileged groups in society who lack legitimate means to attain socially approved goals. Marxist theory, by and large, views criminals as victims of an intrinsically unjust and inegalitarian capitalist economic system. But it also calls into question the ways in which crime itself is defined and measured. If crime is defined in terms of such acts as vandalism, theft, and property damage, the disprivileged swell the ranks of criminals. But if the definition of crime is broadened to include acts that result in social harm, then the majority of criminals may well turn out to be members of the business elite and agents of the state itself. In effect, the definition of crime determines the distribution of criminals. Within capitalist society, the elite class have disproportionate power to impose such definitions.

Social constructionist theory focusses on the discourse of criminology. It explores the processes through which deviant and criminal labels are applied to actions and the effects such labelling has on the victims. Contemporary research goes beyond the naming of behaviour to question how professionals at all levels of the criminal justice system, in their routine everyday activities, decide that certain behaviour by certain kinds of people fits the category to which criminal labels apply. Disproportionate arrest of members of visible minority groups is arguably as much a reflection of police prejudices as it is of actual variations in criminal activity.

Feminist theory challenges the entire field of criminology for systematic gender bias that undermines the scientific credibility of the field. None of the major explanations for crime proposed by anomie theory, Marxism, or labelling theory adequately accounts for differences in crime rates between women and men. Criminology is also blinkered in virtually dismissing the major problem of domestic violence, especially violence against women, from its concern. The contemporary areas of debate and struggle in criminology thus centre around such fundamental questions as the definition of crime itself and where or if the boundaries should be drawn around the subject matter of criminology.

Suggested Reading

The study of Robert Blauner, *Alienation and Freedom: The Factory Worker and His Industry* (1964), is a classic in the field of sociology of work. In the introductory chapters he develops a research model based on a combination of the Marxist concept of alienation and the Durkheimian concept of anomie. He then systematically applies this model to four kinds of industrial work. He concludes by relating patterns of technology to the relative experience of alienation and anomie.

Alvin Gouldner's study *Wildcat Strikes* (1965) explores the frustrations that lay behind a series of strikes in a mine. He warns against the simplistic assumption that formal issues raised in a strike, commonly demands for more money, are necessarily at the root of the strike. A Marxist perspective on labour unrest is provided by Leo Panitch and David Swartz in *The Assault on Trade Union Freedoms* (1988). They argue that the state has systematically broken the power of unions in Canada by repressive legislation.

Rosemary Warskett's article "Bank Worker Unionization and the Law" (1988) explores the contradictory role of labour legislation for unions. In part, the laws protect union rights, but they also constrain and rigidify union actions and remove the locus of class struggle from the workplace to the courts.

Eileen Leonard's *Women, Crime, and Society: A Critique of Theoretical Criminology* (1982) provides a comprehensive and critical overview of criminology theory. She develops a perceptive critique of the entire range of current theories and shows that they cannot account for the marked difference in crime rates between men and women.

A classic presentation of the functionalist perspective on crime is by Robert Merton in chapters 6 and 7 of *Social Theory and Social Structure* (1968). Merton develops a model of types of deviance based on the gap between socially desired goals and socially approved means to achieve them. Also in the functionalist tradition is the work of Mike Brake, *The Sociology of Youth Culture and Youth Subcultures: Sex and Drugs and Rock 'n' Roll?* (1980). Brake describes the deviant subcultural values that integrate different youth gangs from working-class and middle-class backgrounds. His data are drawn mostly from Britain.

The Marxist perspective on crime is well presented by David Greenberg, ed., *Crime and Capitalism: Readings in Marxist Criminology* (1981a). The introduction is particularly useful in giving a critical overview of the approach. Eighteen short articles by different authors provide a valuable overview of the criminal justice system. A particularly useful article on adolescent delinquency and gangs is by Greenberg, "Delinquency and the Age Structure of Society." The short book by Ian Taylor, *Crime, Capitalism, and Community: Three Essays in Socialist Criminology* (1983), also provides a valuable introduction to the Marxist approach to crime.

An excellent overview of labelling theory is provided by Edwin Schur in *The Politics of Deviance: Stigma Contests and the Uses of Power* (1980). Schur acknowledges the criticisms of earlier formulations of labelling theory but argues persuasively that this approach is valuable, particularly for understanding crime where there is no clear victim and no clear threat to the interests of the capitalist class.

Two useful studies of policing practices in Canada are R.V. Ericson, *Reproducing Order: A Study of Police Patrol Work* (1982) and John Sewell, *Police: Urban Policing in Canada* (1985). Both books describe what police officers do in the routine performance of their jobs and how the labelling processes work in terms of who is singled out for police checks. For a study of racism in the criminal justice system see Michael Harris, *Justice Denied: The Law Versus Donald Marshall* (1986).

An excellent resource book on women and crime is E. Adelberg and C. Currie, eds., *Too Few To Count: Canadian Women in Conflict with the Law* (1987b). The chapter by Holly Johnson provides valuable statistical data on changing crime rates and on women in Canada convicted of various crimes. Other articles present case studies of the lives of women in trouble with the law and relate their experiences to patriarchal social institutions. A critical essay showing how criminology theory systematically ignores violent crimes against women is Elizabeth Stanko, "Fear of Crime and the Myth of the Safe Home: A Feminist Critique of Criminology" (1988).

Questions

1. What is the basic assumption of Sutherland's theory of differential association? Why does Leonard find it weak?

2. What two factors are central to Merton's anomie theory of crime? How does Greenberg apply this to adolescent gangs? List two applications.

3. How has anomie theory been used to account for the lower crime rates among women compared with men? How is the same theory used to account for rising crime rates among women?

4. Why is armaments production predicted to expand in poorer regions of North America now that the Free Trade Deal is in effect? How does this influence the application of anomie theory?

5. What is the definition of *crime*:
   a) according to Durkheim?
   b) according to Quinney?

6. How can the discipline of criminology be seen as ideology?

7. How does E.P. Thompson modify Quinney's simplistic view of law as established in the interests of the propertied classes, while still accepting Marxist theory?

8. Define *victimless crime*. List three kinds of supposedly victimless crimes.

9. What is entailed in the social constructionist study of deviance? How does this relate to crime rates?

10. List two possible processes by which females may commit as many crimes as men, but have much lower crime rates?

IV

Political Economy: Challenging Capitalism

CHAPTER

8

Karl Marx and the Analysis of Capitalism

Karl Marx (1818–1883) was a profound thinker whose work has had a phenomenal impact upon the twentieth century. His most famous treatise, the three-volume *Capital*, stands as a monumental study of Western industrial society. It is difficult to overstate Marx's importance. It is also very difficult to condense his prolific writings into one short chapter. Much controversy surrounds the interpretation of his ideas: some theorists see an important break between his early philosophical and later economic works, while others stress the underlying continuity. Some see him as an **economic determinist**, others as the forerunner of the mode of analysis concerned with the **social construction of reality**. Analysis is made more difficult by the fact that Marx died before the last volume of *Capital*, particularly his section on class analysis, was complete. Much of this work was pulled together by his colleagues from his notes.

In 1844, Marx announced his intention to publish a critique of politics and political economy, dealing with the interconnection between political economy and the state, law, ethics, and civil life (Sayer 1985, 222–23). This vision was never completed, leaving *Capital* as his major work. Also, many of his early manuscripts were not published until the late 1920s and 1930s. The result, Sayer suggests, is that prevailing interpretations of Marx's writings may have given too much emphasis to the study of economic relations in *Capital*, in isolation from his broader critique of society.

Marxist thought also stirs up often intense political feelings for or against the communist world society that Marx advocated and predicted would come to pass with the collapse of capitalism. Such feelings tend to cloud the assessment of his work itself. It is not possible, therefore, to give a definitive summary statement of Marx's work. The presentation here is very much an introduction to his ideas. It is also slanted toward sociological theory. Economists and political scientists would place their emphasis differently.

Karl Marx (1818–1883).

Historical Materialism

Historical materialism is a theory of history in which the material conditions of life are seen as ultimately determining the course of human history. For Marx, the most fundamental aspect of human existence is the absolute necessity for people to produce the means for their own subsistence. In order to survive, people must produce food and process it to the point where it is edible. In all but the rarest conditions of an ideal climate, people need to produce clothing and shelter and heat for warmth and for cooking. They also need to produce the tools or technology required for such processes. Even the simplest hunting and gathering economies use surprisingly complex implements. People also organize themselves in complex ways to hunt and gather, to process and preserve food, to build shelters, and so on. As the means of providing for material needs become more complex—in herding economies, settled agriculture, trade and industry—so the ways in which people organize themselves around these activities change in both form and complexity.

Marx reasoned that the processes by which people meet their basic subsistence needs constitute the foundation of social organization. Any system of production entails a definite pattern of relations between people. Human production is by nature social. From simple economies to the most technologically complex industrial production, work is a co-operative activity. The way in which people co-operate varies with different modes of production, and this affects all other aspects of social life. **Relations of production** directly influence the prevailing family forms, political structures, religious ideas, and modes of thought. People experience social life as it is organized through relations of production. As they reflect on this experience, they generate the patterns of thought and ideas that come to prevail. For Marx, and theorists inspired by him, it makes sense to begin the analysis of economic and social life with the study of the prevailing mode of production and relations of production associated with it. All other aspects of social life can be understood as reflecting and responding to this underlying form of economic organization.

Modes of Production and Class Relations

Marx briefly traces historical changes in **modes of production**, or ways in which societies transform their material environment to meet subsistence needs. The simplest form is **primitive communism**, with production confined to hunting and gathering. Simple hand tools such as weapons, bowls, and digging sticks are easily made and shared. The key means of production—the flora and fauna in the surrounding territory—are accessible to all. No one has ownership rights to the terrain or its resources.

The second stage is ancient society or **slavery**, which already assumes a higher level of productivity within the society as a whole. There is sufficient surplus production that one class of people, the slave-owners, are supported by the labour of others without producing anything themselves. Slavery is associated with warfare: warring communities capture people from other societies and use them for drudgery and heavy manual labour.

The third stage, **feudalism**, is associated with settled agriculture. Here the predominant means of production are land and the draught animals, machinery, tools, seeds, and so on, required to work it. But this land is not shared equally as under primitive communism. An important division of labour emerges in which a certain stratum of people perform most of the work of cultivating the land while another stratum oversees and controls the land and extracts the surplus produced. The two great strata or classes under feudalism are serfs and nobles. The **serfs**, the people who actually work the land, inherit their position as labourers who are tied to the particular estate on which they are born. They are not free to leave or to work land elsewhere. A hereditary class of **nobles** exercise control over the estates, commonly held in trust under a superior military ruler or king. They extract surplus production from serfs in return for protecting them, maintaining law and order, and providing them with whatever is necessary to cultivate the land. Only land that is too poor to bear the double burden of labourers and landlord is likely to remain in the hands of small **peasant** producers.

Within the feudal mode of production no meaningful distinctions can be drawn between economy and polity or civil society. A person's economic, political, and community statuses—as serf, noble, vassal, or whatever, all coincide. The notion of property or ownership with respect to land also has no meaning. A multiplicity of obligations tie people and land together all the way up through the feudal hierarchy. No one has exclusive proprietary rights. The serfs or tenants who plough the land and gather the crops, their immediate lord to whom they pay dues, and the lord of the lords, can all claim that a particular plot is in a sense "my field." These rights also extend horizontally to the whole village community, without whose consent land cannot be leased or given away (Sayer 1985, 227).

Within feudalism the majority of people have direct access to the means of producing for their own subsistence needs. Serfs work plots of land and keep animals for themselves. But they are also required to work on the estates of the nobility. The extent of their exploitation is obvious, measured by the days on which they labour for the lord and the amount of produce that the lord appropriates.

Marx saw the transition from feudalism to **capitalism**, the fourth mode of production, as the most profoundly important change in the history of society. The emergence of private property, specifically the privatization of means of production, brought about the breakup of the unity of feudal social order. The separation of economic and political spheres of activity, the emergence of

a *civil society* of isolated individuals, and the separation of the state as the sphere of public activity, were all interrelated aspects of the same process. Capitalism brought about the most extreme forms of alienation and exploitation, and at the same time mystified or disguised them beneath the institutions of property and wages.

The term *capitalism* refers to an economic system based on private ownership of **capital**, or the means of production, in the hands of a limited number of people. Capital comprises the funds and the stock of land, machinery, and materials used in production, together with the accumulated wealth that is invested to produce more capital.

The transition from feudalism to capitalism is a process that involves significant changes in people's relationship to land. Land becomes defined as the exclusive, private property of the former landlords. Estates are fenced off and used to produce cash crops such as wheat and wool for sale, with all the benefits going to the new landowners, rather than to meet the subsistence needs of the local community. Former serfs lose their hereditary rights to live and work on the land. In one sense they are "freed" from the shackles of feudal obligations that tied them to the land of their fathers, but by the same token they lose all their former rights and control over what the community produces. The families of serfs who had supported themselves for generations on the land are forcibly pushed off, losing all direct access to the means of producing their own subsistence. They are left with nothing but their capacity to work, their labour power. They can survive only by selling their labour power for wages to whomever will hire them, and by using the money they earn to purchase what they need. The two great classes that emerge within capitalism comprise those who own the means of production and those who do not. As we say in chapter 2, people who sell their labour power are collectively referred to as the *proletariat* or working class, while those who own the means of production and purchase the labour power of others are referred to as the *bourgeoisie* or capitalists.

The concept of **class** has a historically specific meaning in the context of capitalism, referring to a person's status in purely economic terms. Under feudalism, there is no distinction between economic and political status. But in capitalism production is privatized. Strictly "economic" activities become independent of any community control. They begin to appear as a world apart, subject to the "laws of the market." The notion of labour also takes on a historical special meaning as *labour power*, involving the separation of one's capacity to work from the means to use it in production, and hence the necessity of selling that labour power to others for wages. As means of production become separated from community ties and obligations, so people become individualized. It becomes possible to think in terms of the eighteenth-century notion of autonomous subjects or isolated individuals who enter into social contracts with each other. The modern notion of the state also gradually emerges as the arena of general, public concerns, with individuals as citizens of the polity with legal rights (Sayer 1985, 223). This shifting of community interests to the separate sphere of the *polity* and the state is the practical expression of the depoliticization of the community. Concepts such as *class*, *individual*, *economy*, *polity*, *state*, *civil society*, *contracts*, are thus all very modern ideas that only make sense when the unity of the feudal order has been shattered.

This privatization of means of production, its freeing from former political and social obligations so that it can appear as the exclusive possession of individuals, was a very complex process that stretched over centuries. In England, on the eve of the **Industrial Revolution**, the **enclosure** movement spread as landlords claimed the right to fence off huge tracts of land for sheep pastures to produce wool for sale. Some of the former serfs were able to get work as wage-labourers on big farms, tending the cereal crops and the sheep. The rest found themselves destitute. They had no choice but to migrate to the cities and compete with each other for whatever jobs they could get, often working under wretched conditions in the factories that were slowly opening up. Over time, industrial technology and factories became the dominant means of production, with land becoming steadily less important. Marx saw the separation of town and country as a particularly significant division of mental and manual labour, marking the separation of capital and landed property (Sayer 1985, 230). The factories and the industrial technology, like the land, were privately owned by a relatively small class of wealthy people. The mass of people who own neither land nor other capital have to sell their labour power to the owners of factories.

Marx foresaw a fifth mode of production, which he called **advanced communism**, where all the important means of production in a society—farmland, factories, technology, and so on—would be communally controlled. Capitalism emancipated individuals from the servitude of feudalism but also led to their inability to control the productive relations that their activities create. **Communism**, as envisioned by Marx, is a mode of production that has the potential to overcome this alienation. Much more is involved than merely an equitable redistribution of wealth, or a changing of title deeds on property. The goal is to create the conditions within which people can directly control the processes of production and the social relations they entail, so that, ideally, all can develop their individual capacities to the full and mutual benefit of the collective enterprise. When all have access to the means of production, class differences will disappear. Also, when a community of people directly controls the productive forces that their activities create, economic and political activities will no longer be differentiated and a separate state as arbiter of public good would be redundant. Hence, in the sense in which these terms are understood within capitalist society, advanced communism would be both classless and stateless (Sayer 1985, 245–50).

Marx believed that this mode of organizing production would take advantage of all the benefits of technological advances made under capitalism without the devastating costs of inequality, exploitation, and alienation that capitalism entails. But we are getting ahead of ourselves. We need to go back and explore what is so important and distinctive about capitalism as a mode of production, and why it seems in Marxist analysis to be both the key to progress and, at the same time, an inherently destructive system.

Capitalism and Technological Progress

Capitalism, more than any other mode of production, is associated with an ever-accelerating pace of technological change. It is uniquely geared toward the continual reinvestment of profits in innovative technology to enhance labour productivity. All types of economies are oriented toward generating surpluses to make life easier or more comfortable for people. Only under capitalism is there a never-ending compulsion to invest the surplus or profit in accumulating productive forces, rather than to consume it in luxuries or leisure. It is this compulsion to invest, to accumulate capital, and to increase labour productivity that is the engine of economic development. But from where does this compulsion come? To answer this question, we draw upon the work of the contemporary Marxist, Robert Brenner (1977), who elaborates the unique relationship between capitalism and modernization.

Capitalism requires the constant reinvestment of profits in technology in order to increase productivity.

Brenner begins with a critical look at Adam Smith's famous treatise, *The Wealth of Nations* ([1776] 1894). For Smith, the expansion of trade relations promotes division of labour, specialization, and rising productivity. Increasing food demands of large manufacturing centres stimulate rural production, which in turn induces the expansion of manufacturing to supply the countryside. These processes of self-sustaining growth are fuelled by the central values of capitalism: rational individuals in free competition in the marketplace, each striving to maximize profits.

The problem with this theory, suggests Brenner, is not that Adam Smith was wrong, but that he assumed too much. The core values of competition and profit maximization in the market presuppose structural conditions that Smith ignores. The principal condition is that producers are separated from the means of production; that is, from the ability to produce their own subsis-

tence. Labour becomes a commodity that can be freely bought and sold. Subsistence has to be bought in the market. The means of production themselves, such as land and later factories and machines, have to be bought or rented in the market, for they are also commodities. It is only under these conditions—conditions specific to the capitalist mode of production—that people must trade in order to survive. Only then do money and transactions in the market become important. Concerns with competition and profit maximization follow from this. Brenner stresses that the use of money to buy commodities to make more money does not exist under other modes of production, such as slavery, feudalism, or small peasant landholdings.

In feudal economies, the direct producers are still tied to the land. On their own plots they produce crops that have use value for their own subsistence. The landlords can also provide their own means of subsistence through their command of the land and the labourers who work it for them. They market only what is left over after their own needs or wants are filled. The critical difference from capitalism is that neither serf nor lord depends upon markets for survival, and hence at a fundamental level it does not matter whether they beat the competition or maximize profits. There is no immediate pressure to innovate or to increase the productivity of labour.

Under this system, exploitation takes the form of squeezing serfs to extract more **absolute surplus**. In other words, the absolute amount that a particular labourer can produce in a particular period of time remains roughly constant, but more of what is produced is taken for sale in the market. This can be done by cutting the subsistence standards of the workers to have more left over for the market or by cutting the workers' leisure time to extend the length of the working day.

Under both slavery and feudalism, the direct producers themselves have no interest in the productive process. Slaves are maintained by the master; it is not in their interest to produce more for the owner to market. Serfs have their own plots for subsistence; it does not matter to them how much or how little landlords can sell. Under these conditions, when trade expands, it may result only in more intensive squeezing to extract more surplus. The long-term result may actually be a decline in production as serfs lack time to tend their own plots, and soils are exhausted.

Small peasant farmers who own their land are similarly independent of the market. Since they can produce their own means of subsistence, the pressures of competition and profit maximization are largely irrelevant. It is in their own interest to produce a variety of crops and animals to enhance their own subsistence standards of living. They may sell surplus produce in the market to buy luxuries, but they are not dependent upon the market.

Brenner argues that, in order to establish capitalism, it is necessary to break the ability of producers to produce their own means of subsistence. They must be separated from land, so that they have to rent it for cash or buy it in the real estate market. Then they must earn money in the market to survive. Once farmers must pay rent or mortgages, Brenner argues, they must be concerned with competition in the market and with profit maximization. They have to make the average rate of profit on what they produce, because otherwise they will be unable to pay the going rents and will be thrown off the land. Hence, they have to increase their labour productivity to keep up with competitors, which forces them to be concerned with technological innovations.

Large landowners, cultivating their lands with the aid of wage-labourers or rent-paying tenants, must also be concerned with labour productivity. They cannot squeeze the workers indefinitely to extract a greater absolute surplus for themselves, because the workers will go elsewhere. They must focus on **relative surplus**; that is, upon increasing the productivity of workers through **labour-saving technology**. If they do not, they will be unable to pay the going wage rate, and workers will leave. It is actually in the interest of the landowners to invest in their lands so that the tenants or labourers can produce more and pay higher rents.

Brenner concludes that both labour power and means of production must become commodities in the market for market forces to have the impact upon people that they do under capitalism. The ideology of market forces and profit maximization taken for granted by Adam Smith is the *effect* of this capitalist mode of production and not the *cause* of it. Capitalism presupposes some form of class struggle that forcibly separates producers from means of production. The history of capitalism has been, in this sense, the history of class struggle, taking various forms in different times and regions.

Capitalism in Canada

In Canada, the emergence of capitalism and the class struggles associated with it took a very different form than in Europe. As we have seen, capitalism presupposes a large class of people who have no direct access to any means of production and who are thus forced to sell their labour power. But such a class of people did not exist in Canada before the 1850s. It took active government policies and a peculiarly Canadian version of the class struggle to produce it.

Indigenous peoples in Canada practised a hunting and gathering mode of production, supplemented by horticulture and trade, including the fur trade with Europeans. They could support themselves and had little interest in becoming permanent wage-labourers. They had to be forcibly driven from the land by settlers, the buffalo exterminated, and traditional northern hunting grounds disrupted by mining, exploration, and lumber companies, before they would begin to turn to wage-labour for their livelihood.

Attracting immigrants to Canada was not difficult. Masses of displaced and landless people were produced by the enclosure movement and the capitalization of agriculture in Europe, as land belonging to the great estates was fenced off for keeping sheep or growing cereal crops, and the serfs were driven off. These landless people were willing, and indeed desperate, to seek a new life in North America. During the first half of the 1800s, tens of thousands of immigrants came to Canada every year from Ireland alone, fleeing the appalling conditions of enclosures, economic collapse, and famine generated by economic domination from England (Pentland 1959, 459). They joined the multitudes of immigrants leaving similarly wretched conditions throughout Europe. Mass immigration from China and other parts of Asia began toward the end of the nineteenth century. Few European immigrants had any intention of remaining wage-labourers if they had any choice. What they found in Canada was a vast and sparsely populated land. So long as free or cheap land was available, the majority of immigrants preferred to acquire land and to work for themselves rather than for employers.

The problem, from the perspective of members of the business class, eager to develop capitalism in Canada, was how to staunch this outflow from the labour pool (Pentland 1959, 458–59). This was at the root of deliberate policies to make land so expensive that immigrants would be forced to labour for many years to earn even a down payment for a farm. Policies included monopolization of land for speculative purposes all across Canada and grants of huge tracts to absentee proprietors (Teeple 1972, 46). In one day in 1767, for example, the whole of Prince Edward Island was granted to a few dozen absentee landlords. Between 1760 and 1773, Nova Scotia had a population of about 13 000, but 5.4 million acres of the best land were given in grants to individuals and companies based in Britain and the United States. Similar policies were followed in central Canada, sparking riots against land monopolies in 1794 and 1796. On the Prairies there were vast tracts of virgin land, and the Homestead Act granted 160 acres per settler. Yet even here the enormity of land speculation was eventually to stifle settlement and drive land prices far beyond the reach of the average immigrant.

Such policies were far from accidental. The Land Act of 1841 clearly expresses the objective of "creating a labour pool" by the two-pronged approach of promoting massive immigration and making land prohibitively expensive. The land speculators and the class of merchant industrialists who wanted a cheap wage-labour force, to build canals and railways and to work in factories, were the same people, and so indeed were members of the government! The wretched conditions of poverty and unemployment within the developing industrial cities of Canada from the mid-nineteenth century mirrored in many respects the conditions of early *industrialization* in Britain.

Alienation Under Capitalism

A central unifying theme in Marx's early philosophical writings is the concept of **alienation**. This refers to the dehumanizing character of social relations that emerge in their purest form under the capitalist mode of production. Marx saw people as, by nature, producers, engaged in a creative relationship with their physical environment to transform it to their needs. They are also, by nature, social beings, co-operating together in their creative, productive process.

People experience alienation from their human nature when the fundamental relationship to production is broken: when they are denied access to the basic means of producing for their own subsistence needs, when they are separated from the products of their labour so that what they create does not belong to them, and when their social relations with other producers are broken.

Life within hunting and gathering societies is often harsh, but it is not alienating. People relate to the natural world and to each other in a direct and immediate way in meeting their collective subsistence needs. Under feudalism, the tied labourers are exploited but are still not alienated in the same way as under capitalism. They work with the land directly and collectively to produce what they consume. They are exploited to the extent that what they produce as labourers on the estates belongs not to them but to those who control the estates. All the surplus, beyond what is needed for their immediate subsistence, is expropriated. Under harsh landlords, the labourers themselves may be reduced to the meanest level of survival while the leisured, ruling class lives in luxury on what the workers produce. Yet, there is still a human relationship between the two great classes of those who work the land and those who control it. Feudal lords acknowledge a hereditary obligation to sustain the families attached to their estates in the bad years as well as the good, and the labouring families have a hereditary right to use that land for their own needs, generation after generation.

It is only under capitalism that alienation is experienced in its fullest and harshest form, pervading every aspect of human relations. The root cause of alienation is separation of the mass of people from the means of production, leaving them unable to provide for themselves. In order to survive, they must sell that labour power as a commodity to the owners of capital, who will use it for their own productive purposes in return for a cash wage. Almost everything that workers need to survive must be bought for cash in the marketplace. It is during times of high unemployment, or low demand for wage workers relative to supply, that the alienating character of capitalism is most immediately experienced. People can offer their labour power for sale, but there is nothing to oblige employers to buy it. Unwanted workers cannot use their labour power to meet their own subsistence needs because they have no access to any means of production, and they have no hereditary rights to share in what the society as a whole produces.

Under the capitalist mode of production, alienation is experienced in multiple ways. Workers are alienated from the products of their labour. Feudal serfs had a right to a share of the harvest, but factory workers have no claims whatever to their products. They are paid a wage, but everything they produce belongs to the factory owner. In effect, the harder they work and the more they produce, the more impoverished they become, because more and more of their creative effort is taken from them. Workers in developing industrial capitalism are also alienated from the work task itself, which has no intrinsic meaning or sense of purpose. Under such alienating conditions, Marx suggests, people avoid work. They are often forced to work under miserable conditions. People are reduced to becoming appendages to machines; the work rhythms are set not by the changing seasons, or by the human body, but by the machines.

Bad as the conditions of work often were during early industrialization, and still are in many industries, they are a reflection rather than the cause of alienation experienced in social relations of production. The underlying problem is that, under capitalism, human relations of production are reduced to inhuman cash payments. Within the labour market, it is not a whole person who is bought and sold, as in slavery, but her or his labour power—the power to produce. Labour power is purchased by capitalists as needed, and laid off when not needed, with no further responsibilities to meet the subsistence needs of those who provide that labour power or of their dependants. The sole obligation of employers is to pay wages for labour power as and when they need it. People no longer co-operate with each other as full human beings in the production process. Marx suggests that in the capitalist exchange of labour power for wages, the employers are themselves as alienated as the workers, for they too are cut off from human social relations. Private property and money dominate their existence.

It is precisely these inhuman relations of production that make possible the classical economics concepts of *economic men*, *profit maximization*, and *market forces*. In addition, these relations encourage the functionalist conception of human relations as emotionless, narrow, and calculated by market attributes. These concepts do not describe human nature or society in the abstract. They arise out of the historically specific conditions of capitalism.

The Model of Capitalism as an Economic System

So far in this chapter we have alluded to capitalism or to the capitalist system without describing this system itself in detail. But it is the actual workings of capitalism, its internal dynamics and its contradictions, that occupied Marx's central attention in all his later work. His three volumes on *Capital* comprise an extensive analysis of the capitalist system, and his model still forms the basis of the contemporary theory of political economy. A condensed version of his elaborate model is laid out below.

Certain key terms are useful in understanding Marx's model of a capitalist economy. A **commodity** is anything produced for exchange, and not for use by the producer. The production of commodities presupposes a division of labour. It is only as people become specialized in distinct occupations, and cease to produce everything that they need for themselves, that exchange becomes important. **Exchange value** refers to the amount of human labour time that went into the production of a commodity. It measures a social relation between producers. As people exchange what they have produced, they are exchanging the time and skill that each has contributed to the product. **Abstract labour time** refers to labour in general, to the average amount of time that it takes to produce a given commodity in a society with a given level of technology and knowledge.

The Theory of Exchange

The **theory of exchange** is fundamental to Marx's analysis. He begins from the observation that people in every society must labour to produce goods. Commodities exchange in definite proportions in the market. It is usually possible, for example, to calculate roughly how many pairs of shoes a cobbler would have to sell or barter in order to buy a wool coat or a given amount of firewood. Each such commodity also absorbs a definite amount of human labour time. From these basic propositions, Marx derives his **labour theory of value**. The theory posits that the exchange value or price of a commodity is determined not by the laws of supply and demand proposed by classical economists, but by the amount of labour that goes into the commodity.

For Marx, the exchange ratio between commodities is the labour-time ratio. In other words, in order to calculate the true exchange value of one commodity, such as shoes, for another commodity, such as firewood, one has to calculate how much total time went into raising the cow, getting the hide, tanning it into leather, and fashioning it into shoes, compared with the time it takes to care for trees to the appropriate age, cut the timber, saw it into logs, and take them to market. In using labour time as the fundamental measure of value, Marx is not suggesting that lazy people who take twice as long as others to do something will thereby be able to exchange their production for twice as much, or that people who make things quickly will get less. What counts, over the economy as a whole, is how long it takes, on average, to produce commodities, given the prevailing level of technology and skills. Marx refers to this as **socially necessary labour time**; it averages out lazy, unskilled, and unusually quick people. **Skilled labour time** includes teaching and learning in the calculation of socially necessary labour time.

Consider a simple example of exchange within a hunting society. Suppose, in a given community at a given time of year, it takes the average hunter one hour to catch a deer and two hours to trap a beaver. Fair exchange would then be two deer for one beaver. This exchange has nothing to do with the nature of the commodities themselves: the size of the animal, the amount of meat, the relative utility of deer skins over beaver pelts. It is based on the amount of human labour time it takes to catch them. If hunters could not get two deer for one beaver, they would pretty quickly stop "wasting time" catching beaver and start catching deer instead. People would start trapping beaver again when they were sufficiently scarce, or people wanted them enough, that the labour time spent would be compensated by what the beaver could be exchanged for. The classical relations of supply and demand are thus balanced by time. Individual producers decide

how best to allocate their labour time so that what they produce in the course of a day's labour will exchange for the equivalent of a day's labour by other people.

In the traditional exchange process money may be used, but only as a convenient mechanism for keeping tallies on exchanges between many different people, particularly when spread out over time. The fundamental exchange is still one useful commodity for another.

Capitalist exchange entails a subtle but extremely important difference from this traditional exchange process. The basis of exchange is not one commodity for another, but some money for more money by means of a commodity. The objective is not to trade useful items, but to increase the amount of money one started with. Money as such has no use value. One cannot eat money or dress up in it. We want money because we can exchange it for something else. This fact itself makes the desire for money very different from desire for useful commodities. There is a limit to our desire for such commodities. We want only so much food, so much clothing, and so on, and we then lose interest in getting any more. Money is not like that. There is no intrinsic limit to how much we want. Desire for money is, in principle, insatiable. It is this desire that drives capitalist exchange.

Labour Commodity and Surplus Value

In capitalist exchange, labour itself is treated as a commodity. As we have already seen, the means of production are owned by a few people, while labour power is owned by others. As a commodity, labour has a value and, like every other commodity, that value is labour time needed to produce it. This is averaged out as the **subsistence wage**. This value includes not only the cost of maintaining the adult labourer at an acceptable standard of living, but the cost of replacing that labour through raising and educating children. Capitalists use money wages to purchase the commodity of labour power with the objective of using it to make more money.

In Marxist theory, profit comes from surplus value. The only way for the capitalist to make a profit is for labourers to produce goods of more value than the subsistence value of their labour time, for which they are paid in wages. Marx argues that profit does not normally arise through dishonest or underhanded practices. Nor does it come from simply charging more for given commodities. If all commodities, labour power included, were sold at double their previous price, nobody would benefit. The result would be inflation in which money would be worth half its former value.

The one place in the system where profit can routinely be made is in the use of labour power. Human labour can produce more than its own value. The exchange value of labour power, expressed in the subsistence wage, is the time it takes to produce and maintain the worker. Producing and maintaining a worker involves all the costs entailed in raising a child to maturity; training in work skills; feeding, clothing, and housing the worker and the worker's dependants. The exchange value of a commodity is the average time it takes a worker, with a given technology, to make that commodity. The goal of the capitalist is to maximize the productivity of labour power for a given subsistence wage; that is, to maximize the gap between the exchange value of the labour power and the exchange value of the commodities produced. This gap constitutes **surplus value**. For example, if in six hours a worker can produce a commodity with an exchange value equivalent to her or his daily wage, then any commodities produced outside of those six hours produce surplus value for the capitalist. The value of the time expended in producing the additional commodities accrues to the capitalist, not to the workers.

The gap between a day's wages and the resale value of all commodities produced by a worker in a day constitutes, in principle, an objective measure of the degree of exploitation of labour. The actual calculation of surplus value is more complicated than this. Capitalists have to spend money to buy or replace machines and materials, to rent the factory, and to satisfy their own subsistence needs. Surplus value arises over and above these socially necessary exchange values.

If the objective of production were solely to provide useful commodities for people, there would be no problem with hiring labour and then distributing everything produced. But this is not the objective of capitalist exchange. The objective is to make money, to maximize surplus value so that the largest possible amount of money comes back to the owner of capital.

Competition is crucial in the process of creating surplus value. Commodities exchange for the average time it takes to produce them in a given market, with a given level of technology. The goal of the capitalist is always to better this **average labour time**—to get more than the average amount of commodities for a given subsistence wage bill. Those who can better the average rate can make large profits by having more commodities for exchange at the going rate or by undercutting competitors and controlling the market. Those who only make the average rate may break even, but they will not make much profit. Those whose level of production falls below the average rate will go bankrupt. They will have insufficient commodities to sell at the going price to cover their higher-than-average labour time costs.

How can individual capitalists maximize surplus value? Logically there are only three ways to do so. First, the capitalist can extend the working day, trying to harness more and more of the workers' energy. During the early stages of capitalism in Britain, workdays often extended to sixteen and eighteen hours, workweeks to six or seven days, even for children in factories and coal mines. Ultimately, however, this became self-defeating. Workers reach such a point of exhaustion that they can no longer produce anything. Pushed to the extreme, people die. Long before this point is reached, overworked people become markedly slower and less efficient so that overall production actually falls.

The second possibility is depressing real wages. This can be done either by raising prices while wages stay the same, by reducing actual wages while other commodity prices remain the same, or by some combination of lower wages and higher prices. This process also has natural limits. If wages drop so low relative to prices that workers cannot meet subsistence needs or feed and educate their children, people collapse and the labour power available drops both in quantity and quality. Workers are also not totally passive under such conditions, and employers can expect strikes and sabotage if they push these policies too far. As Marx acknowledged, there tends to be an acceptable minimum standard of living for a particular community of people, and employers cannot easily push workers below this level. Individual capitalists cannot indefinitely drive their workers harder than the average, or pay them less than the average wage, because workers will quit their jobs and go to work elsewhere. The exception to this rule occurs wherever workers have limited mobility, as in peripheral regions where unemployment is high or in Third World countries. In such

locations, workers can be exploited more than the average. But there are still absolute limits on how far even these workers can be pushed.

There is a third option that is much more important than the other two because it is, in principle, limitless. That option is to strive to increase the productivity of labour power through labour-saving technology. Machines are important for their usefulness for increasing the productivity of labour power. For a given number of working hours, and at a given level of wages, the proportion of surplus value goes up. In principle, if the introduction of a new machine doubles a worker's output, it would be possible to cut working hours per week by 25 percent and give a 25 percent pay raise to the workers, and still increase profits by about 50 percent once the new machine is paid for.

This process can work in several ways. New technology may speed up production while using the same workers. Alternatively, the technology may simplify the production process so that the time required to train workers is reduced, hence reducing the exchange value or wage costs of the labour power needed. Innovations that improve the quality of commodities are another way of improving the average rate of production. Other producers would require far more time to create a product of the same quality without the technology.

At first glance, it looks as though everybody wins under this scenario. Workers get a better standard of living while capitalists make more profits. In the short run, this is correct. In the long run, however, there is a very serious problem: the process becomes self-defeating. In fact, Marx saw this process as the fundamental contradiction in capitalism and predicted that it would eventually bring about the collapse of the system.

Law of the Falling Rate of Profit

The problem begins from the fact that capitalists are competing among themselves for profits. The first ones to introduce new labour-saving technology can make large profits, since their commodities are cheaper to produce and they are able to undersell competitors in the marketplace. Other capitalists must rapidly introduce similar technology to keep their production costs down, or they will go bankrupt. Smaller or less efficient capitalists, who cannot afford to purchase the new technology, find themselves unable to compete in the marketplace. They have to drop their prices in order to sell their commodities, but they are unable to drop their costs of production. Eventually they become uncompetitive, go bankrupt, and drop out of the market. Those capitalists who remain can buy up the bankrupt person's machines and factories cheaply and can expand their market share with their high-volume, low-cost commodities.

Over time, however, profits start to drop. Eventually all the capitalists remaining in the market are using the new technology. They are all achieving the new rate of production. This becomes the standard or average labour time that sets the exchange value of the commodity. The average commodity price drops to this real exchange value, and nobody makes much profit. The economy will stagnate until some new technological breakthrough permits innovative capitalists, once again, to better the average rate of production and raise profits. A further problem is that, as mechanization increases, capitalists must spend relatively more money on machines than on wages. Since profits are made on the latter, the actual rate of profit starts to fall. The new technology must increase productivity markedly over the older method of production for the capitalist to keep ahead.

Crisis of Overproduction

If this were the only problem with labour-saving technology, it might not be that serious, but there is a more serious problem associated with it. As the technological race increases, machines replace labour at an ever greater rate. The result is unemployment. Unemployed people are not the responsibility of the capitalist. The problem for capitalists is that unemployed people do not have the money needed to purchase the commodities that flood the market. Capitalists find themselves with surplus production that they cannot sell. In this situation, they are forced to operate more and more below capacity but, at the same time, they must make still greater efforts to develop technological innovations that will cut production costs so that they can sell more cheaply. They thus generate still more unemployment.

Labour-saving technology may increase productivity and so make possible an increase in wages in the short run. Expanding production will also give rise to increased demand for labour power, which will work to raise wages above the real subsistence value of labour power. Rising wages, however, reduce surplus value, and so generate a reaction. It becomes potentially more profitable to invest in more labour-saving technology to displace high-priced labour. As unemployment increases, the bargaining power of workers collapses. They start to undercut each other to get jobs, and wages start to fall, either in an absolute amount or relative to rising prices. People displaced by machines or bankrupted when they cannot keep up with competitors form a **lumpenproletariat**. Marx conceptualized the lumpenproletariat as a free-floating mass of people who are "declassed," separated from their class of origin and unable to find a place for themselves in the society. This disintegrated mass of ruined and impoverished people fall easy prey to reactionary or fascist ideologies and movements. Displaced workers struggling to regain a foothold in the working classes, form a **reserve army of labour**, their competition for jobs serving to depress wages still further. In the long run, Marx suggests, these processes work to force down the average wage across the market to subsistence value. Workers may make temporary gains in their standard of living, but these gains will always be insecure and threatened by the prospect of technological change that will make their work obsolete. Contradictions of capitalism look formidable. There is the tendency toward a falling rate of profit, as expensive technology replaces labour. Secondly, there is the tendency toward increasing concentration of capital and the resulting **polarization of classes** as members of the petite bourgeoisie are bankrupted and join the proletariat. Thirdly, there is the tendency toward the increasing poverty of the masses as unemployment forces wages down. Fourthly, there is the crisis of overproduction as unemployed and poorly paid people lack the money to purchase commodities. The remaining capitalists are driven to invent still more labour-saving technology to push down the costs of production in order to undercut competitors in an ever-tighter market. In the process, they produce yet more unemployment, tighter profit ratios, more bankruptcies, and a still bigger glut of commodities that people cannot afford to buy.

In these multiple ways, the competitive relations that develop between two great classes of workers and capitalists, and among capitalists themselves, in the marketplace, fetter the productive potential of new technology. Marx predicted that these internal contradictions within capital-

ism would generate an endless cycle of crises, of booms and slumps characterized by bankruptcies, unemployment, and overproduction. In the long run, the system would collapse due to its own internal problems. Marx expected, however, that social revolution would forcibly overthrow the system long before it reached this stage.

Marx foresaw the possibility of a new form of economic relations that would not be based on competition for profits and so would avoid all the internal contradictions of capitalism. New technology could be communally owned and worked to full capacity, with the products shared communally. As less and less labour time was needed to satisfy people's desire for useful products, relative to their desire for more free time, the portion of the day spent working could drop. In principle, people could work in the mornings, relax in the afternoons, and gather for intellectual, creative, or social activities in the evenings.

Counteracting Factors

An unavoidable question arises in relation to Marx's analysis of the capitalist system. If his theories were correct, why have his predictions not come to pass? How is it that capitalism remains the dominant mode of production a century after he predicted its demise?

Critics of Marx's thesis have pointed to extensive empirical evidence that seems to contradict his predictions. Shareholder capitalism appears to have countered the tendency toward the concentration of capital foreseen by Marx. Twentieth-century workers are vastly better off than Marx ever foresaw, in some cases enjoying a standard of living that rivals that of the middle classes. The rise of the middle classes, in particular, appears to contradict Marx's law of the increasing polarization of classes. Democratic politics, the welfare state, and the organization of trade unions have also served to ameliorate the exploitative aspects of capitalism. From this perspective, capitalism appears to have weathered the crises.

Theorists within the Marxist tradition have countered these claims by pointing out that many of the crises that Marx foresaw do plague capitalist economies. The ultimate crisis, they argue, has been avoided so far by a series of counteracting factors. These serve to soften, but do not resolve, the internal contradictions of capitalism.

Central among such factors has been the accelerating rate of technological advance, which has staved off the falling rate of profits. Labour productivity has continued to rise with the aid of computers, robots, fossil fuels, and nuclear energy. An important effect of this accelerated innovation has been the cheapening of the costs of the machines themselves, as labour productivity has risen in heavy industry. Machines can be mass-produced in shorter periods of labour time. Some theorists suggest that bankruptcies and mergers have also significantly reduced the costs of heavy industry. Tax write-offs and other state benefits also help. Technological developments have also led to an explosion in the variety of cheap, mass-produced consumer goods available, which has helped to reduce the intensity of cut-throat competition to sell commodities. In addition, huge military expenditures in the centres of capitalist development have staved off the crisis of overproduction. Weapons constitute a staggering proportion of production. They are bought and blown up or thrown away as obsolete. Newer weapons are then purchased, and production in war industries is maintained.

The worldwide expansion of capitalism, through the economic domination that corporate interests in wealthy countries have been able to exert over underdeveloped countries, has meant that the worst contradictions of capitalism have been shifted from the centres of capitalism to the Third World. Here multinational corporations have been able to protect profits through cheap labour and long working hours. These countries are also sources of cheap raw materials and at the same time provide expanded markets for manufactured goods.

Within the developed centres, revolt has been held off by the lure of mass-produced consumer goods. Material comforts promote acceptance of the status quo, however inegalitarian it may be. Critical awareness is also dulled by processes of legitimation referred to as **ideological hegemony**. This is the capacity of the dominant class to rule not only by control over means of production, but also by control over ideas. When Marx dismissed religion as the opiate of the masses, he had in mind precisely the ways in which religion has been used to legitimate the social order and gross inequalities in wealth as manifestations of God's will. Conceptions of God and big business are still closely associated, as we have seen in the discussion of the Protestant ethic and the spirit of capitalism in chapter 6. Establishment religions generally legitimate the success of the wealthy,

The worldwide expansion of capitalism has led to the exploitation of the people and raw materials in underdeveloped countries.

and at the same time enjoin the poor to endure misery on earth by the promise of rewards in the life after death. As religion has begun to lose its influence over everyday life for many people, other powerful ideological forces have taken its place, in particular the institution of the state and its administrative apparatuses.

The Bourgeois State in Marxist Theory

The **state** in bourgeois society plays a fundamental role in maintaining the social conditions necessary for capitalism to function. The state maintains social order and controls the potential for revolt through monopolizing the legitimate means of force in society. It sustains and legitimates the legal and administrative institutions that protect property rights, as well as contractual obligations essential for capitalist relations of production. It also serves to regulate divisions within the capitalist class, so as to ensure free competition in the market.

In Marxist theory, the state is in essence "nothing more than the form of organization which the bourgeoisie essentially adopts . . . for the mutual guarantee of their property and interests" (Marx and Engels [1846] 1970, 79). However, this relationship is far more complex than one of control. As Sayer expresses it (1985, 241), the state is intrinsically a bourgeois form of social relationship in the sense that it emerges as a separate entity, beside and outside the community, with the privatization of property. This privatization makes it impossible for people as a community to control the material conditions of their collective existence. Social powers are taken from them and vested in a separate apparatus that operates over and above them. The apparatus of the state endeavours to secure communal interests when people are prevented from doing it themselves. The concept of *state* is thus a historically specific category, not a synonym for all forms of government.

Within the affairs of capitalism, the state occupies a paradoxical position that is both central and marginal. Its function is to preserve the conditions for capitalists to act freely as independent and competing individuals, while otherwise not interfering in the marketplace.

The links between the state and members of the bourgeoisie are complex. As a class, the bourgeoisie is peculiarly divided. Its members relate to one another principally as competitors. Different sectors of the class, such as financiers and industrialists, have systematically divergent interests. They have a common interest only in maintaining the conditions within which they can freely compete, specifically in the protection of private property and contractual obligations. The role of the state is to maintain these conditions.

The Base-Superstructure Debate: Materialism Versus Idealism

Marx's analysis of the origins and functioning of the state in bourgeois society is part of his broader thesis that an adequate understanding of all the social institutions and cultures of any soci-

ety must be grounded in analysis of relations of production.

Marx's early philosophical writings grew out of the philosophical traditions of his day, and yet profoundly transformed their meaning. He acknowledged a great intellectual debt to the eighteenth-century philosopher Hegel, and yet at the same time he claimed to have stood Hegel's work on its head. Hegel argues that the human spirit is the guiding force of history. The essence of what it is to be truly human is to strive constantly toward a better future, toward perfection, that would ultimately achieve the merging of humanity with God. It is this spirit that distinguishes people from other animals. In Hegel's view, the unified expression of the collective ideal, over and above individual selfishness is, at any particular stage in history, embodied by the state. For him, the state is the sphere of universal, rational, orderly life.

Marx also sees humanity as struggling toward perfection, but his is a materialist conception in which he reverses Hegel's idea of the causal relations between social structures and ideas. He argues that ideas develop out of and reflect material experience, and can only be understood by reference to this **base**. He sums this up in his famous statement that "it is not human consciousness that determines our existence, but our social existence that determines our consciousness" (Marx [1859] 1975, 452).

Marx praised the work of the philosopher Feuerbach for raising a similar criticism against traditional Christian theology (Marx and Engels [1846] 1970, 39–96). Feuerbach insisted that the starting point in philosophy had to be real people in their material, physical context. The concept of *god* he suggests is really the projection of human self-awareness. There is no pre-existing spiritual entity that creates humanity; rather humanity creates god. Feuerbach believed that people become alienated from themselves when their own projected ideal is held over them as if it were some external force, ordering and judging their actions.

Marx agreed, but he pushed the analysis further to question why people would conceive of god in such an alienating form, as set above and against them. Marx's answer is that people experience alienation in their everyday lives. Powerful forces are indeed set above them. They feel themselves utterly dependent for their existence on feudal lords, or capitalist market forces. It is little wonder that the mass of people would accept such an alienating feudal vision of the "lord god" or that the ruling intelligentsia among the aristocracy and the clergy would propound such doctrines. Marx further suggests that Feuerbach's efforts to criticize such alienating views of god would not be sufficient to make people change their ideas. So long as their material experience of life was alienating, so too would be their vision of god. One would have to change the material base before one could hope to change the thinking of the mass of people. So far, he argued, "philosophers have only interpreted the world in various ways. The point, however, is to change it" (Marx [1845] 1975, 5).

Ideology and False Consciousness

Marx's insistence that ideas reflect material experience raises serious questions about how false ideas can emerge. How can the mass of people be misled by ideological hegemony in capitalist society? How could Hegel have come up with the thesis of ideas determining history if his ideas are a reflection of his own material experience?

Ideology denotes falsity. If we accept Marx's argument that people's actions in, and consciousness of, the world are intrinsically related, then we imply that their consciousness, including ideology, must have some practical adequacy. Their ideas must make sense of their practical everyday activity (Sayer 1983, 8–9). Hence, we cannot explain ideology as merely a consequence of indoctrination or inadequate perception. If ideas are grounded in experience, then there must be something about the nature of experience that is capable of sustaining illusions.

Marx draws a critical distinction between phenomenal forms or *appearance* and essential relations or *essence*. He argues that the essential relations of capitalism are precisely those that produce illusory appearances. A critical example is the experience of exploitation. In feudalism the level of exploitation is obvious to all involved. Serfs know exactly how much time they labour on the big estates for the benefit of the lord, as distinct from working on their own plots to produce for themselves. In capitalism, however, exploita-

tion is mystified in the relationships of wage-labour and private property (Gulalp 1990, 147). Workers appear to contract freely for wages that compensate them for the hours they work for an employer. Profits and interest appear to originate from capital, as legitimate compensation for using the privately owned property of the capitalist. The intrinsically exploitative character of the privatization of material resources of a community, and the appropriation of surplus value from labour power, are not immediately evident. To the extent that everyday conceptions of these relations are merely the conscious expression of the visible movements they will ordinarily be ideological in character (Sayer 1983, ix). Workers typically do not see that capitalism presupposes the violence of the class struggle described above by Brenner, in which the mass of people were forcibly separated from any means of production. What they see is their dependence on businesses to provide them with jobs, and what they commonly feel is gratitude for being given steady work and wages—what Marx termed **false consciousness**. They may see how money, investments, and technology are essential to making profits, but what they typically do not recognize is how processes of extracting surplus value work, so that their own labour power is the true basis of profits. In Marx's view it is a complex work of science to explore beyond immediately visible economic relationships to reveal the underlying relations of class struggle and exploitation that produce this visible experience of benevolent capitalists and grateful workers.

Classical Economics as Ideology

The most difficult aspect of this work is to get beyond the abstract logical models of classical economics that, in Marx's view, mystify relationships between people, including alienation, exploitation, and power, translating them into abstract market forces. Instead of people acting collectively in relation with each other to produce economic inequalities and dependence, the "economy" seems to be the causal agent, doing things to people. Human relations appear to be governed by the forces of competition, supply, demand, price, productivity, and the like, to which both capitalists and workers are subject.

In *The German Ideology*, Marx explains at some length the practices that create such distorted understanding. Three distortions or tricks are involved. The first trick is to separate the ruling ideas from the rulers. We lose sight of the connection between the dominant ideas of capitalism and the ruling class that propounds them. The second step is to order these ideas in terms of some mystical connections or abstract conceptual schemes. Complex mathematical models produced by economists are one example of such schemes. They seem to provide impressive models of how economies work, with all the messy details of what people are doing abstracted out of them. The models are based on concepts like *supply-demand curves*, *prices*, *wages*, *commodities*, and *markets*. The balance of supply and demand determines the price at which commodities exchange in the market, and governs the actions and decisions of "rational economic men." These abstract forces make up the **invisible hand of the market**. The third trick is to treat these abstract models as causal forces that explain behaviour. They appear to function in terms of laws of their own. Whatever people do in specific situations appears to be responses to economic forces (Marx and Engels [1846] 1970, 64; Sayer 1983; Smith 1974a, 45–46). This is a powerful way of controlling people because the logical models do indeed seem to fit people's experience. Once people believe these models, they become obedient to them, and they can be more effectively controlled than if capitalists came right out and stated their class interests. People accept such practices as massive downsizing of business resulting in widespread unemployment as somehow inevitable, the effect of forces beyond anyone's control.

Marx himself did not contest whether these models of classical economics were adequate for describing market forces. The problem for him is that they remain at the level of appearances without exploring the essential processes that give rise to these appearances. Concepts are treated as abstract logical relations rather than historically specific social practices. The models assume precisely what needs to be explained.

Take the concept of *rational economic men*, for example. Marx argues that we cannot simply take for granted that it is human nature to be "profit-maximizers." People only begin to behave like this when they have lost all direct access to the means of providing for their own subsistence needs. When they have to buy and sell labour power for wages, and purchase everything they need in the commodity market, they become intensely concerned with making money. It is not abstract market forces that determine such behaviour, but very real relations of class struggle between people. All this gets covered up when we focus on market forces doing things to people. The classical economists' vision of abstract market forces is very similar to the theological vision of an abstract god that Feuerbach criticized. Both are conceptualized as external to the lives of people, acting over them, doing things to them, punishing and rewarding their behaviour.

Marx dismisses these supposedly explanatory models of market forces and exchange of commodities as **commodity fetishism**. A **fetish** is an inanimate object that is worshipped for its magical powers. Commodities become fetishes in economics. Things appear to rule people instead of people producing things. Exchange appears to occur between things, rather than the exchange of labour power between people. Abstract typifications are treated as having active causal agency while people become objects, their lives determined by the properties of things.

Marx argues that capitalism, more than any other social form, creates illusory appearances, because its survival depends on it. Once it becomes obvious that all the suffering caused by abstract market forces is only a reflection of the concentration of private ownership of the means of production, and the mass of people's forced separation from it, the entire edifice is likely to totter. Marx even goes so far as to suggest that once capitalism is overthrown and replaced by the openly visible, communal sharing of access to the means of production, social science itself will wither away. It would be unnecessary, since people could directly see for themselves what was going on (Cohen 1980).

Dialectical Method

Marx tried to develop a method of research that would help to expose the processes underlying human history and immediate experience. He borrowed the notion of **dialectical method** from Hegel and adapted it to his own purposes. In Hegel's philosophy, the dialectical method is a form of testing and developing logical arguments by first exploring the contradictions that may be present in a particular argument and then devising solutions. Hegel argues that the advancement of human knowledge reflects the recurrent cycles of thesis, antithesis, and synthesis. The **thesis** consists of any philosophical system or theory. Its **antithesis** comprises the logical inconsistencies, internal problems, and unexplained anomalies within the system of thought. These problems force philosophers to attempt to resolve them. **Synthesis** is achieved with the integration of a new system of ideas that resolves the old problems. This provides a new starting point or thesis, until new problems become obvious. The **dialectical** processes of antithesis and synthesis continue until perfection is reached.

Marx applied this dialectical method to material conditions to arrive at his theory of **dialectical materialism**. For him the thesis consists of the existing organization of production. The antithesis comprises the internal contradictions. These are the tensions and practical inconsistencies between productive potential of a given means and how people organize their productive relations. The synthesis breaks these contradictions by establishing new forms of organization capable of unleashing the full potential of the emerging means of production.

In relation to the historical processes of his own time, Marx identified feudalism as the original thesis. It is a mode of economic production that endured for centuries and gave basic security of subsistence to all its members. But it was destined to give way under its own internal contradictions. The productive potential of feudalism was stifled by its social relations. Tied labourers, who were responsible for production, had no incentive to produce more than was necessary for their own subsistence, and those who controlled the estates had little incentive to invest in them. The system could only expand by squeezing the absolute surplus, to the point that production itself was threatened.

Capitalism seemed to resolve the contradictions inherent in feudalism. For all its faults, capitalism succeeded in breaking feudal restraints. Productive potential expanded exponentially under competitive capitalism, and labourers were freed from their hereditary bondage. It was because of this tremendous liberating potential of capitalism that Marx believed it was a necessary intermediate step between feudalism and communism.

When Lenin declared the communist revolution a fait accompli in Russia in 1917, a great many committed Marxist revolutionaries had their doubts. Most of what became the Soviet Union was trapped in a backward feudal mode of production, with only a tiny and mostly foreign bourgeoisie. Lenin argued that a centralized state-capitalist phase was required initially in the Soviet Union to promote development. He hoped that this would lead eventually to the next step of a truly socialist revolution (Resnick and Wolff 1993, 48–49).

Lenin's Marxist critics argued that it would be impossible to advance from feudalism to communism without the intermediate stage of capitalism. They were partially right. The struggle toward economic development in Eastern Europe was long and hard and involved severe internal repression that Marx had not foreseen. In part this reflects historical circumstances. Soviet society was surrounded by hostile capitalist states intent on its destruction, and this impelled the development of a coercive military apparatus (Panitch 1992, 143–44). But this coercive state capitalism itself generated exploitative class interests that blocked any easy route to socialism, while the inflexible collectivized socialist economy proved incapable of achieving the level of industrial and technological development of advanced capitalist societies. The theoretical analysis of this failure and the lessons to be learned from it are critical issues in contemporary Marxist scholarship.

In the West, the political rhetoric and euphoric claims of the triumph of democracy and capitalism that followed the collapse of communist states in Eastern Europe quickly faded as worldwide recession and government debt reached crisis proportions. These conditions are a stark reminder that, while capitalism may have broken the fetters of feudalism, it has its own internal problems and contradictions. Like feudalism, its productive potential is stifled by the relations of production. These relations generate the inherent tendencies toward concentration of capital, falling rate of profit, crises of overproduction, and increasing misery among the masses.

The new synthesis that Marx foresaw was advanced communism. When all members of a community could share in and exercise direct control over the means of advanced industrial production, this would finally remove the shackles on the productive potential of capitalism.

There would no longer be a class of economically dependent labourers separated from the means of production and vulnerable to unemployment and poverty with every advance of labour-saving technology. Production could truly take off. There would be no crisis of overproduction until all the wants of all the people had been satiated. Then the system could settle down at this desired production level with the minimum input of labour, using the best labour-saving technology available. According to Marx, perfection would be reached. It is a utopian vision that is far removed from the reality of any of the so-called communist societies of Eastern Europe.

The Class Struggle

Marx did not expect the transition from capitalism to advanced communism to occur automatically as the inexorable workings of some grand evolutionary scheme. Rather, he saw a dynamic process in which **class struggle** would necessarily play a central role. As we have seen with respect to both Europe and Canada, the development of capitalism was a violent process in which capitalists overthrew the existing relations of production and asserted their private property rights; this drove producers from the land and into the position where they had to sell their labour power for wages. It would take a similar struggle to break private ownership of the productive forces developed under capitalism.

A major problem that confronts Marxist politics, Sayer suggests, is the conflict between means and goals. Because the state is so central to bourgeois society, social struggle will have to take a political form (1985, 251–52). But at the same time, the state is part of what excludes people from directly controlling the circumstances of their lives. The focus on state politics promotes a hierarchical, oligarchic, or elitist, form of organization rather than an egalitarian, democratic form. In principle, socialist parties believed in giving power to the workers to control production, and abolishing the power of capitalists and their hierarchy of supervisors and bosses. But in practice, socialist parties found themselves compelled to work in **autocratic** and bureaucratic ways to function in a capitalist state system. The means they needed to confront the bourgeois state undermined the goals of democratic socialism itself.

Marx believed that the impetus for the struggle to overthrow capitalism would come from the mass of working people disadvantaged by the existing relations of production. But this would not be automatic. Before the struggle could begin, people would have to see through the ideology of rational market forces. They would have to understand the relations of production, and their own position within these relations, and see the potential for change. It would be the role of radical intellectuals to educate working people in these areas. But intellectual revelation alone would not be sufficient. Capitalist contradictions would first have to reach the point where they became part of the immediately experienced reality of the people so that experience and theory would connect. Then the class struggle might seriously begin.

Marx drew a clear distinction between the situation of people as a **class-in-itself** and their conscious realization of their situation as a **class-for-itself**. People who share the same relationship to the means of production constitute a class-in-itself. Only when such people become conscious of this shared class position, and act collectively in their class interests, do they come to form a class-for-itself. This *class consciousness* is a necessary starting point for revolutionary social action.

Contemporary Marxist Theory

Marx is such a complex theorist, and the implications of his work are so far-reaching, that it is simply not possible to sum his theory up in a way that would satisfy all contemporary Marxists. There is no single body of theory, even in the discipline of sociology, that now constitutes "Marxist theory." Marxist-inspired theoretical orientations have developed in several very different directions, especially in recent years, with much internal dissent and debate. Only the flavour of these alternative perspectives can be introduced here.

Marxist Structuralism and Political Economy Theory

The dominant perspective in Marxist theory in sociology is inspired by Marx's model of the capitalist system and its internal dynamics and contradictions. It takes from Marx his central observation that all social relations are determined, in the last instance, by the mode of production. The model of the capitalist system thus provides an explanatory framework that can account for specific characteristics of contemporary capitalist societies. This general orientation is widely referred to as **Marxist structuralism**. It forms the core of political economy theory. Its power as an approach for analysing contemporary Canadian society is explored in the next chapter.

The structuralist political economy perspective has come under increasing criticism in recent years from scholars working within the Marxist framework. Taken to its extreme, the application of Marx's model of the capitalist system as an explanatory scheme risks repeating the mistakes for which Marx himself castigated classical economists, namely, of giving causal force to abstract concepts. The structural contradictions of capitalism seem to produce their determined effects, while active human agency seems redundant. The Marxist historian E.P. Thompson (1978b) has come out strongly against economic-determinist versions of Marxist historicism. He insists that, in a Marxist approach, class does not constitute a *thing* but a *process*.

> Classes do not exist as separate entities; look around, find an enemy class, and then start to struggle. On the contrary, people find themselves in a society structured in determined ways, . . . they identify points of antagonistic interest, they commence to struggle around these issues and in the process of struggling they discover themselves as classes, they come to know this discovery as class-consciousness (Thompson 1978a, 149).

Marxism and Social Constructionist Theory

The social constructionist approach to Marxist analysis draws extensively on Marx's earlier philosophical writings, and the methods that he himself used in the development of his critique of classical economics (Smith 1990b; Sayer 1985; 1989). Marx insisted that an adequate understanding of bourgeois society could not stop at the descriptive models of classical economics. Sayer argues that Marx's seminal work of *Capital* can best be understood not as an economic theory of society and history, but as a historical sociology of economic forms (Sayer 1989, 49). Marx's methodological critique consisted in essence of tracing each of the supposedly abstract logical concepts of economics back to their historically specific roots in social relationships between people. Analysis is grounded in what people actually do, in their immediate material situation of trying to make a living, and how they come to make sense of these experiences for practical purposes. From this perspective, concepts such as property, commodities, profit, and the like, are not merely abstract ideas, nor do they describe structural entities within the economy. Rather, they denote active practices and relationships between people. *Property* is the mystified form of privatizing the productive energies of members of a community embedded in active relationships of class struggle and exploitation of human energies. *Profit* is the visible manifestation of surplus labour power extracted from workers. *Commodities* embody the exchange of labour power between people. The abstract sphere of the economy itself is an expression of active processes that separate creative labour from community control, in turn producing the notion of "isolated individuals" in civil society who are condemned to compete incessantly as "rational economic men." These are all historically specific patterns of social relations.

Much of the contemporary work in sociology that adopts a social constructionist perspective is by theorists who define themselves as Marxists, but who avoid the more deterministic **structuralism** of dominant political economy theory. For this reason we have been careful to avoid treating the political economy perspective in sociology as synonymous with Marxist theory, even though it is based directly on Marx's analysis of capitalism, and is widely identified as "Marxist" theory.

Marxist Feminism and Radical Feminism

Marxist feminism constitutes a third theoretical approach developing out of the Marxist perspective. It uses the analytical tools of historical materialism, rather than Marx's actual writings, as inspiration. Marx himself said very little about women. Mitchell (1972, 24) suggests that if we actually start looking in Marx's work for material under the heading "women," we would probably conclude that Marx was a hopeless male chauvinist. There is little to suggest that Marx ever intended the generic term *mench* or *men* to include *women*. He conceives the proletariat to be, essentially, working *men*. Women enter the picture in so far as they themselves sell their labour power in the marketplace. But their work as women, as housewives, as domestic workers, and as mothers, had little place in Marx's analysis of capitalism and the class struggle in history.

Recent feminist theory takes two basic approaches to Marxist theory. The dominant one, represented in the domestic labour debate, which we examine in the next chapter, tends toward a structuralist approach. It seeks to explicate the position and role of women within the workings of the capitalist system.

An alternative strategy is to try to rework the Marxist concept of class itself, not only to incorporate women as proletariat but also to give more central attention to the dimension of women's work as reproducers—both in the bearing and raising of children as the next generation of workers and the daily maintenance of workers themselves. The neglect of reproduction in Marxist theory is a very large omission in the scheme of things. A classical Marxist theorist would probably argue that the question of reproduction has been subsumed under the more general issue of means of subsistence for workers and their dependants. But this does not satisfy feminists. Classical Marxist structuralism, or political economy theory, is faulted for its unwarranted endorsement of the capitalist standpoint that defines the "main business" of ruling as capital accumulation, and marginalizes all other topics (Smith 1992a, 9–14).

Eisenstein (1984, 146) suggests that the Marxist version of class should be reworked to incorporate the notion of women as a **sexual class**. This does not mean that they are like the proletariat, defined in relation to the mode of production. Rather they are a sexual class in relation to the mode of reproduction. They are a class in that they perform the basic and necessary activities of society: reproduction, child-rearing, nurturing, consuming, domestic labouring, and wage earn-

ing. They are a sexual class because what they do as women, the activities for which they are responsible, and the labour they perform are essential and necessary to the operation of society, more important even than the activities of the proletariat.

The feminist project of re-working Marxist theory to incorporate women's reproductive work draws inspiration from Marx's recognition that it is capitalism itself that breaks the integration of relationships of production and reproduction. The privatization of means of production within capitalism creates the abstraction known as "economic organization," an abstraction that makes no sense within earlier societies (Smith 1992a, 10). Feminist political economy tries to heal this rupture between production, producers, and reproduction by shifting the standpoint of women from periphery to centre stage.

Conclusion

It is not possible to draw any clear conclusions about the contribution of Marxism or Marxist theory to sociology because it is still very much in the process of formulation. Despite the fact that Marx died over a century ago, his ideas are only beginning to be established in mainstream sociology in North America. Marxism came to the fore during the 1960s as a critique of Parsonian functionalism. It is still considered rather avant garde in some sociological circles. The implications of Marxist thought for political economy, for the social construction of reality, and for feminist theory are very much still in the process of being worked out. There is no definitive interpretation of Marx. You should take the arguments presented here as a point of departure and raise questions for yourself.

The next chapter explores Marxist contributions to understanding contemporary Canadian political economy. The broader implications of Marxism, as they relate to the social relations of family, stratification, education, ethnicity, and modernization, are explored in more depth in later chapters as we present the value of Marxist theory as a critique of traditional functionalism in sociology.

Suggested Reading

The booklet by Ernest Mandel, *An Introduction to Marxist Economic Theory* (1969), provides an excellent and very readable introduction to the model of capitalism as an economic system. Mandel covers the three issues of the theory of value and surplus value, capital and capitalism, and neocapitalism, showing how contemporary crises of capitalism are managed. Another concise introduction to Marxist political theory is Karl Marx and Friedrich Engels, *The Communist Manifesto*, edited by Samuel Beer ([1848] 1955). This booklet includes an introduction to Marx's ideas, the full *Communist Manifesto*, and selections from *The Eighteenth Brumaire of Louis Bonaparte* and *Capital*.

Two collections of selected writings by Marx, both edited by Tom Bottomore, give an easy introduction to a variety of Marx's writing. The collection entitled *Karl Marx: Early Writings* (1963) gives selections from his economic and philosophical manuscripts. The second collection, *Karl Marx: Selected Writings in Sociology and Social Philosophy* (1956), covers Marx's materialistic conception of history, precapitalist societies, the sociology of capitalism, and politics.

The article by Dorothy Smith "Feminist Reflections on Political Economy" (1992a) discusses the marginalization of critical issues of domestic economy, reproduction, and child care in traditional political economy theory and proposes a feminist alternative.

Questions

1. How do the modes of production and class relations differ between feudalism and capitalism?

2. How does the Marxist thinker, Brenner, account for the unique compulsion to invest in capitalist economies?

3. Why is the experience of alienation so much more pronounced under capitalism compared with feudalism?

4. What did Adam Smith see as the single most critical factor promoting economic development?

5. What does Brenner see as essential in order for capitalism to develop?

6. In principle, how does capitalist exchange differ from traditional exchange in barter economies?

7. What is the significance of abstract labour time in competition between capitalists?

8. Why is class struggle seen as the fundamental characteristic of capitalism?

9. What combination of factors accounts for the crisis of overproduction in capitalist economies?

10. How can classical economics concepts like *economic man, profit maximization*, and *market forces* be seen as ideological concepts—in the sense of ideology as a means NOT to see and NOT to know what is happening?

CHAPTER

9

The Political Economy of Canada: "The Main Business"

This chapter is designed to explore and to test Marxist theory concerning the workings of the capitalist mode of production by focussing on the Canadian economy. The fundamental question for political economy theory is whether the contradictions of capitalism foreseen by Marx can be, or have been, overcome by **advanced capitalism**, or whether the crises of capitalism will lead to the overthrow of the system by an alienated and exploited proletariat. The main points of Marx's model, discussed at greater length in the preceding chapter, are outlined below to highlight the questions we need to ask.

This chapter is divided into four major sections, each focussing on a specific aspect of Marxist theory. The first section describes the structure of capitalism in Canada. It begins with evidence of the increasing expansion of **corporate capitalism** and the contraction of smaller businesses. It tests the Marxist prediction concerning concentration of capital against the lib-

eral argument that shareholder capitalism will dilute corporate control over the economy. In the second section, we explore the situation of independent primary producers in Canada—the petite bourgeoisie. We test the Marxist prediction that there will be falling rates of profit and bankruptcies among the petite bourgeoisie against the liberal thesis that free enterprise fosters healthy competition in the marketplace.

The third section examines the disparities of wealth between the rich and the poor in Canada. The Marxist thesis holds that most of the wealth generated in capitalist societies will become concentrated in the hands of a small elite class. Meanwhile, there will be an ever-expanding class of impoverished people and a shrinking middle class destined to collapse eventually into poverty. This is tested against the thesis that the welfare state and trade unions will ensure a more equitable redistribution of wealth. We will argue that Marxist predictions fit very closely with the dominant features of contemporary Canadian society, but with two important qualifications. The thesis does not adequately account for the expansion of the middle class of professional people, and it fails to account for the situation of women.

The chapter concludes with a fourth section on the feminist challenge to political economy theory. The dynamics of capitalist society seem very different when viewed from the particular standpoint of women as homemakers and mothers. A central argument in the Marxist feminist thesis is that the focus of traditional political economy theory is too narrow. Political economy mirrors the assumption of classical economics that "the main business" of the economy is to accumulate capital. Consequently, the work of women as homemakers is completely ignored.

Marx and the Contradictions of Capitalism

Marx conceptualized capitalism as based on the private ownership of the means of production in the hands of a small class of capitalists referred to as the bourgeoisie. Others, who do not own

---

Table 9-1

The Contradictions of Capitalism	
1. **Increasing concentration of capital.**	Marx predicts that giant corporations will control the economy as smaller businesses collapse or are bought out. These corporations will constantly increase in size and decrease in number as they merge or are bought out.
2. **Falling rate of profit.**	As more and more money is needed for investment in technology, the returns on investment decline. Surplus value and profits come ultimately from labour power, not from machines.
3. **Polarization of classes.**	Capitalists will get richer and richer with the concentration of control over markets. The middle class of small business people and independent commodity producers will collapse into the working class.
4. **Increasing poverty of the masses.**	Unemployment continually threatens to undermine wage levels. Labour-saving technology results in more and more people competing for fewer jobs. These workers will eventually be joined by bankrupted former members of the small business class. Basic wages will hover around subsistence levels. The gap between poor workers and rich capitalists will get larger.
5. **Recurrent crises of overproduction.**	Due to unemployment and low wages, people lack the money to purchase the goods being produced. Productivity expands faster than markets can absorb the goods.
6. **A treadmill of technological innovation.**	When capitalists cannot sell their products, they must drop their prices. They must increase productivity still further to undercut their competitors. Hence they are driven to develop better labour-saving technology, which will enable them to produce more goods with fewer workers.
7. **Recurrent cycles of booms and slumps.**	Bankruptcies lead to unemployment and overproduction. Technological breakthroughs such as robotics and computers bring temporary affluence, but competitors catch up and the cycle repeats itself.

any means of production, must sell their labour power in the marketplace to capitalists who use that labour power to run their enterprises and to make commodities. The term *capital* refers to the stock of land, buildings, machinery, goods, and money used in the production of commodities. In capitalist exchange, money is used to purchase the machines, raw materials, and labour power needed to create commodities that can be sold for more money, or profit. The source of profit is surplus value, which comes from the difference between the value of wages paid to workers and the value of the commodities that the workers make. The rate of surplus value provides an objective measure of the rate of exploitation of workers.

Marx argued that the **contradictions of capitalism** stem from competitive pressure to make profits. This pressure drives capitalists to maximize the exploitation of labourers through longer working hours, lower wages, and labour-saving technology to reduce costs. In the long run, this is self-defeating since, as the ratio of machines to labour increases, profits drop and unemployment rises, leading to crises of overproduction as people cannot afford to buy products. Capitalism thus seems prone to continual and ever-worsening cycles of booms and slumps. Falling profits, an insatiable drive for new technology, and bankruptcies among the smaller bourgeoisie lead to unemployment, the polarization of classes, and increasing poverty among workers. The system can be held together by a combination of state domination, imperialism, and ideological control by the ruling capitalist class.

These ideas are listed in table 9-1 as a series of predictions that we will test against Canadian data in this chapter.

The Liberal-Bourgeois Thesis

Within Canadian sociology, the work of political economy has been largely a debate with the competing **liberal-bourgeois thesis**. This thesis has its roots in the classical economics of Adam Smith, which state that competition in the marketplace regulates profits: if they are too high, other entrepreneurs will rush in to compete and prices will drop; if profits are too low, entrepreneurs will pull out and invest elsewhere. Competition keeps wages fair as workers will

change to better-paying jobs if the rate is too low or move into high-wage areas and drive the rates down. Overproduction is similarly regulated because entrepreneurs will shift investments to new products for which there is more demand.

The strongest contemporary advocate of this theory of competition is Milton Friedman, a Nobel Prize winner in economics and long a key adviser to the American government and to its allies in Latin America. Friedman (1978) opposes in principle any state intervention in the economy because such interference upsets the delicate balance of supply and demand in the marketplace, the **supply-curve demand**. He sees the minimum wage as regressive, arguing that it increases unemployment as jobs that might have been viable at lower rates of pay become uneconomical. Freedom of competition in a capitalist society is, in his view, the main guarantee of democracy and individual freedom.

Research in the liberal-bourgeois tradition points to evidence that advanced capitalism has largely avoided or overcome the contradictions predicted by Marx. The argument is that the expansion of **shareholder capitalism** has led to a democratization of ownership of capital and has promoted a separation of ownership and control through the **managerial revolution**. A multitude of shareholders own capital while a separate class of managers is hired to run the enterprises. Companies that are owned and managed by capitalists are no longer the norm. The increasing affluence or embourgeoisement among working-class people and the rise of the **welfare state** seem to contradict the Marxist prediction of increasing poverty among the masses. The rise of the middle classes, the sector of well-paid professional people, further counters the prediction of a polarization of classes. A political democracy that gives expression to competing interest groups rounds out this picture of a system that enhances the quality of life for the vast majority of people.

Critics of the liberal-bourgeois thesis point to the rise of corporate monopoly capitalism, which spells the end of competition in the marketplace, to the growing polarization resulting from the collapse of the petite bourgeoisie into the working classes, to huge disparities in wealth and poverty within Canada, and to imperialism abroad. Marxist political economy also looks at the character of the state itself and its role in support of ruling capitalist interests. These comparative data will be systematically reviewed now.

❂ The Structure of Capitalism

Corporate Monopoly Capitalism

The central point in the Marxist response to liberal-bourgeois theory is the simple but devastating observation that the era of free competition in the marketplace has passed. The competitive market system no longer exists, even though economists still use the rhetoric. It has gone for the very reasons that Marx foresaw. In the competitive drive for better labour-saving technology to push down costs of production, the smaller, weaker, less ruthless entrepreneurs are eclipsed in the market by a small number of huge corporations. These corporations are no longer subject to competitive market forces of supply and demand. They dictate what the supply and price will be and, in large measure, control demand through advertising.

It is true that there still is much competition in the marketplace, but this is confined to the weaker sectors of the economy—to small firms, such as garment factories, small restaurants, and businesses run by independent tradespeople, which are labour intensive and operate on low capital investment. Such firms tend to be unstable. One estimate is that small businesses have a life expectancy of about eighteen months, with a stunning number of bankruptcies every year. New businesses continually enter the market but, in recent years, as many as two-thirds go bankrupt (Veltmeyer 1986, 55). Wages and profits in small business are low.

Figures published by Statistics Canada in 1990 indicate that corporate concentration has intensified. By 1987, the top 1 percent of all enterprises controlled 86 percent of all assets and made 75 percent of all profits. The top one-hundredth of 1 percent of all enterprises controlled 56 percent of all assets (Hurtig 1991, 159). Hurtig estimates that since the signing of the Canada–United States Free Trade Agreement in January 1989 corporate concentration has increased, mostly in the form of transnational corporations based in the United States buying out Canadian enterprises.

Veltmeyer documents the staggering extent of **monopoly** and **oligopoly** throughout major industries in Canada. An oligopoly is a situation of shared monopoly, where four or fewer firms dominate the market in a particular industry and can co-operate to control it (Veltmeyer 1987, 25). The tobacco industry, breweries, and motor vehicles are each dominated by four—or fewer—big corporations that control over 90 percent of production. A further twenty manufacturing industries, including petroleum, publishing, iron and steel, and cement, were each dominated by four firms that controlled at least 75 percent of their output. This process of concentration is cumulative, since large firms grow faster than small ones and can accumulate more capital.

The wealth controlled by these firms rivals that of nation-states. World Bank data show that 46 of the top 100 economies in the world are transnational corporations. The total value of the output of these firms exceeds the gross national product of more than 150 countries, and they are expanding at two-to-three times the national rates of growth (Veltmeyer 1987, 76–79). They expand primarily by buying out or merging with existing corporations.

Horizontal Mergers

The dominant form of takeover in the earlier stages of corporate capitalist growth was through **horizontal integration**, the consolidation of firms in the same industry. This gave the corporation enormous power in setting the terms of labour contracts and fixing prices. The Bertrand Report (1981) on *The State of Competition in the Canadian Petroleum Industry* estimated that, through price fixing by the then "big four"—Imperial, Texaco, Shell, and Gulf—Canadians were overcharged by about $12 billion for petroleum products between 1958 and 1978.

In 1910, the Canadian government passed legislation that provided for the "Investigation of Combines, Monopolies, Trusts, and Mergers" that might lead to the decline of "free competition" and therefore to "unfair pricing" (Veltmeyer 1987, 28). Generally, however, the capacity of the federal government to restrict the formation of monopolies has been very limited. Several royal commissions have documented the continuing problem and expressed grave concerns, but mergers have continued largely unchecked. Several significant mergers and buy-outs occurred in the first month of 1989 alone. Molson's brewery merged with Carling O'Keefe, leaving Labatts as the only other large brewery in Canada. Canadian Airlines made an offer to buy out Wardair, leaving only Air Canada for competition. The buy-out of Consolidated Bathurst by an American company, Stone Container, made the latter the dominant manufacturer of paper products in North America. Imperial Oil bought out Texaco, reducing the "big four" to the "big three." Corporate mergers to the value of $57 billion took place in 1988 and 1989 (Hurtig 1991, 160).

Vertical Integration

The most important form of takeover is **vertical integration**, the linking of firms that operate at different stages in the development of a product. These firms then have enormous power over primary producers who provide the raw materials for processors and manufacturers.

The McCain group of companies in New Brunswick, for example, is in a position to control all stages of food processing, brokerage, wholesaling and retailing of potatoes. They own large tracts of land in the province on which farmers work as company employees. They own the potato-processing factory in Florenceville, storage facilities, brokerage, and pricing firms, and also a major trucking line shipping to other parts of the Maritimes and to Ontario and Quebec. Corporation subsidiaries manufacture farm building materials, seeds, fertilizers, and harvesters. The majority of New Brunswick potato farmers may technically be independent commodity producers working their own farms, but in practice they are subject to the dictates of the agribusiness corporation. The McCain company is in a position to enforce contracts with regional farmers on terms very advantageous to itself. Growers are required to deliver potatoes to the company at the company's convenience, pay all storage costs, and make up any shortfall by purchasing additional potatoes. They are also required to follow specific instructions with respect to type of potato grown, amount and time of application of fertilizer, and time of planting and harvesting. The company can withhold payment for potatoes to the amount owing to any of the McCain group of companies. Local banks want contracts signed with processors before they will advance loans to the farmers, as do machinery, seed and feed, and fertilizer dealers (Veltmeyer 1987, 36–38).

Conglomerate Mergers

Conglomerate mergers take the form of links with other companies in fields of production different from that of the parent corporation. Such diversification provides stability as profits in one area can compensate for losses in another. The Thomson empire, for example, controls the big department stores of Hudson's Bay, The Bay, Zeller's, and Fields. There is thus no direct competition between these stores for customers, although managers may be forced to compete with each other for profit ratings. With the takeover of Hudson's Bay, Thomson gained control over significant oil and gas interests, as well as insurance companies and truck lines. Thomson also controls 50 percent of the newspaper market in Canada, his most significant holding being the *Globe and Mail*, plus other papers in the United States and Britain (Veltmeyer 1987, 40). Such conglomerate ownership has significant implications for the control of ideas by the business elites within capitalist society. For example, editors of major newspapers are unlikely to take a critical stand against corporate interests when they are themselves employees of those corporations.

Conglomerate mergers give companies an advantage in dealing with labour disputes.

Companies of this size have a very lopsided advantage in dealing with trade unions or nonunion labour. A six-month strike by newspaper workers at *The Times* in London cost the Thomson corporation an estimated $35 million in 1980, but the corporation as a whole still increased its profits during that year. In effect, such corporations can afford to ride out a very long strike in one sector by subsidies from other sectors. This gives them a very powerful weapon against workers for whom strikes are a massive drain on economic resources and entail the serious risk of failure.

Intercorporate Ownership and Control

A much cheaper but very effective means of gaining control over other companies is to purchase equity in them in the form of a majority of voting shares, or the largest single block of such shares if share ownership is widely dispersed. If a company has its assets divided equally into bonds, nonvoting preferred stock, and voting common stock, the purchase of half the voting common stock, or one-sixth of the total worth of the company, will give effective legal voting control. The purchaser can then form a **holding company**, convert its assets into bonds, nonvoting preferred stock, and voting common stock, sell everything but a little over half of the voting stock, and still retain voting control over the original company or group of companies. The intercorporate empires controlled by two individuals in Canada, Conrad Black and Paul Desmarais and their associates, comprise 350 corporations, plus a further 1500 subsidiaries, with combined assets of $60 billion (Veltmeyer 1987, 53). Three other Canadian families who control giant holding companies are the Thomsons, Westons, and Bronfmans. Apart from these five family empires, the biggest holding companies are Bell Canada and the chartered banks.

It is almost impossible to keep up with all the ramifications and threads of control of such huge holding companies. Takeover bids and efforts to avoid being taken over comprise the arena of modern corporate warfare. The burgeoning business section of the *Globe and Mail* reports almost daily instances of companies suddenly finding that their voting stock is being swallowed up. They may not even know who is trying to buy them out because bidding is done through brokers. The targeted company must get cash quickly to buy up its own shares and block the takeover, or it must capitulate. Share prices shoot up because of aggressive buying. The company trying to stop the takeover buys back the shares at inflated prices. Even the "losers" in a takeover game may make a fortune by selling out their shares at top prices before withdrawing. In this process, cash flow is critical; firms need access to large amounts of money. Banks play a central role in this game of mergers and takeovers, so much so that Peter Newman (1975, 99–101) described them as the heart of the private intelligence network that keeps top Canadian business people in touch with each other.

Interlocking Directorships

Bank directors are commonly in the position to exert enormous influence over corporations through the mechanism of **interlocking directorships**. A *direct interlock* is a situation where a person serves on the board of directors of two different companies. An *indirect interlock* occurs when each of two companies has a director on the board of a third company (Veltmeyer 1987, 60). Clement (1977, 70) shows that there are far fewer elite individuals than there are elite positions. At the time of his study, a mere 274 individuals held a total of 782 positions as directors of big corporations, an average of 2.85 positions per person.

The major interlockers in this system have bank connections. In 1981, 40 directors of the Royal Bank held 431 directorships among them, many in the biggest corporations in Canada. Similarly, 100 top bank directors in Canada held 1110 corporate connections. Just 10 individuals held 237 directorships, linking top industrial corporations, foreign corporations, financial institutions such as trust companies and insurance firms, and large family fortunes (Veltmeyer 1987, 60). Newman (1975, 99–101) argues that "the executive board meetings of the five largest banks represent the greatest source of nongovernmental power in the country." The power of these bankers is wielded through their ability to withhold favours, to keep those whom they consider unsuitable from joining either their own or any other clusters of influence. In effect, they have virtual veto power over entry into the big business establishment in Canada. Such is the extent of corporate concentration and interlocking networks of power. There are fears voiced, however, that even this concentration of financial power may be vulnerable to even larger American banks as they have gained access to the Canadian financial services market with the Free Trade Deal.

Marxist Critique of the Liberal-Bourgeois Thesis

The liberal-bourgeois vision of free competition in the marketplace, regulating prices, profits, and wages, no longer accurately describes the current structure of capital in Canada, if it ever did. Through processes of horizontal and vertical integration and conglomerate mergers, once-competitive enterprises have been amalgamated into huge corporations, with subsectors run by managers. When a corporate empire like Thomson Co. owns Hudson's Bay, Zellers, and Fields, competition among these conglomerates exists only on paper, or in the boardrooms where the performance of managers is compared. Competition among the conglomerates is also muted as it is in their collective interests to manage the market rather than compete to undercut each other's profits. The big players are able to control the market and to determine both supply and price. Even when individual firms have not lost their identity through outright mergers, the control over major decisions in the investment and transfer of capital is concentrated through intercorporate ownership, holding companies, and interlocking directorships. A handful of family empires and the directors of the major chartered banks in Canada dominate the capital market.

The Canada–United States Free Trade Agreement has in a sense opened up competition, especially in retail and services, but this competition is still confined to a small number of giant transnational corporations. The United States–based retail superstore Wal-Mart bought out the Woolco chain in 1994 and began to expand into Canadian markets. The *Globe and Mail* carried many stories of fear among retailers, such as Sears and the Thomson chains, that they will be driven out of business by Wal-Mart's huge size and capacity to offer deep discounts.

The liberal thesis that ownership of capital has been democratized through shareholding has little relevance in the context of corporate capitalism. While hundreds of thousands of Canadians may own a few shares each, only a tiny fraction own sufficient shares in any one corporation to sway decisions. Shareholder meetings represent a **plutocracy**—rule by the wealthy. Usually, they are preplanned affairs in which those present are told what corporate policies will be. The notion that a new class of managers has emerged that runs corporations in the shareholder's interests, also has little substance. They may run day-to-day operations, but they do not make policy decisions on when and where to invest capital, how assets will be used, or which plants to shut down.

Small businesses continually spring up among these corporate giants, but their survival rate is low. Primary producers in farming, fishing, and lumbering all across Canada are fighting a losing battle against big corporations. They cannot keep up with the pace and the costs of the labour-saving technology of big producers and processors. They survive in ever-smaller numbers, dependent on government subsidies and intermittent wagework of the primary producer. The Marxist thesis, that internal contradictions of capitalism would lead to ever-increasing corporate concentration, and to the collapse of the petite bourgeoisie into the proletariat, finds extensive support.

✸ The Petite Bourgeoisie

Marx's prediction concerning the polarization of classes focussed particularly on the petite bourgeoisie, comprising independent producers who own their own means of production but who are not major capitalists. They labour for themselves in small family enterprises, but they are not major employers of labour. Marx predicted that, over time, this small business class would collapse into the proletariat. Unlike corporate capitalists, they would be unable to afford the labour-saving technology that makes possible cheap mass production. Slowly, they would go bankrupt.

In Canada, the petite bourgeoisie comprises independent commodity producers in family-run farming, fishing, and craft enterprises, and another group of small retailers and independent salespeople. The liberal-bourgeois vision of capitalism as founded on entrepreneurship and free enterprise focusses particularly on these small business people. The dream of many workers is that one day they will save enough money to quit their jobs and go into business for themselves. But Canadian data suggest that, as a class, small business people are economically insecure and face a permanently uncertain future (see table 9-2). Large numbers of small businesses start up every year, but the majority fail within two years. Although self-employed people are much more likely than other workers to say that they would choose the same job again, they are much less likely to say they would recommend it to a friend (Archibald 1978, 129). They are too vulnerable to the whims of corporate buyers and sellers.

Table 9-2

Income of Self-Employed Workers by Sex, April 1986		
Income	Male	Female
Less than $ 5 000	12.2	43.7
5 000– 9 999	14.4	20.0
10 000–14 999	14.9	11.9
15 000–19 999	12.1	8.4
20 000–24 999	10.6	4.6
25 000–29 999	7.8	4.2
30 000–34 999	7.2	2.3
35 000–39 999	5.0	1.3
40 000–49 999	6.4	1.2
50 000–59 999	2.7	0.0
60 000 and over	6.8	1.7
Self-employed as % all employed	17.1	8.3

Source: Statistics Canada (1987, 74).

Farming

The situation of **independent commodity producers** in Canada has become increasingly precarious in the face of expanding capital, centralized production, and big bankers. There has been a steady decline in the number of farms in Canada as undercapitalized farms have been forced out of business. Between 1931 and 1961, the **capitalization** of farms—that is, the amount of financial investment that the average farmer needs to operate a farm— rose by 450 percent. Over the same period, the

number of people working in farming dropped by 50 percent, and output per farm worker doubled. Between 1951 and 1981, fully 80 percent of New Brunswick farms disappeared. In 1951, three million acres were being farmed by 26 000 farmers, but by 1981 only one million acres were being farmed by a total of 4000 farmers (Murphy 1987). In Nova Scotia between 1941 and 1981, 87 percent of farms failed as did 74 percent of farms on Prince Edward Island.

Murphy suggests that the invention of mechanical potato harvesters made possible the expansion of farm size in the Maritimes because of the reduced need for manual labour. The pressure to introduce harvesters itself reflected the impact of McCain's food-processing corporation in New Brunswick. The company promoted the mass production of potatoes as raw materials for manufacturing frozen french fries. But as the mechanization of potato harvesting spread, the many small farmers who could not afford such expensive equipment, could not compete in the potato market. Others invested in the new machines but could not carry the exorbitant debt.

As small farms went bankrupt, they were bought up by McCain in New Brunswick and Cavendish Farms in Prince Edward Island. Farms that were too hilly to use the mechanical harvesters went out of production altogether. The result of this process was the creation of an underclass of dispossessed rural dwellers, estimated to comprise as many as one-third of the people living in the rural Maritimes during the 1970s (Veltmeyer 1986, 49). These dispossessed farmers and farm workers became dependent upon what wagework they could find, supplementing their incomes with unemployment insurance and welfare cheques. They swelled the ranks of the poor, socially disorganized, and anomic residents of the rural communities described in chapter 4.

The lot of farmers who have remained in business has not improved either. Despite the doubling of labour productivity, farm incomes generally have fallen and are reflected in declining standards of living. Farmers are largely at the mercy of monopoly processors and distributors. Clement (1981) suggests the term **dependent commodity producers** to refer to the people in this ambiguous class position. Technically they own their own means of production, but they have nevertheless lost their economic independence.

Farm women, in particular, have been active in the desperate struggle to save their family farms.

The circumstances of Saskatchewan wheat farmers are similar to those of maritime farmers. Together with small business people in prairie towns, they share what has been called a "companionship of vultures" (*Globe and Mail*, 11 July 1987, D2) as they wait for someone to go bankrupt so that they might survive by buying the farm and thus expanding their holdings. Small business people, who depend on farm families as clientele for their cafes and stores, likewise face bankruptcy as the local population declines.

Between 1956 and 1986, the Saskatchewan farm population shrank by more than half, as small farmers abandoned the increasingly corporate industry. The average size of farms increased by 6.4 percent just between 1982 and 1987. Those who remain in business face mounting debts for their heavily capitalized irrigation, ploughing, and harvesting machinery. As Marx predicted, the rate of profit is falling as an ever-larger percentage of investment goes into machines. In 1987, 8 percent of Saskatchewan farmers were effectively bankrupt and a further 23 percent were unable to prevent their debts from mounting. One farmer projected a year-end loss of $40 000 on his large grain farm. He already had debts that were costing him $100 000. The family survived on the wife's wagework income (*Globe and Mail*, 11 July 1987, D2). Many farm families have already joined the proletariat, with the wife and often the husband working part-time or seasonally for wages, to supplement the farm income.

Farm women have been especially exploited in the process that ties family farms into capitalism. Their exploitation was total because farm wives commonly did not receive wages; they worked for subsistence. A woman could work for a lifetime on the family farm only to find that everything she produced belonged to her husband. This is precisely what happened to Irene Murdoch, an Alberta farm woman. After her husband petitioned to divorce her, the Supreme Court of Canada ruled in 1975 that she had no right to a share in the farm that she had helped to build up during a twenty-five-year marriage. Reaction to this infamous judicial decision spurred changes to family property laws. Today it is more likely that farms are owned jointly by the husband and wife. The woman's situation, however, may not be substantially better. Formerly she worked for the benefit of her husband. Now both work for the benefit of the mortgage company. They constantly run the risk of losing everything, including their family home, if the farm fails.

Only farms with huge outputs of grain can hope to come out ahead of the falling rate of profit on heavy investments at high interest rates. But the crisis of overproduction is now hitting the industry. Canada has enormous stockpiles of grain, so massive that the Wheat Board is forced to slash prices to sell it. An estimated 500 million people go hungry in the Third World, but they cannot afford to buy our grain. Canada cannot give it away either. If it did, the argument goes, it would promptly bankrupt small farmers in Third World countries by destroying their incentives to grow food for local markets. (We will view this issue further in chapter 10 on development.)

The Canadian state has become directly involved in the marketing of wheat, through the Wheat Marketing Board. The goal was to reduce cutthroat competition between individual farmers and to give some price stability. The Board contracts to purchase grain from farmers at a prearranged price, and then sells it on international markets for the best price it can get. The Free Trade Agreement complicates this arrangement, since in years of low average grain prices, the Wheat Board price looks like an unfair **subsidy**. Ironically, 1994 was a good year in that Canadian export of durum wheat to the United States roughly doubled. The Canadian state claimed that this is an effect of United States export subsidies that encourage farmers to sell their crops abroad rather than locally. United States farmers, however, claimed that Canada is dumping cheap wheat in their market. Some of the complications surrounding the Free Trade Agreement and the issues of subsidies and agricultural marketing boards are discussed in chapter 10.

Supply-management boards have been established in the dairy industry, and in eggs, chicken, and turkey production, with a similar aim of avoiding the ravishes of free-market competition so as to stabilize production and prices (Skogstad 1993). They have greatly aided participating producers who were awarded quotas under the system. But at the same time they have come under much criticism for blocking the entry of other potential producers, encouraging less than optimal productivity, and working against consumers who have to pay higher prices for these commodities. An especially powerful group of consumers are the corporate food processors who manufacture such items as yoghurt, cheese, and prepared meals. They are lobbying hard for greater representation on the boards, or their dismantling altogether. Otherwise they threaten to move their manufacturing plants to the United States where raw materials are cheaper. If the boards are dismantled, however, the almost inevitable result would be the collapse of thousands of small farm producers. There is no easy solution to these contradictions.

As small farmers go deeper into debt or are forced out of business, the social costs to rural communities are enormous. Once-stable, homogeneous communities on the Prairies are being torn apart by acrimonious disputes between older and relatively debt-free farmers who inherited their farms and younger debt-ridden farmers, and also between the specialized grain growers and the mixed producers. Not only farmers suffer. Corporate **rationalization** has killed many small farm-machinery dealerships and bank branches. As grain prices fall and debts rise among farmers, they spend less money, and other local small businesses collapse. People cannot afford to go out so they stay on their isolated farms, and the communities fall apart. Local hockey and baseball leagues collapse as the communities can no longer put teams together. The social anomie that Clark described in the Maritimes (see chapter 4) has thus hit Prairie communities also.

Fishing

Independent producers in the Maritime fishing industry suffered a similar decline to farmers, finding themselves unable to compete with huge factory freezer trawlers, or reduced to a virtual tenant status under contract to fish-processing plants. Small boat owners relied on processors to give them loans for fishing gear, and in return owed them their catch, on terms very advantageous to the processors. The stranglehold of big fishpackers over fishing communities in the Maritimes has a long history. What changed in recent years was the degree of concentration of corporate control in fish factories, and the involvement of the state on the side of corporate capital at the expense of small producers (Sacouman 1985). Sacouman suggests that traditionally there was a roughly equal split in the industry between small producers and corporate giants but this pattern decisively shifted towards corporate capital from the 1960s onward. The rapid expansion of factory freezer trawlers in the North Atlantic coincided with the development of an infrastructure for frozen food marketing, as refrigerators became a common household appliance. The profitability of corporate mass production depends on a number of conditions, but first and foremost is a secure supply of relatively homogeneous raw materials, such as potatoes and wheat (Neis 1991, 153–58). The corporate fishing industry required access to dense and homogeneous fish stocks suitable for automated harvesting and processing. The waters off Newfoundland were characterized by large concentrations of a narrow range of fish species including cod, redfish, and herring, and hence were ideal for corporate exploitation. Trawlers commonly stayed at sea for sixty to ninety days at a time, processing their catches into standardized frozen fish blocks for mass markets. Global fish production expanded dramatically after 1955, to reach a peak of 60 million tons in 1974. Federal and provincial governments invested heavily in the industry, financing the construction of trawlers, and encouraging transnational food conglomerates to set up in Newfoundland.

The very success of corporate enterprise in fishing, however, was also to be its downfall. It was particularly vulnerable to any decline in fish stocks. The rigid technology employed by freezer trawlers was very wasteful of natural resources.

The need for homogeneity was such that even valuable species of fish were often discarded or converted into fish meal (Neis 1991, 157). When fish stocks began to decline in the late 1970s the industry was in trouble. Particularly hard hit were the large, vertically integrated trawler firms like Nickersons, National Sea, and Fisheries Products International. By 1981 these companies were close to bankruptcy, with debts of over $300 million, held principally by the Bank of Nova Scotia, and the Nova Scotia and Newfoundland provincial governments. The state stepped in to regulate resources by extending jurisdiction to 200 miles off the coast. It also helped finance a restructuring of the industry to decentralize processing plants and diversify production, with a mixture of trawlers and the smaller in-shore fishery. Corporate owners still retained control over the industry. Multiplant ownership limited the ability of local workers to strike for better contracts. Commonly, corporations also owned other businesses in the local communities, and had effective control over local housing.

This control and diversification, however, was not sufficient to save the industry from impending ecological disaster. By 1993 fish stocks had become so severely depleted that the Atlantic fishery was closed down completely, with some 30 000 people forced onto a government relief program, 23 000 of them in Newfoundland. As Neis observes, the crisis of capital accumulation in the corporate fishing industry is largely the result of ecological factors, to which the industry itself may have been a major contributor.

Forestry

Intensive capitalization and concentration similarly characterizes forestry in Canada, reflecting the domination of the pulp and paper industry by transnational corporations. Sacouman (1985) notes that formerly there was a relatively equitable split in this industry in the Maritimes with about 50 percent of wood being produced by big corporations and 50 percent by small woodlot owners. Again, provincial and federal initiatives, in alliance with large corporations, shifted this balance against the small producers.

The policies advocated by the Nova Scotia Royal Commission Report on Forestry in 1984 supported the expansion of corporate capital production at the expense of small woodlots (Schneider 1987, 117–18). The report recommended establishing uniform government management of private woodlands to ensure a viable market for industries supplying pesticides, fertilizers, and seedlings. The effect of such policies was to impose a capital-intensive technology on wood production. Small producers are compelled to use expensive inputs such as chemical herbicides and mechanical harvesters rather than manual labour, if they are to have any hope of competing with corporate wood production. Government subsidies to help woodlot owners principally benefit the multinational companies producing the chemicals and seedlings. They otherwise ensure a dependable supply of low-cost, raw materials to foreign-owned pulp companies.

▓ Disparities in Wealth

The third major area of debate between the liberal and the Marxist theses on capitalism concerns the structure of classes in capitalist societies. Marx predicted that a steady polarization of classes would occur, with increasing wealth in fewer and fewer hands at one extreme and increasing poverty at the other. The middle group, the petite bourgeoisie, would eventually collapse into the working classes, unable to keep up in the technological rat race.

Proponents of the liberal perspective challenge this thesis on two counts. Firstly, they argue that under capitalism the members of the working classes have become increasingly better off, enjoying generally higher standards of living, longer and healthier lives, and access to a vast array of cheap consumer goods. This thesis that the working classes are becoming more like the bourgeoisie in their styles of life is sometimes referred to as the embourgeoisement thesis.

Secondly, they argue that Marxist theory fails to account for the spectacular expansion of the middle-class—the professional and managerial classes—under advanced capitalism. Even if we discount the argument that managers have actually taken over from owners of capital in the control of corporations, the expansion of the middle class appears to contradict the Marxist notion of class polarization. It is hard to see how these people can fit unambiguously into the working class.

If contemporary Marxist theory is to retain credibility, it needs to account for these conditions. In the following pages, we test the Marxist theory of the polarization of classes against the liberal challenge embodied in the embourgeoisement thesis and the rise of the middle class.

The Rich

The existence of a numerically tiny but immensely powerful class of ultra-rich individuals, who dominate corporate capitalism in Canada and worldwide, supports Marx's prediction of increasing concentration of wealth. In 1994, *Forbes* magazine listed 358 people around the world as billionaires, people whose personal wealth exceeds a thousand million dollars (U.S.). Topping the world is the Walton family ($23.6 billion), founders of Wal-Mart, the largest American retailer.

The richest Canadians, Kenneth Thomson and the late K.C. Irving, made their fortunes in oil and in newspapers. The Reichmann brothers, before the spectacular collapse of their real estate empire in 1992, came a close third, along with the "supermarket czar" Galen Weston (*Globe and Mail*, 21 Sept. 1987, B14). Conrad Black and Paul Desmarais follow close behind. This handful of men controlled more than 1300 companies in 1987, their empires constantly expanding as they swallowed up more and more companies to diversify their holdings.

The business section of the *Globe and Mail* newspaper and its *Report on Business Magazine* keep us informed on the nouveau riche who make their fortunes in the stock market, mastering pyramiding and **leveraged buy-outs**, or "the art of buying companies with little cash and forcing the target to swallow the subsequent debt" (*Report on Business*, Oct. 1987, 27–28).

Hanging on to the coattails of such men are Canada's top executive class, people—almost always men—who manage the vast corporations that the tycoons acquire. Veltmeyer (1986, 28) describes these executives as men who earn more in one day than most Canadians earn in a year. In 1983, the two top executives of Dome Petroleum received $9.4 million in salaries, equivalent to

$37 000 a day—this in a debt-ridden company bailed out by the federal government in 1984 to the tune of $500 million. In 1993, a year of severe recession and national unemployment rates around 11 percent, Canada's executive class continued to do well, especially in the field of financial services. The top executive of First Marathon Investment dealers received $6.9 million in a mixture of salary and performance-related commissions and bonuses. Two vice-presidents took home $6.4 million and $4 million (*Globe and Mail*, 13 April 1994, B1). The chairman of Time Warner Inc. received $5.3 million (U.S.) in salary, bonuses, and other compensations (*Globe and Mail*, 31 March 1994, B2).

An important way of rewarding top executives is to give them stock or share options. The value of options is the difference between the exercise price (what the executive has to pay) and the market price (what the executive can sell them for on the stock market). Frank Stronach earned $200 000 as chairman of Magna International in 1993. However, after adding a bonus, other compensation, and exercised stock options, his fiscal pay-out in 1994 came to $41 million (*Globe and Mail*, 1 Nov. 1994, B1). Galen Weston, the chairman of Loblaw, received a salary of $290 000 in 1993, but with share options valued at $1 469 502. The president of Loblaw received a salary of $1 050 000 with share options of $3 578 602. Vice-presidents received salaries in the range of half a million dollars with stock options worth about double their salaries. To put them in some perspective, these rewards were paid out in a year when employees in Loblaw's Maritime grocery stores earned about $6 per hour or $12 500 a year, if they were lucky enough to work full-time.

Shareholders of Nova Scotia Power Inc. objected to the company president receiving $197 852 in salary and bonuses in 1993, a year when the company laid off four hundred employees (*Globe and Mail*, 28 April 1994, B8). The president shrugged off the complaints, arguing with some justification that he received less than the heads of other large utilities. He also had no qualms about pension rights worth almost $80 000 a year.

Estimates of just how many people comprise the corporate elite are hard to make because the relevant information is rarely made public. Veltmeyer puts it at about 3 percent of the population, with a core of perhaps 1 percent and a handful of ruling families. In 1990, Carniol estimates that the richest 20 percent of Canadians owned 70 percent of wealth while the poorest 40 percent owned less than 1 percent of wealth in Canada (1993, 105).

Welfare for the Ultra Rich

The popular image of welfare is that it goes to the poor. In reality, however, the largest proportion of government hand-outs, tax breaks, and subsidies goes to the ultra rich, the heads of big corporations.

"The caterers haven't shown up, the musicians are late, and the elevator is broken. We might as well be living in a Third World country."

Drawing by Weber; © 1993 The New Yorker Magazine, Inc.

David Lewis (1972) first popularized the term "corporate welfare bums" in his account of the plethora of grants and subsidies available to corporations through the federal government's Department of Regional and Economic Expansion (DREE). DREE was established to try to promote development in the poorer regions of Canada, but in Lewis's view the department's major practical achievement was to subsidize big companies. Corporations used public money to update equipment in one plant, to close down others, or to relocate at public expense in search of cheaper sources of labour. Among the examples that Lewis gives is Aerovox Canada, a company that was given a grant of $254 000 from DREE to start a new factory in Amherst, Nova Scotia. Aerovox responded by closing down its plant in

Hamilton, Ontario, with the loss of sixty-eight jobs at an average hourly wage of $3.32. Ninety new jobs were created in Amherst at an average wage of $2 per hour. The company was thus paid a quarter of a million dollars to reduce its labour costs. Another example is Celanese Canada, which received grants of $279 000 for modernization and expansion of plants in Drummondville, Montmagny, and Coaticook, Quebec. It responded by shutting down its Montmagny plant and laying off 450 workers. DREE then gave $2 477 000 to two other companies to create 412 new jobs in the old Celanese plant. The Newfoundland government heavily subsidized Eastern Pacific Airways, only to have the company move out of the province, with virtually no notice.

In the early 1980s, federal and provincial governments bailed out the giant fishing conglomerates Nickersons and National Sea to the value of $300 million in an abortive effort to keep them operating. In 1994, the Ontario NDP government paid employers to hire unemployed people and train them, with the only condition that they be hired for at least one year. Critics argued that many companies took advantage of the scheme to pay employees that they would have hired anyway, and contributed only minimal training.

Tax concessions to corporations also amount to large government welfare donations. A Revenue Canada report for 1987 put the figure for amount owed but not paid by corporations at some $10 billion (Hurtig 1991, 154). Corporations are entitled to a wide range of tax writeoffs, exemptions, deferrals, and other concessions, and in addition can often use tax lawyers to find favourable interpretations of complex legislation, so as to minimize their tax liability or force long delays in payment. Hurtig's figures indicate that between 1980 and 1987 inclusive, Canada's banks reported profits of over $7.64 billion and paid federal income taxes at the rate of 2.48 percent. This was over a period when the banks cut more than 10 000 employees from their work forces. From 1981 to 1984, life insurance companies in Canada made total profits of over $3 billion and paid federal income taxes at the rate of 4.3 percent. The metal mining industry paid a combined federal and provincial tax rate of 7.7 percent on profits of well over $2 billion in 1986 and 1987. During the same years, petroleum and coal products industries made profits of over $6 billion and paid taxes of only 9.5 percent. Carniol estimates that the total of all untaxed corporate profits in 1990 equalled $27 billion. In short, these corporations paid far less than the statutory tax rate for business profits, and many times lower rates than individuals. Federal income tax rates for individuals in 1993 was 17 percent for the first $29 590 and 29 percent on income over $59 180, with additional provincial tax at approximately 60 percent of federal tax liability.

Back in 1950 the share of total income taxes paid by corporations and individuals was about equal but since then the corporate share has dropped steadily while the individual share has risen. During the decade between 1980 and 1990, personal income tax as a proportion of all federal government budgetary revenues rose from 40.6 percent to 46.9 percent while corporate income tax fell from 16.6 percent to 10.4 percent (see figure 9-1) (Hurtig 1991, 150). Compared with the gross domestic product, corporate taxes fell from 4.4 percent in 1950 to 1.9 percent in 1990. Government transfer payments back to corporations annually constitute about 65 percent of tax that is collected (ibid., 335).

Figure 9-1

Corporate and Individual Income Tax

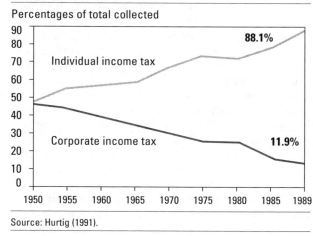

Percentages of total collected

Source: Hurtig (1991).

Within the personal tax system, the inequalities between the rich and the poor are massive. The National Council of Welfare Report (1986) notes that the more than sixty deductions, exemptions, credits, exclusions, and preferential tax rates within the income tax system all result

in the largest tax savings going to the richest earners in the highest tax bracket. Billions of dollars are involved. Carniol indicates that in Ontario in 1990 some 779 individual taxfilers with incomes over $100 000 paid no income tax at all, and a further 13 167 such taxfilers paid less than 10 percent (Carniol 1993, 105).

At the other extreme, people whose earnings are so low that they are below the tax-paying threshold gain nothing from these concessions. A subsequent report on tax expenditures (National Council of Welfare 1987b) explores who benefits most from a dozen different income tax exemptions. The report notes two clear patterns. In every case, the higher the taxfilers' income, the higher their benefit from the tax expenditure. Taxfilers in the lowest income group get a disproportionately small share of benefits. In 1984, the estimated cost to the federal government of all these tax exemptions was close to $245 billion.

The main excuses for not imposing a heavier share of taxes on wealth and profits is that it would discourage entrepreneurship and corporate investment in Canada, or prompt corporations to move to cheaper tax havens, and so leave the Canadian economy worse off.

The Poor

It is a harsh jolt to the imagination when one switches from contemplating the lives of the ultra rich to considering those of the much larger groups of Canadians who live in poverty. Marx made two predictions concerning how capitalism as an economic system produces poverty. The relentless drive toward labour-saving technology in an effort to cut production costs would lead to chronic unemployment. At the same time, the very existence of this class of unemployed people would serve to depress wages to a level at or below subsistence, as people compete against each other for jobs.

Unemployment Figures

For a growing proportion of Canadians in the 1980s, these predictions became reality. By the early 1990s the situation worsened. Unemployment hovered around 10 percent of the labour force for most of the decade, with over one million people actively seeking work but unable to find it. The proportions were higher among early school-leavers and people living in the poorer regions such as the Maritimes. By the beginning of 1994 the rate was 11.6 percent. A small drop in March seemed to reflect more a shrinking in the size of the labour force than any significant increase in the jobs available, as many people gave up even looking for work.

Labour force statistics for people aged sixteen to sixty-four during the years 1988–90 showed that 49 percent experienced some unemployment during this period, 1.5 percent for the entire period (National Council of Welfare 1993a, 6). The real risk of experiencing unemployment is thus much higher than the official rates. In Ontario during this period the offical rate of unemployment averaged 5.5 percent, but 18.3 percent of the working-age population received unemployment insurance for some of the time. Ontario was hurt more than any other province by the 1990–91 downturn in the economy, with welfare rolls jumping 38 percent in one year to a record 929 900 people (National Council of Welfare 1992b, 27).

It is important to recognize that the official Statistics Canada unemployment figures seriously underestimate the actual number of people unemployed, because many are excluded by the rigid definition used. The *unemployed*, as defined by Statistics Canada, include only "those actively seeking paid work during the previous week." This excludes all Native peoples living on reserves, all people who have given up looking for work because there are no jobs in the region, and all women who would like to work but cannot do so because they cannot find day-care for their children. People who can find only a few hours a week of part-time work may think of themselves as unemployed, but Statistics Canada does not include them in the jobless rate. The hidden unemployment figure has been estimated as more than double the official rate.

Everywhere workers are finding their jobs threatened by competition from Third World countries offering cheaper labour power, or by automation. Throughout the 1980s the major concern of unions in contract negotiations was job security. They lost the fight. The early 1990s saw massive layoffs in a wide range of industries. The growing numbers of unemployed and under-employed workers comprises a reserve army of labour, with many people desperate to get a job under any conditions. Their need sets worker against worker, breaking the potential power of strike action as they provide a ready source of strikebreakers. In Cape Breton in August 1987, a furniture manufacturer, thinking of setting up a factory in the region, demanded that would-be employees pay $10 each for job application forms. Employees would also have to agree to work up to sixty hours a week for minimum wages, with only one week's holiday at the end of the year (CBC News, 11 Aug. 1987). He got hundreds of takers.

Subsistence Wages: The Working Poor

Marx's second prediction, that wages would drop to subsistence level or below, has also become a reality for a growing proportion of Canada's labour force. During the 1980s, the average wage in Canada did not keep pace with price increases, so that real incomes fell. In 1993 average wage increases were close to zero. What this means is that many workers experienced a drop in wages, having to accept lower-paying and part-time jobs. Some public sector workers rioted in the Nova Scotia legislature in April 1994 when the government announced plans for a 3 percent cut in salaries, following a three-year wage freeze.

The most commonly used measure of poverty in Canada is the Statistics Canada definition of the *Low-Income Cutoff*, generally referred to as **"the poverty line."** This line is a measure of relative poverty in the Canadian context—indicating how the most vulnerable groups of people are doing relative to other Canadians and people in their community (Johnston 1993, 89). Surveys of family expenditure in 1978 and again in 1982 found that families in Canada spend on average 38.5 percent of their income on the basic necessities of food, clothing, and shelter. Statistics Canada adds 20 percentage points to this average, defining the low-income cutoff as the level of income at which families would have to spend 58.5 percent on necessities. This cutoff varies with size of family and area of residence, since it generally costs more to find housing in towns and cities than in rural areas. The lines are adjusted annually according to the rise in the cost of living. Table 9-3 shows the poverty lines for 1992. They range from $10 331 to $15 175 for an individual and $20 494 to $30 105 for a family of four. There

Table 9-3

Statistics Canada's Low-Income Cutoffs (1986 base) for 1992

Family Size	Community Size				
	Cities of 500 000+	100 000– 499 999	30 000– 99 999	Less than 30 000	Rural Areas
1	$15 175	$13 328	$13 021	$11 870	$10 331
2	20 569	18 068	17 650	16 089	14 005
3	26 146	22 965	22 434	20 450	17 801
4	30 105	26 439	25 830	23 547	20 494
5	32 891	28 888	28 221	25 726	22 392
6	35 703	31 355	30 632	27 924	24 305
7+	38 399	33 727	32 949	30 036	26 142

Source: National Council of Welfare (1994, 3).

are other measures of poverty, based on different cost-of-living estimates, and the Canada Council on Social Development's line that sets poverty as 50 percent of average family income (Johnston 1993, 90), but this Statistics Canada definition is the most stringent and the most often used.

These calculations are essentially subjective. There is no one correct definition of poverty. All the above measures conceptualize poverty as relative to community standards. In 1992, the House of Commons Subcommittee on Poverty considered an alternative proposal to calculate poverty on an absolute measure of minimum need. This measure calculates, for example, that a single parent with two children needed only 80 cents per meal to meet basic caloric needs. By this measure the numbers of people in poverty in Canada would drop by three-quarters. Few people, however, consider such a drastic survival level to be acceptable in a society such as Canada, with a high average standard of living. In this text, the Statistics Canada Low-Income Cutoff is taken as the working definition of poverty.

A National Council of Welfare Report entitled *Poverty Profile 1992* (1994) estimates that in 1992, 16.1 percent of all Canadians, or 4 320 000 people, were living below the poverty line. Provincial figures on those living below the poverty line varied from 13.3 percent in Ontario to 20 percent in Newfoundland. In 1992, the overall poverty rate was 16.8 percent of all Canadians (National Anti-Poverty Organization 1992). Most of these poor people have incomes considerably below the poverty line. The gap between them and the average Canadian is enormous.

Who are the people living below the poverty line? The first myth to dispel is that they are all unemployed. In 1992, 56 percent of poor family heads were employed, about 21 percent of these working full time (National Council of Welfare 1994). In other words, more than half of the families living below the poverty line are families whose major breadwinner's income from employment is so low that it pushes them below acceptable subsistence standards.

Figure 9-2

Depth of Poverty by Family Type, 1992

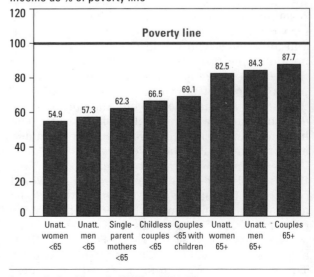

Income as % of poverty line

Source: National Council of Welfare (1994, 44).

In 1992, the poverty line for unattached people in cities of 500 000 or more was calculated at $15 175. An individual working at minimum wage had a gross income of 75 percent of the poverty line. Unemployment insurance is set at a maximum of 60 percent of earnings, the equivalent of 44 percent of the poverty line for a person laid off from a minimum-wage job (National Council of Welfare 1993a, 26). For an adult with one child to support, the minimum wage is below the poverty line in every community in Canada. Families with a child to support are better off on welfare than working for minimum wage, especially when working outside the home necessitates additional expenses such as child care, transportation, and clothing costs, as well as the loss of drug and dental coverage and possibly eviction from subsidized housing.

A second myth to dispel is that all poor children live in single-parent households. While a staggering 64 percent of single-parent families live below the poverty line, the actual numbers of children in poverty are greater in two-parent families (National Council of Welfare 1992a, 59).

Many more people are borderline poor. In 1990, more than half a million families lived on incomes between 100 to 125 percent of the poverty line. Many families just manage to stay above the poverty line with both parents working, but fall below it if one of them loses a job. The poverty rate among families would have doubled in 1987 from 8 to 16 percent, if wives had not been employed (National Council of Welfare 1990b, 40).

Welfare for the Poor

The Canada Assistance Plan of 1966 established a 50–50 cost-sharing arrangement between federal and provincial governments for provision of basic welfare or social assistance. Provinces retained the right to set terms and conditions for eligibility within national guidelines that required that all recipients be treated "with dignity" and be provided with "adequate" assistance to meet their basic shelter (rent, heat, lights, water, sewerage), clothing, personal needs, household replacement, and food needs. Other needs such as short- or long-term care, and aids for rehabilitation and training costs are cost-shared within this plan if they promote self-sufficiency and well-being (Kerr et al. 1993, 67). As welfare rolls

have jumped during the 1980s, successive federal and provincial governments have tried to cut back on spending commitments. In 1989, one in fourteen Canadians, or 7 percent, were receiving welfare. By March 1991 this had risen to 8.5 percent or 2.3 million people. The federal share of the costs in 1988–89 was nearly $5.2 billion. In the 1990 budget the federal government restricted Assistance Plan increases to 5 percent, thus pulling away from the 50–50 agreement. As the recession worsened, provinces have had to take up more and more of the increased costs. Ontario was hurt the most as their welfare rolls jumped by 38 percent in 1991 alone. The federal contribution to the Ontario welfare system declined to an estimated 28 percent of costs in the 1992–93 fiscal year (National Council of Welfare 1992b, 27).

All the provinces have been trying in various ways to cut welfare costs, typically by two-tier systems that give differential amounts for employable and long-term unemployable or disabled people, and particularly low rates for single employable people and younger school-leavers who have not worked away from home. Many provinces are experimenting with "workfare" regulations in which recipients are required to enter training programs and seek work afterward under threat of drastic cuts in welfare rates (National Council of Welfare 1991). In April 1994, the New Brunswick government proposed a scheme whereby people over fifty who have been unemployed for more than a year could receive a guaranteed income of $12 000 a year in return for working at least six months of the year on community aid projects. Some commentators welcome these moves as promoting work incentives, while others see them as a form of indentured servitude that threatens the supply of even minimum-wage jobs.

Welfare rates in all categories are set at levels far below the poverty line. In 1992, the average rate for families with children, and disabled people is 60 percent of the poverty line, dropping to 43 percent of the line for single employable people. New Brunswick had the lowest rate for single people, set at 24 percent of the poverty line in 1992.

In March 1992, 38 percent of all welfare recipients were children under 18, and another 15 percent were single parents, mostly women with young children. About 20 percent of all welfare recipients have disabilities. Over one million children, or 18.2 percent, lived in poverty in Canada in 1992. These included 61.2 percent of children of single-parent mothers.

The Gendered Character of Poverty

Women have a higher risk of living in poverty than men. In 1992, 17.4 percent of women over eighteen years of age were poor compared with 13.1 percent of men (National Council of Welfare 1994). Among elderly people, 23.3 percent of women were poor and 12.4 percent of men. Official figures also exclude a large but unmeasured class of women who live in poverty in male-headed households. A husband is required by law to feed, clothe, and house his wife in times of need, but he is not obliged to give her any money. A parsimonious husband can make life miserable for a dependent housewife, but this would not show up in Statistics Canada data.

The data that are available suggest that the most poverty-prone category of people in Canada are single-parent women. In 1992, 62.3 percent of single-parent mothers with children under 18 lived below the poverty line. There are multiple reasons for this. They bear the heavy burden of raising children with little help and with lack of affordable day-care. Women commonly take time out of the labour force to raise children, and when they are in the labour force they are concentrated in a narrow range of low-paying occupations. In 1988, after years of affirmative action and equal pay legislation, women with full-time, year-round occupations earned on average 65 percent of male earnings.

Poverty among mothers is closely related to education levels. The most severely at risk are teenagers who become pregnant before finishing school. In 1990, 80.3 percent of single-parent mothers who did not graduate from high school lived below the poverty line, compared with 49.1 percent of those who did graduate. The incomes of single-parent mothers generally averaged 60.7 percent of the poverty line (National Council of Welfare 1992a, 36).

When unions break up, children are most likely to remain with their mother. Support payments in 1986 averaged about 18 percent of the gross income of the fathers, leaving most mothers with incomes far below the poverty line. The average amount paid was $368 a month, the median being $260. About half the mothers who received support payments had total incomes of less than $10 000 a year and most were unemployed and relied on welfare (National Council of Welfare 1990b, 72–17).

Put this way, the gender inequity seems glaring but the overall picture is complicated. The mother may remain living in the family home with the children while the father sets up a new home. Also, some 70 percent of men enter a new union, either legal or common-law, compared with only 28 percent of women. These men may be supporting a wife and additional children from this second relationship, as well as making support payments to children from the first marriage. Few men earn sufficient income to keep two families at an average standard of living. When resentment at the breakup of the family is added to financial stress it is not altogether surprising that about a third of ex-partners default on support payments. Increasingly aggressive efforts by governments to go after "dead beat dads" does little to resolve the poverty of single-parent mothers. Most of the payments that are recovered only offset welfare. This helps the government more than the children. Ironically, children can even be worse off financially if support payments bring the family just above welfare levels, because they lose eligibility for welfare and the health and dental benefits that go with it.

The underlying problem that the issue of support payments reflects but does not address is the structured economic dependency of women and children upon male incomes. As the National Council of Welfare expresses it, the vast majority of women are only one man's pay cheque away from poverty. The social organization of work and economic relations are such that it is very difficult for women with young children to find adequate child care and other services needed to enable them to work outside the home, and to earn enough to pay for these services and still support a family above the poverty line.

Other ways of organizing the economy and community support for children are possible. Sweden and Norway have explicit family policies that provide generous benefits for parents in general, and single parents especially, including universal family allowance, a major income-related housing allowance and an "advance maintenance payment" system for single parents. The latter is a tax-free, universal benefit that amounted to $1974 per child under 18 in 1989. All single parents receive these payments in full, and cost is recovered from the noncustodial parent to the maximum specified in child support orders, or the full benefit, whichever is less. There is no disincentive for single parents to take paid jobs because, unlike social assistance, the advance maintenance payment is guaranteed income, which is not reduced by other earnings (National Council of Welfare 1990b, 82).

Quality of Life of the Poor

The stark reality of poverty in Canada is that many people, including the working poor, have insufficient money to meet basic subsistence needs of housing, food, and clothing. The fact that homeless people have no fixed address makes it very difficult to count them, and hence the homeless rate is an estimate based on surveys of people found living on the streets. The City of Toronto Department of Public Health estimated that between 25 000 to 50 000 people were homeless in Toronto in 1992. The report admits that the visible homeless may only be the tip of the iceberg. The Canada Council on Social Development estimated that between 130 000 and 250 000 Canadians needed emergency shelter during 1986. Updated figures for Toronto show that Metro hostels sheltered 2500 people nightly, to a total of 32 000 individuals in 1991. Hostel records showed that most of the people who left the hostels had no place to go. Many more people are on the verge of homelessness, living in temporary, inadequate, or unsafe conditions. The cost of housing is so great, relative to their incomes, that any kind of financial disruption will put them on the streets. A September 1987 survey of eight campgrounds around Toronto showed that about seventy-five homeless families were living in tents. The fragility of many people's hold on housing is shown in the following example. A person earning minimum wage—$5 an hour in 1987—in Toronto could earn $800 a month. The average rent for a one-bedroom apartment in Toronto in 1987 was $854, rising to $966 for two-bedrooms. A single person in a bachelor apartment could expect to pay $616 per month, leaving $184 for food, clothes, and heat. Minimum wage in Toronto is so far below subsistence for a family that they cannot even afford to rent a one-bedroom apartment, let alone have

money left for food, clothes, and other items that most of us consider essentials, like personal care products, bus fares, school supplies, and furniture. "Luxuries" like a night out once in a while, or a holiday, are out of the question. Families break up and the children are put into care because their parent or parents simply cannot find an affordable place to live. Welfare payments for single people who are deemed employable are set far below the cost of even the cheapest single room in any city in Canada. Many single parents pay more than 50 percent of their income for an apartment.

By 1994, severe recession and the crash in real estate values in Toronto changed the relationship between minimum wage and average rents. The minimum wage in Toronto in 1994 was set at $6.70 an hour, or $1072 a month for full-time employment, while the average rent for a one-bedroom apartment was $627, rising to $773 for two bedrooms. What these figures do not show, however, is the steep rise in unemployment in the city as the recession deepened. Most of the people working in minimum-wage service jobs cannot hope to get full-time work, and proportions of people who can find no work at all have risen dramatically since 1990.

The level of desperation is indicated by the rise in use of food banks. Many low-income people who can afford to pay their rent find that they do not have sufficient money left for food. Food banks did not exist before the recession of the early 1980s. In 1994, there are 463 food banks in Canada—about 900 000 children make use of them (*Globe and Mail*, 18 May 1994).

Low-income people are significantly disadvantaged on a wide range of measures of health (National Council of Welfare 1990a, 7–20). Age of death for men is linearly related to income, with men in the lowest income group dying on average six years earlier than men in the highest income group, and women one year earlier (see figure 9-3). Years of life free from activity restrictions due to ill health was more than 14 years shorter for men in the lowest income group compared with the highest (50 years versus 64.3 years). The comparable gap for women was 7.6 years (59.9 years versus 67.5 years). Babies born in the poorest neighbourhoods are twice as likely to die before their first birthday as babies in the richest neighbourhoods. In 1986, the infant death rate in poor areas was 10.5 per 1000 live births and 5.8 in wealthy neighbourhoods.

Figure 9-3

Life Expectancy of Males and Females by Neighbourhood Income, 1986

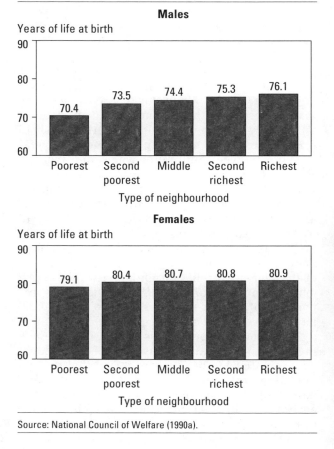

Males

Years of life at birth

Poorest	Second poorest	Middle	Second richest	Richest
70.4	73.5	74.4	75.3	76.1

Type of neighbourhood

Females

Years of life at birth

Poorest	Second poorest	Middle	Second richest	Richest
79.1	80.4	80.7	80.8	80.9

Type of neighbourhood

Source: National Council of Welfare (1990a).

A 1975 report on children attending school in Montreal's impoverished East End notes that 21 percent of the children were malnourished, 22 percent had retarded height and weight development, and 27.5 percent had retarded physical or mental co-ordination. Poor children are more likely to be born premature and underweight, and they are more than twice as likely as other children to miss a month or more of school a year because of illness. Some children live through prairie winters without winter boots or coats. As a result, they are almost constantly sick.

It is amazing that some of these children actually manage to get passing marks at school. Only a minority do well. Poor children are far more likely to fail in school than those from rich families. Quite apart from nutrition and health prob-

lems, they must face the almost daily humiliation of being dressed worse than others, of having teachers criticize what they had for breakfast or for lunch, and of being unable to participate in a multitude of extracurricular activities because they cannot afford the fees, equipment, or uniforms required. Nor can poor families afford to buy books, to travel, or to participate in cultural activities that stimulate learning.

The mothers of these children suffer too, both the anguish of seeing their children go without things that other children take for granted and also from going without themselves. Poor women are prone to nutritional and vitamin deficiency diseases such as scurvy (O'Connell 1983, 61). Data from a 1987 conference on homeless women

Although Canada and the United States have the highest standard of living in the world, the level of child poverty is staggering.

show that such women tend to die seventeen to twenty-one years younger than women who have homes (*Globe and Mail*, 23 Sept. 1987).

Aboriginal peoples living on reservations in Canada have significantly poorer health than other Canadians even in the poorest income brackets. Aboriginal men have a life expectancy of 65.7 years, and women of 73 years—eight to ten years shorter than average Canadians. Infant mortality is 17.2 per 1000 live births in 1986. They are prone to all the "diseases of under-development"—infections, parasitic and respiratory diseases, aggravated by malnutrition (National Council of Welfare 1991, 15).

We have to remind ourselves, when looking at these staggering figures on homeless and hungry people all across Canada and the United States, that these numbers refer to people who are living in the heart of capitalism in countries, that, on average, have the highest standard of living in the world. These data speak of a phenomenal imbalance of wealth. To the obvious questions—Why not redistribute some of the wealth? Why not raise the minimum wage? Why not have a guaranteed annual income that would place everyone above the poverty line?—comes the standard answer that such welfare measures would reduce incentives to work. While nobody suggests that children from rich families will become too comfortable to go out to work, such an argument is used against children from families on welfare (Gregory 1983, 62). Critics maintain that welfare might reduce the pool of cheap labour, or reduce capitalists' incentive to hire people and thus worsen unemployment, or raise corporate taxes and reduce incentives to invest in Canada.

The Poorest

Bad as are the conditions of poverty experienced by the unemployed and the people living on minimum wage in Canada, they cannot begin to compare to those facing the victims of the American and Canadian capitalist system in the underdeveloped Third World. These countries suffer so badly in world markets against advanced capitalist countries that they survive only by offering their labour at starvation rates and by granting greater handouts and tax concessions to corporations than are found in Canada. The levels of subsistence, and hence the minimum-wage rates, in many countries within Africa, Asia, and Latin America fall far below even the level of people living in garages in Los Angeles.

As an example of how Canadian companies contribute to the misery of Third World workers, consider the Bata Corporation, which had set up a shoe factory in the black homeland of KwaZulu in South Africa, about 150 kilometres from Durban. In 1985, Bata paid its black workers about 200 rand a month ($140 Cdn). This compares with a poverty line or "household subsistence level" for the Durban area of about 300 rand. Ottawa's code of conduct for Canadian employers in South Africa set a guideline for wages at nearly 450 rand ($337.50) per month. This would bring wages up to the local "supplemented living level," which itself was barely above subsistence. Yet Bata paid wages well below even the household subsistence level. This measure of absolute poverty calculates the clothing allowance for an adult woman as one plastic raincoat, one pair of overalls, one sweater, three pairs of stockings, one pair of pajamas, and two headscarves, two brassieres, and two pairs of underpants a year. Household equipment is calculated at one bed for two persons, to last for fifteen years; one table for the entire family for twenty years; one mug, knife, fork, and spoon per person to last eight years; and one saucepan, one kettle, and one frying pan per family to last ten years.

The poverty line is more remarkable for what it omits.

> It does not allow a penny for amusement, for sport, hobbies, education, medicine, medical or dental care, holidays, newspapers, stationary, tobacco, sweets, gifts of pocket money or for comforts or luxuries of any kind . . . or for insurance or saving. It is not a human standard of living (*Globe and Mail*, 16 Feb. 1985, 13).

Bata shoes on sale in Canada may well have been made by people whose income from the Bata factory was only two-thirds of this minimum level.

The reason why people work for such pitifully low wages in Third World countries was pointed out by Marx. The workers can sell their labour cheaply or be replaced by labour-saving technology and so receive no wages at all. Workers have no bargaining power whatsoever. In August 1987, some 300 000 black miners in South Africa participated in a three-week strike for higher wages, but they eventually capitulated with nothing more than slightly improved fringe benefits. They were beaten by the argument that if wages went up, labour-substitution technology would quickly follow, with massive layoffs. Unemployment among blacks in South Africa and the surrounding black homelands was so high that, during the miners' strike, the Anglo American Corporation was able to lay off 40 000 employees and hire strikebreakers. Workers are thus trapped in a vicious circle of dependency and low wages, which is very hard to break.

Workers at a Hyundai car factory in South Korea went on strike in July and August 1987 to press for better wages, and the strike quickly spread through 190 other companies. The protest was eventually crushed by state police. Only minimal concessions were granted to the strikers. It was argued that South Korea could only hope to compete on world markets by paying low wages to make cheaper cars and other products. Meanwhile, American car manufacturers are pressuring for tariffs and other trade restrictions to reduce competition from foreign auto producers. The alternative strategy, followed by many corporations, is to close down plants in North America and set up factories in the Third World, where they can combine high technology and low wages.

The Affluent Middle Classes

When the two extremes—the super rich and the very poor—are considered, the data clearly fit the predictions derived from the Marxist model. It is with respect to the middle classes, particularly within advanced capitalist countries, that the fit between evidence and model becomes shaky. Marx predicted the polarization of classes into the capitalist elite and the workers at subsistence wages, but he did not foresee the spectacular rise of the middle classes.

Blue-Collar and Office Workers

The rise of the affluent middle classes is the central focus of the liberal critique of Marxist theory. The **embourgeoisement thesis** holds that workers in many industries are becoming more affluent, their wages rivalling the salaried incomes of the professional and managerial class. Car assembly workers are a favoured example for this the-

sis, together with other skilled tradespeople and skilled industrial workers. Unionized employees can often command high wages, particularly in semi-automated or high-technology industries where labour costs are a declining proportion of overall production costs.

Marxist theorists argue, however, that a decent standard of living for many workers is bought at the very high price of alienation at work, coupled with the growing threats of automation, deskilling, and job loss. Rinehart, in his powerful study *The Tyranny of Work* (1975), asks whether workers are affluent. For the majority of both blue-collar and white-collar workers, the answer is no. Even those workers who are not close to the poverty line are generally only getting by. They are concerned with meeting car and mortgage payments. Their jobs are becoming increasingly deskilled, with no opportunity for learning or advancement. Covert efforts to humanize work are evident in wildcat strikes, sabotage of the production process, output restrictions, and the permanent struggle against pressures to speed up work.

Those who have skilled jobs find themselves increasingly subject to the threat of technological change and automation, both of which downgrade their skills. Typographical workers in the printing industry once were highly paid, skilled workers in great demand. Now the job has been automated, their skills are obsolete, and their job security is gone. A similar fate befell highly skilled hard rock mining workers at the INCO mines in Sudbury. As all aspects of mine work became progressively more mechanized from the 1960s onward, many of the highly skilled jobs such as drilling and blasting were downgraded to routine semiskilled work easily learned by new employees. Once-powerful workers found their skills obsolete and their job security and high pay gone. Maintenance workers, who look after the new machines, are trained only in narrowly specific skills appropriate for one piece of equipment. This ties workers to one machine and minimizes the training time required. They are easily replaceable and hence are cheap (Clement 1981, ch. 8).

Office workers also face the mounting pressures of automation. In offices, this process is almost always associated with increased workloads, speed up, and technological supervision of virtually every movement, keystroke, and error. Gregory (1983) describes the alienation of workers in these "electronic sweatshops," confined all their working hours to one spot, doing keystrokes at a tremendous pace, while a computer at the end of the room keeps count.

Productivity increases tremendously with new machines, but this is not reflected in more breaks, more pay, or shorter workweeks, just more pressure with fewer people doing more work. Meanwhile jobs are devalued, pay is stagnant or declining, and unemployment is rising among secretarial staff.

Archibald (1978, 174) describes at length the experience of depression, bordering upon mental illness, among many blue-collar and office workers. Work is, in a literal sense, dehumanizing. Workers are not paid to be creative or to think. They are paid to do as they are told when they are told. As both Archibald and Gregory acknowledge, the result is often passivity and withdrawal, mixed with frustration and covert defiance. People who have no control over their jobs are likely to withdraw from social and political activity. People who have creative jobs, involving decision making and control over their working lives, are far more likely to become involved as leaders in social and political activities as well. Mainstream theory in sociology compares the different levels of apathy and involvement, develops typologies of class culture, and uses them to account for the class character of democracy. It becomes an instance of ideology, of blaming the victims for the results of the dehumanizing experiences of work.

The Professional and Managerial Class

The working lives of people in professional and managerial middle-class jobs seem far better in comparison. They earn more money, and their work is not machine-paced. They exercise decision-making responsibilities and have generally higher status than blue-collar and office workers. The term *professional* is associated with notions of autonomy and freedom from external controls. The expansion of this middle class of skilled and well-educated workers is at the core of the liberal thesis of embourgeoisement, which envisions the majority of workers in advanced capitalism coming to share the satisfaction and sense of personal freedom associated with professional work.

Marxist theorists, however, dispute this image of affluence and autonomy. The majority of lower-level supervisors find their jobs almost as tightly circumscribed as do workers, only in different ways. They do not determine the guidelines or

objectives of the organizations for which they work but are responsible for ensuring they are carried out. Some suggest that middle-class people working for corporations may be even more alienated than are the working classes. They owe their minds, their thoughts, their whole being to the corporation. They are paid to think like "corporate men." Workers are paid to do as they are told, but they are free to think as they please. They do not have to accept or believe in what they do, nor need they fit the image desired by the corporation to the same extent that managers must (Smith 1977). The minority of women who enter managerial roles find that they have little if any leeway to change the image. They must conform if they are to keep their jobs or get promoted. Many women managers are finding the demands of corporate conformity so repressive that they are quitting their jobs (Maynard and Brouse 1988).

Managers wield considerable power, but that power is borrowed, exercised by proxy from above, and it requires obedience. Essentially their role is to transmit orders from above and to ensure compliance from below. One supervisor described his job as constant checking on people: checking that they arrive on time, that they do not take too long in the washroom or too long for lunch breaks; checking their work; checking that they are not cheating (Terkel 1972, 400).

For the most part, this is lonely work, with managers separated from the comradeship of fellow workers but too trapped in the hierarchy to have friendships with other supervisors. There is always someone above them trying to find fault, and someone below hoping to push them aside and take their job. Managers thus find themselves caught in a squeeze, subject to scrutiny and control from above and pressure from below (Terkel 1972, 405–6).

Workers in the public service sector fare little better. Governments are not geared to competition and profits, but they are geared to restraint and cost cutting, or they risk corporate criticism. Efficiency experts, drawn from management consulting firms to study public sector operations, bring with them the philosophies and loyalties of private business. They also bring the views that the public service is nonproductive, even parasitic, and hence that employment in the public sector should be kept to a minimum. Workers find themselves subject to the same work overload, impossible demands, deteriorating working conditions, and drive for labour-saving technology as in industry (Rinehart 1975, 111).

These alienating pressures on managerial, professional, and administrative staff are reflected in growing unionization within this middle-class sector. Managers do not identify with workers or see themselves as members of the proletariat, yet at the same time they feel the need to organize for their own protection. Lower-level managers, particularly, can find themselves subject to their own programs of efficiency and cost cutting as computer surveillance techniques and computerized work flow reduces the need for human supervisors (Nichols and Beynon 1977). During the major recession of the early 1990s many larger corporations cut deeply into their ranks of middle managers.

The Limitations of the Traditional Marxist Thesis

The Controversial Character of the Middle Class

Traditional political economy theory has proven a powerful explanatory tool with respect to our understanding of the concentration of capital, the decline of small business and primary producers in Canada, the miserable conditions facing the working poor, and the growing reserve army of unemployed and underemployed people and their children. But it has difficulty classifying the large and growing segment of the labour force employed in technical, professional, and managerial roles, particularly those within the service sector.

Marxist arguments to justify categorizing members of the professional and managerial classes as "proletariat" can only be pushed so far. The attempt to push everyone who does not own capital into the proletariat only succeeds at the risk of making this class so broad as to be almost meaningless. It also ignores very real gains in affluence and the inequality of working life within the professional, managerial, and technical sectors.

Veltmeyer, an avowed Marxist structuralist theorist, grapples with these problems in his text on *Canadian Class Structure* (1986, 25) where he debates whether to place the managerial class in the petite bourgeoisie or the proletariat. He acknowledges that the development of capitalism has generated a new form of middle class not envisioned by Marx, a class that falls somewhere between capital and labour. Members of this class sell their labour power but have considerable control over their own conditions of work and often over those of other people. These people are not exploited, strictly speaking, because the wealth that accrues to them from salaries, commissions, or fees is equal to or greater than the value of any wealth or service they create (Veltmeyer 1986, 46–47). Veltmeyer attempts to resolve the ambivalent status of this new middle class in relation to Marxist theory by splitting it into two parts. The lower part, comprising semiprofessionals and office and service sector workers, he places with the proletariat, while the higher sector of managerial and professional workers he places with the business class (Veltmeyer 1986, 25).

Veltmeyer, in effect, conceptualizes semiprofessionals and office workers as sharing the life chances and therefore the status of the manual working class, whereas professionals and managers share the life chances of the capitalist class. Professionals are thus lumped in with capitalist "parasites" who live on the surplus value created by the producing classes while producing nothing themselves. This surplus class or new petite bourgeoisie encompasses a bewildering variety of occupations. Speculators in the stock market may fit unambiguously into the category of parasites, but when it is expanded to include people working in "insurance, real estate, advertising, finance, as well as those in the ideological apparatus (government, law, military, education, and religion)" (Veltmeyer 1986, 58), one begins to feel uneasy.

Something is seriously amiss with a classificatory system that has such a huge jumble in the middle.

Even the broad classifications of bourgeoisie, petite bourgeoisie, and proletariat or wage-worker, cannot be unambiguously applied in all situations. An analysis of Nova Scotia fishing communities (MacDonald and Connelly 1992) showed that people engaged in the fishery frequently shifted class positions between independent capitalist boat owners, crew members on other boats, and employees in fish-processing plants. The class relations between independent fishers and plant owners is further complicated if their wives or children are plant workers. Higher fish prices may mean lower wages for other family members working in the plant.

A number of Marxist theorists have become embroiled in classificatory nightmares, arguing among themselves where to place boundaries. Such sterile arguments are a sure sign that something is wrong with the model that generates the classifications.

It is precisely this kind of Marxist structuralism, with its slavish application of abstract categories onto data, that the Marxist historian E.P. Thompson (1978a) challenges. He advocates a conceptualization of class as a process rather than an entity. Classes do not exist with people slotted into them, as in Veltmeyer's approach. Rather, classes emerge as the outcome of processes of struggle around material interests.

The New Middle Class in Marxist Theory

An important alternative analysis emerging within Marxism suggests that the phenomenon of the rising middle class needs to be understood in relation to processes in the development of advanced capitalism. These processes actually require the expansion of an educated middle-class labour force. They also require that capitalists exert less rather than more control over that labour force (Morgan and Sayer 1988, 26).

Morgan and Sayer draw attention to the fundamental importance of innovation to capitalism. Intensification of labour and deskilling are not the only means toward the goal of profit. Product diversification and the cheapening of the machines needed for production are also alternatives. Particularly in the burgeoning field of electronics, product innovation is an essential element in staying ahead of competition in the rate and quality of production. The relations of production that enable capitalists to deskill and control employees are anathema to the flexibility, creativity, and skill needed to be able to develop innovative ideas and to organize, swiftly and collectively, to translate these ideas into commodities.

Sayer and Walker (1992) extend this critique of the oversimplification of class analysis in traditional Marxist theory. Their comparative analysis of capitalist structures in the United States and Japan suggest that much of what has been considered the inevitable characteristics of capitalism, such as deskilling and cheapening of labour, is specific to the American system of standardized mass production. Japanese capitalism is more extensively geared to small batch production that relies on skilled work teams and close co-operation between management, engineers, and skilled shopfloor workers.

A second important critique is that the marketing process itself is more complex than Marx envisioned. The co-ordination of division of labour in complex economies itself involves complex and necessary labour practices that need to be conceptualized as productive work rather than merely exploitative or parasitic behaviour. An economy made up of noncapitalist worker co-operatives would still need to do it.

An important implication of this critique is that there are major structural divisions within what classical Marxist theory refers to as "the proletariat" that limit the usefulness of this classification. A highly educated, professional sector of the labour force may be developing at the same time that other workers are being deskilled, fragmented, and routinized. Severe shortages of skilled labour can occur at the same time as high unemployment.

The reconceptualization of class relations proposed by Morgan, Sayer, and Walker is rooted in a Marxist analytical framework. Their thesis predicts an increasing polarization within the working class, both nationally and internationally, between skilled workers in high-technology industries and deskilled workers elsewhere. If this thesis wins general acceptance, it seems likely to generate major changes in Marxist analysis of class relations under capitalism.

▣ The Marxist Feminist Challenge to Political Economy

Women: The Marginal Topic

It has long been argued that Marxist theory is unable to deal with the oppression of women because it subsumes the issue under the oppression of the working classes generally. Classical

Marxist analysis can accommodate women who have paid employment on the same terms as men. They can be classified as capitalists (extremely rare) or workers or placed in the middle-cum-working-class masses as office and service workers, technicians, professionals, and semiprofessionals. The main debate centres on whether to classify office work as middle class or working class, and why women generally are ghettoized into low-paying "women's work."

These are important questions, but they apply to, at most, about half the adult female population of Canada. Statistics Canada data for August 1987 showed that only 52 percent of all women in Canada were listed as employed and, of these, 21 percent worked part-time (Statistics Canada 1987, 45). The problem, then, is what to do with the more than half of all women whose sole or predominant occupation is that of homemaker.

Classical Marxist theory left no place for home-making within its analysis. People who do such work—virtually all women—are relegated to the category of nonproductive dependants. House-wives are usually accorded the status of the male to whom they are attached, either husband or father, suddenly to take on a status of their own, often much lower, when they get a job. House-work as such does not have a clear status. A homemaker who is the wife of a billionaire capi-talist is not in the same class as a homemaker married to a propertyless, unskilled, minimum-wage-earner, although even the latter is higher in status than a single-parent welfare recipient.

Until very recently, homemaking was not seen as work at all. A columnist with the *Globe and Mail* business section, in a discussion of the dol-lar value of housework, referred to it disparag-ingly as work "such as feeding the cat and shopping for a new spring wardrobe" (Corcoran, 8 April 1994, B2). It took pioneering studies by feminist theorists in the late 1970s and 1980s to begin to show the amount and the complexity of the work actually encompassed under the label *housework*. Meg Luxton's (1980) study of women's work in the home details just how demanding and how important such work is. Homemaking involves all those activities that maintain the house and service its members, including planning and preparing meals, cleaning and maintaining the house and its contents, and obtaining the materials and supplies needed for that work. In involves financial work of consump-tion management, ensuring that limited financial

resources will cover the subsistence needs of the worker and the worker's family. Shopping for a family on a tight budget, in an era when people are constantly bombarded with advertising con-cerning the multitude of commodities a family supposedly needs, takes considerable skill. Homemaking further involves all the rhythms of motherwork: coping with pregnancy, birth, infancy, training preschoolers, and supporting school-age children. Often it involves juggling several different schedules to accommodate the demands of baby, preschoolers, school time-tables, a husband's work timetable, and the woman's own work. It also includes the emo-tional labour of tension management, continually repairing the damage done to household mem-bers at work and at school. Yet this work still remains a marginal topic, relegated to the sphere outside the labour force or, more usually, outside the economy altogether.

The Domestic Labour Debate

The **domestic labour debate** struggles with ques-tions concerning women's work within the home and its place in the economy. Where and how do domestic workers fit into the capitalist social sys-tem? What is it that domestic workers do? What is the function of that work for capitalism? From the answers to these questions, theorists hope to understand why it is that men seem to have power over women in society.

One approach in this debate conceptualizes domestic labour as essentially a remnant of a feu-dal form of production that has never become integrated into the capitalist system. The relation-ship between wife and husband within marriage has features in common with the relationship between serfs and nobles under feudalism (Delphy 1984). Women labour within families to produce for the subsistence needs of the unit as a whole under the "lordship" of the husband. This mode of production generates its own internal class struggle between women and men, which occurs independently of the class relations of capi-talist production in the wider economy. There seems little reason to expect that such family sex-class relations would disappear with the over-throw of capitalism. The work of housewives is not subject to any of the contractual regulations characteristic of capitalist waged labour. It is not exchanged for wages, and thus has no value within the public market economy (Benston 1969). Benston proposes that these feudal relations of domestic production should be broken by the transfer of all work now done in the home into the public economy. Laundries, restaurants, cleaning services, and day-care centres could theoretically take over all the domestic labour work done by women in private homes. This would draw women into the work force alongside men, as wage-labourers. They would thus escape the feudal bondage of families and have a class status equal to men.

This theory does not explain the persistence of domestic labour as a feudal remnant. If such labour were marginal to capitalism, it should long ago have been swallowed up by capitalist enterprise. Yet domestic labour shows no sign of disappearing.

An alternative approach conceptualizes domestic labour as actively performing a central function for the capitalist system, even as it appears to be outside the market economy. That function is the maintenance and reproduction of labour power (Morton 1972; Dalla Costa and James 1972; Seccombe 1974; 1980). In the language of Marxist theory, domestic labour produces the commodity of labour power for exchange on the labour market. The male wage appears to be exchanged for labour at the work site, but in fact it is exchanged for the labour needed to produce labour power. Women are "paid" at subsistence level to do this work when they are given housekeeping money. This pay is so low that it serves to cheapen the commodity of labour power itself, so that wages can be lower and profits higher (Seccombe 1980). Seccombe suggests that women balance their "average domestic labour time" against the returns they might make from taking wagework and purchasing domestic services from others. Arguing that capital should be required to pay for the labour of producing and reproducing labour power, proponents of this theory demand wages for housework. In April 1994, Statistics Canada calculated the gross value of unpaid housework in Canada to be about $319 billion, a sum equal to about half the total government debt.

This theory does not fully address the problem of why domestic work came to be privatized, invisible, and unpaid (Armstrong and Armstrong 1985, 15). The Armstrongs argue that the privatization of domestic work is fundamental to the workings of the capitalist system. In their view, capitalism is based fundamentally on free wage labour that can be exploited for surplus value. This requires the separation of a public, commodity-production unit from a private subsistence unit. The system of free wage-labour itself seems to presuppose that labour is produced at least in part outside the capitalist market, or outside the production process proper. Hence housework, the work that produces labour power, takes place in the privatized and unpaid location of families. Women, not men, give birth to and nurture babies. Hence, women as mothers cannot participate fully in the labour force, at least for a time. Women's subordinate status follows from this enforced separation. Since capitalism values commodities, women's noncommodity work is devalued. Moreover, the position of women as a reserve army of labour is also necessary for the system to function. They even out fluctuating demands for labour because they can be hired when there is a shortage and pushed back into unpaid domestic work at other times. Hence, the relative exclusion and subordination of women appears as a necessary condition for the capitalist system.

The major contribution of the domestic labour debate is that it has at least made housework visible as a topic within traditional political economy theory. But analysis of housework still remains marginal to political economy. When the topic does attract interest, the focus is often on how to minimize domestic labour or to push as much of it as possible onto the public sector in order to free women up to participate more fully in wage labour.

This continuing marginalization of domestic labour is being challenged by recent socialist feminist theory. Instead of looking at women's domestic work from the standpoint of the dominant capitalist economy, this perspective advocates a new focus that looks at economy from the standpoint of homemakers. It is this emerging perspective that we examine below.

Political Economy from the Standpoint of Women

One of the major theorists to attempt a feminist re-evaluation of political economy is Dorothy Smith. She argues that political economy, as a discipline within social science, is itself embedded in the **ruling apparatus** of capitalism (1992a). The problem, she suggests, is that the discipline takes for granted the assumption that the "main business" of the economy is the accumulation of capital. What is left out is, in effect, all the rest of the economy. Smith points out that the precapitalist era made no distinction between production and reproduction. Producing food, shelter, tools, and so forth, met subsistence needs and provided for the children of those who did the work of production (Smith 1987b, 8). There was a unity between the economy and people's lives. Capitalism rent asunder this unity when production was geared to exchange for profit. The focus of political economy retains this distorted view. This is as true for theorists interested in the domestic labour debate as for the field at large. The agenda remains structured by the ruling apparatus because the ruling apparatus predefines what the main business of political economy is, what it talks about, and what it ignores. The result is the marginalization of central aspects of the economy such as reproduction, subsistence, and maintenance of the family and home.

This theoretical critique is still a highly controversial subject within Marxist academic circles. When Dorothy Smith first presented her paper entitled "Feminist Reflections on Political Economy" in 1987, it provoked powerful defensive reactions from Marxist theorists present, both women and men. Long-accustomed to taking a critical stand against mainstream economics, the challenge that they themselves might be propounding a conservative, mainstream theory is a bitter pill to swallow.

Smith argues that much feminist work in political economy is still within this mainstream agenda in which the main business is making money. Feminists add topics at the margins of the discipline, but the central focus remains. Smith cites the experience of economist Sylvia Ann Hewlett with the Economic Policy Council in the United States. Hewlett tried to set up a committee in 1980 to study problems of women's work, family, and child care, with a view to making recommendations to the President of the United States and to Congress. Virtually no one wanted to serve on the committee because the topics were not seen as the main business of the council (Smith 1992a, 11–12).

The standpoint of the majority of women is outside the main business of making profits. Most of the work that they do is located in parts of the economy other than where the accumulation of

capital takes place. It is this economy that needs to be addressed. What is needed is a redefinition of the term *economy* that does not begin from the accumulation of capital, but from the situation of people in their actual lives. When the main business is redefined as the social reproduction of people's lives, rather than the accumulation of profits, then women's work becomes, not peripheral, but central to the analysis.

This change in focus also radically alters the way in which the work of people within the service sector is analysed. Within traditional political economy, such workers are seen as marginal, living upon the wages of productive workers while not producing anything themselves. However, when the total process of reproduction, and the enhancement of life becomes the definition of the purpose of the economy, people who provide needed services cease to be merely consumers of other people's wages. They actually appear as producers themselves. The dependency relation then appears to work in reverse, with men as a class, as well as children, depending upon the multiple services provided by homemakers, in return for providing a subsistence housekeeping allowance.

Marxist feminist theory advocates a change not only in the definition of economy but also in the methodology used for analysis. It is important to recall that Marx thought that the problem of bias was not in the values of different researchers but in the methods used, methods that obscured the active social practices of the people involved. Marx accused the classical economists of his time of using abstract concepts such as *markets* and *exchange of commodities* to explain behaviour, as if people were pawns of market forces. They treated abstractions as concrete entities that do things to people. This is ideological because it obscures the fact that *people* do things, and that actual human relations produce the patterns that economists then use for explanations.

It is not possible to summarize in any complete way the political economy from the standpoint of women because the perspective is only beginning to emerge. A basic assumption of this approach is that the personal is political: the intimacy of personal relations within families and between colleagues is directly involved in the production of political economy as experienced by women. What is offered below are only suggestions as to the kinds of issues that come into focus when the main business of the economy is defined in terms of the enhancement of the material well-being of people. It challenges the basic value underlying capitalism as a mode of production, namely that profit and accumulation of capital are all that count in economic analysis.

Housework

Homemaking has to be at the heart of a feminist political economy because it is the responsibility of the vast majority of Canadian women, whether or not they are in the paid labour force as well. The standpoint from which women, as women, experience the social world is that of homemaker. Regular housework is described at some length in chapter 14 on the sociology of the family. The focus here is on the hidden economy of social services performed by women at home. There are multiple ways in which the unpaid work of women is appropriated by the state. This appropriation, or exploitation, is especially marked during periods of recession when governments are under pressure from business interests to cut spending. "Savings" in the economy are made through loading more and more work onto women in the home without paying them anything for it and actually firing many who used to do such work for pay.

Armstrong (1984) notes that when governments cut back on hospital services, women take up the slack by doing the nursing at home. They spend far more time in hospitals helping to care for relatives when adequate nursing services are not available. When patients are discharged early to "save" money, women take over their convalescent care at home. When governments cut

back on senior citizens' homes and residential homes for the disabled, justifying the financial cuts by arguing that these people are better off within the community, it is women who take over this chronic care nursing for free. Free, that is, to the government. It may often be at great expense to the women themselves who forfeit hours of time, and often paid jobs, to do this care work. When the state cuts back on day-care services and kindergartens, women in the home do the work. When the state cuts back on teachers, homemakers take up the slack, giving their time to supervise lunches and after-school activities, and doing the extra coaching and remedial work that teachers no longer have time to do. When youth employment opportunities are cut back, women at home take up the slack by providing homes and care for adolescents who would otherwise be independent. When wages are cut back, women make up the difference with their own labour, trying to substitute for purchases by making do, mending, sewing, knitting, managing with broken appliances. Above all, they double and treble their labour in stress management to absorb and contain the damage done to family members by such cutbacks.

All too often it is women who work in the social service sector who lose their paid jobs when the government cuts back. The government, in effect, defines their work as not in the marketplace, and thus saves all their salaries, while women continue to do the work without pay.

Viewed from the standpoint of women in the home, government restraint programs appear as the most extreme example of total exploitation. Women are driven to perform services without any pay at all and are forced to depend upon others for subsistence. Yet this enormous hidden economy of housework, worth millions of dollars in government savings annually, is invisible to traditional political economy with its focus on capital accumulation. It is treated as nonproductive, as not in the economy at all, and those who do such work are seen as nonentities or idle consumers.

The hidden economy of housework is invisible in traditional political economy.

The Formation of Class in Feminist Political Economy

In traditional political economy theory, the class structure can be taken for granted. It exists; it affects people's lives, and it provides a central explanatory framework for what happens in society. Once people are slotted into their places, class position can be treated as a sufficient explanation for their subsequent behaviour. Within this framework, the notion of cultural domination of the ideas of the ruling class becomes critical in explaining the absence of revolt. Workers fail to act in accordance with their objective class position because an alienating culture dopes them into passive acceptance of their situation.

The Marxist feminist analysis advocated by Smith rejects this class **determinism** as ideological in two respects. First, it adopts the assumptions of the ruling apparatus even as it tries to criticize them. Labour is managed precisely through notions of division of labour and of positions that deserve differential rewards. Such notions are used, for example, to account for the lower average pay of employed women compared with men. They are not underpaid but are simply concentrated in the wrong categories. They need to study science and mathematics to compete for the better jobs that men fill. The questions of whether women's work really is as unskilled as it is held to be, or whether service work such as homemaking, day-care, nursing, and teaching actually warrants low pay, disappear from the analysis. The deterministic approach is ideological in a second sense, in that it loses sight of people as active agents in the production of their economic world. *Classes* rather than *people* seem to do things.

From the standpoint of women and women's work, class relations do not simply exist. They have to be continually produced and reproduced. Women are very actively involved in the social construction of class relations through the work they do within the home, and the support work that they do in the myriad of offices where women put together the work of their bosses.

In this production process, families, or more specifically homemakers, become the **subcontracted agencies** of corporations. Women work for the corporations without being paid. Without the work of women in the home, workers would not appear for work everyday. The upper echelons of the work world would not maintain their pinstriped image without a host of services to manage the backstage production; alienated workers would not turn up for shifts day in day out, year in year out, without women to keep the pressure up, to control recalcitrant and reluctant labour, to absorb the tensions, repair the damage done, and organize home life around the schedules of the workplace.

Women reproduce the generations of labour power. Motherwork, even more than the work of teachers, serves to reproduce children trained to fit the school system and the demands of corporate careers. The roots of ideological hegemony begin in the home as mothers train their children in what it takes to get by or to get ahead within the corporate capitalist system and motivate them to conform to its demands. They know they will be judged as mothers by how well or how badly their children perform in this world. They also know that the material well-being of themselves and their children and grandchildren depends directly upon such conformity. The price of nonconformity can be too high if it is not themselves, but their children and their grandchildren, who pay.

Women also reproduce class as consumers when they maintain appropriate lifestyle images in their homes. As Smith (1977) points out, these images, especially for middle-class women, are not of their own making but are created for them in the media. Mothers also know that their children suffer humiliation and personal pain when they cannot keep up with the lifestyle of other children in their school, long before the children are old enough to figure out that consumerism is the con game of corporate capital and that one does not have to feel humiliated because one lives in a garage and wears used clothing. Employed women continue this work of reproducing class when, as teachers and school counsellors, they advise children on what they think it takes to be successful in society.

The Ruling Apparatus of Capitalism

From the standpoint of traditional political economy, the ruling apparatus comprises the **military-industrial-political complex**. Corporate bosses are at the centre, wielding influence and dictating policies and laws in the interests of promoting capital accumulation. They are aided by the agencies that enforce these policies. From the standpoint of women, the ruling apparatus looks very different. It is located primarily in the social service sector that directly influences family life.

Donzelot's analysis of *The Policing of Families* (1979) surveys how families have been managed for capitalism. Physicians and psychiatrists worked with middle-class housewives to advise them on appropriate ways of raising children and sanitizing their houses; the social work professions trained educated women to teach uneducated or working-class women new rules of home economics and child care; probation officers threatened women that their children would be removed by the courts if they failed to make them conform to the rules, including rules of compulsory attendance at school. Male doctors broke the control of women over bearing and raising children and destroyed women's independent medical knowledge (Ehrenreich and English 1979). The professions of social psychology and sociology worked to control families, teaching women that the structural functional model of male and female roles and family forms was biologically and socially necessary and that any other ways of doing things risked **maternal deprivation**, manifest, of course, in children's failure to succeed in schools and careers (Lasch 1977).

Schools have a **hidden curriculum** that reinforces, above all else, a reliance upon accredited experts. These "experts" are the crucial underpinning of the ruling apparatus over women's lives (Illich 1971). All professions act to weaken rather than empower the working class when they uphold the logic that only people with credentials are experts and that others should rely upon their judgment.

For generations, the professions have been the almost exclusive domain of men. Now more women are entering them, but all the lines of argument and the main beliefs have been set up already. They are very hard to break. When one hears Judith Maxwell, head of the Economic Council of Canada, advocating that food be taxed in the interests of economic efficiency, it becomes clear that being female is not sufficient to change the standpoint of theory. Male professors find it hard enough to get their students to see that law does not simply dispense justice, but *capitalist* justice.

Summary

How can women be, in so many ways, at the heart of the system and yet be ignored or treated as a marginal topic? How can the enormity of what they do and their experience of the social reality of capitalism be left out of the picture? How can their work and experience be trivialized, even by women themselves, as somehow outside the main business? Why are they still relegated in sociology texts to a chapter on "the family"?

The problem seems to be that sociology and radical political economy have largely adopted the worldview of the owners of big corporations, even as they criticize them. All the issues considered important and relevant are those relevant to corporations. From the viewpoint of business, women are irrelevant because much of their work is done outside the corporation. Capitalism itself dissolved the unity of work and life, of production and reproduction. Now social scientists themselves take the division for granted. Merely hiring more women workers in corporations or having more "female businessmen" will change nothing, because the focus—the consensus as to what the main business is—remains unchanged.

The debate over the place of women in the economy and, indeed, what constitutes the economy has only just begun in sociology, and nobody quite knows where it will go. The main questions have not yet been answered. In fact, some of them have not even been asked!

Conclusion

How well have the predictions generated by the Marxist model of capitalism stood up to empirical testing? The general answer is very well, but there are serious qualifications. The prediction of the tendency toward increasing concentration of capital into a handful of giant transnational corporations has largely been realized. The tendency toward a falling rate of profit is also a reality in traditional industries, especially in agriculture. The polarization of poverty and immense wealth has also largely been realized, especially when viewed on a world scale. Plant closures, unemployment, booms and slumps, crises of overproduction, and underutilization of capital, are part of the everyday reality in the capitalist world. The harnessing of the state to mitigate these crises, to control labour, to boost the economy with armaments spending, and to defend new markets in Third World countries is similarly very much in evidence.

Marxist predictions have not been borne out with respect to the increasing misery of the masses and the profit margins in high-technology industries. The thesis of increasing misery has much truth for the lumpenproletariat, the sectors of declining primary producers, marginalized, underemployed workers, and the deskilled working class, but it has not held true for the burgeoning middle classes. Marxist theory did not predict the spectacular expansion of the sector of highly educated, professional workers who enjoy high salaries and privileged conditions of autonomy in their work. Efforts to explain this sector away are generally unpersuasive. The problem here may lie not in the overall Marxist thesis but in the failure to recognize the consequences of the capitalist compulsion to develop innovative technology, products, and relations of production to win a competitive edge in world markets. The explosion in scientific knowledge in the last generation and the exponential advances in electronics and computers are so far outpacing the predicted tendency toward declining rates of profit. These processes are supporting an affluent middle class whose position depends upon the continuing acceleration of innovation.

The Marxist model also has radical implications for the traditional analysis of democratic politics in capitalist societies. Miliband's structuralist analysis shows the enormous power of the business elites within the political arena and their control over avenues of communication through which capitalism secures its legitimation. But the requirement of a highly educated and autonomous professional class of workers potentially threatens this control. The kind of education that is a prerequisite for innovative work simultaneously generates the capacity for creative questioning that may challenge the systems of legitimation of capitalism. Whether the affluent lifestyles of the professional class are adequate to buy off the critical challenge remains to be seen.

There is another area in which the frantic pace of growth under capitalism may be stemmed. The limits to what the ecology of the planet can bear may be more critical in the long run than the inherent contradictions of capitalism. We explore the relation between the expansion of capitalism and the destruction of the world environment further in chapter 10 on development.

Marxist theory, which focusses exclusively upon relations of production, has been found wanting in the analysis of the position of women and women's work. Relations of reproduction fall outside the Marxist framework. Consequently, relations of patriarchy disappear from view. Developing perspectives in Marxist feminist theory are only beginning to redress this imbalance.

The future directions of Marxist theory are hard to predict. What seems likely is a move away from traditional structuralist frameworks and toward a focus on the active processes through which relations of capitalism are socially constructed and through which they change.

Suggested Reading

An excellent and very readable source of information on the Canadian corporate economy is Henry Veltmeyer's *Canadian Corporate Power* (1987). Veltmeyer gives a clear and informative overview of Marxist theory on corporate capitalism and includes much valuable information on corporate concentration and monopoly ownership.

Further readings on the decline of small producers are contained in the collection edited by Gary Burrill and Ian McKay, *People, Resources, and Power: Critical Perspectives on Underdevelopment and Primary Industries in the Atlantic Region* (1987). The contributors demonstrate how small producers in agriculture, fishing, forestry, and mining and energy are being crushed by the expansion of corporate capitalism into primary resource industries.

The text by Ralph Miliband, *The State in Capitalist Society* (1969), provides an excellent overview of the relationship between various branches of government and big business within capitalist societies.

For information on the communication industry in Canada, see Wallace Clement, *The Canadian Corporate Elite* (1975), especially chapters 7 to 9. Clement describes the media owners as gatekeepers of ideas, able to include or filter out information as it suits their interests. Useful sources of statistics on media ownership in Canada include Tom Kent, *Royal Commission on Newspapers* (1981) and G.L. Caplan and F. Sauvageau, *Report of the Task Force on Broadcasting Policy* (1986).

An excellent source of theoretical debate and information on the class structure in Canada is Henry Veltmeyer's *Canadian Class Structure* (1986). In the first chapter, Veltmeyer outlines Marxist theory of class. He follows this with a detailed look at the situation of the capitalist class, the middle class, workers, and the poor. The book contains much statistical information in an accessible form.

Other sources of information, especially on poverty and inequality in Canada are the many reports by the National Council of Welfare: *Poor Kids* (1975); *Jobs and Poverty* (1977); *Women and Poverty* (1979b); *The Hidden Welfare System Revisited* (1979a); *Welfare in Canada: The Tangled Safety Net* (1987c); and *Poverty Profile 1992* (1994).

An excellent overview of the domestic labour debate is the collection of essays by Armstrong, Armstrong, Connelly, Miles, and Luxton, *Feminist Marxism or Marxist Feminism: A Debate* (1985). Articles by these authors explore how women's work in the home can be incorporated into a Marxist theory of work in relation to the capitalist system. These articles tend to be technical and somewhat heavy reading. Another source of critical debate on the Marxist treatment of feminist issues is the collection of readings edited by Heather Jon Maroney and Meg Luxton, *Feminism and Political Economy: Women's Work, Women's Struggles* (1987).

Questions

1. How does Adam Smith see capitalist economies as controlling both excessive profits and overproduction?

2. What features does the liberal-bourgeois thesis point to as contradicting Marxist predictions concerning the characteristics of advanced capitalism?

3. Identify the key practices involved in the development of corporate capitalist monopolies through horizontal mergers, vertical integration, conglomerate mergers, and holding companies.

4. What mechanisms does Veltmeyer see as ensuring banks a high degree of influence within corporations?

5. What are the main advantages and disadvantages of supply-management boards in relation to Canadian agricultural products?

6. How is the shift towards corporate concentration in the Atlantic fishing industry implicated in the decline of the industry?

7. What are some of the practices through which members of the corporate elite can become recipients of government "welfare"?

8. How is the "poverty line" defined for the purposes of Statistics Canada?

9. How does the new Marxist theory proposed by Morgan and Sayer account for the rise of an affluent middle class in societies such as Canada?

10. How does Smith propose to redefine political economy in such a way that domestic work becomes central rather than marginal to the economy?

Development: Competing Theories of Economic Change

Within the world community there are enormous disparities in standards of living across regions and countries. Until recently, world economies have been thought of as comprising three blocks—the First World of affluent capitalism, the **Third World** of impoverished and technologically backward regions, and the intermediate economies of socialist societies. These distinctions have become unworkable with the disintegration of the Soviet bloc and growing disparities between countries in the former Third World. The latter are now euphemistically referred to as "developing" countries.

The plethora of competing theories that try to account for economic disparities have direct practical implications for the design of national and international development programs. In this chapter we will focus first on worldwide development issues and then on the specific situation of Canada within the North American trading bloc. The complexities of economic development are daunting and we can only touch on some aspects

of the theoretical debates here. Niels Bohr, winner of the Nobel Prize in physics in 1922, is reputed to have commented that he switched from economics into physics because economics was too complicated. The subject has not become any easier since the 1920s.

World Development

Functionalist Theory: Modernization as Evolution

The functionalist **theory of modernization** conceptualizes societal evolution as a unilinear process of differentiation and specialization towards more complex and centralized organization. Change within the economic sphere requires simultaneous adjustments within political and administrative structures and especially within culture to maintain an integrated social system. Historically, the advancement of science and technology in developed Western societies was preceded by far-reaching changes in religious, political, and family structures.

Values such as the Protestant ethic promoted a focus on work as a religious calling and upon success within worldly activities as a sign of grace. Such values fostered the intensive commitment to work and investment of profits that characterized early capitalists in Europe.

Talcott Parsons argues that technologically backward and advanced societies have quite different cultural values. Traditional societies are typically centred on family and kinship ties, and on local loyalties, and they tend to view change as threatening to their social order. Modern societies, in contrast, emphasize individual achievement, measured in terms of objective, universal standards of performance that are applied impartially to all. Individual differences, specialization, and change are easily accommodated. Hence, a major problem that backward societies must overcome in order to emulate the advances of Western societies is **cultural lag**: the failure of other spheres of society to adapt to the economic changes that technological innovation entails.

This failure to adapt takes many forms. Localized tribal loyalties undermine a stable central government system. Administrative structures become chronically inefficient when staff are selected on the basis of nepotism rather than individual qualifications. Traditional religious values may oppose worldly success values needed for business and accumulation of capital. Above all, extended family ties may hamper individual initiative and stifle geographic and social mobility vital for taking advantage of economic opportunities. Intense family-centred values, or familism, are also associated with high birth rates. When this is combined with the transfer of modern medicines from the developed world to reduce the death rate, the result is crushing overpopulation, which leads inexorably to famine.

The Culture of Poverty

The thesis that a certain constellation of cultural values perpetuates poverty by stifling initiative for change is known as the **culture of poverty thesis**. The same explanation has been applied to account for pockets of poverty within the developed world. It is particularly associated with the early work of Oscar Lewis (1949) and Everett Rogers (1969, ch. 2). Referring to peasants or subsistence farmers in the Third World, Rogers (1969, 19) comments that "they make the economists sigh, the politicians sweat, and the strategists swear, defeating their plans and prophesies all the world over." Their apathy and traditionalism constantly block the implementation of rural development programs.

Reluctance to innovate is associated with a syndrome of cultural traits that includes limited worldviews and low empathy, familism, mutual distrust in interpersonal relations, dependence on and hostility to government authority, fatalism, limited aspirations, lack of deferred gratification, and "perceived limited good." The trait of perceived limited good refers to the belief among peasants that the economic pie is limited and that anyone who gets ahead must be cheating others out of a share. People who do get ahead are viewed with a mixture of envy and scorn, rather than as models to emulate. Each of these cultural traits hampers modernization. These traits lead to ignorance, inability to conceive of a future different from the present, and a belief that no one outside the family can be trusted, including government development workers with new-fangled schemes. Peasants display an apathetic resignation to fate because of their limited sense of control over the future. Money is not saved or invested but is spent immediately or borrowed by other family members.

According to this functionalist thesis, the main solution to backwardness lies in continuing to transfer scientific and technological knowledge from the developed world, combined with concerted efforts to change outdated traditional values that block saving, investment, and rational organization of the economies of these countries (Chirot 1977, 3–4). This was the guiding ideology behind the American Peace Corps and Alliance for Progress, which flowered in the United States under the Kennedy administration in the early 1960s.

The 1960s were years of optimism sparked by the **green revolution**, a package of scientific developments in agriculture that promised to ameliorate famine. The package included high-yield varieties of wheat and rice, chemical fertilizers and pesticides, and large-scale irrigation projects. Together they had the potential to double or to treble yields. The other avenue for hope was the dissemination of contraceptive technology and aggressive campaigns for population control. It was hoped that, with higher agricultural yields and fewer babies to feed, the battle for adequate worldwide nutrition would be won.

These hopes were only partially fulfilled. The green revolution did raise yields, particularly among large farmers who tended to be more progressive. But the mass of small peasant farmers largely failed to adopt the new technology. The end result was an increase in the gap between rich and poor farmers. The syndrome of attitudes associated with the culture of poverty was widely cited to account for the failure of small farmers to innovate.

The goal of population control similarly met with limited success. Among the wealthier, educated classes, family size did decline, but not among the masses. During the period between 1950 and 1972, the population of Asia rose by an estimated 63 percent, Africa by 72 percent, and Latin America by 91 percent. In contrast, in North America, population increased by only 42 percent and Europe by 26 percent (Kalbach 1976, 11). A UN report estimated that the world's population reached 5.67 billion in September 1994 and is expected to reach 6 billion by 1998 (*Globe and Mail*, 14 Sept. 1994, A12).

Various explanations are offered for continuing high rates of population increase in Third World countries. Improved health care and mass immunization have reduced the infant death rate, but continuing fear of infant mortality makes people reluctant to accept sterilization before the birth and survival of large numbers of children. The medical complications and expense associated with all forms of artificial contraception limit their use, while religious and cultural factors, and especially the desire for sons, favour having many children.

The result is that increases in food production are virtually cancelled out by increases in population. In India, for example, between 1950 and 1970 agricultural yields doubled, but this barely kept ahead of the birth rate. In 1985 the worst happened. Drought in Africa precipitated famine on a devastating scale, with hundreds of thousands of people in Ethiopia, Sudan, and Chad starving to death, and millions more barely kept alive in relief camps. Famine struck these regions again in 1987–88. Only massive gifts of food from around the world stood between millions of people and starvation. The only solution, from the perspective of conventional theories, is more of the same: more technology and more cultural change.

In summary, for functionalists the causes of failure to modernize are within the structures and cultures of the backward countries themselves. Research promoted by this theoretical approach has focussed particularly upon technological transfer and aid projects, internal politics and bureaucratic organization within the Third World countries, and the response of local people to small-scale development projects. The long history of frustration and limited results has offered much support for the thesis that deep-rooted structural and cultural changes must precede modernization.

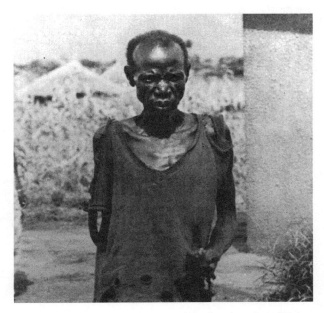

Functionalist theory suggests that economic backwardness in the Third World reflects a culture of poverty.

The Modernization Thesis Discredited

Criticisms generated within the functionalist tradition have focussed upon the limited empirical validity of some of the generalizations outlined above. It is not difficult to point to examples of traditional value orientations in developed countries and evidence of modern value orientations in Third World countries, with no appreciable impact on the level of modernization (Frank 1972). The culture of poverty thesis has been challenged on the grounds that the implied cause and effect should be reversed (Hale 1985, 55). Rather than attitudes causing economic backwardness, it is the condition of economic backwardness that causes the attitudes. Restricted information flow, exploitation, the absolute lack of access to resources needed for agricultural innovation, and the impossibility of saving money in the face of inadequate and irregular incomes are facts of everyday life for peasants in North India, especially small landowners and landless tenant farmers. Such structural factors account both for the failure to innovate and the attitudes that go with such behaviour.

Similarly, with respect to population control, there is evidence that the underlying relation between high birth rates and poverty works in reverse to the usual argument. It is poverty that drives families to have more children, especially male children, to compensate for high death rates and to ensure some means of support in old age. As real economic alternatives emerge for women to support themselves and to raise their standards of living, they choose increasingly to restrict the number of children they have. Attitudes tend to change readily in response to real opportunities for advancement. Functionalism describes the association between attitudes and behaviour, but it does not explain it.

Political Economy Theory: Underdevelopment as Capitalist Exploitation

The strongest challenge to the functionalist theory of modernization has come from the perspective of political economy. Ironically, the main point of this criticism is that functionalist theory has failed to live up to its own insistence that parts should be understood in relation to the total system. The development of any one region or nation can be fully understood only by how it functions in relation to the total system. Political economy theory shifts the focus from the internal structures of poor countries to the functioning of the world economic system in which they are embedded.

The central argument, which we explore below, is that the wealth of some countries and regions and the poverty of others are, and always have been, systematically related. Frank (1972, 3) rejects outright the notion that somehow Third World societies have not yet developed, or that they lack the required cultural or other prerequisites to copy Western development. The Third World, he argues, is not simply **undeveloped**, continuing to exist in some unchanged, traditional pattern. These societies are **underdeveloped**. Their resources have been, and still are being, plundered, and their internal economies are undermined by processes of a world capitalist economic system.

Historically, most now impoverished Third World societies were subject to the destructive impact of **mercantilism**, **colonialism**, and **imperialism**. The economies of many regions of Africa were devastated by the slave trade, while the indigenous societies of Latin America were crushed by European conquerors plundering the regions in search of precious metals. The economies of conquered regions were directed primarily in the interests of the imperial powers, which focussed upon the extraction of resources to fuel imperial development, while simultaneously retarding and distorting the internal development of the regions themselves. Even now, in many parts of Africa, the main roads go from centres to the ports, rather than to other African centres (Hoogvelt 1976). African interregional telephone lines still link up through Britain.

Imperial governments fundamentally transformed indigenous social structures and often divided up territories with no respect for traditional tribal lines. "Divide and rule" tactics often involved favouring selected local elites or encouraging the immigration of ethnic minorities into the colonies, to act as a buffer group between the colonial power and the local people. East Indians, for example, were used in this way in many of the British colonies in Africa. Such people acted as business middlemen, local administrators, and tax collectors for the colonial era, the legacy of tribal conflicts and class disparities along ethnic lines still plagues the new nation-states.

Most colonized countries have now gained political independence, but this has not brought effective economic independence. Their economies are still dominated by forces of the world capitalist economic system over which they have little control. This externalized control through economic pressures is referred to as **neo-imperialism**.

International Capitalism: The Practices of Dependent Development

A major contribution of Gundar Frank's analysis of underdevelopment has been to focus attention on critical mechanisms through which the centres of advanced capitalism are able to exploit dependent economies. These include control over capital, control over patterns of investment, domination of market relations, decisive bargaining power in the labour market, and political clout, including the use of force as a last resort. We will examine these five mechanisms in turn.

Control over Capital

There has been a net outflow of capital from poorer regions such as Latin America to wealthier regions such as the United States for most of this century. This is despite foreign aid payments, which appear to go from rich to poor nations. This outflow takes many forms, one of the most visible of which is debt repayment. Debts have reached crisis proportions in many Latin American and African countries. Interest payments due on loans are so great that they comprise more than one-third of total national income earned from exports in some of the poorest countries of Africa. The situation is so bad that newspaper articles in June 1988, during an economic summit for leading industrialized nations, speculated on how many babies starve to death for each dollar of interest repaid. These are babies who might not have died if debt repayments could have been spent on clean drinking water or minimal health care in desperately poor countries. The debt repayment problem is made worse by currency devaluations forced on debtor nations by the International Monetary Fund.

The outflow of money from poor to rich nations also occurs in less obvious forms. Cheap exports and overpriced imports, often directly controlled by multinational corporations, generate large profits and dividends that flow back to the corporate home base, together with payments for royalties and financial services of all kinds. Multinational empires often also have close ties to banks and hence have preferential access to large investment loans over struggling smaller companies within the host societies. Multinationals are, in any case, relatively independent of banks because they can use profits from one sector of their activities to finance new investments elsewhere. Their commanding control over access to finance capital gives them effective control over investment policy.

Control over Patterns of Investment

Access to capital gives multinational corporate empires almost total control over decisions about where and how to invest. Such decisions are routinely made in the interests of the corporations themselves and focus on export-oriented production rather than on provision of basic public resources such as roads, railways, and electrical power lines and generators that are needed to promote local industry. Export-oriented production also takes away money and other resources that might have been invested in production geared to the needs of the host societies. Corporations have the power to create boom and bust economic cycles, as they can choose to shift centres of production from one region, or from one country, to another, depending on where the greatest profits might be made. Host societies can do virtually nothing about such decisions. Corporate interests have helped to create a new international division of labour, with many countries specializing in production of one or two goods each.

Market Relations

Corporate empires have the capacity to exert decisive control over market relations between poor countries and the world economic system.

Studies have speculated how many babies die for every dollar of debt repaid by Third World nations.

In the first place, an estimated 30 percent of all world trade is no longer in the marketplace but occurs directly between affiliates of multinational corporations (Martin 1982, 95). Martin concludes that the "open market" is a convenient fiction when applied to international trade. **Transfer pricing** refers to the price that a parent company sets in selling supplies to its own branch plants or the price at which the parent company purchases goods produced or assembled by the branch plants. In this internal corporate economy concepts such as *costs* and *benefits* or *profits* do not have fixed values. They are the outcome of accounting practices. Prices can be manipulated to maximize the outflow of profits to corporate headquarters. Underpriced imports may give a competitive edge to an affiliate over local companies. Alternatively, imports may be overpriced to reduce paper profits and local taxes. Either tactic increases the hidden outflow of money from poor to rich. Martin (1982, 109) estimates that such transfer pricing may account for 82.6 percent of capital returns to headquarters.

Vertically integrated companies also directly control the marketing of products. Six multinationals, for example, control 60 percent of the world production of bauxite and 80 percent of aluminum production (Martin 1982, 100). Sometimes a single corporation controls the export of all bauxite produced in one country to its own plants at home. All the bauxite from the Dominican Republic is sent to Alcoa plants in the United States, while all Haiti's bauxite goes to one Reynolds plant in Texas. The economy of an entire country may be dependent upon the export of one or two specialized products that are under the control of one multinational corporation. The country is thus totally vulnerable to the fluctuations in the market price for these products and to the whim of the corporate directors deciding where and how they will market the products.

Labour Market Relations

In the worldwide labour market, the workers in poor countries provide a vast pool of cheap labour. They have little bargaining power and few rights or benefits. Giant companies can potentially shift production to wherever labour is cheapest, and this gives them a powerful bargaining tool for playing off one country against another. In 1976, for example, General Electric was negotiating worldwide to build an assembly plant for televisions (Martin 1982, 93). Hourly wages in Taiwan were 37 cents and in South Korea 52 cents. General Electric was negotiating with Indonesia offering 17 cents per hour. Anti-union legislation may also be a part of the bargaining demands of the corporation. Corporations can force or persuade states to enact legislation to ban strikes, picketing, and other union activities as the price for locating a plant in their region.

Political Force

Should business interests or investments be at risk, large corporations exert substantial political clout. Within the host country itself, the presence of an indigenous capitalist class that benefits directly from foreign capital investments helps to stifle unified opposition. The ultimate back-up for this international system is the military might of the metropolis country. In the early 1970s, when the democratically elected socialist government of Salvador Allende proposed to nationalize the American-owned copper mines of Kennecott and Anaconda in Chile, the corporations were able to mobilize the support of the American government and the CIA to overthrow the regime (Martin 1982, 120–21). International banks, including Canadian banks, co-operated by cutting all credit to Chile. Other international corporations operating in Chile drained their local **subsidiaries** of money and denied supplies of needed resources such as mechanical spare parts, hence bringing the Chilean economy to a halt. International Telephone and Telegraph (ITT) had substantial holdings in Chile and feared nationalization. Corporate directors conspired directly to bring about the downfall of the government through specific forms of armed and funded intervention organized through the American Central Intelligence Agency.

In conclusion, it is important to recognize that dependency theory does not reflect the inexorable working of an invisible hand, with people as mere pawns. It is the result of strategies intended to have specific and foreseen effects. Multinational corporations are oriented toward making profits and increasing their own capital to satisfy large shareholders. Their policies are not designed to raise living standards for the mass of people in the Third World, and it should not be surprising that this is not their major effect.

Dependent Capitalist Development

There is continuing debate within the political economy perspective on how these processes of economic domination work, and whether it is more useful to focus on international trade relations, as Frank does, or modes of production, as traditional Marxist theory does. In practice, as Brenner's analysis shows, the two processes are intimately related.

Brenner (1977) argues that a precondition for capitalism is the separation of the mass of people from the means of producing their own needs. It is this dependence on markets for survival that drives people with capital to invest in new technology to raise productivity and that also drives those without capital prompts others to sell their labour power for wages.

The proletarianization of labour has been largely achieved in most Third World countries. The slums and shanty towns around almost all big cities are flooded with impoverished rural people desperate to sell their labour power at almost any price (Foster-Clark 1978)—but the corollaries of compulsive investment and rising productivity have not followed.

Foster-Clark argues that this is really **dependent capitalism**—imported from outside in a form already fully developed. Impoverished developing countries, struggling to compete in world capitalist markets, face all the contradictions of capitalism full blown: the crises of falling rates of profit, the extreme concentration of capital in huge corporate empires, overproduction, unemployment, and misery as masses of unemployed people the world over compete to sell their labour to investors at the lowest possible wages.

Third World countries are in the worst possible position to try to compete with monopoly capitalists. Companies such as Exxon and General Motors command more wealth than the entire economies of most Third World countries (see table 10-1). Poor countries, trying to develop their economies, are no match for these giants. The best they can hope for is to compete among themselves to attract what investment they can get, with the carrots of cheap labour, cheap raw materials, minimal taxation, and anything else the giant corporations want. This is not the stuff of which balanced and self-sustaining economic growth is made.

In terms of the **dependency theory** model developed by Frank, such poor countries form **hinterlands** for the **metropolis** or centre of capitalism. Hinterlands are the underdeveloped areas that supply cheap labour and cheap raw material or semiprocessed goods to the developed centres. Metropolises are the centres of capitalism, which dominate surrounding regions, extracting their economic surplus. Capital accumulation at the centre siphons off capital from the periphery. Frank conceptualizes the world capitalist system as hierarchically organized with each smaller metropolis forming a hinterland for yet larger centres, with the ultimate metropolis in New York or Tokyo.

Table 10-1

Largest 100 Countries and Companies, 1985*							
Rank 1985	Rank 1976	Name	GNP/Sales (billion $ US)	Rank 1985	Rank 1976	Name	GNP/Sales (billion $ US)
1	1	USA	3 634.6	12	20	Mexico	171.3
2	2	USSR	N/A	13	15	India	162.3
3	3	Japan	1 255.0	14	11	Spain	160.9
4	4	West Germany	613.2	15	18	Iran	157.6
5	5	France	489.4	16	14	Netherlands	132.6
6	6	UK	425.4	17	27	Saudi Arabia	109.4
7	7	Italy	348.4	18	24	*General Motors*	96.4
8	8	Canada	334.1	19	17	Sweden	91.9
9	9	China	281.3	20	21	Switzerland	91.1
10	10	Brazil	187.3	21	23	*Exxon*	86.7
11	13	Australia	182.2	22	42	Korea, Rep of	83.2

Table 10-1 continued

Rank 1985	Rank 1976	Name	GNP/Sales (billion $ US)	Rank 1985	Rank 1976	Name	GNP/Sales (billion $ US)
23	31	*Royal Dutch/Shell*	81.7	62	65	New Zealand	23.3
24	32	Indonesia	80.6	63	77	Israel	22.4
25	19	Belgium	77.6	64	86	*Atlantic Richfield*	22.0
26	28	Argentina	76.2	65	62	Kuwait	21.7
27	12	Poland	75.4	66	57	*Unilever*	21.6
28	16	German Democratic Republic	N/A	67	60	*Chrysler*	21.3
29	36	Nigeria	73.5	68	117	*Matsushita*	20.8
30	33	South Africa	73.4	69	104	*Hitachi*	20.5
31	22	Czechoslovakia	N/A	70	—	*Remex*	20.4
32	25	Austria	64.5	71	—	*Shell Oil*	20.3
33	41	*Mobil*	56.0	72	98	*Elf-Aquitane*	20.1
34	34	Norway	54.7	73	69	Chile	19.8
35	29	Denmark	54.6	74	75	*Franàaise des Petro*	19.3
36	38	*Ford Motor*	52.8	75	55	Portugal	19.1
37	39	Finland	51.2	76	63	Peru	18.8
38	51	Algeria	50.7	77	84	*US Steel*	18.4
39	53	*IBM*	50.1	78	89	Ireland	18.3
40	26	Turkey	47.5	79	106	*Nissan Motor*	18.2
41	35	Venezuela	47.5	80	114	Singapore	18.2
42	40	*Texaco*	46.3	81	68	*Phillips*	18.1
43	54	Thailand	41.9	82	91	*Siemens*	17.8
44	47	*Chevron*	41.7	83	85	*Volkswagenwerk*	17.8
45	30	Yugoslavia	38.9	84	82	*Daimler-Benz*	17.8
46	66	*American Tel & Tel*	34.9	85	97	*Nestlé*	17.2
47	59	Colombia	34.4	86	102	*Petrobas*	16.1
48	49	Philippines	32.8	87	130	*United Technologies*	15.8
49	76	Hong Kong	30.6	88	118	*Phillips Petroleum*	15.7
50	61	Libya	30.5	89	88	*Bayer*	15.6
51	71	Egypt	30.1	90	108	*Tenneco*	15.4
52	44	Greece	29.5	91	80	*BASF*	15.1
53	87	*E.I. du Pont*	29.5	92	120	*Occidental Petroleum*	14.5
54	72	Malaysia	29.3	93	79	*Hoechst*	14.5
55	74	United Arab Emirates	28.8	94	—	*Fiat*	14.5
56	58	*General Electric*	28.3	95	—	*Samsung*	14.2
57	64	Pakistan	27.7	96	112	*Mitsubishi*	14.1
58	67	*Standard Oil (Indiana)*	26.8	97	—	*Hyundai*	14.0
59	—	*IRI*	26.8	98	—	*General Motors (Canada)*	13.9
60	95	*Toyota*	26.0	99	—	*Imperial Chemical*	13.9
61	73	*ENI*	24.5	100	123	*Sun*	13.8

* Countries are ranked by gross national product (GNP) and companies by sales. Countries are shown in roman type, companies in italic. Deficiencies in the data sources kept this table from being truly complete. The World Bank does not list a few countries, such as Taiwan. Others, such as Romania, Hungary, and Bulgaria were in the 1976 list (they would have ranked 37, 43, and 45 respectively in this table) but were missing for lack of data in 1985; consequently, they are omitted from this table, where they would likely have ranked somewhere in the 50s. Similarly, some very large companies, such as National Iran Oil and Renault, were omitted from the *Fortune* list; others ranked in the top 100 in 1985 but not 1976, or vice versa.

Source: Veltmeyer (1987, 78–79). From World Bank (1987); *Fortune*, 4 Aug. 1986.

Frank's model is valuable in countering the notion that the causes of poverty lie within the poorer regions themselves. But it has been widely criticized for invoking a crude functional determinism that cannot account for variation in rates of development. Newly industrializing countries are not all characterized by supercheap labour and state repression (Sayer and Walker 1992, 242). There are also many other countries that have supercheap labour but that show no signs of capitalist development. The dynamics of international division of labour are more complex than Frank's model can accommodate. The view of the world as divided into exporters of primary products who are poor and exporters of manufactured goods who are rich is simply not accurate (Gidengil 1989, 95). The mechanisms that tie Third World labour and production into these arrangements are not explicated, nor is the relative importance of cheap labour pools in resolving the crises of capitalism, compared with other factors (Wood 1989, 123–24).

Key terms such as *metropole* and *hinterland* are also vague, particularly when smaller metropoles are seen as constituting hinterlands for bigger ones. In this era of corporate monopoly capitalism, corporate empires rather than hierarchies of nation-states constitute the metropolises. The biggest twenty-three corporations in the world have their headquarters in the United States, but Canada also is home base to a number of multinationals, as are Japan and many European countries. As we will see, being home base to a multinational corporation does not guarantee wealth or economic development. Many poorer regions of Canada and the United States also find their productive potential siphoned off by corporate empires.

Restructuring Dependent Development

Gidengil (1989) suggests that dependency is best understood not as an explanation for underdevelopment, but as a form of relationship that constrains possibilities for development. Dependent regions or countries are those that lack an autonomous capacity for change and growth. Their development potential is tied to decisions made beyond their borders, and over which they have little or no control. They are integrated into the world economy in a subordinate position and this is reflected in internal structures. Typically,

foreign capitalists form alliances with local power blocs of indigenous capitalists and large landowners, with the local state as mediator (Gulalp 1990, 152–53). Local decision making and development initiatives are tightly constrained by such alliances.

Gulalp suggests that underdeveloped capitalist countries such as in Latin America are most likely to have political democracy within early stages of economic development (1990, 158). Elected governments can maintain popularity among voters by promoting local manufacturing industries to replace foreign imports, subsidizing such enterprises and protecting them from cheap foreign imports by high tariff barriers, and also by instituting state welfare policies. But these democracies are vulnerable to "crises of accumulation." The states cannot generate sufficient revenues to sustain these programs because of very low levels of productivity and profits in local industries. Local manufacturers lack the capital to invest in advanced labour-saving technology, and hence produce goods that are of poorer quality and higher unit costs than foreign manufacturers. They also pay lower wages and provide only a limited tax base. The result is a low standard of living relative to other countries that fosters popular unrest. Indigenous capitalists also have vested interests in forming self-seeking alliances with foreign capitalists that undermine protectionist policies. Military regimes are the likely outcome of such internal conflicts. Since they do not need popular electoral support, they are better able to quell resistance from local people, dismantle the welfare state, abandon protectionist policies, and permit foreign capitalists to exploit local resources and cheap labour. This takeover of the domestic economy by foreign capital is often supported by financial agencies such as the International Monetary Fund. Military regimes may in turn give way to civilian governments in which the local capitalists who are most closely tied in with international business interests come to dominate policy.

These are deeply destructive processes of class struggle that do not fit any simplified model of bourgeoisie versus proletariat. The collapse of internal administrative structures associated with them cannot be resolved by adjustments to backward cultural values. The struggles vary widely across developing societies in different regions. In the Middle East and the Far East, the resources that can be exploited locally, their location in the international system, and the constellation of alliances between local and international capital, vary greatly from the Latin American situation and give rise to different patterns of class struggle. What they have in common are the constraints set by a global economy dominated by centres of advanced capitalism.

Restructuring Advanced Capitalism

Advanced capitalist economies do not form a unified bloc with common policies. They, too, are caught up in the contradictions of capitalism, the endemic crises of accumulation reflected in falling rates of profit, overproduction, and unemployment. Competing factions within the capitalist class struggle to maintain **competitive advantage** in global markets. Alliances with developing countries are an important aspect of these strategies, but they cannot be reduced simply to the drive to deskill and cheapen labour in the hope of undercutting competitors' prices.

There are two major types of competitive strategies: one involves trying to minimize inputs and labour costs in given markets; the other tries to promote innovative product development that gives rise to new consumer markets (Sayer and Walker 1992, ch. 2). The first strategy is associated with "fordism" or the mass production of standardized products. Complex assembly work is fragmented into highly repetitive tasks that can be learned easily and performed quickly. A competitive edge depends on minimizing per unit costs of production and on mass consumer markets. The second strategy is associated with "flexible specialization" geared to smaller-batch production for specialized markets. This requires close working relationships between parent plants and suppliers, and among scientists, design engineers, and skilled shopfloor workers who can shift rapidly in a variety of activities. A competitive edge depends on a continual stream of innovative and quality products that attract consumers.

Standardized assembly work is most easily transferred into Third World countries. Abundant supplies of supercheap labour, low taxes, and lax environmental and working standards promise to minimize production costs. These conditions are not conducive to flexible product innovation, however. The standardized product may be cheap but still lose market share to higher quality alternatives, even at higher unit prices. Sayer and Walker suggest that highly integrated groups of interdependent firms in Japan are well adapted to production based on flexible specialization. Foreign competitors cannot easily copy their innovations. There is little incentive for firms within these Japanese groups of companies to subcontract work to centres of cheap labour.

Patterns of international division of labour reflect these complexities. Regional inequality is endemic to advanced capitalism in that high-technology production flourishes where potential users of innovative products are also concentrated. Innovation in the field of computers, for example, is intimately associated with customers' demands and often involves close consultation with them in both production and marketing. The producers of such products are not scattered across different regions. "Silicon Valleys" tend to be highly localized, although the assembly of standardized components may be dispersed.

Sayer and Walker conclude that an adequate understanding of international development must give much greater attention to the complexities of social division of labour rather than class struggle (1992, 268–70). They suggest that the failure of Marxist theory to come to terms with division of labour undermines our understanding of the mechanisms of capitalism. It also undermines the ability of socialist theory to help socialist economies replace these mechanisms with superior forms of organization. Sayer and Walker suggest that socialist economies in Eastern Europe collapsed in large part because they could not manage the division of labour involved in economic production. In capitalist societies, the relationship between demand for goods and their supply by industry is managed through prices in the market. High demand for limited goods causes their prices to rise, and thus encourages individual manufacturers to shift production from low-demand goods to high-demand goods where they can expect to make greater profits. In centrally planned socialist economies, there is no price mechanism. Planners must guess how much of each kind of produce people in a society will need or want and direct production accordingly. The decisions involved are so impossibly complex that the result is chronic inefficiency, gluts and shortages, and decisions are made on the basis of political influence rather than rational economic factors.

Restructuring Socialist Economies

The disintegration of socialist economies in Eastern Europe, beginning with the demolition of the Berlin wall in 1989, was widely hailed as the triumph of capitalism and democracy over totalitarianism. Masses of people demonstrated in the streets demanding that Western-style political democracy replace the one-party communist system. They also pressured for a free market system to replace discredited centrally planned economies. Hundreds of thousands of East Germans flocked to West Berlin to gaze in awe at the consumer goods in the stores. Polish leader Lech Walesa begged American and Western European businesses to invest in Poland. Economists and business people in the Soviet Union, Czechoslovakia, and Hungary swiftly joined the clamour for foreign investment. People in these countries see the correlation between Western capitalism and high standards of living. Correlation readily becomes interpreted as causation, and capitalism is seen as a potential cure for lower living standards in the Eastern bloc. The hope is that by opening their economies to Western investors and free market principles they, too, will encourage investment, high labour productivity, and the accumulation of wealth.

The euphoria surrounding the dismantling of communist parties and the introduction of *perestroika* and *glasnost*, restructuring and freedom, is now largely spent, amid an increasingly grim reality of economic and political chaos. The class struggles emerging within Soviet society reflect deep contradictions that offer no easy transition to advanced capitalism.

The old system of centralized planning generated an elite of party officials and top-level administrators who wielded enormous power and enjoyed high salaries and other perks. At the same time, the mismatch between supplies and demand within the public sector spawned a powerful mafia of black marketeers, hoarders, and speculators (Kotovsky 1992, 169). Members of these two groups have the capital to take greatest advantage of newly-opened markets and are reputed to be rapidly enriching themselves. But this enrichment has been chiefly through speculative trading ventures rather than production.

Since 1987 in the Soviet Union, factory and farm managers have had direct access to overseas markets. One result has been a boom in the export of consumer goods for sale abroad at lower than world prices. The corollary has been the destruction of linkages between enterprises within the domestic economy and the disappearance of goods in which the society was formerly self-sufficient. In 1991, some 2500 co-operatives were established to compete with the public sector, but Kotovsky (1992, 169) estimates that only 20 percent of them went into production. The rest went into pure commerce, speculating in buying and selling commodities. Such nonproductive investments are generating a small class of nouveau riche, while the mass of people are experiencing a frightening collapse in their standards of living and soaring crime rates.

It is too early to judge the long-term outcome of these new economic policies. But processes that generated economic growth in Western capitalist countries in the past will not necessarily work the same way in the context of contemporary international capitalism. People in the Eastern bloc are facing the same contradictions of global capitalism as the struggling economies of the Third World.

Foreign Aid: Philanthropy or Commercial Interests?

Carty (1982) begins his discussion of the Canadian International Development Agency (CIDA) with a quotation that defines foreign aid as money you take from poor people in a rich country and give to rich people in a poor country. Over the thirty-year period between 1951 and 1981, CIDA contributed approximately $11 billion to finance thousands of projects in over ninety countries. In addition, it shipped millions of tons of food and other supplies for emergency relief. But, Carty (1982, 150) concludes, the Third World is as impoverished, exploited, and oppressed now as it was three decades earlier.

There are several reasons why Canada gives foreign aid: it reflects a philanthropic concern to reduce human suffering, political interests in gaining allies and international influence, and commercial interests in boosting export markets for Canadian goods. Carty argues that commercial interests, backed by a very powerful lobby, have taken precedence. He calculates that fully 60 percent of the total CIDA aid budget was spent within Canada on Canadian goods, commodities, and services, creating over 100 000 jobs in Canada. Much aid is unabashedly oriented toward export promotion. The goal is to hook recipients on Canadian inputs in the form of replacement parts, repairs, and services. Development projects also build the infrastructure of roads, railways, and power supplies required by foreign investors (Carty 1982, 168).

While projects that are potentially beneficial for Canadian exports receive massive financial support, other projects that might help to raise the standard of living of people in poor countries are starved of funds. Commitments for health, welfare, clean water supplies, and education, which might more directly benefit recipient countries, dropped off steadily between 1976 and 1978 in the absence of powerful backers.

The real costs to Canada of CIDA aid may be almost zero once one deducts debt forgiveness on past loans; the transfer of surplus wheat, milk, and rapeseed that we could neither eat nor sell commercially; all the bilateral aid tied to the purchase of Canadian goods and services; loan repayments made to nongovernmental organizations based in Canada, which then spend the funds in Canada; and the projected unemployment benefits the Canadian government might have had to pay if these Canadian beneficiaries were not employed (Carty 1982, 171).

Canada's food aid program, while valuable for strictly emergency relief, has been challenged as actually promoting and perpetuating the emergencies it tries to alleviate. In 1976, some 600 000 tons of international food aid was shipped to Bangladesh, yet scarcely 10 percent of it may have reached the destitute. The rest provided cheap, subsidized food for the influential middle classes. Meanwhile it encouraged government complacency about the food crisis and undermined the local markets for the crops of small producers. Many were forced into bankruptcy.

New strategies developed since 1976 are designed in principle to promote "integrated rural development," with more aid going to the less privileged sectors of sharecroppers and small peasant farmers. But Carty suggests that little has changed in practice. World Bank credit still goes principally to medium and larger farmers for commercial enterprises.

Peasants with medium-sized holdings are often selected as target populations because they have enough land to be integrated into "modern-

ized and monetarized" agricultural systems as good credit risks. On the plus side, productivity increases, but at the cost of transforming peasant producers into commercial agriculturalists. They become part of the **agribusiness** system as consumers of agricultural inputs and as producers of crops suitable for further processing.

Carty concludes that what the Third World really needs is not foreign aid, but a restructuring of international economic relations. Between 1970 and 1979, CIDA disbursed some $2.4 billion in aid, but in this same period the ten recipient countries experienced a trade deficit with Canada of about $2.4 billion. This trade imbalance wiped out even the nominal value of the aid.

Agribusiness and Famine

It is with respect to food production that the interests of multinational corporations engaged in agriculture diverge most obviously from the interests of the mass of people in Third World countries. Policies to maximize profits have been directly implicated in the causes of famine. Lappé (1971, 16) aptly sums up this relationship when she states simply that "land that grows money can't grow food."

"Land that grows money can't grow food." Droughts and famine are caused by human mismanagement, overcultivation, deforestation, and overgrazing.

The problem of using land to grow money began during the colonial era when Western powers took over vast tracts of land in subject countries for plantations. Beckford (1973, 120–22) cites a long list of countries in Asia, the Caribbean, and Latin America that are primarily plantation economies, with the bulk of their agricultural resources devoted to foreign-owned plantations producing crops for sale to overseas markets.

The size of such operations is enormous and is steadily growing as corporations buy more land or push neighbouring farmers out of business. The United Fruit Company in Latin America demanded 5000 acres of the best arable land before it would start a plantation. The company did not use this much land but wanted to hold it in reserve in case they might want to expand in the future. United Fruit controlled 100 percent of the export of bananas from Guatemala in 1966 and 70 percent of banana exports from Costa Rica and Panama (Barnet and Muller 1974). In many instances, the area of land taken over is so vast that it provides the only source of employment for people living in substantial parts of the countries concerned.

Plantation crops include tobacco, rubber, tea, coffee, cocoa, cotton and fibres, sugar, and more recently marijuana, for the North American market. All such crops are grown for export only. They cannot be eaten by local people as staple foods. Even crops such as sugar cane are now being grown in Brazil, not for food, but to produce alcohol as a substitute for gasoline. Many Third World countries depend on these cash crops for their survival. Coffee alone provides the economic livelihood for forty developing countries.

Feder (1976) describes in some detail how this process of takeover and control occurs. Corporations control production, processing, transport, storage, and financing. They either employ local people directly or extend credits and inputs on a contract basis with prearranged terms of sale advantageous to the corporation. A corporation that grew strawberries in Mexico, for example, enjoyed cheap land rentals and cheap wages. When the soil became depleted from overproduction, the company moved to a new location. Impoverished ex-employees remained behind. Most of the benefits of exports do not go to local people, or to labourers on plantations, but to big companies, which remit profits abroad.

The most serious ramification is that local farmers who produce the bulk of subsistence food crops are pushed out onto marginal land where yields are low. Food production falls. Farmers try to compensate by pushing into what was once forest or grazing land. Deforestation and progressive depletion of poor soils result. Food prices rise faster than the prices of export crops, so that foreign exchange earnings are not sufficient to pay for the food imports needed.

Droughts, famine, and environmental bankruptcy are not unpredictable acts of god. They are caused by human mismanagement, overcultivation, deforestation, and overgrazing, which have ruined the soil's ability to absorb water. The topsoil blows off, and droughts and flash floods result.

These processes seem to have triggered the massive famine in Ethiopia. Even at the height of its famine, though, Ethiopia continued to export coffee and meat, largely because it needed the foreign exchange to pay debts. This export production is supported by the Food and Agriculture Organization of the United Nations and by the World Bank.

Patriarchy: The Underdevelopment of Women

Women, the main producers of subsistence food crops throughout the world, have fared the worst from policies that promote cash crops over local food crops. In the international system of stratification, women are at the bottom. They work the hardest, produce the most, but own and earn the least.

The functionalist model of modern society proposed by Parsons explicitly excludes women from economic development. Women are defined as specialized homemakers who are or should be financially dependent upon their husbands. They are conceptualized in functionalist development theory as homebound, family-oriented wives and mothers, concerned with socialization and religious training of children, and hence naturally conservative. They are enjoined to behave in accordance with traditional cultural norms, to stress emotions, diffuse and particularistic family ties, and ascriptive values, while men take care of the instrumental roles (Hale 1985, 53).

But the evidence belies this conceptualization of women's lives in the Third World. Women's unpaid labour is estimated to produce one-third of the world's annual economic product. Their work accounts for more than half the food produced in the Third World and as much as 80 percent of food produced in Africa (Sivard 1985, 5).

Yet women are largely excluded from agricultural development projects sponsored as part of the green revolution. Only men are defined as farmers; women are farm wives. Projects for women may include some information on high-yielding seeds, but rarely are women taught the business side of farming. Even progressive land reform policies, intended to give ownership rights to those who work the land rather than to absentee landlords, have served to weaken rather than strengthen women's rights to land. Their traditional land-use rights are ignored, and land is vested in male household heads (Sen 1985, 27). Western individualistic values are imposed on others. In the Kano River project in Nigeria, communally owned lands were registered only in the name of the "senior owner," almost always a man. Women, along with junior men, lost all their rights (Sen 1985, 35).

Women are systematically disadvantaged with respect to all five of the mechanisms noted by Frank as perpetuating neo-imperialism. Firstly, women have the least access of any Third World group to credit and other financial resources. Because they do not own land legally, they have no collateral (Hale 1985, 58–61). Secondly, investments in agricultural technology are directed toward cash crops, which produce the money to repay loans, rather than toward food that will be eaten locally. Women desperately need appropriate technology to reduce the four to six hours a day needed to search for cooking fuel and to fetch water, but this has a low priority in World Bank objectives. Thirdly, in the markets, women at best scratch out a living in petty trade, which requires minimal capital investment. Fourthly, women also come last in the labour market. Women who work as field labourers in India, for example, are typically paid half the wage rates for men. As jobs such as weeding and threshing are mechanized, men tend to take them over, leaving even fewer jobs for women. In the growth industries for exports, women tend to be concentrated in the most poorly paid sweatshop work where they have no bargaining power (Sen 1985, 28–29). Lastly, any concerted efforts to raise the status of women tend to be resisted with patriarchal force. Sen (1985, 20) particularly stresses the extent to which fears of sexual aggression manipulate and threaten women's lives, especially in the labour market. Male chauvinism and religious fundamentalism serve to reinforce these processes that keep women in subordinated positions.

Development policies have resulted in the position of women in the Third World being systematically underdeveloped. In many regions, their situation frequently deteriorates from one of independent control over subsistence production to that of unpaid labourers begging for money for food from men who control the expanding cash economy (Rogers 1980, ch. 6; Hale 1981, 152).

Feminists demand fundamental changes in the vision of development. Their goal is to make development more people-centred instead of cash-centred. Sen emphasizes that gender subordination, which is integral to Parsons' model of a modern social system, must be eradicated before people-centred development can take place. Such development must begin with women because their work is central to survival (Sen 1985, 13–16). Women have to be empowered before such changes can take place.

Development Efforts as Social Construction

The macrolevel analyses of development policies and programs described above present a picture of frustrated goals and limited achievements. They point to the structures that hamper social change, but generally offer little insight into the active agency of the people involved. The social constructionist approach to development focusses attention on the everyday practices that collectively produce these outcomes, and also the organized practices by which theories are constructed, research undertaken, and results written up and disseminated, so that what passes as factual knowledge about development gets produced.

Feminist work in development has long struggled to redress systematic biases in data collection that contribute to ignorance of the situation of women in the Third World on the part of people charged with designing projects to help them. At the level of powerful international agencies such as UNESCO women were conspicuous only by their absence until well into the 1970s (United Nations 1980). The data available from professional and government agencies as a basis for planning were oriented primarily to male relevancies and particularly the relevancies of market economies (UNESCO 1981). Data on work-force participation, for example, systematically hid the enormous contribution of women in the unpaid subsistence sector. When work is measured in terms of contractual paid labour, women's work is defined so as not to exist. Similarly, when knowledge is measured by years of formal schooling, village women appear to be utterly ignorant. Myths of women as ignorant and idle dependants of men thus become the dominant perspectives in terms of which programs for women are designed. Decades of feminist work have only begun to undermine these statistical images.

After two decades of struggle, women's offices and programs now exist in most of the major international development agencies such as the United Nations, UNESCO, United States Agency for International Development (USAID), The World Bank, Ford Foundation, Canadian International Development Agency (CIDA), and the like. This network of organizations is a major location in which knowledge about women in the Third World is produced (Mueller 1986). But this knowledge is generated by and for development agencies. It is focussed around aid projects, and what is relevant for the aid bureaucracies to know in the technical management of these projects. The documents required for project organization consist of detailed time schedules, budgets, and quantified standards to judge efficiency. All the messy problems of the complex, disorderly, real world conditions in underdeveloped countries become translated into mechanical problems for which there are managerial solutions. These documents provide the basis for project evaluation, supplemented occasionally by brief site visits. They are the products of professionals' and academics' work, and they feed into objective, rational decision making and management work at the headquarters of the international development agencies. These project procedures direct attention away from the local settings in which field workers and residents struggle directly with the overwhelming problems of poverty and underdevelopment. These local people are effectively excluded and silenced.

Mueller (1986) argues that these processes are an important part of the mechanisms that subject Third World countries to relations of ruling by First World agencies. Having more women employed in the development agencies does nothing to resolve this subjection. These women become part of a professional network of knowledge production that sustains a discourse about development in which the Third World comes to be seen only in a relation of dependence to the First World, subject to management and control by the First World agencies. The discourse has succeeded in creating a type of underdevelopment that is politically and economically manageable (Escobar 1984, 388). In the view of some radical critics, the projects sustained by such discourse have not only failed to solve problems of underdevelopment, but actively create more impoverishment and underdevelopment (Mueller 1986, 38).

When we shift the focus from international agencies to the local settings in which development projects take place, another network of practices becomes visible that excludes and silences the people most directly involved, while systematically undermining and dis-organizing the work that they do. A study of development projects designed to improve the living standards of women and children in rural North India made visible some of these failure-producing practices (Hale 1987a; 1987b). The concept of *grass-roots* participation in the implementation of projects is widely supported by development agencies as a response to the criticism that too much control is exerted by external agents. But at village level this is commonly translated into practices that give elite males control and veto power over projects intended for women. Project organizers in the North Indian villages sought the permission of district and village-level councils and village headmen, institutions from which women are systematically excluded. When elite males on the councils disapproved of the projects, they could and did block their implementation. Subsequently, when the programs did begin operations, it was these same male elites who acted as grass-roots overseers, who haggled over which women should host clubs and classes in the village, and who were responsible for verifying that supplies were received and distributed as intended. These men had little personal interest in ensuring that free food and medicines reached children in poorest areas of the village and put great pressure on women workers to divert the supplies elsewhere. Women, as would-be recipients of the services, had no control at all.

Notions of sisterhood, drawn from early feminist scholarship, supported a view of women as relatively undifferentiated, and led to practices that failed to take account of stratification in implementing the schemes. The organization of clubs and classes in the homes of elite women, closely linked with the dominant male faction, effectively ensured that few, if any, women from the poorest households would attend. Village women hired to implement nutrition programs for children were supposed to carry out regular visits to homes in the poorest areas of the villages to check on the health of children. High-status teachers found this task so onerous and distasteful that few ever did it. Helpers who were hired to work with these teachers, however, commonly came from the same lower-class backgrounds as those families most in need of home visiting. They might willingly have done this work, but no attempt was ever made by program organizers to employ them in this manner. As illiterate women, they were defined in advance as too ignorant to be given such responsibilities. In effect, the organizational practices denied lower-class women the competence and authority to speak, even when they were present.

Organizational practices systematically silenced women involved in adult education, both as students and as teachers, serving to perpetuate stereotyped conceptions of the situation and needs of women, and also made possible the subsequent explanations for the limited impact of the schemes in terms of personal inadequacies of the women themselves. The official view that the problems facing village women were those of ignorance, idleness, and apathy, had its counterpart in the view of the teaching role as simply providing information, without needing further skills. Village women with grade eight education were hired as nursery-school and adult-literacy teachers. They were given minimal teacher training, on the assumption that anyone who could read could show others and that women were used to looking after children. The practical problems of the teaching situation were never considered, and when the teachers failed to cope, they were seen as lazy and incompetent.

Women employees within the bureaucracy of the development programs found themselves silenced by systematic practices of subordination and exclusion. Their superiors rarely consulted them on how the projects were running, and when the women offered advice they were not usually heeded. In effect, they were not accorded the authority to speak, or to be listened to. Their views on their own problems, and possible solutions to them, were not made visible within the organization. The only explanations considered were those imposed on them from superiors who had no first-hand experience of village work.

When the focus shifts from operations in the villages to the work-life experiences of women employees in the development bureaucracy, what becomes visible are the organized practices that gave rise to the women's apparent incompetence to do their jobs, particularly the failure of women supervisors to exercise authority. Field research uncovered widespread evidence of neglect of duties by women workers and some blatant corruption, virtually all of which went unpunished. When women supervisors were asked specifically how they had tried to deal with such problems, they gave repeated examples of how their disciplinary actions had been countermanded by senior male bureaucrats. Orders to cut the pay of negligent workers, or to dismiss subordinates caught stealing food supplies were routinely cancelled by more senior males, allegedly in return for bribes or sexual favours. The resulting breakdown in authority relations was treated as fact by onlookers, imposed back upon the situation as an explanation for the failure of various aspects of the project, and then used as justification for arguments that women should be excluded from authority positions because they were inadequate to handle the responsibilities. What was most disturbing was that the women themselves lacked the means to reflect upon, formulate, and articulate their own experiences. They internalized the dominant interpretations of apathy and incompetence, not only as a description of the helplessness that they felt, but as an explanation for it. When questioned on the problems which their programs were encountering, the women blamed themselves and fellow workers as uneducated housewives lacking the competence to do their jobs. None of them offered interpretations in terms of the patriarchal authority relations that were continually dis-organizing their work. The systematically constructed chaos in which these women worked remained unarticulated, even by themselves. The official project evaluation that was sent to headquarters identified the central cause of failure as the decision to hire village women who were previously housewives and who lacked higher education. The managerial solution proposed was to close down the project locally, and start again on a much smaller scale elsewhere with a staff of educated women brought in from outside. Local residents were left to work around the remnants of the failed project.

On a very small scale, the powerlessness of these women in their work mirrors the powerlessness of Third World peoples generally in their relations with foreign development agencies and foreign corporations that control the decisions that influence their lives. The particular experiences of these women in this one project cannot be generalized to other contexts. What is important here is the form of analysis that seeks to translate factual evidence and explanatory theories back into the activities of the people who produce them.

▧ Canadian Development in a World Capitalist System

By most measures Canada ranks as a wealthy, advanced capitalist economy. It has a high average standard of living, and is home base to a number of multinational corporate empires. But these broad generalizations disguise pockets of severe poverty and regional disparities. Canada is also struggling with its own problems of dependent development in a North American context.

Historically, the development of the Canadian economy has been very closely tied to imperial Europe and later to the United States. Until the mid-nineteenth century, Canada enjoyed privileged trading status with Britain, especially for grain; but with the repeal of the Corn Laws, Canadian merchants turned increasingly to the United States as a trading partner. A limited Reciprocity Treaty was signed between Canada and the United States in 1854, promoting free trade between the two countries, but it was abrogated by the U.S. in 1866 in retaliation against the Canadian government for its seeming support of the Confederacy during the American Civil War. The Canadian Confederation was formed in 1867, and, about a decade late, John A. Macdonald's **National Policy** was instituted. This policy established high tariffs against American goods entering Canada. Its primary goal was to pressure American businessmen to invest in Canada and to establish subsidiaries here, in order to avoid tariff barriers. This policy encouraged the development of a **branch-plant economy**. In almost every year since 1900, Canada has absorbed one-third of all

investment capital exported from the United States (Veltmeyer 1987, 77). Canada now has the largest branch-plant economy in the world. By 1987, 49 percent of the top 500 corporations in Canada were foreign-controlled, mostly by Americans, and they earned 50 percent of all manufacturing profits (Hurtig 1991, 55).

The Canadian economy reaped many benefits from these investments but at the price of **dependent development**. Like many newly developing countries, Canada's internal economic structures are constrained by international relationships of dependence that limit autonomous capacity for change and growth (Gidengil 1989). Critical decisions affecting development in Canada are made by centres of corporate enterprise located in the United States, and the benefits of such growth flow disproportionately south of our borders. Trade between Canada and the United States is dominated by multinational corporations. Veltmeyer (1987, 86) estimates that, in 1983, between 75 and 80 percent of all imports and exports involved parent-subsidiary transfers by foreign corporations. In such transactions, transfer-pricing arrangements normally apply, to Canada's net disadvantage.

The distorting effects of this dependent development are revealed in the types of commodities exported and imported. Canada is near the bottom of the industrially advanced capitalist countries on measures involving manufactured exports. Typically, for a branch-plant economy, Canada largely exports raw materials and semi-processed goods and imports manufactured goods. Canada also lags far behind other industrialized countries in the proportion of gross national product spent on research and development. Such research is highly centralized in corporate headquarters located outside Canada.

This is the economic context in which the recent free trade deals were negotiated. The bilateral Canada–United States Free Trade Agreement (CUSFTA) was signed in January 1989 and the trilateral North American Free Trade Agreement (NAFTA) among Canada, the United States, and Mexico was signed in 1993. The negotiations leading up to the 1989 agreement were intense and bitter. The Canadian election in November 1988 was fought almost entirely around this issue, with the Conservative Party, led by Brian Mulroney, strongly in favour and the Liberals and New Democrats strongly against the deal. The money spent by the government, the

Conservative Party, and big business to support the deal has been estimated at $56 million over two years, about ten times what was spent by those campaigning against the deal (Fillmore 1989, 14). Pro-free trade forces spent $3.5 million during the last three weeks of the campaign alone. The re-election of the Mulroney government made the signing a fait accompli. The subsequent trilateral deal was negotiated with relatively little public debate or opposition.

Opponents of the 1989 deal feared that Canada's already shaky control over internal economic structures and resources would be further diluted. If high tariffs under the National Policy encouraged the establishment of American branch plants in Canada, then the dismantling of these tariffs under free trade posed the risk that branch plants would be closed down, and their operations relocated to the parent company, with potentially enormous job losses in Canada. At the same time, the deal made American direct investment in Canada's resource-extraction industries easier, and guaranteed access to all Canada's energy resources on equivalent terms with Canadians. Advantages that Canada might have gained from conserving these resources, or from boosting export prices relative to prices charged to national businesses and consumers would be lost. Control over our primarily natural resources would thus be weakened.

A closely related fear was that Canadian businesses would be unable to compete in North American markets without some protective tariffs. The contradictions of advanced capitalism that led to the increasing concentration and polarization of wealth seemed likely to increase, to the net detriment of Canada. Giant corporations, already dominating American markets, have the capacity to service the entire Canadian market with existing productive capacity, and at per unit costs lower than smaller Canadian competitors could achieve. Under such **imperfect competition** conditions, the logic of free-market competition does not hold.

Canadian businesses start out with many competitive disadvantages relative to American businesses. Fair competition requires a "level playing field" in the sense of approximately equal operating conditions, but between Canadian and American economies, the field is far from level. Canada has a harsher climate, and higher energy and transportation costs, which have particularly severe consequences for agricultural production. Canada also has a higher standard of social services, particularly unemployment insurance, Medicare, and family allowances; it has higher minimum wage rates than apply in the southern United States; and it has a commitment to provincial equalization payments—all of which translate into higher corporate and individual taxes. Higher taxes mean higher production costs and consequently higher prices for equivalent commodities. If these conditions continued unchanged, Canadian businesses might be bankrupted by the unfair competition, or driven south of the border, again with severe loss of jobs in Canada. Before this happened, the Canadian government would likely face intense pressure to cut social services to harmonize with the lower standards in the United States.

Opponents of the deal were also deeply concerned with the implications of free trade in services, particularly financial services such as banking and insurance, and also management and consulting firms, and those engaged in information technology, education, and the like. The Free Trade Deal provided for the right of national treatment to be extended to all firms competing for contracts, explicitly including contracts to supply services on behalf of federal and provincial governments. Canadian cultural industries were exempted from these conditions, but opponents argued that Canadian social institutions would be inexorably Americanized in any case, by the loss of control over services and the downgrading of social security. Canadian nationhood itself seemed in jeopardy.

This severely negative view of free trade propounded by the Left did not prevail, but neither were these fears dispelled. Those who poured their funds into supporting the deal emphasized the advantages and new opportunities that it might bring. But they also argued that under prevailing conditions of economic dependency, Canada had little choice; rejecting the deal in the hope that the status quo would continue was not a viable alternative.

On the positive side, classical economics theory holds that expansion of trade promotes division of labour, specialization, and rising productivity, which in principle makes possible higher wages and lower consumer prices. Conversely, tariffs distort trade and protect inefficient production (Wonnacott 1987). Much trade between Canada and the United States was already free from tariffs in 1989 but there remained important barriers in industries such as textiles, clothing, footwear, and furniture, and multiple nontariff barriers such as quotas, prohibitions on certain imports, and preferential government purchasing of locally produced goods and services. The removal of such protectionist measures promised to force Canadian industry to become more efficient.

Economists such as Paul Wonnacott (1987) of the Institute for International Economics, further argued that free access to the huge American market would increase the potential for **economies of scale** in Canadian manufacturing. Any industry has large overheads and fixed costs—a factory, machinery, skilled workers, an energy supply, production, storage, and transportation facilities, and the like—needed even for low levels of production. In principle, maximum efficiency is achieved when production is increased to the point where all factors of production are fully utilized. But this presupposes sufficiently large markets so that all products can be sold. The small and widely dispersed Canadian market is too confining to promote efficient mass production.

Economies of scale are best realized with specialized production and concentration on long production runs with limited items. Wonnacott uses the example of the Canadian furniture industry to suggest that it would be more efficient to produce huge quantities of one specialized item for a North American consumer market of 250 million people than a variety of products for a national market of 25 million. In principle, profits rise and prices fall, to everyone's benefit. What was required, he argued, was an adjustment period, that was provided for by the slow reduction in tariffs over a ten-year period after the deal came into effect.

Wonnacott's thesis itself presupposes "fordism," a model of standardized mass production with competitiveness based on price cutting, and the corollary of deskilled, cheap labour. It also presupposes that small Canadian firms can find a market niche—offering a product that giant manufacturers are not already geared to produce at maximum efficiency. Competitiveness based on rapid product innovation and customized production for higher-income markets, depends on different principles of production. Such flexible production is potentially less vulnerable to shifts

in consumer demand, but it presupposes the capacity for ongoing research and development, versatile work teams, and integrated groups of companies. Canada's heritage of a branch-plant economy has generated internal business structures with limited capacity to adapt to this alternative organization of production.

Any system of production, however, requires access to markets, and Canada is particularly dependent on the American market. Wonnacott notes that several attempts to develop trade with Europe have not succeeded. Prime Minister Pierre Trudeau tried this policy during the 1970s, but the share of exports to Europe actually declined from 19 percent in 1970 to 15 percent in 1980 and to 7 percent in 1985. A strong argument in favour of accepting the Free Trade Deal was that it would protect Canada from the risk of being shut out of United States markets by their growing **protectionism**, at the same time that protectionism was rising in Europe. The slow pace of international negotiations on a General Agreement on Tariffs and Trade (GATT) made the bilateral agreement with the United States all the more attractive (Rocher 1991). Surveys conducted after the deal was signed suggest that capitalists who supported the deal were not antinationalist, but rather saw Canada's sovereignty as dependent on economic growth and continentalism as their best hope for accomplishing this.

The free trade negotiations took place in a wider context of global changes in the structure of capital and trading blocs that left business and labour feeling vulnerable on both sides of the border. The Canadian labour movement felt threatened by the potential job losses that might accompany the deal, but avoiding the deal in favour of the status quo promised little protection from global trends that were undermining security of jobs and markets. New world competitors were forcing the pace of technological innovation and trade specialization in any case, regardless of what happened with the Canada–United States deal. Oligopolies that once ensured stable investments and market control were losing this control by the mid-1970s as the customized production of innovative products for higher-income markets became a critical competitive strategy (Warskett 1990, 123–25). Even a giant corporation like International Business Machines (IBM) of America could not hold onto its markets (Sayer and Walker 1992, 241–42). The company cut many thousands of skilled jobs in its restructuring program. The freedom of capitalists to shift both financial and physical investments anywhere in the world further undermines job security in Canada and the United States. Low-wage jobs can always be undercut by still lower wages elsewhere. The real target, Warskett suggests, was never really the Free Trade Agreement as such. It was, and still is, the struggle to confront global capital.

Child labour in Mexico provides a low-wage option not available in Canada and undermines job security here and in the United States.

Capital, the State, and the Free Trade Agreements

The North American Free Trade Agreement, encompassing Canada, the United States, and Mexico, and ongoing negotiations with more than thirty other countries in Latin America exemplifies both the central and the marginal character of the state in bourgeois society (Sayer 1985, 39–40). It makes visible in a peculiarly overt and written form the practices by which states maintain the forms of society whose productive activities are governed by market forces. Leading politicians from the three states, together with their professional support staff of bureaucrats, lawyers, and economists, were centrally involved in structuring the highly complex deal—a deal that encompassed over 1000 pages of regulations plus 4300 pages of enabling legislation, and amended twenty-seven major Acts of the Canadian

Parliament. Yet the terms of the agreement are intentionally designed to minimize the power of any of the three governments to intervene in the free play of markets.

Analysts argue that the principles written into the NAFTA are not primarily about either trade or tariffs. They are about the commercialization of society (Calvert and Kuehn 1993; *Peace Research* 1993; *Canadian Forum*, special issue Jan. 1993; Weston et al. 1992). The Agreement institutes a new legal, regulatory, and investment framework for international business. It limits the ability of governments to regulate the economy while shifting a wider range of public sector activities into the private marketplace. It establishes the right of corporations located in any of the three countries to "national treatment" with respect to any business operations, including investments and bidding on contracts. Stringent rules protect corporate interests by providing for extensive compensation to firms for any loss of market opportunity that might accrue from any violation of the agreement by future governments (Santer 1993).

These regulations extend far beyond what is generally thought of as business activities, to commercialize all forms of social services. The chapter on "Mandate of Services" includes sweeping coverage of all possible aspects of provision of services—production, distribution, marketing delivery, transportation connected with the service, and insurance (Calvert and Kuehn 1993, 16). All these aspects are intended to be open to profit-making enterprises. The services considered include education, day-care, insurance, pensions, hospitals and health care—in fact, any conceivable social service that is not specifically designated as an "existing service" provided by government at the time the Agreement was signed. The Agreement has a built-in "ratchet effect" (Calvert and Kuehn 1993, 30) permitting movement only in the one direction of increasing commercialization. Provision of any new services is automatically in the open commercial market, and rights of "national treatment" apply. The Agreement also commits governments to a continual review of exempted or nonconforming services, so that nothing is permanently exempt.

The climate of corporate and business interests is further protected by a greatly expanded definition of "intellectual property." Protection of patents on new products is extended, notably a twenty-year protection on new drugs, and a fifty-year protection on computer programs, now recognized as "literary works" (Dillon 1993). Intellectual property laws also cover interactive computer and audiovisual learning devices, out-of-country cable and satellite transmission of educational programs, courses, and learning aids that have been given patent protection, biotechnology, and multiple other "products" (Dillon 1993, 41). Knowledge itself is now defined as private property. Stringent regulations to control unauthorized use of such property include right of seizure, forfeiture, and destruction of infringed goods.

These principles of government protection for international commerce are now being actively extended across Latin America in fast-paced negotiations (*Peace Research* 1993). The Colombian government agreed to the Intellectual Property Law in 1992 as a preliminary to starting free trade negotiations with the United States. It is also pushing ahead with policies of domestic economic liberalization, the *apertura* model, that United States trade officials emphasized as preconditions for extending the NAFTA. This liberalization includes repayment of foreign debts on schedule and accomplishing the goals set by the World Bank, such as stabilizing currency and reducing inflation, no matter what the domestic social costs.

Countries throughout Latin America are struggling to meet these preconditions. The United States government is encouraging the formation of regional trade blocs, such as the Andean Pact, both to make negotiations easier, and to spread some of the burden for enforcing these policies from United States international financial institutions like the International Monetary Fund.

If the NAFTA is extended across Latin America as planned, it will achieve a number of objectives important to United States business interests. Chief among them is that it will ensure access to Latin American markets on terms favourable to the multinational corporations and subject to United States trade laws. It locks signatory states into binding international agreements designed to make economic restructuring permanent. The commercialization of society that is integral to the NAFTA is effectively binding on future governments. Cameron notes that legally the United States can more easily get out of the agreements than can Canada or Mexico. The American Congress ratified the deals through fast-track legislation that can be overridden by a subse-

quent law passed by Congress. To have the status of an international treaty, standing above domestic legislation, the deals would have had to be ratified by two-thirds of the American Senate (D. Cameron 1993).

The context of negotiations, and part of the explanation for the urgency with which they are being pursued by the United States government is the United States own declining political and business influence in the global economy. It is being challenged, if not overshadowed, by the resurgence of Japan and the European Economic Community. The NAFTA provides special protection for American business by tying Canada and Mexico into a trading bloc that discriminates against external trading partners (D. Cameron 1993; M. Cameron 1993). The NAFTA's chapter on rules of origin sets the proportion or quantity of a product that must originate in North America before it can qualify for preferential, dutyfree entry to the trading bloc. Fuzzy terms like *substantial transformation* and *regional value content* of components have been used to justify **countervailing duties** against Honda cars assembled in Canada but destined for United States markets. Japan has served notice that it intends to challenge the NAFTA rules of origin in the next round of negotiations under the General Agreements on Tariffs and Trade.

The United States economy is increasingly vulnerable to the mobility of capital and competition from low-wage countries, including Mexico and other Latin American countries potentially joining NAFTA. In an effort to protect its interests, the United States government pushed for workers' rights to be officially on the agenda for the next round of GATT talks. This proposal met with concerted opposition from representatives of developing countries, who saw it as a ploy for discriminating against products made in the Third World. What developing countries fear is that industrialized countries will insist on high standards of labour rights, environment protection, and human rights, that poor countries are unable to attain and then use this failure as grounds for trade barriers. Beneath the high-sounding moralisms is a ploy to exclude Third World goods from First World markets—in effect, protectionism for business interests in industrialized countries.

The Uruguay Round of trade talks was signed at Marrakesh on 15 April 1994, after seven years of talks involving 125 countries. Before being implemented, it has been ratified by the legislatures of those countries where it is a requirement, including Canada (*Globe and Mail*, 16 April 1994, B3). Commentators estimate that most of the benefits of this round of talks will flow to industrialized nations. But they project that developing countries will wield much greater influence in the next round of talks, scheduled to begin as soon as the Uruguay Round is ratified.

The Effects of the Free Trade Agreements on Canada

It is impossible to separate the effects of the Canada–United States Free Trade Agreement from the simultaneous effects of the severe recession that hit most of the advanced capitalist countries of Europe and North America in the early 1990s. Few of the positive hopes of liberalized trade, expanding markets, economies of scale, and rising productivity, envisioned by the supporters of free trade have been realized. Many of the dire warnings of opponents of the deal, especially massive job losses, declining investments, and severe cutbacks in Canadian social programs, have come to pass. There is little dispute over the evidence that Canadians generally are worse off in the mid-1990s than they were in the mid-1980s. The only question is the extent to which the free trade deal can be blamed for this decline, or whether the recession might have been worse if compounded with American protectionism. By April 1994 the combined federal-provincial debt had reached $661 billion, or 93 percent of the Gross Domestic Product, a ratio of debt to size of economy widely seen as unsustainable.

Staunch nationalists like Mel Hurtig (1991) and Maude Barlow (1990) directly implicate the Free Trade Deal in the severity of the recession in Canada. Hurtig cites detailed evidence to support his claim that a systematic deindustrialization of Canada has occurred since 1989. Canada lost some 264 000 manufacturing jobs in the first two years of the Agreement and stood dead last of the top thirteen industrial powers in industrial production performance. Since 1987, the average monthly rate of job creation dropped every year from 40 600 in 1987, to 26 300 in 1988, to 13 200 in 1989, to minus 7400 in 1990 (Hurtig 1991, 17). Another estimate puts job losses in Ontario alone

The growth of *maquiladoras*, like this auto part component assembly plant in Mexico, has led to a number of plant closures in Canada.

at 500 000 in three years following the signing of the CUSFTA (Spratt 1992, 8). Profits to Canadian businesses dropped steadily, and business bankruptcies rose. Barlow documents the progressive privatization and deregulation of services such as transportation, telecommunications, and utilities, with the consequences typically being increased foreign ownership, takeovers, bankruptcies, and commercial oligopolies (1990, 33–48).

Foreign investment totalled $88 billion between 30 June 1985 and 30 June 1990, but 92 percent of this investment took the form of foreign takeovers of Canadian businesses, producing no increase in productive capacity or jobs. Moreover, much of this takeover money was from profits generated in Canada. One result of this rash of takeovers is that between 1989 and 1991 corporate debt rose about twice as fast as government debt, with interest costs as a percentage of pretax profits rising from 22 percent to 45 percent (Hurtig 1991, 164). Also typical of dependent economies, the flow of money out of Canada in the form of dividends exceeded money coming into Canada in direct investments by a factor of ten to one (Hurtig 1991, 64–65).

Foreign-owned companies created fewer and poorer jobs and less diversified exports than Canadian-owned companies. For every billion dollars in profits between 1978 to 1984 Canadian companies created 5765 jobs and American-owned companies in Canada created seventeen jobs (Hurtig 1991, 75). Profits from foreign-owned corporations pour out of Canada, much of them in the form of untaxed transfer-pricing. Hurtig cites the case of Canada Safeway, which reported interest expenses of $52.5 million in 1990, mostly the result of assuming a $484-million debt for the parent company in California.

Barlow similarly documents the number of plant closures, particularly in such sectors as textiles, clothing, furniture, and auto parts, which experienced between 25 to 30 percent drop in manufacturing capacity during 1989–90. These industries typically employ low-technology, assembly-line manufacturing processes that can readily be moved to *maquiladoras*, component assembly plants in Mexico, offering labour at $6 per day.

The food-processing industry in Canada is also hard hit by the double problem of high-priced supply-managed farm produce and higher base wages in Canada, and the prospect of cheap American imports. Companies such as Campbell soup, Gerber baby foods, St. Lawrence Starch, Rowntree, Hostess, Hershey, and Kraft are all closing plants in Canada or turning them into warehouses while production shifts south of the border (Barlow 1990, 60). The supply management programs established in dairy, eggs, chicken, and turkey production in Canada are under siege and seem unlikely to long withstand the competition from cheaper American goods now that tariff protection has gone. Even the legitimacy of supply-management is being openly questioned (Skogstad 1993). The end of supply management, however, would probably mean the end of independent family farms. In Canada in 1988, the production of eggs, poultry, and dairy products was spread among some 2500 family farms. In the United States about a dozen integrated companies, located almost exclusively in the low-wage southern states controlled most of the American chicken industry. They can produce chickens at 25 percent below Canadian farm prices, but at high social and humanitarian costs. In these "chicken cities" birds live out their eight-week lives under wretched conditions, crammed into battery cages that are cleaned out at best once a year. Birds have to be heavily drugged with antibiotics to survive under such conditions. In 1994, corporate agribusiness bragged openly about extending this superrationalization of chicken production to the production of pork. Pigs, whose level of intelligence far exceeds that of dogs, are confined in cages too small for them even to turn around. Conveyor belts carry them from birth to slaughter house.

Social Programs

Cutbacks in social programs became increasingly extensive in the early 1990s, much as predicted by opponents to the free trade deals. Again, no one seems to question that the process itself is happening, only whether it would have occurred regardless of the deals, in response to recession and changing views of the appropriate role of government in capitalist society. Four major programs affected are unemployment insurance (UI), family allowances, old age pensions, and Medicare. Unemployment insurance was particularly targeted by the Americans as a potentially unfair government subsidy to business, especially to seasonal businesses such as fishing. Shortly

Corporate agribusiness food-processing techniques have resulted in cruel and inhumane treatment of animals.

after the deal was signed, the Canadian government withdrew its contributions, making it strictly employer-employee funded. New barriers to qualifying for the insurance were introduced, the duration of benefits were reduced, and amounts cut. In April 1994, a federal government task force proposed dropping the employer premiums on the grounds that "a payroll tax is a tax on jobs." UI would become a pure insurance scheme paid for entirely by employees, and with benefits cut to a maximum of twenty-six weeks. The explicit goal of the task force was for Canada to have the lowest payroll taxes of any industrialized country (*Globe and Mail*, 8 April 1994, A1–2).

With the goal of cutting the cost of social programs as part of tax and deficit reduction, old age pensions were de-indexed, and a claw-back provision added to eliminate higher-income pensioners from benefits. Universal family allowances were similarly eliminated in early 1993 and replaced with an income-related scheme that is not fully indexed against inflation.

Medicare, a system of universal, public medical insurance, first established in 1966, is still the jewel in the Canadian system of social programs. Ironically in this case, by the 1990s American business interests began to lobby the United States government to implement a similar scheme, on the grounds that the extremely high cost of private insurance premiums for employee health benefits were rendering them uncompetitive with Canadian businesses. In Canada, however, the future of Medicare is threatened by escalating costs. Efforts to cut costs have resulted in layoffs, privatization, and contracting out of services. Fuller (1993) sees these changes as directly reflecting the NAFTA philosophy of commercialization of services. The potential for profits from health care are high, given that the health industry constitutes about 10 percent of the Gross Domestic Product.

The Canadian health-care system has three main sectors: the public sector of provincial health insurance, hospitals, laboratories, rehabilitation and outpatient care; the quasi-public nonprofit facilities dependent on public funding; and the private sector of clinics, extended care, home care, diagnostic laboratories, and outpatient treatment. Fuller (1993, 16) estimates that the private sector has been growing rapidly as the public sector is being cut back. In 1990, the federal government froze its cash grants to the provinces for two years

and fixed the rate of future growth in payments to the Gross National Product (GNP) minus 3 percent, to begin in 1992. In 1991, Bill C-20 further escalated the reduction in cash transfers. Private health insurance is expanding to cover gaps in services as governments cut back. Private drug plans are particularly important. Blue Cross covers prescription drugs, eyeglasses and contact lenses, dental care, semiprivate hospital rooms, private physiotherapy, ambulance service, and out-of-country medical treatment. Medicare still covers basic health needs.

The Canada Health Act of 1984 entrenched the principles of universality, equal access, comprehensive services, portability across provinces, and public, nonprofit administration of health insurance. In May 1994 the federal government moved to punish British Columbia for extra billing by cutting transfer payments until they stopped the practice. Alberta was also targeted for allowing a two-tier system of private clinics that charge extra fees for early access to certain tests and surgical procedures. The federal government has also taken to emphasizing lower health-care costs in Canada relative to the United States as a competitive business advantage for Canada. However, the clout of the federal government to protect Medicare is being steadily reduced as the value of transfer payments recedes relative to tax transfers. Also, the ratchet effect built into the NAFTA means that as more specialized services are privatized or contracted out, they cannot be re-absorbed into Medicare without compensating all businesses that might lose potential markets.

The Commercialization of Service

Under the NAFTA rules, management consulting firms are increasingly moving into the fields of health and education. They operate in terms of definitions of *efficiency* that focus principally on minimizing operating costs in order to maximize profits. This focus is what makes the contracting out of service management so attractive to cash-strapped governments. But the practices that produce financial efficiency frequently come with important social costs that are not factored into business accounting. Terms such as *efficiency* and *rationalization* cannot be defined apart from the values that determine how they are operationalized in specific contexts. Practices that are efficient in relation to one set of objectives may be totally inefficient for different goals.

Cohen (1988b) describes the management practice of computerizing patient-illness classifications in order to calculate the type and amount of nursing care needed in hospitals. One effect of maximizing the "efficient" use of nursing services is to reduce full-time regular nursing staff to a minimum, where the majority of nurses are on call, their work scheduled in part-time and irregular shifts. Efficiency for the hospital is bought at the cost of severely deteriorating conditions of work for the nurses. Quality of patient care deteriorates as nurses have no discretion to give individuals the extra attention they feel they need. The value of time spent talking to and reassuring worried patients is not readily included in computerized measures of care needed. A poll conducted for the Ontario Nurses Association in 1988 indicated that around 15 percent of Ontario nurses were planning to leave the profession because of excessive patient loads and demoralizing working conditions (*Globe and Mail*, 15 April 1988, A4).

Similar processes are occurring with respect to child care services in Canada. Profit-oriented companies are big business in the United States and the free trade deals guarantee them **right of national treatment**; that is, the right for businesses located outside the country, to be treated in exactly the same manner as local businesses in bidding on any federal and provincial contracts to provide services. The Conservative government's decision in 1988 to direct child-care funding to mothers, rather than to establishing government-run child-care centres, plays directly to a profit-oriented system. No government day-care system can be set up in Canada in the future without compensating all these service firms for loss of potential markets.

Alternatives to the Free Trade Agenda

A major problem in the debates surrounding free trade is that both supporters and opponents tend to be oriented to the same model of economic development, with the main question being whether nationalist or continentalist policies are likely to work best. Largely missing from the public debate are core questions concerning what visions of development we have and whether the continental market-driven form of economic organization can fulfil those visions.

In the middle of the free trade negotiations, in April 1987, the Brundtland Report, entitled *Our Common Future*, was published under the auspices of the United Nations World Commission on Environment and Development. Its core message is that the model of development assumed in the free trade agenda is endangering global survival. Development that is driven by corporate concentration and investment decisions geared to maximizing short-term financial returns is not ecologically sustainable. It is generating environmental damage of staggering magnitude in the Third World and in industrially developed nations.

Current emphasis on cash crops for quick profits encourages mining the soil to maximize immediate outputs rather than conserving it as a future resource. The control of vast acres of land in Third World countries by agribusiness results in the majority of local producers being pushed onto marginal land that cannot sustain intensive production. As the output of subsistence food crops falls, desperate farmers exploit still more marginal lands in a vicious cycle. Rain forests are hacked down for timber and agricultural settlement, but shallow forest soils tend to erode quickly. Watersheds deteriorate, and floods and droughts have a steadily worsening impact. The Brundtland Report estimated that tropical forests were being reduced at the rate of 7 to 10 million hectares annually, while the world's deserts were expanding annually at the rate of 6 million hectares. As habitats are altered, plant, animal, and insect species are decimated.

A preliminary report of the *Project on Environmental Change and Acute Conflict* at the University of Toronto (*Globe and Mail*, 10 May 1994, A19) warns that aggregate data showing worldwide improvements in levels of literacy, health, food production, and population control, obscure critical regional variations. The project's director, Homer-Dixon, agrees with optimists that human ingenuity may be able to overcome resource scarcity through new technology and reformed social institutions. But poor countries most affected by scarcity are least able to promote such ingenuity. Scarcity generates severe political stress in the form of intense rivalries among interest groups and elite factions, and rising social dissatisfaction. Homer-Dixon attributes the vicious ethnic animosity that broke out in Rwanda in 1994 to severe land scarcity, soil depletion, and food production that is declining rapidly relative to increasing population. He might have added that Rwanda has a plantation economy, deriving most of its earnings from the sale of coffee (Beckford 1973, 120–22).

Canada is a technologically advanced society with a high level of ingenuity, but this has not protected us from severe ecological problems, generated by superexploitation of natural resources. Vast stretches of the Prairies are being mined to produce monocrop cereals year after year with the aid of chemical fertilizers and pesticides. The result is soil reduced to the texture of dust. Soil erosion in Canada alone is costing farmers in the region of $1 billion a year. Overirrigation is causing the waterlogging, salinization, and alkalization of soils. In Newfoundland, the precipitous decline in fish stocks off the North Atlantic coast forced the total shutdown of the industry in 1993.

Industrial Pollution

Energy consumption has risen exponentially in the industrialized world over the last quarter century, particularly the consumption of wood, oil, gas, coal, and nuclear power. The burning of fossil fuels creates problems of atmospheric pollution, global warming, acidification, and industrial air pollution. Air pollution is damaging vegetation, corroding buildings and vehicles, and killing lakes and fish. Chlorofluorocarbons used in aerosol sprays, refrigeration, and the manufacture of some plastics, especially styrofoam, are known to damage the earth's ozone layer. Waste disposal companies in developed countries often bypass stringent pollution control legislation at home by pressuring impoverished African countries to take hazardous wastes.

The extension of the Free Trade Deal into Latin America sets up pressures to harmonize environmental standards downwards. The NAFTA permits governments to enforce "generally agreed international environmental or conservation rules or standards" but requires that such measures be "the least trade-restrictive necessary for securing the protection required" (Swenarchuk 1993, 13). Any standards that might be considered a disguised restriction on trade, or that are not fully supported by available scientific evidence, are ruled out. The maquiladoras located in Northern Mexico are described as producing an environmental cesspool, routinely dumping toxic chemicals into rivers, and operating under conditions harmful to the health of employees (Barlow 1990, 67). It is not in the competitive self-interest of other corporations to protect the environment if their comparative costs of production rise as a consequence. At the same time, the principle of government nonintervention in the market that is enshrined in the Free Trade Deal curbs the power of individual governments to impose controls.

The economics of this form of development change abruptly, however, once the "polluter pays" principle is introduced into the equation. This kind of industrial development is not only ecologically unsustainable, but it is also prohibitively expensive when the costs of pollution are calculated into economic models. The firms producing the acidic smog in their coal furnaces would have to pay for all the damage to lakes, rivers, vehicles, buildings, and human health, in the areas reached by the polluted air and acid rain. Under this altered accounting, the economics of conservation and pollution control are many times more cost-efficient than they appear to be now.

Brundtland also notes the staggering costs of urban sprawl created by the concentration of industries in central areas. Urban sprawl, which occurs both in developing and developed economies, results in pollution, housing crises, rising crime rates, and so on. If the industries that locate in urban areas are charged for the full social and environmental costs of urban sprawl, the economics of relocation in smaller centres will look much more appealing. This is particularly true for high service firms where computerized communications systems make geographic decentralization cheap and efficient.

The Brundtland Report's basic conclusion is that we have to call a halt to the kind of economic development that is endangering the survival of the planet. That does not mean we have to stop development. This is not a viable option in a world where the most basic needs of masses of people are not being met. It does mean that the form that such development takes must be altered so as to be ecologically sustainable on a long-term worldwide basis.

Mainstream economics, North American style, still has a long way to go to deal with the problems raised in the report. In practice, environmental costs, like social welfare costs, are generally left out of business equations. They form **hidden diseconomies** or real costs that, if actually paid by the companies responsible for the pollution, would greatly reduce their profits, and might well turn these apparent profits into deficits. But such costs are not counted by corporations because normally it is not the corporations that pay them. The people and other creatures whose lives are damaged or destroyed by the pollution pay the price.

With this shift in focus, the question of unfair subsidies appears in a very different light from the perspective of the free trade debate. When North American companies are permitted to operate without practising energy conservation and without pollution control devices, they are being very heavily subsidized by taxpayers who pay for road repairs and acid rain damage. The economics of using trucks rather than railways reverses when these hidden subsidies are taken away. Further, companies locating in metropolitan centres are being heavily subsidized when the costs of urban sprawl are paid by taxpayers. If and when all these hidden subsidies are removed, the economic advantages of relocating in peripheral areas, like Cape Breton or the interior of British Columbia, might be very considerable.

Traditional economists such as Paul Wonnacott argue that government subsidies promote inefficient production. The blind spot of such economists lies in the extremely narrow definition of **subsidy** utilized in the equations. The implicit, and sometimes explicit, assumption of mainstream economics in leaving the hidden diseconomies out of their equations is that industry could not pay such costs without destroying all profitability. Hence, they are best ignored.

From the perspective of political economy theory, the contradictions inherent in advanced capitalism generate these problems, and cannot resolve them. Trainer (1985, 217) suggests that if the system were even to try to practise conservation and to cut back on wasteful production, "there would be economic chaos. Factories would close, businesses would go bankrupt, people would be thrown out of work and there would be extensive social and political disruption." Trainer's message is that nothing short of radical social revolution will solve the problems we face.

Trainer's blanket indictment of capitalism expresses an extreme position. But there is wider support for the conclusion that market forces alone cannot resolve the social and environmental problems that capitalism generates. It is necessary to rethink the ideological underpinnings of

the North American Free Trade Agreement that marginalizes the role of the state. There are few models for conceptualizing a form of capitalism that is subject to political control.

Sweden comes closer than other Western European countries in the state management of capitalism in the 1980s. The government enacted stringent policies to control industrial emissions, and it successfully carried out a ten-year program to reverse acidification of lakes (Melander 1988). Pollution control itself became a billion-dollar business. The pulp and paper industry operates in Sweden under very different rules of forest management than in Canada. The same Swedish-based multinational that practices the worst forms of clear-cutting and resource exploitation in Nova Scotia practices sustainable harvesting and reforestation in Sweden (McMahon 1987, 100–103). The difference lies not in company ideology or commitment to profitability, but the political controls within which capitalism operates.

Political controls in Sweden disallow the kinds of clear-cutting and resource exploitation that are still occurring in Clayoquot Sound, BC.

In July 1988, Sweden passed an Animal Protection Act that governs the conditions of factory farming. To understand how important this is, think back to the description earlier in this chapter of chicken farms in Canada and the southern United States. This kind of inhumane farming is now outlawed in Sweden. Violations of the law are punishable by fines or imprisonment of up to one year. The law includes nine provisions:

1. All cattle are to be entitled to be put out to graze.

2. Poultry are to be let out of cramped battery cages.

3. Sows are no longer to be tethered. They are to have sufficient room to move. Separate bedding, feeding, and voiding places are to be provided.

4. Cows and pigs are to have access to straw and litter in stalls and boxes.

5. Technology must be adapted to the animals, not the reverse. As a result, it must be possible to test new technology from the animal safety and protection viewpoint before it is put into practice.

6. All slaughtering must be as done as humanely as possible.

7. The government is empowered to forbid the use of genetic engineering and growth hormones, which may mutate domestic animals.

8. Permission is necessary for pelt and fur farms.

9. Doping animals for competition and events is prohibited.

The Act explicitly outlawed the use of battery cages for chickens. A background statement on the Act notes that animal protection and the prevention of cruelty to animals are central ethical issues and an essential part of Swedish cultural heritage.

The Swedish government's actions to curb the excesses of capitalism in these examples is a reminder that there is no inexorable system of market forces existing over and above people, to which societies must submit. There is nothing inevitable about "chicken cities" in the southern states, or factory farming, or the destruction of Nova Scotia forests. These things happen because so many political leaders, and the people who vote for them, have come to accept the ideology that such things are inevitable, or that economies will collapse if we even try to change things to become more socially or ecologically responsible.

It is also clear that Canada cannot follow Sweden's example without either abrogating terms of the CUSFTA and NAFTA by imposing tariffs on cheap factory-farm imports from the United States, or by negotiating with our trading partners to adopt similarly high standards of animal husbandry and environmental protection.

The major questions for free trade look very different from this perspective. Will free trade provide a route for moving toward the principles of sustainable development or toward worsening environmental stress? Will market relations become more open to social and political controls? How might the free trade agreements be used to promote continental pollution control and ecologically sustainable agricultural and industrial practices? How can such issues be incorporated into public political debate in Canada and the United States on our common future?

There are no easy answers to these questions, but the quality of life for future generations of Canadians and Americans will depend very heavily on how they are addressed. These questions force us to rethink not only how to achieve development, but also why and in what direction. Is the expansionist, profit-driven notion of development that currently dominates economic and political thinking actually what we collectively need? Or does it offer only the illusion of progress, while covering up a deteriorating quality of life for most of the inhabitants of the planet? We need to look beneath the veneer of economic and technological rationality that drives our society and explore the additional cultural, emotional, and moral dimensions of rational action. Without this wider vision, much of what we call development may be fundamentally irrational.

Suggested Reading

George M. Foster, *Traditional Societies and Technological Change* (1973), gives a sympathetic and perceptive account of problems of development from the perspective of functionalist theory. Foster gives extensive evidence of cultural, social, and psychological barriers to change in traditional societies. He suggests that anthropological analysis of traditional social systems is a valuable aid to promoting technological change.

Everett M. Rogers, *Modernization Among Peasants: The Impact of Communication* (1969), elaborates the concept of culture of poverty in traditional societies. He advocates a top-down model of development through which the better educated and innovative people are first encouraged to adopt new technology, in the hope that subsequently the more backward peasants will copy these role models.

A classic work in Marxist theory of underdevelopment is André Gundar Frank, "Sociology of Development and the Underdevelopment of Sociology" (1972). Frank documents how the economy of Latin America is being systematically plundered by wealthy nations, especially the United States, which take out far more money than they ever put in through loans and investments. An excellent source of information on how Canadian capitalists plunder poor countries is the collection of articles edited by Robert Clarke and Richard Swift, *Ties that Bind: Canada and the Third World* (1982).

A comprehensive study of women and development is Barbara Rogers, *The Domestication of Women: Discrimination in Developing Societies* (1980). Rogers documents how women's interests are damaged by development programs that ignore their needs and give priority to men.

The issue of regional disparities and underdevelopment in Canada is explored in Henry Veltmeyer, "The Capitalist Underdevelopment of Atlantic Canada" (1979). Veltmeyer argues that the relative poverty in Atlantic Canada has been created by corporate capitalist policies designed to extract profits from peripheral areas and to centralized production.

Arguments against free trade are explored in two comprehensive collections of short articles. Duncan Cameron, ed., *The Free Trade Deal* (1988), and E. Finn, ed., *The Facts: The Facts on Free Trade—Canada Don't Trade It Away* (1988). The many articles and commentaries included in these collections explore wide-ranging issues around economic disparities and possible social and cultural costs of free trade. Mel Hurtig's powerfully argued polemic *The Betrayal of Canada* (1991) documents the economic crises facing Canada two years after signing the first Free Trade Agreement.

John Calvert and Larry Kuehn provide a comprehensive and very readable analysis of the principles of commercialization of society and government nonintervention that are embedded in the North American Free Trade Deal in *Pandora's Box, Corporate Power, Free Trade and Canadian Education* (1993).

G.H. Brundtland, *Our Common Future* (1987), documents the extensive destruction of the environment wrought by intensive farming techniques and resource extraction for industry. Brundtland argues persuasively that this form of development is not sustainable in the long term.

Questions

1. What cultural traits are associated with reluctance to innovate, according to the functionalist perspective on development?

2. What factors have reduced the impact of technological advances in agriculture in Third World countries?

3. How are international market relations implicated in the continuing relative poverty of Third World countries?

4. What are the major problems facing Third World economies in Foster-Clark's analysis of "dependent capitalism"?

5. In Gulalp's view, why are political democracies likely to be unstable and short-lived in Third World countries?

6. How does flexible specialization differ from fordism as a strategy for achieving competitive advantage?

7. How is agribusiness implicated in famine in Third World countries?

8. In Mueller's view, how is the work of professionals in development agencies implicated in the failure to address the problems faced by people, and particularly women, in Third World countries?

9. How is the North American Free Trade Agreement implicated in the "commercialization" of society?

10. What is the core message of the 1987 Brundtland Report on economic development?

PART V

Rationality and Bureaucratic Society

Max Weber and Rationality in Western Culture

Max Weber (1864–1920) is a monumental figure in the history of the social sciences. He was a historian, sociologist, and philosopher who left an indelible mark on the philosophy of history and on social science methodology. The scope of his scholarship is enormous. He wrote major books on comparative religions of Europe, India, and China, on the economy and political structures of democracy in Western Europe, on music and musical forms, the rationality of law, and the structure and function of complex bureaucratic organization.

Background

Weber was born almost fifty years after Marx. Much of his work was a reaction to Marx or, more particularly, to the oversimplified versions of Marxist thought that focussed on economic determinism in social life. The two men wrote within very different cultural settings. Marx and his colleague Engels carried out much of their

research and writing in Britain during the early period of industrialization. By this time, the feudal estates had been broken up into grazing pastures. The peasants who formerly farmed these lands had been driven off. Masses of landless and desperately poor people flooded the cities seeking wagework as their only means of survival. They lived under appalling conditions in city slums and worked in the coal mines and expanding textile mills that fuelled the industrial revolution. The emerging merchant-capitalist class effectively challenged the political power and privileges of the declining aristocracy.

Weber lived in Germany during the period when the country was emerging from a collection of divided states into a unified and modern country under Otto von Bismarck. Germany's development was based upon centralized administration and the armaments industry rather than on private capitalism. It promoted a different view of the state and different theories of power and administration than those in Marx's work (Lee

Max Weber (1864–1920).

and Newby 1983, 169). Weber observed the outbreak of World War I and the concurrent collapse of the international socialist movement into nationalist blocs: the European proletariat supported their nation-states rather than the international working-class movement. Weber lived to see the Bolshevik Revolution in Russia in 1917, the collapse of the Spartacist Revolution in Berlin in 1919, and the rise of the Weimar Republic in Germany after the war.

In his personal life, Weber experienced long periods of severe depression. These are reflected in his profound pessimism concerning the future direction of Western civilization. He was intensely aware of the gap between the intended goals and ideals and the often unintended consequences of the means required to attain those goals. Weber himself long defended the ideal of a strong and unified Germany, only to feel contempt for the Kaiser and the policies that led Germany into World War I and eventual military defeat. In his work he argued strongly against any simplified theories of social change, emphasizing instead the complex **probablistic** character of all theories of human action. Human action is the outcome of free will, he argued, and such freedom can never be described through fixed relations of cause and effect.

Weber's Scholarship

Weber struggled to synthesize the very different intellectual traditions that were prevalent in Europe at the time. Among them was **idealism** with its Hegelian emphasis on ideas and values as the distinctive moving force of human history. This was in contrast to Marxist theories of **historical materialism**, which contended that class conflict was the driving force of history and the primary determinant of human fate. The idealists emphasized human freedom and uniqueness, which could never be reduced to deterministic rules. Countering them were the **positivists** who sought to apply the methods of the natural sciences to the study of human behaviour, seeking predictive or deterministic laws of action. Functionalist analysis adopts almost exclusively a positivist approach to sociological research, as does the classical political economy perspective.

Weber tried to reconcile the commitment to notions of individual freedom and religious values with the apparently contradictory commitment to a scientific study of human behaviour and to an emphasis on economic materialism in history. He tried also to reconcile the obvious commitment of all researchers to political goals and values with the demand for objectivity in social science research. Lastly, he tried to reconcile the objectives of democracy, with its commitment to representative government based upon participation of an informed population, and the mechanism of bureaucracy, which seemed essential to democracy and yet at the same time was its greatest threat. It is the mark of Weber's brilliance that he was largely able to achieve these syntheses in his work.

◈ Weber's Methodological Contribution

Methodology in Social Science

Weber's study of methodology in the social sciences provides the foundations for contemporary ethnomethodology and interpretive sociology. Weber sought to synthesize the objective, empirical methods of the natural sciences with the intuitive aspects of the humanities.

Positivism attempts to analyse the social system in terms of causes and effects in the same way that biological systems are analysed. Weber argues that this is impossible. Because people think about what they do, it is inappropriate to apply such lawlike, or **nomothetic**, generalizations to human behaviour. People have purposes; their behaviour is meaningful to them. In biology we do not ask chemicals or microbes why they do things. We just account for what happens by reference to the laws of science. But with people, we do have to ask why. Our actions are determined not only by objective conditions and forces, but also by the subjective meanings that we attach to our actions—in other words, by our own responses for doing something.

Weber also wanted to avoid the opposite trap of idealism—the view that all human behaviour entails unique spiritual events that can only be grasped by intuition or empathy. For idealists, the only explanation possible seems to be **ideographic**: unique, subjective, intuitive. The "science" in social science seems to be impossible.

We seem to be forced to choose between the view that human action is predictable, which implies determinism, or the view that people have free will and hence that their actions are not determined by outside forces and so are not predictable. Weber denies the validity of this apparent dilemma. He argues that meaningful behaviour, or behaviour guided by free will, is not unique and unpredictable or without any pattern or order. Unpredictable or random behaviour would not be meaningful; it would be mindless. Weber resolves the conflict between free will and determinism by arguing that there is no real contradiction between them. Action that is meaningful is, by its very nature, not haphazard, random, or patternless. The scientific study of meaningful behaviour is possible precisely because it is meaningful and therefore organized and predictable. It requires a different kind of explanation from that of the natural sciences, but it is nonetheless amenable to scientific study.

Weber defines sociology as "the science which attempts the interpretive understanding of social action in order thereby to arrive at a causal explanation of its cause and effects" (Ashley and Orenstein 1985, 213). For Weber, then, sociological analysis must do two things. First, it must explore the meaning of actions for the people involved. Second, it has to show how this meaning provides a causal explanation for the behaviour. **Social action** is, by definition, any human conduct that is meaningfully oriented to the past, present, or future expected behaviour of others. People relate to each other in meaningful ways, and it is these shared meanings that define our expectations of others and ourselves.

The Study of Meaning

Weber draws heavily upon the work of his friend and colleague, Georg Simmel (1949; 1950), who first developed the concept of *Verstehen*, or understanding, as crucial to sociological analysis. Sociologists have to become involved in the process of understanding because the actions that they are trying to explain are actions to which people themselves attach meanings. People do what they do because it is meaningful to them. We can hardly ignore what these meanings are when we try to explain what they do. This does not mean that pure intuition is sufficient for analysis. We still need objective evidence. We need to develop techniques for interpreting meaning so that others can repeat the study and check the results.

The question is how do we do this. How can we develop an objective, verifiable, repeatable study of meaningful action? We need to remember that meaningful action is not random, but purposive and therefore organized by the people involved.

Verstehen involves putting ourselves in the position of the people we are studying and trying to reconstruct the interpretations that they might give to their own action (Ashley and Orenstein 1985, 212). We feel we have explained the unusual behaviour of people in general, when we come to the point where we can say with some assurance that if we had similar life experiences and value orientations, and had found ourselves in similar circumstances, we could understand how we ourselves might have behaved in a similar way. This is a tall order, but we can do it precisely because we are studying fellow human beings. This is an advantage that sociologists have over physical scientists. The latter study objects from the outside, but in social science we study people as subjects engaged in meaningful behaviour, and we can approach an interpretive understanding of that behaviour from the inside.

Direct understanding or reconstruction of action is sometimes possible. It is relatively easy to arrive at a rational understanding of logical relations, such as at the reasoning involved in concluding that 2 × 2 = 4, or in concluding that certain facial expressions are a manifestation of anger (Giddens 1971, 148). At other times, in order to make behaviour intelligible, we need to understand people's underlying motives. It is relatively straightforward to understand rational means-end selection, as when people have a clearly stated objective with straightforward means to achieve it. In other contexts, the understanding of motives may require much deeper searching. Weber is well aware that human motives are complex. Similar actions may be done for a variety of underlying motives, while similar motives may be related to different forms of actual behaviour (Giddens 1971, 149). People can also waver between conflicting motives.

Given the complexity of human motivation, Weber argues that explanations in sociology must take the form of **probabilities** rather than the absolute predictions characteristic of the natural sciences. We have achieved an adequate explanation when the motive that we understand to be behind the behaviour in question would reasonably, or with some measure of probability, give rise to the kind of behaviour observed.

Such causal relationships or predictions are inevitably subject to qualifications and exceptions. They reflect the particular historical situation in which people find themselves. For example, Weber argued that the Protestant religion was an important causal influence on the rise of capitalism in Europe. Capitalism also flourished in Japan but clearly not because of Protestantism, although there may have been a similar pattern of values in Japanese culture that triggered capitalistic behaviour (Ashley and Orenstein 1985, 214). Weber's model of typical characteristics of Calvinist values in contrast with typical Catholic values, makes possible broad generalizations about the relationship between religious ethics and business practices in Europe of that period. In the very different climate of the 1990s there may be no such relationship.

Marx, too, recognized the historical character of explanations when he criticized the economists of his time for treating concepts such as supply, demand, commodities, labour power, and so on, as universal categories without realizing that they only exist within and because of the very particular and historically situated pattern of organization of economic relations of capitalism.

Human Agency

Weber's demand for adequacy at the level of meaning led him to challenge functionalist approaches to the study of human society. Functionalism, he argued, is useful in providing a place from which to begin analysis. But the simple analogy between biological systems and social systems soon breaks down. Sociologists need to go beyond functional uniformities to arrive at an interpretive understanding that takes account of the meanings that an action had for the people involved (Giddens 1971, 150).

It is easy for sociologists to be lured into explanations that refer to the social system as a whole, but one must never forget that the conceptual entity *society* is nothing more than the multiple interactions of individuals in a particular setting. Only individual people are agents who actually carry out subjectively understandable action. In functionalist and much Marxist writing, this collection called society tends to take on a **reified** identity of its own. The word is only a convenient descriptive summary. But it is converted into a thing and then is used in explanations as if it were an acting unit with its own consciousness: society does such and such, or society has certain needs, and so on. This is similar to the complaint that Marx raised against the political economy of his day and its tendency to refer to market forces as doing things to people, while losing sight of the fact that people, and only people, do things.

This is not to say that a sociologist should never use concepts that refer to collectives such as states or industrial corporations, but, Weber insists, we must remember that these collectivities are solely the result of organized actions of individual people. People may organize collectively to do something, and we may refer to this collective organization as, for example, a corporation, but corporations as such do nothing.

Weber's second demand, for adequacy at the level of causality, led him to reject the opposite extreme of **psychological reductionism** (Giddens 1971, 151). Psychology is certainly relevant to sociological understanding, as are several other disciplines. But we cannot understand how people are organized collectively or analyse these emergent institutions by examining only the psychological makeup of individuals. Psychology is likely to draw heavily upon sociology in understanding the sociocultural influences that mould individuals.

Weber draws a careful distinction between the related disciplines of sociology and history. For Weber, history is concerned with the causal analysis of particular culturally significant events and personalities. Sociology, on the other hand, deals with the observation and explanation of general patterns of behaviour. History may well draw upon such general explanations to account for unique events. Weber saw himself primarily as a historian, but in his major work, *Economy and Society* ([1922] 1968), he was more concerned with uniformities of socioeconomic organization, in effect, with sociology.

Causal Pluralism

Weber's concern with adequacy at the level of causality also led him to insist on a strategy of **causal pluralism**; that is, on searching for multiple causes for social phenomena. He rejected as misguided and inadequate the efforts of some theorists, and particularly the approach of oversimplified Marxism, which attempt to explain social phenomena in terms of single factors such as economic determinism. Marx criticized Hegel for trying to analyse ideas without any regard for the social conditions in which they emerged. Weber agreed with Marx's criticism, but he also attacked the opposite fallacy committed by many of Marx's disciples who tried to analyse economic forces without regard for the subjectively meaningful response of individuals to their economic circumstances.

For Weber, sociological explanations have to encompass both objective conditions and subjective forces, for it is through subjective understanding and analysis that these objective conditions come to influence human actions as they do. Ideas and values cannot therefore be dismissed as mere by-products of class position, which can be ignored in explanations. Likewise, the economy is not an entity to which people adjust. It is the outcome of people's subjectively meaningful collective behaviour.

Ideal-Type Constructs

Weber advocated **ideal-type** constructs as a method of inquiry that would be adequate at the level of meaning or interpretive understanding of actions and would at the same time make possible objective and replicable analysis. As we saw in chapter 4, ideal-type constructs are theories that accentuate typical characteristics or elements of action. They are not intended to be literal or accurate descriptions of reality, but rather hypothetical models that can be compared with real situations.

Weber argues that this is not so much a new method as a clarification of what social scientists typically do when they try to isolate key elements in a situation. In chapter 4, we examined the model of *Gemeinschaft* and *Gesellschaft* developed by Tönnies to accentuate the distinctive characteristics of preindustrial and urban societies. In chapter 6 we saw the models of mechanical and organic solidarity developed by Durkheim to accentuate typical forms of social cohesion in undifferentiated and specialized societies. Weber himself developed a series of ideal types of social action that he used as frameworks for exploring distinctive patterns of meaning and action among people in industrial capitalist societies. His ideal-type model of bureaucracy will be described at length later in this chapter.

Objectivity in Social Science

Weber demanded that the study of meaningful action be based upon objectively verifiable and repeatable research. This led to his deep concern with the place of values in research and how objectivity might be possible. Values necessarily enter research as aspects of the subject matter. They also enter as features of the researchers' orientation to the study. Researchers reveal their values by selecting from the infinity of possible subjects those that appear to them to be important or of interest. Nonetheless, Weber insists, the methodology and the outcome of research must be objective; that is, it must be independent of the values of the researcher.

Central to his concern with objectivity is Weber's insistence that science itself cannot pass judgment on values. It is impossible to establish values or ideals scientifically or to decide on a scientific basis what ought to be done. All that science can do is evaluate the adequacy of alternative practical means available for the attainment of given ends, the probable costs of selecting one means over another, and the additional or unforeseen consequences that may arise from particular means.

Weber frequently analysed the struggle for revolutionary socialism in these terms (Lee and

Newby 1983, 200). He argued that the very goals of freedom that are part of the ideal of socialism are threatened by the use of force as a means to achieve socialism and by the political repression inevitably associated with the use of force. He also predicted that the consequences of trying to establish a socialist economy within a largely hostile capitalist world would result in multiple difficulties that would undermine the practice of socialism. Thirdly, and most importantly, he predicted that whatever means were used to bring about socialism, the ideals of socialism would be compromised by the organizational means needed to co-ordinate such a society, namely, the bureaucratic state. Through his analysis, Weber could show the probable costs and long-term negative consequences of the struggle for socialism but, as he acknowledged himself, such analysis could never answer the ultimate question of whether the struggle would be worthwhile.

In Canada, the free trade debate provides another example of the limitations of scientific analysis. Social science analysis can add to the debate by showing the probable consequences for various sectors of Canadian and American societies of measures incorporated within the agreement: threatened job losses in some sectors versus the promise of job gains in others; the probable impact upon Canada's cultural industries and social services; and so on. But what such analysis can never determine is whether the end justifies the means, or whether questions of culture or sovereignty should outweigh questions of economic gain, or whether losses to some people count more or less than gains to others. Science cannot answer these questions, which are based on values. At its best, science can only show what the probable costs will be of various means or actions that may be taken toward the attainment of desired goals.

Weber's powerful essays on "Politics as a Vocation" and "Science as a Vocation" address these ethical dilemmas. Weber distinguishes between two fundamental ethics: the **ethic of ultimate ends** and the **ethic of responsibility** (Gerth and Mills 1946, 120). Neither ethic is in and of itself morally superior to the other. The ethic of ultimate ends is essentially religious. Those who pursue such an ethic are so totally committed to their objective that any means are acceptable if they will further this objective. Such people are not swayed by the consequences, however negative, of their means. When members of the Sons of Freedoms sect of the Doukhobours in British Columbia practise arson, for example, they do so in the fervent belief that they are called by God to cleanse the world by fire of idolatry and evil. The immediate negative consequences for themselves or others may be of concern to them, but they do not affect their decision whether or not to commit such an act. The ultimate ethic of purification in the service of God has higher value.

Alternatively, those who accept the ethic of responsibility must take account of the consequences of their actions or means chosen to further their goals. They must calculate at each step the probable consequences of and possible hardships and suffering caused by efforts to obtain their goal. This is particularly true in the face of the recognition that the decisive means for politics is violence. Political authority in any state implies a monopoly of the legitimate use of force. Science cannot answer the question whether, or to what extent, the end justifies the means. Those who imprison Doukhobour women for the crime of arson, and who consider paroling or pardoning them, must weigh the multiple consequences of these actions. They must take responsibility for the probable deaths of the imprisoned women on hunger strike and for the probable property damage in the further acts of arson that may result if the women are freed, and so on.

The recognition that science cannot pass judgment on questions of values led Weber to insist that professors should not teach political positions, any more than religious convictions, to students in the classroom (Gerth and Mills 1946, 145–47). Professors have the same opportunities as other people to air their views in the political arena. They should not use the lecture room for this. Weber was reacting against the practices of the German professors of his day who routinely used their lecterns as pulpits to impose a particular political view of the German state onto students.

Scientific objectivity has nothing to do with ethical neutrality or fence sitting, or taking some middle road. It has to do with commitment to the examination of facts, facts that are often inconvenient for our own or others' opinions. The ultimate questions of values and commitment lie beyond science, in the realms of faith and revelation.

❖ Weber's Substantive Contribution

Types of Action Orientation

Weber's model of types of action orientation outlines four basic kinds of meaningful action or typical orientations that individuals may adopt in relations with each other.

The simplest orientation, **traditional-rational** behaviour, comprises action based on habit. It involves the least amount of conscious thought. Neither the purpose of the actions nor the alternatives are consciously considered. Traditional-rational actions are done because they always have been done that way.

A second orientation, **affective-rational**, is based on emotions. Actions are expressions of emotions, of passions, and they have an immediacy that involves neither calculated weighing of means or consequences nor commitment to values.

A third kind of orientation is **value-rational**. Here the primary focus is upon an overriding ideal, as in religion. Deeply committed people do not ask the consequences of their actions. They do what they believe is right, regardless of the outcome for themselves or others. This is the value orientation that underlies the ethic of ultimate ends.

The fourth and most important basis for authority is **purposive-rational** action. This involves the rational selection, among alternative means, of action that is the most effective for a given end. It includes rational consideration of consequences in relation to other goals. This kind of rationality is easiest to understand and to analyse and is the basic assumption of theory in economics.

It is important to recognize that all four types of orientation are rational. Action in relation to religious values and emotions are equally rational and equally predictable, as are actions based on custom or habit, once the basic orientation itself is known.

This fourfold model of typical action orientations serves to guide research into the meaning of action from the perspective of the participants' own views of that action. The resulting causal explanation suggests the probability of responses of a certain kind, given the action orientation.

Model of Authority

Weber uses this **typology** as a basis for his subsequent model of legitimacy of political authority (see table 11-1). He draws an important distinction between power that is based on authority and power based on brute force. Authority is legitimate in that the subordinates themselves accept that those in authority have a right to rule, and therefore to expect compliance, even if one might not always agree with particular policies. Weber defines authority in practice as the probability that a given order will be obeyed by a specific group of people. He argues that there are three bases of authority: traditional, charismatic, and rational-legal.

Table 11-1

Action Orientation and Legitimate Authority	
Types of Action	Types of Legitimate Authority
Traditional-rational (customs)	Hereditary rulers: kings, queens, tribal patriarchs
Affective-rational (emotions)	Charisma of people with extraordinary gifts or supernatural powers: Jesus, Gandhi, Hitler
Value-rational (beliefs)	Religious dogma: Bible, Koran, Talmud, authority of church elders
Purposive-rational (practical effects)	Rational-legal regulations: bureaucratic rules, formal office, civil law

The simplest and historically the most prevalent basis for authority is **tradition**. Orders are accepted as legitimate when they come from traditional incumbents of hereditary positions. The authority of an elder and patriarch and the divine right of kings rest on such legitimation. Persons exercising power enjoy authority by virtue of their inherited status. Such authority is likely to have force only in relatively stable and unchanging societies.

Authority wielded by **charismatic** figures is very different. Here legitimation is based on the emotional response of followers to a leader who appears to have extraordinary gifts or supernatural virtue and powers. Great figures in history such as Jesus, Hitler, Gandhi, and Joan of Arc have had such charismatic authority and moved thousands and even millions of people to follow them. E.P. Thompson (1963, 421) described the charismatic power of prophets such as Joanna Southcott whose aura of spiritualism and extraordinary revelation drew a large cult following in England at the turn of the eighteenth century. Charisma means that people are so drawn by the dynamism of the particular person that they are willing to follow that individual without questioning the specifics of policies or direction. The inclusion of Hitler in the list of charismatic figures should be a warning that charisma is a force that can move people for evil as well as for good, or for fleeting goals as well as for critical social movements. It is a powerful force for change, but tells nothing about the direction that such change might take.

Weber saw charisma as the most dynamic and free expression of individual creativity, but also the most transitory of all forms of authority. The rise of charismatic figures is associated particularly with periods of trouble and emergency when people are already predisposed to respond to calls for change. A charismatic leader is always a **radical** in challenging established practices and going beyond the rules of everyday life toward new visions.

The problem with authority based on charisma is that it is inherently unstable, lasting only so long as the leader survives and continues to manifest the extraordinary qualities that initially drew the followers. The inevitable death of the leader gives rise to the problem of succession since no successor can hope to command the same charisma. Weber suggests that succession can only take two basic forms. Either it can relapse into hereditary rule based on traditional authority or it can be formalized by elections and rules of organization that shift toward rational-legal authority.

Rational-legal authority is the most important basis for legitimation of power in Weber's model. He saw it as a precondition for the emergence of a modern state and the fundamental legitimation for bureaucratic administration. Rational-legal authority is based on acceptance of the utility of the rules themselves. Orders are obeyed without concern for the personality of the authority figure who set such rules, because the rules themselves are perceived as rational and purposeful.

Martin Luther King, Jr., and Malcolm X were charismatic leaders whose radical visions of the future challenged established American ways.

The Sociology of Power

In his study of political power, Weber sought to elaborate the insights of Marx on the economic basis of class and class struggle. Weber advocated a wider focus on other bases of group identity and organized political action, and hence on alternative bases of power, including the power vested in state administration. These relations, Weber argued, are too complex to be reducible to the single dimension of ownership of the means of production within a society. He developed an alternative model of power that incorporates three distinct, although closely related, dimensions: class, status, and party.

Class

Weber shared with Marx the assumption that ownership or nonownership of the means of production was a major determinant of class position. But he shifts the focus from one of relationships among people in the production process, to relative life chances in the labour market. He defined **class** as the chance to use property, goods, and services for exchange in a competitive market. The most advantaged group in a capitalist economy is made up of the owners of land, factories, and financial capital, while the least advantaged class comprises people with no property and no skills. In between them are the middle classes. They comprise those who have some property—the petite bourgeoisie—and those like the intelligentsia, who have some skills. Weber recognized that the proletariat or working class is split by skill differentials. Those with privileged education or professions have very different life chances in the marketplace and very different access to political power than do blue-collar workers who own no property. Such divisions, he predicted, would limit the emergence of class consciousness, since these different life chances would give rise to different values and perspectives upon the world.

Status

Weber agreed with Marxist theorists that economic relations of class are central determinants of individual life chances. But he also insisted that actual life chances are too complex to be reducible to economics alone. **Status** also plays a critical role. Status, for Weber, refers to social prestige and honour and is reflected, above all, in styles of life (Gerth and Mills 1946, 186–94). Attributes ascribed by birth, such as nobility, race, ethnicity, sex, and religious affiliation may be more immediately influential than objective class position in the development of group identity. The nouveau riche, people who make money in business or in a lottery, may well have the financial attributes of the upper class, such as expensive homes and possessions, but they may

not have the status to gain acceptance from other members of the upper class. They may well be shunned by families with old wealth and breeding. With the passage of time, the offspring of the nouveau riche may gain acceptance within high status circles.

Political action is likely to reflect status group as class. Historical conflict between Catholics and Protestants in Northern Ireland, for example, cannot be reduced to class conflict. Similarly, in Canada, the struggle for a distinctive identity among the Québécois, Native peoples, Doukhobours, and many other ethnic minorities cannot be reduced to relative economic advantage alone. Weber recognized that status is frequently a basis for exclusion or relative disadvantage in the market and that this may well foment group conflict and hostility. He insisted, however, that religious and ethnic identities exert an independent causal influence on group identity, styles of life, and life chances.

The relation between class and status in Weber's sociology is one of mutual influence. Shared class position within the economy may foster distinctive values and orientations toward life that can draw people together. In his study of comparative religions, Weber draws many parallels between economic experience and religious values. Disprivileged people, for example, are oriented toward other-wordly religions that promise salvation and just compensation for suffering on earth. Nobles are attracted to the view of a god of passion, wrath, and cunning who can be bribed with booty from war. Bureaucrats favour a comprehensive, sober religion such as Confucianism in China, which is expressed in terms of disciplined order and abstract values. Merchants are generally sceptical or indifferent to other-wordly religions that preach salvation, preferring worldly and nonprophetic theology. Shared religious orientation can in turn serve to reinforce separate group identities and loyalties, which may then be reflected in politics. For Marx, the economy has primacy, but for Weber, status is a related but distinct and powerful force in the political arena.

Party

The concept of **party** for Weber refers to actively organized relations in the political arena. Parties are oriented toward communal action designed to influence policy in favour of specified goals (Gerth and Mills 1946, 194–95). They may represent interests determined through class or through status, or through a combination of the two. Occasionally they represent neither. They differ widely in terms of both the means used to attain power and the kind of community interests that they represent. Above all, the structure and operation of parties reflect the structures of ruling, whether based on hereditary rule, democratic processes, or military coercion or other forms of violence.

To 'Rationalize' (17th Century) — I THINK THEREFORE I AM.

To 'Rationalize' (20th Century) — I MERGE, THEREFORE YOU AREN'T.

A Culture of Rationality

Weber's study of the rise of rationality in Western European culture, and its formal expression in capitalism and bureaucratic forms of state administration, stands as a major contribution to contemporary sociology. Weber returned again and again in his work to the theme of purposive-rational action and rational-legal authority as embodying the central features of modern industrial society.

Weber saw purposive rationality as the distinguishing characteristic of Western civilization. Other types of action orientation—toward tradition, emotions, or values—are identified by Weber as rational in the sense that they can be understood as organized and meaningful behaviour. But they are qualitatively very different forms of action from the distinctly calculated, goal-oriented strategies that constitute purposive-rational action. The differences are so striking that there is some debate whether the term *rational* should properly be applied only to purposive-rational behaviour. Weber clearly considered the latter to be a superior form of rationality, involving calculated orientation towards the efficient use of available means for attaining clearly thought-out goals. Its predominance in Western culture accounts in large part for the spectacular progress of Western civilization. Weber found this calculated form of rationality to pervade all aspects of Western culture: religion, law, business, administration, politics, art, music, architecture, education, and formal organization—the ultimate expression of which is bureaucracy.

Weber highlighted worldly rationalism in many aspects of Western culture. Western music, for example, pioneered the development of chord patterns and arithmetical relations. Moreover, the formal writing and timing of music for orchestras developed only in the West. Western art moved toward an emphasis on realism and perspective; architecture was dominated by engineering principles, focussing on straight lines and prefabricated buildings rather than intricate designs. Science promoted emphasis on mastering the world.

Rationality also characterized the development of mass education. Weber suggests that this was intimately tied to the demand for trained experts for newly developing rational-legal administration. The education system was oriented to special examinations by means of which incumbents of official positions could be selected on the basis of merit rather than personal considerations. There was also a demand for regular curricula with standardized content.

Rationality found formal expression at all levels of social organization. It was a central principle in the development of Western legal systems as traditional practices and arbitrary local regulations were replaced by a universal, impersonal legal system. Such a system spread over national and international markets and was essential for the development of capitalism. To do business with people across many different regions and societies, capitalists needed the assurance of a unified and calculable system of laws and regulations governing contracts.

The development of rationality in business was visible in several other areas. Rational bookkeeping was critical since it permitted the calculation of profits and losses in terms of money. Capitalism required wage-labourers who were not tied to hereditary obligations to nobles, but who were free to sell their labour power in the market. It also required the absence of restrictions on economic exchange in the market. Capitalism benefited from the development of technology constructed on rational principles, free from religious or cultural sanctions. Weber suggests that Hinduism may have retarded the development of technology in India by vesting it with religious significance and linking it with hereditary caste occupations. In contrast, the more rational religion of Protestantism was important in promoting the development of capitalism in Western Europe.

In *The Protestant Ethic and the Spirit of Capitalism* ([1904] 1930), Weber argued that there was an affinity between the worldly ethic of Calvinism and the rise of capitalism. As we saw in chapter 6, Protestant doctrine held that it was morally proper and a sign of God's grace to amass wealth. At the same time, Calvinism discouraged spending money on idle consumption or to aid the poor, whose destitution was a sign of damnation. No other ethic, Weber suggests, could have been more exactly suited to the needs of capitalism. Calvinism provided the rational and emotional motivation for the calculated accumulation and reinvestment of profit.

Weber did not claim that Protestantism caused capitalism, although critics have accused him of this. Rather, he saw the affinity between the two: a mutually supportive relation in which the religious ethic encourages behaviour conducive to business rationality while, at the same time, the experience of capitalism generates a propensity to accept a supportive religious ethic.

Above all, the development of capitalism required rational-legal administration. Bureaucracy, which embodies this principle to its fullest extent, was, for Weber, the most rational form of large-scale organization. An office within a bureaucracy is impersonal, separated from the private life and attachments of the incumbents, and obligations are due, not to the individual, but to the office itself.

Bureaucracy

Weber's ideal-type model of **bureaucracy** is the most famous and the most influential of all his typologies of social action. There are seven elements to this model (see table 11-2).

Table 11-2

Weber's Model of Bureaucracy
1. Permanent offices guarantee continuous organization of functions, which are bounded by written rules.
2. The rules set out specialized tasks, with appropriate authority and sanctions, so that everyone knows precisely who has responsibility for what.
3. These specialized functions are organized in terms of the principle of hierarchy and levels of graded authority. Lower offices operate under the control and supervision of higher offices.
4. The principle of trained competence ensures that the incumbents of these offices have thorough and expert training, appropriate for their level within the hierarchy.
5. The resources of the organization are strictly separated from those of the individuals who occupy the different offices. This was a critical change from past practice when tax collectors, for example, were required to pay a certain amount from what they collected to the state and live on the surplus.
6. Administrative actions, decisions, and rules are recorded in writing. The combination of written documents and continuous organization of official functions constitutes the office.
7. These rules guarantee impersonality in the operations of the office, allowing neither favours nor patronage.

The Official

Weber elaborated a further model of the position of the official (Gerth and Mills 1946, 198–204). He stressed that the office is a **vocation**, with performance a duty not exploited for personal gain. Prescribed training and examinations are prerequisites for such employment. These promote the rationality in education noted above. Officers have specified obligations and fixed salaries. They are selected on the basis of their technical qualifications and not favouritism, nepotism, or ascribed characteristics. They are appointed rather than elected. Election, suggests

Weber, would compromise the strictness of hierarchical subordination because incumbents would owe loyalties to those who elected them. As appointed officials, they are directly subordinate to the superior who appoints them. Work is a lifetime career, with a fixed salary and the right to a pension. This further serves to reduce susceptibility to bribery or to the temptation to use the office for personal profit. Independence from personal considerations in the discharge of official duties is legally guaranteed by tenure. The result of this form of organization is impartial performance of duties with maximum calculability and reliability.

It should be emphasized that Weber was constructing an ideal-type model of bureaucracy and bureaucratic officials. He was not claiming that any existing bureaucracy would exactly fit all these characteristics. The model is intended to function as a theoretical tool for practical research. It abstracts typical features and their typical interrelations. The extent to which any specific organization conforms to or deviates from this model is a matter for empirical research.

Advantages of Bureaucracy

Bureaucracies have major advantages over other forms of organization, such as honorific administration by courtiers, relatives of the ruler, or amateurs. Bureaucratic organizations have decisive technical superiority. They can operate with precision, speed, and with unambiguous and predictable performance based on rules. They ensure continuity, unity, and strict subordination, which reduces friction between officials. Personal and material costs of administration are reduced to a minimum.

Once fully established, bureaucracy is virtually indestructible. It is *the* means of carrying out community action. It can be made to work for anyone who can control it, because discipline and compliance are built into the structure. The system itself is able to ensure that the staff within the organization cannot squirm out of their responsibilities, for the specialized duties of each office are clearly spelled out. The consequences of bureaucratic power depend on the direction in which it is used. It is at the disposal of varied political and economic interests. As a technical means of organized action, it is vastly superior in effectiveness to any mass action that is not so organized.

Weber argued that bureaucracy was essential to many developments in the modern world. Capitalism needed the precise rules of bureaucracy to organize trade over long periods of time and in foreign countries. A centralized administration was critical for the development of a unified German state. In addition, bureaucracy is indispensable for democracy. As Weber expresses it, the fate of the masses depends on the steady, correct functioning of state administration. It is essential for the equality of treatment implied in democracy. All clients must be treated the same and be subject to the same uniform rules. Such equality presupposes impartial, regulated organization that operates without hatred or passion, without favouritism or prejudice. Weber argued that it is impossible to get rid of bureaucracies, for only such a system provides protection from undependable and amateur administration, favouritism, and corruption.

The Iron Cage

The negative side of bureaucracy lies in its power to compress all human diversity into conformity with its regulations. Bureaucracy threatens to become, in Weber's words, an **iron cage**, imprisoning the human spirit. For Weber, the bureaucratic mode of organization represents the purest expression of purposive-rational action. He never doubted its technical efficiency or its indispensability for rational capitalist enterprise and state administration. Yet he was deeply pessimistic regarding the negative impact of bureaucracy on the quality of modern life. No sphere of social action more completely exemplifies Weber's warning that the means needed to achieve valued ends may have negative consequences that undermine or destroy the very ends themselves. Weber feared that bureaucratic organization threatened the most cherished political goals of the twentieth century: democracy and socialism.

Weber believed that bureaucracy, based on principles of technical expertise and professional secrecy of office, and swollen to millions of functionaries, would come to exercise virtually unassailable power. Democracy, with its goal of social levelling and equality of treatment, could not function without bureaucratic organization, yet this form of administration has the inherent effect of promoting and sustaining a closed group of officials, with the authority of officialdom, raised over public opinion. People would find themselves disempowered against the bureaucratic experts.

Not only ordinary people, but also their elected representatives would be affected. Efficient bureaucracy rests on technical superiority of knowledge. Inevitably, officials would welcome a poorly informed and hence powerless parliament. There are built-in incentives for officials to fight every attempt of parliament to gain knowledge of bureaucratic affairs. Elected ministers depend on bureaucrats for information on which to base policies.

The loyalty of officials lies not with the general public or the electorate, but with the bureaucracy itself. Their vocation is to serve their official duties. In Canada, as in other Western democracies, it is a criminal offence for civil servants within the state administration to divulge internal policy documents to the public. One official in the Department of Indian Affairs who leaked information about proposed cutbacks to Native funding was summarily dismissed.

Socialism, no less than multiparty democracy, is threatened by bureaucratic administration. Socialism may abolish the power of the bourgeoisie through the socialization of the means of economic production, but it cannot abolish the power of the new class of officials. In all probability, Weber thought, officialdom might come to exert even more of a stranglehold on society under socialism because the countervailing forces of entrepreneurs and free enterprise under capitalism would be absent.

Weber argues that it would be illogical to try to control bureaucratic power by making the inner workings of officials subject to the scrutiny of laypeople. This would undermine the efficiency, speed, calculability, and impersonality of the bureaucratic machine itself, and thus undercut the very qualities that make for superior administration.

Weber saw that the inevitable consequence of the smoothly running bureaucratic machine would be the dehumanization of all who come into contact with it. The rigidly defined regulations and responsibilities of an office provide for calculated efficiency but, as a consequence, the individuality of people who must relate to it, either as employees or clients, cannot be admitted. Bureaucracies are oriented toward *formal* rationality: the purposively rational performance

of standardized and routine functions. They are opposed in principle to the *substantive* rationality of individual circumstances. A system designed to treat everyone equally inevitably lacks the flexibility to treat individual cases as unique. Those who do not fit the patterns for which the rules are established cannot receive the specialized services they may need. For them the formally rational system becomes substantively irrational.

Those who work as employees within the bureaucracy are even more rigidly subject to its regulations. They operate as cogs in the machine. The major requirement for their position is unquestioning and strict adherence to written regulations within their narrowly defined areas of jurisdiction. Their individuality has no place within such a system, for it would disrupt the calculated order.

Weber believed that the iron cage spread beyond bureaucracy itself, for this mode of organization is only the extreme expression of the purposive-rational orientation that dominates all aspects of Western civilization itself. Science brings with it the demythification of the universe. As Weber expresses it, "the fate of our times is characterized by rationalization and intellectualization, and above all, by the 'disenchantment of the world' " (Gerth and Mills 1946, 155).

For Weber there is no escape. "To the person who cannot bear the fate of times like a man," Weber offers only the retreat into silence and into the old religions. Weber feels that it is understandable that people should turn to religion in the hope of finding a refuge from scientific rationality and an alternative account of the meaning of life. Those who embrace religious doctrine are unable to face reality as it appears in the light of rational, scientific study. They may find comfort in the church, but only at the price of closing their minds to scientific knowledge, an intellectual sacrifice that Weber finds unacceptable. Such a retreat must inevitably fail to satisfy people because they are compelled to recognize their concomitant loss of intellectual integrity. As Weber sees it, "the arms of the old churches are opened widely and compassionately for [us]," but this emotional escape is only for those who cannot "meet the demands of the day." The iron cage of rationality is the fate of our time.

William Kurelek's painting, *All Things Betray Thee Who Betrayest Me* (1970) expresses the chilling dehumanization that accompanies bureaucracy—the "iron cage" of Western civilization.

The Limitations of Weber's Thought

It is not easy to criticize Weber's thought on intellectual grounds for it seems that all the usual criticisms are synthesized or neutralized by Weber himself. The approach of functionalism, which locates people as socialized members of an overarching system, is subsumed and transcended in Weber's work. The classical structuralist Marxist thesis, which seeks to understand human alienation in the exploitative relations of capitalism, is also incorporated. Marxism offers no ultimate escape from the experience of alienation and dehumanization, for socialism is also an iron cage, albeit of a different sort. Exploitation under capitalism is only replaced by a deeper dehumanization under centralized bureaucratic control. The interpretive focus on individuals as makers of their own social world is, or seems to be, incorporated as well through Weber's emphasis on meaningful understanding. This understanding is subsumed in his ideal-type model of action orientation.

Weber is his own best critic. He acknowledges that the logical conclusions to his own arguments point to a world that he finds unbearable, dehumanized. For long periods of his life he was profoundly depressed and unable to work. This depression can only be partially accounted for in terms of his personal life and psychological makeup. In part it stemmed from the intellectual hell created by his own ideas.

Rational Action Re-examined: The Feminist Challenge

How can we challenge Weber's theory so that we are not condemned to the same disenchantment and despair? A basic problem in Weber's work seems to lie in its starting assumption, in the conceptualization of rationality itself. Weber divides rationality into four distinct types of orientation: traditional, affective, value, and purposive rationality. He claims that Western civilization is characterized by the triumph of the last form as reflected in science, in capitalism, in a worldly success ethic in religion, in rational-legal authority, and ultimately in bureaucratic organizations.

The question Weber does not raise is, how can a civilization, or a mode of organization, be rational if the result is the destruction of the human spirit itself? Weber is deeply aware that the rational choice of means may destroy the intended ends but he does not question the rationality of purposive action dissociated, as it is, from cultural traditions and emotional or spiritual foundations. He sees such separation as necessary for the modern world, whatever its emotional costs.

When Weber separates types of rationality, he is following a long intellectual tradition in Western thought. This tradition commonly draws a distinction between rational and emotional behaviour. Men tend to be thought of as more rational and intellectual while women are conceived of as more emotional and natural or physical. The masculine principle is thus rational. It is perhaps for this reason that Weber slips into the easy characterization of those who retreat into religion as people "who cannot bear the fate of the times like a *man*." The assumption seems to be that, in the modern world, retreat into emotions and religious values is inappropriate for men although perhaps acceptable and even normal for women.

Feminist theory, more clearly than other theoretical approaches in sociology, has challenged the separation of rational and emotional, of masculine and feminine, as an injustice to the nature of both women and men. Despite the enormous scope of his scholarship, and the depth of his insight, Weber nowhere explicitly considers the position of women or their role in the development of Western civilization. He does not seem to question their absence from intellectual debate. In his personal life, it is clear that his mother was a central figure in his own intellectual development and that his wife Marianne was the person who held him together during his years of depression and made it possible for him eventually to begin work again. Yet the role of women remains invisible in his intellectual work on the nature of man and civilization. How can this happen?

The feminist critique points to the major flaw in his starting assumptions of action orientation. He separates types of rationality so that purposive-rational-legal action—the masculine principle—is separated from the emotional and value-oriented dimensions—the feminine principle. Weber's characterization of Western civilization is, implicitly, a profoundly sexist characterization, although he did not perceive it as such.

The malaise in Weber's work is in essence the malaise of Western civilization itself. Weber sees only too clearly the nature of this disorder: the disenchantment inherent in a civilization that elevates purposive-rational action to the highest form. But he is unable to transcend this view. In Marcuse's terms (1964), he remains trapped in **one-dimensional thought**, unable to conceive of viable alternatives that do not entail intellectual retreat.

It is the breakdown of the unity of cultural, emotional, and spiritual elements of purposive action that makes possible the colossal destruction wrought in the name of rational modernization in the pursuit of profit. The decision of a capitalist to exploit other people and the environment, to further the goal of short-term profit, is one that has emotional and moral components, whether these are recognized or not. It is also a decision embedded in a habitual or traditional mode of action in Western culture. Weber's artificial division into types of orientation, with only one dimension given recognition, does not hold up. The alternative view, which is reflected in feminist theory, albeit often in confused and half-understood ways, is that no individual, no action, no organization, no civilization can be truly rational if it does not integrate the "masculine" and the "feminine," such that tradition, emotion, and spirituality are integrated into purposive action.

The practical critiques of Weber's thesis on rationality, which we examine in the next chapter, usually have not gone this far, but they reflect the recognition that purposive-rational action, separated from other considerations, is often irrational, particularly in its practical embodiment in bureaucratic modes of organization. Weber's thesis that bureaucracy is the most efficient mode of organization has been challenged precisely because bureaucracy reduces employees to trained robots and clients to standardized cases where their real circumstances cannot be taken into account.

The Marxist critique within organization theory rejects the notion of rationality as the root of bureaucratic structures. It raises the possibility that the very notion of rationality itself is a form of ideological hegemony to legitimate the exploitation of the mass of employees by those who direct the organization. Rationality is an ideology of the most invidious kind because it seems so neutral, so objective, that even to challenge it seems unreasonable.

As we will see in the following chapter, theorists who have been most influenced by Weber's own methodological concern with interpretive understanding of human action have challenged his thesis as an unjustifiable reification of a system. From the perspective of the social construction of reality, and of ethnomethodology, Weber's model functions as ideology, or as a convenient way of accounting for what people seem to be doing, but not as a causal explanation for behaviour. The model of bureaucracy pays too little attention to the understanding that individuals themselves have of their relationships with each other. Nor does it pay enough attention to what people actually do, as distinct from what they are supposed to be doing according to the formal plan. The formal model is not a literal description of reality, but rather an accounting procedure, a way in which people have learned to talk about what they do to make sense of it.

Conclusion

The legacy of Weber in contemporary sociology is enormous. His concern with promoting a social science methodology that would have interpretive understanding as its central objective is only just coming to fruition with the development of ethnomethodology, which we will discuss in chapter 18.

Weber's substantive and theoretical contribution to sociology was profoundly shaped by his lifelong dialogue with the ghost of Marx. Weber tried to build upon and go beyond the basic conception of the nature of capitalism and class in Marxist theory while rejecting the oversimplified versions of Marxist thought that reduce human behaviour to economic determinism. Weber insisted that emotional life, values, meaning, or culture must be taken into account as critical aspects of all human behaviour, including economic activities. His famous study of *The Protestant Ethic and the Spirit of Capitalism* explores the religious and moral basis of the drive to accumulate wealth, which helped to foster the development of capitalism in Europe. His other historical and comparative studies of religions and sects in Europe, India, and China focus upon the interrelationship between life experiences, based on class position and mode of production, and forms of religious thought. Some of

these ideas are explored in the section on religion in chapter 6.

Weber shared with Marx an emphasis on the economic base of life chances in relation to modes of production, but he broadened this focus to explore the diversity of class experience. Weber recognized that in a complex, industrial society skills in themselves constitute a form of means of production. Those who have skills to sell in the marketplace are in a profoundly different class position from propertyless, unskilled labourers. Weber emphasized the importance of status in the formation of social groups. Status is based on ascriptive criteria of ethnicity, race, sex, age, and the like. For Marx, these were merely secondary reflections of economic class position, but for Weber they appeared as important determinants of life chances in their own right. The fact that these variables work at the level of meaning and emotion, rather than material need, makes them no less important as dimensions of human experience. Weber shared with Durkheim an awareness of the importance of social cohesion, which cannot be reduced to dimensions of class. Weber's contribution to the study of class and ethnicity are explored in chapters 9, 15, and 17.

Weber's distinctive contribution to sociology lies in his analysis of rationality in Western culture and its particular expression in the rise of bureaucratic modes of formal organization in business and government. This aspect of his work is the focus of the next chapter. Weber's model of bureaucracy has profoundly influenced the development of organization theory in sociology. Much of the work in the field is either an elaboration or test of his insights or a critical counterproposal to them. In contemporary postindustrial society, characterized by the corporate concentration of capital, multinational corporations the size of nation-states, and centralized state administrations, these bureaucratic organizations are not merely facts of life, but dominant features of human experience.

Suggested Reading

A very readable selection of writings by Max Weber is provided by Stanislav Andreski, ed., *Max Weber on Capitalism, Bureaucracy and Religion: A Selection of Texts* (1983). Andreski

provides a brief introduction to Weber's writings, followed by selected excerpts from writings on the uniqueness of Western capitalism, cultural factors that impeded the development of capitalism in the ancient world and in Asia, and the rise of Protestantism and rationalism in the West.

Another useful source is the collection of Weber's writings edited by W.G. Runciman, *Weber: Selections in Translation* (1978). See particularly, part 1, "The Foundations of Social Theory," with selections on social organization, classes, status groups, and parties, and chapter 18, "The Development of Bureaucracy and Its Relation to Law."

The selection by H.H. Gerth and C. Wright Mills, *From Max Weber: Essays in Sociology* (1946), is generally very heavy reading, but it provides an excellent introduction to Weber's theory of bureaucracy in part 8, especially the first two selections, "The Characteristics of Bureaucracy" and "The Position of the Official."

Questions

1. How does Weber reconcile the idea that human action is based on free will with the idea that it is predictable?

2. Why does Weber believe that explanations in sociology must take the form of probabilities rather than clear predictions?

3. What is the role of ideal-type constructs in sociological research?

4. How does Weber modify Marx's definition of *class*?

5. Distinguish between the ethic of responsibility and the ethic of ultimate ends.

6. How does rational-legal authority differ from traditional authority?

7. Why does Weber insist that bureaucratic officials should be appointed rather than elected to office?

8. How does Weber account for the historical association between the rise of capitalism and Protestantism?

9. Why did Weber claim that bureaucracy was fundamentally incompatible with democracy?

10. What is the basis of the feminist critique of Weber's notion of purposive-rational action?

CHAPTER

Rationalizing the Irrational: Bureaucratic Conformity or Liberation?

 Weber's analytical model of bureaucracy has been taken up in diverse ways by different theoretical perspectives in sociology. Traditional structural-functionalist analysis has focussed primarily upon questions of function and efficiency in meeting the objective goals of organizations.

Marxist structuralism refocusses the question around deeper issues of power and the apparatus of ruling embedded in the interlocking bureaucratic structures of contemporary society. This approach challenges in fundamental ways the claims to scientific objectivity and neutrality in traditional functionalist models of efficient administration. It explores the central significance of bureaucratic structures as determinants of the hierarchical divisions that we come to recognize as class and also the gendered inequalities produced through the job ghettos and limited roles made available to women within them.

Different approaches within the broad framework of interpretive theory question the taken-for-granted assumption that bureaucratic structures

exist as entities that do things or have effects. They explore alternative views of bureaucracy as socially constructed through the authoritative procedures of officials and through the accounting practices by which people make sense of what they do. Interpretive theory has its roots in Weber's methodological insistence on grounding sociological analysis in the study of meaning, and his rejection of holistic concepts that tend to lose sight of the fact that only people are active agents. Bureaucratic organizations are, after all, nothing more than collections of people trying, more or less competently, to get things done. These organizations cannot exist independently of the meaningful understanding of the people involved.

The complex work of Michel Foucault is used in this chapter to draw together the Marxist structuralist and interpretive perspectives. Foucault believes that our social world comes to be known to us, and to have the form it does, through **discourse** about it; that is, through how we talk about it. However, it is also our lived experience of the social world that creates our knowledge and our mode of talking about it. For Foucault, this circle is virtually closed, as the way we talk or think structures our experience, which structures the knowledge expressed when we talk. As we have seen many times in earlier chapters, people commonly draw on prevailing theories about human behaviour to organize how they talk about their own experiences, which then appears to provide further ethnographic confirmation for the theory itself.

In the last section of this chapter we explore the discourse of radical feminism, a way of thinking that begins from the standpoint of people whose central experience of nurturing children in families is very different from the bureaucratic mode of public life. As women increasingly merge private and public realms in their own lived experience, their emerging knowledge makes possible a radically new discourse. It suggests ways of thinking in which the nature of rationality itself, and with it the entire bureaucratic edifice, is called into question.

Traditional Functionalism: Bureaucracy as Efficient

Parsons' early essay on "Suggestions for a Sociological Approach to the Theory of Organizations" (1956) aptly summarizes the traditional structural-functionalist perspective. Organizations exist as definite structures designed for attaining specific goals. For Parsons, the question of what constitutes a bureaucracy poses few problems. Organizations are, by definition, formal structures set up for specific purposes, with actions co-ordinated to these ends. Efficiency is measured by success in achieving these ends. The structure of organizations consists of the roles of participants and the values that define and legitimate their functions. Mechanisms for implementing goals consist of the *board*, or top level, which makes policy decisions, and the *line* administration, which makes allocative decisions for optimal use of resources in pursuit of goals. *Personnel management* is responsible for co-ordination and integration of subunits, and for ensuring appropriate motivation through coercion, incentives, and therapy. Lastly, the *workers* themselves are

responsible for production. The organization, which interacts with its external environment, is viewed as a single unit with a single goal.

Testing the Model

Empirical research in the functionalist tradition has commonly taken Weber's model of bureaucratic structures as a framework for analysing how particular organizations function. Many of these studies indicate that the model is not always a good predictor of organizational efficiency, and that it needs to be modified to state precisely the conditions under which bureaucracy will or will not work efficiently.

A study by Blau (1955) casts doubt on the Weberian model through evidence that bureaucratic procedures actually cause inefficient behaviour. Blau studied four sections of a state employment agency in the United States. The work involved screening and counselling job applicants, referring them to appropriate job vacancies, and notifying the state unemployment insurance agency of people refusing jobs without good cause. Measures of job performance included number of interviews per month, number of clients referred to jobs, number of placements, and number of notifications to the unemployment insurance office of fraud.

Blau found that the bureaucratic procedures designed to ensure strict performance accountability directly undermined efficiency. Employees geared their work to what counted. They concentrated on shallow, high-speed interviews, and multiple referrals. Handicapped clients or those needing counselling were discarded because they lowered performance ratings. They also cheated on each other, hiding job vacancies to boost their own placement records, and they falsified statistics to inflate placements.

The degree of inefficiency created by those practices only came to light by comparison with one section of the agency where the employees were all army veterans whose jobs were guaranteed. They could afford to ignore performance ratings. They co-operated in their work and shared knowledge of all job openings. They also spent more time counselling applicants because they genuinely cared that these people, many of whom were themselves veterans, find suitable jobs. The result was that this section actually filled more job openings and placed more people than did the other sections. The bureaucratic rules that controlled the work of employees in other sections of the agency actually created inefficiency because they hampered co-operation.

Blau has not been alone in finding that bureaucratic modes of organization cause inefficiency. Merton (1957) drew attention to the "cogs in the machine mentality" of many career bureaucrats who have learned not to think or to act for themselves but to follow prescribed rules rigidly. Such responses may be functional in routine work but are totally dysfunctional in situations requiring innovation.

Burns and Stalker (1961) highlight the same point in their study of twenty Scottish electronics firms. These firms were struggling to diversify their products in a postwar market where their traditional government defence contracts for radar equipment were declining. Most of these firms were organized in ideal-typical bureaucratic forms, with fragmented, carefully designated jobs in production, sales, and design, co-ordinated through a rigidly defined hierarchy of responsibilities. This formal organization proved disastrous for innovation. Everything new was, by definition, outside the jurisdiction of pre-defined offices. Hence more and more decisions were passed up to the top of the hierarchy while those below refused to do anything until they received direct orders. The inevitable result was that the manager was swamped and subordinates paralyzed. The typical bureaucratic response was to set up a new role to handle the new problem, but that person's job depended upon the continuation of the problem! This is a typical case of **goal displacement** found in many studies of bureaucracies, where maintaining one's own department takes priority over the total enterprise. The subgoal tends to become that of enhancing the prestige and resources of one's own section at the expense of others.

The few firms in Burns and Stalker's study that did manage to innovate successfully scrapped the hierarchy and the predefined, fragmented jobs in favour of co-operative teamwork and collective responsibilities.

A study by Dalton (1959, 342–51) documents the perennial conflicts between technical staff and administrators in bureaucracies. Technical staff were supposed to suggest improvements in functioning, but any such proposals were bitterly resented by administrators, who felt that their own expertise and authority were being challenged. The result was resistance, bordering on sabotage of new ideas.

These are all relatively old studies and are quite well known. They point to serious inefficiencies in typical bureaucratic modes of organization and suggest that more flexible, co-operative, and less hierarchical systems work better, at least for tasks that are not totally routinized. Yet bureaucracy is more pervasive than ever. Burns and Stalker found that, in many of the electronic firms, the employees themselves actively resisted attempts to break down the bureaucratic system. They seemed to prefer fixed tasks that left no doubt exactly what the workers were responsible for and what they were not responsible for. They preferred to be left alone to get on with their jobs without any further commitment.

The theoretical question these studies raise is why there should be such resistance to more co-operative, less hierarchical modes of organization. The Weberian argument that bureaucracy is more efficient is not an adequate explanation.

Political Economy Theory: Bureaucracy, Power, and Control

Political economy theory, which is rooted in classical Marxist analysis of the structures of capitalism, challenges traditional functionalism by asking what segment of society finds bureaucracy functional and efficient. It questions the image of organizations or societies as unified systems with goal consensus and explores instead the dimensions of inequality, class, and power within organizations.

Proponents of political economy theory have pointed out that, historically, factories did not emerge as the result of new technology or concerns with efficient mass production (Marglin 1974–75). The factories actually preceded the technology. They emerged as the result of the interest of owners of the raw materials in exerting greater control over workers. The older putting-out system, where workers took raw materials to their homes and brought back finished goods, was not conducive to close control over the pace of work. Factories were created so that workers would be under the constant surveillance and direct control of the bosses. It was very inefficient for the workers, however, because they could no longer integrate child care and other domestic work with production.

It can be argued that all the characteristics of bureaucracy listed by Weber (see p. 289) are required, not for efficiency of production, but for surveillance and control over unwilling workers. They reflect and gloss over antagonistic class interests. Gouldner (1952) addresses several questions concerning Weber's model. What kinds of obligations and responsibilities are established in Weber's model? What aspects of behaviour are rendered predictable and calculated? What aspects of organizations are left conspicuously unpredictable? Gouldner answers that the rules defining workers' obligations are the most predictable, while rules defining workers' rights, or management obligations, are the least predictable. Workers have had to form unions to force the establishment of rules concerning seniority, job security, grievance procedures, sick leave, holidays, and the like. Rules defining conformity are the most rigid at the bottom of the organizational hierarchy, where workers are subjected to clocking in and out. Rules are least rigid at the top. Senior managers have much more leeway to arrive late or to take breaks when they want to. The level of impersonality also varies. It is strongest between ranks, defining how subordinates and superiors are to interact, but least rigid among formal equals, especially at the top of the rank. Gouldner concludes that Weber's model does not represent an abstract model of efficiency at all, but rather the narrow perspectives of management experts.

In his major empirical study of bureaucratization in a gypsum factory, Gouldner (1954) traces the actual stages in the development of rigid rules. Initially, the factory was anything but bureaucratic. It was located in a small rural community where workers and supervisors grew up together. The organization was easy-going, with minimal attention to rules so long as the work got done. Job switching was permitted and, when vacancies arose, promotion of local people was favoured over importing outside experts, even if the locals were less qualified.

All this changed when head office personnel appointed a new boss from outside the factory who was under pressure to improve the organization. Workers resented him. They wanted a local boss and feared the loss of their old privileges. The new boss found himself forced to impose bureaucratic rules to break the resistance of the workers. He could not use the old co-operative relations to motivate workers because he himself was resented by them as an outsider. Hence he relied upon formal rules to back his authority. He displaced their hostility onto superior officers by arguing that the rules came from senior management. Rules were clear and could be rigidly applied to everyone. They permitted spot-checking or supervision at a distance and so lessened the outright expressions of hostility generated by close supervision. Relations between workers and management worsened to the point of a wildcat strike. Ironically, the resolution of the workers' grievances resulted in still more bureaucratization as work roles and responsibilities were even more rigidly defined and delimited. It was clear what workers did and did not have to do, and supervision could become still more impersonal (Gouldner 1965). Gouldner concludes that the main function of bureaucratic rules in the gypsum mine was not to raise efficiency of production, but to impose discipline on reluctant workers. Rules were a symptom of class hostility between workers and bosses.

A historical study into the origins of job structures in the United States steel industry traces the process of job fragmentation and deskilling of workers (Stone 1974). It was not technical advances, but the class struggle between workers and owners of the Carnegie steel mill, that generated these changes. Before 1892, steel was made by teams of skilled workers with unskilled helpers, using the company's equipment and raw materials. Skilled workers were in complete charge of the labour process. They divided the tasks among themselves, set the pace of the work, and determined pay differentials, with overall pay based on the price of steel. By the 1890s, however, demand for steel was rising, and the owners wanted to raise production and their own profits. A new manager used armed men to close down the plant, lock out the workers, and break their union. New machines were installed, which doubled or trebled productivity while wages went up only marginally. Work was reorganized so highly skilled craftsmen were reduced to semi-skilled labourers.

Finally, to break the unified resistance of workers, the owners instituted artificial job ladders. Very minor differences in skill levels were written into distinct job classifications with different pay levels. Workers thus found themselves competing against each other and currying favour with supervisors to get small promotions. Subsequent union contracts cemented these artificial divisions between workers by negotiating bonuses, pay scales, and seniority clauses in line with the new job classifications. The way the work is organized in the steel industry is both produced by the class struggle and used as a weapon in that struggle.

These critical studies change in significant ways the conception of rationality and efficiency on which Weber based his legitimation of bureaucracy. Bureaucratic organizations have been shown in several different contexts to be much less efficient than nonhierarchical, co-operative models, especially when flexibility or innovation is needed. Yet bureaucracy persists. These authors suggest that it persists primarily because it is the most efficient method of controlling reluctant workers while deflecting hostility and opposition. Deskilled, fragmented workers are easily controlled and exploited by managers who monopolize skilled knowledge for themselves. Workers themselves may come to prefer it as a way of minimizing their own commitment to the organization. Bureaucracy is clearly not a neutral mode of organization. It is intimately associated with inequality and power.

Bureaucracy and Oligarchy

Weber did not question the ultimate functional efficiency of bureaucracy for meeting the goals of whoever was in control, and for this he can be justly faulted. What he did see with stunning clarity was the almost unassailable power that bureaucracy confers upon the elites who control it. Weber likewise did not see job fragmentation as related to a deliberate deskilling process. He was, however, very much aware of the political consequences of the resulting concentration of knowledge and technical expertise in the hands of a bureaucratic elite, and the disempowerment of both functionaries within the bureaucratic machine and the mass of people outside it.

It was the sophisticated German bureaucratic apparatus, for example, that was key to the success of the Nazis in accomplishing the "final solution" to the "Jewish problem" (Berger 1993). The extermination of Jews was translated into mundane tasks that numberless functionaries performed without leaving their desks. It became a matter of bureaucratic competence, efficiency, and problem-solving abilities. The railroad bureaucrat, for example, was able to fulfil his functional role by treating the transportation of Jews to death camps as equivalent to transporting any other passengers to any destination. He was responsible only for assuring that their fares were correctly paid.

Weber's recognition of the inherent tendencies toward **oligarchy** within bureaucratic organizations, and the threat that these pose to democracy, has powerfully influenced the development of theory in political sociology. Robert Michels ([1911] 1949) drew extensively upon Weber's work to develop the concept of the **iron law of oligarchy** to explain the processes of concentration of power in ostensibly democratic political parties and trade unions. He shared Weber's conviction that organization is essential for the expression of collective will. A disorganized mass of people can rarely accomplish anything. They are easily subject to suggestion by skilled orators and are easily swayed by the emotions of the moment. Sober and disciplined decision making is virtually impossible in mass meetings. Some form of delegation of responsibilities is thus essential, but then the problem of hierarchy begins to emerge.

In principle, the person who is elected as leader within a democratic organization is the servant of the masses and can be deprived of office at any moment. Perhaps the ideal is rotating office bearers. But leadership responsibilities and roles are complex. They require technical knowledge and experience that can only be learned over time. People with legal or technical training have a distinct advantage in such roles. As they develop expertise, however, a gulf inevitably widens between them and the masses who elected them to office. The mass of the people lacks information to make clear decisions, and mass involvement wastes time and limits flexibility of action.

Exactly as Weber recognized, secrecy constitutes a critical source of power. As the gap in knowledge grows between leaders and the masses, more committee meetings are held in secret, and the rank and file get only summary reports. Government bureaucrats welcome a poorly informed parliament because they gain greater freedom of action and freedom from surveillance. Michels recognized that unions could become more oligarchic than political parties because the leaders control the funds and can determine legal strikes. During negotiations they can also claim to know the market better than do members.

In principle, election to office should make incumbents accountable to the electorate and therefore promote democracy. In practice, as Weber pointed out, elections undermine the values of efficiency, impartiality, and expertise in the operation of bureaucracies. A glaring example of this occurred in Philadelphia, where more than fifty municipal judges, who are elected to office, were accused of accepting bribes. They were reported to have perpetuated racketeering by having a virtual price list for turning a blind eye to crimes. The chancellor of the Philadelphia Bar Association concluded that such racketeering is almost unavoidable in a system where elected judges receive salaries of $80 000 but where their campaigns cost up to $100 000. It was difficult to prove that bribes were anything more than legitimate campaign contributions. Moreover, there seemed to be a great deal of public tolerance for this behaviour. "While it is unclear whether voters are cynical or merely ignorant," every judge who was suspended for accepting bribes was easily re-elected to office (*Globe and Mail*, 31 Dec. 1987, A1–2).

Within political parties and unions, where leaders are elected, the mass of membership tends to become indifferent toward the organization. While a small inner circle allows for speed of action, it means that most members are left out. Long-tenured leaders tend to develop an aura of indispensability; the masses feel incompetent to handle their own affairs.

The main threat to the power of a leader is not the masses, but a take-over bid from a new dominant figure. It is difficult to succeed in such a bid because the established elite has the advantage of material resources, time, and support staff. Often elite figures have a full-time, paid staff to develop propaganda; they control the main supply of information; and their high position leads others to emulate them. They may try to co-opt potential new leaders by giving them high-level posts and then demanding loyalty, or try to discredit them and label their followers disloyal. The mere threat of abdication, combined with the threat that the party will lose the next election or the union will lose in negotiations, may be sufficient to get the masses to toe the line. The trump card is to convince the masses that they are incompetent to run affairs without a leader. Hence, Michels concludes, a radical change of leaders can occur, but it is relatively rare and often unstable.

The short-lived leadership change within the United Steelworkers Union of America, Ontario office, in 1985, seems a classic case of oligarchy at work. A newspaper report (*Globe and Mail*, 9 Nov. 1985) suggests that the union establishment was shocked in 1981 by the election to office of a rank and file member on a platform of union reform. Union staff traditionally had a strong influence on union politics, but the newcomer, a tough militant who led a long strike at INCO in Sudbury two years earlier, broke this pattern. His problem was that, once in office, he was unable to accomplish much reform. He was unable to challenge the political machine of his rivals. He lacked the administrative expertise to crack the entrenched bureaucracy. Four years later, his dreams were broken as he was beaten in the elections by an establishment candidate. The union executive reportedly hired a public relations firm to run their campaign. Slick campaign literature was designed for the executive's candidate, and behind them there was the might of the president's office at Steelworkers headquarters in Pittsburgh.

Michels concludes that the ideal of rule by the masses never occurs and cannot occur. The reality is a circulation of dominant elites. It is perhaps in the face of this level of powerlessness that people come to accept bribery as an effective, if illegitimate, means of exerting influence over officials.

Bureaucracy and Communism

Michels criticizes Marxist theory for failing to take account of administration in theories of power. Socialism, he argues, is not merely a problem of economics, but also of administration. Large amounts of capital require bureaucracy to organize them, and with this comes hierarchy of control and technical expertise. Hence, the iron law of oligarchy re-emerges. The masses, he argues, will always submit to the minority.

Mosca ([1939] 1960) echoes similar sentiments, arguing that there will always be elites who can monopolize power and advantages through control of political party structures or any large-scale bureaucratic administration. The elite has the advantages of publicity, information control, education, specialized training, and qualifications. Elites also have the advantage of a lifetime of experience that they are able to hand down from one generation to another. Pressure from discontented masses does influence leaders but, whenever established leaders are disposed, another elite minority will have to be elected in their place.

In the final months of 1989 and into the 1990s, the peoples of many countries in Eastern Europe were struggling with this problem of how to oust entrenched Communist Party elites and bureaucrats. Mass demonstrations, protests, and strikes precipitated the resignations of established Communist Party elites. But the difficult task that remained was to select new people to fill the resulting power vacuum. Before free elections could be held, parties had to be organized and candidates found. Periodic elections provide a mechanism for the circulation of elites but do not eliminate the need for them. Nor do elections resolve the problem of rigid bureaucratic structures.

The stranglehold of bureaucracy on life in Soviet society was generally recognized even by the strongest supporters of communism. Marx's assumption that a classless society would in principle protect citizens from the ravages of a bureaucratic state clearly was not sustained in practice.

Barry Smart (1983) argues that two events in Europe in 1968—the popular uprisings among students and workers in France in May of that year and the "Prague Spring"—irrevocably shattered the dreams of European socialists. The protest movements in France formed independently of the trade unions and the French Communist Party, the conventional political institutions of opposition. The generally conservative and unsympathetic response of the Communist Party to these demonstrations revealed the barrenness of the institutionalized and hierarchical forms of political protest. In theory, the Communist Party should have been at the forefront of the uprising, championing the rights and interests of the workers. In practice, the party proved to be out of touch and even hostile to a workers'

movement that it did not control. Later that year, the Soviet Union invaded Czechoslovakia to crush the spontaneous social protest movements known as the Prague Spring. Smart argues that this invasion nullified any claim by the government of the Soviet Union to social, economic, political, or moral superiority over capitalist systems.

The massacre of demonstrators in Tiananmen Square in Beijing in June 1989 similarly undermined the legitimacy of Communist Party rule in China. For some three weeks prior to the massacre, several thousand people, led by Beijing University students, camped in the square to pressure for greater democratization in the country. They were denounced as counterrevolutionaries by Communist Party leaders, and the army was ordered to drive them out of the square. Foreign reporters estimate that hundreds of people were shot or crushed by army tanks. The oligarchic structure of the Communist Party was revealed in the power wielded by a handful of old men. It also became evident how effectively the bureaucracy could control information so as to present a version of events that minimized the massacre, exonerated the army and the party, and silenced criticism. China is generally acknowledged as a state relatively impervious to international pressure; to this can be added the fact that Western countries, led by the United States, seem reluctant to alienate so significant a trading partner by tying trade to human rights.

The critical challenge for Marxist theory is to account for the prevalence of Stalinist dictators in communist societies in which theorists had predicted a gradual withering away of state powers. The conventional Marxist response to such repression has been to return to classical texts in an effort to substitute new interpretations of doctrine. In Smart's view, none has yet been able to resolve the crisis of Marxism: the continuing incompatibility between theoretical expectations and patterns of development in Western capitalist societies and the realities in existing communist states. Indeed, in the late 1980s, challenges to communist rule throughout Eastern Europe were so sudden and so sweeping that some commentators were led to proclaim the end of history—the universal triumph of liberal-capitalist democracy (Fukuyama 1989). Ongoing struggles among ultraright nationalists, free-market advocates, and old-guard communists in former republics of the old Soviet Union make such a pronouncement seem premature.

These grandiose claims, however, have a hollow ring. In principle, the basic ideology of capitalism, which stresses free enterprise, individualism, and hostility to big government and state interference, should have worked against the development of a bureaucratic state in Western societies. But it has not. The iron cage of bureaucracy is not so easily escaped. Weber argued that bureaucratic forms of organization are an essential and unavoidable feature of centralized and industrialized societies, regardless of whether they are organized along capitalist or communist lines. Bureaucratic elites wield power by virtue of knowledge and technical superiority. This power base, Weber argues, is far stronger than the raw power of ownership or control over the means of production because it is founded on the legitimating principle of rationality itself. As Weber saw it, purposive-rational organization is inherently bureaucratic and leads inevitably to oligarchy and dehumanization. Neither communist nor democratic procedures would be sufficient to overcome this. New approaches within interpretive theory have begun the work of pushing beyond both functionalist and classical Marxist theories, toward a critical analysis of bureaucracy and how relations of power are rationalized.

Bureaucratic Society

This section draws heavily on the work of Kathy Ferguson (1984) who bases her analysis of **bureaucratic society** on the work of Foucault. In Ferguson's view, bureaucracy, as an all-pervasive mode of social organization, actually creates the kind of social system that structural-functionalist theory describes: a self-maintaining system that reduces people to sets of fragmented roles. In Ferguson's theory, bureaucracy and society become synonymous. The institutionalized sets of roles that bureaucracy makes available to us, together with bureaucratic descriptions of and justifications for these roles or job classifications, structure our social world and shape how we think about it.

Bureaucracy has become so all-pervasive as to leave people with virtually no options. To remove oneself from bureaucracy is to lose almost all important social connections, while to embrace one's role is to lose the dimensions of oneself that do not coincide with organizational roles. The cost of conformity is resignation, while the cost of resistance is disintegration. Whatever course of action one takes is already determined by the organizational environment (Ferguson 1984, 91–92).

For Ferguson (1984, xii), the central issue is bureaucracy itself, a mode of organization that hurts, twists, and damages people and limits human possibility. Bureaucracy represents "the scientific organization of inequality" through which people are dominated and oppressed. At the same time, it legitimates such practices in the name of rationality and efficiency. Conflict-ridden class relations are disguised in the language of administration.

Bureaucracy can be seen as a self-maintaining social system. Whatever the ostensible services that a bureaucracy might have been set up to accomplish, they tend to become secondary to the interests of members in keeping the machinery running. The central concern of bureaucrats tends to be the maintenance of a stable environment with predictable behaviour from functionaries within the organization and from clients and customers outside it.

Ferguson's analysis, however, goes far beyond a description of the system. She takes up the challenge that social constructionism must necessarily examine the mechanisms through which the system is maintained. The primary function of bureaucracy is control, which is maintained in the face of continuing resistance and pressures toward nonconformity. Such maintenance requires the constant renewal of mechanisms that keep the structures intact. These mechanisms include isolating individuals, depersonalizing relations, and distorting communications. The constant appeal to efficiency conceals the control function that hierarchy performs within bureaucracies. Individuals are isolated in their fragmented and delimited roles. Their potential individual contribution is so limited that they are rendered expendable and therefore powerless. The absorption or co-optation of a few key individuals into management creates the illusion of upward mobility and hence promotes loyalty, while supervision, roles, and the hoarding of knowledge control the mass of people.

People interact with others only as role occupants. We come to see each other from the perspective of the organization and the roles we play in it rather than as whole persons. Likewise, in the wider society, people are commonly referred to as if they only existed in terms of standard bureaucratic categories. We come to think of "taxpayers" pitted against "workers" or "citizens" versus "welfare recipients." It is hard to keep sight of the reality that these are not distinct people but common dimensions of experience. The conception of people in terms of fragmented and competing roles tends to perpetuate our dependency on the very organizations that cause this fragmentation.

Bureaucratic language further depersonalizes people and reinforces this role fragmentation. The **language of technics** replaces the language of human action: dialogue, debate, and judgment are replaced by feedback, input, and output. Class conflicts are depersonalized when firing people is described as "reductions in force" or "downsizing" (Ferguson 1984, 15–16). Opposition is pacified by the ideological construction of rational administration as neutral, efficient, and effective. Interpretive theory seeks to deconstruct such bureaucratic language by exploring how such discourses produce their meanings.

The language of technics, for example, was pervasive in the Nazi bureaucratization of the solution to the "Jewish problem" (Berger 1993). Much effort was devoted to constructing a legal definition of the target population that was amenable to precise bureaucratic categorization, requiring precise reactions from functionaries.

The three practices of authorization, routinization, and dehumanization worked to minimize opposition. Authorization norms allow role occupants to avoid taking responsibility for the consequences of their actions. Routinization eliminates the need to make decisions, especially when moral questions arise. Dehumanization consti-

tutes victims as nonpersons reducible to statistical categories. Berger concludes that the "final solution" to the "Jewish problem" was socially constructed through bureaucratic processes that were in themselves quite ordinary or banal.

Resistance

Opposition may be silenced, muted, or distorted by the conceptions of administrative neutrality and efficiency but, in Foucault's view, it can never be totally destroyed. If people really could be reduced to their roles, to their organizational identities, then the mechanisms of bureaucratic control would no longer be necessary. The intensity of control is itself a measure of the pervasiveness of resistance. In practice, people are never reduced to total conformity. The exercise of power generates the very resistance to which it responds. Foucault argues that power relations presuppose resistance.

No matter how efficient bureaucracies may be in promoting conformity and passivity, uncertainties remain. Control is never total. People within the organization may ignore information they receive or distort information that they pass on, and so produce **intelligence failures**. People who direct the organizations fail to achieve intended results because they base their commands on inaccurate and incomplete information. The goals of individual members will never coincide completely with organizational goals. These discrepancies give rise to continual pressures toward resistance.

Bureaucratization is thus not an accomplished entity, but a process, a struggle between control and resistance. Mechanisms of control must be constantly reproduced to overcome the opposition that control itself generates. Yet at the same time, bureaucracies must disguise these efforts to deal with conflict in order to maintain the image of administrative neutrality and efficiency upon which their legitimacy and control depends (Ferguson 1984, 17–21). The result is more and more centralization, more standardization of rules and regulations, and ever-increasing ratios of supervisors or managers to actual workers. Ferguson estimated there was one supervisor for every three to four workers in the United States in 1984. By the mid-1990s this picture has changed dramatically as computerized monitoring has taken over the work of supervision. Electronic surveillance is many times more detailed and intrusive than human supervision could be.

Society as a whole can be conceptualized as a dense network of interlocking organizations that together form a **technical civilization** penetrating all aspects of social life. Each organization acts as a potential resource for other organizations in an overall collaborative network. Foucault (1980, 106) refers to this as a "closely linked grid of disciplinary coercions" that enforce inequality, normalcy, and control. Unions collaborate with corporations to control workers through contracts. Drug companies make deals with the federal government to change patent laws and with medical associations to promote their products. Clusters of organizations act as suppliers, subsidiaries, distributors, and research organizations for each other. Corporations, together with relevant state agencies, provide banking, legal, managerial, advertising, and public relations services for each other. They come together as loose, flexible, very stable networks of interlocking institutions, their minor conflicts contained within a climate of co-operation (Ferguson 1984, 38–42). Increasingly, all such organizations come to resemble each other and utilize shared knowledge of techniques of management. Prisons come to resemble factories, schools, barracks, and hospitals, which in turn come to resemble prisons (Foucault 1977, 229).

Normalization

Foucault emphasizes that this bureaucratic, technical civilization cannot be understood in such purely negative terms as repression or constraint. When we think of power in terms of sovereignty, or as imposed by elites from the top down, then we focus on laws, but disciplinary power is not imposed from above. It is exercised through ordinary, everyday activities, and it actually produces how we think of normal reality. It is characterized by **therapeutic intervention** in everything. Professionals who engage in such intervention justify it in terms of efficiency and technical expertise in the production of **normalized**, productive people. In Foucault's scheme, social work, police, and military become fused. Individual and collective life is controlled through the disciplines of the social sciences and related techniques of administrative law, policy analysis, social work, public administration, and rational planning.

The most intimate aspects of personal life and social relations are subject to the cult of rationality within this therapeutic civilization. Hochschild (1983, 171–77) refers to **emotional labour** in her description of how flight attendants are trained to manage feelings and facial and body expressions to produce the required response in the customer. The flight attendant learns the techniques of emotional management with the aid of instruction manuals. The goal is not genuine communication but eliciting appropriate responses from customers, which will raise profits for the airline.

Corporate executives pay up to $75 an hour to take courses from behavioural psychologists in how to use a well-modulated voice (*Globe and Mail*, 24 Dec. 1987, B1–2). "The goal is to develop a 'voice image' that conveys confidence, trust, warmth, and believability to improve the way others respond." The objective is to "help business clients talk their way to success," measured in terms of being persuasive enough to close deals. In Ferguson's terms, people learn to substitute technique for connectedness, to attach emotions to functions and not to any person. As soon as a new technique is available, experts apply it to whatever is at hand. Bureaucracy is the organized expression of this **managerial mentality**.

This **cult of rationality** in emotion management is never totally successful in reducing all emotions to the plastic responses required. The exercise of such techniques itself generates resistance and withdrawal. Hence, such control requires constant policing and constant repetition, reflected in such practices as annual retraining courses for flight attendants.

The Bureaucratic Construction of Class

Weber's analysis of class in capitalist society modified Marx's thesis by shifting the ground of class and class relations from the question of ownership of means of production to life chances within the marketplace. The move from market capitalism to corporate capitalism has changed the basis of class relations. Ownership of the means of production is no longer a central issue for the vast majority of people. Control over the means of production has become increasingly concentrated in fewer and fewer hands within giant corporate empires and holding companies. Careers within corporate bureaucracies are now the central determinant of class position of the majority of people, with career entry tightly tied to credentials. Location within the bureaucratic hierarchy and the conditions that determine who gets the positions are now the key factors in the social construction of class.

Ferguson identifies the layers produced by rigid and fractionalized job hierarchies within this organizational class system. Directors and executives make policy; the new working class of highly skilled, technical, managerial, and professional workers administer the implementation of these policies; the industrial and clerical working class with lower educational requirements have highly routinized, fragmented work; the bottom level of marginal workers have casual jobs within the secondary labour market. Casual workers are the people who move back and forth between the roles of workers and clients of unemployment and welfare agencies.

The class system within industrial societies has its origin within such corporate bureaucratic entities. The arrangement of jobs within bureaucracies is very deliberate and is justified in terms of efficiency but perpetuated by the need for control. In this respect at least, the lives of the mass of people in advanced capitalist societies may differ little from the experience of life within state socialist societies.

People who occupy different rungs of the bureaucratic class order have substantially different work situations when measured in terms of income, health and safety, trust, and freedom from close supervision. But they share the same system that de-individualizes them and objectifies their activities and relations (Ferguson 1984, 88). The power that bureaucracy exercises over people is so hard to see because that power becomes so totally part of the activities themselves. It is what people do. If power were always oppressive and negative, it would not be so powerful. It is accepted because it seems productive (Foucault 1980, 119).

Subordination within the bureaucratic hierarchy produces character traits displayed by subordinate, dependent, and powerless people, traits that Ferguson suggests closely resemble the stereotype of femininity. Subordinates must be constantly concerned with impression-management because

their well-being depends upon pleasing superiors. Conformity is central to their survival within bureaucracies and is produced by close surveillance. Their career mobility depends upon pleasing superiors and moulding one's behaviour to fit what superiors want. Career manuals warn aspiring junior managers not to make suggestions that challenge the organization's established ways of doing things. Successful innovations by those who fail to conform to expected bureaucratic patterns of behaviour will be resented rather than welcomed, as they threaten the established order.

The higher up the organizational hierarchy, the more important impression-management and conformity is. As Kanter (1977) has pointed out, social similarity becomes a critical measure of trustworthiness among managers where close surveillance is difficult. As a result, people from cultural backgrounds other than the norm, or people who look different, such as blacks and women, find it extremely hard to break into management ranks, no matter what their competence. They do not fit; they cannot be trusted to conform.

Resistance from within bureaucratic organizations is limited and individualistic. Union radicals and activists at all levels tend to attack individual abuses by particular superiors, or aim at particular policy reforms, rather than attacking the system as a whole. They leave the bureaucratic order intact (Ferguson 1984, 120).

Clients, who seek assistance from social service agencies, occupy the lowest rung on the organizational class structure. Often they are omitted from analyses of organizational hierarchies, and yet they are important in the larger class structure of which an organization is part. "There are growing numbers of organizations whose purpose is to process, regulate, license, certify, hide or otherwise control people," and clients are the prime targets (Ferguson 1984, 123). Customers, who purchase goods and services from bureaucracies, have relatively more independence of action than clients, but neither group has much influence over the organizations on which it depends. Professionals who work in advertising, marketing, and sales are concerned with controlling the behaviour and attitudes of customers, much as employees in welfare bureaucracies are concerned with controlling poor people. Ferguson (1984, 123) suggests that the ghettos of the urban poor are becoming increasingly like total institutions, subject to administrative controls that define, monitor, categorize, produce, and supervise the inhabitants' behaviour.

The poor, as clients of service bureaucracies, must learn to conform to the required image: they must learn to please, to present the appropriate responses, to give recognition to administrative authority, to flatter, and to legitimate the bureaucracy and its rules (Ferguson 1984, 144–46). Ferguson describes the immense strain that this places on poor people. They must learn to treat themselves as categories, to read clues, to control themselves, to anticipate demands, to calculate acceptable responses, and to offer them as signs of deservedness. Even to become clients they must first become cases and pass examinations to demonstrate their eligibility and deservedness. If successful, they are rewarded by becoming the obedient subjects of bureaucratic management. The traits of dependence and passivity help to perpetuate their situation by lowering their self-esteem and ability to assert themselves or to organize collectively. A very few individuals can challenge this by tactics of confrontation but, as Ferguson suggests, such strategies work only because they are rare. It is easier for the administration to give in to the few individual agitators than to fight them, but any organized resistance is likely to be short-lived and easily controlled. Welfare bureaucracies provide financial support to client organizations that then must conform to continue receiving support.

The roles available to clients are very limited, and even the ordinary activities of life tend to be redefined in managerial terms. Patients, for example, do not hold dances, they have "dance therapy": they do not play volleyball or cards, they have "recreation therapy" (Ferguson 1984, 137). The most intimate aspects of their personal lives are known to the bureaucracy, while they themselves are not seen as entitled to claim any special knowledge about their situation of poverty, crime, illness, or despair.

Neither Ferguson nor Foucault intend to attack the personal intentions or integrity of caseworkers within bureaucratic agencies. The cause of the problems does not lie in the attitudes, intentions, or personal lack of humanity of these caseworkers, but within the structure of the bureaucracy itself. Both clients and caseworkers are trapped within the same agency and the same fragmented roles. Caseworkers are institutionally constrained regardless of what they think of their clients.

Ferguson describes caseworkers with very different attitudes: some are advocates who care deeply about client rights, some are mediators, and some are narrowly bureaucratic. But these differences in attitudes do not translate into differences in behaviour (Ferguson 1984, 139–40). Their fragmented job responsibilities and the necessity of translating everything in terms of bureaucratic forms and paperwork homogenizes their behaviour. In the end, the differences in attitudes disappear as there is no room for their expression. Work becomes paperwork, with clients ultimately experienced as nuisances in the pressure to complete the forms and get the work done.

In Foucault's terms, power produces the subjectivities. What he means by this is that the very nature of bureaucratic activities produces the attitudes and behaviour of the people—both clients and caseworkers—that in turn perpetuate these bureaucratic activities.

The Bureaucratic Construction of Gender

Bureaucratic practices produce and reproduce **gender-class**, the situation of women in relation to men in society, as part of the social construction of class society. Ferguson (1984, 3–4) suggests that feminism and bureaucracy arose together in Western society. The shift from market to corporate capitalism and the rise of large-scale bureaucracies increased the need for supervision and record keeping, and created opportunities for middle-class women to move from work in the home to paid work in bureaucracies.

Kanter (1977, 3) describes corporations as "people producers." Huge multinationals virtually run the world economy and control most of the jobs. Within such corporations, women perform clerical services while men manage. Women are in organizations but practically never run them. Management theories frequently justify this practice with stereotypes of men as rational and therefore suited for decision-making positions. Conversely, women are viewed as emotional and thus better suited to work as people handlers in personnel departments and reception areas (Kanter 1977, 25).

In her study of women in the British Columbia civil service, Cassin (1979) explores some of the reasons why affirmative action programs to increase the number of female managers are unlikely to be successful. Men in junior roles in the organizational hierarchy tend to interact far more with male managers and so learn how to present themselves and how to discuss their work in terms of its management or policy implications. When they apply for promotion, they know how to present the right image, and they are well known to those who appoint them. Women, in contrast, tend to be outside this old boys' network. This separation is compounded when they have children and have to restrict their after-hours socializing and overtime work. Women are not taught how to present themselves, and they tend to describe their work in terms of professional and technical competence rather than policy implications. They thus generally sound less like managers in promotion interviews and have less experience and a more limited informal knowledge of organizational policies and practices than do men at junior levels.

Kanter describes at length the patriarchal and patrimonial structure of bureaucratic organizations. By **patrimony**, she means the process by which career ranks and other perks are passed down from male mentors in senior management to junior ranking males with whom they have a fatherly relationship. Management teams are constituted through what Kanter (1977, ch. 3) refers to as processes of virtual "homosexual reproduction" within the old boys' networks. The women who are the secretaries of such men are regarded and treated much as wives. Their primary role is to provide multiple personal services and total loyalty to the boss. They may be promoted along with him, but rarely if ever without him or over him.

The real wives of these male managers are also part of the corporate image, formally outside the organization, paid nothing, and discouraged from visiting the office, but with all aspects of their lives dictated by the corporate image required for their husbands to succeed. As Kanter (1977, 107) puts it, men symbolically bring two people to their jobs, while women are seen to bring less than one, because they are expected to maintain all home commitments.

Women managers are still generally excluded from the "old boys' network" that sustains a patrimonial system of promotion.

The very few women who are promoted up the organizational hierarchy function as tokens, their effectiveness undermined by their systematic exclusion from the old boys' networks that sustain men. They are talked about, passed over, and compared in multiple ways that weaken their effectiveness. Extensive literature on women in management gives advice on how women can function more like men in order to succeed. This literature blames failure on such weaknesses as emotionalism, fear of success, lack of experience of team sports, and inability to delegate responsibilities or to discipline subordinates effectively (Fenn 1980; Hennig and Jardim 1981; Larwood and Wood 1977). But, as Kanter points out, it is difficult to play on a team if other team members do not want you on it.

Contemporary studies of women in bureaucracies continue to focus largely on how to break this dual labour market through effective programs or training schemes that will facilitate the promotion of women into senior managerial positions in more than token numbers. A plethora of instruction books give advice to women on how to use and to copy male mentors to develop bureaucratic skills to get ahead. Ferguson rejects this approach as seriously misguided. What she fears most, as we will discuss further, is the co-optation of the women's movement into bureaucratic society. Bureaucracy is a means to human oppression and not to liberation. Ferguson hopes for more radical change than this.

The Deconstruction of Bureaucratic Discourse

There is a serious problem with the deeply depressing picture of bureaucratic society presented above. People appear as cogs in a machine, fractionalized elements within the iron cage. The worst of Weber's nightmare vision of bureaucracy and rationality appears to have come true. Weber himself, however, insisted that only people do things, and that their actions can only be fully understood in terms of the meanings that people themselves bring to what they do. Concepts like *bureaucracies* are abstractions that refer to groups of people who are collectively organized to do something. Bureaucracies as such do nothing. References to bureaucracy and bureaucratic structures may be seen as a way of accounting for what people are doing rather than literal descriptions of what is actually happening.

We have already seen discrepancies in analyses of bureaucratic organizations. Structural functionalists argue that bureaucratic modes of organizing people exist because they are efficient. Political economy theory challenges this by arguing that such organizational practices arose primarily to control people and may actually be very inefficient. Other research is beginning to debunk the argument that bureaucratic modes of organizing people work by deskilling people at the bottom of the hierarchy and concentrating knowledge and hence power at the top. Studies that have looked in depth at what people actually are doing at the bottom show otherwise.

In a study of advanced clerical workers, Reimer (1987) found discrepancies between job descriptions and performance. The job description of clerical workers within the organization chart defines their work as "routine delegated duties" involving limited educational skills or responsibilities. In practice, however, much of the work done by clerical staff requires independent thought, initiative, considerable skills, and comprehensive knowledge of the operations of the organization in which they work. Often, completed tasks are automatically attributed to the manager who delegated the task. The actual skills involved in the routine aspects of clerical work habitually go unnoticed to the extent that even the people doing the work tend to describe what they do in unskilled terms such as "filing" and "sorting." The same work of collecting information done by someone in a more senior rank would be called "researching."

Cassin's (1980) study of women workers in the British Columbia civil service makes similar observations. She points out that many of the clerical staff were actively engaged in managerial work but often without recognizing it themselves. The task of opening and sorting the mail, for example, may sound unskilled, but in practice it requires considerable knowledge and experience. The secretary has to know what must receive immediate attention and what can wait. If a letter contains an inquiry, the secretary needs to know where to find the information to provide the answer and must make it available for the boss. In effect, as secretaries sort mail, they are actually structuring their bosses' jobs, making key prioritizing decisions before the boss even gets involved. If they make mistakes, like putting on the back burner what should have received prompt attention, the ramifications could be serious.

Officially, these managerial skills are nonexistent because the job description does not mention them. Yet at an informal level, these hidden skills are acknowledged. This is revealed in the sometimes bitter observations of secretaries that they taught their boss everything he knows, only to see him promoted while they remain behind to run the office and train another neophyte.

Such practices may be little different when the boss is female. They are built into the very pattern of bureaucratic relations. Subordinates are required to take the role of their superior, to internalize it, and to apply it as a guide for their behaviour. One secretary describes how she continually covers up errors made by her incompetent boss, knowing that this supervisor would blame her for things that go wrong while taking all credit for things that go right (Ferguson 1984, 108).

The Documentary Construction of Reality

How does the actual lived experience of people get so distorted that they come to believe the distortions themselves? Smith (1974b) terms this the **documentary construction of reality**. It is a convenient fiction in job classification that one evaluates jobs and not people, the roles and not the role incumbents. Then anything that does not fit the organization chart—as when both worker and supervisor insist that a junior clerical worker is performing managerial work—can be put down to "person and performance," which is not evaluated because it is defined as not relevant.

What job classification workers do, then, is evaluate the organization chart itself. The reality of what people are actually doing does not enter the picture. So the fiction goes on. A few exceptions can be forced through, under various excuses, but the prevailing fiction, that official job descriptions represent what people do, remains unchallenged.

What can we learn from this? That injustices abound in the hierarchically ordered scale of prestige and differential pay? Yes, certainly. That sexism is rampant, in that it is frequently women whose acknowledged skills are appropriated by their male bosses? This is true as well, but there is more. From the perspective of interpretive theory, what is really important is that we begin to see that the notion of a structured hierarchy of skills and responsibilities itself is only a useful fiction that justifies and mystifies class and power. The organization chart provides an accounting procedure, not a description of what people actually do.

Yet it is precisely these organization charts, these official bureaucratic job descriptions, that provide the descriptive data base from which other people draw their analyses of class structure. Like coroners categorizing deaths (see chapter 2), job classifiers in bureaucracies label what they assume people do, or ought to be doing. They thus produce the labour-force statistics on the percentage of professional, managerial, paraprofessional, clerical, and semi- or unskilled workers. Statistics Canada records these convenient fictions in neat tables, which sociologists then use to produce their accounts of the occupational class structure of Canadian society. If the managerial work of people in nonmanagerial job categories actually gained recognition, along with the nonmanagerial work that some people in supposedly managerial job categories do, the actual class structure of Canadian society might look very different. The gender-class structure would certainly look vastly different. How different we do not know. Our knowledge of what people do comes to us so totally worked up by bureaucratic accounting procedures, guided by

the fiction of organization charts, that what is actually going on is almost impossible to know. We would have to start from scratch.

The issue of unrecognized work goes far beyond the challenge to formal organization charts. As we have seen in earlier chapters, we have good reasons for asking how much teaching housewives do, or how much nursing and social work they do, or how much diagnostic and doctoring work nurses do, how many articles or even doctoral theses are put together by spouses. If we question far enough, our taken-for-granted reality—that housewives do housework and managers manage—may come to seem entirely fictional. The work of exploring behind the social construction of reality has scarcely begun.

Bureaucratization as Social Construction

Foucault views power, not as a commodity or possession in the hands of the state or an elite class, but rather as a process that pervades all levels and all aspects of social life. Networks of disciplinary power are so pervasive as to be virtually synonymous with society itself (Smart 1983, 112). For Foucault, "the increasing organization of everything is the central issue of our time" (Dreyfus and Rabinow 1982, xxii).

To understand power in this sense, it becomes necessary to study the mechanisms, techniques, and procedures at the actual point of application. Rather than viewing power as descending from the top down, Foucault conceptualizes it as ascending from the most intimate personal events of life—the everyday methods of observation, recording, calculation, regulation, and training through which individuals are disciplined and normalized in society. The elites within the ruling class may use such mechanisms for their own purposes, but the mechanisms themselves do not originate within the bourgeoisie and neither do they disappear with the overthrow of the ruling elite. The **apparatus of ruling** remains to re-emerge intact after the political revolution (Smart 1983, 82–87).

The possibility of a **disciplinary society**, a form of power based not on punishment but on intimate knowledge and regulation of individuals, emerged with the development of the human sciences such as psychology and sociology. Rational-technical knowledge and administrative procedures merged in bureaucracies as a tremendously powerful mechanism to control people.

This form of power is potentially far more effective than repression or prohibition because it rouses less resistance, costs less, and is directly tied in with the actual services of educational, military, industrial, and medical organizations through which such power is exercised. To challenge it seems like challenging reason itself. Education, for example, is concerned with developing knowledge that can be used to control people. Students of education learn how to manage classrooms so that children conform to what is expected of them. Such power is legitimated in ways that brute force could never be. It appears as productive and positive: it produces well-behaved, conformist, normalized people who are productive members of society.

Bureaucratic Discourse: Language and Power

One last question remains. How do organizations come to exercise such power over us? They even have the power to create our sense of what is real, including our sense that the organizations themselves are factually real entities. There seems to be a circular process going on. The activities of people whom we refer to as officials in organizations help to create our taken-for-granted factual knowledge about our society, but it is also precisely our taken-for-granted belief in organizations that gives them the power to do so.

Control over the mind is much more powerful than control over the body. Once the way we think is controlled, to the point that we cannot think of any alternative to the present ways of doing things, then we control ourselves. Hence, when Foucault looks for the basis of power in society, he does not look at structures or institutions but rather at knowledge, at how people learn to think. When he refers to knowledge as power, and discourse as political activity, he is referring to how thought controls people.

Education is central to this process. Ferguson suggests that education has come to control and discipline students less through marks than through the definition of knowledge itself, which

is tightly tied to careers. In North American universities, a broad focus on liberal arts is losing ground to professional and technical training, such as social work, criminal justice, public and business administration, and so on. These are highly specialized training programs with little focus on the big picture and little critical content. The very activity of learning and the subject matter being absorbed moulds students into their future bureaucratic roles. Such knowledge, like the role itself, is fragmented and discontinuous. Narrowly specialized expertise with appropriate credentials provides a perfect justification for narrowly specialized and hierarchical bureaucratic roles. Ferguson (1984, 45) refers to this as the "lifeboat mentality." All that concerns students is obtaining credentials in order to find a secure organizational niche. Once they find such a niche, they will not need to be controlled from the outside. They will control themselves from the inside, their subjective consciousness meshing with the organizational definitions of their situation.

A broad focus on liberal arts is losing ground to professional and technical training, creating a "lifeboat mentality" that supports bureaucratic organization.

Foucault connects the two meanings of **discipline**: orderly conduct and a branch of knowledge. From this point of view, social science theories that analyse bureaucratic organizations as efficient and rational systems are political ideologies. In other words, they are part of the domination. When we believe these theories we act accordingly. The discipline of public administration, for example, assumes from the start that organizations are concrete entities, that they are efficient and rational, and that people can be regarded as role incumbents and managed to maximize efficiency. These theories reproduce the viewpoint of managers and give it scientific credibility. At the same time, they reflect how deeply this managerial mentality is rooted in how we think. Structural Marxist theory helps only a little. It draws attention to conflicting class interests in organizations, but we still end up thinking that organizations are efficient, rational systems for capitalists to make profits, and that people are role incumbents.

Interpretive theory tries to argue that organizations do not exist as entities at all. They exist only in thought as ways of accounting for what people are doing. People are not role incumbents except insofar as they learn to think about themselves in such terms. But language is enormously powerful. As soon as you read the word *organization*, you are likely to start thinking about some entity because that is what the word means to us. I might try to talk about "organizational ways of acting," but you will likely translate this straight back into the familiar words *organization* or *bureaucracy* and wonder why I cannot write plain English instead of jargonese.

It is only a very short step from learning to think in terms of organization language to being controlled by it. Smith (1979a) describes this way of talking as "using the oppressor's language." Think about the situation, described in chapter 2 (see p. 39), where a union organization's explanation for why women do not come to meetings is female apathy. In terms of the union's language, a union is a democratic organization set up for the benefit of its members. It is based on voluntary attendance. When we start with this definition, the notion of apathy seems an acceptable explanation for members not bothering to turn up. But when we stop thinking in terms of the organization's language, and start looking at what people are actually doing, the concept of

apathy disappears. We see that meetings are organized at times and in places that make it very hard for women to attend. Women are responsible for caring for children, for getting dinner, and for doing housework after work. This fact actually frees men to go to union meetings. We also begin to see that when women do attend meetings, they are shouted down and ignored and their concerns are not treated as very important. What we see is something that looks much more like patriarchy than apathy, but the language of democratic union organization cannot express this.

It is not organizations as such that control us, but language, knowledge, and the discipline of social science itself. For Foucault it is a closed circle. Language creates our experience; our experience creates the language in which we come to talk about that experience; how we come to talk about it structures our experience, and so on (Ferguson 1984, xiii). The prevailing forms of power and knowledge create the subjective self-consciousness of individuals themselves, including the professionals who create the power and knowledge. There seems to be no way out of this **bureaucratic discourse**.

Bureaucracies and the Social Construction of Knowledge

Interpretive theory explores how our ways of thinking about everyday reality are put together, and particularly how the work of people within complex organizations structures what we come to think of as factual knowledge. Zimmerman's (1974) work is a classic study of what people in one organization do to produce facts, and how what they produce becomes factual knowledge for people in other organizations. Zimmerman studied workers in an unemployment insurance agency who have to determine whether certain individuals are or are not eligible for benefits. An important criterion is that the potential recipient must have actually looked for work during the previous month. But how can this be established? The applicant's word is not trustworthy, nor is the word of family members or friends. The one kind of evidence that insurance workers took as uncontrovertible fact was a piece of paper supplied by another formal organization stating that so-and-so applied for such-and-such a post.

While they challenged every personal source of proof, they refused even to consider the possibility that the informant from the other organization might make up the document or statement as a personal favour. The fiction of impersonal role incumbents could not be challenged without the entire fiction of a factual reality coming apart.

Once someone in an organization has declared a person eligible for services like unemployment insurance, that becomes fact for anyone else in any other organization where such information might be relevant. The same goes for proof of birth date. It must be supplied by a piece of paper from a formal organization. People who need any kind of government service soon learn that they must carry such pieces of paper around to every appointment. As Zimmerman puts it, pieces of paper produced by people in organizations become "fact for all practical purposes" for people in other organizations. Statements made by people are suspect, but statements made by impersonal role incumbents are treated as impersonal, unbiased facts.

Tuchman carries this exploration further in her study *Making News* (1978), where she shows that anything said by officials is treated as factual for the practical purposes of newspaper reporters. Information from such sources is reproduced as straight facts while anything said by people who are not officials is presented as conjectures that may or may not be true. It is very difficult for readers to penetrate to the source of these "fac-

tual" statements because they are not presented in a way that encourages questioning.

Smith (1979a) has analysed how different accounts of a street riot appear when given by the police rather than by the people in the street. The accounts of bystanders tend to be written in very personal and local ways: "I was standing here and saw and heard this and I thought that. . . ." The account attributed to the police, however, tends to be quite different. The distinct observations and thoughts or conclusions of different individuals in different places, who happened to be working as police, all get merged into one official police account, which is impersonal, abstract, and not tied to any one person's observations or location. Again, what people say is just personal opinion, whereas what role incumbents say is fact.

Feminist Discourse and the Possibility of Resistance

For Foucault, the circle of social control through language and experience is never complete. People can never be totally reduced to the sum of their roles. Hence there is always resistance. The exercise of power generates its own resistance. But this resistance is muted and partial. It tends to be expressed by powerless people who live on the periphery of the bureaucratic order. Foucault himself focussed upon the criminal and the insane, the misfits for whom clinics and prisons are invented. These are the people most able to see the gap between their experience and how it is described by officials. But their protest is subdued. It lacks legitimacy; it is not sanctioned. We tend not to consider such people worth listening to.

Ferguson, however, suggests there is another voice of protest and resistance that is less easily dismissed: the voice of feminism. She argues that the different voice of women has the potential to break this closed circle of experience and discourse because women are marginal to these bureaucratic structures and yet at the same time are educated, resourceful, and increasingly visible.

Women have the potential to provide a radical alternative because the traditional standpoint of women has been outside bureaucratic organizations. Women have been more centrally con-

"Those were the facts, reported objectively. We now return you to your own irrational prejudices."

cerned with reproduction and with nurturing children, which provides them with a radically different experience of human relations. Women, as caregivers, nurturers, and providers for the needs of others, are necessarily oriented toward co-operative and nonhierarchical relations. Bureaucratic organizations of hierarchically ordered, narrowly specified roles and responsibilities are anathema to women's primary experience of life as mothers, daughters, and wives. Boys, suggests Ferguson (1984, 160) learn to separate themselves from mothering to identify with the more aloof, separate, and specialized roles of fathers as breadwinners, while daughters never fully make this separation.

As women are emerging from the private life of the home to join public life as employees in ever-increasing numbers, they bring with them the potential for a radically alternative view of collective organization more in keeping with their experience. Ferguson and others (i.e., Gilligan 1982) suggest that radical feminist discourse focusses upon nurturing, concern, and connectedness with others. It incorporates a different definition of rationality in which emotion is viewed as something that people do. Emotion is not the opposite of reason. It is central to reason itself as a way of experiencing the world. An emotionless person is fundamentally irrational. Emotion is a potential avenue to "the reasonable view" (Ferguson 1984, 200). Feminism also calls for a restructuring of the relations between private and public life so that they cease to be defined as opposites and can be integrated. However, this is unlikely to happen without radically changing the character of family or workplace or both. As Parsons' work implies, family-oriented values cannot enter the workplace without changing the bureaucratic model of neutral, universalistic, and specific pattern variables appropriate for fragmented, hierarchical roles.

Ferguson points to an alternative mode of organization in such feminist projects as bookstores, health collectives, newsletters, shelters, crisis centres, and the like, which are able to minimize ties with bureaucratic organizations. There are occasional glimpses of what might be possible as professional women in law and medicine pool their practices and organize flexible working hours and client-sharing in order to integrate work and family care. Feminist projects, in principle, are committed to internally decentralized and antibureaucratic organization; they rely

on personal, face-to-face relations rather than formal rules; and they encourage egalitarian rather than hierarchical relations. They see skills and information as resources to be shared rather than hoarded (Ferguson 1984, 189–90). Should such modes of organization seem fanciful or inefficient, we should remember that bureaucracies have also been shown to be very inefficient, especially in contexts that require innovation. Bureaucratic structures are oriented more to control and exploitation of a reluctant work force than to efficiency in achieving other goals.

Professional women bring alternative, antibureaucratic concepts to the workplace.

An example of feminist principles of organization in action is the Icelandic Woman's Alliance or Kvennalistinn. The alliance took shape in the early 1980s as the conviction grew among Icelandic women that it would take a women's party to get women's issues to the centre of the political agenda. The party won enough seats in the April 1987 elections to hold the balance of power in Iceland's parliament. The party's organizational structure is explicitly in accord with feminist principles described above. There is no formal leader. Leadership functions are rotated among members. An active mentorship policy ensures that large numbers of women are trained to act as representatives for the party in meetings and campaign debates. No office holder may serve longer than six to eight years. The Alliance operates by consensus, not by majority vote. Members have to work at issues together until some compromise can be found to include all of them. This ensures that individuals cannot dominate or control issues within the party. The party actually refused to join a ruling coalition in 1987 when it became clear that it would have been forced to abandon key principles and so weaken its position as an alternative voice.

Socialist Feminism

Measured against such alternative visions, the discourse of the radical left often fails. The goal of socialist revolution, when defined in economic class terms, only promises to repeat the problems in a different form. Smith and Malnarich (1983) hint at the limitations of traditional Marxist thought when they ask, Where are the women in socialist and communist political organizations? Unions have historically regarded women as competitors rather than partners. In contemporary leftist organizations, women comprise about half the membership but are excluded from almost all leadership positions. They are not included in theoretical work. They are absent from political education and propaganda structures and from journal and newspaper editorial boards, and they are rarely involved in political analysis.

Why is this so? Smith and Malnarich reject the organization language that offers apathy as the explanation. They point to the triple workload of women militants. Like men in the movement, women often combine wagework with political work, but they also do housework: the caring and nurturing work; the production and reproduction of people; the financial, material, and emotional maintenance of the family. Smith and Malnarich suggest that militant men are mostly too busy to help out at home, and they almost never share responsibilities fully. Smith and Malnarich root the problem in socialist ideology itself, which defines family and personal life as a private, non-political matter and ignores the interconnection between production and reproduction. In effect, socialists are reproducing capitalist relations in their own organization. They define the working

class as those who sell their labour, thus excluding women and children and perpetuating the fragmentation within the working class itself.

The implication of this study is that traditional Marxism needs to merge with feminism before it can hope to offer an alternative that will not turn out to be more of the same with new masters. This, of course, raises the question of the type of feminism with which Marxism should be aligned.

Liberal Feminism: The Risk of Co-optation

In Ferguson's view, the central threat to feminism is the risk of co-optation. She suggests that earlier waves of feminism were defused by the expanding bureaucratic society. The first wave radically challenged the **cult of domesticity**, which rationalized the exclusion of women from the public world. Women argued that their domestic skills and experience provided ideal training for careers in politics, teaching, social services, and other spheres of life. This radicalism, however, became muted into **liberalism** and **consumerism**. The collective movement among women was abandoned in favour of defining female independence in terms of personal fulfilment (Ferguson 1984, 49–51, 179–82). Meanwhile, the demands placed on private life to satisfy all human needs steadily increased as public, bureaucratized life became more emotionally barren.

The second wave of feminism pressured for equality in terms of legal rights. Ferguson suggests that late capitalism's answer to this challenge has been more bureaucracy and the cult of rationality. Feminism raises a radical critique against bureaucracy as an inhuman form of organization, but this critique risks being reduced to a concern with eliminating barriers to women's equal representation in executive positions. This focus on individualism and equality rights for women is important in changing the predominantly male character of bureaucracies, but it promises little real change in the structures that create oppression. The problem is how to be heard in a bureaucratic society when bureaucracy itself appears as the problem.

Ferguson challenges the legal equality approach to feminism on two counts. First, she rejects the belief in individual upward mobility as "the illusion of the epoch" (Ferguson 1984, 183–92). The message of all the how-to books for women is fundamentally the same: conformity. Women are taught to see their careers in totally bureaucratic images, that is, in terms of hierarchy and fast-track mobility rather than in terms of the intrinsic meaning or value of actions. People are seen as competitors for scarce resources, and co-operation is defined in largely instrumental terms. The price of individual mobility is thus absolute capitulation to the bureaucratic system, with no prospect for change.

The second illusion for Ferguson is the focus on abstract legal rights. On the one hand, this is essential to guarantee access of women to institutions and to legal protection. But on the other hand, it can lead to acceptance of the bureaucratic game. Women are absorbed into the structures rather than fighting against them. The gender-class job ghettos may begin to crack, but the bureaucratic class hierarchy itself remains largely intact. Feminist critiques can slip into concerns for integration on equal terms with men in a system that fundamentally "hurts, twists, and damages people and human possibilities" (Ferguson 1984, xii).

There are signs of this in Canada as women's issues become translated in terms of career equality with men and bureaucratized, institutionalized child care by experts. In 1987 when the federal government announced small increases in financial support for day-care, a strong feminist voice argued that this money should be channelled into training day-care workers and setting up accredited centres. Beneath this important concern for standards and for places is the unspoken assumption that quality care can and should be measured in terms of formal credentials and government-licensed institutions. The natural expertise of mothers who have raised their own children and who earn money by caring for the children of others is discounted in favour of institutionalized credentials. The people who will teach the new credentials come from the disciplines—early childhood education, child psychology, social work—that were so feared by Foucault and Ferguson. The real need for child care might be translated into total bureaucratic control, with children required to be placed in day-care from very early ages, as they are now required to attend school, unless their parents are trained child-care specialists. There is the risk that careers for women and bureaucratized day-care for children will silence the last bastion of authentic alternative discourse in this world where "the increasing organization of everything is the central issue of our time" (Foucault in Dreyfus and Rabinow 1982, xxii).

This bureaucratic interference in the lives of people now has the potential to precede birth. In 1993, a Royal Commission in Canada examined the implications of issues involved in new reproductive technologies. Scientists now have the technology to screen "test tube baby" embryos genetically before they are implanted in their mothers' wombs. Those whose genes indicate that they will develop inherited abnormalities, such as hemophilia, are discarded. One doctor involved in the development of this technology argues that, in the future, couples who choose not to avail themselves of this screening procedure, and who give birth to disabled children, should be held criminally negligent (Pappert 1989).

Some critics suggest that resistance to the bureaucratic co-optation of feminism itself implies a return to the cult of domesticity and women being limited to the private sphere. It is clear, however, that neither of these options is acceptable. What we need is a more fundamental re-integration of private and public spheres so as to obliterate the artificial barriers between family and productive work, between women and men, between childhood and adulthood. The objective is not to bureaucratize families so as to minimize their interference with traditional careers, but to humanize other spheres of life.

Much of the work to date in women's studies has focussed on making visible women's domestic work. Smith (1987b) urges us to look beyond this traditional focus to recognize that what women are doing is far, far more important than mere domestic work. In this deeply fragmented, irrational culture, what women are doing is nothing less than holding the entire system together.

Men's Liberation

There remains one more potential voice of radical resistance to our bureaucratized world: the voice of **men's liberation**. It is a voice as yet far more deeply subjugated than feminism. In a world so obviously patriarchal, with men in general so obviously occupying superior positions over women in all spheres of life, it is hard even to conceive that men might need liberation. Many men fail to see what else they could want, except perhaps to have their cake and eat it; that is, to retain their dominance within all formal institutions while having richer private lives as well. But the need for men's liberation cannot be so easily dismissed.

The evidence of wife battering and child abuse and the mounting complaints by women that men typically fail to take any responsibility for emotional relationships, plus the evidence of increasing violence on the streets, can be viewed in two not incompatible ways. Women can be seen as victims of patriarchal power, vented increasingly against those women who do not follow traditional roles. Alternatively, such trends can be seen as evidence of the overwhelmingly destructive nature of the bureaucratized world in which most men make their lives. They indicate how severely men are being hurt, twisted, blunted, and dehumanized.

Men's liberation seeks to redefine what it means to be male and to challenge the separation of men from those aspects of life that involve nurturing, caregiving, and reproduction of life itself. It strives for a radical change of structures that now reward competition, aggression, manipulation, and mastery over the material world, and the absence of emotion, at the expense of what it means to be human.

From this perspective, radical feminism and men's liberation have the same goal: the radical demolition of the bureaucratized, hierarchical, specialized, rule-bound, conformist society. Weber's formal rationality has become what he feared it would: an emotional wasteland, an iron cage. The radical critique reveals the fundamental irrationality of Western civilization. This critique demands the unity of cultural, emotional, and spiritual elements of purposive action and rejects their segregation into private and public, or feminine and masculine, spheres of life. A social order based on fragmentation does not and cannot provide a meaningful life for the majority of people.

Conclusion

Weber's vision of bureaucracy as an iron cage that imprisons people remains centrally relevant to contemporary industrial society, both communist and capitalist. Bureaucratic organization seems so pervasive that trying to avoid its influence would be tantamount to withdrawing from society itself. Sociological analysis is still far from grasping the full complexity of the processes involved in such organization.

Bureaucratic society has not emerged entirely as Weber conceptualized. Functionalist theory is based on Weber's ideal-type model of bureaucracy as a system of regulations that ensures the efficient co-ordination of specialized activities for given ends. This model has been discredited by evidence that the rigid formal structures associated with bureaucracy undermine co-operation and stifle initiative and innovation. Yet functionalist analysis cannot be easily dismissed. It may be the most popular perspective in sociology precisely because it comes closest to expressing how people feel about themselves in bureaucratic society. The functionalist model of society, which sees individual role incumbents as socialized to conform to expected norms of behaviour, articulates for people their everyday experience of fragmented and ordered lives that bureaucratic processes generate.

The Marxist structuralist tradition places capitalist relations of production at the centre of analysis. The most important contribution of this perspective has been to demonstrate that bureaucratic modes of organization have more to do with capitalist control over a reluctant work force than with efficiency of performance. This strength, however, may also be its limitation. The focus on capitalism has been criticized as too rigid to explore the complexity of bureaucratic power relations that do not stem from ownership of the means of production in the classic sense.

Emerging forms of analysis in the interpretive tradition push this criticism still further. Relations of power and control remain central to the analysis of bureaucratic society, but they are conceptualized in a radically different way from that of Marxist theory. Power is seen as flowing not from the elite down, but from the bottom up. Power is realized in the everyday activities of people at work, in the details of how records are kept and forms are filled in, in how language is structured, and in the forms of talk through which we make sense of what people do. Interpretive theory challenges the myth of the machine, the external bureaucratic structure that engulfs people. Yet at the same time, the theory manifests the awesome power of language and bureaucratic thought, through which rationality itself becomes a trap.

The social sciences form part of the relations of power to the extent that their theories legitimate and perpetuate forms of language and thought that trap people. Theories provide accounts of what people do in terms of external structures that are rational and efficient or powerful and inevitable. To challenge such accounts seems to challenge reason. The possibility of resistance lies in new forms of discourse and rad-ically different conceptions of power and human potential. Contemporary sociology is perhaps both part of the problem and part of the solution. It contributes to the iron cage of bureaucratic rationality. At the same time, if offers the capacity to analyse and to question and thus the possibility of resistance and change.

Suggested Reading

A dated but very straightforward statement of the functionalist view of bureaucracy is the article by Talcott Parsons, "Suggestions for a Sociological Approach to the Theory of Organizations" (1956). Parsons presents a short, clear model of how such organizations should work.

An old but brief and clear critique of Weber's model of bureaucracy from the perspective of structuralist Marxism is by Alvin Gouldner, "On Weber's Analysis of Bureaucratic Rules" (1952). Gouldner shows how the meticulous statement of regulations and duties that characterize the ideal-type bureaucracy applies only to the obligations that workers owe to an organization. The rules specifying the duties and responsibilities of the organization toward the worker are rarely spelled out so clearly. Unions had to fight for these in separate contracts.

Stephen Marglin's article, "What Bosses Do" (1974–75), argues that the rise of factories, where workers were brought together under the supervision of a boss, long preceded the invention of heavy machinery that made collective factory work necessary. He argues that the purpose of factories was to control workers, not to make efficient use of new technology.

The book by Kathy Ferguson, *The Feminist Case Against Bureaucracy* (1984), is an excellent feminist study of Foucault's view of bureaucratic society. This book is very heavy reading and not easy to understand. It is perhaps best used as a reference work for additional information on certain sections of her analysis that are referred to in this chapter.

A more readable and entertaining look at life within a bureaucracy is Rosabeth Moss Kanter's *Men and Women of the Corporation* (1977). Kanter delights in showing up the status games that go on in relations between male bosses and their female secretaries and among male managers vying for prestigious office space. Kanter also provides a very perceptive view of how bureaucracy carries over into the private family lives of employees.

For a view of how bureaucracies help to create what passes as knowledge, see Gail Tuchman, *Making News: A Study of the Social Construction of Reality* (1978). Tuchman describes how reporters rely very heavily upon official spokespersons from bureaucracies to provide much of what they report as factual information.

Questions

1. How does Blau's study of a state employment agency suggest that precise measures of job performance can inhibit efficiency?

2. What practices are involved in *goal displacement* in organizations?

3. How does the Marxist historian, Marglin, challenge the notion that factories were organized to utilize the technology of steam engines?

4. What does the Marxist Gouldner see as the true function of bureaucratic rules and regulations within capitalist organizations?

5. Why does Michels claim that election to formal office is insufficient to undermine *the iron law of oligarchy* in political parties?

6. What is Foucault referring to with the notion of *technical civilization*?

7. How is bureaucracy implicated in the social construction of gender differences?

8. How are organization charts implicated in analysis of the class structure of a society?

9. What are the two meanings that Foucault associates with the term *discipline* and how does he link them in his study of power relations?

10. In Ferguson's view, how might women be in a privileged position to see beyond the apparent rationality of bureaucratic organization?

Traditional Theory Under Attack

Talcott Parsons and Functionalist Theory

Functionalist theory, particularly as elaborated by Talcott Parsons (1902–1979), was generally accepted in North America as the orthodox approach to the study of society during the 1950s and 1960s and was claimed by some to be virtually equivalent to sociology as a whole. It remains the mainstream theoretical approach in the United States. The study of society as a functioning system, comprising interdependent institutions that each perform specialized functions for the social whole, still dominates the format of most introductory texts in sociology. Only in the last decade or so has more critical political economy theory begun to achieve equivalent stature in Canada.

The core ideas of functionalism are contained in the analogy that Herbert Spencer drew between social systems and biological organisms. Biological organisms are first and foremost bounded systems; that is, they are distinct entities or bodies that maintain themselves in a state of relative equilibrium or balance. They have built-in self-regulating mechanisms that keep the body in a relatively stable state, continually compensating for environmental changes. The human body, for example, maintains the same basic temperature and has a very narrow range of tolerance for fluctuations in this temperature. If too hot, we automatically begin to sweat, and the resulting evaporation cools us. If too cold, we begin to shiver, our body hair becomes more erect, and body temperature rises. Similarly, a complex enzyme system triggered by insulin keeps the blood sugar level in balance, continually compensating for extra sugar absorbed from food and sugar used up in exercise. Biological sciences explore these balancing mechanisms while medical sciences seek to intervene during extreme situations of illness or injury when the natural equilibrium breaks down.

In order to maintain themselves in a state of equilibrium or health, organisms have basic needs that must be met. We all know that green plants need some minimal access to light, water, and water-soluble minerals in order to survive. The human body, at a minimum, needs food, water,

Talcott Parsons (1902–1979).

shelter, and a tolerable temperature range for survival. A host of higher-order needs must be met for our bodies to function at full capacity. All organisms are made up of specialized parts that have specific functions for the body as a whole. If any one part is missing or malfunctioning, it has repercussions for the rest. A central concern of biological sciences is to explore these specialized functions and how the various parts work together. Bodies can be conceptualized as made up of numerous subsystems, such as the digestive system, the nervous system, the blood circulatory system, and so on, which are themselves comprised of multiple subparts. All must work together in co-ordinated ways for the organism to function in a healthy way. Most of us are not conscious of these subsystems working, except when something abnormal happens. Then we turn to the medical and biological sciences for explanations.

The Analogy Between Biological and Social Systems

Functionalism as a social science seeks to analyse societies in ways analogous to the biological study of organisms. The society itself is conceptualized as a bounded, self-maintaining system, comprising numerous specialized parts that must function together in co-ordinated ways. These multiple parts and subparts of societies, such as families, religion, education, and political and economic structures, are analysed in terms of their functions or contributions to the operation of the whole system. Each of these parts can in turn be analysed as a system, with system prerequisites and regulating mechanisms.

Certain operating assumptions in the biological sciences have also been taken over in functional analysis in sociology. The first basic assumption is that organisms are best analysed as **functional unities** rather than as disconnected bits. While it may be very valuable for individual researchers to focus on specialized parts, it is important never to lose sight of the fact that these parts operate only within the environment of the body as a whole.

A second working assumption is **universal functionalism**. Any characteristic of an organism is assumed to have some necessary function that it performs for the body as a whole. Scientists may not yet know what the function of a particular tiny element of a cell or an enzyme might be, but that quest itself becomes a meaningful focus for future research.

The third working assumption, which is closely related to the second, is **functional indispensability**. Each and every element of an organism is assumed to have its own unique and specialized function that the organism would miss if that part were absent or damaged. The argument goes that if organisms did have vestigial or accidental parts that served no useful function, such parts would in all likelihood atrophy and disappear over time. The persistence of certain characteristics is itself an important indication that they serve some useful function.

In functionalist theory in sociology, these same basic assumptions of functional unity, universal functionalism, and functional indispensability guide research questions. A society is analysed as essentially a social system that cannot be reduced to fragmented groups of people. In this sense, the whole is greater than the sum of the parts. Recurrent characteristics of societies are assumed to perform necessary functions, and an adequate explanation for their persistence consists of discovering and explicating what these functions are. They may be obvious or *manifest functions*, which are widely acknowledged by society's members, or *latent functions*, which may not be consciously recognized by many people but which nonetheless meet important social needs. For functionalists, the value of sociological research lies in disclosing these latent functions, hence increasing our understanding of why certain elements of our society have the characteristics they do.

Durkheim and Erikson's analyses of the latent function of crime in the maintenance of group boundaries and distinctive identities, described in chapter 7, are good examples of the functionalist approach. Coser's (1956) insightful analysis of the social functions of conflict is another example. He shows that, like pain in an organism, conflict gives advance warning of strains within the social system and encourages adaptations or innovations that reduce the conflict and so increase levels of comfort and well-being in society. Two-party or multiparty political systems are especially functional for airing conflicts early and dealing with them in constructive and integrative ways rather than allowing them to build up to an explosive point. The universal characteristic of stratification in societies has also drawn particular attention from functionalist theorists. Their basic explanation is that some system of inequality of rewards meets the essential function of motivating the more able and committed people in a society to strive for the more difficult and socially important jobs. In each of these examples, functional analysis shifts the focus of inquiry from the origins of certain patterns in society to why they persist. The operating assumption for research is that social structures continue because they serve some immediate useful purpose for the society.

The term *useful* itself deserves further consideration since it raises the question, useful for what? Functionalist theorists answer this question essentially the same way biologists do. Different features of society are functional when they help in some way, either manifest or latent, to maintain a stable and integrated social whole, that is, to maintain the state of dynamic equilibrium.

Functionalism promised to provide a truly scientific approach to the study of society. It enabled sociology in a sense to come of age and to join the other natural sciences such as biology, adopting analogous research strategies in the study of social systems. Sociology promised in principle to achieve a unification of all the sciences. The practical value of sociology is that it promised to provide the basic research knowledge required for promoting a harmonious and integrated social order. In a world torn apart by wars and facing the upheavals of the scientific-technological revolution of the twentieth century, such a science was urgently sought and readily accepted.

Parsons' Model of a Social System

Variants of the functionalist approach had long proven their usefulness in anthropology for the study of small, relatively isolated tribal societies. But it was Talcott Parsons who unquestionably deserves credit for systematizing and elaborating functionalism for application to advanced industrial societies. Parsons is credited, more than any other social theorist, with developing the scientific credibility of sociology. Through his efforts, sociologists began to play an advisory role to governments (Buxton 1985, ch. 7).

Early in his career, Parsons undertook the intellectually enormous task of trying to synthesize major theories of society into a comprehensive framework around the notion of a system of social action. In his book *The Structure of Social Action* ([1937] 1968), he insisted that such a unifying system had to begin with a **voluntaristic theory** of action. People in society are not like cells in a body, preprogrammed to behave in fixed ways. People make free choices. With rare exceptions, people feel that they do what they do voluntarily, and yet the outcome of these individual actions and choices is a stable social system. How is this possible?

In his second major study, *The Social System* (1951), Parsons formulated a basic model of society, its major parts, and how they are integrated in patterned ways. The model begins with individual actors as the basic building blocks. The critical problem that Parsons grapples with is order. How is order possible in a social system made up of individuals who are capable of making free choices? How can choices be, at the same time, free and yet predictable in an orderly way? The answer, for Parsons, lies in Durkheim's conception of the *conscience collective*: order is produced by moral or normative consensus. Parsons himself criticizes Durkheim for downplaying the central importance or normative consensus in industrial society and for failing to explain the basis of compliance to norms, except through fear of sanctions.

For Parsons, the basis of compliance, and hence the key to the problem of how order is sustained, lies in the internalization of norms. Actors co-operate because they internalize proper courses of action as well as the related values that make them feel shame or loss of self-respect if they fail to live up to these moral values. Knowledge that others share these values and will also react negatively to noncompliance further confirms people in their desire to conform (Heritage 1984, ch. 2). From this perspective, norms are internalized as **need dispositions**. This means that people tend to want to act in conformity with norms and feel dissatisfied if they cannot do so. Norms can be treated as causes of action. Individual actors make choices in the context of particular situations with given means, with ends in view, and with underlying values. These voluntary choices take the form of patterned and predictable behaviour because of the internalization of shared norms at the fundamental level of individual personalities. Ostensibly subjective individual choices become amenable to objective or external scientific analysis in terms of the patterns of values that constrain and determine conduct.

Values can be said to be institutionalized as part of the normative order of society when they are widely internalized. They are institutionalized when the vast majority of society's members choose to conform, feel guilt or shame if they do not conform, expect such conformity of each other, and react negatively with criticisms or punishment when these expectations are not met. We discussed this process, which Berger (1963, 68–78) refers to as "circles of social control," in chapter 2 (see figure 2-1). The innermost circle of control is the internalized desire to conform and internalized guilt, bolstered by approval or disapproval of our friends and close associates. Eventually, economic sanctions come into play as we risk not being hired, losing our jobs, or losing out on benefits when others disapprove of us. Force comes into play only as a last resort.

Roles and the Social System

Shared values alone are insufficient to produce a stable social system of functionally interrelated parts. More detailed sets of behavioural prescriptions are required. These give precise directions for how to behave in different situations and are provided by the **institutionalization** of typical roles. In the Parsonian model, society comprises a system of roles. Roles are typical ways of behaving in predefined situations and exist independently of any individual in a particular situation. We learn how to behave in such roles, which are predefined for us in varying degrees of detail.

Parsons' voluntaristic theory of action begins with the study of actors and behaviour in typical situations, rather than with the study of total individuals. The social context sets the actor's role.

As we saw in chapter 2, the process by which we learn the behavioural expectations of different roles and the underlying values that motivate conformity to them is termed *socialization*. Socialization is a lifelong process in which we learn by modelling ourselves on others. As children, we learn first by watching our parents as role models. We later expand our horizons to others whom we want to emulate. As with core societal values, we come to internalize these behavioural expectations and to want to conform to them as part of a basic need to belong and to be approved of. As adults we learn a great variety of different roles, but the process is essentially the same. What society expects of us we come to expect of ourselves. In a sense we become our roles; they become part of us and how we identify ourselves. Hence we feel a sense of duty to fulfil our roles and pangs of guilt if we fail to live up to them.

Individuals perform a series of roles over a lifetime. They also perform a number of distinct and partially connected roles at any one time. Imagine, for a moment, that you are a parent, a classroom teacher, a town councillor, the director of a fund-raising committee, and a member of a local homeowners' association. In some situations, you may find yourself wearing several hats at once. This might occur if there happens to be a petition from the homeowners' association to the town council about where to locate a proposed school playing field for which you are a fundraiser. All of these roles have to be integrated. According to Parsons, the personality comprises the system that integrates the various roles that one person plays.

Role Theory

A branch of functional analysis loosely referred to as **role theory** (Biddle and Thomas 1966) concerns itself with our interactive behaviour. The study of **role sets** analyses overlapping roles and reciprocal expectations for behaviour in specific situations. The terminology here can be confusing. Sometimes the role set consists of the variety of roles played by one person. More commonly, role sets refer to the variety of roles played by different people that interact or impinge upon each other in a given situation. In either case, the theoretical issues raised are similar.

Different roles are associated with different behavioural expectations that may not always be compatible. A familiar example is that of a school. Overlapping roles include those of students, teachers, parents, head teachers and other administrators, school boards, and support staff such as secretaries, cooks, and caretakers. Sometimes one person may play several of these roles at once, as in the case of a school secretary who is also the parent of a student at the school, or a teacher who may also be a parent and a member of the school board. More commonly, these roles will be played by different people. Each of these positions comprises a set of typical behaviour expectations, and the incumbents of each role have expectations concerning each of the overlapping roles. **Role strain** occurs when incumbents of related roles have differing sets of expectations. For example, parents and teachers may differ in their conception of the teaching role and appropriate classroom behaviour. These potential strains are usually minimized by **role segregation**, a separation in time and space that partially insulates any one role from the others. Parents generally enter classrooms and meet with teachers only at specified and delimited times. School board personnel similarly set policies but do not participate in the day-to-day running of the classroom, unless serious breaches of role expectations occur.

A different kind of role strain occurs within individual actors trying to balance the demands of simultaneous roles that they play in different situations. The role sets of career person and parent, for example, entail different and competing expectations. Again, this potential strain is reduced by segregation of roles in time and space. At certain times of the day and in certain places, the role demands of the job take precedence; at other times, those of parenting are more important. Problems occur only when the role segregation breaks down, as when children are sick and require parenting during the workday or when a parent is trying to work at home. Such strains may be reduced by a subset of rules permitting time off work for extraordinary parenting problems or by the careful segregation of one room in

the house for the office. A wealth of detailed case studies in the role theory tradition has documented the reciprocal expectations and rules concerning contingencies of behaviour that permit such complex sets of roles to function smoothly.

Parsons thus bases his model on internalized moral consensus, which guides choices, and internalized expectations for behaviour in typical situations. Both of these are learned through socialization. He then turns his attention to the construction of an elaborate model of the total action system.

The Social System in a General Scheme of Action

Parsons (1978, 18) defines social action as consisting of "the structures and processes by which human beings form meaningful intentions and more or less successfully, implement them in concrete situations." He conceptualizes this action system as comprising four primary subsystems that are hierarchically organized in relation to each other: the cultural system, the social system, the personality system, and the behavioural organism. Together they form what Parsons terms the **"cybernetic hierarchy"**; that is, a hierarchy of systems of control and communication in human action. Each of these four subsystems of action are referred to as systems in their own right or as subsystems with reference to the total action system.

The **cultural system** is the broadest of all the subsystems of action. It forms the top of the hierarchy of control. It comprises the system of beliefs, rituals, values, and symbols—including language as a symbol system—through which people confront ultimate questions about reality, the meaning of good and evil, of suffering and death. Culture is thus fundamentally religious. A cultural system is normally broader than any one society. Many societies, for example, share a common Christian culture. In areas containing many societies, distinct cultural systems, such as Muslim and Christian, for example, may intermingle. In his abstract model, Parsons does not consider the possibility that a stable society may encompass more than one cultural system.

The **social system** operates at the second level in the **hierarchy** of control. It institutionalizes overarching cultural values into structures and processes that collectively organize action. Norms translate cultural values into specific regulations that define the status, rights, and obligations of members. Through such structures, the social system manages the potential for conflict and disorganization between elements in the action system and so maintains social order. The critical function of the social system is to integrate the cultural system with the personality systems of members and the physical requirements of the behavioural organism. The cultural system functions reciprocally to legitimate these societal-level institutions.

A **society** is a particular type of social system, characterized by what Parsons (1978, 22, 29) terms "territorial integrity and self-sufficiency." A society is a large-scale social system that controls behaviour within a given territory, has relatively clear membership status, and is capable of meeting all the life needs of members at all stages of life. In terms of such a definition, Canada can be considered both a society and a social system. A monastery of celibate monks is a social system but not a society because it has to recruit members from outside. The distinction between society and social system is ambiguous in practice. It is unclear whether communities such as a province or a Hutterite colony, for example, constitute a society or merely a social system. The argument tends to focus on relative territorial control, relative self-sufficiency, or relative clarity of membership status. To the extent that Canada is not economically self-sufficient, even its status as a society could be questioned. In practice, these terms are often used interchangeably, although social system is reserved for settings that are obviously not self-sufficient.

The third system in Parsons' scheme of social action is the **personality system**. Individual personalities are in some sense unique, but they are also constrained and patterned by the social and cultural systems in which they develop. Personality is the learned component of the behaving individual, with socialization as the critical process in the formation of personality. The social system integrates the personality system and the cultural system through the organized processes of learning, developing, and maintaining adequate motivation for participating in socially valued and controlled patterns of action (Parsons 1978, 25). Individual value commitments are formed by the shared cultural system while individual motivations are harnessed primarily by internalized loyalties and obligations to the family system. The

fundamental function of the personality system within the action system is orientation toward the attainment of goals. The personality system serves the social system through the performance of roles in collectively organized actions.

The fourth subsystem in social action is the behavioural organism. The **behavioural organism** provides the energy for all the higher-level systems and also grounds the action system in the physical environment. The social system integrates the behavioural organism into the action system through organizing the processes that meet the basic requirements of food and shelter and the allocation of resources among producers and consumers.

System Prerequisites

The action system as a whole and each of its subsystems are conceptualized by Parsons as meeting a set of four **prerequisites** on which the balance of each system depends. These prerequisites are **latency** or **pattern maintenance**, **integration**, **goal attainment**, and **adaptation**. With respect to the total action system, the cultural subsystem meets the function of latency or pattern maintenance, serving as a reference system of values and meanings in terms of which the other elements in the system are patterned. The social system meets the function of integration, organizing and co-ordinating the elements in the system. The personality system meets the function of goal attainment, providing the fundamental motivating drive for action. The behavioural organism meets the function of adaptation, relating the action system to the physical environment that constrains action. These four functions—goal attainment, adaptation, integration, and latency—are often referred to as Parsons' **GAIL model** (see figure 13-1).

Figure 13-1
Parsons' GAIL Model

Goal Attainment • set priorities • mobilize members	**Adaptation** • get resources • distribute where needed
Latency • manage tensions • motivate performance	**Integration** • co-ordinate activities • keep people informed

Each subsystem of the action system has to meet the same set of four **system prerequisites**. Within the social system, for example, the function of goal attainment is performed by political structures, including pressure groups, political parties, and governing bodies such as parliament. It is through such structures that priorities and future directions of the society are sorted out. Economic structures perform the function of adaptation, both developing and distributing resources through such agencies as farms, factories, and the marketplace. The function of integration is provided by law and administration. They serve to co-ordinate activities, regulate contracts, and generally pull the parts of the social system together. Latency or pattern maintenance is performed by such institutions as schools, churches, and families, which socialize the younger generation, motivate conformity, and support people emotionally.

Within each subsystem there are yet smaller subsystems that have to meet the same prerequisites through various internal structures. The subsystem of a school, for example, needs a governing body to determine goals, including priorities for teaching and budget estimates. Schools also require adaptive mechanisms to get needed funds for salaries, supplies, equipment, and maintenance. This may be primarily from government allocations, private school fees, parental contributions, or fund-raising drives. Schools also need internal administrative structures to co-ordinate activities. Lastly, schools need staff who are committed to the work of latency, instilling in both teachers and students a continuing commitment to the school's educational values and the preservation of school discipline.

Family systems can similarly be analysed in terms of how these four basic needs are met. All families need to have some mechanisms or some person responsible for making key decisions on such matters as major financial investments, where to live, and so on. Someone in every family must also perform the basic breadwinner role, earning the resources on which family members depend for their survival. Someone must co-ordinate activities and ensure that supplies are bought, meals prepared, clothes cleaned, and so on, to be ready as needed by different family members. Families also need to manage the inevitable tensions between the sexes and generations if the family is to continue to hold together as a functioning unit.

Parsons' overarching model is a series of systems with subsystems that have sub-subsystems, and so on. They can be visualized as a series of boxes within the larger box of the action system. The social system box contains important institutional subsystem boxes, each of which has to fulfil the same basic GAIL functions (see figure 13-2).

This model looks very impressive in the abstract, but critics complain that the distinctions are very fuzzy in practice. It is far from clear which box specific items fall into. Is the economy purely involved in the adaptation function or is it also a part of the goal attainment or pattern maintenance functions? Is family primarily oriented to pattern maintenance or more properly also part of the integration, goal attainment, and adaptation functions? There are no easy answers to these questions. Parsons' theoretical writings tend to be at a high level of abstraction where such questions are not raised. Parsons' major contribution to theory lies, perhaps, in his overall vision of social life in terms of interacting systems, rather than in the convoluted abstract models that he builds.

Pattern Variables

The last major dimension of Parsons' overall conception of action systems is his systematization of typical dilemmas of choice in any given role. In any specific behaviour by an individual there is potentially a vast array of orientations toward action that might be adopted. Parsons argues that these can be organized into four options, each associated with one of two opposing sets: traditional or modern. These patterned sets of dichotomous options are what he terms **pattern variables**. The traditional or family set comprises the orientations of affectivity, particularism, ascription, and diffuse obligations, while the modern or occupational set comprises affective neutrality, universalism, achieved characteristics, and specific obligations. Parsons conceptualizes any role relationship as analysable in terms of these two sets of action orientations. Table 13-1 shows the two sets of pattern variables.

The first variable is **affectivity** or **affective neutrality**. This concerns the amount of emotion that should properly be displayed in a role. Relations between family and friends are expected to involve some emotional warmth, while relations with clients in a business or professional situation are expected to be formal or affectively neutral. People may rightfully get upset if such expectations are not met in either context.

Table 13-1

The Pattern Variables

Traditional or Family Set	Modern or Occupational Set
Affectivity • show emotional involvement	**Affective neutrality** • remain emotionally neutral
Particularism • judge relative to age, experience, effort, enthusiasm	**Universalism** • judge relative to objective standards of excellence
Ascription • give special consideration to relatives, friends	**Achievement** • consider only specific qualifications
Diffuseness • co-operate, help, and support in as many ways as possible	**Specificity** • strictly limit involvement
Self • give priority to personal interests over what others want	**Collectivity** • give priority to group interests over personal preferences

Figure 13-2

Structure of General Action Systems

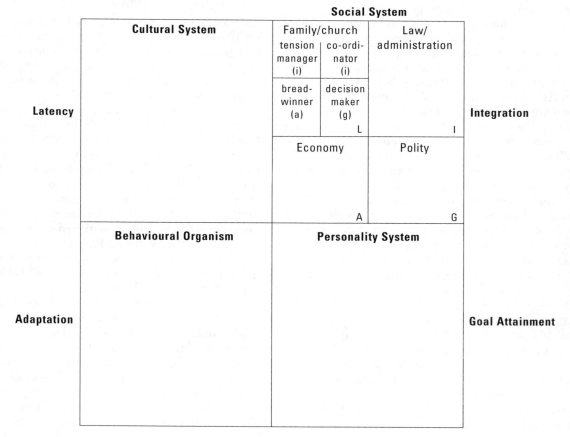

The second variable concerns whether **particularistic** or **universalistic standards** of evaluation for role performance are appropriate. Particularism refers to special treatment based on the relationship of the person or the group to oneself. Friends are not measured against objective standards. But in the business world, or when hiring a lawyer or going to a medical doctor, objective universalistic standards are appropriate. Professionals are judged relative to the universally defined standards of their profession and not by whether or not one likes the individual personally.

A third variable concerns appropriate criteria for assessing an actor, whether by **ascriptive characteristics** or **achieved characteristics**. Ascription refers to "who one is," and those characteristics that we are born with, such as family of origin, sex, appearance, racial or ethnic background. Achievements are those characteristics that we earn by learning special skills or gaining credentials. The first set of characteristics is more important for family or social contacts, the second for business contacts.

A fourth pattern variable concerns the nature of obligations involved in an interaction, whether **diffuse** or **specific**. Obligations toward family and friends tend to be diffuse; friends and relatives call upon each other for a variety of services and support. Business and professional relations are confined to the precise task at hand; neither party to the relationship has any right to ask for or to expect anything more.

A last dimension of role relations is self versus collectivity. This concerns whether the action in question is oriented primarily toward individual interest or toward group goals and interests. Parsons himself accorded this variable less importance in his general model because it was less clearly a dichotomous choice. Individual and group interests frequently overlap, and aspects of both may be involved in any specific role interaction. One does not always have to choose between them.

Parent-child and professional-client relationships are presented by Parsons as polar opposite types of action orientation. Ideally, the relationship of a parent to a child is emotionally affective; evaluations are particularistic with full considerations given to the special situation and abilities of the particular child; assessments are based on ascriptive criteria; role obligations are diffuse. Totally opposite expectations prevail in a professional-client relation such as that between doctors and their patients. Both doctors and their patients are required to maintain a stand of affective neutrality toward each other. One's judgment of a doctor is appropriately in terms of universalistic criteria of the profession and the doctor's professional qualifications and abilities, and not whether the doctor is male or female, an old family friend, or a newcomer. Finally, obligations are confined to the specific issue of providing medical advice.

A fundamental assumption made by Parsons, which is explored further in chapter 14, is that the basic pattern variables and their associated action orientations within families and within the world of industry and business are diametrically opposed. Hence, conflict between them is virtually inevitable whenever the two spheres overlap. This potential conflict is avoided in advanced industrial societies by the specialization and segregation of family roles from work roles. This segregation involves not only time and space but also, characteristically, personnel. Men take primary responsibility for work roles while women take responsibility for the diffuse, emotionally charged role of nurturing children. Parsons is not saying that it is impossible for a person to combine the two roles, but that it is difficult and that social norms prescribe in advance which role—family or work—will take primacy when conflicts arise. The segregation of male and female roles found in nearly all societies is thus seen as meeting a basic functional need. Parsons argues that biological differences between men and women, associated with childbirth, breast-feeding, and different average muscular strength, naturally predispose men to specialize in work roles outside the home and women to specialize in child care and homemaking.

A wealth of research in the role-theory tradition has analysed typical patterns of role relations in various situations in terms of Parsons' pattern variables and has examined reactions to violations of these expectations. Parsons himself (1961) did an interesting analysis of the role of elementary school teacher, usually filled by a woman. Parsons argues that a female teacher helps to prepare young children for the transition from the pattern variables appropriate for relations between themselves and their mother at home, to the impersonal pattern variables of the work world. Such a teacher shows affectivity or emotional warmth toward the children and responds to their ascriptive characteristics, and

Challenging the functionalist view of family roles, this father provides day-care for three other children so he can stay at home with his son.

yet at the same time introduces them to universalistic standards of performance and to more limited, specific role obligations than they are used to with their parents.

Modernization

Parsons maintains that entire societies can be analysed in terms of how they meet the basic GAIL prerequisites and the prevailing orientations toward pattern variables. For Parsons, modernization involves a progressive differentiation of structures by which each of the four prerequisites are met. In traditional societies, the kin group is primarily responsible for meeting all of these needs. The **patriarch** or family head tends to set the major goals for the rest of the members. The adaptation function—the economy—is embedded in kin and family groups. The family and the patriarch are primarily responsible for societal integration, with power relations organized along age-sex lines. Family socialization is likewise of primary importance in teaching the values and skills that assure the maintenance of established patterns of behaviour from one generation to another.

In modern societies, however, the role of the family has receded to only a partial responsibility for the fourth function. Societal goals are set by specialized role incumbents such as politicians and bureaucrats. Economic activities have moved outside the family circle into factories and corporations. Patriarchs have lost much of their former authority, and societal integration is maintained by specialized legal systems and the civil service. The fundamental teaching roles involved in pattern maintenance have also moved outside the family into the realms of schools, churches, and law enforcement agencies. Families now specialize in early childhood socialization and tension management through emotional support of members.

Parsons argues further that traditional and modern societies differ in fundamental ways in types of action orientation. Traditional societies, based on kinship, are oriented primarily toward affective, particularistic, ascriptive, and diffuse role relationships. A very different set of pattern variables prevails in advanced industrial societies, characterized as they are by differentiation and specialization of roles. Universalistic standards and evaluation of contacts on the basis of achievement are functional requirements in technologically complex roles. Specialized roles necessarily carry only specific obligations, which in turn promote affectively neutral relationships.

Nowhere are these patterns more apparent than in the realm of public administration. Traditional societies, suggests Parsons, often adopt the formal structures of bureaucracy from advanced industrial societies but not the cultural patterns. The result is nepotism, graft, and inefficiency as personnel selection is made on the basis of family connections and other ascriptive criteria rather than on the basis of skills, and the new role incumbents are then expected to favour friends and family in dispensing patronage from their office. Efficient bureaucracy is functionally necessary for advanced industrial activities. This efficiency requires that appointments be made on the basis of expertise and that operations be impartial. The logical implications of the Parsonian model are thus that the modernization process requires both structural and cultural changes in traditional societies, to promote differentiation and specialization of formal structures and to give primacy to a different set of pattern variables.

It is clear that Parsons developed an extremely elaborate model of the structure of social action. For more than two decades this model has dominated sociological research. It has been so influential that alternative perspectives still tend to identify their own position in opposition to it.

Problems with Functionalist Theory

Serious criticisms have been raised against functionalism, both as a general theoretical approach and with respect to specific elements of Parsons' model. These theoretical issues are addressed here, with particular reference to the alternative approaches of political economy and ethnomethodology.

When sociologists try to explain the existence of certain structures or patterns in society by reference to the functions that these structures perform for the social whole, they are implicitly suggesting that the structures exist because they are necessary. Families perform the basic function of socializing children, thus we have families; stratification performs the function of motivating

talented people to strive for important jobs, thus we have stratification. This is, of course, an oversimplification of the argument but it helps to reveal the problem, which Merton (1967) calls the *fallacy of functional indispensability*.

Merton points out that there may very well be, and in fact usually are, functional alternatives to these structures. Societies do need some way to socialize children, but there are potentially other ways of doing this than in families. For example, small agricultural communes in Israel experimented successfully with raising children in group homes without having families as we know them (Spiro 1958). Societies do have to motivate people somehow to take difficult jobs, but perhaps there are other motivations besides money. Merton suggests that we can reasonably expect to find some structures or patterns in society to meet important needs. But identifying these structures is not the same as explaining why we have the specific types of structures—the kind of families or the kind of social stratification—that we find in our society.

Hempel (1970, 127) makes the same point but carries it further. Society may need something, but this does not necessarily mean that it will get it. Durkheim argues, for example, that in order to have social cohesion we need social justice and full employment so that everyone feels they are valued members of the community. But we are a very long way from satisfying either need.

Another problem with functionalist arguments is the difficulty in defining what is necessary for society to function. In biology, it is a fairly straightforward matter to define health and sickness and hence to claim that certain states are necessary for the healthy functioning of the organism. But it is much more difficult to define what a healthy or sick society looks like. One might argue that Canada is sick because we do not have full employment, but there are a great many people in the business community who would not share this opinion. With such uncertainty as to what constitutes a need, the functionalist argument that structures exist because they are necessary becomes untenable.

Hempel points to yet another snag in the argument: the time ordering seems to be wrong. Something exists now because of some effect it will have in the future. Consider the statement, "birds have wings in order to fly." This is a functionalist argument. It seems to imply that birds got together one day, decided flying would be nice, and so started developing wings! The fact that birds have wings enables them to fly, but that does not explain how wings developed. If wanting to fly were sufficient cause for having wings, we would all have them. Functionalism describes the *effects* of certain structures, but it does not go very far toward explaining how or why these structures exist. Biologists delve deep into the structure of genes and genetic inheritance to explain the processes and mechanisms by which complex structures like wings are perpetuated in bird species. This goes a long way beyond explaining wings by showing how they function. Hempel concludes that functionalism is a useful descriptive approach, but it does not explain much about social structures.

It is important not to overstate this criticism. Describing the effects or functions that particular structures have is itself a difficult and useful achievement, particularly when these effects are latent or not recognized by many people. This restricted version of functionalism is valuable, provided we recognize its limitations. Functionalists who are largely content with this level of analysis have produced many insightful studies.

One such study is Merton's (1967, 125–35) analysis of the latent functions of political rackets run by party bosses in America. He asks why political rackets run by party bosses persist. Patronage, bribery, graft, and the protection of criminals clearly violate established moral codes. They persist, Merton argues, because they satisfy subgroups' needs that cannot be met by culturally approved social structures. First, the party boss consolidates what is often widely dispersed power to the point where he can actually get things done. Second, he can get around bureaucratic red tape to ensure provision of social services for people otherwise lost in the technicalities. Third, the boss can provide privileges to big business, by acting to control and regulate unbridled competition, without being subject to public scrutiny and control. He is especially important in providing aid to businesses that provide illicit services and hence that are not protected by regular government controls. Fourth, the party patronage controlled by the boss provides avenues for upward social mobility for ambitious individuals who lack legitimate avenues to attain success. Hence, political rackets cannot be understood merely as self-aggrandizement for power-hungry individuals who could be cleaned out of the system. Political

rackets constitute the organized provision of services to subgroups that are otherwise excluded from or handicapped in the race to get ahead. These are important latent functions that the socially approved political structures cannot adequately meet. Hence, the political rackets persist.

Serious criticisms remain, however, even when the claims for functional analysis are confined to the level of descriptive insights. Merton draws attention to two related problems, which he terms the *fallacy of functional unity* and the *fallacy of universalism*. In biology, the assumption of functional unity holds that every element within a biological organism is functional or useful for the good of the entire organism. The assumption of universalism holds that each and every element found within an organism must perform some necessary function. Merton argues that, however reasonable such assumptions sound in the context of a biological organism, they constitute fallacies when applied to elements within social systems.

The general argument that structures exist because they are functional for the social system assumes that the system operates as a unitary whole. Merton argues that given structures may be beneficial or functional for certain groups in society but not necessarily for others. A high rate of unemployment, for example, is functional for reducing wage demands and so enhancing the competitive advantage of business, but it is not functional for the groups of people who are unemployed or for their family members. Neither is it functional for other small businesses that depend on selling goods to families of unemployed people. At best, one might be able to talk about a net balance of functional advantage. But Merton pushes the criticism further to insist that functionalism should routinely take account of **dysfunctions**; that is, the possibility that some structures have a net balance of negative consequences for a society or for large numbers of its members.

Traditional functionalism begins from the premise that recurrent characteristics in a society, like elements within a biological organism, can be explained by reference to the functions that they perform for the maintenance of the system as a whole. But carried to its logical extreme, this position can lead to what look like absurd claims. One can argue that suicide is functional for relieving tensions; wife battering is functional for enhancing male dominance; war is functional for generating high profits and high employment.

These claims themselves are not false. Suicide, war, unemployment, crime, do have advantages for certain people. The problem lies in the assumption that they benefit the society as a whole. The key question for critics of functionalism is, functional for whom? The corollary, of course, is, dysfunctional for whom? When the issues raised by functionalism are reformulated in this way, important dimensions of power and conflict of interest are introduced into the analysis.

A recurrent criticism of functional analysis, and particularly of Parsons' model of a social system, has been that it does not deal adequately with power. Parsons tends to assume that power generally takes the form of authority, which is used in the interests of system adjustment. Not surprisingly, this formulation has been hard to sustain.

Marxist critics argue that corporate bosses wield enormous power over the economy and over political decisions. The mass of workers may view the exercise of such power as arbitrary and illegitimate, but they are unable to oppose it effectively. The result of confrontations between bosses and workers may be disorder and alienation rather than orderly system adjustment. The power exercised by men over women in families has similarly been challenged by feminists as illegitimate. The exercise of patriarchal powers may lead to family breakdown and divorce rather than to stable marriage.

Functionalism started out with great promise as a unifying scientific approach toward sociological analysis, but it seems not to have lived up to expectations. The major contributions of this perspective lie in two broad areas. First, it recognizes the fundamental interdependence of different parts of society. It increases sensitivity to the fact that change in any one part of society affects all other interrelated structures as well. Second, and perhaps more importantly, functionalism has encouraged a wealth of descriptive research that has documented latent or hitherto unsuspected effects of recurrent patterns of behaviour.

The elaborate typologies of system needs and pattern variables worked out by Parsons have, on the whole, not proven particularly useful. System needs are notoriously difficult to establish. Attempts to classify structures as performing one need or another are often not successful. Additionally, each pattern variable is better understood as a continuum rather than a dichotomy and also as varying widely with circumstances rather than as a fixed orientation for given roles.

In summary, the problems associated with traditional functionalist analysis are serious. The system of explanation for the persistence of structures in terms of their functions for the social system is logically flawed. It does not deal adequately with dysfunctions or negative aspects of social structures, nor does it provide an adequate basis for the analysis of power, conflict, and disunity in society. It has thus gained the disrepute of being reactionary and conservative, providing ideological justification for the status quo.

Critical Reformulations of Functionalist Theory

In this section we explore the efforts of theorists, particularly in the Marxist and ethnomethodological traditions, to reformulate functionalism into a potentially more adequate and descriptively useful approach.

A revised model of functionalist analysis proposed by Stinchcombe (1968, 80–100) first addresses the question of the flawed explanatory logic of traditional functionalism. Hempel and others may argue that functionalism cannot go beyond descriptive statements, but the fact remains that most functionalist analysis still aims to do more than describe functions. The tendency is always there to argue that certain structures may exist because they serve certain functions. In other words, some theorists use the functions, or effect, as explanations for the existence of the structures.

Stinchcombe suggests that these logical problems can be resolved if two important changes are made in traditional functionalist analysis. The first change is the explicit recognition and incorporation of intent into the explanation. It makes sense to argue that existing structures are caused by their future consequences if you explain that certain individuals or groups of people intentionally select and reinforce certain structures because they find the effects of such structures beneficial. The second change is that such an explanation needs to examine the mechanisms by which such structures are selectively reinforced and preserved over time. Stinchcombe calls such processes **feedback mechanisms**. In the biological sciences, the exploration of the precise mechanisms and feedback loops by which an equilibrium is achieved is a central part of any explanation of the functions that parts perform for the whole. But to date, functional analysis in sociology has tended to assume equilibrium, without demonstrating the mechanisms through which such effects are sustained. In short, for Stinchcombe, adequate functional explanations should show that structures exist and are perpetuated over time because they are deliberately reinforced by individuals or groups who find their effects beneficial and who have access to mechanisms that are effective in such reinforcement.

Stinchcombe only hints at what some of these mechanisms might be. Some structures may persist simply because no one has any particular interest in stopping them, and because they work sufficiently well that no one has much incentive to seek alternatives. It simply costs too much time and effort to change things. Other structures may be less generally appreciated by all members of the society and hence have to be defended by more overt means. These means might include: control over the socialization of young people to ensure that they are instilled with the proper values; access to mass media, which influence how people think and what they know about; and influence over the selection of successors to policy-making situations in society and control of the rules under which successors work.

Marxist Functionalism

Stinchcombe's reformulation of functional analysis directly incorporates notions of power and the unequal ability of different individuals and groups in society to reinforce those social structures that they find beneficial. Stinchcombe (1968, 94) in fact defines the power of a class in terms of its relative effectiveness as a cause of social structures. In this respect, he explicitly relates his ideas to Marxist analysis and to the Marxist assertion that the dominant culture of a society is the culture of the dominant class. The reason why elites are able to perpetuate their values and mode of organization of society is that they have privileged access to and control over all the key mechanisms that reinforce structures. Elites are in a particularly advantageous position to influence the mechanisms that produce the

semblance of moral consensus central to the Parsonian model of the social system. Not only do they control and direct most mass media outlets, they also pay professional people to defend and disseminate appropriate values. Members of the elite are also in the best position to select their own successors and to ensure that their values are perpetuated in the future operation of important organizations in society.

The notion of **Marxist functionalism** proposed by Stinchcombe retains the more insightful aspects of functionalist theory. In particular, he retains both the concept of society as comprising an interrelated system of parts and the mode of analysis that describes and explains the persistence of structures by reference to their consequences. He also emphasizes purposive action as the foundation of his model. The crucial change from the Parsonian model is that Stinchcombe introduces the concepts of class and unequal power. He replaces the notion of societywide normative consensus with the view that dominant ideas are those perpetuated by the actions of the members of an elite class.

Richard Quinney's analysis of law functioning to protect the interests of the capitalist class, which was outlined in chapter 7, is a prime example of Marxist functionalism. Society is conceptualized as a system of interdependent parts, but it is explicitly a capitalist system. The parts function to protect the elite class and to control and suppress class conflict, which might disrupt this system.

The risk in Quinney's approach is that he repeats earlier logical flaws in functional analysis, namely the fallacies of universal functionalism, functional unity, and functional indispensability. Everything exists because it is functional for the capitalist system—unemployment is functional for profits, welfare is functional for controlling potential revolt—and the description of some effect provides an explanation for the persistence of such structures. Stinchcombe's reformulation of the logic of functionalism still applies here. An adequate explanation still requires detailed analyses of the feedback mechanisms: who controls them, how they operate, how potential opposition or change is prevented. The capitalist system persists, not because of its own inner momentum, but because people with powerful vested interests take actions to reinforce it on an ongoing basis.

A closely related criticism of functionalism stems more directly from the analytical work of

Marx himself than from subsequent political economy theory. When Marx challenged the ideas of the classical economists of his time, he asked a difficult question: What kind of actual social relations must be experienced in order for this kind of economic model to be formulated? Ideas, in other words, do not arise from nowhere. They arise from people's attempts to make sense of their own limited experience. When this same kind of question is asked of Parsons' work, it challenges the claim that his model of a social system is abstract, scientific, and universally applicable. Critics would argue that concepts such as GAIL functions and pattern variables originate within, and refer to the historically specific circumstances of, capitalism. They make sense only in relation to the impersonal capitalist system of commodity production for money.

This criticism can be made clearer if we examine Parsons' analysis of, first, the differences between family and occupational subsystems and, second, the medical profession. Prior to capitalism, there was no clear break between family and work roles for most people. They commonly merged together in household enterprises. Under feudalism, landowners had clearly established personal obligations to provide for the peasant families that were attached to their estates. It was only with the advent of the capitalist wage-labour system that owners of the means of production freed themselves from hereditary obligations toward workers. It was capitalism that segregated production from the home and reduced personal relations to inhuman cash payment in the labour market. It is precisely such a system that is captured in Parsons' concepts of affective neutrality and impersonal and specific role obligations. These concepts cannot be applied universally to all economic systems.

Similarly, there is nothing inevitable about the nature of medicine that would give rise to Parsons' characterization of the doctor-patient relationship as involving affectively neutral, universalistic, achievement-oriented, and specific role obligations. For centuries the opposite was the case. Healing was practised by women whose skills were passed on for generations. The art of healing was integrated into total caring for the person. It was a neighbourly service where the healer knew her patients and their families. She knew about the disappointments, anxieties, and the overwork that could mimic illness or induce it (Ehrenreich and English 1979, ch. 2). Healing

was a diverse and creative process that involved many little kindnesses and encouragements and an understanding of the patients' fears and strengths. But under capitalism, the "art of healing" became the "science of medicine," practised by men as a commodity to be sold at a high price. Male practitioners went to tremendous lengths to protect their commodity, undermining the natural healing of women by burning them as witches and by outlawing midwifery and the practice of medicine by those without credentials. Since women were systematically barred from medical schools until late in the nineteenth century, they were effectively prevented from practising medicine. This set of historically specific practices produced the image of doctors described by Parsons.

Under capitalism, the "art of healing" became the "science of medicine." To protect this field as a male domain, women with natural healing skills were burned as witches or hanged.

Parsons' model and the analyses that flow from it are thus faulted for justifying, under the guise of scientific objectivity, a particularly inhuman form of social relations. By treating such relations as universal, abstract truths about society, Parsons glosses over the historically specific and particular social organization that gives rise to the relationships that he encapsulates in his model.

Some have argued that the Parsonian model is, and was intended to be, an important tool in the legitimation and hence perpetuation of the capitalist nation-state (Buxton 1985). Professional social science functions as a powerful mechanism for social control. Parsons defines professionals as a disinterested or affectively neutral class of experts, operating in terms of universalistic standards of science, committed to the specific objectives of research rather than diffuse political obligations, and dedicated to collective societal well-being rather than self-interest. Hence they command authority as impartial advisers to government. Functionalist theorists have advised the business and political elites how to neutralize destabilizing features of change and so bolster the system. Functionalism also provides a means not to see the underlying realities of class, power, and exploitation within the capitalist system. Buxton goes so far as to suggest that Parsons himself might have been aware of the ideological character of his theory, or certainly that many of his followers who adopted and promoted functionalism in social analysis saw it as a means to reduce class tensions.

Psychoanalysis and Socialization

The basic assumption of the functionalist equilibrium model is the internalization of social norms. Individuals, it is argued, come to accept the norms and values of society as their own, and hence they voluntarily regulate themselves in conformity with expectations. The major problem with this perspective is that it does not explain deviance. People appear to conform because they are preprogrammed to act only in conformist ways, much like ants in an anthill.

Dennis Wrong (1961) argues that such reasoning is blatantly naïve. In reality, people can never be socialized to this extent. Human nature is far too complex for that. Wrong draws on **psychoanalytic theories** to suggest that socialization at best achieves only a veneer of conformity over individual self-will, and this conscious self-will is itself only a veneer over much deeper unconscious or semiconscious passions and desires that forever threaten to overwhelm orderly, conformist behaviour.

In psychoanalytic terminology, the **id** comprises the vast reservoir of life forces—sexual passions, drives, and energy—of which the individual is at best only partially aware. The con-

scious self or **ego** seeks to express and to realize these fundamental drives and passions. They are only superficially held in check by the **superego** of learned social norms and values. This model is illustrated in figure 13-3. Intensive and rigid socialization, such as the kind that puritanical religious sects seek to impose, may succeed in repressing socially unacceptable sexual drives and passions. Socialization may even succeed in pushing them out of the conscious mind altogether, but it can never eliminate them totally. A permanent tension is set up within the individual psyche between repressed drives, guilt, and social conditioning, with the latter continually at risk of being overwhelmed by deep emotional forces. When people are viewed from this perspective, the functionalist vision of societal equilibrium achieved by internalization of norms appears fragile indeed.

Figure 13-3

Model of the Human Mind in Psychoanalytic Theory

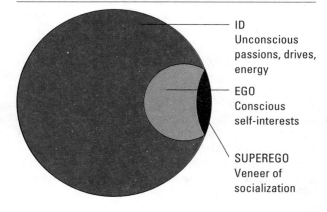

ID
Unconscious
passions, drives,
energy

EGO
Conscious
self-interests

SUPEREGO
Veneer of
socialization

The Ethnomethodological Critique

The approach of ethnomethodology—particularly the work of Garfinkel, who was a student of Parsons—offers a different kind of challenge to the functionalist notion of a voluntaristic theory of action. Heritage (1984) draws attention to the illusory character of this supposedly voluntary choice. In practice, actors seem to be left with no choice at all because the script is already written. Parsons characterizes people as role-players with internalized norms and fixed expectations. These role-players are assumed to share their interpretation of the situation and their knowledge of appropriate rules for behaviour. In effect, says Garfinkel, they are "judgmental dopes" (Heritage 1984, 108). They appear to make no judgments of their own. Like mindless robots, they simply follow rules programmed into them.

The alternative perspective of ethnomethodology allows for a much greater fluidity in behaviour. For a start, in real situations we assume that other people are making responsible and meaningful choices in their actions, such that each of us can and do hold ourselves and other people accountable for behaviour. Furthermore, real situations are not predefined. A constant problem in deciding how we should behave or respond to the behaviour of others is in determining what is going on in the first place. Our actions and those of other people define the situation, not the other way around.

Boughey (1978, 171) gives an example of this in his description of cards night at a church. Six rambunctious men were laughing and joking as they played poker. After a particularly raucous outburst, a woman from a nearby table admonished them, "Shshsh! You're in church, you know!" One poker-player waved her off with the response, "Naah! But this is cards!" In effect, all the participants in this scene were **defining the situation**. We might conclude that, since the players were so raucous, they must have given priority to the role of "card-playing" rather than to that of "being in church." Conversely, if the men had quietened down after the admonishment, we might conclude that, after a temporary lapse, they followed the behavioural prescriptions appropriate for the role of being in church. The important point is that a functionalist could only tell after the fact what was going on by the kind of behaviour displayed. Boughey and the enthomethodologists are interested in how people actively choose and create the situation for themselves by choosing how they are going to behave.

Heritage (1984, ch. 5) gives an example of a situation in which one person meets another and greets her. The norm states that greetings should be reciprocated. If the other person does indeed return the greeting, then everything appears normal. But if she is silent, then the situation is not normal, and a chain of guesses as to what else is going on is immediately set off: maybe she didn't hear; she was deep in thought; she deliberately snubbed me; she wasn't who I thought she was; she doesn't remember me; my new hairpiece sure fooled her. There is no passive actor responding in learned ways to a predefined situation. Rather, there is a person actively involved in creating what is happening and what will happen next.

In chapter 18, we will see some examples of the infinitely detailed and careful research that ethnomethodologists carry out in order to explore how people actively make sense of and create the social world and reproduce it as intelligible for each other. What is significant here is the important criticism that this approach raises against traditional functionalist analysis. The basic functionalist assumption of internalized norms and expectations of behaviour is shown to be insufficient as an explanation for social order.

Conclusion

What remains of functionalist analysis when these criticisms are taken into account? The model of society as a system rather than a collection of disconnected parts remains a central assumption of sociological analysis. Functionalism draws attention to the mutual influence of interdependent elements of society. It also focusses attention on voluntary or purposive action and the importance of typical roles and expectations in guiding behaviour. Functionalism has prompted much valuable descriptive research into the effects of given structures or patterns of behaviour on society.

The weaknesses of functionalism lie in its rigidity, the tendency to assume that existing structures are necessary, because functional, without considering alternatives and especially without considering dysfunctions or damaging effects that given structures may have for less powerful sectors of society. Functionalism typically fails to recognize the essential fluidity and creativity in people's relations with each other. At the system level, functionalism can be faulted for failure to deal adequately with issues of power, conflict, and exploitation in society, except in terms of institutionalized pressure groups. This has marked functionalism as a conservative ideology in the eyes of more critical theorists.

The following four chapters explore the impact of functional analysis on research in a variety of substantive areas, particularly as they apply to Canadian society. These insights are tested against the critical reformulations proposed by Marxist and ethnomethodological perspectives and feminist theory.

Suggested Reading

The most convenient and accessible selection of Parsons' writing is contained in Peter Hamilton's collection, *Readings from Talcott Parsons* (1985). A broadly descriptive article in the collection is "Age and Sex in the Social Structure of the United States." It would be instructive to compare the division of sex roles within different age groups in the 1950s, as outlined by Parsons, with that of the present. In the article "Illness and the Role of the Physician: A Sociological Perspective," illness, particularly mental illness, is treated as a type of deviant behaviour in terms of the sick person's failure to fulfil expectations connected with his or her roles in society. Sickness itself is viewed as a social role in relation to a set of distinctive norms defining appropriate behaviour, such as exclusion from certain normal obligations. The therapist is seen as not just applying technical knowledge to problem cases, but as restoring equilibrium to the social system.

Another broadly descriptive article by Parsons is "The School Class as a Social System: Some of its Functions in American Society" (1961). This article examines the ways in which aspects of the structure of primary and secondary school classes function to adapt young people to adult roles. The students' transformation from family members to members of the wider society is analysed in terms of Parsons' pattern variables.

A brief but demanding exposition of Parsons' scheme of the components of society can be found in his book *Societies: Evolutionary and Comparative Perspectives* (1966).

Questions

1. Distinguish between *manifest* and *latent* functions.

2. How do *need dispositions* influence behaviour, according to Parsons?

3. What four subsystems are involved in Parsons' notion of the *cybernetic hierarchy*?

4. What are the different societal functions of the adaptation system and the latency system in Parsons' GAIL model?

5. What are the pattern variables typically associated with the family subsystem?

6. In Parsons' model, what constellation of pattern variables are typically associated with traditional, preindustrial societies?

7. What critical argument does Merton use to challenge the *fallacy of functional indispensability* that underlies much work in functionalist theory?

8. What two important modifications are proposed by Stinchcombe to resolve problems with the functionalist argument that institutions exist because they are functional for society?

9. How does feminist work on women as healers challenge the Parsonian model of pattern variables as historically specific rather than universal?

10. In what respect does Garfinkel's critique of Parsons' model of social action imply that all people are "judgmental dopes"?

CHAPTER 14

The Family: The Site of Love, Exploitation, and Oppression

As we saw in chapter 13, functionalist theory views society as an integrated and self-maintaining system, analogous to a living organism. Like an organism, it is composed of numerous organs or institutions that are structured to meet the specialized needs or prerequisites of the social system as a whole. The system normally exists in a state of dynamic equilibrium. Built-in mechanisms balance change in one part of the system with complementary changes in other parts, so that the order of the whole is maintained despite major changes in structure. Within subsystems of action, or institutions, are individual roles, which comprise typical patterns of action. The entire system is held together by the mechanisms of **normative consensus** and shared role expectations. These values and expectations for behaviour are internalized by members of society through the complex process of socialization.

The family is an institution that plays a vital part within this functionalist model of society.

Functionalists argue that the family is extremely important, indeed indispensable, for the survival of society. For many theorists, society itself can be conceptualized as made up of families linked together. The family is a universal institution; no known society has existed without it. The central integrative process of socialization—the internalization of behaviour patterns and values—occurs primarily within the family. Institutions such as school and church also play a part in the socialization process, but this is generally only after the newborn infant has developed into a socially functioning child. The few documented cases of feral children, or those who have survived in the wild or in extreme isolation without family contact, indicate that these children's behaviour is less than human. Even after they have been intensively trained in clinics, these children have not been able to learn to talk or to think in terms of the symbolic meaning systems that distinguish humans from other animals. Functionalists suggest that, without families, there would be no humanity and hence no society. Functionalists accord no other social institution such central importance. For this reason, the study of sociology of the family offers the strongest test of the contributions and the limitations of the functionalist perspective.

Functionalist Theories of the Family

Any institution can be studied from two related perspectives: the contribution of that institution to the functioning of society as a whole or the institution's internal functioning as a subsystem in its own right, with its own set of prerequisites for maintaining a dynamic equilibrium.

The four main functions that the family unit performs for society are: reproduction of society's members; socialization of new members, especially the newborn and young children; regulation of sexual relations; and economic co-operation to sustain adults and their offspring. The family constitutes the basic emotional or expressive social unit, providing nurturing, protection, and affection for members, controlling their behaviour, and channelling fundamental sexual and reproductive drives into socially acceptable forms. Although reproduction and sexual relations can and do take place outside of families, they are only socially legitimated within families. Reiss suggests that this is because the family context best ensures the nurturance of the newborn, with kinship groups on both the father's and the mother's side acknowledging a relationship with, and some responsibility for, the child (Reiss 1976, ch. 2).

The family occurs in a great variety of forms in different societies. There are **extended families**, in which several generations of kin live in the same dwelling usually under the authority of the most senior male or the most senior female in a matriarchal society, and **nuclear families** consisting of isolated couples with their dependent children. Legitimate sexual relations include **monogamy** (one man with one woman) or forms of **polygamy** (more than one spouse). The more common form of polygamy is **polygyny** (one man having two or more wives), but some societies practise **polyandry** (one woman having more than one husband). Whatever the particular arrangement favoured in a given society, functionalists argue that there is an essential core that is universal. This core was defined by George Murdock (1949, 2):

> The family is a social group characterized by common residence, economic co-operation, and reproduction. It includes adults of both sexes, at least two of whom maintain a socially approved sexual relationship, and one or more children, own or adopted, of the sexually cohabiting adults.

Not all members of a society conform to this pattern of living at any one time, but most people spend a significant part of their lives in a family situation. In Canada, most people marry and have children, and most of these children will do the same when they are adults. Kinship ties remain extremely important to people throughout life, even for those individuals who do not form families of their own.

The nuclear family is seen by functionalists as having a biological base.

The nuclear family core of two sexually cohabiting adults of the opposite sex, together with their dependent children, is seen by functionalists as having an essential biological foundation (Goode 1982, 15–32). This thesis incorporates the core ideas of **sociobiology**, a branch of sociology closely associated with functionalism, which studies the biological bases of social behaviour. Functionalists argue that the vital institution of family is rooted in sexual drives and the imperative of reproduction and in the sociological imperative of transforming the biological organism of a newborn baby into a human or social being. Unlike many animals, the argument goes, human babies are born with relatively few instincts. They rely upon a complex brain to learn, through symbols and abstractions, the essentials of survival in society. This necessitates a long period of social dependency that lasts well into adolescence and beyond in industrial society. Because of this, there is a relatively long period during which the nurturing mother depends upon care and support of other adults, usually the husband/father, to meet her economic needs while she is engaged in child care.

Many biological drives predispose humans for male-female pair bonding. Goode suggests that, despite the fact that there is some homosexuality, people are preprogrammed for heterosexuality. The constancy of the human sex drive, far more intense than is needed for reproduction itself, promotes long-term, stable relations between men and women. The biologically based impulse of jealousy reinforces this pair bonding through the urge to regard one's mate as one's exclusive sexual property. Another very general biological drive is territoriality, the natural desire to settle in one location and defend it from others. This is combined with a biologically determined reproductive strategy of having few offspring and caring intensively for them, rather than producing many offspring at once and leaving them to fend for themselves. All these traits create strong impulses in humans to form families.

Functionalists argue that sexual differences promote heterosexual bonding. Only women undergo menstruation, pregnancy, and lactation, and hence they are biologically predisposed to perform the task of caring for children. Breastfeeding intensifies the bond between mother and child. Women are relatively weak during pregnancy and just after birth; hence natural choice as well as efficiency dictate that they will stay close to home and children. Males, on the other hand, have greater strength and aggressiveness, which gave them the edge in early hunting societies and hence provided a biological basis for early male dominance. Lionel Tiger (1977) argues that "man the hunter" was preprogrammed for aggression and dominance over females and also for strong male bonding in hunting packs. This predisposition for male bonding gives man an advantage in politics and in business. Tiger argues that women are preprogrammed to be submissive and to be oriented toward their chil-

dren rather than to form bonds with other women. These biological predispositions favour the sex-role division of labour within families, with women concentrating on nurturing roles within the home while men concentrate on the role of economic provider.

Functionalists posit that sociological factors stemming from the nature of work in industrial societies strongly reinforce this biologically based tendency toward sex-role division of labour within families. As we saw in chapter 13, Parsons argues that family and industry are based on diametrically opposed patterns of action orientation and hence must be separated if both are to function effectively. Family life is based on emotional ties between members; membership is dependent on ascriptive characteristics and not qualifications; individuals are judged by particularistic values as unique family members; and there are diffuse obligations to meet each others' needs in multiple ways. Industry necessarily operates in terms of totally different patterns. Relations among people in industry are emotionally neutral; membership is ideally determined by achievements; judgments are based upon universalistic criteria of standards of performance; and obligations are specific to the particular transaction. The specialization of sex roles, with women concentrating upon the internal affairs of the family while men concentrate upon occupational roles, best serves to minimize confusion of values across the two spheres.

In functionalist analysis, the family constitutes a social system with its own internal needs that must be met if the family is to maintain its equilibrium. Individual families, like society as a whole, must meet the four basic prerequisites of goal attainment, adaptation, integration, and latency or pattern maintenance. Parsons and Bales (1956, ch. 1) analyse how families function internally to divide up roles along sex-specific lines. Bales maintains that small groups typically develop two kinds of leaders: an **instrumental leader** who gets tasks done and an **expressive leader** who supports and encourages group members and smooths over tensions. Parsons proposes that, within families, one adult, typically the male, performs instrumental tasks, while the female performs the expressive roles. In terms of system prerequisites, instrumental roles include goal attainment and adaptation. The man typically represents the family to the external social system, making the key decisions that set family goals and earning the resources needed for the family to adapt to its surroundings and survive. Expressive roles are oriented toward the internal needs of the family, meeting the prerequisites of integration and latency by supporting and nurturing people, smoothing over tensions, and teaching the family values and patterns of behaviour to the children. Parsons argues that these functional imperatives reinforce, if they do not totally mandate, sex-role division of labour within families.

Spencer (1976, ch. 11) speculates on what might happen if a particular husband and wife decided to change this pattern. In order to challenge male control over goals and adaptation decisions, she argues, a couple must first acknowledge their present functions. Western societies generally mandate a certain pattern of sex-role specialization, such that the male is obliged to support and defend his wife and children. Thus society penalizes the male if both partners want to stay home. If men and women want equal work opportunities, both must take equal responsibility for support of the family. If the wife were to become the chief breadwinner, Spencer argues, then she would have to have authority within the household. If her job required her to move, then the rest of the family would have to move with good grace. If she pays the bills, she would have to decide the family budget. If she is to be fit and awake for her job, then her dependants would have to protect her health, her mood, her rest, and so on, by obeying her requests. Spencer notes that these are the prerogatives now enjoyed by men and resented by women. She concludes that traditional roles are designed to protect children and are functionally necessary, at least to some degree.

Functionalists also argue that the typical nuclear family pattern, consisting of a married couple with their children, is mandated by the requirements of industrial society. Industrialization is founded on free labour markets and a flexible, mobile work force. Workers and their families must be willing to move as and where the breadwinner's work demands. The nuclear group is much more mobile than the extended family group, which is commonly tied to landed property.

In summary, functionalism appears to offer a comprehensive theory that accounts for all the essential features of family as we know it in industrialized society. The heterosexual pair bonding at the core of any family system stems from biological imperatives—not merely the sex drive, but the need for long-term nurturing of newborn infants and children. The sex-role division of labour within families and the segregation of women's domestic nurturing work from male instrumental roles in the work force are rooted both in biological predispositions and in the very distinctive values and behaviour orientations of family life and occupational roles in industrial society. The authority of males in the home in terms of the allocation of money also reflects the imperatives of the breadwinner role that men normally hold. The demands for a mobile work force account for the predominantly isolated nuclear family residence pattern. The explanation seems complete. It suggests that efforts to change family life or sex roles in any significant way are impractical.

Critique of Functionalist Theory

The functionalist theory of the family has come under considerable attack, however, primarily for elevating a historically specific form of family into a universal principle. The theory ignores the wide diversity of family forms. Such diversity renders a rigidly defined notion of the family, such as that proposed by Murdock (1949), useless. Functionalist views of the family have been challenged, especially by Marxist and feminist theorists, as an ideology that seeks to justify the status quo while ignoring the ways in which family life is constrained by interests associated with capitalism and patriarchy. These are interests that benefit in multiple ways from exploiting the cheap labour of women in the home. Functionalism supports that exploitation by legitimating it as if it were unavoidable and universal. The traditional functionalist model of the family has been criticized particularly for a false universalism that implies that all the functions associated with family life are necessarily met by a single institution in which all functional elements are combined. In Eichler's view, such theorizing is flawed by four major biases: monolithic, conservative, sexist, and microstructural (Eichler 1988a, chs. 1–4). In this section we briefly examine each of these biases in turn.

Monolithic Bias

The **monolithic bias** is inherent in Murdock's definition of the family, which functionalists tend to treat as a given. A host of alternative family forms that have existed in other societies, and that are emerging in contemporary industrial societies such as Canada, are simply ignored or treated as problematic deviations. Anthropologists have long been familiar with examples of cultural patterns in other societies that violate some or all elements of Murdock's supposedly universal family form.

The Nayars of South India had, until the beginning of the twentieth century, a family form that incorporated none of the attributes considered essential by functionalists. Family life was not organized around sexually cohabiting pairs. There was no economic co-operation between women and their sexual partners, and the children of such liaisons had no socially recognized relationship with their biological fathers. They might not even know who their father was. Nayar families were organized around the female line. The joint family comprised the mother, her siblings, and her own and her sisters' children. A brief ceremony took place before girls reached puberty that linked each girl with a man from her own social rank. The ritual functioned only to establish female adult sexual status. From then on, women were free to have sexual relations with whomever they chose. Children lived in their mother's joint family home. Men did not live with their sexual partners; they continued to live in their own mother's household. All property belonging to the joint family was inherited through the mother's line. The mother's eldest brother commonly managed the property, but he did not own it and could not dispose of it. His principal relationship with children was as uncle to his sisters' offspring (Liddle and Joshi 1986, 28, 51–52).

Other studies suggest that in Jamaica, and in poor black communities in the United States, nuclear families are also not the norm. The stable relationship is between a woman and her children, while she has only temporary and sequential relations with male partners (Reiss, 1976, 14–15).

Functionalists have responded to these challenges to the universality of the family by proposing various redefinitions around the mother-child dyad or, more commonly, by dismissing variations as rare aberrations that prove the general rule (Reiss 1976, ch. 2). The Nayar culture can be viewed as an anthropological anomaly that developed in the exceptional circumstances of extensive migration of males in search of work as soldiers. The fact that this type of family broke down in the early twentieth century during British rule in India indicates that it was not a viable form. Critics doubt whether such a system could work in any larger society. The female-headed households among poor blacks do not represent a cultural ideal so much as the collapse of normal family life in the face of the abject poverty and chronic unemployment of black males. The ideal remains permanent marriage and stable fatherhood.

But charges of monolithic bias cannot be avoided simply by dismissing these family forms as aberrations. Eichler challenges the monolithic bias squarely within the North American society that functionalist theory is designed to explain. She argues that the image of family as the monogamous nuclear group comprising husband, wife, and their biological children applies to only a minority of structures that participants themselves regard as family. The argument that most individuals may have lived in a nuclear family at some time in their lives does not alter the fact that the majority of people in Canada are not now living in such families. Functionalists arbitrarily exclude from their definition of family a multitude of other arrangements: common-law couples (see table 14-1); commuting couples where spouses have careers in different places and meet only on weekends or holidays; couples who do not have children; couples whose children live elsewhere; **reconstituted families** where one or both spouses may have children living elsewhere; single-parent families; homosexual couples; and so on.

Eichler suggests that, if functionalists insist on having one definition to cover all forms of family, it would have to look something like the following: A family is a social group that may or may not include adults of both sexes, may or may not have children born in wedlock, or originating in the marriage, may or may not be living in a common residence, may or may not be sexually cohabiting, and may or may not include love, attraction, economic support, and so on (Eichler 1988a, 4).

Eichler proposes that the attempt to define the family should be abandoned in favour of an alternative approach that empirically researches the dimensions of family life. The important dimensions that Eichler (1988a, 6) singles out are procreation, socialization of children, sexual relations, residence patterns, economic co-operation, and emotional support. Functionalists assume that members of a family will be high on all

Table 14-1

Age Group	1981		1986		1991	
	Men	Women	Men	Women	Men	Women
Total	356 610	356 610	486 945	486 945	725 945	725 945
15–19	8 340	32 450	4 655	21 535	6 570	26 135
20–24	83 080	109 625	81 630	123 500	89 195	138 485
25–29	88 120	77 675	122 670	116 085	163 840	169 060
30–34	61 160	47 865	90 335	76 730	140 410	130 900
35–39	38 715	29 325	65 010	52 670	101 305	91 980
40–44	24 230	18 715	42 395	33 950	76 735	65 490
45–49	17 630	13 275	26 525	21 110	53 570	42 130
50–54	13 315	10 290	19 215	14 430	34 155	24 310
55–59	9 080	7 450	13 710	10 410	24 020	14 680
60–64	5 740	4 770	9 245	7 625	16 330	9 710
65+	7 200	5 170	11 555	8 895	19 815	13 065

Number of Persons Living in Common-law Unions, by Age Group and Sex, Canada, 1981, 1986, and 1991

Source: Reproduced by authority of the Ministry of Industry, 1994. Adapted from Statistics Canada (1994a), *Age, Sex, Marital Status, and Common-law Status*, Cat. 92-325E.

Gay rights activists in Toronto lobby for social benefits for same-sex couples under the banner "We Are Family."

dimensions. A husband and wife will have children together, socialize them, have sexual relations with each other, live together, co-operate economically, and give each other emotional support. This global assumption is false. Eichler addresses each dimension in turn, suggesting how it needs to be reconceptualized in terms of a range of behaviour options that vary widely, depending on circumstances.

The dimension of *procreation*, for example, has been radically affected by the number of couples choosing to remain childless and by the high rate of divorce and remarriage. Eichler (1988a, 243) cites evidence that, in Canada in 1985, one in three marriages ended in divorce. Statistics Canada data indicates that between 15 to 20 percent of brides or grooms in 1985 were previously married. We can estimate that between a quarter to a third of all Canadian children grow up in reconstituted families where one of the adults with whom they live is not their biological parent.

The dimension of *socialization* is likewise a variable. A child may be socialized by both biological parents together, or by one parent alone, or one parent with one step-parent, or one parent and step-parent in one house and another parent and step-parent in a second house, or some other combination of possible arrangements. It also cannot be assumed that simply because a parent lives in the same house as a child that that parent is involved in socialization. It is quite possible and probably common for one parent to do most of the socialization work while the other does very little. Similarly, we cannot assume that when parents are divorced, the absentee parent is necessarily not involved in socialization. It may well be that divorced fathers give more time and attention to children than do fathers in two-parent households who take it for granted that the mother will do all the child-rearing work. Even the assumption that socialization gets done by parents can be questioned in a society in which very large numbers of young children spend most of their waking time in child-care centres, or with nannies, and in the company of television.

The notion that *sexual relations* take place only between married or cohabiting partners can readily be challenged. Lifelong chastity in marriage may be the exception rather than the rule. This, in turn, has important implications for procreation. It cannot simply be assumed that all children are the biological offspring of the mother's spouse.

Residence patterns also vary widely. In divorced and reconstituted families, children may have two separate family homes and commute between them. It is possible, although rare in our society, for children to have one residence while the parents rotate. Many two-career families have two or even three separate homes, one near the husband's and/or the wife's work and another family home elsewhere. Many more couples may live in one place during the winter and another during the summer.

Economic co-operation cannot be treated as given within a family. Functionalists conceive of the husband-breadwinner providing economic resources for the homemaking wife and their children, but many other arrangements are common. A sole breadwinner may pool all income for joint family use, or may keep some or most of the money for private use and give only a housekeeping allowance to the spouse. In extreme cases, the nonemployed spouse may get no money at all: the breadwinner keeps everything and makes all decisions about what to buy. Two-income families have another set of possible arrangements; this is compounded when there are adult, income-earning children living at home.

The last dimension of family interaction, *emotional relations*, may vary all the way from close, loving, and mutually supportive ties to shallow and detached relations with little emotional involvement. In extreme though by no means uncommon situations, emotional relations may be characterized by abuse, violence, and hatred.

Traditional functionalist theory is not adequate to explore the dimensions of family life because the theoretical structure itself is too rigid. The monolithic bias is so pervasive that most sociology of the family textbooks, even in the 1980s,

ignore the huge number of reconstituted families and all other forms of living arrangements not organized around heterosexually cohabiting pairs (see figure 14-1). All other family forms are pre-defined as "problem families" regardless of how participants feel about them. We know little or nothing about the internal economies of families, because functionalism does not go beyond treating families as economic units. Most textbooks ignore the issue of family violence entirely or at best treat it as an aberration. This is notwithstanding the evidence of extensive wife battering and the physical and sexual abuse of children. Eichler suggests that, far from being an aberration, emotional stress and violence may be normal occurrences in families. The situation of enforced intimacy between people of different sexes, different careers, different incomes, and markedly different ages would normally be seen as conducive to high stress in any context other then families. Why would we expect families to be immune?

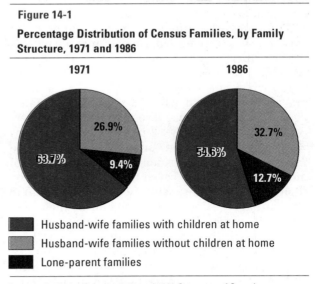

Figure 14-1

Percentage Distribution of Census Families, by Family Structure, 1971 and 1986

1971   1986

1971: 26.9%, 63.7%, 9.4%

1986: 32.7%, 54.6%, 12.7%

■ Husband-wife families with children at home
▨ Husband-wife families without children at home
■ Lone-parent families

Source: Statistics Canada, 1971 and 1986 Censuses of Canada.

Conservative Bias

Other biases compound the distortions arising from a monolithic focus. Eichler criticizes traditional sociology of the family literature for its **conservative bias**, reflected in a pervasive failure to focus upon changes that are transforming family life. Demographic variables are high on the list of critical changes. People in Canada are having fewer children than in the past and are living much longer. Declining fertility rates mean that most women experience pregnancy only twice in their lives. A full-time mothering role is no longer a lifetime expectation. Over half the adult women in Canada are employed outside the home. Even for the stereotypical family, the period of "Mom, Dad, and the kids" may cover only a limited stage in the family life cycle. Couples who have one or two children in their early twenties can look forward to twenty to thirty years of working lives after their children have left home. They can also realistically expect ten or more years of life after retirement.

Changes in longevity have been dramatic and are having a profound impact on family life. Eichler (1988a, 42) notes that, in 1931, the average life expectancy for a male at birth was 60.0 years, but this had risen to 70.2 years by 1986. The rise in life expectancy for women was even larger: from 62.1 years in 1932 to 78.3 years in 1986. Thus, women, on average, outlive men by over eight years, and they also tend to marry men who are older than themselves.

The combined effect of women's longer life expectancy and men's older age of marriage leads to very different experiences for women and men (Eichler 1988a, 42–43). Figures for 1986 show that 74 percent of men aged 65 and over were married, compared with 42 percent of women aged 65 and older who were married, and 46 percent widowed. Roughly 12 percent of both groups were single, separated, or divorced (see figure 14-2). These differences mean that the majority of men can expect to be cared for in their old age by their younger wives, while women of the same age can rarely expect to be cared for by their husbands. It would take a dramatic change in marriage patterns to redress this imbalance, but there is no evidence that this is happening.

Eichler points out that the pattern of long widowhood for women is particularly problematic because of the uneven distribution of earnings and pensions between women and men. Women who have worked as homemakers all their lives have no individual pension entitlements when their husbands die, other than the universal old age pensions paid by the government. Women generally spend more years outside the paid labour force than men to care for children. Even when they do work full-time, they earn signifi-

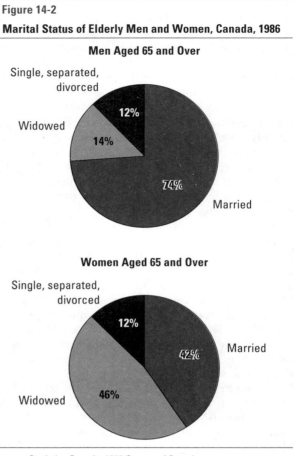

Figure 14-2

Marital Status of Elderly Men and Women, Canada, 1986

Men Aged 65 and Over

Single, separated, divorced 12%
Widowed 14%
Married 74%

Women Aged 65 and Over

Single, separated, divorced 12%
Married 42%
Widowed 46%

Source: Statistics Canada, 1986 Census of Canada.

cantly less money than men. Low earnings translate into low pensions. Poverty rates rise steeply for women in the older age groups, where most are widowed. The 1992 poverty rates are shown in figure 14-3.

The rise in average life expectancies also means that a greater proportion of people are living into their eighties and nineties. What this means is that people who are themselves elderly and retired commonly have parents who require care. These responsibilities fall particularly heavily upon women, since it tends to be women rather than men who do the caring work within families. Many women around sixty-five years of age may find themselves caring for their own very elderly mother, and perhaps their father and in-laws, as well as for their older, retired husband. This is a great deal of work to do at an age when the woman herself might have expected to

Figure 14-3

Poverty Rates, 1992

Poverty Rates for Persons by Age and Sex, 1992

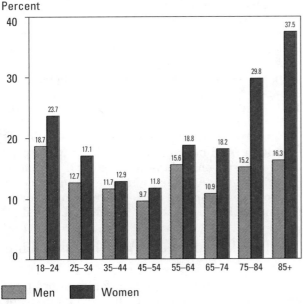

Percent

Men Women

Poverty Rates by Family Type and Age of Head, 1992

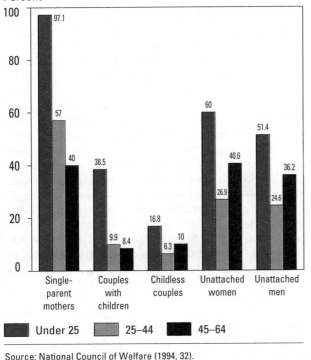

Percent

Under 25   25–44   45–64

Source: National Council of Welfare (1994, 32).

be able to retire from the obligations of looking after other people.

All of these are very dramatic changes from family life in Canada only a few generations earlier, yet they receive little attention in functionalist theory.

Sexist Bias

The **sexist bias** in family sociology is reflected in the pervasive stereotyping of female and male roles around images of the pregnant woman and man the hunter. Such images are largely irrelevant in an era when few women have more than two pregnancies, and the vast majority of men neither hunt nor have jobs that require hard physical labour. This stereotyping perpetuates the myth that women are only marginally involved in the work force and that men are marginally involved in homelife and child-rearing. Still worse, functionalist theory elevates such myths to the level of functional imperatives, conveying the impression that alternative lifestyles threaten the equilibrium of family and occupational subsystems, and hence threaten society itself.

Microstructural Bias

Lastly, the **microstructural bias** in functionalist theory is reflected in a primary focus on the internal workings of individual family units. Most sociology of the family textbooks give little consideration to the impact of the wider political economy and the nature of government policies as they affect family life. Functionalists tend to discuss family problems as if they arose from inadequacies in the role of performance of individual members, rather than from external pressures on people. The microstructural bias is inherent in each of the other biases described above. We cannot understand what is happening to families apart from studying the political economy in relation to which people organize their personal lives.

Marxist Theories of the Family

The Marxist approach to sociology of the family challenges the microstructural bias of traditional functionalist theory. Marxists argue that both the organization of economic production in the wider society and the way people earn their living critically influence the organization of family life. The family form that functionalists assert as universal represents only one historically specific form, prevalent only at a certain stage in the development of capitalism and only for members of a certain social class. Marxist feminists accept this broad analysis of the relationship between modes of production and family forms but give special attention to the impact of the economy on women's roles within the family. They challenge Parsons' notion of a separation between the **private realm** of family life and the **public realm** of industry. They claim that the demands of capitalism intrude into the most intimate personal relations of family life. Homemakers work for the corporations as much as employees do. The only difference is that the homemakers' work is not acknowledged and is not paid for.

The Marxist Theory of Patriarchy

The Marxist perspective draws its initial inspiration from an early essay by Engels ([1884] 1978), a long-time colleague of Marx. Engels speculates that the earliest form of family was probably communal, based on relatively free sexual relations and organized around matriarchal households, reflecting the known biological relation between mother and child. The family form among the Nayars, described earlier, closely resembles the model that Engels had in mind.

Engels argues that this original matriarchal family form was probably undermined by two factors: the knowledge of paternity and male control over private property. Awareness of the male role in conception represented a profound leap of knowledge, Engels suggests, with important implications for power within the family, especially when combined with control over property. As the means of subsistence changed from hunting and gathering to more settled herding and agriculture, men gained control over land and domestic herds and thus over the economic surplus. As men gained wealth, they wanted to control inheritance through the male line. This necessitated control over women's sexuality and over their offspring. Monogamy and patriarchy emerged together, Engels suggests. Monogamy was strictly required for women; men could still enjoy relative sexual freedom. This inequality gave rise to prostitution. Engels comments that "the overthrow of mother right was the world historic defeat of the female sex. The man seized

the reins of the house also, the woman was degraded, enthralled, the slave of man's lust, a mere instrument for breeding children" (Engels [1884] 1978, 736).

Engels suggests that inegalitarian family forms would disappear only under two possible situations. The first was where people were so poor that men would have no property to inherit or pass on. The second was under a system of communal ownership of the means of production and equal employment of women in a socialist society. This would remove forever the basis of male power over women.

Engels' essay, and particularly his theory of the transition from matriarchy to patriarchy, is speculative, based on little anthropological evidence. But his argument concerning the importance of control over property as a determinant of male dominance in the household is widely accepted.

Capitalism and Family Forms in Canada

In a series of essays, Dorothy Smith (1977, 1979b, 1983b) traces changing forms of property ownership associated with the development of capitalism in Canada. She examines how these changes transformed relations between women and men in the home. During the early homesteading period, she argues, a husband and wife shared all property. They depended on each other and worked together to produce everything they needed to survive. There was no separation between domestic and productive work. Men cleared and ploughed land for crops while women maintained gardens, kept chickens, pigs, and cows, helped in the harvest, and preserved the food. Women owned not only what they produced, but also whatever money they could make by selling surplus vegetables, eggs, and butter in the market. Thus, a basic economic and social equality existed between wife and husband.

This equality changed in a subtle but significant way with the transition from subsistence homesteading to cash production. Land speculation led to escalating prices, and settlers required heavy mortgages to buy land and equipment. This meant that they were no longer merely producing food for the subsistence needs of their families. Their survival depended on producing cash crops like wheat from which to earn the money to pay bank loans. Laws of property, debt, and credit endowed only the husband with full economic status in a marriage. Land was held as collateral for loans and mortgages made to him. The result, suggests Smith, was drudgery and tyranny for farm wives, who were totally subordinated to their husbands. They laboured on the homesteads, but all their labour went to pay off bank loans. When the mortgage was finally paid off, the farm belonged legally only to the husband. Women owned nothing. All the results of their labour were appropriated by their husbands.

The powerlessness of farm wives was underlined by the Supreme Court of Canada decision in 1975 concerning Irene Murdoch. She had worked on the family farm for twenty-five years with her husband but, after their divorce, the court decreed that she had no legal right to any of the farm property. Women who worked with their husbands in other kinds of small business enterprises found themselves in essentially the same situation. They had no assurance of a share in the assets of a business to which they had contributed. It took a national outcry from women's organizations after the Murdoch decision to change the law to give women a share in marital property and family business.

As capitalism had advanced, the petite bourgeoisie—people who earn their living by means of family farms and family-run businesses—had declined. In the current era of corporate monopoly capitalism, the vast majority of Canadian families depend upon employment in large corporations and state bureaucracies. This dependence on wages and salaries from work done outside the home and beyond the control of family members has critical implications for the working lives of those adults who still remain within the home. Typically, men were the first to leave the home to work for wages. Women continued to do domestic work and to care for children, but they were cut off from the productive enterprise. Production was no longer centred around the home but took place in factories to which they did not have access. Marxists argue that this historically specific change in the development of capitalism produced the separate role of housewife and the model of the private family segregated from the occupational world. This is the same model that Parsons treats as a universal principle.

Marxist feminist theorists argue that women's work in the home remains crucial to the productive enterprise. The ties that bind homemakers to the corporations are less immediately visible than those binding employees but, nonetheless, almost all aspects of their working days are dictated by corporate demands. Women's labour within the home is appropriated by corporations in multiple ways, but this relation tends to be covered up by the misleading notion of the homemaker's work as a private service to her breadwinner husband. Smith argues that this "private service" by homemakers for their husbands and children may ultimately be responsible for holding together the entire system of capitalist relations of production. Smith rejects the simplistic version of Marxist theory that claims that class structure determines family structure. She insists that we must examine what people do in their everyday lives to produce the relations that we subsequently come to see as the class structure. Women's work in the home is an integral part of the processes through which class relations are produced and maintained on a daily basis. It is these work processes that we briefly explore below.

The Social Construction of Class Relations in the Home

Whether or not women work outside the home, they maintain the responsibility for homework. This responsibility and the ways in which women's homework is appropriated by capitalism vary with the social class or occupation of employed family members, which may include the women themselves. A working-class wife has to put a home together, often under conditions of poverty and inadequate housing. Her labour is vital in the struggle for some measure of comfort on a limited income. Her efforts make it possible for people to survive on incomes that may barely meet subsistence needs. Her fundamental work for the corporation is to keep her husband working under these conditions. Corporations know well that married men make more stable workers than single men because of their responsibility to support their families. It is less easy for married men to leave if they do not like the working conditions. The working-class wife supports the capitalist system against her husband because she depends so heavily upon his wages to provide for herself and her children. She cannot let him quit. An unemployed man may commonly be punished by his wife, through nagging, criticism, and humiliation, to pressure him back into the work force.

Luxton (1980, ch. 3) describes with stark realism the harsh lives of women married to miners in the single-industry town of Flin Flon in northern Manitoba. The working lives of these housewives remain totally tied to the rhythms of their husbands' work. A housewife must get up long before the mine whistle goes, to get her husband up, fed, and ready for work, and she must be there to greet him with his dinner when he returns. When he is working shifts, she must alter her entire schedule to meet his and yet still maintain the school schedules of their children. She must keep the children quiet and out of the way when he is sleeping, do her housework only when it will not disturb him, provide meals when he wants them, and in effect manage the family so that he turns up regularly for work. In a sense, she is as much an employee of the mine as he is, but she does not get paid.

The appropriation of the labour of middle-class women by capitalism takes a different form. In material terms, their lives may be more comfortable and their homemaking responsibilities easier to meet than those of working-class housewives because they do not have to struggle against poverty. But the wives of men who hold managerial and executive positions within corporations may have less personal autonomy as they find themselves more trapped by the demands of the corporation. Smith (1977) argues that, while a working-class man has a job within a corporation, a man in a more senior rank plays a role for the corporation. He must meet the image of a corporation man, and it is his wife's duty to maintain this image and to mould their children to fit it. The family home becomes something of a subcontracted agency of the corporation. The housewife works to produce the image that the corporation wants. The image that is on display is largely set by the media and disseminated in glossy magazines and television advertising; the housewife herself has little control over it. It is subtly but rigidly enforced within the corporate hierarchy. An executive whose personal and family appearance does not conform to the corporate mould tends to be viewed with suspicion and overlooked for promotion.

Middle-class women routinely support the careers of their husbands by relieving them of household and child-care responsibilities.

The corporate man is then free to display his undivided loyalty to the corporation by spending long hours of overtime at the office on evenings and weekends and travelling on business whenever requested. In the highly competitive corporate world, such behaviour is often essential for mobility up the corporate hierarchy. The support work that wives do often begins very early in men's corporate careers. A wife may work to support her husband through college. Subsequently, she may help his career by entertaining his business associates and doing unpaid secretarial work. The wife of a professor often helps with the research, sorting, and editing involved in writing, although the resulting work bears only his name. Corporations thus appropriate the labour time of the wives of their executives and professional staff through the support services that wives are routinely expected to provide for their husbands. The competence of wives, especially wives of executives, to perform these support roles can be so important that some corporations have insisted on interviewing not only the male applicants for senior positions, but their wives as well (Kanter 1977).

A middle-class homemaker further serves the corporation through absorbing the tensions generated by the career demands made on her husband. In this there is a catch-22; when she supports and repairs him and sends him back refreshed, she is in fact supporting the external system that oppresses him. But, like her working-class counterpart, she has little choice. To be a good homemaker, she must make her husband's success visible. She cannot afford to let him fail.

Corporations also appropriate the mothering work of middle-class women. Middle-class status is inherited not through property, but through careers, and mothering work is essential to this process. The academic streaming of children begins very early in the education process, and a mother who wants her children to succeed in future corporate careers must groom them even in infancy so that they will perform well from the first days of kindergarten. Her children's failure in school will be seen as evidence that she does not love them enough.

In times of economic recession, women's unpaid labour in the home absorbs the resulting social problems. As unemployment rises, women are disproportionately affected, laid off more frequently, and pushed into part-time work. They bear the increased burden of the emotional stress felt by workers who risk being unemployed or who may be squeezed out in corporate mergers. As we saw in chapter 9, women in the home must absorb the extra work no longer being done by professionals when social services are cut back for the elderly, the handicapped, and the sick. (Armstrong 1984, ch. 7).

In these multiple ways, homemakers work for the corporate capitalist system—work for which they receive no pay and rarely any acknowledgment. The enormity of their exploitation is hidden under the myth of private family life. Until the women's movement began to have some impact, all the work that women did in the home was not even identified as work. It was considered merely "a labour of love" (Luxton 1980).

Research in the Marxist feminist tradition has documented the processes through which relations of political economy intrude into the most intimate relations of love and marriage. Luxton's study of Flin Flon shows how courtship and marriage are affected by the economy of this single-industry mining town, in which there are few well-paying jobs for women. Marriage is the only viable option for adult women in the town. This reality pervades the dating game and sexual activities. Boys have the chance to earn good money working in the mine while girls do not. Girls therefore trade sexual favours for a good time and economic rewards. Boys pay for the date and expect, sooner rather than later, that the girl will "come across." This same dependency continues after marriage and is made all the more evident if pregnancy has forced a quick wedding. Both the woman and the man feel trapped by her dependence on his wages.

Luxton (1980, ch. 6) suggests that this economic reality is at the root of much domestic violence. She describes the explosive tensions that revolve around the fact that he earns the money and she spends it. Men who come home drained and exhausted from a day's work at the mine often feel they have a right to control the household because they are responsible for its subsistence. Many of the women whom Luxton interviewed described how they took the brunt of their husband's resentment against his job. One woman summed it up this way: "He puts up with shit every day at work and he only works because he has to support me and the kids. Weren't for us he'd be off trapping on his own—no boss" (Luxton 1980, 70). Women blame themselves, feeling guilty for having induced male hostility and

aggression by being a burden. Women absorb the tensions. In extreme cases they absorb violence and beatings. More commonly, they deny themselves even basic needs because they cannot escape the sense of guilt that they are spending "his" money on themselves. This is the reality that is glossed over in the abstract functionalist category of "tension management."

Such dependent relationships may only be marginally improved for most women who take up employment outside the home. Having their own income allows women some independence, but the reality is that few women can hope to earn enough to support themselves and their children above the poverty line. With the exception of a minority of professional women, a male wage is still essential to support an average middle-class family lifestyle.

In summary, Marxist feminists argue that family relations and domestic work are embedded in the political economy of corporate capitalism. Homemakers are agents of tension management and pattern maintenance for corporations, but their work is not acknowledged and not paid for. They remain outside the corporations and so cannot influence any of the decisions that direct their lives. Smith (1977) sees this as the root of depression and mental illness among women. Women are oppressed in a nameless way by a system from which they appear to be entirely separated and yet which comes to rule the most intimate aspects of their lives. This thesis avoids the monolithic and conservative biases evident in functionalist theory by analysing family structures in their historical and class contexts. Family forms in Canada changed markedly with transformations in capitalism from early homesteading, through cash cropping and small business, to the current form of monopoly capitalism. The thesis also incorporates an analysis of the processes through which people socially construct the realities of family life in the situation in which they find themselves.

The Radical Feminist Critique: Capitalism or Patriarchy?

The **radical feminist** perspective shares with Marxism an appreciation of the impact of capitalism on family life, but challenges the narrow, deterministic focus on political economy as the cause of family structures. These theorists argue that this tunnel vision of traditional Marxists gives inadequate attention to relations of patriarchy or gender hierarchy that cannot be subsumed under capitalism. In particular, they challenge the more deterministic version of Marxist theory, sometimes referred to as Marxist structuralism, that explains family structures by reference to their functions for the capitalist system.

Marxists would argue, for example, that the privatization of women in the home occurs because it is functional for capitalism (Armstrong and Armstrong 1985). Capitalism is based on free wage-labour that requires the separation of a public, commodity-production unit from a private subsistence unit in which free labourers are reproduced and maintained. Hence the subordination of women appears to be a necessary condition for the capitalist system. Structuralist Marxists also describe the position of women as a reserve army of labour, which can be stored cheaply within the home, as necessary for the capitalist system. The implications of this thesis are that the **privatization** of women was not evident in the precapitalist era. It arose with capitalism and will decline with the transition to socialism.

Radical feminists argue that the evidence does not support this thesis. In precapitalist Europe, the economy may have centred around domestic production in which women were involved, but this did not ensure gender equality, either in family practice or in religious and social ideologies. In many parts of contemporary Asia, in both Hindu and Muslim cultures, the traditions of **purdah**, which include an emphasis on the extreme subjugation and segregation of women within the home, still persist. The origins of the purdah system long predate the emergence of capitalism. If anything, this extreme privatization of women has begun to break down under capitalism, as more women gain access to education and professional employment outside the home.

The Marxist thesis shows how capitalism accommodates and uses existing inequalities between women and men in the household, but this is not sufficient to explain why such inequalities developed in the first place or why they persist (Miles 1985). We still need to explain why capitalism developed in such a way as to bolster men's power over women. We need to explain why the sexual division of labour appears as it does. Why is it, almost invariably, women and not men who are engaged in unpaid domestic labour? Marx tends to treat this as the biological nature of things, but it is by no means biologically determined that women must do the domestic work beyond the actual physical acts of giving birth and breast-feeding. Why is it mostly women who bear the double burden of domestic work and a paid job? Why do husbands continue to do so little domestic work in comparison with their wives, even when wives are employed full-time? Why is it that the issue of whether a wife should be employed takes on the connotations of a threat to male power and status? Reference to the needs of capitalism does not seem to explain this. Marxist theory would actually predict the opposite response, that men would generally welcome any reduction in the economic burden of a dependent wife.

The prevalence of domestic violence is also not adequately explained within the Marxist thesis. Economic dependence helps to explain the vulnerability of women to male power, but it does not explain why so many wives are battered in the first place (Miles 1985, 47). Nor does economic dependence account for other forms of male violence against women and children, such as rape, incest, and sexual harassment. It cannot explain practices such as burning widows alive on the funeral pyres of their husband, foot-binding, genital mutilation, and **dowry murders**, which are prevalent in some non-Western societies.

Radical feminists assert that Marxist theory describes but does not explain male supremacy inside and outside the home. The exploitation of workers under capitalism and the oppression of women by men are not equivalent concepts (Eisenstein 1979, 22). Relations of patriarchy have to be addressed directly. In trying to subsume issues of patriarchy under the blanket explanation of capitalism, Marxist theory functions as an ideology. It can serve to legitimate male domination over women by displacing responsibility onto the economy.

This misuse of Marxist theory was powerfully illustrated at a meeting of the Canadian Asian Studies Association in response to a paper describing women's oppression in Pakistan under President Zia's "Islamization" program (Rafiq 1988; Hale 1988b). Part of the paper referred to Islamic law concerning rape. A woman who claims she has been raped requires no less than four male witnesses, all of impeccable character, before she can press charges in court. Otherwise, her case will be dismissed, and she herself can be sentenced to public flogging for having engaged in unlawful sex. Men in the audience reinterpreted this paper in terms of the capitalist mode of production, debating how it was in the interests of the capitalist class to keep women at home as cheap labour. In this determinist, structuralist version of Marxism, the men who commit the violence disappear: it is the system that appears to do things. A woman's experience of being raped, with those who violate her not only immune to punishment, but able to have her flogged for even mentioning what they had done to her, was excluded from the debate. It became trivialized as a form of false consciousness, while the concerns of men with their own class oppression took precedence. Radical feminist theory addresses this failure to analyse the oppression of women by placing the issue of patriarchy at the centre of sociology of the family.

The Roots of Male Power

O'Brien (1981) challenges the original thesis proposed by Engels that links male power and control over property. Engels argues that, with the development of settled agriculture and herding, men controlled the means of production and hence the wealth of society. Men sought control over women in order to ensure that their property would be inherited by their own biological children. Thus, the institution of monogamy for women became important. O'Brien suggests that this thesis has too many unquestioned assumptions. Why did men gain control over property in the first place? Why did it have to be inherited through the male line? Why did it have to be inherited individually rather than by the community as a whole? Among the **matrilineal** Nayar in South India, land and animals were communally owned by the mother's joint family and inherited by her children. Men did not have the right to own or to dispose of such property. Why and how did men come to wrest control from the original matriarchal communal families?

O'Brien proposes that the basic causal relationship between control over property and control over women's sexuality should be reversed. Men, she suggests, seek to control property in order to control women's sexual and reproductive

powers, not the other way around. The material base of the gender hierarchy is the means of reproduction of children rather than production of material goods. When a women has sexual freedom, a man has no way of knowing which, if any, of her children he fathered. Paternity is reduced to an abstract idea. O'Brien argues that male alienation from birth, and thus from human continuity through children, is profound. This alienation can only be partially overcome by the institution of monogamy, through which a man asserts an exclusive right of sexual access to a particular woman.

Male power over women is not automatic, but is the result of continual struggle, in which final victory is impossible. Men can struggle to control women, but it is women who control reproduction. Male control over a woman's reproductive powers, and hence male appropriation of her children as his own, is always uncertain. It depends upon absolute faith in her chastity or upon the strictest possible control over her, including her seclusion from other men. It depends also on trust in other men. But such trust is tenuous, especially in the context of war, competition, and hierarchical divisions among men. Male dominance over other men in war is often expressed through sexual violation of the women "belonging" to the enemy.

O'Brien situates the origin of the private family, and the split between the private realm of women and the public realm of men, in this male struggle for exclusive sexual access to women, rather than in the development of capitalism. The economic dependence of women on men and the inability of women to support themselves and their children apart from a man are essential mechanisms for male control over women. The inheritance of property from father to son is also of paramount importance in the social assertion of the principle of paternity over biological maternity. Male control over property and inheritance thus remains central in O'Brien's thesis, but for different reasons than Engels proposes.

The major difference between the two formulations becomes evident in predicting the behaviour of males who own no property. Engels predicts that when men have no property to control or to transmit to children, they will have no interest in controlling women. O'Brien predicts that such men will still try to control women's sexual and reproductive powers through any other means at their disposal, including sexual violence.

The history of the mother-centred Nayar house-holds gives insight into the nature of the struggle for control over family property and women's reproductive powers. The Nayar family organization did not disappear as an inevitable result of developments in agriculture industrialization. It was deliberately and systematically undermined by the British Imperial government in India.

The British passed a series of laws between 1868 and 1933 that broke up the matrilineal households and imposed a monogamous, male-headed marriage system. The first law held that a man had to provide for his wife and children, a law that had no meaning in the Nayar situation. The next law declared that the wife and children had the right of maintenance by the husband. Again this had little effect because the Nayar did not register marriages. Then followed various Nayar Regulation Laws that decreed that the brief ceremony that took place when a girl reached puberty constituted a legal marriage that could only be dissolved through a legal divorce. The man gained the right to inherit the property of his wife rather than sharing in the communal property of his mother's household. Further laws declared that all property held in common in the matrilineal household could be broken up and inherited and that a man's heirs were no longer his sister's children but his wife's children. The laws were part of a long struggle for supremacy between men and women within the Nayar communities, and they are still bitterly resented and resisted by the Nayar women. Males gained the advantage under the British, both through the laws and through access to an English education, which enabled men but not women to obtain administrative posts in the British colonial service. Men thereby gained personal income and economic independence from the communal household, and they were granted the legal right to dispose of this private property as they wished (Liddle and Joshi 1986, 28–29).

In Canada, male power over women and property was similarly imposed through patriarchal laws. It was not the inevitable outcome of capitalist farming that dispossessed women homesteaders, but specific laws that required a man to have single, unencumbered title to real estate for it to stand as collateral for mortgages and loans. It was only after the Irene Murdoch case in 1975 that these laws were revised to permit and subsequently to require joint ownership by husband and wife of family property used as collateral. Native women were dispossessed by the British North America Act which decreed that any Native woman who married a non-Native forfeited all her rights to Native status and to band property. It was 1984 before this law was changed, and then only after it had been challenged before the World Court.

Given that ownership of property is such an important mechanism in male control over the sexual and reproductive powers of women, it follows that women's paid employment outside the home threatens that control. Radical feminist theory argues that men fear the expansion of income-earning opportunities for their wives, even though this relieves them of the economic burden of a dependent family. The theory predicts that men will strive to minimize the level of economic independence and also that they will strive to reassert control through other mechanisms including domestic violence and medical and legal control over reproduction.

Limits to Economic Freedom for Women

Liddle and Joshi (1986, part IV) argue that class hierarchy in the labour force is built upon and reinforces gender hierarchy. Women are employed but predominantly within low-paid job ghettos. Their incomes supplement their husbands' earnings but do not supercede them. Few women earn sufficient money to provide for themselves and their children at an average standard of living. They still depend on a male wage earner.

The unequal division of domestic labour within the home is cited by Liddle and Joshi as a primary mechanism ensuring the continued economic and familial dominance of men. Even when women are employed in full-time jobs outside the home, they commonly bear almost the entire responsibility for domestic work. Men, by and large, refuse to do this work, or at best contribute only in the least onerous areas. Men appropriate women's labour in the home to restore their own energies. They return to work relaxed and refreshed, while women return to work exhausted from doing three jobs: domestic work, child care, and the work for which they are paid. Then women are penalized in the labour market for having less strength and energy and making slower career progress than men.

Child care outside the home is limited and expensive, so that only women who earn above-average incomes can afford it. The majority of women are faced with the choice of taking long periods of time out of the paid labour force to care for young children or of working themselves to exhaustion trying to do everything. Women who take such time out, or who begin to develop a career only in their late thirties or early forties, present no competition to men who are far advanced in their positions.

Few women earn enough money to support themselves and their children.

This inequality in the labour force stemming from women's responsibility for domestic work becomes apparent whenever marriages break down. Wives are legally entitled to an equitable share in family property, but husbands take their income-earning capacity with them. All too often, women find themselves left with half a house, but without the income to maintain it.

This artificial separation between the realms of public and private, the world of men and the world of women and children, creates its own dynamic that tends to reinforce male efforts to control and possess women. The public realm is associated with rational and technical concerns of production, and the private family with meeting emotional needs. Men come to depend on women in the home to meet their ongoing need for nurturing or mothering, in addition to their need for women to procreate and to nurture their children. This may be especially so in societies where men are discouraged from being nurturing themselves and where they spend their working lives in a public realm, which is characterized by competitive, fragmented, impersonal, and emotionally neutral or nonaffective relationships. Long after children have been born and raised, men may still seek to possess women in order to ensure that their own nurturing needs are met. This need for personal nurturing may be so overwhelming for some men that they become jealous of their own children and the attention they are given by the nurturer-mother.

Domestic Violence

The threat and the reality of domestic violence, in all its forms, is another powerful mechanism for asserting male control over women and children. Until recently, wife beating had both religious and legal approval. The Roman Catholic law of chastisement enjoined a husband to beat his wife for her moral betterment. This injunction was carried over to British common law and Canadian and American law and only began to be challenged toward the end of the nineteenth century. Fathers were also endowed with the religious prescription and legal right to discipline their children using physical force.

In addition to physical battering, children are also victims of sexual abuse. Estimates of such abuse vary widely depending on the measurements used (Badgley 1984, 114). The rate most commonly cited is that one in five girls and one in ten boys have experienced unwanted sexual attention. Guessing rates by pitting the findings of different sources against each other is a largely futile exercise. But the fact that physical and sexual abuse of children occurs in a significant number of families is not in dispute. Why does such behaviour occur?

The Marxist thesis attributes the violence primarily to the frustration experienced by men who are employed or are trapped in low-paid, alienating jobs. Radical feminists dispute this explanation as inadequate to account for the extent of wife battery and incest. An American study (Shupe, Stacey, and Hazlewood 1987, 22–21) cites evidence that the social background of wife batterers in selected counselling sessions and police records mirrored the population at large with respect to age, education, race, ethnicity, religion, and occupation. The one exception was that the percentage of unemployed men among the batterers was double the national average. Unemployed men seem more likely to batter, perhaps because they have lost the economic basis of their control over their wives, but this does not alter the evidence that men from all strata of the population—including doctors, lawyers, politicians, ministers, and police officers—beat their wives. Similarly, many of the men who commit incest are "pillars of the community" in other respects.

Various psychological explanations have been put forward to account for wife battering. They include the common argument that it is a symptom of other emotional problems that can stem from trauma from abuse as a child, learned behaviour from watching an abusive father, lack of communication skills with the spouse, low self-esteem, lack of emotional controls, and the need to express repressed anger and frustration (Adams 1988). Radical feminists argue that such explanations only offer excuses for the batterer to continue the behaviour. They also do not account for why the batterer's behaviour is directed at his wife. Batterers rarely assault anyone other than their wives. They do not habitually lose emotional control or lack of communication skills in other contexts.

Radical feminists argue that one has to examine the practical gains that accrue to the batterer from his violence; that is, fear and submission in his victim and compliance with his wishes (Adams 1988; Ptacek 1988). Wife battering is essentially a controlling behaviour designed to create and maintain an imbalance of power in the household. Battery and sexual abuse of children are the extreme expressions of male assertion of property rights over women and children. Less extreme forms of such controlling behaviour include verbal and non-verbal intimidation and psychological abuse, pressure tactics like withholding financial support, accusations or threats of infidelity, ultimatums and deadlines that force

a woman to comply with her husband's wishes (Adams 1988, 191–94). Such persistent humiliation can be pushed to the point where competent, professional women have their self-esteem destroyed (Forward and Torres 1987, 15–85).

Government agencies provide some support for women who are the victims of abuse, but violence against women is deep-rooted in our society.

Not all expressions of violence are by husbands against wives. Some wives abuse their husbands, but it is currently impossible even to guess at the rate. It would appear that much of the violence directed by wives toward husbands is defensive or retaliatory. The relatively small number of unprovoked attacks on men by female partners seems often to involve jealous ex-wives and ex-girlfriends. Firestone (1971, ch. 6) suggests that many women are so intensely socialized to see their own self-worth in terms of being a sexual partner for a male that, when their relationship breaks down and the male begins to see another woman, their sense of self-worth and identity are shattered. Occasionally these feelings may turn to rage and hatred. Such responses, however, are not equivalent in form or intent to the systematic, repeated brutality that constitutes wife battering. While it may be true that much abuse experienced by husbands goes unreported, the same is true of abused wives. We do know that the overwhelming majority of people who are injured in domestic violence are female. There is a vast body of evidence of systematic, severe, intimidating force used by men against women, while there is no such evidence for women against husbands (Dobash and Dobash 1988, 60–62).

The problems of wife battering and sexual abuse of children are very deep-rooted in our society. They reflect both the identification of masculine sexuality with aggression and the pervasive socialization of males to be aggressive. They also reflect the patriarchal structures of family life that accord authority, power, and control to the father figure. Such power carries with it the inherent risk of corruption. Thirdly, they highlight the emotional shallowness of relations among men, which leaves the family as the only source of human warmth and sensuality. But this source is itself constrained and distorted by the emphasis on exclusivity, possession, authority, and control. Wives and children bear the emotional brunt of these distorted relations.

Custody Battles: Shared Parenting or Patriarchal Control?

Divorce is a fact of life in Canadian society (see table 14-2), but its frequency does not lessen the traumatic effect on the parties involved. Divorce invariably means a significant drop in the income of single-parent families headed by women. Divorced fathers who do not want to pay child support face no effective pressure to do so. The default rate on court-ordered support payments has been estimated to be between 80 and 90 percent (Crean 1989, 20). While the court generally awards custody of children to mothers, about half the fathers who contest custody win their case, often in the face of evidence of minimal previous involvement in nurturing and despite evidence of

Table 14-2

Number of Divorces, Canada, 1950–91

Year	Number of Divorces	Year	Number of Divorces
1950	5 386	1971	29 685
1951	5 270	1972	32 389
1952	5 650	1973	36 704
1953	6 160	1974	45 019
1954	5 923	1975	50 611
1955	6 053	1976	54 207
1956	6 002	1977	55 370
1957	6 688	1978	57 155
1958	6 279	1979	59 474
1959	6 543	1980	62 019
1960	6 980	1981	67 671
1961	6 563	1982	70 436
1962	6 768	1983	68 567
1963	7 686	1984	65 172
1964	8 623	1985	61 980
1965	8 974	1986	78 160
1966	10 239	1987	90 872
1967	11 165	1988	79 872
1968	11 343	1989	81 009
1969	26 093	1990	78 488
1970	29 775	1991	77 031

Source: Reproduced by authority of the Minister of Industry, 1994. Adapted from Statistics Canada (1994h), *Marriage and Conjugal Life in Canada*, Cat. 91-534E, table 18, p. 47.

physical or sexual abuse (Chesler 1991). Sexual abuse of children is difficult to prove, and mothers who raise the issue not only risk having their credibility challenged in court, but jeopardize their own custody claims by being labelled as an unfriendly parent who is trying to block rightful access by the father.

Custody battles over children and the demand for mandatory joint legal custody following divorce are forming a new arena of struggle between principles of feminism and patriarchy. Of particular concern to feminists are the threatening implications of seemingly progressive legislation aimed at ensuring the rights of divorced fathers in relation to their children. Mandatory joint custody legislation was passed in thirty-six American states between 1980 and 1988.

Across Canada, joint custody is an option but not a presumption. The Ontario Divorce Act of

1985 closely parallels the Ontario Children's Law Reform Act which states that the courts may award custody or access to one or more persons, but without any policy legislation favouring joint or sole custody. In each case "the best interests of the child" are paramount. A private member's bill introduced in the Ontario legislature in January 1988 sought to commit the province to mandatory joint custody, but the bill was not passed. Opponents emphasized the distinction between shared parenting and joint legal custody.

Medical and Legal Control over Reproduction

The struggle for control over women's reproductive power continues in the public arenas of medicine and law. In Canada, the medical profession has almost entirely succeeded in wresting technical control over childbirth from women (Burtch 1988). Formerly, O'Brien suggests (1981, 10), childbirth was an affirmation of sisterhood, a rite shared by the mother-to-be, the midwife, and other women friends who attended the birth in the community. However, as a government-financed health-care system developed, and as the traditional healing arts were professionalized and institutionalized, midwives were shut out. It became normal for childbirth to take place in an antiseptic hospital delivery room under the control of predominantly male obstetricians. Until very recently, it was normal for the mother to be drugged into semiconsciousness, her feet tied up in stirrups, while the baby was pulled out with forceps. While some accuse feminists of romanticizing simpler childbirths, feminists insist that the issue is male supremacy or, specifically, the supremacy of male doctors over mothers and midwives. Available evidence indicates that the mortality rate for home births with a midwife is as low or lower than physician-attended births in hospitals. Yet medical control remained absolute. Midwifery did not die out in Canada but it had no legal status. Women who attended home births could face criminal charges, especially if the newborn died. By law, a doctor had to be in attendance at a birth. As recently as April 1989, a Montreal doctor was suspended for six months for letting a midwife deliver the baby of one of his patients, without him being in the room.

Only in the 1990s has this control over birth by the medical profession begun to weaken, partly in response to pressure from the women's movement, and partly to cut medical costs. The province of Ontario led the way in 1986 with a decision to establish midwifery as a self-regulated profession. Five years later, the Midwifery Act was proclaimed, permitting midwives to work in maternity wards. On January 1, 1994, midwives were granted the right to admit women to hospital, deliver babies, and send them home, without consulting a doctor (*Globe and Mail*, 14 May 1994). In 1994, Quebec passed legislation approving midwifery in eight free-standing birthing centres but they met fierce opposition from doctors because they are not based in hospitals. By 1994, only one centre was still operating.

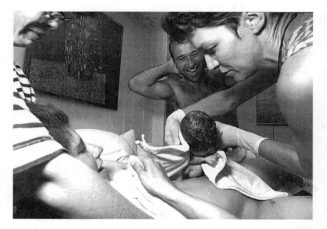

Midwives can now deliver babies in Ontario, allowing women to take back some medical control over childbirth.

Recent developments in reproductive technology, including test-tube babies, embryo transplants, surrogate motherhood, and assisted insemination, further this process of control over birth by predominantly male scientists. This medico-scientific takeover of birth is being combined with increasing legislative controls over the lives of pregnant women. Court-ordered stays in hospital and cesarean sections against the mother's will have already occurred in Canada (*Globe and Mail*, 1 Aug. 1986, D1–2). A Vancouver lawyer hired to fight one such case commented that one should not underestimate the male fixation on having the perfect son and heir, or what a man might do if a woman pregnant with his child was perceived to be disobeying orders that related to having that perfect baby. The desperation of some men to find a **surrogate mother** for artificial insemination with their sperm, and the amount they are prepared to pay for this service (around $15 000 U.S. plus expenses), underline how important biological reproduction is to many men.

The Canadian Royal Commission on New Reproductive Technologies, which issued its formal report in December of 1993, came out strongly against the commercialization of any aspect of human reproduction, including the sale of sperm or fetal tissue. The report also stressed the importance of a pregnant woman's autonomy and right to bodily integrity. It opposed any judicial intervention in pregnancy, favouring voluntary care and assistance to pregnant women instead (Canada, Royal Commission on New Reproductive Technologies 1993, 24). However, the Commission also favoured the establishment of a federal regulatory and licensing body for reproductive technology, and proposed strict limits on the availability of treatment that is still considered experimental. It recommended that in-vitro fertilization technology for preconception arrangements, for postmenopausal women, and for profit should be banned. Commercial fertilization clinics would also be banned. If such recommendations are adopted, women's choices would remain tightly controlled by professional decision-makers with all other commercial avenues for treatment blocked within Canada.

The Abortion Debate: Pro-life or Pro-patriarchy?

The abortion issue is at the centre of the political struggle surrounding reproductive rights in Canada and the United States. In January 1988 the Supreme Court of Canada struck down Canada's existing abortion law as unconstitutional because it was being applied in an arbitrary and discriminatory manner. There were huge geographic disparities in accessibility, and women experienced long and sometimes dangerous delays in having abortions approved. The Supreme Court decision added fuel to the political struggle between the opposing forces.

New legislation on abortion proposed by the Mulroney government in 1989 marginally passed a House of Commons vote but was defeated in the senate on 31 January 1991. Since then Canada has had no legislation governing abortions. The Medical Services Act of Nova Scotia, which pro-

hibited the performance of abortions outside of hospitals, was also struck down in October of 1990. The Morgentaler abortion clinic in Halifax was thus declared lawful. In the summer of 1994, Morgentaler challenged a similar law in New Brunswick by opening a free-standing abortion clinic in Fredericton. Another clinic is planned for Prince Edward Island, the only province in which no abortions are available, even in hospitals. The struggle continues around whether Medicare will cover the cost of abortions performed in clinics.

The issue of a woman's right to an abortion never seems to be settled once and for all. Physicians who are known to perform abortions continue to have their careers and their lives threatened by anti-abortion activists. On the surface, the anti-abortion lobby speaks to a humanistic concern for the sanctity of human life and a reluctance to kill that potential life for motives of convenience. But opponents of the lobby fear that the "pro-life" label obscures a political agenda that is fiercely antifeminist (Eichler 1985b; Dubinsky 1985). In principle, Eichler argues, the pro-life stand should be consistent with supporting every effort to minimize unwanted pregnancies and to maximize all forms of social support that would encourage pregnant women to keep their babies. But, in practice, the lobby groups fighting hardest to have abortion declared illegal are publicly against most of the policies intended to help women with children.

The anti-abortion movement in the United States campaigned strenuously to bring about the defeat of the Equal Rights Amendment, which would have prohibited discrimination on the basis of sex (Eisenstein 1984). They actively opposed welfare payments to mothers, public day-care programs, and **affirmative action** policies to promote employment for women. A similar lobby group in Canada, REAL women (Realistic Equal Active for Life), is anti-abortion and is also against welfare and against enshrining equality provisions for women in the Charter of Rights and Freedoms. The REAL women platform opposes abortion under all circumstances; opposes the contraceptive pill as suppressing maternal instincts; opposes sex education in schools as inciting immorality; opposes welfare and public day-care as undermining family responsibilities; opposes affirmative action for women in employment because this creates competition with male breadwinners; opposes feminist counsellors in homes for battered women because they advocate the breakup of the family; opposes the National Action Committee on the Status of Women as antifamily and antihousewife; and favours the right of a woman to be a full-time homemaker and the obligation of her husband to support her.

This agenda is a clear example of the politics of the "New Right." At the root of the New Right political agenda is a concern with the preservation of the traditional patriarchal family form, centred around the private family home. Women perform the expressive roles of full-time homemaker, mother, and nurturer of the family members, while men are responsible for public instrumental roles as providers. Policies to promote women's employment, state welfare, and public day-care are all seen as threatening such families by relieving men of their primary provider role. To the extent that women's domestic work and men's family responsibilities ensure a cheaply maintained, rested, committed, and stable work force, such policies also threaten capitalist interests. The New Right fears that contraception and abortion rights trivialize the mother role, reduce male commitment or obligation to support mothers and children, and hence undercut the social foundations of a stable family and work force.

The clash between New Right politics and feminism essentially revolves around the different views of the ideal family. Conservatives frequently claim that feminism leads to the breakdown of the family. The family they have in mind is the traditional patriarchal form that ensures male authority and female domesticity and dependence. The feminist movement advocates a very different form based on a consensual and egalitarian union that maximizes freedom of choice in the division of roles and responsibilities between spouses.

The National Action Committee on the Status of Women (NAC) is an umbrella organization that represents a broad range of feminist concerns. Its policy platform challenges the economic exploitation of women in the home and in the labour force and challenges the mechanisms of male oppression of women through economic dependence, the domestic burden, family violence, and medico-legal controls over women's reproductive freedom. Specific policies favoured by NAC include affirmative action in employment, universal, affordable child care, transition houses for battered women, income support for women and children to escape the dependency that makes women vulnerable to domestic violence, and protection of women's reproductive choice through safer and more effective contraception, maximum support services for pregnant women, and abortion as a back-up. In this context, abortion rights symbolize the inviolable right of women to control their own reproductive power.

The vision of family at the root of the feminist political agenda is a consensual union between equal partners, free from relations of dependency and without any forced sex-role division of labour between private and public, expressive and instrumental tasks. This vision of family equality presupposes a transformation in the position of women in the labour force and in the ways in which work time is organized. The feminist platform shares with the nascent men's liberation movement a belief that the alienation of men from children can be overcome not through possession of women and children, but through participation as equals in the nurturing process. If men as parents are to assume equal responsibilities with women for domestic and child-care work, then the ways in which men as workers are exploited by capitalism will also have to be transformed.

The abortion debate has become a focal point for struggle around these two very different conceptions of family. Both sides claim to be defending the true interests of women and children. Eisenstein (1984, ch. 7) suggests that the New Right political agenda appeals to many women because it addresses their real material conditions in a patriarchal and capitalist society. The reality is that the mass of women with children are dependent on male breadwinners for their survival. The women's movement, combined with developments in capitalism, has widened opportunities for women beyond traditional domestic roles, but this opportunity is largely illusory. Women predominate in low-paid job ghettos. Rising divorce rates mean that many women must struggle in abject poverty as single parents. The superwoman image of professionals who manage to combine careers and domestic and child-care responsibilities has limited appeal for women who already feel overburdened. Feminism threatens their security without being able to bring about the radical social and economic change needed to provide women with real alternatives.

The Limitations of Radical Feminism

The weakness of radical feminist analysis of family life stems from its overly narrow focus. The perspective has drawn attention to widespread and serious problems of violence and abuse within families, which have been overlooked or downplayed by other approaches. But radical feminist research also tends to overstate the case for patriarchy to the extent that the abnormal becomes the norm. Some sources speculate, for example, that as many as one girl in two and one boy in three are victims of incest, an estimate that encompasses virtually every family in Canada. When concepts are pushed to this extreme, it becomes impossible to make distinctions between different experiences of family life. Radical feminism runs the risk of generating its own form of monolithic bias.

We know that, however pervasive the hidden problems might be, not all people experience family life as abusive. Most people do get married, and most of those who get divorced subsequently remarry. The majority of women and men thus appear to find marriage worth the struggle, or at least feel that it is more rewarding than living alone.

There is evidence of widespread changes in family roles. Husbands and fathers are increasingly getting involved in domestic work and in the nurturing of children, albeit generally not at the same level of responsibility as women. The combination of shorter working hours, free weekends, and changing conceptions of fatherhood means that children and fathers are more closely involved with each other than in the past. The real suffering of many fathers who are separated from their children by divorce cannot be subsumed under the blanket explanations of desire for revenge and legal control over their ex-wives.

The problem for radical feminist theory is to account for these different experiences. The pioneering work of feminist research into family violence means that we can no longer discount the 10 to 20 percent of families characterized by wife battery and other forms of abuse. But neither can we discount the majority of families where couples manage to establish mutually supportive relations and where children can look to both fathers and mothers for nurturance and emotional support. We need more research into the processes that account for this variation.

We are still far from understanding the factors that encourage egalitarian marriages and shared parenting as opposed to patriarchy and rigid role differentiation. Such analysis will need to take into account the context of political economy and the processes that exploit people and help to perpetuate role differentiation and yet simultaneously provide opportunities for women to be financially independent. The analysis will also need to take into account the emotional stress generated by patriarchal family forms and the evidence that men who abuse wives and children were commonly abused themselves when young. Abuse may generate the emotional insecurity that finds expression in the drive for domination and possession in marriage. From this perspective, patriarchy appears less as the expression of male power than of chronic insecurity, powerlessness, and fear. This remains speculation. Feminist theory has opened up the debate by focussing attention on issues that have been ignored by mainstream theories. But the research needed to explain the conflicting patterns of egalitarian and patriarchal families, and nurturing and abusive family relations, is still in its infancy.

Conclusion

Family life may be the most difficult area of sociology to study. It is so familiar and so emotionally charged that it is hard for us to distance ourselves from it. Sociological analysis has moved a long way from the original functionalist view that sex-role divisions within the nuclear family were natural, rational, and efficient adaptations to industrial society. But functionalist formulations still dominate most sociological textbooks. Monolithic, conservative, sexist, and microstructural biases in functionalist analysis of the family are being eliminated only with difficulty. Research in the Marxist tradition shows how different family forms are embedded in economic relations that exploit both women and men and set constraints on their lives. Feminist theory reveals other aspects of the family as the central arena for the struggle between competing principles of gender equality and patriarchy. The processes that influence the outcome of these struggles are still far from understood.

Suggested Reading

An excellent source of statistical information on families in Canada is Margrit Eichler, *Families in Canada Today: Recent Changes and their Policy Consequences*, 2nd ed. (1988a). Eichler takes a very critical approach to traditional sociology of the family and provides quantities of data to back her argument that family life in Canada is diverse and rapidly changing.

For the functionalist perspective, a particularly useful source is the short text by William J. Goode, *The Family*, 2nd ed. (1982). He presents an easily readable account of the functions that families perform for the society as a whole.

For the Marxist feminist approach, an excellent book is Meg Luxton, *More than a Labour of Love* (1980). Luxton presents an in-depth description of the lives of three generations of women in a small mining town in northern Manitoba. She conveys through the words of the women themselves how deeply their family lives are influenced by the economic reality of their dependence on male wages.

For a radical feminist perspective, an excellent source book is the collection of articles edited by Yllö and Bograd, *Feminist Perspectives on Wife Abuse* (1988). Articles here by Dobash and Dobash, Adams, and Saunders give insight into the experience of wife battery and the difficult problems of doing research and analysis in this area.

Questions

1. List four critical functions of family according to functionalist theory.

2. a) List two respects in which Nayar family form deviates from the functionalist view of universal family form.
   b) How does functionalist theory typically discount this deviation?
   c) How does feminist theory challenge the functionalist account of the collapse of Nayar family form?

3. What procedure or methodology does Eichler recommend to avoid "monolithic" bias in research on family life?

4. Regarding conservative bias, what two critical factors are commonly cited as radically altering family structure?

5. What functionalist bias is particularly addressed by Marxist theory of family?

6. What single factor is seen by Engels as accounting for monogamy for women?

7. According to Engels, what two conditions are necessary to eliminate inequality within families?

8. In Smith's historical survey, why did women's farm labour change from equality to drudgery and tyranny under the capitalist mode of production?

9. List three ways in which the labour of middle-class homemakers can be seen as appropriated by corporations.

10. How is mothering-work implicated in ideological hegemony with respect to capitalism?

Stratification: Meritocracy as Ideology

Inequality is a pervasive feature of social life. It may be manifested in disparities in access to money and other material resources in the power to manipulate events in one's own interest, in the prestige enjoyed in relations with others, and in the overall quality of life. The extent of these disparities varies widely across societies. In an industrially advanced economy such as Canada's, very few people are so poor or disadvantaged that their physical survival is threatened by starvation or lack of rudimentary shelter and sanitation. Yet, as we have seen in earlier chapters, Canada does have a visible and growing underclass of homeless and destitute people who rely on food banks and hostels for a meagre survival. At the other extreme, Canada has a class of super-rich, comprising mostly members of the corporate elite, some of whom rank among the richest people in the world.

Various forms of inequality commonly go together, suggesting that there are important causal relationships between them. Powerful people are often rich, command high prestige, and enjoy pleasurable, even luxurious, lifestyles. The poor are often powerless, scorned, and live in misery. Yet there is no inevitable association between these elements. Winning a lottery, for example, may bring wealth and leisure but not necessarily influence or prestige. A large income may not improve the quality of life if it is earned at the expense of chronic anxiety in the high-pressure corporate rat race. In terms of influence, even poor people can exercise power, especially if they are politically united.

Societies vary greatly in the degree of opportunity for **mobility**; that is, the likelihood that people born poor may eventually become wealthy and influential or that people born rich may fall in status. Canadians tend to think of their society as relatively open, offering opportunities for mobility through individual effort and achievement. But we know that social position is very commonly inherited. Children tend to attain a similar social position to that of their parents or to move slightly upwards or downwards. Members of certain groups are disproportionately better or worse off than others. Children from white Anglo-Saxon Protestant (WASP) backgrounds have very different life chances on average than children of Native Indian or black parents. Why is this so?

Children of Native peoples have very different life chances than do children from WASP backgrounds.

The explanations for inequality offered by different sociological theories reveal core assumptions concerning the nature of social order. Traditional functionalism stresses individual merit. It posits that inequality reflects rewards for individual contributions to the functioning of society. Marxists stress the importance of control over critical means of production for accumulating wealth in industrial society. Variations in income among the mass of working people reflect the relative utility of different workers for the owners of capital. Interpretive theory looks within the grand schemes of functioning social systems, capitalism, and patriarchy to explore what people do in their everyday relations to produce the patterns of inequality that we subsequently perceive as merit, class, or gender hierarchies. Feminist theory focusses on disparities in wealth, power, prestige, and leisure between women and men, arguing that men, on average, are advantaged in all of these respects. These disparities reflect patriarchy, or the power of men over women, which is distinct from, although associated with, capitalism. These theoretical perspectives, and their relative strengths and limitations, are examined below.

Functionalist Theory: Stratification as Meritocracy

The traditional functionalist theory of **stratification** begins from the basic observation that no society is classless. There must be a universal necessity for such stratification. It must perform some function for the social system as a whole, a function so important that no society can do without it.

Davis and Moore (1945) provide one of the clearest functionalist explanations for why stratification occurs. Their central concern is with inequality of positions in society, not the characteristics of the individuals in those positions. The basic theoretical question is why roles themselves differ in prestige and rewards. They find the answer in the functional requirement of placing and motivating individuals in any social structure. A social system must distribute members into social positions and must instil in members the desire to perform the attached duties once in the position. This is a continuous challenge because people are constantly being born, aging, retiring, and dying. Competitive systems such as our own stress motives to achieve the positions; noncompetitive systems, such as socialist societies, stress motives to perform the duties. Both systems, however, require motivation.

Roles differ enormously in the demands they place on people. If all roles were equally important, and everyone were able to do all of them, then placement would be no problem. However, some jobs are more agreeable, some serve more important social functions, some require more talent and training, and some require that duties be performed more diligently. Therefore, say Davis and Moore, a differential reward system is necessary. These differential inducements form part of the social order and produce stratification. Rewards may include sustenance and comfort provided by economic incentives; self-respect and ego development provided by prestige and power; and recreation and diversion made possible by more leisure time. These rewards are built into positions and constitute the rights that are related to the duties of the roles. Inequality is thus necessary, inevitable, and justifiable.

Two primary factors determine the relative rank of different positions: their importance for the society and the scarcity of personnel for the positions. Important jobs need sufficient rewards to ensure competent performance, but if such jobs are easily filled, great rewards will not be needed. Garbage collector and janitor, for example, are important jobs, but they are relatively easy to fill and so are not highly rewarded. On the other hand, important jobs that require both talent and long training must be well rewarded. No one would go through the training and do the work of a modern medical doctor, the argument goes, unless the position carried great material reward and prestige.

Variations among societies in the income received by the highest- and lowest-paid members are primarily explained by the degree of specialization of roles. Highly industrialized societies such as Canada have an immense variety of specialized occupations, each of them associated with small graduations in income and prestige. Simpler, less industrialized societies have a more limited range of occupations, which tend to require less specialized training. There are fewer gradations of income and prestige. The nature of functional emphasis—whether sacred or secular—also affects rewards. Industrialized societies place greater emphasis on science and technology than on religion, and so scientists and technicians get higher pay. In other societies where science is relatively undeveloped, religious leaders may have far greater influence, prestige, and material rewards than do scientists.

In summary, functionalists argue that stratification is justified on the basis of merit. The critical moral issue for functionalist theory is not equality of rewards, but rather equality of opportunity to compete for them. The true battle is over merit versus inherited advantage.

Critique of Functionalism

Equal Opportunity

Much of the research generated by the functionalist thesis of stratification has focussed on questions of social mobility and differential opportunities for access to positions that carry the highest rewards. Research in the sociology of education has cast doubts on the notion that rewards are based on merit. Tumin (1973) challenges the argument that only a limited amount of talent is available within a population to be trained in appropriate skills for important jobs. He maintains that stratification itself limits the talent pool. We can never know what talents are available among children born to impoverished and disprivileged homes when poverty so pervasively affects their relationship with the school system. Rich children have all the advantages and hence do better in school, get the credentials for better jobs, and in turn give advantages to their own children (see chapter 16).

Unequal distribution of motivation to succeed, so important to functionalist theory, is itself a direct product of stratification. Poverty breeds hopelessness. Imagination, curiosity, and aspiration are systematically blunted when children experience powerlessness and humiliation at first hand. It is hard to develop one's full potential under such conditions. The result is low credentials, poorly rewarded jobs, and another generation of children who are stunted and trapped in the poverty cycle.

The argument that conversion of talent into skills requires sacrifices during the training period, and hence merits rewards, again treats the effects of stratification as its cause. Poor families cannot afford to buy books and school supplies or to pay for dance or music lessons, and so on, without cutting back on food money. Poor families cannot afford to keep children in school after the minimum school-leaving age or to send them to university without great sacrifices. The expenses involved are not sacrifices for wealthy parents in the professions. Pay differentials between the unskilled work available at school-leaving age and the professional careers available to university graduates more than compensate students who defer the gratification of an early job. Tumin estimates that any loss of income is usually regained within seven to ten years of employment. After this, the lifetime earnings of graduates greatly surpass those of untrained people (see table 15-1).

Table 15-1

Average Income of Full-year, Full-time Workers by Level of Education and Sex, 1991		
Education	Men	Women
Grade 0 to 8	$27 116	$18 138
Some secondary education	32 348	20 709
High-school graduation	33 583	23 265
Some postsecondary	35 845	24 891
Postsecondary diploma	37 887	26 951
University degree	56 522	40 537

Source: Reproduced by authority of the Minister of Industry, 1994. Statistics Canada (1994d), *Earnings of Men and Women*, Cat. 13-217, pp. 36–37.

Unequal Importance

The second pillar of the functionalist thesis on stratification is that the most important jobs in society must be the most rewarded, particularly when they require special skills. But, Tumin asks, how is importance to be measured? A typical answer is that importance is calculated in terms of a position's indispensability for society, but it is not difficult to find exceptions to this rule. Farming, for example, is important for survival in any society, and it requires skills that take a lifetime to learn, but it is not well rewarded. In terms of industry, during wartime it proved easier to dispense with supervisors than to spare factory workers, but this relative indispensability is not translated into wages.

The real problem is conceptual. Relative importance is a value judgment that is inextricably tied to relative financial rewards. In other words, the argument is circular. Those jobs that are better paid tend to be regarded as more important, regardless of their actual contribution to society or the actual skill levels required for the work.

Women and Stratification

This kind of circularity is especially evident in relation to work habitually done by women. As a sex, women have lower social status than men, so that work identified as "women's work" tends to have low status. The skills and responsibilities involved in such work tend to be downplayed or ignored. Then the lower average earnings of women in the labour force are justified on the grounds that women are concentrated in low-status work. The circle is completed when women themselves internalize such evaluations of what they do, and the low pay associated with it, as justifying the lower status of women generally.

The most extreme example of these processes occurs in relation to homemaking. This is a critical, multidimensional job that, like farming, takes a lifetime to learn. But it goes unpaid and commands such low status that people habitually apologize for doing it. Up until recently, homemaking was not even defined as work.

Within the paid labour market generally, skills associated with women's work are undervalued and underpaid. Nursing, for example, is a high-stress, extremely important job that requires a great deal of responsibility. The survival and recovery time of patients often depend more upon the quality of nursing care than on intermittent doctors' visits. The job demands long hours, shift work, and advanced technical skills that require a university degree and years of practical experience. But one would never know this judging from the salary and status that nurses command.

On some university campuses, the starting salary for secretarial staff (virtually all women) is several dollars per hour below that for people who mow lawns (virtually all men). It would be very difficult to argue that lawn mowing is either more important or more highly skilled than the work that secretaries do. The skills of advanced clerical workers are commonly ignored by bureaucratic classification systems that characterize such work as routine delegated tasks.

Women and men might do virtually identical work, but the work done by women tends to be called by a different name and to command lower status and salaries than the work associated with men. Positions like seamstress versus tailor, or cook versus chef, readily come to mind. In Muslim countries, where the work of buying household supplies is habitually done by men, it is seen as requiring important decision-making authority. When the same work is habitually done by women, as in our society, it tends to be thought of as a mundane routine.

Relative Scarcity of Personnel

The functionalist thesis claims that relative scarcity of personnel raises rewards. Jobs that are easily filled need not be paid well. Women who compete with each other for limited jobs in the traditional women's occupations know this well. Tumin (1973), however, points out that scarcity is often artificially constructed in order to protect incomes. For example, predominantly male unions have historically tried to bar women and immigrants from access to unionized jobs, arguing that these groups would lower wages. Women were also barred from entry into universities and hence from any profession that required a university degree. Professions have commonly been in a position to restrict access through their control over accreditation.

Historically, male unions took an active role to ensure that women were confined to low-paying, subordinate positions.

First-year admissions into medical schools in Canada were sharply reduced in the early 1980s and again in 1993 to an overall cut of 14 percent (Ryten 1994). Also, in 1993 for the first time, the number of women enrolled in first-year medicine exceeded the number of men, reflecting a 29 percent drop in the number of men admitted since the early eighties. These limitations on enrolments have the approval both of provincial governments and physicians' lobby groups, but for different reasons. Provincial governments hope to reduce the "oversupply" of doctors suggested by some reports on medical personnel and thereby to save money on Medicare payments. Physicians, on the other hand, lobbied successfully for cuts in enrolments and for restrictions on the licensing of immigrant doctors in order to limit the number of physicians and thus ensure their continued high salaries. Medical associations can then pressure for a fee schedule increase on the grounds of doctors' stressful work and the long hours they put in. Women doctors are more willing to trade high incomes for shorter working hours in group practices, but the male-dominated profession seems unlikely to encourage this.

Another common practice in limiting access to positions is to raise the qualifications needed to get into a job, thus putting up hurdles to stifle competition from below. Jobs in business and management, for example, which even a decade ago only required high-school graduation, now increasingly require university degrees. This effectively blocks competition from those who have learned their skills from work experience but do not have paper credentials.

Motivation

The last pillar of the functionalist argument is that differential rewards, and hence stratification, are necessary in order to motivate people to fill the more demanding positions. These rewards include money or material goods, leisure, respect, and prestige. Tumin's challenge to this thesis is that there are other kinds of motivators that could achieve the same results. An important one is work satisfaction. Positions that require training are usually the most interesting and the least routine. Tumin questions whether such positions need high pay to attract candidates and to ensure competent job performance. Other motives for job performance include the sense of a job well done, prestige from a social duty performed well, or increased leisure hours if the work is particularly demanding or difficult. Women commonly flock to jobs that give them the same time off and holidays as the schools so that they can cope with the extra work and responsibility of having children at home and not have to face the major expense of day-care.

Another question is whether money is, in fact, entirely effective as an **extrinsic reward**. In capitalist society, money is emphasized but people attracted by high salaries are just as likely to peddle their services elsewhere to the highest bidder. High salaries do not command loyalty. Senior executives, on average, remain only about four years with any one firm. There is an old joke about people in politics: they are the best politicians that money can buy. The question is whether people who can be bought with money actually do make good politicians or good anything else.

In summary, Tumin's critique points to the fallacies of unity, indispensability, and universal functionalism. Disparities in material rewards may be demonstrably valuable for certain sectors of society, but they can simultaneously be damaging for others. Large differences in income may be useful for motivating people, but they are not indispensable. People can and frequently do commit themselves to doing important work out of a sense of responsibility for others, or for the pleasure and excitement of the work, without demanding high incomes in return. Many persisting differences in prestige, wealth, and power do not serve useful functions for society at all. Functional importance of different positions is a value judgment. Stratification itself limits talent and restricts educational opportunities while other techniques restrict access and cause scarcity to drive up incomes. Training for skilled jobs either is not, or need not be, a sacrifice. People can be motivated to fill positions on the basis of intrinsic job satisfactions and the prestige of the office, without gross inequalities in standards of living.

Marxist Theory: Inequality as Class Exploitation

Marxists agree with traditional functionalists that stratification does perform very important societal functions, but they argue that these functions specifically help to perpetuate capitalism as an economic system. The central Marxist argument is that stratification functions to preserve a system of expropriation of wage labour from the mass of people. Profits from this expropriation accrue to an elite minority of owners of capital. Stratification is at the same time profoundly functional for capitalists and dysfunctional for the interests of the majority of people who must sell their labour. This perspective rejects the **meritocracy thesis** as an ideological distortion that, rather than questioning the structure of the system within which people are forced to compete, blames the individuals who do not get to the top of the reward system.

The Structure of Unequal Opportunities

Marxist analysis begins from the premise that because of the structured inequality of positions in society there is no possibility of equality of opportunity for the masses. A simplified model of a social system illustrates the problem (Himelfarb and Richardson 1979, 174). Assume a perfectly closed society in which there are 1000 positions, 10 percent of which are elite and the remaining 90 percent ordinary. Then assume that each of these 1000 role incumbents has one child. What will happen to these children as they come to take over from their parents? In a society based absolutely upon inherited advantage, the 100 elite children will take over from the 100 elite parents, with no elite positions left for anyone else. The 900 children of people in the ordinary jobs will remain at the same level.

What will happen in the opposite case, where there is no inherited advantage and everyone has an equal chance to get an elite job? Only 10 percent of all positions, or 100 jobs are elite. With perfect equality, 10 percent of elite children, or 10 children, will get elite positions and the rest will have ordinary jobs. Ten percent, or 90 of the 900 ordinary children will get remaining elite positions, with the other 810, or 90 percent, remaining where they are. It is clear that, when there are few really good or elite positions to be had, it makes little practical difference to the masses whether they are filled by inherited advantage or absolute equality. Most people will not get such positions in either case.

Any real change in opportunity for ordinary people will require a change in the structure of positions so that there are many more good jobs to be had. After World War II there were huge increases in the United States in middle-class technical, managerial, and white-collar jobs, as well as pink-collar jobs for women. This expansion is the root of the American Dream, the myth that anyone can achieve upward mobility if they have enough drive and talent. After the war, children whose parents had struggled through the

Great Depression found that there were many more well-paying jobs to be had. Children from elite homes enjoyed their usual advantage, but there were still many good positions opening up for others. Subsequently the picture changed. With recession came widespread unemployment and cutbacks in the economy. Fewer jobs meant that more children would not get positions equal to those of their parents, no matter how hard they tried. The structure of the job market and the distribution of wealth have to change in order to turn this around.

How does capitalism as a system function to give rise to the structure of the job market? This structure is largely treated as a given within traditional functionalist theory, so that the only question of interest is why existing jobs are rewarded differently. But for Marxists, the changing pattern of the job market itself requires explanation. Bowles and Gintis (1976, 10) insist that capitalist production is not simply a technical process, but is also a social process in which the central problem for employers is to maintain a set of social relations and organizational forms that will enable them to exploit wage-labourers to extract a profit. The objective of the system is to get the most production for the least wages; that is, to get workers to produce commodities of greater market value than the wages that they receive. Extremes of wealth and poverty are necessarily built into how this system works, and individual differences in abilities or effort count for little.

The problem for capitalism as a system is how to prevent revolt. Marxists ask how it is possible to maintain an inegalitarian system in relative equilibrium. What are the mechanisms that minimize the risk of workers forming coalitions to drive up wages or to wrest direct control over the means of production for themselves? The stability of the capitalist system is by no means assured. It has to be actively worked at.

Credentialism as Ideology

An important component assuring the stability of capitalism is force. Capitalists have the power to hire and fire people, and they can also call upon coercive laws to keep labour in line and to weaken unions. But naked force is itself inherently unstable in that it generates hostility and revolt. What is essential to the long-term stability of the system is that workers themselves come to accept the inequalities as just, or at least as inevitable, and therefore become resigned to them, even if they do not actively support them. The system of stratification or differential prestige ranking among workers serves this function, particularly when it is bolstered by the meritocratic ideology of traditional functionalism.

The stratification system, suggest Bowles and Gintis (1976, 81–85), is a direct reflection of capitalist policies of **divide and rule**. Its function is to fragment workers. In its cruder form, ascriptive criteria of race, ethnicity, and sex are manipulated to justify differential rewards. In the United States, older white males, particularly WASPs, are favoured for supervisory positions while immigrants, blacks, and women are given low-paid subordinate jobs. Those in superior positions are encouraged to see themselves as coming from better stock, while subordinates internalize their relative inferiority. The risk of coalitions to form a united front against capitalist employers is thus minimized.

Now that such ascriptive criteria are becoming increasingly discredited as a basis for legitimating inequalities, **credentialism** has come to take their place. This is precisely the meritocratic thesis of functionalism. Marxists agree that motivating people to strive for higher credentials does indeed perform an important function for capitalist society, but it is that of justifying inequality. People with different credentials readily come to see themselves as meriting different rewards. This effectively fragments wage-labourers and lessens the possibility of revolt. Those with relatively low credentials come to see themselves as meriting only limited rewards. Bowles and Gintis (1976, 81) argue forcefully that this is not merely a side effect of stratification but is its primary and intended purpose. Capitalists, they argue, will accede to higher wages for certain groups only when this increases social distance between groups of workers and strengthens capitalist control. Capitalists need to cement the loyalty of supervisors to the organization rather than to workers. Hence managers receive higher pay and privileges, regardless of relative scarcity of personnel.

It is important to recognize that Marxism reverses the cause-and-effect relation between credentials and rewards accepted by traditional functionalists. Functionalists, as we saw above, argue that certain jobs need people with higher skills and credentials. Since these people are in relatively scarce supply, the function of higher pay is to attract them to these difficult and important jobs. Marxists argue the reverse. Capitalism requires that workers be fragmented and stratified in order to minimize the risk of coalitions to challenge the controlling position of the capitalist class. Therefore, largely irrelevant criteria, such as race, ethnicity, sex, and credentials, are used as excuses to reward people differently and so divide them from each other. The function of focussing on credentials is to divide and rule workers by artificially stratifying them.

This is such a turn-around from how we are accustomed to think about credentials and rewards that it deserves further scrutiny. Bowles and Gintis categorically deny that schooling and credentials are actually needed for most jobs that currently demand them. True, there has been an explosion in public education in North America in recent decades, with ever-greater proportions of young people completing high school and seeking postsecondary education. True, on average, there is a **linear relation** between years of formal schooling and economic rewards: the more schooling, the more pay. But, this is not due to any essential requirement that better-paid jobs be filled by people with higher abilities. If such were the case, one would expect a very high correlation between measured intelligence and economic success. We do not find this. When measured intelligence and academic ability are controlled, the relation between years of schooling and pay remains virtually unaltered. It seems to be the piece of paper that counts, not the ability level (Bowles and Gintis 1976, 107).

The history of the Ontario Public School system offers a classic illustration of the triumph of credentialism over work experience (Cassin 1992). At the time when individual schools were consolidated into school districts, women predominated as both rural and primary school teachers. Most of them had graduated from high school and had two years of Normal School training. After consolidation, a new credential structure deemed that university studies in specific subjects were more important than experience for salary and promotion. Teachers with the most experience, predominantly women, were placed at the bottom of the teaching hierarchy. During times of retrenchment in the 1930s and 1970s, teachers with secondary school certification in specific subject areas, mostly men, were granted access to teaching positions in primary schools even though they had no experience or training in primary-level teaching. They coped in large measure because women teachers on the job taught them everything they knew. Conversely, primary school teachers were barred from applying for positions in secondary schools, no matter how experienced they were, if they lacked the formal subject-area credentials.

The Deskilling of Work

Further support for the argument that the function of the growing emphasis on credentials is to fragment workers rather than to meet essential job requirements is that there is little evidence of any major increase in the complexity of jobs in advanced capitalist societies. If anything, the process seems to be working in reverse. Once-skilled jobs are being systematically **deskilled**; that is, they are broken down into simple component operations that can be easily learned. This process has been going on for a long time, dating back at least to the era of **Taylorism**, or **scientific management**, in the last decades of the nineteenth century (Braverman 1974, ch. 4). The expressed goal of Taylor's time-and-motion studies was to break the power that skilled craftsmen wielded through their control over knowledge of the work process. Work was minutely analysed and broken down into component parts, each of which could be assigned to a different worker. Only the boss retained knowledge of the whole process. Taylorism served two functions for capitalism. It fragmented workers and cheapened labour costs. Employers thus deliberately created the mass of repetitive and unskilled jobs that traditional functionalists point to as deserving only low pay and low prestige.

Braverman argues that this deskilling process has continued unabated, with more and more skilled and even professional occupations being degraded into fragmented, repetitive tasks. Workers are continually being replaced by machines, their skills rendered obsolete. Assembly lines and automation have replaced proud crafts. The impetus for deskilling work was not that average workers were unable to learn the jobs. The problem for capitalists has been that skilled workers are harder to control. They can use their knowledge and skills as bargaining chips to get concessions. They also tend to think of themselves as more deserving of rewards. In effect, they threaten profits. People doing simple, fragmented tasks have minimal bargaining power and come cheaper.

INCO in Sudbury successfully broke the skills and power of mine workers by introducing new technology to automate work. Highly skilled people, who commanded high salaries and prestige among other workers, found their jobs disappearing (Clement 1981, ch. 10). Children of men who once had skilled jobs at the mine can no longer expect to get similar positions in Sudbury, no matter how motivated and well-educated they might be.

This deskilling, fragmenting, and routinizing of work is not an inevitable consequence of modern technology. It is the result of the kinds of technology that owners of capital opt to promote and how they use it. Teams of skilled workers can put together entire cars themselves as readily and efficiently as can be done on assembly lines. The president of Volvo in Sweden experimented with precisely such teamwork during a period of relatively full employment when he found he could not keep workers in fragmented assembly-line jobs (Gyllenhammer 1977). The function of job fragmentation is not to ensure greater technical efficiency but to break down workers' power, cheapen their labour, and so raise profits.

There is a serious problem for the capitalist system, however, with reducing all jobs to unskilled, repetitive, minimum-wage work: how to prevent coalitions of workers from forming to overthrow the system. The answer in the steel industry was to introduce artificial job ladders. In effect, the owners created a system of stratification to fragment the workers. Petty differences were exploited, linked to credentials such as years of experience and apprenticeship certificates, and used to justify small differences in prestige and piece-rate payments. Workers competed with each other to get the better jobs, and the unions cemented these different pay scales in formal contracts. This was exactly what management wanted. If such petty differences in the job ladder can be linked to race and ethnic differences, so much the better.

Skilled Labour Under Capitalism

Braverman's thesis on the systematic deskilling of work has recently come under criticism from other Marxist theorists for oversimplifying labour-market processes in advanced capitalism (Morgan and Sayer 1988; Sayer and Walker 1992). The strategy of deskilling and thus cheapening and controlling the work force may enhance profits in long-established mass production industries, but it may spell economic disaster in high-technology industries where rapid product innovation is occurring. Morgan and Sayer argue that in such industries competitive advantage and profit maximization depend not on producing a standard product more cheaply than competitors, but on high quality and product innovation. Traditional firms that opt for a cheap, deskilled labour force that is tightly controlled will not be able to keep up in the race for product innovation and so will likely face bankruptcy. Rapid innovation requires a work force that is highly educated in science and advanced technology, and a management team capable of directing rapid and complex organizational changes. Highly skilled, innovative workers cannot be controlled by the tactics of Taylorism (Morgan and Sayer 1988, 26).

From this viewpoint, it makes sense for capitalists to fund applied university research and graduate programs, especially in the sciences, engineering, and business management. More is at stake than empty credentialism, or a desire to divide and rule the work force. Business interests have promoted a series of public and private reports over the last decade debating whether North American high-school and college students are adequately prepared in mathematics and sciences (Darrah 1994, 64). A central concern is that Japanese capitalists may be outperforming Americans in high-technology industries because of better-educated workers.

Sayer and Walker's (1992) comparative study of the structure of American and Japanese corporations suggests that very different patterns of work-force stratification have been developed in the two countries. Major Japanese corporations have reduced or eliminated the hierarchical job ladders and the proliferation of small distinctions in tasks and pay scales described by Bowles and Gintis. These have been replaced with three broad classifications incorporating a variety of jobs. Individual workers are encouraged to learn wide-ranging skills so that they can switch easily between jobs and so maximize flexibility in production. Hence, these corporations place a high premium on worker loyalty, and they foster it with guarantees of job security and salaries linked to length of service rather than location on a job ladder. These firms also promote contact, information exchange, and co-operation among production workers on the shopfloors, engineers, and managers. The intent of such management styles is to maximize the speed and the quality of product innovation, with production workers better able to understand new product designs, and engineers better able to recognize and correct production flaws. This kind of production system is not compatible with the strategy of shipping components to cheap labour assembly plants in the Third World.

The core argument in Sayer and Walker's analysis is that more than one possible structure of labour relations is compatible with advanced capitalism. The seemingly inexorable process of deskilling and cheapening labour described by Braverman is not inevitable. It is a historically specific pattern associated with a certain period of American capitalism and a certain kind of production. It is profitable mainly in association with a highly standardized product and long, mass production runs.

One consequence of a mix of mass production and high-technology industries is that processes of deskilling jobs and upgrading skills may occur simultaneously in different sectors of an economy, resulting in very uneven patterns of high unemployment generally, combined with shortages of skilled labour. Declining real incomes may be the lot of the mass of workers who compete for deskilled jobs while an elite of university graduates in the sciences, engineering, and applied management may be in high demand and able to command high salaries.

Summary

Political economy theory sets out to debunk the **technocratic-meritocratic thesis** of stratification as an ideological smokescreen that legitimates and therefore helps to perpetuate inequality and exploitation. It challenges functionalist theory for ignoring the processes through which capitalism structures the job market, deskills many jobs, fragments workers, and breaks their bargaining power, and then justifies low pay on the grounds that they are doing unskilled work. Advanced capitalism, organized around multinational corporations, produces an extremely unequal structure of job opportunities beyond the control of individual workers. Explanations for stratification that focus on individual efforts and abilities obscure these larger structural processes that constrain individual life chances.

Traditional structural Marxist theory, exemplified in the work of Bowles and Gintis, and Braverman, has been challenged in recent Marxist work for an oversimplified economic determinism. It is giving way to a more dynamic class analysis that explores the diversity of ways in which labour can be managed and exploited for profits in advanced capitalism. But the core argument remains that social inequality is a product of profit-driven corporate interests. Only such effort and ability as directly feeds these profits are likely to be rewarded.

The Social Construction of Stratification

In both functionalist and political economy perspectives on stratification, such key concepts as *jobs*, *duties*, *responsibilities*, *skills*, and *credentials* are taken for granted as common-sense aspects of work. Social constructionist theory challenges each of these concepts and the pattern of reasoning that underlies them. These concepts are embedded in the professional discourse that has emerged around employment equity policies, and the ongoing political debates concerning whether North American workers are adequately prepared for work that is being transformed by technological and organizational innovations.

Central to this discourse is the notion of jobs. Jobs are conceptualized as separate from the persons hired to do them and the quality of individual performances. A job constitutes an identifiable set of duties or tasks, associated with a defined bundle of skills required to get the tasks done. Individual jobs make different contributions to the overall organization or enterprise of which they are a part. Jobs, the value of their contribution, and associated pay scales, are analysed as structural features of organizations. Within this discourse, workers are decomposed into job incumbents with typical profiles or bundles of skills. Skilled workers appear to move freely between workplaces, carrying their skills like baggage.

This way of thinking about jobs fits readily into the functionalist theory of meritocracy discussed above. The vision of equity in employment that emerges within this discourse focusses on the routine application of standard procedures. Tasks and skills are identified, and pay scales set, prior to anyone being hired. The aura of neutrality and objectivity is further assured by hiring external consultants to design an employment equity policy for a specific organization. Independent management teams are assumed to be unbiased because they do not directly profit from the implementation of the schemes they design. So long as hiring practices also follow objective procedures, matching workers' skill bundles to task-requirement bundles, equity on the basis of merit seems assured. The problem for employers is to attract appropriately qualified individuals, while educational institutions are enjoined to equip students with the skills called for in a given work force.

Social constructionist analysis suggests that the appearance of neutrality and objectivity is illusory. Employment equity policies are an aspect of management oriented principally to the justification of pay differentials. Systemic, or structured, inequality in the treatment of employees is embedded within them. Workers appear to be, and indeed *are* treated the same in ways that are authorized, sanctioned, and accepted practices of organization, and yet that have the consequence of inequality (Cassin 1991, 4).

The central argument is that while the discourse of jobs appears to reflect common-sense understanding of work, it fundamentally misrepresents the nature of work. The distinction between work as what people do, and jobs as disembodied sets of tasks obscures what people actually have to do to accomplish completed tasks and the knowledge that goes into such accomplishment.

The assumption that jobs can be decomposed into bundles of separate skills that can be listed does not correspond to how people experience the simultaneity of their work. In practice, workers are commonly required to juggle many tasks simultaneously, and amid constant interruptions. In the computer assembly plants studied by Darrah (1994) workers were expected to work on several units at once, depending on the availability of parts, and to repair several units at different stages in diagnostic cycles, as well as responding to other workplace demands. Individually, simple tasks required complex memory work under such

conditions, but memory work was not part of the job description. Secretarial work is also routinely carried on in the context of continual interruptions from a wide range of disparate sources, including supervisors, bosses, a host of people flowing in and out of the office exchanging information, asking questions, wanting services, raising complaints, and telephones ringing, that all need to be attended to in the same limited space of time available to do the word processing, filing, and other paperwork expected. Listing tasks individually and measuring the skill required to do each one in turn gives a seriously inadequate picture of the complexity of the work being accomplished.

The notion that specific skills can be clearly identified as required for specific tasks obscures the difficulty involved in making such connections, and the potentially disparate ways in which similar work may be accomplished by different people. In his study of computer assembly workers, Darrah (1994) found little consensus as to which individual tasks or which skills were central to getting the work done, beyond the most basic level of some manual dexterity. Production managers based their hiring requirements on standard job descriptions that they borrowed from other local firms. This explained why system repair technicians were called upon to display knowledge of electronic principles such as Ohm's Law. Once on the job, both technicians and managers concurred that such knowledge was irrelevant. Management stressed literacy skills as essential for workers to communicate clearly between shifts, but in practice few of them had such skills. Communications did sometimes get scrambled, but the plant kept running, so presumably literacy was not as essential a skill as managers implied. Troubleshooting was identified as a single skill by engineers, supervisors, and machine operators alike, but in practice operators dealt with trouble in a wide variey of ways, using memory, reasoning, co-operation, and random guesswork. There was no single skill that could be labelled *problem solving.*

Workers further described many other aspects of their work that they found essential to getting the work done, but that did not appear in any specified skills list. These included developing strategies for dealing with aging and frequently recalcitrant machinery, strategies for conveying acceptable impressions of work commitment in front of management, and ways of training new supervisors to provide appropriate support before they were transferred out of the plant. All the supervisors saw was their work in training the operators.

The Community of Practice

An important asset in problem solving and in getting the routine work done proved to be support networks among workers. Darrah found that computer assembly workers compensated for gaps in their own abilities by pooling their heterogeneous skills to help each other. The main challenge facing a newly hired operator was to develop a network of helpers who would assist when inevitable problems arose. The conceptualization of jobs as performed by individual workers with bundles of skills makes this "community of practice" invisible (Darrah 1994, 82; Lave and Wenger 1991). The shift in focus from job to work group raises the possibility that overall plant performance may depend less on attracting individually skilled workers than developing a co-operative work environment, in which workers can routinely help and learn from each other.

The focus on workplace also facilitates a shift in emphasis for skills that workers bring with them to opportunities for learning on the job. It was in this regard that Darrah found blatant contradictions between the management's overt demand for skilled workers and systemic, organizational barriers to skill development. Management claimed to want educated workers who could "see the big picture" and understand the overall system of production. Yet workers complained repeatedly of being blocked in their efforts to learn more. Supervisors routinely prohibited any documentation that would allow workers to learn more and possibly advance their careers. Repair technicians were barred from having schematic drawings of the computers they repaired on the grounds that it was their job merely to replace faulty circuit boards. It was someone else's job to repair the boards. In one instance, production workers were granted a tour of the firm's customer service department in an adjacent building. They found that much of the work overlapped, particularly with respect to faulty products that customers had returned. Both departments reported the exchange of ideas valuable, but the production manager banned further excursions because he feared workers might use them to transfer to another depart-

ment. These routine practices of information control reflected in structure and intent the deskilling practices referred to by Braverman (1974). Only the rhetoric of senior management had changed. Supervisors still boasted of controlling workers through ignorance.

Job Description as Ideological Practice

The gaps between jobs as task bundles described in job evaluation schemes and work as experienced by people cannot be bridged merely by adding elements to the bundle. The process of description itself is flawed. Descriptions appear to arise directly out of job design as objective statements, but these descriptive practices are themselves embedded in a managerial discourse that takes for granted distinctions between mental and manual labour, or between design and execution of tasks, and that also assumes the gendered character of work. Cassin (1991, 31–32) compares the following typical description of clerical work with what an equivalent description of managerial work would look like. Firstly, with respect to clerical work:

> Typically, employees are engaged in preparing, transcribing, systematizing and maintaining records, reports and communications by manual processes, or by operating various machinery and equipment; conducting analytical and investigative duties; determining the nature of enquiries and dealing with callers and customers in a service capacity/performing a variety of related admin support tasks under guidance and direction of Supervisory/ Mgt personnel.

An equivalent description of management work might be as follows:

> Typically (mgt) employees are engaged in talking on telephones, attending formal and informal meetings (32), chairing formal and informal meetings, touring company facilities, presiding over honorary occasions, representing the company in a variety of capacities, reading, answering and writing reports, correspondence and other documentation, responding to requests of various kinds from subordinates, colleagues, customers, superiors.

As Cassin remarks, the first description appears reasonable while the latter appears ludicrous. We are used to managerial work being described by terms like: plan, organize, co-ordinate, control, and decide. Such terms describe mental processes, not physical descriptions of what managers can be seen to be doing. Clerical work could also be described in terms of mental processes—the planning, organizing, co-ordinating, and decision-making work involved. But all this managerial work is obscured by descriptions framed in terms of manual performance of tasks. Clerical descriptions focus on essentially "empty" functions that give no indication of the knowledge involved in doing any of the work, the contexts in which such work gets done, or the organizational relevance of this work. It is such omission that accomplishes the view of clerical work as contributing only limited value to organizations and thus warranting limited pay. Conversely, the inclusion of organizational context and relevance is what creates the basis for designating managerial work.

Cassin's central point is that clerical work is inherently managerial and administrative work. The routine designations "managerial," "administrative," and "clerical" work and occupations, are by and large distinctions within the same domain of work (1991, 30). Job evaluation schemes are premised on the assumption that jobs are to be defined by their differences, rather than by their sameness to each other. But this premise obscures the essentially collaborative and overlapping character of work. The "sealing off" of clerical work from managerial work also contributes to the construction of a domain of gender-segregated jobs—women's work—before there are any incumbents in the positions.

The close co-operation between clerical and managerial work, and the fine line dividing them is reflected in the work of the *Conditional Sales and Rental Clerk Position* in a Consumer's Gas Company (Cassin 1991, 58–59). The woman holding this position was responsible for determining the credit worthiness of customers and authorizing sales up to a value of $1500. Considerable judgment, knowledge of credit practices and sales contracts, and interactional abilities were involved in this work. The clerk prepared a report on credit worthiness, formed a judgment, and then sought approval from her supervisor. She represented the company to the customers—finding out what they wanted, offering explanations, and dealing with people variously angry, frightened, threatened, and abusive. Her work was a very significant contribution to the company. Indeed, sales could not take place without her. Yet none of this was visible in her job description, which focussed on the routine completion of paperwork. The fine line separating clerical from managerial designation was drawn at the point where the supervisor approved or questioned the final judgment. Seen from this viewpoint, the separation of mental from manual labour did not result in the deskilling of clerical *work*, but a downgrading of the job.

Similar research by Reimer (1987) documents how clerical staff routinely organize the work of their superiors, collecting materials, setting priorities, arranging agendas, dealing with correspondence, and the like. Complex judgments are involved in this work, which presuppose comprehensive knowledge of an organization. Yet their work was conceptualized by both themselves and others as comprising routine, delegated tasks, variously referred to as answering mail, typing or word processing, filing, and finding things. Even the advanced computerized technology and software packages that secretaries now manage are more likely to be described as "making their work easier" than as enhancing it (Cassin 1991, 58).

Invisibility of Skills as Social Construction

The invisibility of managerial forms of work performed by subordinates does not arise from accidental oversight, and cannot be corrected merely by pointing it out. Institutionalized invisibility is

"You're a man of the world, Miss Wallis.
Tell me, what are sexist remarks really like?"

accomplished through organized sets of relationships that also accomplish relations of class and gender. Documents are central to these processes of recording, recognizing, and attributing work within formal organizations. They provide a way of tracking how the division between mental and manual, design and execution is organizationally sustained.

The work of nursing is a stereotypically female occupation, which, although it is recognized as a profession, is accorded relatively low status within the medical hierarchy of hospitals, and significantly lower pay than other medical personnel. Nurses routinely perform aspects of managerial, administrative, educational, and diagnostic work as part of patient care, yet only a small part of such work is documented (Gregor 1994). The dividing line in the hospital hierarchy was graphically recorded in the hospital studied by Gregor in a pamphlet called "Your Medical Team." This pamphlet, which was given to each new patient as part of the process of admission, described the qualifications and responsibilities of medical personnel a patient might encounter. It included attending physician, resident physician, intern, clinical clerk, and head nurse. The qualifications, ranking, work organization, and responsibilities of nurses below the level of head nurse were not mentioned. In effect, the people most directly involved in the daily care of patients did not appear as members of the medical team.

Institutional recognition of the educative work performed by nurses was accorded specifically to pre-operative education provided to patients on the surgical ward. Nurses were required to document that such work had been done by entering it into their patients' charts on a form entitled "Pre-op Patient Education Check List." Its content was also documented in a teaching manual "Before and After Surgery" to be used by nurses in instructing patients.

The educative work actually done by nurses extended far beyond this required minimum, but it received no official recognition, and even the nurses themselves generally failed to name it. Gregor records talk between nurses and patients in which nurses explained aspects of diagnosis and treatment, informed patients about various tests, clarified the meaning of symptoms, advised patients how to aid recovery, and explained aspects of hospital administration. Patient care could hardly have proceeded without such talk,

but all that nurses were doing officially was "administering medication" or "checking the intravenous." The omission has potentially far-reaching implications in a period when hospital administration is being contracted out to management consulting firms. The computerized calculation of nursing staff ratios and time needed for patient care routinely incorporates only the officially sanctioned tasks listed in job descriptions.

The invisibility of educative work performed by nurses was further obscured by the fact that much of it contravened the recognized medical hierarchy. Nurses routinely advised less experienced health-care workers and physicians on appropriate pieces of equipment, how various kinds of medical work processes could be initiated through use of requisition forms, where to find such forms, and how to fill them in. Nurses also became involved in aspects of the diagnosis and treatment of patients. This often took the form of a "problems list" by which nurses informed hospital physicians about medical work that needed their attention. Such lists were prepared daily, usually by night nurses, and modified during the day as old problems were solved and new ones identified. Examples included "patient vomited 500cc. leave I.V. in?" or "re-order senecot—no bowel movement." The critical difference between the problems list and the pre-operative, education check list described above, was that it was not officially sanctioned. The lists were written on plain paper and never found their way into hospital records. In other instances, nurses were observed contacting a physician to explain a patient's problem, then suggesting the appropriate drug treatment and the normal dosage. The resulting prescription, however, carried only the physician's name. The collaborative character of the work process is actively hidden from view. As with the example of the clerical worker discussed above, the knowledge and judgment used by the subordinate worker was rendered invisible. Only the superior was officially recognized as making the decision, while the subordinate appeared merely to carry out orders. The suppression of the active involvement of subordinates in forming decisions is part of the set of practices that sustains the organizational hierarchy.

The organization of work within the hospital limited the opportunities for nurses to learn more about diagnoses and treatment plans in ways that paralleled the experience of computer assembly workers decribed above. Physicians routinely scheduled their rounds at the same time of day as nurses changed their work shifts. Even when physicians did come during the day, it was also not their practice to invite nurses to come with them when they went to see a patient. Such organizational practices, Gregor suggests, had the function, and perhaps also the direct intent of maintaining the status of the physician as authoritative knower in matters of patient care.

Maintaining the Fictions

The view of work as hierarchically ordered sets of task bundles that merit differential rewards, does not come naturally. It has to be worked at. The incorporation of workers' representatives on committees charged with designing job evaluation systems constitutes an important mechanism in gaining commitment to the schemes and in training workers to think in the appropriate conceptual framework (Cassin 1992, 68–73). Participants in these committees learn the job evaluation system, learn about jobs from this perspective, and learn to make and to defend judgments and decisions made within the constraints of job evaluation. Cassin suggests that an intensive orientation process is required to "break in" new members to a thinking process that belies common-sense experience of work.

Job descriptions define who is authorized to know certain aspects of work and these relations of hierarchy are continually reproduced and reinforced through displays of superordination and subordination. Gregor describes how nurses maintained the fiction of "doctor's orders" in relations with patients when they were quite capable of giving advice directly, and in fact even when they had initiated the doctor's order in question. In one of many examples, a patient asked a nurse how long she should wait before taking the bandages off her leg. The nurse responded with "You will have to ask your doctor" followed by questions such as "When will he come to see you next?" and "When is your next appointment?" After it became clear that the doctor had visited the patient, omitted any mention of removing bandages, and would not be seeing the patient for another six weeks, the nurse said it would be okay to soak the bandages off after ten days. How much nurses told patients depended primarily on the personality of the attending physician and

what he would allow, not on what the nurses knew. Experienced nurses quickly warned incoming nurses what to expect in this regard.

The costs of this socially constructed hierarchy on those in subordinate positions are high. The most obvious cost is financial. The fine line separating managerial from managed can mark large differences in income. More subtle, but equally destructive are the costs in terms of social well-being and mental health. Blue-collar workers located at the bottom of the job-status hierarchy are much more likely to experience feelings of powerlessness and self-depreciation that closely mirror the symptoms of reactive depression (Archibald 1978, 177–80).

Summary

Social constructionist theory complements in many respects the political economy analysis of stratification in the work force. Both critique the artificiality of job ladders, and the lost potential for co-operation and pooling of knowledge that such distinctions tend to create. But constructionist analysis focusses attention on the routine practices through which **doing hierarchy** comes to be accepted and legitimated in common-sense reasoning as merited. In challenging the discourse of jobs and job evaluation, it also calls into question the extent to which distinctions between mental and manual labour, design and execution of tasks, can be sustained in everyday experience of work.

Feminist Theory and Stratification

Women are subordinated to men in Canadian society on just about every measure of social status—the average incomes they earn, ownership of property, control over capital, participation in politics, representation in managerial, administrative, and decision-making bodies. Women's contributions to society in general and to the world of work in particular, are not accorded the same value or recognition as those associated with men. Feminist theory addresses this systemic gender inequity and the generalized inadequacy of mainstream theories to account for it.

Statistics on the gender composition of different occupations in Canada present extensive evidence of the lower status of women generally in the work force. The proportion of adult women in the labour force more than doubled between 1941 and 1981, and it continues to rise (see figure 15-1). But women are heavily overrepresented in the reserve army of part-time, seasonal, and cheap labour.

In labour-market theory, the market is generally understood as divided into two sectors. Jobs in the primary sector are characterized by relatively good wages and working conditions and opportunities for promotion, whereas jobs in the secondary sector are short-term, low-paid, and dead end. White males hold the majority of jobs in the primary sector, while females form the large majority of workers in the secondary sector,

along with many men from visible minorities (Armstrong and Armstrong 1990, 62).

Women are concentrated in a small number of occupations—clerical, service, sales, health and teaching—with three-quarters of employed women in the first three of these categories. When women enter professions they are overrepresented in low-status and low-paid categories. They are far more likely to be the dental hygienists, librarians, therapists, and dieticians, than the dentists, doctors, lawyers, engineers, or university professors (see table 15-2). These patterns are changing, but very slowly.

An important impetus for change has been the implementation of the equality rights section of the Canadian Charter of Rights and Freedoms in 1985, the federal Employment Equity Act passed in 1986, and particularly the section of the Act

---

Figure 15-1

Labour Force Participation Rates for Women and Men Over 15 Years of Age, Canada 1911–93*

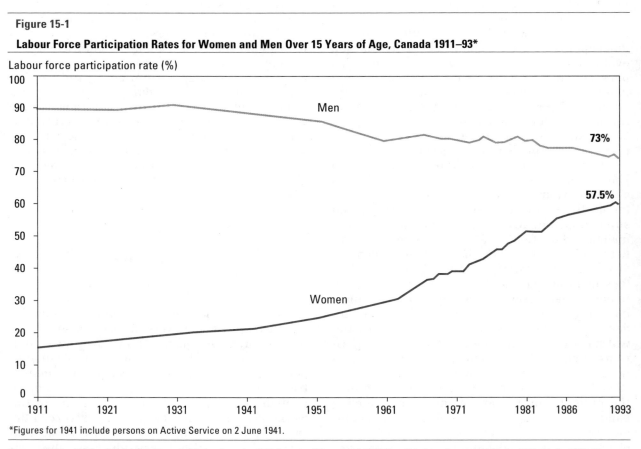

Labour force participation rate (%)

*Figures for 1941 include persons on Active Service on 2 June 1941.

Source: Eichler (1988a, 95). Adapted from Statistics Canada, 1961 Census of Canada, Vol. III (Part 1) Labour Force, table 1, for 1911–61; for 1966–79: Cat. 71-201 Historical Labour Force Statistics, pp. 151, 153, 158; for 1981–84: Historical Labour Force Statistics, 1984, Cat. 71-201, p. 220, D767895, p. 225, D768005; for 1985–86, Cat. 71-001; for 1986–93, Cat. 71-201.

Table 15-2

Female Workers in Selected Professional and Technical Occupations, 1971 and 1981

Occupation	Female % of Occupation		% of all Female Workers	
	1971	1981	1971	1981
Dental hygienists, assistants, and technicians	76.6	81.1	0.3	0.4
Social workers	53.4	62.6	0.2	0.4
Librarians and archivists	76.4	80.2	0.2	0.3
Physiotherapists, occupational and other therapists	81.6	84.6	0.2	0.2
University teachers	16.7	24.6	0.1	0.2
Physicians and surgeons	10.1	17.1	0.1	0.1
Pharmacists	23.1	41.3	0.1	0.1
Psychologists	47.2	52.0	0.1	0.1
Dieticians and nutritionists	95.3	94.0	0.1	0.1
Lawyers and notaries	4.8	15.1	—*	0.1
Industrial engineers	3.3	12.2	—	0.1
Dentists	4.7	7.9	—	—
Total	29.0	39.4	1.5	2.1

*— means less than 0.1 percent.

Source: Armstrong and Armstrong (1984). Adapted from *1971 Census*, vol. 3.2, table 8; and from *1981 Census, Labour Force–Occupational Trends* (Cat. 92-920), table 1.

concerned with the Federal Contractors Program. The Act requires that all federally regulated companies (banks, transport, and communications companies) set up **employment equity** programs and file annual public reports on the demographic composition of their work force, including data on salaries and promotion for women and minorities.

The first reports filed in 1988 revealed major inequities in pay scales for women and men and restricted employment opportunities for disabled people and visible minorities. Women were concentrated in the majority of jobs paying less than $25 000 while men predominated in jobs that paid more than $35 000. Women were rarely represented in the very high-paying jobs. Roughly 10 percent of the 13 800 male employees with Air Canada, for example, earned more thn $70 000. Only 4 out of the 6300 women working for the corporation earned that much (*Globe and Mail*, 22 Oct. 1988).

The Act has come under heavy criticism from advocacy groups for not incorporating penalties for failure to practice employment equity. The Act leaves it up to individual members of disadvantaged groups to challenge these companies in court, using human rights legislation. But such action requires considerable time, money, and effort, and legal expertise, as well as proof that failure to hire or to promote a particular individual was due to discrimination and not to some other factor.

The section dealing with federal contractors does have some teeth, in that every company that has 100 or more employees, and that wants to bid on a federal government contract of more than $200 000, must prove its commitment to gender and minority equity in terms of hiring, training, salary, and promotions. No equity plan, no federal contract (Kates 1988). These companies are under pressure to promote women and minorities into managerial positions, and also to keep them. Before the Act, Kates suggests, a request for maternity leave was an instant ticket to a dead career, but companies are now more prepared to offer flexible policies in order to retain women in senior positions.

Employment equity policies and associated job evaluation schemes have had some successes in redressing overt discrimination in hiring practices, and in winning pay increases for categories of women workers found to be paid significantly less than men in closely comparable jobs. But the impact of such cases on the overall pattern of income differentials between women and men in the work force is small. As we have seen above in the social constructionist critique of job evaluation schemes, systemic discrimination remains largely invisible. Job descriptions are gendered at basic common-sense levels of practical reasoning. Hiring and promotion procedures that follow strict rules of gender neutrality and objectivity, still have gendered outcomes. Compensation for work done appears to be gender-neutral, based entirely on objective job characteristics, yet the pervasive outcome is that work primarily done by women is accorded less worth than work primarily done by men (Cassin 1991, 1–2).

The initial concentration of women and men in different entry-level job categories has cumulative implications for progression and career advancement. In order to appear qualified for promotion into managerial positions, junior personnel need to display knowledge and experience in policy areas, and decision-making capabilities. But, as we have seen above, clerical, sales, and service jobs are normally described in ways that obscure such experience. Personnel managers use job descriptions to structure performance appraisals, orienting questions around recognized task-related competences. Resulting evaluation procedures and interviews may give no scope for workers to display the managerial knowledge they might have. Jobs in which women are concentrated generally offer little scope for discretion, advancement, authority, or higher salaries. Clerical positions qualify women to compete for other clerical positions, but not for administrative or management positions, even at entry level. Affirmative action programs designed to get more women into management appear to offer privileged and unfair competition to women. The structural barriers that make affirmative action necessary, remain invisible.

Feminist Challenge to Traditional Theory

Functionalist perspectives on stratification and effort, and socially learned differences in occupational choices by individual women and men serve to legitimate rather than challenge gendered inequality. Job evaluation schemes to date largely mirror functionalist assumptions. Traditional political economy theory, although much more critical of stratification, has mostly ignored its gendered character. The working class is generally conceptualized as an undifferentiated whole in labour-market theory, with marginal attention to women (Brittan and Maynard 1984, 56). Inequality between workers is broadly accounted for in terms of the interests of the capitalist class in fragmenting working-class solidarity so that some segments can be exploited for cheap labour while others control them.

This thesis, however, does not explain why women are so consistently singled out for super-exploitation at the bottom of the job and wage heap (Armstrong and Armstrong 1990, 66). Nor does it explain why male workers have for so long seen it as legitimate that fellow workers should be in subordinate, lower paid, and often insecure and temporary work, because they happen to be female (Beechey 1977). It is hard to blame capitalism for the pattern of women's economic subordination

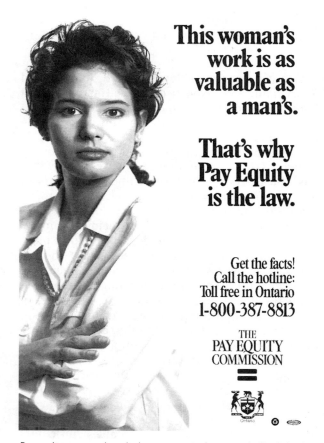

This woman's work is as valuable as a man's.

That's why Pay Equity is the law.

Get the facts!
Call the hotline:
Toll free in Ontario
1-800-387-8813

THE
PAY EQUITY
COMMISSION

Pay equity programs have had some success, but systemic discrimination is largely invisible.

that long predates it. Capitalists can and do take advantage of this subordination, exploiting women as a pool of cheaper labour, controlling male workers by the threat that they can be replaced by cheaper women, and buying the compliance of men to the wage-labour hierarchy by appearing to favour them with differential rewards (Hartmann 1979). Such arguments, however, fall far short of claiming that capitalism causes gender inequality.

Historically, capitalism was associated with improvements in the relative social status of women by providing some opportunity for women to earn an income independently of men. Capitalists also stand to benefit from the increasing numbers of married women entering the labour force, in ways that go beyond exploitation of cheap labour. Wage-earning women expand the market for consumer goods of all kinds and open up market opportunities in the service sector to supplement domestic labour with day-care, take-out food, and domestic cleaning services.

A different order of explanation seems to be needed to explain the subordination of women in the labour force that goes beyond the structuralist argument that the pattern persists because it is in the interests of capital. Such an argument functions as ideological justification for patriarchy in that it obscures more fundamental relations of male power and oppression of women (Brittan and Maynard 1984, 52–55; Cockburn 1981, 54; Hartmann 1979). Hartmann focusses attention directly on how male workers, individually and collectively through unions, have acted to exclude women from well-paid jobs, preserving them as male strongholds. She traces what she sees as "centuries of patriarchal social relationships" in which men pushed women into subordinate economic roles. In Canada, women always worked alongside men in developing homesteads and family farms, yet patriarchal laws dispossessed them, vesting ownership rights in men. Men commonly kept that control even after death by willing the farms to their sons. During the early development of factories, men resisted factory labour, preferring their greater independence in agricultural work. Women and children were available as "more docile and malleable" labour, itself reflecting their long-term subordination to men in agriculture. As industrialization progressed, men dominated the skilled trades while women filled less important positions as casual labourers and assistants.

The potential problem with this arrangement was that the cheap labour of women might undercut men's jobs and wages, especially in a tight job market. Male-dominated unions took active steps to control this threat. Hartmann documents systematic actions by male unions to exclude women from membership and to prevent them from entering apprenticeships, and gaining the skills required for equal status jobs. Fear of job competition does not account for this pattern, since the same men who excluded women and girls from learning trades, offered such training to boys. In principle, both male and female workers could have joined together in unions to demand equal pay for women and men, and thus eliminate the threat of cheaper female labour. But this rarely happened. More commonly, male unionists used their organizational force to eliminate women from factories. In one example, male spinners even plotted to set fire to a factory in which girls were working at wages below those of male unionists.

Such overt discrimination against women in the work force has been virtually eliminated in Canada. Women and men who do the same work within the same organization are guaranteed equal pay. Women have been joining unions in steadily increasing numbers. The Canadian Labour Congress fully endorsed equality rights for women in employment, and unions have become active in pushing labour benefits for women workers, including improved maternity benefits. But there remains much overt and covert resistance to the acceptance of women as colleagues in traditionally male occupations. Companies that have actively instituted policies to hire more women managers to comply with the Employment Equity Act and qualify for government contracts, have also had to address the sexist attitudes of some male managers. In one report of an interview with a woman applicant for a management position with the Canadian Imperial Bank of Commerce, a male manager displayed such attitudes when he asked her if she were married or had any marital plans, and then commented later that she was not all that attractive. The senior manager at the bank commented "John's good, but he's got a problem with women. It will cost him" (Kates 1988).

In practice, however, it is women in management who more often bear the costs of male resistance to their presence on the team. This resistance undermines women's effectiveness as managers, which then becomes attributed to the women themselves as evidence of their relative incompetence, compared with men. The veiled hostility of male managers, especially younger ones who feel they are competing directly with women for promotion, may take such forms as withholding important information, sidelining women managers at meetings, creating behind-the-scenes barriers to co-operation, deliberately sabotaging projects, or transferring a bad worker to the woman's department to foul things up. Sexist comments betray male discomfort at having to work with women, even when this is denied. Token women managers are subjected to constant scrutiny, rating them lower than male colleagues regardless of their actual job records and blocking appointments and promotions that would give them authority over men.

The difficulties that many women managers experience in gaining informal acceptance among male members of management teams carry implications that go far beyond personal enjoyment of work. Darrah's (1994) research, described above, indicates the importance of newly hired workers developing a network of helpers who can assist when problems arise. It is this community of practice that makes it routinely possible for workers to compensate for individual weaknesses and enhance their overall competence. When women managers are not part of the informal social networks among male managers at the pub, the golf course, and elsewhere, they lose critically important opportunities for gaining insider knowledge of what is happening, how to present themselves and their work, how to discuss its policy relevance

and not merely its technical adequacy, and so on. All these factors directly impact on their apparent potential for promotion (Cassin 1979; Kates 1988). On top of all this, women may find themselves pressured to underplay their abilities in front of male colleagues who feel threatened by competent women. Displays of subservience and deference to male views and male authority may be essential to gain a minimum of co-operation from such colleagues, and to avoid open harassment (Liddle and Joshi 1986, 178–80). Such compromises help to sustain the myth of women's relative incompetence, which further reduces the probability of their receiving recognition and promotion.

Domestic Division of Labour and Social Inequality

The most severe impediments to gender equality within the workplace may lie outside the workplace itself, in the very uneven distribution of domestic responsibilities between women and men. Most research in Canada and elsewhere concurs that even when married women are employed full-time, they still do the bulk of domestic work and child care. The class hierarchy presupposes the gender hierarchy in the sense that the organization of work and working hours assumes that workers are generally not involved in domestic labour or child care. Such work is presumed to be done by someone else. The class privileges of professional women similarly depend upon the gender subordination of other women who will perform domestic service work and child care so cheaply that they absorb only a portion of

SALLY FORTH

Reprinted with special permission of King Features Syndicate.

the money that professional women themselves earn (Liddle and Joshi 1986, 150–51).

The greatest impediment to women's success in corporate careers remains the very long, sixty-five-hour workweeks commonly expected of young executives on the fast track (Kates 1988). Men have traditionally been able to put in such long hours primarily because their wives have absorbed the bulk of their domestic responsibilities. But few women have spouses or other adults at home who can take up most of the domestic and mothering work. Men have a career advantage in this regard, but at a high price. Men who value home life and parenting lose out in their careers relative to traditional men in a corporate culture where being at the office during evenings and weekends, and willingness to uproot and to travel on corporate business, are taken as measures of career commitment.

Few women feel able or willing to pay such a high price for a career. An article in the *Globe and Mail* business magazine entitled "Thanks, But No Thanks" (Maynard and Brouse 1988) describes the lives of women who graduated with masters of business administration degrees from the University of Western Ontario. They got good, although not top, jobs as corporate business executives and were "keenly watched and courted [as] the standard bearers in women's drive for equality at work." They found themselves burned out and under extreme stress in the face of inhuman demands to give 110 percent to clients and 120 percent to children, to work from 7:30 A.M. to 6:30 P.M. and on weekends, and to travel for the company. Added to this was the desperate struggle to find and keep adequate day-care and the guilt that their children were victims of their relentless career demands. It was as if the companies were deliberately pushing women beyond human limits to prove they could not be equal to men and should give up and go home. According to the article, many of them did just that, or they started their own businesses. A few companies have moved some way towards reducing such strain, particularly under the pressure to make public their adherence to employment equity. But this has stopped at the level of maternity leave provisions and some flexibility in working hours. In August 1994, the Canadian Bar Association approved motions stating that time off for family responsibilities should not normally delay a lawyer's eligibility for partnership in a firm or affect the right to equitable pay (*Globe and Mail*,

22 Aug. 1994, B1-9). They also endorsed a motion that law firms should apply flexible treatment to men and women with children. They backed off, however, from making it a "legal duty" that firms accommodate such lawyers and from endorsing equal pay for women working shorter hours because of children. The lawyers prided themselves as "definitely leading all the other professions" on the issue.

Equality Rights as Ideology

The equality rights provisions in the Charter or in employment equity policies do nothing to redress such experiences. The principle of equality based on *sameness* in the treatment of women and men in the workplace ignores the additional demands of home and child care that are socially defined as women's responsibility. The strain of trying to do too much is readily attributed back to individual women as their personal inadequacy. It has prompted some feminist advocates like Betty Friedan (1981) to eschew earlier arguments that housewives were not living up to their potential, and to advocate motherhood as a valid career option.

Eisenstein (1984) rejects such "feminist revisionism" in favour of a conceptual shift in the meaning of equality. Feminism, she argues, shows up fundamental contradictions in the liberal philosophy of equal opportunity and merited hierarchy. The ideology of equal opportunity covers up an unequal system that privileges men by their ascribed sexual status. Affirmative action policies that try in very minor and insignificant ways to redress this systemic privileging of men are attacked within liberalism as discrimination against men. The feminist movement threatens the foundations of liberal individualism by making visible women's situation as members of a sexual class. Women as child-bearers and child-rearers face major systemic disadvantages that cannot be alleviated by abstract notions of equal opportunity.

True gender equality, Eisenstein argues, will be achieved only when child-bearing and child-rearing become socially inconsequential; that is, when they do not restrict women's choices, and do not result in women being segregated in the institution of private, domesticated motherhood, or forced into economic dependence on men, or into secondary wage-earner status. Such equality implies far-reaching social and political changes that are not envisioned in current equality rights provisions within the Canadian Charter.

What would such a world look like? It might include, among other policies: reproductive freedom; new visions of child care and health care; statutory parenting leave that would acknowledge both the special needs of childbirth and the equal parenting responsibilities of mothers and fathers; flexible working hours; a fundamental rethinking of the notions of worker or employee to include the presumption of domestic and child-care responsibilities as intrinsic to the experience of work; economic independence for mothers that presupposes profound changes in the conceptualization of private family and social responsibility. These suggestions are only a beginning: the theory of true gender equality and what it would entail for society has scarcely begun to be developed. The absence, or gross inadequacy, of such policies in most industrial societies, attests to how patriarchal these societies are.

Conclusion

This exploration of stratification in capitalist society has taken us a long way from traditional functionalist analysis with its certainty of differential skill and requirements and merited differences in prestige and rewards. As the concepts used in analyses change, so also does the nature of the reality being talked about. Where traditional functionalists talk of "stratification," for example, Marxists talk of "class." *Class* essentially refers to power based on relationship to the means of production; stratification is essentially a prestige ranking. For traditional functionalists, stratification is based on innate individual differences in abilities and motivation but, seen from the political economy perspective, it refers primarily to the relative utility of different positions for the capitalist system at any one time (Boughey 1978, 130). Good jobs can quickly crumble into nothing once they cease to be useful to corporate employers. Members of the prestigious upper middle class of corporate executives have been finding this out to their cost during the 1980s and 1990s. Cutbacks in middle management positions have left many unemployed.

The dimension of power or powerlessness is central to the Marxist analysis, not the differences in income or lifestyle that occupy traditional func-

tionalists. It certainly helps to have scarce skills that are high in demand, but it does not alter the fact that shifting labour-market demands, or new technologies, or just an overabundance of other people with similar skills can rapidly wipe out any advantage. Distinctions between professional, middle class, working class, and lower class begin to look unimportant under such conditions. What they have in common is insecurity and dependency in the labour market.

Marxist theorists acknowledge the need for skills and professional training, and the need to attract particularly able, qualified, and dependable people to certain jobs. However, they use different criteria to answer the moral question of what differential rewards should be. Personal need and labour time, rather than importance and scarcity, are the key variables. The well-known Marxist motto is "To each according to need and from each according to ability." True justice requires equality in power, prestige, and property. People deserve equal power to influence government in their own society, equal dignity as human beings, and equal access to a good standard of living (Boughey 1978, 130). People do not automatically warrant a higher standard of living just because they happen to be born brighter, or with wealthy parents, or because they lucked into an elite job. In theory, people could be rewarded for the labour time they give to their jobs. The time taken to develop skills can be calculated into the amount. So can the extra time involved in doing quality work. Those who support more dependants should take home proportionately more money. These are the principles that underlie current state salary policies in China.

Social constructionist theory introduces a qualitatively different dimension into this analysis of stratification. It focusses attention on the practices through which people work up and accept notions of jobs and skills as common-sense features of work. Like Marxism, it draws attention to the often arbitrary character of hierarchical divisions between jobs. It explores how such divisions are accomplished, particularly in the professional discourse of management experts in the field of job evaluation. It explores also how people adopt such accounts as "the way things are" and act accordingly.

Feminist theory, often in close association with social constructionism, makes visible how these practices are gendered. It explores, moreover, how a gender hierarchy, built on inegalitarian division of domestic labour, is presupposed in the organization of labour relations. Reform of institutionalized patriarchy requires fundamental changes in the organization of society, changes that go far beyond a shift in attitudes or procedures to establish formal equity in the evaluation of male and female job applicants.

Suggested Reading

An excellent source of statistical information on inequality in Canada is Henry Veltmeyer, *Canadian Class Structure* (1986). Veltmeyer takes a strong, structuralist Marxist approach to inequality, showing how capitalism works to create a class of super-rich at the top of the Canadian hierarchy and a class of poor and sometimes destitute people at the bottom.

For a clear presentation of functionalist theory of stratification, the article by Davis and Moore, "Some Principles of Stratification" (1945) is excellent. It is an older publication, but the main argument is very clear, without being hedged or qualified to avoid criticism. The rebuttal by Melvin Tumin, "Critical Analysis of 'Some Principles of Stratification'" (1953) is also very straightforward.

For the Marxist approach an excellent book is Harry Braverman, *Labour and Monopoly Capital* (1974). This descriptive and readable book presents a strong argument for the importance to capitalism of deskilling workers.

For the ethnomethodological perspective, any of the studies by Erving Goffman are valuable. They are all very readable descriptions of how everyday life is managed in ordinary interactions. One short book by Goffman is *Interaction Ritual* (1967).

Charles Darrah's article "Skill Requirements at Work" (1994) provides an insightful social constructionist analysis of work that challenges the adequacy of common-sense notions of skill, and also draws attention to the importance of interpersonal networks in generating and transmitting crucial work-related knowledge. The article also discusses how the deskilling practices of management seriously hamper the efforts of workers to learn more about their work.

It should have become apparent throughout this debate that education is related in critical, although contradictory, ways to stratification. Schools and colleges, with their technological-meritocratic principles, have become central arenas within which relations of stratification are worked out. It is to the analysis of the education system that we now turn.

From the perspective of radical feminism, Heidi Hartmann, "Capitalist Patriarchy and Job Segregation by Sex" (1979), presents a groundbreaking study of how male unions systematically limited the job opportunities open to women. A journalistic article by Rona Maynard and Cynthia Brouse, "Thanks, But No Thanks" (1988) documents the high stress experienced by women in corporate executive careers.

Questions

1. What do Davis and Moore see as the functional prerequisites that generate stratification in all known societies?

2. How can Tumin argue that, in a sense, equality and opportunity are inherently in conflict?

3. How does Tumin critique the argument that differential financial rewards are essential to motivate people to do important and difficult jobs?

4. What structural changes lie behind the American Dream that anyone can achieve upward mobility through talent and effort?

5. How does Marxist theory challenge the relationship between credentials and financial rewards?

6. In Braverman's classical Marxist theory, what is the functional importance of job ladders in industry? How might such structures be dysfunctional for competitive advantage in high-technology industries?

7. How does the notion of work as a *community of practice* undermine the notion that specific jobs require specific skills?

8. How do the job descriptions of clerical and managerial work function as ideological practices that distort understanding of what people are actually doing?

9. How can the incorporation of workers' representatives in job evaluation committees serve to further distort rather than enhance understanding of what workers actually do?

10. How is domestic division of labour directly implicated in gender inequality in paid work?

16

Education: Does It Moderate or Perpetuate Social Inequality?

Compulsory public schooling for children is a central feature of all industrialized societies. In Canada, the beginnings of a public school system can be traced back to the early 1840s in Ontario (MacDonald 1988, 102–3). In 1846, a general board of education was set up to examine the state of education in the province and to make recommendations for developing a common school system. In 1850 an Act was passed to regulate the classification of teachers and to establish boards of public instruction for each county to certify teachers and to select textbooks. In 1871, free, compulsory education was established. Children between the ages of seven and twelve had to attend school four months per year. In 1919, the school-leaving age was raised to sixteen. Secondary school fees were abolished two years later. Other provinces slowly followed Ontario's lead.

In contemporary Canada, schooling is compulsory between the ages of six and sixteen, although many children are enrolled in formal educational institutions at an earlier age and remain in school past the legal school-leaving age. Statistics Canada data indicate that the numbers of children enrolled in pre-elementary education increased by 9 percent between 1977 and 1984, and a further 9 percent by 1991 to a total of 466 123 children in 1991. During the same period the proportions of people aged 15 to 19 still in full-time education rose from 64.5 percent to 77.4 percent. Many people continue their formal education in a postsecondary institution. Full-time postsecondary enrolment grew by 33 percent between 1981–82 and 1991–92 to a total of nearly 900 000, with 62 percent of these at university.

Why has compulsory and advanced education achieved such importance in industrial societies like Canada? What forms does education take? What are the explanations for inequalities among different social groups in access to and achievement in education? These are some of the central questions we examine in this chapter.

Theories of education are very closely linked to the theories of stratification explored in the previous chapter. In industrial society, careers have become more important than inherited wealth in determining the standard of living of the majority of people. These careers, in turn, depend on access to education. As in the previous chapter, we present the traditional functionalist perspective first, followed by the Marxist structuralist critique. Both of these approaches are challenged by contemporary efforts to reformulate theories of education in less deterministic ways. Such challenges give central attention to the social construction of schooling in daily interaction in classrooms and to feminist efforts to radically transform the curriculum and teaching methods.

Functionalism: The Liberal Theory of Education

Next to the family, education ranks as the most important institution within the traditional functionalist model of the social system. Education is responsible for developing moral or normative consensus, which is at the centre of social integration and pattern maintenance. It is also critical for giving young people the skills that will enable them to adapt to rapidly changing economic conditions.

The Ideal of Liberal Education

The nineteenth-century philosopher and reformer John Dewey advocated a free and universal school system as vitally important for democracy and for developing industrial society. He believed that schools have a central role to play in the psychic and moral development of the individual. By helping to develop the cognitive and psychomotor skills of students, schools also offer each individual the chance to compete openly for privileges in society (Bowles and Gintis 1976, 20–23). Dewey saw universal education as a powerful mechanism for reducing extremes of wealth and poverty and for fostering equality. In his view, universal schooling was not only desirable in itself, but it was also an efficient way to train a skilled labour force. It would be, therefore, eminently compatible with capitalism.

This vision of the education system as democratic, just, and efficient stands at the heart of the functionalist view of stratification in industrial society. Functionalism focusses primarily on the objectives of socializing young people in the skills and moral commitment necessary for them to take over adult roles within the social system. The goal is to ensure the continuity of the system itself. Functionalists define equality of opportunity primarily in terms of meritocracy. The desired outcome of schooling, therefore, is that the more able and motivated students are allocated to the more difficult and important social roles.

The Functions of Schools

Parsons' essay, "The School Class as a Social System" (1961), provides a statement of the basic assumptions underlying the functionalist theory of education. In this essay, Parsons argues that families are not adequate to prepare children for adult roles in advanced industrial societies, primarily because the values and commitments appropriate for kinship roles conflict with those of the workplace. A primary function of schools is to help children to make the transition from the value orientations of family life to the affectively neutral, universalistic, and achievement-oriented values of the work world.

Parsons suggests that it is significant that close to nine out of ten elementary school teachers are women. The nurturing orientation that these teachers provide gives young children some continuity with the mother role and absorbs the strain of achievement and differential ranking. Children can relate to their female teacher and try to please her as they do their mothers. They have the same teacher for a whole year in all subjects. At the same time, the teacher is not a mother but is in an occupation. Each year children have a new teacher. This reinforces particularistic role identification. They also learn that the teacher judges them according to their achievements. Parsons further suggests that it is significant that traditionally a high proportion of American school teachers are unmarried. They thus avoid the contradictory demands of maternal and occupational roles for women.

Senior classes are differentiated into specialized subject areas, each taught by a different teacher. The majority of these teachers are men. Specialization by male teachers reduces attachment to any one teacher and promotes and reinforces the masculine image of affective neutrality and specificity. Hence children learn the pattern variables appropriate for adult sex roles.

At the same time, schools socialize children in required commitments and capabilities for adult roles. *Commitment* comprises two broad aspects: societal values and performance of specific roles. The two components of *capabilities* are skills to perform the task and role responsibility; that is, the ability to live up to the expectations of others. The school is thus crucial for the allocation of young people into future roles on the basis of achievement. At the elementary level, where cognitive skills appear relatively simple, the moral component of responsible citizenship takes precedence. Students are graded both for achievement and for "responsible good behaviour" such as respectfulness and co-operativeness in class. Parsons sees these as fundamental moral skills, important for future leadership and initiative. Stratification on the basis of cognitive skills is translated into college preparatory streaming at grade 9. Parsons admits that the ascriptive characteristics of class of origin influence this streaming, but he concludes that the main force is still achievement.

Parsons' essay is a masterpiece in displaying the working assumptions of the functionalist approach. The first assumption is *functional indispensability*. Parsons conveys the impression that all aspects of American schools in the 1950s had important functions within the education system and could not be easily replaced. He further accepts the basic assumption of *functional unity*. Any established patterns are regarded as good for the educational system, for society as a whole, and for individual members. There is no question in his model that practices such as the early streaming of children on the basis of behaviour rather than cognitive abilities might not be functional for all sectors of society. The third basic assumption, *universal functionalism*, is evident in Parsons' effort to find a valuable purpose for every detail that he notices. Nothing is dismissed as an irrelevant or useless habit left over from earlier times or from other life situations.

The main problem with this approach is that almost any change in the status quo is problematic. We are left with the impression that any change in the school system, such as using male teachers in elementary grades or married women

specialists in later grades, or having mixed playground activities for girls and boys together, would be psychologically disturbing for the students. Contemporary functionalist theories have largely discarded Parsons' assumptions concerning the importance of such details as spinsterhood for elementary teachers, but in other respects his essay still expresses the core ideas of functionalism.

The main functions of the school system, as highlighted by Parsons, can be summarized as follows:

1. to teach the values of achievement, universalistic standards of judgment, and emotional neutrality appropriate for specialized occupational roles;

2. to train in specific skills and knowledge appropriate for occupational roles;

3. to ensure the appropriate selection and allocation of young adults to occupational roles in accordance with merit, as measured by universal standards of achievement;

4. to legitimate inequalities in material rewards in democratic society through principles of merit established in the school grading system;

5. to develop stable social relations with age peers outside the family;

6. to inculcate appropriate sex-role identification.

The functionalist approach to the sociology of education has largely accepted this list of functions defining the roles that schooling plays in society, particularly in preparing children for the job market. The main focus of the debate has been on the extent to which schools are able to meet the moral goals set out by Dewey: to provide equality of opportunity to all children for personal and intellectual development and academic attainment across different social classes, races, and ethnic groups. More recently, the importance of sexual equality has also been recognized. The growing consensus is that, notwithstanding concerted efforts at educational reform, schools are failing miserably with respect to the goal of equality.

Equality and Educational Opportunity

The concept of *equality* in education has been understood in several contradictory ways. During the early era of the common school system, emphasis was placed on **equality of condition** or sameness. A common curriculum was planned for all children as a standardized, age-graded program of studies without reference to individual differences in interests or abilities. Later the interpretation of equality shifted to emphasize **equality of opportunity** for all children to develop their individual potential. A variety of curricula were planned to reflect the different needs, capacities, and interests of students, and their different occupational futures. Differential treatment is justified on the basis of merit. Specialized and advanced education would be open to all children who qualify on the basis of effort and ability.

The acknowledged difficulty with offering differentiated programs is that they can become a source of inequality of opportunity. Children risk becoming trapped in educational streams that limit their future options. A third approach shifted the focus to *equality of outcome*. A range of educational opportunites, resources, and different teaching methods were designed to meet the special needs of individual children, with the goal that all students would succeed in school to the best of their innate abilites.

Each of these approaches tries to grapple with the evidence of persistent and marked differences in the formal educational attainment of students from different backgrounds. These cannot be accounted for solely by variations in intellectual ability. Porter, Porter, and Blishen (1982) conducted an extensive survey of 2571 Ontario students in grades 8, 10, and 12 to explore the relationship between the backgrounds of students and their aspirations to attend university. The researchers found a direct and strong relation between the father's occupational status and the student's aspiration to graduate from grade 13 and to enter university (see figure 16-1). The higher the occupational status of the father, the more likely the student was to want to complete grade 13. Seventy-six percent of students whose fathers were in the higher professional category intended to go on to university, compared with 46 percent of students whose fathers had unskilled jobs. This gap could only be partially accounted for by the different ability levels of students. The researchers found that social class background was a more powerful indicator of aspiration to graduate from university than was measured mental ability (Porter, Porter, and Blishen 1982, 61).

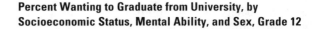

Figure 16-1

Percent Wanting to Graduate from University, by Socioeconomic Status, Mental Ability, and Sex, Grade 12

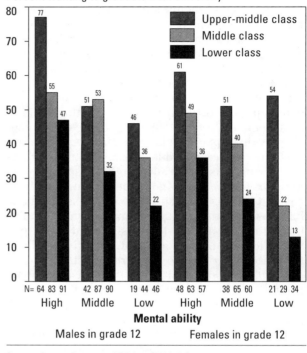

Source: Porter, Porter, and Blishen (1982, 61).

Among the high-ability boys, 77 percent of those with upper-middle-class backgrounds aspired to graduate from university. The corresponding figure for lower-class boys was 47 percent. At the other extreme, among the low-ability boys, 46 percent of those with upper-class backgrounds aspired to university. By contrast, only 22 percent of low-ability boys with lower-class backgrounds wanted to graduate from university. Thus, there is a 24 to 30 percentage-point difference in proportions of boys aspiring to university that can be accounted for by the effect of social class background. Grade 12 girls show similar differences in aspirations by social class. Among girls with high mental ability, 61 percent of the upper-middle-class girls aspired to university compared with only 36 percent of lower-class girls, a difference of 25 percentage points.

When grade 12 boys and girls are compared, boys have higher aspirations than girls across most categories of social class and mental ability. The exceptions occur among middle-ability and low-ability students within the upper-middle class where girls equal or exceed boys in aspirations.

These findings concerning the link between social class and aspirations for higher education closely mirror the results of research conducted in the 1950s in the United States by Tumin (1973, 46–54). This similarity suggests that the intervening twenty years of educational reforms had little effect on class bias in educational attainment. However, the differences between the sexes in the Ontario data are significantly less than in Tumin's data. Tumin found that, in every category of class and mental ability, boys had consistently higher educational aspirations than girls. The rise in aspirations among upper-middle-class girls in the Ontario data is striking.

A follow-up study of the Ontario grade 12 students confirmed the predicted relation between social class background and actual attendance at university, particularly among the high-ability students. In this group, 74 percent of the upper-middle-class students went to university compared with 62 percent of the middle-class and 59 percent of the lower-class students. Low-ability students showed similar differences in their rate of attendance by social class. Among the medium-ability group, however, there was an insignificant difference in attendance rates among the three classes.

In summary, the data suggest that the occupational class status of the father has a significant effect on the likelihood of children aspiring to and attending university. The influence of social class exceeds that of mental ability, especially for boys. Students whose fathers are professionals are particularly likely to intend to go to university, even when their mental ability is low. Girls generally lag behind boys in their aspirations to attend university, although the differences seem to be decreasing, particularly within upper-middle-class families.

Functionalist Explanations for Class and Gender Bias in Educational Attainment

Functionalists view education as a system that provides for the appropriate allocation of young people into occupational roles on the basis of ability. How, then, do they explain the large num-

bers of high-ability students choosing not to attend university? Porter, Porter, and Blishen (1982, 25–29) draw upon the classical functionalist ideas of socialization and self-concept to explore the class and sex differences that are associated with the wasted talent. As we have seen in earlier chapters, socialization is the process through which children learn appropriate social roles and rules of behaviour for the groups in which they find themselves. These rules reflect those of the wider social settings of neighbourhood, social class, and religious group within which families are located. Through interacting with others, children learn to conform to the behaviour that others expect and learn to expect approval and esteem from others for such conformity. Of great importance to children is the approval of significant others. These people first consist of immediate family members and later the children's peers and teachers. Porter, Porter, and Blishen predict that the roots of ambition lie in the early socialization process when the influence of parents is likely to be paramount.

Self-Concept

Self-concept, the image that we hold of ourselves, is closely related to socialization. Children develop a sense of who they are through coming to see themselves as they appear to others. Boys and girls growing up in different social classes come to develop different conceptions of themselves and their abilities. These self-concepts may not accurately reflect innate mental abilities, but they powerfully influence what children believe they can do, and therefore what they are willing to try.

Porter, Porter, and Blishen devised a series of questions to measure students' self-concepts and to determine who acted as their significant others. Their data suggest that parents seem to be more significant then either teachers or peers in influencing educational aspirations for the majority of children. In every social class, and for both sexes, a greater proportion of students aspired to university when parental influence was high, than when it was low. The high or low influence of peers made relatively little difference. Teachers appeared to have even less influence than peers on future educational plans.

The researchers found large differences between social classes in the amount of direct assistance that parents gave children with schoolwork. At the grade 10 level, they found a difference of 27 percentage points between upper-middle and lower-class boys, and 13 percentage points between upper-middle-and lower-class girls in this regard. By grade 12 these differences rose to 34 and 41 percentage points respectively.

Self-concept of ability seems to be powerfully linked to parental influence and to school performance but minimally linked to measures of mental ability or to teacher's influence (Porter, Porter, and Blishen 1982, 125–29). Self-concept seems to account for the generally lower educational aspirations of girls relative to boys. The researchers found that girls had a lower self-concept of their own ability than boys for every measure used. Their striking finding was that girls achieved consistently better grade point averages in school than boys for every level of mental ability, and yet they had consistently lower self-concepts of their abilities than boys for every category of ability and performance. Girls, it seems, may be held back by their own low conceptions of themselves.

The researchers link the low self-concept of girls to a combination of socialization and realistic appraisal of the roles they see females perform, both of which are inconsistent with academic success and achievement. Girls, they suggest, are socialized to be overly dependent on the opinions of others and to be submissive. They are more likely to accede to the demands of female teachers and to perform well in school. But because they are not encouraged to be independent, they do not develop confidence in their ability to cope with their environment, and they receive less encouragement from parents to continue their education. They are taught to realize their ambitions through marriage and to passively accept the social status of their husbands.

Boys, on the other hand, are socialized to be independent and autonomous from their mothers, so they resist female teachers in early grades. But, as they near school-leaving age, they are under pressure to qualify for university, as this is linked to future male occupations. They encounter more male teachers in high school and new subjects associated with males in our culture. Thus, boys perform less well than girls throughout school but have higher self-concepts and are significantly more likely to go on to higher education.

If this analysis of the differential socialization and lower self-concepts of girls relative to boys

accurately accounts for the 1971 data, it would appear that dramatic changes have occurred in gender socialization in one generation. In 1971, when Porter, Porter, and Blishen did their study, females comprised only 37.7 percent of full-time undergraduate enrolment. But by 1987–88, 50.3 percent of all full-time undergraduates were women, rising to over 53 percent by 1991–92 (see figure 16-2). The proportions in graduate programs remained stable between 1981 and 1991 with roughly three women to every four men enrolled. These figures suggest that the pattern found by Porter, Porter, and Blishen—that girls generally lack sufficient self-confidence in their abilities to develop high educational aspirations—no longer holds in the 1990s. We need new studies of family socialization to understand what changes have taken place and whether girls are attending university in numbers equal to boys because of, or in spite of, prevailing patterns of socialization.

Figure 16-2

Full-time University Enrolment, by Level and Sex, Canada, 1981–82 and 1991–92

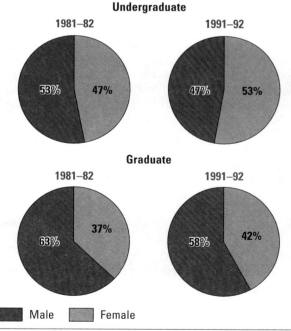

Source: Reproduced by authority of the Minister of Industry, 1994. Statistics Canada (1994e), *Education in Canada: A Statistical Review*, Cat. 81-229, p. 51.

The more general findings of Porter, Porter, and Blishen concerning differential educational aspirations and attainment by social class have not been challenged by any more recent data. The researchers conclude that different patterns of family socialization by social class constitute the primary cause of wasted talents in the education system. Parents are of central importance as significant others for children and are therefore significant in promoting or reducing educational aspirations. Upper-middle-class parents are more likely to take an interest in, and to help with, their children's schooling and to emphasize success in education as a factor in their approval and esteem. They promote higher aspirations in their children (see figure 16-3).

Figure 16-3

Program by Socioeconomic Status, Grade 12

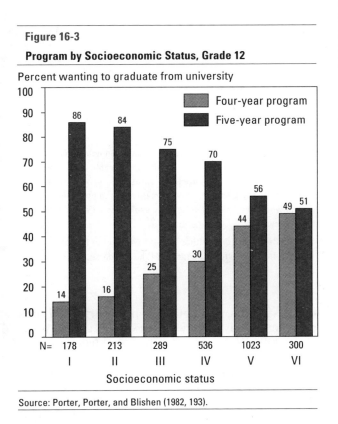

Source: Porter, Porter, and Blishen (1982, 193).

Schools may try to develop teaching methods to counter the negative influence of lower-class backgrounds on students, but the real solution seems to lie in changing the norms and values of lower- and lower-middle-class parents. Schools provide an avenue for upward social mobility, particularly in Canada. It is up to the students themselves to choose to take advantage of the opportunities provided.

The Political Economy of Education: Schooling in Capitalist Society

The Marxist structuralist perspective is rooted in very different conceptions of stratification in capitalist society and of the associated role of education. It focusses primarily on the structure of the school system rather than on the aspirations of individual students. Differences in aspirations are regarded as the effects rather than the causes of inequality in education. Functionalists blame lower-class students for not wanting to take advantage of opportunities for higher education and social mobility. Marxists argue that the school system is structured in such a way as virtually to ensure their failure. In focussing on individual aspirations rather than underlying structures, functionalist theory acts as an ideology; that is, a means not to see what is really going on in the school system.

In this section we draw heavily on the work of Samuel Bowles and Herbert Gintis to illustrate the broad outlines of the Marxist structuralist perspective on education. Their study, *Schooling in Capitalist America* (1976), is widely cited as a seminal work that inspired a decade of Marxist-oriented research in education.

In a summary statement of their theory, Bowles and Gintis (1988) point to the contradictions between democracy and capitalism. Political democracy is based on rights invested in the person. The central problems for democracy concern how to maximize participation in decision-making, shield minorities against majority prejudice, and protect majorities against undue influence of an unrepresentative minority. The economic system is based on the principle of rights invested in property. The central problems are how to minimize participation of the majority (the workers), protect a specific minority (capitalists and managers) against the will of the majority, and subject the majority to the will of an unrepresentative minority.

Schools are caught in the middle. They are part of the democratic state system, but they are responsible for educating young people to fit into the economic system. Bowles and Gintis (1976, 54) argue that most of the problems in the school system stem from this contradiction between a democratic political system and a totalitarian economic system. The liberal conception of education, first put forward by Dewey, emphasizes three fundamental goals: (1) developing the full potential of individual students with respect to cognitive, physical, emotional, critical, and aesthetic powers; (2) promoting equality through common public schools that would overcome disadvantaged social backgrounds; and (3) ensuring social continuity through preparing young people for integration into adult social roles. Bowles and Gintis argue that these three goals are fundamentally incompatible. Schools cannot promote full personal development and social equality while integrating students into alienating and hierarchically ordered roles within the economy.

The problems are compounded by the compulsion within advanced capitalist economies to develop labour-saving technology that will either displace workers altogether or deskill them in order to cheapen their wage-labour and so raise profits. Bowles and Gintis accept the main theme of Braverman's *Labor and Monopoly Capital* (1974), which predicts that the vast majority of skilled craftworkers, clerical staff, and even professionals will be systematically deskilled and fragmented by technological advances. The resulting class structure will be characterized by a mass of low-skilled workers, controlled by a small class of supervisors and managers, with a very small elite class of highly skilled professionals and executives who run the huge corporations in the interests of the owners of capital. A principal function of schooling in relation to such a system is to prepare the mass of children to fit into a largely deskilled, fragmented, and hierarchical class system. Their natural abilities and desire for autonomy need to be suppressed rather than enhanced to make them comply.

Seen from this perspective, both the evidence of an apparent waste of talented lower-class children who drop out of school, and the lack of fit between mental ability and postsecondary education, take on new meanings (see table 16-1). Schools perpetuate class inequality because this is precisely what they are intended to do. Lower-class children are channelled into dead-end voca-

Table 16-1

Labour Force Participation and Unemployment Rate by Education and Sex, May 1994*

Level of Education	Unemployment Rate	
	Male	Female
0–8 years	16.4	16.3
Some secondary education	16.8	15.0
High-school graduate	9.9	9.8
Some postsecondary	12.7	13.2
Postsecondary diploma	9.2	8.6
University degree	5.5	5.7
Total	11.0	10.2

Level of Education	Participation Rate	
	Male	Female
0–8 years	41.7	19.3
Some secondary education	64.3	42.5
High-school graduate	81.6	63.9
Some postsecondary	80.9	70.6
Postsecondary diploma	84.8	70.9
University degree	86.3	80.5
Total	74.0	57.6

*The table shows relatively small differences in unemployment rates between males and females with comparable levels of education. Although there are large differences in official participation rates. The participation rate measures the proportions of people who are employed or actively seeking work at the time of the survey.

Source: Reproduced by authority of the Minister of Industry, 1994. Adapted from Statistics Canada (1994b), *Canada Year Book 1992*, table 5, p. B-16.

tional streams, drop out of school early, and thus provide a ready supply of workers to fill the mass of unskilled jobs. Middle-class children, regardless of ability, stay in the education system long enough to get credentials that qualify them for better-paid positions. Bowles and Gintis argue that the main function of such credentials is to make distinctions between workers, and particularly to legitimate the higher pay and status of supervisors relative to workers. Very few of the people who achieve higher credentials actually find they need what they learned to do their jobs.

Bowles and Gintis (1976, 97–100) cite many examples to back up their argument that the relation between credentials and rewards is largely arbitrary. People who earn credentials, but who lack other attributes of superior status, tend not to get high economic rewards. For example, the economic returns on schooling—average increments in salary for each additional year of formal education—are twice as high for white males as for blacks and women in the United States. White males of upper-class background experience returns on education 66 percent higher than white males of lower-class background. Even when years of experience on the job are identical, white males are likely to have higher earnings than blacks and women. Body image is also important. Bowles and Gintis cite the results of one study that suggested that height was a more important determinant of earnings than either grade point average or a cum laude degree. Another survey of 15 000 executives found that those who were overweight were paid significantly less, the penalty being as much as $1000 a pound. People are much less likely to challenge the prestige, authority, and higher earnings of distinguished-looking older white males, regardless of their actual abilities, than they would if younger, overweight, black women were promoted to supervisory positions.

From the perspective of traditional functionalism, such patterns are irrational—inexplicable holdovers of ascriptive criteria in what should be the impersonal and achievement-oriented bureaucratic world of business. But from the Marxist structuralist perspective these patterns serve to reinforce the status consciousness that fragments workers.

Structural Correspondence Theory

Structural correspondence theory argues that there is a close correspondence between how relationships are structured within schools and within the work force. Schools reproduce the social relations required for production. Bowles and Gintis (1976, ch. 6) trace historical parallels between significant changes in the American capitalist economy and developments in the school system. The origin of the common schools in the mid-1830s in the United States coincided with the expansion of the factory system and the widespread labour unrest associated with it. What the factory owners desperately needed was not a skilled labour force, but a disciplined one. Common schools enforced military discipline and values of order, neatness, politeness, and punctuality that served to transform an ill-disciplined

Common schools enforced military discipline and moral education well suited for training a docile and disciplined factory work force.

immigrant and farming populations into a docile and disciplined factory work force.

The subsequent progressive education movement, and greatly increased enrolment in public schools, coincided in the United States with the expansion of corporate capitalism between about 1890 and 1930 (Bowles and Gintis 1976, ch. 7). Corporate bosses needed a mass of middle-ranking employees who could be trusted to work without direct supervision in clerical, sales, bookkeeping, and junior supervisory roles. These employees also had to be divided socially from the lower-level workers whom they supervised. More than obedience and punctuality was required. These employees had to internalize an identification with the employer and the corporation. It was this kind of stratified work force that the mass high schools produced. Schools expanded greatly in size and became bureaucratic, hierarchical, and competitive, ousting the once uniform curriculum of the common schools.

Social relations within vocational and college-track classes came to conform to different norms, consistent with the kinds of jobs for which children were being prepared. Vocational streams emphasized close supervision and obedience to rules, whereas college-track classes encouraged a more open atmosphere emphasizing internalization of norms, independent activities, and limited supervision. Near the top of the educational hierarchy, four-year colleges came to emphasize creative and critical thinking congruent with careers at senior levels of corporate hierarchies.

A classic in this research is the study by Jean Anyon (1980) into how social studies and language arts were taught in five elementary schools located in different communities in the eastern United States. The research describes marked variation in patterns of classroom interaction by the social class background of those attending school. Instruction in the elite school for the children of executives emphasized the development of analytical reasoning and leadership skills. Lessons were creative. Students made presentations to the class and criticized each other's work. In the middle-class school, lessons were very different. Language arts, for example, was reduced to grammar. Teachers checked for right answers rather than for critical understanding of the questions. In lower-class schools, children seemed to be taught primarily to follow rules set out by the teacher for completing the exercise. Their work was evaluated not by whether the answers were right, but whether the rules had been followed.

These differences reflect and reinforce the family backgrounds from which the different streams of children are drawn. Working-class parents favour stricter educational methods, directly reflecting their own knowledge that submission to authority is essential to getting and holding a steady job. Their children form the majority of pupils in vocational education streams. Professional and self-employed parents prefer a more open atmosphere with greater emphasis on motivational controls rewarding students for achievements rather than for obedience and good behaviour. Such an atmosphere is more consistent with their position in the labour force. Their children are mostly destined for college-track classes.

A third phase in the development of the education system, marked by the expansion of higher education in the 1960s, coincided with the effective domination of the capitalist economy by corporate and state sectors (Bowles and Gintis 1976, ch. 8). Self-employed entrepreneurs were relegated to increasingly peripheral roles. White-collar and professional employment expanded but became more fragmented and compartmentalized. The expansion of community colleges and diploma courses came in response to this shifting job market, producing what Bowles and Gintis refer to as skilled, subprofessional, white-collar workers. This category includes lower-level supervisors, secretaries, and paraprofessionals in dentistry, law, teaching, and medicine.

Liberal functionalists would largely agree with such an analysis, but Marxist structuralist theory goes further to draw attention to the changing social relations of higher education. Bowles and Gintis ask why the stress on free inquiry and liberal arts in higher education gave way to an emphasis on vocationalized and compartmentalized packages of credits. Why did the student politicization of the 1960s occur? Why has there been an overexpansion of graduates? The main answer they give is that free inquiry was appropriate for the entrepreneurial class, but not for corporate employees, except at the highest levels. Student radicals were drawn mostly from members of the declining entrepreneurial class who resented the loss of autonomy over their working lives. Mass higher education produced a surplus army of people with bachelors degrees and subprofessional qualifications, and this served to break their bargaining power in the labour market. Corporations thus gained access to a highly skilled work force, while salaries and other concessions could be held to a minimum. Corporate profits were protected. The training of elites has now shifted further up into graduate and postgraduate education. Free inquiry tends to be stressed only at this heady level.

The pressure on universities to serve industry has now become more overt. It takes the form of cutbacks in public funding to force these institutions into greater direct co-operation with corporations. The result is that university autonomy is undermined, funding in less marketable liberal arts and humanities programs is threatened, and, even in the favoured science and engineering faculties, pure research is subordinated to short-term profit motives. Bowles and Gintis suggest that community colleges have already largely succumbed to pressure to produce the labour force that corporations want. They offer the veneer of higher education for lower-class students but, in reality, they may be little more than "high schools with ashtrays," channelling students into dead-end vocational programs (Bowles and Gintis 1976, 211).

Educational Reform: The Losing Battle?

Proposals for educational reform are compromised by the corporate context in which they are evaluated and implemented. Alternative, non-bureaucratic forms of schooling designed to promote the creative potential of children have operated in many pilot projects. They tend to be very successful in their own terms, and are described with great enthusiasm by teachers and students, but rarely do they expand beyond isolated schools for small numbers of privileged students. Bowles and Gintis blame reformers, not for their objectives, but for their narrow focus on schools while failing to target the wider economy that schools mirror.

The educational reformer Ivan Illich has long railed against the stultifying character of the North American public school system, which incarcerates students in classrooms, cuts them off from the real world, and teaches them to distrust their own knowledge and experience and to rely on experts (Illich 1971). "Knowledge" is treated as a packaged commodity that becomes the private property of those who attain credentials, while those who lack such paper credentials are predefined as incompetent. Illich proposes an alternative system of education in which students would recover responsibility for their own teaching and learning through watching people at work and learning alongside them. For Bowles and Gintis (1976, 255–62), the main problem with this vision of a deschooled society is that it treats the socialization agency of the school as the basic explanatory variable. But dismantling schools will not cure the effects of capitalism that cause schools to function as they do. Individuals cannot be held personally responsible for their own deschooling when schooling is obligatory for ten years and is the major means of access to a livelihood.

Schooling for Contemporary Capitalism

Critics of the structural **correspondence theory** suggest that Bowles and Gintis oversimplified the relationship between schools and capitalism. The rise of common schools in Upper Canada preceded the expansion of factories by some twenty-five years, discrediting the argument that their original purpose was to train workers for industrial capitalism (MacDonald 1988; Curtis 1987). The Ontario School Act of 1943 followed soon after the rebellions in Upper Canada in 1837–38 and seems to have been centrally concerned with promoting values of patriotism and citizenship in children. This was not incompatible with training a disciplined factory work force, but it did require a balancing of interests between democracy and capitalism.

The assertion that vocational schools were intended to prepare children for failure and entry into unskilled, dead-end jobs is also overstated. Automation and the systematic deskilling of the work force have played an important role in increasing profits to capitalists in mass-production industries. But the thesis that all capitalists want deskilled, cheap labour ignores the importance of rapid product innovation and a highly flexible, adaptive labour force in competitive global capitalism. The expansion of higher education since the 1960s, and the funds that capitalists have donated to certain university faculties, cannot be totally dismissed as credentialism. Authoritarian classrooms and standardized curriculum packages are not functional for the production of creative, innovative workers.

The signing of the North American Free Trade Agreement (NAFTA) in 1993 promises to usher in a new era of structural correspondence between the Canadian education system and global capitalism, characterized by the commercialization of society (Calvert and Kuehn 1993). Many aspects of education reflect a shift from a publicly funded social service to a private, profit-oriented system. Under NAFTA rules, once any aspect of the provision of educational services is opened to private contract, it cannot subsequently return to government control without all relevant United States firms being compensated for loss of market opportunity. Profit-making postsecondary training firms are expanding rapidly in Canada while funding for community colleges is being cut. Business colleges now routinely offer courses in keyboarding, computing skills, bookkeeping, and accounting. Any effort by governments to return such courses to the publicly funded community college system could be challenged under NAFTA regulations as unfair practices limiting markets for private firms.

The difference between public-service and private-profit educational institutions is, in any case, narrowing. In the language of administrators and new university presidents, education is increasingly being described as a product that managers market. Students are consumers and corporations are stakeholders. University administrators are corporate managers with objectives to run universities like a business, selling a product for which they must attract revenue or close down. Corporations are encouraged to rent university facilities for research in return for copyrights and patents. By 1993, fifteen universities and an estimated 800 researchers were linked with over 170 companies in joint research projects. Universities compete with each other to attract funding deals with corporations, as government revenues are frozen or reduced.

Provision of food services in schools is already being privatized with giant corporations like Burger King and McDonald's running school cafeterias. United States companies are also guaranteed **right of national treatment** in the publishing and distribution of textbooks. Intellectual property rights have been established over a wide range of educational materials including cable and satellite transmission of proprietary educational programs, courses, and learning aids that have patent protection. Educational television is fast becoming big business with companies providing equipment to schools in return for showing programs that carry commercials. The company Youth News Network incorporates a computer chip into its equipment to monitor how often a show is viewed, for how long, and at what volume, to be sure teachers don't "cheat" and spend time teaching instead of watching the show (Calvert and Kuehn 1993, 101).

The corporate agenda impacts on educational programs in multiple ways. Business groups are able to exert increasing pressure on high-school and university curriculum planning, arguing that Canada's global competitiveness depends on schools training children in business-oriented skills. In community colleges in particular, overt constraints are placed on teaching in the interest of serving business. Muller (1989) documents how any new programs introduced in community colleges in British Columbia are constrained to conform to local business interests. Standardized forms and procedures govern how new programs are to be presented to the provincial government. These forms require the signatures of relevant employers in the locality of the college—who might be expected to hire students graduating from such programs—to indicate that they have been consulted and have given their approval. Community college management standardizes the curriculum so it is no longer the prerogative of individual instructors. It is even possible for a student to take an instructor to court for breach of contract if the published course curriculum does not appear to have been strictly followed. Student services staff are explicitly directed to guide students toward training for which there are immediate jobs in the local market (Muller 1990). Instructors are also required by college management to keep up with any and all technological innovations, such as computer-designed instruction, that industry wants. Muller concludes that community college management, in effect, works for local industry, while being financed by the state.

Publishing companies exercise significant control over the context of the texts that are made available to teachers (Apple 1986, ch. 4). Acquisitions editors and decision makers in these companies are mostly males with a background in marketing. They focus principally on what they think will sell. The goal is to produce texts with standard content that will be used for years in multiple schools. Apple stresses the urgent need for detailed research into the routine daily work processes and the politics of publishing companies that produce textbooks.

Teachers are increasingly under pressure to use curriculum packages, with heavy emphasis on the preparation of worksheets and the standardized testing and evaluation of students. One effect of such packaged teaching, Apple suggests is to deskill teachers, reducing them to technicians rather than professionals who control their own activities (Apple 1986, ch. 2). Apple fears that the growing emphasis upon teaching computer literacy in schools will exacerbate the trend toward standardization and depersonalization of classrooms. Computer manufacturers foist machines onto schools, even offering a free machine for every classroom, in the hope that parents will be motivated to buy school-compatible models for their children to practise on at home. Computers come with standard software packages for classroom instruction. Rarely do these programs incorporate the richness of the professional experience of teachers. Nor do they include the "soft" curriculum of liberal arts. Humanities, ethnic studies, culture, history, politics are all likely to lose out to the mathematical and technical subjects that are readily adaptable to computers. Teachers may find themselves reduced to technicians running programs.

The influx of computers also seems likely to exacerbate class differences between schools. Rich schools can afford multiple machines for personal instruction, and wealthy parents are able to buy computers for home use. Poorly endowed schools and poorer students are not able to have these advantages. Apple argues, too, that elite children are more likely to learn the intellectually stimulating aspects of programming, while lower-class children are trained to use computers for drill and practice sessions.

Cutbacks in government funding for schools influence the social relations of schooling for teachers no less than for the children from poor families. Dorothy Smith and the Wollestonecraft Research Group (1979) document how cutbacks in school funding affect the everyday work of teachers and produce the classroom rigidities for which teachers are subsequently held responsible. When there is not enough science equipment for all pupils to conduct their own experiments, teachers have to demonstrate the experiments while pupils watch passively. Larger classrooms mean that small-group work and seminars become less and less possible. Children who receive less hands-on experience and less attention get bored and distracted, discipline problems increase, and authoritarianism increases. Teachers do not have time to go through batches of essays or independent projects, so they assign fewer of them and rely more on uniform examinations. Teachers give more and more of their personal time to make up the shortfall in staffing until they burn out and leave the profession or become resigned to lower standards and autocratic methods. The schooling patterns criticized by Bowles and Gintis then take shape. The manifest function of budget cutbacks is to save taxpayers' money. The effect is increasingly authoritarian and rigid classrooms. The contrasts between the creative teaching in schools for elite children and the uninspired, autocratic styles of teaching in lower-class schools may well have more to do with teachers trying to cope with large classes and minimal teaching aids in lower-class schools than with any deliberate intention by such teachers to reproduce relations of class.

Standardized teaching practices are also becoming the norm in undergraduate university programs, although overt controls are less in evidence. Increasing enrolments in the face of limited budgets mean huge lecture halls, oppressive one-way teaching techniques, programmed assignments, and a reduction in individual projects. Students in lower-level sociology and psychology courses are more likely to be tested by multiple-choice examinations, marked by computers, which require rigid conformity to prepro-grammed textbook answers. Fighting such trends requires tremendous effort on the part of professors who have to mark several hundred individual essays. Creative undergraduate research becomes progressively less possible as classes of a hundred or more students descend on libraries that can only afford one copy of each book and that have cut journal subscriptions to save money and space. These are the ways in which the social reality of undergraduate education for middle-level corporate conformity is socially constructed.

Schooling for Oppressive Social Relations

A central argument within the Marxist theory of education is that the school system within capitalist societies is designed to mould children to accept and submit to hierarchical and inegalitarian class relations within capitalist societies. Schools for children at the bottom of the social hierarchy exhibit these oppressive characteristics the most clearly. Bowles and Gintis claim that within American public schools, relations between administrators and teachers, teachers and teachers, teachers and students, students and students, and also between students and their work, all replicate the hierarchical and fragmented division of labour within corporations (Bowles and Gintis 1976, 131). The content of the curriculum may be designed to teach the values of democratic citizenship, equality, freedom of speech, and so on. But the hierarchical relations within schools teach a very different lesson of submission to a rigid, rule-bound, and autocratic system. The usual liberal argument condoning such patterns is that students are children. They have not reached the stage of adult maturity when democratic rights of free choice would be appropriate.

Schools resemble factories in multiple ways. The architecture of the buildings, with separate rooms, offices, and recreation areas, arranged differently for staff, teachers, secretaries, and students, reproduces in concrete form the division of labour of the school. The seating arrangement in classrooms, with students in rows facing the front area controlled by the teacher, reinforces the hierarchy in which the teacher has authority and the students submit. The lessons of authority and submission are reported in the routines and rituals of the classroom that require students to speak only when spoken to and to leave and enter classrooms only when bells sound. Through such practices, children become inured to the discipline of the workplace. They develop the types of personal demeanor and self-image that fit them for future occupational roles in factories and bureaucracies. They learn to accept vertical lines of authority. They learn to accept the curriculum package offered. They learn to be motivated primarily through the extrinsic rewards of the grading system rather than the intrinsic pleasures of learning. Students are also fragmented through the insidious emphasis on competition and continual ranking and evaluation (Bowles and Gintis 1988, 2–3; 1976, 131).

The educational reformer, Paolo Freire, similarly decries the destructive impact of education on lower-class children, based on his observation of education in the slums of Brazil and ghetto schools in America (1970). He describes what he refers to as a banking concept of education. Students in classrooms are treated as objects rather than as acting subjects. They are containers to be filled by the teacher. The more meekly the receptacles permit themselves to be filled, the better students they are. In this system the teacher teaches and the students are taught; the teacher knows everything and the students know nothing; the teacher thinks and the students are thought about; the teacher talks and students listen; the teacher chooses and enforces the choice and the students comply. In the process, schools perpetuate oppression by reinforcing subordination, passivity, and apathy among students. Teachers are created by and in turn reproduce the **culture of domination**. Students learn to respond with fatalism and docility towards authority and to direct their anger against comrades, rather than against their dominators. Their overwhelming aspiration is to take the place of the dominator and to boss others in their turn.

Education for Native Peoples

These descriptions of oppressive schooling may seem far removed from the everyday experience of Canadian university students who are used to the college-preparatory track of Canadian high schools. But for members of socially disadvantaged groups in ghetto classrooms in Canada, the parallels can be only too glaring. The following section, which focusses on an aspect of Canadian

Native school experience, tries to bring this reality closer to home.

The traditional education of Native children took place through total involvement in community life. Children learned through sharing the lives of adults, through watching, listening, and learning by participation in the domestic, economic, political, and ceremonial life of the community. Formal schooling for Indian children in Canada was first provided by missionaries and later by government schools. Attendance at these schools became compulsory. Children from isolated bands were taken away from their communities and placed in residential schools. The explicit goal of residential schools was **assimilation**, or moulding Native children into whites. Native parents had no voice in what was taught. The language of instruction was English or French, and children were commonly punished for using their own language in school. This overtly imperialistic form of schooling was later replaced by smaller schools located within the band communities, particularly for the elementary grades. This shift toward educating Native students within their home communities was an important change, but much of the hidden curriculum of cultural domination remained intact. The description that follows is drawn from two anthropological studies of schools located within two Kwakiutl Indian villages situated along the northwest coast of British Columbia (Wolcott 1967; Rohner 1967). It is supplemented by an overview of formal education in an American Indian community (Wax, Wax, and Dumont 1964).

The hidden curriculum was manifest in the explicit assumption of many white educators in Native schools that only what the schools taught was worth knowing. Wax, Wax, and Dumont (1964, 67) refer to this attitude as the **vacuum ideology**. Teachers emphasized what they saw as the meager experience of Native children outside school and catalogued their multiple deficiencies relative to white children. The Native children's home experiences, the stories they heard from their parents, the skills of hunting, fishing, and trapping that they learned from parents were simple ignored because they fell outside the school curriculum. Teachers generally knew nothing of Native culture, values, or language, and had no respect for them either.

Teachers commonly lamented the overwhelming passivity of Native children, but this may well

The hidden curriculum of the culture of domination was evident in both residential and reserve schools for Native children.

have been a symptom of the dehumanizing character of the schools and the breakdown in communication between teachers and pupils (Wax, Wax, and Dumont 1964, 98–99; Wolcott 1967, 92). The older the children grew, the shyer they seemed to become, so that by the eighth grade they were mute to all interrogation. Upper elementary grades were characterized by silent classrooms, the silence providing a shield behind which an unprepared, unwilling student could retreat. The teachers became ridiculous, futile figures, and they responded by condescension and dislike toward Native students. Students would arrive late for school and would drift home at midday, start some task, and not return. They refused any active participation in classroom work. They expected boredom and even asked for highly repetitive work like copying. They had learned to equate the classroom with endless repetition, and they reacted against any variation in routines attempted by a new teacher. Their typical response was, "We didn't come to school for this, we came to do our schoolwork" (Wolcott 1967, 100).

This overt passivity within the classroom was combined with covert, horizontal violence against each other, which Freire observed among the oppressed people in Brazil (Wolcott 1967, 93). Younger children complained of being mercilessly teased, tortured, and bullied by classmates, behind the teacher's back. Some children absented themselves for days in fear. The only advice their mothers could give was to keep out of the way of the bigger children and not provoke them.

The school curriculum seemed irrelevant to the lives of adolescents on the reserves. Not only did it do nothing to prepare them for future jobs in their village, but it also actually conflicted with their informal education gained through participating in adult activities. Pupils resented attending school when they could otherwise be doing vital things like helping their fathers with fishing and clam digging.

The quality of academic performance in these reservation schools, measured in terms of universalistic grade standards, was abysmal (Wolcott 1967, 111; Rohner 1967, 110). The teachers, trained to respond to universalistic standards, found it almost impossible to adjust. When they administered normal intelligence tests, the Native students performed at near idiocy level. It was a hard shock for teachers, despite their knowledge that such tests are culturally biased. Teacher attitudes generally were highly unfavourable toward Native people. The village school studied by Rohner (1967, 105) had a turnover of eight teachers in fourteen years. Four of the eight had generated great hostility within the village. One had become so afraid of villagers that he had nailed up all the windows of his home and had refused to let his children play in the village. Another was so hated by the Native peoples that the superintendent had to remove him. Parents were equally intimidated by the teachers and were reduced to silence whenever they attended parent-teacher meetings. They asked only that the school open every day, start on time, and keep the pupils busy. Discipline problems were to be resolved by the teacher (Wolcott 1967, 86).

Given these kinds of school experiences, it would be miraculous if more than a small minority of Native pupils made it through to high-school graduation. Marxist structuralists would argue that they were being educated for failure. The oppressive school system defined all aspects of Native culture and traditional knowledge as irrelevant. It judged the students by white cultural standards and found them so ignorant that they were ranked as borderline mental defectives. Pupils learned to expect nothing but boredom and endless repetition in school, an expectation that exactly fits the menial, low-paying jobs that Native adults commonly attain in white capitalist society.

Since these studies were conducted there have been concerted efforts to address these problems. Many Native communities, in co-operation with the federal government, have begun to take control over their own education, and many universities in Canada and the United States have introduced Native Studies programs into their arts curriculum. The strategies seem to be working, evidenced in significantly higher numbers of Native students pursuing some form of postsecondary education in recent years. Enrolment of Native students in all postsecondary institutions nearly doubled between 1985–86 and 1992–93 from 11 170 to 21 566 students (see table 16-2). Enrolment in university increased from a mere 60 Native students in 1960–61 to 5800 in 1985–86. The proportions, however, still remain well below those for Canadians as a whole (see figure 16-4).

Figure 16-4

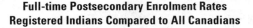

Postsecondary Participation Rate: A Comparison

Full-time Postsecondary Enrolment Rates Registered Indians Compared to All Canadians

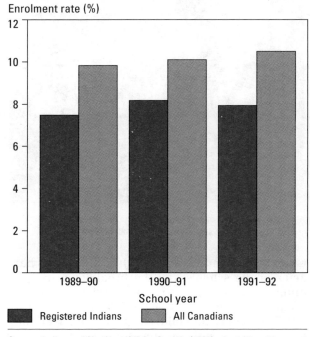

Source: Indian and Northern Affairs Canada (1993), chart 17, p. 42.

Table 16-2

Enrolment in University and Postsecondary Institutions for the Registered Indian Population, Canada, 1960–61 to 1992–93

School Year	University Enrolment	Postsecondary Enrolment[1]
1960–61	60	n/a
1965–66	131	n/a
1970–71	432	n/a
1975–76	2071	n/a
1980–81	4455	n/a
1985–86	5800	11 170
1986–87	n/a	13 196
1987–88	n/a	14 242
1988–89	n/a	15 572[2]
1989–90	n/a	18 535
1990–91	n/a	21 300
1991–92	n/a	21 442
1992–93	n/a	21 566

Notes:

[1] Includes Bill C-31 population. Total number of registered Indians funded by DIAND enrolled in postsecondary institutions also includes the number enrolled at university.

[2] Since 1988–89, numbers include students in the University and College Entry Program (UCEP).

Source: Indian and Northern Affairs Canada (1993), table 16, p. 41.

Status Indians are eligible for financial assistance to attend university under the Postsecondary Student Assistance Program, but this funding was capped in 1989. This freeze on funding coincided with a significant increase in the numbers of Native students eligible under the program. The implementation of Bill C-31 granted recognition of aboriginal status to women who had formerly lost it by marrying men who were not status Indians. These women and their children now also qualify for financial assistance as defined within treaties. Band councils now have to make difficult decisions about how to allocate limited funds among a larger group of competing claimants.

Schooling and Poverty

Poverty exacerbates the problems of racism, language, and cultural divisions against which Native peoples struggle. Children in poverty, who comprised an estimated 18.2 percent of all children in Canada in 1992, face problems of ill health, malnutrition, and daily humiliation as a routine part of their educational experience (National Council of Welfare 1994). A study by the National Council of Welfare (1975) documents that poor children are more likely than others to be born premature and underweight, to contract childhood diseases, and to miss one to three months of school in a year because of illness.

The social effect of poverty on children, and their isolation from others in the classroom, may be less visible than inadequate clothing and ill health, but they are equally damaging to the children's educational aspirations and sense of well-being. Poor children face the humiliation of not being able to bring in money for special school events or excursions. They cannot afford to buy art supplies, sports equipment or uniforms, or instruments for the school band, and so they cannot join in many of the extracurricular activities open to other children. The list of barriers goes on and on (Gabriel 1986). Humiliation fosters withdrawal, defeat, and resentment. It drains them of the motivation to give their best efforts. Poor children lack money for school books and basic supplies, which makes it hard for them to keep up with homework. Cutbacks in school budgets often mean that teachers cannot provide books for all students and cannot permit them to take books home because they must be stored away and used in other classes. Poor children are also more likely to live in inadequate and overcrowded homes where they may have no quiet place to study. Teachers used to be able to supervise quiet study periods after school hours, but with budget and staff cutbacks, such "frills" are eliminated.

Poor children in senior classes may lack the time and energy for schoolwork because they take long hours of employment at minimum wage. If school counsellors suggest they would be better off quitting school to join the army or take a typing job, they are likely to agree. Realistically they see little possibility of mobility into professional occupations when all the people around them only have low-paying semiskilled jobs. **Headstart programs** for children in deprived areas may end up only making things worse because they raise unrealistic expectations, resulting in bitter disappointment for adolescents faced with limited opportunities.

The Limitations of Political Economy Theory

The major criticism of classical political economy theory of education concerns its reductionist and deterministic formulation. Ironically, an approach that began as a radical critique of traditional functionalism depends in practice on the same logic. The structure of parts are explained by their functions for the social system as a whole. The difference is that, in Marxist theory, the system is specifically capitalist. The explanation invokes rigid historical **reductionism**. All changes in the school system since its inception in the 1840s are explained as responses to the needs of capitalism (Aronowitz and Giroux 1985, 71, 117; Cole 1988, 7–37; Moore 1988, 58–61; Apple 1988, 124).

A significant problem with this form of explanation is that it presupposes a passive view of humanity. Human agency plays little part in the analysis. Teachers and students are reduced to mere pawns of the capitalist system (Aronowitz and Giroux 1985, 71). According to Marxist structuralists, schools legitimate inequality and limit personal development to aid in the process whereby youths are resigned to their fate (Bowles and Gintis 1976, 266; Cole 1988, 35). From the perspective of social constructionist theory, Aronowitz and Giroux endorse the Marxist critique of capitalism, but challenge the oversimplified version that tries to reduce all explanations of human behaviour to position in the class structure. They argue (1985, ch. 2) that it is essential to recognize the role of teachers as professionals who are actively involved in the creation of what constitutes education. Teachers are not mere technicians who deliver standard curriculum packages and who function to preserve a hierarchical social order. For the best of them the opposite is closer to the truth, as teachers struggle to break the hold of inherited disadvantages, and push their students to develop enquiring minds and go on to academic careers. Historically, teachers have been active in professional associations that have fought for better working conditions, and for a greater say in what and how teachers teach and who evaluates them, and for control at the level of classroom practice (Apple 1986, 75). Students, too, are active in shaping the social relations of classrooms. The classic study by Willis (1981) documents how "the lads" in working-class schools in Britain actively resisted the efforts of teachers, imposing their own anti-school values on the classroom that mirrored the factory-floor culture of working-class men (see chapter 5). When Bowles and Gintis blame schools for reproducing class relations of capitalism, they may be attacking the wrong target, blaming schools for reproducing a culture that teachers are vainly trying to break.

Critics point out that, despite the Marxist commitment of Bowles and Gintis, the outcome of their theory is politically reactionary. It supports the status quo in that it leaves no space for individual or collective action to change the situation. The only viable option seems to be resignation or radical pessimism (Aronowitz and Giroux 1985, 79; Cole 1988, 35). More significantly, this ostensibly Marxist argument has been appropriated by spokespeople for the right wing in the United States. Conservatives are in full agreement with the view of Bowles and Gintis that schools are an adjunct to the labour market. They complain only that schools do not do this preparatory work well enough. The left wing seems to have no alternative to offer and to be constrained to silence (Aronowitz and Giroux 1985, 5–6). Aronowitz and Giroux (1985, 128) suggest that, despite their diametrically opposing political values, the philosophies of Marxist structuralism and capitalism share an uncritical acceptance of **scientism**: a reliance on simple cause and effect explanatory models that tend to reduce people to objects at the mercy of structural economic forces.

In this critique, we have referred to Marxist structuralism rather than Marxist theory in general, because there are important developments within contemporary Marxist theory that retain a radical critical perspective while rejecting the deterministic aspects of structuralism. This perspective shifts the focus of research from macro-studies of capitalism to the everyday interaction within the classroom of teachers and students.

How is it that capitalists are somehow able to dictate how people should relate to each other within classrooms? How do administrators, teachers, and students make sense of what is happening? How do they respond to such pressures? Why do they put up with them? When and how do they resist? These kinds of questions prompt a very different kind of research from that prevailing in either functionalist or Marxist structuralist approaches. Rather than mass surveys or sweeping historical overviews, **cultural**

Marxism and the **social construction of reality** perspectives favour research into the intimate details of interpersonal relations within classrooms. It is these relations that we explore below.

The Social Construction of Schooling*

Proponents of the social construction of reality do not view classrooms as the effects of social structures. Classrooms are the location within which the **social structures** of class, gender, or race are produced. The causal processes involved are the meaningful interactions between people in intimate everyday activities. Many studies of classrooms are beginning to piece together the mechanisms that produce what Bowles and Gintis identify as the social relations of capitalism.

The Social Construction of "Academic Ability" and "Merit"

Research in both the functionalist and political economy traditions has demonstrated how children are streamed on the basis of apparent capabilities and commitments, beginning in kindergarten or first grade; how pervasively such streaming carries over into senior classes when children are directed into vocational and academic programs; and the close correlation between such streaming and the social class backgrounds of the children. But we still have little understanding of how this happens. We need to get beyond the circular reasoning that capitalist society needs to reproduce and to justify class divisions. Social constructionist research explores the practices that accomplish what teachers come to recognize as "bright middle-class children" and also the common-sense reasoning through which the behaviour of young children becomes coded into categories such as "academically gifted" or "not very bright."

Observations and analysis of conversations between mothers and children in Toronto play-schools (Noble 1982; 1990) reveal the complex

---

* The draft of this section on social constructionist approaches to education was prepared by Dr Peter Weeks as an extension of his work on the microsociology of everyday life for chapter 18 of this text.

interactional practices through which these mothers produced the school readiness of their children. This mothering work involved training children in how to think in terms of abstract concepts and how to interact with other children and adult authority figures in ways that would fit them into the organization of school classrooms. Mothers continually prompted children into elaborating their sentences, introducing proper nouns and adjectives that were largely redundant in the immediate context. For example, one child displayed a small cut and explained, "I hit it here." Mother adds, "You hit your knee on the step."

Mothers also routinely took advantage of children's topics and activities to build mini-lesson structures into their interaction. A child playing with beads shows one to her mother and says, "Look what I got." Mother replies, "You've got beads. What colour are they?" More than a simple conversation is involved in such exchanges. The mother already knows the answer to the question and the child knows that the mother knows. The child is being encouraged and taught to display knowledge for adult evaluation (Noble 1982, 21).

Another mother playing alongside her child with a farm animals puzzle continually named and talked about each animal in turn, and also continually stressed the abstract category frame, "These are all <u>animals</u>, animals that live on the farm. Now let's put all the <u>animals</u> back in their place." When all the pieces were in place the mother asked, "How are all of these the same?" If the child failed to get the right answer, the mother might have prompted, "They are all _____." Another day the exercise will be run through again. Mothers showed by their intonational stress, and the energy directed to making it fun, just how favoured such games are.

Conversations with kindergarten teachers revealed how important such mother-child interactions can be in the subsequent evaluation of children as precocious and "ready for academic work" or "not very bright." Children in kindergarten were encouraged to engage in "free play," but not all play was regarded equally. Children who chose "mere play," like slides and sand box, were seen by teachers as not ready to go on to academic work. Children who "spontaneously" chose the ostensibly more mentally demanding matching and categorizing equipment were seen as ready to move ahead (Noble 1982, 12).

Children whose mothers had convincingly presented puzzle-matching games as fun have a distinct advantage. It was important for teacher evaluations that children respond to the instructional "question-answer-evaluation" sequence. When a teacher asks a child, "That's a nice truck. How many wheels does it have?" the child who does not respond appears as "not very bright" or "not very verbal" compared with the child who immediately responds with the number. The interpretive framework used by the teacher takes for granted that the child has been test-broken into this instructional sequence, but this presupposes years of prior exposure to such question-answer "games" and the interactional awareness that they **must** respond.

In another kindergarten classroom, the teacher displayed a picture of rain coming out of a cloud and asked, "What other word do you think of when you think of the word *rain*?" (Noble 1982, 29). Children offered a range of experiential associations like "raincoat," "umbrella," and "boots," but they were all passed over until the answer "weather" was offered. Children who have been sensitized in advance to their mothers preferring category words like "These are all animals" have a distinct advantage. Similarly, children who fill their sentences with proper nouns and adjectives appear brighter and more verbally advanced than children who do not bother to state the obvious.

A requirement of the organization of kindergarten classrooms is that children know they must drop their own activities and attend to the relevances of the teacher, and with appropriate posture and facial displays. Noble gives the example of children dropping whatever else they are doing to sit in a circle when the teacher announces that it is circle time for reading (1982, 16–18). Years of prior work, of subordinating bodies so that instruction can take place, are required for children to appear to do this "naturally" and so to appear bright and interested in what the teacher is doing. Parents may carry out this intensive one-on-one work over years, first positioning infants in front of objects they want the infant to focus on, screening other objects from view, and even pinning down limbs to enforce appropriate looking and listening. If this bodily learning is not already in place when a child enters school, it is difficult for a teacher to remedy it, even in very small groups. Noble describes scenes of kindergarten teachers struggling to restrain children in circles so that storytime could begin, and forcibly holding one child's head so he would pay attention to instructions.

Noble suggests that mothers with conventional middle-class backgrounds are far more likely to be familiar with such child development work than parents with lower-class backgrounds, and to have more time and resources with which to accomplish it. This observation, however, begs the further questions of how mothers acquire these child-developing competences and the conditions under which motherwork gets done.

Intelligence as Interactional Competence

Differences in levels of **interactional competence** among kindergarten children are directly reflected in supposedly formal or objective tests of intelligence. Noble (1990) gives three examples of test questions in the Wechsler Preschool and Primary Scale of Intelligence (WPPSI) (see table 16-3). An answer is assigned a score of 0 if unacceptable; 1 for a response that is appropriate but vague, experiential, or idiosyncratic; and 2 for a "better" answer that is more general, precise, and categorical.

According to Noble, what counts as intelligence includes:

1. being rule-governed, i.e., oriented to standard and conventional forms rather than personal and idiosyncratic ones;

2. being able to take a generalized position, external to yourself, and think in terms of the needs and interests of organizational entities beyond yourself;

3. being able to orient only to information given and solve questions asked only within the frame provided (Noble 1990, 55).

Table 16-3

Test Questions in the Wechsler Preschool and Primary Scale of Intelligence (WPPSI)	

Example 1: Vocabulary Section

What is a knife?

Something to cut with . . . a weapon	2 points
Something to kill with	1 point
I have one . . . I play with it	0 points

Evidently, the 0 option is hopelessly experiential and does not treat *knife* as a general category. 1 is too restricted in terms of range of uses to count for the full 2 points.

Example 2: Similarities Section

Why shouldn't you play with matches?

So people won't get hurt . . . so your house won't burn down	2 points
You get burned . . . you can hurt yourself	1 point
You'll get a spanking	0 points

Though all these answers involve reasoning processes, some count more than others. While the 2 point answer is generalized in taking account of persons and property, the 0 option represents a refusal to take an adult view of morality.

Example 3: Comprehension Section

Why should children who are sick stay home?

So the class won't get the germs	2 points
So you don't get sicker	1 point
Their mommies get mad if they go out	0 points

To get the 2 points, the child again must take a generalized perspective, considering the interests of the organization (the school) rather than merely one's own.

Source: Adapted from Noble (1990, 54).

A child must know that general, categorical, and precise answers are preferred by adult testers over personal, experiential answers, in order to appear intelligent.

A similar study explores children's common-sense reasoning by asking them how they decided on their answers to a reading test (MacKay 1974a, 183–84). One stimulus sentence was about an animal that had been out in the rain. The "correct answer" was a picture of a room with dotted wallpaper walls and a floor imprinted with a trail of animal tracks. One child misperceived the picture to be the outside of a house, with the dotted wallpaper being snow flakes. She consequently chose the "wrong" answer and scored zero. But her explanation clearly demonstrates interpretive skills in coming up with reasonable accounts of the world.

These interpretive studies reveal "brightness" as an interactional accomplishment rather than a measure of "real" intellectual capabilities. Teachers usually describe students in terms of cognitive attributes such as "bright" or "highly verbal" or else "nonverbal" or "not having a clue." But while these appear to be common-sense to teachers, Noble asserts that these are "ideological formulations" (1990, 45). In effect they are "class-defining practices."

Streaming as Practical Accomplishment

Teachers exercise a monopoly of professional competence to determine the academic ability and appropriate educational stream of children in school. How these allocative decisions are made influences the future career opportunities of children. Interpretive approaches to education have tried to make visible the common-sense reasoning practices through which teachers accomplish streaming as visibly and accountably appropriate.

Studies that use a **labelling theory** approach show how teachers' practices in categorizing children as they enter kindergarten can shape the children's entire school careers. Labelling theory, if you recall from chapter 7, was first developed in relation to studies of deviance. It explores the thesis that deviance is not inherent in any particular action, but in the judgments of witnesses. Those judgments determine how the person committing a "deviant" act comes to be treated thereafter.

Rist (1977) outlines a four-step process by which initial evaluations affect future options beginning with (1) the various evaluative mechanisms, both formal and informal, (2) how students react to them, (3) outcomes for personal interaction, particularly between teachers and students, and (4) the consequences of having a certain evaluative tag for the options available to students in the school (Rist 1977, 293). Rist argues that through such processes, failure in school becomes a self-fulfilling prophesy as teacher expectations are operationalized in the classroom to produce what the teacher had initially assumed.

Rist carried out a longitudinal study of an inner-city American urban ghetto school following the progress of children in kindergarten through to second grade. Within eight days of beginning kindergarten the teacher permanently assigned each child to a seat at one of the three tables for the remainder of the school year, based on her perception of their academic promise. Her judgments were based on immediate experience of interacting with the children in class for the first few days, together with knowledge of their older siblings, and information from admission forms and school social workers indicating which children were welfare recipients. The children assigned to Table 1, nearest the teacher, were generally more talkative to the teacher and more familiar with standard American English, and they participated well as group members.

One can speculate that children who had been coached in their prekindergarten years to use elaborate sentences with proper nouns and adjectives, who are cued in to the compulsory instructional form of question-answer-evaluation sequences, who know that abstract, category terms are preferred over personal associations in question-answer games, who choose matching and categorizing toys over the sandbox, and who have learned to subordinate their bodies and facial expressions to adult relevances, are far more likely to end up at Table 1. It was also clear in Rist's study that the children assigned to Table 1 were neat and clean in appearance and of higher average socioeconomic backgrounds than the children assigned to Table 3.

Once assigned to Table 1, these children were designated as "fast learners" and received more teaching time and attention while the "slow learners" at Table 3 were taught less frequently, subjected to more control, and received less support from the teacher. The gap in completion of academic material between the two groups widened during the course of the school year. Objective measures of past performance seemed to confirm the appropriateness of initial labelling on the eighth day of kindergarten. Two years later, the children from Table 1 in kindergarten were almost all together in Table 1 of grade 2, labelled as the "Tigers" or the winners, and they were still receiving more teaching time than other groups.

Another study of teachers' labelling practices (Becker 1977) confirms the high correlation between assessments of ability and socioeconomic backgrounds. He records a typical teacher's assessment of "slum" children:

> They don't have the right kind of study habits. They can't seem to apply themselves as well. Of course, it's not their fault; they aren't brought up right. After all, the parents in a neighbourhood like that really aren't interested. . . . But as I say, those children don't learn very quickly. A great many of them don't seem to be really interested in getting an education. . . . It's hard to get anything done with children like that.

Children from upper-class neighbourhoods seemed to respond much more readily than slum children to ideas and suggestions from teachers and concentrated more on lessons. To get attention in a chemistry class in the slum area school, teachers felt they had to do flashy demonstrations with lots of noise and smoke.

Maintaining the Home-School Relation

Each of these studies, by Noble, Rist, and Becker, repeats the same observation that the behaviour of children in kindergarten is closely correlated with socioeconomic status. The children who fit most readily into the social organization of schools are "middle-class" children. But we still have limited understanding of how differences in parenting practices by social class are accomplished. We need more research into the organization of peoples' lives and the meanings that people bring to the situations they find themselves in—to the grinding effects of poverty and the dis-organizing practices that continually threaten to disrupt what poor people manage to put together. The teacher's comment that parents in poor neighbourhoods "really aren't interested"

A child's *mind* is an *open* book.

As a parent, it is your responsibility to fill the pages of a child's mind with wonder and joy. Reading together is a delightful way of accomp- | lishing this and a means of ensuring that your child's future remains an open book.

Prepare a young mind for tomorrow. Open a book today.

ABC
CANADA
Literacy Foundation
Fondation pour l'alphabétisation

Distribution of this message was made possible by the Canadian Advertising Foundation

Literacy support groups attempt to redress the imbalance of different parenting practices.

in the lives of their children is a summary term for ignorance rather than an explanation of differences in parenting work.

Intensive parenting work is also involved in accomplishing the appearance of being an "interested" parent (Noble 1982, 39–67). "Support" for school is not merely a matter of positive attitudes; it involves real resources of time, energy, and skills. Parents require tacit knowledge of what kind of support work and what kind of communication is appropriate. Managing parent-teacher interactions requires skills in picking up cues from teachers, knowing acceptable ways of asking questions about a child's progress or about what goes on in the classroom, and ways of expressing concern that will be interpreted by teachers as cooperative, responsible, and emotionally stable rather than hostile, unreasonable or overprotective. These are class-related skills. Middle-class mothers are likely to have far more experience of interacting as equals with people in professional careers than do working-class mothers.

The teaching profession generally claims expertise in the specific field of cognitive development with parents responsible for auxiliary work. Noble describes parent-teacher meetings as often providing a forum for teachers and principals to disseminate professional views on child-management to parents, with parents being held accountable for the socioemotional development. Parents can establish their presence as "interested" by asking about their child's "adjustment problems" in the classroom, and otherwise deferring to the teacher's professional expertise. Teachers, in turn, may be influenced to notice and to give more attention to a particular child in order to have something to talk to an "interested" parent about. But the parent-teacher relationship must be handled carefully if it is to result in protecting and improving children's chances at school.

Many working-class parents do not know how to play the parent-teacher game, do not feel at ease in contact with the school, and do not know how to raise topics with teachers. They withdraw under the weight of accumulated small intimidations and join the ranks of parents who appear "not interested" in their children. Parents who openly confront teachers and challenge their expertise may be regarded as "trouble-makers" with "personal problems," and they may well generate retaliation against their children in the classroom. Parents need to know how streaming works operationally. Objections to disadvantageous streaming decisions are more likely to be successful when parents do not attack test scores or teachers directly, but use the jargon of testing to focus on discrepancies.

In summary, the relationships between teachers as professionals and both children and parents from middle-class backgrounds work more smoothly than relationships with working-class families. Noble's work tries to make visible the interactional and discourse skills that accomplish this relation. Becker interprets his data as teacher reactions to cultural variations associated with social-class backgrounds, but much more than mere prejudice is involved.

Kindergarten teachers in Noble's study had to depend on children's willingness to sit quietly in a circle in order to read stories to them. On bad

days, virtually one-on-one bodily monitoring was needed, with an adult blocking getaways and physically separating children from their toys before circle time could begin (Noble 1982, 16). A wide range of interactional competences, bodily subordination, and attending to adult relevances have to be assumed before lessons can happen.

HERMAN

"I think you'll find my test results are a pretty good indication of your abilities as a teacher."

Lessons as Social Accomplishments

Lessons do not happen naturally by themselves, either for students or for teachers. A branch of ethnomethodology known as **conversation analysis** researches detailed features of student-teacher interaction in lessons, using the technique of audio- and video-recordings. The questions explored include: the organization of turn-taking (McHoul 1978); teacher strategies to maximize participation of the class as a cohort (Payne and Hustler 1980); the detection and handling of deviance (Hester 1991); the overall organization of lessons from beginning to end (MacKay 1974a; Mehan 1979); and collaboration in students' writing stories employing computers (Heap 1986).

Weeks's study of primary-school oral reading lessons (1985) makes visible the error-correction sequences by which teachers alert a student that there is a problem and present an opportunity for the student to come up with the correct word. Complex interpretive practices or working assumptions are involved in both teacher and student getting the correction completed. The teacher may only hint at a problem with a brief "hm hm." The student has to have sufficient interpretive skills to pick up on the hint, figure out what the problem is, which word is wrong, and what to do about it. After a two-second pause the student enunciates another word, in a rising tone that indicates uncertainty or waiting for confirmation. The teacher's second "hm hm," with a different tone from before, means something quite different from the first utterance—a positive evaluation of the student's answer. Following this, the student resumes reading aloud from the text.

Highly complex but tacit interactional competences are assumed between teacher and student, and other members of the reading group, to get through this self-correction instructional sequence. Other correction techniques involve the teacher giving explicit directions like "Watch for the period!"—but even then the student has to know what to do with it. It is clearly not enough just to watch for a period; the reader has to manage proper intonation and to make a break at the right place. Students who are not attuned to such cues will not be able to follow the lesson.

Other studies explore the turn-taking organization of classrooms, and how teachers maintain authority by such practices as controlling the turn-taking, selecting specific students for next turns, who then have to return the "floor" to the teacher rather than hold onto it or select other students to speak (McHoul 1978). Teachers may organize lessons by posing a question that students lack the resources to answer at the beginning, but that they come to answer in the end through processes of hinting and filling in (Hammersley 1990). Teachers also commonly use "undirected questions" addressed to the class-as-a-whole, such as "Who knows the distance between Toronto and Montreal?" Such seemingly open invitations to respond are accompanied by the practice of students raising hands to bid for a turn, with the teacher as arbiter among competing bids.

It is through such practices that teachers organize the collectivity of students as a **cohort**—as one collective party to the talk with the teacher acting as the other party (Payne and Hustler 1980, 56). Students are thus led to take the teacher as

their single focus of attention, with any one student being a potential target for the teacher's next question. Such practices also discourage students from talking to each other, except for prompting each other with candidate answers. Students who have not mastered the proper posture and facial expressions for conveying attention to the teacher are likely to be targeted.

Other research suggests that teachers tend to use positive evaluations like "That's right," "Okay," or "Well done" quite frequently, while avoiding negative ones by such tactics as offering cues to correct answers, and asking other members of the class if they agree or have other suggestions (McHoul 1990). This can be seen as another way of accomplishing "cohorting" by opening opportunities for wider student participation, and using each answer as an occasion for further instruction (Weeks 1994). When such tacit cohorting work and turn-taking practices fail to elicit appropriate responses from students, as in the slum schools described by Becker (1977), or the Native schools described in the previous section, teaching may be experienced as very difficult, if not impossible.

The Limitations of Social Constructionism

Interpretive perspectives open up the "black box" of schooling to show the complex interaction between background factors like social class and the routine practices of the school. We begin to see the practices that constitute what is traditionally understood as cultural deprivation, and how the social structural characteristics of inequality are accomplished through intimate everyday interaction in classrooms.

The potential strength of this approach can also become its weakness. Explanations that focus on the intimate behaviour of individuals in classrooms risk losing sight of the structural contexts in which such interactions are embedded. Individual mothers, teachers, and students appear as blameworthy for failing to prepare students adequately for school, or for failing to adapt classroom instruction to compensate for different behavioural profiles. It remains important to recognize how structures of capitalism—the commercialization of education and the impact of corporate agendas on curriculum budget cutbacks, intensification of teachers' work, standardized curriculum and evaluation packages imposed on teachers, and the like—constrain teaching and learning in critical ways. The special contribution of the interpretive perspective is that it provides ways of seeing how these seemingly external structural factors work, through the activities of people at the level of everyday interaction.

Feminist Theory in Education

Until the beginning of the twentieth century women in Canada were largely excluded from all forms of higher education, and most had little for-

mal schooling beyond learning to read and write. By the 1990s, the pattern was dramatically different. Women and men are equally likely to graduate from high school and enter undergraduate programs; however, they remain concentrated in different fields of study. Women are overrepresented in arts, nursing, and domestic science programs, and significantly underrepresented in mathematics, physical sciences, computer science, and technology (see figure 16-5 and table 16-4).

Feminist research in education has focussed attention on the different experiences of girls and boys in the school system. Much of this research has adopted the theoretical perspectives and methodology of social constructionism, recording detailed observation of classroom interaction to

Figure 16-5

Percentage Distribution of Full-time Fall Enrolment in Postsecondary Career Programs by Sex and Program Field, Canada, 1990–91

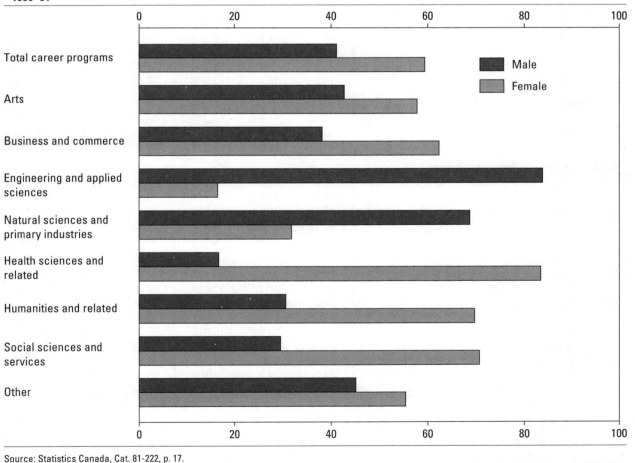

Source: Statistics Canada, Cat. 81-222, p. 17.

Table 16-4

Field of Study	1983–84			1991–92		
	Percent Male	Percent Female	Total	Percent Male	Percent Female	Total
Agricultural and biological sciences						
Agriculture	62.9	37.1	4 713	54.5	45.5	3 511
Biology	50.2	49.8	9 639	44.9	55.1	17 200
Household science	3.6	96.4	3 513	9.2	90.8	3 651
Veterinary medicine	45.9	54.1	1 053	35.7	64.3	1 187
Zoology	54.4	45.6	781	43.2	56.8	1 017
Education						
Education	25.6	74.4	27 431	25.3	74.7	37 777
Physical education	47.7	52.3	12 260	51.5	48.5	15 428
Engineering and applied sciences						
Architecture	70.0	30.0	2 220	64.0	36.0	2 344
Engineering	90.2	9.8	37 724	84.0	16.0	39 897
Forestry	88.4	11.6	1 335	80.9	19.1	1 325
Fine arts	39.7	60.3	13 872	38.3	61.7	16 459
Health professions						
Dental studies and research	73.8	26.2	1 982	59.7	40.3	1 749
Medical studies and research	58.2	41.8	8 411	54.8	45.2	8 389
Nursing	3.2	96.8	6 634	6.6	93.4	7 428
Pharmacy	32.8	67.2	2 696	38.5	61.5	3 183
Rehabilitation medicine	10.6	89.4	2 510	16.0	84.0	3 796
Humanities						
History	58.6	41.4	4 745	54.4	45.6	11 844
Languages	28.0	72.0	12 757	26.7	73.3	18 352
Other	51.7	48.2	9 858	46.9	53.1	13 401
Mathematics and physical sciences						
Chemistry	67.7	32.3	3 052	60.8	39.2	3 938
Geology	79.3	20.7	3 249	72.4	27.6	1 201
Mathematics	64.6	35.4	8 262	60.9	39.1	9 063
Computer science	72.7	27.3	12 250	79.8	20.2	9 039
Physics	88.2	11.8	2 407	83.0	17.0	2 753
Social sciences						
Business and commerce	58.8	41.2	48 835	54.1	45.9	57 382
Economics	68.8	31.2	10 009	67.8	32.2	12 278
Geography	64.1	35.9	4 466	60.0	40.0	7 680
Law	55.8	44.2	9 892	48.8	51.2	11 284
Political science	63.1	36.9	6 712	56.0	44.0	12 933
Psychology	27.4	72.6	13 187	23.9	76.1	23 184
Social work	18.3	81.7	4 227	16.9	83.1	5 587
Sociology	34.0	66.0	6 157	29.2	70.8	13 404
Grand Total*	52.6	47.4	397 351	49.8	56.2	485 418

*Individual totals will not add up to grand total because certain smaller fields, labelled "other," are omitted from this table.

Source: Reproduced by authority of the Minister of Industry, 1994. Adapted from Statistics Canada (1994e), *Education in Canada: A Statistical Review*, Cat. 81-229, table 13, pp. 84–87.

explore the practices through which gender differentiation is accomplished. Richer's (1979) study of an Ontario kindergarten class displays multiple ways in which the teacher emphasized gender distinctions. Gender was repeatedly used to organize classroom activites. Boys and girls were asked to line up separately before moving from one activity to another, to go to the library, the gymnasium, or the dining room, and to get ready to go home. Boys and girls hung their outdoor clothing in separate areas. Commonly they were pitted against each other by such comments as "Who can do this the fastest, boys or girls?" In co-ordination exercises commands were routinely given separately to boys and girls: "Boys, put your fingers on your nose; girls, put your hands in your laps; boys, touch your toes," etc. When any of the children responded to an activity intended for the other sex, the teacher commonly drew attention to it with a comment like "Are you a girl? I thought all along you were a boy" (Richer 1979, 201).

Observations of classroom interaction suggest that teachers may respond differently to girls and boys, and in ways that encourage boys to dominate classroom space while subtly devaluing the girls. Sadker and Sadker (1987, 144) found that teachers in the classes they observed tended to accept answers shouted out by boys who did not raise their hands and wait to be given a turn. When girls behaved similarly they were more likely to be reprimanded. Observations of elementary grades suggest that girls tend to be quieter and more obedient whereas boys are more likely to bounce around, ask questions, and be aggressive. One of the consequences seems to be that teachers generally find girls easier to deal with, so concentrate more attention on boys. Boys are likely to receive more disapproval, scolding, and other forms of negative attention than do girls, but they are also likely to receive more attention and praise (Huston 1983, 439; Basow 1986, 126). Teachers also admitted to finding boys more fun to teach (Schneider and Coutts 1979; Russell 1987, 240). Russell's observations of grade 12 classes revealed that teachers were one-and-one-half to five times more likely to direct questions to boys than to girls. Girls dominated verbal interaction with the teacher in only 7 percent of the classes, while boys dominated in about 63 percent. In only about 30 percent of classes did teachers seem to select girls and boys equally in turn-taking interaction.

Observational studies also suggest that teachers tend to hold different expectations about the academic abilities of girls and boys. When girls outperformed boys in early grades, teachers explained their "overachievement" as a result of their docility and conscientiousness, subtly devaluing their work (Russell 1987, 241). Conversely, when girls fell behind boys in high-school mathematics and science courses, teachers were inclined to treat this as "natural" and consistent with their lower expectations for girls in these subjects. Girls were more likely to be advised to drop such subjects than coached to improve their performance (Shapiro 1990, 57). High-school counsellors routinely encouraged high-achieving girls into "women's work" such as social work, teaching, and secretarial positions rather than into better-paid male-dominated business and professional positions (Russell 1987). Years of exposure to such classroom practices may accomplish what Porter, Porter, and Blishen (1982, 125–29) describe as the lower self-esteem of girls and lower self-assessment of their abilities than boys, even when they outperformed boys on school tests.

An explosion of feminist studies of classroom practices and school textbooks since the 1970s, combined with political lobbying, has produced significant changes in the Canadian school system (Mackie 1991, 162–65). Much effort has gone into changing the content of textbooks and school curricula to include nonsexist materials and present women in a wider variety of nonsex-typed activities (Gaskell and McLaren 1987, 8). Efforts are also being made by universities to encourage more girls in high school to consider careers in science and engineering (Armour 1988).

The question is whether such remedial actions will be sufficient to overcome wider social pressures beyond the schools. Richer (1988) carried out a comparative study of cohorts of students in an Ottawa elementary school before and after a seven-year consciousness-raising program in the school. The school established a "positive action committee" that provided films and reading materials for teachers on issues of gender and organized several seminars on teaching practices. In 1979, and again in 1986, children in grades 1 through 6 were asked to draw a picture of themselves engaged in their favourite activity. Comparison of the pictures showed virtually no drop in sex stereotyping. In 1986, fully 97 percent of boys' drawings and 87 percent of girls' drawings depicted sex-segregated activities. Richer concludes that influences outside the school have a greater impact on children than classroom teachers.

More detailed studies of classroom interaction are beginning to uncover ways in which students actively resist efforts by teachers to challenge gender and class stereotypes. Girls from a lower-class district in England collectively sabotaged lessons by tacitly and even blatantly withdrawing their attention (McRobbie 1978). When asked what they did during math lessons, they gave such answers as "carve boys' names on my desk," "comb my hair under the lid of the desk," "put makeup on, or look in my mirror." McRobbie suggests that while parents and teachers do try to encourage girls to study more to get a good job, the girls' own immediate experience of the types of jobs open to women like them does little to induce them to focus on schoolwork. They know that their chance for a decent home and money to support their children depends primarily upon the superior wages of a man. Hence, from as young as thirteen and fourteen years, their preoccupation is with boyfriends and going steady. Success in the classroom consists of asserting their "femaleness" and spending vast amounts of time discussing boyfriends in loud voices that disrupt the class.

This is irrational behaviour from the perspective of the teachers who, at least initially in their careers, are committed to trying to break this pattern and open new options for the girls. But it is fully rational from the perspective of the working-class girls themselves in the face of their expectations for their own future. Actually, it may be the teachers who are being unrealistic and irrational in assuming that they can somehow change the life chances for more than a minority of these girls. It is little wonder that many teachers become more realistic with experience and opt for a more class-biased curriculum to which the girls will respond. In a sense schools fail the girls, but in another sense girls fail the schools. The process of class and gender formation is thus mutually constructed within the everyday struggles of the classroom.

Feminism in the Universities

As noted above, women are entering Canadian universities in greater numbers than ever before, equalling the numbers of men at undergraduate level. Feminist research, however, suggests that women students generally experience university campuses as very much "male turf," with resentment, petty harassment, and depreciation of women commonplace.

A study by Hall and Sandler (1984) suggests that female students generally, and especially those who enrol in the traditional male bastions of physical sciences and engineering, face a "chilly campus climate" that is not conducive to learning. Women students tend to receive less attention and less feedback than male students from the predominantly male faculty. They are more likely to experience disparaging comments about their work or their commitment to studies, or comments that focus on their appearance rather than their performance. They are likely to be counselled into lower career goals than men. As graduates, they are less likely to be included as co-researchers with faculty in academic publications. Women who interrupt their studies, or attend part-time while raising children, are not taken seriously. A commentary written by a female geology student some ten years after this article was published suggests that little has changed (*Globe and Mail*, 13 July 1994). The student recounts being the butt of a series of more and more threatening practical "jokes" in the geology labs, combined with a constant barrage of insulting remarks about women in general. Repeated sexual comments and innuendoes from one of her chemistry professors were directed at female students in the class.

Males dominate classroom and seminar discussions. Male styles of communication are highly assertive, combined with physical gestures that express ease, dominance, and control. They are more likely to interrupt other speakers and to control the topic of conversation. In laboratory classes, female students routinely complain that men take control over the equipment, relegating female students to note-takers. Females tend to be more personal in their communications, offering more self-disclosure rather than impersonal and abstract styles of speech. This style is disparaged as less intelligent. Women are more reticent in taking over conversations and tend to encourage other speakers. They often feel that they are imposing on advisers rather than that they have a right to ask questions.

Athletic activities by women get less support and attention than do male sports teams. Women are demeaned when campus organizations screen pornographic movies as fund-raisers and when student newspapers publish sexist articles and advertisements. Women who live in residences often face petty harassment from men in the guise of fun. In 1989, a rash of such actions and verbal assaults directed at female students, and feminists in particular, made headlines in Canadian newspapers. At Queen's University some male students mocked a campaign against date rape on campus by displaying posters bearing slogans such as "No Means Tie Her Up" and "No Means Kick Her in the Teeth" (*Globe and Mail*, 11 Nov. 1989, D1–2; 17 Nov. 1989). Engineering students' newspapers at Queen's and the University of Alberta, in particular, have been criticized for sexist content "that portrays women in a thoroughly demeaning and abusive manner" (*Globe and Mail*, 13 Dec. 1989, A5).

On 6 December 1989, a man armed with a semi-automatic rifle entered the enginering building at the University of Montreal. He massacred fourteen women engineering students before turning the gun on himself. In a three-page suicide note found on his body, the man expressed his hatred of feminists, claiming that they had ruined his life. In the days that followed, seven male students at the University of Toronto set off firecrackers outside the women's residence, spreading panic. Following this experience, adminstrations on many campuses took steps to institute or strengthen policies against sexual harassment, to curtail the sexist content of engineering newspapers, and to set up programs to support and promote women in sciences and engineering. We have yet to see how effective these initiatives wil be.

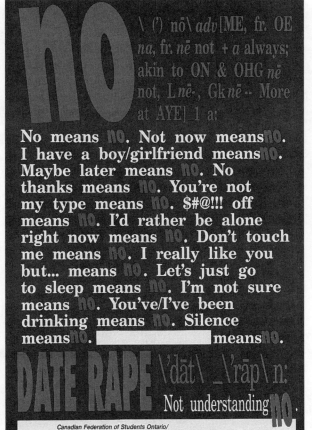

The "No Means No" campaign spells out sexual harassment in no uncertain terms.

A plaque commemorates the women massacred at l'Ecole Polytechnique, the Université de Montréal's engineering school.

Feminist Pedagogy

Feminists also criticize traditional methods of teaching within universities as perpetuating a masculine orientation to learning that alienates women students. They echo the work of Paolo Freire in challenging oppressive and hierarchical approaches to knowledge as truths handed down from authority figures. Emphasis in lectures and seminars on competition, confrontation, and winning debates in a public forum, intimidate and silence many women, along with other students outside the dominant white middle-class male group, who lack a sense of social mastery, or lack the will to put others down. Belenky et al. (1985) suggest that women generally respond better to "connected teaching" that emphasizes creative reflection on personal experience, and that confirms not merely that women can learn, but that they already know something through personal experience.

The problem they highlight is that hierarchical methods of teaching are so closely associated with authority and professional competence that lecturers who are committed to involving students as equals in the classroom, and who affirm the value of knowledge based on personal experience, risk appearing weak and incompetent to their students (Bezucha 1985; Friedman 1985). Female professors can find themselves simultaneously challenged and resented by students, whichever approach they take. Students who accept authority, high standards, discipline, and toughness from male professors, often deeply resent the same demands from female professors. It violates their sense that females should not be in authority positions over them. Feminist pedagogy also clashes with the hierarchical structure of universities, and the necessity of grading students on classroom performance.

Feminist Theory and Resistance

As we noted in chapter 5, the introduction of women's courses into the curriculum of Canadian universities in the 1970s met with strong opposition, bordering on rage (Smith 1992d, 208). The women professors who were trying to develop the courses were subject to personal insults and their professional competence was called into question. Traditions of rational debate did not seem to extend to consideration of women's studies. By the mid-1990s, most Canadian universities have established some courses spread across the arts curriculum, but women's studies programs still tend to be seen as frills, given second-rate status and limited funds. Students aspiring to professional and corporate careers are discouraged from taking such courses. A common strategy for sidelining feminist courses, Bezucha suggests

(1985, 90), is for established professors to support hiring a few women to teach designated women's studies courses, and then to use this to justify not including anything on women in the content of their own courses. Ignorance of feminist theory and research is studiously maintained. This studied ignorance is not emptiness or mere absence of knowledge. It is an active refusal to learn (Aronowitz and Giroux 1985, 159).

Students who are exposed to feminist theory develop their own forms of resistance, as their established frameworks of meaning are challenged. One response is to deny the validity of any evidence that goes against the dominant view of reality. Culley describes the common reactions of students, both female and male, when exposed for the first time to readily available statistics on education, employment categories, and income levels of women compared to men:

> Who published those statistics?" (U.S. Department of Labor.) "When was that?" (Any time before yesterday is pre-history.) "Those figures must be based on women who work part time." Or, "A lot of women choose not to work, you know, are they in there?" Then soon after, "You can't get anywhere hating men, you can't blame them." And quietly to themselves or to each other, "I heard she's divorced, she's probably a lesbian or something" (1985, 212).

Culley suggests that it is important for teachers to let students express these defensive efforts to distance, discount, and deny. Only then can these responses be examined and questioned. Other professors who teach feminist theory describe instances of outright hostility from some students who actively try to disrupt classes by joking, chatting loudly, jeering, and attacking the credibility and professional competence of the professor (Bezucha 1985, 214; McIntyre 1986).

For all the difficulties encountered, feminist theory and research has made a significant impact across the arts curriculum. Traditional approaches may still be dominant but they have lost their taken-for-granted character. As radical pedagogy, feminism is potentially an agent of change through both the process and the content of teaching. Charlotte Bunch (1983) describes how she left university teaching to work full-time in the women's movement but later returned to university because she had become convinced that the development of feminist theory is essential to political action. Theory is not just a body of facts and opinions. It involves the development of explanations that can guide actions.

Bunch proposes a four-part model of theory. The first part is *description*. Changing people's perceptions of the world through new descriptions of reality is usually a prerequisite for changing that reality. In the 1960s, few people would have thought of American women as oppressed, but now the injustices and oppression experienced by women are widely recognized. Feminist work, which described that oppression in a number of different ways, played a critical role in making it visible. The second element of theory is *analysis*. Analysis involves trying to understand why the reality described in feminist work exists and what perpetuates it. The third element is *vision*. The work of envisioning what should exist involves examining our basic assumptions about human nature and relationships. The fourth element of theory is *strategy*. Theoretical understanding of how social relations work is essential to planning ways of changing those relations. Teaching feminist theory thus involves teaching the basic skills of critical literacy—how to read, analyse, and think about ideas—and challenging students to develop their own ideas and to analyse the assumptions behind their actions.

Conclusion

Compulsory schooling has a profound effect on children's lives and upon their life chances after leaving school. This much is beyond dispute. It also seems clear that children with different class, gender, and ethnic characteristics experience schooling and higher education in very different ways, and end up with markedly unequal levels of educational attainment and formal credentials. Different perspectives in sociology struggle with the questions of how and why schooling affects children in these ways.

Functionalist and political economy perspectives agree that schools perform the function of selecting and allocating children for adult roles within the economy, but they focus on very different factors in their analysis of how this selection

process works. Functionalists suggest that, by and large, schools do provide equal opportunities for all children to reach their full academic potential and to strive for social mobility. They locate the causes of unequal attainment by class and by sex primarily in socialization processes that occur within families, largely outside the influence of schools. Political economy theory, in contrast, locates the causes of low aspirations and unequal attainment in capitalism. This perspective takes for granted the argument that capitalists seek to standardize and deskill work in the interests of cheapening labour and increasing profits. Scope for creativity seems confined to the elite who direct the huge corporations. This political economy is held responsible for structuring schools in the corporate image.

The social constructionist perspective begins from the assumption that people, in their everyday interactions, create the social world and give it the patterns and the meanings that we come to see as the structures of capitalism. Research into intimate interaction within classrooms explores how students react to and against the pressures of school, in terms of how they themselves foresee the utility or irrelevance of education for their future lives. Teachers also struggle to retain some autonomy in their working lives, amid pressures to adopt packaged curricula, textbooks, and technical devices pushed by corporate interests, often acting in concert with school boards and college management.

The central debate within this perspective concerns how far it is possible for people to retain autonomy of thought and action in the face of the established ways of thinking within the prevailing culture. Teachers are criticized by radicals, and increasingly also by members of the business class, for not developing the capacity for creative and innovative thinking in their students. Yet, they themselves work in contexts that seem increasingly designed to minimize their own capacity for creative teaching. Feminist pedagogy is one form of teaching that takes seriously the possibility of challenging and changing established social relations by developing the power of critical reflection in students. The question for the future is whether this power will be neutralized and accommodated in the service of greater profits, or whether people will use it to push for more fundamental change.

Suggested Reading

An excellent study of education from the functionalist perspective is by John Porter, Marion Porter, and Bernard Blishen, *Stations and Callings: Making It Through the School System* (1982). Chapter 1 of this book discusses the theory of equality and educational opportunity, exploring the different interpretations that can be placed on the notion of equal opportunity. Chapter 3 outlines in a clear and precise form the basic ideas of socialization and self-concept in functionalist and symbolic interaction theory. The authors then incorporate these concepts into an elaborate explanatory model that guides their research into educational aspirations. The text includes many easily understandable statistical graphs and tables.

The main text that presents the structuralist Marxist perspective is by Samuel Bowles and Herbert Gintis, *Schooling in Capitalist America* (1976). A briefer introduction to the ideas debated at length in the text is provided in a collection of articles edited by Mike Cole, *Bowles and Gintis Revisited: Correspondence and Contradiction in Educational Theory* (1988). In the prologue and chapters 12 and 13, they address some of the criticisms raised against structuralist Marxist theory. Chapters 1 and 3 provide a brief but useful overview of criticisms of the work of Bowles and Gintis.

A good introduction to the social construction of reality approach, and one that complements the work of Bowles and Gintis, is by Jean Anyon, "Social Class and the Hidden Curriculum of Work" (1980). She describes in detail the very different teaching techniques that she observed in elementary school classes in working-class, middle-class, and elite school districts. A classic study in the rejection of school values by working-class children is P. Willis, *Learning to Labour: How Working Class Kids Get Working Class Jobs* (1981). Willis shows how boys have absorbed the shopfloor culture of their working-class fathers, including sexist and racist values, and utilize them to support their rejection of school. A similar study by Angela McRobbie, "Working-class Girls and the Culture of Femininity" (1978) describes how these girls reject the school culture in favour of their paramount concern with sexuality and attracting boyfriends.

Michael Apple's work, *Teachers and Texts: A Political Economy of Class and Gender Relations in Education* (1986), explores the contemporary work of teachers. Apple documents the pressures that threaten to reduce the role of teachers from autonomous professionals to deskilled technicians, constrained to use standardized curriculum packages.

A good overview of the feminist approach to education is provided by a collection of articles edited by Jane Gaskell and Arlene Tigar McLaren, *Women and Education: A Canadian Perspective* (1987). Among other useful updates, the collection includes a reprint of the classic article by Dorothy Smith, "An Analysis of Ideological Structures and How Women Are Excluded: Considerations for Academic Women" (1975).

Questions

1. What does Parsons see as the functional importance of women teachers in primary education?

2. Distinguish between *equality of condition*, *equality of opportunity*, and *equality of outcome*.

3. In what sense can the goals of liberal education—the development of individual potential, equality, and social continuity—be seen as internally contradictory?

4. How does structural correspondence theory account for the shift in higher education from broad liberal arts to packages of credits?

5. What principles does the educational reformer Ivan Illich advocate in his vision of

a deschooled society, and why is this vision rejected as unrealistic by the Marxist theorists Bowles and Gintis?

6. How is the North American Free Trade Deal implicated in the structural correspondence between schooling and global capitalism?

7. What problems are highlighted by the notion of *a vacuum ideology* in reference to the policies of white educators towards Native peoples?

8. In what respects is intelligence an interactional accomplishment rather than a measure of intellectual capabilities?

9. What practices are involved in parents accomplishing themselves as "interested" in their children's education from the perspective of teachers?

10. What teaching practices are implicated in promoting the passivity of girls relative to boys in typical classroom interaction?

17

Race and Ethnic Relations: Creating the Vertical Mosaic

The analysis of racial and ethnic relations in society presents a major challenge to theories of social order, both functionalist and Marxist. The subject is very closely tied to conceptions of family, stratification, and education, which we have traced in the previous three chapters. Concepts of ethnic and racial identity are commonly associated with ancestry, kinship ties, and socialization. Secondly, the pattern of stratification in Canada forms what Porter (1965) has called a **vertical mosaic**, with different racial and ethnic groups organized vertically with respect to class location. People of white Anglo-Saxon Protestant origin prevail at the top of the hierarchy while Native peoples are at the bottom. Various other Europeans and nonwhites range in between. Thirdly, the system of education, as we saw in chapter 16, reflects and perpetuates this vertical mosaic. The coincidence of ethnicity, race, and class is by no means peculiar to Canada. It seems to be a recurrent feature of industrial societies, although specific characteristics of the mosaic vary from one country to another.

Traditional Functionalism: Consensus or Conflict?

Shared culture or ethnic identity plays a pivotal role in traditional functionalist theory. Moral consensus is seen as providing the foundation of social order. Such consensus is internalized through early childhood socialization within the family, and reinforced through religion and education. Components of culture include language, history, symbol systems, values, behavioural norms, expectations, and attitudes—in effect, the totality of what Durkheim refers to as the *conscience collective* of a community of people.

In functionalist theory, our cultural community or ethnic group is fundamental to our personal identity. Those whom we identify with as "our people" or "our community," when asked who we are, are typically an ethnic group. Ethnic identity is seen as ascriptive, or largely biological-based, deeply rooted in primordial ties of kinship, blood, and common territory. Such ties invoke an emotional intensity akin to sacredness (Shils 1957, 142; Horowitz 1985, 57). Ethnicity constitutes one of the givens of social existence, a givenness that stems from being born in a particular religious community, speaking a particular language, and following particular social practices (Geertz 1973, 259). Membership itself is virtually imperative; opting out of the affiliation is very difficult, especially because it implies renouncing obligations to other members. Offspring of mixed parentage experience some degree of marginality or partial belonging to two exclusive groups. Occasionally, they become a grouping in themselves, like the Métis. If effect, the defining characteristics of an ethnic group are very close to those of a social system as a whole. This closeness is intentional within functionalist theory: this perspective assumes that no social system could function without such a core of common culture.

The concept of **race**, as distinct from **ethnicity**, refers to people's visible and inherited physical differences that are socially noticed. In principle, racial diversity should not give rise to the same interaction problems as ethnic diversity, since race does not constitute any threat to cultural consensus. In practice, however, race tends to be confounded with ethnicity, since members of any given ethnic group tend to see themselves as racially homogeneous. They regard a person of visibly different racial stock as being outside their own ethnic group. Distinct racial characteristics thus heighten the tendency to avoid **out-groups**, or people perceived to be outside one's own cultural group.

The functionalist focus on internalization of culture and ethnic identity leads to the assumption that ethnocentrism and prejudice against other ethnic groups are normal and probably unavoidable attitudes. **Ethnocentrism** refers to an exaggerated view of the qualities and correctness of the culture of our own group. It is only an extreme form of internalizing the values that define our group vis-à-vis out-groups. **Stereotypes** are simplified versions of other groups, mental cartoons that we form by generalizing too much or by exaggerating the characteristics of ethnic groups on the basis of too little information. **Prejudice** is the logical mirror image of ethnocentrism. It involves prejudging in negative terms the characteristics that we assume are shared by members of other ethnic groups. **Racism** applies such prejudices toward groups that we perceive to be different on the basis of inescapable genetic characteristics. These ethnocentric, stereotypical, prejudiced, and racist attitudes are themselves part of the cultural assumptions of a group, which may be learned through socialization. Socialization also provides us with shared notions of the relative status of our own and other groups within the society.

In theory, an increased focus on universalistic achievements criteria in industrial societies should bring about a lessening of ascriptive ethnic identifications, but this has not happened. Richmond (1988, 7–9) suggests that heightened feelings of ethnicity, nationalism, and ethnocentrism are the almost inevitable consequences of the rapid pace of modernization. The global character of modern economics creates enormous pressures on people to migrate within and between industrialized countries and from the less developed and poorer countries to those whose economies are expanding. People try to cope with the stress of such upheavals by closing in upon themselves, seeking emotional and social support in ethnic and racial group solidarity.

Implications for Political Organization

The functionalist analysis of ethnic identification and strained interaction with out-groups has far-reaching implications for political organization. Given the disruptive character of ethnic differences, functionalism posits that the only viable options for the maintenance of social order are **domination**, **separation**, or total **assimilation** of ethnic minorities. The first two options are seen as mechanisms to control and contain conflict. The ideal is full assimilation because this resolves the source of the tension and so eliminates the need for control.

The presence of immigrants or ethnic minorities within a society is necessarily problematic. By definition, they lie outside the boundaries of the cultural consensus of the majority. Minorities cannot be trusted to have internalized either the appropriate values or the typical behaviours associated with different social roles. Predictably, therefore, interaction will be strained and restricted, and social controls will be weakened. In the absence of cultural homogeneity and the subtle controls of internalized values, force necessarily plays a greater role in the maintenance of order, which in turn presupposes domination by one cultural group (Kuper 1969, 14; Van den Berghe 1969, 76–78). Social interaction will be closest with those who share the same culture. Relations with outsiders will be restricted to those areas where common understanding can be assumed. The only safe meeting ground for different ethnic groups is likely to be the impersonal marketplace. Harmony is most readily sustained when distinct ethnic groups have both economic and legal autonomy, so that each group controls its own members' lives (Kuper 1969, 16; Van den Berghe 1969, 75).

The third option of harmonious assimilation requires that minority ethnic groups adopt the lifestyles, language, values, and customs of the dominant group. Structural integration should follow as immigrant or minority ethnic groups enter the social organization of the dominant group. Gordon (1964) suggests that groups tend to lose language and culture first, but to hold on to religion. Intermarriage is the last to go. The final stage is such total amalgamation that ethnic background is forgotten.

A general assumption that derives from traditional functionalist theory is that ethnically and racially mixed societies, such as Canada, are inherently unstable and prone to divisions and conflicts. Metta Spencer (1976, ch. 9) makes explicit these theoretical assumptions in her synthesis of functionalist theories of ethnicity. She predicts that there will always be claims of minority groups for recognition, equality, or freedom, and at least one ethnic group unhappy with its treatment or position within, or rather at the margins of, the society. A brief overview of Canadian social and political history provides much evidence to support functionalist models of minority group relations.

Domination

The first model, where one ethnic group exercises institutional domination over another, characterizes the experience of Native peoples in Canada. As the fur trade declined and white set-tlers pushed westward onto the Prairies, the Native peoples were driven off their lands onto small reserves. The Indian Act of 1896 established the legal, political, and economic dominance of the federal government over these reserves. The Minister of Indian Affairs had the authority to attend all band council meetings, to veto any bylaws that the bands might pass, to control their finances, to approve all expenditures, and to dictate land sales.

True to predictions based on functionalist theory, this option of institutionalized domination by one ethnic group over others has not led to stability in Canada. This essentially colonial relationship between the Canadian federal government and Native peoples has been a constant source of resentment and strife. The struggle gained national attention in June 1988 with the violent confrontation between Quebec police and Mohawk warriors at Oka. Native political leaders all across Canada continue to press for greater recognition of their status as distinct Nations within Canada, and for increased economic and legal autonomy.

Separation

The second model, of institutional separation, applies in some respects to the situation of French-speaking Quebec within Confederation. The experience of Quebec illustrates the fragility of such an arrangement. Canada seems to be in constant danger of either separating into two autonomous nations or reverting to the first option of quasi-colonial domination.

John Porter (1979a, 106) writes enthusiastically of the special relationship of "binationalism of French and English Canada as the founding principle of Confederation." This relationship only makes sense, he suggests, because of very specific historical conditions. The fact that 80 percent of French Canadians live in Quebec gives them a homeland that was conquered. This helps to make sense of, and to give impetus to, the notions of separation and eventual formation of a French state.

In practice, the ideal of "separate but equal" status implied in the separation model has never been a reality. The French ethnic group, even within Quebec, has until very recently formed a class with deprived status. French elites within the church and the state in Quebec collaborated with the federal government in return for protected status, but the mass of unilingual francophones occupied the low ranks in the class structure. Professional and business elites in Quebec have been predominantly English Canadians or Americans, and the language of business has clearly been English. The few Québécois who attained professional occupational status had to function in English.

The Royal Commission on Bilingualism and Biculturalism, established in 1963, concluded that either Canada would break up or there would have to be a new set of conditions for Quebec's future existence (Porter 1979a, 107). Subsequent policies to institutionalize bilingualism in the federal civil service, together with concessions, especially in social welfare legislation, have moved toward providing special status for Quebec in Canada. But strife continues.

The Parti Québécois first came to power in 1976, dedicated to achieving independent nationhood for Quebec. The 1980 referendum on sovereignty association was only narrowly voted down. Subsequent efforts by the Canadian federal government to gain Quebec's support for constitutional reform in the proposed Meech Lake Accord in 1987 and the subsequent Charlottetown Accord in 1992 both failed. In September 1994, the Parti Québécois was again elected. The party's central electoral promise was that a referendum on the separation of Quebec from Canada would be held within a year. Quebec's history gives much supporting evidence for the functionalist thesis that ethnic pluralism in separate communities living side by side is inherently unstable and destined to be associated with continual conflict and stress.

As with Quebec, the survival of other ethnic communities as separate entities within Canada reflect very specific historical circumstances of economy and geography. At the turn of this century, the Canadian government tried to attract peasants from Europe to settle the Prairies by offering subsidized passage, and promising ethnic tolerance or pluralism (Baker 1977, 117). Ukrainians, Slavs, Doukhobours, and Hutterites were attracted by the promises of land and cultural integrity. They settled in sparsely populated regions in the western provinces where there was little need for assimilation. On occasion, nonetheless, these communities were pressured to change, to learn English, and to swear allegiance to the British Crown. The general expectation within the government of the time was that all ethnic minorities, French and aboriginal peoples included, would eventually assimilate.

Integration Through Assimilation

The functionalist thesis suggests that this third option—acculturation, assimilation, and loss of distinct ethnic identity—is the most likely to be viable in the long run. It promises to remove the basic source of conflict rather than merely controlling and containing it. From this perspective, policies supporting multiculturalism are suspect in that they encourage a particularistic emphasis on descent groups, rather than a universalistic focus on principles of citizenship and individual human rights (Porter 1979a, 128). Carried to the extreme, Porter argues, such an emphasis on ethnicity in politics might lead to a nightmarish system of quotas being imposed on all large organizations to enforce proportional representation of each descent group—whites, people of colour, males and females, people of English, French, Native, or Chinese origin, and on and on. Strict equality on the basis of ethnic groups would undermine principles of merited individual achievement. Enforcement would depend on emphasizing visibly distinct group characteristics, forcing individuals to identify themselves as a member of some ethnic subgroup in order to qualify for a position under the quota system. The likely outcome would be intensified hostility and rivalry between groups.

Porter concedes that assimilation requires that minorities conform to dominant Anglo-Canadian values, but he argues that this only amounts to conformity to the values of modernization, namely the values of rationality and science, universalism and achievement.

Others draw different policy implications from the functionalist thesis, suggesting that liberal states must recognize and accommodate the primordial strength of ethnic group identity. Official recognition and protection of minority cultures and languages is compatible with universalistic principles of promoting the self-defining activities of individuals, and promoting diversity of opinion that is healthy for liberal democracy (Taylor 1992).

Multicultural policies rest on the assumption that it is possible to separate culture as private or personal identity from integration in wider social,

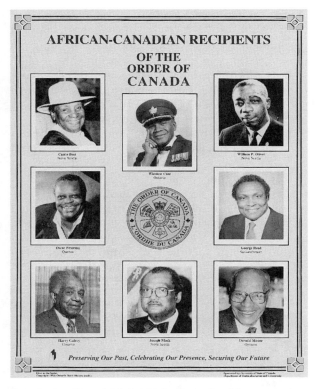

AFRICAN-CANADIAN RECIPIENTS
OF THE
ORDER OF
CANADA

Preserving Our Past, Celebrating Our Presence, Securing Our Future

Some functionalists maintain that it is healthy for liberal democracies to support ethnic group identity rather than assimilation.

economic, and political institutions of democratic society. The intent of granting recognition to ethnic minorities is that it would promote ethnic harmony and integration at the societal level, but this goal is not easily achieved. Legitimating the politics of cultural survival has merits, Rorty suggests (1994, 159–60), in acknowledging the hostilities that tend to become inflamed as various groups compete for public funds and attention, all within what passes as mutual respect. Critics argue that multiculturalism only promotes separatism, and that assimilation remains the only viable option for national integration.

The functionalist perspective on culture and ethnicity dominates both sociological and popular accounts of ethnic and racial strife. Pavlowitch (1994), for example, accounts for the violent breakup of Yugoslavia as the inevitable outcome of the state being built across a zone of ethnic fault lines. Modern nation-states, he argues, are built on ethnic communities, a collective characterized by cultural and historical affinities. Yugoslavia was dualistic from the start and doomed to

collapse as soon as external empires and strong state control weakened. Similar arguments prevailed in journalistic accounts of the outbreak of civil war between ethnic Tutsi and Hutu in Rwanda during 1994. A similar fate is predicted for neighbouring Burundi. Only the close comparisons between the violence in Yugoslavia and Rwanda muted popular interpretations of the Rwandan conflict in terms of primitive tribalism as opposed to modern universalistic cultural values. The history of ethnic relations in Canada provides copious support for the functionalist prediction that whenever there are ethnic divisions within a society there will be strife.

Limitations of Traditional Functionalism

The body of evidence that can be cited in support of the functionalist view of ethnicity is immense. Nevertheless, the theoretical underpinnings of functionalism have come under increasing criticism as based on a fundamentally flawed conceptualization of ethnic identity that seriously distorts our understanding of intergroup conflict. The more one tries to pin down the key concepts of *ethnic group* and *culture*, the more elusive they become.

Statistics Canada has tried various ways to measure the ethnic group composition of the Canadian population to provide basic data for multicultural policies (Pryor et al. 1992). Since funding is often based on numbers, some method of counting is important. But the statisticians have had to struggle with a conceptual maze of confused referents. A multiplicity of possible indicators including subjective group identification, objective place of origin, ancestry, place of residence, culture, race, religion and language, permit multiple response possibilities for any one individual. Over the past four decades, wording has changed repeatedly from the initial focus on "coming from elsewhere" with the exception of aboriginal peoples, to ethnic group of male ancestor on first coming to this continent, and then to a plurality of ethnic groups for different ancestors on both male and female side. In 1986, the reference to "on first coming to this continent" was dropped to allow subjective sense of affiliation, and the option "black" was added. Before 1986, the response "Canadian" was permitted as a write-in response, but with no explicit reference to it. Subsequent experiments with different wording to give "Canadian" as an example of possible ethnic identities, or as an explicit markbox, produced strikingly different responses. Also, as wordings became more complex to try to measure the difference between ethnic origin and ethnic identity, the nonresponse rate increased. Pryor concludes that there is no way to measure ethnic group identity because the concept itself is too fluid. People may be motivated to select "Canadian" for a variety of reasons, and these motives and hence identity claims can change over time.

The policy of multiculturalism presupposes that *culture* can be separated from other aspects of social and political identity, but there are no clear criteria for making such a distinction. The definition of *cultural group*, even within functionalist theory, has been defined as narrowly as language, or as broadly as a "total way of life," with the favoured definition having major policy implications (Rorty 1994, 155). Does recognition of "Irish Canadian" as an ethnic group, for example, imply that parochial Catholic schools should receive public funding? Or that curriculum should be modified to reflect Catholic teaching on such issues as abortion or euthanasia? What implications would this have for all other ethnic and religious minorities? Recognition of the distinct cultural identity of Quebec within Canada tends to revolve around language, but separatists believe that economic, political, and legal self-determination is a precondition for cultural survival in a broader sense of an integrated way of life that goes beyond remaining francophone (Rorty 1994, 156). Acadians in New Brunswick have voiced similar concern that their cultural identity may be weakened by the introduction of French immersion for anglophone children. Anglophones may learn to speak French without sharing Acadian culture.

The key concepts of *acculturation* and *assimilation* have proven similarly impossible to pin down once one shifts from the level of simplified abstractions to practical instances and policies. It is not possible to specify the set of norms and values that constitute the dominant Canadian culture that minorities are supposed to adopt. It breaks into a myriad of subcultural variations. Consider the diversity of lifestyles, values, religion, language, history, community, and self-concepts among upper-, middle-, and lower-class people,

elderly, middle-aged, and young people, men and women, those of left, right, and centrist political persuasions. Even within the dominant English language there is so much variation that professionals at conferences may as well be speaking Greek as English for all the sense that the average person could make of it. The theoretical notion of common socialization seems unworkable.

In summary, the failure of concerted efforts to observe and measure key concepts in the functionalist theory of ethnicity leads to the conclusion that the theory itself is seriously flawed. The theory relies on static or essentialist definitions of culture and ethnic group. People are assumed to "have" identifiable sets of attitudes, values, and behavioural traits that are absorbed through primary group socialization, and that converge into distinct ethnic subgroups. But this conceptualization misses both the fluidity and the context-dependent character of ethnic identity.

The Political Economy of Race and Ethnic Relations

The political economy perspective shifts the focus from enumeration of elements of culture to the boundary relations between groups of people and relations of inequality, power, and exploitation that structure the conditions within which ethnic consciousness develops. Culture is understood as representing a way of life that a group of people develops in order to adapt to external conditions, rather than a primordial given of social existence (Li 1990, 8). Cultural patterns thus reflect the changing economic and social conditions in which people live. Although a functionalist style of research may well reveal major differences between ethnic groups on issues like orientation to education and to occupations, the political economy view is that such patterns are to be expected, given the very different location of ethnic groups in the vertical mosaic.

The central concern in political economy analysis is with the economic institutions that organize groups hierarchically within the class system, and the power of the dominant ethnic class to define the location of subordinate groups (Li 1990). The internal class structures of particular societies are formed within an overarching world capitalist system that has been shaped historically by the institutions of colonialism, imperialism, slavery, and indentured and migrant labour shifting between the periphery and the centres of industrial capitalism.

In classical Marxist analysis, the rise of racist theories claiming the biological superiority of white over nonwhite races is rooted in colonial expansion (Cox ([1948] 1970). Cox argues that such **biological theories** found favour among scientists and anthropologists because they provided a justification for the subjugation of indigenous peoples by more economically powerful invaders. Colonial rulers could see themselves as taking on "the white man's burden" in imposing supposedly superior forms of social organization over colonized peoples. Racist doctrines continued thereafter to legitimate the superexploitation of nonwhite people as slaves, indentured labourers, and cheap migrant labour for corporate interests.

Historically, the British colonial government exercised power over the structural incorporation of different ethnic groups within Canada. The policies with respect to aboriginal peoples and to the French colonists, as well as the regulation of immigration, in large measure produced the vertical mosaic of ethnic groups now evident in Canada. The imposition of the Indian Act that defined the status and nonstatus of Indians, had nothing to do with people's cultural attributes (Li 1990, 6) but everything to do with the economic interests of the colonizers. The current location of Native peoples on the lowest rungs of the Canadian capitalist system can be traced back directly to their brutal exploitation and the plunder of their economic resources from the time when white settlers began to compete with Native peoples for land and other resources. It may well have been inevitable that Native hunting and gathering economies would decline with the influx of white settlers (Stanley 1964, 3–5). But there was nothing inevitable about the nature of the treaties imposed upon many Native bands or about the fact that, while European settlers were allocated 160 acres of farmland per family, Native families were allocated 10 acres or less. Nor was it inevitable that Indian reserves were located on lands unsuitable for agriculture. These conditions were socially constructed by the very uneven bargaining power of the negotiators. In the few instances where Indians settled on good farmland and began to cultivate it, they were

pushed off to make way for white settlers. Later, when gold and other minerals were found in the North or when hydro-electric power projects were set up, Native lands were expropriated with minimal compensation. Such events reflect the fact that Native peoples are not represented within the centres of economic and political control in Canadian society where such decisions are made, and hence that their interests are not taken into account.

Kellough describes how the first Indian Act of 1896 legalized the colonial subordination of Native peoples by giving the Minister of Indian Affairs authority over laws and reserve land. The ministry had total authority over what land should be sold for what price. The National Indian Brotherhood estimated that as much as half the original reserve allotment in Canada was lost through land sales to benefit railways, coal corporations, farms, and recreation developers between 1900 and 1930. All the profits from the sales went to pay the salaries of Indian Affairs personnel (Kellough 1980, 348).

During the late 1960s, the Indian Affairs budget exceeded $62 million per year, but only $1.5 million was spent on economic development. More recently, the rhetoric has changed in favour of promoting development for Native peoples, but success has been limited. Tentative efforts to develop the business potential of wild rice cultivation have been destroyed by hydro-electric developments, with Native peoples receiving little compensation. Traditional hunting grounds and trap lines have also been destroyed by oil and gas exploration. Native land claims have been stalled indefinitely in Canadian courts. In the face of such historical experience, it is perhaps surprising that violent confrontations such as that which happened at Oka have not occurred more frequently.

A Marxist analysis of relations between English Canada and the French-speaking settlers in Quebec similarly focusses attention on the long history of economic exploitation and inequality. The British business class dominated the economy, controlling much of the wealth, while French-speaking people were subjugated within their own province. Within the vertical class mosaic of Quebec, monolingual anglophones on average held the top positions and commanded the highest incomes. Senior executive positions within the companies tended to be filled by British people brought in from elsewhere. The language of business was English and the French were required to adapt. Bilingual anglophones who dealt more directly with the French community were concentrated in lower rungs of management, and earned lower incomes, on average, than did their wholly anglophone bosses. Below them again was the class of bilingual francophone workers, while monolingual francophones were concentrated in the less desirable, low-paying jobs, or otherwise trapped in marginal, primary occupations in farming and fishing. From the Marxist perspective, the anger and resentment felt by generations of Québécois subjected to this internal colonialism is a sufficient explanation for the rise of nationalism in Quebec. Conflict over language or cultural differences are symptoms of this more fundamental conflict over power and access to resources. The Quebec government's controversial language law (Bill 101), passed in 1977 making French the language of business and work in Quebec, went some way towards guaranteeing job opportunities for French-speaking workers, but could not by itself dismantle an entrenched ethnic-class system. Figures published in 1994 indicated that francophones in Canada still earn less, on average, than anglophones.

Capital and Migrant Labour

The presence and location of other ethnic minorities within the Canadian class structure is closely linked to the interests of capital in attracting and controlling certain kinds of migrant labour to meet periodic and specialized labour demands. This, in turn, was linked to the wider context of international capitalism and the collapse of local economies that left hundreds of thousands of people willing and even desperate to migrate to seek work abroad.

The way in which different groups were incorporated depended in large measure on three factors: the historical period in which specific groups of settlers came; the extent to which the dominant class needed settlers for economic development; and the power of different settler groups, based on available resources and how well they could mobilize to use them (Baker 1977). From this perspective, the formation of class and ethnic relations within the Canadian state are historically identical. The one cannot be understood except in terms of the other. British immigrants generally came to dominate the Canadian middle and upper classes because this was precisely how the immigration process was organized. This pattern did not simply happen by itself or come about without human intervention as the result of the functioning of the capitalist system.

Ng (1988a, 8) describes the work of immigration societies set up in most major cities of Canada in the nineteenth century to organize patterns of immigration. Mainly upper-class women reformers actively organized the emigration of working-class girls from Britain to serve as domestics and wives in Canada. The avowed goal of the reformers was to ensure the white character and Christian morality of the dominant group. In the 1890s, peasant farmers of central European stock were encouraged to migrate in large numbers to settle the Prairies, and hence the ethnic-class composition of that area was formed. Unskilled labourers were encouraged to come to build railroads and canals. They emigrated from countries in which the collapse of the domestic economy had created large pools of destitute people seeking their livelihood anywhere they could find it. So the ethnic classes of Irish navvies and Chinese coolies emerged within Canada.

Subsequent policies were designed to perpetuate these social relations to production for migrating people. Land prices were artificially inflated beyond the means of these migrants so that they remained wage-labourers rather than becoming independent farmers. Chinese women were not permitted to immigrate; this helped to ensure a gender-class of temporary Chinese male migrants.

The Immigration Act that came into effect in 1978 divides immigrants into three categories. The **independent immigrant** category, which includes "assisted relatives," comprises people whose entry into Canada is subject to economic requirements and criteria measured by a point system. People gain points according to their level of education, job skills, and ability to meet current labour shortages in Canada. The category of **business-class immigrants** comprises people who have capital to invest in Canadian industries and businesses and can provide guarantees that they will create employment opportunities in Canada. A third category of **sponsored** or **family-class immigrants** includes people who do not accrue enough points by themselves but who are sponsored into Canada by a close relative. In addition, people can apply for **refugee status** and be assessed by a different set of criteria.

This immigration policy is generating a particular form of ethnic-class relations within Canada (Ng 1988b, 16). The formal wording of the classifications do not refer to the gender, ethnic origin, or class position of individuals. But the criteria used to determine entry, based on language proficiency, educational attainment, Canadian labour-force requirements, and investment potential, have built-in sex, race, and class biases. People from Western Europe have a clear advantage in the points system, along with members of the highly educated, English-speaking elite from parts of Asia. Currently, business people with capital to invest in Canada are in high demand. The migration of Hong Kong Chinese businessmen is encouraged. This has resulted in the formation of an ethnic class within the Canadian economy very different from that of their Chinese predecessors.

Figure 17-1

Annual Levels of Immigration, 1901–91

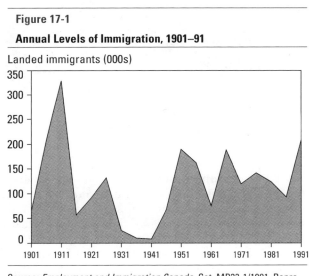

Landed immigrants (000s)

Source: *Employment and Immigration Canada,* Cat. MP22-1/1991. Reproduced by authority of the Minister of Industry, 1994. Statistics Canada (1994c), *Canada's Changing Immigrant Population,* Cat. 96-311E, p. 6.

The "Racialization" of Class Consciousness

State policies, organized in the interests of capital, structure the class relations within which racial and ethnic conflicts emerge. These conflicts have the effect of dividing workers against each other and obscuring awareness of class. Different migrant groups find themselves in conflict with each other and with indigenous or more long-settled groups for scarce resources such as jobs, housing, and educational opportunities (Rex and Moore 1967; Brittan and Maynard 1984, 35–36). Indigenous workers may win concessions from capitalists that are not necessarily extended to migrants. Discrimination in employment means that minority group workers are more willing to take the worst jobs that more established workers refuse to do. Racism as quality of relations between groups is thus inextricably bound up with class relations (Miles 1985).

In the Maritimes, British immigrants splintered into English, Scottish, and Irish subgroups as they struggled for ascendancy over land, tenancies, fishing rights, control over fish processing, and so on. They became so divided by the 1930s that they came to see themselves as belonging to different races (Ng 1988a, 12). Marriages across religious groups such as Baptists and Roman Catholics were formally registered as "interracial." By the late 1980s, the main focus of competition had shifted to jobs in the civil service, with the policy of bilingualism in government service pitting English-speaking groups generally against the French-speaking Acadians.

Some Marxist theorists push this class analysis further to suggest that it is in the interests of capitalists to foment ethnic divisions precisely because they weaken class solidarity. It facilitates the superexploitation of the most subjugated groups, especially those with racially distinct characteristics. They can more easily be separated from other workers and squeezed without other workers jumping to their protection. The term *racialization* has been proposed as a way of drawing attention to the ways in which groups are singled out for unequal treatment on the basis of real or imagined cultural or racial characteristics that are fundamentally irrelevant to the economic interests that underlie such treatment (Bolaria and Li 1988).

The power of such divisions to deflect hostility from the capitalist class onto fellow workers is cited as an important factor in the overall stability of the exploitative class system itself. Race consciousness in some of the inner cities of the United States serves to divide black, Latino, Asian, and Korean groups against each other in the struggle for survival. In the Los Angeles riots that followed the acquittal of a police officer from a charge of assaulting a black suspect, black anger exploded at Korean shopkeepers rather than the white business class (Marable 1993).

In other contexts, as conditions change, government policies may shift towards more active multiculturalism. But such policies are also open to the interpretation that they are forms of managing and containing race and ethnic divisions through exerting fiscal control over their expression (Li 1990, 12).

Restructuring Marxist Theory

The shift in focus within Marxist theory from analysis of class interest and struggles over resources to the manipulation of racial and ethnic group politics has also fostered a shift in the conceptualization of race and ethnic group identities. Earlier structuralist Marxist formulations, like functionalism, take the existence of race and ethnic group as given. Relations between them shifted from culture to struggle over economic resources. In the final analysis, class location determined race and ethnic group relations, with the interests of the dominant capitalist class playing a central role in the formation of prevailing ideologies.

But this **class reductionism** has come under increasing criticism for its inherent rigidity and determinism. The notion of the structural necessity of ethnic divisions among the working class for the stability of capitalism is also unconvincing. Such divisions arguably hamper the free flow of capital and labour and constrict business interests rather than promote them. Preoccupation with the analysis of white racism in these early theoretical formulations was valuable in focussing theoretical debate on questions of power and inequality. But as an analytical framework it has proven too rigid to deal with the complexity of group identity politics. It failed to provide a theoretical framework for analysing the active involvement of people in forming their own political identities (Solomos and Back 1994, 149). What is needed, Solomos and Back argue, is a fundamental restructuring of Marxist theory to encompass an elaborated analysis of wider social and cultural processes. The current shift within Marxist theory is toward a conceptualization of race and ethnicity as social constructions, the perspective that we consider now.

The Social Construction of Race and Ethnic Identities

The social constructionist perspective on race and ethnic relations incorporates two important aspects of Marxist analysis: the concern with class relations within capitalism and the institutional frameworks that structure how migrant peoples are incorporated into host societies. What distinguishes it is a fundamental reconceptualization of what is meant by terms such as *race* or *ethnic* group.

The social constructionist perspective challenges what is meant by *race* or *ethnic* group.

At the beginning of this chapter, we gave a functionalist definition of ethnic group as based on primordial attachments of kinship, blood, and home territory that are experienced as a part of self-identity and associated with intense emotions. Within the social constructionist framework, all aspects of this definition are called into question. Key concepts such as *ethnicity* and *ethnic groups* are changed from nouns into verbs, from observable entities to ethnicizing processes through which ethnic identity claims emerge. What ethnicity means to different people in different historical situations is not fixed, but continually modified and negotiated, revised and revitalized (Eller and Coughlan 1993). People can and do make choices among possible ethnic identity claims (Waters 1990). As we have seen above, even simple word changes in a census form can prompt major shifts in how people identify themselves. The degree of saliency given to such claims is highly variable. There is no certainty that ethnicity will be associated with any strong emotional attachments. Ethnic-group ties between people do not persist automatically. If they are maintained, it is because they are actively worked at (Hoben and Hefner 1990, 18). The assumption that ethnicity constitutes a primordial attachment obscures all of the ethnicization processes involved. It takes as given what needs to be explained, namely, how ethnicization emerges in different historical situations.

The tenuousness of cultural underpinnings of ethnicization become evident when researchers, or group members themselves, try to pin down or quantify the relevant attributes (Rorty 1994). Internal group self-definitions and extragroup characterizations continually shift in response to changing political contexts and the ebb and flow of those sought or seeking membership. The terminology used to characterize Negroes in the United States has shifted from coloured people, to blacks, to Afro-Americans, and to African-Americans as claims for primacy of racial or cultural identity have shifted.

Often profound disagreements emerge over what constitutes the supposedly shared cultural norms. As we saw in the chapter on religion, people felt able to identify themselves as Mennonites so long as they were not called upon to specify what this meant. But efforts to formalize elements of Mennonite membership, either in terms of specific religious beliefs, family origins, or emotions, rapidly proved divisive (Winland 1993). Such underpinnings were best left vague. Ethnicization claims based on shared texts are often problematic because of the wide variety of interpretations of those texts, interpretations that can be openly contradictory. For example, Israel grants automatic citizenship to Jews under the law of return, but it is by no means obvious in practice how to determine who is entitled to make such a claim, and on what grounds. People as disparate as black Africans from Ethiopia, ultra-orthodox followers of the Talmud, and atheists from the United States have pressured such claims. The self-presentation of Israel as a Jewish state is itself oriented to fund-raising abroad and hence necessarily flexible (Rorty 1994, 159). Ethnicization claims based on shared histories must similarly contend with dramatic differences among those whom the claim tries to encompass.

The vagueness of such constructs begins to make sense when we reverse the causal association traditionally drawn between culture and ethnic group. It is the formation of political groups that produces ethnicity rather than ethnicity that produces groups. From this perspective, ethnicity is a political process, emerging and coalescing within political struggles. It is these struggles that generate the emotional intensity that can then be reflected back into ethnic-group identity. In the process of laying claim to status as an "ethnic" group, people may activate old realities and resources that were relatively dormant but that can in some sense be constituted as aspects of "heritage." When such "objective" indicators are lacking, people can often construct them, actively creating new cultural resources around which to coalesce (Eller and Coughlan 1993, 189). Such ethnicization is often focussed around claims concerning the distribution of scarce resources, such as affirmative action programs, quota systems, or even certain social services. During the colonial period in Africa, for example, new ethnic groups emerged through the efforts of local political entrepreneurs looking for a political base on which to establish their own careers (Kasfir 1979, cited in Eller and Coughlan 1993, 188).

Political Economy and Ethnicization

The ethnicization of different groups in a society occur within a broader context of struggles over economic and political resources. Within Canada, the history of colonialism, treaty rights with various Native groups, immigration policies, bilingualism and more recently multiculturalism, constitute the institutional frameworks within which various groups negotiate ethnicity claims. The aboriginal peoples of Canada came to be Native Indians through processes of colonization and subjugation that "destroyed, re-organized, fragmented and homogenised the myriad tribal groups across the land" (Ng 1988a, 7). As we saw above, struggles over access to and control over economic resources lay behind the coalescing of British immigrants as the dominant capitalist class in one region, and their fragmentation into English, Irish, Scottish, and Welsh in other regions, where migrants from different parts of the British Isles competed for economic space.

Ethnicization, however, involves more active processes of identity negotiation than is generally recognized within the more traditional Marxist perspective. It cannot be reduced to class location. Crean and Rioux (1983) analyse Québécois nationalism and francophone cultural identity as pre-eminently an act of resistance to the homogenizing forces of global capitalism. American corporate giants are able to saturate mass media, promoting standardized entertainment and mass-produced goods, and extolling values of materialism and competitive individualism. Québécois identity is emerging as an expression of local experience and local life-worlds. It is an active refusal to become homogenized, and as such reflects the "innovative, self-creative capacity of people and [their] collective imagination" (Crean and Rioux 1983, 18).

Discourse Analysis and the Politics of Authenticity

When ethnicity is defined in terms of primordial ties of blood and heritage culture, then these contemporary political movements are problematic. The creative resurrection of long dormant items of culture, and the active invention of cultural indicators, can be discredited as inauthentic. This has generated intense and acrimonious debate among scholars, particularly with respect to Native cultural expression. Clifton (1990) and colleagues maintain that much of what is claimed as "Indianness" is simply invented. Notions such as "ecological natives" who recognized the sanctity of mother earth and who worshipped the earth goddess are contrasted with greedy, civilized white men who raped and pillaged her. Clifton argues that there is minimal anthropological evidence to support myths of any pan-Indian mother earth symbolism. He argues that such images originate not within Indian cultures at all, but within the myth of the "noble savage" that pervades Western culture. This myth contrasts modern man with an idealized humanity uncorrupted by civilization. Indigenous peoples of North America became readily associated with such mythical humanity in the largely fictional writings of white explorers. Yet other theorists cite evidence that Indian rituals and ceremonies are more likely borrowed from or grafted upon Euro-American myths of cultural primitivism combined with Catholic missionary stories (Gill 1990). Images of Indians living in a state of equality,

harmony, and joyous spontaneity before the coming of the white man are challenged by anthropological evidence of conflicts and wars among tribes, and evidence of slavery as institutionalized within some Northwest Coast Indian societies.

Images of Indians in braids, feather headdresses, and leather moccasins may similarly be largely the invention of Europeans (Francis 1992). European artists travelled across the continent as tourists, bent on capturing what they believed were a vanishing race of noble savages. Edward Curtis carefully staged his photographs, with the aid of props like wigs, clothing, and doctored photographs to eliminate evidence of white culture, so as to portray Indians as he thought they had existed before the white man came. Since the 1960s we have been inundated with books and films celebrating the spiritual side of Indian life—their ceremonials and the wisdom of their elders. Such films, Francis suggests (1992, 58), reflect the desire of non-Natives to project onto Natives the values and the sense of sacredness that they find lacking in their own society. A number of publications acclaimed as written by Native authors turned out to have been written by non-Natives. These include the hugely successful books by Grey Owl, the trapper turned conservationist. Grey Owl claimed to be part Apache, born in Mexico, but records show that he was born and raised in England. Francis concludes that the image of Indians held in the white world is the image that whites wish Indians to be. The stereotype does not reflect the real world, but it does powerfully influence how Indians and whites present themselves to each other. Indians come to adopt the white man's image of Indians in order to claim authentic ethnicity in relations with white society.

The problem with the kind of analysis represented by Clifton and Gill is that it presupposes some authentic Indian heritage against which current claims can be objectively assessed. From the perspective of social constructionist theory, however, this itself is a myth. Ethnicity is always an ongoing construction, not a projection of the past. The focus on the authenticity or otherwise of historical "facts" is to miss the point that ethnicization is about contemporary social relations, not about history (Hornborg 1994).

Hornborg analyses the co-operation between environmentalists and Nova Scotia Mi'kmaq to stop the building of a gravel pit on Kelly Mountain

Whites mingle with Indians at this potlatch ceremony in Alert Bay, BC. Historically, European explorers readily interpreted Indian culture in terms of Western myths of the noble savage.

in 1989. The Mi'kmaq argued that the mountain has spiritual significance for them as the sacred abode of the Mi'kmaq god Kluskap, and the site of his prophesied return. Environmentalists also adopted the notion of the "spiritual impact" of the quarry into their own message. As Hornborg acknowledges, the image of the ecological Native is a projection from non-Native writers like James Fenimore Cooper, but this does not mean that its adoption as an emblem within Native discourse is inauthentic (1994, 252–53). Mi'kmaq leaders were openly aware of these processes, and recognized the real opportunity presented by the Kelly Mountain drama to fill their own sense of ethnic identity with new meaning. The emerging view of the proposed quarry as a violation of their spirituality involved an active process of

reflexive self-identity creation. It is this emerging awareness that the Mi'kmaq leaders projected through the mass media in ceremonies organized around drumming, dancing, and chanting.

The discourse of ethnicity, like all discourses, continually changes in relation to what will be accepted as credible, particularly in the public media. The image of the ecological Native holds special potency today as it speaks to the collective sense of guilt in white society about environmental damage wrought by uncontrolled industrialization. For the Mi'kmaq who became involved in the struggle, Hornborg suggests, it was a profoundly important integrative process, providing a means of expressing ethnic identity that overrode many internal divisions. As one of the Mi'kmaq leaders expressed it, "Some people think that Mi'kmaq religion and culture is gone, but we are Mi'kmaq and what we are doing is our culture" (Hornborg 1994, 253).

Claims to ethnic authenticity and challenges to such claims occur at multiple levels among group members, as well as with outsiders. In their encounters with the media, the Mi'kmaq presented themselves collectively as authentic ecological Natives, standing against the materialist greed of white society. At another level, however, the traditional Mi'kmaq Grand Council claimed authenticity against the band chiefs and council who were derogated as having adopted a white mentality. At yet another level, traditionalists within the Grand Council claimed superior authenticity relative to the "Catholics," sometimes also referred to as the "academics." At a fourth level, the more militant traditionalists identified themselves as more authentically Mi'kmaq warriors, modelled on the Mohawk Warriors at Oka, compared with the pacifists. At each level, Hornborg suggests, the claim of authenticity was made by those less able to get funding from the dominant white capitalist society. The inauthentic were those who compromised with funding authorities. The band chiefs and council received funding from the Department of Indian Affairs while the Grand Council did not; the Catholics were better positioned to get funding from such agencies as churches and universities than the traditionalists; the pacifists were more able to qualify for funds under various multicultural programs. A very similar pattern of questioning authenticity occurred among the non-Native environmentalists. Those who adopted the current discourse of "sustainable development" and who made successful claims for funding were challenged by more marginal unfunded groups as inauthentic, or having sold out. Greenness, Hornborg suggests, is as contestable an identity as Indianness (1994, 256).

The fundamental meaning of authentic as against corrupted self-identity claims, Hornborg concludes, concerns the expression of local life-worlds of concrete, embodied social relations, as distinct from the disembodied and decontextualized abstractions of capitalism. Ethnicization speaks to these local life-worlds. This is as true of the Québécois discourse of francophone nationalism as it is of Mi'kmaq spiritual identity, and of Canadian cultural nationalism speaking out against continental North American free trade agreements.

The Politics of Knowledge Production

The ethnicization of any group takes place within a context of broader societal discourse about dominant and minority groups. As we have seen, how Native peoples of Canada come to formulate their own sense of group identity is not entirely of their own choosing. It emerges at least in part as a reaction to, adaptation to, or exploitation of elements of prevailing public discourses within which their own claims gain credibility. All other visible minority and migrant groups of people similarly confront a public discourse around race and ethnic relations in which their position in the society is described. It bears repeating here that whatever historical relations or heritage claims may be contained in discourses about ethnicity, the message is not principally about history, but about contemporary relations.

Discourse analysis within the field of race and ethnic relations draws attention to the forms of political discourse that sustain mundane or common-sense everyday **racism** in Western societies. A prominent exponent of discourse analysis, Teum Van Dijk (1993) focusses on the texts and talk of white leaders, particularly politicians, in the cultural construction of the subordination of nonwhites. He stresses that only fragments of beliefs are usually expressed in discourse; underlying belief systems have to be inferred. Denial of racism, and other forms of face-saving expressions, are currently the stock in trade of politicians. After World War II, the foundations of empire and colonialism were shaken, and the United Nations Declaration of Human Rights set the tone for a different way of talking about peoples in former colonies. Blatant statements of derogation and inferiorization of colonized peoples has given way to more subtle discourse. The criterion that Van Dijk adopts for distinguishing true antiracism from the merely apparent is the consistency of discourse. The presence of disclaimers provides a clue to subtle forms of racism, such as: "We are very tolerant, but . . . they abuse us" or "We have done our best, but . . . now it is up to them."

Other disclaimers include the pervasive emphasis on negative or criminal properties of minority group members as a prelude to get-tough policies to restrict immigration or refugees. Another disclaimer is the attribution of social problems to minorities in the absence of any discussion of gross inequalities, unemployment, bad housing, and failing social services that underlie such problems. In contemporary discourse on relations with minority groups, racism is being replaced by ethnicism—an emphasis on seemingly neutral notions of cultural differences between groups. But these differences are pathologized, as when mother-centred black families are defined as the source of problems among blacks in the United States, or when minorities are described as suffering from "handicaps" that ill-equip them to take advantage of new opportunities. Such discourse fosters the view of minorities as the cause of their own victimization, and provides support and justification for discriminatory policies. A similar mode of political discourse involves attributing racist attitudes to the population at large, particularly the lower classes, as in the comment, "If you ask the man in the street 'Are we being too strict on immigration?' the answer is a strong NO. We are being extaordinarily generous" (Van Dijk 1993, 73). Again, such discourse supports get-tough policies on immigration on the dubious grounds that "it is necessary to stop immigration or we will get racist."

The discourses of political leaders can be very influential in the construction of public opinion about minorities because the large majority of people in any society may have limited personal experience of them. Many Canadians may have little opportunity to mix with Native peoples or immigrants, particularly if they live in homogeneous small towns and villages. Much of what we think we know about minorities is based on information that comes to us second hand from media reports. The choice of words can be significant in impression formation. When groups of people running away from a war or police brutality in their home countries are described as "illegal aliens" in newspapers, it invokes emotions that set "us" against "them." An alternative choice of words might have evoked sympathy.

Shifting public opinion about the descendants of people who have come to Canada from Japan provides a powerful example of the politics of public discourse. Sunahara (1981) describes how anti-Japanese feeling in British Columbia before World War II made possible the internment of Japanese Canadians, and how a change in popular opinion after the war fostered demands for restitution and apology. What she does not explore is how such popular feelings were socially produced. Before the war, Japan was a rising world power competing with the imperial-

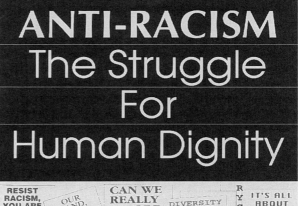

The discourses of political leaders can be very influential in the construction of public opinion about minorities.

ist powers in Europe and North America. After the war, Japan became a trading partner of significance to Canada. The very different political discourses about Japan played a strong role in shifting public opinions.

A media-driven panic about waves of immigration and hoards of refugees occurred during 1987–88 when Bill C-55, a policy to restrict the flow of refugees into Canada, was being debated in the federal parliament. Notwithstanding some dissenting voices, the general impression created by the media was that Canada was being swamped by hoards of bogus refugees pouring in to take unfair advantage of Canada's generosity. An oft-repeated image was that of 174 East Indians, mostly Sikhs, landing at the tiny village of Charlesville, Nova Scotia, in July 1987. People were encouraged to watch the coastline for "invaders." It was hard to remind oneself that the supposed "flood" of refugees constituted less than two percent of the immigrants that came to Canada annually, under the regular immigration policy. It is through such practices as these that public discourse about the characteristics and location of various kinds of migrant peoples within Canada is constructed (see figure 17-2).

Sociology as Ideological Discourse

Sociological theories of race and ethnic relations are not politically neutral, nor merely of academic interest. Academic discourse carries the aura of science, and is readily incorporated into government policies, and into the professional work of committees, institutions, and bureaucracies of government administration. Van Dijk (1993, ch. 5) devotes special attention to the analysis of sociology textbooks and what he sees as discourses of academic racism embedded in the materials on race and ethnic relations that students are typically required to study. These accounts, he suggests, are commonly written in

Figure 17-2

Immigrants as a Percentage of Census Metropolitan Areas, 1991

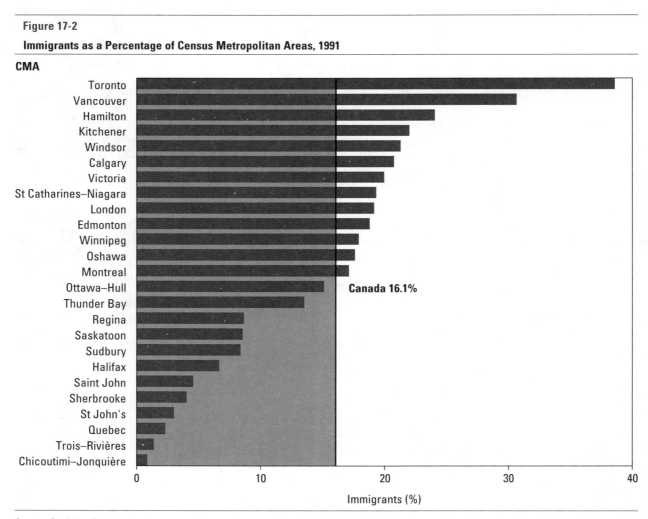

Source: Statistics Canada, *Immigration and Citizenship*. 1991 Census of Canada, Cat. 93-316. Reproduced by authority of the Minister of Industry, 1994. Statistics Canada (1994c), *Canada's Changing Immigrant Population*, Cat. 96-311E, p. 10.

The media can "construct" public discourse about the characteristics and location of immigrants.

Ellen Terry Cole of the Canadian Jewish Congress and Dr Alan Li of the Chinese Canadian National Council collaborated on an antiracism guide that takes a hard look at federal government injustices. Behind them, the Chinese Railway Workers Monument honours the 17 000 men from Kwangtung province, China, who helped build the Canadian Pacific Railway—4000 of them were killed during its construction.

forms that ignore, deny, minimize, and excuse racist attitudes and practices.

He challenges a series of definitions of key terms, in each case drawing attention to what they omit, and consequently, to the hidden assumptions that they support. When *racism* is defined as "believing in biological explanations for behaviour," this excludes an understanding of racism as the property of dominance relations in society. People who both practice and benefit from the subordination of people with particular racial characteristics can, by the above definition, present themselves as not racist. Similarly, when *prejudice* is defined as "unwarranted, fixed opinions," systemic inequality disappears from the picture. When *affirmative action* policies are defined in terms of "allocating places to minorities with lower grades," this excludes from view the evidence that prior education of nonwhite students is often vastly worse than that of white students, and that white students were preferentially and even exclusively admitted to the relevant positions prior to affirmative action policies being instituted.

The use of the passive tense such as "were subjugated" in descriptions of colonialism directs attention away from the issue of who subjugated whom. The adoption of ahistorical generalizations such as "ethnic antagonisms" as euphemisms for racism similarly shifts attention and culpability away from the dominant groups in such relationships. Such discourse conveys the impression that prejudice is ubiquitous within all ethnic groups, natural, and therefore excusable. Inequalities in power and dominance relations are ignored. The prevailing functionalist analysis of ethnicism as rooted in primordial emotional ties can readily be used to justify segregation, ethnic cleansing, and outright war. Marxist analysis also lends justification to ethnic antagonisms as the inevitable outcome of struggles over scarce resources. The traditional structuralist Marxist view that racism exists or persists because it is functional for capitalism exonerates whites from culpability for the deprived status and oppression of minorities. The system produces it, not the white racists themselves (Brittan and Maynard 1984, 35–70).

The next section of this chapter uses many of the tools of discourse analysis to examine the application of feminist analysis to race and ethnic relations.

Feminist Theory in Race and Ethnic Relations

At the Canadian Learned Societies Conference in 1988, heated debate was generated on the extent of racism within the women's movement, particularly among academic feminists (Das Gupta 1989, 1). The main contention of black and Native panelists was that as feminist studies became institutionalized in various universities, a stratum of privileged white, middle-class women emerged who claimed to speak for all women, but whose scholarship both excluded and misrepresented the experiences of women of colour.

This criticism has not been easy to accept. Mainstream feminist theory developed as a critique of traditional social science while in practice representing the partial and biased viewpoints of men to the virtual exclusion of women's experience. Now feminist theory itself is challenged for promoting a false universalism, claiming to speak from the standpoint of women, but all the while failing to address the experiences of women of colour, or of imposing white, Eurocentric perspectives on those experiences. Some of the grounds for this contention, and current efforts to address these concerns, are explored below.

The growing body of writings by feminist women of colour, often self-identified collectively as "black" women, draws attention to the triple oppression inherent in **gendered ethnic-class** relations. In common with constructionist theory, these women emphasize that these three aspects of their lives cannot adequately be understood as distinct or parallel phenomena. They are experienced simultaneously in all their social relations.

The central notion of patriarchy itself becomes problematic from the perspective of black women, since it implies a structural opposition between black women and black men. Feminist anti-male politics pushes black feminists into a forced choice—to be feminist first or black first (Carby 1982, 213). But such a choice does not address the gendered racist experience of black women's lives. Patriarchy, as a concept, largely fails to account for the oppression of black men, and their historical subordination to white women, as well as to white men.

In multiple other ways, the central theoretical frameworks developed within mainstream feminist work have been found inadequate to address the experiences of women of colour. Feminist theory has challenged demeaning conceptions of womanhood embodied in ideals of femininity, the presumed delicacy and daintiness of women, their need to be helped, and their dependency on men. But such notions of womanhood were never applied to black women. Carby (1982, 214) cites the anger of Sojourner Truth, a black slave woman and pioneering feminist, at how her womanhood and her motherhood were denied. At a time when white women were helped into carriages, lifted over ditches, and given the best places to sit, she did hard physical labour in the fields; she ploughed and planted and harvested alongside black men, and bore thirteen children, only to see them sold into slavery. The gendered identity of black women bears little in common with the constructions of white femininity that is the focus of mainstream feminist writing. Black women who have looked to academic feminism to find images of themselves have found very little (Thornhill 1989).

Feminist theory has also focussed criticism on the patriarchal nuclear family form as the site of women's oppression, with women confined to the private sphere as homemakers, dependent upon a male breadwinner. But this family form bears little resemblance to the family lives of black American or Caribbean women. For such women, the institution of family and kinship has often served as the site of resistance to slavery and racism. The feminist struggle to change the economic dependency of women on men has little meaning for black American and Caribbean women who are often the main breadwinners in their families. This, in turn, is a direct reflection of racist labour market practices. It was often easier for black women to find employment as domestics and cleaners, than for black men to find wage labour. Ironically, the very characteristics that distinguish black family forms from the patriarchal nuclear model have been pathologized in research on the family as generating delinquency and social breakdown within black culture.

A dominant theme within feminist theory is the exploitative character of relations of reproduction, the conflict between homemaker responsibilities and careers for women, and the struggles between women and men over the double shift. But these theories rarely acknowledge the importance of black women's domestic labour in mediating these contradictions for white women. It is black women who have commonly acted as domestics and caregivers to children in rich, white family homes, often at the expense of caring for their own children. Feminist literature has given little attention to the class relations between professional white women and the often nonwhite women who provide domestic labour. Nor has it widely addressed the racist character of such class relations, the humiliating condescension of white women towards their servants, and not uncommonly the threat of sexual exploitation that these servants experienced from white males in the houses where they worked. The sexuality of black women was not socially constructed within black families, as much as within their roles as domestic servants and labourers.

Black feminist writings also rail against the incipient racism and Eurocentrism of mainstream feminist theory directed towards Third World women generally. The cultural patterns of Western industrial societies are typically used as measures of progressive and liberated feminism, against which Third World women are characterized as backward and unliberated. Western feminist writings are replete with sweeping generalizations about the sexism of these societies in comparison with the supposedly more liberated West. One Native American feminist recalls her outrage at the blatant assumptions of sexism made by a white feminist student who was conducting research on Native American families (Moraga and Anzaldua 1981, 51). Third World women writers complain that the major concerns of local women on health, clean water, and agricultural credit, are totally neglected by Western feminist researchers intent on pursuing their own theoretical interests in exposing patriarchy.

The central focus of Carby's critique is not only that such research assumptions are misguided and implicitly racist, but also that they ignore the active role of European colonizers in many parts of the world in undermining the social, economic, and political status of indigenous women, imposing class and gender relations that were notably less egalitarian. The promotion of cash crops in Africa and Asia, combined with the virtually unquestioned assumptions that "farmers" were male, undermined women's traditional rights to land for subsistence farming and worsened their economic position relative to men. In societies where women traditionally wielded political authority, their status was systematically eroded. British colonizers in Nigeria, for example, subverted the indigenous Igbo political structures that accorded decision-making authority and economic power to women, replacing them with colonial structures that denied Igbo women any means of representation.

Mohawk women in Canada experienced a similar denial of their indigenous roles as elders and decision-makers within their communities. The British North American Act that defined Native Status for purposes of government and treaty rights took away the status of any Native woman who married a non-Native. It was not until 1985 that this Act was changed. Chipewyan women were also readily defined as beasts of burden by fur traders in Canada (Bourgeault 1989, 99). Like black women, the gendered identity of Native women was constructed by the colonizers in very different ways from how those same colonizers constructed white women. In conclusion, there is little evidence from colonial history to support any claims by white feminists that European cultural influences promoted the liberation of women in the former colonies.

The Canadian State and Gender-Ethnic-Class Formation

Canadian immigration policies are directly implicated in the construction of gendered ethnic-class relations within Canada. The immigration societies established in the nineteenth century specifically favoured the immigration of white, working-class girls from England to serve as domestics and wives in Canada, in order to preserve the white and Christian character of the dominant settler group (Ng 1988a, 8; Arat-Koc 1989, 45). Only as this source of cheap domestic labour dried up and demand for domestic servants escalated, have immigration policies shifted in favour of domestic servants from other ethnic groups. In the postwar period, the Department of Immigration in Canada became actively involved in the recruitment and control of domestic workers from the Caribbean (Caliste 1989; Arat-Koc 1989). Prior to 1962, domestic service constituted one of the few ways by which black women from the Caribbean could enter Canada. The discriminatory conditions under which they were admitted can readily be described as institutionalized racism. Restrictions were openly supported on the grounds that black women could not be assimilated and were not a "permanent asset" to Canada. In an effort to meet the insatiable demand for domestics in Canada, the Domestic Worker Program was instituted in 1955 with the aim of importing domestic workers from the Caribbean. Under this scheme, only single women of good health, between eighteen and forty years of age, and with no children, were allowed into Canada as landed immigrants on

442 ☒ TRADITIONAL THEORY UNDER ATTACK

condition that they would spend at least one year as domestic servants before choosing other types of work (Arat-Koc 1989, 45–46). In their desperation to find employment, women with children were forced to conceal these children and leave them behind with relatives. By the mid-1960s, roughly 1000 women a year were entering Canada under this scheme, but conditions of domestic service were so miserable that most of them sought other work as soon as they fulfilled their one-year obligation. To solve this problem the Canadian government started issuing temporary work permits in 1973 that only allowed these workers to remain in Canada for a specified period of time, doing a specific type of work, for a specific employer. They needed special permission from immigration authorities to change employers, and could not leave domestic service without also leaving Canada. As foreign workers with only visitor status, these women are denied basic rights of citizenship. They have the status only of bonded labour. Canada Pension Plan and Unemployment Insurance contributions are deducted from their salaries even though they are expressly excluded from benefiting under such programs because of their temporary status. In November 1981, changes in the Temporary Employment Authorization Program enabled foreign domestics who have worked in Canada continuously for two years to apply for landed immigrant status without leaving the country. But this gives no guarantee that landed immigrant status will be granted. They have to demonstrate a "potential for self-sufficiency." But domestic skills are accorded only very few points on official measures of vocational preparation, and ironically, given the demand for domestic workers, they receive only low points in the Occupational Demand Category (Arat-Koc 1989, 49). Women who do qualify for landed immigrant status are eligible to sponsor relatives. Those women who concealed the fact that they had children in order to get jobs under the restrictive legislation, however, risk being deported on the grounds that they falsified their initial immigration documents (Caliste 1989, 145). These immigration policies have worked to create in Canada's major cities a gender-ethnic-class of poor black women trapped in low-paid employment.

At the other end of the vertical mosaic, a very different gender-ethnic-class is emerging. Wives and children of Hong Kong Chinese businessmen have set up domicile in Canada with the intent of qualifying for Canadian citizenship after a three-year period. These wives can subsequently ensure the right of entry of their husbands into Canada when ownership of Hong Kong reverts to Communist China in 1997. Meanwhile, these husbands can continue to run their businesses in Hong Kong where they can routinely expect to earn huge profits on their investments (Smart 1988). A new class of ultra-rich Chinese women is thus slowly emerging in large Canadian cities.

The immigration category under which many women enter Canada, especially from the Third World, is sponsored or family class. These women enter as the dependants of men who already have landed immigrant status in Canada. Ng reports that women are frequently classified as family class even when they have been in the paid labour force in their home countries (1988b, 16). The husband is classified as the wage earner with the wife as his dependant. Asian women seeking to enter Britain as the wives or brides of residents have reported deeply offensive questioning by British Embassy staff about their wedding night, and vaginal examinations, ostensibly to prove their marital status (Parmar 1982, 245).

This pattern where males are considered the primary immigrants and females their dependants is particularly pronounced with respect to the admission of refugees. A report on refugees by the National Action Committee on the Status of Women (NAC) (1987, 1) estimates that, during the 1980s, women and children constituted 75 to 80 percent of all refugees and displaced persons in different parts of the world. Women flee their home countries for many of the same reasons as men, but they also face additional persecution as women. During wartime, many are widowed and must support their children alone. While fleeing from their homes or surviving in refugee camps, women are also particularly vulnerable to sexual abuse, especially when they do not have the protection of a man. Yet the outstanding feature of Canadian refugee applications is that about 80 percent of them are made by men (National Action Committee on the Status of Women 1987, 2). Most women "refugees" in Canada are sponsored by husbands who have made a previous successful refugee claim. Very few female refugees receive asylum in Canada without the agency of a husband. This means that most of the women who are here are members of a relatively small proportion of family units that survive refugee-creating situations intact.

Women with children who wish to claim refugee status face many barriers. It is often extremely difficult for them to travel in order to get to designated centres in their home countries where they might file a claim for refugee status. The life experiences that drive women to flee their homeland may also not fit the formal criteria for establishing refugee claims, which are typically written with men in mind. A brief to the Canadian Government by NAC (1987b, 3) questions whether an Asian woman running away from an arranged marriage would be considered to have a legitimate claim of persecution, even when the woman feared being beaten or burned to death for failing to provide an adequate dowry. The NAC brief cited the case of an Islamic woman persecuted for showing too much hair in public. Islamic authorities fixed a veil to her head with thumbtacks, whipped her, and threatened that she would be raped and shot if she were to be seen unsuitably dressed again. Would such a woman or multiple other women who fear punishment for disobeying dress codes be seen as legitimate refugee claimants by Canadian immigration officials? Are such women being persecuted for the nonviolent expression of political opinions, or would their dissent be interpreted as personal rather than political?

NAC lobbied the federal government to recognize persecution based on sex as just cause for a refugee claim and to agree to accept more female-headed families from refugee camps. In 1988, the Canadian government responded by selecting twenty-five such women, a minuscule proportion of all refugees accepted. For practical purposes, the working definition of *immigrant* and *refugee* is male, with women qualifying only as their sponsored dependants.

The legal designation of "sponsored immigrant" has significant consequences for the treatment women receive once they arrive in Canada. Sponsored immigrants are not entitled to social assistance and they can be deported if they are deemed to be a financial burden on the Canadian state. This policy forces many immigrant women into complete dependence on their male sponsors and contributes to their isolation in sometimes unpleasant and even abusive family situations (Wilson 1978; Ng 1988b, 17). Lack of access to government-subsidized language and job-training programs also pressures many immigrant women into low-paid and marginal employment. A combination of discriminatory immigration policies,

the vested economic and political interests that support such policies, and the way they are implemented over time, produces the gendered ethnic-class character of the Canadian vertical mosaic.

Institutional Ethnography: The Accomplishment of Gender-Ethnic-Class

Technically, the term *immigrant women* refers to all women who have landed immigrant status in Canada, and they may be located anywhere in the occupational hierarchy from professional to unskilled service work. The image that typically comes to mind is not that of an educated, English-speaking professional, but rather a member of a visible minority group, usually from the Third World, who works as an office cleaner or in a garment factory. The term *immigrant woman* is socially constituted in terms of labour-market relations (Ng 1988b, 15). An English-speaking, professional woman from India may never feel like a stranger in Canada, while others who have been here fifty years still feel like immigrants.

Ng's (1986; 1988b) study of a nonprofit employment agency set up to help immigrant women, reveals some of the practices through which the location of visible minority women in the labour force comes about. The agency applied for and received government funding to carry out three activities: to assist immigrant women find jobs; to act as agents for employers looking for workers; and to socialize women as to what was expected of them.

The government funding contract set rigid boundaries defining whom the agency could help and how they were to act. The agency had originally intended to help all immigrant women, but the funding contract specified counsellors for West Indian-, Chinese-, Italian-, and Spanish-speaking people. Later, when the agency asked for additional counsellors to serve Vietnamese, Portuguese, and East Indian women, the request was not granted. Formal membership in the designated ethnic group thus became a decisive factor in whether assistance would be granted.

Funding regulations also required detailed statistics on job placements, to be recorded in special forms. Counselling interviews initially intended to help immigrant women with their problems, became subordinated to the necessity of filling in the forms. All other matters became secondary.

Agency workers were also under pressure to display a high ratio of job placements to applicants, in order to qualify for continuing funding. Hence, they had to have a steady flow of job openings, which necessitated forming a stable network of contacts with employers most likely to hire immigrant women. These were typically large establishments like office cleaning companies and garment factories that paid minimum wages for repetitive, low-skilled work, precisely the jobs stereotypically associated with "immigrant women."

Lastly, agency workers had to keep their placement numbers high by talking their women clients into taking these jobs, and instructing them in such matters as what to say in job interviews, and the importance of punctuality, cleanliness, and the like. The agency had intended to help immigrant women, but it ended up functioning as an agency of the state, managing the segregated labour market in ways that perpetuated the low status of these women (Ng 1988b, 12).

The stereotype of "ethnic" housewives as confused and incompetent women can similarly be understood as arising from organized practices within Canada, rather than from the inherent characteristics of immigrant women themselves (Ng 1981). Since housework is not defined as a job, immigrant housewives are accorded the status of dependants. Thus, they do not qualify for language and job training provided for immigrant breadwinners. Children of immigrants are required to go to school in Canada, but adults can only attend community college programs, for which they must pay fees. Housewives do not earn money and so can only go with the approval and financial support of husbands.

If these women were treated differently when they arrived in Canada, they would not display the kind of behaviour viewed as characteristic of them as types of women. These characteristics are not attributes of the women themselves, but are effects of the treatment they receive. A volunteer agency funded with a different set of criteria, and with different application forms to fill in, could produce a very different reality. One could imagine agencies geared to matching immigrant women with counsellors whose job it would be to teach them basic language, shopping, bus-riding, and car-driving skills. Such coping mechanisms do not imply the total cultural assimilation of

basic beliefs and sentiments envisioned in the functionalist model, but merely a practical working knowledge of how the society of the locality in which they live is organized. This itself would alter their characteristics as commodities within the labour force. They would no longer have the credentials typical of workers destined as office cleaners. Their credentials, and hence their potential location within the labour market, would be transformed.

Common-Sense Racism

Images of West Indian and Asian women that are widely held in both North American and British societies reflect the narrow range of occupations in which such women are concentrated, and at the same time work to perpetuate and to justify such segregated roles. West Indian women are held to be "temperamentally well suited" to domestic service because they are "fond of children" and "know their place" (Caliste 1989, 135). Asian women, on the other hand, are held to be docile, passive, and compliant, to have legendary manual dexterity. They are ideally suited to work in garment factories (Parmar 1982, 260). Parmar describes how such myths are manipulated by Asian governments to attract foreign investment. They are also manipulated by employers to control Asian women employees.

Sweeping generalizations about the supposed cultural norms of Asian women are used to explain and to justify their subordinate status within British society. They are conceptualized as homebound, their lives limited to the kitchen, the children, their religious rituals, and their emotional dependence on their husbands (Parmar 1982, 250). School counsellors consider it a waste of time to encourage Asian girls toward careers and withhold information they routinely give to white girls. British employers play up cultural notions about Asian women's reticence before male strangers both to harass and humiliate them, and to threaten them with public embarrassment if they should contemplate going on strike or walking a picket line (Parmar 1982, 258–61).

Parmar lays much of the blame for these cultural stereotypes on sociological accounts. These accounts, she suggests, promote intolerable overgeneralizations about West Indian and Asian women and advocate cultural explanations for the disadvantaged situation of such women in Western societies, particularly the focus on observance of *purdah* among Hindu and Muslim women. The cultural expectations that women will veil their faces, not speak before male strangers, and remain within their homes, provides at best a superficial excuse for the realities of gendered ethnic-class relations. It ignores the structured barriers to employment opportunities that such women face. As we saw in chapter 10 on development, predictions based on the normative expectations of the culture of purdah proved irrelevant when women in rural India were given real opportunities for paid employment. Assertions about the natural passivity of Asian women ignore the long history of Asian women's active involvement in political resistance and independence struggles in colonized countries. Such assertions also ignore the empowering and supportive aspects of women's networks, conceptualizing them only in negative terms. Generalizations about domesticity as a cultural value ignore the fear generated by racist attacks on Asian women in the streets of Britain. In short, the sociological and anthropological accounts of the lives of women of colour that focus on the overarching notion of culture function as ideology. They become a means not to know and not to see the reality of the situation of women of colour in Western societies.

These ideological discourses feed into the everyday common-sense racism that can be so humiliating to women of colour—the commonplace assumptions that a black woman living in a middle-class neighbourhood must be the maid, or that a black woman in a clothing store may be a thief because she probably cannot afford good clothes (Brown 1977). The pervasiveness of such petty slights is what motivates Brown to claim that racism in Canada is worse than in the United States. She has come to expect that Canadian customs officers will search her baggage with far greater frequency than the baggage of her white friends, and will routinely ask her to prove that the battered camera she carries was actually bought in Toronto. What she finds hardest to take is how white Canadian friends invariably deny that racism exists in Canada, and insist that dozens of such incidents are merely isolated cases to which she is overreacting.

To be poor, black, and a woman in Western societies, is to risk such humiliating encounters on a routine basis. Each incident by itself may perhaps be minor, but cumulatively they can be deeply hurtful to one's sense of self and self-esteem. Women of colour who also struggle against homophobia describe a special sense of victimization and exclusion. A collection of letters and stories by black lesbians starkly convey the hurt, humiliation, bitterness, and sometimes raging anger of these women (Moraga and Anzaldua 1981). For many of these writers, the failure of mainstream feminist theory and practice of the late 1970s to address their issues in an inclusive way was a particularly bitter disappointment.

In conclusion, a central issue within contemporary feminist theory is how to address issues of ethnicity and race relations within a broader analysis of patriarchal relations (Gagnier 1990, 23–24). This calls for a shift in feminist theory away from essentialist conceptions of women and sisterhood implied in earlier formulations of "the standpoint of women," to incorporate a recognition of the diversity of women's experiences, and the historically specific and contingent meaning of gender identity. But at the same time, Gagnier insists, feminist theory cannot lose sight of the larger structural patterns of patriarchy within which the local and particular experiences of women are embedded.

Suggested Reading

The book by Anthony Richmond, *Immigration and Ethnic Conflict* (1988), provides an overview of theoretical and practical issues concerned with ethnic relations in advanced industrial societies. He adopts a mainly structural functionalist approach to the analysis of structural change and adaptation associated with migration and problems of racism and multiculturalism. The book draws upon Richmond's own extensive survey research on ethnic groups and assimilation in Canada.

The study by Edward N. Herberg, *Ethnic Groups in Canada: Adaptations and Transitions* (1989), provides comprehensive statistical data on the multi-ethnic character of Canada. Herberg draws extensively on Statistics Canada census reports from 1871 to 1981 and other published survey research.

The article by John Porter, "Ethnic Pluralism in Canadian Perspective" (1979a), gives an overview of the traditional liberal functionalist perspective on ethnicity. He includes a discussion of the vertical mosaic. Porter also explores the pros and cons of bilingualism and biculturalism from a functionalist perspective.

For a short history of racism in Canada, see D.G. Hill and M. Schiff, *Human Rights in Canada: A Focus on Racism*, 2nd ed. (1986). This booklet documents the often discriminatory and exploitative treatment of racial and ethnic minorities in Canada and the slow progress toward establishing a national policy on human rights.

The article by D. Baker, "Ethnicity, Development and Power: Canada in Comparative Perspective" (1977), provides historical evidence of the link between patterns of immigration in Canada and labour force requirements of the dominant group.

Peter Li's chapter entitled "Race and Ethnicity" in the text that he edited, *Race and Ethnic Relations in Canada* (1990), presents a Marxist analysis of minority group relations that also shifts the focus towards a social con-structionist form of Marxist analysis, rather than traditional structuralist Marxism.

The article by Eller and Coughlan, "The Poverty of Primordialism" (1993) presents a complex but well-argued case for the interpretation of ethnic groups as social constructions rather than primordial givens. Alf Hornborg's article, "Environmentalism, Ethnicity, and Sacred Places" (1994), provides an excellent case study of Mi'kmaq cultural identity formation during a confrontation over a proposal to establish a gravel pit on a mountain that has sacred properties.

The article by Roxana Ng, "The Social Construction of Immigrant Women in Canada" (1986), provides an excellent analysis of the experiences of immigrant women from the social constructionist perspective. Ng shows how many of the characteristics associated with immigrant women cannot be adequately understood as attributes of the women themselves. They are effects of how they are treated in Canada. The collection of articles in the text *Race, Class, Gender: Bonds and Barriers* edited by Jesse Vorst (1989) contains both powerful critiques of feminist analysis of race and ethnic relations, and proposals for more effective scholarship.

Questions

1. What basic premise of functionalist theory suggests that ethnic pluralism is likely to result in social instability and conflict?

2. In Pryor's view, what are the fundamental problems that makes Statistics Canada measures of ethnic diversity so difficult?

3. What historical practices by the British colonial government are directly implicated in the current impoverished conditions on many Native reservations?

4. How are the historical patterns of class relations within Quebec implicated in separatism?

5. According to classical Marxist theory, how might racial tensions and hostilities among workers be functional for capitalism?

6. What is the basic assumption behind the argument that concepts such as *ethnicity* and *ethnic groups* should be thought of as verbs rather than as nouns?

7. In what sense can politics be said to produce ethnic groups rather than ethnicity producing political groups?

8. In constructionist theory, how is concern with the authenticity of ethnic group traditions challenged as theoretically flawed?

9. How does the experience of black women challenge central notions of patriarchy in mainstream feminist theory?

10. In what ways can Canada's policies with respect to refugees be characterized as gendered or sexist?

VII

The Sociology of Knowledge

CHAPTER 18

The Microsociology of Everyday Life

by Peter A.D. Weeks

In his review essay entitled "On the Microfoundations of Macrosociology," Randall Collins (1981) offers the following definitions for two extremes of sociological concern. **Macrosociology** comprises "the analysis of large-scale and long-term social processes, often treated as self-subsistent entities such as 'state,' 'culture,' and 'society.'" **Microsociology** comprises "the detailed analysis of what people do, say, and think in the actual flow of momentary experience." Collins advocates a **microtranslation strategy**, which shows how macrosocial structures can be understood as patterns of repetitive micro-interactions. Terms such as *state* or *class* are a kind of shorthand. He argues that, strictly speaking, there is no such thing as a state, an economy, a culture, a social class. There are only collections of individual people acting in microsituations. Microsituations make up the empirical basis of all other macrosocial structures. Researchers never leave their own microsituations. They compile summaries of microsituations by using a series of coding and translating procedures from which they produce macro-analytical constructs (Collins 1981, 988–89).

Until recently, microsociology received little attention because it fell outside the explanatory frameworks of traditional functionalist and Marxist perspectives. Microlevel interactions were not viewed as causally significant, but only as a reflection of broader social structures. Interpretive perspectives had to battle for recognition. By the 1990s, however, monographs and journal articles that use ethnomethodology and social constructionist analysis are appearing with increasing frequency across all the subfields of sociology. There is also a noticeable shift away from the descriptive, role-theory orientation of symbolic interactionism towards the more detailed ethnomethodological study of the practices by which people produce and sustain a sense of meaning.

The feminist perspective in sociology has also expanded and diversified during roughly the same time period as ethnomethodology. It has strong roots in Marxism, but also a close affinity with ethnomethodology and social constructionist analysis. Feminist analysis draws attention to the intimate politics of personal interactions between women and men through which the relations of patriarchy are expressed and reproduced.

This chapter presents an overview of diverse approaches to the microsociology of everyday life, with the main emphasis on ethnomethodology. Examples from research in the functionalist and Marxist traditions show how micro-experiences as diverse as professional-client relations or work in restaurants can be explained as reflections of the broader structures in which they play a part. We then switch to the meticulously detailed and critical work of **radical microsociology**. The chapter concludes with selected examples from feminist research to show how this heightened awareness of the social construction of reality can be used to explore how the relations of patriarchy are accomplished in intimate personal behaviour.

Microsociology from the Functionalist Perspective

David Orenstein (1985, 106) illustrates the functionalist approach with an example from his personal experience as a neophyte sociology instructor. He was only twenty-one at the time and he feared that students, many of them close to his own age, might not respect him. He tried the following experiment. He dressed in denims and a casual shirt, arrived early for his first lecture period, and sat with the students for a few minutes. Students started talking and commenting on the lateness of the professor. Then Orenstein got up, went to the front, wrote his name on the board, faced the class, and spread out his lecture notes. There was an immediate transformation in the behaviour of the students. They stopped talking in mid-sentence, faced the front of the class, and got their pens ready. To an ignorant onlooker it might have appeared that they had rudely stopped talking, turned their backs on each other, and silently stared at this young man in jeans. Why? Were they rude? Was he strange? Were his clothes or his behaviour abnormal? No. The socio-

logical explanation, says Orenstein, is that all the students in the class knew the culturally shared rules for behaviour in a given situation. They knew what to expect and how to act because they had been socialized into North American society and so had shared knowledge of many different social situations and the appropriate behaviours in each. They could differentiate between such situations as cafeteria, bar, classroom, dancehall, library, or grocery store, and alter their behaviour to fit the appropriate expectations.

Orenstein's introductory text is devoted almost exclusively to an elaboration of the process of socialization, the ways in which we learn cultural roles. He refers to the values governing what we should or should not do in different situations as **prescriptive** and **proscriptive norms** respectively. He notes that we also learn emotional behaviour; that is, what to feel and when to feel it. We learn that it is not acceptable to cheer at funerals or to get too ecstatic over an A grade if our friend has done badly. Even the expression of romantic love is learned behaviour. A teenage girl is expected to have a boyfriend. On the other hand, if a girl and boy, aged thirteen and fourteen, were to express undying love for each other and commit suicide if this love were thwarted, we would consider them emotionally disturbed, unless, of course, we were reading *Romeo and Juliet*.

Orenstein's analysis of micro-events in terms of learned expectations for appropriate role behaviour summarizes the dominant American tradition in sociology. In principle, every situation comprises roles with predefined expectations that people need to know in order to participate. These expectations include exactly what one has a right to ask of other people, how to judge their performance, who is permitted to play what roles, and whether or not it is appropriate to express emotions toward others in the situation.

Work roles are particularly well-defined because work situations typically entail interaction between a number of specialized roles, oriented to the achievement of specified broader functions. Talcott Parsons' (1951, 454–79) analysis of professional-client interaction, particularly that between medical doctor and patient, in many respects sets the standard for such research. In the process of training, a physician learns not only the technical knowledge of medicine, but also a set of attitudes and rules that governs professional interaction with others in related roles as patients, colleagues, nurses, and staff. Above all, doctors must learn to be neutral and objective and to avoid emotional attachment to patients. They must also learn that they are expected to put the welfare of patients above their own interests. Decisions about surgery must be based solely on a medical assessment of the patient's conditions and not on a doctor's desire to finance a vacation in the Caribbean.

Clear guidelines establish the limits of any relationship between doctor and patient. Parsons argues that such guidelines or norms are functional, because they facilitate the physician's penetration into the personal affairs of the patient, which is essential for effective treatment, while protecting the patient from exploitation. When people are sick, they are particularly vulnerable to emotional, sexual, and financial manipulation. They must expose private parts of their bodies and divulge information that is potentially damaging. The rules governing the practice of medicine protect the patient from exploitation and also protect the doctor from excessive or inappropriate demands from the sick person.

The doctor-patient relation shows how interaction between two people in the privacy of an office is structured in precise detail by the predefined norms of behaviour for persons playing the roles. Each person enters the setting with clear and mutually shared expectations as to how each is supposed to behave vis-à-vis the other. Deviations will be subject to sanctions, including the threat of formal reprimand for professional misconduct. These predefined rules for behaviour can be directly explained as necessary for the smooth and adequate functioning of the health-care system. Adjacent roles of nurse, receptionist, orderly, and so on, can be analysed in similar ways to build up a picture of the total functioning system.

William Foote Whyte's pioneering study, *Human Relations in the Restaurant Industry* (1948), analyses the micro-interactions between people in all the different roles that make up the functioning system of a restaurant. Whyte begins his study with a description of the functions of waitress, dining-room manager, kitchen worker, and service-pantry worker, beginning well before the restaurant opens its doors to customers. We learn the functional **prerequisites** of the restaurant system: "the food must move, and it must move in the right time." Delays must be avoided,

plates must be clean, customers must be served what they ordered, and so on. We also see how the restaurant business functions to handle feeding and food ceremonials in complex industrial society. The ongoing development of civilization, Whyte argues, requires a corresponding growth and development of the restaurant industry. Centralized means of mass feeding play an important role in keeping the system working when industrialization requires that most people work in factories or offices, often located far from their homes. Indeed, without the restaurant industry, Whyte (1948, 9) argues, our industrial society would cease to function.

Within this functional setting, Whyte describes the human structure of the restaurant, the patterned interactions between people of different statuses, co-ordinated so as to achieve the integration of production with service. Typical of a functionalist approach, he views the relationships between customer and waitress, waitress and supervisor, waitress and service-pantry worker, as interdependent parts of a social system, such that changes in any one part lead to compensatory changes in other areas. The seemingly idiosyncratic behaviours of individuals are explained as examples of threats to the kitchen hierarchy. Occasional frictions are used to illustrate the operation of the supply system—the continual flow of food from pantry through to kitchen workers to waitresses and finally to diners—and the necessity of appropriate role performance by everyone in the supply train. Episodes when waitresses burst into tears are explained in reference to role strains between them and kitchen staff when the supply system is under pressure. The use of written orders placed on spindles facilitates smoother interaction between the two status groups of waitresses bringing orders and countermen filling them. This is particularly important since the situation of females giving orders to males potentially violates wider expectations of interaction norms according to which males are dominant and females subordinate.

Whyte's study gives us an intimate account of the emotional ups and downs of people interacting in the different roles that make up a restaurant. But the overarching interest is in how people are moulded into the roles that they play within the social system. Those who cannot make the necessary adjustments, like bad actors in a play, are required to leave the scene.

The Limitations of Functionalist Analysis

The central problem with the functionalist approach to microsociology is that it shifts the active agency in social life from living people to inanimate and abstract structures. Functionalists run the risk of **reifying** society when they conceive of social rules as existing outside and above ongoing human activity and what people themselves do. People appear as "cultural dopes," programmed to play their roles as if they were puppets, with social structures pulling the strings. It may be that people often do feel trapped and manipulated in their personal lives, but we still need to explain how these feelings come about. As we will see, theorists who adopt the interpretive perspective in sociology argue that functionalism provides only a descriptive account of everyday experience. It does not explain it.

It is through continual processes of mutually negotiating the sense of what is happening now, and what will happen next, that people produce the patterns that functionalists subsequently observe as a particular role.

Microsociology in the Political Economy Tradition

Analysis of micro-experiences from the structuralist Marxist or political economy perspective adopts a more explicitly top-down approach than even functionalist theory. The Marxist perspective rejects the basic assumption of functionalism that social systems can be understood by reference to normative consensus, or shared expectations governing the performance of predefined roles. Important explanatory variables are found at the macrostructural level of the capitalist system as a whole. Production for profit, private ownership of the means of production, dependent wage labour, exploitation, and class conflict are the key elements in this system. What happens at the microlevel of interpersonal interaction, including the expressed norms and values of participants, reflects their class position in this system of production. Microlevel interactions are effects, not causes, of how the system works.

The debate over the culture of poverty thesis, treated more fully in chapter 10, provides a classic example of the difference between functionalist and Marxist approaches to microsociology. Functionalists direct attention to the attitudes and values of poor people to account for why they are trapped in the roles they play. Such attitudes include: rejecting the value of hard work as a means to getting ahead; spending money or going into debt to get what they want rather than saving for it; seeing whatever happens to themselves or others as based on luck or cheating rather than effort; an inability to imagine themselves in different roles; a tendency to distrust the motives of everyone outside immediate family networks; and a "handout mentality," in which they look to others to solve their problems. In more technical terms, this pattern of values can be described as lack of achievement motivation, limited aspirations, fatalism, lack of **deferred gratification**, familism, low empathy, and dependence on and hostility to authority. Such values are appropriate for only the most menial jobs, which have minimal responsibilities and low wages.

In Marxist theory, however, the cause and effect relation between values and social position is reversed. Exploitative relations of capitalism give rise to an underclass of chronically unemployed or underemployed people, with incomes barely meeting subsistence needs. People trapped in the bottom social class develop distinctive values as a means of coping with a reality in which they are denied genuine opportunities to better themselves. Their experience of being cheated and exploited generates their distrust and hostility toward those who have power. A significant transformation in the structure of opportunities open to them is a necessary precondition for changing these adaptive reactions. For Marxist theorists, there seems little point in researching how poor people think or behave. What matters is to research how the structures of capitalism operate to produce and perpetuate the poverty class.

The limited research that has addressed microexperiences from the perspective of political economy has typically sought to demonstrate how class position and class relations structure personal lives. Archibald (1978) reviews much of this material to show how working-class people cope with and adjust to **alienation**; that is, to the experience of being powerless to control the conditions of their working lives and of being trapped in meaningless and humiliating jobs. Significantly, Archibald entitles his book *Social Psychology as Political Economy*, suggesting that he views this level of analysis as more appropriate for the discipline of psychology than sociology. He gives descriptions of people coping with the low self-esteem and misery that come from doing mindlessly boring and routine jobs. The symptoms of reactive depression—daydreaming, withdrawal, and learned helplessness—often experienced by such workers reflect in many respects the symptoms associated with mental illness or schizophrenia (Archibald 1978, 178).

The Limitations of Political Economy Analysis

Traditional political economy theory is even more dependent than functionalism on explanations of structures being the active agents in human behaviour. Archibald (1985, 61–62) makes this very clear when he insists that adequate causal explanations in sociology must be at the level of macrostructures because individuals do not act as "free agents." He argues that Marx himself referred to individuals merely as dependants or accessories of their collectivities or class position, and even as "herd animals." Individuals, suggests Archibald, generally do not think or act differently from other members of their class. The few who do are by definition anomalies and are largely irrelevant to our understanding of broader social processes and social change. Hence, Archibald argues strongly for the principle of **methodological holism** rather than **methodological individualism**. The principle of methodological holism asserts that social experiences need to be explained in terms of forces that operate at the level of the social system as a whole.

It is important to note that we are painting this picture with a broad brush. Not all theorists who identify themselves with the Marxist tradition feel comfortable with this conclusion. The Marxist historian E.P. Thompson (1963) has argued that, while macrostructures such as the system of economic production set the context in which people experience their lives, reference to such structures is not sufficient to explain the formation of classes. For Thompson, classes are actively produced by working people through the processes of subjective experience, conflict, and struggle, which bring them into active relations with oth-

ers. His own historical research seeks to understand, through the study of ongoing relations between people, how classes arose. More traditional Marxist critics, however, accuse Thompson of reducing objective structural conditions and economic forces to the level of **psychologism**, attempting to explain them in terms of subjective personal experiences and individual choices and attitudes (Wood 1982, 64). Thompson denies this, arguing that he sees the patterns of relations between people, which arise in their struggle for shares of material goods, as genuinely social forces, albeit at the microsociological level.

The central problem with the critique of Thompson's analysis as psychologism is that it runs the same risk of reifying society that we encounter with respect to functionalism. People appear as puppets while inanimate structures appear as the agents pulling the strings. Wood (1982, 65) points out the irony that critics of Thompson, who accuse him of trying to reduce history to the level of personal experiences and choices, end up talking about macrostructures as if they were people. The *working class* does things. *It* has interests. *It* sometimes fails to understand what its true interests are. Notions of **subjectivism** and **voluntarism** seem to have simply shifted upwards to the aggregate level of the working class, as if "it" were some living entity with subjective feelings and capable of voluntary choices.

In summary, traditional political economy theory focusses on class relations rather than typical role expectations to explain the micro-experiences of everyday life. But it generally shares with functionalism the common assumption that critical explanatory mechanisms cannot be found at the level of mundane interactions. Such mechanisms have to be sought in the broader macrostructures of the social system as a whole. It is this fundamental assumption that is challenged by interpretive theory.

Microsociology from the Interpretive Perspective

Interpretive theory shifts the focus of explanation from macrostructures to micro-interactions. This approach developed primarily out of dissatisfaction with functionalism, particularly with the image of people as programmed puppets obedient to pre-determined role expectations.

Critics of functionalism suggest that people normally operate with very little conscious awareness of their roles. They tend to take a great deal for granted, performing their routines without having to call to mind at each point what norms they should be following. Sometimes people are aware of the rules, and they attempt to conform to them but, at the same time, they try to indicate their lack of commitment to, perhaps even their disdain for, the role they are playing. This is what Erving Goffman (1961b) calls **role distancing**. Whether committed or cynical, individuals on many occasions improvise their performances, attempting to cope with uncertainty about what is going on, with disagreements about what should be happening, and with competing expectations of their various role partners.

It is too simplistic to try to account for smooth interaction in terms of learned role expectations. A great deal of work—improvising, joking, interpreting, second guessing, and manipulating—must go on for any particular performance to be carried off. What we need to study in any given situation, therefore, is precisely how people collectively accomplish the work of creating and sustaining a particular definition of the situation, so that they perceive each other to be playing a specific role rather than some other possible one.

Emerson's (1970) research on gynaecological examinations illustrates in detail the work that goes into maintaining doctor-patient relations. In Parsons' account, described earlier, the rules seem nonproblematic; the doctor should be emotionally detached, altruistic, and committed to viewing illness in an objective way. Emerson, however, asks how such abstract rules are actually practised. She argues that maintenance of the definition of the situation of a gynaecological examination requires much effort and skill on the part of the doctor and nurse to guide the patient through this precarious scene. In theory, doctors should be able to conduct gynaecological check-ups in the same matter-of-fact manner that they would carry out an examination of the ear. But in the actual microsituation, this is not possible.

Emerson argues that the situation involves several role definitions simultaneously, and they each have to be managed if the encounter is to work. From a purely medical perspective, the woman is merely a gynaecological specimen. But she is also a woman who is striving to retain her personal dignity while having her sexual parts penetrated by metal instruments. If her emotional stress is not attended to, she may become so physically tense that it will be impossible to conduct the examination without causing considerable pain. If pain is added to humiliation, the "specimen" may get up and leave the office.

The woman cannot be treated merely as a specimen. But the sexual aspects of the encounter cannot have prominence either, for this would also jeopardize the exam. It is the task of the doctor, with the active assistance of the nurse, to balance the various interacting roles. These people have to try to reassure the woman that her personhood and her sexuality are being respected and that her embarrassment is quite normal. She must be reassured that, while she is not regarded as a specimen, she is being treated as one in the sense that she is being examined and not sexually violated. These different levels of meaning are active at the same time, and the balance between treating the woman as a medical specimen and as a person is not struck once and for all. Rather, "it is created anew at every moment." It can, and sometimes does, go wrong. In 1988, fourteen women complained to the Nova Scotia Medical Board that a particular gynaecologist had handled them so roughly, and had made sufficiently inappropriate comments, that they had come to feel they were being sexually assaulted rather than examined. The review board's response to the complaints was that there was a communication problem between the doctor and the women (CBC Radio, "Maritime Magazine," 18 Sept. 1988).

Seen from the interpretive perspective, functionalists fail to link their macroscopic concepts of functioning systems to the detailed examination of mundane interaction. They reify society; that is, they treat social rules as if they existed as factual entities outside of human activity. Interpretive theorists stress that we are constantly engaged in processes of interpretation, defining, and redefining the situation in which we find ourselves. We must constantly ask ourselves questions. Who am I to them? What are we doing together? In effect, we are actively engaged in the construction of reality.

Ethnomethodology

Interpretive perspectives explore how the variety of expectations concerning social behaviour are actively negotiated by participants. Ethnomethodology pushes the questioning still further. How does the notion of *role* itself arise? How do participants come to decide collectively that it is this role and not some other possible role that is being played at this particular time? How is it that sociologists as outside observers come to decide that a specific role is or ought to be going on at a particular moment in time?

Ethnomethodology focusses on how members of a given society or community use their common-sense knowledge and their **background understandings** to make sense to themselves, and to one another, of their activities, the situation they are in, and the wider social structure in which any particular activity is embedded. The complexities of the gynaecological examination described above can only occur if all the people present share basic background knowledge about what such an examination is. It is normally taken for granted, for example, that the patient knows more or less what is going to happen and what is expected of her. A routine ten-minute examination would take all day if the doctor had to explain to each patient why she had to go into the examination room, get undressed, lie on the table, place her feet in the stirrups, be examined in a particular way, and so on.

The distinctive approach of ethnomethodology becomes clearer when we contrast it with the reasoning involved in traditional sociological research. Typically, researchers interview participants in a situation to ask them what is happening, and then accept these accounts as valid explanations of what is indeed going on. Ethnomethodologists try to get behind the participants' accounts to find out what kind of reasoning the participants are using to come up with their accounts. The term *ethnomethodology* is derived from the Greek words *ethno* meaning people or members of a society, and *methodos* meaning way, and it refers to members' ways of making sense of the social world around them. Harold Garfinkel (1967, vii) offers the following definition:

> Ethnomethodological studies analyse everyday activities as members' methods for making those same activities visibly-rational-and-reportable-for-all-practical-purposes, i.e., "accountable" as organizations of commonplace everyday activities.

This definition is such a departure from traditional ways of thinking that it deserves further explanation. Garfinkel strings words together with hyphens because he wants to break our usual way of thinking. We are actually being asked to think backwards. The way most of us tend to think is that, first, some activity happens; second, we think about it and decide what is happening and what kind of practical relevance it might have; then, third, we form some account of it such that we can tell an observer "this is what is happening."

Garfinkel argues that the sequence actually works in reverse. It is the process of forming an account that actually produces for us the sense that something is happening. Otherwise nothing much would be happening, or at least nothing recognizable. This is a two-sided process. On the one hand we, as members of a society, have to be able to formulate accounts so that the vague blur of people milling around us becomes recognizable as persons involved in discrete activities. On the other hand, as members we have to know how to behave or to talk in ways that we can reasonably expect other members to recognize.

These are actually very complex processes, and we need a great deal of background understanding about our society or our community to accomplish them successfully. A deceptively simple example is that of a queue or service line-up. What are members' methods of producing a queue? How do people recognize or signal to each other that they are in a queue and are not just standing around? Perhaps people have simply been socialized to expect queues in certain places, and so they invoke common-sense understandings to recognize them. The notion of queue-forming is certainly more established in some cultures than others. Many a hapless British tourist in Canada has found this out after queuing expectantly to board a bus or train, only to be swept aside as the local people surge forward in a mass. However, even when the common-sense notion of queuing is shared, it is by no means obvious when and where queues do or do not exist. In crowded airports or shops, or in front of busy service counters, for example, people may be spread out sideways as well as in front of and behind each other. Yet, this may constitute a queue in that members are collectively aware of the ordering, of who is in front of whom, even when they are arranged in a bunch.

Ethnomethodologists study exactly how we organize the details of what we are doing to create and sustain our collective understanding that this is the distinctive kind of social order we call a queue. This does not mean that people always follow the rules of queuing when there is a line-up. But it does mean that failure to conform, as when someone pushes to the front, is recognizable by the people involved as a violation, and hence as requiring some explanation or **accountability**. Once people have formed the notion that what is going on is queuing, then just about any behaviour that seems consistent with this is likely to be considered accounted for. You assume, for example, that a man standing behind another in a line-up is himself queuing up. He might actually be lost, or spying on people, or even just standing around waiting to find out what other people are standing around for. But you are unlikely to question his motives, unless you are watching some kind of mystery thriller. However, any behaviour that does not conform to the behaviour of queuing immediately threatens our notion of what is going on, and so requires some account. We tend to search for or to demand some valid excuse that will confirm for us that, yes, this is a queue, but that person is not in it because of some particular reason. Once too many people seem not to be keeping in the proper order, our notion that this is a queue is likely to fall apart.

Ethnomethodologists focus on what they term **practical reasoning**, or the methods by which ordinary people, in their everyday affairs, mutually create and sustain their common-sense notions of what is going on. It is people's capacity to do this that makes it possible for sociologists to talk about the notion of **social structures**. It is pointless for sociologists to discuss roles and social structures as if their existence could be taken for granted, before they have understood how ordinary people manage to create and sustain these notions.

In going about our everyday lives, we generally do not reflect upon how we manage to accomplish activities like forming a queue. We tend to adopt what ethnomethodologists refer to as the **natural attitude**. We simply take it for granted that everyone knows how to do such things, unless they are severely mentally handicapped or have suddenly arrived in our milieu from a culture so totally different that we cannot expect them to share even our simplest common-sense understandings. Yet these understandings are absolutely essential if we are to maintain any sense of a meaningful social world in which we can participate. Ethnomethodologists therefore insist that sociologists, in order to study how society works, must suspend this natural attitude and reflect on precisely the processes that ordinary people take for granted. Roles need to be studied, not as social facts that are treated as given, but rather as processes or ongoing accomplishments that emerge through our everyday, practical reasoning.

In summary, ethnomethodology enquires into the methods whereby we, as members of a society or community, organize our activities so that we, as well as sociologists, come to recognize the patterns that we think of as social structures. By suspending the natural attitude and thus viewing ordinary social activities such as talking or queuing as if they were "anthropologically strange" or problematic, we can begin to explore the many taken-for-granted practices and rules for practical reasoning through which our world becomes socially constructed. As we will see, this kind of research strategy gives rise to a radically different conception of society and very different methods of studying it. Many of the concepts and the terms used in such research appear strange when first encountered. The reason is that we are being forced to think about processes that seem so mundane we are scarcely aware they exist.

The best way to get a feeling for this research is to get involved in it. In this chapter we review several ethnomethodological studies of how people accomplish everyday activities and what practical reasoning processes they use. These studies should help you to explore how your own everyday activities are accomplished.

Harold Garfinkel is the recognized founder and still a leading proponent of ethnomethodology as an approach to doing sociology. He completed his doctoral studies at Harvard University under leading structural functionalist Talcott Parsons. But Garfinkel became increasingly disillusioned with the functionalist approach. As we saw earlier in this chapter, functionalism seeks to explain social order from the top down in terms of a pre-existing common culture that defines our norms and social structures. Individuals learn this normative order through socialization and feel committed or pressured to conform to it. Garfinkel advocates a bottom-up approach that studies how people, in their practical everyday interactions, create or build up the patterns that we subsequently come to recognize as distinctive social structures and social activities. A classical statement of the principles of Garfinkel's approach, and his early experiments designed to explore mundane reasoning, are contained in his text *Studies in Ethnomethodology* (1967).

Background Understandings and Indexicality

Garfinkel developed his now famous technique of breaching experiments to explore how people create social order in everyday interaction. The ways in which order is produced are exposed by finding out what would disrupt given social scenes. Experimenters begin with the stable features of the scene and ask what can be done to make trouble.

One procedure for disrupting and thus exposing the practical reasoning that underlies social order is to demand that the meaning of common-sense remarks be explained. In the two examples given below (from Garfinkel 1967, 42–43), (S) refers to the subject trying to have a normal conversation; (E) refers to the experimenter or eth-nomethodologist requesting that the subject explain his or her commonplace remarks.

(S) Hi Ray. How is your girl friend feeling?
(E) What do you mean, "How is she feeling?" Do you mean physical or mental?
(S) I mean how is she feeling? What's the matter with you? (He looked peeved.)
(E) Nothing. Just explain a little clearer what do you mean?
(S) Skip it. How are your Med School applications coming?
(E) What do you mean, "How are they?"
(S) You know what I mean.
(E) I really don't.
(S) What's the matter with you? Are you sick?

On Friday night my husband and I were watching television. My husband remarked that he was tired. I asked, "How are you tired? Physically, mentally, or just bored?"

(S) I don't know, I guess physically mainly.
(E) You mean that your muscles ache or your bones?
(S) I guess so. Don't be so technical.

(After more watching.)

(S) All these old movies have the same kind of old iron bedstead in them.
(E) What do you mean? Do you mean all old movies, or some of them, or just the ones you have seen?
(S) What's the matter with you? You know what I mean.
(E) I wish you would be more specific.
(S) You know what I mean! Drop dead!

In both cases the subjects clearly expected that the experimenters would rely upon common background understandings to make sense of their utterances. Garfinkel suggests that such expectations are essential features of all spoken interaction. When the experimenters did not use their background understandings, the subjects almost immediately expressed anger and indignation. As Garfinkel expresses it, people feel they are morally entitled to have their talk treated as intelligible, and they react with swift and powerful sanctions when it is not.

Another set of experiments explores the **index-ical** or context-dependent character of conversations. When we talk, we invariably include only brief references to, or indications of, the context and subject matter. We expect other participants to fill in the rest—the background understandings that make talk possible. Garfinkel illustrated this by asking his students to take a scrap of a conversation in which they had participated and note in the left-hand column what had actually been said and in the right-hand column what they and their partners understood they were talking about. One such analysis is given in figure 18-1.

It is quickly apparent from the fragment of conversation in figure 18-1 that there were many matters that the partners understood but did not mention. These were the background understandings that both partners required in order to carry on a meaningful exchange. For example, the statement, "Dana succeeded in putting a penny in the parking meter," would hardly be intelligible without the background knowledge that Dana was a young child. Otherwise, we might surmise that Dana was a severely handicapped adult. Similarly, the reference to Dana being "picked up" only makes sense when we have the background understanding that Dana, as a young child, is too short to reach most parking meter slots. In another context, the reference to being picked up might have a totally different meaning, like getting into a vehicle that has stopped, going out on a date, or accepting an offer to go off somewhere, possibly for a sexual encounter.

Conversations are always indexical; their sense is always context-dependent. Actions and words can only briefly refer to the background understandings that participants in the conversation must invoke in order to understand what is being said. If every participant in every conversation insisted on having all elements of that conversation explicated, talk would be impossible.

Figure 18-1

The Indexical Nature of Conversation

Husband:	Dana succeeded in putting a penny in a parking meter today without being picked up.	This afternoon as I was bringing Dana, our four-year-old son, home from the nursery school, he succeeded in reaching high enough to put a penny in a parking meter when we parked in a meter parking zone, whereas before he always had to be picked up to reach that high.
Wife:	Did you take him to the record store?	Since he put a penny in a meter that means that you stopped while he was with you. I know that you stopped at the record store either on the way to get him or on the way back. Was it on the way back, so that he was with you or did you stop there on the way to get him and somewhere else on the way back?
Husband:	No, to the shoe repair shop.	No, I stopped at the record store on the way to get him and stopped at the shoe repair shop on the way home when he was with me.
Wife:	What for?	I know of one reason why you might have stopped at the shoe repair shop. Why did you in fact?
Husband:	I got some new shoe laces for my shoes.	As you will remember I broke a shoe lace on one of my brown oxfords the other day so I stopped to get some new laces.
Wife:	Your loafers need new heels badly.	Something else you could have gotten that I was thinking of. You could have taken in your black loafers which need heels badly. You'd better get them taken care of pretty soon.

Source: Garfinkel (1967).

The mix of background understandings required to carry on conversations is the stuff of which many cartoons and jokes are made. What strikes us as funny is the invoking of meanings and contexts other than the one that we know should be applied.

The recognition that ordinary interaction is indexical, its meaning dependent upon context and background understandings, means that no social event can ever be totally unambiguous. Ethnomethodology, however, starts with the observation that most social actions and communications have an orderly character. Members of a community are competent at selecting precisely those aspects of the relevant context required to make sense of the interaction. In the jargon of ethnomethodology, it is **members' competences** that make order possible. If someone says to you, "Mary is out to lunch," you generally know which Mary this refers to, and whether the intended meaning is that she has gone elsewhere to eat lunch or she is showing signs of mental incompetence. You may both grin at the statement to show that you know the alternative meanings, but you nonetheless know, and know in common, what the intended meaning is. The ability to invoke correct background understandings is part of what is involved in being recognized as part of a group. In this sense, meaning is not subjective, but *intersubjective*, or dependent upon and defined by shared background knowledge.

Indexicality has important implications for research methods in sociology, especially for survey research in which questionnaires are commonly used. Researchers gamble when they assume that respondents all invoke the same context and the same background understandings in

HERMAN

"It's not even on the map."

answering questions as the researchers intended. Respondents take a similar gamble when they assume the researchers will invoke the appropriate background understanding to know what they meant by their answers. We saw an example of this in chapter 3 when a white English woman

The indexicality of these doctors' shoptalk could affect a researcher's observations.

refused to answer questions about her relations with black and Asian immigrants living nearby. She feared that, in interpreting her remarks, researchers would invoke the background understanding of racial prejudice rather than the specific context, which she herself experienced, of sexual taunts and propositions from large groups of single men in adjacent houses.

A further implication of indexicality is that researchers who rely on observations to collect their data must first learn a great deal of insider knowledge before they can accurately interpret the meanings of actions. Observed interaction between insiders in an unfamiliar occupational setting, for example, may come across as largely incomprehensible **shoptalk** when one does not have the necessary background knowledge to interpret it correctly. More seriously, researchers in unfamiliar contexts may be guilty of imposing their own irrelevant or incorrect background understandings, and thus producing false accounts of what happened. We saw examples of this in chapter 3 when anthropologists with different theoretical backgrounds were able to produce markedly different accounts of life in ostensibly the same village setting.

The Documentary Method of Interpretation

The search for patterns in the vague flux of everyday interaction is a critical component of members' methods of making sense of what is going on around them. Garfinkel refers to this process of imposing patterns as the **documentary method of interpretation**. In our practical everyday reasoning, Garfinkel suggests, we assume that there is some underlying pattern. Hence we habitually search for such a pattern in any new situation. We know that activities and conversations are indexical, that surface appearances refer to background understandings that we are expected to know and to use in order to make sense of what is going on. Surface appearances provide clues to the underlying pattern. Once we deduce a pattern, we use it to interpret other details of ongoing activities as instances of that supposed pattern. As we noted in our earlier example, people standing around can be accounted for as queuing, which implies an underlying pattern of "first come first served, and newcomer stand at the back." Any actions that violate this expectation then call the assumed pattern of queuing into question, unless the violation can be accounted for in terms of permissible exceptions. This reasoning process is thus circular, continually moving between surface appearances and hypothesized underlying pattern. Each becomes defined and redefined in terms of the other.

Figure 18-2 gives a simple example of this **reflexive** process. When we notice such an element in a book, we almost automatically assume that it is not some random doodling that is on the page by accident. We assume it is a picture, and a picture of something. One possibility is that the pattern underlying the specific lines of the drawing might be a duck. With this in mind, we interpret the protuberances on the left as the bill and the small indentation on the right of the figure as irrelevant. But if we adopt the idea that the pattern is a rabbit, then the same features are interpreted differently. The features on the left are ears, and the small indentation on the right now has relevance as the rabbit's mouth. The same surface appearances can thus be seen as instances of totally different features, once a new underlying pattern comes to mind (Heritage 1984, 86–87). If you stare at the pattern long enough, you may be able to come up with other interpretations that would assign yet other meanings to the surface appearances. There is also the possibility that the lines are nothing but random doodling and have no meaning at all, but this interpretation is likely to be the least satisfying. Almost any pattern tends to be more believable than no pattern at all.

Figure 18-2

The Reflexive Nature of Perception

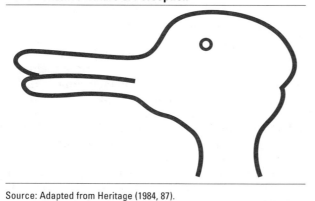

Source: Adapted from Heritage (1984, 87).

A counselling experiment, briefly mentioned in chapter 2, was designed by Garfinkel to illustrate how tenaciously people strive to find underlying patterns and also how they utilize these patterns to reinterpret surface features of their experience. In the experiment, psychiatry students were told that they were trying out a new technique in personal counselling in which the counsellor would give a yes or no answer to any question asked but would not otherwise elaborate. Students were asked to comment on the advice they received. What the students did not know was that the "answers" were simply random. What interested Garfinkel was the practical reasoning that students used to make sense of these utterances and how long it would take them to realize that they were in fact random, or literally senseless. The beginning of one of these interchanges is given below (Garfinkel 1967, 80–81) (S and E refer to subject and experimenter).

(S) Ok, this is the situation that I am presented with. I happen to be of the Jewish faith and I have been dating a Gentile girl now for about two months. My dad is not directly opposed to this situation, but I feel at the same time that he is not exactly pleased with it. Mother feels that as long as Dad is not directly opposed to this situation that I should go ahead and continue dating until he makes some direct statement to the contrary. My reason for feeling why he is not too pleased with this is that he has never said don't date her, but at the same time he will come up with digs and sayings that make me feel very ill at ease about dating the girl. My question is, do you feel under the present circumstances that I should continue or stop dating this girl? Let me put that in a positive way. Do you feel that I should continue dating this girl?

(E) My answer is no.

(S) No. Well, that is kind of interesting. I kinda feel that there is really no great animosity between Dad and I but, well, perhaps he feels that greater dislike will grow out of this. I suppose or maybe it is easier for an outsider to see certain things that I am blind to at this moment.

I would like to ask my second question now.

(E) Okay.

(S) Do you feel that I should have a further discussion with Dad about this situation or not? Should I have further discussion with Dad over this subject about dating the Gentile girl?

(E) My answer is yes.

(S) Well I feel that is reasonable but I really don't know what to say to him. I mean he seems to be not really too understanding. In other words he seems to be afraid really to discuss the situation. I mean at least it appears that way to me so far. But I guess if it is worthwhile to me, if I really want to continue to date her that I will go on and have this discussion with Dad. I really don't know what to say because I mean I am dating her. I am not in love with her or anything but I really never know what is going to come out. I guess we should have a discussion based on what the future possibilities might be and how he would feel about that. He may not be too strongly opposed now because we are only dating, but perhaps he sees future complications that he would really like to get off his chest at the moment. I am ready for my third question now.

If after having my conversation with Dad and he says to continue dating her, but at the same time gives me an impression that he is really not, he really does not want me to date her, but he is only doing it because he wants to be a good Dad, should under these conditions, should I still date the girl?

(E) My answer is yes.

(S) Well I am actually surprised at the answer. I expected a no answer on that. Perhaps this is because you are not quite aware of my dad and his reactions and he seems to be the type of person that is sensitive and therefore he is very careful in the way he will handle things. Even though he might have said go ahead and date her I perhaps would feel guilty in knowing that he really did not want me to continue to date her. Though I don't know that it would actually help the situation any. So, well, perhaps we will look into this further and that is another question.

In practice, all the students managed to get through the nonsensical exchange with the coun-

sellor, to make sense of it, and to reinterpret current and previous answers to give them the appearance of consistent advice even when they were blatantly contradictory. The students typically heard the random utterances as answers that were motivated by their questions. One of the basic principles of any normal conversation, Garfinkel suggests, is that utterances immediately following any question will be an answer to that question. Students applied this practical reasoning by construing whatever followed each of their questions as prompted by the question and as an answer to it.

A second principle of any normal conversation is that people expect that what they say will be treated as meaningful and that other participants will draw upon their background understandings to make sense of what has been said. Remember the earlier experiments in which people rapidly became indignant when the experimenter asked that common-sense remarks be explained. In the counsellor experiment, students went to great lengths to treat the random utterances as meaningful and were almost always successful, to the degree that they claimed they could see "what the adviser had in mind." Students drew very heavily upon background understandings to infer what the counsellor might have meant. They displayed the basic expectation of normal conversation: that statements are indexical or context-dependent and that the context is inferred but not explicated in the statements. Students went back through the conversation as the context that would make sense of the particular answer received.

Garfinkel further points out how students displayed the retrospective-prospective character of normal conversations. We have already seen that normal conversation becomes impossible if people demand that every statement be fully explicated before the talk continues. In normal conversation we anticipate that a future statement will help to clarify what has previously been said. Hence, rather than stopping to ask for an explanation, we continue to talk on the basis of our working interpretation of what the conversation is about, and we use the next statement to test or to revise our interpretation. Students in the counsellor experiment did this continuously. They thought back over the preceding part of the conversation to come up with working interpretations of what the counsellor might have meant and then formulated their next question on the basis of this. The following yes or no was immediately incorporated in a retroactive reshuffling of plausible interpretations of the conversation to be consistent with the new response. This modified interpretation then set the stage for the next question.

In managing their one-sided conversation with the counsellor, students displayed their competence in applying the documentary method of interpretation, a further basic principle of all normal conversation. They assumed throughout that any utterance by the counsellor signalled an underlying pattern. They searched for the pattern that would be consistent with the surface appearance of what the counsellor had said, referred to the pattern to reinterpret details of the exchange, used it to formulate new questions, revised their working assumptions concerning the underlying pattern as soon as they had the new answer, performed all necessary reinterpretation of details, and carried on.

When Garfinkel spells out for us everything these students had to do in order to carry on a ten-minute conversation, the complexity is staggering. Even the students were amazed when they learned how much and how actively they had contributed to making sense out of the random utterances they had heard. Yet this is what we, as competent members of society, accomplish everyday in ordinary conversations.

Practical Reasoning and the Social Construction of Order

Ethnomethodological research explores how the documentary method of interpretation underlies all sense of order in social life. Order does not exist. It is accompanied by the same kind of practical reasoning processes that the students used to make sense of nonsensical advice. The undefined flux of experience becomes recognizable as instances of underlying patterns and hence is made accountable as certain kinds of events. Actions that appear to us as normal are those that can readily be interpreted as instances of typical underlying patterns. Behaviour that is out of order is problematic until it comes to be reinterpreted as instances of some alternative pattern.

As we saw in chapter 7, the labelling of a particular person as a deviant is an interpretive scheme that can be readily invoked to account for actions that otherwise appear out of order. By the same documentary reasoning processes, all other details of the person's life may be reinterpreted

to fit the new pattern of accounting, so as to confirm that this person was deviant all along. Mental health personnel, police officers, and judges all draw on their sense of an underlying pattern of typical deviant behaviour to interpret details of surface appearances and make judgments about individual cases. The deviant label provides such an all-encompassing accounting scheme that it may be very difficult to break. In a classic study by Rosenhan (1973), researchers who faked hallucinations to gain admission to a mental hospital found it impossible to convince hospital staff afterwards that they were "normal." Their protestations that they were normal and had merely faked symptoms to gain admission were not believed. Even the fact that they took research notes was seen as a symptom of a deviant mental state rather than a normal research activity. They were eventually discharged as schizophrenics in remission rather than as people who were "normal all along."

Another classic application of ethnomethodology is Zimmerman's (1974) account of the sense-making practices of officials in a public assistance agency, which we looked at in chapter 12. Applicants present themselves as eligible for assistance, but officials are trained to be sceptical of all such claims. Assertions made by clients were viewed as reflecting underlying self-interests in getting money and hence intrinsically biased. Conversely, the caseworkers also assumed that bureaucratic organizations embody impartial, objective work practices, and hence that any piece of paper bearing the letterhead of such an organization and the signature of an incumbent official could be accepted as conveying statements of fact. Caseworkers refused even to consider the possibility that such official papers might themselves be open to doubt, or in need of further investigation.

Much of the surface appearance of social reality comes to us not through direct experience but through documents. These documents, which may be written or on tape or film, are produced by professionals and people in positions of authority within organizations. Ethnomethodological research explores how the manner in which such documents are constructed influences the practical reasoning processes of their audiences.

A study of the news media (Jalbert 1984) draws attention to the normally loaded categories in which various parties to a conflict are presented and particularly to the subtle use of grammatical devices that create the underlying patterns that audiences use in interpreting details of the events. For example, the actions of one party to a conflict may be expressed in the active grammatical voice while the actions of the other party are expressed in the passive voice. The effect is to convey the impression that responsibility for the conflict rests with the former. Eichler (1980, 23–26) shows how patriarchal assumptions about the distribution of power in societies are typically coded into anthropological accounts of women's activities. She cites Ford's (1970, 102) discussion of customary activities of women during their menstrual periods:

> Societies vary markedly, however, in the degree to which they curtail a menstruating woman's participation in social life. In a few societies, the only restriction placed upon her activities is that she may not engage in sexual intercourse. In a few other societies, menstruation involves strict seclusion and isolation. The majority of primitive peoples surround the woman with specific restrictions, leaving her free to move about with certain exceptions. Always she is forbidden sexual intercourse, frequently she may not go into the gardens, and may not participate in religious ceremonies.

The passive voice used in this passage powerfully conveys the view of women as passive victims of restrictions placed on them. They are not active agents in deciding their own behaviour. Eichler shows how the same evidence could have been written up very differently if the anthropologist had started with the underlying view of women as decision-makers within their societies. Described in the active grammatical voice: "women *refrain* from certain activities during their menstrual periods . . . always the woman *refuses* to engage in sexual intercourse; frequently, she *will not* enter the gardens or *refuses* to cook for men . . . she *may refuse* to participate in certain religious ceremonies" [italics added]. This version conveys the same facts but totally different information about the power relations and decision-making processes in the society, and the relative position of women. Neither version is necessarily the more factually correct.

The ideal, Eichler suggests, is that we write about both sexes in the active voice, acknowledging that both women and men are subjects in the social world and not passive victims of it. This implies much more sensitivity to the niceties of the generic *he* versus *he/she*. It requires a new form of data collection in which we discover what the world looks like from a victim's standpoint and the "resistance, helplessness, fear, rage or mute acceptance" of the situation that the person may feel (Eichler 1988b, 89).

Conversation Analysis

Conversation analysis is a branch of ethnomethodology that focusses on the detailed features of talk and their role in creating and sustaining our sense of social order. Conventional macrosociology tends to ignore talk altogether, or to treat it as a passive medium through which major social structural variables relate to one another. When researchers use questionnaires and interviews, they take for granted the mutual intelligibility of such written and verbal interaction. But, as we have seen in the discussion of indexicality, the achievement of mutual understanding is far from automatic. Ethnomethodologists analyse conversations to discover how people convey such multiple messages as whether an utterance is to be taken literally or figuratively, whether it is a statement or a question that requires a response, whether what one is saying or hearing is comprehensible or requires some qualifiers or additional explanations, when one person's turn is up and another may legitimately take up the conversation, how a topic change or conversation end is signalled. These are only a few of the multitude of questions raised by theorists who focus on conversation analysis. Talk is perhaps one of the most basic building blocks of our intelligible social world. The more closely we look into how talk is collectively structured and managed, the more we come to appreciate how complex it is.

Conversation analysis typically relies upon tape-recordings of conversations. Specialized transcripts are made that are designed to capture hearable details of talk—intonation, pauses, the stretching of vowels, and the overlapping of turns—all of which may be significant for making the talk comprehensible. Video-recordings are now used to study the nonverbal aspects of talk. The elements of talk are so complex that most researchers still prefer to work only with verbal transcripts, or even with telephone conversations where there is no visible component of interaction. People in everyday life organize their conversations in incredible detail. The use of recordings makes possible repeated and detailed examination and reinterpretation of data while eliminating any risk of distortion arising from the limitations of respondents' memories (Heritage 1984, 238). Recordings also avoid the problem, which plagues conventional sociology, that data are coded into preset categories in ways unknown to the researcher.

Conversation analysis focusses on members' methods of producing recognizable forms of talk and understandable **utterances**. In other words, it analyses how people get their meanings across to others in conversations and how they continually recognize and repair the instances when the meaning has not been completely clear. Transcripts of conversations, interviews, court hearings, lessons, and the like, are analysed to discover the very general features of how talk is structured. Researchers look for the context-free features of these speech-exchange systems. These are features or structures that are common to all conversation, regardless of topic or situation and the age, sex, social class, or ethnicity of the participants. In a sense, these universal features can be viewed as the machinery through which people communicate verbally for all sorts of purposes.

One critical aspect of this machinery is the organization of turn-taking. Generally, in a conversation, one party talks at a time, and the transitions between speakers' turns usually occur with little or no gap or overlap. This is despite the fact that the order in which the participants speak and the length of the conversation as a whole are not preprogrammed. Even where there are violations of these features, such as when two people start to talk at the same time, systematic repair mechanisms come quickly into play to restore order.

This turn-taking machinery is worked out by the participants in the immediate ongoing setting of the talk. Such organization depends on the participants listening carefully to one another so as to figure out just the right moment to start speaking without interrupting. Despite the fact that the alternations of talk are improvised moment by moment, people are able to produce a recognizable order in their talk that can be detected by close listening and analysis (Sacks, Schegloff, and Jefferson 1974). Similar machinery of talk governs the familiar activities of opening up conversations and bringing them to a close. The interpretive practices and improvised manoeuvres involved give a structure to conversations that goes far beyond simply starting to speak or instantly shutting up.

A further common aspect of the machinery of talk is that utterances occur in pairs. Questions, for example, are expected to be followed immediately with answers, summonses are followed with acknowledgments, and greetings with return greetings. These are adjacency pairs; a first pair-part of one type is expected to be followed immediately by a second pair-part of the same type. The moment that one participant in a conversation says a first pair-part, by asking a question or offering a greeting, the situation of the talk has changed, because the people involved know that they are accountable for coming up with appropriate responses. If they do not do so, their failure will be immediately noticeable and will require some explanation. For example, when A greets B, A's greeting has a prospective character in the sense that it changes how B's next utterance will be heard. If B returns the greeting, then it acts as an acknowledgment that A and B are mutually involved in the interaction. But, if B fails to respond, B's silence will be "hearable" as a silence and will require some explanation. It is not the same situation as silence if A's greeting had not occurred. The silence is out of order and A, together with other listeners, will need to think about whether B's silence is intelligible as, for example, an insult or a failure to hear A's greeting (Heritage 1984, 106–9).

The management of conversations is intimately associated with the social construction of status and power relations. West found that male physicians usually interrupt their patients far more than patients interrupt them. Female physicians,

The management of conversations is intimately associated with the social construction of status and power relations.

however, are interrupted by patients as much or more than vice versa. West concludes from these data that gender can have primacy over the status of physician "when the doctor is a lady" (West 1984, 102). Studies such as these give valuable insight into how the microworld of everyday interaction both reflects and reproduces the wider system of inequality and power.

The techniques of conversation analysis have similarly been applied to other settings such as courtrooms (Atkinson and Drew 1979), doctor-patient interviews (Heath 1981), service encounters (Merritt 1976), and even the Watergate hearings (Molotch and Boden 1985). These studies give a new perspective on the microsociological bases of control over information, biases in decision making, and the exercise of power.

Ethnomethodological Studies of Work

Recent developments in ethnomethodology are moving beyond the analysis of conversations to explore the intimate details of practical reasoning that make possible the joint activities of people at work. The kinds of work processes studied range from improvised jazz performances (Sudnow 1978) and the order of service in a queue to discoveries in astrophysics (Garfinkel, Lynch, and Livingston 1981) and research in a chemistry laboratory (Lynch 1985).

This research approach is so strikingly different from conventional sociology of occupations that our primary objective here will be to clarify the kind of questions that the ethnomethodology of work raises, rather than to present an overview of findings. The analysis of conversations described above may give you a hint about these differences. Conventional sociology tends to focus on the content of what people say, the answers they give to questions, and what information we might learn from them. Ethnomethodology, in contrast, focusses on the mechanisms that make orderly talk possible, regardless of what people are talking about. Similarly, in the study of work, conventional sociology of occupations tends to tell us a great deal about the occupation in question and the lives of the workers. What we do not learn is exactly how people do what they are doing (Heritage 1984, 293–99). Earlier in this chapter, while looking at functionalist approaches, we learned about people working in restaurants, but we learned almost nothing about how one

does the work of serving. On the basis of Whyte's study we could not apply for a job and claim to be competent waitresses or waiters. What we are missing is the information that might be supplied by someone on the job helping us and saying, "This is what you do. . . . Watch me." Ethnomethodology explores "the missing what."

An excellent example of the contrast between symbolic interactionist and ethnomethodological studies of work is Becker's (1951) study of professional musicians and Sudnow's (1978; 1979) ethnomethodological studies of jazz improvisation. Becker focusses on musicians' work as a service occupation in which the players have personal contact with members of their audience who exert pressure on how they do their work, particularly on the musical selections they are asked to play. Becker's specific interests are:

1. the conceptions that musicians have of themselves and of the nonmusicians for whom they work and the conflict they feel to be inherent in this relation;

2. the basic consensus underlying the reactions of both commercial and jazz musicians to this conflict; and

3. the feelings of isolation musicians have from the larger society and the way they segregate themselves from audience and community (1951, 249).

His analysis is based on eighteen months of interviews and participant observation as a jazz pianist. He describes how musicians think of themselves as artists who possess a mysterious gift that sets them apart from outsiders, whom they regard as "squares." The musicians feel that the audience, who are mostly squares, has no right to dictate what they should play. But since the audience is the major source of their income, they are faced with the dilemma of whether to "go commercial," which implies abandoning the creative principle but making a good living, or to stay with what they consider good jazz but make a precarious living. Commercial musicians look down on the audience, but they choose to sacrifice self-respect and the respect of their peers in order to enjoy the advantages of steady work and higher income (Becker 1951, 254).

In the actual playing situation, the musicians segregate themselves from the audience as much as possible by playing on a platform and positioning the piano to act as a physical barrier that reduces direct interaction with, and therefore undesirable influence from, the audience. Becker concludes that generally musicians are hostile towards audiences and that they tend to associate mostly among themselves.

Ethnomethodological studies of musicians by Becker and Sudnow examine the practical activity of making music.

This study is in many ways a fascinating account of the lives of musicians. But an important aspect has been ignored. We learn about the musicians' roles, their relations with the audience, their career choices, and their distinctive subculture, but we learn nothing about their actual musical activities, despite the fact that Becker was a participant musician. We are no more competent to play jazz piano in a band at the end of reading Becker's study than we were at the beginning. We do not learn even the most elementary information, such as how all the members of the band manage to start playing at the same time. Garfinkel (1976, 36) sums up the problems with Becker's study thus:

> We learn from Becker . . . that there are jazz musicians, where they work, whom they work with, what they earn, how they get their jobs, what the audience size and composition is . . . but . . . nowhere in the article can it be read and no interrogation of the article can supply that it is just in those places, with just those persons . . . at just those times, under the circumstances at hand, these parties must in and of their local work make music together. The curiosity of the reportage . . . is that Becker's article omits entirely . . . and

exactly what the parties are doing that makes of what they are doing for each other recognizably, just so, just what, just this that is going on, namely, their making music!

In contrast, Sudnow (1978) raises the question of how jazz musicians actually manage to play. His study focusses on the stages he went through learning to play jazz piano. He also discusses the frantic character of playing with other people when they set the pace at which his hands had to move. Sudnow argues that aspects of tempo and rhythm are integral parts of any social interaction. We have to pay attention to how people notice changes in tempo and how these are accomplished (Sudnow 1979, 117).

Ethnomethodological studies of musicians focus on the practical activity of playing music. In a study of band members, for example, an ethnomethodologist would explore the intimate details of the interaction between members that makes it possible for them to play together, to keep time, to pace their collective movements. One of the basic things we need to know in order to play in a band is how the members jointly manage to keep in time. A conductor might help, provided we know that when he or she lifts the baton and flicks it, some, though not necessarily all, of the musicians start playing. For amateur orchestras, however, simply following the conductor may not be enough, as can be jarringly obvious when they have to start a new piece or change tempo. For a small jazz group or any small musical group without a conductor, the question of when to start and how to keep together is more complicated. As a new band member, we would have to learn what the gestures are, what to watch out for, and how to listen to other players.

Ethnomethodology explores how bands rehearse or prepare for performances, and what their everyday shop practices are (Weeks 1982; 1988). We listen in on their shoptalk and glimpse just what kind of interpretive thinking is required to go from the underlying pattern, that this is the piece being played, to make sense of the surface features of given instructions. We will also learn how musicians fake it when something goes wrong: how they cover for someone who has come in on a wrong note, how they blend in and slur a beat to catch up, and how they make what are initially wrong notes sound intentional and leading to the right notes after all, so that the performance keeps going and the audience does not notice the error.

If we are studying professional musicians, we can usually assume that they have mastered the techniques of how to play their instruments to get the sounds required, once they have understood the instructions. But a band leader in a junior school cannot make such assumptions. Here the shoptalk might be much more explicit, like "Trumpeter, take a big breath right here so you have enough air left for the d-a-a, and that goes for the singers too. Violinist, get your bow right up so you will have enough of it left to hold the note. Move it slo-o-wly." We might see the trumpeter drawing a balloon shape in the music notebook and the singers writing a large B with an arrow at the same place. The violinist might write "up-sl." If we attend the school performance after reading an ethnomethodological account of rehearsals, we would have a much better idea of just how the band leader and the students together manage to do what they are doing. This is the goal of the ethnomethodology of work studies.

Ethnomethodological studies of professional scientists at work explore the practical everyday reasoning through which scientists collectively arrive at the belief that they have made a discovery. Garfinkel, Lynch, and Livingston (1981) examined tape-recordings and notebooks made by astronomers when they discovered optical pulsars. Conventional accounts of the discovery make no mention of the work that went into it or how the scientists involved managed to convince themselves that they had found something. Garfinkel, Lynch, and Livingston (1981, 139–40) describe what we learn from one conventional account:

1. the pulsar is depicted as the cause of everything seen and said about it;

2. the pulsar is described as *existing prior to and independently of* any specific method of detecting it;

3. the account is in the third person, that is, it is impersonal with nothing of [the scientists'] personal presence included;

4. the scientists through proper lucid methods came upon the pulsar that was otherwise hidden due to ignorance, sloppy work, etc.

In other words, the report takes for granted that the pulsars were there all along and that appropriate research procedures made their presence obvious.

When ethnomethodologists explore the tape-recordings and notebooks made by the scientists involved, however, we get a strikingly different view of the scientists' work. We hear their shoptalk as they discuss among themselves how to interpret the ambiguous readings they were getting from their research equipment. Before the "discovery" was made, it was by no means obvious how to interpret these surface appearances. Many different underlying patterns could be and were proposed to account for these details, with the option of optical pulsars only one among several interpretive schemes. The scientists had to talk themselves into believing that what they were seeing were pulsars. Perhaps if the shoptalk had gone differently, the conclusions drawn about what they were looking at would have been different, and pulsars would not have been discovered at all.

The Limitations of Ethnomethodology

In summary, ethnomethodology focusses on the ways in which we, in our everyday lives, use our common-sense knowledge and background understandings to make sense to ourselves and to each other of what is going on around us. Our sense of reality, including all the familiar features of our society, is created through such practical everyday reasoning. The vague flux of people milling around us only becomes visible as discrete activities because we actively search for patterns that might account for what we notice. Talk is meaningful only because we continually search for underlying patterns to which utterances might refer. Order is visible in activities and conversations only as a result of such reflexive practical reasoning, which moves continually from experiences to the interpretive schemes that seem to account for them to new experiences and to revisions of the interpretive scheme.

The central contribution of ethnomethodology is its focus on the methods by which people create a sense of what is happening in intimate, everyday interactions, and how they construct their own actions in order to make what they are doing sensible to others. These sense-making processes form the basis of all social life. The problem that this approach leaves largely unresolved is how to build from micro second-by-second experiences outwards to the broader social structures that people come to experience, somehow, as constraints upon their lives. These constraints are embodied in such notions as *typical expectations*, *power*, and *class*. Collins (1981, 986–89) conceptualizes macrostructures as aggregates of micro-experiences stretched out from seconds to days, months, and years, with the numbers of people involved growing from one or two to increasingly larger groups. He suggests that concepts of physical space, the amount of time that social processes take, and the number of people involved are true **macrovariables**; that is, they are variables that cannot be reduced to micro-elements. But the problem remains that much more than an exercise in addition seems to be needed to get from microsecond, sense-making practices to what people come to experience and to talk about as social structures. Ethnomethodology has uncovered the microfoundations of these macro-experiences, but the linkages and the building mechanisms remain obscure.

What seems to be needed is a theoretical approach that is rooted in ethnomethodology but that works outwards to explore how people bring macrostructures into being. This new approach is loosely referred to as the **social construction of reality**. As a body of theory, it explores how members' methods for making sense of experience continually sustain and reproduce the larger social world. This larger world is experienced as external constraints on people's lives, yet it exists not as a given but as an ongoing accomplishment.

Feminist Theory and the Social Construction of Reality: The Personal as Political

Feminist theory is currently at the forefront of explorations into the social construction of reality. There are important reasons for this. First, the everyday lives of most women are not experienced as embedded in the formal organizations of society—administration, government, and so on—that are the central foci of dominant sociology. Women's lives are experienced as embedded

in what Smith (1987a, 7) refers to as the "local particularities of home and family." Smith herself, as a sociology graduate and a mother of young children, found it almost impossible to reconcile the abstract theoretical debates of academic sociology with her local and particular world of feeding, cleaning, bedding down, and playing with small children—the parks they went to together, the friends they had, the neighbours, the children's sicknesses and visits to the doctor, or walks down the road to look at the scenery and at the bugs under the leaves.

This is still the world inhabited primarily, although not exclusively, by women. It is a mode of being that is not readily captured by the abstractions of traditional macrostudies in sociology. Smith concluded that there must be something wrong with the academic sociology she was studying and trying to teach if it failed to connect with the world of her own immediate experience. She worked to develop a new way of doing sociol-

Dorothy Smith pioneered the introduction of women's studies courses in Canadian universities. She developed a way of doing sociology that begins with people in their everyday lives and moves outwards to the macrostructures of society.

ogy that begins with people in their everyday lives and moves outwards.

As we saw in chapter 2, feminist theory, beginning from the standpoint of women in the particularities of everyday life, emphasizes that the personal is political. Intimate encounters between women and children and men, intimate decisions about who will do what in day-to-day relations, are fundamentally implicated in sustaining and reproducing what feminists refer to as the structures of patriarchy. At the same time, theorists working within dominant sociological perspectives have had considerable difficulty incorporating notions of patriarchal structures into their work or even recognizing that they exist. They have generally not been taken for granted as social facts in the functionalist sense of external constraints. Learning to see them is a struggle.

Dorothy Smith is concerned with showing how micro-experiences, the intimate particularities of everyday life, produce the macrostructures of a patriarchal world. She begins with the insights of ethnomethodology into how talk is put together and the devices used by men, apparently with women's consent, that serve to maintain male control over the topics of conversation (Smith 1987a, 33–36). These devices include not picking up topics raised by women, or reattributing such topics to a man, and the polite pauses when a woman speaks followed by a swift return to the "real" conversation being held by men. Such micropractices produce a world dominated intellectually by men in which women's experience does not appear as the source of authoritative expression (Smith 1987a, 51). The patriarchal worldview is reproduced in what is written about and read, and hence in what becomes part of the formal macrostructures of academic disciplines. As Smith described it, men tend to take seriously only what other men say. What other men write becomes established as the standard for the discipline, against which new writing, including that done by women scholars, is evaluated.

Again at the microlevel of sense-making practices, Smith (1987a, 831) describes studies that explore how people accomplish evaluations of other people. Identical descriptions of academic backgrounds and qualifications are evaluated quite differently when they appear to be those of a woman rather than a man. These sense-making practices, in the conversations of people on hiring committees, help to accomplish the macrostruc-

tural reality of where woman and men come to be located in universities and other organizations. These are part of the active microprocesses that produce the reality of women in junior positions being evaluated by men in senior positions, in terms of standards set in advance by men—a "factual" reality experienced by women as external constraint.

Dixon (1976) uncovers the microlevel sense-making processes through which the social construction of radical professors as "incompetent academics," unworthy of tenure, was socially accomplished in many North American social science departments. These processes are part of the members' practices that socially accomplish what Marxists refer to as the dominance of ideas of the ruling class. Since the early 1970s the targets of such degradation practices have changed, but the techniques remain.

Smith shows how the ways in which academic talk is managed in sociology become built into the dominant ideas and methods of the discipline. Academic sociologists do not write and talk about what they are doing as if they were ordinary people doing their jobs. Instead, they adopt a detached, abstract mode of "professional talk." This is a mode of scientific shoptalk that invokes membership in the particular profession and conveys the image of the scientist as outside any particular location. It serves at the same time to accomplish the reduction of the people being talked about to the level of objects for discussion. In academic sociology, people are thought about as if they were specimens, role incumbents, or instances of abstract models. Smith refers to this as the **imperialism of rationality**.

It is this mode of talking, Smith suggests (1987a, 71–72), that makes it possible for professionals to relate to battered wives as objects for discussion—precisely the mode of relating that makes wife battery possible. It is also the mode of talking that socially accomplishes the perspective that macrostructures are causal agents and that people are objects of them. Earlier in this chapter we saw how this worked in Eichler's illustration of how anthropologists typically use the passive voice to describe what women do. Women thus do not appear as subjects actively creating their social world. They are merely examples of culture at work. Eichler includes stronger examples. An anthropological description of how kinship ties strengthen group cohesion in primitive societies stresses the importance of the genetic interrelatedness among adult males (Shaw 1985, 197–98). In writing in this form, Shaw has conceptualized the group as consisting only of males, with assorted wives who have no effect whatever on group cohesion and solidarity (Eichler 1988b, 25). Here we begin to see how functionalism and patriarchy in social science are socially accomplished in the ways in which we do our research and write our reports.

Smith (1987a, 151–80) proposes an alternative way of doing and writing sociology, which she terms **institutional ethnography**. It begins with the particular activities of people in particular localities and explores how these practical activities are co-ordinated to bring our world into being. It shares with traditional ethnomethodology the need to see exactly what work is done to accomplish the accountable order. At the same time, the method draws upon the insights of Karl Marx, who insisted that all social life is essentially practical, and hence that understanding must begin with the study and comprehension of practical human activities. The method goes beyond the boundaries of traditional ethnomethodology in explicating the wider set of social relations in which the local activities of any one participant are embedded and in terms of which they are organized.

As an example of this method, Smith focusses on the social construction of the school system and class differences within it. She begins with the particular situation of mothers describing how their day's work within the home is put together. We see how a child's success in school is socially produced by mothering work, including the "monitoring and repair sequences" by which mothers check on homework and try to fix it after deciding what teachers want. We see the work processes involved in being what teachers mean by "concerned parents." Smith illustrates how the practical work of mothers in the home is organized by relations outside it, the demands of scheduling the departures and arrivals of children and husband to fit the timetables of school and job, the ongoing accomplishment of shopping, cooking, and mealtimes, and of keeping children clean so they will pass the monitoring activities of school health officials.

Smith shows how the monitoring sequences of teachers in classrooms produce the status of particular children as proceeding normally or not. We realize how the teacher's work of managing a classroom and accomplishing a reading lesson is directly related to and dependent upon the ongoing mothering work that accomplishes the readiness of children to act in ways that make possible such activities. Smith also illustrates how relations of class and inequality are socially accomplished in the practical struggles of poor women, living in places without even indoor plumbing, to accomplish the appropriate level of preparedness of their children for school. She discusses the struggle of single-parents to accomplish the skilled and time-consuming practices of monitoring and repair sequences appropriate for competent mothering. It is through such everyday practices that our world as hierarchically ordered is brought into being. These relations are explored in detail in chapter 16 of this text, which is concerned with education and the social construction of class.

The Limitations of Feminist Microsociology

As sociologists, we can explicate how our social world is socially accomplished through the everyday activities of people in local, particular settings. But this cannot work magic. The apparatuses of ruling are still there, even when we see how they are accomplished. Critics of ethnomethodology point out that while Garfinkel's breaching experiments show how our sense of reality is accomplished, they do not thereby change that reality. The power relations embedded in them are not reducible to the reasoning processes themselves. Smith (1987a) points to the social organization of talk, which excludes or trivializes what women contribute, the social organization of written talk in texts, which constructs women as objects of study, the social organization of evaluation, which accomplishes how what is written comes to be judged, and its translation into who is appointed to what positions.

Research oriented to explicating the subjectively experienced world of women, to show how schooling is imposed upon mothers, and how they might act collectively vis-à-vis this mode of organizing, is central to Smith's own vision of what a sociology for women might be like. But, speaking from her own experience, she comments that "such bold contravention of professional constraints would be a one-time-only operation" (Smith 1987a, 219). Such research proposals have to be evaluated in order to get funding. In the particular location of government funding agencies, the ongoing accomplishment of evaluation of research proposals is based on very particular standards, not those of feminist sociology. Smith's ideal of a research centre organized to create a sociology from the standpoint of women could not survive, for the very simple reason that it could not get funded. Time and again the social organization of funding, the way in which voluntary organizations are required to act in order to get money, and the forms through which they have to account for what they are doing, make it impossible to do what they intended to do. Smith's central point is that microsociological analysis is not of itself sufficient to understand power relations at the macrosocietal level. It can make visible the strategies used in the relations of ruling, but the strategies are not in themselves the foundations of patriarchy.

Conclusion

The critical value of microsociology is that it provides a means of discovering how social relations are produced through the everyday activities of individual people. Macrostructures comprise collections of individual people acting in certain kinds of microsituations. What gets done is accomplished by people, not by abstract systems. But the warning sounded by Smith with respect to the feminist exploration of power in personal relationships holds for all forms of micro-analysis. Recognizing the interpersonal foundations of social organization does not make the organization disappear. The apparatus of ruling is still there. People have come to think about society as if it consisted of structures in which they are embedded. This conception expresses their real experience of constraint in their everyday relations with others.

Suggested Reading

An excellent theoretical analysis of the relations between micro- and macrosociology is provided by Randall Collins in "On the Microfoundations of Macrosociology" (1981). Since this is not an easy article, it is best to read it over for the general ideas without worrying about the details of the debate. Dorothy Smith's work also tends to be highly complex and written for advanced students. A refreshing exception is her book *The Everyday World as Problematic: A Feminist Sociology* (1987a). Smith gives multiple examples of how the everyday lives of women are socially constructed, both in the intimate details of interaction and in relation to wider social organizations in which such interactions are embedded. Her work effectively bridges microfoundations and macrostructures.

David Orenstein's introduction to sociology, *The Sociological Quest: Principles of Sociology* (1985), is limited to the functionalist perspective, but it presents an excellent overview of theories of socialization and role playing. He uses multiple examples that are readily familiar to students.

For a good introduction to a Marxist approach in microsociology, see W. Peter Archibald, *Social Psychology as Political Economy* (1978). He describes with passion how the intimate daily lives of workers are influenced by capitalism. See particularly chapters 7 to 9 in the section entitled "A Political Economic Approach to Some Pressing Social Psychological Problems."

The early text by Harold Garfinkel, *Studies in Ethnomethodology* (1967), provides an excellent introduction to ethnomethodology. Garfinkel's theoretical discussions are complex, but his descriptions of experiments are fascinating and straightforward. See particularly chapters 2 and 3.

For the application of ethnomethodology to practical situations, see Egon Bittner, "The Police on Skid Row: A Study of Peace-Keeping" (1967). Bittner shows how police officers make their everyday decisions about what behaviour will be treated as ordinary and why other similar actions may be treated as reportable offences. Candace West, "When the Doctor is a 'Lady': Power, Status and Gender in Physician-Patient Encounters" (1984), shows how individuals continually negotiate their sense of what is going on in a doctor's office.

Questions

1. How does functionalist theory account for the marked shift in behaviour of students as a new instructor introduces himself to a university class?

2. What is involved in the debate between methodological holism and methodological individualism in Marxist analysis of micro-interactions?

3. How does the interpretive perspective on doctor-patient interactions change the focus of questions from the functionalist analysis of these relations?

4. What is implied in the ethnomethodological claim that conversations are always *indexical*? How is this implicated in the analysis of *shoptalk*?

5. List the practices that students used to manage conversation in the counselling experiment.

6. Give two examples of how adjacency pairs serve to structure conversations and to clarify mutuality of understanding in conversations.

7. How does an ethnomethodological account of the work of professional musicians differ methodologically from a symbolic interactionist account of the same work?

8. How does the study of the discovery of optical pulsars illustrate Garfinkel's admonition that we have to think backwards in order to understand accounts of events?

9. What is entailed in the methodology of *institutional ethnography*?

10. How is patriarchy maintained through the typical structuring of talk in male/female interaction?

CHAPTER

Culture and Communications: Struggles over Meaning

Culture is "species specific." All animals communicate with each other, but only humans have developed the capacity to communicate through symbols and so to develop systems of meaning. Language is the most important symbol system, but gestures and rituals also convey meanings that go far beyond the immediate utterances and actions. **Culture**, in its most fundamental sense, is concerned with the generation and circulation of meaning. Language both expresses, and makes possible, culture. Culture is a basic element in society. The concept of *culture* encompasses the symbol systems through which humans create and communicate the meanings, beliefs, and values that are the foundations of social order, as well as what we think of as the high culture of arts and humanities.

Such a dauntingly abstract concept is not too easy to pin down. Widely divergent studies—ethnographies of whole societies, subcultures and youth groups, humanities and religion, language, mass media, and audience studies—are all studies of culture. Cultural anthropology uses the concept in its broadest sense to encompass the way of life of a people—everything that an individual would need to know in order to function as a competent member of a given society, including knowledge of technology and material artifacts. At the other extreme, culture is narrowed to refer to the best achievements of intellectual work—literature and philosophy, art and music. Williams (1982, 9) aptly describes the sociology of culture as more of a miscellaneous heading than a coherent body of research. But Williams traces some practical convergence between these two extremes in the study of "signifying practices" that range from language and arts to mass media and popular culture, and studies of ideology (1982, 13). We will follow roughly that convention in this chapter.

Functionalist Theory: Culture and Societal Integration

The functionalist approach to the study of culture developed out of the classical writings of Durkheim and Weber, and their synthesis in the work of Talcott Parsons. From Durkheim, Parsons draws the importance of culture as the shared beliefs and sentiments that form the basis of moral order. The ritual practices that express collective culture function to unite people together in a community. From Max Weber's work, Parsons draws the importance of grounding sociological explanation in the meanings and intentions of actors in a situation. The prevailing culture—the beliefs, values, and customs of the actors—provide the basis for predicting typical patterns of action. As we saw in chapter 11, Weber's study of *The Protestant Ethic and the Spirit of Capitalism* (1904) is essentially a study of how culture influences economic action.

Parsons, in collaboration with Shils (1951b), developed a synthesis of the ideas of Durkheim and Weber into a concept of a cultural system, as part of a general scheme of social action. Of the four subsystems of social action—biological, personality, social, and cultural—the cultural system is the highest and most important. A shared system of culture is a basic prerequisite for social order. A common culture provides standards that structure interaction so that it becomes possible for any one actor to know what to expect in the behaviour and responses of others. Actors must be able to generalize from particular situations, and must be assured that actions, gestures, or symbols that they use themselves will have more or less the same meaning for others.

Parsons' general theory of action and his conceptualization of cultural systems are defined in sufficiently abstract terms to be applicable, in principle, to any kind of society. Nonetheless, there are important differences between simple and complex industrialized societies. It makes sense within the context of small and relatively undifferentiated societies to approach culture in a holistic way as a total way of life, but such a view is difficult to operationalize when considering complex societies. Increasing differentiation gives rise to a distinct class of people who specialize in intellectual work (Billington et al. 1991,

7). This in turn leads to a new concept of culture that distinguishes between the "high" culture of literature and philosophy, art and music, which constitute the humanities, and the storytelling, myths, drumming, dancing, and singing associated with popular culture.

Contemporary functionalist theory has by and large followed the model of cultural systems synthesized by Parsons, in which social integration is based on a shared system of beliefs and sentiments. Research in this tradition has concentrated on the study of mass culture, the beliefs, sentiments and ritual practices of ordinary people, and how they function to support social order. For example, as we have seen in chapter 4, the rapid pace of industrialization and urbanism prompted widespread fears of a breakdown in community cohesion that would give rise to atomized, isolated, alienated, and disenchanted individuals, who would be prey to the normlessness and chaos that Durkheim calls anomie (Billington et al. 1991, 12). The most pessimistic view of mass society held that rootless and lonely people would be easy prey for totalitarian social and political movements, such as the rise of National Socialism in Germany.

These fears prompted concern with how to promote collective values and sentiments of nationhood within highly diversified pluralist societies. The rise of mass media is seen as particularly important in the shaping of mass culture. Technical forms of mass communication, including newspapers, radio, and especially television, have the capacity to reach enormous numbers of people simultaneously. Marshall McLuhan saw television as able to create a future world society as a "global village" (McLuhan 1964). As a medium of communication, television can reach all regions of the globe virtually simultaneously, programs can be dubbed in any language, and literacy is not required.

The following overview of functionalist studies of culture begins with a detailed analysis of language as the foundation of all culture. It looks at research into some of the rituals that structure everyday life in complex industrial societies such as Canada. It concludes with studies that seek to define a distinctively national Canadian culture that might distinguish it from Britain and the United States, despite the shared dominant language of English, and the potential role of mass media in promoting national culture.

Integration Through Language

Language is a structured system of grammar and symbolic representations that carry determined cultural meanings. Any one individual must conform to this structure in order to be understood. The work of the French linguist Ferdinand de Saussure ([1916] 1964) on the structure of language is widely cited as a model for studying many other forms of communication that work in ways similar to language in transmitting meanings, including myths, customs, rituals, eating habits, gestures, photographs, films, television, and the like.

Saussure conceptualizes language as fundamentally a system of signs. A sign is something that stands for, or is a symbol of, something else, and that is recognized by other users of the language or sign system. A sign has two parts: the **signifier**, which is the physical form of the sign—in language the sound or the word—and the **signified**, which is the mental concept referred to. The relationship between signifier and signified is essentially arbitrary and socially constructed. There is no inherent relationship between the sound of a word and what it stands for. The word for *mother*, for example, is very different in different language systems. Whatever meaning the word *mother* has, is attributed culturally. Moreover, Saussure argues, the meaning of any one word within a system of language can be defined only in relationship to other words, as different from related words. *Mother* has its meaning only in relation to *child* and *father*. Meaning, therefore, occurs only within an overall system of meaning, or language, not in isolation.

Saussure sees language as the ground of all culture, the structure that frames and enables the production of meaning (Turner 1990, 13). Language does not merely name an already organized and coherent reality, Saussure insists. Its role is far more powerful and complex—namely, to organize and construct what we see as reality. The way we see the world is determined by the cultural conventions through which we conceptualize the images we receive. We live in symbolic universes, our taken-for-granted views of reality constituting a "sacred canopy" that defines the very nature of our existence, why things *are* the way they are (Wuthnow et al. 1984, 86; Berger 1967; Berger and Luckmann 1966, 93–94). The myriad categories, classifications, types, labels, and definitions coded into language transform the formless, unorganized experiences of life into a meaningful social reality, a reality that is in some respects always unique to a given language system. The Inuktitut language, for example, names many qualities and textures of snow, whereas English speakers can articulate only the most general form—*snow*.

The structure of language differs according to whether a community is close-knit or loose-knit (Douglas 1970). In close-knit communities, where members know each other well, people can talk in very condensed or restricted ways and be understood, whereas among strangers a more elaborate or detailed form of communication is required to get meaning across. Douglas suggests that restricted talk helps to produce a sense of community, since it forces members to utilize their commonly held group assumptions to decode what is said, thus bringing these assumptions to life and reaffirming them. This process works independently of direct intention of the people involved (Wuthnow et al. 1984, 103–4; Douglas 1970, 22–25).

The power accorded to language as the ground of culture is recognized in contemporary Canadian politics in the emphasis given to the institutionalization and preservation of the two founding languages of French and English. Québécois culture is conflated with the French language, the survival of the former seen as dependent upon the vitality of the latter. From this perspective, Québécois people who do not develop, or who lose the capacity to speak French are seen as no longer truly Québécois. First Nations peoples all across Canada are similarly struggling to revitalize their languages as a basic step in the recovery of cultural identities shattered by colonialism. Many other heritage languages are being actively promoted and taught in schools and colleges across Canada as part of a commitment to a multicultural society.

Communication Studies

Semiotics—the methodology, concepts, and terminology used by linguists to study languages—has been widely adapted as a model for studying other aspects of culture (Turner 1990, 16, 22–23). Culture shares the three characteristics of language: it is a symbolic system of shared meanings. Culture is symbolic in that it points to levels of meaning that go beyond surface actions and gestures; secondly, culture forms a system that is structured externally to individual users; and thirdly, elements of culture have meaning only through their recognition by a community of users.

The structuralist anthropologist Claude Levi-Strauss adopts this model of culture to analyse the meanings of myths and customs in simpler societies. Roland Barthes (1973) applies it to the analysis of codes and conventions employed in such activities as films, sports, and eating habits in contemporary Western societies. A famous example of Barthes' work is his analysis of a photograph in the magazine *Paris Match* of a black soldier saluting a French flag (Barthes 1967, 89–90). Barthes suggests that the photograph itself acts as a sign with meaning in the context of the news story in which it appears. The flag symbolizes France; saluting the flag is a gesture that symbolizes nationalism and loyalty; the man's clothing symbolizes the armed forces, and

related notions of duty, service, and obedience. All these signs are available to be used by the newspaper in conveying meaning for readers. Individual photographs, like talk, are essentially unique, but the codes, or shared meaning system by which their message is communicated, is seen as highly structured. Turner (1990, 34–37) uses Barthes' analytical model to "read" newspaper photographs of Oliver North during the Iran-Contra investigation. The location of the American flag in a picture, the image of military or civilian clothing, and the facial pose, with eyes looking up or downcast, all convey meanings, both emotional and factual. The correct "reading" of such signs presupposes a system of codes that is shared by the producer and the intended readers. In effect, these codes constitute another, nonverbal, level of cultural language.

An entire branch of sociology, known as communication studies, has developed around the application of the methodology and terms of

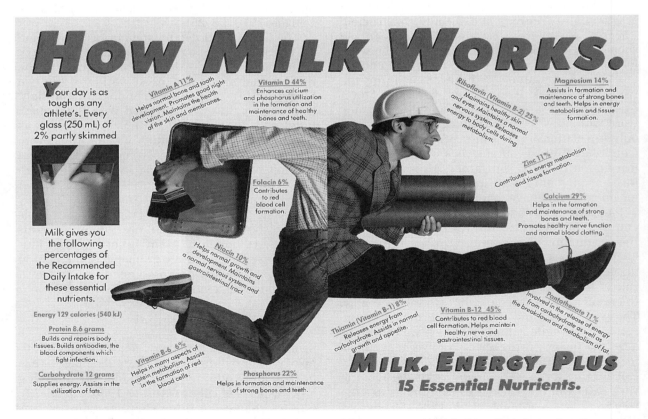

Advertisers use signifiers to create images associated with their products. Here milk is promoted as a health food that will supply enough energy to get the consumer through a tough day.

semiotics to multiple gestures and rituals of social life (Fiske 1982). The notion of a "text" has been broadened to cover any cultural practices—gestures, dress, writing, speech, photography, film, television, and the like. The notion of "sign" is the smallest unit of communication within a language system, variously applied to such elements as a sound, a musical note, a gesture, or an item of clothing. Our selection and combination of items of clothing constitute a combination of visible signs, that have meaning for other people we meet. In choosing our clothes, we participate in a system of communication. We signify ourselves through the signs available within our culture, selecting and combining them with reference to codes and conventions, in order to structure the range of possible meanings they are likely to generate when read by others.

There can be multiple levels of meaning depending on the cultural competencies of readers. Barthes suggests, for example, that the *Paris Match* photograph of the black soldier saluting the French flag has a second-order signification, or connotation for people who know something of French history, namely, French imperialism and the subservience of the colonized races.

A familiar example of this signifying process is advertising (Turner 1990, 21). What advertisers do is use signifiers already conventionally related to a mental concept that they wish to attach to their product and then juxtapose them in images. Turner describes advertisements for "Ski yogurt" that show the product being eaten by people engaged in sailboarding, hang-gliding, surfing, and skiing, to develop the notion of yogurt as associated with youth, fitness, and health. Yogurt thus becomes a lifestyle product as much as a food. In similar ways, the goods we choose to buy do not merely fill material needs. They serve to encode our social surroundings and convey meanings about who and what we are (Douglas 1979).

Integration Through Rituals

It is a small step from the application of semiotics to visual displays in photographs and advertising to seeing all forms of ritualized behaviour and displays in society as structured by symbolic codes that can be "read" to communicate complex levels of meaning. Mary Douglas makes these connections explicit in her extensive research into

ritual in contemporary North American society. She acknowledges her intellectual debt to Durkheim but, like Parsons, argues that the model of societal integration through shared beliefs and practices applies to complex no less than simpler societies.

Douglas's research begins from the basic assumption that culture is rooted in everyday social relations—in daily cleanliness rituals and the organization of eating as much as in sweeping worldviews (Wuthnow et al. 1984, 82). Her most famous work is the study of rituals surrounding dirt (1966) and how these are linked to a symbolic system of pollution and purity, and from purity to questions of the sacred and the holy. She argues that dirt and what makes things dirty or clean provides a basis for understanding the moral order of society and the means by which society periodically renews and reaffirms its basic social relations and collective sentiments (Wuthnow et al. 1984, 84). Her basic question is why the ugh and the ick of dirt, and the compulsion to clean things up? Matter is not simply dirty in and of itself. Food, for example, is clean when on a plate, but dirty when on one's shirt; leftover dinner is dirty when on the floor, but clean when put into a waste bin that is still on the floor, only in a different place. It does not seem to be the bits of food in themselves that elicit the response "dirty" but their location. Dirt, Douglas concludes, is matter out of place. This in turn implies two conditions: a set of ordered relations and a contravention of that order. Dirt is the by-product of a systematic ordering and classification of matter. The organization of the world into distinct countries and regions, is similarly associated with ideas of dirt and pollution. Travellers in almost all countries are advised to regard the water and food in other countries as dirty, and to take precautions against it. Here it is the people rather than the matter that are out of place.

The idea of dirt is linked to moral rules, and at a deeper level, to the very definition of things, to a symbolic universe that both defines and orders the nature of our existence and legitimates our experiences. For Douglas, like Durkheim, social order is also moral order. Activities like sorting, tidying, cleaning and putting things in their place, act to reinforce both the structure of social reality and moral sentiments. When things get out of place we feel socially obligated to reset the structure of things, and therefore reinforce the fabric of social and moral order (Wuthnow et al. 1984, 87). Douglas draws close parallels between our propensity to see cleanliness as a matter of hygiene with similar purity rituals in primitive societies, which are seen as magic and religion (1966, 44). We tell ourselves that our practices are hygienic while theirs are symbolic; we kill germs while they ward off evil spirits. But, Douglas suggests, our fear of pollution is like fear of moral deviance or crime. Both involve things and behaviour out of place and as such threaten the larger moral structure. Our reaction to dirt, as to crime, is one of the basic social mechanisms that renew and redefine social rules and boundaries. We are particularly likely to get worked up about dirt, or crime, or other pollution, and to start to "clean things up" in times of social crisis. Douglas links heightened fears of environmental pollution in the United States to the crisis of Vietnam and the weakening of the hegemony of the United States in international politics.

Douglas (1979), Sahlins (1976), and others provide similar analyses of food as symbolic code in North American society, building on the classic study by Levi-Strauss ([1970] 1990) into food and mythology in nonindustrialized societies. Given the central importance of food in human life, it is not surprising that powerful rituals, symbolic meanings, and moral taboos are associated with it. Complex ritualized practices govern when and how we eat, the different kinds of foods appropriate for morning, noon, and evening meals, the order in which foods are presented (e.g., savory before sweet), and what combinations are permissible. Complex rituals construct how different foods are properly eaten, whether with knife, fork, spoon, chopsticks, or fingers. Seating arrangements around family tables and during formal meals reflect the status hierarchy within the group.

Other complex symbolic rules construct the relative status of what is deemed edible; for example, steak, pork chops, or fish fingers carry different symbolic messages when one has guests for dinner. Other proteins such as meat from horses, dogs, and cats, are generally considered taboo in North America, although they are acceptable in other cultures. Extensive tourism and migration in the late twentieth century have significantly expanded what North Americans consider to be good food, but this is still within fairly defined limits. The horror with which most of us might respond to the idea of eating a dog indicates that a powerful moral order underlies the cultural organization of food. It is not merely a matter of taste. Meat from dead humans is almost universally considered taboo. Sahlins suggests that the relationship of animals to people, as family pets, servants, or "livestock," and whether they are named or talked to, is closely connected to their acceptability as food. Food taboos thus serve to reflect and reinforce important social relations and relations of production in society.

Integration Through National Sentiments

Parsons' conception of an integrated cultural system as the basis for all social action, was particularly influential in North American sociology in promoting a search for the integrative values of modern American culture (Bellah et al. 1985). Robert Brym suggests that this focus had an impact on Canadian sociology principally through the very close academic ties between American and Canadian departments of sociology during the 1960s. Most of the faculty members were either recruited from, or trained in, universities in the United States (Brym 1989, ch. 1). American sociologists tended to see the United States as the best example of political and economic modernity, and they sought to explain this in terms of the distinctive culture that arose from the common experience of frontier settlement by rugged individualists, many of them Protestant noncon-

Culture is rooted in everyday social relations—complex symbolic rules are associated with food.

formists fleeing persecution in Europe. This promoted a system of cultural values that emphasized individualism, free enterprise, private property, and rejection of religious authority, tempered by a highly abstract "civil religion" embodied in the Declaration of Independence, and presidential oaths of office (Bellah 1990).

Canadian sociologists trained in the American functionalist tradition sought to discover similar unifying principles in Canadian society. To theorists like Clark, Lipset, and Porter, Canadian society seemed more conservative than the United States, with Canadians having a noticeably greater tendency to respect authority and hierarchy, and to accept state control over the economy. Theorists suggested that such cultural differences developed in response to harsher geographic frontiers, the migration of very large numbers of Loyalists to Canada after the American revolution of 1776, and the colonial government's concern to control the population and to put down liberal democratic rebellions in Upper and Lower Canada in 1837, so as to lessen the risk of United States territorial expansion northwards. In addition, while emigrants to America tended to be members of nonconformist Protestant sects, the majority of Canadians were Roman Catholic or Anglican, relatively hierarchical and authoritarian churches that inculcated deep respect for authority (Clark 1968; Lipset 1967; 1976; 1985; Porter 1965; 1979b).

Lipset (1963) adapted Parsons' model of pattern variables to compare American and Canadian societies on five main orientations to action (Brym 1989, 28). Lipset concluded that Canadians are (1) more elitist and accepting of class divisions, (2) less entrepreneurial or achievement-oriented, (3) less willing to take risks, (4) more collectively than self-oriented, and (5) more accepting of differences among people (Brym 1989, 28). Such differences, particularly the lower achievement drive, seemed to explain the more limited propensity for economic development in Canada compared to the United States. Horowitz (1968) suggested further that French Canada inherited a feudal political culture, and English Canada, while sharing some of the liberalism that influenced the United States, also had a strong element of toryism associated with the British aristocratic and Loyalist values. Liberalism views society as an agglomeration of individuals, while toryism views it as a corporate entity of hierarchi-

Unlike the United States, Canadian culture has allowed for the emergence of a third party of social democrats, such as the government headed by Premier Michael Harcourt in BC.

cally ordered classes. The combination of liberalism and toryism, Horowitz suggests, has made it possible for a weak third party of social democrats to emerge in Canada but not in the United States. Social democrats soften the emphasis on free enterprise inherent in liberalism with elements of feudal obligation of aristocrats towards commoners inherent in toryism. These historical, political, and religious characteristics are seen as defining a distinctively Canadian national cultural system, notwithstanding the dominant English language that Canada has in common with the United States and Britain.

Integration Through Mass Media

In functionalist theory, mass media, along with other institutions of socialization such as school and church, are seen as functioning to promote a unifying national culture.

The formal organization of mass media, particularly radio and television, has developed somewhat differently in Canada and the United States, reflecting some of the cultural distinctions noted above. A greater fear of a dictatorial state, combined with a heavy emphasis on individualism and entrepreneurship, encouraged the development in the United States of a "free press" model of media ownership based on private property and revenues from advertising. In Canada, as in Britain, the government has become heavily involved in media through public broadcasting, as well as through subsidies to the arts and publishing in Canada.

In both countries, the media are credited with performing important integrative functions for the nations as a whole. The prevailing functionalist conception of American mass communications since the 1960s characterizes it as both reflecting and reinforcing shared societal values of tolerance and incorporation of difference. The diversity of media outlets provides mechanisms through which all points of view in American society could contribute to the melting pot of cultural values. At the same time, the core values of individualism, free enterprise, and entrepreneurship are directly embodied in the pattern of private ownership and competition between the multiple channels for advertising revenues (Turner 1990, 200). In Canada, the Canadian Broadcasting Corporation is enjoined to operate in ways that will promote national unity and respect for the two founding languages of English and French and other heritage cultures. It also plays a powerful role in developing consensus around critical political issues such as free trade and constitutional debates.

Apart from any intentional transmission of cultural values, mass media have the capacity to promote societal integration simply as a by-product of their mass character. Millions of people may view the same television programs and this shared experience provides basis for conversations in school yards and over coffee, a ground for common beliefs and sentiments that can be shared with strangers (Fiske 1987, 285). Fiske concludes that television is a "cultural enabler" providing a means for the mass of people to participate in the processes of production and circulation of meanings that constitute culture. Hobson (1982) describes the importance of daytime radio for housewives in Britain. It serves to order the largely structureless experience of doing housework, dividing the day up into a series of time sequences around which women organize their daily routines. Disc jockeys often direct their discourse to this audience of housewives, breaking the isolation and creating a sense of community with millions of other women who may be listening in as they do their housework. These programs both reflect and reinforce cul-

THEORY OF EVOLUTION (UPDATED)

tural norms surrounding housework, as women's work, and usually done by women who spend all day in their home.

The Limitations of Functionalist Analyses of Culture

Parsons' model includes individual actors who make choices. But in his cultural system, individual choices appear to be determined by the overarching system of values and expectations. Active human agency is lost behind structured conformity to the cultural system. This is especially so when grammar, with its rigid rules, is used as a model for culture in general.

A further problem within the Parsonian conception of the cultural system is the primacy accorded to values in determining behaviour. It implies that people who adopt different courses of action must have very different value systems. This is the main theme behind the culture of poverty debate, for example. Lower-class people are seen as failing to take advantage of opportunities because they have internalized a deviant and disabling set of subcultural values. Repeated studies of lower-class people, however, suggest that they often do share middle-class aspirations and values (Swidler 1986, 275). Such research suggests that the structure of opportunities and the distribution of material and cognitive resources may have more to do with limiting choice than deviant values.

The strength accorded to culture as an integrative force also raises a number of unanswered questions concerning how such uniformity comes to be imposed in societies characterized by major divisions along class and ethnic lines. It implies relations of power and structured inequality in access to and control over resources through which to structure culture, which are not addressed within functionalist theory.

The Political Economy of Culture: Ideology and Control

Traditional Marxist theory downplays the importance of culture in social action as a secondary effect of economic relations. The mode of production forms the base, which determines, in the final analysis, the superstructure of prevailing ideas and values. Although culture may play a role in people's acceptance of the status quo, its explanatory power is weak.

Robert Brym (1989) adopts the political economy perspective when he challenges cultural interpretations of Canadian society on the grounds that all the patterns of social, political, and economic behaviour to which cultural explanations have been applied, can be more adequately accounted for by material, political, and economic constraints. Brym argues that while the cultural differences highlighted between United States and Canadian societies might have some tenuous validity at the level of description, they have minimal explanatory value. A lower level of entrepreneurship in Canada compared to the United States can be better explained by Canada's branch-plant economy and the stifling effects of foreign control over Canadian manufacturing industries, than by more limited achievement drive or propensity for risk-taking; processes of capital concentration and centralization better explain the patterns of uneven economic development within Canada than proportions of Catholics or Protestants in the population; the presence of a third party of social democrats is better explained by the structure of the voting system in Canada than by a cultural legacy of aristocratic toryism; any evidence of greater ethnic inequality in Canada can be better explained by immigration policies and a restricted school system than cultural values placed on ethnic differences.

Where Brym does see the impact of culture is, ironically, in the development of social sciences in Canada, which he sees as dominated by American functionalism. Brym explains this cultural dominance in terms of the political and economic constraints under which Canadian sociology developed, and in particular the heavy dependence on American personnel and such bastions of American capitalism as the Rockefeller, Carnegie, and Ford Foundations. The fledgling sociology department at McGill received a large grant from the Rockefeller Foundation in 1929 to study unemployment in Montreal. The Carnegie Endowment gave funds to several Canadian universities to study Canadian frontier settlement. Universities in the United States similarly looked to these capitalist benefactors for funds, and not surprisingly, they reflected worldviews compatible with capitalism. During the great expansion of its sociology departments between 1960 to 1975, Canada depended very heavily on American recruits, American theories, data, and textbooks. This process restructured intellectual agendas, promoting variants of functionalism across all the social sciences.

Ideology, Power, and Consent

All Marxist theory concurs in viewing the organization of forces of production and resulting class relations as critical. A branch of Marxist theory that developed in Europe, variously however, known as **The Frankfurt School** or as **critical theory**, has developed Marxist analysis of culture in a very different direction. The central problem that theorists such as Habermas, Althusser, and Gramsci address is why the expected socialist revolution prophesied by Marx in the mid-nineteenth century did not occur as expected (Agger 1991, 107–8). They try to reconstruct the logic and methods of Marxism to fit twentieth-century conditions of advanced capitalism in which the capitalist system has clearly become very effective at forestalling crises and promoting mass support. They were particularly influenced by a vision of mass society in which individuals seemed powerless against the economic and technical forces and the mass culture produced by advanced capitalism (Billington et al. 1991, 14–18). Some of the founding theorists in the Frankfurt School—Adorno, Horkheimer, and Marcuse—were themselves refugees from National Socialism in Germany. They had reason to fear the apparent ease with which the masses had accepted totalitarianism, military rule, and anti-Semitism. Detached and anomic individuals from broken or harsh and unloving families seemed especially vulnerable to such mass indoctrination.

In particular, the Frankfurt theorists believed that Marx underestimated the extent to which culture could be used within advanced capitalism to win the complicity of workers in a highly exploitative economic system. From the perspective of critical theory, culture is ideology (Fiske 1987, 256). It reflects the processes by which members of a society come to absorb and internalize ways of looking at reality that support the interests of the dominant class. Critical theory challenges the earlier Marxist view of culture as merely the effect of economic relations, stressing instead the relative autonomy of culture, and its independent capacity to influence economic and political relations. Althusser (1971) argues that such institutions as the legal system, schools, and mass media, or what he calls "the ideological apparatuses of the state," are as significant as economic structures in the perpetuation of capitalism. Furthermore, while these apparatuses or institutions may appear to operate independently of each other, in practice they work together in promoting ideology (Althusser 1971; Fiske 1987, 256–57). Althusser concurs with Saussure's argument that language exercises a determining influence over what we perceive as "real," and he argues further that language is inherently ideological. Ideology is a structure of thought and consciousness, a conceptual framework in terms of which we all think and act, and experience the world and ourselves (Billington et al. 1991, 25; Turner 1990, 26).

Ideology not only produces culture, it produces our consciousness of ourselves, our very subjectivity. Ideology is truly successful when it is invisible to the people who absorb it. It is not an argument that elites are trying to force others to accept. It is what other people themselves think and feel. It is common sense, internalized into our unconscious and taken for granted. When this argument is pushed to its logical conclusion, then the very idea of an individual with an essential self disappears as a fiction, an impossibility. In its place is a social being who possesses a socially produced sense of identity—a *subjectivity*. We experience our identities as freely chosen, or at least as natural, but this is a myth, and a very powerful myth supporting the notions of individualism and free enterprise that underlie capitalism. This socially constructed self-consciousness is so deeply incor-

porated into our being that no scientific analysis of the exploitative relations of capitalism or objective class interests can undermine it.

In summary, for Althusser, there is no room for individual human agency in relation to culture, because the individual is determined by culture. Cultural change seems virtually impossible, and ideological struggle futile. The frightening closure of this analysis of ideology drove Althusser himself towards suicidal depression.

Other Marxists have rejected Althusser's extreme structuralism as too deterministic, and have proposed a more flexible and open conception of ideology. This new approach, which is sometimes referred to as **culturalism** or **cultural Marxism**, builds on the work of the Italian Marxist Antonio Gramsci.

Gramsci conceptualized culture as the site of continual struggle over meaning between dominant and subordinate classes, never a finished victory or a static set of beliefs that can be taken as given. The dominant class attempts to "naturalize" the meanings that serve their interests into the common sense of the society as a whole, while the subordinate classes resist, and try to make different meanings that serve their interests (Fiske 1987, 255). A classic example of such struggle is the portrayal of contract negotiations between union and management where each side tries to win popular support through the mass media by presenting their stand as reasonable and in the interest of the wider society while the other side is being intransigent and rapacious. The "winner" is not determined in advance.

Gramsci developed the concept of **hegemony** to refer to the way in which the consent of the subordinate classes to the wider capitalist system is achieved. He argues that while some coercion is inevitable, given differences in power, hegemony is principally achieved by means of winning the active consent of subordinated classes. To achieve cultural leadership, the dominant group has to negotiate with opposing groups or classes, and these negotiations must lead to some genuine accommodation (Turner 1990, 211–12). As a result, the cultural meanings that prevail in capitalist societies are never totally the meanings of the dominant capitalist class. Popular or mass culture is a contradictory mixture of meanings—it is both dominated and oppositional, determined and spontaneous, continually being negotiated and struggled over (ibid.). Canadian political elites could by no means be certain that the corporate business orientation towards free trade deals, cutbacks in government spending, and the like, will gain mass support or even mass acquiescence.

Turner suggests that this approach has important advantages over earlier versions of Althusser's deterministic structuralism. It restores human agency to the analysis of culture, and avoids simplistic notions that class position determines how and what people think. It has served to focus research interests within Marxist theory on popular culture. Important questions raised within this perspective are: What are the processes through which the dominance or the "naturalizing" of elite values as common sense are achieved? How deeply do elite values penetrate the consciousness of the mass of people? How are they resisted or challenged?

Mass Media and the Manufacturing of Consent

The traditional Marxist approach to cultural analysis, strongly influenced by Althusser, focussed on the political economy of the communications industry. The central argument is that the class background and class interests of those who control the economic resources needed by the media determine the content of the message. The media are in a position to wield enormous power with respect to the manufacture and dissemination of mass culture, but are not accountable to the mass of people. They owe allegiance principally to those who pay the piper—the corporate owners and advertisers, and the capitalist state that operates to protect those interests.

The corporate empires of billionaire capitalist families such as the Irvings and the Thomsons and multimillionnaire Conrad Black dominate the communications industry in Canada, controlling extensive newspaper chains, magazines, and radio and television stations. The Irving family controls all the English-language newspapers in New Brunswick, as well as CHSJ radio station and CHSJ-TV station in Saint John. Thomson Corporation controls 189 newspapers, 56 in Canada—including the influential *Globe and Mail*—and 133 in the United States. The Kent Commission, set up in 1980 to explore the implications of the concentration of media ownership in Canada, strongly criticized such concentration

as against public interest. It recommended that the Irvings in particular be forced to sell at least some of the newspaper or television channels to ensure some competition in the media within the Maritimes. No action was ever taken by any level of government to act on such recommendations.

Behind the corporate empires that own media outlets, is another layer of big business influence, that of corporate advertisers. They exert their influence vicariously through their power to withhold or withdraw revenues from media outlets that promote views with which they do not agree. Few media outlets are sufficiently independent of advertising revenues to risk offending corporate clients.

The mass media function as **gatekeepers**, selecting and screening information from the viewpoint of corporate elites (Clement 1975, ch. 7–9). They have the power to determine whether or not certain ideas and information will reach a wide public audience, how such information will be presented, the sources deemed credible, and the opinions seen as worthy of quotation.

Noam Chomsky documents particularly dramatic examples of selective news coverage in the North American media that manufactured public consent for wars in the interests of global capitalism (Chomsky 1988; Achbar 1994). Most people

As gatekeepers, the mass media can control public information. Cable TV czar Ted Rogers recently took over Maclean Hunter, a major communications company.

in the United States and Canada know something about the genocide that occurred in Cambodia in the 1970s, but little or nothing about similar genocide occurring in East Timor during the same period. The main reason, Chomsky argues, is that the Khmer Rouge regime under Pol Pot was identified as procommunist and anticapitalist, while the Indonesian government that invaded East Timor was an ally that supported United States capitalist interests in the region. In 1991, a tyrant who threatened United States oil interests in the Middle East was demonized and pilloried in the media as a prelude to manufacturing consent for the Gulf War. Equally tyrannical military rulers in Latin America who support American business interests are routinely ignored. We are likely to get the same patterns of coverage in all branches of the media, except perhaps from small, alternative media outlets.

The corporate interests behind mass media are also typically reflected in the slant that is placed on information provided. Labour unrest and strikes that run counter to business interests are typically portrayed as subversive, against the national interest, damaging to the public, irresponsible, unfair, and so on. Media coverage of the CANDU nuclear power program in Canada overwhelmingly cited probusiness spokespersons and opinions, while extensive documentation of the environmental threats posed by this industry was either ignored or belittled in brief coverage (Clow 1993).

The constant focus in mass media on political and state offices as the seat of power also works to mask the central influence of business and financial elites. Reporting news as discrete events similarly encourages acceptance of the social structure as "the way it is," stifling critical thought or questioning. Emphasis on entertainment displays life as individual dramas determined by human nature or fate rather than economic structures. All such tactics can be seen as serving the ideological function of disguising the workings of capitalism and so promoting false consciousness in the masses.

Newspaper owners commonly deny that they exercise any direct editorial control over their papers, and reporters also, typically, deny direct interference in what they write. But, as Clement points out, such direct control is unnecessary when owners have the power to select their editors and staff (1975, ch. 9). Clement cites the example of newspaper tycoon Paul Desmarais, who took over *La Presse* in Quebec and promptly purged its staff of all dissidents. A similar purge took place at *The Globe and Mail* after it was acquired by Thomson in 1980. Changes at the *Globe* that, in the words of its publisher, "better serve the interests of [the paper's] elite audience" included sharp reductions in news space and personnel and dismantling the labour and women's beats, while vastly expanding business coverage, reshaping delivery routes to eliminate "undesirable" [poor] subscribers, and adding glossy magazines to appeal to upscale advertisers. Many columnists who had contributed to the *Globe*'s "mix of voices" departed (Heinricks 1989, 16). In May 1989, for example, the paper dropped the weekly column by David Suzuki, which regularly revealed the damage done to the environment by unbridled industrial expansion. Suzuki's column was dropped ostensibly because its concerns were "too narrow."

Conrad Black has been particularly outspoken about his interest in owning newspapers. He reportedly has said that he doesn't see much point in owning newspapers if he can't use them to get his point of view across and influence affairs of state (*Globe and Mail*, 25 July 1987, D8). He apparently agreed not to get directly involved in the editorial policy of the magazine *Saturday Night* when he bought it, but he chose an old friend, John Fraser, to run it.

Rethinking Hegemony

This traditional political economy analysis of media as an arm of capitalism, has been challenged within contemporary Marxist theory for an oversimplification of culture. The approach implies a deterministic explanation of class

GABLE, The Globe and Mail

manipulation and exploitation that obscures complex interrelationships between producers, texts, and audiences (Curran and Seaton 1985, 282). The Centre for Contemporary Cultural Studies (CCCS) at the University of Birmingham in Britain is widely acknowledged as the centre of Marxist cultural studies (Hall et al. 1980; Fiske 1987; Turner 1990; Grossberg et al. 1991; Sherwood et al. 1993). Theorists associated with this school of "cultural studies" have sought to develop Gramsci's conceptualization of culture as an area of struggle, involving both accommodation and resistance, in which the outcome is not determined in advance.

Fiske (1987, 254–55) identifies the basic Marxist assumptions that underlie the CCCS research. Firstly, meanings and how they are made are seen as indivisibly linked to social structures and adequately explained only with reference to those structures and their history. Reciprocally, social structures are themselves held in place by the meanings that culture produces. Also underlying this approach is the assumption that capitalist societies are deeply divided, primarily along class lines, but there are also divisions of gender, race, age, occupation, and the like. Society is not an organic whole. Furthermore, social relations are understood in terms of social power, structures of domination, and subordination, which are continual sites of conflict and struggle. These structural divisions are centrally important in determining how mass communications are produced and interpreted.

Stuart Hall, one of the founders of Marxist cultural studies in Britain, argues that the structures and relations of capitalism determine the prevailing frameworks of knowledge (1980, 130). Perspectives derived from this basis are then *encoded* into mass media texts. Encoding uses a set of codes, which must be sufficiently commonplace to have shared meanings for producers and intended audiences. The texts are then transmitted to a mass audience who must *decode* the message. There may well be discrepancies or misinterpretations between encoded meaning and decoded interpretation, but Hall suggests that this occurs only within a limited range. Codes may carry more than one potential meaning but not all meanings are equal, since any culture tends to impose dominant or preferred meanings. Hall proposes three hypothetical positions from which decodings may be constructed—preferred, negotiated, and oppositional.

In the preferred response, both producers and viewers or readers are operating within the dominant hegemonic worldview. A negotiated reading is one that acknowledges the legitimacy of the hegemonic definitions of reality at the grand level but makes exceptions to the rule to fit local situations. Hall gives the familiar example of people who agree at the level of national interest that wages should be checked to combat inflation, but make an exception for their own wage negotiations (1980, 137). An oppositional reading is one that decodes messages at the national level in a globally contrary way. An example would be when a message that portrays wage restraint as in the "national interest" is read as "class interest." Fiske (1987, 284) argues that the social relations of capitalism always involve a political dimension because all such relations are determined more or less directly by the unequal distribution of power. Hence, all meanings arise, in part, from a political base, in terms of which the struggle for meanings takes place.

Textual analysis within Marxist cultural studies seeks to "crack open" the codes of mass communication, to show how media produce and perpetuate the status quo. Studies of television programs have sought to demonstrate how contradictions and divisions within society are smoothed over (Turner 1990, 95–100). Antagonistic class relations are neutralized, by a series of translations in which inequality becomes personal differences, political opposition becomes disorder, and power becomes authority. When journalists claim to be objective, neutral and impartial, and to operate autonomously from government or business interference, this makes it more difficult for audiences to see through the biases, or to recognize how restricted news coverage actually is.

Ethnographic Studies of Class and Culture

Ethnographic research within Marxist cultural studies has focussed particularly on working-class subcultures in an effort to document processes of resistance and opposition to the dominant hegemonic ideology. The irony is that even this opposition works in practice to perpetuate the class structure of capitalism and to preserve the status quo of inequality and exploitation. The study by Paul Willis, *Learning to Labour* (1981), has been particularly influential in this regard. Willis participated extensively in the lives of working-class boys in England during their last year of school and into the first six months of work, supplementing his observations with group discussions, informal interviews, and diaries. He documents how the boys lived their school lives, and how completely they managed to invert its values through such practices as truancy, being asleep in class, being in class and doing no work, being in the wrong class, and actively ridiculing anyone who took school work seriously. Willis viewed the refusal to compete as a radical act—a refusal by members of the working class to collude in its own educational suppression (Willis 1981, 128; Turner 1990, 176–77). The structural effect of this opposition to the culture of the school, however, is to perpetuate the cycle of working-class youths entering low-paid, working-class jobs. In the 1990s, with the steady decline in manual labouring work in Britain, it is likely to lead to a future of chronic unemployment.

The typical subcultural dress, music, and behavioural styles of working-class boys in Britain

Ironically, the effect of opposition to the culture of school works to perpetuate the class structure of capitalism.

(the spiked hair, black leather, heavy boots, loud discordant music, and threatening speech and posture associated with punks and skinheads) are interpreted within Marxist cultural studies as expressions of opposition to middle-class lifestyles that these boys cannot hope to achieve (Hebdige 1979; Cohen 1980).

Strengths and Weaknesses in the Marxist Theory of Culture

Classic Marxist analysis draws attention to relations of power and class interests that are inherent in mass culture, both in the content of mass media and in how audiences interpret that content (Grossberg et al. 1991, 23). What functionalists accept as shared meaning systems are reinterpreted within Marxist theory as expressions of ideological hegemony. This has led to some heated academic debates between the two schools of theory, with each side accusing the other of bias and oversimplification (Sherwood et al. 1993, 373).

Contemporary research within cultural Marxism suggests that neither the class-interest model nor the shared-values model is adequate to understand how people respond to mass communication. It has not been possible to predict how people will interpret television programs on the basis of their class position. Similarly, researchers who interpreted the subcultural practices of working-class boys as expressions of resistance to capitalism have acknowledged in retrospect that they may have imputed political values and commitments that the boys themselves did not hold (Hebdige 1988).

Greater appreciation of the complexity of the processes involved in reading mass communications has generated a shift within cultural Marxism towards a more social constructionist analysis of how people construct and disseminate meaning.

The Social Construction of Meaning

The social constructionist approach to the study of culture tries to escape the rigidity of either class or cultural determinism by focussing on how meanings are produced, sustained, and changed through social practices. The work of Foucault forms an important intellectual bridge between classical structuralist Marxism and social constructionist theory. In common with Marxist theory, Foucault rejects Saussure's semiotics approach to language and meaning as too abstract and ahistorical. He insists that cultural meanings have to be understood as specific to particular historical periods and prevailing economic and political relations. He also agrees with Marxists that power relations are built into language. What he rejects is the notion that power can be reduced to relations of production. He proposed an alternative conception of power in which control over knowledge rather than economic resources is crucial.

Foucault shifts the analysis of culture to centre stage. He is especially interested in the historical rise of the "disciplines" that make up the social sciences, and how professionals working within these disciplines developed their **discourses**, or ways of thinking and talking about social phenomena. Foucault combines the two meanings of the term *discipline*—a body of knowledge, and a system of regulation and control—into a theory of "power-knowledge" in which discourse becomes simultaneously a claim to expertise and a mechanism for controlling social behaviour through controlling how people think.

In *Discipline and Punish* (1977), Foucault analyses the historical development of the discourse of criminology as a social science discipline, documenting the shift in conceptualization of crime from disobedience that must be punished, to the notion of delinquency as a personality disturbance that could be treated and "normalized" through the therapeutic practices of probation officers, psychiatrists, and other professionals. This shift in discourse around crime marked a shift in power. Formerly, the monarch exercised control over death, from the top down, but this shifted to the power exercised by professionals, to control life by normalizing behaviour from the bottom up, through multiple agencies. In *The History of Sexuality* (1970) Foucault similarly traces the emergence of a discourse around sexuality within the health and education professions, that associates sexuality with repression, personality disorders, and a multiplicity of behavioural problems. As with criminology, this discourse is associated with a shift in power to physicians, educators, and psychologists concerned with surveillance, normal-

ization, and control of bodies. Discourse is thus a political activity. It legitimates practices of power in terms of efficiency and rationality, based on technical superiority and knowledge. Resistance is muted because it seems irrational.

Foucault's work has encouraged research into professional discourses as the site of struggles over meaning and competing claims to power. His contemporary Donzelot (1979), for example, explores how discourses on hygiene within the medical profession enhanced the status of mothers relative to fathers in the home, and simultaneously legitimated the authority of physicians and social workers to intervene in the once private sanctuary of the home.

The Limitations of Foucault's Work: Derrida and Deconstruction

Foucault's approach to the study of meaning has come under criticism for being too rigid and implicitly elitist in his conceptualization of discourse (Weedon et al. 1980b, 214; Doran 1993, 18). Ironically, while Foucault criticizes Marxism for a top-down analysis of power, he in turn adopts a top-down analysis of discourse. Critics accuse him of seeing all discourse as produced by professionals and imposed over others, without considering how ordinary people produce discourses in everyday communications. Foucault emphasizes the importance of resistance, but fails to analyse how people actually do resist and struggle against professional interpretations of their lives.

Jacques Derrida, a student of Foucault, challenges the view of discourses and texts as carrying definitive meanings. Derrida is the acknowledged founder of the school of philosophy and literary theory known loosely as poststructuralism or **deconstructionism**. Derrida's deconstructionist approach to literature has implications that challenge the basic assumption of both functionalist and classical Marxist theories, namely, that culture can be analysed as structured systems of meaning and values, founded on a common language. Derrida denies the possibility of ever arriving at a clear reading of the meaning of communication. The meaning of any text, written, spoken, or even in our unspoken thoughts, is fundamentally "undecidable," subject to an endless play of possible interpretations that no individual, or social analyst, can hope to pin down.

Derrida, like Saussure, sees language as a system of signs, with a sign being something that stands for, or is a symbol of, something else. Where Derrida differs from Saussure is that he pushes the notion of difference, and the arbitrary nature of words, toward a radically new meaning. He coins the term *differAnce* to convey this altered meaning. The capital letter "A" in this word is used intentionally to highlight Derrida's distinctive spelling. It is derived from the French verb *differer*, but is intended to combine two distinct concepts: to differ and to defer. Words differ in meaning and they also defer meaning. Derrida focusses on the gap between the sign (the signifier) and what it stands for (the signified), a gap that can never be bridged. The only way we could know the exact meaning of a word would be to have the thing itself that the word, as sign, refers to, and then we would not need the sign at all. Plato's concept of *tree* is a well-known example of this gap in meaning. What does the signifier *tree* refer to? One could point to a specific example, like the apple tree in my garden, and say "That is a tree," but does that cover the totality of everything that is meant by the concept of *tree*? The answer has to be no. There are millions of other objects to which the concept *tree* might correctly be applied, which may bear only minimal resemblance to my apple tree, including the green plastic object that I hang decorations on at Christmas. The concept of *tree* or *treeness* cannot be summed up by pointing to one object, or even a set of objects. *Tree* is a relatively straightforward concept compared with other terms. Consider the difficulty of trying to point to what is signified by the concept of *culture*. Human communication is an endless play of interpretation, uncertainty, and reformulation. This endless play of meaning, far from being a negative characteristic to be overcome, creates an openness that makes philosophy possible in the first place (Derrida 1974, 17, 31; Neel 1988, 118).

The classic notion of logic assumes not only that any given word has an exact meaning, but also that an exact word exists for any concept, such that we can say exactly what we mean, no more and no less. In Derrida's view this is an illusion. Words inevitably carry far more meaning than the one intended, because they bear traces of all the contexts of their previous usage (Derrida 1974, 167). Try as we might, we cannot slough off this baggage that language carries. The "trace" itself does not exist as an entity.

Derrida, in his work in literary criticism, plays around with writing. His goal is not to repeat or rephrase what the author is "really" saying, as some all-sufficient vision of truth, but to deconstruct the text to see how it works—to make the baggage visible, what it excludes, suppresses, alludes to, fills in, and the ever-present structural possibilities of miscarrying.

In *Grammatology* (1974, 42–44, 62–70) and in *Margins of Philosophy* (1982, 316–21), Derrida explores what he sees as the essential qualities of writing: Written texts can long outlive their authors and there is an inexhaustible variety of ways in which unknown future readers might read them. Written signs can break with their contexts. Whole documents can be carried off, or paragraphs and sentences extracted from their context, which necessarily rearranges all the associations and possible interpretations that the original had. Consider what I am doing here with Derrida's writings, taking sentences and brief paragraphs extracted from five separate books, originally written in French, summarizing them and suggesting that "this is what Derrida means"! Derrida himself has no control over what I do with his texts once he has written them. His work, like mine, or that of any other author, is open to an endless play of repetitions, reformulation, and interpretation that cannot possibly be controlled (Neel 1988, 112–13). There is no absolute meaning that he or I can point to as the exact meaning, precisely what is signified.

Writing, moreover, occurs as "graft." It is always grafted onto other texts, the endless stream of other writing that has been and will be linked with the topics at hand (Derrida 1982, 320–21). These, too, stick to the current text as baggage, as that which this text tries to distinguish itself from. As readers, we encounter any text with all this multiplicity of associations, all the previous contexts in which we have encountered the same words, all the other texts we are familiar with, and the multitude of specific contexts in which the reading occurs. All this goes into our "reading" of what the current text "means." My understanding of what Derrida meant is a composite of what he wrote himself, what others have said about him, and other texts I have read about language and culture. It does not and cannot stand on its own. The absolutely uncontaminated, totally "correct" meaning of Derrida's texts, or any text, is truly undecidable.

Derrida argues further that problems with controlling the meaning of written texts apply equally to speaking. We commonly think that speaking is closer to thinking, and so a more accurate medium for saying what we mean. But no sooner are words uttered than they are available for interpretation, repetition, and reformulation, even by those who did not hear them. Verbal statements are even more vulnerable than written ones since, unless they were tape-recorded, there is no record of the total conversation in which given utterances occurred, no way of checking the precise wording used, and no possibility of editing. It can be very intimidating to speak in front of others and have one's unguarded utterances deconstructed.

This fear may underlie the myth of the "strong silent type" who "knows" but does not say anything, but Derrida does not permit this retreat into silence. He stresses repeatedly that there can be no meaning outside of language. When we think, we think in words. As soon as we try to formulate our thoughts coherently, even to ourselves, the trouble starts. We are likely to find that we really do not know what we mean, or "what we want to say" if we knew how to say/write it.

Valverde's (1987) analysis of feminist articles in mainstream women's magazines brings out the complexity of any deconstructionist reading of a text. Valverde identifies the initial intent of feminist authors as spreading information to women who are not normally reached by explicitly feminist publications, but she suggests that the context of glamour and pornographic magazines will inevitably distort the messages. When women's magazines like *Vogue* and *Cosmopolitan* embed feminist "think-pieces" in a sea of glamorous fashion pictures, readers will think of them as "fashionable ideas for fashionable women," rather than as a serious challenge to women as objects of beauty and subjects of consumption. A photograph of feminist Gloria Steinem in a black swimsuit, with a discussion of her diet problems, reduces her to just another Cosmo girl. When a pornographic magazine like *Forum* runs a feminist article critiquing policies to censor erotica, it co-opts feminism into supporting media that systematically degrade women. Valverde concludes that debates about feminist tactics and ethics must be informed by analysis of the strategies used by media to co-opt and subvert feminist messages.

The deeper problem is that Valverde's own deconstructive reading of texts can be further deconstructed. She presumes to know that *Vogue* and *Cosmo* readers will use the framework of hegemonic consumerism to interpret feminist articles, but she herself bought the fall issue of *Vogue* to look at the furs, and yet ends up thinking very analytically about the set of feminist articles she found therein. Other *Cosmo* readers might identify with a feminist in a swimsuit as "just like a Cosmo girl" and be more open to reading her work than if they think of her as totally unlike themselves. Readers of *Forum* may be brought up with a jolt by a feminist article that distinguishes erotica from violent and degrading treatment of women, and that includes a critique of heterosexism.

In short, there are multiple possible readings of these feminist articles—their surface appearances, their context amid glamorous and pornographic materials, the opposition reading that Valverde herself offers, the retrospective, future re-reading or re-thinking of the articles under the influence of other commentaries in other contexts, including perhaps the effects of Valverde's own article. Deconstructive analysis does not merely describe how other texts produce their effects. The textual deconstruction materially alters the nature of what is being described in the very process of describing it. Readers of Valverde's article will not read magazines in entirely the same way in future. But neither will all Valverde's readers read or re-read the relevant articles in the same way as Valverde reads them, just as I am not reading into Valverde's article exactly the meanings that I think she is trying to convey.

Meaning as Social Practice

The central problem for sociology that Derrida's work leaves unresolved is how meaning is established outside the endless play of words. For language to be mutually comprehensible among members of a society, meaning cannot be arbitrary. Individuals are not free to alter the meanings of words at will. Derrida cannot avoid making the assumption that people share conventional meanings for language in order to write anything. For signs to exist there must be mechanisms outside of language that fix and sustain conventional meanings, both within social practices and at the level of individuals, and we have to go beyond Derrida to explore these social determinants (Weedon et al. 1980b, 196–97).

Derrida's ideas are encouraging the shift within cultural studies away from an exclusive concern with texts, and toward a focus on the plurality of audiences and readers, and how they interpret communications from a multiplicity of subcultural standpoints (Brunsdon 1989; McRobbie 1991, 137). A central idea taken from Derrida's work is that reading is always an active process, not a passive absorption of messages. Classical textual analysis, as we have seen above, seeks to crack the codes and display how journalists and others construct their texts to privilege certain meanings. But as yet we have limited insight into how different audiences do this active work of cracking codes, and how they draw on intertextual meanings from diverse individual and subcultural experiences to insert meaning into texts.

A number of studies of audience reactions that began from a Marxist perspective of class analysis have suggested that class background is not an adequate predictor of responses. David Morley (1980) tested the reactions of twenty-six mixed occupational groups to the British television current affairs program *Nationwide*. He found an unexpected variety of readings, and very unexpected cross-class similarities between bank managers and apprentices, university students and shop stewards. Responses were influenced more by conversations among the people gathered together to watch the program than by the class backgrounds of individual members (Turner 1990, 132–36).

Subsequent studies have taken a more ethnographic approach, studying audiences in the natural settings of their homes. They reveal a great complexity of responses in which people draw on many aspects of their everyday lives to weave distinctive meanings into the television programs that they watch. They are never merely "a television audience" (Morley 1986; Hobson 1982; Buckingham 1987). Both Buckingham and Hobson compared audience reactions with how producers initially conceived of the programs. What they found was that producers generally knew very little about their audiences, imputing to them simplified and even childlike responses that were far off the mark. Audiences on the whole were quite sophisticated readers of televi-

sion. Even young children clearly understood the constructed nature of the programs, if not the precise coding mechanisms utilized. They were aware that the secrets of the program were carefully "doled" out and enjoyed speculating on how the plot would work out in subsequent episodes.

Audience studies such as these are open to the criticism that even the idea of "an ethnography" of television audiences is problematic (Hartley 1988, 236; Turner 1990, 158). Audiences are not subcultures, but at best only disconnected fragments of culture, with the action of watching television artificially separated from the community of experiences on which people draw to make television meaningful. Morley actively created audiences when he collected unconnected strangers together to watch a program they might not otherwise have looked at. Television producers have little idea of who watches their productions or how people will react to them. The notion of "an audience" is a fiction invented by academics who want to study it, and by the television industry and regulatory bodies who see themselves as servicing it. It is a product of their discourses. It directs attention away from the actual audience and back to the discourses that call it into being—the critics, the programs, and the government policies and regulations (Turner 1990, 166).

The approach of *institutional ethnography* avoids some of the difficulties of audience studies by focussing on very specific groups of people in organized settings. It tries to make visible exactly what people do to produce an accountable order or meaning as part of their everyday, practical activities (Smith 1987a, 150–80). It draws theoretically upon both discourse analysis and ethnomethodological studies of actor's practices in making sense.

Of particular interest for cultural studies is the research on journalists as professionals, and what they do to produce news. Fishman (1980) documents the specific methods that journalists use in order to organize the world into something coherent that they can write about, while working under rigid practical constraints that include having to write from two to six stories every day, to meet publication deadlines, and news space limitations. They are forced to develop work routines that rely very heavily on bureaucratically organized agencies and personnel that are already in socially structured positions to gather information about phenomena of interest, and that have prescheduled activities that concentrate sources of information in short periods. Typically, they develop a sequence of related activities that they follow each day. A reporter on the "police beat," for example, routinely calls at the sheriff's office, checks the file box of overnight cases, checks the arrest reports, and calls at the police headquarters, all before checking in at the city editor's desk. Bureaucratic accounts, produced by officials who are expected and authorized to know, are treated as factual for the practical purposes of journalism. The result is that staff reporters routinely reproduce a bureaucratically organized view of society. Different methods would produce very different kinds of news.

The Limitations of Social Constructionism

Textual analysis assumes that mass media produce what a society comes to know about itself. The problem with this approach is that we still do not know how readers or television viewers actually insert meaning into such journalists' texts. Analysts assert their own competence to deconstruct texts and show how they are put together, yet assume that everyone else who reads newspapers or watches television naively absorbs what-

ever messages are encoded within it. Fishman can deconstruct newspaper reports as manufactured by noting how editors cobble together disparate items into themes, and how journalists rely on bureaucratic schedules to detect "events." He is under no illusion that such accounts represent the full truth of the matter. On the contrary, he argues strongly that concepts such as "crime waves" are fabrications used by editors to give some coherence to disparate items of news, notwithstanding evidence of declining crime statistics (1980, 4–6). It is not unreasonable to assume that other readers are also capable of reading between the lines of a text, and viewing news as "concocted" rather than factual truth. We can also reasonably assume that people generally, like journalists, cobble together versions of society around themes that link disparate items of experience, picking out some bits and ignoring or discounting others.

What we cannot take for granted is that all people automatically accept journalists' accounts as factual, no matter how skilfully such journalists may manipulate the codes for unbiased viewpoints. If Canadians in general routinely accepted accounts given by leading newspapers, television broadcasters, and politicians, the Charlottetown Accord would have won overwhelming acceptance in 1992 instead of being decisively rejected.

Evidence suggests that Canadians do not always accept journalists' accounts of events as factual.

Derrida's critique of discourse analysis still stands. The meaning of texts is inherently undecidable. The alternative critique of Derrida's approach also still stands. Meanings may have multiple interpretations, but they are not arbitrary and individuals are not free to interpret communications or to change the meanings of words any way they wish. Sociological analysis of audiences and how they read texts is still in its infancy.

Feminist Theory: Culture from the Margins

Feminist theories of culture have sought to expose the gendered character of culture and to challenge it. They bring to attention the absence of consideration of women in both theory and research, and explore the differences that their inclusion produces. They also try to articulate a subordinated women's culture, highlighting alternative standpoints, myths, beliefs, and values. Feminism as theory and as social movement is actively influencing the dominant culture.

The Discourses of Gendered Culture

The history of professional discourse in Western social sciences surrounding sexuality and culture has been profoundly influenced by the work of Sigmund Freud and the school of psychoanalysis that he founded. Freud argues that the unconscious mind is governed by primary biological drives and it is the control of these drives that is the foundation of social order and culture. The most basic or primal drive in infants is the drive to possess their mother. She is the source of life support and the satisfaction of basic physical needs and pleasures, and she is the first love object. Freud surmises that in the first months of life, an infant may have no clear sense of itself as distinct from the mother's body, as lacking her. It is not yet a conscious subject, only a mixture of chaotic, fragmented sensory experiences. It is in the process of coming to recognize itself as separate from the mother's body that the infant begins to develop true self-consciousness as a subject, and to enter the social, symbolic, and cultural world (Freud 1905).

The father, or perhaps more accurately the relationship between infant and symbolic father-figure, plays a crucial role in this process. In all infants, the mother is the focus of infantile sexual drives. The problem for boys is that this primal sexual desire to possess their mother brings them into immediate conflict with their father, and so gives rise to the *oedipus complex*. Even the expression of this desire raises profound anxiety that the more powerful father would retaliate and castrate the boy. The oedipus complex is resolved, Freud suggests, by mechanisms of repression and displacement. The unacceptable desire for the mother is repressed into the unconscious mind, and the powerful primal energies associated with it are displaced onto other, more acceptable motivations. Boys learn to identify with their fathers, and to channel their sexual drives into non-incestuous, heterosexual love objects. They are reconciled emotionally by the promise of sexual possession of a woman of their own in adulthood.

Infant girls also desire to sexually possess their mother but for them it is physically impossible because they lack a penis. They are castrated before birth. Freud suggests that this primal awareness of their sexual powerlessness, relative to boys, and their biological, rather than social inability to satisfy their most basic drive to possess their mother, is responsible for the relative passivity of girls, and their envy of and submission to boys who possess what they lack—a penis. Girls cannot ever obtain their primal desire for sexual power, except vicariously, through pregnancy and giving birth to a male child.

The conscious mind is aware only of the culturally acceptable ideas and emotions onto which the repressed psychic energy has been displaced. But the original primal drives remain within the unconscious. Psychoanalytic methods make it possible to retrieve them, through the language in which patients recount dreams, memories, fantasies, and free associations. Freud thus sees language as a channel to the unconscious mind, through associative chains of meaning (Weedon et al. 1980b, 201).

These processes of repression and displacement through which the unconscious and subjectivity are formed constitute, for Freud, the origin of culture, the fundamental imposition of social order on biological drives. The "superego" of moral constraints, sometimes referred to as the

Law of the Father, is imposed over the unconscious, and over the conscious, willful self, the "ego." Culture emerges through control over sexuality within the family, and male sexual power over the female.

The distinction into male and female is the most basic of the binary concepts that characterize culture, linked with other classifications such as presence/absence, active/passive, positive/negative, culture/nature, self/other, sacred/profane, public/private, and the like. In all these binary oppositions, the second or subordinate term is defined through its relation to the primary term, and in all cases the secondary term is identified with the female. Woman is "not-man," defined by what she lacks. In Freudian theory, all options open to a woman are circumscribed by this relation. In principle, she can accept her castration, and achieve true femininity as the object of male desire, or she can deny it and consider herself phallic like a man or she can reject all sexuality and become frigid. None of these options offers a positive identity for women (Grosz 1989, 133).

Freud's theories have had a profound impact on discourses within the social sciences and the humanities. The anthropologist Claude Levi-Strauss, for example, accepts the oedipus complex as the principal universal feature of human culture, linked to the universal prohibition against incest, to the principle of exogamy or marriage outside the kinship group, and to the consequent exchange of women across kin groups (Franklin et al. 1991, 9).

Lacan's Re-reading of Freud

The post-Freudian psychoanalyst Jacques Lacan replaces Freud's neurological model of the unconscious with a linguistic model, borrowing heavily on the work of Saussure (Grosz 1990, 96-97). He suggests that the unconscious is structured through language, and that linguistic analysis provides a way of understanding it. The content of the unconscious mind is composed of symbols, fragments of language, signifiers that have had their associated meanings or signifieds repressed, and hence cannot be consciously thought. The processes through which an infant comes to recognize itself as separate from the mother figure, as lacking her, and as competing for her with the father figure, are essentially

symbolic, not instinctual processes. It is not the penis, as physical organ, that establishes the crucial distinction between male and female, but the cultural meanings associated with it, what Lacan calls the *phallus*.

For Lacan, as for Freud, this symbolic order of cultural meanings embodied in language is inherently patriarchal. Infantile needs, demands and desires are organized according to patriarchal social formations. As children learn language, they learn their positions within this symbolic order, especially their positions as male or female. The phallus symbolizes the power that will accrue eventually to the boy child, but never to the girl. For Lacan, our individual subjectivity or sense of identity is not a given, or a starting point for analysis of behaviour. Nor is it produced by each unique individual. Rather, subjectivity is socially constructed—an effect of language.

The unconscious mind, the repository of repressed symbolic meanings, expresses and distorts itself in the conscious mind, through language. Lacan draws direct parallels between the mechanisms of repression and displacement in Freudian theory, and the metaphoric structure of meaning in language. Metaphors carry meanings that are not directly expressed, but implied through associations. Metonyms similarly substitute an attribute for a main reference, as when the word *crown* substitutes for *king*. Linguistic analysis thus provides a tool for psychoanalysis in probing unconscious systems of meaning (Grosz 1989, 24). Derrida's analysis of texts as the endless play of traces and associations that can

Feminist psychoanalysis challenges Freud's phallocentric theory, especially as it relates to the oedipus complex and power within the family.

never be fully defined, provides for Lacan, a model for exploring unconscious meanings carried metaphorically in conscious thought.

The Feminist Response

Much of the work in feminist theory of culture seeks to expose the patriarchal ideology inherent in the discourses of psychoanalysis, revealing what Freud, Lacan, and others claim as general theories of masculine and feminine subjectivities. The problem is that while certain aspects of psychoanalytic theory are blatantly patriarchal, other aspects can be readily incorporated into feminist thinking, particularly notions of the inherent bisexuality of human nature, and the rooting of gender identity in early childhood experience. Lacan's reformulation of Freud's theories in terms of language rather than innate biological drives appeals to many feminists as a way of challenging notions of natural sexuality and phallocentric ideology. But on the other hand, Lacan's formulation of the linguistic basis of psychoanalysis is as phallocentric as Freud's original account, and may be no less resistant to change (Grosz 1990, 144).

Feminists like Mitchell, Kristeva, and Irigaray see psychoanalytic theory, at least in the modified form proposed by Lacan, as an important contribution to the understanding of gendered culture. If gendered identity is socially constructed through language, then it follows that even the most deeply felt emotional experiences of femininity are not natural in the sense of innate characteristics of physiology (Turner 1990, 28). The symbolic privileging of the phallus in Freud and Lacan's theories may be determined by historically specific, patriarchal family forms and wider social relations, rather than the outcome of primal sexual drives. The core of Mitchell's defence of Freud is that he did not intend his analysis as a prescription of what women and femininity should be, but a description of what patriarchal culture demands of women (Mitchell 1975, 301–2; Grosz 1990, 19–20). Mitchell advocates psychoanalysis as a useful tool in understanding the formation of subjectivity and oppression.

The French feminists Julia Kristeva and Luce Irigaray both use psychoanalytic theories and methods to explore the buried pre-oedipal bedrock underlying paternal, phallic, symbolic law, although they carry it in different directions (Grosz 1989, 100–4). Kristeva suggests that within each subject there is a play of masculine and feminine that is repressed in the oedipal stage at which gender identity is formed. Irigaray is more concerned with developing an autonomous space for women to define their own identity *as women*, an identity that is not defined as "not-man," but as truly another sex. Traditional psychoanalysis focusses primarily on the mother-son relation, reducing it to a smothering maternity that must be overcome. Girls must renounce their initial homosexual attachment to the mother to be initiated into the social order and into relations of sexual exchange between men. Irigaray rejects the necessity of this crippling phallocentric maternity, and the separation demanded between one woman and another. But she recognizes that the displacement of the father's central place in the oedipal triangle, and the formation of a female genealogy of descent would require a complete reorganization of social order and a new system of language (Grosz 1989, 122–23).

Each of these theorists struggles endlessly with language. They are critically aware that the key words they use carry baggage of patriarchal connotations and associations. They struggle to talk about motherhood in a way that does *not* carry patriarchal ways of thinking about maternity as distinct from its binary opposite of paternity; or to discuss a corporeal sexuality for women that is not phallic-centred; or to define an otherness or "alterity" for women that is not different from, not in opposition to, and not complementing its binary opposite—"men." All of this makes these writers very difficult to read.

These theorists draw extensively on the techniques of linguistic analysis and textual deconstruction associated with Saussure and Derrida. They share Saussure's recognition that words only have meaning in relation to an entire system of words to which they are similar and yet different from, and Derrida's recognition that individual words cannot escape the endless play of associations and traces. Irigaray acknowledges that, ultimately, what she wants to achieve is unattainable—a pure woman-centred language in which to talk about women's experiences without any patriarchal connotations does not exist. Its construction would require changing the entire social order from which language emerges. In the meantime, she blurs the distinctions between poetry, fiction, and what passes as scientific knowledge, constantly deconstructing texts to reveal their phallic-centred underpinnings. Psychoanalysis itself can be seen as a form of textual analysis, revealing the unconscious underpinnings of conscious text.

Irigaray argues that the whole of Western thought, including the idea of God, can be seen as a strategy for alleviating man's consciousness of and guilt about the debt of life, body, nourishment, and social existence he owes to his mother. Culture substitutes for this debt an image of self-made, self-created man, with God as man's self-reflecting Other, usurping women's creativity to become the creator (Grosz 1989, 120–21). Mary O'Brien (1981) similarly explores the possibility of a theoretical reversal of gendered hierarchy in psychoanalytic theory, arguing that male envy of female reproductive power is more significant psychologically than penis envy. Infants directly experience the power of mothers to suckle their young, or see them swelling in pregnancy with a younger sibling, while the father's role is at best obscure, and may be totally unknown to most children. O'Brien suggests that phallocentric Western culture emerged as an attempt by males to compensate through the symbolic order for their primordial experience of powerlessness and alienation from birth and human continuity. Institutions such as marriage, and the pervasive subordination of women to men, reflect this same male drive to achieve their desire for reproductive power vicariously, through possession of a wife and her children.

Such feminist re-reading of the subtext of Western culture, however, can still be readily absorbed into classical psychoanalytic theory. It does not challenge the core argument that it is precisely male alienation from nature and suffocating maternity that makes culture possible. It is pre-eminently the father, and the male child, that accomplish the break from nature into cultural, symbolic, and social life.

The Limitations of Feminist Psychoanalysis

Sceptics remain unconvinced that feminist re-interpretations of psychoanalytic theories can significantly overcome its phallocentric base. Weedon et al. (1980b, 208) raise an important caveat to feminist efforts to appropriate Lacan's thesis. They argue that the psychoanalytic theory of the origin of subjectivity, language, and culture in primal sexual drives is not compatible with a notion of subjectivity as contingent upon changeable historical conditions. Lacan himself sees the development of language as structured by the resolution of the universal oedipus complex in the unconscious mind. It is this deeper root of gendered subjectivity that needs to be challenged in order to establish an alternative theory of subjectivity as historically contingent and constituted within language.

The major contribution of feminist reworking of psychoanalysis for the broader study of Western culture has been to expose its ideological character, to reveal the pervasive phallocentric roots of discourses that claim scientific neutrality. The implications of this systemic privileging of masculine standpoints, and the difference that a feminist viewpoint can make, are explored below.

Gendered Ethnography

Studies of working-class subcultures that have used a cultural Marxist approach have overwhelmingly focussed on boys (McRobbie 1991, 1). Culture is defined almost entirely with reference to masculine behaviour, styles, and values. Girls, if they appear at all, are portrayed only in marginalized and stereotypical ways. The problem is not merely that male researchers choose to study young men rather than young women. It is that the terms of reference are so narrowly defined that entire dimensions of the boys' lives are left out. We see the boys on the streets and in schools, but there is a structured absence of attention to family and domestic life. We do not know how these boys behave when they go home after a weekend on drugs, or how their studied flight from the "family trap" takes place at the expense of women, especially their mothers and girlfriends.

The brutally patriarchal orientation to sexuality displayed by these boys is commonly ignored. Marxist researchers like Cohen (1980), Corrigan (1979), Willis (1981), and Hebdige (1979) highlight and even celebrate the aggressive masculinity through which the lads kick against the oppressive structures of capitalism. They ignore how the language of these macho styles is degrading to women. Angela McRobbie highlights how these texts are littered with references of the utmost brutality (1991, 21–22). One teacher's authority is undermined by her being labelled a "cunt." Boredom in the classroom is alleviated by replacing the teacher's official language with a litany of sexual "obscenities." The lads demonstrate their disgust for and fear of menstruation by substituting "jam rag" for towel at every opportunity. Crude violence underpins their descriptions of sexual intercourse as "having a good maul on her." Willis does not comment on how images of sexual power and domination are used by the lads as ways of kicking the system. McRobbie comments further on how Willis fails to integrate his observations on working-class machismo—male pride in physical labour and contempt for "pen-pushing"—into the softer sphere of the family where fathers, sons, and boyfriends expect to be, and are, emotionally serviced. The shopfloor culture of toughness and resilience is often used against women and girls in the form of both wife and girlfriend battering.

In her own study of teenage mothers, McRobbie describes how it was not uncommon for girls to be hit by their skinhead boyfriends (1991, 225). A teenage mother on welfare might find a place to live, only to be quickly followed by her boyfriend, and his brothers and friends, with the girl and her baby being the least important members of the household. As boyfriends moved in they would claim welfare benefits in the family's name while the young mothers often went hungry and had to borrow to buy baby milk and other necessities. McRobbie abandoned her research when she became too frightened of the girls' skinhead boyfriends and the climate of fear in the Birmingham streets in which these boys made their presence felt.

Mass Media and Patriarchal Culture

Feminist studies of mass media, not surprisingly, record a prevailing discourse that overwhelmingly privileges male viewpoints. By and large, the mainstream media replicate the conventional subordination of women. Two surveys of selected Canadian newspapers, conducted in 1990 and 1991 showed that women were pervasively underrepresented in news coverage, bylines, and employment, referred to in stereotyped ways, marginalized and subordinated to male concerns and story-lines (Media Watch 1991). Women constitute more than half the population but on aver-

age were mentioned in newspaper reports less than one-fifth of the time. In Canada's largest paper in national circulation, *The Globe and Mail*, women received only 9 percent of the references in 1991. Women's issues are not considered newsworthy and women are not sought out as valued sources of information or opinions. Women reporters generally have less than 30 percent of the bylines in Canadian newspapers, the proportions actually dropping slightly between 1990 and 1991. This is despite the fact that half the journalism school graduates in Canada are now women. When women were referred to in Canadian papers, they were typically subsumed under male generics such as "man" and "he," situated in relation to men ("his wife" or "Donald Trump and Ivana") rather than as having an independent identity, and described in ways that drew attention to their clothing and body parts.

A study of children's readers used in junior grades in Ontario schools in 1986 (Batcher and Winter 1987) found that fictional stories were most frequently about boys, and nonfictional material overwhelmingly about men. While girls were allowed a modicum of representation, women were scarcely there at all. In story plots, men's activities were highly varied and allowed opportunities to excel. Girls and women were confined to limited activities, including such things as being a loyal friend, being sick, or bossing the neighbourhood, almost none of which involved striving for achievement. In these stories females were essentially relegated to the status of "nothing special." The authors conclude that after thousands of pages of reading, they felt immersed in a medium that they called The Old Metaphor (TOM). TOM is a male-dominated view of the world in which binary either/or thinking prevails: "Men name things, and thereby call them into creation. Men decide the future of the world and 'men's' (meaning people's) place in it" (Batcher and Winter 1987, 36). Girls and women are always "other," and what they might become if allowed a full existence is never explored. There are many affirmations of manhood in these readers but few if any affirmations of womanhood.

Studies of Hollywood cinema similarly document the pervasive privileging of male rather than female perspectives. The camera explores the female body as an object of desire for men, but rarely the male body as an object of desire for women (Turner 1990, 109). Women are represented as objects of male gaze rather than as subjects with their own standpoints.

In the ideological construction of "woman" in advertising, similarly, women are invited to respond to the advertisements through the imagined fetishes of men—the legs, the lips, the silky skin—which sell cosmetics and fashion (Winship 1980). At the hard end of advertising is pornography, the multibillion-dollar cultural industry that sells women to men for sex. Feminist artists and filmmakers in Canada sought to expose the brutality of hard-core pornography in the National Film Board film, *Not a Love Story*. The irony is that this film, too, is open to the criticism that it adopts the viewpoint of the voyeur rather than the viewpoint of the women involved. The camera focusses in on closeups of the women's bodies and sexual parts just as the men paying their money in the peep shows would see them. We do not see the female models' view of the men staring in (Rich 1983). In the end, this film may have as pornographic an impact on viewers as the real things, perhaps more so since the images are wrapped up in a story-line that legitimates staring at them.

From Structure to Interpretation: Dethroning the Text

Structuralist analysis of patriarchal culture, like that for Marxist analysis of capitalism, implies an inescapable determinism in which human agency is lost. Women appear as the passive victims of overdetermining ideological structures. But the emergence of the women's movement and feminist theory itself belie this victimology. More recently, feminist theories of culture are shifting from a Foucauldian analysis of discourse to incorporate Derrida's insights into active reading and the essential indeterminacy of texts.

In her analysis of *Just Seventeen*, a British magazine for teenage girls, McRobbie combines textual analysis with a focus on active reading and the contexts in which reading occurs. This is particularly evident in her treatment of the problem pages—the "agony aunt" advice columns in which staff would respond to letters from teenage readers. McRobbie documents how answers to letters changed from a strong moralistic tone in the sixties to a more candid and realistic approach. Melanie McFadyean (1988), the

magazine's "agony aunt" for five years, took her work very seriously, seeing herself as a counsellor for teenagers experiencing problems with families, school, their own sexuality, sexual abuse, pregnancy, and the like. McRobbie, however, shifts the focus to how teenagers read these advice columns, how they are giggled over and passed along the back rows of classrooms, and how girls would get together during school lunch hours to write the letters. This strong element of joking challenges McFadyean's image of thousands of girls writing about their misery and sufferings in isolation.

These columns may nonetheless form a privileged site for the creation of discourses around female sexuality. McRobbie draws upon Foucault's analysis of the history of sexuality (1970) to suggest that these columns feign a private intimacy while in practice encouraging a flood of sexual voices, pressuring teenage girls to write in and to describe their anxieties, fears, and sexual insecurities, so that they can participate in the discourses. Once out in the open they are more easily controlled. Teenage girls have no power in this context. While they write the thousands of letters, editors select what gets published and the advice and knowledge provided. Even progressive discourse may play a policing role, especially in separating what is normal from abnormal sexuality.

The problem remains that any analysis of the content of a text does not provide information about the multiplicity of potential readings. Fiske (1987, 271–80) notes how the media presentation of Madonna is full of images that support a patriarchal reading of submission or subordination to men and sexual lust. But it is equally possible to read Madonna videos as a site of resistance and self-definition that can be free from the power of the male. More traditional feminist analysis, which has focussed on the hegemony of patriarchal discourse, has difficulty accounting for sudden and major changes in the reading of familiar cultural symbols. One of the most pervasive is the image of public power as male. What happens when a woman has the position of power, as Margaret Thatcher had as Prime Minister of England for more than a decade? Predictably, she should have experienced great difficulty mediating the contradictions between femininity and leadership. In practice, the "Iron Lady" had little difficulty in finding and drawing upon very familiar forms of female authority such as the cultural image of Britannia, and the image of a strict governess with unchallenged rights of censure, or the strict mother—a very familiar form of female authority—that she wielded to great effect in her cabinet (Franklin et al. 1991, 32). Traditionally, militarism and authoritarianism are associated with masculinity, but again Thatcher appeared to have little difficulty calling upon women's fear of male violence, and support for the family, to gain support for a right-wing agenda of law and order, and cutbacks on social services in the name of greater independence for families. If Margaret Thatcher could call on these cultural images within British society to bolster her rule, then presumably they have always been open to such alternative readings to back up the leadership claims of women in other roles. This recognition of the potential for multiple readings of cultural symbols suggests that given appropriate conditions, cultural change can occur very rapidly.

The Limitations of Feminist Theories of Culture

Feminist theories of culture struggle with similar theoretical problems as Marxist and social constructionist perspectives. There is extensive evidence supporting the structuralist analysis of the dominant culture as patriarchal. Prevailing social science discourses and mass media presentations reflect patriarchal images of men and women, dividing the social world into categories of male—masculine, dominant, acting subjects inhabiting the public realm—and female—feminine, submissive, passive objects of male attention inhabiting the private realm of family and children. These conceptions of masculine and feminine are also deeply embedded in subjective self-identities of people, and invested with strong emotions.

The problem for feminist analysis is that in the process of exposing and condemning patriarchy, it may unwittingly become part of the processes that reproduce it. The study of culture is especially difficult because it is so hard to separate description from the phenomenon. Members of any given culture know what the prevailing discourses are, and are able to recite and reproduce these discourses. But there may be a large gap between what women think other women think, and what they themselves and other women actually DO think.

A study in rural India, for example, tested predictions generated from the prevailing culture of "purdah" concerning how village women would respond to the prospect of jobs in a development project (Hale 1988a). According to the cultural ideals, village women valued domestic seclusion very highly as a mark of status and moral purity. They would not seek jobs outside the home unless they were desperately poor, and they would regard other employed women with a mixture of pity and suspicion. The exceptions might be well-educated and Westernized city women. All such predictions proved false. Village women from all social classes jumped at the chance to get a job, and admitted that they envied those who succeeded. These same village women still insisted that domestic seclusion was the prevailing cultural norm. They imputed these beliefs to others while not sharing them themselves.

Feminist analysis of culture risks doing the same thing, imputing cultural norms and attitudes to women that most women do not hold. Feminist work in exposing patriarchal discourse has played an essential role in breaking down its pervasive and taken-for-granted character, and has created space in which alternative discourses have been able to emerge that express the subjective experiences of women. The risk is that this process may itself help to cement the arbitrary category "woman" into taken-for-granted status. This categorization collapses the multiple differences between women from different class, educational, racial, ethnic, and subcultural backgrounds, while exaggerating the differences between women and men in similar circumstances. It also perpetuates the notions of binary oppositions in culture such as male/female, culture/nature, public/private, and the like, that are associated with patriarchal discourse (Parr 1990, 8; Hamilton forthcoming).

Conclusion

Within the broad field of cultural studies, the problem of the relationship between structure and human agency remains unresolved. Discourse analysis has revealed the historically contingent character of taken-for-granted knowledge, and the relations of power embedded within it. Analysis of the practices involved in normalizing and privileging certain discourses over others is beginning to make visible the mechanisms by which both professionals and producers of mass media construct and sustain their accounts. We still have much to learn, however, about how people, in their everyday lives, structure their reading. Once we recognize the polysemy of texts, the multiplicity of possible meanings that can be read into any aspects of culture, then the question of how people individually and collectively arrive at and communicate specific meanings becomes critical. The sociology of culture has only begun to explore the everyday practices that establish and challenge meaning.

Suggested Reading

Excerpts from the work of Talcott Parsons in Alexander and Seidman's edited collection on *Culture and Society* (1990, 159–79) gives a useful formal statement of the functionalist theory of culture. Wuthnow et al. (1994, 77–132) provide an excellent overview of the work of Mary Douglas and her analysis of dirt and social order.

For the political economy perspective, Clement devotes three chapters to mass media in his study of *The Canadian Corporate Elite* (1975, chs. 7–9), exploring the power of corporate owners to screen information that reaches the Canadian public. Achbar's documentary text on the work of Noam Chomsky (1994) gives many vivid accounts of how the American media have systematically distorted international news to manufacture consent for capitalist imperialism. Willis's study *Learning to Labour* (1981)

remains a classic ethnography of the culture of working-class boys and how it works to perpetuate their class position within capitalism.

For social constructionist analysis, Valverde's discussion of sex-trade workers in her article "Too Much Heat, Not Enough Light" (1987) and Ruby's analysis of the National Film Board film *Not a Love Story* in "Anti-Porn: Soft Issue, Hard World" (1983) give fascinating examples of alternative readings of texts. Mark Fishman's study *Manufacturing the News* (1980) provides a detailed ethnography of how the work of producing news gets done.

Angela McRobbie's collection of articles in *Feminism and Youth Culture* (1991) offers a very readable and hard-hitting critique of male-centred studies of subcultures, and excellent examples of ethnographic work and analysis from a feminist perspective.

Questions

1. What does Mary Douglas see as the significance of "dirt" in cultural order?

2. List several ways in which mass media in Canada can be seen as functioning to promote societal integration.

3. What is the central historical problem for Marxist theory that is addressed by members of the Frankfurt School of critical theory?

4. In principle, how does the approach of cultural Marxism differ from the earlier work of Althusser?

5. How does the oppositional culture of lower-class youths studied by Paul Willis serve to perpetuate their lower-class status?

6. What is Derrida referring to with the concept of *trace*? Why does the trace make it so difficult to say exactly what one means?

7. Why is it impossible, even in principle, for a deconstructive analysis to give a decisive meaning for any text?

8. What parallels does Lacan draw between metaphors in language and psychoanalytic theory?

9. How is Freud's notion of penis envy challenged in the feminist work of Irigaray and O'Brien?

10. How is feminist analysis of mass media open to deconstructive critique?

CHAPTER 20

Postmodern Sociology and the Sociology of Postmodernism

You are likely to enjoy this section if you are the kind of person who enjoys intellectual conundrums like the following: "How do you know that table exists?" "Because I can see it!" "Ah, but you cannot see the back legs or the part behind the chair. How do you know they exist?" "Because my toe hurts when I kick it." "Ah, all that proves is that your toe hurts!"

Postmodernism is not easily defined because it is used differently in different contexts. In sociology, there is no agreement on whether postmodernism should be thought of as a particular period of time, a tendency within a period, a broad philosophical category, or even who or what fits clearly into the definition (Brodribb 1993, 10). Some of the theorists we have discussed in this text, including Foucault, Derrida, Lacan, Baudrillard, and Barthes, are often referred to as postmodernists, but both Foucault and Derrida rejected the label. Other theorists argue that postmodernism merely dresses up old ideas and even premodern concerns in new language. Yet the term

pervades contemporary theorizing. The goal of this introductory chapter is to give a feel for the issues and the controversies emerging around the notion of postmodernism.

Rosenthal (1992, 84–85) traces the origins of the term to literary critics and artists in New York in the 1950s and sixties. Later, it was adopted by European intellectuals, in particular Jean-Francois Lyotard (1984). It thus has two very different connotations: a genre of artistic styles and a set of philosophical tenets. The characteristics of postmodern art provide a useful avenue for understanding the application of the term to developing trends in the social sciences and philosophy.

Postmodern art and architecture arose as a reaction against the excesses of modern art. Modern art, as Rosenthal describes it, aimed to outrage. While popular culture was easy to like, modern art was dissonant, grating, and user-unfriendly. Modern artists projected an image of themselves as tortured and misunderstood, struggling against a vulgar, commercial age. They sought to express a sense of eternal and immutable order beneath the fragmentation of modern life. By the late 1960s it had reached its most extreme form, expressed in nearly all-black paintings, or one-colour canvases with a stripe. The acquisition of one such painting by the National Gallery of Canada in 1993 created quite a storm of controversy. Mark Rothko's painting entitled *No. 16* is a huge canvas, measuring roughly 3 metres by 2.5 metres and features two white rectangles on a red background. It was purchased for $1.8 million. Modernist architecture is similarly characterized by stark "ice-cube" forms of glass and steel, which "attempt to find order within the fragmented, chaotic, ruptured character of modern experience" (Rosenthal 1992, 88).

Mark Rothko's painting, *No. 16*, expresses the search for order within a fragmented modern society. Postmodern art challenges this purity of form.

© Mark Rothko 1994/VIS*ART Copyright Inc.

Postmodern art and architecture try to break away from such stark *essentialism* or purity of form to express all that modern art suppressed—the decentred, the contingent, the unstable, the fragmentary (Rosenthal 1992, 90–93). In architecture, a multitude of styles are playfully merged together in a pastiche. Greek columns, Roman porticos, and Italian renaissance decor might all be juxtaposed in a high-rise building. In postmodern art, all images seem to refer back to other images, culture bending back on itself in a perpetual futureless present. Everything seems to be held up to ridicule. The real and the simulated are so mixed up that it is hard to tell one from the other. Music videos convey the image of screaming teenagers at a heavy-metal concert and then suggest the sound is really coming from a tape-recorder and an old Elvis performance. In the film *Paris Is Burning* we see drag queens impersonating trim, young executives, or is it young men impersonating drag queens impersonating young male executives? The "real" Madonna seems to be a pastiche of all the images of women she can adopt and parody. We no longer know if what we are seeing and hearing is real or really just a performance.

When these themes of pastiche, parody, and merging of real and simulated realities are transposed into philosophy and social science, they are used to challenge notions of essentialism and claims to absolute truth. The main targets of postmodernist critical theory are grand theories or *metanarratives* of society that claim to discover the patterns underneath the chaotic appearance of diversity, contingency, and confusion. The Western intellectual tradition is full of such grand theories, and we have explored several in this text. Social Darwinism, for example, conceptualized the evolution of all human society in terms of the survival of the fittest in the relentless struggle of competition, innovation, and adaptation. Weber characterizes Western civilization as embodying the triumph of rational-legal thought over tradition and superstition. Feminist thought in this tradition sees history as patriarchy. Marxist theory is perhaps the most influential of all Western metanarratives, conceiving of all history as the expression of class struggle, culminating in the ultimate triumph of scientific socialism. While the themes differ, their underlying forms are the same: they strive for a single grand theory or "totalizing story" that would subordinate all other explanations. Also characteristic of these grand theories is the attempt to define social reality in terms of fundamental dichotomies that subsume diversity under basic themes. We have many such dichotomies in this text: male/female, man/nature, nature/culture, mind/body, human/machine, self/other, public/private, reason/emotion, sacred/profane, folk/urban, *Gemeinschaft/ Gesellschaft*, primitive/complex, bourgeois/proletariat . . . the list is endless. The structuralist anthropologist Claude Levi-Strauss conceptualized all cultures as the working out of such fundamental oppositions.

Postmodernist theory rejects all such metanarratives and essentialist categories as myths that distort and obscure a reality characterized by heterogeneity, diversity, fluidity and contingency. A number of the leading postmodernist thinkers, including Lyotard, Foucault, and Baudrillard, began their intellectual careers as Marxists but became disillusioned with its determinism and reductionism, and the failure of neo-Marxist theory to come to terms with the collapse of communism (Larrain 1994, 290). Faith in the ability of science to provide objective, factual knowledge was also undermined by challenges to scientific practice as itself resting on presuppositions or paradigms that define what is worth researching, what constitutes evidence, how such evidence is to be read, and what are acceptable solutions (Kuhn 1970; Feyerabend 1975). If one concedes that there is no possibility of representation without presupposition, then science seems to become a matter of interpretation, subordinate to the humanities and social sciences that explore theories of interpretation (Madison 1988, 46). What was once taken-for-granted as objective truths have been denounced by feminists as particularistic and pervasively sexist (Harding 1986). Once truth becomes redefined as "assertions from a viewpoint" then multiple viewpoints would seem to promote multiple truths that are partial and contingent, changing with historical and local circumstances (Agger 1991, 115–16).

Lyotard (1984) encapsulates postmodernist thought in his argument that we cannot talk about a totalizing idea of reason, for "there is no reason, only reasons." All universals, such as the Marxist theory of history, are illusions that suppress differences and conceal self-aggrandizing motives. Lyotard maintains that there are no large stories about the world, only small stories from the subject positions of individuals and diverse social groups that examine the social world from multiple perspectives of class, race, gender, and a myriad of other group affiliations.

These different subject positions cannot be subsumed under some unifying perspective, nor can we decide which group is more oppressed or more deserving of liberation. Feminists have challenged almost all aspects of traditional social science knowledge as embodying the perspectives of men under the guise of universal statements about humanity. But feminism in turn is challenged by postmodernist theory as itself introducing a new form of essentialism under the category of "woman" that distorts and suppresses difference. Feminist postmodernism tries to address this critique by greater attention to differences among women, and to the ethnocentrism, racism, and heterosexism inherent in earlier feminist theory (Gagnier 1990, 22). Gagnier cites the example of the late poet Audre Lorde, "a forty-nine-year-old Black lesbian feminist socialist mother of two, including one boy, and a member of an interracial couple" to make the point that one's allegiance can never simply be to "woman." Postmodern alliances, Gagnier suggests, look like affinities rather than identities; they are characterized by fluidity—the ability to mobilize and disperse in a continuous array of micronarratives.

Postmodernism and Social Experience

Postmodernism as a cultural and intellectual movement reflects a pervasive loss of certainty that goes far deeper than academic debates on the excesses of scientific claims to truth (Rosenthal 1992, 96–97). Few people now believe in progress through scientific knowledge: we are too aware of impending ecological catastrophe. The heroic myths of communism have taken a severe beating, but at the same time capitalism is in a worldwide recession, with many people believing that their children are likely to be worse off than themselves. Increasingly, profits seem not to be based on tangible production but on fictions about things that might be produced—through speculation on the stock and futures markets, and through paper empires, bought with borrowed money, that have come crashing down with accelerating frequency in the early 1990s. Feminist ideals of a new moral order based on nurturing relationships have generally not been translated into governments and political parties headed by women. Widespread cynicism fills the vacuum left by these receding myths.

Our knowledge of reality is increasingly presented to us through mass media reports in which we cannot distinguish with any certainty between the real and the fictional, the live and the re-runs. We receive "live" reports of the Gulf War produced by reporters sitting in a hotel in Bahrain or even in the backrooms of the White House in Washington. Media coverage of the Quebec elections in the summer of 1994 illustrates the force and the circularity of language games. Journalists wrote their obligatory daily reports of the campaigning, structured around the pronouncements of politicians, who quoted their speechwriters, who scanned the media to find out what it was important to say. People read the journalists to formulate opinions for the opinion pollsters that tomorrow's journalists would quote. Whatever the polls or the speechwriters might say became woven into the interpretive paradigm already in place in the medium for which the journalists prepared their reports.

Postmodernist analysis pushes beyond a scepticism towards media reports. Reality itself is a plurality of language games, with no one language game truer or superior to the others (Van Reijen and Veerman 1988, 278; Lyotard 1984, 37, 40). There is no true account, against which individual reports can be measured. There is no distinction between real and simulation. The real IS simulated. This is the core of Baudrillard's (1988) analysis of American society in *Simulacra and Simulations*. Disneyland, he suggests, is there to conceal the fact that it is the "real" country, all of "real" America, which is Disneyland: "Disneyland is presented as imaginary in order to make us believe that the rest is real, when in fact all of Los Angeles and the America surrounding it are no longer real, but of the order of the hyper-real and of simulation. It is no longer a question of a false representation of reality (ideology), but of concealing the fact that the real is no longer real, and thus of saving the reality principle" (1988, 172). A conference held in New York to discuss the end of the world, only misses the reality that New York already is the end of the world. Prophesies about a Third World War only miss the hyper-reality that the Third World War has already happened and both communist and Western capitalist states have already exterminated their own societies (Baudrillard 1987, 226). For postmodernists like Baudrillard, behind the mask of false appearances is not a real world but an absence. There is no hidden meaning, only the endless play of signs and media images (Kellner 1988, 62; Larrain 1994, 310). This vision is both liberating and frightening. It is also paralyzing.

Postmodernism Revisited: New Wave or Oxymoron?

The debates emerging around postmodernism are as fragmented and diverse as the postmodern vision itself. Those excited by postmodernism welcome its iconoclasm, its attack on claims to absolute truth and reason. Connell (1991, 71) sums up its intellectual promise as follows:

> Postmodernism is a medicine, a specific cure for certain kinds of intellectual arrogance. It is good for ice-cube architecture, political tunnel vision and monolithic social theories. It may help discomfit the pompous and patriarchal priesthoods of the Great Tradition, of whichever edition. It is good for undermining a priori claims to be in possession of the one perspective from which social reality can be unlocked or decoded. For all people contending against such claims, postmodernism may appear a breath of fresh air.

Those who fear postmodernism see an inherent conservatism in the intellectual position that suspects even those who suspect the established system. Sceptical theories that deny the possibility of truth challenges even the possibility of solving societal problems or working towards a better future (Larrain 1994, 312–13). It seems to paralyze opposition.

Yet, others point to self-contradictory elements in the postmodernist assertion that on the one hand there is no reality and on the other that reality is an infantile Disneyland simulation. Such an argument presumes its own validity even as it denies the possibility of truth (Habermas 1987a, 97). Also, if we take seriously Lyotard's assertion that there are no universal stories about the world, only small stories from local subject positions, then the question arises, from whose subject position does Los Angeles appear as Disneyland? Who do the postmodernists speak for? Callinicos (1985), among others, suggests it is the vision of disaffected intellectuals, particularly ex-Marxists who have lost faith in the validity of their former vision of society and economy and who now feel useless.

Marxism and Postmodernism

The core of the Marxist critique of postmodernism is the sense that it cannot speak for people who suffer oppression. In reducing all social relations to language games, postmodernism seems to deny the reality of experiences of colonialism, violence, exploitation, and corruption (Connell 1992, 72). But war and bombs are not language games. Beneath the fabricated stories, the simulated air strikes, and euphemisms like "collateral damage" that pervaded media coverage of the Gulf War is a different order of reality—the hundreds of thousands of shattered lives, dead people, and destroyed homes. While textual analysis of the language games is crucial to understanding how consensus was constructed in North American society in support of the war, such analysis is not itself sufficient (Rosenthal 1992, 103). To take a position for or against the war we need to know the history and politics of the Middle East, long-term British and American involvement in the region, and strategic interests around control of oil that contributed to the crisis. From the perspective of postmodernism, however, any provision of further information would merely create another text, whose meaning would be relative to previously available texts. The basis for taking a stand only recedes further.

The postmodernist insistence on the validity of heterogeneous subject positions denies any superiority to Western colonialist interpretations of history, and yet at the same time it does not address the reality of colonialism that has silenced subjugated peoples and blurred the distinction between authentic and imperialist culture. Edward Said (1978) points out that the very concepts of *Eastern* or *Oriental* only have meaning within a Western discourse. The status of writers as Oriental or Third World is produced in advance by the West, and Western discourse sets the context in which what they say will be heard. Asian women writers, for example, find it difficult to criticize patriarchal practices freely in their own societies lest it read like complicity in racist international discourse that defines their cultures as backward and premodern relative to the West (Ahmed 1982, 527). Marxist critics argue that an appeal to cultural relativism is not sufficient to give subjugated people a voice. What is needed is a transformation in relations of power.

Feminism and Postmodernism

The relationship between feminist theory and postmodernism is equally contradictory. Many feminists embrace postmodernism for dethroning masculine discourse as monolithic truth, and for discrediting reality claims about the supposed naturalness of male and female (Nicholson 1990). Postmodernism's celebration of difference and multiple subject positions creates intellectual space for the voices of women, and for diversity of women's subject positions by class, age, ethnicity, colour, and sexual orientation (Gagnier 1990). At the same time, however, postmodernism seems to challenge the core of feminist theory by opposing the very category 'woman' as essentialist and denying the reality of patriarchal oppression (Brodribb 1993). In effect, Brodribb suggests, these theorists claim to speak on behalf of women while not taking seriously what feminists are saying, and indeed denying even the existence of women as women. She echoes Hartsock's (1990, 163) suspicions concerning how it is that postmodernist theories emerged to challenge notions of subjecthood, reason, and the reality of structures of power, just at the moment when women and other subjugated minorities are finding their voices, forming their own theories about the world, and pressing for material and structural change. The Disneyland vision of unreality may, in any case, have little in common with the subject position of women embedded in the practical everyday work of caring for children, feeding families, washing clothes, cleaning rooms, emptying ashtrays, and serving muffins and coffee when the postmodern philosophers take a break. Matter, the material and maternal world, is not so easily dismissed.

Conclusion

In summary, it is far too soon to attempt to assess the possible impact of postmodernist thought on the future of sociology. In some respects, the ideas are not so avant-garde. The notion that ideas are real and the world of the senses mere appearance is as old as Plato. The notion of multiple subject positions is also not new. In the mid-1990s, concern with imperial domination is less pressing than the identity politics of a multiplicity of ethnic subgroups fragmenting into premodern tribal warfare. But this does not detract from the importance of the postmodernist critique of grand theorizing, and the centrality of discourse in structuring social relations. The challenge is to draw on the critical strengths of postmodernism while redressing its limitations.

This text is postmodernist in that it subjects each of the metanarratives of contemporary sociology to scrutiny, focussing attention on how these theoretical perspectives are built up, and their implicit guiding assumptions. It takes seriously the postmodernist claim that there can be no presuppositionless representation of reality, and hence that we need to make visible precisely what presuppositions are being made by different theoretical perspectives in the selection and interpretation of evidence.

This text is also postmodernist in that it tries to deconstruct sociological writings, to reveal the values and interests embedded in them, in this text, no less than the texts it reviews. It follows Agger's insistence that we need to raise assumptions to the surface, opening them up to readers, so as to politicize and democratize the process of reading itself (Agger 1991, 114–15). The goal in each of the book's chapters is to show how theoretical assumptions affect what we see as evidence. The meaning of evidence is always, in some measure, undecidable, because whenever we change how we look at evidence, we change what it means. The text offers many instances in which data that are taken to be factual from one theoretical perspective, are disclaimed as flawed interpretation from another. Featherstone (1985, 1988) credits postmodernism with shifting the study of culture from peripheral topic to centre stage, reconceptualizing sociology as fundamentally concerned with the study of how meaning is socially constructed. Agger (1991, 119–21) similarly credits postmodernism and poststructuralism with "reauthorizing" sociological texts, pushing authors and readers to be reflexive, to make visible the presuppositions necessarily embedded in texts. This text has also tried, however, to go beyond the closed circle of textual analysis to explore how meanings are socially constructed by people in their practical, everyday activities, and the power relations embedded in these actions.

Feyerabend proposes (1970) that the only way to avoid the dogmatism of preconceived theories is to juxtapose any one theory against alternatives that conceptualize experience in very different ways. The ideal is to develop theories that are so fundamentally different that even what is taken to be reality is called into question. Postmodernism offers this challenge.

Suggested Reading

Rosenthal's (1992) article "What Was Post-Modernism?" offers a humorous introduction to postmodernism, while critiquing it from a Marxist perspective. Regenia Gagnier's article on "Feminist Postmodernism: The End of Feminism or the End of Theory?" (1990) offers a more positive appraisal of the value of postmodernist theory for feminist analysis.

Questions

1. What special features distinguish postmodernist architecture from "modern"?

2. What does postmodernist art struggle to express, in opposition to the essentialism of modern art?

3. How is the rise of postmodernist theory in the social sciences linked to historical Marxist critique?

4. In what ways can postmodernist theory in the social sciences be seen as arising from specific aspects of contemporary social experience?

5. In what respects can postmodernism be challenged as inherently conservative?

6. In what respect can the postmodernist critique of essentialist views of reality itself be challenged as self-contradictory?

7. What is the core of the Marxist critique of the postmodernist analysis of media coverage of events like the Gulf War?

8. How can a similar Marxist critique be levelled against the notion of cultural relativism?

9. In what respects is the relationship between feminist theory and postmodernism internally contradictory?

10. In what respect can it be argued that postmodernism is as old as platonic philosophy?

Glossary

There are many terms in sociology that do not have standard meanings. They are used differently depending on the theoretical perspective of the writer. The definitions suggested below provide a guide to the meaning of terms as they are used in this text. They are not definitive in the sense of specifying how such terms are utilized in all sociological writing. Many theoretical concepts require extensive explanation to capture their full meaning. The best way to understand terms in sociology is to see how they are used in context. There is little value in trying to memorize definitions.

Absolute surplus For Marx, the amount of surplus production available when workers are driven to work as hard as possible and given the lowest possible standard of living.

Abstract labour time Marx uses this term to refer to the average amount of time it takes to produce a given commodity in a society with a given level of technology and knowledge.

Accounting/Accountability In ethnomethodology, these terms refer to the ways in which people use their common-sense knowledge and background understandings to make sense to themselves and to one another of what is going on.

Acculturation The process through which newcomers learn and adopt the prevailing attitudes and values of the group or society that they are entering.

Achieved characteristics Characteristics that one earns by learning skills or gaining credentials.

Actor In functionalism, the conception of a person as a role player within a system of roles.

Adaptation Parsons uses this term to refer to securing needed resources for an activity and distributing them among the people involved.

Adjacency pairs This term is used in conversation analysis to refer to aspects of the structure of typical, orderly conversations. One expects that a certain kind of comment by a participant in a conversation will immediately be followed by a corresponding comment from another participant (i.e., that a question will be followed by an answer).

Advanced capitalism For Marxist theorists, an economic order in which national and international markets are dominated by huge corporations rather than characterized by competition among entrepreneurs.

Advanced communism An economic system where all the important means of production in a society—land, factories, technology—are communally owned. Everyone shares access to them and everyone labours collectively according to their ability to meet the collective needs of the community.

Affective-rational action A term used by Weber to refer to action oriented to emotions.

Affectivity/Affective neutrality Parsons uses these terms to refer to the amount of emotion that should properly be displayed in a given role.

Affirmative action Action taken as part of a policy designed to increase the representation of members of specified groups deemed to be disadvantaged or underrepresented in certain positions relative to their numbers within the population as a whole.

Agency The capacity of individual people to act in consciously chosen ways to influence social structures.

Agribusiness The network of international corporations that controls production, processing, transport, storage, and financing of agriculture.

Alienation Marx uses this term to refer to the dehumanizing character of social relations, particularly under capitalism. The term is used more generally to describe a syndrome or combination of characteristics including powerlessness, meaninglessness, isolation, and self-estrangement.

Altruism Regard for others as a principle of action. Also, a readiness to put the interests of other members of society or those of society as a whole over personal interests.

Altruistic suicide The form of suicide committed by people who are so intensely integrated into their social group or community that they are willing to sacrifice themselves for the good of that community.

Anomic division of labour For Durkheim, a forced specialization that is experienced as unjust or as not regulated by reference to a clear and meaningful system of values.

Anomic suicide The form of suicide committed by people who have lost any clear sense of values that regulate and give meaning to their lives.

Anomie In general this refers to a breakdown in moral order. Durkheim uses the term to refer to the experience of a relative absence or confusion of values and a corresponding lack of meaningful regulations or a clear position and objectives in life.

Anomie theory of crime A theory developed by Merton, which attributes variations in propensity for criminal behaviour to the discrepancy between culturally valued goals and access to socially approved means to achieve them.

Anti-Semitism Prejudice against Jews.

Antithesis See Dialectic; Dialectical materialism.

Apparatus of ruling A term developed by Smith to refer to the organized activities that form part of the overall mechanisms for control in a society, including the activities of individual people who work in government offices and the forms and regulations that guide their behaviour.

Ascriptive characteristics/Ascription Refers to the characteristics with which we are born, such as age, sex, height, and racial or ethnic background.

Assimilation The process through which individuals or groups of people lose their distinctive ethnic or minority group patterns of behaviour and values and adopt the values and behavioural expectations of the dominant group.

Autocracy Rule from above, without democratic participation.

Automation Mechanical or electronic control of a process.

Average labour time For Marx, the typical amount of time it takes a worker to produce a particular commodity with the technology that prevails in a given society.

Background understandings In ethnomethodology, the knowledge that competent participants in an activity or conversation can be expected to have, which allows the activity or conversation to be understandable to them without any further explanation.

Base A term used by Marx to refer to the social relations of production.

Behavioural organism For Parsons, the human biological organism, which provides the fundamental energy and drive for activity and which also links the social system with the physical environment.

Berdache A term used in anthropology to refer to people whose social identity is neither male nor female, but encompasses aspects of both.

Biological theory of race The theory that people with different skin colours evolved from distinct subspecies of humans and that they have innately different levels of intelligence and other attributes.

Bourgeoisie Those who own capital, or the means of production, and who hire wage-labourers to produce commodities for sale in order to make profits; capitalists.

Branch-plant economy A society in which a significant proportion of all business enterprises are branch plants; that is, subsidiaries of multinational corporations with headquarters in another country.

Breaching experiments A methodological approach in ethnomethodology that involves disturbing what the researcher thinks might be an unquestioned or taken-for-granted rule of normal behaviour in order to test the extent to which that normal behaviour is subsequently disturbed.

Bureaucracy Generally, a formal organization characterized by a hierarchical chain of command and precisely delimited roles and responsibilities governed by written rules. For Foucault and Ferguson, bureaucracy constitutes the scientific organization of inequality through which people are dominated and oppressed. See Disciplinary society; Iron cage.

Bureaucratic discourse Foucault uses the term to refer to a form of talk that translates all human concerns and human interaction into narrow technical language relevant for organizational purposes and for predefined classifications that relate to the specialized work of officials.

Bureaucratic language Description of human interaction in terms of technical jargon referring to regulations defining responsibilities of role incumbents in organizations, often for the purpose of obfuscation.

Bureaucratic society For Foucault, a society in which bureaucracy is the all-pervasive mode of social organization. See Disciplinary society.

Business-class immigrant A category within the Immigration Act that refers to people who have capital to invest in Canadian industries and businesses and can provide guarantees that they will create employment opportunities in Canada.

Calvinism Weber uses the term to refer to the religious doctrine of John Calvin, which advocates a sober, frugal lifestyle and a disciplined obligation to work as a means to serve God. It emphasizes the doctrine of predestination: that salvation is attainable by God's grace alone and that the identity of those who will be saved is known by God from the beginning of life.

Capital The stock with which a company or person enters into business. The means of production. The accumulated wealth that is used in producing commodities.

Capitalism A system of production in which capital, or the means of production, is privately owned by a small, elite class of people. The mass of people have no direct access to means of producing for their own needs. They depend on selling their capacity to labour to those who own the means of production.

Capitalists Owners of capital or the means of production who hire wage-labourers to produce commodities for sale. The bourgeoisie.

Capitalization The expansion in the amount of wealth invested in a business in order for it to remain competitive. Undercapitalized enterprises are those with insufficient investment in technology to remain competitive in the market.

Causal pluralism For Weber, a research strategy that involves searching for multiple causes for social phenomena.

Causality A relationship of cause and effect that is assumed to exist between two or more variables.

Census/Census data Data obtained through comprehensive surveys of the entire population of a country, carried out with government funding and commonly with the force of law to compel people to answer the questions.

Charismatic authority For Weber, authority legitimated by the extraordinary gifts or supernatural powers that the leader appears to have.

Chicago School (The) A theoretical and methodological approach to urban sociology associated with the University of Chicago during the late 1920s and 1930s. An approach that emphasized the three variables of size, density, and cultural heterogeneity as critical determinants of the character of social life.

Circles of social control The mechanisms by which conformity is produced, including guilt, desire for approval, economic sanctions, and force.

Class Generally, the location in a hierarchically stratified work force, commonly divided into a set of ranked categories, on the basis of relative income and level of education or skill required. Alternatively, the location within a bureaucratic organization as defined by job classification schemes. Marx defined class as location in relation to the means of production, mostly as owners and nonowners, with some intermediate classes. Weber expanded Marx's definition to refer to differential life chances and the chance to use property, goods, and services for exchange in a competitive market.

Class-for-itself In Marxist theory, the collectivity of members of a class who recognize their shared class position and come together to act in their class interests.

Class-in-itself Marx uses the term as a theoretical concept referring to all people who share the same relationship to the means of production (i.e., capitalists as the class of all owners).

Class reductionism The thesis that inequalities associated with gender, ethnicity, or race can be explained by class interests.

Class struggle The conflict between those who own the means of production and those who do not. For Marx this is a dynamic process of struggle by which working people most disadvantaged by the existing relations of production struggle to change those relations.

Cohort Persons banded together for the purposes of analysis, particularly on the basis of being born during the same period of time.

Colonialism The process of establishing settlements in a conquered territory with the administration of such settlements fully or partially subject to control by the conquering state.

Commodity Anything produced for exchange and not for use by the producer.

Commodity fetishism The tendency to attribute causal agency to commodities exchanged in the marketplace, as if the commodities determined relations between people.

Common-sense understandings Assumptions about how and why things work the way they do, based on immediate, personal experience.

Communism See Advanced communism; Primitive communism.

Community A body of people living in the same locality. Alternatively, a sense of identity and belonging shared among people living in the same locality. Also, the set of social relations found in a particular bounded area.

Competitive advantage Special conditions prevailing in certain areas that enable businesses to produce certain kinds of commodities more cheaply than they can be produced elsewhere.

Conflict theory The study of society, or specific elements of society, conceptualized as made up of parts held together by hierarchical relations of power and dependency. Conflict is seen as endemic.

Conformist A category in Merton's anomie theory of crime. One who accepts socially valued goals and socially approved means to achieve them.

Conglomerate mergers The consolidation of diverse industries within one corporation.

Conscience collective For Durkheim, the totality of beliefs and sentiments common to the average citizens of the same society. The French term is translated into English in two ways. *Collective conscience* refers to the collective sense of what is morally right and wrong. *Collective consciousness* refers to a sense of belonging and commitment to a collectivity or community of people.

Consensus In cultural Marxism, a kind of one-dimensional or group thinking manipulated by mass media and the professions to ensure that the values and behaviour expectations of the ruling class will prevail. See Ideological hegemony.

Conservative bias Generally, being disposed to maintain existing social institutions and to oppose efforts to change or reform them.

Conspicuous consumption A term referring to buying and displaying expensive items in order to demonstrate wealth and so enhance one's social status.

Consumerism The high value placed on the ownership or purchase of goods as a means of attaining personal happiness and as a measure of personal success and well-being.

Content analysis A methodological approach that involves the organized counting of content of written materials in relation to predefined categories that are determined by the theoretical hypothesis.

Contradictions of capitalism For Marx, the thesis that the capitalist system of production necessarily works in such a way that it generates problems that become steadily more disruptive for production as the system evolves. Eventually, capitalism is destined to collapse under its own internal problems.

Conversation analysis A theoretical approach within the broad perspective of ethnomethodology that explores the typical ways in which talk is structured by participants.

Corporate capitalism An economic system in which huge business enterprises are able to dominate the market and substantially influence or determine the supply and price of many commodities.

Correlation A statistical term referring to the degree to which change in one variable is associated with change in another variable.

Correspondence theory This theory, developed by Bowles and Gintis, posits that the pattern of social relations established in one institution (i.e., schools) parallels in critical respects the pattern of social relations established in another institution (i.e., industry).

Counterculture A system of norms and values held by members of a subgroup or class within a society that contradicts or opposes a significant number of the norms and values that prevail within the society as a whole.

Countervailing duties Import taxes that one country imposes on certain commodities from another country to compensate for subsidies that the exporting country has given to producers of the commodities.

Credentialism In Marxist theory, the thesis that formal qualifications are emphasized by capitalists to create artificial division and competition among workers rather than because such qualifications are essential for performance of particular jobs.

Critical literacy The capacity to reflect upon and to question the content of what one reads.

Critical theory Any sociological theory or research that challenges the legitimacy of the established social order and that seeks to understand the workings of that society as a basis for action to change it.

Cult of domesticity A set of attitudes and values that justifies the segregation of women in the private realm of the home.

Cult of rationality Justification of everything by reference to the supposedly objective principles of scientific and technical efficiency.

Cultural lag The failure or excessive slowness of prevailing values and norms in a society to adapt to economic changes associated with technological innovation.

Cultural Marxism Closely associated with the social construction of reality perspective, this is a variant of Marxist theory that emphasizes ideological hegemony rather than the determining force of capitalist structures in explaining social relations in capitalist societies.

Cultural system In functionalism, the system of beliefs, rituals, values, and symbols, including language as a symbol system, through which people confront ultimate questions about reality, the meaning of good and evil, suffering, and death.

Culturalism See Cultural Marxism.

Culture The set of shared ideas about what constitutes ideal behaviour within a given society.

Culture of domination A system of values and behavioural expectations that condones or legitimates subordination of the mass of people to autocratic rule.

Culture of poverty thesis The thesis that poverty is caused or perpetuated by the attitudes and values of poor people, which inhibit them from taking action to ameliorate their situation.

Cybernetic hierarchy For Parsons, a hierarchy of systems of control and communication in human action.

Deconstructionism The detailed investigation of how texts are organized or internally constructed so as to achieve their meaning.

Deferred gratification Foregoing immediate pleasures or rewards in order to work toward greater future rewards.

Defining the situation In symbolic interaction and ethnomethodology, the process of negotiating the meaning of what seems to be going on.

Demography/Demographic The study of vital statistics of a population, including such information as population size, births, marriages, deaths, migration, and so on.

Dependency theory A theory that the poverty evident in the Third World and in poorer regions of developed economies is generated and perpetuated through systematic exploitation by developed capitalist economies.

Dependent capitalism The experience of capitalist development in Third World countries caught in an already highly advanced corporate capitalist world system.

Dependent commodity producers A class of workers who own their own means of production of certain commodities but who are controlled by the corporate monopoly processors and distributors who dominate the market for what they produce. See also Petite bourgeoisie.

Dependent development The restricted pattern of development within a region or country where the economy is controlled externally by capitalist metropolises that develop the locality only as a resource hinterland. See Dependency theory.

Dependent variable The variable that is assumed to depend on or be caused by other variables included in research.

Deskilling The process of breaking down a complex operation or activity into simple component operations that can be easily learned.

Determinism Any thesis that sees human activity as caused or controlled by forces independent of human choice or will. See Economic determinism.

Deviance Behaviour that does not conform to behavioural expectations prevailing in a given group or community.

Deviant subculture See Subcultural theory of deviance.

Dialectic Recurrent cycles of thesis, antithesis, and synthesis. Thesis refers to the original idea, philosophy, or system of thought. Antithesis represents the logical inconsistencies, problems, and anomalies within the thesis. The synthesis is a new system of ideas, thoughts, or philosophy that resolves these contradictions.

Dialectical materialism The application of dialectical reasoning to the organization of production. Thesis represents the existing organization of production. The antithesis refers to the tensions or problems that impede or shackle the full productive potential of this organization. The synthesis is a new form of organization of production that overcomes these problems and unleashes the full productive potential of the available means of production.

Dialectical method The application of dialectical thinking to a given problem, clarifying the original situation, explicating the contradictions inherent in it, and seeking a synthesis or new approach that will resolve these contradictions.

Differential association theory A theory that attributes variation in propensity for criminal behaviour to relative closeness of involvement with others whose subcultural values condone criminal behaviour.

Differential opportunity theory A theory that attributes variation in propensity for criminal behaviour to the relative availability of legitimate or illegitimate means to achieve valued goals. See Innovator.

Differentiation Generally, the process of becoming less alike as the result of performing more specialized social roles. Spencer used this term to refer to the breakdown of simple, unspecialized structures into many separate parts.

Diffuse obligations The perceived right of others, such as close family members, to expect a variety of services and support.

Disciplinary society The term is used by Foucault to refer to social order maintained through power based on intimate knowledge and regulation of individuals rather than on punitive sanctions.

Discipline Foucault uses this term to refer both to orderly conduct and to a branch of knowledge.

Discourse For Foucault, how we come to talk about our social world, which determines how it comes to be known to us and to have the form that it does.

Distributive justice The quality of fairness in the distribution of rewards or resources among participants in a situation or activity.

Divide and rule The policy of encouraging schisms within a mass of subordinate people to reduce the likelihood of concerted action by subordinates, making them easier to control.

Documentary construction of reality For Smith, a theoretical approach that focusses on how the seemingly neutral language of bureaucratic forms and categories actively structures social relations and what comes to be seen as factual information.

Documentary method of interpretation In ethnomethodology, the active search for patterns in the vague flux of everyday interaction, as a fundamental element of practical, everyday reasoning. This search is based on the premise that there is always an underlying pattern to everyday activity or conversation. Surface appearances are treated as evidence of, or as documenting, this presumed underlying pattern.

Dogmatism An assertion of opinion that is authoritarian.

Doing hierarchy In ethnomethodology, the actual practices of people in ongoing social interaction that produce and reproduce the experience of some individuals as inferior or superior to others.

Domestic labour debate A body of theory concerned with where and how homemakers fit into the capitalist economic system.

Dominant culture The set of values and behavioural expectations that prevails in a given society and that legitimates and supports the activities that directly benefit the dominant class. In capitalist society, the dominant culture is that which legitimates the activities of the capitalist class in the pursuit of profit.

Dominant values The values of the powerful class that tend to prevail within a society.

Domination In ethnic relations, the state of one ethnic group exerting regularized and institutionalized rule over other ethnic groups.

Double standard The standard for behaviour that is applied unevenly within a group or community such that given behaviour will be criticized and condemned if practised by one sector of a community but considered acceptable when practised by others.

Dowry murder A new bride murdered by her husband or his family because the amount of goods or money that the woman brought to the marriage is deemed inadequate. Dowry murder allows the husband to remarry to collect additional dowry.

Dramaturgical model Goffman's theoretical approach that studies how people creatively act out particular social roles in a manner analogous to how actors in a play creatively interpret their script.

Dynamic equilibrium In functionalist theory, the maintenance of balance and order between elements of a society by systematically adjusting for change in one element by complementary changes in other related elements.

Dysfunctions Effects or consequences of any given structure or pattern of behaviour that are damaging for some other element or for people in the wider social system.

Ecological fallacy A logically false or misleading argument that attempts to draw inferences about individuals from aggregate data.

Economic determinism A form of theorizing that reifies the abstract concept of an economic system, such that the system of production is held to cause or to determine all major aspects of social life, without reference to human agency.

Economies of scale A principle of economics that asserts that as the size of a business enterprise increases, the cost of producing any one unit of output decreases.

Ego In psychoanalytic theory, the conscious self that seeks to express and to realize fundamental drives and passions.

Egoism For Durkheim, a value system that places self-interest at the centre. Also, systematic selfishness, reflecting the absence of a sense of social bonds and commitment to other people.

Egoistic suicide The form of suicide committed by individuals who have lost any sense of social bonds linking them to other people.

Embourgeoisement thesis The thesis that, under capitalism, working-class people will become or are becoming steadily wealthier to the point that their lifestyles closely resemble those of professional middle-class people.

Emotional labour The work of managing facial expressions and manipulating the emotional responses of clients as part of one's job.

Empiricism A commitment to and quest for knowledge based on observation and experiment.

Employment equity Legislation and policies designed to ensure that women and men employed in jobs of equivalent levels of skill, responsibility, difficulty, etc., receive equivalent levels of pay.

Enclosure Feudal landlords' practice of fencing off huge tracts of arable land for sheep pastures thereby depriving serfs of access to land for subsistence crops.

Enumeration In survey research, the process of counting the total membership of a particular set of people from which a sample is to be drawn.

Equality of condition A policy that stresses sameness. In education, it means that a standardized age-graded curriculum be available for all students regardless of individual ability or interests.

Equality of opportunity A policy that, in principle, gives all individuals an equivalent chance to compete for social positions that carry relatively higher rewards. See Meritocracy thesis.

Equilibrium In functionalism, the maintenance of balance and order between elements of a society over long periods of time.

Ethic of responsibility For Weber, moral principles that take account of the probable consequences of actions.

Ethic of ultimate ends A term used by Weber to refer to morality based on obedience to religious doctrine or to what is perceived as the will of God, or some absolute value, regardless of the consequences.

Ethnic/Ethnicity Identity as a member of a distinctive cultural group associated with a particular country or region of origin. Social constructionists argue that ethnicity is used as an ideology that blames differences and inequalities caused by discriminatory treatment of certain people on intrinsic personal characteristics of the victims.

Ethnocentrism A belief that one's culture or way of life is superior to others. An exaggerated view of the quality and correctness of the culture of one's own groups. A self-centred view of social life lacking respect for the different perspectives or values of other people.

Ethnomethodology A theoretical approach that focusses on micro-interactions and explores the methods or practical reasoning that individuals use to make sense of what is going on around them. Ethnomethodologists argue that the process of formulating an account of what is happening produces reality for the practical purposes of participants.

Evolution A theory positing that societies developed from simple undifferentiated societies into highly complex industrial societies in a way analogous to evolution in the natural world where single-cell organisms evolved into complex advanced organisms.

Exchange value For Marx, the amount of human labour time that goes into the production of a commodity. The value of one commodity relative to another is measured by the labour time needed to make the commodities.

Experiment A methodological approach that, ideally, holds constant everything that might influence the phenomenon of interest and then allows one variable to change in a controlled manner. Any subsequent change observed in the phenomenon of interest is then attributed to the influence of the manipulated variable.

Expressive leader One who is primarily responsible for relieving tensions and smoothing social relations in a group.

Extended family A family in which several generations of kin live in the same home.

Extrinsic rewards Payment or other benefits received for doing some activity. The opposite of intrinsic rewards.

Fact Datum. That which is known as the result of empirical investigation conducted according to objective scientific methods of observation and experiment. Also, that which is attested to be correct by an appropriate official within a formal organization. See also Social facts.

False consciousness The condition of some members of the working class who fail to understand their true or objective long-term class interests to the extent that they are predisposed to support a system of production that exploits them.

Familism Particularly close attachment to kin, and high value placed on family membership, combined with generally shallow relations with nonkin.

Family-class immigrant See Sponsored immigrant.

Family wage The policy of paying male workers sufficient wages to support their wives and children.

Feedback mechanisms The processes through which given structures or patterns of behaviour are selectively reinforced and perpetuated over time.

Feminist movement Collective protest and political action to ameliorate the subordinate situation of women in society.

Feminist theory A perspective that takes as its starting point the situation and experiences of women in questioning the adequacy of any analysis of human behaviour. See also Marxist feminism; Radical feminism.

Fetish An inanimate object worshipped for its supposed magical powers. See Commodity fetishism.

Feudalism/Feudal system An economic system in which land is the primary means of production. Land is owned by a hereditary elite of nobles or lords and is worked by a hereditary class of labourers or serfs who are tied to the land.

Folk society An ideal-type model of isolated rural society.

Fragmentation The subdivision of tasks or responsibilities among workers such that each worker performs highly repetitive and monotonous actions devoid of any intrinsic interest or sense of importance.

Frankfurt School (The) See Critical theory.

Function For functionalists, the basic needs or conditions that must be met by a social system in order to maintain itself in a state of equilibrium. Also, the particular contribution of parts of a social system to the maintenance of the whole system.

Functional indispensability For Parsons, the assumption, borrowed from biology, that every element found within a social system is indispensable for the functioning of that system. Hence, no element can be removed or changed without some negative effect for the system as a whole.

Functional unity For Parsons, the assumption, borrowed from biology, that every element found within a social system has effects or consequences that are good for the entire system.

Functionalism/Structural functionalism The study of society as a functioning system comprising interdependent institutions or patterned relations that are stable over time, and that perform specialized functions for the whole. The central focus is on how order is maintained between elements of society. Any given pattern of relations or structures within society is explained by reference to the effects or functions that such patterns have for the wider whole.

GAIL model See System prerequisites.

Gatekeepers People who are in a strategic position to transmit or screen out information, especially in the media.

Gemeinschaft A theoretical model of a society as a community of people united by relations of kinship, a strong sense of community identification, and shared values and norms. A community.

Gender Culturally learned differences in behaviour of males and females.

Gender-class Socially constructed location of women and men relative to the organization of the activities of production and reproduction. See also Sexual class, which is often used synonymously with gender-class.

Gender-ethnic-class Location within the occupational hierarchy based on the combination of gender, ethnic background, and marketable job skills.

Gender-role socialization The process by which children are taught and internalize behaviour deemed appropriate for their particular sex.

Gender roles Markedly distinct and nonoverlapping roles for typical activities for women and men.

Generalized other A group or class of people whose overall responses to us play an integral part in the development of our own sense of self-identity. Similarly, a class or team of people whose reactions we try to anticipate.

Gesellschaft A theoretical model of an association of people related only by transitory and superficial contacts that are formal, contractual, and specified in character. An association.

Goal attainment For Parsons, establishing priorities among competing goals and mobilizing members involved in a given activity to attain them.

Goal displacement The tendency for groups or organizations set up to achieve some specific objective to shift priorities from this original objective to a concern with maintaining the group or organization itself.

Green revolution A package of scientific developments in agriculture that promises to increase yields.

Headstart program A policy of providing enriched learning experiences for young children from economically and culturally deprived families to help them keep up with the achievements of more advantaged children.

Hegemony Relations of ruling through which the consent of subordinate classes to capitalism is achieved, particularly through control over how people think.

Heterosexism The institutionalized organization of social relations that assumes that all women will be tied to men, usually in relations of sexual and economic interdependence.

Hidden curriculum That which is taught by the form of teaching rather than by the explicit content of lessons.

Hidden diseconomies The costs or negative consequences of economic activities that are not counted in corporate cost-benefit analyses, because members of the wider society, rather than the enterprise engaging in the activities, suffer from, and pay for, these consequences.

Hierarchy Graded or ranked positions within a society or organization.

Hinterland Underdeveloped areas that supply cheap labour and cheap raw materials or semiprocessed goods to developed centres.

Historical materialism For Marx, the thesis that the processes by which people meet their basic subsistance needs constitute the foundation of social organization. Hence, the analysis of social life should begin with the study of prevailing modes of production and the relations that these generate between people.

Historical sociology The study of how human actions generate social structures over time.

Holding company A company that holds sufficient shares in multiple other companies to control their executive boards.

Horizontal integration A corporation that owns or controls all or most stages in the production of a specific commodity, including production and supply of all raw materials, manufacturing, distribution, and retail sales.

Human relations school of management A style of management that gives priority to generating a friendly and relaxed social atmosphere in the workplace, on the assumption that contented workers are more productive. The term can be used pejoratively to refer to management styles that manipulate a friendly social atmosphere among subordinates to divert attention from the deeper reality of exploitation.

Humanism For Durkheim, a form of religion or spirituality in which the central value is devotion to humanity rather than to a divinity.

Hypothesis A prediction made on the basis of a theory.

I and Me Terms used by Mead to refer to two aspects of the individual. The I is the impulsive, spontaneous aspects of self. The Me is learned identity, incorporating the common attitudes and meanings of the group to which one belongs.

Id In psychoanalytic theory, the vast reservoir of unconscious and semiconscious drives and passions, especially sexual drives, that underlie and energize our conscious activities.

Idealism A philosophy that emphasizes ideas and values as the distinctive moving force of human history. The view that all human behaviour entails unique spiritual events that can only be grasped by intuition, not by objective scientific method.

Ideal-type model A theoretical model that is designed to highlight the typical characteristics of the kind of social organization being studied.

Ideographic Explanations based on unique, subjective, intuitive accounts.

Ideological hegemony The capacity of the dominant class to rule through control over prevailing ideas or culture. It ensures that the mass of people accept as legitimate the activities that directly benefit the dominant class.

Ideology Systems of values that justify certain kinds of action or ways of life, sometimes to the detriment of other people. Belief systems that strongly influence the way we see social reality. They tend to sensitize us in certain ways and blind us in others. Dorothy Smith uses the term to describe a method of inquiry about society that results in a systematic means not to see and not to know what is actually happening.

Imperfect competition In economic theory this refers to a situation in which a few giant producers or purchasers of a commodity are able to dominate the market and to act in collusion rather than in competition.

Imperialism The practice of one state extending its sovereignty over another by force, usually for the purpose of economic exploitation.

Imperialism of rationality A form of control over, or manipulation of, people. It is exercised by presenting certain kinds of behaviour as consistent with reason or scientific knowledge, such that any disagreement or resistance seems irrational.

Inclusive language Nonsexist language. Gender-neutral language that does not use masculine nouns and pronouns generally to include feminine forms.

Independent commodity producers A class of workers who own their own means of production of certain commodities, generally referring to people engaged in farming, fishing, and the like. See also Petite bourgeoisie.

Independent immigrant A category under the Immigration Act that refers to people whose entry into Canada is subject to economic requirements and criteria measured by a point system.

Independent variable A factor included in research as a possible cause of some phenomenon of interest. It is treated as known or given for the purpose of the research and not as itself requiring explanation.

Indexicality In ethnomethodology, the context-dependent character of the meaning of words or actions. The thesis that words or gestures always stand for or indicate a broader background and that this background understanding is essential for words to have meanings.

Indicator An observable feature that is used in research to measure a particular concept.

Industrial Revolution The period of transition associated with the eighteenth century in Europe when the primary means of production changed from land to machines located in factories.

Industrialization Mechanization. The transition from dependence on human and animal energy to fossil fuels. Usually associated with a shift in primary means of production from land to machines located in factories.

Inner city A general term referring to the central residential areas within large cities, usually characterized by high density housing.

Innovator A component of Merton's anomie theory of crime. One who accepts socially valued goals but adopts socially disapproved means to achieve them.

Institutional ethnography A theoretical and methodological approach that studies the active processes through which people construct their social reality through their everyday working activities in a local setting (ethnography). It then links these local dynamics to the wider institutional context that shapes them.

Institutionalization The establishment of certain patterns of behaviour as typical and expected to the point that they are generally taken for granted as appropriate by most members of a society.

Institutions Typical ways of structuring social relations around specific functions or needs of a society.

Instrumental leader One who is concerned with and who directs task performance in a group.

Integration Generally, to combine parts into a whole or to combine individuals into cohesive collectives. Spencer uses this term to refer to the evolutionary process of developing a central co-ordinating agency, such as state administration, to regulate relations between specialized elements of society. Parsons uses the term to refer to co-ordinating the behaviour of different members or role incumbents in a particular activity and maintaining orderly interrelations between role players.

Intelligence failure Loss of effective control in organizations resulting from distorted or inadequate information.

Interactional competence See Background understandings.

Interlocking directorships A situation where one person serves on the board of directors of two or more companies.

Internalization The process of learning group values and behavioural expectations and wanting to conform to them from an inner sense that they are morally right.

Interpretive theory A paradigm that focusses on micro-interactions and how people present themselves to each other and come to understand the surface and underlying meanings of their interaction. The perspective includes symbolic interaction and the dramaturgical model. Ethnomethodology is sometimes included with the interpretive perspective although it is distinct from traditional symbolic interaction. See Verstehen.

Intersubjectivity The capacity of knowing what another person actually intended.

Interviewer bias The interviewer's preconceived opinions or personal characteristics that influence the interaction with the respondent and influence in a measurable way the information being sought.

Invisible hand of the market The thesis that the competition between the mass of sellers, trying to get the best price for their commodities, and the mass of buyers, trying to buy commodities at the cheapest price, will produce the best outcome in the long run without external planning.

Iron cage Weber's vision of bureaucracy as an all-powerful system of organization that would regulate all aspects of individual life.

Iron law of oligarchy The process whereby power within any organization comes to be wielded by a tiny elite minority. A process hypothesized to occur regardless of democratic principles or procedures.

Isolation Absence of a sense of social bonds or belonging with other people. Particularly loss of a sense of loyalty or commitment to one's workplace. See Alienation.

Kin universe The average number of kin with whom an individual remains in regular contact.

Labelling theory An approach that focusses on how stereotypes or fixed mental images are applied to certain kinds of people, particularly by officials in positions of power, and the effects that this application has on the self-concepts and future behaviour of the people so labelled.

Labour-saving technology Machines designed to perform work previously done by people.

Labour theory of value For Marx, the theory that the average labour time that goes into the production of a commodity, with a given level of technology, determines the exchange value of that commodity.

Laissez-faire system An economic system that operates without any government control or regulation. Advocacy of such a system.

Latency See Pattern maintenance.

Latent functions Those effects or consequences of any given structure or pattern of behaviour that are important for maintaining social order but that are not directly recognized by people involved in the behaviour.

Leveraged buy-outs The practice of borrowing money to buy a controlling interest in a firm in the hope that assets so gained will generate sufficient profits to pay off the debt.

Liberalism Generally, a belief in the values of free enterprise and equality of opportunity for individuals to compete for social and economic rewards on the basis of merit. Used in a positive sense, it refers to a willingness to help individuals to overcome disadvantages or to open up opportunities for disadvantaged individuals. Critics use the term to refer to people who advocate piecemeal reform of the social system rather than radical or major changes to social structures. Critics also use the term to describe the tendency to blame inequality on personal merit or personal failings without acknowledging the structural constraints that disadvantage many groups.

Liberal-bourgeois thesis A theory that emphasizes the positive aspects of capitalism as an economic system. It is considered by Marxists to constitute the ideology of the bourgeoisie. Also, a thesis that associates capitalism with free enterprise and competitive markets that potentially provide opportunities for all people to improve their standard of living. See Liberalism.

Liberal feminism Feminist theory that focusses on establishing equal treatment for women and men as individuals in law, employment, and other public roles.

Liberation theology A religious doctrine that holds that the call to achieve social justice is central to the Christian message. See Social Gospel movement.

Linear relation An apparent relationship between two variables such that any change in the value of one variable is associated with an equivalent change in another variable.

Looking-glass self For Cooley, the way in which people reflect on how they appear to other people who are important to them, how their appearance is being judged by such people, and the effect of such reflection in feelings of pride or shame.

Lumpenproletariat In Marxist theory, unemployed workers who form a reserve army of cheap labour power to be used by capitalists as they require additional labour power.

Macrosociology The analysis of large-scale and long-term social processes, often treated as self-sufficient entities such as state, class, culture, and so on.

Macrovariable A variable that cannot be reduced to micro-elements.

Managerial mentality The thesis that organizations are rational and efficient entities and that people can be regarded as role incumbents and managed to maximize efficiency of co-operative activities. Generally, the endorsement of the viewpoint of managers.

Managerial revolution The thesis that ownership of corporations has become separated from control over them. The belief that managers rather than capitalists run corporations.

Manifest functions The consequences of any given structure or pattern of behaviour that are openly recognized and intended by the people involved in the behaviour.

Marginal workers A class of workers who are frequently unemployed or who can find work only in a succession of temporary and low-paid jobs.

Marxist feminism Feminist theory that focusses on the role of economy and private property in the subordination of women to men.

Marxist functionalism The modification of functionalist analysis to incorporate notions of power and unequal ability of different individuals and groups to selectively reinforce those social structures that they find beneficial.

Marxist structuralism The theory that utilizes the model of the capitalist system and its internal contradictions as an explanatory framework to account for specific characteristics of contemporary capitalist society.

Maternal deprivation theory The theory that young children require extensive physical and social contact with their mothers in order to become psychologically well adjusted and hence that all evidence for adult maladjustment, particularly delinquent behaviour, can be explained by inadequate maternal attention.

Matriarchy Social organization in which the mother is the head of the family.

Matrilineal Ancestry and inheritance through the mother's line.

Me See I and Me.

Meaninglessness Absence of a sense of involvement in a worthwhile activity. The term refers particularly to fragmented work where one individual's contribution is so small as to seem worthless. See Alienation.

Mechanical solidarity Durkheim used this term to describe a form of cohesion that is based fundamentally on sameness.

Members' competences See Background understandings.

Men's liberation A social and political movement concerned with challenging stereotypes of masculinity and the associated sex roles that confine men to the public occupational realm.

Mercantilism Trade, particularly referring to the historical period when European countries effectively dominated world trade and amassed great wealth at the expense of less developed countries.

Meritocracy Inequality in social rewards based on individual differences in ability and effort.

Meritocracy thesis In functionalist theory, the thesis that hierarchy and social inequality are accounted for by the need to motivate the more talented and competent individuals to occupy the more important and difficult roles in society.

Metaphysical stage A stage in Comte's model of the evolution of societies. Societies in the metaphysical stage are characterized by a prevailing belief in a single deity. Phenomena are explained by reference to abstract forces or ultimate reality rather than to a multiplicity of spirits.

Methodism A puritanical religious doctrine that stresses spiritual egalitarianism, grace through penitence, strictness in religious practice and moral behaviour, and submission to authority.

Methodological holism The principle that social experiences must be explained in terms of forces that operate at the level of the social system as a whole.

Methodological individualism The theory that social experiences can be reduced to the characteristics of individual people. See Psychological reductionism.

Metropolis The centre of capitalism, which dominates surrounding regions, extracting their economic resources.

Microhistory The study of how personal interaction is shaped over time.

Microsociology The detailed analysis of what people do, say, and think in the actual flow of momentary experience.

Microstructural bias A tendency to concentrate on the internal workings of organizations rather than to examine the effects of wider political and economic forces on them.

Microtranslation strategy The attempt to show how large-scale social structures can be understood as patterns of repetitive micro-interactions.

Military-industrial complex The thesis that there is a close affinity between the interests of the elites within the military and industry.

Military-industrial-political complex The thesis that there is a close affinity between the personnel and the interests of elites within the military and industry and senior ranks of the civil service and government ministries.

Misogyny Hatred of women.

Mobility Geographic mobility refers to movement from one locality to another. Social mobility refers to a change in relative status, either up or down the social class hierarchy.

Mode of production Marx uses this term to refer to the prevailing way in which a society transforms the material environment to meet subsistence needs.

Monogamy Having only one mate. Marriage between one man and one woman.

Monolithic bias The assertion that a particular phenomenon is uniform throughout, allowing no variation.

Monopoly Exclusive possession of the trade in some commodity by one individual or one corporation.

Morality Durkheim uses the term to refer to the expression of the relationship between individuals and society.

Multinational corporations Business enterprises that operate in one or more countries in addition to the country housing the corporate headquarters.

Multivariate analysis An aspect of survey research in which statistical techniques are used to see how sets of variables interact in combination.

National Policy The policy instituted by John A. Macdonald in 1878 to establish high tariffs against American goods entering Canada in order to encourage industrialization in Canada. The effect was that American businesses invested in branch plants within Canada.

Natural attitude This term is used in ethnomethodology to refer to people's tendency to assume that social interaction is meaningful, without their reflecting on how such meaning comes to be perceived and sustained.

Natural laws Statement of a causal relationship between physical phenomena, held to be universally true under given conditions.

Need dispositions Parsons uses this term to refer to the way people tend to act in conformity with norms and feel dissatisfied when they cannot do so. Individual choices take the form of patterned behaviour because of the internalization of shared norms.

Neo-imperialism The practice of one country exerting effective control over the economy of another country and exploiting its resources even though it has formal independence.

Noble Under the feudal system, one who controls the estate on which serfs work.

Nomothetic Lawlike generalizations. Deterministic cause and effect relations.

Normalization Foucault uses this term to refer to a manipulated conformity managed by rational social science principles and legitimated by reference to models of healthy psychological and social adjustment. See Therapeutic intervention.

Normative consensus In functionalist theory, this refers to a social group's shared acceptance of a set of values and behavioural expectations as legitimate and appropriate. The establishment of normative consensus is considered critical in the maintenance of a stable social order to which members willingly conform.

Norms Typical expectations for behaviour in given situations that are seen as legitimate and appropriate.

Nuclear family A family unit comprising two sexually cohabiting adults of the opposite sex together with their dependent children.

Objectivity The attempt to present and to deal with facts, uncoloured by the feelings, opinions, and viewpoints of the person presenting them. Objective evidence is that which is accepted as factual and independent of the subjective opinions or theories of any observer.

Oligarchy Rule by a few people at the top without democratic participation.

Oligopoly Concentrated possession of the trade in some commodity by a few individuals or a few corporations.

One-dimensional thought The inability to conceive of viable alternative ways of organizing social relations. Acceptance of the status quo and of the prevailing ways of thinking as the only credible option.

Order theory Closely related to systems theory, a perspective in which the central focus is on how a stable balance is maintained between elements of a social system.

Organic solidarity Durkheim uses this term to refer to a form of cohesion based upon specialization and interdependence.

Other For Mead, those people whose responses to us play an integral part in the development of our own sense of self-identity.

Out-group A group of people considered sufficiently different as to be outside one's own cultural group.

Outsiders Nonconformists. People whose lifestyles or characteristics visibly violate at least some of the norms that define membership within a given community. See Symbolic brackets.

Paradigm A broad theoretical perspective that may encompass several more specific but related stories. A pattern.

Participant observation A methodological approach in which the researcher shares as fully as possible in the everyday activities of the people being studied in order to understand their lives through personal experience.

Participatory management A form of management in which workers are permitted some involvement in making decisions, usually as a way of winning their support for the implementation of such decisions.

Particularism/Particularistic standards For Parsons, evaluation based on the particular abilities, interests, and efforts of an individual.

Party Weber uses the term to refer to organized relations within the political arena, designed to influence policy in favour of a tribe or family.

Patriarch Father and ruler of a tribe or family.

Patriarchy A social system based on male dominance and female subordination.

Patrimony Property inherited from one's father. Also used to refer to a system of senior male mentors conferring rank or privileges onto specifically chosen junior males.

Pattern maintenance Parsons uses the term to refer to the mechanisms to manage tensions and ensure that individual role players in an activity have the skills and motivation needed to perform their given role(s) appropriately. Latency.

Pattern variables For Parsons, a patterned set of dichotomous options that systematize typical dilemmas of choice in any given role.

Pay equity Equal pay for equal work means that women and men who do identical work should receive identical pay. Equal pay for work of equal value means that workers in different jobs should receive the same pay when their work involves the same level of skill, responsibility, or difficulty.

Peasant A person who works the land to produce food and other materials for immediate consumption rather than for sale or exchange. In discussions of feudalism, the term is often synonymous with serf. Generally, one who works the land.

Personal troubles Mills uses the term to refer to the private matters that lie within an individual's character and immediate relationships.

Personality system Parsons uses the term to refer to the learned component of individual behaviour. Socialization is a critical process in its formation.

Petite bourgeoisie Marx uses the term to describe the class of people who own their own means of production and work for themselves but who hire little or no additional wage-labour.

Phenomenology A theory of the methods or grounds of knowledge based on the premise that all knowledge constitutes interpretations of basic sense experience. The study of how sensory information becomes interpreted as meaningful.

Piece-rate payment A system of payment based on the number of items or units of work completed, rather than on the length of time worked.

Plutocracy A ruling class of wealthy persons. Rule by the wealthy.

Polarization of classes Marx's thesis that, under capitalism, wealth will become progressively more concentrated in the hands of a tiny elite class of capitalists as the mass of people become steadily more impoverished.

Political economy theory A theoretical perspective in which the central explanatory framework for analysing society is the Marxist model of capitalism. The dynamics of the capitalist economy are seen as the fundamental determinants of political structures and action.

Polyandry One woman having more than one husband at the same time. Wife sharing.

Polygamy Having more than one spouse at the same time.

Polygyny One man having more than one wife at the same time. Husband sharing.

Positive society The third stage of Comte's model of the evolution of societies. Positive society is characterized by a commitment to scientific rationality. Scientists rather than priests are the intellectual and spiritual leaders, and explanations take the form of regular lawlike connections between phenomena based on observation and experiment.

Positivism/Positivist A scientific approach to the study of society that seeks to emulate the methodology of the physical sciences. Emphasis is placed on quantitative, objective data rather than on subjective or impressionistic research. Conclusions are based upon observation and experiments that are assumed to provide factual, objective evidence, independent of the theories or opinions of any observer. Also, the search for deterministic or lawlike relations of cause and effect governing human behaviour. The philosophical assumption that observation and experimentation constitute the only valid human knowledge. In ethnomethodology the term refers to an ideology that accords the subjective interpretations of sense experience by other people.

Postmodernism A complex term that refers to architectural styles that incorporate a pastiche or merging of multiple styles in one building. In sociological theory, a perspective that rejects the search for grand theories or unifying explanations for society, conceptualizing social reality as heterogeneous, fluid, and contingent.

Poverty line A level of income below which people are defined as poor. Commonly calculated on the basis of the proportion of total income required to meet basic subsistence needs of food, shelter, and clothing in a particular society.

Powerlessness Lack of control over factors directly affecting one's life, particularly lack of control over one's work and fear of unemployment. See Alienation.

Practical reasoning In ethnomethodology, the methods by which ordinary people, in their everyday practical affairs, mutually create and sustain their common-sense notions of what is going on.

Precontractual basis of contract Durkheim uses the term to refer to a collective commitment to shared values that are a moral precondition for orderly contractual relations. It refers, in particular, to a commitment to respect for individual differences and human rights.

Predestination See Calvinism.

Prejudice Prejudging, usually in negative terms, the characteristics that are assumed to be shared by members of another group. Preconceived opinion or bias against or in favour of a person or thing. Commonly used to refer to negative opinions of people regarded as outside one's one cultural group.

Prerequisites Those needs or functions that must be met within any social system for that system to maintain a state of balance or equilibrium.

Presentation of self The image that we try to create for ourselves in the eyes of other people whose opinion we value.

Prescriptive norms Shared behavioural expectations concerning what one should do or how one ought to behave in a given situation.

Primitive communism An economic system characterized by a simple hunting and gathering technology where the means of production—the local plants and animals—are accessible to all, and no one has ownership rights to the terrain or to its resources

Private realm In functionalism, the aspects of society perceived as oriented toward personal life, particularly family and leisure activities.

Privatization In the domestic labour debate, this refers to the process of separating domestic work, and the people—mostly women—who perform it, from other productive activities.

Probability The recognition that social phenomena have multiple causes and involve elements of free choice that cannot be predicted with certainty but can be explored with respect to the likelihood of their occurrence.

Procedural norms Rules that govern how a particular activity, such as contract negotiations, should proceed.

Profane Durkheim uses this term to describe that which does not belong to the sacred. Mundane, ordinary.

Proletariat Wage-labourers who survive by selling their labour power. Those who do not own any means to produce for themselves.

Proscriptive norms Shared behavioural expectations concerning what one should not do or what is unacceptable behaviour in a given situation.

Protectionism The situation where duties are applied to imported goods to raise their sale price relative to the price of equivalent local goods, usually to compensate for higher local production costs.

Protestant ethic Weber uses this term to refer to the moral value accorded to work as a spiritual duty and a sign of God's grace. This value system emphasizes accumulation of wealth as a sign of grace; poverty, laziness, and idle luxury are seen as signs of moral depravity and damnation.

Psychoanalysis A body of theory that focusses on infantile sexual drives and their repression within the nuclear family as the foundations of adult personality.

Psychological reductionism The attempt to explain collective social processes by reference only to the psychological processes within the individuals involved.

Psychologism See Psychological reductionism.

Public issues Mills uses this term to refer to the broad social forces that affect the life experiences of many people in similar circumstances.

Public realm In functionalism, aspects of society, particularly economic and political institutions, that are perceived to be oriented toward the society as a whole.

Purdah A cultural tradition among East Indians that emphasizes the seclusion of women in the home, as part of a pattern of restrictions on their behaviour. Literally, a curtain, especially one serving to screen women from the sight of strangers.

Puritanism A doctrine that emphasizes extreme strictness in moral behaviour such that frivolity, idleness, and luxury, and sex other than for procreation are condemned.

Purposive-rational action Weber uses this term to describe action based on calculation of the most effective means to achieve a particular desired outcome, balanced against probable costs.

Qualitative methods Methods that are not based on quantitative procedures. These methods are used to explore small settings in depth with the goal of gaining insight that may form the basis for generalizations.

Quantitative methods A methodological approach that counts instances of specified aspects of human behaviour in order to derive broad generalizations about patterns of experience.

Questionnaires A formulated series of questions used in survey research.

Race A concept that refers to people's visible and inherited physical differences that are socially noticed. It is commonly associated with differences in skin colour.

Racism Prejudicial attitudes toward groups perceived to be different on the basis of inescapable genetic characteristics. Feelings of antagonism, commonly associated with hostile and discriminatory behaviour toward people of a different race or visibly distinct descent group.

Radical One who advocates fundamental change that goes to the root of the existing social order as distinct from one advocating piecemeal changes.

Radical feminism Feminist theory that focusses on control over sexuality and relations of reproduction.

Radical microsociology The study of everyday life in second-by-second detail, using such techniques as audio- and video-recordings to permit the detailed analysis of conversations and nonverbal interaction.

Rationalization Cost-benefit analysis generally, with both costs and benefits defined primarily in narrow and technical terms rather than incorporating all social and emotional costs and benefits. Also, concentrating production in one or a few large enterprises with the objective of minimizing unit production costs. An aspect of the strategy of maximizing economies of scale.

Rational-legal authority Weber uses the term to describe authority legitimated by reference to the practical utility of the rules themselves.

Rebel A category in Merton's anomie theory of crime. One who replaces socially valued goals with alternative goals and who adopts alternative means to achieve these new goals.

Recipe knowledge Awareness of typical patterns of actions, learned through socialization, that provide a basis for interpreting the meaning of particular actions.

Reconstituted family A family produced by combining some members of two previously separate families, usually produced by the second marriage or one or both spouses who bring children from a previous marriage or partnership.

Reductionism The tendency to explain complex phenomena by reference to a single cause. The attempt to explain complex social processes by reference only to some lower level of analysis Ii.e., to explain social phenomena by individual psychology). See Psychological reductionism.

Reflexive/Reflexivity In ethnomethodology, the assumption that there is a mutually determining relationship between appearances and underlying patterns. What one notices about an object or event is contingent upon what one assumes it to be. Similarly, what one assumes it to be is contingent upon the details that one notices.

Refugee status Status that can be accorded those fleeing to a foreign country to escape persecution.

Regulation Durkheim uses the term to refer to values and rules that restrain individual self-interest for the good of the social whole.

Reification The tendency to impute causal force or motives to abstract concepts such as society or markets instead of to the activities of people.

Relations of production Refers to how people organize to produce goods.

Relations of reproduction Refers to how people organize to produce children and raise them to maturity.

Relative deprivation The subjective experience of poverty or loss in comparison with other people rather than in terms of an absolute measure of penury.

Relative surplus Marx uses this term to refer to the amount of surplus production available after payment of wages, when the productivity of workers is increased through labour-saving technology.

Religion Durkheim describes religion as a unified system of beliefs and practices, relative to sacred things, which unite into a single moral community—a church—all adherents.

Repressive law Durkheim uses the term to refer to law that is essentially religious in character and that is concerned with punishing offenders who have transgressed the shared values of the community.

Reserve army of labour Marx uses the term to refer to those people who can be drawn into the labour market when needed by capitalists but let go, often to return to unpaid domestic work, when no longer needed.

Restitutive law Durkheim uses this term to refer to law that is concerned with the regulation of contracts and the re-establishment of reciprocal obligations between members of a society.

Retreatist A category in Merton's anomie theory of crime. One who rejects or gives up on socially approved goals and who fails to conform to behavioural expectations.

Right of national treatment Part of the free trade agreement between the American and Canadian governments. Any enterprise based in one country but doing business in the other would be subject to the same regulations as those that apply to local enterprise.

Ritualist A category in Merton's anomie theory of crime. One who rejects or gives up socially valued goals but conforms to behavioural expectations.

Role A typical pattern of behaviour in a predefined situation or status. In ethnomethodology, interpreting behaviour after the fact so as to render it meaningful or accountable, rather than random.

Role distancing Goffman uses the term to refer to a way of performing a social role so as to convey to onlookers the impression that this is not an activity to which one is wholeheartedly committed.

Role model A person whom others strive to emulate in the performance of a particular role.

Role segregation A separation of roles in time and space, which partly insulates one role from others.

Role set The set of all roles with which a person interacts in the process of playing a specific role. Alternatively, the set of all the different roles that any one person plays simultaneously.

Role strain The conflicting expectations and demands that the person playing a specific role experiences from other people in the wider set of related roles. Also, the conflicting expectations and demands that people experience when playing several different roles simultaneously.

Role-taking Mead uses the term to describe the way in which children develop an image of themselves through trying to see themselves as they appear to others.

Role theory In functionalism, the theory concerned with the patterns of interaction established in the performance of typical activities or functions in society.

Ruling apparatus The totality of processes through which the work of governing a society occurs, including the work of employees in local offices and the forms and documents around which their work is organized.

Sacred For Durkheim, that which is set apart by a community of people as the expression or symbol of highest spiritual value. Often, but not necessarily, that which is consecrated to a deity.

Sample A separated part of a population or type of situation being studied, which is used in research to illustrate the qualities of the population from which the part is drawn.

Science A search for knowledge that tries to test tentative assumptions or explanations through the systematic search for evidence.

Scientific management A principle of management of manual work based on the fragmentation of tasks into their smallest component actions, each of which can be precisely regulated through time and motion studies to achieve the maximum possible speed of performance. Sometimes referred to as Taylorism, after Frederick Taylor, the engineer who first developed the system.

Scientism A reliance on simple cause-and-effect explanatory models that imply that external forces rather than human agency determine human experience.

Secondary analysis Analysis that uses data collected in previous research for some other purpose.

Secondary deviance Used in labelling theory to refer to deviance caused or prompted by the sense of being considered a deviant person by other people.

Self The image of oneself comprising both spontaneous feelings and learned attributes.

Self-estrangement Absence of a sense of personal involvement or pride in what one does and hence a detachment from it. See Alienation.

Semiproletarianization The situation of people who were formerly self-sufficient producers but who have to take part-time wagework to survive.

Separation In the context of ethnic relations, this term refers to two or more distinct ethnic groups living within the same nation-state but maintaining separate political, economic, and cultural institutions and having minimal interaction.

Serf A tied labourer on a feudal estate. A person whose service is attached to the land and transferred with it.

Sets of roles See Role set.

Sex Biological differences in reproductive capacities of males and females.

Sex roles Activities that are defined within a particular culture as the typical responsibility only of women or only of men.

Sexism/Sexist bias Stereotyped and usually derogatory attitudes or discriminatory behaviour toward people of one sex, commonly but not necessarily toward people of the opposite sex.

Sexual class Location of women and men relative to the organization of the activities of reproduction involving conception, pregnancy, childbirth, nurturing, consuming, domestic labour, and wage earning.

Shareholder capitalism The thesis that ownership of capital is becoming democratized through large numbers of people owning shares.

Shoptalk The shorthand jargon that can be used in conversations between people who share specialized background understandings.

Significant others People whose relationship to us and whose opinions of us are important.

Signified The mental concept to which a signifier refers; e.g., a picture of a suitcase with an arrow (signifier) refers to the baggage claim area in an airport (signified).

Signifier The physical form of a sign. In language, the sound or the word.

Skilled labour time A concept developed by Marx to refer to the time it takes for a skilled person to produce a commodity. It includes the average time taken to learn the skill, including the teacher's time.

Slavery Economic organization in which some persons are the legal property of another or others and are bound to labour for them.

Small groups laboratories Rooms that, in order to facilitate experiments, are designed to permit a researcher to control a wide variety of factors that might influence interaction within a small group of people.

Social action In functionalism, the structures and processes by which people form meaningful intentions and, more or less successfully, implement them in concrete situations. Weber used the term to refer to any human conduct that is meaningfully oriented to the past, present, or future expected behaviour of others.

Social construction of reality/Social constructionism A theoretical perspective, loosely associated with Marxist theory, that explores how the immediate practical activities of people in their everyday working lives produce the patterns that we subsequently come to recognize as social structures.

Social facts Durkheim uses this term to refer to social phenomena that are experienced as external to the individual and as constraints on the individual's behaviour.

Social Gospel movement A movement that stresses the doctrine of collective social responsibility and the links between Christianity and socialism. Concepts of sin and salvation are interpreted in social rather than individual terms.

Social order In ethnomethodology, the active processes of creating and sustaining notions of underlying patterns in the otherwise undefined flux of experience. It is accomplished through practical, everyday reasoning.

Social structures A broad macrosociological term, referring to large-scale and long-term patterns of organization in a society. Roughly equivalent to social institutions. In ethnomethodology, the outcome of practical reasoning processes engaged in by sociologists and others, to account for what seems to be going on. See Institutions.

Social system In functionalism, the structures and processes that collectively organize action and manage the potential for conflict and disorganization to maintain order over time.

Socialism A political and economic theory that advocates collective responsibility for the well-being of members of a society.

Socialist feminism Feminist theory that focusses on the linkages between the economy and domestic division of labour.

Socialization The lifelong process through which we learn the values and expected patterns of behaviour appropriate for particular social groups and specific roles. This learning process is particularly intense in infancy but continues throughout life as we change roles and group membership.

Socially necessary labour time See Abstract labour time.

Society Generally, the multiple interactions of individuals in a particular setting. A set of forces exerted by people over one another and over themselves. In functionalism, the term refers to a relatively self-sufficient, functioning social system comprising interdependent parts—polity, economy, family, administration, and so on—that each perform specialized functions for the whole. Parsons uses the term to refer to a large-scale social system that controls behaviour within a given territory, has relatively clear membership status, and is capable of meeting all the life needs of members from birth to death.

Sociobiology The study of the biological bases of social behaviour.

Sociological imagination The capacity to understand the relationships between elements of society and their impact on individual lives. The ability to use information in a critical way to achieve an understanding of what is going on in the world and what may be happening within one's own life experience.

Sociology The scientific study of society. The study of relations of social life. Mills uses the term to refer to the study of the major parts or structures of society (polity, economy, church, family, and so on), how these are interrelated, how they came to be as they appear, how they are changing, and the qualities or characteristics of the people involved. Weber uses this term to refer to the science that attempts the interpretive understanding of social action to arrive at an explanation of its cause and effects.

Solidarity Durkheim uses the term to refer to the emotional experience of cohesion and bonding between individuals so that they feel integrated into a social whole.

Specific obligations The perceived right of others to expect only a narrow range of services confined to the precise task at hand, such as in a business contract.

Sponsored immigrant A category within the Immigration Act that refers to people who are permitted to enter Canada as the dependants of a resident of Canada who agrees to take financial responsibility for them.

State Within the social construction of reality approach, the term is used to refer to the whole spectrum of government, including the behaviour of people at all levels of the civil service and related bureaucracies, agencies, departments, and offices.

Status Generally, the position that one occupies in a society. Weber uses the term to refer to social prestige and honour accruing to a person or office.

Status degradation ceremonies A term used by Garfinkel to refer to rites or actions that publicly signal a drop in social status of a person from a normal member of a group or community to a deviant or stigmatized person.

Stereotypes Simplified versions of other groups of people. Such mental cartoons are formed by generalizing too much or exaggerating people's characteristics on the basis of too little information.

Stigma/Stigmatization Disgrace attaching to some act or characteristic.

Stratification The hierarchical organization of people in occupations that are differentially rewarded in terms of income, prestige, and authority. A general ranking or pattern of inequality in a society, commonly measured in terms of occupation, income, and education.

Structural correspondence theory See Correspondence theory.

Structural functionalism See Functionalism.

Structuralism See Marxist structuralism.

Structure See Social structures.

Structuring The process in time through which actions at any one time set constraints upon subsequent actions.

Subcontracted agency An organization that is used by another to supply goods or to perform work. The term is used figuratively to refer to domestic workers who provide a variety of goods and services for the benefit of corporations, even though not regulated by a specific contract.

Subcultural theory of deviance Growing out of Merton's anomie theory of crime, this theory posits that deviance and crime reflect the values of the subculture of which the deviant is a member.

Subculture A distinctive subset of values and behavioural expectations shared by a particular subgroup within a society.

Subjectivism Any approach that explains human activity solely by reference to individual motivation without considering broader structural forces and constraints.

Subsidiary A company controlled by another company that owns a majority of its shares.

Subsidy Money contributed to an enterprise by the state.

Subsistence Provision of the necessities of life but with little surplus for luxuries or profit.

Subsistence wage The minimum wage required to cover the cost of sustaining workers and reproducing the next generation, given prevailing standards of living and education required by such workers.

Substantive norms Rules that govern what activities should be done (i.e., the responsibilities of participants in a contract).

Suburbs Residential areas in outlying districts of cities, usually characterized by relatively low-density housing.

Superego In psychoanalysis, the veneer of learned values and behavioural expectations that control drives and passions.

Superstructure For Marx, all aspects of culture, ideas, religion, legal, and political institutions, and so on, that are seen as determined by the prevailing mode of production in that society.

Supply-curve demand The relationship between supply of a commodity in the market and the demand for it, mediated by the price.

Surplus value For Marx, the difference between the value of the wages paid and the value of the commodities produced by the worker.

Surrogate mother A woman who becomes pregnant in order to produce a child for someone else.

Survey research A methodological approach that utilizes questionnaires or structured interviews in which a series of questions are asked of a sample of people. Answers are then analysed with the aid of computers to provide broad comparative information.

Survival of the fittest The thesis that those biological organisms and societies that survive and prosper are the fittest or best adapted to their environment.

Symbolic brackets Erikson uses the term to refer to the culturally defined limits of acceptable behaviour that distinguish members of a community from nonmembers.

Symbolic interaction A theoretical approach within the interpretive perspective. It focusses on micro-interactions and how people use gestures and language to convey typical meanings in interaction with others who share a common cultural background.

Synthesis See Dialectic; Dialectical materialism.

System A complex whole. A set of connected parts.

System prerequisites For Parsons, the basic requirements of pattern maintenance, integration, goal attainment, and adaptation found in any ongoing social system and subsystem.

Systems theory The study of society as a whole or of specific elements of society as functionally interrelated elements, analogous to a biological organism or an organ within such an organism. The central focus is on how a stable balance is maintained between elements.

Taboo Sacred ban or prohibition.

Taylorism See Scientific management.

Technical civilization A vision of society as comprising a dense network of interlocking bureaucratic organizations penetrating all aspects of social life. See Bureaucratic society; Disciplinary society.

Technics/Language of technics The use of computer terminology to refer to human interaction (i.e., feedback, input, output instead of dialogue, debate, judgment).

Technocratic-meritocratic thesis The theory that hierarchy and social inequality in industrial societies reflect differential competence of individuals with respect to science and technology. See Meritocracy thesis.

Text See Textual analysis.

Textual analysis A methodological approach that involves the detailed study of particular pieces of writing to reveal how meaning is constructed by the text.

Theological stage A stage in Comte's model of the evolution of societies. In the theological stage, societies are dominated by primitive religious thought, and explanations for phenomena are expressed primarily in terms of supernatural forces.

Theory of exchange In Marxist analysis, the theory that the exchange value of a commodity is determined by the amount of labour that goes into a commodity. Under capitalism, the basis of exchange is money, rather than another commodity.

Theory of modernization A theory originating in Spencer's model of societal evolution. It sees societies evolving toward increased differentiation and specialization in political, cultural, economic, and social areas.

Therapeutic intervention For Foucault, the process of manipulating conformity and consensus in society through technical means developed in the social sciences and justified by reference to efficiency and healthy psychological and social adjustment.

Thesis See Dialectic; Dialectical materialism.

Third World The impoverished and technologically backward regions of Latin America, Africa, and Asia.

Totem Any natural object, especially a local animal or plant, that is recognized as the symbol or emblem of a clan or sometimes of an individual.

Traditional authority For Weber, authority legitimated by custom, such as that of hereditary rulers.

Traditional-rational action Weber uses the term to refer to action that is based on habit.

Transfer pricing The prices charged when goods and services are exchanged between a parent corporation and one of its subsidiaries or between two subsidiaries of the same parent corporation.

Typify/Typifications Sets of shared assumptions concerning what is normal behaviour for people in related roles or social positions. See Background understandings.

Typology A theoretical model defining different categories or elements of a phenomenon.

Underdeveloped society A society in which critical economic resources have been and still are being plundered and the internal economy undermined by processes within the world capitalist economic system.

Undeveloped society A society in which the economy continues to function in an unchanged, traditional pattern without benefit of technological advance.

Universal functionalism Parsons uses the term to refer to the assumption, borrowed from biology, that every element found within a social system must perform some function for the whole society.

Universalism/Universalistic standards For Parsons, evaluation based on objective criteria that apply equally to any person performing a given activity.

Unobtrusive measures Measures that avoid the possibility of influencing the phenomenon being measured.

Utterances In ethnomethodology, sounds made by a person before they have been interpreted as having any meaning.

Vacuum ideology An attitude that children from minority cultures learn virtually nothing worth knowing outside of school.

Value-rational action Weber's term for action based on beliefs.

Values The beliefs shared among members of a group or society concerning qualities thought to be desirable or esteemed.

Variable Any phenomenon that has more than one value.

Verstehen The interpretation of behaviour as involving meaningful intentions. A methodological approach that involves trying to reconstruct the interpretations that the people being studied might give to their own actions.

Vertical integration Enterprises that operate at different stages in the production of a particular commodity and are consolidated into one corporation.

Vertical mosaic A pattern of stratification in which members of different racial and ethnic groups are arranged vertically with respect to each other in terms of class position.

Victimless crimes Transactional crimes where the persons involved participate willingly in exchanging goods and services and do not see themselves as either criminals or victims. Crimes against morality where there are no clear victims.

Vocation For Weber, performance of the responsibilities of an office as a duty, not for personal gain.

Voluntarism An explanation for action that refers to the rational and free choice of the actor.

Voluntaristic theory For Parsons, a theory of social action that explains social order by reference to mutual agreement or consensus between actors.

Welfare state A state that provides a range of social services for workers, including such benefits as health care, unemployment insurance, welfare payments, pensions, and the like. Such services ameliorate the effects of cyclical ups and downs in the economy as well as helping workers survive personal crises.

White-collar crime Violations of the law committed by professional and business people.

Worked up An expression used by Smith to describe the state of raw sense data having been categorized and organized in terms of an interpretive framework in the process of communicating it.

References

Aberle, D.F., A.K. Cohen, A.K. Davis, M.J. Levy Jr., and F.X. Sutton. 1950. "The Functional Prerequisites of a Society." *Ethics* 60 (Jan.): 100–11.

Abrahamson, M. 1978, "Sudden Wealth, Gratification, and Attainment: Durkheim's Anomie of Affluence Reconsidered." *American Sociological Review* 45: 49–57.

Abrams, P. 1982. *Historical Sociology.* Shepton Mallet, Somerset: Open Book Publishers.

Achbar, M. 1994. *Manufacturing Consent: Noam Chomsky and the Media—The Companion Book to the Award-winning Film by Peter Wintonick and Mark Achbar.* Montreal: Black Rose Books.

Adams, D. 1988. "Treatment Models of Men Who Batter: A Profeminist Analysis." In *Feminist Perspectives on Wife Abuse.* Ed. K. Yllö and M. Bograd. Beverly Hills: Sage, 176–99.

Adelberg, E., and C. Currie. 1987a. "In Their Own Words." In *Too Few to Count: Canadian Women in Conflict with the Law.* Ed. E. Adelberg and C. Currie. Vancouver: Press Gang, 67–102.

Adelberg, E., and C. Currie. 1987b. *Too Few To Count: Canadian Women in Conflict with the Law.* Vancouver: Press Gang.

Adorno, T.W., E. Frenkel-Brunswik, D.J. Levinson, and S.R. Nevitt. [1950] 1968. *The Authoritarian Personality.* New York: Norton.

Agger, B. 1991. "Critical Theory, Poststructuralism, Postmodernism: Their Sociological Relevance." *American Review of Sociology* 17: 105–31.

Ahmed, L. 1982. "Western Ethnocentrism and Perceptions of the Harem." *Feminist Studies* 8, 3: 521–34.

Ahmed, L. 1989. "Feminism and Cross-Cultural Inquiry: The Terms of the Discourse in Islam." In *Coming to Terms: Feminism, Theory, Politics.* Ed. E. Weed. London: Routledge.

Alderman, T. 1974. "And What Do You Do for a Living?" *Canadian Magazine,* 12 Oct.: 2–13.

Alexander, B.K. 1990. *Peaceful Measures: Canada's Way Out of the "War on Drugs."* Toronto: University of Toronto Press.

Alexander, J.C., and S. Seidman, eds. 1990. *Culture and Society: Contemporary Debates.* New York: Cambridge University Press.

Allen, R. 1975. "The Social Gospel and the Reform Tradition in Canada 1890–1928." In *Prophesy and Protest: Social Movements in Twentieth-Century Canada.* Toronto: Gage, 45–61.

Althusser, L. 1969. *For Marx.* Trans. B. Brewster. London: New Left Books.

Althusser, L. 1971. "Ideology and Ideological State Apparatuses." In *Lenin and Philosophy and Other Essays.* London: New Left Books, 127–86.

Andreski, S., ed. 1983. *Max Weber on Capitalism, Bureaucracy and Religion: A Selection of Texts.* London: George Allen and Unwin.

Anyon, J. 1980. "Social Class and the Hidden Curriculum of Work." *Journal of Education* 162, 1 (Winter): 67–92.

Apple, M. 1986. *Teachers and Texts: A Political Economy of Class and Gender Relations in Education.* London: Routledge & Kegan Paul.

Apple, M. 1988. "Facing the Complexity of Power: For a Parallelist Position in Critical Educational Studies." In *Bowles and Gintis Revisited: Correspondence and Contradiction.* Ed. M. Cole. London: Falmer Press, 112–30.

Arat-Koc, S. 1989. "In the Privacy of Our Own Home: Foreign Domestic Workers as Solution to the Crisis in the Domestic Sphere in Canada." *Studies in Political Economy* 28 (Spring): 33–56.

Archibald, W.P. 1978. *Social Psychology as Political Economy.* Toronto: McGraw-Hill Ryerson.

Archibald, W.P. 1985. "Agency and Alienation: Marx's Theories of Individuation and History." *Studies in Political Economy* 16: 61–75.

Armour, M.A. 1988. "The WISEST Approach." *New Trial* 43 (Autumn): 21–23.

Armstrong, P. 1984. *Labour Pains: Women's Work in Crisis.* Toronto: Women's Press.

Armstrong, P., and H. Armstrong. 1984. *The Double Ghetto: Canadian Women and Their Segregated Work.* Rev. ed. Toronto: McClelland & Stewart.

Armstrong, P., and H. Armstrong. 1985. "Beyond Sexless Class and Classless Sex: Towards Feminist Marxism." In *Feminist Marxism or Marxist Feminism: A Debate.* Ed. P. Armstrong, H. Armstrong, P. Connelly, A. Miles, and M. Luxton. Toronto: Garamond, 1–38.

Armstrong, P., and H. Armstrong. 1990. *Theorizing Women's Work.* Toronto: Garamond.

Armstrong, P., and H. Armstrong. 1992. "Lessons from Pay Equity." In *Feminism in Action.* Ed. M.P. Connelly and P. Armstrong. Toronto: Canadian Scholars Press, 295–316.

Armstrong, P., H. Armstrong, P. Connelly, A. Miles, and M. Luxton. 1985. *Feminist Marxism or Marxist Feminism: A Debate.* Toronto: Garamond.

Aronowitz, S., and H.A. Giroux. 1985. *Education Under Siege: The Conservative, Liberal, and Radical Debate Over Schooling.* Hadley, MA: Bergin and Garvey.

Ashley, D., and M. Orenstein. 1985. *Sociological Theory: Classical Statements.* Boston: Allyn & Bacon.

Assmann, H. 1993. "Liberation Theology: Looking Forward." *Religion: State and Society* 21, 1: 39–52.

Atkinson, J.M., and P. Drew. 1979. *Order in Court: The Organization of Verbal Interaction in Judicial Settings.* Atlantic Highlands, NJ: Humanities Press.

Backhouse, C. 1991. *Petticoats and Prejudice: Women and Law in Nineteenth-Century Canada.* Toronto: Women's Press.

Badgley, R.F., chair. 1984. *Sexual Offences Against Children.* Vol. 1. Ottawa: Canadian Government Publishing Centre.

Baines, B. 1988. "Women and the Law." In *Changing Patterns: Women in Canada.* Ed. S. Burt, L. Code, and L. Dorney. Toronto: McClelland & Stewart, 157–83.

Baker, D. 1977. "Ethnicity, Development and Power: Canada in Comparative Perspective." In *Identities: The Impact of Ethnicity on Canadian Society.* Ed. W. Isajiw. Toronto: Peter Martin.

Barker, M., et al. 1986. "Methods for Cultural Studies Students." In the Introduction to *Contemporary Cultural Studies.* Ed. D. Punter. London: Longman.

Barlow, M. 1990; 1991. *Parcel of Rogues: How Free Trade is Failing Canada.* Toronto: Key Porter.

Barnet, R., and R. Muller. 1974. *Global Reach.* New York: Simon & Schuster.

Barthes, R. 1967. *Elements of Semiology.* London: Cape.

Barthes, R. 1971. "The Rhetoric of the Image." *Cultural Studies* 1.

Barthes, R. 1973. *Mythologies.* London: Paladin.

Basow, S.A. 1986. *Gender Stereotypes: Traditions and Alternatives.* 2nd ed. Monterey, CA: Brooks/Cole.

Batcher, E., and A. Winter. 1987. "'Nothing Special': The Portrayal of Girls and Women in Current Junior Grade Readers." *Canadian Woman Studies: Women and Media* 8, 1 (Spring).

Batsleer, J., T. Davies, R. O'Rourke, and C. Weedon. 1985. *Rewriting English: Cultural Politics of Gender and Class.* London: Methuen.

Baudrillard, J. 1985. "The Ecstasy of Communication." In *Post-Modern Culture.* Ed. H. Foster. London: Pluto Press.

Baudrillard, J. 1987. *Cool Memories.* Paris: Edition Galilee.

Baudrillard, J. 1988. "Simulacra and Simulations." In *Selected Writings.* Ed. M. Poster. Cambridge, Eng.: Polity Press.

Baum, G. 1979. "Christianity and Socialism." *Canadian Dimension* 13, 5 (Jan.–Feb.): 30–35.

Baum, G. 1981. "Liberation Theology and 'the Super- natural'." *The Ecumenist* 19, 6 (Sept.–Oct.): 81–87.

Bauman, Z. 1988. "Is There a Postmodern Sociology?" *Theory, Culture and Society* 5: 217–37.

Beauvoir, S. de. 1953. *The Second Sex.* New York: Knopf.

Becker, H.S. 1951. "The Professional Jazz Musician and His Audience." *American Journal of Sociology* 57: 136–44.

Becker, H.S. 1963. *The Outsiders: Studies in the Sociology of Deviance.* New York: Free Press.

Becker, H.S. 1977. "Social Class Variations in the Teacher- Pupil Relationship." In *School and Society.* Ed. B.R. Cosin et al. 2nd ed. London: Routledge & Kegan Paul.

Beckford, G.L. 1973. "The Economics of Agricultural Resource Use and Development in Plantation Econo- mies." In *Underdevelopment and Development: The Third World Today.* Ed. H. Bernstein. Harmondsworth, Eng.: Penguin, 115–51.

Beechey, V. 1977. "Some Notes on Female Wage Labour in Capitalist Production." *Capital and Class* 3 (Autumn).

Beechey, V., and J. Donald, eds. 1985. *Subjectivity and Social Relations.* Milton Keynes, Eng.: Open University Press.

Belenky, M.F., B.M. Clinchy, N.R. Goldberger, and J.M. Tarule. 1985. *Women's Ways of Knowing.* New York: Basic Books.

Bell, S.J. 1994. "An Empirical Approach to Theoretical Perspectives on Sentencing in a Young Offender Court." *Canadian Review of Sociology and Anthropology* 31, 1 (Feb.): 35–64.

Bellah, R., et al. 1985. *Habits of the Heart: Individualism and Commitment in American Life.* Berkeley, CA: University of California Press.

Bellah, R. 1990. "Civil Religion in America." In *Culture and Society: Contemporary Debates.* Ed. J.C. Alexander and S. Seidman. New York: Cambridge University Press, 262–72.

Bem, S.L. 1974. "The Measurement of Psychological Androgyny." *Journal of Consulting and Clinical Psychology* 42, 2: 155–62.

Benn, M. 1991. "How to Make Dirty Money Squeaky Clean." *New Internationalist* (Oct.): 20–21.

Benston, M. 1969. "The Political Economy of Women's Liberation." *Monthly Review* 21, 4 (Sept.): 13–27.

Berger, P.L. 1963. *Invitation to Sociology: A Humanistic Perspective.* New York: Anchor Books.

Berger, P.L. 1967. *The Sacred Canopy.* Garden City, NY: Doubleday.

Berger, P.L., and T. Luckmann. 1966. *The Social Construction of Reality.* Garden City, NY: Doubleday.

Berger, R.J. 1993. "The 'Banality of Evil' Reframed: The Social Construction of the 'Final Solution' to the 'Jewish Problem.'" *The Sociological Quarterly* 34, 4: 597–618.

Betto, F. 1993. "Did Liberation Theology Collapse with the Berlin Wall?" *Religion, State, and Society* 21, 1: 33–38.

Bezucha, R.J. 1985. "Feminist Pedagogy as a Subversive Activity." In *Gendered Subjects: The Dynamics of Feminist Teaching.* Ed. M. Culley and C. Portuges. London: Routledge & Kegan Paul.

Biddle, B.J., and E.J. Thomas, eds. 1966. *Role Theory: Concepts and Research.* New York: John Wiley and Sons.

Bierstedt, R. 1966. *Emile Durkheim.* New York: Dell.

Billington, R., S. Strawbridge, L. Greensides, A. Fitzimons. 1991. *Culture and Society: A Sociology of Culture.* London: Macmillan.

Bissett-Johnson, A. 1988. "Murdoch Case." In *The Canadian Encyclopedia.* 2nd ed. Vol 3. Edmonton: Hurtig, 1405.

Bittner, E. 1967. "The Police on Skid Row: A Study of Peace-Keeping." *American Journal of Sociology* 32: 699–715.

Bland, L. 1985. "In the Name of Protection: The Policing of Women in the First World War." In *Women-In-Law: Explorations in Law, Family, and Sexuality.* Ed. J. Brophy and C. Smart. London: Routledge & Kegan Paul, 23–49.

Blau, P.M. 1955. *The Dynamics of Bureaucracy.* Chicago: University of Chicago Press.

Blauner, R. 1964. *Alienation and Freedom: The Factory Worker and His Industry.* Chicago: University of Chicago Press.

Bolaria, B.S., and P. Li. 1988. *Racial Oppression in Canada.* 2nd ed. Toronto: Garamond.

Bottomore, T.B., ed. 1956. *Karl Marx: Selected Writings in Sociology and Social Philosophy.* New York: McGraw-Hill.

Bottomore, T.B., ed. 1963. *Karl Marx: Early Writings*. New York: McGraw-Hill.

Boughey, H. 1978. *The Insights of Sociology: An Introduction*. Boston: Allyn & Bacon.

Bourgeault, R. 1989. "Race, Class and Gender: Colonial Domination of Indian Women." In *Race, Class, Gender: Bonds and Barriers*. Ed. J. Vorst et al. Toronto: Between the Lines (for the Society for Socialist Studies, Winnipeg).

Bowles, S., and H. Gintis. 1976. *Schooling in Capitalist America*. New York: Basic Books.

Bowles, S., and H. Gintis. 1988. "Prologue: The Correspondence Principle." In *Bowles and Gintis Revisited: Correspondence and Contradiction*. Ed. M. Cole. London: Falmer Press, 1–4.

Boyd, S.B. 1993. "Investigating Gender Bias in Canadian Child Custody Law: Reflections on Questions and Methods." In *Investigating Gender Bias: Law, Courts, and the Legal Profession*. Ed. J. Brockman and D. Chunn. Toronto: Thompson Educational, 169–90.

Boyle, C., and S.W. Rowley. 1987. "Sexual Assault and Family Violence: Reflections on Bias." In *Equality and Judicial Neutrality*. Ed. S. Martin and K. Mahoney. Toronto: Carswell, 312–26.

Brake, M. 1980. *The Sociology of Youth Culture and Youth Subcultures: Sex and Drugs and Rock 'n' Roll?* London: Routledge & Kegan Paul.

Braverman, H. 1974. *Labor and Monopoly Capital: The Degradation of Work in the Twentieth Century*. New York: Monthly Review Press.

Breckenridge, J. 1985. "Equal Pay's Unequal Effect." *Report on Business Magazine* (Dec.).

Brenner, R. 1977. "The Origins of Capitalist Development: A Critique of Neo-Smithian Marxism." *New Left Review* 104 (July–Aug.): 25–92.

Briggs, J.L. 1970. *Never in Anger: Portrait of an Eskimo Family*. Cambridge, MA: Harvard University Press.

Brittan, A. 1989. *Masculinity and Power*. Oxford: Basil Blackwell.

Brittan, A., and M. Maynard. 1984. *Sexism, Racism and Oppression*. Oxford: Basil Blackwell.

Brockman, J., and D. Chunn. 1993. *Investigating Gender Bias: Law, Courts, and the Legal Profession*. Toronto: Thompson Educational.

Brodribb, S. 1993. *Nothing Mat(t)ers: A Feminist Critique of Postmodernism*. Toronto: Lorimer.

Broverman, I.K., D.M. Broverman, F.E. Clarkson, P.S. Rosencrantz, and S. Vogel. 1970. "Sex Role Stereotypes and Clinical Judgments." *Journal of Consulting and Clinical Psychology* 34 (Jan.): 1–7.

Brown, R.T. 1977. "Racism in Canada: So You Think It's Just a Few Punks in Subway Stations." *Last Post* (April): 29–37.

Brundtland, G.H. 1987. *Our Common Future*. Geneva: World Commission on Environment and Development. United Nations.

Brunsdon, C. 1989. In *Rethinking the Audience*. Ed. E. Seiter. Chapel Hill, NC: University of North Carolina Press, ch. 4.

Brym, R.J., with B. Fox. 1989. *From Culture to Power: The Sociology of English Canada*. Toronto: Oxford University Press.

Buckingham, D. 1987. *Public Secrets: Eastenders and its Audience*. London: British Film Industry.

Bunch, C. 1975. "Not for Lesbians Only." *Quest* 11, 2 (Fall): 245–48.

Bunch, C. 1983. "Not by Degrees: Feminist Theory and Education." In *Learning Our Way: Essays in Feminist Education*. Ed. C. Bunch and S. Pollack. Trumansburg, NY: Crossing Press, 248–60.

Burns, T., and G.N. Stalker. 1961. *The Management of Innovation*. London: Tavistock.

Burridge, K. 1969. *New Heaven New Earth: A Study of Millenarian Activities*. Toronto: Copp Clark.

Burrill, G., and I. McKay, eds. 1987. *People, Resources, and Power: Critical Perspectives on Underdevelopment and Primary Industries in the Atlantic Region*. Fredericton: Acadiensis Press.

Burtch, B.E. 1988. "Midwifery and the State: The New Midwifery in Canada." In *Gender and Society: Creating a Canadian Women's Sociology*. Ed. A.T. McLaren. Toronto: Copp Clark Pitman, 349–71.

Butler, D., and K. Brookfield. 1992. "Justice Delayed: Pay Equity and the Federal Public Service." Professional Institute for Public Service Canada National Office. 17 Nov. Mimeographed.

Buxton, W. 1985. *Talcott Parsons and the Capitalist Nation State: Political Sociology as a Strategic Vocation*. Toronto: University of Toronto Press.

Calhoun, J.B. 1963. "Population Density and Social Pathology." In *The Urban Condition*. Ed. L. Duhl. New York: Basic Books, 33–43.

Caliste, A. 1989. "Canada's Immigration Policy and Domestics from the Caribbean: The Second Domestic Scheme." In *Race, Class, Gender: Bonds and Barriers*. Ed. J. Vorst et al. Toronto: Between the Lines (for the Society for Socialist Studies, Winnipeg), 133–65.

Callinicos, A. 1985. "Postmodernism, Poststructuralism, Post-Marxism?" *Theory, Culture and Society* 2, 3: 85–101.

Calvert, J., with L. Kuehn. 1993. *Pandora's Box, Corporate Power, Free Trade and Canadian Education*. Our Schools/Our Selves Education Foundation. Monograph series no. 13 (July/Aug.).

Cameron, D. 1993. "One America." *Canadian Forum* (Jan.): 9–10.

Cameron, D., ed. 1988. *The Free Trade Deal*. Toronto: Lorimer.

Cameron, M. 1993. "Developing a Bloc Mentality." *Canadian Forum* (Jan.): 15–16.

Campbell, E.Q. 1975. *Socialization, Culture and Personality*. Dubuque, IA: Wm. C. Brown.

Canada. House of Commons. Standing Committee on Health, Welfare and Social Affairs. 1982. *Wife Battering: Report on Violence in the Family*. Ottawa: Queen's Printer. May.

Canada. House of Commons. 1989. "A Review of the Post-secondary Student Assistance Program of the Department of Indian Affairs and Northern Development."

First Report of the Standing Committee on Aboriginal Affairs. June.

Canada. Royal Commission on New Reproductive Technologies. 1993. *Proceed with Care: Final Report of the Royal Commission on New Reproductive Technologies*. Ottawa: Canada Communication Group—Publishing.

Canadian AIDS Society. n.d. "Homophobia, Heterosexism and AIDS: Creating a More Effective Response to AIDS." Ottawa.

Caplan, G.L., and F. Sauvageau. 1986. *Report of the Task Force on Broadcasting Policy*. Ottawa: Ministry of Supply and Services.

Carby, H.V. 1982. "White Woman Listen! Black Feminism and the Boundaries of Sisterhood." In *The Empire Strikes Back: Race and Racism in 70s Britain*. Centre for Contemporary Cultural Studies. London: Hutchinson, 212–35.

Carey, A. 1967. "The Hawthorne Studies: A Radical Critique." *American Sociological Review* 32: 403–16.

Carniol, B. 1993. "Resisting Cuts to Social Programs." *Canadian Review of Social Policy* 31 (Spring): 105–7.

Carty, R. 1982. "Giving for Gain: Foreign Aid and CIDA." In *Ties that Bind: Canada and the Third World*. Ed. R. Clarke and R. Swift. Toronto: Between the Lines.

Cassin, A.M. 1979. *Advancement Opportunities in the British Columbia Public Service*. British Columbia Economic Analysis and Research Bureau. Ministry of Industry and Small Business Development.

Cassin, A.M. 1980. "The Routine Production of Inequality: Implications for Affirmative Action." Paper, Ontario Institute for Studies in Education.

Cassin, A.M. 1991. "Women, Work, Jobs and Value: The Routine Production of Inequality—A Report with Special Reference to Consumers Gas." Expert testimony before Ontario Pay Equity Tribunal. March.

Cassin, A.M. 1992. Expert testimony before Supreme Court of Ontario on behalf of the Federation of Women Teachers' Association of Ontario in the case between Margaret Tomen, Applicant, and Ontario Public School Teachers' Federation and Ontario Teachers' Federation, Respondents.

Chance, N.A. 1966. *The Eskimo of North America*. New York: Holt, Rinehart & Winston.

Chatterji, S.A. 1988. *The Indian Woman's Search for an Identity*. New Delhi: Vikas Publishing House.

Chesler, P. 1991. *Mothers on Trial: The Battle for Children and Custody*. New York: Harcourt Brace.

Chirot, D. 1977. *Social Change in the Twentieth Century*. New York: Harcourt Brace Jovanovich.

Chodorow, N. 1978. *The Reproduction of Mothering: Psychoanalysis and the Sociology of Gender*. Berkeley, CA: University of California Press.

Chomsky, N. 1988. *Manufacturing Consent: The Political Economy of the Mass Media*. New York: Pantheon.

Churchill, W. 1992. *Fantasies of the Master Race: Literature, Cinema, and the Colonization of American Indians*. Monroe, MA: Common Courage Press.

Cicourel, A.V. 1974. *Theory and Method in a Study of Argentine Fertility*. New York: Wiley.

Clairmont, D.H., and D.W. Magill. 1974. *Africville: The Life and Death of a Canadian Black Community*. Toronto: McClelland & Stewart.

Clark, L.M.G., and D.L. Lewis. 1977. *Rape: The Price of Coercive Sexuality*. Toronto: Women's Press.

Clark, S.D. 1968. *The Developing Canadian Community*. 2nd ed. Toronto: University of Toronto Press.

Clark, S.D. 1978. *The New Urban Poor*. Toronto: McGraw-Hill Ryerson.

Clarke, R., and R. Swift, eds. 1982. *Ties that Bind: Canada and the Third World*. Toronto: Between the Lines.

Clement, W. 1975. *The Canadian Corporate Elite*. Toronto: McClelland & Stewart.

Clement, W. 1977. *Continental Corporate Power*. Toronto: McClelland & Stewart.

Clement, W. 1981. *Hardrock Mining: Industrial Relations and Technological Change at INCO*. Toronto: McClelland & Stewart.

Clifton, J.A. 1990. "The Indian Story: A Cultural Fiction." In *The Invented Indian: Cultural Fictions and Government Policies*. New Brunswick, NJ: Transaction, 29–48.

Clough, P.T. 1991. *The End(s) of Ethnography*. Newbury Park, CA: Sage.

Clow, M., with S. Machum. 1993. *Stifling Debate: Canadian Newspapers and Nuclear Power*. Halifax: Fernwood.

Cloward, R., and L. Ohlin. 1960. *Delinquency and Opportunity: A Theory of Delinquent Gangs*. Chicago: Free Press.

Coch, L., and J.R.P. French Jr. 1949. "Overcoming Resistance to Change." *Human Relations* 1: 512–32.

Cockburn, A., and Cohen, A. 1991. "Explosive Mix." *New Internationalist* (Oct.): 14–15.

Cockburn, C. 1981. "The Material of Male Power." *Feminist Review* 9 (Autumn): 41–59.

Cohen, A.K. 1955. *Delinquent Boys: The Culture of the Gang*. New York: Free Press.

Cohen, G.A. 1980. "Karl Marx and the Withering Away of Social Science." In *Karl Marx's Theory of History: A Defense*. Princeton: Princeton University Press, 326–44.

Cohen, M.G. 1988a. "Services: The Vanishing Opportunity." In *The Free Trade Deal*. Ed. D. Cameron. Toronto: Lorimer, 140–55.

Cohen, M.G. 1988b. "U.S. Firms Eager to Run Our Institutions—For Profit: Americanizing Services." In *The Facts: The Facts on Free Trade—Canada: Don't Trade It Away*. Ed. E. Finn. Canadian Union of Public Employees 10, 2 (Spring).

Cohen, P. 1980. "Subcultural Conflict and Working-Class Community." In *Culture, Media, Language*. Ed. S. Hall, D. Hobson, A. Lowe, and P. Willis. London: Hutchinson, 78–87.

Cohen, S. 1972. *Folk Devils and Moral Panics: The Creation of the Mods and Rockers*. London: MacGibbon & Kee.

Cole, M. ed. 1988. *Bowles and Gintis Revisited: Correspondence and Contradiction*. London: Falmer Press.

Coleman, A. 1984. "Trouble in Utopia." *Geographical Journal* 50, 3.

Coleman, A. 1985. *Utopia on Trial.* London: Hilary Shipman.

Collins, R. 1981. "On the Microfoundations of Macrosociology." *American Journal of Sociology* 86: 984–1014.

Collins, R. 1982. *Sociological Insight: An Introduction to Non-Obvious Sociology.* Oxford: Oxford University Press.

Connell, R.W. 1987. *Gender and Power: Society, the Person and Sexual Politics.* Palo Alto, CA: Stanford University Press.

Connell, R.W. 1991. "A Thumbnail Dipped in Tar or: Can We Write Sociology From The Fringe Of The World?" In *Social Analysis: Special Edition on Postmodern Theorising* 30: 68–76. Ed. A. Yeatman.

Cooley, C.H. 1964. *Human Nature and the Social Order.* New York: Schocken.

Corrigan, P. 1979. *Schooling the Smash Street Kids.* London: Macmillan.

Coser, L.A. 1956. *The Functions of Social Conflict.* Glencoe, IL: Free Press.

Cowie, J., V. Cowie, and E. Slater. 1968. *Delinquency in Girls.* London: Heinemann.

Cox, O.C. [1948] 1970. *Caste, Class and Race.* New York: Monthly Review Press.

Crean, S. 1989. "In the Name of the Fathers: Joint Custody and the Anti-Feminist Backlash." *This Magazine* 22, 7 (Feb.): 19–25.

Crean, S., and M. Rioux. 1983. *Two Nations: An Essay on the Culture and Politics of Canada and Quebec in a World of American Pre-eminence.* Toronto: Lorimer.

Crimshaw, J. 1986. *Feminist Philosophies: Women's Perspectives on Philosophical Traditions.* Hertfordshire: Wheatsheaf Books.

Culley, M. 1985. "Anger and Authority in the Introductory Women's Studies Classroom." In *Gendered Subjects: The Dynamics of Feminist Teaching.* Ed. M. Culley and C. Portuges. London: Routledge & Kegan Paul, 209–18.

Curran, J., and J. Seaton. 1985. *Power Without Responsibility: The Press and Broadcasting in Britain.* 2nd ed. London: Methuen.

Currie, E. 1974. "Beyond Criminology." *Issues in Criminology* 9 (Spring): 133–42.

Curtis, B. 1987. "Preconditions of the Canadian State: Educational Reform and the Construction of a Public in Upper Canada, 1837–1846." In *The Benevolent State: The Growth of Welfare in Canada.* Ed. A. Moscovitch and J. Albert. Toronto: Garamond.

Dalla Costa, M., and S. James. 1972. *The Power of Women and the Subversion of the Community.* Bristol, Eng.: Falling Wall Press.

Dalton, M. 1959. *Men Who Manage.* New York: Wiley.

Daly, M. 1973. *Beyond God the Father: Toward a Philosophy of Women's Liberation.* Boston: Beacon Press.

Daly, M. 1978. *Gyn/Ecology: The Metaethics of Radical Feminism.* Boston: Beacon Press.

Daniel, F. 1992. *The Imaginary Indian: The Image of the Indian in Canadian Culture.* Vancouver: Arsenal Pulp Press.

Daniels, A.K. 1972. "The Social Construction of Military Psychiatric Diagnoses." In *Symbolic Interaction: A Reader in Social Psychology* Ed. J.G. Manis and B.N. Meltzer. Boston: Allyn & Bacon.

Darrah, C. 1994. "Skill Requirements at Work: Rhetoric versus Reality." *Work and Occupations* 21, 1 (Feb.): 64–84.

Das Gupta, T. 1989. "Introduction." In *Race, Class, Gender: Bonds and Barriers.* Ed. J. Vorst et al. Toronto: Between the Lines (for the Society for Socialist Studies, Winnipeg).

David, D.S., and R. Brannon, eds. 1976. *The Forty-Nine Percent Majority: The Male Sex Role.* New York: Random House.

Davis, K., and W.E. Moore. 1945. "Some Principles of Stratification." *American Sociological Review* 10, 2: 242–49.

Dawkins, R. 1976. *The Selfish Gene.* London: Oxford University Press.

DeKeseredy, W.S., and R. Hinch. 1991. *Woman Abuse: Sociological Perspectives.* Toronto: Thompson Educational.

Delphy, C. 1984. *Close to Home: A Materialist Analysis of Women's Oppression.* London: Hutchinson.

Denis, W.B. 1990. "The Politics of Language." In *Race and Ethnic Relations in Canada.* Ed. Peter Li. Toronto: Oxford University Press, ch. 7.

Denzin, N.K. 1992. *Symbolic Interactionism and Cultural Studies: The Politics of Interpretation.* Cambridge, MA: Blackwell.

Derrida, J. 1974. *Of Grammatology.* Trans. G.C. Spivak. Baltimore, MD: Johns Hopkins University Press.

Derrida, J. 1978. *Writing and Difference.* Trans. A. Bass. Chicago: University of Chicago Press.

Derrida, J. 1982. *Margins of Philosophy.* Trans. A. Bass. Chicago: Chicago University Press.

Diamond, S. 1985. "Pornography: Image and Reality." In *Women Against Censorship.* Ed. V. Burstyn. Vancouver: Douglas & McIntyre, 40–57.

Dillon, J. 1993. "Intellectual Property." *Canadian Forum* (Jan.): 11–12.

Dinnerstein, D. 1976. *The Mermaid and the Minotaur: Sexual Arrangements and Human Malaise.* New York: Harper & Row.

Dixon, M. 1976. *Things Which Are Done in Secret.* Montreal: Black Rose Books.

Dobash, R.E., and R.P. Dobash. 1988. "Research as Social Action: The Struggle for Battered Women." In *Feminist Perspectives on Wife Abuse.* Ed. K. Yllö and M. Bograd. Beverly Hills: Sage, 51–74.

Donzelot, J. 1979. *The Policing of Families.* New York: Pantheon.

Doob, A., and J. Meen. 1993. "An Exploration of Changes in Dispositions for Young Offenders in Toronto." *Canadian Journal of Criminology* 35, 1: 19–29.

Dooley, D. 1984. *Social Research Methods.* Englewood Cliffs, NJ: Prentice-Hall.

Doran, C. 1993. "Codifying Women's Bodies? Towards a Genealogy of British Victimology." Department of Sociology, University of New Brunswick at Saint John. May. Mimeographed.

Douglas, J. 1967. *The Social Meaning of Suicide.* Princeton: Princeton University Press.

Douglas, M. 1966. *Purity and Danger: An Analysis of the Concepts of Pollution and Taboo.* New York: Pantheon.

Douglas, M. 1970. *Natural Symbols: Explorations in Cosmology.* New York: Pantheon.

Douglas, M. 1979. *World of Goods: Toward an Anthropology of Consumption*. London: Allen Lane.

Dreyfus, H.L., and P. Rabinow. 1982. *Michel Foucault: Beyond Structuralism and the Hermeneutics*. Chicago: University of Chicago Press.

Driedger, L. 1991. *The Urban Factor: Sociology of Canadian Cities*. Toronto: Oxford University Press.

Dubinsky, K. 1985. "Lament for a 'Patriarchy Lost'? Anti-Feminism, Anti-Abortion, and REAL Women in Canada." *Feminist Perspectives Series. No. 1*. Ottawa: Canadian Research Institute for the Advancement of Women.

Duelli Klein, R. 1980. "How To Do What We Want To Do: Thoughts About Feminist Methodology." In *Theories of Women's Studies*. Ed. G. Bowles and R. Duelli Klein. Berkeley, CA: University of California Press.

Durkheim, E. [1893] 1964. *The Division of Labour in Society*. New York: Free Press.

Durkheim, E. [1895] 1964. *The Rules of Sociological Method*. 8th ed. Trans. S.A. Solvay and J.H. Mueller. New York: Free Press.

Durkheim, E. [1897] 1951. *Suicide*. Glencoe, IL: Free Press.

Durkheim, E. [1915] 1976. *The Elementary Forms of Religious Life*. London: Allyn & Unwin.

Dworkin, A. 1980. "Pornography: A Hatred Without Bounds." *New Directions for Women* (Nov.–Dec.): 20.

Ehrenreich, B., and D. English. 1979. *For Her Own Good: 150 Years of Experts' Advice to Women*. Garden City, NY: Anchor Books.

Eichler, M. 1980. *The Double Standard: A Feminist Critique of Feminist Social Science*. London: Croom Helm.

Eichler, M. 1985a. "And the Work Never Ends: Feminist Contributions." *Canadian Review of Sociology and Anthropology* 22, 5 (Dec.): 619–44.

Eichler, M. 1985b. "The Pro-Family Movement: Are They for or Against Families?" *Feminist Perspectives Series*. Ottawa: Canadian Research Institute for the Advancement of Women.

Eichler, M. 1988a. *Families in Canada Today: Recent Changes and Their Policy Consequences*. 2nd ed. Toronto: Gage.

Eichler, M. 1988b. *Nonsexist Research Methods: A Practical Guide*. Boston: Allen & Unwin.

Eisenstein, Z.R. 1979. "Developing a Theory of Capitalist Patriarchy and Socialist Feminism." In *Capitalist Patriarchy and the Case for Socialist Feminism*. Ed. Z.R. Eisenstein. New York: Monthly Review Press, 5–40.

Eisenstein, Z.R. 1984. *Feminism and Sexual Equality: Crisis in Liberal America*. New York: Monthly Review Press.

Elias, N. 1970. *What Is Sociology?* London: Hutchinson.

Eller, J.D., and R.M. Coughlan. 1993. "The Poverty of Primordialism: The Demystification of Ethnic Attachments." *Ethnic and Racial Studies* 16, 2 (April): 183–201.

Ellis, J. 1980. "Ideology and Subjectivity." In *Culture, Media, Language*. Ed. S. Hall, D. Hobson, A. Lowe, and P. Willis. London: Hutchinson, 187–94.

Emerson, J. 1970. "Behavior in Private Places: Sustaining Definitions of Reality in Gynecological Examinations." In *Recent Sociology*. Vol. 2. *Patterns of Communicative Behavior*. Ed. H. Dreitzel. New York: Macmillan.

Engels, F. [1884] 1978. "The Origins of the Family, Private Property, and the State." In *The Marx-Engels Reader*. 2nd ed. Ed. R.C. Tucker. New York: W.W. Norton, 734–59.

Ericson, R.V. 1982. *Reproducing Order: A Study of Police Patrol Work*. Toronto: University of Toronto Press.

Erikson, K.T. 1962. "Notes on the Sociology of Deviance." *Social Problems* 9 (Spring): 309–14.

Erikson, K.T. 1966. *Wayward Puritans: A Study in the Sociology of Deviance*. New York: John Wiley and Sons.

Escobar, A. 1984–85. "Discourse and Power in Development: Michel Foucault and the Relevance of His Work to the Third World." *Alternatives* 10: 377–400.

Falardeau, J.C. 1964. "The Seventeenth-Century Parish in French Canada." In *French-Canadian Society*. Vol. 1. Ed. M. Rioux and Y. Martin. Toronto: McClelland & Stewart, 19–32.

Faludi, S. 1991. *Backlash: The Undeclared War Against American Women*. New York: Doubleday Anchor Books.

Fasteau, M.F. 1974. *The Male Machine*. New York: McGraw-Hill.

Featherstone, M. 1985. "The Fate of Modernity: An Introduction." *Theory, Culture and Society* 2, 3: 1–5.

Featherstone, M. 1988. "In Pursuit of the Postmodern: An Introduction." *Theory, Culture and Society* 5, 2–3 (June): 195–216.

Feder, E. 1976. "How Agribusiness Operates in Under-developed Agricultures." *Development and Change* 7, 4 (Oct.): 413–43.

Fenn, M. 1980. *In the Spotlight: Women Executives in a Changing Environment*. Englewood Cliffs, NJ: Prentice-Hall.

Ferguson, K.E. 1984. *The Feminist Case Against Bureaucracy*. Philadelphia: Temple University Press.

Feyerabend, P.K. 1970. "How To Be a Good Empiricist: A Plea for Tolerance in Matters Epistemological." In *Readings in the Philosophy of Science*. Ed. B.A. Brody. Englewood Cliffs, NJ: Prentice-Hall.

Feyerabend, P.K. 1975. *Against Method: Outline of an Anarchistic Theory of Knowledge*. London: Verso.

Fillmore, N. 1989. "The Big Oink: How Business Won the Free Trade Battle." *This Magazine* 22, 8 (March–April): 13–20.

Findlay, B. 1975. "Shrink! Shrank! Shriek!" In *Women Look at Psychiatry*. Ed. D.E. Smith and S.J. David. Vancouver: Press Gang.

Fine, G.A. 1992. "The Dirty Play of Little Boys." In *Men's Lives*. Ed. M.S. Kimmel and M.A. Messner. 2nd ed. New York: Macmillan, 135–43.

Finn, E., ed. 1988. *The Facts: The Facts on Free Trade—Canada: Don't Trade It Away*. Canadian Union of Public Employees. 10, 2 (Spring).

Firestone, S. 1971. *The Dialectic of Sex*. London: The Women's Press.

Fishman, M. 1980. *Manufacturing the News*. Austin, TX: University of Texas Press.

Fishman, P.M. 1978. "Interaction: The Work Women Do." *Social Problems* 25: 397–406.

Fiske, J. 1982. *Introduction to Communication Studies*. London: Methuen.

Fiske, J. 1987. "British Cultural Studies and Television." In *Channels of Discourse: Television and Contemporary Criticism*. Ed. R. Allen. Chapel Hill, NC: University of North Carolina Press, ch. 8.

Flanders, A., and A. Fox. 1969. "Collective Bargaining: From Donovan to Durkheim." In *Management and Unions*. Ed. A. Flanders. London: Faber & Faber.

Ford, C.S. 1970. "Some Primitive Societies." In *Sex Roles in Changing Society*. Ed. G.H. Seward and R. Williamson. New York: Random House.

Forward, S., and J. Torres. 1987. *Men Who Hate Women and the Women Who Love Them*. New York: Bantam.

Foster, G.M. 1973. *Traditional Societies and Technological Change*. 2nd ed. New York: Harper & Row.

Foster-Clark, A. 1978. "The Modes of Production Controversy." *New Left Review* 107 (Jan.–Feb.): 47–77.

Foucault, M. 1970. *The History of Sexuality*. London: Allen Lane.

Foucault, M. 1977. *Discipline and Punishment: The Birth of the Prison*. London: Allen Lane.

Foucault, M. 1978. *The History of Sexuality*. Vol. 1. New York: Vintage.

Foucault, M. 1979. *Michel Foucault: Power, Truth, Strategy*. Ed. M. Morris and P. Patton. Sydney: Feral Publications.

Foucault, M. 1980. *Power/Knowledge: Selected Interviews and Other Writings 1972–1977*. Ed. C. Gordon. New York: Pantheon.

Fox, B., ed. 1980. *Hidden in the Household: Women's Domestic Labour Under Capitalism*. Toronto: Women's Press.

Francis, Daniel. 1992. *The Imagery Indian: The Image of the Indian in Canadian Culture*. Vancouver: Arsenal Pulp Press.

Frank, A.G. 1972. "Sociology of Development and the Underdevelopment of Sociology." In *Dependence and Underdevelopment: Latin America's Political Economy*. Ed. J.D. Cockcroft, A.G. Frank, and D.L. Johnson. New York: Doubleday, 321–97.

Frank, B. 1987. "Hegemonic Heterosexual Masculinity." *Studies in Political Economy* 24 (Autumn): 159–70.

Frank, B. 1992. "Hegemonic Heterosexual Masculinity: Sports, Looks and a Woman, That's What Every Guy Needs to be Masculine." Paper presented at 26th Annual Meeting of Atlantic Association of Sociologists and Anthropologists. Session on Violence and Social Control in the Home, Workplace, Community and Institutions. ISER Conference Paper #3, ISER, Memorial University of Newfoundland.

Franklin, S., C. Lury, and J. Stacey, eds. 1991. *Off-Centre: Feminism and Cultural Studies*. Cultural Studies, Birmingham Series. London: HarperCollins Academic.

Fraser, N., and L. Nicholson. 1988. "Social Criticism Without Philosophy: An Encounter Between Feminism and Postmodernism." *Theory, Culture and Society* 5: 373–94.

Freeman, D. 1983. *Margaret Mead and Samoa: The Making and Unmaking of an Anthropological Myth*. Cambridge, MA: Harvard University Press.

Freire, P. 1970. *Pedagogy of the Oppressed*. New York: Seabury.

French, J.R.P., J. Israel, and D. As. 1960. "An Experiment on Participation in a Norwegian Factory: Interpersonal Dimension on Decision-making." *Human Relations* 13: 3–19.

Freud, S. 1905. *The Standard Edition of the Complete Psychological Works of Sigmund Freud*. Vol. 7. *The Three Essays on the Theory of Sexuality*. London: The Hogarth Press.

Freud, S. [1905] 1976. "Three Essays on the Theory of Sexuality." In J. Strachey, trans. and ed. *The Complete Psychological Works*. Vol. 7. New York: Norton.

Friedan, B. 1981. *The Second Stage*. Fort Worth, TX: Summit.

Friedman, M. 1978. *Capitalism and Freedom*. Chicago: University of Chicago Press.

Friedman, S.S. 1985. "Authority in the Feminist Classroom: A Contradiction in Terms?" In *Gendered Subjects: The Dynamics of Feminist Teaching*. Ed. M. Culley and C. Portuges. Boston: Routledge & Kegan Paul, 203–9.

Frisby, D., and D. Sayer. 1986. *Society*. New York: Tavistock.

Fukuyama, F. 1989. "The End of History?" *The National Interest* (Summer).

Fuller, C. 1993. "A Matter of Life and Death: NAFTA and Medicare." *Canadian Forum* (Oct.): 14–19.

Furlong, K., and D. Moggach. 1990. "Efficiency, Competition, and Full Employment in Canadian Free Trade Literature." *Studies in Political Economy* 33 (Autumn): 135–59.

Fyvel, T.R. 1963. *The Insecure Offenders*. London: Chatto & Windus.

Gabriel, J. 1986. "School and Stratification." Honours thesis, St. Thomas University.

Gagnier, R. 1990. "Feminist Postmodernism: The End of Feminism or the End of Theory?" In *Theoretical Perspectives on Sexual Difference*. Ed. D.L. Rhode. New Haven: Yale University Press, 21–30.

Game, A. 1991. *Undoing the Social: Towards a Deconstructive Sociology*. Milton Keynes, Eng.: Open University Press.

Gans, H.J. 1962. *The Urban Villagers*. Glencoe, IL: Free Press.

Garfinkel, H. 1956. "Conditions of Successful Degradation Ceremonies." *American Journal of Sociology* 61 (March): 420–24.

Garfinkel, H. 1967. *Studies in Ethnomethodology*. Englewood Cliffs, NJ: Prentice-Hall.

Garfinkel, H. 1976. "Manual for Studies of Naturally Organized Activities." Unpublished manuscript, Department of Sociology, University of California.

Garfinkel, H., M. Lynch, and E. Livingston. 1981. "The Work of Discovering Science Construed with Materials from the Optically Discovered Pulsar." *Philosophy of the Social Sciences* 1: 131–58.

Garigue, P. 1956. "French-Canadian Kinship and Urban Life." *American Anthropologist* 58: 1090–101.

Garigue, P. 1964. "Change and Continuity in Rural French Canada." In *French-Canadian Society*. Vol. 1. Ed. M.

Rioux and Y. Martin. Toronto: McClelland & Stewart, 123–37.

Gaskell, J. 1986. "Conceptions of Skill and the Work of Women: Some Historical and Political Issues." In *The Politics of Diversity: Feminism, Marxism, and Nationalism*. Ed. R. Hamilton and M. Barrett. Montreal: Book Centre.

Gaskell, J. 1988. "The Reproduction of Family Life: Perspectives of Male and Female Adolescents." In *Gender and Society: Creating a Canadian Women's Sociology*. Ed. A.T. McLaren. Toronto: Copp Clark Pitman, 146–68.

Gaskell, J., A. McLaren, and M. Novogrodsky. 1989. *Claiming an Education: Feminism and Canadian Schools*. Toronto: Our Schools/Our Selves Education Foundation.

Gaskell, J., and A.T. McLaren, eds. 1987. *Women and Education: A Canadian Perspective*. Calgary: Detselig.

Geertz, C. 1973. *The Interpretation of Cultures*. New York: International Universities Press.

Geller, G. 1987. "Young Women in Conflict with the Law." In *Too Few to Count: Canadian Women in Conflict with the Law*. Ed. E. Adelberg and C. Currie. Vancouver: Press Gang.

Gérin, L. 1964. "The French-Canadian Family: Its Strengths and Weaknesses." In *French-Canadian Society*. Vol. 1. Ed. M. Rioux and Y. Martin. Toronto: McClelland & Stewart, 32–57.

Gerth, H.H., and C.W. Mills. 1946. From *Max Weber: Essays in Sociology*. New York: Oxford University Press.

Giddens, A. 1971. *Capitalism and Modern Social Theory*. London: Cambridge University Press.

Giddens, A. 1979. *Central Problems in Social Theory*. London: Macmillan.

Giddens, A. 1982. *Sociology: A Brief but Critical Introduction*. New York: Harcourt Brace Jovanovich.

Giddens, A. 1991. *Modernity and Self-Identity: Self and Society in the Late Modern Age*. Cambridge, Eng.: Polity Press.

Gidengil, E. 1989. "Diversity Within Unity: On Analyzing Regional Dependency." *Studies in Political Economy* 29 (Summer): 91–122.

Gill, S. 1982. *Native American Religions: An Introduction*. Belmont, CA: Wadsworth.

Gill, S. 1990. "Mother Earth: An American Myth." In *The Invented Indian: Cultural Fictions and Government Policies*. Ed. J.A. Clifton. New Brunswick, NJ: Transaction, 129–43.

Gilligan, C. 1982. *In a Different Voice*. Cambridge, MA: Harvard University Press.

Gittens, M., and D. Cole. 1994. *Racism Behind Bars: The Treatment of Black and Other Racial Minority Prisoners in Ontario Prisons*. Interim Report of the Commission on Systemic Racism in the Ontario Criminal Justice System. Toronto: Publications Ontario.

Goffman, E. 1959. *The Presentation of Self in Everyday Life*. Garden City, NY: Doubleday.

Goffman, E. 1961a. *Asylums*. Harmondsworth, Eng.: Penguin.

Goffman, E. 1961b. "Role Distance." In *Encounters: Two Studies in the Sociology of Interaction*. New York: Bobbs-Merrill.

Goffman, E. 1963. *Stigma: Notes on the Management of Spoiled Identity*. Englewood Cliffs, NJ: Prentice-Hall.

Goffman, E. 1967. *Interaction Ritual: Essays on Face-to-Face Behavior*. Garden City, NY: Doubleday.

Goffman, E. 1969. *Strategic Interaction*. Philadelphia: University of Pennsylvania Press.

Gold, R. 1951–52. "Janitors Versus Tenants: A Status Income Dilemma." *American Journal Sociology* 57: 486–93.

Goldberg, S. 1973. *The Inevitability of Patriarchy*. New York: William Morrow.

Gonos, G. 1980. "The Class Position of Goffman's Sociology: Social Origins of an American Structuralism." In *The View from Goffman*. Ed. J. Ditton. London: Macmillan, 134–69.

Goode, W.J. 1982. *The Family*. 2nd ed. Englewood Cliffs, NJ: Prentice-Hall.

Goodman, P. 1956. *Growing Up Absurd*. New York: Random House.

Gordon, M.M. 1964. *Assimilation in American Life*. New York: Oxford University Press.

Gouldner, A.W. 1952. "On Weber's Analysis of Bureaucratic Rules." In *Reader in Bureaucracy*. Ed. R.K. Merton, A.P. Gray, B. Hockey, and H.C. Selvin. New York: Free Press, 48–51.

Gouldner, A.W. 1954. *Patterns of Industrial Bureaucracy*. New York: Free Press.

Gouldner, A.W. 1965. *Wildcat Strikes*. New York: Free Press.

Gouldner, A.W. 1970. *The Coming Crisis of Western Sociology*. New York: Avon.

Grabb, E.G. 1984. *Social Inequality: Classical and Contemporary Theorists*. Toronto: Holt, Rinehart & Winston.

Gramsci, A. 1971. *Selections from the Prison Notebooks*. Ed. and trans. Q. Hoare and G. Nowell-Smith. New York: International Publishers.

Grant, G. 1984. *Lament for a Nation: The Defeat of Canadian Nationalism*. Ottawa: Carleton University Press.

Gray, S. 1987. "Sharing the Shop Floor." In *Women and Men: Interdisciplinary Readings on Gender*. Ed. G. Hofmann Nemiroff. Toronto: Fitzhenry & Whiteside, 377–402.

Green, B. 1979. "The Christian Left in English Canada." *Canadian Dimension* 13, 5 (Jan.–Feb.): 38–42.

Greenberg, D.F., ed., 1981a. *Crime and Capitalism: Readings in Marxist Criminology*. Palo Alto, CA: Mayfield.

Greenberg, D.F. 1981b. "Delinquency and the Age Structure of Society." In *Crime and Capitalism: Readings in Marxist Criminology*. Palo Alto, CA: Mayfield.

Greenglass, E. 1992. "Socialization of Girls and Boys: How Gender Roles Are Acquired." In *Sociology for Canadians: A Reader*. 2nd ed. Ed. A. Himelfarb and C.J. Richardson. Toronto: McGraw-Hill Ryerson, 203–12.

Gregor, F.M. 1994. "The Social Organization of Nurses' Educative Work." Ph.D. thesis, Dalhousie University, Halifax, NS.

Gregory, J. 1983. "The Electronic Sweatshop." In *Perspectives on Women in the 1980s*. Ed. J. Turner and L. Emery. Winnipeg: University of Manitoba Press, 99–112.

Grossberg, L., C. Nelson, and P. Treichler, eds. 1991. *Cultural Studies*. New York: Routledge.

Grosz, E. 1989. *Sexual Subversions: Three French Feminists*. Boston: Allen & Unwin.

Grosz, E. 1990. *Jacques Lacan: A Feminist Introduction*. London: Routledge.

Guindon, H. 1964. "The Social Evolution of Quebec Reconsidered." In *French-Canadian Society*. Vol. 1. Ed. M. Rioux and Y. Martin. Toronto: McClelland & Stewart, 137–61.

Gulalp, H. 1990. "The State and Democracy in Underdeveloped Capitalist Formations." *Studies in Political Economy* 32 (Summer): 145–66.

Gyllenhammer, P. 1977. *People at Work*. Reading, MA: Addison-Wesley.

Habermas, J. 1987a. *The Philosophical Discourse of Modernity*. Cambridge, MA: MIT Press.

Habermas, J. 1987b. *The Theory of Communicative Action*. Vol. 2. *Lifeworld and System: A Critique of Functionalist Reason*. Boston: Beacon Press.

Hale, S.M. 1981. Review of B. Rogers, *The Domestication of Women: Discrimination in Developing Societies*. London: Tavistock: 1980. In *Atlantis* 7, 1 (Autumn): 151–52.

Hale, S.M. 1985. "Integrating Women in Developmental Models and Theories." *Atlantis* 11, 1 (Autumn): 45–63.

Hale, S.M. 1987a. "The Documentary Construction of Female Mismanagement." *Canadian Review of Sociology and Anthropology* 24, 4 (Nov.): 489–513.

Hale, S.M. 1987b. *The Elusive Promise: The Struggle of Women Development Workers in Rural North India*. Montreal: Centre for Developing-Area Studies, McGill University.

Hale, S.M. 1988a. "Male Culture and Purdah for Women: The Social Construction of What Women Think Women Think." *Canadian Review of Sociology and Anthropology* 25, 2 (May): 276–98.

Hale, S.M. 1988b. "Using the Oppressor's Language in the Study of Women and Development." *Women and Language* 11, 2 (Winter): 38–43.

Hall, E.T. 1966. *The Hidden Dimension*. Garden City, NY: Doubleday.

Hall, R.M., and B.R. Sandler. 1984. "Out of the Classroom: A Chilly Campus Climate for Women?" Project on the Status and Education of Women. Washington, DC: Association of American Colleges.

Hall, S. 1977. "Culture, the Media, and the 'Ideological Effect.'" In *Mass Communication and Society*. Ed. J. Curran, M. Gurevitch, and J. Woollacott. London: Arnold, 315–49.

Hall, S. 1980. "Encoding/Decoding." In *Culture, Media, Language*. Ed. S. Hall, D. Hobson, A. Lowe, and P. Willis. London: Hutchinson, 128–38.

Hall, S. 1982. "The Rediscovery of 'Ideology': The Return of the 'Repressed' in Media Studies." In *Culture, Society and the Media*. Ed. M. Gurevitch, T. Bennet, J. Curran, and J. Woollacott. London: Methuen, 56–90.

Hall, S., D. Hobson, A. Lowe, and P. Willis, eds. 1980. *Culture, Media, Language*. London: Hutchinson.

Hall, S., and T. Jefferson, eds. 1976. *Resistance Through Rituals*. London: Hutchinson.

Hamilton, P., ed. 1985. *Readings from Talcott Parsons*. London: Tavistock.

Hamilton, R. Forthcoming. *Half the Sky: Feminist Perspectives on Canadian Society*. Toronto: Copp Clark.

Hammersley, M. 1990. *Classroom Ethnography: Empirical and Methodological Essays*. Toronto: OISE Press.

Harding, S. 1986. *The Science Question in Feminism*. Ithaca, NY: Cornell University Press.

Harland, R. 1987. *Superstructuralism: The Philosophy of Structuralism and Post Structuralism*. New York: Methuen.

Harlow, H.F. 1962. "The Heterosexual Affectional System in Monkeys." *American Psychologist* 17: 1–9.

Harlow, H.F. 1965. "Sexual Behavior in the Rhesus Monkey." In *Sex and Behavior*. Ed. F.A. Beach. New York: Wiley.

Harper, D. 1979. "Life on the Road." In *Images of Information*. Ed. J. Wagner. Beverly Hills: Sage, 25–42.

Harris, M. 1986. *Justice Denied: The Law Versus Donald Marshall*. Toronto: Macmillan.

Hartley, J. 1982. *Understanding News*. London: Methuen.

Hartley, J. 1988. "The Real World of Audiences." *Critical Studies in Mass Communication* (Sept.): 234–38.

Hartmann, H. 1979. "Capitalist Patriarchy and Job Segregation by Sex." In *Capitalist Patriarchy and the Case for Socialist Feminism*. Ed. Z. Eisenstein. New York: Monthly Review Press, 206–47.

Hartmann, H.I. 1984. "The Unhappy Marriage of Marxism and Feminism: Towards a More Progressive Union." In *Feminist Frameworks: Alternative Theoretical Accounts of the Relations Between Women and Men*. 2nd ed. Ed. A.M. Jaggar and P.S. Rothenberg. New York: McGraw-Hill, 171–89.

Hartsock, N. 1990. "Foucault on Power: A Theory for Women?" In *Feminist Postmodernism*. New York: Routledge.

Heap, J.L. 1986. "Classroom Talk: A Criticism of McHoul." Paper, Department of Sociology, Ontario Institute for Studies in Education.

Heap, J.L., and S. Moore. 1986. *Collaboration in Word Processing*. Toronto: Queen's Printer for Ontario.

Heath, C. 1981. "The Opening Sequence in Doctor-Patient Interaction." In *Medical Work: Realities and Routines*. Ed. P. Atkinson and C. Heath. Farnborough, Eng.: Gower, 71–90.

Hebdige, D. 1979. *Subculture: The Meaning of Style*. London: Methuen.

Hebdige, D. 1988. *Hiding in the Light: On Images and Things*. London: Routledge.

Heinricks, G. 1989. "Whose News? Business Circles the Globe." *This Magazine* (Sept.): 14–21.

Hempel, C.G. 1970. "The Logic of Functional Analysis." In *Readings in the Philosophy of Science*. Ed. B.A. Brody. Englewood Cliffs, NJ: Prentice-Hall.

Hennig, M., and A. Jardim. 1981. *The Managerial Woman*. New York: Anchor Books.

Henripin, J. 1968. *Tendances et facteurs de la fecondité au Canada*. Ottawa: Statistics Canada.

Henry, J. 1971. *Pathways to Madness*. New York: Random House.

Herberg, E.N. 1989. *Ethnic Groups in Canada: Adaptations and Transitions*. Scarborough, ON: Nelson.

Heritage, J. 1984. *Garfinkel and Ethnomethodology*. Oxford: Polity Press in association with Basil Blackwell.

Hester, S. 1991. "The Social Facts of Deviance in Schools: A Study of Mundane Reason." *British Journal of Sociology* 42, 2 (Sept.): 443–63.

Hill, D.G., and M. Schiff. 1986. *Human Rights in Canada: A Focus on Racism*. 2nd ed. Ottawa: Canadian Labour Congress and Human Rights Research and Education Centre, University of Ottawa.

Himelfarb, A., and C.J. Richardson. 1979. *People, Power, and Process: Sociology for Canadians*. Toronto: McGraw-Hill Ryerson.

Himelfarb, A., and C.J. Richardson. 1992. *Sociology for Canadians: A Reader*. Toronto: McGraw-Hill Ryerson.

Hitchcock, G., and D. Hughes. 1989. *Research and the Teacher: A Qualitative Introduction to School-Based Research*. London: Routledge.

Hoben, A., and R. Hefner. 1990. "The Integrative Revolution Revisited." *World Development* 19, 1: 17–30.

Hobson, D. 1982. *Crossroads: The Drama of a Soap Opera*. London: Methuen.

Hochschild, A. 1973. *The Unexpected Community*. Englewood Cliffs, NJ: Prentice-Hall.

Hochschild, A. 1983. *The Managed Heart*. Berkeley, CA: University of California Press.

Hodge, G., and M.A. Qadeer. 1983. *Towns and Villages in Canada: The Importance of Being Unimportant*. Toronto: Butterworths.

Hoebel, A. 1960. *The Cheyennes: Indians of the Great Plains*. New York: Holt, Rinehart & Winston.

Hoffman, L.W. 1977. "Changes in Family Roles, Socialization and Sex Differences." *American Psychologist* 32: 644–67.

Hoogvelt, A.M. 1976. *The Sociology of Developing Societies*. London: Macmillan.

Hornborg, A. 1994. "Environmentalism, Ethnicity and Sacred Places: Reflections on Modernity, Discourse and Power." *Canadian Review of Sociology and Anthropology* 31, 3 (Aug.): 245–67.

Horowitz, D.L. 1985. *Ethnic Groups in Conflict*. Berkeley, CA: University of California Press.

Horowitz, I.L. 1968. "The Life and Death of Project Camelot." In *Professing Sociology: Studies in the Life Cycle of Social Science*. Chicago: Aldine.

Horwitz, A.V. 1984. "The Economy and Social Pathology." *Annual Review of Sociology* 10: 95–119.

Hostetler, J.A., and G.E. Huntington. 1965. *The Hutterites in North America*. New York: Holt, Rinehart & Winston.

Huff, D. 1954. *How To Lie with Statistics*. New York: W.W. Norton.

Humphreys, L. 1970. *The Tearoom Trade*. Chicago: Aldine.

Hurtig, M. 1991. *The Betrayal of Canada*. Toronto: Stoddart.

Huston, A.C. 1983. "Sex Typing." In *Handbook of Child Psychology*. Ed. P.H. Mussen. Vol. 4. Ed. E.M. Hetherington. New York: John Wiley & Sons, 387–467.

Illich, I. 1971. *Deschooling Society*. New York: Harper & Row.

Illich, I. 1983. *Gender*. London: Marion Boyars.

Indian and Northern Affairs Canada. 1993. *1993 Basic Departmental Data*. Ottawa: Department of Indian Affairs and Northern Development.

Iverson, N., and R. Matthews. 1968. *Communities in Decline: An Examination of Household Resettlement in Newfoundland*. St. John's: Institute of Social and Economic Development.

Jaggar, A.M., and P.S. Rothenberg. 1984. *Feminist Frameworks: Alternative Theoretical Accounts of the Relations Between Women and Men*. 2nd ed. New York: McGraw-Hill.

Jalbert, P. 1984. "'News Speak' About the Lebanon War." *Journal of Palestine Studies* 14, 1 (Fall): 16–35.

Jamieson, S.M. 1968. *Times of Trouble: Labour Unrest and Industrial Conflict in Canada, 1900–1966*. Ottawa: Information Canada.

Johnson, H. 1987. "Getting the Facts Straight: A Statistical Overview." In *Too Few to Count: Canadian Women in Conflict with the Law*. Ed. E. Adelberg and C. Currie. Vancouver: Press Gang.

Johnston, P. 1993. "The Threat to Canada's Poverty Lines: Implications and Strategy." *Canadian Review of Social Policy* 31 (Spring): 89–93.

Jong, E. 1981. *Witches*. New York: Harry N. Adams.

Jungueira, J.C. 1979. "The Re-emergence of the Christian Left in Latin America." *Canadian Dimension* 13, 5 (Jan.–Feb.): 46–49.

Kalbach, W. 1976. "Canada: A Demographic Analysis." In *Introduction to Canadian Society*. Ed. G.N. Ramu and S. Johnson. Toronto: Macmillan.

Kanter, R.M. 1977. *Men and Women of the Corporation*. New York: Basic Books.

Kasfir, N. 1979. "Explaining Ethnic Political Participation." *World Politics* 31: 365–88.

Kates, J. 1988. "The Quiet Revolution." *Report on Business Magazine* (July): 58–64.

Katz, J.N. 1990. "The Invention of Heterosexuality." *Socialist Review* 1: 7–34.

Keat, R., and J. Urry. 1982. *Social Theory as Science*. 2nd ed. London: Routledge & Kegan Paul.

Kehoe, A.B. 1990. "Primal Gaia: Primitivists and Plastic Medicine Men." In *The Invented Indian: Cultural Fictions and Government Policies*. Ed. J.A. Clifton. New Brunswick, NJ: Transaction, 193–210.

Kellner, D. 1988. *Jean Baudrillard: From Marxism to Postmodernism and Beyond*. Cambridge, Eng.: Polity Press.

Kellough, G. 1980. "From Colonialism to Economic Imperialism: The Experience of the Canadian Indian." In *Structured Inequality in Canada*. Ed. J. Harp and J.R. Hofley. Scarborough, ON: Prentice-Hall, 343–77.

Kelly, L. 1988. "How Women Define Their Experiences of Violence." In *Feminist Perspectives on Wife Abuse*. Ed. K. Yllö and M. Bograd. Beverly Hills: Sage, 114–32.

Kent, T., chair. 1981. *Report of the Royal Commission on Newspapers*. Hull: Ministry of Supply and Services.

Kerr, M., D. Miller, and B. Viloria. 1993. "Has the Response to 'Persons in Need' Changed in Saskatchewan Since the NDP Returned to Power?" *Canadian Review of Social Policy* 31 (Spring): 67–73.

Kessler, S.J., and W. McKenna. 1978. *Gender: An Ethnomethodological Approach*. Chicago: University of Chicago Press.

Khayatt, M.D. 1990. "Legalized Invisibility: The Effect of Bill 7 on Lesbian Teachers." *Women's Studies International Forum* 13, 3: 185–93.

Khayatt, M.D. 1992. *Lesbian Teachers: An Invisible Presence*. Albany, NY: State University of New York.

Kinsey, A.C., W.B. Pomeroy, and C.E. Martin. 1948. *Sexual Behavior in the Human Male*. Philadelphia: Saunders.

Kinsman, G. 1986. "Whores Fight Back: Valerie Scott of CORP on Empowering Prostitutes." *Rites* (May): 8–9, 19.

Kinsman, G. 1987a. "Men Loving Men: The Challenge of Gay Liberation." In *Beyond Patriarchy: Essays by Men on Pleasure, Power and Change*. Ed. M. Kaufman. Toronto: Oxford University Press, 103–19.

Kinsman, G. 1987b. *The Regulation of Desire: Sexuality in Canada*. Montreal: Black Rose Books.

Kinsman, G. 1991. "'Homosexuality' Historically Reconsidered Challenges Heterosexual Hegemony." *The Journal of Historical Sociology* 4, 2 (June): 91–111.

Kinsman, G. 1992. "Managing AIDS Organizing: 'Consultation,' 'Partnership,' and the National AIDS Strategy." In *Organizing Dissent: Contemporary Social Movements in Theory and Practice*. Ed. W.K. Carroll. Toronto: Garamond, 215–31.

Kirby, S., and K. McKenna. 1989. *Experience, Research, Social Change: Methods from the Margins*. Toronto: Garamond.

Kline, M. 1989. "Women's Oppression and Racism: A Critique of the 'Feminist Standpoint.'" In *Race, Class, Gender: Bonds and Barriers*. Ed. J. Vorst et al. Toronto: Between the Lines (for the Society for Socialist Studies, Winnipeg).

Kolbenschlag, M. 1979. *Kiss Sleeping Beauty Good-bye: Breaking the Spell of Feminine Myths and Models*. Garden City, NY: Doubleday.

Kotovsky, G. 1992. "The Former Soviet Union in the Era of Primitive Accumulation and Kleptocratic Rule." *Studies in Political Economy* 38 (Summer): 167–74.

Kuhn, T.S. 1970. "The Function of Dogma in Scientific Research." In *Readings in the Philosophy of Science*. Ed. B.A. Brody. Englewood Cliffs, NJ: Prentice-Hall, 356–73.

Kuper, L. 1969. "Plural Societies: Perspectives and Problems." In *Pluralism in Africa*. Ed. L. Kuper and M.G. Smith. Berkeley: University of California Press, 7–26.

Kuyek, J.N. 1979. *The Phone Book: Working at the Bell*. Kitchener, ON: Between the Lines.

Lacan, J. 1972. "The Insistence of the Letter in the Unconscious." In *The Structuralists: From Marx to Levi-Strauss*. Ed. R. DeGeorge and F. DeGeorge. Garden City, NY: Anchor Books, 287–324.

Laing, R.D. 1965. *The Divided Self*. Harmondsworth, Eng.: Penguin.

Lambert, W.E. 1967. "A Social Psychology of Bilingualism." *Journal of Social Issues* 23, 2: 91–109.

Landsberger, H.A. 1958. *Hawthorne Revisited: Management and the Worker, Its Critics, and Developments in Human Relations in Industry*. Ithaca, NY: Cornell University Press.

Lapierre, L., and H. Aylwin. 1985. *Canadian Youth: Perspectives on Their Health*. Cat. 82-545E. Ottawa: Ministry of Supply and Services.

Lappé, F.M. 1971. *Diet for a Small Planet*. New York: Ballantine.

LaPrairie, C.P. 1984. "Selected Criminal Justice and Sociodemographic Data on Native Women." *Canadian Journal of Criminology* 26, 2: 161–69.

Larner, C. 1984. *Witchcraft and Religion: The Politics of Popular Belief*. Oxford: Basil Blackwell.

Larrain, J. 1994. "The Postmodern Critique of Ideology." *The Sociological Review* 42, 2 (May): 289–314.

Larwood, L., and M.M. Wood. 1977. *Women in Management*. Lexington, MA: Lexington Books.

Lasch, C. 1977. *Haven in a Heartless World*. New York: Basic Books.

Lave, J., and E. Wenger. 1991. *Situated Learning: Legitimate Peripheral Participation*. New York: Cambridge University Press.

Lavigne, M. 1986. "Feminist Reflections on the Fertility of Women in Quebec." In *The Politics of Diversity: Feminism, Marxism, and Nationalism*. Ed. R. Hamilton and M. Barrett. Montreal: Book Centre, 303–21.

Lawless, E.J. 1991. "Rescripting Their Lives and Narratives: Spiritual Life Stories of Pentecostal Women Preachers." *Journal of Feminist Studies in Religion* 7, 1 (Spring): 53–72.

Lecky, W. 1891. *History of England in the Eighteenth Century*. Vol. 2. n.p.

Lee, D., and H. Newby. 1983. *The Problem of Sociology*. London: Hutchinson.

Lehne, G.K. 1976. "Homophobia Among Men." In *The Forty-Nine Percent Majority: The Male Sex Role*. Ed. D.S. David and R. Brannon. New York: Random House, 66–92.

Lemert, E.M. 1951. *Social Pathology: A Systematic Approach to the Theory of Sociopathic Behavior*. New York: McGraw-Hill.

Lengermann, P.M., and Niebrugge-Brantley, J. 1990. "Feminist Sociological Theory: The Near-Future Prospects." In *Frontiers of Social Theory: The New Synthesis*. Ed. G. Ritzer. New York: Columbia University Press, 316–44.

Leonard, E.B. 1982. *Women, Crime, and Society: A Critique of Theoretical Criminology*. New York: Longman.

Leschied, A.W., and P. Jaffe. 1991. "Dispositions as Indicators of Conflicting Social Purposes Under the JDA and YOA." In *The Young Offenders Act: A Revolution in Canadian Juvenile Justice*. Ed. A.W. Leschied et al. Toronto: University of Toronto Press.

Levi-Strauss, C. 1969. *Elementary Structures of Kinship*. Boston: Beacon Press.

Levi-Strauss, C. [1970] 1990. *The Raw and the Cooked*. Vol. 1. *Mythologiques*. Trans. J. Weightman and D. Weightman. Chicago: University of Chicago Press.

Lewis, D. 1972. *Louder Voices: The Corporate Welfare Bums*. Toronto: James Lewis and Samuel.

Lewis, O. 1949. *Life in a Mexican Village: Tepoztlan Restudied*. Urbana, IL: University of Illinois Press.

Leyton, E. 1986. *Hunting Humans: The Rise of the Modern Multiple Murderer*. Toronto: McClelland & Stewart.

Li, P.S. 1990. "Race and Ethnicity." In *Race and Ethnic Relations in Canada*. Ed. Peter Li. Toronto: Oxford University Press, ch. 1.

Liddle, J., and R. Joshi. 1986. *Daughters of Independence: Gender, Caste and Class in India*. New Delhi: Zed Books.

Lieberman, S. 1956. "The Effect of Changes in Roles on the Attitudes of Role Occupants." *Human Relations* 9: 385–402.

Lipset, S.M. 1967. "Values, Education, and Entrepreneurship." In *Elites in Latin America*. Ed. S. Lipset and A. Solari. New York: Oxford University Press, 3–60.

Lipset, S.M. 1976. "Radicalism in North America: A Comparative View of the Party Systems in Canada and the United States." *Transactions of the Royal Society of Canada (Series IV)* 14: 19–55.

Lipset, S.M. 1985. "Canada and the United States: The Cultural Dimension." In *Canada and the United States*. Ed. C. Doran and J. Sigler. Scarborough, ON: Prentice-Hall, 109–60.

Lombroso, C. 1895. *The Female Offender*. New York: Fisher Unwin.

Lorimer, J., and M. Phillips. 1971. *Working People: Life in a Downtown City Neighbourhood*. Toronto: James Lewis and Samuel.

Loseke, D.R. 1987. "The Construction of Social Problems: The Case of Wife Abuse." *Symbolic Interaction* 10, 2: 229–43.

Lucas, R.A. 1971. *Minetown, Milltown, Railtown*. Toronto: University of Toronto Press.

Lumpkin, K., and D. Douglas. 1937. *Child Workers in America*. New York: International Publishers.

Luxton, M. 1980. *More than a Labour of Love: Three Generations of Women's Work in the Home*. Toronto: Women's Press.

Lynch, M. 1985. *Art and Artifact in Laboratory Science: A Study of Shop Work and Shop Talk in a Research Laboratory*. Boston: Routledge & Kegan Paul.

Lynn, D.B. 1974. *The Father: His Role in Child Development*. Monterey, CA: Wadsworth.

Lyotard, J.F. 1984. *The Postmodern Condition: A Report on Knowledge*. Manchester: Manchester University Press.

Lyttleton, N. 1990. "Men's Liberation, Men Against Sexism and Major Dividing Lines." In *Women and Men*. Ed. G. Hofmann Nemiroff. Fitzhenry & Whiteside, 472–77.

Maccoby, E., and C.N. Jacklin. 1974. *The Psychology of Sex Differences*. Palo Alto, CA: Stanford University Press.

MacDonald, G. 1993. Faculty seminar, St Thomas University.

MacDonald, M., and M.P. Connelly. 1992. "Class and Gender in Fishing Communities in Nova Scotia." In *Feminism in Action: Studies in Political Economy*. Ed. M.P. Connelly and P. Armstrong. Toronto: Canadian Scholars' Press, 23–46.

MacDonald, P. 1988. "Historical School Reform and the Correspondence Principle." In *Bowles and Gintis Revisited: Correspondence and Contradiction*. Ed. M. Cole. London: Falmer Press, 86–111.

Machum, S. 1992. "The Impact of Agribusiness on Women's Work in the Household, On-the-farm and Off-the farm: A New Brunswick Case Study." Master's thesis, Department of Sociology and Social Anthropology, Dalhousie University.

MacKay, R.W. 1974a. "Conceptions of Children and Models of Socialization." In *Ethnomethodology: Selected Readings*. Ed. R. Turner. Harmondsworth, Eng.: Penguin, 180–93.

MacKay, R.W. 1974b. "Standardized Tests: Objective/ Objectified Measures of 'Competence.'" In *Language Use and School Performance*. Ed. A. Cicourel et al. New York: Academic, 218–47.

Mackenzie, S. 1986a. "Feminist Geography." *The Canadian Geographer* 30, 3: 268–70.

Mackenzie, S. 1986b. "Women's Response to Economic Restructuring: Changing Gender Changing Space." In *The Politics of Diversity: Feminism, Marxism, and Nationalism*. Ed. R. Hamilton and M. Barrett. Montreal: Book Centre, 81–100.

Mackenzie, S. 1987a. "Neglected Spaces in Peripheral Places: Homeworkers and the Creation of a New Economic Centre." *Cahiers de géographie du Québec* 31, 83 (Sept.): 247–60.

Mackenzie, S. 1987b. "The Politics of Restructuring: Gender and Economy in De-industrialized Areas." Paper presented to the Canadian Association of Geographers, Hamilton, ON.

Mackie, M. 1991. *Gender Relations in Canada: Further Explorations*. Toronto: Butterworths.

Mackinnon, C.A. 1989. *Toward a Feminist Theory of the State*. Cambridge, MA: Harvard University Press.

Madison, G.B. 1988. *The Hermeneutics of Postmodernity: Figures and Themes*. Bloomington, IN: Indiana University Press.

Mandel, E. 1969. *An Introduction to Marxist Economic Theory*. New York: Pathfinder Press.

Marable, M. 1993. "Beyond Racial Identity Politics: Towards a Liberation Theory for Multicultural Democracy." *Race and Class* 35, 1: 113–30.

Marchak, P. 1985. "Canadian Political Economy." *Canadian Review of Sociology and Anthropology* 22, 5 (Dec.): 673–709.

Marcuse, H. 1964. *One-Dimensional Man*. Boston: Beacon Press.

Marglin, S.A. 1974–75. "What Bosses Do." *Review of Radical Political Economy* 6: 60–112; 7: 20–37.

Markwart, A.E., and R. Corrado. 1989. "Is the Young Offenders Act More Punitive?" In *Young Offender Dispositions*. Ed. L. Beaulieu. Toronto: Wall and Emerson, 7–17.

Maroney, H.J., and M. Luxton, eds. 1987. *Feminism and Political Economy: Women's Work, Women's Struggles*. Toronto: Methuen.

Martin, D. 1982. "Facing the Octopus: The Transnational Corporation." In *Ties that Bind: Canada and the Third World*. Ed. R. Swift and R. Clark. Toronto: Between the Lines, 87–148.

Marx, K. [1845] 1975. "Thesis on Feuerbach." In *Karl Marx, Frederick Engels: Collected Works*. Vol. 5. New York: International Publishers, 3–7.

Marx, K. [1859] 1975. "'Preface' to a Contribution to the Critique of Political Economy." In *Karl Marx: Early Writings*. Harmondsworth, Eng.: Penguin.

Marx, K. 1967. *Capital*. Vol. 1. *A Critical Analysis of Capitalist Production* [1867]. Vol. 2. *The Process of Circulation of Capital* [1885]; Vol. 3. *The Process of Capitalist Production as a Whole* [1894]. Ed. F. Engels. New York: International Publishers.

Marx, K., and F. Engels. [1846] 1970. *The German Ideology*. New York: International Publishers.

Marx, K., and F. Engels. [1848] 1955. *The Communist Manifesto*. Ed. S.H. Beer. New York: Appleton-Century-Crofts.

Mayhew, H. 1968. *London Labour and the London Poor*. New York: Dover.

Maynard, R., with C. Brouse. 1988. "Thanks, But No Thanks." *Report on Business Magazine* (Feb.): 26–34.

Mayo, E. [1933] 1960. *The Human Problems of an Industrial Civilization*. New York: Viking.

McAteer, M. 1989. "Women in the Clergy: Numbers Keep Growing." *Toronto Star*, 21 Oct., M29.

McFadyean, M. 1988. "Agony Aunts and Advice Columns." *The New Statesman and Society* 19 Aug.

McGahan, P. 1982. *Urban Sociology in Canada*. Toronto: Butterworths.

McHoul, A.W. 1978. "The Organization of Turns at Formal Talk in the Classroom." *Language and Society* 7: 183–213.

McHoul, A.W. 1990. "The Organization of Repair in Classroom Talk." *Language and Society* 19: 349–77.

McIntyre, S. 1986. "Gender Bias Within the Law School." Memo to all members of the Faculty Board. Queen's University, 28 July.

McKendy, J.P. 1992. "Ideological Practices and the Management of Emotions: The Case of 'Wife Abusers.'" *Critical Sociology* 19, 2: 61–80.

McLoughlin, M. 1987. "The Pleasures of Reading." BA diss., North East London Polytechnic.

McLuhan, M. 1964. *Understanding Media: The Extensions of Man*. Toronto: McGraw-Hill.

McMahon, S. 1987. "The New Forest in Nova Scotia." In *People, Resources, and Power: Critical Perspectives on Underdevelopment and Primary Industries in the Atlantic Region*. Ed. G. Burrill and I. McKay. Fredericton: Acadiensis Press, 99–105.

McRobbie, A. 1978. "Working-Class Girls and the Culture of Femininity." In *Women Take Issue: Aspects of Women's Subordination*. London: Hutchinson, 96–108.

McRobbie, A. 1981. "Settling Accounts with Subcultures: A Feminist Critique." In *Culture, Ideology and Social Process: A Reader*. Ed. T. Benne, G. Martin, C. Mercer, and J. Woollacott. London: Open University Press, 112–24.

McRobbie, A. 1991. *Feminism and Youth Culture*. Houndsmills: MacMillan Education.

Mead, G.H. 1934. *Mind, Self, and Society*. Chicago: University of Chicago Press.

Mead, M. 1928. *Coming of Age in Samoa: A Psychological Study of Primitive Youth for Western Civilization*. New York: Blue Ribbon Books.

Mead, M. 1935. *Sex and Temperament in Three Primitive Societies*. New York: William Morrow.

Media Watch, Vancouver BC. 1991. "Two Years of Sexism in Canadian Newspapers: A Study of 15 Newspapers." *Resources for Feminist Research* 20, 1/2 (Spring): 21–22.

Mehan, H. 1979. *Learning Lessons: Social Organization in the Classroom*. Cambridge, MA: Harvard University Press.

Mehan, H. 1992. "Understanding Inequality in Schools: The Contribution of Interpretive Studies." *Sociology of Education* 65 (Jan.): 1–20.

Meis, M. 1983. "Toward a Methodology for Feminist Research." In *Theories of Women's Studies*. Ed. G. Bowles and R. Duelli Klein. London: Routledge & Kegan Paul.

Melander, T. 1988. *Saving Lakes*. Trans. C. Thorn. Gothenburg, Sweden: Informator AB.

Mellor, P.A. 1993. "Reflexive Traditions: Anthony Giddens, High Modernity and the Contours of Contemporary Religiosity." *Religious Studies* 29, 1 (March): 111–27.

Merritt, M. 1976. "On Questions Following Questions in Service Encounters." *Language in Society* 5: 315–57.

Merton, R.K. 1957. "Bureaucratic Structure and Personality." In *Social Theory and Social Structure*. Ed. R.K. Merton. Glencoe, IL: Free Press, 249–60.

Merton, R.K. 1967. *On Theoretical Sociology: Five Essays, Old and New*. New York: Free Press.

Merton, R.K. 1968. *Social Theory and Social Structure*. Enlarged ed. New York: Free Press.

Messner, M. 1992. "Boyhood, Organized Sports, and the Construction of Masculinities." In *Men's Lives*. Ed. M.S. Kimmel and M.A. Messner. 2nd ed. New York: Macmillan, 161–73.

Michels, R. [1911] 1949. *Political Parties*. Glencoe, IL: Free Press.

Michelson, W. 1970. *Man and His Urban Environment: A Sociological Approach*. Reading, MA: Addison-Wesley.

Michelson, W. 1988. "Divergent Convergence: The Daily Routines of Employed Spouses as a Public Affairs Agenda." In *Life Spaces: Gender, Household, Employment*. Ed. C. Andrew and B.M. Milroy. Vancouver: University of British Columbia Press, 81–102.

Midnight Sun. 1988. "Sex/Gender Systems in Native North America." In *Living the Spirit: A Gay American Indian Anthology*. Ed. W. Roscoe and comp. Gay American Indians. New York: St. Martin's Press, 32–47.

Miles, A. 1985. "Economism and Feminism: Hidden in the Household. A Comment on the Domestic Labour Debate." In *Feminist Marxism or Marxist Feminism*. Ed. P. Armstrong, H. Armstrong, P. Connelly, A. Miles, and M. Luxton. Toronto: Garamond.

Miliband, R. 1969. *The State in Capitalist Society*. New York: Basic Books.

Miller, W.B. 1958. "Lower Class Culture as a Generating Milieu of Gang Delinquency." *Journal of Social Issues* 14, 2: 5–19.

Mills, C.W. 1959. *The Sociological Imagination*. New York: Oxford University Press.

Miner, H. 1939. *St. Denis: A French-Canadian Parish*. Chicago: University of Chicago Press.

Miner, H. 1964. "Changes in Rural French-Canadian Culture." In *French-Canadian Society*. Vol. 1. Ed. M. Rioux and Y. Martin. Toronto: McClelland & Stewart, 63–75.

Mitchell, J. 1972. "Marxism and Women's Revolution." *Social Praxis* 1, 1.

Mitchell, J. 1975. *Psychoanalysis and Feminism*. New York: Random House.

Molotch, H.L., and D. Boden. 1985. "Talking Social Structure: Domination and the Watergate Hearings." *American Sociological Review* 50: 273–88.

Moore, R. 1988. "The Correspondence Principle and the Marxist Sociology of Education." In *Bowles and Gintis: Correspondence and Contradiction*. Ed. M. Cole. London: Falmer Press, 51–85.

Moraga, C., and G. Anzaldua, eds. 1981. *This Bridge Called My Back*. New York: Kitchen Table—Women of Color Press.

Morgan, E. 1972. *The Descent of Woman*. New York: Stein & Day.

Morgan, K., and A. Sayer. 1988. *Microcircuits of Capital: "Sunrise" Industry and Uneven Development*. Cambridge, Eng.: Polity Press.

Morley, D. 1980. *The "Nationwide" Audience: Structure and Decoding*. London: British Film Institute.

Morley, D. 1986. *Family Television: Cultural Power and Domestic Leisure*. London: Comedia.

Morris, A. 1987. *Women, Crime and Criminal Justice*. Oxford: Basil Blackwell.

Morris, R. 1964. "Female Delinquency and Relational Problems." *Social Forces* 42 (Oct.): 82–88.

Morton, P. 1972. "Women's Work Is Never Done." In *Women Unite!* Toronto: Women's Press, 45–69.

Mosca, G. [1939] 1960. *The Ruling Class*. New York: McGraw-Hill.

Mueller, A. 1986. "The Bureaucratization of Feminist Knowledge: The Case of Women in Development." *Resources for Feminist Research* 15, 1 (March): 36–38.

Muller, J. 1989. "Ruling Through Texts: Developing a Social Service Training Program for a Community College." *Community Development Journal* 24, 4 (Oct.): 273–82.

Muller, J. 1990. "Co-ordinating the Re-organization of Ruling Relations: Management's Use of Human Resource Development for the New Brunswick Community Colleges." In *Political Economy of Community Colleges: Training Workers for Capital*. Ed. J. Muller. Toronto: Garamond.

Murdock, G.P. 1949. *Social Structure*. New York: Free Press.

Murphy, T. 1987. "Potato Capitalism: McCain and Industrial Farming in New Brunswick." In *People, Resources, and Power: Critical Perspectives on Underdevelopment and Primary Industries in the Atlantic Region*. Ed. G. Burrill and I. McKay. Fredericton: Acadiensis Press, 19–29.

National Action Committee on the Status of Women. 1987. "Refugee Women and Bill C-55." Prepared by the NAC Foreign Policy Committee. Sept.

National Anti-Poverty Organization. 1992. *Poverty Statistics at a Glance*. Ottawa: NAPO.

National Council of Welfare. 1975. *Poor Kids. A Report by the National Council of Welfare on Children in Poverty in Canada*. Ottawa: National Council of Welfare.

National Council of Welfare. 1977. *Jobs and Poverty. A Report by the National Council of Welfare on Canada's Working Poor*. Ottawa: National Council of Welfare.

National Council of Welfare. 1978. *Bearing the Burden, Sharing the Burden. A Report by the National Council of Welfare on Taxation and the Distribution of Income*. Ottawa: National Council of Welfare.

National Council of Welfare. 1979a. *The Hidden Welfare System Revisited. A Report by the National Council of Welfare on the Growth in Tax Expenditures*. Ottawa: National Council of Welfare.

National Council of Welfare. 1979b. *Women and Poverty*. Ottawa: National Council of Welfare.

National Council of Welfare. 1982. *Revised 1982 Poverty Lines*. Ottawa: National Council of Welfare.

National Council of Welfare. 1986. *The Impact of the 1985 and 1986 Budgets on Disposable Income*. Ottawa: National Council of Welfare.

National Council of Welfare. 1987a. *The Hidden Welfare System: Exemptions, Deductions and Credits*. Ottawa: National Council of Welfare.

National Council of Welfare. 1987b. *Tax Expenditures: Who Gets What*. Ottawa: National Council of Welfare.

National Council of Welfare. 1987c. *Welfare in Canada: The Tangled Safety Net*. Ottawa: National Council of Welfare.

National Council of Welfare. 1987d. *What To Look for and Look Out for in Tax Reform*. Ottawa: National Council of Welfare.

National Council of Welfare. 1988a. *Child Care: A Better Alternative*. Ottawa: National Council of Welfare.

National Council of Welfare. 1988b. *Poverty Profile 1988*. Ottawa: National Council of Welfare.

National Council of Welfare. 1989. *1989 Poverty Lines: Estimates of the National Council of Welfare*. Ottawa: National Council of Welfare.

National Council of Welfare. 1990a. *Health, Health Care and Medicare*. Ottawa: National Council of Welfare.

National Council of Welfare. 1990b. *Women and Poverty Revisited*. Ottawa: National Council of Welfare.

National Council of Welfare. 1991. *The Canada Assistance Plan: No Time for Cuts*. Ottawa: National Council of Welfare.

National Council of Welfare. 1992a. *Poverty Profile 1980–1990*. Ottawa: National Council of Welfare.

National Council of Welfare. 1992b. *Welfare Reform*. Ottawa: National Council of Welfare.

National Council of Welfare. 1993a. *Welfare Incomes 1992*. Ottawa: National Council of Welfare.

National Council of Welfare. 1993b. *Incentives and Disincentives to Work.* Ottawa: National Council of Welfare.

National Council of Welfare. 1994. *Poverty Profile 1992.* Ottawa: National Council of Welfare.

Neel, J. 1988. *Plato, Derrida, and Writing.* Edwardsville: Southern Illinois University Press.

Neis, B. 1991. "Flexible Specialization: What's That Got To Do with the Price of Fish?" *Studies in Political Economy* 36 (Fall): 145–75.

Neuringer, C., and D.J. Lettieri. 1982. *Suicidal Women: Their Thinking and Feeling Patterns.* New York: Gardiner.

Newman, P. 1975. *The Canadian Establishment.* Toronto: McClelland & Stewart.

Neyer, J. 1960. "Individualism and Socialism in Durkheim." In *Essays on Sociology and Philosophy by Emile Durkheim et al.* Ed. K.H. Wolff. New York: Harper & Row.

Ng, R. 1981. "Constituting Ethnic Phenomenon: An Account from the Perspective of Immigrant Women." *Canadian Ethnic Studies* 13, 1: 97–108.

Ng, R. 1986. "The Social Construction of Immigrant Women in Canada." In *The Politics of Diversity: Feminism, Marxism, and Nationalism.* Ed. R. Hamilton and M. Barrett. Montreal: Book Centre, 269–86.

Ng, R. 1988a. "Ethnicity, Gender, Class and Canadian State Formation." Paper presented at Ontario Institute for Studies in Education, 24 Feb.

Ng, R. 1988b. *The Politics of Community Services: Immigrant Women, Class, and State.* Toronto: Garamond.

Nichols, T., and H. Beynon. 1977. *Living with Capitalism: Class Relations and the Modern Factory.* London: Routledge & Kegan Paul.

Nicholson, J. 1984. *Men and Women: How Different Are They?* Oxford: Oxford University Press.

Nicholson, L.J., ed. 1990. *Feminism/Postmodernism.* New York: Routledge.

Niezen, R. 1993. "Power and Dignity: The Social Consequences of Hydro-electric Development for the James Bay Cree." *Canadian Review of Sociology and Anthropology* 30, 4 (Nov.): 510–29.

Noble, J. 1982. "Fitting the Child to the Classroom: What Mothers Do." Paper prepared for Project 3648. Department of Sociology in Education, Ontario Institute for Studies in Education, Toronto.

Noble, J. 1990. "Social Class and the Under-Fives: Making the 'Differences' Visible." *Our Schools/Our Selves* 2, 2 (April): 42–61.

O'Brien, M. 1981. *The Politics of Reproduction.* London: Routledge & Kegan Paul.

O'Connell, D. 1983. "Poverty: The Feminine Complaint." In *Perspectives on Women in the 1980s.* Ed. J. Turner and L. Emery. Winnipeg: University of Manitoba Press, 41–65.

Oakley, A. 1981. *Subject Women.* New York: Pantheon.

Opie, A. 1992. "Qualitative Research, Appropriation of the 'Other' and Empowerment." *Feminist Review* 40 (Spring): 52–69.

Orbach, S. 1979. *Fat Is a Feminist Issue: A Self-Help Guide for Compulsive Eaters.* New York: Berkley Books.

Orenstein, D. 1985. *The Sociological Quest: Principles of Sociology.* St. Paul, MN: West.

Pala, A.O. 1977. "Definitions of Women and Development: An African Perspective." *Signs: Journal of Women in Culture and Society* 3, 1 (Autumn).

Panitch, L. 1992. "Beyond Communism and Social Democracy." *Studies in Political Economy* 38 (Summer): 139–54.

Panitch, L., and D. Swartz. 1988. *The Assault on Trade Union Freedoms.* Toronto: Garamond.

Paper, J. 1989. *Offering Smoke: The Sacred Pipe and Native American Religion.* Edmonton: University of Alberta Press.

Paper, J. 1993. "Methodological Controversies in the Study of Native American Religions." *Studies in Religion* 22, 3: 365–77.

Pappert, A. 1989. "Social Debate Rages Over Unlimited Scope of Test Tube Babies." Part 1 of series The Reproductive Revolution. *Toronto Star*, 7–12 Oct.

Park, R. 1936. "Human Ecology." *American Journal of Sociology* 42: 1–15.

Park, R.E., and E.W. Burgess, eds. 1916. *The City.* Chicago: University of Chicago Press.

Parkhill, T. Forthcoming 1995. *Weaving Ourselves into the Land: Charles Godfrey Leland, "Indians," and the Study of Native American Religions.* Albany, NY: SUNY Press.

Parmar, P. 1982. "Gender, Race and Class: Asian Women in Resistance." In *The Empire Strikes Back: Race and Racism in 70s Britain.* Centre for Contemporary Cultural Studies. London: Hutchinson, 236–75.

Parr, J. 1990. *The Gender of Breadwinners: Women, Men and Change in Two Industrial Towns, 1880–1950.* Toronto: University of Toronto Press.

Parsons, T. [1937] 1968. *The Structure of Social Action.* New York: Macmillan.

Parsons, T. [1949] 1964. *Essays in Sociological Theory.* New York: Free Press.

Parsons, T. 1951. *The Social System.* New York: Free Press.

Parsons, T. 1956. "Suggestions for a Sociological Approach to the Theory of Organizations." *Administrative Science Quarterly* (June): 63–69.

Parsons, T. 1961. "The School Class as a Social System: Some of its Functions in American Society." In *Education, Economy and Society.* Ed. A.H. Halsey, J. Floud, and C.A. Anderson. New York: Free Press.

Parsons, T. 1966. *Societies: Evolutionary and Comparative Perspectives.* Englewood Cliffs, NJ: Prentice-Hall.

Parsons, T. 1978. "The Concept of Society: The Components and Their Interrelations." In *Contemporary Sociological Theories.* Ed. A. Wells. Santa Monica, CA: Goodyear, 18–31.

Parsons, T., and E. Shils. 1951. *Towards a General Theory of Action.* Cambridge, MA: Harvard University Press.

Parsons, T., and R.F. Bales, eds. 1956. *Family, Socialization, and Interaction Process.* London: Routledge & Kegan Paul.

Pavlowitch, S.K. 1994. "Who Is 'Balkanizing' Whom? The Misunderstandings Between the Debris of Yugoslavia and an Unprepared West." *Daedalus* 123, 2 (Spring): 203–23.

Payne, G.C.F. 1976. "Making a Lesson Happen: An Ethnomethodological Analysis." In *The Process of Schooling: A Sociological Reader*. Ed. M. Hammersley and P. Woods. London: Routledge & Kegan Paul.

Payne, G.C.F., and D.E. Hustler. 1980. "Teaching the Class: The Practical Management of a Cohort." *The British Journal of Sociology of Education* 1, 1: 49–66.

Peace Research (no specific author). 1993. "The Implications of Free Trade and the NAFTA for Latin America." (Abridged version of "Free Trade: Manifest Destiny Without Gunboats," *Free or Fair Trade* 1, 2 [Dec.]). *Peace Research* 25, 1 (Feb.): 77–84.

Pentland, H.C. 1959. "The Development of a Capitalist Labour Market in Canada." *Canadian Journal of Economics and Political Science* 25, 4 (Nov.): 450–61.

Philbrook, T. 1966. *Fisherman, Logger, Merchant, Miner: Social Change and Industrialism in Three Newfoundland Communities*. St Johns: Institute of Social and Economic Research.

Piddington, R. 1965. "The Kinship Network Among French Canadians." *International Journal of Comparative Sociology* 6: 145–65.

Pollak, O. 1950. *The Criminality of Women*. Philadelphia: University of Pennsylvania Press.

Pope, W. 1976. *Durkheim's Suicide: A Classic Analysed*. Chicago: University of Chicago Press.

Porter, J. 1965. *The Vertical Mosaic: An Analysis of Social Class and Power in Canada*. Toronto: University of Toronto Press.

Porter, J. 1979a. "Ethnic Pluralism in Canadian Perspective." In *The Measure of Canadian Society: Education, Equality and Opportunity*. Toronto: Gage, 103–37.

Porter, J. 1979b. *The Measure of Canadian Society: Education, Equality and Opportunity*. Toronto: Gage.

Porter, J., M. Porter, and B.R. Blishen. 1982. *Stations and Callings: Making it Through the School System*. Toronto: Methuen.

Prentice, A., et al. 1988. *Canadian Women: A History*. Toronto: Harcourt Brace Jovanovich.

Pryor, E.T., G.J. Goldman, M.J. Sheridan, and P.M. White. 1992. "Measuring Ethnicity in 'Canadian': An Evolving Indigenous Category?" *Ethnic and Racial Studies* 15, 2 (April): 214–36.

Psathas, G. 1980. "Early Goffman and the Analysis of Face-to-Face Interaction in *Strategic Interaction*." In *The View From Goffman*. Ed. J. Ditton. London: Macmillan, 52–79.

Ptacek, J. 1988. "Why Do Men Batter Their Wives?" In *Feminist Perspectives on Wife Abuse*. Ed. K. Yllö and M. Bograd. Beverly Hills: Sage, 133–57.

Quinney, R. 1975. "Crime Control in Capitalist Society: A Critical Philosophy of Legal Order." In *Critical Criminology*. Ed. I. Taylor, P. Walton, and J. Young. London: Routledge & Kegan Paul.

Radway, J. 1987. *Reading the Romance: Women Patriarchy and Popular Literature*. London: Verso.

Rafiq, F. 1988. "Women in Islam with Reference to Pakistan." Paper presented at Canadian Asian Studies Association meeting, Windsor, 9 June.

Rance, S. 1991. "Growing the Stuff." *New Internationalist* (Oct.): 10–13.

Ransom, D. 1991. "The Needle and the Damage Done." *New Internationalist* (Oct.): 4–7.

Razack, S. 1991. *Canadian Feminism and the Law: The Women's Legal Education and Action Fund and the Pursuit of Equality*. Toronto: Second Story Press.

Redfield, R. 1930. *Tepoztlan–A Mexican Village: A Study of Folk Life*. Chicago: University of Chicago Press.

Redfield, R. 1947. "The Folk Society." *American Journal of Sociology* 52 (Jan.): 293–303.

Redfield, R. 1964. "French-Canadian Culture in St-Denis." In *French-Canadian Society*. Vol. 1. Ed. M. Rioux and Y. Martin. Toronto: McClelland & Stewart, 57–62.

Reimer, M.A. 1987. "The Social Organization of the Labour Process: A Case Study of the Documentary Management of Clerical Labour in the Public Service." Ph.d. thesis, Ontario Institute for Studies in Education.

Reiss, I. 1976. *Family Systems in America*. 2nd ed. Hinsdale, IL: Dryden Press.

Resnick, S., and R. Wolff. 1993. "State Capitalism in the USSR? A High-Stakes Debate." *Rethinking Marxism* 6, 2 (Summer): 46–67.

Rex, J., and R. Moore. 1967. *Race, Community, and Conflict*. Oxford: Oxford University Press.

Rheingold, H., and K. Cook. 1975. "The Content of Boys' and Girls' Rooms as an Index of Parent Behavior." *Child Development* 46: 459–63.

Rich, A. 1980. "Compulsory Heterosexuality and Lesbian Existence." *Signs* 5, 4: 638–40.

Rich, B.R. 1983. "Anti-Porn: Soft Issue, Hard World." *Feminist Review* 13 (Feb.): 56–67.

Richardson, R.J., and B. Wellman. 1985. "Structural Analysis." *Canadian Review of Sociology and Anthropology* 22, 5 (Dec.): 771–93.

Richer, S. 1979. "Sex-Role Socialization and Early Schooling." *Canadian Review of Sociology and Anthropology* 16: 195–205.

Richer, S. 1988. "Schooling and the Gendered Subject: An Exercise in Planned Social Change." *Canadian Review of Sociology and Anthropology* 25: 98–107.

Richmond, A.H. 1988. *Immigration and Ethnic Conflict*. London: Macmillan.

Richmond, A.H., M. Lyon, S. Hale, and R. King. 1973. *Migration and Race Relations in an English City*. London: Oxford University Press.

Rinehart, J.W. 1975. *The Tyranny of Work*. Don Mills, ON: Academic.

Rioux, M. 1964. "Remarks on the Socio-Cultural Development of French Canada." In *French-Canadian Society*. Vol. 1. Ed. M. Rioux and Y. Martin. Toronto: McClelland & Stewart.

Rioux, M., and Y. Martin, eds. 1964. *French-Canadian Society*. Vol. 1. Toronto: McClelland & Stewart.

Rist, R.C. 1973. *The Urban School: A Factory for Failure*. Cambridge, MA: MIT Press.

Rist, R.C. 1977. "On Understanding the Process of Schooling: The Contributions of Labelling Theory." In *Power and Ideology in Education*. Ed. J. Karabel and A.H. Halsey. New York: Oxford University Press, 292–305.

Robbins, D., and P. Cohen. 1978. *Knuckle Sandwich*. Harmondsworth, Eng.: Penguin.

Roberts, J.V. 1990. *Sexual Assault Legislation in Canada: An Evaluation*. Report No. 4. Ottawa: Department of Justice.

Rocher, F. 1991. "Canadian Business, Free Trade and the Rhetoric of Economic Continentalism." *Studies in Political Economy* 35 (Summer): 135–54.

Rogers, B. 1980. *The Domestication of Women: Discrimination in Developing Societies*. London: Tavistock.

Rogers, E.M. 1969. *Modernization Among Peasants: The Impact of Communication*. New York: Holt, Rinehart & Winston.

Rohner, R.P. 1967. *The People of Gilford: A Contemporary Kwakiutl Village*. Ottawa: National Museums of Canada.

Rorty, A.O. 1994. "The Hidden Politics of Cultural Identification." *Political Theory* 22, 1 (Feb.): 152–66.

Roscoe, W. 1988. "The Zuni Man-Woman." *Outlook* 1, 2 (Summer): 56–67.

Rosenhan, D.L. 1973. "Being Sane in Insane Places." *Science* 179 (Jan.): 250–58.

Rosenthal, M. 1992. "What Was Post-Modernism?" *Socialist Review* 22, 2 (July–Sept.): 83–105.

Rosenthal, R., and K. Fode. 1963. "The Effects of Experimenter Bias on the Performance of the Albino Rat." *Behavioural Science* 8: 183–89.

Rothfield, P. 1991. "Alternative Epistemologies: Politics and Feminism." In *Social Analysis: Special Edition on Postmodern Theorising* 30: 54–67. Ed. A. Yeatman.

Ruether, R.R. 1975. *New Woman New Earth: Sexist Ideologies and Human Liberation*. New York: Seabury.

Runciman, W.G., ed. 1978. *Weber: Selections in Translation*. Cambridge, Eng.: Cambridge University Press.

Russell, S. 1987. "The Hidden Curriculum of School: Reproducing Gender and Class Hierarchies." In *Feminism and Political Economy: Women's Work, Women's Struggles*. Ed. H.J. Maroney and M. Luxton. Toronto: Methuen, 229–46.

Ryten, E. 1994. "Getting into Medical School in the Nineties: Who's In? Who's Out?" *ACMC Forum* 26, 4 (June–July): 13–26.

Sacks, H. 1972. "Notes on Police Assessment of Moral Character." In *Studies in Interaction*. Ed. D. Sudnow. New York: Free Press.

Sacks, H., E. Schegloff, and G. Jefferson. 1974. "Simplest Systematics for the Organization of Turn-Taking for Conversation." *Language* 50: 696–735.

Sacouman, R.J. 1980. "The Semi-proletarianization of the Domestic Mode of Production and the Underdevelopment of Rural Areas in Maritime Canada." Unpublished paper.

Sacouman, R.J. 1981. "The 'Peripheral' Maritimes and Canada-wide Marxist Political Economy." *Studies in Political Economy* 6 (Autumn): 135–50.

Sacouman, R.J. 1985. "Restructuring Conflict and the Question of Class and Gender Alliances in Primary Producer Struggles in the Maritimes, 1965–1985." Lecture at University of New Brunswick. 28 Nov.

Sadker, M., and D. Sadker. 1987. "Sexism in the Schoolroom of the '80s." In *Gender Roles: Doing What Comes Naturally*. Ed. E.D. Salamon and B.W. Robinson. Toronto: Methuen, 143–47.

Sahlins, M. 1976. *Culture and Practical Reason*. Chicago: University of Chicago Press.

Said, E. 1978. *Orientalism*. London: Penguin.

Said, E. 1981. *Covering Islam: How the Media and the Experts Determine How We See the Rest of the World*. New York: Pantheon.

Saint Exupéry, A. de. [1943] 1971. *Le Petit Prince*. New York: Harcourt, Brace and World.

Santer, M. 1993. "A Tool to Dismantle the Public Sector." *Canadian Forum* (Jan.): 15–16.

Saunders, D.G. 1988. "Wife Abuse, Husband Abuse, or Mutual Combat? A Feminist Perspective on the Empirical Findings." In *Feminist Perspectives on Wife Abuse*. Ed. K. Ylló and M. Bograd. Beverly Hills: Sage.

Saussure, F. de. [1916] 1964. *Course in General Linguistics*. New York: McGraw-Hill.

Sayer, A., and R. Walker. 1992. *The New Social Economy: Reworking the Division of Labour*. Cambridge, MA: Blackwell.

Sayer, D. 1983. *Marx's Method, Ideology, Science and Critique in Capital*. Sussex, NJ: Harvester/Humanities Press.

Sayer, D. 1985. "The Critique of Politics and Political Economy: Capitalism, Communism and the State in Marx's Writings of the Mid-1840s." *Sociological Review* 33, 2: 221–53.

Sayer, D., ed. 1989. *Readings from Karl Marx*. London: Routledge.

Schneider, A. 1987. "Underdeveloping Nova Scotia's Forests and the Role of Corporate Counter-Intelligence." In *People, Resources, and Power: Critical Perspectives on Underdevelopment and Primary Industries in the Atlantic Region*. Ed. G. Burrill and I. McKay. Fredericton: Acadiensis Press, 117–22.

Schneider, F.W., and L.M. Coutts. 1979. "Teacher Orientations Towards Masculine and Feminine: Role of Sex of Teacher and Sex Composition of School." *Canadian Journal of Behavioral Science* 11: 99–111.

Schur, E. 1965. *Crimes Without Victims*. Englewood Cliffs, NJ: Prentice-Hall.

Schur, E. 1971. *Labelling Deviant Behavior: Its Sociological Implications*. New York: Harper & Row.

Schur, E. 1980. *The Politics of Deviance: Stigma Contests and the Uses of Power*. Englewood Cliffs, NJ: Prentice-Hall.

Schur, E.M., and H.A. Bedau. 1974. *Victimless Crimes: Two Sides of a Controversy*. Englewood Cliffs, NJ: Prentice-Hall.

Schutz, A. 1967. *Collected Papers*. New York: Free Press.

Schwendinger, H., and J. Schwendinger. 1975. "Defenders of Order or Guardians of Human Rights?" In *Critical Criminology*. Ed. I. Taylor, P. Walton, and J. Young. London: Routledge & Kegan Paul, 113–46.

Scott, V. 1987. "C-49: A New Wave of Oppression." In *Good Girls/Bad Girls: Sex Trade Workers and Feminists Face to Face*. Ed. L. Bell. Toronto: Women's Press, 100–3.

Seccombe, W. 1974. "The Housewife and Her Labour Under Capitalism." *New Left Review* 83 (Jan.–Feb.): 3–24.

Seccombe, W. 1980. "Domestic Labour and the Working-Class Household." In *Hidden in the Household: Women's Domestic Labour Under Capitalism*. Ed. B. Fox. Toronto: Women's Press, 25–100.

Sen, G. 1985. *Development, Crises, and Alternative Visions: Third World Women's Perspectives*. New Delhi: Development Alternatives with Women for a New Era (DAWN).

Sewell, J. 1985. *Police: Urban Policing in Canada*. Toronto: Lorimer.

Shapiro, L. 1990. "Guns and Dolls." *Newsweek* 28 May: 56–62.

Sharrock, W.W. 1987. "Individual and Society." In *Classic Disputes in Sociology*. Ed. R.J. Anderson, J.A. Hughes, and W.W. Sharrock. London: Allen & Unwin, 126–55.

Shaw, C.R. [1930] 1966. *The Jack-Roller: A Delinquent Boy's Own Story*. Chicago: University of Chicago Press.

Shaw, R.P. 1985. "Humanity's Propensity for Warfare: A Sociological Perspective." *Canadian Review of Sociology and Anthropology* 22, 2: 158–83.

Sherwood, S.J., P. Smith, and J.C. Alexander. 1993. "The British Are Coming . . . Again! The Hidden Agenda of 'Cultural Studies.'" *Contemporary Sociology* 22, 3 (May): 370–75.

Shils, E. 1957. "Primordial, Personal, Sacred and Civil Ties." *British Journal of Sociology* 8, 2: 130–45.

Shulman, N. 1976. "Role Differentiation in Urban Networks." *Sociological Focus* 9: 149–58.

Shupe, A., W.A. Stacey, and L.R. Hazlewood. 1987. *Violent Men, Violent Couples*. Toronto: Lexington Books.

Simard, J-J. 1990. "White Ghosts, Red Shadows: The Reduction of North American Natives." In *The Invented Indian: Cultural Fictions and Government Policies*. Ed. J.A. Clifton. New Brunswick, NJ: Transaction, ch. 17.

Simmel, G. 1949. "The Sociology of Sociability." *American Journal of Sociology* (Nov.): 254–61.

Simmel, G. 1950. "The Metropolis and Mental Life." In *The Sociology of George Simmel*. Glencoe, IL: Free Press, 409–24.

Sivard, R.L. 1985. *Women: A World Survey*. Washington: World Priorities.

Skogstad, G. 1993. "Policy Under Siege: Supply Management in Agricultural Marketing." *Canadian Public Administration* 36, 1 (Spring): 1–23.

Smart, B. 1983. *Foucault: Marxism and Critique*. London: Routledge & Kegan Paul.

Smart, C. 1977. "Criminological Theory: Its Ideology and Implications Concerning Women." *British Journal of Sociology* 28, 1 (March): 89–100.

Smart, C. 1984. *The Ties That Bind: Law, Marriage and the Reproduction of Patriarchal Relations*. London: Routledge & Kegan Paul.

Smart, C. 1989. *Feminism and the Power of Law*. London: Routledge.

Smart, J. 1988. "Immigration and Household Formation: The Emergence of Female-Centred Households Among Hong Kong Business Immigrants." Paper presented to the Canadian Asian Studies Association. Windsor. June.

Smillie, B.G. 1979. "The Social Gospel." *Canadian Dimension* 13, 5 (Jan.–Feb.): 35–37.

Smith, A. [1776] 1894. *The Wealth of Nations*. London: Macmillan.

Smith, D.E. 1974a. "The Ideological Practice of Sociology." *Catalyst* 8 (Winter): 39–54.

Smith, D.E. 1974b. "The Social Construction of Documentary Reality." *Sociological Inquiry* 44, 4: 257–68.

Smith, D.E. 1975. "An Analysis of Ideological Structures and How Women Are Excluded: Considerations for Academic Women." *Canadian Review of Sociology and Anthropology* 12, 4: 353–69.

Smith, D.E. 1977. "Women, the Family, and Corporate Capitalism." In *Women in Canada*. Ed. M. Stephenson. Don Mills, ON: General, 32–48.

Smith, D.E. 1979a. "Using the Oppressor's Language." *Resources for Feminist Research*. Special publication no. 5 (Spring).

Smith, D.E. 1979b. "Women's Inequality and the Family." Department of Sociology, Ontario Institute for Studies in Education. Mimeographed.

Smith, D.E. 1983a. "No One Commits Suicide: Textual Analysis of Ideological Practices." *Human Studies* 6: 309–59.

Smith, D.E. 1983b. "Women, Class and Family." In *The Socialist Register*. Ed. R. Miliband and J. Saville. London: Merlin.

Smith, D.E. 1987a. *The Everyday World as Problematic: A Feminist Sociology*. Toronto: University of Toronto Press.

Smith, D.E. 1987b. "Feminist Reflections on Political Economy." Paper presented at the Learned Societies. Hamilton, ON.

Smith, D.E. 1990a. "Femininity as Discourse." In *Texts, Facts, and Femininity: Exploring the Relations of Ruling*. Ed. D.E. Smith. New York: Routledge, 159–208.

Smith, D.E. 1990b. "On Sociological Description: A Method from Marx." In *Texts, Facts, and Femininity: Exploring the Relations of Ruling*. Ed. D.E. Smith. New York: Routledge, 86–119.

Smith, D.E. 1990c. *The Conceptual Practices of Power: A Feminist Sociology of Knowledge*. Toronto: University of Toronto Press.

Smith, D.E. 1990d. *Texts, Facts and Femininity: Exploring the Relations of Ruling*. London: Routledge & Kegan Paul.

Smith, D.E. 1992a. "Feminist Reflections on Political Eonomy." In *Feminism in Action: Studies in Political Economy*. Ed. M.P. Connelly and P. Armstrong. Toronto: Canadian Scholars Press, 1–23.

Smith, D.E. 1992b. "Remaking A Life, Remaking Sociology: Reflections of a Feminist." In *Fragile Truths: 25 Years of Sociology in Canada*. Ed. W.K. Carroll (and others). Ottawa: Carleton University Press, 125–30.

Smith, D.E. 1992c. "Sociology from Women's Experience: A Reaffirmation." *Sociological Theory* 10, 1: 88–98.

Smith, D.E. 1992d. "Whistling Women: Reflections on Rage and Rationality." In *Fragile Truths: 25 Years of Sociology in Canada*. Ed. W.K. Carroll (and others). Ottawa: Carleton University Press, 207–26.

Smith, D.E., and G. Malnarich. 1983. "Where Are the Women? A Critique of Socialist and Communist Political

Organization." Paper presented at the Conference on Marxism: The Next Two Decades. University of Manitoba.

Smith, D.E., and the Wollestonecraft Research Group. 1979. "Educational Cutbacks and the Workload of Elementary Teachers." *Women in the Educational Workforce*. Status of Women Tabloid. Canadian Teachers' Federation. Sept.

Smith, G.W. 1990. "Political Activist as Ethnographer." *Social Problems* 37, 4 (Nov.): 629–48.

Smith, G.W. 1992. "The Ideology of 'Fag': Barriers to Education for Gay Students." Ontario Institute for Studies in Education. Mimeographed.

Smith, J., and W. Fried. 1974. *The Uses of the American Prison: Political Theory and Penal Practice*. Lexington, MA: Lexington Books.

Snodgrass, J. 1982. *The Jack-Roller at Seventy: A Fifty-Year Follow-Up*. Lexington, MA: Lexington Books.

Solomos, J., and L. Back. 1994. "Conceptualising Racism: Social Theory, Politics and Research." *Sociology* 28, 1 (Feb.): 143–61.

Spencer, M. 1976. *Foundations of Modern Sociology*. Englewood Cliffs, NJ: Prentice-Hall.

Spiro, M.E. 1958. *Children of the Kibbutz*. Cambridge, MA: Harvard University Press.

Spitzer, S. 1975. "Toward a Marxian Theory of Deviance." *Social Problems* 22 (June): 638–51.

Spratt, S. 1992. "The Selfishness of 'Free' Trade." *Perception* 16, 4 (Fall): 8.

Stack, S. 1982. "Suicide: A Decade Review of the Sociological Literature." *Deviant Behavior: An Interdisciplinary Journal* 4: 41–66.

Stanko, E.A. 1988. "Fear of Crime and the Myth of the Safe Home: A Feminist Critique of Criminology." In *Feminist Perspectives on Wife Abuse*. Ed. K. Yllö and M. Bograd. Beverly Hills: Sage.

Stanley, G.F.C. 1964. *Louis Riel: Patriot or Rebel?* Canadian Historical Association Booklet no. 2. Ottawa: Canadian Historical Association.

Statistics Canada. 1984. *Canada's Native People*. Cat. 99-937. Ottawa: Ministry of Supply and Services.

Statistics Canada. 1985. *Education in Canada: A Statistical Review for 1984–85*. Ottawa: Ministry of Supply and Services.

Statistics Canada. 1985–86. *Women in the Labour Force*. Ottawa: Ministry of Supply and Services.

Statistics Canada. 1986. *Canadian Crime Statistics*. Cat. 85-205. Ottawa: Ministry of Supply and Services.

Statistics Canada. 1987. *The Labour Force*. Cat. 71-001. Ottawa: Ministry of Supply and Services.

Statistics Canada. 1989a. *Education in Canada: A Statistical Review for 1987–88*. Cat. 81-229. Ottawa: Ministry of Supply and Services.

Statistics Canada. 1989b. *The Labour Force: August 1989*. Cat. 71-001. Ottawa: Ministry of Supply and Services.

Statistics Canada. 1994a. *Age, Sex, Marital Status, and Common-law Status*. Cat. 92-325E. Ottawa: Ministry of Industry.

Statistics Canada. 1994b. *Canada Year Book 1992*. Cat. 11-402E. Ottawa: Ministry of Industry.

Statistics Canada. 1994c. *Canada's Changing Immigrant Population*. Cat. 96-311E. Ottawa: Ministry of Industry.

Statistics Canada. 1994d. *Earnings of Men and Women*. Cat. 13-217. Ottawa: Ministry of Industry.

Statistics Canada. 1994e. *Education in Canada: A Statistical Review*. Cat. 81-229. Ottawa: Ministry of Industry.

Statistics Canada. 1994f. *Employment and Immigration Canada*. Cat. MP22-1/1991. Ottawa: Ministry of Industry.

Statistics Canada. 1994g. *Immigration and Citizenship*. Cat. 93-316. Ottawa: Ministry of Industry.

Statistics Canada. 1994h. *Marriage and Conjugal Life in Canada*. Cat. 91-534E. Ottawa: Ministry of Industry.

Stillman, D. 1980. "The Devastating Effect of Plant Closures." In *The Big Business Reader*. Ed. M. Green and R. Massie. New York: Pilgrim Press, 72–88.

Stinchcombe, A.I. 1968. *Constructing Social Theories*. New York: Harcourt Brace and World.

Stone, K. 1974. "The Origins of Job Structures in the Steel Industry." *Review of Radical Political Economics* 6, 2 (Summer): 113–73.

Stone, S.D. 1993. "Getting the Message Out: Feminists, the Press and Violence Against Women." *Canadian Review of Sociology and Anthropology* 30, 3 (Aug.): 377–400.

Sudnow, D. 1978. *Ways of the Hand: The Organization of Improvised Conduct*. Cambridge, MA: Harvard University Press.

Sudnow, D. 1979. *Talk's Body: A Mediation Between Two Keyboards*. Harmondsworth, Eng.: Penguin.

Sunahara, A.G. 1981. *The Politics of Racism: The Uprooting of Japanese Canadians During the Second World War*. Toronto: Lorimer.

Suter, B. 1976. "Suicide and Women." In *Between Survival and Suicide*. Ed. B.B. Wolman and H.H. Krauss. New York: Gardiner.

Sutherland, E.H. 1937. *The Professional Thief*. Chicago: University of Chicago Press.

Sutherland, E.H. 1939. *Principles of Criminology*. Philadelphia: Lippincott.

Sutherland, E.H. [1949] 1961. *White Collar Crime*. New York: Dryden.

Sutherland, E.H., and D. Cressey. 1960. *Principles of Criminology*. Philadelphia: Lippincott.

Suttles, G.D. 1968. *The Social Order of the Slum*. Chicago: University of Chicago Press.

Suttles, G.D. 1972. *The Social Construction of Communities*. Chicago: University of Chicago Press.

Swenarchuk, M. 1993. "NAFTA and the Environment." *Canadian Forum* (Jan.): 13–14.

Swidler, A. 1986. "Culture in Action: Symbols and Strategies." *American Sociological Review* 51: 273–86.

Synnott, A. 1992. "Little Angels, Little Devils: A Sociology of Children." In *Sociology for Canadians: A Reader*. 2nd ed. Ed. A. Himelfarb and C.J. Richardson. Toronto: McGraw-Hill Ryerson, 191–202 .

Taylor, C. 1992. *Multiculturalism and the Politics of Recognition*. Princeton, NJ: Princeton University Press.

Taylor, I. 1983. *Crime, Capitalism, and Community: Three Essays in Socialist Criminology*. Toronto: Butterworths.

Taylor, I., P. Walton, and J. Young, eds. 1975. *Critical Criminology.* London: Routledge & Kegan Paul.

Teeple, G. 1972. "Land, Labour, and Capital in Pre-Confederation Canada." In *Capitalism and the National Question in Canada.* Ed. G. Teeple. Toronto: University of Toronto Press, 43–66.

Terkel, S. 1972. *Working: People Talk About What They Do All Day and How They Feel About What They Do.* New York: Pantheon.

Thomas, W.I., and F. Znaniecki. [1919] 1971. *The Polish Peasant in Europe and America.* New York: Octagon Books.

Thompson, E.P. 1963. *The Making of the English Working Class.* Harmondsworth, Eng.: Penguin.

Thompson, E.P. 1975. *Whigs and Hunters: The Origins of the Black Act.* London: Allen Lane.

Thompson, E.P. 1978a. "Eighteenth-Century English Society: Class Struggle Without Class." *Social History* 3, 2 (May).

Thompson, E.P. 1978b. *The Poverty of Theory.* London: Merlin Press.

Thornhill, E. 1989. "Focus on Black Women!" In *Race, Class, Gender: Bonds and Barriers.* Ed. J. Vorst et al. Toronto: Between the Lines (for the Society for Socialist Studies, Winnipeg), 26–36.

Thrasher, F.M. 1963. *The Gang: A Study of 1,313 Gangs in Chicago.* Chicago: University of Chicago Press.

Tiger, L. 1969. *Men in Groups.* New York: Random House.

Tiger, L. 1977. "The Possible Biological Origins of Sexual Discrimination." In *Biosocial Man.* Ed. D. Brothwell. London: Eugenics Society, 23–40.

Tompkins, P., and C. Bird. 1973. *The Secret Life of Plants.* New York: Avon.

Tong, R. 1989. *Feminist Thought: A Comprehensive Introduction.* Boulder, CO: Westview Press.

Tönnies, F. [1887] 1957. *Community and Society.* New York: Harper & Row.

Trainer, E.F. 1985. *Abandon Affluence!* London: Zed Books.

Tuchman, G. 1978. *Making News: A Study in the Social Construction of Reality.* New York: Free Press.

Tumin, M. 1953. "Critical Analysis of 'Some Principles of Stratification'." *American Sociological Review* 18, 4.

Tumin, M. 1973. *Patterns of Sociology.* Boston: Little Brown.

Turner, G. 1990. *British Cultural Studies: An Introduction.* Boston: Unwin Hyman.

Turner, R., ed. 1974. *Ethnomethodology: Selected Readings.* Harmondsworth, Eng.: Penguin.

Turner, T. 1991. "I Want It Now." *New Internationalist* (Oct.): 8–9.

UNESCO. 1981. *Women and Development: Indicators of Their Changing Roles.* UNESCO Socio-Economic Studies, No. 3. Paris: UNESCO.

United Nations. 1980. *Report of the World Conference of the United Nations Decade for Women: Equality, Development and Peace.* Copenhagen. July 14–30. New York: United Nations.

Valverde, M. 1987. "Too Much Heat, Not Enough Light." In *Good Girls/Bad Girls: Sex Trade Workers and Feminists Face to Face.* Ed. L. Bell. Toronto: Women's Press, 27–32.

Van den Berghe, P.L. 1969. "Pluralism and the Polity: A Theoretical Exploration." In *Pluralism in Africa.* Ed. L. Kuper and M.G. Smith. Berkeley, CA: University of California Press.

Van Dijk, T.A. 1993. *Elite Discourse and Racism.* Vol. 6. Sage Series on Race and Ethnic Relations. London: Sage.

Van Gelder, L., and C. Carmichael. 1975. "But What About Our Sons?" *Ms* 4: 52–56.

Van Reijen, W., and D. Veerman. 1988. "An Interview with Jean-François Lyotard." *Theory, Culture and Society* 5, 2–3.

Veblen, T. 1928. *The Theory of the Leisure Class.* New York: Vanguard.

Veltmeyer, H. 1979. "The Capitalist Underdevelopment of Atlantic Canada." In *Underdevelopment and Social Movements in Atlantic Canada.* Ed. R.J. Brym and R.J. Sacouman. Toronto: New Hogtown Press, 17–35.

Veltmeyer, H. 1986. *Canadian Class Structure.* Toronto: Garamond.

Veltmeyer, H. 1987. *Canadian Corporate Power.* Toronto: Garamond.

Vorst, J., et al., eds. 1989. *Race, Class, Gender: Bonds and Barriers.* Toronto: Between the Lines (for the Society for Socialist Studies, Winnipeg).

Wainwright, H. 1992. "The New Left After Communism." *Studies in Political Economy* 38 (Summer): 155–66.

Walker, G. 1990a. "The Conceptual Politics of Struggle: Wife Battering, the Women's Movement, and the State." *Studies in Political Economy* 33: 63–90.

Walker, G. 1990b. *Family Violence and the Women's Movement: The Conceptual Politics of Struggle.* Toronto: University of Toronto Press.

Walkowitz, J.R. 1983. "Male Vice and Female Virtue: Feminism and the Politics of Prostitution in Nineteenth-Century Britain." In *Powers of Desire: The Politics of Sexuality.* Ed. A. Snitow, C. Stansell, and S. Thompson. New York: Monthly Review Press, 419–38.

Warskett, G. 1990. "Capital's Strength and Labour's Weakness under Free Trade." *Studies in Political Economy* 33 (Autumn): 113–34.

Warskett, R. 1988. "Bank Worker Unionization and the Law." *Studies in Political Economy* 25 (Spring): 41–73.

Waters, M.C. 1990. *Ethnic Opinions.* Berkeley, CA: University of California Press.

Wax, M.L., R.H. Wax, and R.V. Dumont Jr. 1964. "Formal Education in an American Indian Community." *Social Problems* 11, 4 (Spring) Supplement: 1–126.

Webb, E.J., D.T. Campbell, R.D. Schwartz, and L. Sechrest. 1966. *Unobtrusive Measures: Nonreactive Research in the Social Sciences.* Chicago: Rand McNally.

Weber, M. [1904] 1930. *The Protestant Ethic and the Spirit of Capitalism.* London: Unwin University Books.

Weber, M. [1922] 1964. *The Sociology of Religion.* Trans. E. Fischoff. Boston: Beacon Press.

Weber, M. [1922] 1968. *Economy and Society: An Outline of Interpretive Sociology.* Trans. G. Roth and G. Wittich. New York: Bedminister Press.

Weber, M. 1949. *The Methodology of Social Sciences.* Trans. E. Shils and A.M. Henderson. Glencoe, IL: Free Press.

Weedon, C., A. Tolson, and F. Mort. 1980a. "Introduction to Language Studies at the Centre." In *Culture, Media, Language.* Ed. S. Hall, D. Hobson, A. Lowe, and P. Willis. London: Hutchinson, 177–85.

Weedon, C., A. Tolson, and F. Mort. 1980b. "Theories of Language and Subjectivity." In *Culture, Media, Language.* Ed. S. Hall, D. Hobson, A. Lowe, and P. Willis. London: Hutchinson, 196–216.

Weeks, P.A.D. 1982. "An Ethnomethodological Study of Collective Music-Making." Unpublished Ph.D. thesis, Ontario Institute for Studies in Education.

Weeks, P.A.D. 1985. "Error-Correction Techniques and Sequences in Instructional Settings: Toward a Comparative Framework." *Human Studies* 8: 195–233.

Weeks, P.A.D. 1988. "Musical Time as a Practical Accomplishment: A Change of Tempo." Paper presented to the Society for Phenomenology and the Human Sciences, Toronto.

Weeks, P.A.D. 1994. "The Quest for Reasonableness and Reasoning in a Mathematics Lesson." Paper, Department of Sociology, University of Manchester.

Weitzman, L.J., D. Eifler, E. Hokada, and C. Ross. 1972. "Sex-role Socialization in Picture Books for Preschool Children." *American Journal of Sociology* 77 (May): 1125–50.

Wellman, B. 1978. "The Community Question: The Intimate Networks of East Yorkers." University of Toronto Centre for Urban and Community Studies and Department of Sociology.

West, C. 1984. "When the Doctor is a 'Lady': Power, Status and Gender in Physician-Patient Encounters." *Symbolic Interaction* 7: 87–106.

West, C., and D.H. Zimmerman. 1987. "Doing Gender." *Gender & Society* 1, 2 (June): 125–51.

Weston, A., A. Piazze-McMahon, and E. Dosman. 1992. *Free Trade with a Human Face? The Social Dimensions of CUSFTA and the Proposed NAFTA.* Ottawa: The North-South Institute.

White, J. 1980. *Women and Unions.* Ottawa: Supply and Services Canada (for the Canadian Advisory Council on the Status of Women).

Whyte, W.F. 1943. *Street Corner Society.* Chicago: University of Chicago Press.

Whyte, W.F. 1948. *Human Relations in the Restaurant Industry.* New York: McGraw-Hill.

Williams, R. 1982. *The Sociology of Culture.* New York: Schocken.

Willis, P. 1981. *Learning to Labour: How Working Class Kids Get Working Class Jobs.* New York: Columbia University Press.

Wilson, A. 1978. *Finding a Voice: Asian Women in Britain.* London: Virago.

Wilson, S.J. 1986. *Women, the Family and the Economy.* 2nd ed. Toronto: McGraw-Hill Ryerson.

Winland, D.N. 1993. "The Quest for Mennonite Peoplehood: Ethno-religious Identity and the Dilemma of Definitions." *Canadian Review of Sociology and Anthropology* 30, 1: 110–38.

Winship, J. 1980. "Sexuality for Sale." In *Culture, Media, Language.* Ed. S. Hall, D. Hobson, A. Lowe, and P. Willis. London: Hutchinson, 217–23.

Winship, J. 1987. *Inside Women's Magazines.* London: Pandora.

Wirth, L. 1938. "Urbanism as a Way of Life." *American Journal of Sociology* 44, 1: 1–24.

Wolcott, H.F. 1967. *A Kwakiutl Village and School.* Toronto: Holt, Rinehart & Winston.

Wonnacott, P. 1987. *The United States and Canada: The Quest for Free Trade. An Examination of Selected Issues.* Policy Analyses in International Economics vol. 16. Washington, DC: Institute for International Economics.

Wood, E.M. 1982. "The Politics of Theory and the Concept of Class: E.P. Thompson and His Critics." *Studies in Political Economy* 9 (Fall): 45–76.

Wood, P.J. 1989. "Marxism and the Maritimes: On the Determinants of Regional Capitalist Development." *Studies in Political Economy* 29 (Summer): 123–53.

World Bank. 1987. *World Development Report.* New York: Oxford University Press.

Wrong, D. 1961. "The Oversocialized Conception of Man in Modern Sociology." *American Sociological Review* 26 (April): 183–93.

Wuthnow, R., J.D. Hunter, A. Bergesen, and E. Kurzweil. 1984. *Cultural Analysis: The Work of Peter L. Berger, Mary Douglas, Michel Foucault, and Jurgen Habermas.* London: Routledge & Kegan Paul.

Yinger, J.M. 1957. *Religion, Society, and the Individual: An Introduction to the Sociology of Religion.* New York: Macmillan.

Yllö, K., and M. Bograd, eds. 1988. *Feminist Perspectives on Wife Abuse.* Beverly Hills: Sage.

Young, M., and P. Willmott. 1957. *Family and Kinship in East London.* London: Routledge & Kegan Paul.

Zimmerman, D.H. 1974. "Fact as a Practical Accomplishment." In *Ethnomethodology: Selected Readings.* Ed. R. Turner. Harmondsworth, Eng.: Penguin.

Credits

An honest attempt has been made to secure permission for all material used, and if there are errors or omissions, these are wholly unintentional and the Publisher will be grateful to learn of them.

Photo Illustrations

Chapter 1
pp. 1 and 4, FFAW/CAW photo • p. 5, George Wirt for CARE Canada • p. 6, National Archives of Canada/C8070 • p. 7, *The Globe and Mail*/Fred Lum • p. 8, *Regina Leader-Post*/Cam Cardow

Chapter 2
p. 14, Architectural Review London • p. 19, Dick Hemingway • p. 20, Dick Hemingway • p. 31, HERMAN copyright 1981 Jim Unger. Reprinted with permission of Universal Press Syndicate. All rights reserved. • p. 37, Dick Hemingway

Chapter 3
p. 48, PEANUTS reprinted by permission of UFS, Inc. • p. 55, Library of Congress • p. 56, *The Globe and Mail*/Brian Gable. Reprinted with permission from *The Globe and Mail*.

Chapter 4
pp. 61 and 66, Hugh Allan • p. 70, National Archives of Canada/PA 140823 • p. 75, Central Mortgage and Housing Corporation • p. 77, Calgary Herald Print Collection, Glenbow Archives, Calgary • p. 82, Public Archives of Nova Scotia, photo by Bob Brooks

Chapter 5
p. 90, Graham Harrop • p. 91, *The Markham Economist and Sun* • p. 97, © Danny Ogilvie • p. 102, Canapress • p. 105, *The Toronto Star*/P. Gower • p. 115, Drawing by Cheney; © The New Yorker Magazine, Inc.

Chapter 6
p. 119, Robert Galbraith • p. 124, Library of Congress • p. 132, T. Pugh • p. 137, Public Archives of Canada/C16786 • p. 141, © Punch/Rothco • p. 144, Courtesy of the Royal British Columbia Museum/PN254

Chapter 7
p. 156, © Gayle Hurmuses 1993 • p. 158, Manitoba Archives • p. 167, Robert Galbraith • p. 168, Public Archives of Canada/C47396 © Tak Toyota, Slocan, BC • p. 175, © Punch/Rothco • p. 177, © 1992 Schmidt Photography. Reprinted by permission of Joyce Milgaard. • p. 184, *The Globe and Mail*/Brian Gable. Reprinted with permission from *The Globe and Mail*.

Chapter 8
p. 189, T. Pugh • p. 192, National Archives/306-NT-176423 • p. 195, *The Toronto Star*/K. Faught • p. 201, Reprinted by permission of United Electrical, Radio, and Machine Workers of America, from *UE News*. • p. 204, Public Archives of Canada/C29847/International Labour Organization

Chapter 9
p. 217, © Gayle Hurmuses 1993 • p. 221, T. Pugh • p. 225, Drawing by Weber; © 1993 The New Yorker Magazine, Inc. • p. 232, AP/Wide World Photos • p. 241, Dick Hemingway

Chapter 10
p. 249, Photo courtesy of CARE Canada • p. 251, Courtesy Save the Children Canada • p. 258, Courtesy Save the Children Canada • p. 266, *The Toronto Star*/ B. Weil • p. 268, *The Toronto Star*/ B. Weil • p. 269, Animal Alliance of Canada/Andrea Maenza • p. 273, Western Canada Wilderness Committee

Chapter 11
p. 277, Dick Hemingway • p. 280, Library of Congress • p. 286, Library of Congress • p. 288, *The Globe and Mail*/Brian Gable. Reprinted with permission from *The Globe and Mail*. • p. 291, Don Wright, *The Palm Beach Post* • p. 292, Reproduction courtesy of The Isaacs Gallery, Toronto, from the Estate of William Kurelek

Chapter 12
p. 304, *The Globe and Mail*/Brian Gable. Reprinted with permission from *The Globe and Mail*. • p. 309, Dick Hemingway • p. 312, Mohawk College, Hamilton, ON • p. 314, © Punch/Rothco • p. 315, Mohawk College, Hamilton, ON

Chapter 13
pp. 321 and 332, *The Toronto Star*/ R. Bull • p. 324, Courtesy of the Harvard University Archives

Chapter 14
p. 342, Dick Hemingway • p. 346, © Danny Ogilvie • p. 357, Dick Hemingway • p. 358, Ministry of the Solicitor General, Ontario • p. 360, Fahmida Bhabha

Chapter 15
p. 366, Western Canada Pictorial Index • p. 369, National Archives of Canada/PA42949 • p. 377, © Punch/Rothco • p. 382, Pay Equity Commission, Ontario • p. 384, SALLY FORTH reprinted with special permission of King Features syndicate

Chapter 16
p. 397, Ontario Archives • p. 403, Calgary Herald Print Collection, Glenbow Archives, Calgary • p. 410, ABC Canada Literacy Commission • p. 411, HERMAN

copyright 1981 Jim Unger. Reprinted with permission of Universal Press Syndicate. All rights reserved. • p. 417 (left), Canadian Federation of Students Ontario • p. 417 (right) Courtesy of Brian Young

Chapter 17
p. 427, Ontario Black History Society • p. 432, Dick Hemingway • p. 435, Courtesy of the Royal British Columbia Museum/PN10083 • p. 437, Ontario Anti-Racism Secretariat • p. 439 (left), Ontario Ministry of Industry and Tourism • p. 439 (right) *The Toronto Star*/T. Bock

Chapter 18
pp. 447 and 464, Dick Hemingway • p. 459 (top), HERMAN copyright 1981 Jim Unger. Reprinted with permission of Universal Press Syndicate. All rights reserved. • p. 459 (bottom), Dick Hemingway • p. 466, Ontario Black History Society • p. 468, Liza McCoy

Chapter 19
p. 476, Courtesy of The Ontario Milk Marketing Board • p. 478, Dick Hemingway • p. 479, Photo by Alex Waterhouse Hayward, Courtesy of the government of British Columbia • p. 480, *The Globe and Mail*/Brian Gable. Reprinted with permission from *The Globe and Mail.* • p. 483, Russell Monk • p. 484, *The Globe and Mail*/Brian Gable. Reprinted with permission from *The Globe and Mail.* • p. 486, Dick Hemingway • p. 491, Global Communications • p. 493, *The Markham Economist and Sun*

Chapter 20
p. 502, National Gallery of Canada, Ottawa. © Mark Rothko 1994/VIS*ART Copyright Inc.

Figures, Tables, and Excerpts

Figure 2-1, Peter Berger, *An Invitation to Sociology* (New York: Doubleday, 1963). Reprinted with permission. • Figure 2-3, Illustrations from *Le Petit Prince* by Antoine de Saint-Exupéry, copyright 1943 by Harcourt Brace & Company and renewed 1971 by Consuelo de Saint-Exupéry, reprinted by permission of the publisher. • Table 4-1, Adapted from J. Henripin, *Tendances et facteurs de la fecondité au Canada* (Ottawa, 1968). • Tables 6-1 and 6-2, Lapierre and Aylwin, *Canadian Youth: Perspectives on Their Health*, Cat. 82-545E. • Figure 6-1, Statistics Canada, Cat. 84-202, 84-206, and 84-528. • Table 7-1, Reprinted with the permission of The Free Press, a Division of Simon & Schuster, from *Social Theory and Social Structure* by Robert K. Merton © 1957 by The Free Press; copyright renewed 1985 by Robert K. Merton. • Figure 7-1, Statistics Canada (1986), *Canadian Crime Statistics*, Annual, Cat. 85-205. • Table 9-2, Statistics Canada

(1987, 74). • Figure 9-1, M. Hurtig, *The Betrayal of Canada* (Toronto: Stoddart, 1991). • Table 9-3, National Council of Welfare (1994, 3). • Figure 9-2, National Council of Welfare (1994, 44). • Figure 9-3, National Council of Welfare (1990a). • Table 10-1, Reprinted from *Canadian Corporate Power* by Henry Veltmeyer (Toronto: Garamond, 1987), 78-79. • Table 14-1, Statistics Canada (1994a), *Age, Sex, Marital Status, and Common-law Status*, Cat. 92-325E. • Figure 14-1, Statistics Canada, 1971 and 1986 Censuses of Canada • Figure 14-2, Statistics Canada, 1986 Census of Canada • Figure 14-3, National Council of Welfare (1994, 32) • Table 14-2, Adapted from Statistics Canada (1994h), *Marriage and Conjugal Life in Canada*, Cat. 91-534E. • Table 15-1, Statistics Canada (1994d), *Earnings of Men and Women*, Cat. 13-217. • Figure 15-1, Adapted from Statistics Canada, 1961 Census of Canada, Vol. III (Part 1) Labour Force, table 1, for 1911–61; for 1966–79: Cat. 71-201 Historical Labour Force Statistics, pp. 151, 153, 158; for 1981–84: Historical Labour Force Statistics, 1984, Cat. 71-201, p. 220, D767895, p. 225, D768005; for 1985–86, Cat. 71-001; for 1986–93, Cat. 71-201. • Table 15-2, Adapted from 1971 Census, vol. 3.2, table 8 and 1981 Census, Labour Force–Occupational Trends, Cat. 92-920, table l. • Figures 16-1 and 16-3, Porter, Porter, and Blishen, *Stations and Callings* (Toronto: Nelson Canada, 1982), pp. 61, 193. Reprinted with permission of the authors. • Figure 16-2, Statistics Canada (1994e), *Education in Canada: A Statistical Review*, Cat. 81-229. • Table 16-1, Statistics Canada (1994b), *Canada Year Book 1992*, table 5, p. B-16. • Table 16-2, Indian and Northern Affairs Canada (1993), table 16, p. 41. • Figure 16-4, Indian and Northern Affairs Canada (1993), chart 17, p. 42. • Table 16-3, Adapted from Noble (1990, 54). • Figure 16-5, Statistics Canada, Cat. 81-222, p. 17. • Table 16-4, Adapted from Statistics Canada (1994e), *Education in Canada: A Statistical Review*, Cat. 81-229, table 13, pp. 84–87. • Figure 17-1, Statistics Canada, *Employment and Immigration Canada*, Cat. MP22-1/1991, and Statistics Canada (1994c), *Canada's Changing Immigrant Population*, Cat. 96-311, p. 6. • Figure 17-2, Statistics Canada, *Immigration and Citizenship*. 1991 Census of Canada, Cat. 93-316 and Statistics Canada (1994c), *Canada's Changing Immigrant Population*, Cat. 96-311E, p. 10. • Figure 18-1 and quotes on pp. 457 and 460–61, Harold Garfinkel, *Studies in Ethnomethodology* © 1967, pp. 38–39, 42–44, 80–81. • Figure 18-2, From *Philosophical Investigations* by Wittgenstein, copyright Basil Blackwell.

Note: Readers wishing additional information on data provided through the co-operation of Statistics Canada may obtain copies of related publications by mail from: Publication Sales, Statistics Canada, Ottawa, ON, K1A 0T6, or by calling (613) 951-7277or toll-free 800-267-6677. Readers may also facsimile their order by dialing (613) 951-1584.

Name Index

Subject Index